Texas DTPA Forms & Practice

by David G. Tekell

HIGHLIGHTS

In the new Edition of *Texas DTPA Forms & Practice*, author David G. Tekell has collected and organized into individual chapters the materials regarding three common grounds for DTPA actions, to make it easier for you to find the law and tools you need to successfully tackle a case involving new and used motor vehicles (Chapter 14); business opportunities and franchises (Chapter 15); and manufactured housing (Chapter 16). The highlights of the new Edition include:

Revised and Updated Text
Overview of consumer rights in relation to "products and services" [§3.03]
Commercial real property leases: relationship between landlord and tenant [§5.25]

Updated DTPA Desk Book, including additions to the "laundry list" and other relevant statutory revisions enacted during the 2015 legislative session.

New and/or Substantially Revised Forms:
- Plaintiff's Original Petition: Used Motor Vehicle - Misrepresented/Undisclosed Condition [Form 14.07[b]]
- Defendant's Original Answer With Affirmative Defenses - Sale of Used Motor Vehicle [Form 14.08[a]]
- Plaintiff's Interrogatories to Defendant - Car Dealer [Form 14.09.1[a]]
- Plaintiff's Interrogatories To Defendant - Car Manufacturer (Recall) [Form 14.09.1[b]]
- Defendant's Interrogatories to Plaintiff re: Claim of Misrepresented Defective Vehicle [Form 14.09.1[c]]
- Plaintiff's Request for Production to Car Dealer/Seller [Form 14.09.2[a]]
- Defendant's Request for Production to Plaintiff [Form 14.09.2[b]]
- Defendant's Answer, with Specific Denials, Verified Denials and Affirmative Defenses—Texas Business Opportunities Act [Form 15.07[a]]
- Request for Production -- Franchisee to Franchisor re Misrepresentations Regarding Territory and Profits [Form 15.08.2[a]]
- Request for Production - Defendant-Franchisor to Franchisee re Misrepresentation in Sale of Franchise [Form 15.08.2[b]]
- Plaintiff's Original Petition Against Manufactured Home Retailer for Refusal to Refund Deposit [Form 16.04[b]]
- Interrogatories to Defendant-Manufactured Home Dealer re Misrepresentations at Time of Sale [Form 16.05.1[a]]
- Interrogatories to Defendant-Manufactured Home Dealer for Wrongfully Withholding Deposit [Form 16.05.1[b]]
- Request for Production to Defendant-Manufacturer [Form 16.05.2[a]]
- Request for Production to Defendant re Wrongfully Withholding Deposit [Form 16.05.2[b]]

James Publishing

We Welcome Your Feedback

Our most useful source of improvements is feedback from our subscribers, so if you have any comments, we would appreciate hearing from you.

Revision Editor
James Publishing, Inc.
3505 Cadillac Avenue, Suite P-101
Costa Mesa, California 92626

Visit us on the Internet at www.jamespublishing.com.

Texas DTPA Forms & Practice

David G. Tekell

Contact us at (866) 72-JAMES or visit www.jamespublishing.com

Texas DTPA Forms & Practice

Copyright © 1989 - 2016

James Publishing, Inc.

ISBN 978-0-938065-87-6

All rights reserved.

This publication is intended to provide accurate and authoritative information about the subject matter covered. It is sold with the understanding that the publisher does not render legal or other professional services. If legal advice or other expert assistance is required, seek the services of a competent professional.

Persons using this publication in dealing with specific legal matters should exercise their own independent judgment and research original sources or authority and local court rules.

The publisher and the author make no representations concerning the contents of this publication and disclaim any warranties of merchantability or fitness for a particular purpose.

We view the publication of this work as the beginning of a dialogue with our readers. Periodic revisions to it will give us the opportunity to incorporate your suggested changes. Call us at (866) 72-JAMES or send your comments to:

> Revision Editor
> James Publishing, Inc.
> 3505 Cadillac Ave.
> Suite P-101
> Costa Mesa, CA 92626

Revision 13, 12/2013
Revision 14, 04/2016

STAFF

Managing Editor:	Lisa Dunne, Esq.
Production Manager:	Amishi Sanghvi

About the Author

DAVID G. TEKELL

(**J.D.**, University of California—Hastings College of the Law, 1986; B.S. Business Administration, University of Southern California, 1983.)

Mr. Tekell is a practicing trial lawyer and an Adjunct Professor at Baylor University School of Law where he teaches Consumer Protection. He has over 25 years of experience handling consumer law cases on both sides of the docket. After interning with Chief Judge Walter S. Smith, Jr. of the United States District Court for the Western District of Texas, Waco Division during his last semester of law school in 1986, Mr. Tekell worked with Waco's largest defense firm, trying cases in both federal and state courts. In 1987, Mr. Tekell defended one of the first "vanishing premium" life insurance fraud cases filed in Texas. In 1990, he began handling "vanishing premium" life insurance fraud cases from the plaintiff's side. In 1995, he represented the plaintiffs in the landmark case of *Ferguson v. Crown Life Insurance Company*, which resulted in one of the largest consumer law verdicts ever issued in Travis County at the time. That case was subsequently appealed and reported as *Crown Life Ins. Co. v. Casteel*, 22 S.W.3d 378 (Tex. 2000).

From 1996 to 2005, Mr. Tekell served as co-lead class counsel in several national class actions against life insurance companies for "vanishing premium" life insurance sales practices and lead class counsel against other national companies for deceptive trade practices. He has been a frequent author and speaker on life insurance sales practices and class action litigation. Throughout his career, Mr. Tekell has maintained an active docket of individual consumer law cases, trying many of them to jury verdicts. He is board certified in Consumer and Commercial Law (2004) and in Personal Injury Trial Law (2004) by the Texas Board of Legal Specialization. Currently, Mr. Tekell is managing partner of the law firm Tekell & Atkins, L.L.P. in Waco, Texas.

Past Authors

DAVID F. BRAGG

(**J.D.**, cum laude Baylor University School of Law, 1974).

For eight years, Mr. Bragg served as an Assistant Attorney General of Texas and then Chief of the Attorney General's Consumer Protection and Antitrust Division. Mr. Bragg was a co-author of Texas Consumer Litigation (1st and 2nd Editions). In addition to authoring numerous articles on various legal subjects and three State Bar video tapes on trial practice, Mr. Bragg has served as Chairman of the State Bar's Consumer Law Section and is a former President of Texas Consumer Association. In 1991, Mr. Bragg was appointed by Governor Ann Richards to be her "Citizen Trustee" on nursing homes and authored a report entitled, *Make Texas A Good Place to Grow Old*. Mr. Bragg frequently serves as a faculty member of the State Bar of Texas and University of Texas Continuing Legal Education programs and lectures throughout the State on subjects related to trial strategy, nursing home abuse and neglect and deceptive trade practices litigation. Mr. Bragg has been in private practice since 1981 and is a member of the firm of Bragg Chumlea McQuality, with offices in Austin and Dallas.

MICHAEL CURRY

(**J.D.**, with honors, University of Texas School of Law, 1976).

Following graduation from law school, Mr. Curry served as a briefing attorney for the Supreme Court of Texas. He was then appointed an Assistant Attorney General of Texas in the Consumer Protection and Antitrust Division until he entered private practice in 1979. Mr. Curry has served as Chairman of the State Bar of Texas Consumer Law Section, and as an Adjunct Professor of Law at the University of Texas School of Law since 1985. Mr. Curry was the Editor of TEXAS CONSUMER LITIGATION (2nd Edition), has authored numerous law review and continuing legal education articles on subjects related to deceptive trade practices, Insurance Code litigation, negotiation and ADR.

Mr. Curry, a full-time professional mediator, has mediated over 2,000 cases across the State, including complex personal injury, construction, DTPA, malpractice, insurance, employment and regulatory disputes. He has been recognized as an AAM Certified Advanced Mediator. He is a member of the Association of Attorney-Mediators and the Association for Conflict Resolution. He is a Fellow of the Center for Public Policy Dispute Resolution. He is on the approved mediator lists for the federal district courts in the Western District of Texas (Austin, San Antonio, El Paso, Waco) and for the state district courts in Austin and San Antonio. He maintains a web site at www.mcmediate.com.

Table of Contents

Chapter 1		Initial Client Contacts (Plaintiff)
Chapter 2		Initial Client Contacts (Defendant)
Chapter 3		Giving Notice and Responding to an Offer
Chapter 4		Responding to the Notice
Chapter 5		Plaintiff's Pleadings
Chapter 6		Defendant's Pleadings
Chapter 7		Discovery
Chapter 8		Pre-Trial Proceedings
Chapter 9		Trial: Part One Voir Dire to Close of Evidence
Chapter 10		Trial: Part Two Court's Charge to Judgment
Chapter 11		Insurance Code Actions
Chapter 12		Residential Construction
Chapter 13		Real Estate
Chapter 14		New and Used Motor Vehicles
Chapter 15		Business Opportunities and Franchises
Chapter 16		Manufactured Housing

Expanded Table of Contents

Chapter 1
Initial Client Contacts (Plaintiff)

§1.01 General Considerations
§1.02 The Deceptive Trade Practices Act: An Overview
   §1.02.1 Application and Effective Dates
   §1.02.2 Construction of the DTPA
   §1.02.3 Cumulative Remedies
      §1.02.3.1 Limitations
   §1.02.4 Plaintiff Must be a Consumer
      §1.02.4.1 "Consumer" Defined
      §1.02.4.2 Consumer Status of Intended and Incidental Beneficiaries
      §1.02.4.3 Assignability of DTPA Claims
      §1.02.4.4 Survival of Action Following Death of Consumer
   §1.02.5 "Goods"
   §1.02.6 "Services"
   §1.02.7 Who Can Be Sued?
      §1.02.7.1 Goods or Services Must Form Basis of Complaint
      §1.02.7.2 Engaged in Trade or Commerce
      §1.02.7.3 Exemptions
         §1.02.7.3.1 Professional Services
         §1.02.7.3.2 Personal Injury Claims
         §1.02.7.3.3 Large Transactions Exemptions
      §1.02.7.4 Preemption
      §1.02.7.5 Real Estate Agents and Brokers
   §1.02.8 False, Misleading or Deceptive Acts or Practices
      §1.02.8.1 "Mere Breach of Contract"
      §1.02.8.2 Implied Representations
      §1.02.8.3 Parol Evidence Rule Inapplicable
   §1.02.9 Breach of Warranty
      §1.02.9.1 Express Warranties
      §1.02.9.2 Implied Warranties
         §1.02.9.2.1 New Home Construction
         §1.02.9.2.2 Commercial Leasing/Construction
         §1.02.9.2.3 Implied Warranty for Services
         §1.02.9.2.4 No Implied Warranty Recognized
   §1.02.10 Unconscionability

§1.02.11 Chapter 541 of Texas Insurance Code
§1.02.12 Other Statutory Causes of Action—Tie-in Statutes
  §1.02.12.1 Debt Collection Practices
    [a] FORM: Letter to creditor to end collection calls
§1.02.13 Causation
§1.02.14 Damages Under the DTPA
  §1.02.14.1 Economic Damages
  §1.02.14.2 Additional Recovery for "Knowingly" and "Intentional" Violations
    §1.02.14.2.1 Recovery for Mental Anguish Damages
    §1.02.14.2.2 Recovery for Additional Damages
  §1.02.14.3 Offset Necessary
  §1.02.14.4 Combining Elements or Causes of Action
  §1.02.14.5 Restitution Under the DTPA
§1.02.15 Attorney's Fees
  §1.02.15.1 Consumer Must Prevail
  §1.02.15.2 The Evolution of DTPA Attorney's Fees
  §1.02.15.3 Evolution of the Contingent Fee
  §1.02.15.4 The Contingent Fee Meets the "Reasonable and Necessary" Fee
  §1.02.15.5 Reasonable Attorney's Fees Under the DTPA Before *Arthur Andersen*
  §1.02.15.6 Reasonable Attorney's Fees Under the DTPA After *Arthur Andersen*
  §1.02.15.7 Attorney's Fees Must Be Segregated
§1.03 Initial Client Interview and Questionnaire
  [a] FORM: Letter setting appointment, enclosing questionnaire
  [b] FORM: Client questionnaire (plaintiff)
§1.04 Checklists for Initial Interview
  [a] CHECKLIST: Purchase of goods or services
  [b] CHECKLIST: Investments
  [c] CHECKLIST: Lender liability
  [d] CHECKLIST: Lease of commercial real property
§1.05 Contacting the Previous Attorney
  [a] FORM: Letter to previous attorney
§1.06 Conflicts of Interest
§1.07 Attorney–Client Contracts
  [a] FORM: Letter enclosing contract
  [b] FORM: Contingency fee agreement
  [c] FORM: Hourly agreement
§1.08 Fee Division Agreements (including referral fees)
  [a] FORM: Client authorization for division of fee
  [b] FORM: Agreement to divide attorney's fee (referring attorney)
  [c] FORM: Agreement to divide attorney's fees (co-counsel)
§1.09 Beginning the Case
  [a] FORM: Letter—what to expect
  [b] FORM: Alternative paragraph (residential construction governed by RCLA and not RCCA)

Chapter 2

Initial Client Contacts (Defendant)

§2.01 General Considerations
§2.02 Defenses Available in DTPA Cases
    §2.02.1 Common Law Defenses Do Not Apply
    §2.02.2 Professional Services Exemption
    §2.02.3 Real Estate Brokers and Agents Exemption
    §2.02.4 Waiver
        [a] FORM: Waiver of consumer rights
    §2.02.5 "As Is" Clause or Agreement
    §2.02.6 Independent Investigation
    §2.02.7 Statutory Defenses
    §2.02.8 Media Exemption
    §2.02.9 Contribution and Indemnity
    §2.02.10 Responsible Third Party
    §2.02.11 Settlement Credit
    §2.02.12 Large Transactions Exemption
§2.03 Client Questionnaire (Defendant)
    [a] FORM: Client questionnaire (defendant)
§2.04 Checklists for Initial Interview
    [a] CHECKLIST: Sale of goods or services
    [b] CHECKLIST: Lease of commercial real property
§2.05 Attorney-Client Agreements
    [a] FORM: Letter agreement with respect to legal services
    [b] FORM: Letter enclosing attorney-client agreement
    [c] FORM: Attorney-client hourly fee agreement

Chapter 3

Giving Notice and Responding to an Offer

§3.01 General Considerations
§3.02 Notice Letter: DTPA
§3.03 Products or Services
§3.04 Elements of a Notice Letter
    [a] FORM: Notice letter (general form)
    [b] FORM: Notice letter: defective product (rescission and damages)
    [c] FORM: Notice letter: defective product or service (damages)
§§3.05 - 3.08 [Reserved]
§3.09 Client Communications Concerning the Notice Letter
    [a] FORM: Letter to client transmitting notice letter
    [b] FORM: Letter to client: claim rejected
§3.10 Evaluating a Settlement Offer
    [a] FORM: Letter to client evaluating a settlement offer
    [b] FORM: Letter to client evaluating a settlement offer (residential construction)

[c] FORM: Letter accepting the settlement offer
[d] FORM: Letter accepting the offer to repair
[e] FORM: Letter rejecting the settlement offer
[f] FORM: Letter rejecting offer to repair

Chapter 4

Responding to the Notice

§4.01 Evaluating the Notice Letter
    [a] FORM: Letter requesting inspection of goods
§4.02 Initial Evaluation of DTPA Notice Letter
    [a] FORM: Letter to client analyzing claim
    [b] FORM: Letter requesting additional time
§4.03 Requesting Additional Information
    [a] FORM: Letter requesting additional information (general)
    [b] FORM: Alternative questions: residential construction defects
§4.04 Responding to the Notice Letter
    [a] FORM: General statement denying liability
§4.05 Offering the Full Amount
    [a] FORM: Offer of settlement: full amount of claim
§4.06 Offering Less Than the Amount Sought
    [a] FORM: Offer of settlement: less than the amount sought
§4.07 Rejecting the Claim
    [a] FORM: Letter rejecting claim
§4.08 Effect of Consumer's Rejection of Settlement Offer
    [a] FORM: Affidavit of rejection of settlement offer

Chapter 5

Plaintiff's Pleadings (General)

§5.01 Contents of Petition
  §5.01.1 Expedited Actions [effective March 1, 2013]
§5.02 Original Petition
    [a] FORM: Petition (general form)
§5.03 Citation
§5.04 The Function of Pleadings
§5.05 Service of Citation on Individuals and Partnerships
    [a] FORM: Citation on individual
    [b] FORM: Citation on general partnership
    [c] FORM: Citation on limited partnership [Service on registered agent]
§5.06 Service of Citation on Corporations and Insurance Companies
    [a] FORM: Service on Texas corporation
    [b] FORM: Service on Texas insurance company

§5.07 Service on the Secretary of State
    [a] FORM: Citation on Secretary of State—no agent for service
    [b] FORM: Citation on Secretary of State—engages in business in Texas
    [c] FORM: Citation on Secretary of State—former resident
    [d] FORM: Citation on Secretary of State—claim arises from business

  §5.07.1 Service on the Commissioner of Insurance
    [a] FORM: Citation on Commissioner of Insurance—non-admitted insurer doing business in Texas

§5.08 Long Arm Jurisdiction
    [a] FORM: Citation based on long arm jurisdiction

§5.09 Obtaining Proof of Service

§5.10 Citation on Person in Charge of Business
    [a] FORM: Citation when currently engaged in business
    [b] FORM: Notice of service to nonresident

§5.11 Service on Certain Employees or Agents

§5.12 Alleging Statutory Authority

§5.13 Notice and Conditions Precedent
    [a] FORM: Notice given
    [b] FORM: Notice not given

§5.14 Venue
    [a] FORM: General venue
    [b] FORM: DTPA venue
    [c] FORM: Breach of warranty by manufacturer
    [d] FORM: Venue proper as to other defendant

§5.15 Knowing Conduct
    [a] FORM: Knowing conduct (general form)
    [b] FORM: Knowing conduct, breach of warranty

  §5.15.1 Intentional Conduct
    [a] FORM: Intentional conduct, general
    [b] FORM: Intentional conduct, breach of warranty

§5.16 Economic Damages
    [a] FORM: Economic damages (product)
    [b] FORM: Economic damages (unimproved land)
    [c] FORM: Economic damages (residential construction)
    [d] FORM: Economic damages (investment)

§5.17 Additional Statutory Damages; Exemplary Damages
    [a] FORM: Additional damages (personal injury; wrongful death)
    [b] FORM: Exemplary damages

§5.18 Pleading Specific Actions
    [a] REFERENCE TABLE OF CAUSES OF ACTION AND REMEDIES

§5.19 [Reserved]

§5.20 Misrepresentation in Sale of Business Goods
    [a] FORM: Business goods

§5.21 Commercial Construction
    [a] FORM: Defective Commercial Construction

§5.22 [Reserved]

§5.23　Banking, Lending
　　　[a]　FORM: Unauthorized withdrawal of funds
　　　[b]　FORM: False representation to extend credit
§5.24　[Reserved]
§5.25　Commercial Real Property Lease
　　　[a]　FORM: Commercial lease of real property
§5.26　Unfair Debt Collection Practices
　　　[a]　FORM: Petition for unfair debt collection practices
　　　[b]　FORM: Petition against bank on auto lease
§5.27　Application for Injunctive Relief
　　　[a]　FORM: Petition for injunctive relief (general form)
　　　[b]　FORM: Temporary restraining order (general form)
　　　[c]　FORM: Application for temporary injunction (threatened foreclosure)
　　　[d]　FORM: Temporary Injunction
§5.28　Pleading Discovery Rule to Avoid Limitations
　　　[a]　FORM: Allegation invoking the discovery rule
§5.29　Petition for Unfair Debt Collection Practices
　　　[a]　FORM: Petition for unfair debt collection practices
　　　[b]　FORM: Petition against bank on auto lease
§5.30　Professional Services
　　　[a]　FORM: Petition for attorney's misrepresentations
§5.31　Residential Repair Services
　　　[a]　FORM: Misrepresentation re services performed

Chapter 6

Defendant's Pleadings

§6.01　Pleas in Abatement
　§6.01.1　Inadequate Notice of Claim
　　　[a]　FORM:　Plea in abatement (inadequate notice of claim)
　　　[b]　FORM:　Order on plea in abatement
　§6.01.2　Refusal to Allow Inspection
　　　[a]　FORM:　Plea in abatement: no opportunity to inspect
　　　[b]　FORM:　Order on plea in abatement
　§6.01.3　Plea in Abatement—Mediation/Arbitration Agreements
　　　[a]　FORM:　Plea in abatement: mediation/arbitration
　　　[b]　FORM:　Order on plea in abatement
§6.02　[Reserved]
§6.03　Motion to Transfer Venue
　　　[a]　FORM:　Motion to transfer venue
　　　[b]　FORM:　Affidavit in support of motion to transfer venue
　　　[c]　FORM:　Order sustaining motion to transfer venue
§6.04　Original Answer
　　　[a]　FORM:　Original answer (general form)
§6.05　Special Exceptions: Inadequacy of Pleadings

§6.06 Affirmative Defenses: DTPA
    [a] FORM: Original answer with affirmative defenses
§6.07 Affirmative Defense: Waiver
    [a] FORM: Affirmative defense: waiver
§6.08 Affirmative Defenses: Residential Construction
§6.09 Affirmative Defense: Professional Opinion
    [a] FORM: Affirmative defense: professional opinion
  §6.09.1 Affirmative Defense: Claim Arises Out of Written Contract
    [a] FORM: Affirmative defense: claim arises out of written contract
  §6.09.2 Affirmative Defense: Transaction Exceeds DTPA's Dollar Limit
    [a] FORM: Affirmative defense: consideration paid exceeds DTPA's transactional cap
  §6.09.3 Affirmative Defense: "As Is" Purchases
    [a] FORM: Affirmative defense: "as is" real estate purchase
  §6.09.4 Affirmative Defense: Independent Investigation
    [a] FORM: Affirmative defense: independent investigation
  §6.09.5 Affirmative Defense: Reasonable Settlement Offer
    [a] FORM: Affirmative defense: reasonable settlement offer
  §6.09.6 Affirmative Defense: Texas CRPC Chapter 33
    [a] FORM: Damages recovered must be reduced by value of settlement
§6.10 Counterclaim for Bad Faith and Harassment
    [a] FORM: Counterclaim for bad faith, harassment
§6.11 Leave to Designate Responsible Third Party
    [a] FORM: Motion for leave to designate responsible third party

Chapter 7
Discovery

§7.01 General Considerations
§7.02 Informal Discovery
§7.03 Corporation Information
§7.04 Assumed Names
§7.05 Financial Institutions
§7.06 Insurance Companies
§7.07 Insurance Agents
§7.08 Realtors
§7.09 Real Estate Inspectors
§7.10 Prior Lawsuits
§7.11 Prior Claims or Complaints
§7.12 Construction Information
§7.13 Manufactured Housing
§7.14 Formal Discovery
§7.15 [Reserved]
§7.16 Scope of Discovery
§7.17 Specific Discoverable Matters

§7.18   Potential Fact Witnesses and Parties
§7.19   Expert Witnesses
§7.20   Documents
§7.21   Tax Returns
§7.22   Financial Records
§7.23   Photographs
§7.24   Indemnity, Insuring and Settlement Agreements
§7.25   Medical Records
§7.26   Statements
§7.27   Wealth of Parties
§7.28   Other Claims
§7.29   Insurance Company Files
§7.30   Land
§7.31   Exemptions from Discovery
§7.32   Work Product
§7.33   Other Privileged Information
§7.34   Subpoenas
    [a]   FORM: Subpoena
§7.35   Forms of Discovery
§7.36   Discovery Control Plan
§7.37   Level 1 Discovery
§7.38   Level 2 Discovery
§7.39   Level 3 Discovery
§7.40   Modification of Discovery Control Plan
    [a]   FORM: Motion to modify discovery control plan
    [b]   FORM: Order modifying discovery control plan
§7.41   Discovery Agreements
    [a]   FORM: Rule 11 Agreement
  §7.41.1   Requests for Disclosure
    [a]   FORM: Request for Disclosure (general form)
    [b]   FORM: Request for Disclosure (short form)
    [c]   FORM: Supplemental Request for Disclosure (Level 1 expedited actions)
§7.42   Interrogatories
§7.43   Drafting Interrogatories
    [a]   FORM: Interrogatories (general form)
§7.44   Additional General Questions to Plaintiff
    [a]   FORM: Additional questions (to plaintiff)
§7.45   Additional Questions for Specific Cases
    [a]   FORM: Defective product (to defendant)
    [b]   FORM: Defective product (to plaintiff)
    [c]   FORM: Lender liability: unauthorized withdrawal of funds (to defendant)
    [d]   FORM: Lender liability: unauthorized withdrawal of funds (to plaintiff)
    [e]   FORM: Lender liability: false representation to extend credit (to defendant)
    [f]   FORM: Lender liability: false representation to extend credit (to plaintiff)
    [g]   FORM: Commercial lease (to defendant)
    [h]   FORM: Commercial lease (to plaintiff)
    [i]   FORM: Unfair debt collection practices (to defendant)

§7.46 Requests for Production of Documents and Things
§7.47 Drafting Requests for Production
    [a] FORM: Request for Production (general form)
§7.47.1 Additional Requests for Specific Cases
    [a] FORM: Defective product (to defendant retailer)
    [b] FORM: Defective product (to plaintiff)
    [c] FORM: Unfair debt collection practices (to defendant)
§7.48 Requests for Admission
§7.49 Drafting Requests for Admission
    [a] FORM: Requests for Admission (general form)
    [b] FORM: Unfair debt collection practices (to defendant)
§7.50 Responding to Written Discovery Requests
   §7.50.1 Depositions on Written Questions
      [a] FORM: Notice of deposition of written questions
§7.51 Oral Depositions
§7.52 Notice of Oral Deposition
    [a] FORM: Notice of Oral Deposition (individual)
    [b] FORM: Notice of Oral Deposition (organization)
   §7.52.1 Depositions Before Suit
      [a] FORM: Petition for Pre-Suit Deposition
      [b] FORM: Order for Deposition Before Suit
§7.53 Deposition Checklists
§7.54 Preparing the Client for Deposition
    [a] FORM: Deposition Preparation Memorandum (plaintiff)
    [b] FORM: Deposition Preparation Memorandum (defendant)

Chapter 8

Pre-Trial Proceedings

§8.01 General Considerations
   §8.01.1 Mediation
      [a] FORM: Motion to compel mediation
      [b] FORM: Order on motion to compel mediation
      [c] FORM: Mediation Settlement Agreement
   §8.01.2 When to Use Mediation
   §8.01.3 Preparing for Mediation
   §8.01.4 The Mediation Process
     §8.01.4.1 Avoiding Ethical Traps in Negotiation
   §8.01.5 Arbitration
   §8.01.6 Applicable Law
   §8.01.7 Defenses to Arbitration Agreement
     §8.01.7.1 Unconscionability
     §8.01.7.2 Waiver or Estoppel by Litigation
     §8.01.7.3 Plaintiff or Defendant Not a Party to the Agreement
     §8.01.7.4 Arbitration Procedure Under Texas Arbitration Act

§8.01.8 Appeal of Arbitrator's Decision
    [a] FORM: Motion to Compel Arbitration
    [b] FORM: Order Compelling Arbitration

§8.02 Offer of Settlement
  §8.02.1 Invoking the Rule
    [a] FORM: Declaration for Application of Offer of Settlement Rule
  §8.02.2 Making Settlement Offer
    [a] FORM: Offer of Settlement
  §8.02.3 Awarding Litigation Costs
  §8.02.4 "Litigation Costs"

§8.03 Obtaining Trial Setting and Giving Notice
    [a] FORM: Letter requesting trial setting
    [b] FORM: Certification of trial readiness
    [c] FORM: Letter providing notice of setting to parties
    [d] FORM: Letter providing notice of setting to witnesses

§8.04 Evidence by Affidavit

§8.05 Cost and necessity of services
    [a] FORM: Affidavit concerning cost and necessity of services

§8.06 Controverting Affidavit Concerning Cost and Necessity of Services
    [a] FORM: Counteraffidavit concerning cost and necessity of services
    [b] FORM: Request for leave of court to file counteraffidavit
    [c] FORM: Order granting leave to file counteraffidavit

§8.07 Business and Medical Records
    [a] FORM: Business or medical records affidavit

§8.08 Use of Criminal Convictions for Impeachment
    [a] FORM: Request for notice of use of criminal convictions for impeachment

§8.09 Visiting Judges
    [a] FORM: Objection to assignment of visiting judge

§8.10 Motions in Limine
  §8.10.1 Travis County Local Rule
  §8.10.2 Procedure
    [a] FORM: Motion in limine (general form)
    [b] FORM: Specific matters for plaintiff's motion in limine
    [c] FORM: Specific matters for defendant's motion in limine
    [d] FORM: Order on motion in limine

§8.11 Judicial Notice
    [a] FORM: Motion for court to take judicial notice
    [b] FORM: Order taking judicial notice

§8.12 Pre-Trial Conference
    [a] FORM: Motion for pre-trial conference
    [b] FORM: Order on pre-trial conference (general form)
    [c] FORM: Scheduling order

§8.13 Summary Judgment
    [a] FORM: Motion for Summary Judgment on Independent Investigation
    [b] FORM: Response to Motion for Summary Judgment: Independent Investigation

Chapter 9

Trial: Part One Voir Dire to Close of Evidence

- §9.01 Jury Selection
- §9.02 Challenges to Jurors
- §9.03 Exemptions from Jury Service
- §9.04 Voir Dire Examination
- §9.05 Scope of Voir Dire Examination
- §9.06 Sources of Information on Jurors
- §9.07 Collecting the Information
- §9.08 General Voir Dire Questions
- §9.09 Communicating Concepts
- §9.10 Introducing the Participants
- §9.11 Opening Statement (Plaintiff)
- §9.12 Opening Statement (Defendant)
- §9.13 Objections in Voir Dire
  - [a] CHECKLIST: Voir dire objections
- §9.14 Preserving Error
- §9.15 The Case-in-Chief
- §9.16 Order of Testimony
- §9.17 Direct Examination
- §9.18 Cross Examination
- §9.19 Objections to Evidence
  - [a] CHECKLIST: Objections to evidence
- §9.20 Proof of Attorney's Fees
  - §9.20.1 Keep Detailed Accurate Records
  - §9.20.2 Draft Fee Agreement to Support Award
  - §9.20.3 Present Attorneys as Expert Witnesses
    - §9.20.3.1 Independent Expert
    - §9.20.3.2 Trial Counsel as Witness
  - §9.20.4 Segregate DRPA Fees From Non-Recoverable Attorney's Fees
  - §9.20.5 Present *Arthur Andersen* Factors to Jury
  - §9.20.6 Contingency Fee and Lodestar Evidence
  - §9.20.7 Contingency Fee, Percentage of Recovery
  - §9.20.8 Attorney's Fees for Appeals
  - §9.20.9 Uncontroverted Testimony May Establish Amount of Recoverable Attorney's Fees as a Matter of Law
  - §9.20.10 FORM: Outline for Narrative Testimony on Attorney's Fees

Chapter 10

Trial: Part Two Court's Charge to Judgment

- §10.01 The Court's Charge
  - §10.01.1 Supported by Pleadings and Evidence
  - §10.01.2 Governing Rules

§10.01.3 Case Example
§10.01.4 Form of the Jury Questions
    [a] FORM: Requested special charge
    [b] FORM: Ruling on requested question, instruction or definition

§10.02 General Definitions and Instructions
    [a] FORM: Producing cause
    [b] FORM: Market value
    [c] FORM: Good and workmanlike manner
    [d] FORM: Uninhabitable
    [e] FORM: Unconscionable action or course of action
    [f] FORM: Express warranty
    [g] FORM: Knowingly
    [h] FORM: Intentionally
    [i] FORM: Corporate agents
    [j] FORM: Alter ego
    [k] FORM: Agency

§10.03 DTPA "Laundry List" Questions
    [a] FORM: False, misleading, or deceptive act or practice
        [a.1] FORM: Broad form jury questions
        [a.2] FORM: Separate form jury questions
    [b] FORM: Description of goods or services
    [c] FORM: Quality or style of goods or services
    [d] FORM: Misrepresented and unlawful agreements
    [e] FORM: Work or services performed
    [f] FORM: Failure to disclose
    [g] FORM: Failure to disclose (Alternate)

§10.04 Breach of Duty of Good Faith and Fair Dealing
    [a] FORM: Breach of duty of good faith and fair dealing—cancellation of insurance coverage
    [b] FORM: Breach of duty of good faith and fair dealing—claim denial or delay

§10.05 Negligent Misrepresentation
    [a] FORM: Negligent misrepresentation

§10.06 Fraud
    [a] FORM: Common law fraud: general question
    [b] FORM: Common law fraud instruction: fraud by affirmative misrepresentation
    [c] FORM: Common law fraud instruction: misrepresentation
    [d] FORM: Common law fraud instruction: duty to disclose
    [e] FORM: Common law fraud instruction: duty to disclose whole truth
    [f] FORM: Statutory fraud in real estate or stock transaction: misrepresentation
    [g] FORM: Statutory fraud in real estate or stock transaction: false promise

§10.07 Breach of Warranty
    [a] FORM: Breach of warranty (broad form)
    [b] FORM: Breach of warranty (separate form)
    [c] FORM: Breach of warranty of merchantability
    [d] FORM: Breach of implied warranty on services
    [e] FORM: Breach of warranty of habitability and workmanship (new house) (governed by RCLA and not RCCA)
    [f] FORM: Breach of warranty of suitability of commercial lease space

§10.08 Unconscionability
    [a] FORM: Unconscionable action or course of action

§10.09 Chapter 541 of the Insurance Code
    [a] FORM: Chapter 541 of the Insurance Code (broad form)
    [b] FORM: Chapter 541 of the Insurance Code (separate form)

§10.10 Damages
    [a] FORM: Damages (general form)
    [b] FORM: Damages (alternative form)
    [c] FORM: Restoration of money or property

§10.11 Specific Elements of Damages
    [a] FORM: Cost to repair
    [b] FORM: Loss of use
    [c] FORM: Loss of value—benefit of the bargain
    [d] FORM: Stigma damages
    [e] FORM: Mental anguish

§10.12 "Knowing" and "Intentional" Conduct
    [a] FORM: "Knowing" conduct
    [b] FORM: "Intentional" conduct

§10.13 Additional and Exemplary Damages
    [a] FORM: Additional or exemplary damages
    [b] FORM: Exemplary damages predicate
    [c] FORM: Exemplary damages amount

§10.14 Attorneys' Fees
    [a] FORM: Attorneys' fees

§10.15 Defenses to DTPA and Residential Construction Actions
    [a] FORM: Third Party Information
    [b] FORM: Unreasonable rejection of settlement offer
    [c] FORM: No opportunity to repair
    [d] FORM: Negligence of another person

§10.16 Statute of Limitations
    [a] FORM: Discovery Rule

§10.17 Proportionate Responsibility
    [a] FORM: Proportionate responsibility

§10.18 Sample DTPA Charge
    [a] FORM: Sample DTPA charge

§10.19 Jury Arguments

§10.20 General Legal Principles

§10.21 Contents of Jury Arguments

§10.22 Preserving Error

§10.23 Improper Jury Arguments

§10.24 Contents and Structure of Jury Argument

§10.25 Motions for Judgment
    [a] FORM: Motion for judgment on the jury verdict
    [b] FORM: Defendant's motion for judgment on jury verdict
    [c] FORM: Plaintiff's motion for judgment disregarding certain jury findings—attorney's fees

§10.26 Final Judgments
    [a] FORM: Final judgment for damages and attorneys' fees
    [b] FORM: Final judgment for restoration of money or property and rescission
    [c] FORM: Final judgment for defendant's attorney's fees
    [d] FORM: Alternative judgment for attorney's fees

Chapter 11

Insurance Code Actions

§11.01 Introduction
§11.02 Texas Insurance Code Chapter 541
    §11.02.1 Standing Under the DTPA and Chapter 541
§11.03 Broad Grounds for Private Cause of Action Under Chapter 541
    §11.03.1 Misrepresentation of Insurance Policy
    §11.03.2 Unfair Settlement Practices as Grounds for Action
    §11.03.3 Damages and Attorney's Fees Under Chapter 541
§11.04 Duty of Good Faith and Fair Dealing
§11.05 Interpretation of Insurance Contracts
§11.06 Defenses Under Chapter 541
    §11.06.1 Settlement Offer Defense
    §11.06.2 Limitations
    §11.06.3 ERISA Preemption
        §11.06.3.1 Attorney's Fees and ERISA
    §11.06.4 Counterclaim for Frivolous Action
§11.07 Providing Pre-Suit Notice Under Chapter 541
    [a] FORM: Notice letter: Chapter 541
§11.08 Plaintiff's Pleadings—Insurance Actions
    [a] FORM: Petition (Insurance Code Chapter 541)
    [b] FORM: Petition asserting ambiguity, breach of contract and Chapter 541 violations
§11.09 Defendant's Pleadings—Insurance Actions
    [a] FORM: Original Answer with specific denials, verified denials and affirmative defenses Insurance Code action
§11.10 Discovery—Insurance Code Actions
    §11.10.1 Interrogatories—Insurance Actions
        [a] FORM: Insurance Code claim: denial of disability insurance benefits
        [b] FORM: —Insurance Code claim: homeowner's policy (to defendant)
        [c] FORM: —Insurance Code claim: homeowner's policy (to plaintiff)
    §11.10.2 Requests for Production—Insurance Actions
        [a] FORM: —Denial of insurance claim (to defendant insurance company)
        [b] FORM: —Insurance claim (to plaintiff)

Chapter 12

Residential Construction

§12.01 History of Texas Residential Construction Law
§12.02 Applicability of the DTPA to New Home Construction
§12.03 Common Law Implied Warranties
    §12.03.1 New Home Construction
    §12.03.2 Repairs or Modifications to Existing Homes

§12.04 Residential Construction Commission Act (Historical)
    §12.04.1   RCCA—New Homes Purchased Prior to September 1, 2003
    §12.04.2   RCCA—New Homes Constructed between September 1, 2003 and June 1, 2005
    §12.04.3   RCCA—New Homes Constructed between June 1, 2005 and September 1, 2010
    §12.04.4   RCCA—2009 Sunset
    §12.04.5   RCCA—Third-Party Warranty Companies

§12.05 Residential Construction Liability Act ("RCLA")
    §12.05.1   RCLA—Definitions and Scope of Coverage
    §12.05.2   RCLA—Affirmative Defenses Available to Contractor
    §12.05.3   RCLA—Notice and Offer of Settlement Provisions
    §12.05.4   RCLA—Consequences of Failing to Provide Inspection or to Accept a Settlement Offer
    §12.05.5   RCLA—Consequences of Failing to Make Reasonable Settlement Offer or Initiate Repairs
    §12.05.6   RCLA—When Pre-Filing Notice Is Not Required
    §12.05.7   RCLA—Abatement for Failure to Give Pre-Suit Notice
    §12.05.8   RCLA—Limitations on Damages

§12.06 Forms
    §12.06.1 Checklists for Initial Interview
        [a]   CHECKLIST: Purchase of new residence (Plaintiff)
        [b]   CHECKLIST: Sale of new residence (Defendant)
    §12.06.2   Pre-Suit Notice Letters in Residential Construction Cases
        [a]   FORM: Notice letter to builder/seller
        [b]   FORM: Notice letter to engineer, architect
        [c]   FORM: Notice letter on a home warranty claim
        [d]   FORM: Notice letter to real estate broker/agent
    §12.06.3   Responses to Residential Construction Notice Letter
        [a]   FORM: Letter requesting opportunity to inspect and photograph defects
        [b]   FORM: Letter to builder analyzing the notice letter
        [c]   FORM: Letter to subcontractor giving notice of claim
        [d]   FORM: Offer of settlement: repair of construction defects
        [e]   FORM: Offer of settlement: pay for repairs
    §12.06.4   Petitions
        [a]   FORM: New house purchased from builder/seller (RCCA warranties)
    §12.06.5   Defendant's Responsive Pleadings
        [a]   FORM: Plea in abatement (inadequate notice of claim)
        [b]   FORM: Order on plea in abatement
        [c]   FORM: Plea in abatement: no opportunity to inspect
        [d]   FORM: Order on plea in abatement
        [e]   FORM: Original answer with affirmative defenses (residential construction)
    §12.06.6   Discovery in Residential Construction Cases
        [a]   FORM: Interrogatories to defendant
        [b]   FORM: Interrogatories to plaintiff
        [c]   FORM: Requests for Production to defendant (foundation repair)
        [d]   FORM: Requests for Production to plaintiff

Chapter 13
Real Estate

§13.01 General Considerations
§13.02 Texas Law Affecting Real Estate Sales
    §13.02.1 Applicability of DTPA to Real Estate Transactions
    §13.02.2 Disclosures Required in Sale of Existing Residence
    §13.02.3 Statutory Real Estate Fraud
    §13.02.4 Standards of Conduct for Real Estate Brokers and Agents
    §13.02.5 Real Estate Brokers' and Agents' Exemptions from Liability
    §13.02.6 Affirmative Defense: "As Is" Purchase
    §13.02.7 Real Estate Funds to Satisfy Judgments
    §13.02.8 Real Estate Inspectors
    §13.02.9 Real Estate Inspector Recovery Fund
§13.03 Checklists for Initial Interview
    [a] CHECKLIST: Purchase of existing residence
    [b] CHECKLIST: Purchase of raw land (Plaintiff)
    [c] CHECKLIST: Sale of raw land (Defendant)
§13.04 Pre-Suit Notice Letters
    [a] FORM: Notice letter: raw land—no potable water on land
    [b] FORM: Notice letter: raw land in flood zone
§13.05 Sample Petitions
    [a] FORM: Unimproved land
    [b] FORM: Alternative claim for rescission and restitution
    [c] FORM: Existing house purchased from owner (failure to disclose defects)
    [d] FORM: Used house, suit against real estate agent
    [e] FORM: Used house, suit against real estate inspector
§13.06 Sample Affirmative Defenses in Real Estate Cases
    [a] FORM: Affirmative defense: transaction size limitation
    [b] FORM: Affirmative defense: real estate agent exemption
    [c] FORM: Affirmative defense: "as is" real estate purchase
    [d] FORM: Affirmative defense: independent investigation
§13.07 Sample Motions for Real Estate Recovery Trust Account
    [a] FORM: Motion for order directing payment out of the Real Estate Recovery Trust Account
    [b] FORM: Affidavit of custodian of official records, Texas Real Estate Commission
    [c] FORM: Order directing payment out of Real Estate Recovery Trust Account
§13.08 Discovery Requests for Real Estate Actions
    §13.08.1 Interrogatories
        [a] FORM: Plaintiff's interrogatories to defendant (sale of unimproved land)
        [b] FORM: Defendant's interrogatories to plaintiff (sale of unimproved land)
        [c] FORM: Plaintiff's interrogatories to defendant (sale of existing residence)
        [d] FORM: Defendant's interrogatories to plaintiff (sale of existing residence)
    §13.08.2 Requests for Production
        [a] FORM: Plaintiff's Requests for Production to defendant (sale of unimproved land)

- [b] FORM: Defendant's Requests for Production to plaintiff (sale of unimproved land)
- [c] FORM: Plaintiff's Requests for Production to real estate agent defendant (sale of existing residence)
- [d] FORM: Real estate agent defendant's Request for Production to plaintiff (sale of existing residence)

Chapter 14

New and Used Motor Vehicles

§14.01 General Considerations
§14.02 Specific Laundry List Provisions Applicable to Motor Vehicles
§14.03 Other Texas Laws Governing Sale of Motor Vehicles
    §14.03.1 Texas Lemon Law
    §14.03.2 Regulation of Motor Vehicle Advertising
    §14.03.3 Warranty Considerations
    §14.03.4 FTC Used Car Rule
§14.04 Defenses
§14.05 Initial Client Checklist
    [a] CHECKLIST: Purchase of new or used motor vehicle
§14.06 Pre-Suit Notice Letter to Seller of Motor Vehicle
    [a] FORM: —Notice letter (demanding rescission and/or damages)
§14.07 Plaintiff's Pleadings—New or Used Motor Vehicle
    [a] FORM: —New vehicle (with Holder-in-Due-Course Rule claim)
    [b] FORM: —Used motor vehicle (misrepresented/undisclosed condition)
§14.08 Defendant's Pleadings—Sale of New or Used Motor Vehicle
    [a] FORM: —Original answer with affirmative defenses—Sale of Used Motor Vehicle
§14.09 Discovery—Motor Vehicle Sales
    §14.09.1 Interrogatories
        [a] FORM: —Plaintiff's interrogatories to defendant car dealer
        [b] FORM: —Plaintiff's interrogatories to defendant manufacturer (recall)
        [c] FORM: —Defendant's interrogatories to plaintiff (claim of misrepresented defective vehicle)
    §14.09.2 Requests for Production
        [a] FORM: —Plaintiff's requests for production to defendant dealer/seller
        [b] FORM:— Defendant's requests for production to plaintiff

Chapter 15

Business Opportunities and Franchises

§15.01 Business Opportunities and Franchises—General Overview
§15.02 Texas Business Opportunity Act
§15.03 F.T.C. Franchise Rule Exemption
§15.04 Other Theories of Liability
§15.05 Pre-Suit Notice Letter to Seller of Business Opportunity
    [a] FORM: —Notice letter: business opportunity
§15.06 Plaintiff's Pleadings—Texas Business Opportunities Act
    [a] FORM: —DTPA, Texas Business Opportunity Act tie-in violations, fraud and bad faith
    [b] FORM: —Franchise investment
    [c] FORM: —Purchase of existing franchise
§15.07 Defendant's Pleadings—Sale of Franchise
    [a] FORM: —Original answer with specific denials, verified denials and affirmative defenses—Texas Business Opportunities Act Action
§15.08 Discovery—Business Opportunity Actions
    §15.08.1 Interrogatories
        [a] FORM: —Franchise investments (to defendant)
        [b] FORM: —Franchise investments (to plaintiff)
    §15.08.2 Requests for Production
        [a] FORM: —Franchisee to franchisor (misrepresentations regarding territory and profits)
        [b] FORM: —Franchisor to franchisee (misrepresentations in sale of franchise)

Chapter 16

Manufactured Housing

§16.01 Texas Manufactured Housing Standards Act
    §16.01.1 Warranty Actions
    §16.01.2 Tie-In Statute Violation
    §16.01.3 Notice/Abatement
    §16.01.4 Manufactured Homeowners Recovery Fund
    §16.01.5 Action for Wrongfully Withheld Deposit
§16.02 Initial Client Checklist
    [a] CHECKLIST: —Manufactured housing
§16.03 Pre-suit Notice Letters
    [a] FORM: —Notice letter: manufactured housing
    [b] FORM: —Manufactured Homeowners' Recovery Trust Fund claim
    [c] FORM: —First demand for return of deposit
    [d] FORM: —Second demand for treble deposit and attorney's fees
§16.04 Sample Petitions—Manufactured Housing
    [a] FORM: —Manufactured home defects in workmanship and repairs

        [b] FORM: —Manufactured home retailer (refusal to refund deposit)
§16.05 Discovery in Manufactured Housing Cases
    §16.05.1 Interrogatories
        [a] FORM: —Interrogatories to defendant mobile home manufacturer
        [b] FORM: —Interrogatories to defendant wrongfully withholding deposit
    §16.05.2 Requests for Production
        [a] FORM: —Requests for Production to defendant manufacturer
        [b] FORM: —Requests for Production to defendant retailer (wrongfully withheld deposit)

Appendix - Desk Book

Table of Cases

Index

Chapter 1

Initial Client Contacts (Plaintiff)

§1.01 General Considerations
§1.02 The Deceptive Trade Practices Act: An Overview
  §1.02.1 Application and Effective Dates
  §1.02.2 Construction of the DTPA
  §1.02.3 Cumulative Remedies
    §1.02.3.1 Limitations
  §1.02.4 Plaintiff Must be a Consumer
    §1.02.4.1 "Consumer" Defined
    §1.02.4.2 Consumer Status of Intended and Incidental Beneficiaries
    §1.02.4.3 Assignability of DTPA Claims
    §1.02.4.4 Survival of Action Following Death of Consumer
  §1.02.5 "Goods"
  §1.02.6 "Services"
  §1.02.7 Who Can Be Sued?
    §1.02.7.1 Goods or Services Must Form Basis of Complaint
    §1.02.7.2 Engaged in Trade or Commerce
    §1.02.7.3 Exemptions
      §1.02.7.3.1 Professional Services
      §1.02.7.3.2 Personal Injury Claims
      §1.02.7.3.3 Large Transactions Exemptions
    §1.02.7.4 Preemption
    §1.02.7.5 Real Estate Agents and Brokers
  §1.02.8 False, Misleading or Deceptive Acts or Practices
    §1.02.8.1 "Mere Breach of Contract"
    §1.02.8.2 Implied Representations
    §1.02.8.3 Parol Evidence Rule Inapplicable
  §1.02.9 Breach of Warranty
    §1.02.9.1 Express Warranties
    §1.02.9.2 Implied Warranties
      §1.02.9.2.1 New Home Construction
      §1.02.9.2.2 Commercial Leasing/Construction

§1.02.9.2.3 Implied Warranty for Services
§1.02.9.2.4 No Implied Warranty Recognized
§1.02.10 Unconscionability
§1.02.11 Chapter 541 of Texas Insurance Code
§1.02.12 Other Statutory Causes of Action—Tie-in Statutes
  §1.02.12.1 Debt Collection Practices
    [a] FORM: Letter to creditor to end collection calls
§1.02.13 Causation
§1.02.14 Damages Under the DTPA
  §1.02.14.1 Economic Damages
  §1.02.14.2 Additional Recovery for "Knowingly" and "Intentional" Violations
    §1.02.14.2.1 Recovery of Mental Anguish Damages
    §1.02.14.2.2 Recovery for Additional Damages
  §1.02.14.3 Offset Necessary
  §1.02.14.4 Combining Elements or Causes of Action
  §1.02.14.5 Restitution Under the DTPA
§1.02.15 Attorney's Fees
  §1.02.15.1 Consumer Must Prevail
  §1.02.15.2 The Evolution of DTPA Attorney's Fees
  §1.02.15.3 Evolution of the Contingent Fee
  §1.02.15.4 The Contingent Fee Meets the "Reasonable and Necessary" Fee
  §1.02.15.5 Reasonable Attorney's Fees Under the DTPA Before *Arthur Andersen*
  §1.02.15.6 Reasonable Attorney's Fees Under the DTPA After *Arthur Andersen*
  §1.02.15.7 Attorney's Fees Must Be Segregated
§1.03 Initial Client Interview and Questionnaire
  [a] FORM: Letter setting appointment, enclosing questionnaire
  [b] FORM: Client questionnaire (plaintiff)
§1.04 Checklists for Initial Interview
  [a] CHECKLIST: Purchase of goods or services
  [b] CHECKLIST: Investments
  [c] CHECKLIST: Lender liability
  [d] CHECKLIST: Lease of commercial real property
§1.05 Contacting the Previous Attorney
  [a] FORM: Letter to previous attorney
§1.06 Conflicts of Interest
§1.07 Attorney–Client Contracts
  [a] FORM: Letter enclosing contract
  [b] FORM: Contingency fee agreement
  [c] FORM: Hourly agreement

§1.08 Fee Division Agreements (including referral fees)
 [a] FORM: Client authorization for division of fee
 [b] FORM: Agreement to divide attorney's fee (referring attorney)
 [c] FORM: Agreement to divide attorney's fees (co-counsel)

§1.09 Beginning the Case
 [a] FORM: Letter—what to expect
 [b] FORM: Alternative paragraph (residential construction governed by RCLA and not RCCA)

§1.01 General Considerations

The first contact with a prospective DTPA client is an important process of consideration and analysis. The process may end abruptly, even over the telephone, with a decision to reject the case or the client. The process may, on the other hand, be the first step in a long term relationship. Obviously, it is essential that the first contact be handled thoroughly and managed well.

There is no such thing as a "typical" DTPA client, since people who have DTPA claims run the gamut from very wealthy to very poor, intelligent to ignorant, and sophisticated to naïve. We all are consumers. Even those of us who sell spend a good part of our lives consuming. The diversity of DTPA plaintiffs means that an attorney should entertain very few assumptions about the "type" of person who has a DTPA claim.

The first meeting or meetings with the client must answer basic questions about the case and the parties. Much of the information required can be obtained over the telephone so that valuable office time is not spent on a case that obviously should be rejected. In some cases, only a face to face meeting will reveal sufficient facts to enable an attorney to make an intelligent decision about a case. Regardless of when the information is obtained, each of these five areas must be fully discussed and explored during the initial contacts with the prospective client.

(a) *Who is the client?*

As soon as possible, and preferably in the first meeting, the attorney must determine whether this particular client creates a conflict of interest because of other cases or clients that already are in the office. An individual can be checked easily for conflicts. It is more difficult to ascertain whether a conflict of interest exists when the prospective client is a corporation with a board of directors, shareholders and officers, or a partnership with numerous members. Taken a step further, a particular witness who may be necessary to a case may create either a conflict of interest or a situation that is unworkable, at best. Obviously, in learning who the client is, it is important to learn the identities of the people who are associated with the client and all of the participants in the transaction.

Conflicts of interest are only one of the areas to consider in evaluating the client. The client's personality is equally important. If the attorney and client are unable to establish a favorable rapport during the first meeting, the client should, in all likelihood, be turned away. When personalities clash, it is difficult, if not impossible, to establish and maintain the trust, confidence and open communication essential to an attorney-client relationship. The client's personality and demeanor also will affect the merits of the case. If the attorney finds the client to be untrustworthy, or to lack credibility, the jury probably will as well.

(b) *Who is the prospective defendant?*

Aside from conflicts of interest, the most important fact to be learned about the defendant is whether he or she is solvent. There are limited funds from which judgments can be satisfied against certain insolvent defendants, *e.g.*, the Real Estate Recovery Fund. All of these funds have limited funds available for the satisfaction of judgments. Consequently, regardless of the type of case, if the defendant is uninsured and has insufficient assets to pay a judgment, the case should, in most instances, be rejected. There are exceptions.

The first exception that may allow a case against an insolvent defendant to be taken is when the client is seeking relief from a debt which is owed to the defendant. Some houses are sold through owner financing. If the house is defective, then the client may be entitled to an offset against the debt owed on the house. Also, many lender liability cases have as their primary objective the reduction or elimination of debt. That is, the losses caused by the wrongful conduct of the lender will be offset against the debt owed by the client to the lender. It is important to note that in either instance, if the case is taken on a contingent fee, the attorney's fee will be a percentage of the debt which is cancelled, a fact which may require the client to borrow money to pay the fee.

The second exception that will allow a case to be taken against an insolvent defendant is presented when extraordinary relief is required in order to stop threatened conduct. Wrongful foreclosure, certain debt collection practices, and other such claims are examples. These types of cases, however, normally would be handled on an hourly fee basis.

(c) *What are the facts?*

Within a short period of time, all of the key facts about the client's claim need to be learned so that the client's case can be evaluated intelligently, and so that an informed decision can be made on the merits of the case.

It is human nature for prospective clients to present their claims in the best light possible. Some facts about a case can be so appealing that the attorney is drawn into the client's enthusiasm before serious consideration is given to what the other side has to say. In order to keep the interview as objective as possible, it is generally helpful to ask the prospective client to "argue" the opponent's case by asking very specific questions about what the other side will claim. There are two sides to every controversy. Depending on the nature of the case, if the client is unable to come up with a plausible summary of the other side's contentions, then it is likely that the client has lost the ability to be objective. The attorney must be prepared to present the probable arguments that the other side will make in order to elicit facts necessary to meet those contentions and so that the client will have a realistic view of the strengths and weaknesses of the case.

Clearly, it is rarely, if ever, in an attorney's interest to take on a case that lacks any significant potential for an effective legal remedy. Even so, there was a time in Texas law when the tendency was to interview the client, file a petition and rely on discovery to weed out the good cases from the bad. If that practice was ever acceptable, those days are gone. Today, the sanctions for initiating unfounded lawsuits are too severe to file a lawsuit and ask questions later. For example, with respect to litigation generally, TEX. R. CIV. P. 13 provides:

> The signatures of attorneys or parties constitute a certificate by them that they have read the pleading, motion, or other paper; that to the best of their knowledge, information and belief *formed after reasonable inquiry* the instrument is not groundless and brought in bad faith or groundless and brought for the purpose of harassment. (Emphasis added).

The sanctions for violating Rule 13 range from an order to pay attorney's fees and costs to contempt of court. *See* TEX. R. CIV. P. 13, 215(2)(b); *see also, Texas Rule of Professional Conduct* 3.01. With respect to the DTPA in particular, DTPA §17.50(c) (as amended in 1995) provides:

> On a finding by the court that an action under this section was groundless in fact

or law or brought in bad faith, or brought for the purpose of harassment, the court *shall* award to the defendant reasonable and necessary attorneys' fees and court costs. (Emphasis added).

For these reasons, even in those rare cases when the precipitous filing of a lawsuit appears to be in the client's interest, the action is risky, at best. There is no substitute for getting as much information as possible as early as possible in the relationship with a prospective client.

(d) *What are the client's expectations?*

People frequently enter an attorney's office with unrealistic expectations about what the attorney can do for them. The media has done such a thorough job of reporting occasionally large jury verdicts that some prospective clients believe that they can get whatever they want as long as they get the right lawyer.

Prospective clients with DTPA claims are particularly likely to have exaggerated ideas of the attorney's ability to make things rights. The prospective client may have heard of mandatory treble damages and believe they still are available. Very few non-lawyers have ever heard of "measures of damages" that limit a client's recovery to provable losses; even fewer people are aware that individuals who have perfectly valid claims are likely to actually recover less than their true losses, assuming there is any recovery at all.

In 1989, the Consumer Law Section of the State Bar of Texas conducted a survey of all jury trials involving DTPA claims in a thirty-four county area. Among other things, the survey found that parties who assert DTPA claims lose more frequently than they win. *See Survey of Jury Trials Under the Deceptive Trade Practices Act*, Consumer Law Section, State Bar of Texas, March 21, 1989, as reported in 14 CAVEAT VENDOR 35 (1989). Significantly, since these cases actually went to trial, presumably there was some evidence in each of them that the plaintiff had a viable claim.

The time to dispel unrealistic expectations is during the initial interview, and certainly before an attorney and client agreement is signed.

(e) *What are the terms on which the case will be handled?*

An additional question which must be resolved during the first contacts with a prospective client are the financial terms on which the case will be handled.

Many DTPA clients are unable to afford or unwilling to pay an attorney's hourly rate. If a case is to be handled for this type of client, then it must be taken on a contingent or "modified" contingent fee. DTPA cases do not lend themselves easily to contingent fee arrangements. For example, in a "typical" defective construction case involving a new home, one of the largest elements of damages is the cost to repair the defects. If the case is settled for the amount of the repair costs, then the net recovery for the client will be less than the actual dollars needed to fix the client's house. Even if attorneys' fees are added to the settlement, they rarely will equal the amount of the contingent fee; generally, they will approximate the fee that would have been earned on an hourly basis. In this respect, DTPA cases are unlike personal injury cases where "soft" damages like pain and suffering are nearly always included in a settlement or recovery. Because of this difference, when DTPA cases are handled on a straight contingent fee, the attorney will be forced to take either all or a portion of his or her fee from money that the client needs to complete repairs, or accept a fee that represents an hourly fee for work on the case. In other words, the contingent fee becomes a "contingent hourly fee," the worst of all possible arrangements for an attorney.

In order to compensate for this difference between personal injury and DTPA cases that are handled on a contingent fee, many DTPA attorneys charge the client an initial retainer that is non-refundable. In this way, the attorney does not bear all of the risk associated with the litigation. Additionally, if the case is ultimately settled for actual damages and the equivalent of an hourly fee, the net recovery to the attorney will be more than just a deferred hourly fee.

Although cases which are taken on a contingent fee would appear to present the greatest risk for the attorney when the initial analysis is flawed, a client who has paid substantial hourly fees for a case that ultimately is dropped may present an even greater problem for the attorney than merely uncompensated time.

If the case is taken on an hourly fee arrangement, care must be taken to explain to the client the range of fees that can be anticipated. The client should be advised that the attorney will not have full control over the hours that are spent on the case. For example, the defendant may decide to take depositions of individuals that the client feels are unimportant; nevertheless, the attorney must be present for each deposition and each additional hour spent is an hour that must be charged.

When the fee arrangements for the case are being negotiated, it also is essential to determine whether another attorney has previously been retained by the client to work on the claim. If another attorney has been involved, the new attorney must insure that the previous relationship has been severed so that there will be no inadvertent interference with an ongoing attorney-client relationship. The new attorney must also determine that there are no attorneys' fees, expenses or contingent interests payable to the prior attorney.

§1.02 The Deceptive Trade Practices Act: An Overview

[For a discussion of DTPA defenses, see §2.02 infra]

The Deceptive Trade Practices Act—Consumer Protection Act, or "DTPA" as it is commonly known, was enacted in 1973 for the purpose of providing special protection to Texas consumers who are victims of four types of conduct: (1) false, misleading or deceptive acts or practices, (2) breaches of express or implied warranties, (3) unconscionable actions or courses of action, and (4) violation of the DTPA's counterpart in the Insurance Code, Chapter 541. See generally, TEX. BUS. & COM. CODE §§17.46-17.63 (the "DTPA").

§1.02.1 Application and Effective Dates

The DTPA has been amended many times and so, when reviewing case law interpreting the DTPA, it is important to remember which version of the DTPA was before the court. For instance, as originally enacted in 1973, the DTPA provided for mandatory trebling of all damages, regardless of whether a "knowing" finding was made. *See Woods v. Littleton*, 554 S.W.2d 662, 667 (Tex. 1977). Subsequent amendments limited the automatic trebling to just the first $1,000 of damages. After 1995, "additional" (or treble) damages are only available upon a finding that the deceptive act or practice was committed "knowingly." *See* §1.02.14.3, *infra*. Most of the amendments provide that their application is limited to those causes of action which accrue in their entirety after the date of the amendment. *See, e.g.,* 1979 TEX. GEN. LAWS Ch. 603 §9. The 1989 amendments, however, apply to any action commenced on or after September 1, 1989 unless statutory notice was given prior to that date, and suit was filed within 120 days after the date of delivery or mailing of the notice. 1989 TEX. GEN. LAWS Ch. 380 §§6,7.

In 1995, the legislature substantially overhauled the DTPA and Article 21.21 §16 [now Chapter 541] of the Insurance Code. The 1995 amendments applied to all causes of action that accrued after September 1, 1995. *See generally, In re: Alford Chevrolet-Geo*, 997 S.W.2d 173, 179 (Tex. 1999). These amendments also applied to all lawsuits filed on or after September 1, 1996, no matter when the cause of action accrued. While certain provisions of the DTPA have been amended or added since 1995, the 1995 amendments were arguably the most significant and affected almost every aspect of the statute. For this reason, many of the references in this book make a distinction between pre-1995 and post-1995 claims.

§1.02.2 Construction of the DTPA

DTPA §17.44 provides:

> This subchapter shall be liberally construed and applied to promote its underlying purposes, which are to protect consumers against false, misleading, and deceptive business practices, unconscionable actions, and breaches of warranty and to provide efficient and economical procedures to secure such protection.

The 1995 amendments renumbered §17.44 quoted above as §17.44(a), and added a second paragraph which provides:

> (b) Chapter 27, Property Code, prevails over this subchapter to the extent of any conflict.

Chapter 27 of the Property Code applies to all causes of action for defects in new residential construction and residential remodeling. TEX. PROP. CODE §27.001 *et seq*. The DTPA and Chapter 27 differ in several important respects; therefore, in those cases to which the limitations of Chapter 27 apply, it "preempts" the DTPA when there is a conflict between the statutes. If there is no conflict, then both statutes apply.

The liberal construction mandate directs the courts to interpret the DTPA in such a manner, "to provide efficient and economical procedures to secure...protection" against deceptive acts and practices. In part, this mandate reflects the holding in *Nobility Homes of Texas, Inc. v. Shivers*, 557 S.W.2d 77, 83 (Tex. 1977) (quoting with approval a 1962 New York appellate court decision) which recognized that limiting a consumer's cause of action to the person immediately before him in the chain of distribution created unnecessary expense and was not economical:

> It is true that in many cases the manufacturer will ultimately be held accountable for the falsity of his representations, but only after an unduly wasteful process of litigation. Thus, if the consumer or ultimate business user sues and recovers for breach of warranty from his immediate seller and if the latter in turn, sues and recovers against his supplier in recoupment of his damages and costs, eventually, after several separate actions by those in the chain of distribution, the manufacturer may finally be obliged "to shoulder the responsibility which should have been his in the first instance."

In *Amstadt v. U.S. Brass Corporation*, 919 S.W.2d 644 (Tex. 1996), although the court did not overrule *Nobility Homes,* it declined to follow it by holding that the DTPA does not create liability on the part of "upstream" manufacturers and distributors of consumer products when the false representations made by such persons are not communicated to the ultimate consumer.

§1.02.3 Cumulative Remedies

The remedies provided under the DTPA are intended to be in addition to other remedies provided by law. DTPA §17.43. *See Latham v. Castillo*, 972 S.W2d 66 (Tex. 1998) (holding that clients' claim that their lawyer acted unconscionably was not a legal malpractice claim but a separate claim with different elements than a malpractice claim).

§1.02.3.1 Limitations

There is a two year statute of limitations applicable to claims made under the DTPA. DTPA §17.565. The limitations period begins when the false, misleading or deceptive act or practice occurred, or, when "the consumer discovered or in the exercise of reasonable diligence should have discovered the occurrence of the false, misleading or deceptive act or practice." DTPA §17.565. The two years limitation period may be extended by 180 days if the plaintiff proves that his or her failure to timely commence the action "was caused by the defendant's knowingly engaging in conduct solely calculated to induce the plaintiff from or postpone commencement of the action." DTPA §17.565.

§1.02.4 Plaintiff Must be a Consumer

§1.02.4.1 "Consumer" Defined

One must be a "consumer" to maintain an action under the DTPA. A consumer is generally defined as "an individual, partnership, corporation, this state, or a subdivision or agency of this state who seeks or acquires by purchase or lease, any goods or services." DTPA §17.45(4). The burden of proof is on the plaintiff to prove that he or she qualifies as a consumer. *Farmers and Merchants State Bank v. Ferguson*, 617 S.W.2d 918 (Tex. 1981). Texas courts of appeals have uniformly held that consumer status is a question of law for the court to decide from the evidence. *See Fix v. Flagstar Bank, FSB*, 242 S.W.3d 147, 159-160 (Tex. App.—Fort Worth 2007, pet. den'd.); *Rivera v. South Green Ltd. P'ship*, 208 S.W.3d 12, 21 (Tex. App.—Houston [14th Dist.] 2006, pet. den'd.); *Bohls v. Oakes*, 75 S.W.2d 473, 478-479 (Tex. App.—San Antonio 2002, pet. den'd.); *Allied Towing Service v. Mitchell*, 833 S.W.2d 577 (Tex. App. Dallas 1992, no writ); *Reed v. Israel Nat'l. Oil Co., Ltd.*, 681 S.W.2d 228 (Tex. App.—Houston [1st Dist.] 1984, no writ); *Netterville v. Interfirst Bank*, 718 S.W.2d 921 (Tex. App.—Beaumont 1986, writ dism'd); *Commercial Escrow Co. v. Rockport Rebel, Inc.*, 778 S.W.2d 532 (Tex. App.—Corpus Christi 1989, writ denied). However, when the underlying facts necessary to determine consumer status are disputed, there is a question of fact for the trier-of-fact to decide. *Roof Sys., Inc. v. Johns Manville Corp.*, 130 S.W.3d 430, 440 (Tex. App.—Houston [14th Dist.] 2004, no pet.).

Exception: Everyone potentially is a consumer with one exception: A "business consumer that has assets of $25,000,000 or more, or that is owned or controlled by a corporation or entity with assets of $25,000,000 or more." DTPA §17.45(4). A "business consumer" is one who is "an individual, partnership or corporation who seeks or acquires by purchase or lease, any goods or services for commercial or business use." DTPA §17.45(10). Because requiring each consumer to prove that he is not a millionaire would be inefficient, the Texas Supreme Court has held that the defendant has the burden to plead and prove this exception as an affirmative defense. *Eckman v. Centennial Sav. Bank*, 784 S.W.2d 672 (Tex. 1990) (business consumer exception is an affirmative defense).

The Texas Supreme Court has recognized two requirements for consumer standing: (1) a person must seek or acquire goods or services by purchase or lease and (2) the goods or services must form the basis of the complaint. *Cameron v. Terrell & Garrett, Inc.*, 618 S.W.2d 535 (Tex. 1981). When the consumer actively shops for and pays money or other consideration for the good or services made the basis of his complaint, his status as a consumer under this definition is obvious. But the definition of "consumer" is broader and includes a person who is merely seeking goods or services when a deceptive act or practice is committed. It is not necessary for qualification as a consumer that the transaction be consummated. *Sherman Simon Enter., Inc. v. Lorac Serv. Corp.*, 724 S.W.2d 13 (Tex. 1987). *See also Williams v. Hills Fitness Center, Inc.*, 705 S.W.2d 189 (Tex. App.—Texarkana 1985, writ ref'd n.r.e.) (prospective patron of fitness center seeking its services when she was injured during pre-enrollment visit was a consumer under the DTPA). As the court described in *Williams v. Hills Fitness Center*, the DTPA's definition of consumer includes both "the proverbial lady who tries on every hat in the millinery shop and buys none, as well as the lady who buys." *Id.* at 191.

Texas courts have historically taken an expansive view of whether goods or services form the basis of the consumer's complaint. *See, e.g., Knight v. International Harvester Credit Corp.*, 627 S.W.2d 382 (Tex. 1982) (purchase of dump truck included financing arrangement with lender assignee of retail installment contract; *Flenniken v. Longview Bank & Trust Co.*, 661 S.W.2d 705 (Tex. 1983) (home construction transaction included financing arrangement between builder and lender); *Arthur Anderson and Co. v. Perry Equip. Corp.*, 945 S.W.2d 812 (Tex. 1997) (auditors who provided financial statements to seller); *Dewitt County Elec. Coop., Inc. v. Parks*, 1 S.W.3d 96 (Tex. 1999) (representations by electricity provider regarding its easement were actionable as part of the homeowners' transaction to acquire electricity).

A consumer transaction does not necessarily end at the time of purchase. Thus, in *Melody Homes Mfg. Co. v. Barnes*, 741 S.W.2d 349 (Tex. 1987) the Texas Supreme Court held that the purchasers of a mobile home remained "consumers" as to repair work performed by the seller over two years after the purchase. And, in *Flenniken v. Longview Bank & Trust Co.*, the court held that the defendant's unconscionable conduct occurring after the parties entered into a contract was actionable.

§1.02.4.2 Consumer Status of Intended and Incidental Beneficiaries

Consumer status under the DTPA is not determined by contractual privity. *Cameron v. Terrell & Garrett, Inc.*, 618 S.W.2d 535 (Tex. 1981). A consumer can "acquire" goods or services, even though he did not seek them, purchase them or pay for them. *See, e.g., Arthur Anderson and Co. v. Perry Equip. Corp.*, 945 S.W.2d 812 (Tex. 1997) (consumer does not have to be actual purchaser of goods or services if consumer is beneficiary of those goods or services); *Kennedy v. Sale*, 689 S.W.2d 890 (Tex. 1985) (employee is a consumer as to group insurance purchased by employer for employees' benefit). *Compare Brandon v. American Sterilizer Co.*, 880 S.W.2d 488, 492 (Tex. App.—Austin 1994, no writ) (employee is not a consumer when equipment purchase was primarily for benefit of employer).

One who "acquires" goods or services need not do so voluntarily in order to qualify as a consumer. Thus, an evicted tenant whose property was confiscated and sent to a storage facility for storage was a consumer of the storage facility's services. *Nelson v. Schanzer*, 788 S.W.2d 81 (Tex. App.—Houston [14th Dist.] 1990, writ den'd.); *see also Allied Towing Service v. Mitchell*, 833 S.W.2d 577 (Tex. App.—Dallas, 1992, no writ) (party whose car was wrongfully towed and who paid for its release involuntarily acquired services and was, therefore, a consumer); *D/FW Commercial Roofing Co., Inc. v. Mehra*, 854 S.W.2d 182 (Tex. App.—Dallas 1993, no writ) (tenant was consumer of roof repairs purchased by landlord).

A third party beneficiary of a contract may qualify as a consumer of goods or services as long as the transaction was specifically required by or intended to benefit the third party and the good or service was rendered to benefit the third party. Thus, when one spouse contracts for the construction of a home in which both spouses are to reside, the non-contracting spouse is a "consumer" under the DTPA. *Bohls v. Oakes*, 75 S.W.3d 473, 479 (Tex. App.—San Antonio 2002, pet. denied). In *Bohls*, the court held that the relevant inquiries to be made in determining consumer status are (1) to whom the representations were made, (2) who suffered damages from the representations, and (3) who was affected by the defendant's alleged misconduct. *Bohls v. Oakes*, 75 S.W.3d 479.

Children will be deemed consumers of products or services purchased for their benefit by their parents. In *Birchfield v. Texarkana Mem. Hosp.*, 747 S.W.2d 361 (Tex. 1987), a minor's parents sued on their daughter's behalf to recover damages caused by hospital personnel who improperly administered supplemental oxygen to the child shortly after her birth. The hospital contended on appeal that the infant did not qualify as a consumer. The Texas Supreme Court rejected this argument, reasoning that the infant acquired goods and services sold by the hospital and therefore established her standing for purposes of the DTPA. *See also Wellborn v. Sears, Roebuck & Co.*, 970 F.2d 1420 (5th Cir. 1992) (child killed while skateboarding under garage door who was intended beneficiary of garage door opener purchase by his mother was a consumer under the DTPA.)

Merely incidental beneficiaries of a transaction will not be deemed consumers. *See, e.g., Chamrad v. Volvo Cars of North Am.*, 145 F.3d 671 (5th Cir. 1998) (permissive driver was not consumer of fiancee's car where he was only incidental beneficiary of its purchase). Employees will not be consumers with respect to products or services purchased by their employer for the benefit of the employer's business and which benefited the employee only incidentally. *See, e.g., Brandon v. American Sterilizer Co.*, 880 S.W.2d 488, 492 (Tex. App.—Austin 1994, no writ) (nurse not a consumer of equipment repair services purchased by hospital); *Lara v. Lile*, 828 S.W.2d 536, 542 (Tex. App.—Corpus Christi 1992, writ denied) (construction worker was not consumer of employer's concrete delivery service); *Clark Equip. Co. v. Pitner*, 923 S.W.2d 117, 128 (Tex. App.—Houston [14th Dist.] 1996, writ den'd.) (employee was not consumer of defective forklift purchased by his employer). Nevertheless, if it is shown that the employer purchased the product or service primarily for the employee's benefit, consumer status will be found. *See, e.g., Kennedy v. Sale*, supra.; *Lewis & Lambert Metal Contractors v.*

Jackson, 914 S.W.2d 584, 588 (Tex. App.—Dallas 1994), *vacated without reference to merits by*, 938 S.W.2d 716 (Tex. 1997) (hospital employees injured by toxic gas exposure were consumers of hospital's ventilation repair contractor when repairs were performed at the request of employees).

§1.02.4.3 Assignability of DTPA Claims

The DTPA is silent on whether a consumer can effectively assign his claims to another. The Texas Supreme Court has held that DTPA claims generally, and DTPA claims for breach of warranty in particular, cannot be assigned by an aggrieved consumer to someone else. *PPG Indus. v. JMB/Houston Ctrs. Ltd. P'ship*, 146 S.W.3d 79, 92 (Tex. 2004). The court expressly reserved from its decision whether causes of action specifically created by the DTPA, such as claims for false going-out-of-business sales or price-gouging during a disaster, could be assigned. *Id.*

§1.02.4.4 Survival of Action Following Death of Consumer

The courts of appeal are divided on the question of whether a cause of action under the DTPA survives the death of the consumer. In *Thomes v. Porter*, 761 S.W.2d 592, 593-594 (Tex. App.—Fort Worth 1988, no writ), the Fort Worth court of appeals held that a DTPA cause of action for statutory damages and damages for claims other than personal injuries survives the death of the consumer. *See also Mahan Volkswagen v. Hall*, 648 S.W.2d 324, 332-33 (Tex. App.—Houston [1st Dist.], 1982, writ ref'd n.r.e.) (holding that DTPA claims survive the death of the consumer). The San Antonio court of appeals, sitting *en banc,* rejected *Thomes* and its reasoning in *Mendoza v. American National Ins. Co.*, 932 S.W.2d 605, 608 (Tex. App.—San Antonio 1996, no writ), and held that a DTPA cause of action does not survive. The question of survival of a DTPA cause of action was certified to the Supreme Court of Texas by the Fifth Circuit Court of Appeals in *Wellborn v. Sears, Roebuck & Co.*, 970 F.2d 1420 (5th Cir. 1992); however, the case was settled before the Supreme Court answered the question. When presented with a second opportunity to follow *Thomes*, the San Antonio court of appeals again held that a DTPA cause of action does not survive. *Lukasik v. San Antonio Blue Haven Pools, Inc.*, 21 S.W.3rd 394, 402 (Tex. App.—San Antonio 2000, no pet.). The Texas Supreme Court expressly left open the question of survivability in *PPG Indus. v. JMB/Houston Ctrs. Ltd. P'ship*, 146 S.W.3d 79, 92 (Tex. 2004).

§1.02.5 "Goods"

The term "goods" is defined in the DTPA as "tangible chattels or real property purchased or leased for use." DTPA §17.45(1). The Dallas Court of Appeals has defined "tangible chattels" as "those items of personal property which may be seen, weighed, measured, felt, or touched." *United Postage Corp. v. Kammeyer*, 581 S.W.2d 716 (Tex. Civ. App.—Dallas 1979, no writ). The courts have identified certain types of "intangible" property which do not qualify as goods. *See Riverside Nat'l Bank v. Lewis*, 603 S.W.2d 169 (Tex. 1980) (money); *Snyders Smart Shop, Inc. v. Santi, Inc.*, 590 S.W.2d 167 (Tex. Civ. App.—Corpus Christi 1981, no writ) (accounts receivable); *Portland Sav. & Loan Assn. v. Bevil*, 619 S.W.2d 241 (Tex. Civ. App.—Corpus Christi 1981, no writ) (securities); *Kilgore Fed. Sav. & Loan v. Donnelly*, 624 S.W.2d 933 (Tex. Civ. App.—Tyler 1981, no writ) (savings certificates). *In Wheeler v. Box*, 671 S.W.2d 75 (Tex.

App.—Dallas 1984, no writ) the court held that purchasers of a franchise were consumers. The court reasoned that although the business entity was intangible, it encompassed both tangible personal property and services, thus bringing the transaction within the ambit of the DTPA. *See also Hennessey v. Skinner*, 698 S.W.2d 382 (Tex. App.—Houston [14th Dist.] 1985, no writ) (the DTPA was clearly intended to cover mixed purchases of goods and services on the one hand and non-DTPA items on the other).

In *Bailey v. Gulf States Utilities Co.*, 27 S.W.3d 713 (Tex. App.—Beaumont 2000, no pet.), the defendant argued that electricity is "intangible" and is, therefore, not a "good," which is defined in the DTPA as a "tangible chattel." The court of appeals noted that the Texas Supreme Court previously has held that electricity is a "product" in the context of tort law. *See Houston Lighting & Power Co. v. Reynolds*, 765 S.W.2d 784, 785 (Tex. 1988). The court then reasoned that since electricity is a thing which can be measured (through a meter), it should be considered a "good" under the DTPA.

"Real property" is included within the definition of "goods," but real property is not otherwise defined. In *Chastain v. Koonce*, 700 S.W.2d 579, 584 (Tex. 1985), the Texas Supreme Court gave the term real property an expansive definition and concluded that it meant "the land, its fixtures, and all its accompanying exercisable rights." A contract for the construction of a house is a clearly a transaction involving goods or services. *Flenniken v. Longview Bank & Trust Co.*, 661 S.W.2d 705 (Tex. 1983).

The "for use" requirement was considered in *Big H Auto Auction, Inc. v. Saenz Motor*, 665 S.W.2d 756 (Tex. 1984). The question before the court was whether goods purchased for resale constituted goods purchased "for use" as required by §17.45 of the DTPA. Relying upon legislative history and the mandate of liberal construction, the court held that goods purchased for resale were purchased "for use," thereby qualifying the plaintiff as a consumer.

§1.02.6 "Services"

"Services" is defined by the DTPA to mean, "work, labor or service provided or leased for use, including services furnished in connection with the sale or repair of goods." DTPA §17.45(2). In *Riverside Nat'l Bank v. Lewis*, 603 S.W.2d 169 (Tex. 1980), the Supreme Court held that the mere lending of money does not constitute a service. Other cases, however, have established that if the purchaser's objective in borrowing the money is to purchase goods or services, then the transaction involves more than the "mere extension of credit" and consumer standing is conferred. *Knight v. International Harvester Credit Corp.*, 627 S.W.2d 382 (Tex. 1982); *Flenniken v. Longview Bank & Trust Co.*, 661 S.W.2d 705 (Tex. 1983). Banking services other than the "mere extension of credit" also have been held to qualify as "services." *See, e.g., La Sara Grain Co. v. First Nat. Bank of Mercedes*, 673 S.W.2d 558 (Tex. 1984) (checking account services).

The 1995 amendments exclude from the DTPA a claim for damages "based on the rendering of a professional service, the essence of which is the providing of advice, judgment, opinion, or similar professional skill." DTPA §17.49(c), as amended 1995. For a detailed discussion of this exclusion, see §2.02.01 *infra*.

§1.02.7 Who Can Be Sued?

It is critically important to recognize that the DTPA standing requirement focuses on the consumer's relationship to the transaction, not the consumer's relationship to the defendants. *Cameron v. Terrell and Garrett, Inc.*, 618

S.W.2d 535 (Tex. 1981). Accordingly, direct privity with the defendant is not required. *Id.* The plaintiff need not seek or acquire goods or services from the defendant to be a consumer, provided that the plaintiff sought or acquired goods or services from another party to the transaction. *Id.*; *see also Knight v. International Harvester Credit Corp.*, 627 S.W.2d 382 (Tex. 1982); *Flenniken v. Longview Bank & Trust Co.*, 661 S.W.2d 705 (Tex. 1983).

The only expressed limitation in the DTPA on who is and is not an appropriate defendant is that the defendant be a "person." DTPA §17.50(a). The term "person" is broadly defined to include almost any type of entity. DTPA §17.45(3). As written the DTPA simply requires that the defendant's conduct actionable under the DTPA be a producing cause of damages to a consumer. DTPA §17.50(a). When that actionable conduct is a laundry list violation, the DTPA further requires that the consumer rely on the defendant's laundry list violation to her detriment. DTPA §17.50(a)(1).

Early on, the Supreme Court noted the broad coverage of the DTPA:

> Section 17.45(4), defining "consumer" ... only describes the class of persons entitled to bring suit under Section 17.50; it does not define the class of persons subject to liability under the DTPA. The range of possible defendants is limited only by the exemptions provided in Section 17.49.

Flenniken v. Longview Bank & Trust Co., 661 S.W.2d 705, 706 (Tex. 1983). Thus, for example, non-merchants (persons not in the business of selling goods or services) are not excluded from the DTPA. *Pennington v. Singleton*, 606 S.W.2d 682 (Tex. 1980). Likewise, agents acting on behalf of another are not excluded from the statute. *Miller v. Keyser*, 90 S.W.3d 712 (Tex. 2002); *Weitzel v. Barnes*, 691 S.W. 2d 598 (Tex. 1985). Indeed, even those who do not furnish goods or services to the plaintiff, but who commit a deceptive trade practice in the course of a sale by another party, are subject to liability under the Act, regardless of the lack of privity of contract between the plaintiff and the defendant. *See Cameron v. Terrell & Garrett, Inc.*, 618 S.W.2d 535 (Tex. 1981) (seller's agent who misrepresented the size of the house subject to suit by buyer).

§1.02.7.1 Goods or Services Must Form Basis of Complaint

There is no requirement that the defendant be a person from whom the consumer sought to purchase goods or services or from whom the consumer actually acquired goods or services. As such, the courts have consistently held that, as long as goods or services "form the basis of the complaint," a consumer's DTPA action may be maintained against any defendant who engaged in deceptive acts or practices to the detriment of the consumer. *Cameron v. Terrell & Garrett, Inc., supra*. If the consumer sought or acquired goods or services in a transaction, lenders and others who benefited from that transaction will be proper defendants for conduct actionable under the DTPA. *See, e.g., Knight v. International Harvester Credit Corp.*, 627 S.W.2d 382 (Tex. 1982) (lender assignee of retail installment contract for purchase of dump truck was proper defendant for its DTPA violations); *Flenniken v. Longview Bank & Trust Co.*, 661 S.W.2d 705 (Tex. 1983) (bank who purchased mechanic's lien contract from builder and then improperly foreclosed was proper defendant); *Arthur Anderson and Co. v. Perry Equip. Corp.*, 945 S.W.2d 812 (Tex. 1997) (auditors who provided financial statements to seller).

While the expansive view of the consumer's transaction will include defendants who are not in privity with the plaintiff, it will not make independent defendants vicariously liable for each other's conduct. *Qantel Bus. Sys., Inc. v. Custom Controls Co.*, 761 S.W.2d 302 (Tex. 1988).

§1.02.7.2 Engaged in Trade or Commerce

In *Amstadt v. U.S. Brass Corp.*, 919 S.W.2d 644 (Tex. 1996) the Texas Supreme Court announced a new doctrine that provides limitations on who can be sued under the DTPA. *Amstadt* involved the sale of residential plumbing pipes that were installed in new homes built in the Houston area. False representations about the quality and durability of the pipes were made to everyone in the chain of distribution, except the ultimate consumer. The evidence established that the pipes would not have been used by the consumers' homebuilders had the false representations not been made. In *Amstadt*, the court announced an "in-connection-with" requirement which means that a consumer cannot sue an upstream manufacturer or supplier under the DTPA unless the false representations are communicated to the consumer. Without such direct communication, in the court's view, the upstream manufacturers and distributors are insufficiently "connected to" the transaction to have DTPA liability to the consumer. In so holding, the court abandoned *sub silentio* the policy enunciated in *Nobility Homes of Texas, Inc. v. Shivers*, 557 S.W.2d 77 (Tex. 1977), of permitting a direct action against the party responsible for the damage, rather than requiring successive claims up the distribution chain. *See also Nissan Motor Co. v. Armstrong*, 145 S.W.3d 131 (Tex. 2004) (automobile manufacturer could not be sued by the second owner of a vehicle when the manufacturer had no involvement or pecuniary interest in the purchase by the second owner and there was no evidence of any manufacturer warranty or representation to that purchaser).

The Texas Supreme Court has recognized, in dicta, that the "in-connection-with" requirement announced in *Amstadt* extended to warranty claims as well as laundry-list and unconscionability claims. *PPG Industries, Inc. v. JMB/Houston Centers Limited Partnership*, 146 S.W.3d 79, 89 (Tex. 2004). Thus, an upstream seller of goods may not be a proper defendant in a DTPA breach of implied warranty claim, even though it may be a proper defendant in a UCC breach of implied warranty action. *Id.* (implicitly overruling *Gupta v. Ritter Homes, Inc.*, 646 S.W.2d 168, 169 (Tex. 1983) on that point).

§1.02.7.3 Exemptions

There are several express exemptions provided by the DTPA in §17.49. The first three are aimed at particular classes of defendants. The exemption in §17.49(a) protects owners or employees of newspapers, magazines, telephone directories, broadcast stations and billboards. The exemption does not apply, however, if the owner or employee knew that the information disseminated was false, misleading or deceptive, or if the owner or employee had a financial interest in the sale or distribution of the unlawfully advertised product. *See* DTPA §17.49(a); *see generally Miller v. Keyser*, 90 S.W.3d 712 (Tex. 2002*); Mother and Unborn Baby Care v. State*, 749 S.W.2d 533 (Tex. App.—Fort Worth 1988, writ denied). A second exemption has even more limited application. This exemption protects persons who are sued because of conduct that has been specifically approved by the Federal Trade Commission. DTPA §17.49(b).

§1.02.7.3.1 Professional Services

Added in 1995, DTPA §17.49(c) now exempts "claims for damages based on the rendering of professional services, the essence of which is the providing of advice, judgment, opinion, or similar professional skill" from the DTPA. Section 17.49(d) makes this "professional services" exemption applicable to the professional's employer or principal. The intent of these amendments may have been to protect attorneys, doctors and other professionals and their employers from claims under the DTPA; however, the same legislature enacted four exceptions to this exemption which almost completely negate any protection otherwise offered by the "professional services" exemption. These exceptions preserve DTPA claims against professionals based on:

1. an express misrepresentation of a material fact that cannot be characterized as advice, judgment, or opinion;

2. a failure to disclose information in violation of §17.46(b)(23);

3. an unconscionable action or course of action that cannot be characterized as advice, judgment, or opinion; or,

4. breach of an express warranty that cannot be characterized as advice, judgment, or opinion.

DTPA §17.49(c)(1) through (4).

These exceptions make it clear that the DTPA will still be applicable to claims against professionals where the professional has made false representations of fact. For instance, in *Latham v. Castillo*, 972 S.W.2d 66 (Tex. 1998) (decided under pre-1995 DTPA), the defendant attorney was accused of misrepresenting the fact that he had filed suit for the plaintiffs when in fact he had not. The professional services exemption would not prevent the consumers from maintaining that suit for misrepresenting a material fact or for an unconscionable action or course of action. Even so, Texas courts disfavor the fracturing of professional malpractice claims into other causes of action. Care must distinguish a misrepresentation claim from a mere professional negligence claim.

The professional services exemption from DTPA liability is an affirmative defense that must be pleaded and proven by the defendant. *Finger v. Ray*, 326 S.W.3d 285, 298 (Tex. App.—Houston [1st Dist.] 2010, no pet.).

§1.02.7.3.2 Personal Injury Claims

Prior to the 1995 amendments to the DTPA, consumers could use the DTPA to recover all of their personal injury damages caused by a DTPA violation along with attorney's fees and perhaps treble damages. After the 1995 amendments, DTPA §17.49(e) now provides that "[e]xcept as provided Subsections (b) and (h), Section 17.50, nothing [in the DTPA] shall apply to a cause of action for bodily injury, death or infliction of mental anguish." The obvious intent and effect was to limit the applicability of the DTPA in personal injury claims.

Even so, the two exceptions given still allow a consumer a certain amount of relief under the DTPA. The personal injury exemption does not preclude relief under §17.50(b), which provides for recovery of *economic* damages and, in appropriate circumstances, compensation for mental anguish and treble damages. Lost wages and medical expenses are examples of "economic damages" still recoverable under the DTPA, despite the 1995 amendments to §17.49. *See* §1.02.14.1, *infra*. If the consumer shows that the defendant's conduct was committed "knowingly" or "intentionally," the consumer will also be able to recover mental anguish damages under the DTPA §17.50(b). See §1.02.14.2, *infra*.

A second exception to the personal injury exemption is for tie-in statute violations. *See* §1.02.12, *infra*. DTPA §17.50(h) still provides for recovery of all *actual* damages for a violation a tie-in statute that would include compensation for any personal injuries sustained as a result.

PRACTICE POINT:

While the "personal injury" exemption prevents the recovery of attorney's fees for a tort-based personal injury claim, the existence of other economic damages and the reduced "producing cause" standard of causation (see §1.02.13) may warrant using the DTPA for claims where a straight tort theory may not be enough to provide the consumer with a strong cause of action.

Example: Tom's house catches on fire because the air conditioning repairman incorrectly installed his new condenser unit. Tom trips and falls as he runs to escape the fire and is injured. Tom can still bring a breach of implied warranty claim through the DTPA against the air conditioning repair shop to recover the medical expenses incurred by Tom and his lost earnings while he is off of work. If the breach of implied warranty is found to have been committed knowingly, he may recover mental anguish damages as well. While a negligence claim may also lie against the repairman, the lower "producing cause" standard may make it easier to establish legal causation of Tom's personal injuries which were not directly caused by the fire.

§1.02.7.3.3 Large Transactions Exemptions

DTPA §17.49(f), another 1995 addition, provides an exemption for claims arising out of certain contracts exceeding $100,000 in consideration to be paid by the consumer. The exemption is substantially limited, however, by the requirement that the consumer be represented by legal counsel who has not been hired or referred by the defendant. Transactions involving the consumer's residence are also not included in the exemption.

DTPA §17.49(g) exempts from DTPA coverage consumer transactions involving more than $500,000 in consideration, regardless of whether the consumer is represented by legal counsel. Again, transactions involving the consumer's residence are not included in the exemption.

The purpose behind these two "large transaction" exemptions appears to be to deny DTPA remedies to more affluent consumers, presumably because they have more access to legal counsel and other sources of advice and information about the proposed transaction, and are less likely to be misled into an unfavorable bargain. These amendments were added in 1995 and the threshold amounts—$100,000 and $500,000—have not changed since then. Thus, price inflation will continue to increase the effect of this exemption in the future.

§1.02.7.4 Preemption

The attempts to assert some form of preemption of the DTPA by virtue of heavy state or federal involvement with the defendant's line of business have been generally unsuccessful. *See, e.g., Brown v. American Transfer & Storage Co.*, 601 S.W.2d 931 (Tex. 1980)

(Carmack amendment's limitations on claims for damages for goods shipped in interstate commerce held not to always apply); *Riverside Nat'l Bank v. Lewis*, 603 S.W.2d 169 (Tex. 1980) (federal laws providing for regulation of unfair and deceptive trade practices by banks do not preempt DTPA); *Southwestern Bell Tel. Co. v. Von Nash*, 586 S.W.2d 647 (Tex. App.—Austin 1979, writ ref'd n.r.e.) (state regulated telephone utility not exempt); *Frizzell v. Cook*, 790 S.W.2d 41 (Tex. App.—San Antonio 1990, writ denied) (Texas Securities Act does not preempt a consumer's DTPA claim for misrepresentations related to investment and counseling services); *Boales v. Brighton Builders, Inc.*, 29 S.W.3d 159 (Tex. App.—Houston [14th Dist.] 2000, no pet.) (Water Code does not preempt a claim that a utility district misrepresented facts that induced homeowners to purchase homes within the district.)

The preemption argument has had mixed results in the area of mobile home litigation. On the federal level, mobile home construction and safety standards are regulated by the National Manufactured Home Construction and Safety Act, 42 U.S.C. §5401 *et seq. MacMillan v. Redman Homes, Inc.*, 818 S.W.2d 87 (Tex. App.—San Antonio 1991, writ denied), held that a products liability action which sought to impose liability for unreasonably dangerous levels of formaldehyde in a mobile home's ambient air conflicted directly with federal regulations on the subject; therefore, the state action was barred. In *Redman Homes v. Ivy*, 920 S.W.2d 664, 666-667 (Tex. 1996), while recognizing the correctness of the *MacMillan* decision, the Texas Supreme Court held that the plaintiff's breach of warranty and deceptive trade practices claims were not preempted by federal law because they did not contend that *Redman* should have adhered to a construction or safety standard that was higher than or different from what the federal statute imposes.

The Texas Supreme Court has held that the Employee Retirement Income Security Act of 1974 (ERISA), 29 U.S.C.A. §§1001-1461 (1985) preempts DTPA and Article 21.21 claims for unfair settlement practices in connection with insurance issued pursuant to an employee benefit plan. *Cathey v. Metropolitan Life Ins. Co.*, 805 S.W.2d 387 (Tex. 1991); *see also Gorman v. Life Ins. Co. of No. Am.*, 811 S.W.2d 542 (Tex. 1991); *Pan Am. Life Ins. Co. v. Erbauer Constr. Co.*, 805 S.W.2d 395 (Tex. 1991); *Forbau v. Aetna Life Ins. Co.*, 876 S.W.2d 132 (Tex. 1994).

Further, the Texas Supreme Court has held that the Federal Arbitration Act preempts application of the "no-waiver" provision in DTPA §17.42. *Jack B. Anglin Company, Inc. v. Tipps*, 842 S.W.2d 266 (Tex. 1992); *see also Capital Income Properties—LXXX v. Blackmon*, 843 S.W.2d 22 (Tex. 1992). In *Abbott Lab. (Ross Lab. Div.) v. Segura*, 907 S.W.2d 503 (Tex. 1995), the court held that the bar to indirect purchaser recovery under the Texas Free Enterprise and Antitrust Act also bars indirect purchasers from recovering under the DTPA for conduct which involves alleged violations of the Antitrust Act. In *Worthy v. Collagen Corp.*, 967 S.W.2d 360 (Tex. 1998), the court held that a DTPA action against the manufacturer for damages resulting from a class III medical device with pre-marketing approval from the FDA was preempted by the Food, Drug and Cosmetic Act. However, the FDCA did not oust state courts of jurisdiction over claims involving certain non-prescription drugs. *Mills v. Warner Lambert Co.*, 157 S.W.3d 424 (Tex. 2005). In *Epps v. Ayer*, 859 S.W.2d 107 (Tex. App.—Eastland 1993, writ denied), the court held that the Texas Smoke Detector Statute preempts the DTPA.

§1.02.7.5 Real Estate Agents and Brokers

It has long been the law that a real estate broker is liable for false representations of fact under the DTPA. *Cameron v. Terrell & Garrett, Inc.*, 618 S.W.2d 535 (Tex. 1981). In *Cameron*, a real estate broker was held liable for misrepresenting the number of square feet in a house. In 2011, the DTPA was amended to provide a partial exemption for licensed real estate brokers and agents. *See* §13.02.5 *infra*. Although the exemption may affect causes of action based on a broker's "advice, judgment, opinion or similar professional skill," it does not reduce a broker's or agent's liability for making false representations of fact or failing to disclose material facts known to him or her. DTPA §17.49(i)(1)-(3).

§1.02.8 False, Misleading or, Deceptive Acts or Practices

The first cause of action created by §17.50 is for false, misleading or deceptive acts or practices as enumerated in §17.46(b). The list of 32 acts and practices deemed "false, misleading or deceptive" is referred to as "the laundry list." Of these 32 acts and practices contained in the laundry list, subsection (5) (misrepresenting the characteristics, uses or benefits of a good or service), subsection (7) (misrepresenting the standard, quality or grade of good or service), subsection (12) (misrepresenting the terms of a written agreement), and subsection (24) (failing to disclose known information) are the most commonly used in most DTPA cases.

The party asserting the DTPA claim must prove that the false, misleading or deceptive act or practice was, "relied on by a consumer to the consumer's detriment." DTPA §17.50(1)(B).

Historically, the Texas Supreme Court has declined invitations to construe the laundry list narrowly. *Pennington v. Singleton*, 606 S.W.2d 682 (Tex. 1980). *See also Smith v. Baldwin*, 611 S.W.2d 611 (Tex. 1980) in which the Court held that §17.46(b)(7) applies not only to existing goods or services but to representations concerning goods or services not yet in existence.

In *Pennington v. Singleton*, 606 S.W.2d 682, 687 (Tex. 1980) the Court noted that "[m]isrepresentations, so long as they are of a material fact and not merely 'puffing' or opinion, are nevertheless actionable even though they are broad descriptions . . . ." Although dicta, this statement has ripened into a recognized limitation on laundry list claims involving misrepresentations. *See Helena Chemical Co. v. Wilkins*, 47 S.W.3d 486 (Tex. 2001) (noting that the puffing defense has not been extended to non-disclosure or unconscionable conduct). For example, in *Douglas v. Delp*, 987 S.W.2d 879 (Tex. 1999), the Court held that a lawyer's representation that an agreement presented for signature by his client would protect that client's interest was "too vague under the facts of this case to support DTPA liability" and was at most "nonactionable opinion." *Id.* at 886. *See also Bradford v. Vento*, 48 S.W.3d (Tex. 2001) (holding that a representation was too vague to be actionable but not mentioning the word "puffing"). The puffing defense is discussed further at §2.02 *infra*.

Although several laundry list items incorporate a scienter requirement, most do not. The Texas Supreme Court has repeatedly held that it is improper to impose a knowledge or intent requirement as a basis for liability under §17.46(b) where it does not otherwise exist. *See Miller v. Keyser*, 90 S.W.3d 712 (Tex. 2002); *Eagle Properties, Ltd. v. Scharbauer*, 807 S.W.2d 714 (Tex. 1990); *Weit-*

zel v. Barnes, 691 S.W.2d 598 (Tex. 1985); *Pennington v. Singleton*, 606 S.W.2d 682 (Tex. 1980); *Smith v. Baldwin*, 611 S.W.2d 611 (Tex. 1980). When the consumer invokes a laundry list provision containing an intent requirement, then that element must be proved. *See, e.g., Doe v. Boys Clubs*, 907 S.W.2d 472 (Tex. 1995) (discussing DTPA §17.46(b)(23), now (24)); *Willowbrook Foods, Inc. v. Grinnell Corp.*, 147 S.W.3d 492 (Tex. App.—San Antonio 2004, no pet.).

Several of the laundry list items expressly refer to "goods," or "services." The Texas Supreme Court, expanding its earlier decision in *Transport Ins. Co. v. Faircloth*, 898 S.W.2d 269 (Tex. 1995), held that those laundry list subsections are actionable only by consumers. *Crown Life Ins. Co. v. Casteel*, 22 S.W.3d 378 (Tex. 2000). Thus, while consumer status generally is not required to bring an action under Article 21.21 for violations of §17.46(b), misrepresentations of "goods" or "services" are actionable only by consumers. *Id.*

The Texas Supreme Court has held that, in order for a false representation to be actionable, it must be communicated to the consumer; the fact that false representations may have been made "upstream" does not create liability. *Amstadt v. U. S. Brass Corporation*, 919 S.W.2d 644, 649 (Tex. 1996). In *U.S. Brass Corporation*, the plaintiffs were homeowners whose plumbing systems had failed. The manufacturers of the systems made false representations about the systems to local governments and homebuilders, some of whom used the systems in the homes purchased by the plaintiffs. None of the false representations made to third parties were communicated to the plaintiffs. In rejecting liability for the manufacturers under the DTPA, the court held:

> Although the DTPA was designed to supplement common-law causes of action, we are not persuaded that the Legislature intended the DTPA to reach upstream manufacturers and suppliers when their misrepresentations are not communicated to the consumer. Despite its broad, overlapping prohibitions, we must keep in mind why the Legislature created this simple, nontechnical cause of action: to protect consumers in consumer transactions. Consistent with that intent, we hold that the defendant's deceptive conduct must occur in connection with a consumer transaction[.]

Amstadt v. U. S. Brass Corporation, 919 S.W.2d 649.

§1.02.8.1 "Mere Breach of Contract"

The Texas Supreme Court long ago observed that a "mere breach of contract" does not constitute a violation of the DTPA. *La Sara Grain Co. v. First National Bank of Mercedes*, 673 S.W.2d 558, 565 (Tex. 1984); *See, Ashford Development, Inc. v. USLife Real Estate Services*, 661 S.W.2d 933 (Tex. 1983) (allegation of breach of contract did not constitute a deceptive trade practice). However, the Court has never explained exactly when (or why) the mere breach of contract rule applies in DTPA cases. Clearly the rule does not apply to all conduct that breaches a contract since the Court also has held that the breach of a promise to construct a home in accordance with Veterans Administration standards violates the DTPA. *Smith v. Baldwin*, 611 S.W.2d 611 (Tex. 1980).

In *Crawford v. Ace Sign, Inc.*, 917 S.W.2d 12 (Tex. 1996), a business owner met with Crawford, a sales representative of Southwestern Bell Yellow Pages, to discuss payment on the 1988-89 yellow page advertisement and possible renewal for the next year's directory. The Court accepted as true the following facts: Crawford told the owner that if full payment was made "up front" for the 1989-90 year, (a) the business's yellow page advertisement would appear in the directory, and (b) the owner could expect his business to grow at least 70 to 80%. A written contract, containing contractual limitations on liability, was executed and the owner paid the full contract amount in advance. The advertisement did not appear in the directory. The trial court rendered a summary judgment holding that Ace Sign, Inc. could assert only a breach of contract cause of action and that the available remedies were limited by the express language of the contract. The court of appeals reversed, holding that there was a fact issue concerning misrepresentations made by the sales representative. The Texas Supreme Court reversed the court of appeals and held that (1) nonperformance of a contract is not actionable under the DTPA, and (2) a representation by a party that it will fulfill its contractual duty to perform and a subsequent failure to do so does not violate the DTPA. *Crawford v. Ace Sign, Inc., supra*. The Court observed that to permit the representation to be actionable under the DTPA "would convert every breach of contract into a DTPA claim." *Id*. at 14. The Court also reasoned that the sales representative's statements "did not cause any harm. ... The failure to run the advertisement ... actually caused the lost profits." *Id*.

The Court subsequently distinguished *false* pre-contractual misrepresentations of the type at issue in *Crawford* from *fraudulent* misrepresentations that induce the execution of a contract. *See Formosa Plastics Corp. USA v. Presidio Eng'rs & Contrs.*, 960 S.W.2d 41 (Tex. 1998). In *Formosa*, the defendant fraudulently induced the plaintiff to enter into the contract by making promises about a portion of its performance that it had no intention of keeping. The Court held that a claim of fraudulent inducement was a tort, not a simple breach of contract. Importantly, the Court held that the plaintiff could recover tort damages "irrespective of whether the fraudulent representations are later subsumed in a contract or whether the plaintiff only suffers an economic loss related to the subject matter of the contract." *Id*. at 47.

The court rejected the argument that the "mere breach of contract" rule precluded a claim under §(b)(12) because the contractual provision in question was void. The court reversed, holding that the indemnity provision was not void. The court further opined that while the "mere breach of contract" rule would not automatically foreclose a DTPA action where all or part of the contract is void by operation of law, the fact that a portion of the contract is void, standing alone, does not constitute a violation of §(b) (12). The provision prohibits, for example, a representation that the contract confers or involves rights that are prohibited by law. The contractual indemnity provision itself did not constitute such a representation, but was only an agreement to indemnify.

In *Tony Gullo Motors I, L.P. v. Chapa*, 212 S.W.3d 299 (Tex. 2006), the Texas Supreme Court clarified (or perhaps confused, depending on your point of view) the "mere breach of contract" exception to DTPA coverage. There, Ms. Chapa sued her car dealer for fraud, breach of contract and DTPA violations when the salesman represented she was buying and would receive a Toyota Highlander "Limited" model, when in fact she was delivered a base model worth significantly less. *Id*. at 305. The court found her complaint fell outside of the "mere breach of contract" restriction because she alleged, like the plaintiff in *Formosa Plastics, supra*, that the defendant dealership *never intended* to deliver a Highlander Limited model as represented. As in *Formosa Plastics, supra*, the court held that, in such instances, the plaintiff can maintain a fraudulent inducement claim outside of and in addition to her breach of contract claim. *Id*. at 304-5. The court went on to say that the initial misrepresentation as to the intent to deliver the Highlander Limited model was actionable under the DTPA:

> Similarly, while the failure to deliver a Highlander Limited would not alone violate the DTPA, [footnote omitted] Chapa's claim was that Gullo Motors represented she would get one model when in fact she was going to get another. While failure to comply would violate only the contract, the initial misrepresentation violates the DTPA. [footnote omitted.]

Id. at 305. This line of cases reflects that there is no bright-line rule governing every conceivable situation. However, two guidelines seem to emerge for the application of the "mere breach of contract" rule:

1. False representations, promises or warranties pertaining to a past, present, or future fact or state of affairs, whether made prior or subsequent to the contract or incorporated into the contract, potentially are actionable under the DTPA. *See, e.g. Pennington v. Singleton*, 606 S.W.2d 602 (Tex. 1980) (statement that used boat was in "excellent condition"); *Donwerth v. Preston II Chrysler-Dodge*, 775 S.W.2d 634 (Tex. 1989) (statement that there was nothing wrong with the car's brakes); *Howell Crude Oil Co. v. Donna Refinery*, 928 S.W.2d 100, 109 (Tex. App.—Houston [14th Dist.] 1996, no writ reported) (statement that contract with third party existed when it did not); *Jim Walter Homes, Inc. v. Valencia*, 690 S.W.2d 239 (Tex. 1985), (statement that house would be built in a good and workmanlike manner); *Hurst v. Sears, Roebuck & Co.*, 647 S.W.2d 249 (Tex. 1983) (statement which implicitly promised to comply with governmental standards in installing an air conditioning system); *Royal Globe Ins. Co. v. Bar Consultants*, 577 S.W.2d 688 (Tex. 1979) (statement that insurance policy would cover vandalism); *Southwestern Bell Telephone Co. v. FDP Corp*, 811 S.W.2d 572 (Tex. 1991) (statement that advertisement would be published correctly); *First Title Co. of Waco v. Garrett*, 860 S.W.2d 74 (Tex. 1993) (representation in a title commitment that there were no restrictive covenants); *Smith v. Baldwin, supra* (promise in the contract to build the home in a good and workmanlike manner in accordance with Veterans Administration standards); *Honeywell v. Imperial Condominium Ass'n*, 716 S.W.2d 75 (Tex. App.—Dallas 1986, no writ) (pre-contractual representations about future services incorporated into contract); *Cronin v. Bacon*, 837 S.W.2d 265 (Tex. App.—Fort Worth 1992, writ denied) (representation before and after contract but before final payment had been made that consumer's horse had been bred to identified stallion); *Latham v. Castillo*, 972 S.W.2d 66 (Tex. 1998) (representation by lawyer that lawsuit had been filed within the limitations period when it had not).

2. If the "representation" is nothing more than a contractual obligation or an assurance or promise that the defendant will do that which is promised in the contract, and if the consumer's complaint is only that the defendant failed to do what the contract promised, i.e. a simple non-performance as opposed to defective performance, then the consumer is limited to breach of contract remedies. *Crawford v. Ace Sign, Inc. supra.; Holloway v. Dannenmaier*, 581 S.W.2d 765, 766 (Tex. Civ. App.—Fort Worth 1979, writ dism'd) (failure to return security deposit as promised in the lease); *Rocky Mountain Helicopters v. Lubbock County Hosp. Dist.*, 987 S.W.2d 50 (Tex. 1998) (failure to com-

ply with an indemnification agreement). If, however, the pre-contractual statements were made with the intent to not perform or deliver as promised, the other party may have a common law cause of action for fraud and a cognizable claim under the DTPA. *See Formosa Plastics v. Presidio Engineers*, 960 S.W.2d 41 (Tex. 1998); *Tony Gullo Motors I. L.P. v. Chapa*, 212 S.W.3d 299 (Tex. 2006).

In summary, conduct that constitutes a breach of contract can also qualify as a deceptive trade practice. The fact that the defendant has breached the contract does not preclude a DTPA claim. Actionable misconduct is not laundered clean because that conduct (be it a misrepresentation, broken promise or breach of warranty) also constitutes a breach of contract. Such conduct is more than a "mere breach of contract." But nonperformance under a contract—as opposed to defective performance—is not actionable under the DTPA. And, that nonperformance is not transformed into a deceptive trade practice by the defendant's pre-contractual representation or assurance that it will perform as promised or by its announcement after the contract that it will not.

There are, of course, other post-contractual duties that may apply by virtue of TEX. INS. CODE CHAPTER 541 or when there is a special relationship between the parties.

§1.02.8.2 Implied Representations

A representation may be implied from the circumstances of the transaction. Thus, for example, in *Hurst v. Sears, Roebuck & Co.*, 647 S.W.2d 249 (Tex. 1983) a jury found that the defendant represented that it would secure a city permit to install a cooling system and would get the work inspected by city inspectors. It was undisputed that this was not done. The Texas Supreme Court held that a §17.46(b)(7) violation was established in that by representing that it would obtain a city permit there was an implied representation that the work would be done according to city standards. *Id.* at 252; *see also Douglas v. Delp*, 987 S.W.2d 879 (Tex. 1999) (the Court assumed without deciding that a lawyer's advice to his client to sign a document inferred that the agreement presented for signature would protect that client's interests); *Apple Imports, Inc. v. Koole*, 945 S.W.2d 895 (Tex. App.—Austin 1997, writ den'd.) (dealership impliedly represented it would not sell consumer's trade-in vehicle until new car purchase was completed); *Orkin Exterminating Co., Inc. v. Lesassier*, 688 S.W.2d 651 (Tex. App.—Beaumont 1985, no writ); *RRTM Restaurant Corp. v. Keeping*, 766 S.W.2d 804 (Tex. App.—Dallas 1988, writ den'd).

§1.02.8.3 Parol Evidence Rule Inapplicable

The parol evidence rule does not prevent proof of an oral representation as to the quality of goods even when a written contract gives the buyer the right to inspect those goods. *Weitzel v. Barnes*, 691 S.W.2d 598 (Tex. 1985). *See Alvarado v. Bolton*, 749 S.W.2ds 47 (Tex. 1988).

§1.02.9 Breach of Warranty

The DTPA does not create warranties. *La Sara Grain v. First Nat'l Bank of Mercedes*, 673 S.W.2d 558 (Tex. 1984). Purchasers must look outside the DTPA for law establishing a warranty. Section 17.50(a)(2) does, however, permit consumers with a cause of action for breach of warranty to assert that claim under the DTPA. Not all breach of warranty claims are actionable under the DTPA. The plaintiff must still qualify as a consumer and the breach of warranty claim must arise in connection with the plaintiff's transaction in the goods or services at issue. *Amstadt v. U.S. Brass Corp.*, 919 S.W.2d 644, 649 (Tex. 1996).

The concept of "warranty" has always been defined broadly, so broadly that it is frequently lamented: "to say warranty is to say nothing definite as to legal effect." *La Sara Grain v. First Nat'l. Bank of Mercedes*, 673 S.W.2d 558, 565 (Tex. 1984) (*quoting* K. LLEWELYN, CASES AND MATERIAL ON THE LAW OF SALES 211 (1930). A typical definition of warranty is set forth in *Detroit Automatic Scale Co. v. G.B.R. Smith Milling Co.*, 217 S.W. 198, 199 (Tex. Civ. App.—Dallas 1919, no writ): "'Warranty' is said to be an express or implied agreement by which the seller undertakes to vouch for the title, quality or condition of the thing sold [citation omitted]. Warranties usually go to the qualities, quantity, capacity, condition (or) fitness of property for the purposes for which it is sold."

There are at least eight types of warranties that may arise in DTPA cases which, if breached, are actionable under DTPA §17.50(a)(2):

(a) Implied warranty of merchantability of goods. TEX. BUS. & COM. CODE §2.314 (sale), §2A.212 (lease).

(b) Implied warranty of fitness of goods for a particular purpose. TEX. BUS. & COM. CODE §2.314 (sale); §2A.213 (lease).

(c) Implied warranty of good and workmanlike performance of services. *Melody Home Manufacturing Co. v. Barnes*, 741 S.W.2d 349 (Tex. 1987); *Thrall v. Renno*, 695 S.W.2d 84, 87 (Tex. App.—San Antonio 1985, writ ref'd n.r.e.).

(d) Implied warranties of habitability and workmanship with respect to new home construction. *Humber v. Morton*, 426 S.W.2d 554 (Tex. 1968); *Gupta v. Ritter Homes, Inc.*, 646 S.W.2d 168 (Tex. 1983).

(e) Implied warranty that real estate development services will be performed in a good and workmanlike manner. *Luker v. Arnold*, 843 S.W.2d 108 (Tex. App.—Fort Worth 1992, no writ); *but see Parkway Co. v. Woodruff* 901 S.W.2d 434 (Tex. 1995).

(f) Implied warranty of suitability of commercial lease space. *Davidow v. Inwood North Professional Group — Phase I*, 747 S.W.2d 373 (Tex. 1988).

(g) Implied warranty of title of goods. TEX BUS. & COM. CODE §2.312.

(h) Express warranty on goods (TEX BUS. & COM. CODE §2.313) and services. *Woods v. Littleton*, 554 S.W.2d 662 (Tex. 1977).

§1.02.9.1 Express Warranties

A seller of real property or a provider of services may extend express warranties in the same manner as a vendor of goods. Thus, any representation of fact or promise as to the title, quality, or condition of existing or future goods or services will constitute an express warranty. *See McCrea v. Cubilla Condominium Corp.*, 685 S.W.2d 755, 757 (Tex. App.—Hous. [1st Dist.] 1985, writ ref'd n.r.e.); c.f. *Harroll v. McDuffie*, 128 S.W. 1149, 1151 (Tex. Civ. App. 1910, no writ); TEX BUS. & COM. CODE §2.313 (Tex. UCC). It is not necessary that any particular words such as "warrant" or "guarantee" be used, and a specific intent to create a warranty is unnecessary; pure expressions of the seller's opinion, however, will generally not suffice. *See* TEX BUS. & COM. CODE §2.313; *Harroll v.*

McDuffie, supra; Ellis v. Riddick, 78 S.W. 719, 722 (Tex. Civ. App. 1904, no writ). When the seller has superior knowledge about the object of the sale, the courts will narrowly construe the "opinion exception" to the warranty rule. *See United States Pipe and Foundry Co. v. Waco*, 108 S.W.2d 432, 435-37 (Tex. 1937) cert. den. 302 US 749; *Valley Datsun v. Martinez*, 578 S.W.2d 485 (Tex. Civ. App.—Corpus Christi 1979, no writ) (holding the "slightest divergence from mere praise" to qualify as a warranty when the seller has superior knowledge).

A distinction has been drawn between delivery of products or services which do not conform to the representations or promises made about them and the complete failure to deliver the product. The former is a breach of warranty while the latter is a breach of contract. *Southwestern Bell Tel. v. FDP Corp.*, 811 S.W.2d 572 (Tex. 1991); *Donnelley Marketing v. Lionel Sosa, Inc.*, 716 S.W.2d 598 (Tex. App.—Corpus Christi 1986, no writ).

In *Southwestern Bell Tel. v. FDP Corp.*, 811 S.W.2d 572 (Tex. 1991) the court held that a limitation of remedies found in the written advertising contract between the parties governed an express oral warranty and did not contravene §17.42 of the DTPA, which prohibits waiver of a consumer's statutory rights. The court went on to hold, however, that such a disclaimer would not be effective against a laundry list violation.

All warranties are not created equal. Certain warranties do not warrant the condition or quality of the goods or service but warrant only a party's future performance in the event the product or service is faulty. Thus, for example, in *Bunting v. Fodor*, 586 S.W.2d 144 (Tex. App.—Houston [1st Dist.] 1979, no writ) the court held that a warranty stating that a "short block" installed in a vehicle was "guaranteed for 90 days or 4,000 miles whichever came first" was not breached by a defect in material or workmanship; in the court's view, the warranty only imposed an obligation to repair any defect. *See PPG Industries v. JMB/Houston Centers*, 146 S.W.3d 79, 96 (Tex. 2004); *Austin Co. v. Vaughn Bldg. Corp.*, 643 S.W.2d 113, 115 (Tex. 1982); *also see Preston v. Sears, Roebuck & Co.*, 573 S.W.2d 560 (Tex. Civ. App.—Texarkana 1978, writ ref'd n.r.e.); *Stewart Title Guar. Co. v. Cheatham*, 764 S.W.2d 315, 318-319 (Tex. App.—Texarkana 1988, writ denied).

The Supreme Court has held that privity of contract is not required in a suit for breach of an *implied* warranty in order to recover purely economic losses. *Nobility Homes, Inc. of Texas, Inc. v. Shivers*, 557 S.W.2d 77, 81 (Tex. 1977); *Garcia v. Texas Instruments, Inc.*, 610 S.W.2d 456, 465 (Tex. 1980). The Supreme Court has not yet spoken on whether privity of contract is required for breach of an express warranty when purely economic losses are involved, and, there is a split among the courts of appeal. *See, e.g., U.S. Tire-Tech, Inc. v. Boeran*, 110 S.W.3d 194, 197-198 (Tex. App.—Houston [1st Dist.] 2003) (adopting the more current view that privity is not required): *Edwards v. Schuh*, 5 S.W.3d 829, 833 (Tex. App.—Austin 1999, no pet.) ("Privity is not required to enforce an express warranty under the DTPA."); *Church & Dwight Co. v. Huey*, 961 S.W.2d 560, 568 (Tex. App.—San Antonio 1997, pet. denied); *Nat'l Bugmobiles, Inc. v. Jobi Prop.*, 773 S.W.2d 616, 622 (Tex. App.—Corpus Christi 1989, writ denied); *Indust-Ri-Chem Lab., Inc. v. Par-Pak Co.*, 602 S.W.2d 282, 287-88 (Tex. Civ. App.—Dallas 1980, no writ). Nevertheless, the concept of privity is alive and well for breach of warranty claims—express or implied—asserted by consumers under the DTPA. *See PPG Industries v. JMB/Houston Centers Limited Partnership*, 146 S.W.3d 79, 89 (Tex. 2004) (observing breach of warranty claim must arise in connection with the plaintiff's transaction in the goods or services at issue).

§1.02.9.2 Implied Warranties

Implied warranties are created as a matter of law in furtherance of the public good. *Melody Home Mfg. Go. v. Barnes*, 741 S.W.2d 349, 353 (Tex. 1987); *La Sara Grain v. First Nat'l Bank of Mercedes*, 673 S.W.2d 558, 565 (Tex. 1984). In this respect, implied warranties differ from express warranties, which reflect the intentions of the parties evidenced by affirmations, promises or the use of models, descriptions or samples. Nonetheless, implied warranties almost always reflect what is in fact intended and expected by the parties in the great majority of transactions. For example, most buyers reasonably expect that a new home is habitable, that new goods are fit for the ordinary purpose for which such goods are used, and that repairs will be or have been done in a good and workmanlike manner. And if a seller or service provider were asked on the date of the agreement (as opposed to the date of the breach), he or she would agree that this is his or her intention and expectation, as well. In short, if express warranties reflect the expressed intentions of the parties, implied warranties reflect the unexpressed intentions of the parties. These intentions are so prevalent and so reasonable that the law assumes their existence and makes it difficult or impossible for them to be disclaimed. Perhaps part of the justification for this view is the assumption that no reasonable buyer in anything but a grossly unequal bargaining situation would agree to receive new goods or services which fail to meet the standards of the marketplace.

§1.02.9.2.1 New Home Construction

In *Humber v. Morton*, 426 S.W.2d 554, 555 (Tex. 1968), the Texas Supreme Court rejected and discredited the common law doctrine of *caveat emptor* and recognized two implied warranties in the sale of a new house: (1) the house was constructed in a good and workmanlike manner, and (2) was suitable for human habitation. *See also Evans v. J. Stiles, Inc.*, 689 S.W.2d 399 (Tex. 1985). The *Humber* warranties implied into the sale of new homes were superseded by the Residential Construction Commission Act between 2005 and 2010. After that law was repealed by sunset, the *Humber* implied warranties reemerged. *See* §12.03, *infra*, for a thorough discussion of the *Humber* warranties.

§1.02.9.2.2 Commercial Leasing/ Construction

In *Davidow v. Inwood North Prof'l Group— Phase I,* 747 S.W.2d 373 (Tex. 1988), the implied warranty of suitability was extended to leases of commercial property. The Court held that there is an implied warranty that the leased commercial premises are suitable for the intended purpose. *Id.* at 377. The Court made two additional significant holdings: (1) that the tenant's obligation to pay rent and the landlord's obligation under the implied warranty are mutually dependent, i.e. the landlord's breach of warranty justifies non-payment of rent, and (2) that if the landlord and tenant expressly agree that the tenant will be responsible for certain defects, that agreement will control. In *Gym-N-I Playgrounds, Inc. v. Snider*, 220 S.W.3d 905, 912 (Tex. 2007), the Court held that the implied warranty of suitability can be waived by the tenant in the lease. There, the lease conspicuously stated that the tenant accepted the leased premises "as is" and that the landlord "has not made and does not make any representations as to the commercial suitability" and makes no warranties, express or implied, including the warranty of suitability.

§1.02.9.2.3 Implied Warranty for Services

In 1987, the Supreme Court held that an implied warranty of good and workmanlike performance arises in consumer transactions involving the repair or modification of existing goods. *Melody Home Manufacturing Co. v. Barnes*, 741 S.W.2d 355, 354 (Tex. 1987). *Melody Home* involved a mobile home which was built poorly. The defects were of such a nature that the buyers could have sued under the *Humber* warranties. *Melody Home Manufacturing Co. v. Barnes*, 741 S.W.2d 352. Instead of suing immediately, however, the buyers elected to request that the manufacturer make the necessary repairs. The repair work was done poorly, as well, and resulted in even more damage to the home.

In addition to recognizing an implied warranty in repair transactions, the court further held that the implied warranty could not be waived. The court wrote:

> When disclaimers are permitted, adhesion contracts—standardized contract forms offered to consumers of goods and services on an essentially "take it or leave it" basis which limit the duties and liabilities of the stronger party—become commonplace. [Citations omitted.] The consumer continues to expect that the service will be performed in a good and workmanlike manner regardless of the small print in the contract. A disclaimer allows the service provider to circumvent this expectation and encourages shoddy workmanship. To the extent that it conflicts with this opinion, we overrule *G-W-L, Inc. v. Robichaux*, 643 S.W.2d 392.

Melody Home Manufacturing Co. v. Barnes, 741 S.W.2d 355. Although *Robichaux* dealt with the *Humber* implied warranties, and *Melody Home* involved a newly recognized implied warranty on service transactions, the meaning of the last sentence in the quoted language appears clear: The *Humber* implied warranties may not be waived as previously permitted by *Robichaux*.

Even so, the court modified this holding to allow written warranty provisions to *supersede* the implied warranty remedy if "the parties' agreement sufficiently describes the manner, performance or quality" of the services. *Gonzales v. Southwest Olshan Found. Repair Co., LLC*, 400 S.W.3d 52, 56 (Tex. 2013) (foundation repair company's written warranty promised lifetime adjustments and all work to be performed in a good and workmanlike manner). In either instance, the consumer is provided with a remedy enforceable through the DTPA for non-conforming services. *Id.*

What is the "good and workmanlike" standard? The courts have recognized that there is no real difference between the "good and workmanlike" standard and the "negligence" standard. *Coulson v. Lake L.B.J. Mun. Util. Dist.*, 734 S.W.2d 649, 651 (Tex. 1987); See *Archibald v. Act III Arabians*, 755 S.W.2d 84, 86 (Tex. 1988) (Wallace, J. concurring). The *Melody Home* warranty focuses on performance and thus is not a "classic" warranty, which focuses on results. The one obvious difference between a breach of warranty claim under the DTPA and a common law negligence claim is causation; producing cause applies to the former and proximate cause to the latter. See *Archibald v. Act III Arabians, supra*.

§1.02.9.2.4 No Implied Warranty Recognized

The Texas Supreme Court has indicated that implied warranties in service transactions will not be created "in the absence of a demonstrated, compelling need," that is, when other adequate remedies are unavailable to the consumer. *Rocky Mountain Helicopters, Inc. v. Lubbock County Hosp. Dist.*, 987 S.W.2d 50 (Tex. 1998) (refusing to recognize an implied warranty that services incidental to helicopter maintenance will be performed in a good and workmanlike manner). On this basis, the Court has refused to acknowledge an implied warranty that professional services will be rendered in a good and workmanlike manner. *Dennis v. Allison*, 698 S.W.2d 94 (Tex. 1985); *Murphy v. Campbell*, 964 S.W.2d 265 (Tex. 1997) (holding that there is no warranty implied in accounting services and expressing agreement with the statement that "Texas law does not recognize a cause of action for breach of an implied warranty of professional services").

There are several areas where the courts have refused to imply the existence of a warranty. These transactions include: the sale of a used house by a non-builder, *Gupta v. Ritter Homes, Inc.*, 646 S.W.2d 168, 169 (Tex. 1983); a patient physically abused by her psychiatrist, *Dennis v. Allison*, 698 S.W.2d 94, 96 (Tex. 1985); property purchased at a foreclosure sale, *Diversified, Inc. v. Gibraltar Sav. Asso.*, 762 S.W.2d 620, 622 (Tex. App.—Houston [14th Dist.] 1988, no writ); *Diversified, Inc. v. Walker*, 702 S.W.2d 717, 723 (Tex. App.—Houston [1st Dist.] 1985, writ ref'd n.r.e.); a bank's handling of a checking account, *La Sara Grain v. First Nat'l. Bank of Mercedes*, 673 S.W. 2d 558, 565 (Tex. 1984); future development of a subdivision by a real estate developer, *Parkway Co. v. Woodruff*, 901 S.W.2d 434 (Tex. 1995); accounting services, *Murphy v. Campbell*, 964 S.W.2d 265 (Tex. 1997); and installation and maintenance of alarm system, *Arthur's Garage v. Racal-Chubb Sec.*, 997 S.W.2d 803 (Tex. App.—Dallas 1999, no writ) (dicta).

§1.02.10 Unconscionability

The DTPA provides a cause of action for "any unconscionable action or course of action by any person." DTPA §17.50(a)(3). Before the 1995 amendments were enacted, this phrase meant an act or practice which to a person's detriment, (1) takes advantage of the lack of knowledge, ability, experience or capacity of a person to a grossly unfair degree; or (2) results in a gross disparity between the value received and the consideration paid, in a transaction involving the transfer of consideration. In 1995, the DTPA's provision on unconscionability was amended to delete the second part of the definition dealing with gross disparities in value.

An "unconscionable action or course of action" includes all manner of actions and inactions. Misrepresentations may form the basis for the unconscionability. *See, e.g., Latham v. Castillo*, 972 S.W.2d 66 (Tex. 1998) (representation by a lawyer to client that client's lawsuit had been filed within limitations when it had not); *Rendon v. Sanchez*, 737 S.W.2d 122 (Tex. App.—San Antonio 1987, no writ) (exaggeration of the profitability of a business); *Brown v. Galleria Area Ford, Inc.*, 752 S.W.2d 114, 116 (Tex. 1988) (misleading representation of ownership of dealership). Unconscionability may exist even without specific misrepresentations. *See, e.g., Bennett v. Bailey*, 597 S.W.2d 532 (Tex. Civ. App.—Eastland 1980, writ ref'd n.r.e.) (persuading lonely widow to buy $29,000 worth of dance lessons). The most common example of this latter type of unconscionability is a transaction involving a "gross disparity" between the price paid and consideration received. *See Kinerd v. Colonial Leasing Co.*, 800 S.W.2d 187 (Tex. 1990). A failure to act, such as a failure to return a down payment can be unconscionable. *See, e.g., R.S. Assoc. Gen. Bldg. Contractors v. Devona*, 610 S.W.2d 190 (Tex. Civ. App.—Houston [1st Dist.]

1980, writ ref'd n.r.e.). A defendant's failure to disclose material information can also form the basis for an unconscionability claim. *See, e.g., Aetna Casualty & Surety. Co. v. Martin Surgical Supply Co.*, 689 S.W.2d 263 (Tex. App.—Houston [1st Dist.] 1985, writ ref'd n.r.e.); *Nationwide Mut. Ins. Co. v. Holmes*, 842 S.W.2d 335 (Tex. App.—San Antonio, 1992, writ denied).

It is unclear whether the unconscionable conduct must occur contemporaneously with the sale to be actionable. *Compare Flenniken v. Longview Bank & Trust Co.*, 661 S.W.2d 705 (Tex. 1993) (no) *with Parkway Co. v. Woodruff*, 901 S.W.2d 434 (Tex. 1995) (yes). *See also Chastain v. Koonce*, 700 S.W.2d 579 (Tex. 1995); *cf., Latham v. Castillo*, 972 S.W.2d 66 (Tex. 1998) (misrepresentation during course of attorney client relationship); *Trinity Universal Ins. Co. v. Bleeker*, 966 S.W.2d 489 (Tex. 1998) (lawyer's failure to disclose settlement offer to client could not be basis of unconscionability action where there was no evidence that offer would have been accepted and, therefore, no evidence of producing cause).

In *Chastain v. Koonce*, 700 S.W.2d 579 (Tex. 1985) the Supreme Court addressed the meaning of the term "grossly unfair," and held that the term "gross" should be given its "ordinary meaning of glaringly noticeable, flagrant, complete and unmitigated." *Id.* at 584; *accord, State Farm Lloyds v. Nicolau*, 951 S.W.2d 444 (1997); *Brown v. Galleria Area Ford, Inc.*, 752 S.W.2d 114, 116 (Tex. 1988); *see also Williams v. Trail Dust Steak House, Inc.*, 727 S.W.2d 812 (Tex. App.—Fort Worth 1987, no writ) (holding that a finding of unconscionability should not be conditioned upon proof that the defendant acted with knowledge, *citing Chastain v. Koonce*); *Miller v. Soliz*, 648 S.W.2d 734, 738 (Tex. Civ. App.—Corpus Christi 1983, no writ) (intent is not an element of §17.50(b)(3)).

Prior to the 1995 amendments, it was only necessary to produce evidence under *either* definition of §17.45(5) to establish the existence of an unconscionable action. DTPA §17.45(5); *Kennemore v. Bennett*, 755 S.W.2d 89 (Tex. 1988). After the 1995 amendments, gross disparities between price and value are not actionable under the DTPA except when there is price gouging during a natural disaster. *See* DTPA §17.45(5), §17.46(b)(25), as amended 1995.

§1.02.11 Chapter 541 of Texas Insurance Code

The DTPA provides a consumer a cause of action for a violation of Chapter 541 of the Texas Insurance Code. DTPA §17.50(a)(4). Chapter 541, Subchapter B, prohibits a wide range of false advertising and unfair methods of competition in the sale of insurance, including misrepresenting the terms and benefits available under an insurance policy and using unfair and deceptive tactics in the handling of insurance claims. Because Chapter 541 provides its own private cause of action, a DTPA consumer can maintain suit under both the DTPA and Chapter 541 and then elect the remedy which provides the best recovery.

The contours of Chapter 541 are discussed in detail in Chapter 11, *infra*.

§1.02.12 Other Statutory Causes of Action—Tie-in Statutes

Statutory reference: DTPA §17.50(h), as amended 1995, reads:

Notwithstanding any other provision of this subchapter, if a claimant is granted the right to bring a cause of action under this subchapter by another law, the claimant is not limited to the recovery of economic damages only, but may recover any actual damages incurred by the claimant, without regard to whether the conduct of the defendant was committed intentionally. For the purpose of the recovery of damages for a cause of action described by this subsection only, a reference in this subchapter to economic damages means actual damages. In applying Subsection (b)(1) to an award of damages under this subsection, the trier of fact is authorized to award a total of not more than three times actual damages, in accordance with this subsection.

A number of statutes, often called "tie-in statutes," provide that violations of the statutes are actionable under the DTPA. These statutes typically deal with special types of transactions (*e.g.* the purchase of a mobile home or a timeshare) and declare specific types of conduct in those transactions illegal. By making a violation of these statutes a violation of the DTPA, the legislature was able to create certain uniformity to consumer litigation in Texas. In several of these statutes, *e.g.* the Debt Collection Practices Act, the types of damages that a claimant would be expected to suffer generally do not fit within the restrictive definition of "economic damages" now in the DTPA. *See* DTPA §17.50(b)(1), *as amended* 1995. For example, the most significant element of damages that a person who is hounded illegally by a debt collector would be expected to suffer is mental anguish. As amended, the DTPA would allow a recovery of mental anguish damages only if the unlawful conduct was committed "knowingly." DTPA §17.50(b)(1), as amended 1995. Without the exception provided by §17.50(h), many of these special statutes would have been rendered less effective, a result which the legislature did not intend. The exception in §17.50(h) is intended to preserve the viability of the statutes that historically have used the DTPA as the remedy for violation.

The following statutes specifically reference the Deceptive Trade Practices—Consumer Protection Act so that a victim of conduct prohibited by these statutes can use the remedies under the DTPA. In some cases, the statute itself provides a private cause of action for damages, injunctive relief or attorney's fees. Even if the statute provides its own remedy, a claimant bringing a cause of action under one of these statutes can plead the violation as a violation of the DTPA and thereby avoid the restrictions on recovery of actual damages incorporated in the 1995 DTPA amendments.

The summaries of the statutes following the table are intended to give a general idea of their coverage, prohibitions and requirements. The reader is cautioned to consult each statute to determine its applicability.

Statute	Citation
Beach Property Disclosure	Tex. Nat. Res. Code §61.025
Business Opportunity Act	Tex. Bus. & Com. Code Chapter 51
Cigarette Stamps and Tax	Tex. Tax Code §154.4095
Contest and Gift Giveaway Act	Tex. Bus. & Com. Code Chapter 621
Credit Reporting Agencies	Tex. Bus. & Com. Code Chapter 20

Statute	Citation
Credit Service Organizations	TEX. FIN. CODE CHAPTER 393
Debt Collection Practices Act	TEX. FIN. CODE CHAPTER 392
Executory Contracts for Sale of Real Estate (Contracts for Deed)	TEX. PROP. CODE CHAPTER 5, SUBCHAPTER D
Health Spa Act	TEX. OCC. CODE CHAPTER 702
Homestead: Sham Sales & Home Improvement Contracts	TEX. PROP. CODE §§41.006 & 41.007
Home Solicitations Act	TEX. BUS. & COM. CODE CHAPTER 601
Identity Theft Enforcement and Prevention Act	TEX. BUS. & COM. CODE CHAPTER 521
Insurance	TEX. INS. CODE CHAPTER 541
Invention Development Services	TEX. BUS. & COM. CODE CHAPTER 52
Lemon Law (New Motor Vehicle Warranties)	TEX. OCC. CODE CHAPTER 2301, SUBCHAPTER M
Manufactured Housing Standards Act	TEX. OCC. CODE CHAPTER 1201
Membership Camping Resort Act	TEX. PROP. CODE CHAPTER 222
Motor Fuel Sales and Delivery	TEX. AG. CODE §17.152
Notary Public Representation as Attorney at Law	TEX. GOV'T CODE §406.017
Optometry Act	TEX. OCC. CODE CHAPTER 351
Personnel Services	TEX. OCC. CODE CHAPTER 2501
Private Post-Secondary Educational Institutions	TEX. ED. CODE CHAPTER 61, SUBCHAPTER G
Private Security Act	TEX. OCC. CODE CHAPTER 1702
Rebate Response Grace Period	TEX. BUS. & COM. CODE CHAPTER 605
Rental-Purchase Agreements	TEX. BUS. & COM. CODE CHAPTER 92
Residential Service Company Act	TEX. OCC. CODE CHAPTER 1303
Self-Service Storage Facility Liens	TEX. PROP. CODE CHAPTER 59
Spam E-Mail Regulation	TEX. BUS. & COM. CODE CHAPTER 321
Speech-Language Pathologists and Audiologists	TEX. OCC. CODE CHAPTER 401
Talent Agency Registration Act	TEX. OCC. CODE CHAPTER 2105
Telephone Solicitation	TEX. BUS. & COM. CODE CHAPTER 302
Timeshare Act	TEX. PROP. CODE CHAPTER 221
Treatment Facilities Marketing Practices Act	TEX. HEALTH & SAFETY CODE CHAPTER 164

Beach Property Disclosure, TEX. NAT. RES. CODE §61.025

Chapter 61 of the Natural Resources Code regulates the use and maintenance of public beaches. Section 61.025 of that Act requires a seller of property located in close proximity to a beach fronting on the Gulf of Mexico to disclose in the sales contract that the public has the right to use an easement over the beach up to the vegetation line. It must further be disclosed that the law prohibits the erection of structures that interfere with the use of the beach. Non-disclosure is grounds for termination of the contract and constitutes a deceptive trade practice.

Business Opportunity Act, TEX. BUS. & COM. CHAPTER 51

"Business Opportunity" is defined to include the sale or lease of goods or services to be used by the purchaser to begin a business. To be a "business opportunity," the seller must represent that the purchaser is likely to earn a profit and that the seller will either assist the purchaser in finding a location, provide a sales, production or marketing program or buy back product, equipment or supplies.

The Act requires that the seller be registered with the secretary of state. Additionally, prior to the sale, a seller must provide the purchaser with an extensive disclosure statement which includes ownership, earnings and financial information. The form of a business opportunity contract are set forth and include the terms of payment, delivery dates for goods, equipment or supplies and a description of the services the seller has undertaken to perform. The Act generally prohibits actions taken to deceive a consumer and more specifically proscribes the misrepresentation or omission of material facts, including undocumented representations concerning earning potential and other statements inconsistent with the required disclosure. Any violation of the Act is actionable under the DTPA. TEX. BUS. & COM. CODE §51.302.

Cigarette Tax and Stamps Regulation, TEX. TAX CODE §154.4095

This statute regulates the taxation of cigarette sales and prohibits the sale of cigarettes that do not comply with the Cigarette Labeling and Advertising Act (15 U.S.C. §§1331 *et seq.*) and other import, export and purity regulations from federal and state law. The sale of a package of cigarettes that does not meet this regulation is a deceptive trade practice.

Contest and Gift Giveaway Act, TEX. BUS. & COM. CHAPTER 621

This statute regulates advertising which utilizes gifts, prizes and drawings as an inducement to attend a sales presentation or make a purchase.

The Act requires that any advertising or promotion offering a gift fully disclose any consideration, charge or expense that the consumer must pay, any item that the consumer must purchase and any sales presentation that the consumer must attend in order to receive the gift. Further, misrepresentation of the characteristics, benefits or quality of the gift, non-disclosure of its retail value, misrepresentation of the gift as a contest prize or other use of the term "gift" in a misleading manner is prohibited.

Notifications that a person has won or will receive or has a chance to receive a prize must disclose any required attendance at a sales presentation and cannot be conditioned on the purchase of a good or service unrelated to the prize or on the payment of any charge or expense except travel expense to or from the sales location or certain refundable deposits.

"Matched contests" whereby winning numbers are preselected, and "drawings" whereby the winner is determined from all entries received are heavily regulated by the Act. Among the requirements are: disclosure of the odds of winning and the retail value of each prize offered, statement of the beginning and ending dates of the contest period and maintenance of a record of the contest including the identity of all contestants and winners. Misrepresentations of the nature, characteristics, quality or value of the prizes and other misleading conduct is prohibited.

A violation of the Act is a deceptive trade practice.

Credit Reporting Agencies, TEX. BUS. & COM. CODE CHAPTER 20

This chapter establishes procedures that a consumer reporting agency must follow in responding to consumer complaints. Similar to the requirements of the Fair Credit Reporting Act, 15 U.S.C. §§1681 *et seq.*, the chapter provides that if the accuracy of information contained in a consumer's file is disputed by the consumer, the consumer reporting agency must reinvestigate the disputed information free of charge and record the current status of the information within 30 business days. If inaccurate or unverifiable information is discovered after a reinvestigation, the agency must promptly delete that information from the file and provide the revised report to the consumer.

In addition, this chapter requires that a credit reporting agency must provide for, on the properly authenticated request from a consumer, a 45-day "security alert" (informing users of the report that the consumer's identity may have been used fraudulently) within 24 hours, and a timely "security freeze" (a refusal to provide the consumer's credit report to a requestor without the consumer's express consent) within five business days. A credit reporting agency must also honor a security freeze placed on a consumer's file by another consumer reporting agency.

This chapter provides its own private cause of action. For a willful violation, an aggrieved consumer may obtain the greater of three times actual damages or $1,000, plus attorney's fees and costs. For a negligent violation, the consumer can obtain the greater of actual damages or $500, plus attorney's fees and costs. TEX. BUS. & COM. CODE §20.09. The violation of any provision in this chapter is a false, misleading or deceptive act or practice actionable under the DTPA. TEX. BUS. & COM. CODE §20.12.

Credit Service Organizations, TEX. FIN. CHAPTER 393

A "credit service organization" means a person who provides advice or assistance to a consumer to improve the consumer's credit history or rating or to obtain an extension of credit for the consumer. There are several exemptions, chief among which are financial institutions, non-profit organizations and real estate brokers. Credit service organizations must be registered and, under some circumstances, must file a surety bond. The statute requires organizations to provide the consumer with written disclosures (including the services to be performed and the consumer's rights to information in the consumer's files) prior to the execution of the contract and prescribes mandatory contract terms (including a statement of the services to be performed, time for performance, total payments to be made by the consumer, and a right to cancel the contract within three days). The statute generally prohibits false and misleading conduct, including misleading guarantees about the likelihood of erasing bad credit or obtaining loans, and additionally proscribes misrepresentations about the consumer's credit worthiness or credit standing. The statute also regulates when and for what the consumer may be charged. An organization's breach of contract constitutes a violation of the statute.

The chapter creates a cause of action for injured consumers and additionally provides that a violation constitutes a deceptive trade practice actionable under the DTPA. TEX. FIN. CODE §393.001.

Debt Collection Practices Act, TEX. FIN. CHAPTER 392 (SEE §1.02.12.1, *infra*)

Under this statute a "debt collector" is any person who directly or indirectly acts to collect or solicits for collection consumer debts or who sells forms or systems to be used in the collection of consumer debts. This definition is broader than the Federal Fair Debt Collection Practices Act (15 U.S.C.A. §1692), which applies only to third-party debt collectors, *i.e.* those who are in the business of collecting debts for others. A consumer debt is a debt arising out a purchase for personal, family or household purposes.

The Act prohibits the use of threats or coercion (including improper threats to have the debtor arrested, harmed, accused of fraud, charged with a crime or otherwise subjected to action prohibited by law) and harassment or abuse (including the use of profane language, failing to disclose the name of the person calling or making repeated or continuous telephone calls). The Act also proscribes unfair conduct (such as the collection of interest, charges or fees not authorized by the agreement or legally chargeable to the consumer) and fraudulent, deceptive or misleading representations (such as using false identities, falsely representing that the collector has information or something of value for the consumer to obtain information, misrepresenting the character, extent or amount of a consumer debt, creating a false impression of government affiliation, falsely representing that a debt will be increased by fees or charges).

The Act also requires Credit Bureaus and third-party debt collectors (including attorneys whose staff regularly solicits debts for collection or makes contact with debtors for the collection of debts) to post a $10,000 bond and provides a mechanism for the retrieval and correction of consumer's information in the credit bureau or third-party debt collector's files.

The Act creates a cause of action for violations of its provisions; available relief includes actual damages, injunctive relief, limited civil penalties and attorney's fees. Additionally, a violation of the Act is a deceptive trade practice actionable under the DTPA. TEX. FIN. CODE §392.404.

Executory Contracts for Sale of Real Estate, TEX. PROP. CODE CHAPTER 5, SUBCHAPTER D

Executory contracts for the sale of real property are transactions where the buyer gets a deed only after full payment has been made. This is distinguished from a transaction where the buyer receives a deed at closing encumbered by a deed of trust pending full payment. This subchapter of the Property Code requires that before a contract is signed, the seller must furnish the buyer with a survey and a copy of any encumbrances. Additionally, the seller must provide a disclosure statement providing information about the property, including whether there is potable water, electrical and sewer service available, whether the property is in the floodplain, who maintains the road and whether back taxes are owed.

Additionally, this subchapter requires that the seller provide the buyer with a tax certificate from each taxing unit that collects ad valorem taxes on the property as well as a legible copy of any insurance policy covering the property prior to signing the contract. TEX. PROP. CODE §5.070. The seller must also provide an annual accounting statement to the buyer each year by January 31. TEX. PROP CODE §5.077.

The seller's failure to provide the required information before executing the contract is declared to be a deceptive trade practice actionable under the DTPA and entitles the purchaser to rescind the contract. TEX. PROP. CODE §5.069.

Health Spa Act, TEX. OCC. CODE CHAPTER 702

A health spa, for purposes of this Act, is a business that sells memberships that entitle members to receive instruction in a program of physical exercise or to use facilities for that purpose. Health spa operators must obtain a certificate of registration and in most circumstances must post security and escrow membership prepayments. The Act sets forth rules concerning contract provisions, contract enforceability, cancellation, refunds, and the liability of holders in due course. Misrepresentation of the staff qualifications, services, facilities, results obtained through fitness programs, membership rights and discounts are prohibited.

The Act creates a cause of action for consumers injured by prohibited practices, as well as an enforcement action by public officials. Additionally, the Act provides that a violation of its provisions constitutes a deceptive trade practice under the DTPA. TEX. OCC. CODE §702.403. The secretary of state is granted rule-making authority to assure compliance with the Act. Those administrative rules may be found at 1 TEX. ADMIN. CODE §102.1.

Homestead: Sham Sales and Home Improvement Contracts, TEX. PROP. CODE §§41.006 & 41.007

Title 5 of the Property Code deals with property exempt from creditors' claims. Efforts to take a homestead as security by structuring the loan to appear to be a sale and lease back of a homestead is prohibited by §41.006 of the Property Code. The taking of a deed in connection with such a transaction is declared to be a deceptive trade practice under the DTPA.

Section 41.001(b)(3) authorizes an encumbrance on a homestead for work and material used to improve the property. Section 41.007 requires that a home improvement contract contain a conspicuous warning to the homeowner that includes the statement that, "[i]f you sign this contract and you fail to meet the terms and conditions of this contract, you may lose your legal ownership rights in your home." The failure to include the required language is a deceptive trade practice under the DTPA.

Home Solicitations Act, TEX. BUS. & COM. CHAPTER 601

Although this statute has been codified under the heading "Cancellation of Certain Consumer Transactions," it is still unofficially referred to as the Home Solicitations Act because it pertains primarily to door-to-door sales. Generally, for a sale to be governed by the statute it must have been personally solicited by the merchant and agreed to by the consumer at a location other than the merchant's place of business. The consumer is given the right to cancel the transaction within three business days of the date of the agreement and the merchant must give the consumer written notice, in a form prescribed by the statute, of the consumer's right to cancel. The statute spells out in some detail the procedure for cancellation and the rights of the parties before and after cancellation.

A violation of the provisions of the statute is a deceptive trade practice under the DTPA. TEX. BUS. & COM. CODE §39.001.

Identity Theft Enforcement and Prevention Act, TEX. BUS. & COM. CODE CHAPTER 521

This Act prohibits a person from obtaining, possessing, transferring, or using personal identifying information of another person without that person's consent and with intent to obtain a good, a service, insurance, an extension of credit, or any other thing of value in that person's name. It also requires businesses to implement and maintain reasonable safeguards to handle records containing sensitive personal information collected in the regular course of business to prevent their public disclosure. It also requires a business that experiences a breach of data security to notify the persons whose personal identifying data was acquired through the breach as soon as possible. The Act provides for enforcement and collection of civil penalties by the Attorney General for its violation, but does not provide for a private cause of action. The Act further provides a mechanism for a victim of identity theft to obtain a sealed court order declaring the person to be a victim of identity theft. The court order can then be used by the victim to request that businesses or governmental agencies correct records or accounts that were affected by the identity theft.

The violation of this Act is a deceptive trade practice actionable under the DTPA TEX. BUS. & COM. CODE §521.152.

Insurance, TEX. INS. CODE CHAPTER 541

As discussed in detail at §1.02.11, *supra*, violations of Insurance Code provisions prohibiting deceptive and unfair practices in the sale of insurance and handling of claims are expressly actionable under the DTPA pursuant to DTPA §17.50 (a)(3).

Invention Development Services, TEX. REV. CIV. STAT. art. 9020

"Invention Development Services" means actions (e.g., evaluation, marketing, promoting, or the pursuit of a patent application) taken by or for an invention developer of a licensee or buyer of an intellectual property right in an invention. An "invention" includes a discovery, design, product or idea, whether patentable or not. Excluded from coverage of the Act are government agencies, non-profit organizations, attorneys and persons whose only fee for the invention development services is a portion of the income received by the consumer of those services.

The Act requires certain disclosures (e.g., the total number of customers of the developer and the number who have received income in excess of the fees paid to the developer), dictates certain contract terms (e.g., a full description of the services, a statement of projected customer earnings and the basis for that projection, and a statement of the time schedule for performance), and provides a three-day cancellation period during which the developer cannot receive money from the consumer. A contract that does not substantially comply with the Act is voidable at the option of the consumer. Developers must be bonded.

The Act creates a cause of action for affected consumers; alternatively, the Act provides that any violation of the Act or failure to make the required disclosures is a deceptive trade practice under the DTPA. TEX. BUS. & COM. CODE §52.153.

Lemon Law (New Car Warranties), TEX. OCC. CODE CHAPTER 2301, SUBCHAPTER M

The statutes governing the sale of motor vehicles in Texas have been recodifiied into the Texas Occupations Code. These regulations generally require automobile dealers to perform the delivery, preparation, and warranty obligations placed on a franchised dealer under the manufacturer's agreements. TEX. OCC. CODE §2301.353. Additionally, these provisions prohibit a dealer from using false, misleading or deceptive advertising and from requiring a purchaser of a new vehicle to purchase equipment or accessories not ordered or desired by the purchaser. TEX. OCC. CODE §2301.352.

Chapter 2301, Subchapter M, popularly referred to as the "Lemon Law," deals with new car warranty obligations. The provisions of this law reinforce the duty of the manufacturer, converter or distributor to make those repairs necessary to conform a vehicle to the manufacturer's new car warranty. The Lemon Law provides that if the responsible party is unable to correct any defect or condition that either creates a serious safety hazard or substantially impairs the use or market value of the motor vehicle after a reasonable number of attempts, the consumer is to be given a comparable replacement vehicle or permitted to return the vehicle and receive a refund of the purchase price (less reasonable allowance for use of the vehicle) and reimbursement of incidental expenses. The Director of the Board of the Texas Department of Motor Vehicles is empowered to order the relief after a hearing and to promulgate administrative rules. TEX. OCC. CODE §2301.602.

Section 2301.607 provides that the provisions of this subchapter are available under the DTPA against a manufacturer, converter or distributor after the consumer has exhausted his administrative remedies but not against a seller (retailer).

The regulations of the Texas Department of Transportation Motor Vehicle Division may be found at 43 TEX. ADMIN. CODE Part 110, Chapter 215, Subchapter G.

For a full discussion of the Texas Lemon Law and other remedies available under the DTPA in the purchase of new and used motor vehicles, see Chapter 14, *New and Used Motor Vehicles.*

Manufactured Housing Standards Act, TEX. OCC. CODE CHAPTER 1201

Manufactured housing is a prefabricated home which, in the past, has been commonly referred to as a mobile home. The Act sets forth comprehensive manufactured housing licensing, training, construction, labeling and installation standards. Sellers of used homes and manufacturers of new homes must give a written warranty of habitability and proper construction, respectively. TEX. OCC. CODE §§1201.455, 1201.351. Additionally, a retailer must give a written warranty that the installation of a new home will be properly done as must an installer for subsequent relocations. TEX. OCC. CODE §§1201.352, 1201.361.

The Act provides for administrative remedies and establishes a recovery fund for consumers. The failure to give the warranties and notices required or the failure to otherwise comply with the Act is a deceptive trade practice under the DTPA. TEX. OCC. CODE §1201.603. The failure to comply with the warranties is likewise actionable; however, the Act sets forth an abatement period during which the home is to be inspected by the state agency and during which the manufacturer, installer or retailer is given an opportunity to perform the service required by the report. TEX. OCC. CODE §1201.602. Administrative provisions promulgated under the Act may be found at 10 TEX. ADMIN. CODE §80.1 *et seq.*

For a full discussion of the Texas Manufactured Housing Act and other remedies available under the DTPA in the purchase of manufactured housing and mobile homes, see Chapter 16, *Manufactured Housing.*

Membership Camping Resort Act, TEX. PROP. CHAPTER 222

A "membership camping resort" is a camping site for which a purchaser receives a membership right to use the camping site and its amenities. This type of site is to be distinguished from a mobile home or recreational trailer park open to the public on a fee for use basis without membership contracts. Camping resort operators and membership brokers must be registered with the Secretary of State. The Act requires extensive disclosure in any advertising promotion (including complete disclosure of promotion rules and that membership in the resort will be solicited) and a separate disclosure statement prior to the contract (including a description of the amenities, membership interest and membership rights). Mandatory contract terms are set forth and a three day cancellation period is required.

The Act declares prohibited conduct to be a deceptive trade practice under the DTPA, including the following: making false or misleading statements concerning camping sites or amenities, predicting specific increases in value of a membership interest without a reasonable basis and making misleading statements concerning a purchaser's right to use other membership camping sites or amenities. TEX. PROP. CODE §222.011.

Motor Fuel Sales and Delivery, Tex. Ag. Code §17.152

This section requires motor fuel dealers and distributors to accurately certify, and service stations and other retailers to accurately post, the motor fuel rating and mixture for gasoline sold to the public and to retain the delivery documents evidencing the purchase. This article gives purchasers who have suffered damages as a result of a violation of its provisions a cause of action and further declares that a violation of these provisions is a deceptive trade practice under the DTPA.

Notary Public Representation as Attorney at Law, TEX. GOV'T CODE §406.017

This section of the statute regulating notary public deals with the concern that Spanish-speaking consumers may confuse a notary public with a lawyer. A notary public who is not an attorney and who advertises his or her services in a language other than English must include statutory language advising consumers that the notary is not an attorney. Failure to comply with the statute is a deceptive trade practice actionable under the DTPA.

Optometry Act, TEX. OCC. CODE CHAPTER 2501

The Act licenses therapeutic optometrists and prohibits those without a license to practice optometry. False and misleading advertising is prohibited. More specifically, advertisements of prescription lenses must disclose that a doctor's prescription is required, and if price is advertised, must indicate whether a doctor's examination is included. Advertisements must also disclose limitations on duration of the offer and quantity of the goods. Manufacturers and sellers of ophthalmic goods are prohibited from attempting to control or influence the professional judgment of an optometrist by, for example, making payments to optometrists for services not actually rendered.

The Act creates a cause of action for those injured by violations of its prohibitions and additionally declares those violations to be actionable under the DTPA. TEX. OCC. CODE §351.604.

Personnel Services, TEX. OCC. CODE CHAPTER 2501

"Personnel Service" means attempting to procure for a fee permanent employment for a person or a permanent employee for a business, including, for example, executive search services, out-placement services, job-listing services, and personnel-consulting services. The owner of a personnel service must obtain a certificate of authority and must file a bond to operate the service. This chapter prohibits owners, operators, employees and agents of a personnel service from a long list of activities, including charging the consumer before an offer of employment has been accepted, splitting fees received from the consumer with the employer, making false promises or misrepresentations, failing to disclose in any advertisement that the ad has been placed by a private personnel service or advertising a position without a job order from the employer. Additionally, the chapter prohibits the employer from making false statements or omissions of fact for the purpose of obtaining employees through a personnel service or splitting fees or payments made to a personnel service.

The chapter creates a cause of action for persons adversely affected by a violation and provides, further, that a violation of the Act is a deceptive trade practice actionable under the DTPA. TEX. OCC. CODE §2501.204. Administrative rules promulgated under the Act may be found at 16 TEX. ADMIN. CODE §63.1.

Private Post-Secondary Educational Institutions, TEX. ED. CODE CHAPTER 61, SUBCHAPTER G

This subchapter of the part of the Education Code governing institutions regulated by the Texas Higher Education Coordinating Board prohibits the offering and advertising of college-credit courses, college degrees and graduate-level courses and degrees from a post-secondary educational institution unless it has obtained a certificate of authority to do so from the Board. A violation of the provisions of this subchapter is a deceptive act or practice actionable under the DTPA. TEX. ED. CODE §61.320.

Private Security Act, TEX. OCC. CODE CHAPTER 1702

The Texas Private Security Act establishes the Texas Private Security Board and sets forth the licensing requirements of private security providers, such as security guards, private guard services, alarm systems vendors, private investigators, locksmiths and armored car operators. The Act prohibits a person from providing or offering to provide such services to the public without a license and prohibits the employment of an unlicensed person to provide such services. A person who performs or offers to perform an activity regulated under this chapter, but who is not licensed or otherwise authorized under this chapter to perform the activity, commits a false, misleading, or deceptive act or practice actionable under the DTPA. TEX. OCC. CODE §1702.3835.

Rebate Response Grace Period, TEX. BUS. & COM. CODE CHAPTER 605

This chapter requires manufacturers and retailers offering a rebate to pay the rebate offered within 30 days after receipt of the consumer's submission of the required forms, unless a longer time is specified in the rebate offer. Additionally, this chapter requires that an otherwise qualified rebate consumer who timely but incorrectly submits the rebate documentation must be paid the rebate or given notice and an opportunity to cure the submission within 30 days. Although class actions are prohibited, the chapter provides that a violation of the chapter is a false, misleading or deceptive act actionable under the DTPA. TEX. BUS. & COM. CODE §605.004.

Rental-Purchase Agreements, TEX. BUS. & COM. CODE CHAPTER 92

A "rental-purchase agreement" is one which (1) grants a consumer the use of personal, family or household goods for an initial period of four months or less, (2) is automatically renewable after the initial period and (3) permits the consumer to become the owner of the merchandise. This subchapter of the Code provides for the form and content of the agreement by requiring disclosures about the merchandise (e.g. whether it is new or used) and the consumer's rights (e.g. the amount of the payments and rights of reinstatement), prohibiting waivers of rights and the imposition of certain fees and expenditures (e.g. waivers of defenses and counterclaims and the unfair imposition of late charges).

The consumer who is damaged by a violation is granted a cause of action; additionally, a violation of this subchapter is a deceptive trade practice under the DTPA. TEX. BUS. & COM. CODE §§92.201, 92.202.

Residential Service Company Act, TEX. OCC. CODE CHAPTER 1303

A "residential service company" undertakes to maintain repair or replace appliances or home components or systems such as structural components or plumbing systems. The Act excludes from its coverage builder warranties, home warranty insurance and service or maintenance contracts by the manufacturers and sellers of products. The Act requires residential service companies to be licensed and bonded. The Act generally prohibits false or misleading advertising. Additionally, a service company is required to provide the consumer "evidence of coverage" in an approved format which must, among other things, set forth the services or benefits to which the holder is entitled and any limitations thereon. Payment of commissions or rebates by a service company to agents of the owner or prospective owner to procure a service contract are prohibited.

The Act creates a private cause of action against the service company and also provides that such violation is an actionable deceptive trade practice subject to suit by consumers under the DTPA. TEX. OCC. CODE §1303.405.

Self-Service Storage Facility Liens, TEX. PROP. CODE CHAPTER 59

A "self-service storage facility" is real property rented for the exclusive use of storage of property and which is cared for and controlled by the tenant. This portion of the Property Code regulates the rental of self-storage units and the creation and enforcement of liens on stored property. The lessor is given a lien on all property in a self-service storage facility for the payment of charges that remain unpaid. The Code requires disclosure in the contract if the lessor seeks to have the right to seize and sell the lessee's property. The Code prescribes the contents of notice that must be given before any property is seized and the manner of the sale and disposition of the proceeds. The lessee is given a right of redemption before the sale.

The Code provides that a person injured by a violation of its provisions may sue for damages under the DTPA. TEX. PROP. CODE §59.005

Spam E-Mail Regulation, TEX. BUS. & COM. CODE CHAPTER 321

This chapter of the Business and Commerce Code prohibits the transmission of unsolicited commercial e-mail that falsifies the electronic mail transmission or routing information, contains false, deceptive, or misleading information in the subject line, or uses another person's Internet domain name without the other person's consent. It also requires the sender of unsolicited commercial e-mail to include "ADV:" or, for sexually explicit material, "ADV: ADULT ADVERTISEMENT" in the message header. It also requires the sender of commercial e-mail to provide an "unsubscribe" reply address to be honored within three days of the unsubscribe reply and prohibits the sale or transfer of e-mail addresses of those persons who have requested to be removed from the e-mail list.

This chapter provides both a private civil action for damages as well as a civil penalty collectable by the Attorney General's office. The private cause of action provides for the recovery of actual damages or a civil penalty of the lesser of $10 per message received or $25,000 per day, plus attorney's fees. In addition, a violation of the chapter is actionable as a false, misleading, or deceptive act or practice under the DTPA. TEX. BUS.& COM. CODE §321.103.

Speech-Language Pathologists and Audiologists, TEX. OCC. CODE CHAPTER 401

The practices of Audiology and Speech-Language Pathology are governed by the provisions of this chapter and the rules and regulations of the Texas Board of Audiology and Speech-Language Pathology Examiners. A person may not practice speech-language pathology or audiology or represent that the person is a speech-language pathologist or audiologist unless the person holds a license issued by the Board under this chapter. A violation of this prohibition is actionable as a false, misleading, or deceptive act or practice under the DTPA. TEX. OCC. CODE §401.501.

Talent Agency Registration Act, TEX. OCC. CODE CHAPTER 2105

A "talent agency" is a business that attempts to obtain employment for "artists," e.g. actors, musicians, writers, and models. The Act requires the operators of talent agencies to obtain a certificate of registration and post a surety bond. The Act prohibits talent agencies from charging a registration or advance fee, cannot require the artist to use the services of any specific photographer, acting or modeling school, advertisement service or publication and cannot share fees with a person who is not registered under the Act. The artist must be given a fully completed copy of the contract and has three business days to cancel.

A violation of the Act is a deceptive trade practice under the DTPA. TEX. OCC. CODE §2105.201. Administrative rules promulgated under the Act may be found at 16 TEX. ADMIN. CODE §78.1

Telephone Solicitation, TEX. BUS. & COM. CODE CHAPTER 302

"Telephone Solicitation" means a telephone call made by a seller or salesperson (including an automatic dialing or recorded message device) to induce a person to purchase, rent, claim or receive an item. The term includes a call made by a purchaser in response to a solicitation. There are several exemptions that apply when a seller engages in a telephone solicitation on its own behalf. These exemptions include persons regulated by other laws (e.g., the Securities Act), sellers of newspapers, magazines and cable television service, non-profit organizations, sellers to a business which will resell the item, and some solicitations made to current or former customers.

Sellers must be registered and bonded. The registration statement requires a long list of disclosures including disclosures of ownership information, prior convictions, judgments and bankruptcies, sales literature and telephone scripts, descriptions of any gifts, prizes or premiums to be offered and information about the items to be sold. Additionally, the statute requires the seller to provide much of this information to the consumer at the time of the solicitation and prior to consummation of the sale.

A violation of these provisions is a deceptive trade practice under the DTPA. TEX. BUS. & COM. CODE §302.303; *see also* TEX. BUS. & COM. CODE CHAPTER 301 (dealing with telephone solicitation and providing for public enforcement) and TEX. UTIL. CODE §55.121 *et. seq.* (governing automatic dial announcing devices).

Timeshare Act, TEX. PROP. CODE CHAPTER 221

A "timeshare use" is the right to use an accommodation or amenity for a period on a recurring basis but under which the consumer does not receive a freehold estate or an estate for years in the property. Under a typical timeshare arrangement, a consumer acquires the right to use a property (e.g., resort condominium) for a specified time (e.g., one week) out of each year. The Act represents an attempt to comprehensively regulate timeshare interests, including the creation, registration, ownership and conveyance of such interests.

The Act requires disclosures with any promotion in connection with the sale of timeshare interests. These disclosures must include a statement as to the purpose of the promotion, the name of the seller, the rules of the promotion, the method of awarding prizes and their value. Additionally, prior to the signing of a contract, the seller must give an extensive disclosure, including a description of the accommodations and amenities, the budget for the operation of the timeshare properties, pending lawsuits or unsatisfied judgments against the seller, and any other material circumstances concerning a timeshare interest. The Act sets forth mandatory contract provisions including disclosure of the consumer's five-day right to cancel.

The Act provides a list of activities defined as deceptive trade practices under the DTPA including the following: failing to disclose required information, making false or misleading statements concerning the characteristics of the accommodations or the period of time they will be available, predicting increases in the value of the timeshare without a reasonable basis and failing to provide the annual timeshare fee and expense statement. TEX. PROP. CODE §221.071. Administrative regulations pertaining to timeshares may be found at 22 TEX. ADMIN. CODE §543.1 *et seq.*

Treatment Facilities Marketing Practices Act, TEX. HEALTH & SAFETY CODE CHAPTER 164

This Act regulates the marketing of mental health services. Specific disclosures are required by the Act to be made to patients and prospective patients, including the treatment facility's estimated average daily charge for inpatient treatment with an explanation that the patient may be billed separately for services provided by mental health professionals, the identity of the attending physician or mental health professional, and the current "patient's bill of rights" as adopted by the Texas Department of Mental Health and Mental Retardation, the Texas Commission on Alcohol and Drug Abuse, or the Texas Department of Health that sets out restrictions to the patient's freedom that may be imposed on the patient during the patient's stay in a treatment facility. The facility must also give accurate information and not misrepresent the consequences of the patient leaving the facility against medical advice.

The Act prohibits advertising the services of a treatment facility through promises of cure or guarantees of treatment results that cannot be substantiated, advertising the availability of intervention and assessment services unless and until the services are available and are provided by mental health professionals licensed or certified to provide the particular service, and representing that a referral service is a qualified mental health referral service when it is not. The Act further requires the up-front disclosure of any affiliation between a treatment facility and its soliciting agents, employees, or contractors.

Any violation of the Act is actionable under the DTPA as either a public or private remedy. TEX. HEALTH & SAFETY CODE §164.013.

§1.02.12.1 Debt Collection Practices

Recent events have led to an explosion of new and sophisticated collection actions by debt collectors and thus the increased importance of the Texas Debt Collections Practices Act, TEXAS FINANCE CODE Chapter 392 ("TDCPA"), as a tie-in statute to the DTPA. Between 1985 and 2007, the average household debt in the United States rose from approximately 60% of annual disposable income to more than 125%. See FEDERAL TRADE COMMISSION, COLLECTING CONSUMER DEBTS: THE CHALLENGES OF CHANGE—A WORKSHOP REPORT (2009) (available at www.ftc.gov/bcp/workshops/debtcollection/dcwr.pdf) ("FTC 2009 WORKSHOP REPORT"), p. 11. During this same time frame, the nature of consumer debt drastically changed. Revolving credit card accounts issued by multi-national banks have become the most common credit arrangement for today's consumers who often having several credit card accounts open at the same time.

Relaxed or non-existent usury restrictions in South Dakota and a few other states have encouraged many of these banks to relocate their credit card operations to those states. These banks can now charge excessively high interest rates and impose a panoply of imaginative penalties on consumers who do not pay their credit card bills by the correct deadline. Stein, Robin, "PBS Frontline: The Ascendancy of the Credit Card Industry" (November 2004) (available at www.pbs.org/wgbh/pages/frontline/shows/credit/more/rise.htm). The contractual basis for these interest rate fees and other penalties is contained in the fine print of multiple-page credit card agreements that no unsophisticated consumer could be expected to read, much less comprehend. Thus, just as consumer credit has become more available to the marginally qualified, the products themselves have become increasingly incomprehensible and dangerous. It is no wonder then that when many consumers are hit with an unanticipated medical bill or work lay-off, these consumers find themselves trapped in a cycle of upwardly spiraling credit card debt without the ability to timely meet their payment obligations.

Between December 2007 and June 2009, the United States economy experienced the longest recession since World War II. During this time, consumers were hard hit by a triple whammy of unemployment or under-employment, drastic reduction in the value of their homes and the decimation of their retirement savings in the stock market. Overlapping this economic downturn, the increased availability of credit cards and home mortgage loans resulted in a steady increase of consumer debt, both in terms of total debt dollars and per capita household debt. FTC 2009 WORKSHOP REPORT, *op cit.*, p. 12. The downturn in the U.S. economy in 2008 and 2009 thus triggered record levels of credit card defaults and charge-offs.

What inevitably follows for most credit card consumers unable to meet these obligations is an encounter with the debt-collection industry. While the character of consumer debt has changed much in the past 35 years, so has the third-party debt collection industry. Technological innovations and nationwide consolidation of consumer credit information has made debt collection a growth industry in the United States. FTC 2009 WORKSHOP REPORT, p. 14-15. Computers now spit out personalized dun letters on a programmed schedule. Auto-dialers and cheap long-distance telephone rates now make it profitable for out-of-state debt collectors to call Texas consumers at their homes and work places and through relatives to hassle and berate them into paying delinquent debts.

More and more, these functions are performed by debt consolidators or "debt buyers" whose business model is to purchase a portfolio of charged-off debt for literally pennies on the dollar, thereafter keeping any amounts collected as profits. FTC 2009 WORKSHOP REPORT, p. 13-14. The financial incentives to skirt or completely disregard the federal and state laws in place to regulate debt collection activities is great, with the penalties and potential for civil liability rationalized as part of the price of doing business.

The Federal Debt Collection Practices Act ("FDCPA"), 15 U.S.C. §§1692-1692p, prohibits debt collectors from engaging in unfair, deceptive and abusive acts or practices and sets forth certain affirmative standards to which debt collectors must adhere during the course of contact with consumers in the course of collecting a debt. The FDCPA is enforceable by the Federal Trade Commission but also provides a private cause of action for damages, civil penalties and attorney's fees. However, the FDCPA's private cause of action is limited to "actual damages" shown and a civil penalty of no more than $1,000.00 for any individual civil action. The FDCPA does not preempt state law to the extent state law is not inconsistent with the FDCPA or provides a greater protection. 15 U.S.C. §1692n. Thus, in Texas, consumers also have additional access to the private cause of action provided by the TDCPA.

The TDCPA is a tie-in statute. A Texas consumer may bring a cause of action for a violation of TDCPA through the DTPA, accessing its private cause of action for damages, additional damages and mandatory attorney's fees. TEX. FIN CODE § 392.404; DTPA §17.50(h). The plaintiff must still establish "consumer" status in order to sustain a DTPA claim for a tie-in violation of the TDCPA. *Dodecka v. Garcia*, ___ S.W.3d ___ 2011 Tex. App. LEXIS 8101 (Tex. App.—San Antonio, Oct. 12, 2011, no writ) (credit card customer does not have "consumer" status as to attorney bringing suit on a credit card debt).

Like the FDCPA, the TDCPA prohibits the use of threats or coercion, harassment or abuse, unfair or unconscionable means and fraudulent deceptive or misleading misrepresentations in connection with the collection of a consumer debt. A "consumer debt" is limited to an obligation or alleged obligation which is primarily for personal, family or household purposes arising from a transaction. TEX. FINANCE CODE §392.001(2).

The TDCPA is somewhat broader than the FDCPA in that it applies to both "debt collectors" and "third party debt collectors." Under the FDCPA, "debt collector" is defined as any person whose principal business purpose is debt collection or who "regularly collects" debts owed or due to "another." Thus, the FDCPA generally does not apply to creditors collecting their own debt. Thus, attorneys can be debt collectors under the FDCPA. *Heintz v. Jenkins*, 514 U.S. 291, 115 S.Ct. 1489 (1995).

In the TDCPA, a "third party debt collector" is defined to mean a "debt collector" under the

FDCPA, except that attorneys are specifically excluded. TEX. FINANCE CODE §392.001(7). Then, under the TDCPA, "debt collector" means any person "who directly or indirectly engages in debt collection" and would thus include creditors or debt buyers who engage in debt collection for their own debts.

Like the FDCPA, the TDCPA prohibits a wide range of offensive conduct in the collection of debts, including the following:

a) Threats or coercion. TEX. FIN. CODE §392.301.

b) Harassment or abuse. TEX. FIN. CODE §392.302.

c) Unfair or unconscionable means. TEX. FIN. CODE §392.303.

d) Fraudulent, deceptive or misleading representations. TEX. FIN. CODE §392.304.

As an additional restriction found in the FDCPA, the TDCPA requires that third-party debt collectors may not engage in debt collection in Texas until they have obtained and filed with the Texas Secretary of State a $10,000 surety bond in favor of persons damaged by a violation of Chapter 392. TEX. FIN. CODE §392.101. It is thus a violation of the TDCPA to engage in debt collection in Texas without a surety bond.

The TDCPA also requires that a third-party debt collector report a consumer's dispute of a debt to a credit bureau or investigate the dispute itself. The third-party debt collector must also report back to the consumer concerning the result of its investigation and correct any records it finds to be in error. TEX. FIN. CODE §392.202.

Like the FDCPA, the TDCPA provides an affirmative defense for debt collectors who can show that the debt collection complaint resulted from a bona fide error that occurred notwithstanding the use of reasonable procedures adopted to avoid the error. TEX. FINANCE CODE §392.401; *compare* 15 U.S.C. §1692k(c) (same). The defense is waived if it is not pled affirmatively by the defendant. *Waterfield Mortgage Co., Inc. v. Rodriguez*, 929 S.W.2d 641 (Tex. App.—San Antonio 1996, no writ). Under federal law, a mistake in interpreting the law, even if made in good faith, will not be a defense to a violation. *Jerman v. Carlisle, McNellie, Rini, Kramer and Ulrich LPA*, 559 U.S. 573, 130 S.Ct. 1605, 1620-21 (2010).

[a] FORM: Letter to creditor to end collection calls

With certain specific exceptions, it is a violation of the FDCPA for a debt collector to contact a consumer after the consumer has given notice to the debt collector that the consumer refuses to pay the debt and wishes all further communications to cease. 15 U.S.C. §1692c(c). It is also a violation of the FDCPA for the debt collector to contact the consumer directly after receiving notice that the consumer is represented by an attorney. 15 U.S.C. §1692c(a)(2). The following letter may be used as a means to stop a debt collector from further communicating with the consumer while the attorney attempts to negotiate a settlement. Any communications received after the letter is sent may be the basis of an action for civil penalties, damages and attorney's fees under the FDCPA.

_____ (Date)

Certified Mail _____

Return Receipt Requested

Creditor

Creditor Address

Creditor City, State Zip

Re: Our Client: _____ <client name>

Your Account No.: _____ <account number>

Dear Sir or Madam:

I have been retained by _____[*client*] to represent him in connection with the above-referenced account. Please cease and desist any further collection efforts on this account. Please direct all future correspondence regarding this matter to me.

Please provide written verification of the debt, including a copy of the original contract or note and a full payment history to this office at your earliest opportunity. Your prompt attention to this matter will be of benefit to all involved.

Yours very truly,

_____

Attorney for Consumer

§1.02.13 Causation

In order to recover damages under the DTPA, the defendant's conduct must be a "producing cause" of actual damages. DTPA §17.50(a). *Prudential Insurance Co. v. Jefferson Associates, Ltd.*, 896 S.W.2d 156, 161 (Tex. 1995). "Producing cause" is defined as "a cause that was a substantial factor in bringing about an injury, and without which the injury would not have occurred." *Ford Motor Co. v. Ledesma*, 242 S.W.3d 32, 46 (Tex. 2007). "Producing cause" is similar to the more familiar legal standard of "proximate cause" in that both standards require actual causation in fact, *i.e.*, the injury would not have occurred "but for" the wrongful conduct. *Id.*; *Jefferson*, 896 S.W.2d at 161; *Smith v. Hennessey & Associates, Inc.*, 103 S.W.3d 567,

569 (Tex. App.—San Antonio 2003). The distinction between producing cause and proximate cause is that proximate cause includes an element of foreseeability. *Hyundai Motor Co. v. Rodriguez,* 995 S.W.2d 661 (Tex. 1999). In *Archibald v. Act III Arabians,* 755 S.W.2d 84 (Tex. 1988), the jury found that that the defendant's breach of the implied warranty that services would be provided in a good and workmanlike manner was a producing cause of the plaintiff's damages, but failed to find that the defendant's negligence was a proximate cause of the same damages. In his dissent, Justice Gonzalez noted that the only discernible difference between these causes of action was the lower threshold of causation required by the "producing cause" standard. *Id.* at 88, (Gonzalez, J., dissenting).

Regardless of how clearly liability is proven, if the element of causation is missing, then the DTPA cause of action must fail. *See e.g. Gourrier v. Joe Meyers Motors,* 115 S.W.3d 570, 576-577 (Tex. App.—Houston [14th Dist.] 2002) (seller's misrepresentation of its ability to sell automobile and breach of the warranty of title not a producing cause of damages where consumer used automobile for three years, driving it 80,000 miles, and did not learn of the title problems until he stopped making payments on the car).

Proof of causation may require expert testimony. In *Wolfson v. BIC Corp.,* 95 S.W.3d 527, 534 (Tex. App.—Houston [1st Dist.] 2002), the personal representative of a consumer's estate sued alleging that a defective lighter exploded and caused the consumer to suffer fatal burns in a fire. Following the rules of *E.I. du Pont de Nemours & Co. v. Robinson,* 923 S.W.2d 549, 558 (Tex. 1995), the court upheld the trial court's exclusion of an expert witness' testimony on causation, and further held that without expert testimony on causation, there could be no DTPA recovery.

§1.02.14 Damages Under the DTPA

From its enactment until the 1995 amendments, the DTPA provided that an injured consumer could obtain "the amount of actual damages found by the trier of fact." DTPA §17.50(b)(1). "Actual damages," undefined in the statute, were construed by the courts to mean those damages recoverable at common law. *Kish v. Van Note,* 692 S.W.2d 463 (Tex. 1985). Case law further held that any element of damages available at common law could be used in a DTPA case. *W O. Bankston Nissan, Inc. v. Walters,* 754 S.W.2d 127 (Tex. 1988). And in order to ensure that a consumer was fully compensated, the Supreme Court held that a consumer could select whichever common law measure provided the greatest amount of recovery. *Leyendecker & Assoc., Inc. v. Wechter,* 683 S.W.2d 369 (Tex. 1984). As the Supreme Court said in *Kish,* "[t]he amount of actual damages recoverable under the DTPA is determined by the total loss sustained as a result of the deceptive trade practice." *Kish v. Van Note,* 692 S.W.2d 466.

In the 1995 amendments, the Legislature changed the statutory recovery granted to consumers in Section 17.50 from "actual damages" to "economic damages." The most obvious non-economic damages excluded from recovery by this change are the general damages typical of personal injury claims, such as damages for pain and suffering, physical impairment and physical disfigurement. Damages for mental anguish are still recoverable; however, a knowing or "intentional" finding is now required as a predicate.

The 1995 amendments made no attempt to limit the elements that the courts have recognized as constituting pecuniary loss in DTPA cases; therefore, the elements of economic damages historically recoverable under the

DTPA should be as recoverable after the 1995 amendments as they were before.

When a jury verdict contains more than one acceptable measure of damages, an election of remedies by the consumer is required. *Kish v. Van Note*, 692 S.W. 2d 463, 466-67 (Tex. 1985). However, if the consumer fails to elect between alternative measures of damages, the court must render judgment on those findings, which will afford the greatest recovery so as to give the consumer all of the relief to which he may be entitled. *Birchfield v. Texarkana Memorial Hosp.*, 747 S.W.2d 361, 367 (Tex. 1987); TEX. R. CIV. P. 301. However, a party is not entitled to a double recovery and upon request before entry of judgment, the plaintiff must elect its remedy. *Waite Hill Servs. v. World Class Metal Works*, 959 S.W.2d 182 (Tex. 1998).

§1.02.14.1 Economic Damages

In all cases, the DTPA now allows for the recovery of "economic damages." The DTPA expressly defines "economic damages" as "compensatory damages for pecuniary loss, including costs of repair and replacement. The term does not include exemplary damages or damages for physical pain and mental anguish, loss of consortium, disfigurement, physical impairment, or loss of companionship and society." DTPA §17.45(11).

Prior to 1995, DTPA §17.50 allowed for the broader recovery of "actual damages," and not just "economic damages." The 1995 amendments also added the personal injury exemption in §17.49(e). The combined effect of these two amendments is to preclude a consumer from recovering general personal injury damages such as physical pain and mental anguish, loss of consortium, physical impairment, disfigurement and loss of companionship and society. *See* DTPA §17.45(11). However, certain other personal injury damages such as lost wages and medical expenses remain recoverable, despite these amendments.

Mental anguish damages, previously considered as "actual damages" recoverable under the DTPA, are now treated differently after the 1995 amendments. Generally, mental anguish damages are only recoverable if the defendant's conduct was committed "knowingly" or "intentionally." DTPA §17.50(b)(1); *see* §1.02.__, *infra*. "Actual damages" remain recoverable under §17.50(h) for tie-in statute violations.

Some examples of the types and measures of "economic damages" under the DTPA are:

(1) **Reliance Damages/Out-of-Pocket Loss.** The out-of-pocket rule measures the difference in value between the consideration parted with by the consumer (e.g., the purchase price) and the actual value of the goods or services purchased. *Leyendecker & Associates, Inc. v. Wechter*, 683 S.W.2d 369 (Tex. 1984); *Henry S. Miller Co. v. Bynum*, 836 S.W.2d 160, 163 (Tex. 1992) (Phillips, C.J., concurring); *see, e.g., Cameron v. Terrell & Garrett, Inc.*, 618 S.W.2d 535 (Tex. 1981); *Pennington v. Singleton*, 606 S.W.2d 682 (Tex. 1980); *Gupta v. Ritter Homes, Inc.*, 646 S.W.2d 168 (Tex. 1983); *Smith v. Baldwin*, 611 S.W.2d 611 (Tex. 1980). If the goods or services are deemed to have no value, a sum of money equal to the amount of the purchase price can be recovered, not as recovery of the purchase price per se but rather under the out-of-pocket rule when the value of the good or service as delivered is zero. *Chrysler Corp. v. Schuenemann*, 618 S.W.2d 799 (Tex. Civ. App.—Houston [1st Dist.] 1981, writ ref'd n.r.e.). *See Lubbock Mortg. & Inv. Co., Inc. v. Thomas*, 626

S.W.2d 611 (Tex. App.-El Paso 1981, no writ); *Smith v. Kinslow*, 598 S.W.2d 910 (Tex. Civ. App.—Dallas 1980, no writ); *Lone Star Ford, Inc. v. McGlashan*, 681 S.W.2d 720 (Tex. App.—Houston [1st Dist.] 1984, no writ).

(2) **Expectancy Damages/Benefit of the Bargain.** The benefit of the bargain rule (sometimes referred to as the "loss of bargain" rule) measures the consumer's damage by the difference between the value of the product as represented and its actual value. *Gulf States Utilities Co. v. Low*, 79 S.W.3d 561, 566-567 (Tex. 2002). The consumer may use the measure that provides the greatest recovery.

(3) **Personal Property Damages/Difference in or Loss of Value.** There is a "general" measure for damages to personal property, which is the difference in market value immediately before and immediately after the injury, at the place where the damage occurred. *Thomas v. Oldham*, 895 S.W.2d 352, 359 (Tex. 1995).

(4) **Cost of Repair.** A consumer may recover the reasonable cost of necessary repairs to the defective goods. *See Nobility Homes of Texas, Inc. v. Shivers*, 557 S.W.2d 77, 78 n. 1 (Tex. 1977); *Raye v. Fred Oakley Motors, Inc.*, 646 S.W.2d 288 (Tex. App.—Dallas 1983, writ ref'd n.r.e.); *Jordan Ford, Inc. v. Alsbury*, 625 S.W.2d 1 (Tex. Civ. App.—San Antonio 1981, no writ); *Harrison v. Dallas Court Reporting College*, 589 S.W.2d 813 (Tex. Civ. App.—Dallas 1979, no writ); *see also Sparkman v. Presley Olds-Cadillac, Inc.*, 616 S.W.2d 264, 265, fn. 1 (Tex. Civ. App.—San Antonio 1981, writ ref'd n.r.e.). One court has held that cost of repairs may be recovered in lieu of difference in market value, except where considerable economic waste would result. *Jim Walter Homes, Inc. v. Castillo*, 616 S.W.2d 630, 635 (Tex. Civ. App.—Corpus Christi 1981, no writ).

(5) **Loss of Use.** In *Luna v. North Star Dodge Sales, Inc.*, 667 S.W.2d 115 (Tex. 1984) the Texas Supreme Court held that the reasonable rental value of a substitute automobile is sufficient evidence to support an award of actual damages. The period of compensatory loss of use will be the amount of time the plaintiff was deprived of the loss of use of the automobile. The evidence put before the jury may be a reasonable rental value by the day, week or month. *Id.* at 119. The Court also held that the consumer need not actually rent a replacement automobile or show any amounts expended for alternative transportation. *See also Metro Ford Truck Sales, Inc. v. Davis*, 709 S.W.2d 785 (Tex. App.—Fort Worth 1986, writ ref.d n.r.e.).

(6) **Expenses Incurred.** It has been held that in order to recover expenses incurred as a consequence of the defendant's conduct, they must be established to be both reasonable and necessary. *See Oakes v. Guerra*, 603 S.W.2d 371 (Tex. Civ. App.—Amarillo 1980, no writ); *Carrow v. Bayliner Marine Corp.*, 781 S.W.2d 691 (Tex. App.—Austin 1989, no writ).

(7) **Medical Expenses and Lost Earnings.** Medical expenses for the treatment of personal injuries and lost earnings and earnings capacity should be recoverable under the DTPA as pecuniary losses. *See Lucas v. United States*, 757 S.W.2d 687, 701 (Tex. 1988) (Phillips, C.J. dissenting) (referring to medical expenses and lost earnings are "economic, pecuniary damages").

(8) **Lost Profits.** Lost profits are recoverable if shown by competent evidence with reasonable certainty. At a minimum, opinions or lost-profit estimates must be based on objective facts, figures or data from which the lost-profits amount may be ascertained. *Helena Chem. Co. v. Wilkins*, 47 S.W.3d 486, 504 (Tex. 2001).

(9) **Loss of Credit.** Damage to one's credit rating or ability to secure credit is recoverable under the DTPA. *Smith v. Herco, Inc.*, 900 S.W.2d 852 (Tex. App.—Corpus Christi 1995, writ denied).

(10) **Lost Time.** The value of the consumer's time spent repairing or replacing nonconforming goods or correcting problems is a proper element of damages. *See Village Mobile Homes, Inc. v. Porter*, 716 S.W.2d 543, 549-50 (Tex. App.—Austin 1986, writ ref'd n.r.e.).

§1.02.14.2 Additional Recovery for "Knowing" and "Intentional" Violations

In most instances, proof of scienter—knowledge or intentionality—is not a predicate to recovering economic damages under the DTPA. But if the deceptive act or practice is found to have been committed "knowingly" or "intentionally," DTPA §17.50 allows for the recovery of two additional measures of damages: damages for mental anguish and discretionary "additional damages."

"Knowingly" is defined in §17.45(9) as follows:

> Knowingly means actual awareness, at the time of the act or practice complained of, of the falsity, deception, or unfairness of the act or practice giving rise to the consumer's claim or, in an action brought under Subdivision (2) of Subsection (a) of Section 17.50, actual awareness of the act or practice constituting the breach of warranty, but actual awareness may be inferred where objective manifestations indicate that a person acted with actual awareness.

The Texas Supreme Court has held that "actual awareness" means more than that a person knows what he is doing. Instead, it means "that a person knows that what he is doing is false, deceptive, or unfair." *St. Paul Surplus Lines Ins. Co. v. Dal-Worth Tank Co.*, 974 S.W.2d 51, 54 (Tex. 1998). In the Court's view, to establish knowing conduct, the evidence must support the conclusion that at some point the defendant thought to himself, "I know this is false, deceptive, or unfair to him, but I'm going to do it, anyway." *Id.*

A "knowingly" finding serves a dual role:

> If the trier of fact finds that the conduct of the defendant was committed knowingly, the consumer may also recover damages for mental anguish, as found by the trier of fact, and the trier of fact may award not more than three times the amount of economic damages.

DTPA §17.50(b)(1). In order to multiply the mental anguish damages, the trier of fact must now find that the conduct was committed "intentionally." Intentionally is defined as:

> ... actual awareness of the falsity, deception, or unfairness of the act or practice, or the condition, defect or failure

constituting a breach of warranty giving rise to the consumer's claim, coupled with the specific intent that the consumer act in detrimental reliance on the falsity or deception or in detrimental ignorance of the unfairness. Intention may be inferred from objective manifestations that indicate that the person acted intentionally or from facts showing that a defendant acted with flagrant disregard of prudent and fair business practices to the extent that the defendant should be treated as having acted intentionally.

DTPA §17.45(13).

Although the exact meaning of the term "intentionally" is not clear, it appears that there are three methods by which intentional conduct may be proved. First, intentional conduct may be proved by direct evidence of (1) actual knowledge of wrongdoing and (2) an intent to induce the consumer to act or refrain from acting because of the wrongdoing. Second, the two elements of intentional conduct may be based on inferences drawn from objective manifestations which indicate that a person acted intentionally. Third, the two elements of intentional conduct may be proved by showing a "flagrant disregard of prudent and fair business practices." In other words, if a person acts with flagrant disregard of such practices, then "the defendant should be treated as having acted intentionally."

The statute is unclear with respect to what is required to prove an "intentional" breach of warranty. Clearly, there must be a showing that there was an actual awareness of the condition, defect or failure constituting the breach of warranty. It is unclear, however, whether anything further needs to be shown. That is, the definition of "intentional" includes a second prong of a "specific intent that the consumer act in detrimental reliance on the falsity or deception, or in detrimental ignorance of the unfairness." DTPA §17.45(13), as amended 1995. Neither false representations nor ignorance of unfairness have anything to do with a breach of warranty.

When a warranty is breached intentionally, it may be and usually is done without deception. A warranty claim is made, and the warrantor denies the claim. And yet, the definition suggests that the legislature wanted something else to be shown, over and above "knowing" conduct. The legislature easily could have written the amendment to say that an "intentional" breach of warranty means a breach that is done by a person who, at the time of the breach, knows he or she had an obligation to perform under the warranty; however, the person chose not to do so. Given the present wording of the amendment, it is suggested that the only thing which must be shown is "actual awareness" of the condition, defect or failure in order to establish an intentional breach of warranty.

§1.02.14.2.1 Recovery of Mental Anguish Damages

As noted above, damages for mental anguish are recoverable, in addition to economic damages, when the DTPA violation was committed "knowingly" or "intentionally."

Even if the consumer is successful in proving that the defendant's conduct was committed "knowingly" or "intentionally," any recovery of damages for mental anguish must still be supported by sufficient evidence. While admitting that there is no clear definition of mental anguish, the Texas Supreme Court has set forth a two tiered test for evaluating the legal sufficiency of the evidence to support a jury finding. First,

> [a]n award of mental anguish damages will survive a legal sufficiency challenge when the plaintiffs have introduced direct evidence of the nature, duration, and severity of their mental anguish, thus establishing a substantial disruption of the plaintiff's daily routine.

Parkway Co. v. Woodruff, 901 S.W.2d 434, 444 (Tex. 1995). Alternatively, when there is no such direct evidence there must be other evidence from which "a high degree of mental pain and distress" that is more than "mere worry, anxiety, vexation, embarrassment, or anger" can be inferred. *Id.*

In *Parkway*, the Court held that the homeowners' reaction to the repetitive flooding of their home did not rise past a level of "mere emotions," and the flooding itself was not the type of event from which mental anguish could be inferred. *Id.*; *see also Gunn Infinity, Inc. v. O'Byrne*, 996 S.W.2d 854 (Tex. 1999) (car purchaser's testimony that the car made him sick and he got teased a lot by his friends was insufficient to support an award of mental anguish damages); *Saenz v. Fidelity & Guaranty Ins. Underwriters*, 925 S.W.2d 607 (Tex. 1996) (testimony that insured "worried a lot" about future medical expenses and his inability to afford them did not rise to the level of compensable mental anguish).

In contrast, the evidence of mental anguish in *Latham v. Castillo*, 972 S.W.2d 66 (Tex. 1998), was sufficient to support a recovery under the DTPA. There, the plaintiffs testified that the discovery that their lawyer had been lying about having filed suit for the death of their daughter caused them to be physically ill, sick, nervous, mad, heartbroken and devastated, and caused them to throw up. *Id.* at 71.

In *Serv. Corp. Int'l. v. Guerra*, 348 S.W.3d 221 (Tex. 2011), the Court compared the legal sufficiency of mental anguish evidence between family members affected by the same conduct. There, the plaintiffs were the surviving widow and daughter of a man whose corpse was moved from one grave to another without the family's knowledge or permission. The cemetery operator then made false statements to the family about its actions. Based on the sufficiency of the evidence presented, the widow was allowed to recover damages for her mental anguish, while the daughter was not. The Court observed that, while cases involving the mishandling of a corpse have been recognized to produce compensable mental anguish damages, the plaintiffs were nevertheless required to provide sufficient evidence of the nature, duration and severity of the mental anguish. *Id.* at 231. The widow's testimony that she lost sleep, had headaches and burning in her stomach, took medication for anxiety and depression and continually worried about what might happen to her body once she died was held to be legally sufficient to support the jury's award of mental anguish damages. *Id.* at 233. In contrast, the daughters' testimony that they had sleepless nights worrying, that they were not at peace and that they were "always wondering" was held insufficient as a matter of law to support the jury's finding of compensable mental anguish damages. *Id.*; *see also Burleson State Bank v. Plunkett*, 27 S.W.3d 605 (Tex. App.—Waco 2000, no pet.) (evidence that plaintiff was unable to sleep, suffered from headaches, diarrhea, vomiting, and depression was sufficient to support a $10,000 damage award for mental anguish); *Norwest Mortgage, Inc. v. Salinas*, 999 S.W.2d 846 (Tex. App.—Corpus Christi 1999, no pet.) (evidence that plaintiff was unable to sleep, suffered severe stomach cramps, had difficulty eating and found it difficult to concentrate at work, sought medical help and took prescription sleeping pills was sufficient to support mental anguish damage award of $71,000).

§1.02.14.2.2 —Recovery for Additional Damages

DTPA §17.50(b)(1) provides for the recovery of additional (sometimes referred to as "treble") damages if the trier of fact determines the defendant's actionable conduct was committed knowingly or intentionally. Since 1995, there are no longer any automatic treble damages under the DTPA. Now, the amount of the award of additional damages is discretionary with the trier of fact. In a jury trial, current practice is to submit an additional damages question to the jury with no explanation that the amount of additional damages is capped by law. *See* §10.12. If the jury awards more than the statutory cap, the trial judge will reduce the amount awarded to the highest allowable amount.

The amount of the cap may have been unwittingly changed by the Texas Supreme Court in 2006. Currently, as amended in 1995, §17.50(b)(1) provides, in part, that a prevailing consumer may obtain:

> the amount of economic damages found by the trier of fact. If the trier of fact finds the conduct of the defendant was committed knowingly ... the trier of fact may award not more than three times the amount of economic damages...

DTPA §17.50(b)(1). A fair reading of this language seems to allow the recovery of *additional* damages of three times the amount of economic damages. However, interpreting almost exactly the same language from the 1979 amendments, the Texas Supreme Court held, in *Jim Walter Homes, Inc. v. Valencia*, 690 S.W.2d 239 (Tex. 1985), that the clear legislative intent from this language was to limit additional damages to just two times "actual" (now replaced by "economic") damages. Thus, the consumer could recover treble damages in total, but could not recover treble, additional damages along with actual damages, or quadruple damages. *Id.* at 241-42.

That this same interpretation of §17.50(b)(1) would apply after the 1995 amendments has been taken for granted. *See, e.g., Dal-Chrome Co. v. Brenntag Sw., Inc.*, 183 S.W.3d 133, 143-44 (Tex. App.—Dallas 2006, no pet.) (reducing award of quadruple economic damages to treble economic damages under post-1995 law). Then, in *Tony Gullo Motors I, L.P. v. Chapa*, 212 S.W.3d 299 (Tex. 2006), the Texas Supreme Court assumed, in the context of comparing the recovery of additional damages under the DTPA with exemplary damages for common law fraud, that §17.50(b)(1) in fact allowed quadruple damages—economic damages plus additional damages of three times economic damages. The court did not discuss its long-standing precedent in *Valencia* and the cases following it.

The discussion in *Chapa*, interpreting the DTPA to allow quadruple damages, may be dismissed as inadvertent dicta. *See* Note and Comment, *Not More than Dicta? Whether the DTPA's Additional Damages Can Quadruple Economic and Mental Anguish Damages Under* Tony Gullo Motors I, L.P. v. Chapa, 63 Baylor L. Rev. 934 (2011). Since *Chapa*, the courts have shown the confusion created on the issue. *Compare Bossier Chrysler-Dodge II, Inc. v. Riley*, 221 S.W.3d 749, 752 (Tex. App.—Waco 2007, pet. denied) and *Lin v. Metro Allied Ins. Agency*, 305 S.W.3d 1, 3-4 (Tex. App.—Houston [1st Dist. 2007] (mem. op.), *rev'd per curiam on other grounds*, 304 S.W.3d 830 (Tex. 2009), *with Texas Mut. Ins. Co. v. Morris*, 287 S.W.3d 401, 434 (Tex. App.—Houston [14th Dist.] 2009), *rev'd per curiam on other grounds*, 383 S.W.3d 146 (Tex. 2012) **[23]** and *Ramsey v. Spray*, No. 2-08-129-CV, 2009 Tex. App. LEXIS 9737, 2009 WL 5064539, at *1 (Tex. App.—Fort

Worth Dec. 23, 2009, pet. denied). For the time being, *Chapa* stands as at least some authority that additional damages of three times economic damages are recoverable in addition to economic damages otherwise found by the trier of fact. For the time being, *Chapa* stands as solid authority that additional damages of three times economic damages are recoverable in addition to economic damages otherwise found by the trier of fact.

For determining the limit on DTPA additional damages, determining which damages multiplied—whether by three or by four—depends on whether the defendant's conduct was committed "knowingly" or "intentionally." In cases in which mental anguish damages are awarded and the trier of fact finds that the defendant's conduct was committed "knowingly," additional damages are limited to the multiple of the amount of economic damages only. However, if there also is a finding that the unlawful conduct was committed "intentionally," additional damages may be awarded up to the multiple of the sum of economic damages and mental anguish damages. DTPA §17.50(b)(1). In computing additional damages, the court may not consider attorney's fees, costs, or prejudgment interest. DTPA §17.50(c).

§1.02.14.3 Offset Necessary

The amount of actual damages in pre-1995 DTPA lawsuits subject to mandatory trebling is the net damages determined by deducting all allowable offsets from the actual damages found by the trier of fact. *Smith v. Baldwin*, 611 S.W.2d 611 (Tex. 1980); *Durham v. St. John*, 645 S.W.2d 261 (Tex. 1983); *Building Concepts, Inc. v. Duncan*, 667 S.W.2d 897 (Tex. App.—Houston [14th Dist.] 1984, writ ref'd n.r.e.).

§1.02.14.4 Combining Elements or Causes of Action

A consumer may not recover both multiple damages for insufficient value and full restoration of the purchase price. *Smith v. Kinslow*, 598 S.W.2d 910 (Tex. Civ. App.—Dallas 1980, no writ). However, a consumer may recover partial rescission and additional damages when a double recovery will not result. *See Whirlpool Corp. v. Texical, Inc.*, 649 S.W.2d 55 (Tex. App.—Corpus Christi 1982, no writ).

When a common law action is combined with an action under the DTPA the damages caused by the DTPA violation should be separated from other damages so that the court can determine which sums are subject to trebling. *Cf. Frank B. Hall & Co. v. Beach, Inc.*, 733 S.W.2d 251 (Tex. App.—Corpus Christi 1987, writ ref'd n.r.e.). *Birchfield v. Texarkana Memorial Hospital*, 747 S.W.2d 361 (Tex. 1987).

As a result of the 1989 amendments to the DTPA, multiple damages rules governing actions under the DTPA for personal injury or death were altered. Generally, in those cases, the recovery of additional damages is subject to the rules set forth in Chapter 41 of the Civil Practice and Remedies Code. *See* TEX. CIV. PRAC. & REM. CODE §41.001 *et seq*. Thus, the "knowing" threshold for recovery of additional damages was replaced in those cases by the requirement that fraud, malice, or gross negligence be proven. TEX. CIV. PRAC. & REM. CODE §41.003(a). The maximum recovery was no longer three times the amount of actual damages; instead the "exemplary damages awarded against a defendant may not exceed four times the amount of actual damages or $200,000, whichever is greater." TEX. CIV. PRAC. & REM. CODE §41.007. The 1995 amendments provide that Chapter 41 of the

Texas Civil Practice and Remedies Code does not apply to actions under the DTPA. DTPA §17.50(g), as amended 1995.

§1.02.14.5 Restitution Under the DTPA

As an alternative to actual damages, a consumer may obtain a court-ordered return of money (or property) acquired in violation of the DTPA, pursuant to §17.50(b)(3). This often overlooked remedy provides an alternative especially (but not exclusively) useful in cases in which damages are not reasonably susceptible to proof. *See, e.g., United Postage Corp. v. Kammeyer*, 581 S.W.2d 716 (Tex. Civ. App.—Dallas 1979, no writ); *see also David McDavid Pontiac, Inc. v. Nix*, 681 S.W.2d 831 (Tex. App.—Dallas 1984, writ ref'd n.r.e.); *Carrow v. Bayliner Marine Corp.*, 781 S.W.2d 691 (Tex. App.—Austin 1989, no writ); *Freeman Oldsmobile Mazda Co. v. Pinson*, 580 S.W.2d 112 (Tex. Civ. App.—Eastland 1979, writ ref'd n.r.e.); *Jim Walter Homes, Inc. v. Samuel*, 701 S.W.2d 351 (Tex. App.—Beaumont 1985, no writ).

§1.02.15 Attorney's Fees

Attorney's fees are recoverable under the DTPA:

> "Each consumer who prevails shall be awarded court costs and reasonable and necessary attorney's fees."

DTPA §17.50(d). Attorney's fees also are available under Chapter 541 of the Texas Insurance Code:

> "In a suit filed under this section, any plaintiff who prevails may obtain: (a) the amount of actual damages plus court costs and reasonable and necessary attorney's fees."

TEX. INS. CODE §541.152.

§1.02.15.1 Consumer Must Prevail

As noted, the DTPA provides that in order for a consumer to recover attorney's fees, the consumer must "prevail." This means that in a suit for damages, the consumer must obtain a judgment for damages; otherwise, attorney's fees will be denied. *Harrison v. Dallas Court Reporting College, Inc.*, 589 S.W.2d 813 (Tex. App.—Dallas 1979, no writ). A consumer can "prevail," however, even if the consumer's judgment for actual damages is offset entirely by a judgment in favor of the defendant on the defendant's claim. *McKinley v. Drozd*, 685 S.W.2d 7 (Tex. 1984); *Matthews v. Candlewood Builders, Inc.*, 685 S.W.2d 649 (Tex. 1985). Of course, attorney's fees are recoverable if the consumer prevails in a suit for any of the remedies listed in the statute, including rescission. DTPA §17.50(d).

In contrast, a claimant whose DTPA recovery is completely offset by settlements with other parties does not "prevail" and is not entitled to recovery attorney's fees from the non-settling defendant *Osborne v. Jauregui, Inc.*, 252 S.W.3d 70 (Tex. App.—Austin 2008, pet. den'd.) (en banc); *Buccaneer Homes of Ala., Inc. v. Pelis*, 43 S.W.3d 586, 590 (Tex. App.—Houston [1st Dist.] 2001, no pet.); *Hamra v Gulden*, 898 S.W.2d 16, 19 (Tex. App.—Dallas 1995, writ dism'd w.o.j.); *Blizzard v. Nationwide Mut. Fire Ins. Co.*, 756 S.W.2d 801, 806 (Tex. App.—Dallas 1988, no writ). See § 2.02.11 *infra*.

Attorney's fees also are proper when a DTPA case has been submitted to arbitration if the consumer prevails. *Monday v. Cox*, 881 S.W.2d 381 (Tex. App.—San Antonio 1994, writ denied).

Once a consumer prevails under the DTPA, then the recovery of attorney's fees is mandatory. *Joseph v. PPG Indus., Inc.*, 674 S.W.2d 862 (Tex. App.—Austin 1984, writ ref'd n.r.e.).

§1.02.15.2 The Evolution of DTPA Attorney's Fees

As originally enacted, the DTPA allowed a consumer who prevailed to obtain, "attorney's fees reasonable in relation to the amount of work expended." DTPA §17.50(b)(1) (1973 Supp.). This language was necessary because of the prevailing rule that held that attorney's fees had to bear some reasonable relationship to the amount of the recovery. *See e.g., Capitol Life Ins. Co. v. Rutherford*, 468 S.W.2d 535, 537 (Tex. Civ. App.—Houston [1st Dist.] no writ). Under the DTPA as originally enacted, the focus was on the amount of work needed to get relief for the consumer. *See, e.g., Jack Roach Ford v. DeUrdanavia*, 659 S.W.2d 725 (Tex. App.—Houston [14th Dist.] 1983, no writ) (evidence held sufficient to support award of attorney's fees of $28,500 where actual damages were $500). Because the initial focus of the statute was on the "amount of work expended," evidence showing that a contingent fee agreement was "reasonable" was insufficient to prove the amount of fees that a consumer should recover. *King v. Ladd*, 624 S.W.2d 195 (Tex. Civ. App.—El Paso 1981, no writ). In fact, the terms of a contingent fee contract between the consumer and his attorney were deemed "irrelevant." *First Bankers Ins. Co. v. Howell*, 446 S.W.2d 711, 714 (Tex. Civ. App.—Amarillo 1979, no writ).

In 1979, the attorney's fees provision of the DTPA was changed to provide that attorney's fees must be "reasonable and necessary." DTPA §17.50(d) (1979 Supp.). The amendment did not change the amount of fees that could be recovered; instead, the amendment changed the type of evidence that could be used to support the fees claimed. Under the amended language, all of the facts traditionally used to determine whether attorney's fees are reasonable could be considered. These factors include:

(1) The nature of the case, its difficulties, complexities, and importance, and the nature of the services required to be rendered by counsel;

(2) The amount of money involved, the client's interest at stake, the amount of time devoted by the attorney and the benefit derived by the client; and

(3) The responsibility imposed upon counsel, and the skill and experience reasonably needed to perform the services.

See Houston Lighting & Power Co. v. Russo Properties, Inc., 710 S.W.2d 711, 715-716 (Tex. App.—Houston [1st Dist.] 1986, no writ) *quoting with approval, Tuthill v. Southwestern Public Serv. Co.*, 614 S.W.2d 205, 212-213 (Tex. Civ. App.—Amarillo 1981, writ ref'd n.r.e.). *See also* TEXAS DISCIPLINARY RULES OF PROFESSIONAL CONDUCT §1.04(b) which lists eight factors to be considered: (1) the time and labor required, the novelty and difficulty of the questions involved, and the skill requisite to perform the legal services properly; (2) the likelihood, if apparent to the client, that the acceptance of the particular employment will preclude other employment by the lawyer; (3) the fee customarily charged in the locality for similar legal services; (4) the amount involved and the results obtained; (5) the time limitations imposed by the circumstances; (6) the nature and length of the professional relationship with the client; (7) the experience, reputation, and ability of the lawyer or lawyers performing the services; and (8) whether the fee is fixed or contingent on results obtained or uncertain of collection before the legal services have been rendered.

§1.02.15.3 Evolultion of the Contingent Fee

In *March v. Thiery*, 729 S.W.2d 889 (Tex. App.—Corpus Christi 1987, no writ), the court of appeals specifically approved an attorney's fee award based on a percentage of the damages. Before discussing this case, however, a brief detour into the evolution of contingent fee agreements may be helpful.

Contingent fees were not favored in English law. Labeled as "champerty," the arrangement was defined by Blackstone as:

> a bargain with a plaintiff or defendant... to divide the land or other matter sued for between them, if they prevail at law; whereupon the champertor is to carry on the party's suit at his own expense.

(4) WILLIAM BLACKSTONE, LAWS OF ENGLAND, 134-135. Blackstone regarded champertors as "pests of civil society, that are perpetually endeavoring to disturb the repose of their neighbours." *Id* at 135. Needless to say, the practice was illegal.

From the earliest days, however, Texas courts took a different view. In *Butterworth v. Kinsey*, 14 Tex. 495 (1855), the court held that there was no prohibition against one person suing on an obligation given to another; thus, the plaintiff, who had agreed to collect a debt owed to the defendant for a percentage of the debt, could recover his agreed upon fee once the debt was paid. Since the old English doctrine of champerty applied to lawyers and non-lawyers alike, the *Butterworth* decision was important even though the debt collector in *Butterworth* was not a lawyer.

The propriety of using a contingent fee in Texas as a means of compensating a lawyer was considered, apparently for the first time, in *Bentinck v. Franklin*, 38 Tex. 458 (1873). In *Bentwick*, a dispute over title to land, the lawyer for Bentwick was to be paid a percentage of the land recovered in the event Bentwick prevailed. The court approved of the fee arrangement:

> A law which would prevent the officious intermeddling in the suits of others, in no way concerning parties so interfering, might be a salutary law in any state or community; but it cannot be denied that cases often present themselves to the profession in which a good man may do a service to humanity by espousing the cause of the weak against the strong.

Bentwich v. Franklin and Galveston City Co., 38 Tex. 473. The Court also distinguished the conditions in England that gave rise to the statutes against champerty: "In a country where all the lands embraced in what was once three kingdoms are owned by about eleven thousand persons, who form a strong landed aristocracy, such a statute...might serve to keep the land titles within these aristocratic limits; but in this country we have land for the millions; and if a lawyer helps his client to recover lands from the possession of another, and even takes a part of the land for his fee, if the right of his client is clear to the land, we are unable to see any immorality or breach of professional ethics in the transaction." *Bentinck v. Franklin and Galveston City Co.*, 38 Tex. 473.

Today, of course, contingent fees are approved explicitly by §1.04(d) of the Texas

Disciplinary Rules of Professional Conduct and are used in a wide variety of lawsuits including debt collection, personal injury claims, estate contests, suits to recover land, insurance claims and deceptive trade practices.

§1.02.15.4 The Contingent Fee Meets the "Reasonable and Necessary" Fee

Historically, a contingent fee means that the lawyer is paid a percentage *of the amount awarded to or collected by the client.* That is, if the damages awarded to the client are $90,000, a one-third contingent fee agreement would mean that the client is paid $60,000 and the lawyer is paid $30,000.

Long after contingent fees had been approved, a variety of state statutes were enacted authorizing a party to recover attorney's fees in specific types of litigation. The list of such statutes is long. Justice O'Connor has identified two hundred and four individual statutory provisions authorizing the recovery of attorney's fees in claims ranging from deceptive trade practices to family disputes to violations of the Water Code. O'CONNOR, O'CONNOR'S ANNOTATED CIVIL PRACTICE & REMEDIES CODE PLUS 153-166 (1997). The most notable of these statutes is now codified in §38.001 *et seq.* of the Civil Practice and Remedies Code. Among other things, this statute authorizes a person to recover attorney's fees in a suit on an oral or written contract. TEX. CIV. PRAC. & REM. CODE §38.001(8). Significantly, the statute must be liberally construed to achieve its underlying purposes. TEX. CIV. PRAC. & REM. CODE §38.005.

It has been held that the purpose of statutes such as that found in the Civil Practice and Remedies Code is to insure that the client is made whole and receives a reasonable fee for his attorney as well. *Rauscher Pierce Refsnes, Inc. v. Koenig,* 794 S.W.2d 514, 516 (Tex. App.—Corpus Christi 1990, writ denied). When the statutory purpose of making the claimant whole is combined with judicial recognition of contingent fees as reasonable, the result is a line of cases in which courts allowed a party to recover not only his damages but also a percentage of those damages as his attorney's fees. Thus, if the client's damages are $90,000 and a reasonable contingent fee is one-third (or $30,000), the total recovery awarded would be $120,000. *See, e.g., Texas Farmers Ins. Co. v. Hernandez,* 649 S.W.2d 121, 124-125 (Tex. App.—Amarillo 1983, writ ref'd n.r.e); *Hochheim Prairie Farm Mut. Ins. v. Burnett,* 698 S.W.2d 271 (Tex. App.—Dallas 1985, no writ); *Aetna Casualty & Surety. Co. v. Taff,* 502 S.W.2d 903, 904 (Tex. App.—Waco 1973, writ ref'd n.r.e.); *see also, Kerrville HRH, Inc. v. Kerrville,* 803 S.W.2d 377, 387-388 (Tex. App.—San Antonio 1990, writ denied) (suit under the "actionable fraud statute," TEX. BUS. & COM. CODE §27.01, which also allows recovery of reasonable attorney's fees).

In *Goodyear Tire and Rubber Co. v. Portilla,* 836 S.W.2d 664, 671-672 (Tex. App.—Corpus Christi 1992), *aff'd,* 879 S.W.2d 47 (Tex. 1994), the plaintiff unsuccessfully tried to carry the contingent fee formula one step further. The plaintiff argued that if the client's actual damages are $90,000 and a reasonable attorney's fee would be $30,000, then the combined total is $120,000 and the truly reasonable attorney's fee would be $40,000 (or one-third of the combined total). The court rejected this argument finding that it was an effort to recover "attorney's fees on attorney's fees."

§1.02.15.5 Reasonable Attorney's Fees Under the DTPA Before *Arthur Andersen*

Since its enactment, there has been no doubt that hourly attorney's fees are recoverable under the DTPA. When DTPA cases are handled on a contingent fee basis, however, a contingent hourly fee is less than desirable. As a result, an effort was made to incorporate the contingent fee as the measure of fees in DTPA cases. As noted above, a separate attorney's fees award calculated as a percentage of the plaintiff's damages, was recognized in DTPA litigation in *March v. Thiery*, 729 S.W.2d 889, 897 (Tex. App.—Corpus Christi 1987, no writ). The court's opinion in *March* merely followed the holdings of other courts of appeal under the general attorney's fees statute discussed above. In fact, each of the cases cited by the court as authority for its holding were cases decided under the general statute. *See Liberty Mut. Ins. Co. v. Allen*, 669 S.W.2d 750, 755 (Tex. App.—Houston [1st Dist.] 1983, writ ref'd n.r.e.); *Hochheim Prairie Farm Mut. Ins. Co. v. Burnett*, 698 S.W.2d 271, 277-278 (Tex. App.—Fort Worth 1985, no writ); *Texas Farmers Ins. Co. v. Hernandez*, 649 S.W.2d 121 (Tex. App.—Amarillo 1983, writ ref'd n.r.e.).

The first foreshadowing of Supreme Court discontent with the *March* rule appeared in *Great Am. Ins. Co. v. North Austin Mun. Util. Dist. No. 1*, 908 S.W.2d 415, 428 (Tex. 1995). The court of appeals had affirmed a trial court judgment for the plaintiff in which attorney's fees were calculated based on one-third of the amount of the total "recovery." Since the total recovery included prejudgment interest and attorney's fees, the Supreme Court held that this calculation improperly inflated the amount of attorney's fees; accordingly, the attorney's fees were reduced to one-third the amount of damages (which were fixed by law at the amount of a bond). Although the case *appeared* to approve of calculating attorney's fees based on one-third of the amount of the plaintiff's damages, the Court was careful to note the following:

> Great American did not object to the form of [the attorney's fees] question on any basis other than its failure to segregate damages arising from the various parties and claims. We address the segregation issue but otherwise *do not express an opinion* as to the propriety of this question under section 38.001 of the Texas Civil Practice and Remedies Code.

Great Am. Ins. Co. v. Austin Utility Dist. No. 1, 908 S.W.2d 415, 428 (Tex. 1995) (emphasis added).

§1.02.15.6 Reasonable Attorney's Fees Under the DTPA After *Arthur Andersen*

In *Arthur Andersen v. Perry Equip. Corp.*, 945 S.W.2d 812, 818 (Tex. 1997), the Supreme Court did not cite but clearly disapproved of the holdings of the courts of appeal which allowed recovery of attorney's fees merely upon proof of the contingent fee agreement between the plaintiff and his attorney. In *Arthur Andersen*, the trial court asked the jury to find reasonable attorney's fees in three ways: in dollars and cents, as a percentage of the plaintiff's recovery, and as a combination of dollars and cents and percentage of recovery. On appeal, Arthur Andersen argued that under a fee shifting statute like the DTPA, a defendant is forced to compensate the plaintiff not only for attorney's fees incurred in prosecuting the lawsuit at hand, but also for matters unrelated to the case. In other words, a contingent fee not only is intended to pay for the lawyer's time but also for those cases that are not won (and no fee is paid) and for the increased financial risk of getting no fee at all if the case is lost. Although the Supreme Court expressed some sympathy with this view, the main fault the Court identified was the plaintiff's failure to present evidence on any of the items listed in the Disciplinary Rules of Professional Conduct, which define what a "reasonable" fee is.

It is unclear whether the Court intended to disallow an attorney's fee that the jury calculates, at least in part, on a percentage of the damages awarded to the plaintiff. The Court appeared to leave room for some flexibility on the part of the jury:

> While we do not doubt that many plaintiffs must contract for a contingent fee to secure the services of a lawyer, we do not believe that the DTPA authorizes the shifting of the plaintiff's entire contingent fee to the defendant *without consideration of the factors required by the Rules of Professional Conduct.*

Arthur Andersen v. Perry Equip. Corp., 945 S.W.2d 818 (emphasis added). Further, the Court approved of the admissibility of the contingent fee agreement into evidence for "consideration" by the fact finder. *Id.* At the conclusion of the opinion, two black letter rules emerged. First, under the DTPA, the plaintiff must prove that the amount of fees was both reasonably incurred and necessary to the presentation *of the case at bar*; and, second, the jury must be asked to award the fees in a specific dollar amount, not as a percentage of the judgment.

§1.02.15.7 Attorney's Fees Must Be Segregated

In practice, DTPA claims are often joined with claims under other theories of law which do not provide for recovery of attorney's fees. When the plaintiff has a legal basis to recover her attorney's fees under each claim under the other theories of law, there is little chance of the plaintiff improperly recovering attorney's fees. However, when DTPA claims are joined with fraud, negligent misrepresentation and other tort-based claims, the plaintiff's attorney's fees incurred in pursuing these non-DTPA claims are not recoverable. As such, the plaintiff is required to segregate the attorney's fees incurred pursuing her DTPA claim from those incurred in pursuing claims for which no recovery of attorney's fees is allowed. *Stewart Title Guaranty Co. v. Sterling,* 822 S.W.2d 1, 10 (Tex. 1991).

Furthermore, if the plaintiff settles her claims against one or more of several defendants prior to trial, the attorney's fees incurred in pursuing her claims against the settling defendants must be segregated and excluded from the attorney's fees sought to be awarded at trial. That was the case in *Stewart Title Guaranty Co. v. Sterling*. There, the plaintiffs had settled with two defendants but proceeded to trial against Stewart Title. When they presented their jury issue on attorney's fees, Stewart Title objected that there was no breakdown or allocation of the fees incurred in the prosecution of the plaintiff's case against Stewart Title. *Id.* at 10. In fact, the record reflected that "a large majority" of the attorney's fees for plaintiff were incurred as a result of "fighting" with the settling defendants. *Id.* at 12. As such, the court held that it was incumbent upon the plaintiff to segregate proof of attorney's fees incurred in pursuing the defendant at trial from the settling defendants. *Id.*

The *Stewart Title* court, in dicta, recognized a broad exception to the plaintiff's duty to segregate recoverable from unrecoverable attorney's fees. Quoting from two lower courts, the Supreme Court recognized:

> Therefore, when the causes of action involved in the suit are dependent upon the same set of facts or circumstances and thus are "intertwined to the point of being inseparable," the party suing for attorney's fees may recover the entire amount covering all claims.

Id. at 11, *quoting from Gill Sav. Ass'n. v. Chair King, Inc.*, 783 S.W.2d 674, 680 (Tex. App.—Houston and [14th Dist.] 1989), *modified*, 797 S.W.2d 31 (Tex. 1990); *see also Flint & Assoc. v. Intercontinental Pipe & Steel, Inc.*, 739 S.W.2d 622, 624-25 (Tex. App.—Dallas 1987, writ denied). Out of this statement arose the current "inextricably intertwined" exception to the duty to segregate recoverable attorney's fees from unrecoverable attorney's fees.

As the court in *Tony Gullo Motors I, L.P. v. Chapa*, 212 S.W.3d 299 (Tex. 2006), observed, there are at least 100 cases addressing the "inextricably intertwined" exception from *Sterling* since 1991, often with conflicting results. *Chapa*, 212 S.W.3d at 312 fn. 72; *see, e.g., Pegasus Energy Group, Inc. v. Cheyenne Petroleum Co.*, 3 S.W.3d 112, 131 (Tex. App.—Corpus Christi 1999, pet. denied) (research and representation involved in establishing and presenting fraud claim were intertwined with main claim of breach of contract); *and Young v. Neatherlin*, 102 S.W.3d 415, 420-21 (Tex. App.—Houston [14th Dist.] 2003, no pet.) (claims for declaratory relief and breach of contract not inextricably intertwined with claims for quantum meruit, fraud, and negligent misrepresentation). It had become an exception which swallowed the rule. *See* TEXAS PATTERN JURY CHARGES §110.43, Comment (State Bar of Texas 2006).

In *Chapa*, the Texas Supreme Court pulled back considerably from the "inextricably intertwined" exception. There, Ms. Chapa's claims arose out of the purchase of a new Toyota. She brought suit against the dealership for breach of contract, fraud and DTPA violations. She recovered and obtained jury findings on all three claims, including exemplary damages on her fraud claim in the amount of $250,000. As recognized by the Beaumont Court of Appeals below, many appellate courts following *Sterling* had focused on the similarities in the *facts* which the plaintiff was required to prove for each cause of action. *Id.* at 313. The court in *Chapa*, however, moved the focus from the underlying facts to the *actual work done* on various aspects of the case:

> It is certainly true that Chapa's fraud, contract and DTPA claims were all "dependent upon the same set of facts or circumstances," but that does not mean they all required the same research, discovery, proof, or legal expertise. Nor are unrecoverable fees rendered recoverable merely because they are nominal; there is no such exception in any contract, statute, or "the American Rule." To the extent *Sterling* suggested that a common set of underlying facts necessarily made all claims arising therefrom "inseparable" and all legal fees recoverable, it went too far.

Id. at 313. Whether the plaintiff meets the now significantly limited "inextricably intertwined" exception to the duty to segregate attorney's fees is a question of law for the court to decide. *Chapa* at 312; *Sterling* at 12. The court also reiterated that the remedy for failing to segregate evidence of recoverable attorney's fees from evidence of unrecoverable attorney's fees was to remand the case to the trial court for a new trial on attorney's fees. *Chapa* at 315.

What about attorney time and effort spent defending a DTPA plaintiff from a counterclaim? The court recently made it clear that fees incurred in defending a counterclaim are recoverable on the claim supporting an award of attorney's fees. *Varner v. Cardenas*, 218 S.W.3d 68, 69 (Tex. 2007) (suit on a note, counterclaim for breach of contract). Because the counterclaim would have prevented full recovery on the plaintiffs' claim, the attorney's efforts in defense of the counterclaim were recoverable. *Id.*

After *Chapa*, a plaintiff may not simply rely upon the existence of common facts underlying her DTPA claims and her fraud or other tort claims to avoid the duty to segregate proof of attorney's fees. Even so, the Court stopped short of requiring detailed time records to support the evidence of segregation. The Court recognized that its new standard "does not require more precise proof for attorney's fees than for any other claims or expenses." *Id.* at 314. Recognizing that the bulk of the attorney's services (drafting, discovery, voir dire, trial, etc.) perform "double service" for recoverable and unrecoverable claims, the Court suggested that a simple opinion from the attorney stating that, "for example, 95% of their drafting time would have been necessary even if there had been no fraud claim" would suffice to discharge the duty to segregate. *Id.*

In *El Apple I, Ltd. v. Olivas*, 370 S.W.3d 757, 763 (Tex. 2012), the Texas Supreme Court addressed the type of proof needed for a court to award attorney's fees under the Texas Commission on Human Rights Act. The court stated that "when applying for a fee under the lodestar method, the applicant must provide sufficient details of the work performed before the court can make a meaningful review of the fee request. For the purposes of lodestar calculations, this evidence includes, at a minimum, documentation of the services performed, who performed them and at what hourly rate, when they were performed, and how much time the work required." *Id.* at 764. While not a DTPA case, *El Apple* may signal the need for timesheets and other time records to prove an amount of attorney's fees calculated on an hourly basis.

The failure to segregate attorney's fees can be and frequently is waived by the defendant by not timely objecting. *Matthews v. Candlewood Builders, Inc.*, 685 S.W.2d 649, 650 (Tex. 1985). So, when does the defendant have to make his objection to the plaintiff's failure to segregate? Prior to *Sterling*, some courts required the defendant to object to the failure to segregate at the time the proof of attorney's fees was offered into evidence in order to preserve the error. *See Stewart Title Guaranty Co. v. Sterling*, 772 S.W.2d 242, 248-49 (Tex. App.—Houston [14th Dist.] 1989), *rev'd.* 822 S.W.2d 1, 10 (Tex. 1991); *Houts v. Barton*, 657 S.W.2d 924, 926-27 (Tex. App.—Houston [1st Dist.] 1983, no writ). However, the court in *Sterling* held that an objection to the jury question on attorney's fees at the charge conference is sufficient to preserve the error. *Stewart Title Guaranty Co. v. Sterling*, 822 S.W.2d at 12. In practice, the objection at that point—after the evidence has been closed—does not give the plaintiff an opportunity to cure the deficiency without re-opening the evidence.

It remains to be seen whether the plaintiff must be allowed to re-open the evidence in order to segregate attorney's fees when the opposing party waits until after the close of the evidence to object. However, because evidence of unsegregated attorney's fees is sufficient to require a jury issue, the refusal to submit the jury issue based upon that objection would be reversible error. *Id.* at 12 (evidence of unsegregated fees more than a scintilla of evidence of segregated fees); *Hyundai Motor Co. v. Rodri-*

guez, 995 S.W.2d 661, 663 (Tex. 1999), *citing Tex R. Civ. P.* Rule 278. Since the remedy on appeal would only be a remand and re-trial on attorney's fees, judicial economy would be best served by allowing the plaintiff to re-open on the issue of segregated attorney's fees.

PRACTICE POINT:

Practical impact of Chapa

After *Chapa*, with its focus on the nuts and bolts of the lawyer's work in preparing a case for trial, it is highly unlikely that a court will ever conclude, given a timely objection, that *none* of the plaintiff's attorney's fees could be attributable to the pursuit and preparation of unrecoverable claims. You should, therefore, always offer evidence of how much of the attorney's work in preparing the case for trial and trying it was required by the claims on which attorney's fees are recoverable. Even if it is nothing more than an opinion that, say, 99% of the work you did benefited the plaintiff's DTPA claims, this evidence should discharge the duty to segregate as outlined in *Chapa. Id.* at 314. If you face a valid objection at the jury charge stage that you did not properly segregate, move the court to re-open the evidence to do so. *See Tex. R. Civ. P.* Rule 270. Until there is adequate law upholding this procedure, point out that it would be reversible error to refuse to submit the jury question on attorney's fees and that remand and re-trial is the likely remedy should the court of appeals uphold the objection.

§1.03 Initial Client Interview and Questionnaire

It is not unusual for DTPA clients to have had little or no experience with attorneys or the legal system. Few clients will know precisely the information that the attorney needs to evaluate the case. An effective initial interview is a carefully structured interview. If an attorney approaches such an interview with nothing more than a blank legal pad, then valuable time will be wasted in follow-up conversations with the client to obtain information that was overlooked or forgotten in the first meeting.

Some of the information required for the evaluation and pursuit of a client's claim should be gathered by the client before the first interview and merely reported to the attorney. Other information should be gathered during discussions with the client so that the facts can be developed thoroughly.

The following sections begin with a form letter reminding the client of the date of the initial conference and transmitting a client questionnaire.

The second form is a "client questionnaire" which is intended to be completed entirely by the client, preferably before the initial interview. Since the questionnaire requires some research (names, address, etc.) as well as some reflection (*e.g.* whether mental anguish symptoms have been present) ideally the questionnaire should be mailed to the prospective client several days before the actual meeting is to occur. There are alternative first pages for the questionnaire, depending on whether the client is an individual or a business consumer.

The next series of forms are "checklists" that are intended to serve as a guide during the actual interview. The interview must, if at all possible, produce sufficient information for an analysis of the merits of the claim. Additionally, the initial interview should reveal those facts and circumstances which suggests a need for immediate action. For example, if a foreclosure is threatened or if the statute of limitations is about to run, the manner in which the file is handled initially will be considerably different than if there are no such emergencies.

The checklists are intended to be *suggestive* of topics that should be explored. The checklists are not exhaustive lists of each and every question that must be asked. Instead of adhering rigorously to each question, the checklists should be used as a general framework around which a comprehensive discussion can take place.

Lastly, if the client indicates on the questionnaire or during the interview that another attorney has been involved in the claim, §1.05 should be consulted.

[a] FORM: Letter setting appointment, enclosing questionnaire

```
(Date)

(Inside address)

Re: [Name of prospective defendant]

Dear _____:

Thank you for contacting our firm concerning your complaint
against the above referenced company. I look forward to meeting
with you in person at _____.m. on _____, 20____ to
discuss your claim in depth.

So that we may make the most of our meeting, I have enclosed
a questionnaire for you to complete. I realize that there are a
large number of questions; however, it is essential that we have
this information so we can properly evaluate your claim. Please
follow the instructions carefully and make sure that you have pro-
vided all of the information requested. If any of the questions
are unclear, please call me.

Lastly, please remember to bring with you to our meeting all of
the documents which you have that relate to your claim.

Again, thank you for the confidence you have shown in our firm.
I look forward to meeting with you.

_____   Sincerely,


_____   [Signature of attorney]
```

The questionnaire which follows is intended for use by those clients who have a claim that they wish to assert against another person, *e.g.,* a client who is to be the plaintiff or counter-plaintiff in a lawsuit. As noted earlier, alternative first page(s) for the questionnaire may be used, depending on whether the client is an individual or business consumer.

The forms which follow include various attorney-client agreements which can be used in DTPA litigation.

[b] FORM: Client questionnaire (plaintiff)

Instructions

It is essential that we obtain all of the information asked about in the following questions so that we may properly evaluate your claim. For several of the questions, we have provided space on this form for your answers. For many of the questions, it will be necessary to write your answers on separate pages.

We will spend some time reviewing the questionnaire at our initial meeting, therefore, if you do not understand what is being asked, either call us or make a note so we can discuss it when we meet.

Your cooperation in answering these questions is deeply appreciated.

[Individual]

CLIENT QUESTIONNAIRE

A. *Information about you:*

1. Name _____
2. Address _____

_____
                                                                                 zip code

3. Telephone: (Day) _____ (Night) _____
4. Spouse's name _____
5. Children's _____

   names and ages
6. Occupation _____
7. Spouse's occupation _____

_____

[Business]

CLIENT QUESTIONNAIRE

A. *Information about you and your company*:

1. Name of Business _____
2. Address _____

    _____
    zip code
3. Telephone _____
4. Type of organization:

    ____ Sole proprietor   ____ Partnership

    ____ Limited Partnership   ____ Professional Association

    ____ Corporation
5. Your name _____
6. Your address _____

    _____
    zip code
7. Telephone: _____ (Night) _____
8. Who owns the business? (Give name, address and percentage of ownership)

    _____

    _____

    _____

    _____
9. If your business is a corporation:

    (a) What are the names of the members of the Board of Directors?

    _____

    _____

    _____

    _____

    (b) Who are the officers of the corporation?
    President: _____
    Vice-President: _____

Secretary: _____

Treasurer: _____

(c) Are the corporation's franchise tax payments current?

___ Yes

___ No

10. If your business is a partnership:

(a) Who is the managing partner(s)?

_____
_____
_____

(b) Who are all of the partners and what percentage interest is owned by each?

_____
_____
_____
_____

11. What type of business are you involved in?

_____

B. *Other attorneys*:

Please answer the following questions in this section if you have talked to another attorney about your claim:

1. What is the name, address and telephone number of the attorneys to whom you have spoken about your claim:

_____
_____

2. Was any written or verbal agreement made with any attorney concerning your claim? ___ Yes ___ No

If you have answered "yes" to question number 2 above,

(a) Is the agreement still in effect?

___ Yes ___ No

(b) If the agreement is not still in effect, why not?

_____
_____

3. Have you been or do you expect to be billed by the attorney for any fees or expenses?

_____ Yes _____ No

C. *Prior legal involvement:*

1. Have you been involved in any prior lawsuits?

   _____ Yes _____ No

2. If you answered question number 1 "yes," please list on a separate page all prior lawsuits in which you have been involved and include the following information for each:

   (a) the names of the parties to the lawsuit

   (b) the type of case

   (c) the outcome of the case

   (d) the name of your attorney in the case

D. *Nature of your claim*:

In a few sentences, please describe the type of claim that you have.

E. *Opposing party(ies)*

On a separate page, please list the full name, address (with zip code) and telephone number of *every person* against whom you believe you have a claim that we should pursue. Include in your list a brief statement as to why you believe you have a claim against each person.

F. *Fact witnesses*

On a separate page, please list the full name, address (with zip code) and telephone number of *every person* who has *any* knowledge or information about your case or any of the damages you have suffered, regardless of how little or how much the person knows, *and* describe briefly those facts known to each person.

G. *Expert witnesses*

On a separate page, please list the full name, address and telephone number of any experts to whom you have talked about your claim. After each name, please put the person's area of expertise. And, if the expert has provided you with any type of written report, please bring the report to our conference.

H. *Damages*

List each loss you have suffered, describing (1) what the loss is and (2) the amount of the loss. If you do not know the amount of the loss, please estimate the amount as best you can.

Item/Description	Amount
_____	$_____
_____	$_____
_____	$_____
_____	$_____
_____	$_____

_____ $_____
_____ $_____
_____ $_____

I. *Mental anguish*

Many times our clients have suffered mental anguish as a result of the transactions in which they have been involved. Take a few minutes and think through the following questions and then answer each one to the best of your ability.

(1) Have you been examined or treated by a physician, psychologist or other health care professional for depression, anxiety, or other psychological symptoms which were caused, in whole or in part, by the conduct of the opposing party?

_____ Yes _____ No

(2) If you have answered part (a) "Yes," list the name, address and telephone number of the health care professional(s) who provided the examination or treatment.

_____
_____
_____
_____

(3) Are you taking any kind of medication for the treatment or control of the psychological symptoms? If so, what is the name of the medication, the dosage and the frequency with which it is taken?

_____
_____
_____

(4) Regardless of whether you have been treated or examined by a health care professional, have you experienced any of the following symptoms which you think are or were caused by the conduct of the opposing party(ies). If "Yes," place a check mark by the symptom:

_____ Change in sleep patterns (sleep more, sleep less)

_____ Change in eating habits (eat more, eat less)

_____ Frequent feelings of depression, inadequacy, failure

_____ Change in relationship with spouse or children (irritable, less intimacy, etc.)

_____ Change in ability to concentrate on daily routine

_____ Other changes in behavior (please specify below):

_____

J. Diary of events

This is the last question, but it is the most time consuming of all and, quite possibly, the most important of all.

Beginning with the first event or conversation that you recall about your case, write a detailed account of your claim, including each thing that has happened and each thing that has been said or done to you and each thing that has been said or done by you. Include dates as best you can remember. If you do not recall an exact date, estimate when it was. If you remember the exact words of conversations, use them. If you do not recall the exact words used, then write out the substance of the words spoken. Give special attention to all of your conversations and correspondence with the other side. The more detailed your diary is, the better.

Be sure to include in your diary every act or omission of the other side that you feel caused you harm or damages.

Please write legibly. Use as many pages as are necessary.

The diary does not need to be completed by the time of our meeting; however, if you are able to complete it by that time, it will be very helpful.

§1.04 Checklists for Initial Interview

The following sections contain interview checklists for the following types of consumer and business transactions:

[a] Purchase of goods or services (general)

[b] Investments

[c] Lender liability

[d] Lease of commercial real property

[a] CHECKLIST: Purchase of goods or services (general)

Client _____ Date of Interview _____

The purchase

- ❑ What was purchased
- ❑ When
- ❑ Where did the solicitation take place

[If the solicitation occurred in "a residence" then the Home Solicitation Transactions Act may be triggered. See TEX. BUS. & COM. CODE Chapter 601.]

- ❏ Who was the seller
- ❏ Who was the salesperson
- ❏ What was the purchase price
    - Down payment
    - Monthly payments
    - Was there third party financing
    - Term of loan
    - Interest rate
    - Are payments current? If not, how far behind

[If payments are not current then the prospective defendant may file suit against the client for the default in an inconvenient forum upon receipt of the pre-filing demand letter; therefore, consideration should be given to filing a "preemptive" common law claim against the seller to fix venue and to insure that the client is the plaintiff.]

- ❏ Why was the good/service purchased
- ❏ Why was it purchased from this seller
    - Advertising
    - Sales pitch
    - Prior dealings between parties
    - Other
- ❏ Was a written contract for the purchase used
- ❏ If a contract was used, is there an arbitration clause

[An arbitration clause may be enforceable if the Federal Arbitration Act applies to the transaction. See 9 U.S.C. §1, *et seq.*]

- ❏ If a contract was used, is there a holder-in-due course clause

[The Federal Trade Commission "holder-in-due course" and the "purchase money loan" rules extend liability for the seller's conduct to anyone who purchases the consumer's contract (if the purchase is for personal, family or household purposes) by requiring a holder in due course provision in the contract. See 16 C.F.R. 433.2(a); *also see Home Savings Association v. Guerra*, 733 S.W.2d 134 (Tex. 1987).]

❑ Were any models or samples used in the sale

[Models and samples may create express warranties. See TEX. BUS. & COM. CODE §2.313(a)(3).]

❑ Were any written warranties given

[If express warranties were given, then federal law limits the effectiveness of disclaimers of implied warranties on goods purchased for personal, family or household purposes. See 15 U.S.C. §2308 ("Magnuson-Moss Warranty-Federal Trade Commission Act").]

❑ What was said about the quality, quantity or benefits of the good/service

❑ Was the seller in the business of selling this good/service

[The implied warranty of merchantability is created only by a person who is in the business of selling goods of the type that were purchased. TEX. BUS. & COM. CODE §2.314(a).]

❑ Was any important information about the product/service not disclosed to the client

Complaint about product/service

❑ What is the defect or deficiency in the product/service

❑ When was the defect discovered

[The discovery rule applies to avoid the statute of limitations only if the client exercised "reasonable diligence." See DTPA §17.565.]

❑ How was the defect discovered

❑ Has the defect been repaired before

❑ Has the seller been notified of the defect; if so, how and when

❑ If seller has been notified, what was the response, if any

❑ Have repairs been attempted; if so, how and when

❑ Have any alterations been made to product or service since its delivery

[Alterations to the product or service since the date of its delivery may affect the seller's liability under express and implied warranties. Also, alterations or use of "goods" after the discovery of defects may prevent rescission or revocation of acceptance. See e.g. TEX. BUS. & COM. CODE §2.608.]

❑ Have any repairs been performed by any third parties

[Third party repairs may raise questions as to who is responsible for the condition of the product or service.]

Use of product/service

- ❑ What benefit has been derived from the use of product/service

[The seller may be entitled to a credit for the benefit, if rescission is sought.]

- ❑ If product/service has not been used, what has been the consequence to the client
- ❑ Has another product/service been purchased or leased as a replacement
- ❑ If another product/service has been acquired, when and for how much

Damages

- ❑ What is needed to fix the product/service
- ❑ If product/service cannot be fixed, what type of replacement is available
- ❑ How long was the product/service not used
- ❑ Discuss each item of loss in questionnaire

Expectations of client

- ❑ What does client expect to accomplish through litigation

Explanations to client

- ❑ Anticipated cost of lawsuit
- ❑ Attorney and client agreement
- ❑ Requirements of discovery
- ❑ Must be present at depositions and trial
- ❑ Outcome of litigation is unpredictable

Documents to obtain from client

[Client should be advised to deliver *all* documents that in any way relate to transaction; however, the following list is illustrative of the type of documents that must be provided if they exist.]

- ❏ Advertising seen
- ❏ Point of sale brochures or documents
- ❏ Contract or receipts
- ❏ Warranties provided
- ❏ Service orders
- ❏ Any document provided to or signed by client in connection with sale
- ❏ Letters to or from anyone involved in transaction
- ❏ Reports of experts
- ❏ All documents reflecting losses from transaction

[b] CHECKLIST: Investments

Client _____ Date of Interview _____

The investment

- ❏ Type of investment
- ❏ Was client to be active or passive investor

[If the investment is passive, it is necessary to determine whether the Texas Securities Act applies. *See* TEX. REV. CIV. STAT. art. 581 - I *et seq.*]

- ❏ When was investment made
- ❏ What amount was invested by client
- ❏ Did client receive any tangible property or services in exchange for investment

[This question may determine whether "goods" or "services" were purchased as defined by DTPA in order to satisfy the DTPA standing requirement.]

- ❏ Was the client required to pay at least $500 in initial consideration for the investment
- ❏ Did the seller represent that the client would earn or was likely to earn a profit in excess of the initial consideration

- ❏ Did the seller agree to provide locations for the use or operation of the products, equipment or supplies sold
- ❏ Did the seller agree to provide a sales, production or marketing program
- ❏ Did the seller agree to buy back any products from the client

[The preceding series of questions are intended to explore the possible application of the Texas Business Opportunity Act to the transaction. *See* TEX. BUS. & COM. CODE Chapter 51. If an affirmative answer is given to any of the questions, the statute should be consulted.]

- ❏ What evidence of ownership did client receive after investing
- ❏ Did client make the investment alone or were others also involved in investment

The seller

- ❏ Who was the seller; if the seller was a business entity, who were all of the principals involved in the business
- ❏ Was there any kind of special relationship of trust and confidence between the seller and client

[If an affirmative answer is given, the possible existence of a fiduciary duty should be explored in depth.]

- ❏ What was the seller's compensation from the investment
- ❏ Is the seller licensed by any governmental agency

[If a governmental agency has licensed the seller, the agency's enabling statute and rules and regulations should be consulted to determined possible additional causes of action.]

The promoter (salesperson)

- ❏ Who was the promoter
- ❏ Was there any kind of special relationship of trust and confidence between promoter and client
- ❏ What was the promoter's compensation from the investment
- ❏ Is the promoter licensed by any governmental agency

Representations about investment

- ❏ What representations were made about the investment, by whom and when
- ❏ What representations did client believe
- ❏ What representations were not true
- ❏ Were any important facts not disclosed to client by seller or promoter; if so,
    - What was not disclosed
    - How did client discover the information that was not disclosed
- ❏ Was client provided any written information about the investment
- ❏ Was any media advertising involved in the sale of the investment
- ❏ Did client sign any documents in connection with the investment; if so,
    - Did documents contain any waivers
    - Did documents contain any arbitration clauses

[The Federal Arbitration Act may apply to the transaction to make arbitration mandatory and binding. See 9 U.S.C. §1 et seq.]

- ❏ Why did client decide to make the investment

Result of investment

- ❏ Why did investment fail
- ❏ Was seller or promoter responsible for investment's lack of success; if so
    - What did seller or promoter do to effect the investment
- ❏ Did client's conduct contribute to investment's failure; if so
    - What did client do to effect investment
- ❏ When the investment failed, what did client do, if anything, to reduce or mitigate damages

Complaint to seller or promoter

- ❑ Did client complain verbally to seller or promoter; if so
  - What did client tell seller or promoter
  - What was promoter or seller's response
- ❑ Has client written to seller or promoter about the investment; if so
  - When was letter written
  - Did letter contain a statement of the claim and a demand for payment of damages and attorney's fees
  - What was the response to the letter from the seller or promoter

Complaint to government agency

- ❑ Has client complained to any government agency; if so
  - When was complaint made
  - Which agency took the complaint
  - What has been done by agency about the complaint

[Any government agency with regulatory authority over the seller or promoter should be, contacted to determine if there is any file information about the seller or promoter that is public record. See §7.02 *et seq., infra.*]

Expectations of client

- ❑ What does client expect to accomplish through litigation

Explanations to client

- ❑ Anticipated cost of litigation
- ❑ Attorney and client agreement
- ❑ Requirements of discovery, assistance with case
- ❑ Required attendance at depositions, trial
- ❑ Outcome of litigation is unpredictable

Documents to obtain from client

[Client should be advised to bring *all* documents that in any way relate to transaction; however, the following list is illustrative of the type of documents that must be provided if they exist.]

- ❑ Advertising seen
- ❑ Point of sale brochures or documents
- ❑ Disclosure statement
- ❑ Prospectus
- ❑ Projected income/expense
- ❑ Any document provided to or signed by client in connection with sale
- ❑ All contracts or agreements
- ❑ Letters to or from anyone involved in transaction
- ❑ Reports of experts
- ❑ All documents reflecting losses from transaction

[c] CHECKLIST: Lender liability

[NOTE: With the exception of unauthorized withdrawal of funds, and other, similar UCC violations, lender liability cases typically involve unique fact situations. It is recommended that the case illustrations cited below be reviewed prior to the interview to insure that the concepts on which liability are based are thoroughly understood. Additionally, lender liability cases may involve questions relating to the breach of a duty of good faith and fair dealing. *See generally, Arnold v. Nat'l County Mutual Fire Ins. Co.,* 725 S.W.2d 165 (Tex. 1987); *Plaza Nat'l Bank v. Walker,* 767 S.W2d 276 (Tex. App.—Beaumont 1989, writ denied); TEX. BUS. & COM. CODE §1.203.]

Client _____ Date of Interview _____

The institution

- ❑ What is the full name of the financial institution
- ❑ Has the institution been involved in any reorganization, "take over," or related activity involving the FDIC or FSLIC

[If the FDIC or FSLIC has assumed control of the bank subsequent to the time of the alleged unlawful conduct, it is likely that the claim of the client has been or will be assigned to the receivership estate of the institution and there will be little, if any, recovery possible on the claim.]

- ❑ What is the name and title of the officer with whom the client dealt
- ❑ How long has client been a customer of the institution
- ❑ What are the types and account numbers of all accounts client has or has had at the institution
- ❑ If client has a checking account, has it ever been overdrawn
- ❑ Has client ever had overdraft protection at the institution
- ❑ With respect to the client's loan history at the institution, for each loan:
  - Type of loan
  - Amount
  - Method of payment
  - If not paid off, amount due
  - If paid off, date paid off
  - Was loan ever delinquent
- ❑ Is any money belonging to the client on deposit at the institution at this time

[Money that is on deposit may be subject to offset for delinquent loans. When legal action is taken against the bank, the bank may move on account(s) if there is any justification for doing so.]

Unauthorized withdrawals from account

Case illustration: Benjamin Franklin Sav. Ass'n v. Kotrla, 751 S.W.2d 218 (Tex. App.—Houston [14th Dist.] 1988, no writ); *La Sara Grain Co. v. First Nat'l Bank of Mercedes*, 673 S.W.2d 558 (Tex. 1984).

- ❑ Who was authorized to withdraw funds
- ❑ Was signature card given to institution
- ❑ If client is a corporation, was corporate resolution given to institution

- ❑ When was money withdrawn without authority
- ❑ How much money was withdrawn
- ❑ How was money withdrawn (check, bank draft, etc.)
- ❑ Who told institution to disburse funds and was this person ever authorized to withdraw funds
- ❑ What has institution said as to the reason the funds were disbursed
- ❑ What were the consequences to client of the unauthorized withdrawal of funds

Broken promise to extend credit

- ❑ For what purpose was the credit needed
- ❑ Was institution told the purpose of and need for the credit
- ❑ Who represented that credit would be extended
    - What was this person's position with the institution
    - What was this person's lending authority
    - Was committee approval required for the loan; if so, was it given
- ❑ How much credit was to be made available
- ❑ What were the conditions for the credit
- ❑ Were conditions met
- ❑ What did client do in reliance on the promise to extend credit
- ❑ When did client learn that credit would not be extended
- ❑ Did client have the means or ability to make other arrangements for credit when client learned of denial
- ❑ What were the consequences of the credit not being made available

Economic duress; control

Case illustration: State National Bank of El Paso v. Farah Manufacturing Company, Inc., 678 S.W.2d 661 (Tex. App.—El Paso 1984, writ dism'd).

- ❑ Has the institution assumed an active role in the management of the client's business by:

    - requiring that any decisions be approved by the institution

    - determining who will run client's business (selection of officers, board members, managers, etc.)

    - requiring client to keep certain funds tied up with the institution

    - requiring client to spend funds in a certain manner

[The types of control that a bank can exercise over a customer, as well as the types of duress, are many and varied. The client should be questioned closely along these lines to determine whether such control or duress exists by encouraging the client narrate his history of dealings with the bank.]

Wrongful foreclosure

[The requirements for a lawful foreclosure are set forth in Tex. Prop. Code §51.001 *et. seq.*]

- ❑ Legal description of property
- ❑ Property address
- ❑ Date property was purchased
- ❑ Amount of original loan
- ❑ Interest rate(s) on loan
- ❑ Unpaid principal balance of loan
- ❑ Amount of monthly payments
- ❑ Number of payments that were late
- ❑ Was client told that default could be cured; if so

    - How could client cure default

    - Did client attempt to cure default

    - Did bank refuse to allow cure of default

- ❑ What notices of default did client receive
- ❑ Did client receive notice by certified mail that the property would be sold at least 21 days before the sale
- ❑ Was notice of sale posted at courthouse at least 21 days before sale
- ❑ Was notice of sale filed with county clerk at least 21 days before sale
- ❑ Where did the sale take place
- ❑ Was property sold between the hours of 10:00 a.m. and 4:00 p.m. on the first Tuesday of the month
- ❑ Who conducted the sale
- ❑ If trustee did not conduct sale, did trustee resign and was a substitute trustee appointed before sale
- ❑ How much was property sold for at foreclosure
- ❑ Who purchased the property at foreclosure
- ❑ What was the fair market value of the property at the time of the foreclosure sale
- ❑ What is the most recent appraisal that the bank has on the property, and what amount is shown on that appraisal for the value of the property
- ❑ Has client been notified of any deficiency; if so
  - How much is the deficiency
  - Has debt been forgiven
- ❑ At any time during or after notice was received, was client incapacitated in any way; if so
  - Did foreclosing institution or trustee know of incapacity
- ❑ If the institution delayed in its foreclosure and during the delay period the property decreased in value, was the client willing for the institution to foreclose at an earlier date

Expectations of client

- ❑ What does client expect to accomplish through litigation

Explanations to client

- ❑ Anticipated cost of litigation
- ❑ Attorney-client agreement
- ❑ Requirements of discovery, assistance with case
- ❑ Required attendance at depositions, trial
- ❑ Outcome of litigation is unpredictable

Documents to obtain from client

[Client should be advised to bring all documents that in any way relate to transaction; however, the following list is illustrative of the type of documents that must be provided if they exist.]

- ❑ Advertising seen
- ❑ Financial institution brochures or account explanations
- ❑ Loan agreements
- ❑ Signature card; corporate resolution
- ❑ Account activity statements
- ❑ Deed, deed of trust
- ❑ Property appraisals
- ❑ Any document provided to or signed by client in connection with transaction
- ❑ Closing statement
- ❑ Notices or letters to or from anyone involved in transaction
- ❑ Reports of experts
- ❑ All documents reflecting losses from transaction

[d] CHECKLIST: Lease of commercial real property

Client _____ Date of Interview _____

The lease

- ❑ What is the address of the leased property
- ❑ When was the property first leased
- ❑ Was the lease in writing
- ❑ What is the term of the lease
- ❑ What was the purpose for which the property was leased
- ❑ What is the amount of the rent
- ❑ Was the amount of the rent negotiated or was it fixed

[The possibility that known defects were the subject of a negotiated rent payment should be explored.]

- ❑ Is the amount of rent paid by the client the same as the rent charged to others; if not, why
- ❑ What was the amount of the security deposit
- ❑ Are all rent payments current
  - If not, how delinquent is the client
  - Why did the client cease making payments

[A tenant may withhold rent payments if the property is unsuitable for its intended purpose. See *Davidow v. Inwood North Professional Group-Phase I*, 747 S.W. 2d 373 (Tex. 1988).]

- ❑ Has either the client or the landlord given notice of termination of the lease to the other; if yes, when
- ❑ Does the client still occupy the property
- ❑ Has the landlord taken any action to exclude the client from the property, *e.g.*, changing door locks, cutting off utilities
- ❑ Has client abandoned the property

Representations made

- ❏ At the time the property was leased, was the landlord told the purpose for which the property was being leased
- ❏ At the time the property was leased, were any representations made to the client about the characteristics, uses or qualities of the property

Property management

- ❏ Who manages the property
  - On premises manager
  - Management company
  - Owner
- ❏ Who collects the rent
- ❏ Has the client's claim been discussed with the manager; if yes, what was said
- ❏ Has the landlord been responsive to complaints in the past by client or others

Defects in property

- ❏ At the time the property was rented, was the client aware of any defects in the property that are related to the claim made
- ❏ What are the known defects in the property at this time
- ❏ What is the cause of the known defects in the property
- ❏ How did the client become aware of the defects
- ❏ Has client caused any damage to property, other than normal wear and tear; if yes, what and when

Complaints made

- ❏ Does the lease require written notice of defects in the property
- ❏ Has the client complained about the condition of the property to the landlord
- ❏ At the time the client gave notice of the defects, was the client current on rent payments

[When an implied warranty of suitability has been breached, the tenant can withhold rent until the condition has been cured. See *Davidow v. Inwood North Professional Group-Phase I, supra*.]

- ❏ If complaints were made, what was the landlord's response to the complaints
- ❏ Have any other tenants complained about the condition of property

[Evidence of complaints from third parties may establish grounds for a "knowing" violation, thereby increasing the landlord's exposure in a lawsuit. See DTPA §17.45(9); §17.50(b)(1).]

Losses caused by defects

- ❏ In what way have the defects in the property caused the client losses
- ❏ Is the property unsuitable for its intended use because of the defects
- ❏ Has client obtained alternative facilities
- ❏ Has any of client's personal property been affected by the defects in property
- ❏ Have the defects in the property caused any loss or interruption of business

Repairs

- ❏ Since the client moved into the property, have any repairs been made to the property; if yes, what type of repairs and when
- ❏ Since the client moved into the property, has the property been maintained regularly; if yes, what maintenance work has been done and when
- ❏ Since the client moved into the property, have any improvements been made to the property

[These questions are intended to explore how well or poorly the property has been managed generally.]

Compliance with lease

- ❏ Has client violated the lease in any respect

Expectations of client

- ❑ What does client expect to accomplish through litigation
- ❑ Does client want to terminate lease

Explanations to client

- ❑ Attorney-client agreement
- ❑ Expenses of litigation
- ❑ Uncertainty of litigation
- ❑ Requirements of discovery
- ❑ Must be present at depositions and trial

Documents to obtain from client

[Client should be advised to bring all documents that in any way relate to transaction; however, the following list is illustrative of the type of documents that must be provided if they exist.]

- ❑ Lease application
- ❑ Lease
- ❑ Correspondence, notices received from landlord
- ❑ Correspondence, notices sent to landlord
- ❑ Complaints from other tenants
- ❑ Photographs of defects

§1.05 Contacting the Previous Attorney

Some DTPA cases come into an attorney's office after having been discussed with and possibly worked on by a previous attorney. For several reasons, it is essential that the previous attorney be contacted.

The previous attorney should be asked directly whether he or she has any continuing contractual interest in the case. If a contingent fee contract was executed with the former attorney, the agreement must either be canceled or the case rejected so that the new attorney does not subject the client to double fees. Additionally, if the client has already made an agreement with the former attorney, any effort by the new attorney to sign an agreement with the client may be seen as a tortious interference with the existing contract.

If there is no continuing relationship between the client and the previous attorney, the contact still should be made to determine whether any fees or expenses are owed.

Lastly, the previous attorney can be an important source of information about the client and the merits of the client's claim.

The primary channel of communication between the attorneys involved normally will be over the telephone; however, with respect to the existence of an attorney and client agreement, or any debt for fees and expenses that may be owed, some form of written communication is advisable to avoid any misunderstandings.

[a] FORM: Letter to previous attorney

(Date)

(Inside address)

Re: [Name of client]

Dear   :

[As we have discussed] we have been contacted by the above named person for the purpose of providing legal representation on a claim against [name of prospective defendant(s)].

We were told that you previously were consulted on this claim. If you have a continuing contractual interest in the claim, we must, as you know, decline employment. Also, if any fees or expenses are owed to you as a result of your work on the claim, we would prefer to see those taken care of before we become involved.

Please advise us in writing whether you have any continuing financial interest in this matter.

Your kind attention to this request will be appreciated.

           Sincerely,

           [Signature of attorney]

§1.06 Conflicts of Interest

Another consideration which must be examined in connection with the decision to take on a new client is whether the new client will create a conflict of interest as a result of existing or past clients of the firm. Conflicts of interest can arise in many ways, *see, e.g.,* TEXAS RULES OF PROFESSIONAL CONDUCT 1.06-1.09, however, they generally arise out of situations in which an attorney's loyalty is or appears to be divided or compromised.

Attention should also be given to the identity of any key witnesses in the case. If the attorney has an adversarial relationship with any person who is an important witness, or, if the attorney is close to a person who may appear as a witness for the other side, then a practical, if not ethical, conflict may require that the case be turned away.

§1.07 Attorney–Client Contracts

The financial arrangements with respect to how a lawsuit will be handled must be resolved in the early stages of the attorney-client relationship:

> "When the lawyer has not regularly represented the client, the basis or rate of the fee shall be communicated to the client, preferably in writing, before or within a reasonable time after commencing the representation."

See TEXAS RULE OF PROFESSIONAL CONDUCT 1.04(c). In addition to the ethical consideration, contingent fee agreements in DTPA cases must be in writing and signed by the attorney and the client. TEX. GOV'T CODE §82.065; *see also, Gano v. Jamail,* 678 S.W.2d 152 (Tex. App.—Houston [14th Dist.] 1984, no writ).

Obviously, the client must be given the opportunity to read the contract and ask questions about its meaning before being asked to agree to its terms. If the circumstances allow, the contract should be mailed to the client in advance so that there will be no question as to the client's opportunity to read the document.

There are stringent new requirements whenever two or more lawyers in different law firms are going to divide a fee, whether as a result of joint representation or a "referral fee." These requirements are discussed in §1.08 *infra*. Since fee division agreements require the client's written authorization, the authorization can be included in the contract. *See* TEXAS RULES OF PROFESSIONAL CONDUCT 1.04(f).

An attorney-client agreement (or any other document) may not include any language by which the attorney attempts in advance to exonerate himself from or limit his liability to his client for his malpractice. TEXAS RULE OF PROFESSIONAL CONDUCT 1.08(g).

The forms which follow include various attorney-client agreements which can be used in DTPA and other litigation.

[a] FORM: Letter enclosing contract

(Date)

(Inside address)

Re: [Name of prospective defendant]

Dear _____:

Thank you for the confidence you have shown in our firm by retaining us to represent you in your claim against [name of prospective defendant].

As you may know, in most cases, lawsuits are long-term engagements. Very few cases are or can be resolved quickly. For this reason, you need to be prepared for some time to pass before any significant progress is made.

I have enclosed our attorney-client contract, which we discussed. Please read this document carefully. If you have any questions about the contract, please call me. Once you are satisfied with the contract sign it and return it [along with the retainer] to me. We cannot begin working on your case until we have received the signed contract [and retainer] from you.

Again, thank you for the confidence you have shown in our firm. We look forward to working with and for you.

Sincerely,

[Signature of attorney]

[b] FORM: Contingency fee agreement

ATTORNEY AND CLIENT AGREEMENT AND ASSIGNMENT OF INTEREST

This is an employment agreement, an appointment of an attorney-in-fact, and an assignment of interest between the law firm of _____ ("Attorneys") and _____ ("Client").

1. *Scope of Employment.* Attorneys will represent Client with respect to all claims against _____ arising out of _____.

2. *Attorney-in-Fact.* Client hereby constitutes and appoints Attorneys to be Client's attorney-in-fact and authorizes them to investigate, try, compromise, settle and receive in Client's name all damages, Attorney's fees and other money due Client on Client's claims. Client further constitutes and appoints Attorneys to be Client's attorney-in-fact to sign all legal instruments, pleadings, drafts, authorizations and papers as shall be reasonably necessary to investigate, try or settle Client's claims, and to reduce to pos-

session any and all money or other things of value due to Client as a result of Client's claims, as fully as Client could do in person.

3. *Assignment of Interest*. In consideration of the legal services to be provided under this agreement, Client hereby assigns and grants to Attorneys a vested and present interest in _____ percent (_____%) of all money, property or other interests that are collected, whether from the proceeds of any suit and judgment or from a settlement. If a lawsuit is tried and the judgment is appealed or it is necessary to retry the lawsuit, then Client hereby assigns and grants to Attorneys a vested and present interest in _____ percent (_____%) of all money, property or other interests that are collected, whether from the proceeds or any suit and judgment or from a settlement. If the legal services provided under this agreement result in money saved or value obtained by Client through offset or the forgiveness of any obligation, then the amount of such offset or forgiveness shall be included in the amount "collected" under this agreement.

4. *Attorney's Fees*. This is a "contingent fee" agreement. This means that all of Attorney's fees will be payable out of the money, property or other interests actually collected (or obligation forgiven or offset) whether from a judgment after trial or by settlement. In the event that Attorneys are able to recover Attorney's fees in addition to Client's damages, then Attorney's fees will be either a percentage of the combined total of Attorney's fees and damages (as specified in paragraph 3) or the amount of Attorney's fees recovered, whichever is greater. Provided, however, that if Client's claim is such that the fee allowed the attorney is set by law, the amount payable under this contract to Attorneys shall be limited to the maximum so allowed by law.

5. *Retainer*. Client agrees to pay to Attorneys, upon execution of this agreement, a non-refundable retainer in the amount of $_____. In the event Attorney's fees are recovered, the amount of this retainer shall be credited against the Attorney's fees that otherwise are payable.

6. *Costs*. All out-of-pocket expenses incurred by Attorneys in the handling of Client's claims will be reimbursed by Client on a monthly basis. "Out-of-pocket" expenses means _____.

7. *Cost Deposit*. Client will pay a cost deposit in the amount of $_____, which funds will be deposited into Attorney's trust account. These funds will be used to pay the costs described in paragraph 6. If and when the funds have been exhausted, Client agrees to make additional cost deposits in the same amount as the initial deposit.

[8. *Division of Attorney's Fees.* If appropriate, insert form paragraph contained in §1.08[a] *infra.*]

[9]. *Withdrawal from agreement.* Client authorizes Attorneys to withdraw from this agreement at any time upon the happening of any of the following events:

   (a) After due investigation of the facts, research of the law applicable to Client's claims, and an assessment of the prospective defendant's [s'] ability to pay a judgment, Attorney's determine that further pursuit of Client's claims does not have a reasonable likelihood of success; or

   (b) Client fails to cooperate in discovery. Attorneys have advised Client that in any lawsuit the other side has the right, among other things, to take depositions, to ask interrogatories that Client must answer under oath, to make requests for admissions of fact and to request that certain documents be produced, all of which must be done by a certain date. These activities are called "discovery." If, after reasonable notice, Client fails or refuses to assist Attorneys in responding to discovery on a timely basis, or fails to appear for deposition, then this failure or refusal shall be deemed a failure to cooperate under this subparagraph.

[10]. *No oral modifications.* Client agrees that this Attorney and Client Agreement will not be modified by any oral agreement; instead, all modifications of this agreement must be in writing and signed by both Attorneys and Client.

[11]. *Nature of litigation.* Attorneys have advised Client that the outcome of the trial of a lawsuit is impossible to predict, even though Attorneys and Client believe that the claims are well supported and justified. Thus, Client understands that regardless of how strong the claims appear, it is impossible to guarantee or even predict with certainty that the trial will be successful.

[12]. *Settlement.* Attorneys will not settle Client's claims without Client's authorization. Client will not settle Client's claim without Attorney's authorization.

[13]. *Agreement binding.* Client agrees that this Attorney and Client Agreement shall be binding on Client, as well as any and all successors, heirs, executors, or assigns of Client.

[14]. *Texas law applies.* This agreement shall be interpreted and construed according to the laws of the State of Texas.

[15]. *Place of performance*. This agreement is to be performed in _____ County, although the litigation involved may be tried in a different County.

[16]. *Effective date*. This agreement becomes effective on the date that this agreement is signed by Client.

SIGNED AND AGREED TO ON THE DATE SHOWN.

By_____   By_____
        "Attorneys"   "Client"

Date Signed by Client: _____

[c] FORM: Hourly agreement

ATTORNEY-CLIENT AGREEMENT

This is an employment agreement, and an appointment of an attorney-in-fact, between the law firm of _____, ("Attorneys") and _____ ("Client").

1. *Scope of Employment*. Attorneys will represent Client with respect to _____

2. *Attorney-in-Fact*. Client hereby constitutes and appoints Attorneys to be Client's attorney-in-fact and authorizes them to investigate, try, compromise, settle and receive in Client's name all damages, attorneys' fees and other money due Client on Client's claims. Client further constitutes and appoints Attorneys to be Client's attorney-in-fact to sign all legal instruments, pleadings, drafts, authorizations and papers as shall be reasonably necessary to investigate, try or settle Client's claims, and to reduce to possession any and all money or other things of value due to Client as a result of Client's claims, as fully as Client could do so in person.

3. *Retainer*. Client agrees to pay to Attorneys, upon the execution of this document, a [non-refundable] retainer in the amount of $_____, which retainer will be used to pay the attorneys' fees and expenses described in the following paragraphs. If the retainer is exhausted prior to the resolution of Client's claims, client will be billed for the remaining fees. If Client's claims are resolved prior to the exhaustion of the retainer, the balance will not be refunded to Client.

4. *Attorneys' Fees*. All Attorneys' fees will be billed at the following rates:

    (a) Partners: $_____ per hour

    (b) Associates: $_____ per hour

    (c) Paralegals: $_____ per hour

    (d) Law Clerks: $_____ per hour

All legal fees will be billed monthly and are payable upon receipt. If applicable laws allow Attorneys to seek to recover such fees from a third party, Attorneys will do so. Client understands and agrees, however, that such legal fees are due and payable when billed whether or not such fees can be recovered for Client at a later date. Any attorneys' fees which are recovered from a third party will be paid over to Client, so long as all fees due and payable under this agreement have been paid.

5. *Costs*. All out-of-pocket expenses incurred by Attorneys in the handling of Client's claims will be reimbursed by Client on a monthly basis. Copies made in Attorneys' offices will be billed at the rate of $_____ per page. Documents which are transmitted electronically by FAX or some similar method will be billed at the rate of $_____ per page. All other costs will be billed in the exact amount incurred.

[6. *Insert the paragraph on division of fees in §1.08 infra, if there will be a division of fees*:]

[7]. *Withdrawal From Agreement*. Client authorizes Attorneys to withdraw from this agreement at any time upon the happening of any of the following events:

    (a) Client fails to pay attorneys' fees or to reimburse expenses when they are due, after reasonable notice; or

    (b) Client fails to cooperate in discovery. Attorneys have advised Client that in any lawsuit the other side has the right, among other things, to take depositions, to ask interrogatories which Client must answer under oath, to make requests for admissions of fact, and to request that certain documents be produced, all of which must be done by a certain date. These activities are called "discovery." If, after reasonable notice, Client fails to assist Attorneys in responding to discovery, or, if Client fails to appear for deposition, then this failure shall be deemed a failure to cooperate under this subparagraph.

[8]. *No Oral Modifications*. Client agrees that this Attorney-Client Agreement will not be modified by any oral agreement; instead, all modifications of this agreement must be in writing and signed by both Attorneys and Client.

[9]. *Nature of Litigation*. Attorneys have advised Client that the outcome of the trial of a lawsuit is impossible to predict, even though Attorneys and Client believe that the claims are well supported and justified. Thus, Client understands that, regardless of how strong the claims appear, it is impossible to guarantee or even predict with certainty that the trial will be successful.

[10]. *Settlement*. Attorneys will not settle Client's claims without Client's authorization.

[11]. *Agreement Binding*. Client agrees that this Attorney-Client Agreement shall be binding on Client, his or her successors, heirs, executors, or assigns.

[12]. *Texas Law Applies*. This agreement shall be interpreted and construed according to the laws of the State of Texas.

[13]. *Place of Performance*. This agreement is to be performed in _____ County, Texas, although the litigation involved may be tried in a different County.

[14]. *Effective Date*. This agreement becomes effective on the date that this agreement is signed by Client.

SIGNED AND AGREED TO ON THE DATE SHOWN.

_____   _____
       "Attorneys"   "Client"

Date Signed:_____   Date Signed:_____

§1.08 Fee Division Agreements (including referral fees)

Whenever lawyers from different firms are involved with the same client's case, whether it is litigation or otherwise, the fees paid by the client typically will be divided between the lawyers. In addition to cases in which more than one lawyer actively represent the client, historically, referral fee agreements were customary in many parts of the state under which a forwarding lawyer would be paid a percentage of the fee simply for making the referral. Such agreements provided a strong, financial incentive for one lawyer to direct a client to another lawyer who was more highly specialized or skilled in the particular field of law in which the client was involved. The payment of referral fees (or fees to a "forwarding lawyer") was condoned by the Rules of Professional Conduct under certain circumstances, with few requirements to make the fee agreements valid. *See* TEX. RULES OF PROFESSIONAL CONDUCT 1.04(f)(1)(ii) (1990). Effective March 1, 2005, whether the matter involves lawyers from different firms actively representing the interests of one client, or whether a fee is to be paid to a forwarding lawyer, there are stringent requirements for arrangements for the division of fees. *See generally* TEX. RULES OF PROFESSIONAL CONDUCT §1.04(f); Texas Supreme Court Misc. Docket No. 05-9013 (January 28, 2005); 67 TEXAS BAR JOURNAL No. 10 at 838-841.

The substantial support of the bar for tightening the rules for the payment of referral fees reflects a reaction, in part, to the extensive media advertising done by relatively few lawyers (sometimes out-of-state), the purpose of which simply was to identify and secure clients. The advertising lawyers then routinely and automatically referred the clients to other lawyers or law firms who actually handled the cases. The advertising lawyers rarely, if ever, handled anyone's case; instead, they made their money from referral fees, generated from the clients they secured from advertising.

Contrary to the assertions made by some, there is no evidence that traditional referral fees ever caused financial harm to clients or made litigation more expensive, since the fees always were paid out of the contingent share of the recovery already assigned by clients to their attorneys. If anyone was "harmed," it was the lawyers who did all the work but then had to pay a large percentage of their fees to the forwarding lawyers who had no responsibility for or involvement in the cases. Even so, the referral fee system flourished because the lawyers who paid the referral fees believed it to be in their best interests to make it worthwhile for forwarding lawyers to continue to send them cases.

Regardless of the merits or problems of traditional referral fees or any other arrangement in which fees are divided between lawyers, there are stringent rules that must be followed if fees are to be divided.

A division or arrangement for division of a fee between lawyers who are not in the same firm is permissible only if:

> "(1) the division is: (i) in proportion to the professional services performed by each lawyer; *or* (ii) made between lawyers who assume joint responsibility for the representation; *and* (2) the client consents in writing to the terms of the arrangement prior to the time of the association or referral proposed, including (i) the identity of all lawyers or law firms who will participate in the fee-sharing agreement, and (ii) whether fees will be divided based on the proportion of services performed or by lawyers agreeing to assume joint responsibility for the representation; and (iii) the share of the fee that each lawyer or law firm will receive, or, if the division is based on

the proportion of services performed, the basis on which the division will be made; *and* (3) the aggregate fee does not violate paragraph (a) (which prohibits unconscionable fees)."

TEX. RULES OF PROFESSIONAL CONDUCT §1.04(f). Stated simply, the written consent of the client is required (in the form required by the rule) *whenever* the fee paid by a client will be divided between lawyers in different firms. In addition, if the fee is a traditional referral fee, it can be paid only if the forwarding lawyer "assumes joint responsibility for the representation." If more than one lawyer is actively representing the same client in the same matter, then the fee can be divided only if it is in proportion to the professional services provided.

The phrase "joint responsibility" is not defined in the rule; however, it contemplates that there are both "ethical and perhaps financial responsibility for the representation." *See Comment 13*, 67 TEX. BAR JOURNAL No. 10, page 840 (November, 2004). The ethical responsibility is to make reasonable efforts to assure that the representation *and* client communication are adequate. Adequacy of representation is satisfied only if the forwarding or associating attorney conducts a reasonable investigation of the client's legal matter and refers the matter to a lawyer whom the referring or associating lawyer reasonably believes is competent to handle it. *Id.*, p. 840-841.

Assuring adequate attorney-client communication requires the referring or associating attorney to monitor the matter throughout the representation and ensure that the client is informed of those matters that come to the lawyer's attention and that a reasonable lawyer would believe the client should be aware. *Id.*, p. 841. The monitoring requirement does not require the referring lawyer to attend hearings, depositions and other such proceedings; instead, it only requires that the lawyer be reasonably informed of the matter, respond to client questions, and assist the handling lawyer when necessary. *Id.*, p. 841.

Referral fee agreements in DTPA cases generally should be avoided. Most DTPA cases do not involve claims for "soft" damages such as mental anguish. Instead, DTPA cases involve damages that are intended to compensate a client for actual dollars that will have to be spent to fix the problem that precipitated the complaint. If an attorney takes one-third of the cost to repair a foundation as his or her fee, then the client is left without enough money to do the repair work. Because of the lean nature of some DTPA damages claims, a number of DTPA cases are settled by the opposing party agreeing to pay actual "hard" damages, e.g., cost of repair and residual loss of value, as well as the plaintiff's attorneys' fees, based on the number of hours the plaintiff's attorney has in the case. Under some circumstances, attorneys will agree to this approach in order to promote settlement. If, however, a referral fee must be paid out of the hourly fee actually recovered, then the attorney will end up losing money on the case. For these reasons, in DTPA cases, the payment of referral fees is the exception and not the rule.

In those cases when a referral fee is appropriate, it is important to note that an agreement to pay a referral fee is unenforceable and against public policy unless full disclosure concerning the payment of the fee is made to the client and the client consents to the payment of the fee. *Lemond v. Jamail*, 763 S.W.2d 910 (Tex. App.—Houston [1st Dist.] 1988, writ denied). The forms which follow are intended to insure full disclosure to and proper authorization by the client.

[a] FORM: Client authorization for division of fee

The following paragraph should be inserted into the appropriate attorney client agreement contained in §1.07 supra:

> (a) Client authorizes Attorneys to agree to a division of attorney's fees with [*insert name of attorney and firm*]_____.

Insert the following additional paragraph when two or more lawyers from different firms will work actively on the matter:

> (b) I authorize Attorneys to divide the attorney's fees with the attorney and law firm identified in the preceding sub-paragraph in proportion to the professional services performed by each lawyer. [*Describe the basis on which the division will be made, e.g.* The fee division will be based on each lawyer's hourly rate and the number of hours each lawyer works on the case].

[or]

Insert the following when a fee is to be paid to a forwarding lawyer:

> (b) I authorize Attorneys to divide the attorney's fees to be paid under this agreement with the attorney and law firm identified in sub-paragraph (a). This authorization is based on my understanding and agreement that the attorney and law firm so identified have agreed to assume joint responsibility for this matter. Further, [describe the share of the fee that will be paid to each lawyer, e.g. the attorney's fee will be paid as follows: _____ will receive ____% and _____ will receive ____%].

[b] FORM: Agreement to divide attorney's fee (referring attorney)

(Date)

(Inside address)

Re: [Client's name]

Dear _____:

Thank you for referring the above referenced case to our firm. After meeting with _____ and discussing the matter at length, we have agreed to take the case.

This letter will confirm our agreement to divide the attorney's fees recovered in this case with you. The fee will be divided by paying to you ____% of the recovered fee. In exchange for the payment of this fee, you assume joint responsibility for this matter as required by Texas Rule of Professional Conduct §1.04. It is understood that if no attorneys' fees are recovered, then there will be nothing to divide under this agreement.

Enclosed is a copy of our contract with our client.

Again, thank you for referring this matter to our firm.

                Sincerely,

                [*Signature of handling attorney*]

cc: [client]

[c] FORM: Agreement to divide attorney's fees (co-counsel)

(Date)

(Inside address)

Re: [Client/ matter name]

Dear _____:

This letter is intended to memorialize our fee agreement in the above referenced matter.

We have agreed to work as co-counsel on behalf of the above referenced client. Based on this agreement, we have agreed to divide the attorney's fees that will be paid as follows: [*insert the basis on which the fees will be divided, e.g.* each of us will divide the fees to be paid proportionate to the number of hours each of us works on this matter, as reflected in our billings to the client. We further agree that if bills submitted to the client are not paid in full, each of us will divide the fees that are paid based on our proportionate share of the total number of hours billed.]

[Enclosed is an executed copy of the contract with our client].

If this letter accurately reflects our agreement, please sign in the space provided below and return a signed copy to me.

                [*Signature of attorney*]

                [*Signature of co-counsel*]

§1.09 Beginning the Case

After the attorney and client relationship has been established, and the questionnaire has been completed as well as the gathering of all other necessary, preliminary information, the case is ready to begin. So that the client will have a written document explaining how a case progresses, to which reference can be made as the case moves along, it is sometimes helpful to provide a letter of explanation to a new client.

[a] FORM: Letter—what to expect

```
[Date]

[Inside address]

Re: [Name of defendant]

Dear _____:
```

The purpose of this letter is to provide you with some information on what to expect in the coming months as your case progresses.

The handling of your case begins with a "notice" letter. This letter must be sent in order to satisfy the requirements of state law. The other side has sixty days within which to respond to the letter by offering to settle the case for either the full amount stated or a smaller amount that is acceptable to you. Very few cases are settled on a demand letter. If the response to the demand letter is not acceptable, then a lawsuit will be prepared and filed.

[NOTE: The following paragraph should be replaced by that contained in $[b] in cases involving defective residential construction.]

Once the other side receives the demand letter, you may be requested to allow an inspection of the _____. We are required to provide a reasonable opportunity for such an inspection, if it is requested.

After a lawsuit is filed, the other side has approximately thirty days after the lawsuit papers are served to file an answer to the lawsuit. The answer will, most likely, be a short, one or two sentence denial of your claim. The filing of the answer signals the date upon which we can begin "discovery" in your case.

"Discovery" in a lawsuit is a process by which various legal procedures are used to learn everything the other side knows about the lawsuit, who their witnesses will be and what they will say at the trial. Among the more common discovery "tools" which are available to us are *interrogatories* (questions which we send to the other side in writing and which must be answered under oath); *requests for production of documents* (a list of documents we want the other side to produce for inspection and copying); *requests for admission of facts* (written statements of fact which the other side must admit or deny in writing); and *depositions* (the actual taking of live testimony from the other side's witnesses). We can and should expect the other side to use these tools on us as well. In addition to preparing the case for trial, there are two additional purposes of discovery: First, by requiring the parties to answer specific questions and produce certain documents, it is possible to "narrow" the issues in the case so that unnecessary time and money is not spent on unimportant matters. Second, discovery allows the parties to know exactly what they are up against so that reasonable settlement discussions can occur.

Once the discovery process is near completion, the case can be set for trial. Your case will be placed on a docket (calendar) for a specific day. [In Travis County, the cases are called to trial in the order in which they are placed on the docket.] When we place a case on the docket for trial, we try to select a date that makes it likely we will actually go to trial on the date selected; however, there are no guarantees that we will be reached on that date. In most cases, we will not know for sure whether we will go to trial until the Monday of the week the case is set. If our case is not reached for trial on the date we have selected, we must reset the case and go through the process again.

When disputes cannot be resolved amicably and there is a sufficient amount at stake, a civil lawsuit is the only remedy available. Unfortunately, regardless of how strongly we feel about the case, it still must be tried before a jury of people from the community that you have never seen before and will probably never see again. Because of the relatively brief period of time that the jury is exposed to a case, it is impossible to predict the outcome of a jury trial. Even with the unpredictability of a jury trial, it still is the best remedy available to us.

Please understand that a lawsuit also will cause some inconvenience to you and the people who agree to testify for us either in deposition, at trial or both. Courts operate on tight schedules. When the Court directs us to be at a hearing or when we are required to respond to discovery, we have little choice in the matter. Your indulgence and cooperation will be appreciated. Your indulgence and cooperation also are essential to the success of your case.

Our primary purpose during this litigation is to serve your best interests. When a question arises that you feel is important, please feel free to call.

Sincerely,

[Signature of attorney]

[b] FORM: —Alternative paragraph (residential construction governed by RCLA and not RCCA)

[Replace the third paragraph in the preceding letter with the following:]

If the other side requests it within thirty-five (35) days after the receipt of our demand letter, we must agree to allow an inspection of the defects in the house. We also are required to allow the other side to "document" the inspection by videotape, photographs or whatever reasonable method is desired. Within forty-five (45) days after the other side receives our demand letter, they may make an offer to repair the defects. If such an offer is made and it is later deemed by the court to be a "reasonable offer," it will limit your rights to recover more in any lawsuit we file. The penalty for failing to accept a "reasonable offer" timely made or to allow the other side to make the offered repairs is that you will be limited to recovering nothing more than the fair market value of the offer of repair and the attorney's fees incurred before the offer was rejected.

Chapter 2

Initial Client Contacts (Defendant)

§2.01 General Considerations
§2.02 Defenses Available in DTPA Cases
    §2.02.1 Common Law Defenses Do Not Apply
    §2.02.2 Professional Services Exemption
    §2.02.3 Real Estate Brokers and Agents Exemption
    §2.02.4 Waiver
        [a] FORM: Waiver of consumer rights
    §2.02.5 "As Is" Clause or Agreement
    §2.02.6 Independent Investigation
    §2.02.7 Statutory Defenses
    §2.02.8 Media Exemption
    §2.02.9 Contribution and Indemnity
    §2.02.10 Responsible Third Party
    §2.02.11 Settlement Credit
    §2.02.12 Large Transactions Exemption
§2.03 Client Questionnaire (Defendant)
    [a] FORM: Client questionnaire (defendant)
§2.04 Checklists for Initial Interview
    [a] CHECKLIST: Sale of goods or services
    [b] CHECKLIST: Lease of commercial real property
§2.05 Attorney-Client Agreements
    [a] FORM: Letter agreement with respect to legal services
    [b] FORM: Letter enclosing attorney-client agreement
    [c] FORM: Attorney-client hourly fee agreement

§2.01 General Considerations

A prospective defendant in a DTPA lawsuit typically is under considerably more time pressure than the prospective plaintiff. A notice letter may be the first indication the recipient has that a claim exists, and unless the claim is analyzed thoroughly within the time period allowed by law, important legal rights may be lost. For example, the consumer's DTPA claim can be barred entirely or substantially limited by an adequate response to the notice letter so long as the response is made within sixty days after the letter is received. *See e.g.* DTPA §17.505(c), (d); *see also* §4.01 *infra*. The benefits of a prompt response to a notice letter are even more pronounced if the consumer's claim involves residential construction. If the client has taken some time to try and work out the complaint before contacting the attorney, the time pressures may even be greater.

If the client is not a new client, then much of the preliminary work in establishing the attorney-client relationship already will have been done. When the client is new, however, all of the information and discussions necessary to establish the relationship as well as an analysis of the demand must be undertaken within the period of time allowed for a response to the notice letter. In this sense, the use of efficient forms and checklists is even more important than if the client is a prospective plaintiff.

The initial meeting with the prospective defendant must, at least, answer the following questions:

- Who is the client?

- Who is the claimant?

- What are the facts of the transaction?

- Are there any third parties that may share liability for the claim?

- What is the client's level of understanding the litigation process?

- What are the terms on which the case will be handled?

(a) *Who is the client?*

As with the prospective plaintiff in a DTPA lawsuit (*see* §1.01 *supra*), it is essential to determine whether a conflict of interest would be created by representing the prospective client. If the client is a business entity, the identity of all of the principals must be ascertained. Further, some reflection should be given to the identity of any expert or other fact witnesses that may be needed in the case since a "conflict" with any of these individuals may be difficult to reconcile even though there would be no technical prohibition against taking the case. For example, if an expert witness is assisting the attorney on another case in the office, it may be difficult to effectively attack the expert's conclusions and opinions if he or she has been retained by the plaintiff to testify against the prospective client.

It also is important to determine whether the prospective client's personality is such that he or she can be worked with over a long period of time. Some thought should be given to whether the client is likely to create a favorable impression on a jury. Attorneys do not win DTPA cases. Clients win DTPA cases. The prospects for a successful defense are increased measurably by the client's ability to project a favorable image. As previously mentioned, if the client is a corporate entity, it is necessary to ascertain whether the corporate veil may be pierced by the plaintiff in order to create personal liability for the owner or owners of the corporation. Generally, this requires determining whether all corporate formalities have been observed, the extent to which shareholders of the corporation also exercise control over corporate affairs, whether corporate and individual property have been kept separate, and whether the corporation has been used for personal purposes. *See Castleberry v. Branscum*, 721 S.W. 2d 270 (Tex. 1986).

(b) *Who is the claimant?*

The identity of the claimant is important not only in checking for conflicts of interest, but also in evaluating the strength of the claim. As stated in the preceding section, attorneys do not win DTPA cases; clients win DTPA cases. For this reason, if the claimant is likely to be an unusually sympathetic or credible person in the jury's eyes, then the client's exposure may be increased beyond what it otherwise would be. On the other hand, if the claimant is a scoundrel, and this can be shown to a jury, the client's exposure may be reduced considerably.

(c) *What are the facts of the transaction?*

More than likely, the client needs an attorney because a demand letter already has been received. During the sixty days following the receipt of the letter, the client must be advised whether a settlement offer should be made. By the time the prospective client and the attorney meet face to face, a substantial amount of the response time may already have elapsed. An immediate determination must be made as to whether the demands of existing clients and cases allow sufficient time for the investigation that must be completed. If the facts of the transaction are complex and the time for investigation is relatively little, the facts may compel the attorney to turn down the case because of its immediate needs.

(d) *Are there any third parties who may share liability for the claim?*

In many DTPA cases, particularly those which involve the sale of goods or services, there are third parties who are either directly or indirectly involved in the transaction. For example, if a product is defective, the manufacturer of the product may be fully or partially responsible for the consumer's damages. And, if a house is badly built, the architect, engineer or subcontractors who worked on the house may be liable so that the contractor client would have a cross action to recover some or all of the losses that ultimately are paid to the consumer. The existence of such claims, as well as the identity of those persons who may be subject to a cross action should be determined, if possible, in the initial meeting.

(e) *What is the client's level of understanding of litigation and its consequences?*

New litigation clients frequently have a distorted or incomplete understanding of the process of litigation. For example, many people believe that if they have done nothing wrong then they should not be required to pay any money to defend an unjust claim. If the client has not experienced litigation before, or does not fully understand the process, the consequences of being sued must be fully explained in the first meeting. That is, the client must understand some very basic, legal facts of life:

- Anyone can file a lawsuit, whether the claim is valid or not.

- Once a person has been sued, if no answer is filed then a default judgment can be taken even though the person sued believes he is innocent.

- If a lawsuit is filed and the defendant has no insurance, the person sued must pay for a defense to the case even though he believes the plaintiff has no valid claim.

- There are occasional instances when the cost of defense so far exceeds the amount of the claim that it makes better "economic sense" to pay the claim than pay for the defense.

- It will be up to a judge and jury to determine whether the plaintiff has a valid claim.

- Over ninety percent of the cases that are filed are disposed of prior to trial.

Of course, the uncertainties and expense of litigation affect the plaintiff equally; however, unless the client fully understands each of these points, so that informed decisions about the case can be made, there will be frustration, inevitably, in the legal work that is done.

(f) *What are the terms on which the case will be handled?*

There are very few defense cases that are handled on any basis other than an hourly fee; however, there are different types of hourly fee structures. For example, if the attorney uses law clerks, paralegals, associates or other such personnel in handling cases, the billing rates for each should be explained so that a comprehensive fee agreement can be reached.

A more difficult fee question is presented when the client has a viable counterclaim against the prospective plaintiff, which, if successful, would produce a greater recovery than the plaintiff's claim. In such cases, the attorney and client may want to negotiate a fee structure in which a reduced hourly fee is charged in exchange for an assignment of a percentage of any net recovery against the plaintiff.

The client should also be advised that, in some aspects of the defense, the attorney will have little control over the hours that are spent on the case. For example, the plaintiff may decide to take depositions of individuals that the client feels are unimportant, or the plaintiff may designate witnesses whose value in proving the plaintiff's case is marginal, and yet, whose depositions must be taken. Even though the client may believe the witnesses are unimportant, the attorney still must be present for each such deposition, and each hour that is spent is an additional hour that must be charged.

§2.02 Defenses Available in DTPA Cases

[For an overview of DTPA causes of action, see §1.02 supra.]

§2.02.1 Common Law Defenses Do Not Apply

It is well settled that common law defenses do not apply to actions under either the DTPA or Insurance Code Chapter 541. *Kennemore v. Bennett*, 755 S.W.2d 89 (Tex. 1988); *Alvarado v. Bolton*, 749 S.W.2d 47 (Tex. 1988); *Weitzel v. Barnes*, 691 S.W.2d 598 (Tex. 1985); *Smith v. Baldwin*, 611 S.W.2d 611 (Tex. 1980). However, this rule does not excuse consumers from the common law duty to mitigate their damages. *Gunn Infiniti, Inc. v. O'Byrne*, 996 S.W.2d 854 (Tex. 1999); *Arthur Anderson & Co. v. Perry Equipment Corp.*, 945 S.W.2d 812 (Tex. 1997).

One "defense" to misrepresentation suits that is available is the common law defense of "puffing." This defense was permitted by the court of appeals in *Autohaus, Inc. v. Aguilar,*

794 S.W.2d 459 (Tex. App.—Dallas 1990), writ denied *per curiam*, 800 S.W.2d 853 (Tex. 1991). In denying Aguilar's application for writ of error, the Supreme Court noted that it was not approving or disapproving the court of appeals' analysis of the puffing issue. *Id.* at 854. But in *Doe v. Boys Clubs*, 907 S.W.2d 472 (Tex. 1995), the court held that a representation that a club provided a "wholesome environment" was not actionable under the DTPA as a matter of law, citing a common law fraud case dealing with the "puffing" defense. Since then it has become accepted that the defense of "puffing" is available in cases alleging violations of DTPA §17.46(b)(5) and (b)(7). *See Helena Chem. Co. v. Wilkins*, 47 S.W.3d 486 (Tex. 2001) (recognizing puffing defense but holding that defendant's statements about its seed product, *e.g.* "excellent yield potential" were specific representations and not puffing). The Supreme Court has noted that no court has extended the puffing defense to non-disclosure or unconscionable conduct. *Id.* At least one Court of Appeals has applied the "puffing" defense to a breach of warranty action under the DTPA. *See, Humble Nat'l Bank v. DCV, Inc.*, 933 S.W.2d 224 (Tex. App.—Hou. [14th Dist.] 1996, writ denied) (holding the phrases "tradition of excellence" and "we know our customer" to be mere puffing and too vague to qualify as warranties). Other decisions involving puffing: *Prudential Ins. Co. of Am. v. Jefferson Assocs.*, 896 S.W.2d 156, 163 (Tex. 1995) (description of building as "superb" and "super fine" and "one of the finest little properties in the city of Austin" was puffing); *Douglas v. Delp*, 987 S.W.2d 879 (Tex. 1999) (a lawyer's representation that an agreement presented for signature by his client would protect that client's interest was "nonactionable opinion"); *Bradford v. Vento*, 48 S.W.3d (Tex. 2001) (holding that a representation was too vague to be actionable but not mentioning the word "puffing"); *Kessler v. Fanning*, 953 S.W.2d 515 (Tex. App.—Fort Worth 1997, no writ) (representation of "no previous structural repair" and "no improper drainage" not mere opinion puffing); *Milt Ferguson Motor Co. v. Zeretzke*, 827 S.W.2d 349 (Tex. App.—San Antonio 1991, no writ) ("good, excellent motor vehicle" and "a good car... would have no problems" were not puffing); *Padgett v. Bert Ogden Motor's, Inc.*, 869 S.W.2d 532 (Tex. App.—Corpus Christi, 1993, writ denied) ("completely repaired" and "completely fixed" were not puffing). *But see* W. Keeton, PROSSER & KEETON ON THE LAW OF TORTS, 757 (5th Ed., 1984) (discrediting the puffing defense). In order to determine whether a representation is actionable or merely "puffing," courts generally consider three factors: (1) the specificity of the alleged misrepresentation, (2) the relative knowledge of the buyer and seller, and (3) whether the representation pertains to a past or future event or condition. *Munters Corporation v. Swissco-Young Industries, Inc.*, 100 S.W.3d 292, 298 (Tex. App.— Houston 2002).

§2.02.2 Professional Services Exemption

In 1995, the DTPA was amended to exempt certain "professional services" from the statute. DTPA §17.49(c). Specifically, the DTPA does not provide liability for a claim for damages "based on the rendering of a professional service, the essence of which is the providing of advice, judgment, opinion, or similar professional skill." DTPA §17.49(c); *see, e.g., Stafford v. Lunsford*, 53 S.W.3d 906 (Tex. App.—Houston [1st Dist.] 2001, no pet.) (failure to advise client to record a document was a professional service exempted from the DTPA). The exclusion is limited in that it does not apply to (1) an express misrepresentation of a material fact that cannot be characterized as advice, judgment, or opinion; (2) a failure to disclose information in violation of DTPA §17.46(b)(24); (3) an unconscionable action or course of action that cannot be characterized as advice, judgment, or opinion; or, (4) the breach of an express warranty that cannot be characterized as advice, judgment or opinion. DTPA §17.49(c). If the exclusion applies, it includes any person who may be vicariously liable for the conduct of the "professional." DTPA §17.49(d).

The term "professional" is undefined in the DTPA, and so the scope of the exemption has been left for the courts to decide. One commentator has observed that the professional services exemption clearly applies to doctors, lawyers, accountants and realtors, and should be extended to bankers, stockbrokers, engineers and insurance agents. Skeels, D., "The DTPA's Professional Services Exemption: Let 'em Be Doctors and Lawyers and Such," 55 BAYLOR L. REV. 783, 812 (2003). A common and ordinary meaning of "professional" includes a person who, "[is] engaged in a specific activity as a source of livelihood," or "[has] great skill or experience in a particular field or activity." THE AMERICAN HERITAGE DICTIONARY OF THE ENGLISH LANGUAGE 1045 (1981). The common definition is so broad that the exclusion would easily swallow the statute if the term "professional" is used to define the scope of the exclusion.

The better view is that the scope of the exclusion is defined by the requirement in §17.49(c) that the "essence" of the professional service involve "the providing of advice, judgment, opinion or similar professional skill." DTPA §17.49(c). To illustrate, it would be difficult to imagine a consumer transaction in which a dialogue between the consumer and "professional" service provider occurs that does not involve some form of advice, opinion or judgment. For example, when an automobile breaks down, most consumers seek a mechanic's opinion on the cause of the breakdown as well as the mechanic's advice or judgment on the repairs that are required. The exclusion should not apply, however, because the "essence" of the mechanic's service is repairing the automobile, not giving advice.

The mere fact that a "professional" makes a statement in a consumer transaction does not mean that the exclusion applies. For example, in *Nast v. State Farm Fire and Casualty Co.*, 82 S.W.3d 114 (Tex. App.—San Antonio 2002, no pet.), an insurance agent falsely represented to his clients of eighteen years that they did not qualify for flood insurance, and upon being questioned about someone selling flood insurance to neighbors, the agent further represented that it was a "shyster" who had been selling insurance that would not pay claims. The plaintiffs' house flooded, the agent was sued, and he asserted the "professional service" exclusion in the DTPA. The court held that to qualify as a professional service, "the task must arise out of acts particular to the individual's specialized vocation... An act is not a professional service merely because it is performed by a professional; rather, it must be necessary for the professional to use his specialized knowledge or training. *Nast v. State Farm Fire and Casualty Co.*, 82 S.W.3d 122. The court concluded that the exclusion did not apply because whether someone was qualified for flood insurance was a fact — not "advice, opinion or judgment," as was the claim that the seller of the flood insurance was a "shyster."

Prior to the professional services exemption, it had long been held that the DTPA applies to lawyers, depending on the conduct alleged. *See e.g. De Bakey v. Staggs*, 605 S.W.2d 631, 633 (Tex. Civ. App.—Houston [1st Dist.] 1980, *writ ref'd n.r.e. per curiam*, 612 S.W.2d 924 (Tex. 1981) (unconscionability). But a legal malpractice case cannot be "recast" as a DTPA claim in order to take advantage of the benefits in proof and attorney's fees that the DTPA may have over the common law cause of action. *Aiken v. Hancock*, 115 S.W.3d 26 (Tex. App.—San Antonio 2003, pet. denied) ("Texas law does not permit a plaintiff to fracture legal malpractice claims"); *Deutsch v. Hoover, Bax & Slovacek, LLP*, 97 S.W.3d 179, 189 (Tex. App.—Houston [14th Dist.] 2002); *Goffney v. Rabson*, 56 S.W.3d 186, 188-194 (Tex. App.—Houston [14th Dist.] 2001, pet. denied).

And, although the DTPA has been applied to health care providers in limited circumstances, *see e.g. Sorokolit v. Rhodes*, 889 S.W.2d 239 (Tex. 1994) (DTPA applies to knowing misrepresentations or knowing breaches of express warranties by a health care provider), a plaintiff is not permitted to "recast" a medical negligence claim into a claim under the DTPA. *See Walden v. Jeffery*, 907 S.W.2d 446 (Tex. 1995) (plaintiff's claim of ill-fitting dentures barred by MLIIA); *Gormley v. Stover*, 907 S.W.2d 448 (Tex. 1995) (representations of successful surgery nothing more than "recast" negligence claim); *Earle v. Ratliff*, 998 S.W.2d 882 (Tex. 1999) (misrepresenting and concealing the truth about the necessity and likely success of surgery barred by MLIIA)*; Murphy v. Russell*, 167 S.W.3d 835 (Tex. 2005*)* (expressly representing and warranting that general anesthesia would not be used); *see, Diversicare General Partner Inc. v. Rubio*, 185 S.W.3d 842 (Tex. 2005) (a nursing home's negligence in failing to provide adequate supervision and nursing services to prevent a sexual assault by another patient constituted a health care liability claim governed by the MLIIA.); *Boothe v. Dixon*, 180 S.W.3d 915 (Tex.App.—Dallas 2005, no pet.) (misrepresentations as to care; distinguishing *Sorokolit*).

In a legal malpractice setting, the prohibition against recasting a claim appears to apply equally to a defendant's effort to "recast" a DTPA claim as one for negligence in order to avoid the lesser burden of proof and recovery of attorney's fees allowed by the DTPA. In *Latham v. Castillo*, 972 S.W.2d 66 (Tex. 1998), clients sued an attorney for failing to timely file a medical malpractice action. The plaintiff claimed a violation of the DTPA as well as breach of contract, and fraudulent misrepresentation. In upholding the plaintiffs' right to proceed with their DTPA cause of action, the court reasoned:

> "If the Castillos had only alleged that Latham negligently failed to timely file their claim, their claim would properly be one for legal malpractice. However, the Castillos alleged and presented some evidence that Latham affirmatively misrepresented to them that he had filed and was actively prosecuting their claim. It is the difference between negligent conduct and deceptive conduct. To recase this claim as one for legal malpractice is to ignore this distinction. The Legislature enacted the DTPA to curtail this type of deceptive conduct."

Id. at 69; *see also Deutsch v. Hoover, Bax & Slovacek, LLP*, 97 S.W.3d 189-190 (allegations regarding conflicts of interest are breach of fiduciary duty claims and are independent of legal malpractice claims).

The rule against "recasting" causes of action has also been applied to prevent a person from recasting a "mere breach of contract" claim into a DTPA claim. *See* §1.02.8.1 *supra*; *Crawford v. Ace Sign*, 917 S.W.2d 12, 13-15 (Tex. 1996).

As a result of the 1995 amendments, by implication, it is now clear that the DTPA applies equally to professionals when they engage in any of the five, specific types of conduct prohibited by the statute. DTPA §17.49(c).

The exclusion of professional services is an affirmative defense which must be pleaded and proved; otherwise, it is waived. *Head v. U.S. Inspect DFW, Inc.*, 159 S.W.3d 731, 739 (Tex. App.—Fort Worth 2005, pet. den'd.);

see Gibson v. Ellis, 58 S.W.3d 818 (Tex. App.—Dallas 2001, no pet.).

§2.02.3 Real Estate Brokers and Agents Exemption

In 2011, the DTPA was amended to add an exemption for liability arising from an act or omission of a licensed real estate broker or salesperson. DTPA §17.49(h) as amended in 2011. Like the professional services exemption (*see* §2.02.2, *supra*.), the real estate agent exemption does not preclude a DTPA violation based on: (1) an express misrepresentation of a material fact that cannot be characterized as advice, judgment, or opinion; (2) a failure to disclose information in violation of §17.46(b)(24); or (3) an unconscionable action or course of action that cannot be characterized as advice, judgment, or opinion. DTPA §17.49(h) as amended in 2011. The real estate agent exemption is only effective for acts or omissions occurring after its effective date of May 28, 2011.

§2.02.4 Waiver

A waiver under the DTPA is valid and may be enforced if:

(1) the waiver is in writing and is signed by the consumer;

(2) the consumer is not in a significantly disparate bargaining position;

(3) the consumer is represented by legal counsel in seeking or acquiring the goods or services; and

(4) the waiver is in the form specified by the DTPA.

DTPA §17.42(a), (c).

Waiver, obviously, is an affirmative defense, which must be pleaded and proved by the person asserting the defense. TEX. R. CIV. P. 94.

The waiver provision is intended to allow parties of essentially equal bargaining strength to conduct business free of any concerns that their conduct may later be measured by a "consumer protection" statute. Most ordinary consumer transactions, *e.g.* purchasing an automobile or a house or a service will not trigger the waiver provision because the consumer normally either will not be represented by independent counsel or the consumer will be in a significantly disparate bargaining position with the seller.

The waiver now allowed by the DTPA is not effective if the consumer's legal counsel was directly or indirectly identified, suggested, or selected by a defendant or an agent of the defendant. DTPA §17.42(b). Further, the waiver may be modified so that only certain provisions of the DTPA are waived. DTPA §17.42(d).

A waiver or other provision that limits liability or damages will be effective as to warranties even if the waiver language does not comply with DTPA §17.42 because the DTPA does not *create* warranties, but only gives remedies for their breach. *Southwestern Bell Tel. Co. v. FDP Corp.*, 811 S.W.2d 572 (Tex. 1991). Since warranties do not originate with the DTPA, they may be limited or disclaimed by language that does not comply with the DTPA. But the same is not true for non-warranty claims under the DTPA. The Texas Supreme Court has held that non-warranty representations and unconscionability claims are not affected by such liability limitation clauses. *Helena Chem. Co. v. Wilkins*, 47 S.W.3d 486 (Tex. 2001); *Southwestern Bell Tel. Co. v. FDP Corp.*, 811 S.W.2d 572 (Tex. 1991).

[a] FORM: Waiver of consumer rights

[NOTE: The waiver to be signed by a consumer must be in at least 10 point type, must bear a heading of "Waiver of Consumer Rights" (or similar wording), and must be in substantially the following form. See DTPA §17.42(c), as amended 1995].

WAIVER OF CONSUMER RIGHTS

I WAIVE MY RIGHTS UNDER THE DECEPTIVE TRADE PRACTICES - CONSUMER PROTECTION ACT, SECTION 17.41 ET SEQ., BUSINESS & COMMERCE CODE, A LAW THAT GIVES CONSUMERS SPECIAL RIGHTS AND PROTECTIONS. AFTER CONSULTATION WITH AN ATTORNEY OF MY OWN SELECTION, I VOLUNTARILY CONSENT TO THIS WAIVER.

Signature of consumer

[NOTE: A waiver signed by a consumer is not a defense to an action by the Attorney General's office. DTPA §17.42(e), as amended 1995.]

§2.02.5 "As Is" Clause or Agreement

Although the DTPA requires only that the defendant's actions be *a* producing cause of damages, sometimes the actions of the consumer or a third party break the chain of causation and become the sole producing cause of the damages in question. In *Prudential Ins. Co. v. Jefferson Assoc.*, 896 S.W.2d 156 (Tex. 1995) the consumer purchased a building, the contract for which contained a comprehensive "as is" clause. This clause provided, among other things, that "[p]urchaser acknowledges that it is not relying upon any representation, statement, or other assertion with respect to the Property condition, but is relying upon its examination of the Property." The Court held that the "as is" clause defeated causation which is essential to the recovery of damages under the DTPA.

In the opinion of the majority, the clause did not constitute a waiver of DTPA rights; instead, the clause was a "statement that no basis exists for the assertion of such rights." The majority also stated that an "as is" agreement is not determinative, and suggested that it will not be given effect if fraudulently induced, if it was an incidental part of the basis of the bargain between the parties, or if the parties were of unequal bargaining power. *See also, Erwin v. Smiley*, 975 S.W.2d 335 (Tex. App.—Eastland 1998, writ denied) ("as is" clause in residential sale negated the buyer's assertion that the sellers were the cause of the damage as a matter of law.); *compare, Pairett v. Gutierrez*, 969 S.W.2d 512 (Tex. App.—Austin 1998, writ denied).

It is important to note that an "as is" clause in a contract normally would not negate causation as a matter of law under *Prudential Ins. Co. of Am. v. Jefferson Assocs.*, 896 S.W.2d 156 (Tex. 1995). In *Prudential*, which involved the sale of a commercial building, the parties negotiated a contract at arms length which contained the following provision:

"As a material part of the consideration for this Agreement, Seller and Purchaser agree that Purchaser is taking the Property

"AS IS" with any and all latent and patent defects and that there is no warranty by Seller that the Property is fit for a particular purpose. Purchaser acknowledges that it is not relying upon any representation, statement or other assertion with respect to the Property condition, but is relying upon its examination of Property. Purchaser takes the Property under the express understanding that there are no express or implied warranties (except for limited warranties of title set forth in the closing documents). Provisions of this Section 15 shall survive closing."

Prudential Ins. Co. of Am. v. Jefferson Assocs., 896 S.W.2d 160. By contrast, a typical earnest money contract used in the sale of a house says the following in boilerplate language:

"ACCEPTANCE OF PROPERTY CONDITION: Buyer accepts the Property in its present condition; provided Seller, at Seller's expense, shall complete the following specific repairs...."

Obviously, the clause examined in *Prudential* was specific and comprehensive; the clause in the earnest money contract is general boilerplate. The clause in *Prudential* specifically disclaims reliance on any representations; the clause in the typical earnest money contract does not. Thus, *Prudential* does not support the contention that the general, boilerplate paragraph in an earnest money contract negates causation as a matter of law. Unlike *Prudential* the "as is" clause in an earnest money contract says nothing about reliance on a person's representations about a house. As the Court said in *Prudential*:

"The nature of the transaction and the circumstances surrounding the agreement must be considered. Where the 'as is' clause is an important part of the basis of the bargain, *not an incidental or 'boilerplate' provision*, and is entered into by parties of relatively equal bargaining position, a buyer's affirmation and agreement that he is not relying on representations by the seller should be given effect."

Prudential Ins. Co. of Am. v. Jefferson Assocs., 896 S.W.2d 162 (emphasis added).

In *Oakwood Mobile Homes, Inc. v. Cabler*, 73 S.W.3d 363 (Tex. App.—El Paso 2002, pet. denied), the seller of a new mobile home represented to the buyers that his company would fix anything in the home that the purchasers wanted fixed. The buyers testified that this was an important promise to them because the home they were purchasing was a substitute for the new home they had ordered and there were a number of things wrong with it. When the seller refused to make all of the necessary repairs, the buyers sued. The seller defended, in part, by claiming that a clause in one of the sales documents which stated, in essence, that no oral statements or promises would be enforced, precluded a claim by the buyers on anything other than the home's warranty. Distinguishing *Prudential*, the court held that the oral promises were enforceable under the DTPA, in spite of the disclaimers in the sales documents.

The doctrine of merger, under which a deed extinguishes prior contractual obligations, is a common law defense that does not apply to defeat warranties under the DTPA. *Alvarado v. Bolton*, 749 S.W.2d 47 (Tex. 1988); *see, Geodyne Energy Income Production Partnership I-E v. Newton Corp.*, 161 S.W.3d 482 (Tex. 2005) ("the merger doctrine may not prevent proof of prior misrepresentations under the Deceptive Trade Practices-Consumer Protection Act") (dicta).

§2.02.6 Independent Investigation

While "producing cause" has always been the legal causation standard for all DTPA liability [§17.50(a)], the DTPA was amended in 1995 to further require that a "laundry list" violation be "relied on by a consumer to the consumer's detriment." DTPA §17.50(a)(1)(B). Introduction of the element of "reliance" raises several issues which have received increased attention in the years since the 1995 amendments. Does the reliance have to be reasonable or justifiable? Did the consumer (or should the consumer be required to) conduct his own investigation into the represented facts? Did the consumer discover or should the consumer have discovered the falsity of the representations alleged?

The 1995 amendment clearly does not expressly require that the consumer's reliance be reasonable or justifiable. *Id.* Nor is any such requirement found in the cause of action for statutory fraud in real estate and stock transactions. *Cf.* Tex. Bus. & Com. Code §27.01(a)(1)(B) (using simply "relied on"). In fact, under Texas law, the general rule for common law fraud is that a consumer's reliance need not be either "reasonable" or "justifiable" in order to support a finding of fraud:

> "It is not the rule that a person injured by the fraudulent and false representations of another is held to the exercise of diligence to suspect and discover the falsity of such statements. In the absence of knowledge to the contrary, he would have a right to rely and act upon such statements, and certainly the wrongdoer in such a Case cannot be heard to complain that the other should have disbelieved his solemn statements."

Koral Industries, Inc. v. Security-Connecticut Life Ins. Co., 802 S.W.2d 650, 651 (Tex. 1990) *quoting Western Cottage Piano & Organ Co. v. Anderson*, 101 S.W. 1061, 1064 (Tex. Civ. App.—Ft. Worth 1907, writ denied); *see also Matis v. Golden*, 228 S.W.3d 301 (Tex. App.—Waco 2007, no writ); *G. Prop. Mgmt. v. MultiVest Fin. Servs. of Tex., Inc.*, 219 S.W.3d 37, 48 (Tex. App.—San Antonio 2006, no writ).

On the other hand, Texas courts have spoken of requiring that reliance be reasonable when the consumer's reliance is based upon silence, *American Tobacco Co., Inc. v. Grinnell*, 951 S.W.2d 420, 436 (Tex. 1997), and in cases where the misrepresentations are not made to a specific person, *Ernst & Young, L.L.P. v. Pacific Mutual Life Ins. Co.*, 51 S.W.3d 573, 577 (Tex. 2001). *See also Texas First National Bank v. Ng*, 167 S.W.3d 842, 856 (fn. 24 (Tex. App.—Houston [14th Dist.] 2005 petition granted, judgment vacated without reference to merits) (observing confusion and possible split in Texas authority).

The current Texas Pattern Jury Charge does not require a finding of reasonableness or justification for the element of reliance in common law fraud. *See* 4 Texas Pattern Jury Charges §105.2 (2006). Given the statutory mandate for liberal construction and promotion of an efficient and economical procedure to secure consumer protection, DTPA §17.44(a), neither the element of reasonableness nor of justification should be read into the statute by implication. Thus, it should not be a defense to a DTPA claim that a consumer was unreasonable or unjustified in relying upon the defendant's misrepresentation.

Leaving aside for the moment the question of whether a consumer *should have* discovered the truth of the matter before entering a transaction, what if he *actually discovers* the truth before entering the transaction through his own investigation? Sometimes referenced to as the "independent investigation" defense, the consumer's investigation and discovery of the truth is best understood as simply a negation of the element of reliance. The independent investigation defense finds its support from a statement quoted from a pre-1940 text, *Black on Rescission and Cancellation (2d)*, quoted by the Tyler Court of Appeals in 1969 as follows:

"Where false and fraudulent representations are made concerning the subject-matter of a contract, but the person to whom they are made, before closing the contract (or before the time for payment arrives) inspects and examines the subject of the contract, or conducts an independent investigation into the matters covered by the representations, which is sufficient to inform him of the truth, and which is not interfered with or rendered nugatory by any act of the other party, it is presumed that he places his reliance on the information acquired by such investigation and on his own judgment based on such facts, and not on the representations made to him, and therefore he cannot have relief because his bargain proves unsatisfactory to him."

...

"It is not necessary to the application of this rule that the party in question should have made the investigation in person. The same result follows if he employs a third person, in whom he has confidence, to make the test or examination, and receive his report and relies on it, as where a person purchases a tax title to lands on the advice of his attorney, whom he employs to investigate the public records, and who makes an extended search, or where, before concluding the bargain, he has an examination made by an expert skilled in the particular business or process to which the subject-matter relates." (Emphasis added.)

Marcus v. Kinabrew, 438 S.W.2d 431, 432-33 (Tex. App.—Tyler 1969, no writ) *quoting Whitsel v. Hoover*, 120 S.W.2d 930, 934 (Tex. Civ. App.—Amarillo 1938, writ dis'd. f.w.o.j.).

In *Bartlett v. Schmidt*, 33 S.W.3d 35 (Tex. App.—Corpus Christi 2000, pet. denied), the court, in dicta, seemed to extend the "independent investigation" defense further than necessary. There, the plaintiff sued for fraud and negligent misrepresentation in a real estate transaction when deed restrictions restricting the property to residential use only were enforced against his commercial development, despite representations that there were no such restrictions on the property. The restrictions were contained in a deed which plaintiff and his attorney were given, examined and concluded did not apply. Perhaps painting more broadly than necessary, the Corpus Christi Court of Appeals reversed the jury verdict based upon the authority of *Marcus v. Kinabrew, supra*, observing:

"The common thread of the decisions reaching this conclusion [an independent investigation negates reliance] is that, regardless of the result of his investigation, the buyer's decision to undertake such an investigation indicates that he or she is not relying on the seller's representations about the property. The record shows that Schmidt [the plaintiff] undertook such an investigation. Prior to his purchase of the property, Schmidt asked third parties to review conveyancing documents specifically to assure that no restrictions would interfere with his development of the property for his intended purpose. He did this after specifically asking Bartlett [defendant] about the very same thing. He did not rely upon Bartlett's representations in making his decision to purchase the property..."

"Accordingly, as a matter of law, Schmidt cannot recover for either negligent misrepresentation or fraud."

Bartlett v. Schmidt, 33 S.W.3d at 38. (Emphasis added). In *Dubow v. Dragon*, 746 S.W.2d 857 (Tex. App.—Dallas 1988, no writ), the summary judgment in favor of the defendants on the basis that the plaintiffs' "careful inspection" of the house prior to closing was found to be a superseding and intervening cause of their damages as a matter of law. There, the plaintiffs signed a contract modification stating:

> "*After careful inspection of the house, and with professional opinions, we feel that the house will need extensive on-going maintenance because of the site positioning, foundation and drainage. See attached Inspection Report. We will take the home as is, WITH ALL CONTINGENCIES REMOVED.*" (Emphasis in original).

Id. at 860. Based upon this statement, the Dallas Court of Appeals, in this pre-1995 law case, concluded that producing cause was negated as a matter of law, because the problems were discovered and the price reduced. *Id.*

Dubow v. Dragon has been distinguished more often than it has been followed. In *Blackstock v. Dudley*, 12 S.W.3d 131, 133-34 (Tex. App.—Amarillo 1999, no writ), the plaintiffs obtained a professional home inspection, but it did not discover the existing plumbing problems the defendant sellers misrepresented and failed to disclose. On appeal, the court rejected the defendants' claim that the plaintiffs' reliance upon a professional home inspection was a new and independent cause, negating any producing cause as a matter of law because the plaintiffs did not discover the true facts with their investigation. *Id.*

A consumer's own investigation of the real property being purchased will not automatically negate reliance on the seller's misrepresentations and thereby break the causation chain. Thus, in *Fernandez v. Schultz*, 15 S.W.3d 648 (Tex. App.—Dallas 2000, no pet.) the purchasers obtained a pre-closing inspection report which found termites on the home's exterior. After the closing, more extensive termite activity on the home's interior was discovered and a DTPA suit was brought alleging that the seller had covered up evidence of active termites in the interior of the house. The court of appeals rejected the seller's argument that the buyer's inspection constituted a new and independent basis for the purchase of the property.

The court noted that while the buyer's inspector's report may have been a producing cause of the purchase, the seller's concealment of the interior termite activity was also a producing cause, and was not superseded by the inspection report. There was no evidence that the consumers relied solely on their inspector's report in deciding whether or not to purchase the property.

The line of cases holding that the plaintiffs' "independent investigation" negates reliance or producing cause was criticized by the 14th Court of Appeals in *Warehouse Associates Corporate Ctr. II, Inc. v. Celotex Corp.*, 192 S.W.3d 225, 244-45 (Tex. App.—Houston [14th Dist.] 2006, petition den'd). There, the court noted that *Bartlett*, *Marcus* and the cases they cite holding that a buyer's independent investigation alone negates reliance and producing cause are contrary to Texas law on that issue, and reversed a summary judgment on the "independent investigation" defense. *Id.* Even so, it appears that the "independent investigation" defense is gaining acceptance in appropriate cases.

In reality, the "independent investigation" defense is not an affirmative defense, but an inferential rebuttal issue which negates reliance and producing cause, much like "sole cause" negates "proximate cause" in general negligence. *See Dillard v. Texas Electric Cooperative*, 157 S.W.3d 429, 432 (Tex. 2005). It simply recognizes the logical maxim that a person cannot maintain he believed false information was true when he knew it was false. That logic, however, cannot be extended to support the proposition that conducting an investigation which *might* or *should* render the true facts known to the consumer—but does not—nevertheless negates reliance on the defendant's misrepresentations. At best, such an investigation is factual evidence which might discount the consumer's claims of reliance, but does not negate those claims as a matter of law. Otherwise, the concepts of "reasonable" and "justifiable" reliance are improperly reintroduced into the analysis which, as demonstrated above, are not proper considerations in a DTPA case.

§2.02.7 Statutory Defenses

Both the DTPA and Chapter 541 of the Texas Insurance Code (formerly Article 21.21) contain statutory defenses to liability and damages. A common defense in both statutes deals with the situation in which the defendant makes a settlement offer in response to a demand letter. If the defendant tenders to the consumer an amount which is the same, substantially the same, or more than the actual damages found by the trier of fact, then the plaintiff may not recover an amount that exceeds the lesser of (1) the amount tendered in the settlement offer, or (2) the amount of actual damages found by the trier of fact. *See* DTPA §17.5052(g); TEX. INS. CODE §541.159.

The DTPA contains a defense in bar to a cause of action if the defendant tenders to the consumer the amount of damages, expenses, and attorneys' fees demanded in the pre-suit notice. *See* DTPA §17.506(d). *Lester v. Logan*, 893 S.W.2d 570 (Tex. App.—Corpus Christi 1994) writ denied per curiam 907 S.W.2d 452 (offer of $3,230 was not substantially the same as $6,196 damages found by jury). This provision is not contained in Chapter 541 of the Texas Insurance Code. Similarly, Chapter 541 does not contain the so-called third-party misinformation defense found in the DTPA. *See* DTPA §17.506(a). This defense, rarely invoked, permits a defendant to avoid liability by disclosing up front to the consumer the source of the information provided to consumers about goods or services.

If the plaintiff files suit without giving notice (unless the statute of limitations is about to run), the defendant is entitled to have the suit abated. *See* §6.01 *infra*.

Both the DTPA and Chapter 541 also provide that the defendant can recover his or her attorneys' fees and court costs on a finding by the court that the action was groundless or brought in bad faith or for the purpose of harassment. *See* DTPA §17.50(c); TEX. INS. CODE §541.153. In *Donwerth v. Preston II Chrysler-Dodge, Inc.*, 775 S.W.2d 634 (Tex. 1989) the Texas Supreme Court confirmed that the trial court, not the jury, determines the questions of groundlessness, harassment, and bad faith. To establish harassment, the defendant must prove that the action was brought solely for that purpose. "Groundlessness" under the DTPA has the same meaning as groundless under Texas Rule of Civil Procedure 13. *Id; see McCain v. NME Hosps., Inc.*, 856 S.W.2d 751 (Tex. App.—Dallas 1993, no writ).

There is a two-year statute of limitations for actions brought under the DTPA or Chapter 541. See DTPA §17.565; TEX. INS. CODE §541.162. However the statute of limitations does not begin to run until the consumer either "discovered or in the exercise of reasonable diligence, should have discovered the false, misleading, or deceptive act or practice." DTPA §17.565; *see*, TEX. INS. CODE §541.162(2) ("unfair method of competition or unfair or deceptive act or practice). The Texas Supreme Court has placed the burden of proving the date of discovery on the consumer. *Willis v. Maverick*, 760 S.W.2d 642, 647 (Tex. 1988). Common law tolling provisions do not apply to DTPA cases. *See Underkofler v. Vanasek*, 53 S.W.3d 343 (Tex. 2001) (holding that the limitations tolling provision applicable to legal malpractice actions does not apply to DTPA cases); *Pecan Valley Nut Co., Inc v. E.I. du Pont de Nemours & Co.*, 15 S.W.3d 244 (Tex. App.—Eastland 2000, no pet.) (common law "inherently undiscoverable" requirement does not apply to DTPA discovery rule).

In *Smith v. Gray*, 882 S.W.2d 103 (Tex. App.—Amarillo 1994, no writ) the court held that DTPA §17.565 tolls the running of the limitations period until a consumer discovered or through reasonable diligence should have discovered the nature of the injury, not when a consumer discovered that the defendants were the wrongdoers. The Texas Supreme Court denied the application for writ of error but noted that "the court neither approves or disapproves of the court of appeals analysis of the statute of limitations under the DTPA. Smith v. Gray, 907 S.W.2d 444 (Tex. 1995). See also Holmes v. P.K. Pipe & Tubing, Inc., 856 S.W.2d 530 (Tex. App.—Houston [1st Dist.] 1993, no writ) (DTPA action accrues upon discovery of misconduct, not upon discovery that misconduct caused damages.)

Lastly, the 1995 amendments impose a maximum dollar limit on transactions that are subject to the DTPA. After the effective date of the amendments, the DTPA will not apply to "a transaction, a project, or a set of transactions relating to the same project, involving a total consideration by the consumer of more than $500,000, other than a cause of action involving a consumer's residence." DTPA §17.49(g), as amended 1995.

§2.02.8 Media Exemption

The DTPA contains a limited exemption for owners or employees of regularly published media when the plaintiff's claim is based on false representations that appear in the media:

> "Nothing in this subchapter shall apply to the owner or employees of a regularly published newspaper, magazine, or telephone directory, or broadcast station, or billboard, wherein any advertisement in violation of this subchapter is published or disseminated unless it is established that the owner or employees of the advertising medium have knowledge of the false, deceptive or misleading acts or practices declared to be unlawful by this subchapter, or had a direct and substantial financial interest in the sale or distribution of the unlawfully advertised good or service.

> Financial interest as used in this section relates to an expectation which would be the direct result of such advertisement."

DTPA §17.49(a).

The exemption for employees applies only to *media* employees, not to employees of other enterprises who are acting on behalf of their employers. *Miller v. Keyser*, 90 S.W.3d 712, 719 (Tex. 2002).

§2.02.9 Contribution and Indemnity

Section 17.555 provides that a person who is sued under the DTPA may seek contribution or indemnity from the person actually responsible for the consumer's damages. In *Plas-Tex, Inc. v. U.S. Steel Corp.*, 772 S.W.2d 442, 446 (Tex. 1989) the Texas Supreme Court held that this section incorporates into the DTPA the "existing principles of contribution and indemnity law." *See also Swafford v. View-Caps Water Supply Corp.*, 617 S.W.2d 674 (Tex. 1981); *Stewart Title Guar. Co. v. Sterling*, 822 S.W.2d 1 (Tex. 1991); *First Title Co. of Waco, et al v. Garrett*, 860 S.W.2d 74 (Tex. 1993); *C & H Nationwide, Inc. v. Thompson*, 903 S.W.2d 315 (Tex. 1994); *Blackstock v. Dudley*, 12 S.W.3d 131 (Tex. Amarillo 1999, no pet.).

Chapter 33 of the Civil Practice & Remedies Code was amended by the 1995 legislative session in order to make Chapter 33 directly applicable to suits under the DTPA. TEX. CIV. PRAC. & REM. CODE §33.002(a)(2), as amended 1995.

§2.02.10 Responsible Third Party

In addition to contribution and indemnity and other third-party actions, a defendant may designate a third party as being responsible for all or part of the consumer's damages:

(a) A defendant may seek to designate a person as a responsible third party by filing a motion for leave to designate that person as a responsible third party. The motion must be filed on or before the 60th day before the trial date unless the court finds good cause to allow the motion to be filed at a later date.

(b) Nothing in this section affects the third-party practice as previously recognized in the rules and statutes of this state with regard to the assertion by a defendant of rights to contribution or indemnity. Nothing in this section affects the filing of cross-claims or counterclaims.

TEX. CIV. PRAC. & REM. CODE §33.004.

If a defendant designates a third party as responsible, then the plaintiff-consumer can join that person as a defendant even if limitations has run so long as joinder occurs not later than 60 days after that person is designated as a responsible third party. TEX. CIV. PRAC. & REM. CODE §33.004(e).

The court must grant leave to file the designation unless another party objects within 15 days after the date the motion is served. TEX. CIV. PRAC. & REM. CODE §33.004(f). If an objection is made, the objecting party must prove that the pleading fails to allege sufficient facts concerning the alleged responsibility of the person to satisfy the pleading requirements of the Texas Rules of Civil Procedure. TEX. CIV. PRAC. & REM. CODE §33.004(g)(1). The defendant must be given the opportunity to replead. TEX. CIV. PRAC. & REM. CODE §33.004(g)(2).

After an adequate time for discovery, a party may move to strike the designation of the responsible third party on the ground that there is no evidence that the designated third party is responsible for any portion of the consumer's alleged injury or damage. The court shall grant the motion unless a defendant produces sufficient evidence to raise a genuine issue of fact regarding the designated person's responsibility for the claimant's injury or damage. TEX. CIV. PRAC. & REM. CODE §33.004(l).

Although rare in consumer cases, in the event that an unknown third party committed a criminal act that was a cause of the loss or injury that is the subject of the lawsuit, the unknown third party, denominated as "Jane Doe" or "John Doe," may be designated. TEX. CIV. PRAC. & REM. CODE §33.004(j), (k). The pleadings of the defendant must allege sufficient facts to show the unknown person's responsibility, and must provide all identifying characteristics of the unknown person, all of which must be done within 60 days after the filing of the defendant's answer. TEX. CIV. PRAC. & REM. CODE §33.004(j)(1), (2).

§2.02.11 Settlement Credit

As noted above, Chapter 33 of the Civil Practice & Remedies Code is now directly applicable to suits under the DTPA. TEX. CIV. PRAC. & REM. CODE §33.002(a)(2), as amended 1995. Section 33.012(b) provides that the claimant's recovery shall be reduced by the sum of all settlements. The "settlements" which qualify for this settlement credit are not otherwise defined; however, the statute defines "settling person" as "a person who has, at any time, paid or promised to pay money or anything of monetary value to a claimant in consideration of potential liability with respect to the personal injury, property damage, death, or other harm for which recovery of damages is sought." TEX. CIV. PRAC. & REM. CODE § 33.011(5). Here, the settlement is not limited by any particular cause of action asserted, but rather the harm for which recovery is sought. Thus, if the claimant has settled with a person against whom a claim for the same alleged harm, the settlement credit should apply, regardless of whether the claim was asserted as a DTPA claim or under some other form of liability.

The non-settling defendant has the burden of pleading and proving its right to settlement credit. *Mobil Oil Corp. v. Ellender*, 968 S.W.2d 917, 927 (Tex. 1998). If the non-settling party presents sufficient evidence of the settlement, the burden then shifts to the plaintiff to tender evidence allocating the settlement amount applicable to the plaintiff. *Crown Life Ins. Co. v. Casteel*, 22 S.W.3d 378, 392 (Tex. 2000). If the plaintiff cannot satisfy this burden, then the non-settling party is entitled to a credit equaling the entire settlement amount. *Ellender*, 968 S.W.2d at 928.

The settlement credit may have an impact on the recoverability of attorney's fees under the DTPA. While a DTPA plaintiff "prevails" and is thus entitled to recover attorney's fees despite a complete off-set of his recovery by the defendant's counterclaim (*McKinley v. Drozd*, 685 S.W.2d 7 (Tex. 1984); *Matthews v. Candlewood Builders, Inc.*, 685 S.W.2d 649 (Tex. 1985)), a claimant whose DTPA recovery is completely offset by the settlement credit does not "prevail" and is not entitled to recovery attorney's fees from the non-settling defendant. *Osborne v. Jauregui, Inc.*, 252 S.W.3d 70 (Tex. App.—Austin 2008, pet. den'd.) (en banc); *Buccaneer Homes of Ala., Inc. v. Pelis*, 43 S.W.3d 586, 590 (Tex. App.—Houston [1st Dist.] 2001, no pet.); *Hamra v Gulden*, 898 S.W.2d 16, 19 (Tex. App.—Dallas 1995, writ dism'd w.o.j.); *Blizzard v. Nationwide Mut. Fire Ins. Co.*, 756 S.W.2d 801, 806 (Tex. App.—Dallas 1988, no writ).

§2.02.12 Large Transactions Exemptions

DTPA §17.49(f) and §17.49(g) provide two additional exemptions for larger transactions. The first is an exemption for claims arising out of certain contracts exceeding $100,000 in consideration to be paid by the consumer. The exemption in §17.49(f) is substantially limited, however, by the requirement that the consumer be represented by legal counsel who has not been hired or referred by the defendant. Transactions involving the consumer's residence are also not included in the exemption. Under §17.49(f), the transaction is exempted from the DTPA if:

(1) there is a written contract that covers the transaction;

(2) the subject matter of the contract involves a total consideration paid by the consumer of $100,000 or more;

(3) in negotiating the contract, the consumer was represented by legal counsel who was not directly or indirectly identified, suggested, or selected by the defendant or an agent of the defendant; and,

(4) the contract does not involve the consumer's residence.

DTPA §17.49(f).

DTPA §17.49(g) exempts from DTPA coverage consumer transactions involving more than $500,000 in consideration, regardless of whether the consumer is represented by legal counsel. Again, transactions involving the consumer's residence are not included in the exemption.

The purpose behind these two "large transaction" exemptions appears to be to deny DTPA remedies to more affluent consumers, presumably because they have more access to legal counsel and other sources of advice and information about the proposed transaction and are less likely to be misled into an unfavorable bargain. These amendments were added in 1995 and the threshold amounts—$100,000 and $500,000—have not changed since then. Thus, price inflation will continue to increase the effect of this exemption in the future.

§2.03 Client Questionnaire (Defendant)

The routine use of a client questionnaire is equally important when the client is or will be a defendant in a DTPA lawsuit as it is when the client is the plaintiff. In most cases the prospective defendant will be a business person somewhat more accustomed to lawyers and legal proceedings. Even so, the need to obtain basic information still exists and the client must be convinced to spend whatever time is required to provide full answers to the questions.

[a] FORM: Client questionnaire (defendant)

Instructions

```
It is essential that we obtain all of the information asked
about in the following questions so that we may properly evaluate
the claim that has been made against you. For several of the ques-
tions, we have provided space on this form for your answers. For
many of the questions, it will be necessary to write your answers
on separate pages.

We will spend some time reviewing the questionnaire at our ini-
tial meeting; therefore, if you do not understand what is being
asked, we will discuss it when we meet.

Your cooperation in answering these questions is deeply appre-
ciated.

                       CLIENT QUESTIONNAIRE

   A. Information about you and your company:

1. Name of business  _____

2. Address  _____
                                                           zip code

3. Telephone: _____ (Day)  _____ (Night)

4. Type of organization:
     ____  Sole proprietorship
     ____  Partnership
     ____  Limited partnership
     ____  Limited liability partnership
     ____  Professional association
     ____  Corporation
```

5. Your name _____

6. Your address _____
   zip code

7. Who owns the business? (Give name, address and percentage of ownership) _____

8. If your business is a corporation:

   (a) What are the names of the members of the Board of Directors?
   _____

   (b) Who are the officers of the corporation?
   _____

   President: _____

   Vice-President: _____

   Secretary: _____

   Treasurer: _____

   (c) Is the corporate minute book current?

   _____ Yes _____ No

   (d) Does the corporation have regular annual meetings?

   _____ Yes _____ No

   (e) Is the property of the corporation kept separate from personal property?

   _____ Yes _____ No

   (f) Are corporate funds ever used for personal purposes?

   _____ Yes _____ No

   (g) Who controls the day to day operation of the corporation?
   _____

   (h) Does the corporation have sufficient assets with which to pay the full amount of the claim that has been made if payment is ordered by the court?

   _____ Yes _____ No

(i) Are the corporation's franchise tax payments current?

_____ Yes _____ No

9. If your business is a partnership:

   (a) Who is the managing partner(s)? _____
   _____

   (b) Who are all of the partners and what percentage interest is owned by each? _____
   _____
   _____
   _____

10. What type of business are you involved in?
    _____

11. How long have you been in business?
    _____

12. Insurance coverage:

    (a) Do you have insurance or a bond that you believe may apply to the claim that has been made against you?

    _____ Yes _____ No

    (b) If you have answered "yes," have you notified the insurance carrier, agent or bonding company?

    _____ Yes _____ No

B. *Other attorneys*:

Please answer the questions in this section if you have another attorney who has or still handles legal matters for you:

1. What is the name, address and telephone number of the attorney? _____
   _____
   _____

2. What is the reason that you have decided to discuss this matter with our firm instead of this attorney? _____
   _____
   _____

C. *Prior legal involvement*:

1. Have you been involved in prior lawsuits (other than routine collection cases)? _____ Yes _____ No

2. If you have answered question number I "yes," on a separate page, please list all prior lawsuits in which you have been involved, other than routine collection cases, and include the following information for each:

   (a) the names of the parties to the lawsuit

   (b) the type of case

   (c) the outcome of the case

   (d) the name of your attorney in the case

D. *Other possible parties*

On a separate page, please list the full name, address (with zip code) and telephone number of *every person* against whom you believe you may have a claim as a result of the claim that has been made against you. (For example, if a person sells a product that has a defect caused by the manufacturer, the seller may have a claim against the manufacturer if the seller is sued by the buyer.) Include in your list a brief statement as to why you believe you have a claim against each person listed.

E. *Fact witnesses*

On a separate page, please list the full name, address (with zip code) and telephone number of *every person* who has *any* knowledge or information about the claim that has been made against you, regardless of how little or how much the person knows, *and* describe briefly what is known to each person.

F. *Expert witnesses*

On a separate page, please list the full name, address and telephone number of any experts to whom you believe we should talk about the claim which has been made against you. After each name, please put the person's area of expertise. And, if the expert has already been consulted on this matter, please so indicate.

G. *Diary of events*

This is the last question, but it is the most time consuming of all and, quite possibly, the most important.

Beginning with the first event or conversation that you or your personnel, if any, recall about this matter, please write a *detailed* account of your recollections, including each thing that has happened and each thing that has been said or done to you and each thing that has been said or done by you. Include dates as best you can remember. If you do not recall an exact date, estimate when it was. If you remember the exact words of conversations, use them. If you do not recall the exact words used, then write out the substance of the words spoken. Give special attention to all of your conversations and correspondence with the other side. The more detailed the diary is, the better.

Be sure to include in the diary every "defense" you believe we may have to the claims that have been made against you.

Please write legibly. Use as many pages as are necessary.

The diary does not need to be completed by the time of our meeting; however, if you are able to complete it by that time, it will be very helpful.

§2.04 —Checklists for Initial Interview

As mentioned above, the initial interview with the recipient of a DTPA notice letter generally involves greater time pressures than are present when the client is the person making the claim. If a notice letter has been received, it must be answered within the sixty days allowed by law. DTPA §17.505(c). If a lawsuit already has been filed, answer day may not be far away.

At the beginning of the initial interview, the prospective client's answers to the Client Questionnaire should be reviewed.

Particular attention should be given to those questions which have a direct bearing on the client's exposure. For example, when a closely held corporation is the client, the possibility of shareholder liability should be examined. The answers to the questions listed in part 8(c)-(i) of the Client Questionnaire will suggest whether there is a likelihood that the plaintiff can successfully pierce the corporate veil. *See* §2.03[b] *supra*; §10.02[j] *infra*.

Another subject to be discussed specifically in the initial interview is whether the client has any type of insurance coverage or a bond that may apply to the claim. If possible insurance coverage exists, the carrier should be notified immediately in order to give the carrier the opportunity to tender a defense and possible coverage. If the carrier is not notified immediately of the claim, then the carrier may be provided with a defense on the policy. Part 12 of the Client Questionnaire should reveal the existence of insurance; however, some clients are reluctant to make an insurance claim because of a concern that their rates will go up or that the policy will be cancelled. For this reason, possible insurance coverage should be reviewed thoroughly.

The following forms are intended as outlines of topics for discussion during the interview. The questions should be used only as a guide to the interview, since the nature of the claim made will raise a number of questions unique to the case. Additional checklists are provided in the Chapters on Residential Construction (§12.06.01, *infra*) and Real Estate (§13.03, *infra*).

[a] CHECKLIST: Sale of goods or services

Client _____   Date of interview _____

Litigation

- ❑ Has a lawsuit been filed
- ❑ If a lawsuit has been filed, when is answer day

The demand letter

- ❑ When was the demand letter received
- ❑ When is a response to the demand letter due
- ❑ Does the demand letter contain sufficient information to evaluate the claim; if not, what additional information is required

The sale

- ❑ What was sold
- ❑ When
- ❑ Who was the salesperson
- ❑ Other than the salesperson, who else talked to the buyer
- ❑ What was the purchase price
    - Was there any discount given

[If a discount was given, was it because of any explained defect in the product or limitation on liability.]

- ❑ Was the purchase price negotiated
- ❑ Did the buyer explain why the product/service was being purchased; if yes, what was said

[If the seller is aware of the purpose for which a product is being purchased and it is a special purpose, an implied warranty may be created under Tex. Bus. & Com. Code §2.315.]

- ❏ Were any written warranties given
- ❏ What was said about the qualities or benefits of the product/service
- ❏ Was a written contract signed
    - If yes, is there an arbitration clause

[An arbitration clause may be enforceable under the Federal Arbitration Act, 9 U.S.C. §1 *et seq.*]

- ❏ Was this sale in the ordinary course of the client's business
- ❏ Was a model or sample used in the sale

[A model or sample may create an implied warranty under TEX. BUS. & COM. CODE §2.314 if the seller is in the business of selling that product.]

- ❏ Was any information that was given or said to the buyer obtained from a third party, e.g., a manufacturer

[The DTPA contains a defense to liability if certain steps are taken when information is obtained from a third party. *See* DTPA §17.506.]

- ❏ Was buyer advised in writing that the information given to the buyer was obtained from a third party
- ❏ Was any advertising used in the sale of the product/service; if yes, was the advertising general media or point of sale, or other

Complaints from customer

- ❏ Have any complaints been received from the buyer
- ❏ What response was made to the buyer's complaint(s)
- ❏ Has any offer been made to the buyer to settle the complaint

Repairs

- ❏ What repairs have been performed
- ❏ Has service been re-done
- ❏ Was the buyer charged for any repairs
- ❏ Have repairs been performed by any third party

[Under the terms of some express warranties, work done by a third party may void the warranty.]

Condition of product/service

- ❏ Has product/service been inspected; if yes, what were the results of the inspection
- ❏ Is further inspection necessary or would it be helpful
- ❏ What was condition of product/service at time of delivery
- ❏ Has buyer made any alterations after delivery

[Alterations in the product may affect the buyer's right to revoke acceptance or rescission. See TEX. BUS. & COM. CODE §2.608.]

- ❏ Have there been any complaints from third parties about the product/service

[Evidence of complaints from third parties may establish grounds for a "knowing" violation, thereby increasing the client's exposure in a lawsuit. See DTPA §17.45(9); §17.50(b)(1).]

Response to notice

- ❏ Has a response been made to the notice letter
- ❏ What response, if any, does client want to make to the demand
    - Offer of repair
    - Cash
    - Attorneys' fees
    - Other
- ❏ If no notice letter has been received, explain to client the cost/benefit of a plea in abatement to compel a demand

Explanations to client

- ❏ Attorney and client agreement
- ❏ Cost of defense
- ❏ Uncertainty of litigation
- ❏ Requirements of discovery
- ❏ Must be present at some depositions and trial

Documents to obtain from client

[Although client should be cautioned to provide all documents to the attorney that are, in any way, related to the transaction and its aftermath, the following documents must be obtained immediately.]

- ❑ Sales contract, receipt
- ❑ Advertising about product, general media and point of sale
- ❑ Warranty on product
- ❑ Information obtained from third parties about good/service
- ❑ Any correspondence from buyer; notes of conversations with buyer
- ❑ Complaints from other customers about product
- ❑ Correspondence from or to manufacturer about product
- ❑ Any insurance policy that client carries on his business that may apply to claim

[b] CHECKLIST: Lease of commercial real property

Client _____ Date of interview _____

[Before conducting the interview, the provisions of Tex. Prop. Code §92.001 et seq. and §93.001 et seq. should be reviewed.]

Litigation

- ❑ Has a lawsuit been filed
- ❑ If a lawsuit has been filed, when is answer day

The notice letter

- ❑ When was the notice letter received
- ❑ When is the response to the notice letter due
- ❑ Does the notice letter contain sufficient information to evaluate; if not, what additional information is required

The lease

- ❑ What is the address of the leased property
- ❑ When was the property first leased

- ❑ Was the lease in writing
- ❑ What is the term of the lease
- ❑ What was the purpose for which the property was leased
- ❑ What is the amount of the rent
- ❑ Was the amount of the rent negotiated or was it fixed

[The possibility that known defects were the subject of a negotiated rent payment should be explored.]

- ❑ Is the amount of rent paid by the tenant the same as the rent charged to others; if not, why
- ❑ What was the amount of the security deposit, if any
- ❑ Are all rent payments current
    - If not, how delinquent is the tenant
    - Why did the tenant cease making payments

[A tenant may withhold rent payments if the property is unsuitable for its intended purpose. See *Davidow v. Inwood North Professional Group-Phase I*, 747 S.W.2d 373 (TEX. 1988) (commercial lease).]

- ❑ Has either the tenant or the owner given notice of termination of the lease to the other; if yes, when
- ❑ Does the tenant still occupy the property
- ❑ Has client taken any action to exclude the tenant from the property, *e.g.*, changing door locks, cutting off utilities
- ❑ Has the tenant abandoned the property

[A commercial tenant is presumed to have abandoned the property if goods, equipment, or other property, in an amount substantial enough to indicate a probable intent to abandon the premises, is being or has been removed from the premises and the removal is not within the normal course of the tenant's business. TEX. PROP. CODE §93.002(d).]

Representations made

- ❑ At the time the property was leased, was client told the purpose for which the property was being leased
- ❑ At the time the property was leased, were any representations made to the tenant about the characteristics, uses, or qualities of the property

Property management

- ❑ Who manages the property
  - On premises manager
  - Management company
  - Owner
- ❑ Was the tenant given written notice of the name and business street address of the management company, if any
- ❑ Who collects the rent

[If a management company or other person manages the property they should be contacted immediately to determine whether a demand letter or citation has been served on them.]

- ❑ Has the claim that has been made been discussed with the manager by the tenant
  - If yes, what was said
- ❑ Has the claim that has been made been discussed with the manager by the client
  - If yes, what was said
- ❑ Is the client satisfied with the performance of the manager

Defects in property

- ❑ At the time the property was rented, was client aware of any defects in the property that are related to the claim made
- ❑ What are the known defects in the property at this time
- ❑ What is the cause of the known defects in the property
- ❑ How did the client become aware of the defects
- ❑ Has tenant caused any damage to property beyond normal wear and tear; if yes, what and when

Complaints made

- ❑ Before receipt of the demand letter, had tenant made any complaints about the property
- ❑ Does lease require written notice of defects in the property

- ❑ At the time the tenant gave notice of the defects, was the tenant current on rent payments
- ❑ If complaints were made, what was the client's response to the complaints
- ❑ Have any other tenants complained about condition of property

[Evidence of complaints from third parties may establish grounds for a "knowing" violation, thereby increasing client's exposure in lawsuit. See DTPA §17.45(9); §17.50(b)(1).]

Repairs

- ❑ Since the tenant moved into the property, have any repairs been made to the property; if yes, what type of repairs and when
- ❑ Since the tenant moved into the property, has the property been maintained regularly; if yes, what maintenance work has been done and when
- ❑ Since the tenant moved into the property, have any improvements been made to the property

Compliance with lease

- ❑ Has the tenant violated the lease in any respect
- ❑ If the tenant has violated the lease, have violations been brought to the tenant's attention; if yes, when and what was the response

Response to notice letter

- ❑ Has any response been made to notice letter
- ❑ What response does client want to make to notice letter
  - Offer of repair
  - Reduction in rent
  - Termination of lease
  - Cash
  - Attorneys' fees
- ❑ If no notice letter was received before a lawsuit under the DTPA was filed, explain the cost/benefit of a plea in abatement to compel a demand letter

Explanations to client

- ❏ Attorney-client agreement
- ❏ Cost of defense
- ❏ Uncertainty of litigation
- ❏ Requirements of discovery
- ❏ Must be present at depositions and trial

Documents to obtain from client

[Although client should be cautioned to provide all documents that relate, in any way, to the transaction and its aftermath, the following documents *must* be provided immediately.]

- ❏ Lease application
- ❏ Lease
- ❏ Correspondence, notices received from tenant
- ❏ Correspondence, notices sent to tenant
- ❏ Tenant file
- ❏ Complaints from other tenants

§2.05 Attorney-Client Agreements

There are several types of attorney and client agreements that are used in DTPA defense cases. The type of contract used depends more on the identity and experience of the client than on the nature of the case. That is, if the client is a longstanding client for whom numerous legal matters have been handled, no agreement may be required. If, on the other hand, the client is new and generally inexperienced in legal matters, a very detailed attorney and client agreement may be advisable. The fee agreement should be in writing and should be executed, "before or within a reasonable time after commencing the representation. *See* TEXAS RULE OF PROFESSIONAL CONDUCT 1.04(c).

[a] FORM: Letter agreement with respect to legal services

(Date)

(Inside address)

Re: Claim of [name of complainant]

Dear _____:

This letter will confirm our agreement regarding legal services that will be provided to you in the above referenced matter.

In recognition of the fact that various aspects of this matter may be handled by different individuals in our office, our fees will be based on the following schedule:

A. Partners: $_____ per hour

B. Associates: $_____ per hour

C. Paralegals: $_____ per hour

D. Law clerks: $_____ per hour

We will provide you with monthly billing statements itemizing the work that has been done on your behalf. Payment will be due upon receipt of the statement.

As you know, we will be confronted with a number of deadlines in the course of handling this matter that require action on our part. It is essential that we work together to meet these deadlines so that we can preserve the legal rights that you have.

We will keep you informed as the work progresses; however, if, at any time, you have a question or desire additional information, please give me a call.

If this letter correctly reflects our fee agreement, please sign in the space provided below and return a signed copy to me for my files in the enclosed, self-addressed envelope.

Thank you for your cooperation. We look forward to working with you on this matter.

                                        Sincerely,

                                        [Signature of attorney]

[Signature line for client]

[b] FORM: Letter enclosing attorney-client agreement

(Date)

(Inside address)

Re: Attorney-client agreement

Dear _____:

Enclosed is our proposed attorney and client agreement, the terms of which were discussed during our conference.

Please review the agreement to insure that it accurately reflects your understanding of our discussion. If you are in agreement with its provisions, please sign the enclosed copy of the agreement and return it to me for our files.

Although I regret that you find yourself in need of legal services, we look forward to working with you on this matter.

If you have any questions about the agreement, please give me a call.

                        Sincerely,

                        [Signature of attorney]

[Enclose original and one copy of agreement]

[c] FORM: Attorney-client hourly fee agreement

ATTORNEY-CLIENT AGREEMENT

This is an employment agreement, and an appointment of an attorney-in-fact, between _____ ("Attorneys") and _____ ("Client").

1. *Scope of Employment.* Attorneys will represent Client with respect to [describe case to be handled].

2. *Retainer.* Client agrees to deposit with Attorneys, upon the execution of this document, a retainer in the amount of $_____. The fees described in the following paragraph will be billed against this retainer. Whenever the fees charged have exhausted the retainer, Client will deposit an additional retainer in the same amount.

3. *Attorneys' Fees*. All Attorneys' fees will be billed at the following rates:

(a) Partners: $_____ per hour

(b) Associates: $_____ per hour

(c) Paralegals: $_____ per hour

(d) Law Clerks: $_____ per hour

All legal fees will be billed monthly and are payable upon receipt. If applicable laws allow Attorneys to seek to recover such fees from a third party, Attorneys will do so. Nevertheless, Client understands and agrees that such legal fees are due and payable when billed whether or not such fees can be recovered for Client at a later date. Any attorneys' fees which are recovered from a third party will be paid over to Client.

4. *Costs*. All out-of-pocket expenses incurred by Attorneys in the handling of Client's claims will be reimbursed by Client on a monthly basis. Copies made in Attorneys' offices will be billed at the rate of _____ cents per page. Mileage on personal automobiles will be billed at the rate of _____ cents per mile. Copies of documents transmitted over FAX machines will be billed at the rate of $_____ per page if document transmission is performed from Attorneys' offices. All other costs will be billed at the exact amount incurred.

5. *Withdrawal From Agreement*. Client authorizes Attorneys to withdraw from this agreement at any time upon the happening of any of the following events:

(a) Client fails to pay Attorneys' fees or to reimburse expenses when they are due, after reasonable notice; or

(b) Client fails to cooperate in discovery. Attorneys have advised Client that in any lawsuit the other side has the right, among other things, to take depositions, to ask interrogatories which Client must answer under oath, to make requests for admissions of fact, and to request that certain documents be produced, all of which must be done by a certain date. These activities are called "discovery." If, after reasonable notice, Client fails to assist Attorneys in responding to discovery, or, if Client fails to appear for deposition, then this failure shall be deemed a failure to cooperate under this subparagraph.

6. *No Oral Modifications*. Client agrees that this Attorney-Client Agreement will not be modified by any oral agreement; instead, all

modifications of this agreement must be in writing and signed by both Attorneys and Client.

7. *Nature of Litigation.* Attorneys have advised Client that the outcome of the trial of a lawsuit is impossible to predict. Thus, Client understands that, regardless of how strong the defenses may appear, it is impossible to guarantee or even predict with certainty that the trial will be successful.

8. *Agreement Binding.* Client agrees that this Attorney-Client Agreement shall be binding on Client, his successors, heirs, executors, or assigns.

9. *Texas Law Applies.* This agreement shall be interpreted and construed according to the laws of the State of Texas.

10. *Place of Performance.* This agreement is to be performed in County, Texas, although the litigation involved may be tried in a different county.

11. *Effective Date.* This agreement becomes effective on the date that this agreement is signed by Client.

SIGNED AND AGREED TO ON THE DATE SHOWN.

_____   _____
         "Attorneys"   "Client"

Date Signed by Client: _____

Chapter 3

Giving Notice and Responding to an Offer

§3.01　General Considerations
§3.02　Notice Letter: DTPA
§3.03　Products or Services
§3.04　Elements of a Notice Letter
　　　[a]　FORM:　Notice letter (general form)
　　　[b]　FORM:　Notice letter: defective product (rescission and damages)
　　　[c]　FORM:　Notice letter: defective product or service (damages)
§§3.05 - 3.08　　[Reserved]
§3.09　Client Communications Concerning the Notice Letter
　　　[a]　FORM: Letter to client transmitting notice letter
　　　[b]　FORM: Letter to client: claim rejected
§3.10　Evaluating a Settlement Offer
　　　[a]　FORM: Letter to client evaluating a settlement offer
　　　[b]　FORM: Letter to client evaluating a settlement offer (residential construction)
　　　[c]　FORM: Letter accepting the settlement offer
　　　[d]　FORM: Letter accepting the offer to repair
　　　[e]　FORM: Letter rejecting the settlement offer
　　　[f]　FORM: Letter rejecting offer to repair

§3.01 General Considerations

The Deceptive Trade Practices—Consumer Protection Act and Chapter 541 both require that written notice be given to the prospective defendant before suit is filed. This section deals with the particular notice requirements of the DTPA.

The notice provision of the DTPA is found in §17.505(a):

> As a prerequisite to filing a suit seeking damages under Subdivision (1) of Subsection (b) of this subchapter against any person, a consumer shall give written notice to the person at least 60 days before filing the suit advising the person in reasonable detail of the consumer's specific complaint and the amount of economic damages, damages for mental anguish, and expenses, including attorney's fees, if any reasonably incurred by the consumer in asserting the claim against the defendant. During the 60 day period a written request to inspect, in a reasonable manner and at a reasonable time and place, the goods that are the subject of the consumer's action or claim may be presented to the consumer.

DTPA 17.505(a).

The exceptions to the pre-filing notice requirement are (1) when the statute of limitations on a claim will run during the notice period, or, (2) when the DTPA claim is made as a counterclaim in a lawsuit filed against the consumer. *See* DTPA §17.505(b). Further, it is important to note that if the lawsuit seeks a remedy other than damages, *e.g.*, an injunction, restoration of money or property, etc., then pre-filing notice is not required.

In those cases in which DTPA §15.505(b) requires pre-filing notice, if a consumer files a suit for damages without giving notice, the defendant may file a plea in abatement to stop the proceedings until proper notice is given. DTPA §17.505(c). To be effective, the plea in abatement must be filed within thirty days after the date the original answer is filed. DTPA §17.505(c). *See* §6.01 *infra*.

§3.02 Notice Letter: DTPA

Although there is little evidence to suggest that it is effective, the purpose of the notice provisions in the DTPA is to encourage settlement before a DTPA lawsuit is filed. The form of the notice letter should, therefore, be calculated to provide the prospective defendant with sufficient information to evaluate the claim.

Since pre-filing notice is required by the DTPA, it should be sent either by certified mail, return receipt requested, or by hand delivery so that a signed receipt for service can be obtained. At least one court of appeals has held that a notice letter sent by certified mail but returned unclaimed does not satisfy the statute. *Hash v. Hines*, 796 S.W.2d 312 (Tex. App.—Amarillo 1990), rev'd on other grounds, *Hines v. Hash*, 843 S.W.2d 464 (Tex. 1992) (not reaching the issue). If the defendant raises lack of notice as grounds for a plea in abatement, see §6.01 *infra*, then the plaintiff is required to go forward with evidence to show that such notice was, in fact, given, or that it was excused. *Hines v. Hash, supra*. Many consumer purchases involve financing. The "holder-in-due course" and the "purchase money loan" rule of the Federal Trade Commission generally require that any contract used in the sale contain a provision that imposes liability on anyone who purchases the contract from the seller. See §5.16, *infra*. The purpose of the rules is to preserve consumer claims and defenses against those who otherwise could sue to collect the debt regardless of the condition of the product. In these cases, a copy of the notice letter should be sent by certified mail, return receipt requested, to the third party creditor since it probably will be necessary to include this person as a defendant if a DTPA lawsuit is filed.

The sufficiency or validity of a notice letter is a question of law for the court. *See, In Re Alford Chevrolet-Geo,* 997 S.W.2d 173, 176 (Tex. 1999); *Jim Walter Homes, Inc. v. Valencia,* 690 S.W.2d 239, 242 (Tex. 1985); *Williams v. Hills Fitness Center, Inc.,* 705 S.W.2d 189, 191-193 (Tex. App.—Texarkana 1985, writ ref'd n.r.e.); *compare Cielo Dorado Dev. v. Certainteed Corp.,* 744 S.W.2d 10 (Tex. 1988). Section 17.505 does not require that the notice letter detail the DTPA provisions claimed to have been violated. In fact, the sufficiency of the notice letter has been described as a "fairly low threshold." *Richardson v. Foster & Sear,* 257 S.W.3d 782 (Tex. App.—Ft. Worth 2008, no pet.) (pro se plaintiff's rambling, six-page letter which did not cite a single DTPA provision was nevertheless adequate when it gave factual detail of his complaint and specific dollar amounts for economic and mental anguish damages claimed). As long as the notice letter provides sufficient detail of the consumer's specific complaint, the amount of damages claimed and a separate amount for attorney's fees incurred, if any, it will be sufficient to comply with §17.505. *Id.*

The notice letter should be a clear, fair and objective statement of the complaint. The notice letter is not required to include an offer to settle the consumer's claims for an amount less than his losses and attorney's fees. What is required is a notice letter, not a settlement demand. The statute simply requires notice of the claim in reasonable detail with specific amounts stated for the damages claimed and attorney's fees incurred to date.

The letters frequently find their way into evidence, however, as part of the proof that pre-filing notice was sent and received; accordingly, the letters should be written with this possibility in mind. The plaintiff's letter should, when viewed by a third party, be seen as a fair attempt to settle a claim. Even though few cases settle on a notice letter, the practice of grossly overstating the claim in the notice letter as a negotiating tactic is discouraged because it generally reduces the credibility of the complaint. If an overly hostile or hyperbolic letter is introduced into evidence, the plaintiff's credibility will be impacted.

The DTPA notice letter should be written with the following three objectives in mind:

- Satisfying the statutory notice requirement

- Persuading the prospective defendant (or opposing counsel or insurance carrier) that settlement is in everyone's best interest

- Demonstrating to a court or jury who may later see the letter that the client's demand is reasonable in the event the notice letter should make its way into evidence.

The demand letter should be reviewed and approved by the client before it is delivered to insure (1) the accuracy of the factual content of the letter and (2) that the amount of the damages claimed is sufficient to satisfy the client in the unlikely event a check for the full amount is received by return mail, thereby barring the filing of a DTPA lawsuit. *See* DTPA §17.506(d).

§3.03 Products or Services

The most frequent type of consumer transaction involves the purchase or lease of products or services. There are literally millions of such transactions in Texas each day. In fact, in a 1989 survey conducted by the Consumer Law Section, it was determined that defects in products or services were alleged in 66% of all DTPA jury trials in a thirty-four county area. *See Survey of Jury Trials Under the Deceptive Trade Practices Act*, Consumer Law Section, State Bar of Texas, March 21, 1989, *as reported* in 14 CaveaT vendor 35 (1989).

Obviously, the DTPA has valuable remedies for consumers who are damaged by the sale or lease of defective products. There are, however, valuable rights and remedies contained in the Uniform Commercial Code that should not be overlooked. *See* Tex. Bus. & Com. Code §2.601-2.616. Accordingly, a notice letter concerning a defective product should be used not only to satisfy the DTPA, but also to fulfill any notice requirements of the UCC that may be necessary to preserve the remedies provided by the Code. In several respects, the notice provisions of the UCC are more stringent than those of the DTPA. For example, if a buyer wishes to reject goods that have been delivered, it must be done, "within a reasonable time after the delivery or tender." Tex. Bus. & Com. Code §2.602(a). Also, if a buyer fails to specify a defect that is, "ascertainable by reasonable inspection," then, under some circumstances, the buyer cannot rely on the unstated defect as justification for the rejection or to establish a breach of contract. Tex. Bus. & Com. Code §2.605(a). The notice letter may also be used as a means of tendering the rejected goods to the buyer. See Tex. Bus. & Com. Code §2.602(a), (b). If the client needs any of the remedies provided by the UCC, it is, therefore, necessary to examine each of the Code's provisions with respect to rejection and revocation of acceptance in order to make sure that the notice letter is sufficient. *See* Tex. Bus. & Com. Code §§2.601-2.616.

When goods or services are purchased on a "consumer credit contract," i.e., a contract to purchase goods or services for personal, family or household purposes as set forth in Regulation Z, 12 C.F.R. §226.2(a); 15 U.S.C. §1602(h), the Federal Trade Commission "Holder-in-Due-Course" and "Purchase Money Loan" rules may apply. *See* 16 C.F.R. §433.2(a); 16 C.F.R. §433.2. The application of the Holder-in-Due-Course and Purchase Money Loan rules means that the creditor who ends up owning the consumer credit contract is subject to the same claims and defenses that are available to the consumer against the seller. The extended cause of action exists because the F.T.C. rules require that a "consumer credit contract" contain a provision which preserves the claims and defenses. *See, e.g.,* 16 C.F.R. §433.2. An example of the paragraph is contained in paragraph 5(b) of §5.19, Form [a], infra. When the F.T.C. rules apply, however, the creditor's liability is limited to the amount the creditor has been paid. *Home Savings Ass'n v. Guerra*, 733 S.W.2d 134 (Tex. 1987). The value of the holder-in-due-course rule and the purchase money loan rule to consumers is that in proper cases a consumer may recoup payments made for defective products or services. This provision also is valuable when the seller of the product is not financially able to pay all of the damages. Without such provisions in the consumer credit contract, a consumer must pay the underlying debt for the defective product or service without regard to whether the product or service has given any value to the buyer. A form petition is in §14.07[a] *infra*, which illustrates the pleading of these rules in the context of a suit involving a new automobile. When these rules apply, a copy of the notice letter should be sent to the owner of the consumer credit contract.

A notice letter concerning poor or faulty service follows essentially the same format as a notice letter for a defective product; however, since "rescission" is normally not possible in a service transaction, most such letters will be in the nature of a request for a full or partial refund of the price paid, together with any additional damages, expenses, and attorneys' fees that are claimed.

§3.04 Elements of a Notice Letter

Although the format of notice letters varies from case to case and attorney to attorney, each such letter must contain at least three basic elements:

- Notice of representation

- A statement of the claim in reasonable detail

- The amount of actual damages, expenses and attorneys' fees sought, separately stating the amount of economic loss, mental anguish damages claimed, and the expenses (including attorney's fees) that have been incurred.

Many other elements generally are included in a DTPA notice letter. For example, although not required by §17.505, the sections of the DTPA which are violated are often listed or set forth. It also may be advisable to provide notice of the attorney's contingent interest in the case in order to reduce the possibility of a direct settlement of the claim between the client and the prospective defendant. Also, although not required, a threat that litigation may follow if the notice letter is not answered favorably may be included to impress upon the recipient the need for prompt, serious consideration of the demand.

When a bond for performance exists, or, when insurance coverage of the claim is likely in cases involving real estate agents and others who often are insured, it is advisable to request that the insurance carrier or bonding company be notified of the claim. There is no legal effect to making such a request; however, the request may remind a forgetful defendant or nudge a reluctant defendant to do what he or she is required by the insurance policy to do.

The following form provides a general format for a letter containing each of these elements. It would be impossible to draft a form DTPA notice letter for every conceivable DTPA claim. There simply are too many different types of consumer and business transactions. Rather than attempt the impossible, the form notice letters which appear in this chapter are representative of "typical" DTPA claims that are made.

The first form provides the general format that should be appropriate for nearly all DTPA cases. The general form letter in this section is followed by a variety of specific forms for eight different types of consumer transactions.

It is not necessary to use each section contained in the general form letter in every DTPA notice letter; instead, the sections of the general and specific forms should be selected and modified to create a notice letter that is appropriate for the facts and needs of each claim.

[a] FORM: Notice letter (general form)

CERTIFIED MAIL, RETURN RECEIPT REQUESTED

(Date)

(Inside address)

Re: (Client's name)

Dear _____:

[Notice of representation]

Our firm has [or I have] been retained to represent _____ with respect to a claim which he [she] has against you. Please direct all communications concerning this matter to me.

[**Notice of claim**, see specific letters, *infra*]

[Notice of statutory violations]

It is our contention that your conduct constitutes [insert appropriate statutory language, *e.g.*, false, misleading and deceptive acts in violation of §17.46(b)(5) of the Texas Deceptive Trade Practices - Consumer Protection Act].

[**Descriptions of elements of damages**, see specific letters, *infra*]

[Statement of damages and expenses sought]

Based upon the information now available to us, and for purposes of this notice letter, we estimate that our client's damages are as follows:

Economic losses: $_____.

Mental anguish: $_____.

Expenses, including

attorney's fees: $_____.

Of course, we reserve the right to adjust these amounts to conform to the information and additional evidence that will be available to us at the time of trial should litigation be necessary.

[Alternate statement of attorney's fees]

Our client has incurred reasonable and necessary attorney's fees in the pursuit of the claim stated in this letter. The amount of fees incurred as of the date of this letter is $_____ [or _____% of our client's total damages].

[Notice of contingent interest]

Under the contract of employment we have with our client, our firm has [or I have] been assigned an interest in the claim against you.

[Offer of settlement]

The purpose of this letter is to encourage you to resolve our client's claim in a fair and equitable manner without the need for further legal action. In the event you fail to take advantage of this opportunity, we [or I] will have no alternative but to recommend to our client that a lawsuit be filed against you under the Deceptive Trade Practices - Consumer Protection Act. In this lawsuit, rather than seeking only the amount of compensation we are asking of you at this time, we will seek to recover the full measure of damages to which our client is legally entitled and well as our client's expenses and attorney's fees as allowed by law.

[Notice to insurance carrier]

In the event that you have insurance or a bond which you believe may cover all or any part of the claim made in this letter, you are requested to notify your insurance carrier or bonding company immediately.

[Request for response]

If you are interested in resolving this matter without the necessity of litigation, please contact me within sixty days of your receipt of this letter.

[Copy to third party]

A copy of this letter is being sent to [insert name of third party], who, in our opinion, is subject to the same claims and defenses our client has against you.

[NOTE: In sending copies of notice letters to third parties, care must be taken in drafting the notice letter so as to avoid statements that may be actionable as defamatory.]

Sincerely,

[Signature of attorney]

[b] FORM: Notice letter: defective product (rescission and damages)

[Insert the following at "notice of claim," §3.03[a], supra]

As you are aware, on _____, 20___ our client purchased the above-referenced product from your company. At the time of the purchase, our client [insert facts of transaction, e.g., signed a contract and received a brochure which described various qualities and characteristics that our client expected the product to have]. The product does not conform to the descriptions contained in the contract [or brochure] for the reason that it is and has been defective since the date it was purchased.

[In addition, at the time the product was purchased, certain representations about the characteristics and quality of the product were made, including but not limited to the following: [insert representations made]. As the defects listed below demonstrate, these representations were false, misleading and deceptive.]

Among the defects that our client has found in the product are the following: [insert list of defects]. As time passes and additional investigation is done, additional defects may come to light.

Please cancel the transaction by which our client purchased the _____. Upon your agreement to cancel the transaction, our client will return the product to you in exchange for a refund of all money paid by our client to you [less the reasonable rental value of the product during the time that our client actually was able to use it].

[Additionally, it was necessary for our client to finance the transaction. For this reason, interest expense has been incurred in the amount of $ _____ . This interest expense must be included in the amount you agree to pay to our client.]

[c] FORM: Notice letter: defective product or service (damages)

[Insert the following at "notice of claim," §3.03[a] supra]

As you are aware, on _____, 20___ our client purchased the above-referenced product from your company. At the time of the purchase, our client *[insert facts of transaction, e.g.,* signed a contract and received a brochure which described various qualities and characteristics that our client expected the product to have]. The product does not conform to the descriptions contained in the contract [or brochure] for the reason that it is and has been defective since the date it was purchased.

[In addition, at the time the product was purchased, certain representations about the characteristics and quality of the product were made, including but not limited to the following: *[insert representations made]*. As the defects listed below demonstrate, these representations were false, misleading and deceptive.]

Among the defects that our client has found in the product are the following: *[insert list of defects]*. As time passes and additional investigation is done, additional defects may come to light.

The damages which our client has suffered as a result of the defects in the product *[service]* include, but are not limited to, *[insert elements of damages, e.g.,* the amount it will cost our client to repair the product, or alternatively, the difference between what our client paid for the product and its actual value in its defective condition. In addition, our client has been unable to use the product, and will be unable to use it until it is repaired. Our client's inability to use the product has caused consequential damages to our client as well].

§§3.05 - 3.08 [Reserved]

§3.09 Client Communications Concerning the Notice Letter

When a notice letter is sent, it is necessary to communicate the fact that the letter was sent and provide a copy of the letter to the client. Not only does this keep the client advised of the work being done on the matter, it also provides one additional opportunity for the client to review the letter to verify the facts stated and the amount demanded.

Once a response is received to the notice letter, a copy should be forwarded to the client immediately for review since the time for accepting or rejecting any offer that is made is limited. DTPA §17.5052; Tex. Prop. Code §27.004; Tex. Ins. Code §541.154. If the offer is accepted, it should be done so in writing. The same is true for any rejection of the offer. The form letters which follow are intended to complete this cycle of communications with the client and the opposing party.

[a] FORM: Letter to client transmitting notice letter

```
(Date)

(Inside address)

Re: [Opposing party's name]


Dear _____:
```

Enclosed is a copy of the "notice letter" which we have mailed to _____.

We are required by law to allow the other side sixty days from the date the letter is received to respond with an offer of settlement. During this sixty day period, a request to inspect the claimed defects and conditions may be made. We must allow a reasonable opportunity for an inspection.

It is possible that we may receive a request for additional time within which to consider your claim. [It is our practice to allow additional time if the reasons given appear fair and reasonable. If you have any strong objection to our agreeing to a request for additional time to answer the letter, please let me know.]

Although we sincerely hope that the notice letter will produce an acceptable offer of settlement, our experience has been that such a result is unlikely.

As soon as we receive a response to the notice letter, we will send it to you. If no response is received with the time period allowed, we will begin preparing the lawsuit for filing.

       Sincerely,

       [*Signature of attorney*]

[b] FORM: Letter to client: claim rejected

(Date)

(Inside address)

Re:[*Opposing party's name*]

Dear _____:

Enclosed is the response we have received to our notice letter.

As we have discussed, very few cases are settled on a notice letter; instead, most cases which are going to settle do not settle until close to the date they are set for trial. For this reason, I was not surprised that your claim was rejected.

[*If a detailed response was given, add*: Please review the statements made in the response to the letter. It would be very helpful if you would provide me with your analysis of the response. That is, which statements in the letter do you know to be untrue? If there are any such statements, please send me a brief note pointing out the untruthful statements made, as well as your reasons for knowing that the statements are not accurate.]

As soon as the petition has been prepared, we will send a copy to you for your review before it is filed.

Thank you for your continuing cooperation.

       Sincerely,

       [*Signature of attorney*]

§3.10 Evaluating a Settlement Offer

When the prospective defendant makes a settlement offer under the DTPA or the Insurance Code, the plaintiff has thirty days within which to evaluate the offer and accept it or reject it. DTPA §17.5052(e); TEX. INS. CODE §541.158. In residential construction cases, the response time is limited to twenty-five days. TEX. PROP. CODE §27.004(i).

If a settlement offer is made in response to the notice letter, the client must be made fully aware of the consequences of failing to accept it. For example, under the DTPA, if the amount of the offer is the same or substantially the same as the amount of damages ultimately found by the jury, then the client's recovery is limited to the lesser of (a) the amount of damages tendered in the settlement offer, or (b) the amount of damages found by the jury. DTPA §17.5052(g). The court can award attorney's fees to the consumer under these circumstances; however, the amount of the fees is limited to the reasonable and necessary fees incurred before the date and time of the rejected settlement offer. DTPA §17.5052(h). There is an even further limitation on the amount of fees that can be recovered in that if the court finds that the amount of attorney's fees offered in the settlement offer was the same as, substantially the same as or more than the fees actually incurred by the consumer as of the date of the offer, then the consumer may not recover attorney's fees greater than the amount tendered in the settlement offer. DTPA §17.5052(h).

There are similar consequences if a consumer rejects a "reasonable" offer to repair made under the Residential Construction Liability Act.

[a] FORM: Letter to client evaluating a settlement offer

```
(Date)

(Inside address)

Re: [Opposing party's name]

Dear _____:

     Enclosed is a settlement offer we received from _____ on
[insert date letter was received]. We have thirty days from
the date the offer was received to accept or reject the offer.
Although the settlement offer is less than the amount requested,
we need to consider it carefully.

     Under the Deceptive Trade Practices-Consumer Protection Act,
if the amount of your actual damages found by the jury when this
case goes to trial is the "same or substantially the same" as
the amount of the offer that has been made, then your recov-
ery will be limited to the lesser of the amount that has been
offered or the amount found by the jury.

     The offer also must be evaluated in light of the unpredictable
nature of jury trials. There is some risk in rejecting any offer
of settlement, even though the damages you have suffered are
much greater than the amount of the offer.
```

Please give your careful consideration to the offer, and then give me a call so we can discuss how best to proceed.

    Sincerely,

    [*Signature of attorney*]

[b] FORM: Letter to client – evaluating a settlement offer (residential construction)

(Date)

(Inside address)

Re: [*Opposing party's name*]

Dear _____:

Enclosed is an offer to repair the defects in your home which we received from _____ on [insert date letter was received].

We have twenty-five days from the date the offer was received to accept or reject it.

It is very important that we evaluate this offer carefully for the reason that if we make a wrong decision on the offer, the consequences can be severe. [If expert evaluation of the offer is needed, insert: For this reason, I have taken the liberty of sending a copy of the response to [insert name of consulting expert] and have asked that he [she] provide an independent evaluation of the offer for our consideration as soon as possible.

I anticipate receiving a report from our consulting expert within the next seven days. At that time, I will call you so we can discuss the offer, the expert's opinion, and how best to proceed.

    Sincerely,

    [*Signature of attorney*]

[c] FORM: Letter accepting the settlement offer

CERTIFIED MAIL, RETURN RECEIPT REQUESTED

(Date)

(Inside address)

Re: [*Opposing party's name*]

Dear _____:

This is in response to your letter dated _____, 20__.

On behalf of our client, we accept your settlement offer on the following terms:

[1.] Your client will pay to our client $_____.

[2.] Your client also will [insert other things to be done].

[3.] This settlement will be closed on or before _____, 20__.

[4.] You will prepare the settlement documents for our client to execute which will consist of mutual releases, in standard form, of our clients' claims against each other.

If these terms are acceptable to you, please sign in the space provided below, and return a signed copy of this letter to me.

Thank you for your cooperation.

Sincerely,

[*Signature line for opposing counsel*]

[d] FORM: Letter accepting offer to repair

(Date)

(Inside address)

Re: [*Opposing party's name*]

Dear _____:

This is in response to your letter dated _____, 20 __, in which your client has offered to repair the defects in our client's _____.

On behalf of our client, we accept the offer to repair, with the following conditions:

1. The repairs will be performed according to the specifications contained in your letter.

2. The repairs will be completed no later than _____, 20__, and the repairs will be done in a good and workmanlike manner.

3. Your client will pay to our client $_____ as compensation for our client's attorney's fees and expenses.

If the conditions stated above are acceptable to your client, please sign in the space provided below, and return a signed copy of this letter to me.

                        Sincerely,

                        [*Signature of attorney*]

                        [*Signature line for opposing counsel*]

[e] FORM: Letter rejecting settlement offer

(Date)

(Inside address)

Re: [*Opposing party's name*]

Dear _____:

This is in response to your letter dated ____, 20__.

We must reject the offer made in your letter for the reason that it does not fairly compensate our client for his [her] losses in this transaction, and, consequently, does not represent a reasonable settlement offer.

If your client is interested in offering an amount of money that is more in line with our client's actual losses, we will, of course, pass the offer along to our client for the consideration it deserves.

[*or*]

Our client still is willing to resolve this claim amicably. For this reason, we have been authorized by our client to make a counteroffer in the amount of $_____. This counteroffer will remain open for ____ days after which it should be considered withdrawn.

                                      Sincerely,

                                      [*Signature of attorney*]

[f] FORM: Letter rejecting offer to repair

CERTIFIED MAIL, RETURN RECEIPT REQUESTED

(Date)

(Inside address)

Re: [*Client's name*]

Dear _____:

This is in response to your letter dated _____, 20_, in which you offered to repair [some of] the defects stated in our notice letter to you.

We have no alternative but to reject your offer to repair. The reasons for our rejection of the offer are several: [*insert reasons for rejection of offer, e.g.*, your offer is a mere statement that you will make repairs. You have failed to provide any information that would enable our client to evaluate whether the repairs will, in fact, cure the defective construction. For example, our expert advises us that it will be necessary to install piers around the perimeter of the house in order to provide adequate support for the foundation].

Your client's offer is silent on exactly what work will be done; consequently, there is insufficient information in your letter to enable our client [and our consulting expert] to determine the effectiveness of the repairs you plan to make. For these reasons, your client's offer is "unreasonable" as set forth in §27.004(b) of the Texas Property Code, and must, therefore, be rejected.

Sincerely,

[*Signature of attorney*]

(This page intentionally left blank.)

Chapter 4

Responding to the Notice

§4.01 Evaluating the Notice Letter
    [a] FORM: Letter requesting inspection of goods

§4.02 Initial Evaluation of DTPA Notice Letter
    [a] FORM: Letter to client analyzing claim
    [b] FORM: Letter requesting additional time

§4.03 Requesting Additional Information
    [a] FORM: Letter requesting additional information (general)
    [b] FORM: Alternative questions: residential construction defects

§4.04 Responding to the Notice Letter
    [a] FORM: General statement denying liability

§4.05 Offering the Full Amount
    [a] FORM: Offer of settlement: full amount of claim

§4.06 Offering Less Than the Amount Sought
    [a] FORM: Offer of settlement: less than the amount sought

§4.07 Rejecting the Claim
    [a] FORM: Letter rejecting claim

§4.08 Effect of Consumer's Rejection of Settlement Offer
    [a] FORM: Affidavit of rejection of settlement offer

§4.01 Evaluating the Notice Letter

The purpose of a notice letter under either the DTPA or Chapter 541 of the Insurance Code is to afford the parties an opportunity to resolve a claim before lawsuit is filed. Even though no response is required and no sanction exists for failing to respond to a notice letter, the defendant receiving a DTPA or Insurance Code Chapter 541 notice letter may receive a significant legal benefit from making a response. The extent of the benefit depends on (1) the strength of the consumer's claim and (2) the legal adequacy of the response.

Not only does the notice letter provide the defendant a settlement opportunity, it also opens up defenses to the DTPA claim that are not available to defendants who fail to make a timely offer of settlement. As discussed below, a timely settlement offer in response to a DTPA demand letter can be used to preclude the plaintiff from recovering the full amount of damages, additional damages and attorney's fees. The failure to timely set up these defenses in response to the notice letter can be costly to the defendant in the end.

In most cases, the notice letter will be delivered directly to the client. The DTPA provides a sixty day window within which a response can be made. DTPA §17.505(c). Since the time period begins to run from the date the client first receives the letter, it is important to advise clients in advance that if such a letter is received, it should be forwarded to the attorney immediately.

Prior to the 1995 Amendments, the defendant only had a single 60-day opportunity to make a qualifying settlement offer, usually before suit is filed. Now, the defendant has a second opportunity to respond to the notice with a qualifying settlement offer after suit is filed. Under the current scheme, either party to a DTPA action may seek court-ordered mediation within 90 days of service of the first pleading seeking DTPA relief. DTPA §17.5051(a). Time limits are imposed for ruling on the motion (30 days after filing) and holding the mediation (30 days after the order, unless extended by the court). DTPA §17.5051. If no mediation is held, the defendant will have an additional opportunity to make a qualifying settlement offer within 90 days after the filing of the original answer. DTPA §17.5052(b). If mediation is held pursuant to DTPA §17.5051, a qualifying settlement offer may be made within 20 days of the conclusion of mediation. DTPA §17.5052(c).

If the recipient of a notice letter elects to make an offer of settlement, it must include an offer to pay the following amounts of money, *separately stated,* in order to properly set up the DTPA defenses to additional damages and attorney's fees:

(1) an amount of money or other consideration, reduced to its cash value, as settlement of the consumer's claim for damages; and

(2) an amount of money to compensate the consumer for the consumer's reasonable and necessary attorney's fees incurred as of the date of the offer.

DTPA §17.5052(d); Tex. Ins. Code §541.157.

If a settlement offer is made, both parts of the offer must be accepted by the consumer "not later than the 30th day after the date the offer is made." If the offer is not accepted in this manner, then it is deemed rejected. DTPA §17.5052(e); Tex. Ins. Code §541.148.

The defenses available to defendants who make qualifying settlement offers under DTPA §17.5052 and Insurance Code §541.157 substantially limit what the plaintiff could otherwise recover. First, the settlement offer defenses under both the DTPA and Insurance Code Chapter 541 operate to limit the plaintiff's recovery to the lesser of the settlement offer or the damages found by the court or jury as follows:

> If the court finds that the amount tendered in the settlement offer for damages under [the DTPA or Insurance Code Chapter 541] is the same as, substantially the same as, or more than the damages found by the trier of fact, the claimant may not recover as damages any amount in excess of the lesser of:
>
> (1) the amount of damages tendered in the settlement offer; or
>
> (2) the amount of damages found by the trier of fact.

DTPA §17.5052(g); TEX. INS. CODE §541.159. In order to qualify for this defense, the settlement offer made must be greater than or "substantially the same as" the amount of damages found by the trier of fact. It must also be timely made within the deadlines discussed above. This is what is meant by "qualifying settlement offer":

It remains unclear what is necessary for an offer that is lower than the amount of damages found by the trier of fact to nevertheless be "substantially the same as" that amount. Is an offer that is 90% of the amount found "substantially the same as" the amount found? 80%? 70%? 50%? One guideline for this inquiry may be found in the fee-shifting provisions of Texas Civil Practices & Remedies Code Chapter 42, providing for the ability to recover litigation costs, including attorney's fees, incurred in litigation after a qualifying settlement offer has been rejected. There, a judgment of recovery is deemed "significantly less favorable" to the defendant if it is more than 120% of the defendant's settlement offer. TEX. CIV. PRAC. & REM. CODE §42.004. If Chapter 42 has been properly invoked, the defendant would then be required to pay litigation costs. *Id.* Similarly, a judgment of recovery is deemed "significantly less favorable" to the plaintiff if it is less than 80% of the settlement offer made, with similar expense-shifting results to the plaintiff. *Id.* If a settlement offer of 80% of the amount recovered by judgment is "significantly less favorable" in Chapter 42, it seems unlikely that an offer of only 80% of the consumer's damages could be found to be "substantially the same as" that amount under the DTPA. Whether or not an offer of some higher percentage (such as 90%) of the damages found by the trier-of-fact would ever be found to meet this standard, a prudent defendant would not want to test this standard unnecessarily by offering significantly less that could reasonably be expected to be found at trial.

Second, if the court finds that the settlement offer was substantially the same as or more than the amount of damages, it must then make a finding with respect to attorney's fees. That is, the court must determine the reasonable and necessary attorney's fees incurred before the date and time of the rejected settlement offer. The court must then compare its own finding with the amount tendered for attorney's fees in the settlement offer. If the amount tendered is the same as or more than the amount found by the court to be reasonable and necessary, then the consumer may recover only the amount of attorney's fees tendered in the settlement offer. DTPA §17.5052(h); TEX. INS. CODE §541.159(b). If the amount tendered for attorney's fees is not substantially the same as or more than the amount incurred by the consumer as of the date of the settlement offer, the consumer is entitled to recover the amount found by the court to be reasonable. DTPA §17.502(j); TEX. INS. CODE §541.159(d)(2).

Neither the DTPA nor Insurance Code Chapter 541 expressly prohibit contingent attorney's fees. Many DTPA and Insurance Code cases are handled on a contingent fee. Attorney's fees determined as a percentage of the plaintiff's recovery may not increase much from when the attorney-client contract is signed to when the jury returns its verdict. In *Arthur Andersen v. Perry Equip. Corp.*, 945 S.W.2d 812, 818 (Tex. 1997), the Supreme Court disapproved of the practice of allowing recovery of attorney's fees merely upon proof of the contingent fee agreement between the plaintiff and his attorney. As discussed in §1.02.28, *supra*, attorney's fees now must be proved up in specific dollar amounts with reasonableness determined pursuant to the guidelines in the Disciplinary Rules of Professional Conduct, which define a "reasonable" fee. It is therefore unlikely that a court applying the *Arthur Andersen* factors will find that a large contingency fee is reasonable and necessary, even if contractually "incurred" by the plaintiff at the time the rejected settlement offer was made. More likely, the court will determine attorney's fees on an hourly "lodestar" basis for making the determination for the limiting effects of DTPA §17.5052(h) and Insurance Code §541.159(b).

Thirdly, if a recipient of a notice letter tenders to the consumer within 30 days the full amount of the damages claimed and the expenses, including attorneys' fees, reasonably incurred, the response constitutes a complete defense to an action subsequently filed under the DTPA. DTPA §17.506(d). Although it may sound unlikely that a consumer's demand would ever be so low that such a response would be appropriate, many consumers contact businesses directly before consulting with an attorney and before they are aware of the full amount of damages they potentially can recover.

The person making the offer of settlement must be able to perform as offered; and, the cash value of the offer must be substantially correct. If the offer cannot be performed, or, if the cash value is misstated, then the limitations on recovery described above do not apply. DTPA §17.5052(i).

In addition to the legal defenses discussed above, there are several practical benefits to responding to a DTPA or Insurance Code Chapter 541 notice letter. First, a carefully written response provides an opportunity to educate the consumer's attorney on facts about the transaction that may be unknown to the attorney. Second, in the appropriate case, a fair offer of settlement to a consumer may force the consumer to make a hard choice: if the amount of damages is difficult to prove, a modest cash offer may be sufficient to convince the consumer to avoid further legal action. Third, in extreme cases, the response to a notice letter can set up a counterclaim for bad faith and harassment by putting the plaintiff on clear, provable notice that there is no case to be pursued. *See* DTPA §17.50(c).

The DTPA also provides the party receiving a DTPA notice with an opportunity to inspect the goods made the subject of the claim in a reasonable manner at a reasonable time and place. DTPA §17.505(a). Regardless of the type of response which ultimately is made to the consumer, immediately upon receipt of a notice letter involving goods, a written request to inspect the goods should be made.

[a] FORM: Letter requesting inspection of goods

<u>**CERTIFIED MAIL, RETURN RECEIPT REQUESTED**</u>

(Date)

(Inside address)

Re: [Consumer's name]

Dear _____:

This is in response to your letter dated _____, 20__, to _____, our client. We are evaluating your client's claim at this time.

In order to assist us in evaluating your client's claim, we request that you permit our client to inspect the _____ at a time and place that is mutually convenient. We are prepared to conduct the inspection on _____, 20__ at ____ ___.m. If this date and time are not convenient to either you or your client, please let us know and we will make every effort to accommodate your schedules. Please understand, however, that the inspection needs to occur as soon as possible so we may have sufficient time to complete our evaluation of your client's claim before we are required to make a response to your client's notice letter.

This request is made under the authority of Tex. Bus. & Com. Code §17.505(a). We look forward to your prompt response.

Sincerely,

[Signature of attorney]

§4.02 Initial Evaluation of DTPA Notice Letter

A person who receives a DTPA notice letter should be prepared to focus immediately on the transaction that brought about the claim to determine whether the claim should be settled, and if so, on what terms.

As discussed above, the need to respond to a DTPA or Insurance Code Chapter 541 notice letter does not arise simply from the defenses that can be set up by responding with a qualified settlement offer. The cost savings that can be realized if the matter can be terminated with a well drafted, thoughtful response to the notice letter are substantial. If a claim has no validity, the response can demonstrate this fact and possibly, less will have to be spent on attorney's fees. If the claim has validity, postponing the resolution of the claim merely causes the ultimate settlement costs to increase because both sides' attorneys' fees continue to increase with the passage of time.

One of the most difficult jobs for an attorney is to discuss with a client the reasons why it is sometimes better to respond to what is perceived as an unjust demand with an offer to pay money rather than to put up a fight. This is particularly true when the notice letter is written in such a way as to challenge the honest or integrity of the business person to whom it is directed. By responding to the demand with an offer of settlement, the client understandably feels that he or she is admitting improper conduct.

In order to set the stage for an in-depth discussion with the client about the claim, it may be helpful to write a letter to the client setting forth a suggested framework for analyzing the claim. Generally, the letter should address both the legal and economic consequences of the claim. An attorney's knowledge about how a particular client thinks, what the client's "hot buttons" are and the client's general attitude toward consumer complaints may require a carefully tailored letter. The following form is suggested as an example of how such a letter could be written.

[a] FORM: Letter to client analyzing the claim

(Date)

(Inside address)

Re: Notice letter from [consumer's name]

Dear _____:

I have reviewed the enclosed notice letter. The purpose of this letter is to share with you my analysis of the claims made and to suggest some points you may want to consider, if you have not already, as you evaluate the claim.

Please note that our response to the notice letter is due <u>no later than</u> _____, 20___. For this reason, we need to complete the evaluation process as quickly as possible.

A. <u>Legal consequences</u>

A notice letter, such as this, which makes a claim under the Deceptive Trade Practices - Consumer Protection Act, is intended to provide you with basic information about the claim being made so you will have an opportunity to evaluate the claim and decide whether you want to resolve it before a lawsuit is filed.

1. The law requires that you be given an opportunity to inspect the _____ about which the claim is made. We should take advantage of this opportunity. A request for such an inspection has been made already.

2. If the claim has merit in any respect, and the complainant ultimately wins a judgment for any actual damages, you may be required to pay all of the complainant's attorney's fees. I mention this to stress the importance of including economic considerations in your evaluation of the claim.

3. The only way to prevent a lawsuit from being pursued, if the complainant is determined to go to court, is to agree to pay the full amount of the claim and attorney's fees. Obviously, if the claim has no merit, this is not a meaningful option. Even so, if anything less is offered, then a lawsuit can be pursued.

4. If you agree to pay (but the complainant refuses to accept) an amount that is the same as or more than the amount of damages later found by a jury to be the plaintiffs actual damages, then the court can limit the plaintiff's recovery to the lesser of either (1) the amount of damages tendered in the settlement offer; or (2) the amount of damages found by the trier of fact. And, if the court imposes this limitation on damages, the consumer may be limited to recovering the lesser of the attorney's fees found by the court to be reasonable or the amount of attorney's fees offered in the settlement letter.

B. Practical considerations

There are several practical considerations which I am sure you will take into account while you are evaluating the claim:

1. If the claim has little, if any, merit, settling the claim by paying money may establish an unfortunate precedent.

2. If the claim has merit, delaying the resolution of the claim will only increase the ultimate costs, primarily because attorneys' fees on both sides will increase.

3. To properly defend against the claim, we must retrieve all records that relate to the transaction and interview, at length, all personnel who were involved in the transaction. This process should begin immediately if it has not already.

4. If this claim progresses to a lawsuit, and ultimately a trial, at this point the probable outcome is difficult to predict with any degree of certainty.

Sincerely,

[Signature of attorney]

[b] FORM: Letter requesting additional time

There is nothing in the DTPA or Chapter 541 of the Insurance Code which prohibits the parties from agreeing to extend the time within which a response must be made to a notice letter. In the event additional time is required, however, the agreement should be reduced to writing so that it may, if necessary, be filed with the court.

```
(Date)

(Inside address)

Re: Notice letter concerning _____

Dear _____:

    This is in response to your letter dated _____ 20___ con-
cerning a claim made against our client, _____.

    In order to properly evaluate your client's claim, we need an
additional [thirty] days from _____, 20___, the date our
response to your letter would otherwise be required. This time
is needed to enable us to interview the persons involved and to
review the files that our client has on the transaction. [Also,
pursuant to our earlier request, we need to be given the oppor-
tunity to examine the _____ as soon as possible so we can
evaluate its condition.]

    If you are agreeable to giving us this additional time, please
sign in the space indicated below.

    Thank you for your anticipated cooperation.

                            Sincerely,

                            [Signature of attorney]

[Signature line for opposing counsel]
```

§4.03 Requesting Additional Information

When a DTPA notice letter is written in vague, general language, it may be difficult to evaluate the claim. Although the right to inspect the claimed defect provided by DTPA §17.505(a) may supply some of the missing details in the notice letter, one still may be forced to make too many guesses about the claim.

Vague, general notice letters may reflect the fact that the consumer's attorney lacks enough knowledge about the claim to provide anything more than a broad outline. Few attorneys intentionally make notice letters vague in order to hide the facts. Many attorneys, however, will refrain from stating matters as fact unless they are very confident of the evidence to prove the statements out of a fear of losing credibility or weakening the case. Consequently, some notice letters may require follow-up in order to encourage the attorney to speak freely about all of the facts that he or she expects will be proven. If the notice letter is legally deficient, *e.g.* it fails to state an amount of damages, consideration should be given to filing a plea in abatement in order to compel a more complete statement of the claim.

The letter which is set forth below may be used as a means of obtaining prefiling discovery on certain key facts. For example, although the notice letter does not need to contain the date on which the consumer "discovered" the alleged defect, including such a question in the letter may result in an answer that is very helpful in evaluating a case with a potential limitations defense.

[a] FORM: Letter requesting additional information (general)

CERTIFIED MAIL, RETURN RECEIPT REQUESTED

(Date)

(Inside address)

Re: [Consumer's name]

Dear _____ :

Our firm represents with respect _____ to the claim made by your client under the Deceptive Trade Practices - Consumer Protection Act.

As you are aware, the DTPA requires that the notice letter include certain specific elements in order to enable our client to evaluate the claim. The notice letter our client received was deficient because [*insert missing elements of facts of notice letter, e.g. it failed to state the amount of economic damages that are claimed*]. In order to focus your client's attention on certain specific questions we have about the claim that has been made, we respectfully request that your client provide us with answers to the following questions: [*Insert list of questions, e.g.*

1. What is the amount of economic damages that are claimed and how were the damages computed?

2. What was the cause of the claimed defects?

3. Has your client had the _____ repaired or altered in any way by anyone other than the dealer [seller] since the time it was purchased?

4. Have the defects been examined by any independent expert(s) whose findings would assist us in evaluating the condition of the _____ and the cause of the defects?

5. What is the exact manner in which your client computed the damages that he [or she] claims to have suffered?

6. Did your client continue to use the _____ after the claimed defects were discovered?

7. In what manner have the claimed defects interfered with your client's use of the _____?

8. Has your client had to pay any expenses as a result of the claimed defects; if so, please itemize each such expense giving the nature of the expense, the date paid and the amount of the payment?

9. Have you sent a notice letter to anyone else involved in the transaction such as [the manufacturer]?

10. Is your client interested in having the_____ repaired or is your client only interested in being paid money?]

I think you will agree that without answers to these questions, it will be extremely difficult, if not impossible, for our client to evaluate the merits of your client's claims. For this reason, we hope you will agree to answer these questions for us.

Since our response to your notice letter is due on or before _____ 20___, we would appreciate your immediate answers to these questions. If you are unable to answer these questions immediately, we would appreciate you extending the date on which our response to your letter is due to thirty days after the date the answers are provided to us.

[*Insert request for opportunity to inspect the defects. See* §4.01[a], *supra.*]

These questions are asked out of a genuine desire to resolve your client's claims as expeditiously and fairly as possible. If you or your client is unable or unwilling to answer these basic questions about the claim, then we will have no alternative but to assume that your client's claim is in bad faith and is being pursued purely for the purpose of harassment. If a lawsuit is filed before these questions are answered, and without giving our client a reasonable opportunity to evaluate your client's claim, we will have no alternative but to file a plea in abatement to ask the court to require that proper notice be given and to fife a counterclaim for bad faith and harassment.

Thank you for your prompt attention to these questions.

Sincerely,

[Signature of attorney]

[b] FORM: —Alternative questions: residential construction defects

[Insert in letter in preceding section]

1. When did your client first notice the claimed defects?

2. What is the exact location of the claimed defects in the house?

3. Are the conditions about which your client complains continuing to get worse?

4. What effect have the claimed defects had on your client's ability to use the house?

5. Has your client made or attempted any repairs? If yes, what repairs were made or attempted and when?

6. Has your client observed anything that your client believes either caused or contributed to the claimed defects?

7. Have any experts been retained to examine the defects?

8. How did you arrive at the amount of damages stated in the notice letter?

9. Have you received any cost of repair estimates? If yes, what are they?

10. Is your client interested in having the house repaired or is your client interested in being paid money only?

§4.04 Responding to the Notice Letter

A notice letter from a consumer should always be answered, regardless of the contents of the answer. When there is no response whatsoever to the letter, a prospective defendant loses a valuable opportunity to resolve a claim at as small a cost as possible. In many cases, it will be impossible or inadvisable to make the kind of response to a notice letter that will satisfy the consumer. This fact should not discourage a person from making the effort since the savings can be considerable.

The response to a notice letter may include the following elements:

1. A summary evaluation of the merits of the claim;

2. A proposed resolution of the claim; and

3. If any kind of offer of settlement is made, a statement that the offer is not intended as an admission of any kind in a form similar to that contained in §[a] below. *See* DTPA §17.5052(k), as amended 1995.

There are competing considerations with respect to how much evaluation should be contained in the response letter. On the one hand, no evaluation is necessary if an offer of settlement is made in the full amount of the claim. In this case, the response letter should be used more as a public relations tool than a legal document. If the settlement offer is less than the amount of the claim, or zero, then any factual evaluation of the claim will provide a measure of "free" discovery to the other side which may or may not be helpful. Even though the response to the notice letter is not admissible in evidence, (*see* DTPA §17.5052(k), as amended 1995), as a general rule the evaluation of the claim should state only as much detail as required to establish the reasons why the settlement offer is rejected.

[a] FORM: General statement denying liability

[Insert the following statement in the body of the response letter:]

The offer contained in this letter is made for the sole purpose of avoiding further, unnecessary expense associated with your client's claim. The offer is not intended to be and should not be considered by you or your client to be an admission of liability for your client's claim.

§4.05 Offering the Full Amount

If a recipient of a notice letter makes an offer within 30 days of receipt of the notice letter to pay all that the consumer demands, such an offer is a complete defense to a lawsuit subsequently filed against the recipient under the DTPA. DTPA §17.506(d). In those cases in which the amount demanded by the consumer is reasonably close to the amount of damages that the recipient believes the consumer can recover, it may be advisable to offer to pay the full amount.

The response must offer (1) an amount of money or other consideration, reduced to its cash value, as settlement of the consumer's claim for damages; and (2) an amount of money to compensate for the consumer's reasonable and necessary attorney's fees incurred as of the date of the offer. DTPA §17.5052(d). At the time the offer is made, the person making the offer must be able to perform the offer; and, if consideration other than money is offered, the stated cash value of the consideration must be accurate. DTPA §17.5052(i).

[a] FORM: Offer of settlement: full amount of claim

CERTIFIED MAIL, RETURN RECEIPT REQUESTED

(Date)

(Inside address)

Re: Notice letter from

Dear _____:

This is in response to your letter regarding the above referenced client. This letter was received by our client on _____ 20___.

It is important to our client that all customers be satisfied to the extent possible. Our client also realizes that regardless of the merits of the claim, the defense of a lawsuit is very expensive. Accordingly, in response to your client's letter, and on behalf of our client, our client offers to pay the following amounts to your client immediately:

1. $ _____ in settlement of the claim for damages; and

2. $ _____ as attorney's fees.

This offer is contingent only on your client's agreement to execute a full and final release in favor of our client.

[*Insert denial of liability*, §4.04[a] *supra*]

Please respond to this offer within the next thirty days.

Sincerely,

[Signature of attorney]

§4.06 Offering Less Than the Amount Sought

A settlement offer which is less than the amount demanded offers a legal benefit to the person making the offer, so long as it was "the same as, substantially the same as or more than the amount of damages found by the trier of fact." In this situation, the consumer's recovery is limited to the amount offered or the amount found by the trier of fact, whichever is less. DTPA §17.5052(g). See §4.01, supra. Under these circumstances, if the court also finds that the amount of reasonable and necessary attorney's fees incurred by the consumer as of the date of the offer is substantially the same as the amount tendered in the settlement offer, then the consumer is limited to the amount of attorney's fees tendered. DTPA §17.5052 (h).

[a] FORM: Offer of settlement: less than the amount sought

CERTIFIED MAIL, RETURN RECEIPT REQUESTED

(Date)

(Inside address)

Re: Notice letter of

Dear _____ :

This is in response to your letter on behalf of _____. This letter was received by our client on _____.

In response to your notice letter, and on behalf of our client, we tender $ _____ in full settlement of your client's claim. We also agree to pay your attorneys' fees in the amount set forth in your letter.

Our client declines to pay the full amount of your claim for the reason that the amount is clearly excessive even if everything you say is true, which we expressly deny. Further, we have evaluated the claim made by your client and disagree strongly with the "facts" on which your client relies. For example, [*insert factual clarification*].

This offer is contingent on your client executing a full and final release in favor of our client.

[*Insert denial of liability. See §4.04[a], supra*]

Sincerely,

[Signature of attorney]

§4.07 Rejecting the Claim

There are two sound reasons, among others, for rejecting a consumer's claim. First, the claim is unjust and not supported by the facts of the transaction. Second, the possibility exist of establishing a "precedent" of sorts with other consumers so that additional frivolous claims are encouraged. The first reason is a legal consideration; the second reason is a business decision. In some cases, a client simply will refuse to settle on a notice letter and will prefer to pay the attorney for the defense until the case progresses. Since attorneys' fees are recoverable in the DTPA litigation, delaying a decision to settle a valid claim generally only increases the ultimate cost to the client.

Assuming that the client has decided to reject the consumer's claim altogether, that decision should be communicated to opposing counsel within the notice period.

[a] FORM: Letter rejecting claim

```
(Date)
(Inside address)
Re: [Consumer's name]

Dear _____ :

   This is in response to your letter dated _____, 20___ on behalf of your above named client.

   We have evaluated your client's claims and have concluded that they are unfounded. [Insert basis for rejection of claim, e.g. Our client did not engage in the conduct alleged; however, even if everything your client says were true (and we specifically deny it) the amount you have demanded that our client pay is so high that we cannot believe that this claim was made in good faith].

   In the event your client decides to pursue this matter further by filing suit against our client, please be assured that we will defend the suit vigorously and will pursue our client's claim against your client for filing a lawsuit in apparent bad faith and for the purpose of harassment.

   As I am sure you are aware, our client's choices in this situation are difficult. By rejecting your claim, our client is aware that considerable expense may be incurred in defending a lawsuit should your client insist on pursuing this matter further; nevertheless, our client is unwilling to pay any money to your client when the claim is so clearly unjust.

   We encourage your client to think very carefully before pursuing this matter further.

                                   Sincerely,
                                   [Signature of attorney]
```

§4.08 Effect of Consumer's Rejection of Settlement Offer

Unless both parts of the offer (damages and attorney's fees) are accepted by the consumer within thirty days after the offer is made, the offer is deemed rejected. DTPA §17.5052(e). In order to preserve the defenses that arise from the making of such an offer, it is necessary to file with the court a copy of the offer and an affidavit certifying that the offer was rejected (or deemed rejected). DTPA §17.5052(f).

[a] FORM: Affidavit of rejection of settlement offer

[NOTE: The following form contains statutory citations applicable to those causes of action governed by the 1995 amendments. For cases governed by earlier law, the citation should be "§17.505(d)."]

```
                              NO. _____

_____             §      IN THE DISTRICT COURT OF
                       §
vs.                    §      _____ COUNTY, TEXAS
                       §
_____             §      _____ JUDICIAL DISTRICT
```

AFFIDAVIT OF REJECTION OF SETTLEMENT OFFER

_____, defendant, files this affidavit pursuant to Tex. Bus. & Com. Code §17.5052(f):

_____ COUNTY, TEXAS:

BEFORE ME the undersigned authority on this day personally appeared _____, who, after having been by me duly cautioned and sworn, stated to me upon his oath as follows:

1. My name is _____. I am the attorney of record for [defendant] in this lawsuit. I am fully competent to make this affidavit and have personal knowledge of the statements made in it.

2. On _____ 20__, [defendant] received a notice letter from [plaintiff] asserting a claim under the Deceptive Trade Practices - Consumer Protection Act. A true and correct copy of the letter is attached as Exhibit A.

3. On _____, 20__, acting on instructions from [defendant] I prepared and mailed to [plaintiff] a response to the notice letter which contained an offer of settlement. A true and correct copy of the letter containing the offer of settlement is attached as Exhibit B.

4. The offer of settlement was received by [plaintiff] on _____ 20___,

5. The settlement offer was rejected by [plaintiff] [or The settlement offer was not accepted by [plaintiff] within the time allowed by law; therefore, pursuant to TEX. BUS. & COM. CODE §17.5052(e), the offer is deemed rejected].

6. The statements made in this affidavit are true and correct.

[Signature of affiant]

SUBSCRIBED AND SWORN TO before me on this _____ day of 20__, to certify which witness my hand and official seal.

[Signature of notary public]

Respectfully submitted,
[Signature of attorney]

[Certificate of service]

(This page intentionally left blank.)

Chapter 5

Plaintiff's Pleadings (General)

§5.01 Contents of Petition
   §5.01.1 Expedited Actions [effective March 1, 2013]
§5.02 Original Petition
   [a] FORM: Petition (general form)
§5.03 Citation
§5.04 The Function of Pleadings
§5.05 Service of Citation on Individuals and Partnerships
   [a] FORM: Citation on individual
   [b] FORM: Citation on general partnership
   [c] FORM: Citation on limited partnership [Service on registered agent]
§5.06 Service of Citation on Corporations and Insurance Companies
   [a] FORM: Service on Texas corporation
   [b] FORM: Service on Texas insurance company
§5.07 Service on the Secretary of State
   [a] FORM: Citation on Secretary of State—no agent for service
   [b] FORM: Citation on Secretary of State—engages in business in Texas
   [c] FORM: Citation on Secretary of State—former resident
   [d] FORM: Citation on Secretary of State—claim arises from business
   §5.07.1 Service on the Commissioner of Insurance
   [a] FORM: Citation on Commissioner of Insurance—non-admitted insurer doing business in Texas
§5.08 Long Arm Jurisdiction
   [a] FORM: Citation based on long arm jurisdiction
§5.09 Obtaining Proof of Service
§5.10 Citation on Person in Charge of Business
   [a] FORM: Citation when currently engaged in business
   [b] FORM: Notice of service to nonresident
§5.11 Service on Certain Employees or Agents
§5.12 Alleging Statutory Authority
§5.13 Notice and Conditions Precedent
   [a] FORM: —Notice given
   [b] FORM: —Notice not given

§5.14 Venue
  [a] FORM: General venue
  [b] FORM: DTPA venue
  [c] FORM: Breach of warranty by manufacturer
  [d] FORM: Venue proper as to other defendant
§5.15 Knowing Conduct
  [a] FORM: Knowing conduct (general form)
  [b] FORM: Knowing conduct, breach of warranty
  §5.15.1 Intentional Conduct
  [a] FORM: Intentional conduct, general
  [b] FORM: Intentional conduct, breach of warranty
§5.16 Economic Damages
  [a] FORM: Economic damages (product)
  [b] FORM: Economic damages (unimproved land)
  [c] FORM: Economic damages (residential construction)
  [d] FORM: Economic damages (investment)
§5.17 Additional Statutory Damages; Exemplary Damages
  [a] FORM: Additional damages (personal injury; wrongful death)
  [b] FORM: Exemplary damages
§5.18 Pleading Specific Actions
  [a] REFERENCE TABLE OF CAUSES OF ACTION AND REMEDIES
§5.19 [Reserved]
§5.20 Misrepresentation in Sale of Business Goods
  [a] FORM: Business goods
§5.21 Commercial Construction
  [a] FORM: Defective Commercial Construction
§5.22 [Reserved]
§5.23 Banking, Lending
  [a] FORM: Unauthorized withdrawal of funds
  [b] FORM: False representation to extend credit
§5.24 [Reserved]
§5.25 Commercial Real Property Lease
  [a] FORM: Commercial lease of real property
§5.26 Unfair Debt Collection Practices
  [a] FORM: Petition for unfair debt collection practices
  [b] FORM: Petition against bank on auto lease
§5.27 Application for Injunctive Relief
  [a] FORM: Petition for injunctive relief (general form)
  [b] FORM: Temporary restraining order (general form)
  [c] FORM: Application for temporary injunction (threatened foreclosure)
  [d] FORM: Temporary Injunction

§5.28 Pleading Discovery Rule to Avoid Limitations
    [a] FORM: Allegation invoking the discovery rule
§5.29 Petition for Unfair Debt Collection Practices
    [a] FORM: Petition for unfair debt collection practices
    [b] FORM: Petition against bank on auto lease
§5.30 Professional Services
    [a] FORM: Petition for attorney's misrepresentations
§5.31 Residential Repair Services
    [a] FORM: Misrepresentation re services performed

§5.01 Contents of Petition

An original petition in DTPA cases is governed by the general rules of pleading, with two additions. All original petitions must contain:

(a) an allegation in the first numbered paragraph as to whether discovery is intended to be conducted under Level 1, 2, or 3 of Rule 190.1 of the Texas Rules of Civil Procedure;

(b) a short statement of the cause of action sufficient to give fair notice of the claim involved,

(c) a statement that the damages sought exceed the minimum jurisdictional limits, and

(d) A statement about whether the party seeks monetary relief within one of the five scaled categories described in Rule 47(c) (ranging from "less than $100,000" to "over $1,000.000"); and

(e) a demand for judgment for all the other relief to which the party deems himself entitled.

TEX. R. CIV. P. Rules 47(a) - (c); 190.1.

The first addition to the general rules of pleading is that in DTPA cases, pre-filing notice is required unless excused by the statute. *See* §3.01 *supra*. When notice has been given, the facts relating to notice should be pleaded. *See* §5.13 *infra*.

The second addition is that only a "consumer" can maintain an action under the DTPA. DTPA §17.50(a). The facts should be stated in the petition in sufficient detail to establish the DTPA standing requirement.

The specificity with which DTPA or Insurance Code causes of action should be pleaded are tested by the same "fair notice" principles applicable to other petitions. *See e.g., Weitzel v. Barnes,* 691 S.W.2d 598 (Tex. 1985); *Troutman v. Traeco Bldg. Sys., Inc.,* 724 S.W.2d 385 (Tex. 1987). As a rule, pleadings can be quite general and satisfy the fair notice requirement. *See e.g., Holland Mortgage Inv. Corp. v. Bone,* 751 S.W.2d 515 (Tex. App.—Houston [1st Dist.] 1987, no writ).

Of course, if the defendant is of the opinion that the petition is too general, then special exceptions may be employed to require a more detailed statement of the facts. TEX. R. CIV. P. 91; *Troutman v. Traeco Bldg. Sys., Inc., supra.*

Although it is good practice, it is not necessary for the petition to specify the particular statutory provision in the DTPA on which the action is based. *Weitzel v. Barnes, supra* at 601; *Troutman v. Traeco Bldg. Sys., Inc., supra* at 387; *Padre Island Inv. Corp. v. Sorbera,* 677 S.W.2d 90 (Tex. App.—San Antonio 1984, writ dism'd). Including specific statutory references in the petition, however, removes all doubt about whether the jury questions that ultimately are submitted are supported by the pleadings. *See generally, Stone v. Lawyers Title Ins. Corp.,* 554 S.W.2d 183 (Tex. 1977).

§5.01.1 Expedited Actions

In 2011, the Legislature amended section 22,004 of the *Texas Government Code* authorizing the Texas Supreme Court to adopt new rules of procedure to "promote the prompt, efficient, and cost-effective resolution of civil actions" in which the amount in controversy, inclusive of all costs, attorney's fees and damages of any kind, does not exceed $100,000. ACTS 2011, 82ND LEG., CH. 203 (H.B. 274). In response, the Texas

Supreme Court adopted significant amendments to Rules 47 and 190.2, as well as a completely new Rule 169 governing "Expedited Actions." Misc. Docket No. 12-9191 (Texas Supreme Court, Nov. 13. 2012).

These new expedited action rules will have a large impact on the typical consumer cases brought under the DTPA. Because the DTPA is usually the remedy of choice in consumer transactions where less than $100,000 is at issue, most DTPA cases will now fall under the expedited actions procedure.

There are significant limitations on suits governed by the expedited actions rules. Discovery is limited to six hours of deposition time per side, no more than 15 interrogatories, no more than 15 requests for production and no more than 15 requests for admissions. Tex. R. Civ. P. 190.2(b). Deposition time may be extended by agreement between the parties, but to no more than 10 total hours per side without a court order. Tex. R. Civ. P. 190.2(b)(2). The discovery period begins with the filing of suit and ends 180 days after the first request of any kind is served on a party. Tex. R. Civ. P. 190.2(b)(1). Thus, if a request for disclosure or other discovery request is included with the original petition, the discovery period closes 180 days after the suit is served. The court may modify these discovery limitations. Tex. R. Civ. P. 190.5. However, the court is not required to re-open discovery in expedited actions, even if there are new pleadings or late disclosures. *Id.*

In cases governed by the expedited actions procedure, the trial will be short. Each "side" is limited to just five hours to complete jury selection, opening statements, presentation of the evidence, examination and cross-examination of witnesses and closing arguments. Tex. R. Civ. P. 169(d)(3). If two or more parties are substantially aligned, they will be considered on "side" and limited as if they were a single party. Tex. R. Civ. P. 169(d)(3)(A). Neither mediation nor any other alternative dispute resolution may be ordered by the court, either by court order or local rule, unless all parties agree. Tex. R. Civ. P. 169(b)(4). The admissibility of expert testimony may not be challenged before trial, unless in response to a motion for summary judgment or late designation. Tex. R. Civ. P. 169(d)(5).

In cases governed by the expedited actions procedure, the recovery will be limited to no more than $100,000. Tex. R. Civ. P. 169(b).

The expedited actions rules will apply to any action in which only monetary relief of $100,000 or less is sought. Tex. R. Civ. P. 169. Whether the expedited actions procedure applies will usually be governed by the allegations in the plaintiff's petition about how much monetary relief is sought. Rule 47 now requires that all petitions, counterclaims, third-party petitions and cross-claims contain a statement concerning the amount of monetary relief requested. The pleader must choose one of five categories to describe the monetary relief requested: 1) only monetary relief of $100,000 or less; 2) monetary relief of $100,000 or less and non-monetary relief; 3) monetary relief over $100,000 but no more than $500,000; 4) monetary relief over $500,000 but not more than $1,000,000; and 5) monetary relief over $1,000,000. Tex. R. Civ. P. 47(c). The penalty for non-compliance is to prevent the pleading party from engaging in any discovery. Tex. R. Civ. P. 47(d).

The amount of monetary relief requested is determined by adding up all of the claims for damages, costs, attorney's fees, penalties and pre-judgment interest. Tex. R. Civ. P. 47(c)(1), 169(a)(1). This includes exemplary damages and additional damages under the DTPA. *Id.* Care must be taken to calculate all possible scenarios for recovery of monetary relief. A claim for treble damages under the DTPA and even a modest amount of attorney's fees for all levels of appeal may reveal that a recovery is being sought in excess of $100,000. Cross-claims and third-party claims (but not counter-claims) will be aggregated and may take the case out of the expedited actions procedure. TEX. R. CIV. P. 169(a)(1).

There is no mechanism for challenging the pleader's choice of the amount of monetary relief requested. A special exception may still be used to require the pleader to specify the maximum amount of monetary relief requested. TEX. R. CIV. P. 47.

The petition forms (in this chapter and the chapters which follow) have been updated to comply with these new pleading rules. Care should be taken to determine whether the plaintiff's claim for monetary relief exceeds $100,000, inclusive of all damages, exemplary damages, costs, attorney's fees expenses and pre-judgment interest. If not, the expedited action procedures will be applicable. If the plaintiff's total monetary recovery may exceed $100,000, care should be taken to draft the petition accordingly so that the expedited action procedures do not limit the plaintiff's recovery, discovery rights or trial length.

§5.02 Original Petition

The form of an original petition is as much a matter of style as substance, assuming that the requisite elements are present. The following form is general in nature in order to illustrate the format in which the essential allegations in a DTPA petition may be presented.

[a] FORM: Petition (general form)

```
                          NO. _____
_____                §     IN THE DISTRICT COURT OF
                          §
vs.                       §     _____COUNTY, TEXAS
                          §
_____                §     _____ JUDICIAL DISTRICT
```

PLAINTIFF'S ORIGINAL PETITION

TO THE HONORABLE JUDGE OF THE DISTRICT COURT:

NOW COMES _____, Plaintiff herein, complaining of _____, Defendant herein, and for cause of action, would show unto the Court as follows:

I. DISCOVERY CONTROL PLAN DESIGNATION

1.01   By this action, Plaintiff seeks _____ [*insert appropriate designation under Rule 47(c), e.g., only monetary relief of $100,000 or less, including damages of any kind, penalties, costs, expenses, pre-judgment interest, and attorney's fees*]. The damages sought are within the jurisdictional limits of this court.

1.02   Discovery in this case is intended to be conducted under Level _____, pursuant to Rule 190._____, *Texas Rules of Civil Procedure*.

[**NOTE:** For a discussion of the levels of discovery, *see* §7.37-7.39 *infra*.]

II. PARTIES

2.01   _____ is a resident of _____, _____ County, Texas.

2.02   _____ is an individual who resides and may be served with process at _____, _____ County, Texas.

[*See* §5.05, *et seq. infra* for alternative forms]

III. VENUE

3.01   Venue of this action is proper in _____ County, Texas because _____ reside in _____ County, Texas and the events made the basis of this lawsuit and giving rise to Plaintiff's cause of action occurred, in whole or in part, in _____ County, Texas.

[*See* §5.14 *infra* for alternative forms]

IV. NOTICE; CONDITIONS PRECEDENT

4.01   Defendant was given notice in writing of the claims made in this petition including a statement of Plaintiff's economic damages, mental anguish damages and expenses, including attorney's fees, more than sixty days before this suit was filed in the manner and form required by DTPA §17.505(a).

4.02   All conditions precedent to recovery by Plaintiff herein have been performed, have occurred, or have been excused.

[*See* §5.13 *infra* for alternative forms]

V. AGENCY AND JOINT VENTURE

5.01   Unless otherwise stated, whenever it is alleged that Defendant _____ committed an act, failed to perform an act, made a representation or a statement, or failed to make a disclosure, it is alleged that Defendant _____ acted or failed to act through its authorized agents, servants, employees or representatives acting with either expressed, implied, apparent, direct and/or ostensible authority, or _____ subsequently ratified these acts, failures to act, representations, statements or conduct.

5.02   [*If the actions of a particular employee or agent are alleged, consider adding:* [Employee/Agent] _____ was the _____ manager of _____ in _____, _____ County, Texas. It is therefore further alleged that, at all times relevant hereto, [Employee/Agent] _____ acted as the authorized agent of Defendant _____ with either expressed, implied, apparent, direct and/or ostensible authority, or that Defendant _____ subsequently ratified the acts, failures to act, representations, statements or conduct of [Employee/Agent] _____.

5.02   [*If joint venture can be used as a theory for vicarious liability, consider adding:* Further, it is alleged that Defendant was engaged [with joint venturer] in a joint venture for their mutual benefit and acted as each other's agents with all express, implied, direct and/or ostensible authority to so act, and as such are vicariously liable for the acts, omissions, statements and conduct of the other as alleged herein.

VI. FACTS OF CASE

6.01   This lawsuit arises out of the following transaction, acts and events: [*describe facts on which claim is based*].

[*See* §5.18 *et seq. infra* for specific pleading forms]

VII. FIRST CAUSE OF ACTION: DTPA

7.01   Plaintiff is a consumer entitled to bring this action for relief under the Texas Deceptive Trade Practices—Consumer Protection Act (the "DTPA"). The actions of Defendants outlined above constitute [*include any or all applicable:* misrepresentations, breaches of warranties and unconscionable conduct,] actionable under the DTPA.

7.02   Specifically, Defendant committed the following acts in violation of the DTPA "laundry list," one or more of which was a producing cause of damages to Plaintiff:

(a) Representing that the goods or services had characteristics, ingredients, uses or benefits which they did not have;

(b) Representing that goods or services were of a particular standard, quality or grade when they were of another; and

(c) Failing to disclose information concerning goods or services which was known at the time in order to induce the Plaintiff to enter into a transaction which Plaintiff would not have otherwise entered.

[*See* §5.18 *et seq. infra* for specific forms]

7.03   [*Always include for "laundry list" claims:* Plaintiff relied on these representations to his [her] detriment.]

7.04   [*If applicable, add:* Further, Defendant violated the DTPA by breaching one or more warranties.]

[*See* §5.18 *et seq. infra* for specific forms]

7.05   [*If applicable, add:* Further, Defendant violated the DTPA by engaging in unconscionable conduct and/or an unconscionable course of conduct.]

7.06   Defendant's conduct as described herein was a producing cause of damages to Plaintiff.

7.07   Further, Defendant's conduct was committed knowingly, entitling Plaintiff to seek the trebling of his [her] economic damages in accordance with the DTPA. [*See* §5.15 and §5.15.1 *infra* for specific pleading forms]

VIII. SECOND CAUSE OF ACTION: [THEORY TWO]

8.01   [*To make it clear the same facts support the next cause of action, add:* Plaintiff repeats and re-alleges the material factual allegations in the preceding paragraphs.]

8.02   [*Continue with elements of next cause of action.*]

IX. THIRD CAUSE OF ACTION: [THEORY THREE]

9.01   [*If an alternative set of facts are alleged to support another cause of action, introduce them accordingly, e.g.,* Alternatively, should it be determined that the event in question occurred prior to the effective date of the insurance policy with [Defendant One], then the event would nevertheless be covered by insurance policy issued by [Defendant Two].

9.02   [*Continue with elements of next cause of action.*]

X. FOURTH CAUSE OF ACTION:

10.01   Plaintiff repeats and realleges the material factual allegations in the preceding paragraphs.

10.02   [*Continue with all theories of liability alleged.*]

XI. DAMAGES

11.01 Defendant's acts and omissions as described herein have been a producing and/or proximate cause of damages to Plaintiff. Plaintiff has suffered economic damages, including but not limited to: [*insert types of damages*]

[*See* §5.16 *infra* for general damages allegations]

[*See* §5.18 *et seq.* for additional pleading forms]

11.02 These damages are within the jurisdictional limits of this Court.

XII. ADDITIONAL DAMAGES AND PUNITIVE DAMAGES

12.01 Defendant's conduct in violation of the DTPA was committed knowingly, as that term is defined. Accordingly, Plaintiff seeks an award of additional damages under the DTPA in an amount not to exceed three times the amount of his [her] economic damages.

[*See* §5.17 *infra* for alternative forms]

XIII. ATTORNEY'S FEES

13.01 As a result of Defendant's conduct, Plaintiff has been required to obtain the services of the undersigned attorney for the filing, prosecution and trial of this cause, and therefore seeks an award of reasonable and necessary attorney's fees pursuant to applicable law.

WHEREFORE, PREMISES CONSIDERED, Plaintiff respectfully prays that Defendant be cited to appear and answer herein, and that upon final trial hereof, Plaintiff recover from Defendant [*if applicable,* jointly and severally,] all of his economic damages, [*continue as applicable,* mental anguish, additional damages, exemplary damages,] pre-judgment and post-judgment interest as allowed by law, attorney's fees, costs of court and such other and further relief to which he may show himself justly entitled.

Respectfully submitted,

_____

Attorney for Plaintiff

§5.03 Citation

Citation may be served by either (1) "any sheriff or constable or other person authorized by law," or (2) "any person authorized by law or by written order of the court who is not less than eighteen years of age." TEX. R. CIV. P. 103.

There are three methods by which those authorized to do so may serve citation. First, citation may be accomplished by personal service (TEX. R. CIV. P. 106[a][1]); second, citation may be served by registered or certified mail, return receipt requested (TEX. R. CIV. P. 106[a][2]); or third, citation may be by "substituted service," that is, upon motion and affidavit that the other methods have been ineffective, the court may permit an authorized person to deliver citation by leaving it with someone over the age of eighteen at a specified location or in any other "reasonably effective" manner (TEX. R. CIV. P. 106[b]).

§5.04 The Function of Pleadings

A plaintiff's petition serves two functions with respect to service of citation. First, the petition should identify a proper person for service of citation *(see §5.05 et seq. infra)* and second, it should provide sufficient factual information to enable the person charged with serving citation to accomplish the task.

The pleadings should provide either the complete street address, city and county of the person to be served or the complete mailing address (street or post office box, city and zip code), depending on whether service is to be accomplished in person or by mail.

Although the citation should specify a particular address at which the defendant can be served, actual service can be accomplished wherever the defendant can be found in the county, whether or not the petition contains the address. *Garcia v. Gutierrez,* 697 S.W.2d 758 (Tex. App.—Corpus Christi 1985, no writ).

When the defendant is represented by an attorney, a citation served on the attorney is ineffective without the explicit authorization of the defendant. *H. L. McRae Co. v. Hooker Construction Company,* 579 S.W.2d 62 (Tex. App.—Austin 1979, no writ).

§5.05 Service of Citation on Individuals and Partnerships

This section deals with service of citation on persons other than corporations. The natural person to be served with citation depends on whether the defendant is an individual or a legal entity; and, if the defendant is a legal entity, the type of entity. The citation section of the petition should allege those facts which determine the proper person for service.

(1) *Individual.* When the defendant is an individual, he or she normally is served with citation at either his or her residence or regular place of business.

[a] FORM: Citation on individual

2.02 _____ is an individual defendant and may be served with citation at _____, his [her] residence [business] address.

(2) *General partnership.* A general partnership may be served by serving any of its partners, TEX. BUS. ORGS. CODE §5.255, thus authorizing a judgment against the partnership and the partner served. TEX. CIV. PRAC. & REM. CODE §17.022.

[b] FORM: Citation on general partnership

2.02 _____ is a general partnership. _____ is one of the partners and may be served with process at _____, his [her] residence [business] address.

[NOTE: Although all partners in a general partnership are jointly and severally liable for the debts of the partnership (*see* TEX. BUS. ORGS. CODE §152.304(a), if individual partners are to be held liable, each such partner should be sued individually and served with citation (*see* TEX. BUS. ORGS. CODE §152.305.]

(3) *Limited partnership.* Each general partner and the registered agent of a limited partnership are agents on whom citation may be served. TEX. BUS. ORGS. CODE §5.251.

Limited partnerships are required to maintain a registered office and a registered agent for service of process. TEX. REV. CIV. STAT. art. 6132a-1 §1.06(a)(1), (2). The registered agent and address are identified on forms filed with the Secretary of State of Texas.

If a limited partnership fails to appoint a registered agent in Texas or if the agent and general partner cannot, with reasonable diligence, be found, then the Secretary of State of Texas is, by statute, appointed the agent for service of citation. TEX. REV. CIV. STAT. art. 6132a-1 §1.08(b).

[c] FORM: Citation on limited partnership [Service on registered agent]

2.02 _____ is a Texas limited partnership. Citation may be served on _____, the registered agent for the partnership, at the partnership's registered address.

[*or*]

[Service on general partner]

2.02 _____ is a Texas limited partnership. Citation may be served on _____, a general partner of the partnership, at the general partner's residence [business] address.

[or]

[Service on Secretary of State]

2.02 _____ is a Texas limited partnership. The limited partnership has failed to appoint a registered agent for service of citation [or Although _____ has been appointed registered agent for the limited partnership for service of citation, he cannot, with reasonable diligence, be found at the registered office]. Further _____, the general partner of the partnership, with reasonable diligence, cannot be found. For these reasons, citation may be served on this defendant by serving the Secretary of State of Texas at [insert Secretary of State's mailing address for service.] Upon receipt of the citation, the Secretary of State shall forward the citation by registered mail to this defendant at [insert registered agent's address or last registered office address.]

§5.06 Service of Citation on Corporations and Insurance Companies

Corporations are required to maintain a registered office and registered agent, upon whom citation normally is served. TEX. BUS. ORGS. CODE §5.201.

Even so, citation may be served either on the registered agent or the president or any vice-president of the corporation. TEX. BUS. ORGS. CODE §5.255.

Insurance companies admitted to conduct business in Texas are required to appoint an agent for service similar to a corporation's registered agent for service. See TEX. INS. CODE §804.102. Service of process upon a Texas insurance company may be had by serving its president, an "active" vice-president, secretary or "attorney-in-fact" at the principal or home office of the company. Alternatively, service can be accomplished by leaving a copy of the citation at the home office during regular business hours. TEX. INS. CODE §804.101.

[a] FORM: Service on Texas corporation

[Registered agent]

2.02 _____ is a Texas corporation which may be served with process by serving _____, its registered agent, at _____ the corporation's registered address.

[or]

[President or Vice-President]

2.02 _____ is a Texas corporation which may be served with process by serving _____, the corporation's president [*vice-president*], at the principal office of the corporation.

[or]

[b] FORM: Service on Texas insurance company

2.02 _____ is an insurance company organized and existing under the laws of the state of Texas licensed and admitted to do business as a property and casualty insurer in the state of Texas and which may be served through _____, _____ County, Texas, its registered attorney [agent] for service of process in Texas.

§5.07 Service on the Secretary of State

Under specified conditions, the Secretary of State of Texas is, by law, the defendant's agent for service of citation. For nonresidents, the Secretary of State may be served with citation if the nonresident:

(1) is required by statute to designate or maintain a resident agent or engages in business in this state, but has not designated or maintained a resident agent for service of process;

(2) has one or more resident agents for service of process, but two unsuccessful attempts have been made on different business days to serve each agent; or

(3) is not required to designate an agent for service in this state, but becomes a nonresident after a cause of action arises in this state but before the cause is matured by suit in a court of competent jurisdiction.

TEX. CIV. PRAC. & REM. CODE §17.044(a).

The Secretary of State of Texas also is an agent for service of citation for a nonresident, "who engages in business in this state, but does not maintain a regular place of business in this state or a designated agent for service of process, in any proceeding that arises out of the business done in this state and to which the nonresident is a party." TEX. CIV. PRAC. & REM. CODE §17.044(b).

Whenever the Secretary of State is served as an "agent", the facts which justify such service must be set forth in the pleadings and should track the language of the statute conferring authority for service on the Secretary of State.

[a] FORM: Citation on Secretary of State—no agent for service

2.02 _____ is a corporation that is required by law to maintain an agent for service of process but has failed to do so. For this reason, citation should be served on the Secretary of State of Texas under Tex. Civ. Prac. & Rem. Code §17.044(a)(1). A copy of the citation and petition should be mailed by the Secretary of State of Texas to this defendant at _____.

[b] FORM: Citation on Secretary of State—engages in business in Texas

2.02 _____ is a person who engages in business in this state but has not designated or maintained an agent for service of process. For this reason, citation should be served on the Secretary of State of Texas under Tex. Civ. Prac. & Rem. Code §17.044(a)(1). A copy of the citation and the petition should be mailed by the Secretary of State to this defendant at _____.

[c] FORM: Citation on Secretary of State—former resident

2.02 _____ is not required to designate an agent for service of process in this state, but became a nonresident after this cause of action arose in this state and before the cause of action matured by the filing of this suit. For this reason, citation should be served on the Secretary of State of Texas under Tex. Civ. Prac. & Rem. Code §17.044(a)(3). A copy of the citation and petition should be mailed by the Secretary of State to this defendant at [*insert current mailing address*].

[d] FORM: Citation on Secretary of State—claim arises from business

2.02 _____ is a nonresident who engages in business in this state. This defendant does not maintain a regular place of business in this state or a designated agent for service of process. This lawsuit, in which _____ is a party, arises out of the business done in this state. For these reasons, citation should be served on the Secretary of State of Texas under Tex. Civ. Prac. & Rem. Code §17.044(b). A copy of the citation and petition. should be mailed by the Secretary of State to this defendant at [*insert current mailing address*].

§5.07.1 Service on the Commissioner of Insurance

Like the Secretary of State, the Commissioner of Insurance may be deemed the appropriate agent for service of process of certain insurance companies which have failed to appoint or maintain an agent for service within the state of Texas. *See* TEX. INS. CODE Ch. 804, Subch. B. If an "alien" or foreign insurance company engages in business in Texas but does not appoint or maintain an agent for service of process, the Texas Insurance Commissioner will be deemed the agent for service. TEX. INS. CODE §804.103. Similarly, if a "domestic" insurance company does not maintain an appointed agent, or the agent cannot be found with reasonable diligence, the Commissioner will be deemed the agent for service. TEX. INS. CODE §804.102.

When the Commissioner of Insurance is the deemed agent for service of process of an insurance company, the process is served, much like the Secretary of State, by addressing the process to the defendant with its name and address and delivered to the Commissioner or his/her designated representative at the Department of Insurance in Austin during regular business hours. TEX. INS. CODE §804.201. The following form can be used to establish the Commissioner of Insurance as the agent for service of process in the appropriate circumstances.

[a] FORM: Citation on Commissioner of Insurance—non-admitted insurer doing business in Texas

2.02   Defendant _____ is an alien insurance company which engages in business in this state but has not designated or maintained an agent for service of process. For this reason, citation should be served on the Commissioner of Insurance of Texas under Tex. Ins. Code §804.103. Two copies of the citation and the petition should be delivered to the Commissioner of Insurance or his/her designated representative during regular business hours at the Texas Department of Insurance, 333 Guadalupe, P. O. Box 149104, Austin, Travis County, Texas 78714-9104 with instructions to forward the citation and petition to Defendant at [Defendant's address].

§5.08 Long Arm Jurisdiction

When a nonresident is sued, a fundamental question arises as to whether a Texas court can exercise personal jurisdiction over the defendant. There are several grounds upon which long-arm jurisdiction can be exercised; however, the most common basis for the exercise of personal jurisdiction over a nonresident is that the nonresident is "doing business" in Texas. "Doing business" is defined, in part, by statute:

In addition to other acts that may constitute doing business, a nonresident does business in this state if the nonresident:

(1) contracts by mail or otherwise with a Texas resident and either party is to perform the contract in whole or in part in this state;

(2) commits a tort in whole or in part in this state; or

(3) recruits Texas residents, directly or through an intermediary located in this state, for employment inside or outside this state.

TEX. CIV. PRAC. & REM. CODE §17.042. Of course, the statute expressly provides that "other acts" may also satisfy the "doing business" requirement. *Zac Smith & Co. v. Otis Elevator Co.*, 734 S.W.2d 662 (Tex. 1987); *Siskind v. Villa Foundation for Education, Inc.*, 642 S.W.2d 434 (Tex. 1982); *O'Brien v. Lanpar Co.*, 399 S.W.2d 340 (Tex. 1966).

Because of the breadth of the reach of the long-arm statute, Texas has a specific test that it applies to determine if the constitutional limitations on the exercise of state court jurisdiction have been satisfied. *Schlobohm v. Schapiro*, 784 S.W.2d 355 (Tex. 1990). This test has three elements:

1. The nonresident defendant or foreign corporation must purposefully do some act or consummate some transaction in the forum state;

2. The cause of action must arise from, or be connected with, such act or transaction. Even if the cause of action does not arise from a specific contact, jurisdiction may be exercised if the defendant's contacts with Texas are continuing and systematic.

3. The assumption of jurisdiction by the forum state must not offend traditional notions of fair play and substantial justice, consideration being given to the quality, nature, and extent of the activity in the forum state, the benefits and protection of the laws of the forum state afforded the respective parties, and the basic equities of the situation.

Schlobohm v. Schapiro, 784 S.W.2d 358; see also *Guardian Royal Exchange Assurance, Ltd. v. English China Clays*, P.L.C, 815 S.W.2d 223 (Tex. 1991).

When the Secretary of State is served with citation on behalf of a nonresident, the Secretary of State is required to forward a copy of the citation to the nonresident, or, in the case of a former resident who moved before the suit was filed, to either the nonresident or the person in charge of the nonresident's business or to a corporate officer. TEX. CIV. PRAC. & REM. CODE §17.045(b). For this reason, duplicate copies of the petition should be served on the Secretary of State and the pleadings should contain the mailing address to which the Secretary of State will forward citation. *Id.*

[a] FORM: Citation based on long arm jurisdiction

```
2.02           is a foreign corporation, nonresident of
Texas, which has no Certificate of Authority. Although           
engages in business in Texas, no agent has been designated for
service of citation, and it has no regular place of business in
Texas. As set forth in the petition, defendant advertised exten-
sively in this state and solicited, through such advertising, the
purchase which forms the basis of this lawsuit.
```

2.03   Because this lawsuit arises out of defendant's purposeful acts in this state, the assumption of jurisdiction by this court does not offend traditional notions of fair play and substantial justice. Pursuant to TEX. CIV. PRAC. & REM. CODE §17.044(a) and (b), service of citation on this defendant may be accomplished by serving the Secretary of State of Texas who will then forward such citation by certified mail, return receipt requested, to _____ at [insert mailing address of defendant].

§5.09 Obtaining Proof of Service

On request, the Secretary of State will provide an official document certifying under seal the day on which citation was mailed and the day on which the signed return receipt was received. There is a fee for this service; however, it is essential if there is a need to prove actual service on the defendant. The Secretary of State receives a **$40.00** fee for maintaining a record and for forwarding the process, notice or demand. A fee of **$15.00** is collected for the issuance of a Certificate of Service. TEX. GOV'T. CODE *§405.031*.

§5.10 Citation on Person in Charge of Business

When a person is a nonresident who engages in business in Texas but who is not required by statute to designate or maintain a resident agent for service of process, citation may be served on the person in charge of the nonresident's business in Texas. TEX. CIV. PRAC. & REM. CODE §17.043.

If the person in charge of a nonresident's business is served with citation, a copy of the citation and petition as well as a notice of service of the documents must immediately be mailed by registered mail or by certified mail, return receipt requested, to the nonresident or to the nonresident's principal place of business. TEX. CIV. PRAC. & REM. CODE §17.045(c), (d).

[a] FORM: Citation when currently engaged in business

2.02   _____ is a nonresident of Texas and is not required by law to designate or maintain a resident agent for service of process. This defendant is, however engaged in business in this State. Accordingly, citation may be served on _____ who is the person in charge of this defendant's business in Texas at _____ his [her] residence [business] address.

[b] FORM: Notice of service to nonresident

CERTIFIED MAIL, RETURN RECEIPT REQUESTED

```
(Date)

(Inside address)

Re: Cause no. _____ ; _____    vs. _____

Dear _____ :
```

Enclosed is a copy of an Original Petition and Citation which were served on [*person in charge of business in Texas*] on [*date of service*].

```
                              Sincerely,

                              [Signature of attorney]
```

§5.11 Service on Certain Employees or Agents

In very limited circumstances, a clerk or other agent of an individual partnership, or unincorporated association can be served with citation. Essentially, the statutory authority to serve a non-corporate agent or employee is useful when the principal is evading service of process. *See* TEX. CIV. PRAC. & REM. CODE §17.021.

§5.12 Alleging Statutory Authority

A petition should give fair notice that the lawsuit alleges violations of and claim for relief under the DTPA, *see, e.g., Johnson v. Willis*, 596 S.W.2d 251 (Tex. Civ. App.—Waco 1980, writ ref'd n.r.e.), especially since there are statutory defenses to a DTPA action that must be pleaded by the defendant. *See Murray v. O&A Express, Inc.*, 630 S.W.2d 633 (Tex. 1982). *See* §5.02 *supra*.

§5.13 Notice and Conditions Precedent

Pre-filing notice is required in DTPA litigation except under certain, specified conditions. DTPA §17.505. If notice has been given, it should be pleaded. Pleading notice shifts the burden to the defendant to deny under oath that notice was not proper. TEX. R. CIV. P. 93(12). Further, a general allegation that all conditions precedent have been performed or have occurred is sufficient to cast the burden on the defendant to raise specific conditions, such as pre-filing notice, that have not been satisfied. TEX. R. CIV. P. 54. The defendant must timely object to a plaintiff's failure to give notice by filing a plea in abatement within 30 days of filing an answer or the right to notice will be deemed waived. DTPA §17.505(c); *see Hines v. Hash*, 843 S.W.2d 464 (TEX. 1992). If notice has not been given, the reasons for not giving notice should be pleaded.

Pre-filing notice under the DTPA is required only when the suit seeks damages under the statute. DTPA §17.505(a). Thus, a party may file an action not seeking DTPA damages, *e.g.* a suit for injunctive relief, and give the DTPA pre-filing notice at a later time. Then, once the proper notice period has run, the suit that is on file can be amended to include DTPA damages claims. *See Miller v. Presswood,* 743 S.W.2d 275, 281 (Tex. App.—Beaumont 1987, writ denied). If this approach has been taken, then the allegation of notice which is contained in §[a] below will appear in the amended petition which first seeks the recovery of DTPA damages.

[a] FORM: —Notice given

4.01 On _____, 20___, plaintiff gave written notice of his [her] specific complaints concerning the transaction described in this petition along with notice of his [her] economic damages, mental anguish damages, and expenses, including attorneys' fees, in the manner and form required by DTPA §17.505(a). [This notice was received by the defendant on _____.]

4.02 All conditions precedent necessary to maintain this action have been performed or have occurred.

[b] FORM: —Notice not given

4.01 No written notice of the claims made in this petition has been given by plaintiff before this suit was filed because the statute of limitations applicable to this action is expected to expire during the notice period.

4.02 All conditions precedent necessary to maintain this action have been performed or have occurred.

§5.14 Venue

In 1995, the legislature amended DTPA §17.56 twice. As of the 2009 Session, the Legislature has not corrected this anomaly. The first amendment was contained in 1995 Tex. Gen. Laws, Chap. 138 §7:

> Except as provided by Article 5.06-1(8), Insurance Code, an action brought which alleges a claim to relief under Section 17.50 of this subchapter shall be brought as provided by Chapter 15, Civil Practice and Remedies Code.

1995 Tex. Gen. Laws, Chap. 138 §7; DTPA §17.56, as amended 1995. The Insurance Code article referenced in the amended DTPA venue provision dealt with insurance disputes involving uninsured or underinsured motor vehicle accidents and has been recodified at Tex. Ins. Code §1952.110.

The second amendment to DTPA §17.56 was contained in H.B. 668. This amendment provides:

> An action under this subchapter may be brought: (1) in any county in which venue is proper under Chapter 15, Civil Practice

and Remedies Code; or (2) in a county in which the defendant or an authorized agent of the defendant solicited the transaction made the subject of the action at bar.

1995 TEX. GEN. LAWS, Chap. 414 §9. The amendments to §17.56 were for the purpose of having DTPA venue correspond to the new venue rules enacted under the Civil Practice and Remedies Code as part of the "tort reform" legislation package. *See generally,* 1995 TEX. GEN. LAWS. Chap. 138, p. 97E *et seq.*

The general venue rule was amended in 1995 to read as follows:

Except as provided by this subchapter or Subchapter B or C, all lawsuits shall be brought:

(1) in the county in which all or a substantial part of the events or omissions giving rise to the claim arise;

(2) in the county of the defendant's residence at the time the cause of action accrued if the defendant is a natural person;

(3) in the county of the defendant's principal office in this state, if the defendant is not a natural person; or

(4) if Subdivisions (1), (2), and (3) do not apply, in the county in which the plaintiff resided at the time of the accrual of the cause of action.

TEX. CIV. PRAC. & REM. CODE §15.002(a), as amended 1995.

Even though venue may be proper under one of the subdivisions in §15.002, the 1995 amendments to the Code provide further that the court still may transfer venue to another county of "proper venue" if the court finds that:

(1) maintenance of the action in the county of suit would work an injustice to the movant considering the movant's economic and personal hardship;

(2) the balance of interests of all the parties predominates in favor of the action being brought in the other county; and

(3) the transfer of the action would not work an injustice to any other party.

TEX. CIV. PRAC. & REM. CODE §15.002(b), as amended 1995. The trial court is given enormous discretion under subsection (b) in that a court's ruling or decision to grant or deny a transfer under subsection (b), "is not grounds for an appeal or mandamus and is not reversible error." TEX. CIV. PRAC. & REM. CODE §15.002(c).

The 1995 amendments also created new venue rules for suits involving multiple plaintiffs and intervening plaintiffs, *see* TEX. CIV. PRAC. & REM. CODE §15.003; and for suits involving multiple claims when one of the claims has a mandatory venue rule, *see* TEX. CIV. PRAC. & REM. CODE §15.004, as amended 1995; and, lawsuits involving multiple defendants, *see* TEX. CIV. PRAC. & REM. CODE §15.005, as amended 1995, as well as a number of other important changes in the venue rules.

In lawsuits involving defective construction, a venue question may be raised if the lawsuit is filed in a county other than that in which the property is located. The question is based on the venue provision in the Civil Practices and Remedies Code which deals with certain real property actions:

"Actions for recovery of real property or an estate or interest in real property, for partition of real property, to remove encumbrances from the title to real property, *for recovery of damages to real property*, or to quiet title to real property shall be brought in the county in which all or a part of the property is located."

TEX. CIV. PRAC. & REM. CODE §15.011. The argument is that when one seeks to recover damages caused by a cracked foundation, leaky roof, mold, or any other defective condition of the real property, this is a suit "for recovery of damages to real property" and must, therefore, be filed in the county where the property is located. The Austin court of appeals rejected this argument in *Allison v. Fire Insurance Exchange*, 98 S.W.3d 227, 244 (Tex. App.—Austin 2002, pet. granted, jdgm't vacated w.r.m.). According to the court, an analysis of various venue statutes, as well as the purpose of the mandatory venue provided by §15.011, demonstrate that the legislature did not intend for this particular venue provision to be construed so broadly that it would subsume all cases "in which any damages are sought relating to a dwelling, no matter the nature of the action[.]" *Allison v. Fire Insurance Exchange*, 98 S.W.3d 243.

Based on its analysis, the court held that because the plaintiff had brought actions for negligence, negligence per se, breach of contract, deceptive trade practices, and breach of good faith and fair dealing in insurance claims handling, and because the suit did not involve either the recovery of real property or quieting title (or seeking damages for such loss), the mandatory venue language of §15.001 did not apply. *Allison v. Fire Insurance Exchange*, 98 S.W.3d 244.

Venue is a question in a relatively small percentage of cases. In those cases where a motion to transfer venue is likely to be filed, however, venue facts should be alleged specifically in the original petition. Such pleading serves two purposes. First, upon reading the petition, opposing counsel may see that a motion to transfer venue would be unproductive. Second, if a motion to transfer venue is filed, it will not be necessary to amend the petition to allege venue facts.

The forms for pleading venue which follow do not constitute all of the grounds upon which venue can be maintained; instead, the forms provided involve only those grounds most frequently asserted.

[a] FORM: —General venue

```
3.01     Venue of this action is proper in this county because
this cause of action accrued in whole or in part in the county
of suit for the defendant is a natural person and resides in the
county of suit].
```

Authority: TEX. CIV. PRAC. & REM. CODE §15.001.

[b] FORM: —DTPA venue

```
3.01     Venue of this action is proper in this county because
defendant [or an authorized agent of defendant] solicited the
transaction on which this lawsuit is based in the county of suit.
```

Authority: DTPA §17.56(2), as amended 1995.

[c] FORM: —Breach of warranty by manufacturer

3.01 Venue of this action is proper in this county because a substantial part of the events or omissions giving rise to the claim occurred in the county of suit [*or* the manufacturer has its principal office in this state in the county of suit] [*or* the plaintiff resided in the county of suit at the time the cause of action accrued].

Authority: TEX. CIV. PRAC. & REM. CODE §15.033, as amended 1995.

[d] FORM: —Venue proper as to other defendant

3.02 Since venue of this action in this county is proper as to defendant _____ and no mandatory venue provision applies, venue is proper in this county as to all defendants.

Authority: TEX. CIV. PRAC. & REM. CODE §15.005.

§5.15 Knowing Conduct

If the defendant is found to have violated the DTPA or breached a warranty "knowingly," the DTPA authorizes the trier of fact to award additional damages up to three times the amount of actual damages. *See* DTPA §17.50(b)(1). Also, a "knowing" finding will allow the trier of fact to consider an award of mental anguish damages. *See Luna v. North Star Dodge Sales, Inc.*, 667 S.W.2d 115 (Tex. 1984); *Boyles v. Kerr*, 855 S.W.2d 593 (Tex. 1993); *see also State Farm Life Ins. Co. v. Beaston*, 907 S.W.2d 430 (Tex. 1995). The definition of "knowingly" differs in actions for false, misleading and deceptive acts and practices and those for breach of warranty; therefore, the language of the pleadings should be conformed to the language of the statute, depending on the type of action alleged.

The definition of the term "knowingly" reads as follows:

> "Knowingly" means actual awareness, *at the time of the act or practice complained of,* of the falsity, deception or unfairness of the act or practice giving rise to the consumer's claim, or in an action brought under Subdivision (2) of Subsection (a) of Section 17.50, actual awareness of the act, practice, condition, defect, or failure constituting the breach of warranty, but actual awareness may be inferred where objective manifestations indicate that a person acted with actual awareness.

DTPA §17.45(9) (emphasis added). The following forms can be used to allege a "knowing" violation or breach of warranty as a predicate for additional damages and mental anguish damages.

[a] FORM: —Knowing conduct (general form)

7.08   At the time of the acts and practices set forth in paragraph _____ occurred, Defendant had actual awareness that these acts and practices were false, deceptive or unfair in that [insert specific facts showing knowing conduct, e.g. defendant knew of the structural defects in the house at the time it was sold].

[b] FORM: —Knowing conduct, breach of warranty

7.08   Defendant had actual awareness of the act, practice, condition, defect, or failure constituting the breach of warranty complained of in this petition in that [insert specific facts showing knowing conduct, e.g., defendant knew that the automobile had not been properly repaired when it was delivered to plaintiff].

§5.15.1 Intentional Conduct

If the defendant's violation of the DTPA or breach of warranty is found to have been committed "intentionally," the upper limit for additional damages is increased to three times the sum of economic damages and mental anguish damages. DTPA §17.50(b)(1). The following forms can be used to allege an "intentional" violation or breach of warranty as a predicate for this increased limit on additional damages.

[a] FORM: —Intentional conduct, general

7.08   Defendant had an actual awareness of the falsity, deception, [or unfairness] of the acts and practices alleged in this petition. Additionally, Defendant had the specific intent that Plaintiff acted in detrimental reliance on the falsity and deception [or in detrimental ignorance of the unfairness].

[b] FORM: —Intentional conduct, breach of warranty

7.08   Defendant had an actual awareness of the condition [defect or failure] constituting the breach of warranty as alleged in this petition.

[NOTE: The amendment in DTPA §17.45(9) is unclear as to whether anything else must be alleged in order to plead an "intentional" breach of warranty. See §1.02.14.2 supra.]

§5.16 Economic Damages

[For a discussion of damages that are recoverable under the DTPA see §1.02.14 supra.]

It is good practice to plead each type of economic damages sought, although the rules expressly require specific pleading of "special damages" only. TEX. R. CIV. P. 56. Special damages are those which are of such an unusual nature that they normally vary with the circumstances of an individual case. *Sherrod v. Bailey*, 580 S.W.2d 24, 28 (Tex. Civ. App.—Houston [14th Dist.] 1970, writ ref'd n.r.e.). By contrast, general damages are those which so frequently accompany the wrongdoing alleged that the mere allegation of the wrong gives sufficient notice. *Id.*

It is not necessary to plead the measure of damages sought, provided that the petition contains allegations from which the correct measure may be ascertained. *See Davies v. Texas Employers' Ins. Ass'n*, 16 S.W.2d 524, 525 (Tex. Comm'n App. 1929, holding approved); 2 MCDONALD TEXAS CIVIL PRACTICE §8:40 (1992).

The following forms illustrate several manners in which economic damages may be pleaded. Alternative damages allegations are illustrated in §5.18 *et seq. infra.*

[a] FORM: —Economic damages (product)

11.01   The economic damages incurred by plaintiff include the reasonable cost of repairing [*identify the product*], the loss of use of [the product] while in its unrepaired state, and the resulting loss of use.

[b] FORM: —Economic damages (unimproved land)

11.01   The economic damages incurred by plaintiff include the diminished value of the property, and reasonable expenditures made by plaintiff to prepare the property for use as [*describe use to be made of property, e.g.,* a homesite], which use is not feasible due to the undisclosed condition of the property.

[c] FORM: —Economic damages (residential construction)

11.01   The economic damages incurred by plaintiff include the reasonable and necessary cost of repairs to the house, out of pocket expenditures reasonably made by plaintiff for diagnosis of the problems with the house and formulation of a repair proposal, and the residual loss of value of the house remaining after the repairs are made which is due to the stigma associated with structural repairs.

[d] FORM: —Economic damages (investment)

11.01   The economic damages incurred by plaintiff include the amount of money paid for the business investment, less any net profits earned by plaintiff, as well as the reasonable out of pocket expenditures made by plaintiff in operating the business [and the interest expense incurred by plaintiff on the money borrowed to make the investment, less the value of the interest which reasonably could have been earned by plaintiff on the net profits of the business]. Plaintiff also seeks to recover damages for injury to plaintiff's credit reputation.

§5.17 Additional Statutory Damages; Exemplary Damages

[For a discussion of additional damages under the DTPA and Chapter 541 of the Insurance Code, see §1.02.14.2.2, supra]

The general form petition illustrates the allegations appropriate for seeking discretionary additional damages under the DTPA and Insurance Code. See §5.02[a], *supra*. Form [a] below illustrates the allegations in a DTPA lawsuit governed by Chapter 41 of the Civil Practice and Remedies Code. It should be noted, however, that the limitation on recovery of additional damages contained in the suggested allegations does not apply in cases of malice or intentional torts. See TEX. CIV. PRAC. & REM. CODE §41.008.

Form [b] includes the additional pleading necessary when the plaintiff includes a common law cause of action alleging gross negligence, an intentional tort, or other grounds for exemplary damages. See generally, *Transportation Insurance Co. v. Moriel*, 879 S.W.2d 10 (Tex. 1994); *Burk Royalty Co. v. Walls*, 616 S.W.2d 911, 922 (Tex. 1981); *Trenholm v. Ratcliff*, 646 S.W.2d 927 (Tex. 1983); *Arnold v. Nat'l. County Mutual Fire Ins. Co.*, 725 S.W.2d 165 (Tex. 1987); TEX. CIV. PRAC. & REM. CODE Ch. 41. Of course, a consumer cannot recover both exemplary damages and statutory additional damages for the same conduct. See *Birchfield v. Texarkana Memorial Hospital*, 747 S.W.2d 361 (Tex. 1987). Even so, Form [b] can be stated as an alternative to the discretionary additional damages under the DTPA in the same petition.

The recovery of common law exemplary damages, as opposed to additional damages under DTPA §17.50(b)(1), is governed by §41.001 et seq. of the Civil Practice & Remedies Code. This statute provides that exemplary damages may be recovered only if there is "clear and convincing" evidence that the harm suffered by the plaintiff resulted from (a) fraud or (b) malice. TEX. CIV. PRAC. & REM. CODE §41.003(a). In wrongful death actions, exemplary damages may also be recovered upon proof (by clear and convincing evidence) of "gross neglect." Each of these terms is defined in §41.001 of the Code. See also *Transportation Insurance Co. v. Moriel*, 879 S.W.2d 10 (Tex. 1994).

[a] FORM: —Additional damages (personal injury; wrongful death)

12.01   Additionally, plaintiff seeks an award of additional damages, not to exceed four times the amount of plaintiff's actual damages, or $200,000, whichever is greater, which in the opinion of the jury is necessary to punish the defendant and deter similar conduct by defendant and others in the future.

[b] FORM: —Exemplary damages

12.02   The damages suffered by the plaintiff resulted from fraud [or malice] [or gross neglect]. Accordingly, plaintiff [alternatively] seeks exemplary damages, not to exceed $_____, which in the opinion of the jury is necessary to punish the defendant and deter similar conduct in the future by the defendant and others.

§5.18 Pleading Specific Actions

The format of original petitions generally runs from actions that are susceptible to preprinted forms (*e.g.*, collections cases) to those in which each petition is unique (*e.g.*, some lender liability claims). DTPA petitions fall somewhere in the middle. That is, certain parts of the petition are essentially the same in every case while other parts require original writing.

[a] REFERENCE TABLE OF CAUSES OF ACTION AND REMEDIES

CAUSES OF ACTION

Breach of contract: 11.08[a], 11.08[b], 12.06.04[a]

Breach of duty of good faith and fair dealing: 11.08[a], 11.08[b]

Breach of fiduciary duty: 5.21[a]

Chapter 541 Texas Insurance Code: 11.08[a], 11.08[b]

Common law fraud: 5.21[a]

DTPA: express warranty: 5.20, 12.06.04[a],

DTPA: false, misleading, and deceptive: 5.13.05[a], 12.06.04[a], 5.21[a]

DTPA: implied warranty of good workmanship and habitability: 12.06.04[a]

DTPA: unconscionability: 13.05[a], 5.21

Debt Collection Practices Act: 5.25[a], 5.25[b]

Negligent misrepresentation, gross negligence: 5.21[a]

Statutory fraud in sale of real estate: 13.05[a], 13.05[d]

Texas Business Opportunity Act: 15.06[a], [b], [c]

RELIEF SOUGHT

Cost of repair: 12.06.04[a], 14.07[a], 16.04[a]

Damage to credit reputation: 5.21, 5.25[a]

Loss of funds: 15.06[a]

Loss of use: 14.07[a], [b]

Loss of use (temporary housing expenses): 12.06.04[a]

Loss of value: 14.07[a],[b] 16.04[a], 13.05[a]

Loss of value due to stigma: 12.06.04[a]

Lost net profits: 15.06

Mental anguish: 5.21[b]

Out of pocket expenditures: 13.05[a]

Reimbursement for debt incurred: 5.25

Reimbursement for interest expense: 5.21[a]

Rescission and restitution: 13.05[b], [c], 14.07[a]

Restoration of money: 5.21[b]

Return of purchase price: 5.06[a]

Value of failed business: 15.06[b]

Value of lost collateral: 15.06

§5.19 [Reserved]

§5.20 Misrepresentation in Sale of Business Goods

A DTPA petition that asserts a claim based on misrepresentation in the sale of business goods is similar in format to a general DTPA petition. Typically, however, the damages suffered are substantially larger in business transactions, and frequently, the business will specify a particular type, style or brand of goods, either for resale or as an ingredient in goods that the business markets to or uses for its own customers. The following petition illustrates how misrepresentations and breach of warranty in the sale of business goods may be pleaded.

[a] FORM: Business goods

```
                              NO. _____

_____              §    IN THE DISTRICT COURT OF
                        §
vs.                     §    _____ COUNTY, TEXAS
                        §
_____              §    _____ JUDICIAL DISTRICT
```

PLAINTIFF'S ORIGINAL PETITION

NOW COMES _____, Plaintiff herein, complaining of _____, Defendant herein, and for cause of action, would show unto the Court as follows:

I. DISCOVERY CONTROL PLAN DESIGNATION

1.01   By this action, Plaintiff seeks _____ [i*nsert appropriate designation under Rule 47(c), e.g., only monetary relief of $100,000 or less, including damages of any kind, penalties, costs, expenses, prejudgment interest, and attorney's fees*]. The damages sought are within the jurisdictional limits of this court.

1.02   Discovery in this case is intended to be conducted under Level _____, pursuant to Rule 190._____, *Texas Rules of Civil Procedure*.

II. PARTIES

2.01   _____ is a resident of _____, _____ County, Texas.

2.02   _____ is an individual who resides and may be served with process at _____, _____ County, Texas.

III. VENUE

3.01   Venue of this action is proper in _____ County, Texas because _____ reside in _____ County, Texas and the events made the basis of this lawsuit and giving rise to Plaintiff's cause of action occurred, in whole or in part, in _____ County, Texas.

IV. NOTICE; CONDITIONS PRECEDENT

4.01 Defendant was given notice in writing of the claims made in this petition including a statement of Plaintiff's economic damages, mental anguish damages and expenses, including attorney's fees, more than sixty days before this suit was filed in the manner and form required by DTPA §17.505(a).

4.02 All conditions precedent to recovery by Plaintiff herein have been performed, have occurred, or have been excused.

V. AGENCY

5.01 Unless otherwise stated, whenever it is alleged that Defendant _____ committed an act, failed to perform an act, made a representation or a statement, or failed to make a disclosure, it is alleged that Defendant _____ acted or failed to act through its authorized agents, servants, employees or representatives acting with either expressed, implied, apparent, direct and/or ostensible authority, or _____ subsequently ratified these acts, failures to act, representations, statements or conduct.

VI. FACTS OF CASE

6.01 This lawsuit arises out of the following transaction, acts and events: On or about _____, Plaintiff ordered from Defendant the following goods: [*describe goods ordered, e.g.,* 1000 gallons of paint]. At the time of contracting, Defendant had reason to know that the goods ordered were for a particular purpose, [*insert specific purpose of goods, e.g.,* to be painted on the walls of a chip manufacturing facility]. Defendant had reason to know that Plaintiff was relying on Defendant's skill or judgment to furnish suitable goods.

6.02 The goods sold by Defendant to Plaintiff were not the goods ordered from Defendant by Plaintiff. Instead, without notice to or approval from Plaintiff, Defendant substituted a different product. Not only was a different product substituted for the one ordered by Plaintiff, the product which was delivered by Defendant to Plaintiff was defective and was not suitable for the specific purpose for which it was intended and of which Defendant had knowledge.

6.03 [*Describe further facts on which claim is based.*]

VII. CAUSE OF ACTION: DTPA

7.01 Plaintiff repeats and realleges the material factual allegations in the preceding paragraphs.

7.02	Plaintiff is a consumer entitled to bring this action for relief under the Texas Deceptive Trade Practices—Consumer Protection Act (the "DTPA"). The actions of Defendants outlined above constitute misrepresentations, breaches of warranties and unconscionable conduct, actionable under the DTPA.

7.03	Specifically, Defendant committed the following acts in violation of the DTPA "laundry list," one or more of which was a producing cause of damages to Plaintiff:

(a) Representing that the goods or services had characteristics, ingredients, uses or benefits which they did not have;

(b) Representing that goods or services were of a particular standard, quality or grade when they were of another; and

(c) Failing to disclose information concerning goods or services which was known at the time in order to induce the Plaintiff to enter into a transaction which Plaintiff would not have otherwise entered.

7.04	Plaintiff relied on these representations to his [her] detriment.

7.05	Further, Defendant violated the DTPA by breaching one or more express or implied warranties.

7.06	Defendant's conduct as described herein was a producing cause of damages to Plaintiff.

7.07	Further, Defendant's conduct was committed knowingly, entitling Plaintiff to seek the trebling of his [her] actual damages in accordance with the DTPA.

VIII. DAMAGES

8.01	Defendant's acts and omissions as described herein have been a producing cause of damages to Plaintiff.

8.02	Plaintiff has suffered economic damages, including but not limited to:

(a) Past and future lost profits; and

(b) Lost goodwill;

(c) Incidental and consequential damages [*plead incidental and consequential damages with specificity in order to show that they were within the contemplation of the parties at the time of contracting*]; and

(d) Loss of and damage to credit.

8.03 These damages are within the jurisdictional limits of this Court.

IX. ADDITIONAL DAMAGES AND PUNITIVE DAMAGES

9.01 Defendant's conduct in violation of the DTPA was committed knowingly, as that term is defined. Accordingly, Plaintiff seeks an award of additional damages under the DTPA in an amount not to exceed three times the amount of his [her] economic damages.

X. ATTORNEY'S FEES

10.01 As a result of Defendant's conduct, Plaintiff has been required to obtain the services of the undersigned attorney for the filing, prosecution and trial of this cause, and therefore seeks an award of reasonable and necessary attorney's fees pursuant to applicable law.

WHEREFORE, PREMISES CONSIDERED, Plaintiff respectfully prays that Defendant be cited to appear and answer herein, and that upon final trial hereof, Plaintiff recover from Defendant all of his actual damages, additional damages, pre-judgment and post-judgment interest as allowed by law, attorney's fees, costs of court and such other and further relief to which he may show himself justly entitled.

Respectfully submitted,

_____

Attorney for Plaintiff

§5.21 Commercial Construction

The rules for pleading a commercial construction case under the DTPA are the same as pleading a residential construction case; however, the Residential Construction Liability Act is not a factor in the case. Also, the documentation in a commercial construction case is not, necessarily, standardized so that there may be causes of action or defense unique to the case. The following petition illustrates how a commercial construction case may be pleaded:

[a] FORM: Defective Commercial Construction

```
                            NO. _____
_____              §      IN THE DISTRICT COURT OF
                        §
vs.                     §      _____COUNTY, TEXAS
                        §
_____              §      _____ JUDICIAL DISTRICT
```

PLAINTIFF'S ORIGINAL PETITION

TO THE HONORABLE JUDGE OF THE DISTRICT COURT:

NOW COMES _____, Plaintiff herein, complaining of _____, Defendant herein, and for cause of action, would show unto the Court as follows:

I. DISCOVERY CONTROL PLAN DESIGNATION

1.01   By this action, Plaintiff seeks _____ [*insert appropriate designation under Rule 47(c), e.g.*, only monetary relief of $100,000 or less, including damages of any kind, penalties, costs, expenses, prejudgment interest, and attorney's fees]. The damages sought are within the jurisdictional limits of this court.

1.02   Discovery in this case is intended to be conducted under Level _____, pursuant to Rule 190._____, *Texas Rules of Civil Procedure*.

II. PARTIES

2.01   _____ is a resident of _____, _____ County, Texas.

2.02   _____ is an individual who resides and may be served with process at _____, _____ County, Texas.

III. VENUE

3.01   Venue of this action is proper in _____ County, Texas because _____ reside in _____ County, Texas and the events made the basis of this lawsuit and giving rise to Plaintiff's cause of action occurred, in whole or in part, in _____ County, Texas.

IV. NOTICE; CONDITIONS PRECEDENT

4.01   Defendant was given notice in writing of the claims made in this petition including a statement of Plaintiff's economic damages, mental anguish damages and expenses, including attorney's fees, more than sixty days before this suit was filed in the manner and form required by DTPA §17.505(a).

4.02   All conditions precedent to recovery by Plaintiff herein have been performed, have occurred, or have been excused.

V. AGENCY

5.01   Unless otherwise stated, whenever it is alleged that Defendant _____ committed an act, failed to perform an act, made a representation or a statement, or failed to make a disclosure, it is alleged that Defendant _____ acted or failed to act through its authorized agents, servants, employees or representatives acting with either expressed, implied, apparent, direct and/or ostensible authority, or _____ subsequently ratified these acts, failures to act, representations, statements or conduct.

VI. FACTS OF CASE

6.01   This lawsuit arises out of the following transaction, acts and events: On or about _____, Plaintiff closed on the purchase of _____ [insert description of property], which is a commercial building.

6.02   Defendant was the builder and seller of the property. At the time of the sale, Defendant represented and warranted to Plaintiff that the building had been constructed according to plans and specifications, and that the building would be suitable for use as Plaintiff's business location.

6.03   Further, there was and is an implied warranty that the improvements were constructed in a good and workmanlike manner.

6.04   The improvements on the property were not as represented and the warranties were breached. Among the defects in the property (but not limited to these) are and were the following [insert list of major defects in construction, e.g.:

(a) There are two roof leaks with accompanying damage to insulation.

(b) On the northeast side of the building, water is entering from the ground.

(c) On this same side of the building, there are improper fittings between the drainage pipe and the roof gutter drain.

(d) The sprinkler system is not hooked up to the meter of the respective property owner whose property is being served by that part of the system.

(e) There was and is an unrepaired leak in the underground sprinkler system pipe. The system has been shut down because of the leak.]

VII. FIRST CAUSE OF ACTION: DTPA

7.01 Plaintiff repeats and realleges the material factual allegations in the preceding paragraphs.

7.02 Plaintiff is a consumer entitled to bring this action for relief under the Texas Deceptive Trade Practices—Consumer Protection Act (the "DTPA"). The actions of Defendants outlined above constitute misrepresentations, breaches of warranties and unconscionable conduct, actionable under the DTPA.

7.03 Specifically, Defendant committed the following acts in violation of the DTPA "laundry list," one or more of which was a producing cause of damages to Plaintiff:

(a) Representing that the building had characteristics, ingredients, uses or benefits which it did not have;

(b) Representing that the building was of a particular standard, quality or grade when it was of another;

(c) Failing to disclose information concerning the building which was known at the time in order to induce the Plaintiff to enter into a transaction which Plaintiff would not have otherwise entered.

7.04 Plaintiff relied on these representations to his [her] detriment.

7.05 Further, Defendant violated the DTPA by breaching one or more express warranties.

7.06 Further, Defendants took advantage of Plaintiff's lack of knowledge about the condition of the property. Accordingly, Defendants violated the DTPA by engaging in unconscionable conduct and/or an unconscionable course of conduct.

7.07   Defendants' conduct as described herein was a producing cause of damages to Plaintiff.

7.08   Further, Defendants' conduct was committed knowingly, entitling Plaintiff to seek the trebling of his [her] actual damages in accordance with the DTPA.

VIII. SECOND CAUSE OF ACTION: STATUTORY FRAUD

8.01   Plaintiff repeats and realleges the material factual allegations in the preceding paragraphs.

8.02   By the conduct described above, Defendant made one or more false representations of material fact and/or benefitted by not disclosing that a third party's representation of material fact was false, for the purpose of inducing Plaintiff into the contract for the purchase of the property.

8.03   Plaintiff relied upon the false representations of fact and entered into the contract for the purchase of the property, which resulted in actual damages to Plaintiff, for which he [she] sues.

IX. DAMAGES

9.01   Defendant's acts and omissions as described herein have been a producing and/or proximate cause of damages to Plaintiff. Plaintiff has suffered economic damages, including but not limited to: the difference in market value of the building as represented and its actual value at the time it was sold to Plaintiff; the cost of repairing the building; etc. [See §5.16, *supra*, for alternative allegations.]

9.02   These damages are within the jurisdictional limits of this Court.

X. ADDITIONAL DAMAGES AND PUNITIVE DAMAGES

10.01   Defendant's conduct in violation of the DTPA was committed knowingly, as that term is defined. Accordingly, Plaintiff seeks an award of additional damages under the DTPA in an amount not to exceed three times the amount of his [her] economic damages.

10.02   The damages suffered by Plaintiff resulted from fraud. Accordingly, Plaintiff alternatively seeks exemplary damages, not to exceed $_____, which in the opinion of the jury is necessary to punish Defendant and deter similar conduct in the future by Defendant and others.

XI. ATTORNEY'S FEES

11.01 As a result of Defendant's conduct, Plaintiff has been required to obtain the services of the undersigned attorney for the filing, prosecution and trial of this cause, and therefore seeks an award of reasonable and necessary attorney's fees pursuant to applicable law.

WHEREFORE, PREMISES CONSIDERED, Plaintiff respectfully prays that Defendant be cited to appear and answer herein, and that upon final trial hereof, Plaintiff recover from Defendant all of his [her] damages, additional damages, exemplary damages, pre-judgment and post-judgment interest as allowed by law, attorney's fees, costs of court and such other and further relief to which he may show himself justly entitled.

Respectfully submitted,

_____

Attorney for Plaintiff

§5.22 [Reserved]

§5.23 Banking, Lending

Lender liability arises in a variety of banking transactions. Among the more common occurrences which trigger liability are (1) a bank's improper payment of money from a customer's account and (2) a bank's broken promise to extend credit.

The petitions which follow are intended to illustrate these situations.

[a] FORM: —Unauthorized withdrawal of funds

```
                              NO. _____
_____                 §    IN THE DISTRICT COURT OF
                           §
vs.                        §    _____COUNTY, TEXAS
                           §
_____                 §    _____ JUDICIAL DISTRICT
```

PLAINTIFF'S ORIGINAL PETITION

TO THE HONORABLE JUDGE OF THE DISTRICT COURT:

NOW COMES _____, Plaintiff herein, complaining of _____, Defendant herein, and for cause of action, would show unto the Court as follows:

I. DISCOVERY CONTROL PLAN DESIGNATION

1.01   By this action, Plaintiff seeks _____ [*insert appropriate designation under Rule 47(c), e.g.,* only monetary relief of $100,000 or less, including damages of any kind, penalties, costs, expenses, prejudgment interest, and attorney's fees]. The damages sought are within the jurisdictional limits of this court.

1.02   Discovery in this case is intended to be conducted under Level _____, pursuant to Rule 190._____, *Texas Rules of Civil Procedure*.

II. PARTIES

2.01   Plaintiff _____ is a resident of _____, _____ County, Texas.

2.02   _____ Bank Texas, N.A., is a banking corporation with its principal place of business at _____, _____, _____ County, Texas. Service of process may be had on the defendant by serving its President or any Vice-President found at any branch of _____ Bank Texas, N.A., including but not limited to the branch located at _____, _____, _____ County, Texas, or any other branch of _____ Bank Texas, N.A., in _____, _____ County, Texas.

III. VENUE

3.01   Venue of this action is proper in _____ County, Texas because _____ reside in _____ County, Texas and the events made the basis of this lawsuit and giving rise to Plaintiff's cause of action occurred, in whole or in part, in _____ County, Texas.

IV. NOTICE; CONDITIONS PRECEDENT

4.01   Defendant was given notice in writing of the claims made in this petition including a statement of Plaintiff's economic damages, mental anguish damages and expenses, including attorney's fees, more than sixty days before this suit was filed in the manner and form required by DTPA §17.505(a).

4.02   All conditions precedent to recovery by Plaintiff herein have been performed, have occurred, or have been excused.

V. AGENCY

5.01   Unless otherwise stated, whenever it is alleged that Defendant _____ committed an act, failed to perform an act, made a representation or a statement, or failed to make a disclosure, it is alleged that Defendant _____ acted or failed to act through its authorized agents, servants, employees or representatives acting with either expressed, implied, apparent, direct and/or ostensible authority, or _____ subsequently ratified these acts, failures to act, representations, statements or conduct.

VI. FACTS OF CASE

6.01   In _____, 20___, Plaintiff opened a checking account with Defendant bank. The account number is _____. The deposit of funds into the account was controlled by the deposit agreement between Plaintiff and Defendant which agreement required Defendant to safeguard Plaintiff's funds and to disburse them only when authorized by Plaintiff to do so.

6.02   At the time the account was opened, Plaintiff executed a "signature card" which directed Defendant to allow funds to be withdrawn from Plaintiff's account only when Plaintiff's checks were signed in accordance with the signature card. [*If the Plaintiff is a corporation, add*: In addition, at the time the account was opened, Plaintiff presented the bank with a corporate resolution, on a form provided by Defendant, in which Defendant was advised that funds could be withdrawn from Plaintiff's account only when Plaintiff's checks bore the signatures of _____.]

6.03   By providing a signature card [and corporate resolution form] to Plaintiff, Defendant represented that it would disburse money from Plaintiff's account only when authorized by proper signature to do so.

6.04   On _____, 20___, Defendant paid $_____ out of Plaintiff's account to _____. This payment of funds by Defendant was in violation of the written instructions given by Plaintiff to Defendant for the reason that the check by which the funds were paid did not bear the authorized signature[s] for Plaintiff's account.

6.05   Immediately upon discovering that money had been improperly withdrawn from the account, Plaintiff contacted Defendant and demanded that the money be restored to the account. Defendant refused to restore the funds.

6.06   As a result of Defendant's unauthorized withdrawal of funds from Plaintiff's account, [*insert consequential events and losses*].

VII. FIRST CAUSE OF ACTION: DTPA

7.01   Plaintiff repeats and realleges the material factual allegations in the preceding paragraphs.

7.02   Plaintiff is a consumer entitled to bring this action for relief under the Texas Deceptive Trade Practices—Consumer Protection Act (the "DTPA"). The actions of Defendants outlined above constitute misrepresentations, breaches of warranties and unconscionable conduct, actionable under the DTPA.

7.03   Specifically, Defendant committed the following acts in violation of the DTPA "laundry list," one or more of which was a producing cause of damages to Plaintiff:

(a) Defendant represented that funds would be released from Plaintiff's account only upon the presentation of certain authorized signatures, thus representing that its banking or services had characteristics or benefits which they did not have; and/or

(b) Defendant now contends that it had the right to release the funds. Although Plaintiff denies that Defendant had the right to do so, if in fact Defendant had the right to release the funds without presentation of authorized signatures, then Defendant in fact misrepresented Plaintiff's rights under the agreement between the parties.

7.04   Plaintiff relied on these representations to his [her] detriment.

7.05   Defendant's conduct as described herein was a producing cause of damages to Plaintiff.

7.06   Further, Defendant's conduct was committed knowingly, entitling Plaintiff to seek the trebling of his [her] actual damages in accordance with the DTPA.

VIII. SECOND CAUSE OF ACTION:

8.01   Plaintiff repeats and realleges the material factual allegations in the preceding paragraphs.

8.02   Plaintiff entered into one or more contractual agreements with Defendant. Specifically, Plaintiff entered into a written deposit agreement with Defendant Bank.

8.03   Defendant breached the deposit agreement described above by allowing funds to be taken from Plaintiff's account without authority from Plaintiff to do so. This conduct caused direct damages to Plaintiff, as well as consequential damages which were reasonably foreseeable to Defendant at the time the agreement was made.

IX. THIRD CAUSE OF ACTION:

9.01   Plaintiff repeats and realleges the material factual allegations in the preceding paragraphs.

9.02   Defendant owed a duty to Plaintiff to put in place and maintain the safeguards against unauthorized withdrawal of funds that a bank of ordinary prudence would have maintained under the same or similar circumstances.

9.03   Defendant breached this duty and was therefore negligent.

9.04   This negligence was a proximate cause of damages to Plaintiff.

X. DAMAGES

10.01   Defendant's acts and omissions as described herein have been a producing and/or proximate cause of damages to Plaintiff. Plaintiff has suffered economic damages, including but not limited to: the amount of money improperly withdrawn from the account.

10.02   Furthermore, as a result of Defendant's conduct, [*insert consequential damages, e.g.*, Plaintiff had insufficient funds to make the note payments on the vehicle which was used by Plaintiff in his [her] business. As a result of the payments not being made on the vehicle, it was repossessed and sold by the secured creditor. Accordingly, Plaintiff's damages also include the equity Plaintiff had in the vehicle as well as the net profits lost by Plaintiff because of the loss of the vehicle's use in Plaintiff's business]. [*See* §5.16 *supra for alternative allegations*].

10.03   These damages are within the jurisdictional limits of this court.

XI. ADDITIONAL DAMAGES AND PUNITIVE DAMAGES

11.01   Defendant's conduct in violation of the DTPA was committed knowingly, as that term is defined. Accordingly, Plaintiff seeks an award of additional damages under the DTPA in an amount not to exceed three times the amount of his [her] economic damages.

XII. ATTORNEY'S FEES

12.01   As a result of Defendant's conduct, Plaintiff has been required to obtain the services of the undersigned attorney for the filing, prosecution and trial of this cause, and therefore seeks an award of reasonable and necessary attorney's fees pursuant to applicable law.

WHEREFORE, PREMISES CONSIDERED, Plaintiff respectfully prays that Defendant be cited to appear and answer herein, and that upon final trial hereof, Plaintiff recover from Defendant all of his actual damages, additional damages, exemplary damages, prejudgment and post-judgment interest as allowed by law, attorney's fees, costs of court and such other and further relief to which he may show himself justly entitled.

Respectfully submitted,

_____

Attorney for Plaintiff

[b] FORM: —False representation to extend credit

NO. _____

_____   § IN THE DISTRICT COURT OF

§

vs.	§	_____COUNTY, TEXAS
	§	
_____	§	_____ JUDICIAL DISTRICT

PLAINTIFF'S ORIGINAL PETITION

TO THE HONORABLE JUDGE OF THE DISTRICT COURT:

NOW COMES _____, Plaintiff herein, complaining of _____, Defendant herein, and for cause of action, would show unto the Court as follows:

I. DISCOVERY CONTROL PLAN DESIGNATION

1.01   By this action, Plaintiff seeks _____ [*insert appropriate designation under Rule 47(c), e.g.*, only monetary relief of $100,000 or less, including damages of any kind, penalties, costs, expenses, prejudgment interest, and attorney's fees]. The damages sought are within the jurisdictional limits of this court.

1.02   Discovery in this case is intended to be conducted under Level _____, pursuant to Rule 190._____, *Texas Rules of Civil Procedure*.

II. PARTIES

2.01   Plaintiff _____ is a resident of _____, _____ County, Texas.

2.02   _____ Bank Texas, N.A., is a banking corporation with its principal place of business at _____, _____, _____ County, Texas. Service of process may be had on the Defendant by serving its President or any Vice-President found at any branch of _____ Bank Texas, N.A., including but not limited to the branch located at _____, _____, _____ County, Texas, or any other branch of _____ Bank Texas, N.A., in _____, _____ County, Texas.

III. VENUE

3.01   Venue of this action is proper in _____ County, Texas because _____ reside in _____ County, Texas and the events made the basis of this lawsuit and giving rise to Plaintiff's cause of action occurred, in whole or in part, in _____ County, Texas.

IV. NOTICE; CONDITIONS PRECEDENT

4.01   Defendant was given notice in writing of the claims made in this petition including a statement of Plaintiff's economic damages, mental anguish damages and expenses, including attorney's fees, more than sixty days before this suit was filed in the manner and form required by DTPA §17.505(a).

4.02   All conditions precedent to recovery by Plaintiff herein have been performed, have occurred, or have been excused.

V. AGENCY

5.01   Unless otherwise stated, whenever it is alleged that Defendant _____ committed an act, failed to perform an act, made a representation or a statement, or failed to make a disclosure, it is alleged that Defendant _____ acted or failed to act through its authorized agents, servants, employees or representatives acting with either expressed, implied, apparent, direct and/or ostensible authority, or _____ subsequently ratified these acts, failures to act, representations, statements or conduct.

VI. FACTS OF CASE

6.01   In _____, 20__, Plaintiff asked Defendant to loan money to Plaintiff for the purpose of [insert purpose of loan, e.g., refinancing an existing loan with Defendant and meeting other financial obligations associated with Plaintiff's business].

6.02   Defendant, through its duly authorized agent _____, represented to Plaintiff that if Plaintiff would [insert conditions for loan, e.g. pledge certain property as collateral to further secure the existing debt] Defendant would loan Plaintiff $_____.

6.03   In reliance on Defendant's promise to extend credit, Plaintiff [insert acts done by Plaintiff in reliance on loan agreement, e.g., pledged the collateral and did not apply for a loan from other financial institutions].

6.04   In _____, 20__, Plaintiff requested that Defendant fund the loan that it had promised to make. Defendant refused to advance the funds and called the existing note due [or Instead of funding the loan as represented and agreed, Defendant insisted on new conditions for the making of the loan. In particular, Defendant required that Plaintiff [insert new conditions] before any money would be released to Plaintiff].

6.05   As a result of Defendant's failure to fund the loan, Plaintiff, [describe consequences of failure to make loan, e.g.,

Plaintiff did not have adequate funds to timely meet his [her] financial obligations and did not have sufficient time left to arrange for alternative financing].

6.06   As a result, Plaintiff [*describe specific loss, e.g.,* lost the ability to refinance his [her] existing obligations and to meet the new financial obligations incurred by Plaintiff's business].

VII. FIRST CAUSE OF ACTION: DTPA

7.01   Plaintiff repeats and realleges the material factual allegations in the preceding paragraphs.

7.02   Plaintiff is a consumer entitled to bring this action for relief under the Texas Deceptive Trade Practices—Consumer Protection Act (the "DTPA"). The actions of Defendant outlined above constitute misrepresentations and unconscionable conduct actionable under the DTPA.

7.03   Specifically, Defendant committed the following acts in violation of the DTPA "laundry list," one or more of which was a producing cause of damages to Plaintiff:

(a) Defendant's conduct constitutes a representation that its agreement with Plaintiff involved and conferred certain rights, remedies, benefits and obligations which it did not have [*insert facts which establish violation, e.g.,* in that at the time Defendant refused to loan the money to Plaintiff, it represented to Plaintiff and certain of Plaintiff's creditors that Defendant was not obligated to make the loan, a contention which is denied by Plaintiff.

(b) If, however, Defendant is correct that it had no obligation to loan the money, then Defendant misrepresented Plaintiff's rights and remedies and Defendant's obligations under the parties' agreement at the time the agreement was made.

7.04   Plaintiff relied on these representations to his [her] detriment.

7.05   Defendant made the decision not to make the loan to Plaintiff as previously represented; however, Defendant did not disclose this fact to Plaintiff. Instead, Defendant sought to impose new conditions on the loan, knowing that Plaintiff would be unable to meet them. In so doing, Defendant took advantage of Plaintiff's knowledge and capacity to a grossly unfair degree. Accordingly, Defendants violated the DTPA by engaging in unconscionable conduct and/or an unconscionable course of conduct.

7.06   Defendant's conduct as described herein was a producing cause of damages to Plaintiff.

7.07   Further, Defendant's conduct was committed knowingly, entitling Plaintiff to seek the trebling of his [her] actual damages in accordance with the DTPA.

VIII. DAMAGES

8.01   Defendant's acts and omissions as described herein have been a producing cause of damages to Plaintiff. Plaintiff has suffered economic damages, including but not limited to: [*insert elements of damages, e.g.*, the value of Plaintiff's business on the date the loan was denied, the net value (equity) of Plaintiff's property which was pledged as collateral and subsequently foreclosed on and sold by Defendant, and damages for the mental anguish suffered by Plaintiff as a result of Defendant's conduct. [*See* §5.16 *supra for alternative allegations*].

8.02   These damages are within the jurisdictional limits of this court.

IX. ADDITIONAL DAMAGES

9.01   Defendant's conduct in violation of the DTPA was committed knowingly, as that term is defined. Accordingly, Plaintiff seeks an award of additional damages under the DTPA in an amount not to exceed three times the amount of his [her] economic damages.

X. ATTORNEY'S FEES

10.01   As a result of Defendant's conduct, Plaintiff has been required to obtain the services of the undersigned attorney for the filing, prosecution and trial of this cause, and therefore seeks an award of reasonable and necessary attorney's fees pursuant to applicable law.

WHEREFORE, PREMISES CONSIDERED, Plaintiff respectfully prays that Defendant be cited to appear and answer herein, and that upon final trial hereof, Plaintiff recover from Defendant all of his actual damages, additional damages, pre-judgment and post-judgment interest as allowed by law, attorney's fees, costs of court and such other and further relief to which he may show himself justly entitled.

Respectfully submitted,

_____

Attorney for Plaintiff

§5.24 [Reserved]

§5.25 Commercial Real Property Lease

The relationship of landlords and tenants in a residential context is governed almost exclusively by statute. *See* Tex. ProP. Code §92.001, *et seq*. When the suitability of leased property is in issue, the only remedy for residential tenants is that provided by the Landlord-Tenant Act. *See* Tex. ProP. Code §92.157, 92.205, and 92.260. For example, the implied warranty of habitability recognized by the Supreme Court in *Kamarath v. Bennett*, 568 S.W.2d 658 (Tex. 1978) was removed and replaced by a statutory remedy. Tex. ProP. Code §92.061. If a tenant's case is based on false, misleading or deceptive conduct, as defined in the DTPA, then the application of the DTPA is not affected by the Landlord-Tenant Act.

There is an implied warranty of suitability in commercial leases. *Davidow v. Inwood N. Prof'l Group – Phase I*, 747 S.W.2d 373 (Tex. 1988). This implied warranty promises that the leased property will be:

(1) free of latent defects that are vital to the use of the property for its intended purposes; and

(2) maintained in a condition that keeps the property usable.

Id. at 377.

When leased property ceases to be suitable for its intended commercial purpose, a tenant is entitled to cease making rent payments and abandon the premises, unless the lease places the duty to repair the premises on the tenant. *Id.*

In addition to the common law remedy recognized in *Davidow*, a commercial tenant also has a statutory right to sue for damages resulting from the landlord's failure to comply with the lease. Tex. ProP. Code §91.004(a), and to exert a lien against any of the landlord's property in his or her possession, as well as any rent payments that are due, as security for the collection of damages. Tex. ProP. Code §91.004(b). Also, if the landlord prevents a commercial tenant from entering the leased premises, the tenant may have a right to bring an action under the Property Code. Tex. ProP. Code §93.003.

Although the original of a notice letter sent under the DTPA for breach of the warranty of suitability should be sent to the owner of the property, a copy should be sent, by certified mail, return receipt requested, to any on-site manager or management company that is responsible for the day-to-day operation of the property. This is particularly true if the lease designates the manager as the person to whom all notices should be sent.

Additional notice letters tailored to the specifics of the type of transaction involved are provided in the Chapters on Insurance (§11.07, *infra*), Residential Construction (§12.06.2, *infra*) and Real Estate (§13.04, *infra*).

The following form illustrates the pleading of a breach of the implied warranty of commercial suitability, the breach of which is actionable under the DTPA.

[a] FORM: —Commercial lease of real property

```
                        NO. _____
                          §    IN THE DISTRICT COURT OF
_____                §
                          §
vs.                       §    _____ COUNTY, TEXAS
                          §
_____                §    _____ JUDICIAL DISTRICT
```

PLAINTIFF'S ORIGINAL PETITION

TO THE HONORABLE JUDGE OF THE DISTRICT COURT:

NOW COMES _____, Plaintiffs herein, complaining of _____, Defendant herein, and for cause of action, would show unto the Court as follows:

I. DISCOVERY CONTROL PLAN DESIGNATION

1.01   By this action, Plaintiff seeks _____ [*insert appropriate designation under Rule 47(c), e.g.*, only monetary relief of $100,000 or less, including damages of any kind, penalties, costs, expenses, prejudgment interest, and attorney's fees]. The damages sought are within the jurisdictional limits of this court.

1.02   Discovery in this case is intended to be conducted under Level _____, pursuant to Rule 190._____, *Texas Rules of Civil Procedure*.

II. PARTIES

2.01   Plaintiff _____ is a resident of _____, _____ County, Texas.

2.02   Defendant _____ is a Texas corporation which may be served with process by serving _____, its registered agent, at _____, the corporation's registered address.

III. VENUE

3.01   Venue of this action is proper in _____ County, Texas because _____ reside in _____ County, Texas and the events made the basis of this lawsuit and giving rise to Plaintiff's cause of action occurred, in whole or in part, in _____ County, Texas.

IV. NOTICE; CONDITIONS PRECEDENT

4.01   Defendant was given notice in writing of the claims made in this petition including a statement of Plaintiff's economic damages, mental anguish damages and expenses, including attorney's fees, more than sixty days before this suit was filed in the manner and form required by DTPA §17.505(a).

4.02   All conditions precedent to recovery by Plaintiff herein have been performed, have occurred, or have been excused.

V. AGENCY AND VICARIOUS LIABILITY

5.01   Unless otherwise stated, whenever it is alleged that Defendant _____ committed an act, failed to perform an act, made a representation or a statement, or failed to make a disclosure, it is alleged that Defendant _____ acted or failed to act through its authorized agents, servants, employees or representatives acting with either expressed, implied, apparent, direct and/or ostensible authority, or _____ subsequently ratified these acts, failures to act, representations, statements or conduct.

VI. FACTS OF CASE

6.01   Plaintiff is a commercial tenant and Defendant is a commercial landlord, which relationship was established by the execution of a lease, dated _____, 20___, with respect to certain improved real property which is located at [*insert address of property*]. A copy of the lease is attached to this petition as Exhibit A and incorporated at this point as if fully set forth.

6.02   Until the conditions which are described below arose, Plaintiff was current on all lease payments and was not otherwise in default under the lease agreement.

6.03   At the time the lease was signed, Defendant knew that Plaintiff intended to use the property for the purpose of [*insert intended use of property, e.g.*, a physician's office at which, among other things, Plaintiff's patients would be examined and treated].

6.04   At the time the lease was executed, there were no defects in the property known to Plaintiff which would have made the facilities unsuitable for use as a [physician's office].

6.05   In or about _____, 20___, the leased premises became unsuitable for use as a [physician's office] for the reason that at that time [*insert conditions that made property unsuitable, e.g.*, the roof began to leak substantial amounts of water during heavy rains, which caused the carpets throughout the offices to become water soaked. Over time, a mildewed and musty odor developed and became unbearable for Plaintiff's patients and staff].

6.06 Although repeated complaints have been made to Defendant, Defendant has been unable or unwilling to repair the [*insert defects, e.g.*, roof leaks and has been unable or unwilling to remove the musty and mildewed odor from the carpets].

[*If Plaintiff has vacated the property, insert the following:*]

6.07 On or about _____, 20___, Plaintiff was forced to abandon the leased premises [and move to alternative office space]. Plaintiff's abandonment of the leased premises was caused by Defendant's failure to repair the property to a condition that would make it suitable for its intended commercial purpose.

[*If Plaintiff is withholding rent, insert the following*:]

6.08 On or about _____, 20___, Plaintiff began withholding rent payments from Defendant, asserting a lien against such payments for the damages suffered, as is his [her] right under Tex. Prop. Code §91.004(b).

[*If tenant has asserted a lien against the landlord's property, insert the following*:]

6.09 On or about _____, 20___, Plaintiff seized Defendant's non-exempt property which was in Plaintiff's possession and asserted a lien against the property as is his [her] right under Tex. Prop. Code §91.004(b).

VII. FIRST CAUSE OF ACTION: DTPA

7.01 Plaintiff repeats and realleges the material factual allegations in the preceding paragraphs.

7.02 Plaintiff is a consumer entitled to bring this action for relief under the Texas Deceptive Trade Practices—Consumer Protection Act (the "DTPA"). The actions of Defendants outlined above constitute one or breaches of warranties actionable under the DTPA.

7.03 At the time the commercial space was leased to Plaintiff, an implied warranty was created that the property would be suitable for its intended commercial purpose. That is, there was an implied warranty that there were no defects in the facilities that were vital to the use of the premises for their intended commercial purpose, and that the premises would remain in a suitable condition for the duration of the lease.

7.04   By the conduct described above, this warranty was breached which was a producing cause of damages to Plaintiff.

VIII. SECOND CAUSE OF ACTION: BREACH OF CONTRACT

8.01   Plaintiff repeats and realleges the material factual allegations in the preceding paragraphs.

8.02   The lease agreement was a contract between the parties which imposed on Defendant the obligation to [*insert contractual obligations*].

8.03   As set forth above, Defendant's conduct constituted a breach of the lease agreement, which was a direct cause of damages to Plaintiff.

8.04   Plaintiff also suffered certain consequential damages which are described below, which damages were reasonable foreseeable at the time the lease was executed.

IX. DAMAGES

9.01   Defendant's acts and omissions as described herein have been a producing and/or proximate cause of damages to Plaintiff. Plaintiff has suffered economic damages, including but not limited to: [*insert elements of damages, e.g.*, the following necessary expenses: the cost of relocating his [her] office from the leased premises, including moving expenses, utility expenses, the printing of new office forms and stationary, and the cost of announcements to advise existing patients of the new office location. In addition, during the time that the office was being moved, Plaintiff lost _____ days of income from patients who could not be examined or treated by Plaintiff. Plaintiff also incurred overtime charges for employees who were forced to work beyond the hours of their normal workday in order to accomplish the relocation to the new office facilities. The loss of income and increased expenses resulted in lost net profits to Plaintiff.

9.02   These damages are within the jurisdictional limits of this Court.

X. ADDITIONAL DAMAGES AND PUNITIVE DAMAGES

10.01   Defendant's conduct in violation of the DTPA was committed knowingly, as that term is defined. Accordingly, Plaintiff seeks an award of additional damages under the DTPA in an amount not to exceed three times the amount of his [her] economic damages.

XI. ATTORNEY'S FEES

11.01   As a result of Defendant's conduct, Plaintiff has been required to obtain the services of the undersigned attorney for the filing, prosecution and trial of this cause, and therefore seeks an award of reasonable and necessary attorney's fees pursuant to applicable law.

WHEREFORE, PREMISES CONSIDERED, Plaintiff respectfully prays that Defendant be cited to appear and answer herein, and that upon final trial hereof, Plaintiff recover from Defendant all of his actual damages, additional damages, pre-judgment and post-judgment interest as allowed by law, attorney's fees, costs of court, and an order of the court authorizing Plaintiff to foreclose the lien on Defendant's nonexempt property by selling such property at a public or private sale and applying the proceeds of such sale to satisfy Plaintiff's damages, and such other relief to which Plaintiff may be entitled.

Respectfully submitted,

[Signature of attorney]

§5.26 Unfair Debt Collection Practices

The following forms can be used by a consumer to assert claims against a debt collector for unfair debt collection practices in violation of both the FDCPA and the TDCPA. Because violations of the TDCPA are actionable under the DTPA, additional allegations have been included to assert liability under the DTPA through this tie-in statute.

[a] FORM: Petition for unfair debt collection practices

```
                              NO. _____
_____                 §     IN THE DISTRICT COURT OF
                           §
vs.                        §     _____COUNTY, TEXAS
                           §
_____                 §     _____ JUDICIAL DISTRICT
```

PLAINTIFF'S ORIGINAL PETITION

NOW COMES _____, Plaintiff herein, complaining of _____ _____, Defendant herein, and for cause of action, would show unto the Court as follows:

I. DISCOVERY CONTROL PLAN DESIGNATION

1.01   By this action, Plaintiff seeks _____ [*insert appropriate designation under Rule 47(c), e.g.,* only monetary relief of $100,000 or less, including damages of any kind, penalties, costs, expenses, prejudgment interest, and attorney's fees]. The damages sought are within the jurisdictional limits of this court.

1.02   Discovery in this case is intended to be conducted under Level __ [1], pursuant to Rule 190.__[2], *Texas Rules of Civil Procedure*.

II. PARTIES

2.01   _____, Plaintiff, is a resident of _____, _____ County, Texas.

2.02   _____, Defendant, is a [corporation/ individual/partnership, etc.] [incorporated in _____ [state] with its principal place of business in _____ [city], _____ [state]. [Insert service allegations, such as: _____ [name of defendant] has no registered agent for service in Texas and can therefore be served by serving its statutory agent for service, the Texas Secretary of State, P.O. Box 12079, Austin, Texas 78711-2029, who should then forward a copy to _____ [name of defendant] at _____ _____ [address, city, state, zip code].]

[*Continue with similar paragraphs for any additional Defendants*]

III. JURISDICTION & VENUE

3.01   The Court has *in personam* jurisdiction over Defendant pursuant to Section 17.42 of the *Texas Civil Practice and Remedies Code*. By [its/his/her] actions described herein, Defendant has conducted commercial activities within the State of Texas.

3.02   Venue of this action is proper in _____ County, Texas because all or part of the events made the basis of Plaintiff's claims occurred, in whole or in part, in _____ County, Texas and because _____ [name of plaintiff], a consumer under the Federal Debt Collection Practices Act, resides in _____ County, Texas at the time of the commencement of this suit.

IV. CONDITIONS PRECEDENT

4.01   All conditions precedent to recovery by Plaintiff herein have been performed, have occurred, or have been excused.

V. AGENCY [AND JOINT VENTURE]

5.01   Unless otherwise stated, whenever it is alleged that Defendant _____ committed an act, failed to perform an act, made a representation or a statement, or failed to make a disclosure, it is alleged that Defendant _____ acted or failed to act through [its/his/her] authorized agents, servants, employees or representatives acting with either expressed, implied, apparent, direct and/or ostensible authority, or Defendant _____ subsequently ratified these acts, failures to act, representations, statements or conduct.

[*Continue with similar paragraphs for any additional Defendants*]

[*If it is alleged that two or more Defendants acted in concert and should be vicariously liable for each other's actions, continue with the following:*]

5.02   Further, it is alleged that Defendants were engaged in a joint venture for their mutual benefit and acted as each other's agents with all express, implied, direct and/or ostensible authority to so act, and as such are vicariously liable for the acts, omissions, statements and conduct of the other as alleged herein.

VI. FACTS OF CASE

[*Continue with a recitation of the facts giving rise to the plaintiff's cause(s) of action, such as:*]

6.01   In _____, Plaintiff opened a revolving charge account at _____ department store. On or about _____, 2009, Plaintiff purchased a dress using the credit card issued by _____. However, when she got the dress home, she discovered that the dress had a small tear in the fabric. On or about _____, 2009, Plaintiff returned the dress to the store and requested a reversal of the charges on her credit card for the purchase of the dress. At the time, the store clerk indicated to Plaintiff that her request would be honored, and Plaintiff thought no more about the incident for several weeks.

6.02   When Plaintiff received her credit card statement from _____ the next month, she noticed that the charge for the dress was still on her account and had not been reversed or removed. When she called _____ to inquire, she was told that the reversal of charges for returned items might take another "cycle" before it showed up, and that she should deduct the amount of the purchase from the balance on her check for payment of her balance. Plaintiff did as she was instructed and timely paid the balance of her credit card bill, less the amount for the returned dress.

6.03   However, in the following months, the credit card statements sent to Plaintiff continued to show the balance due for the returned dress and now included late fees and interest charges. When Plaintiff called to complain, she was then told that there was no record of her return, that the charges were valid, and that if she did not pay the balance of the credit card statements, with interest and late fees, she would be turned over to a collection agency.

6.04   Beginning on or about _____, 2010, Plaintiff began to receive reminder letters and phone calls from _____ trying to collect the balance of the disputed credit card bill. Beginning in _____, 2010, the tone of these collection efforts changed dramatically. In its effort to collect the disputed credit card debt, Defendant _____ relentlessly called Plaintiff, up to five times a day, and repeatedly sent demand letters threatening legal action. In phone calls to Plaintiff at all times of the day and night, Defendant' agents and representatives repeatedly harassed Plaintiff by calling her names such as "deadbeat," "low life" and "scum," by cursing and using profanity, and by calling back repeatedly after Plaintiff hung up from the calls.

6.05   In addition, in these phone calls, one or more of Defendant's agents made threats of legal action against Plaintiff, including threats to have her house taken away, her car repossessed and to have Plaintiff arrested for non-payment of the disputed bills.

6.06   On or about _____, 2010, Plaintiff notified Defendant _____ in writing that she disputes the validity of the debt and requested that Defendant _____ cease all communication with her.

6.07   Subsequent to receiving Plaintiff's written notice demanding that Defendant _____ cease and desist contacting Plaintiff in attempting to collect the alleged debt, Defendant _____ mailed to Plaintiff yet another letter demanding payment and threatening to pursue legal action, to report the account to all of the major credit bureaus, and to file a lien on her home. This demand letter from Defendant _____ sought to collect the total amount alleged due on the account, an amount of $_____.

6.08   Further, subsequent to receiving Plaintiff's written notice demanding that Defendant _____ cease and desist contacting Plaintiff, on or about _____, 2010, Defendant _____ sent a demand letter to Plaintiff seeking to collect the alleged debt due to _____ [*creditor*] in the amount of $_____. The letter also threatened that the account would be reported to credit reporting agencies.

6.09   On or about _____, 2010, within 30 days from the demand letter from Defendant _____, Plaintiff notified Defendant _____ in writing that she disputes the validity of the debt and demanded that they cease further communications with her. Plaintiff included with the letter to Defendant _____ her letter to Defendant _____ which demanded the cessation of collection efforts.

6.10   On or about _____, 2010, Defendant _____ sent yet another letter to Plaintiff attempting to collect the alleged debt. While this letter stated that Defendant _____ "verified" the amount of the debt, Defendant _____ did not provide Plaintiff any proof of the verification as required.

6.11   Despite Plaintiff's written requests that Defendant _____ cease communications with her, Defendant _____ continued to call Plaintiff at her home in an effort to collect the alleged debt. Defendant _____ called Plaintiff most recently on _____, 2010 and _____, 2010.

6.12   During all time that Defendant _____ attempted to collect an alleged debt from Plaintiff, Defendant _____ had not posted a bond in compliance with Texas Finance Code §392.101.

VII. FIRST CAUSE OF ACTION: VIOLATION OF FAIR DEBT COLLECTIONS PRACTICES ACT

7.01   Plaintiff repeats and realleges the factual allegations in the preceding paragraphs.

7.02   Defendant _____ is a "debt collector" as defined in 15 U.S.C. §1692a(6). Plaintiff is a "consumer" as defined in 15 U.S.C. §1692a(3).

[*Continue with a description of the statutory violations committed, such as:*]

7.03   One or more of Defendant _____'s actions in attempting to collect a debt were in violation of the Fair Debt Collection Practices Act, including:

(a) Engaging in harassment and/or abuse in connection with the collection of a debt [15 U.S.C. §1692d];

(b) Using false and/or misleading representations, threats and improper coercion in connection with the collection of a debt [15 U.S.C §1692e]; and,

(c) Communicating with a consumer with respect to the alleged debt owed after the consumer has given written notice that she wishes the debt collector to cease further communications [15 U.S.C. §1692c].

7.04   One or more of these violations resulted in actual damages to Plaintiff.

VIII. SECOND CAUSE OF ACTION: VIOLATION OF TEXAS DEBT COLLECTIONS PRACTICES ACT

8.01   Plaintiff repeats and realleges the factual allegations in the preceding paragraphs.

8.02   Defendant _____ is a "debt collector" as defined in Texas Finance Code §392.001. Plaintiff is a "consumer" as defined in Texas Finance Code §392.001.

[*Continue with a description of the statutory violations committed, such as:*]

8.03   One or more of Defendant _____'s actions in attempting to collect a debt was in violation of the Texas Debt Collection Practices Act, including:

(a) Engaging in harassment and/or abuse in connection with the collection of a debt [Tex. Fin. Code §392.302];

(b) Using fraudulent, deceptive and/or misleading representations in connection with the collection of a debt [Tex. Fin. Code §392.304];

(c) Using threats and/or coercion in connection with the collection of a debt [Tex. Fin. Code §392.301]; and,

(d) Using unfair and/or unconscionable means in the attempted collection of a debt [Tex. Fin. Code §392.303].

[*Continue, if applicable, with allegations that a third-party debt collector did not post a surety bond with the Texas Secretary of State as required.*]

8.04   Further, Defendant _____, an agent working at the direction of _____ [*creditor and/or co-defendant debt collector*], did not have posted with the Texas Secretary of State a bond required by Texas Finance Code §392.101 when attempting to collect the alleged debt from Plaintiff.

8.05   One or more of these violations resulted in actual damages to Plaintiff.

IX. THIRD CAUSE OF ACTION: DTPA

9.01   Plaintiff repeats and realleges the factual allegations in the preceding paragraphs.

9.02   Plaintiff is a consumer entitled to bring this action for relief under the DTPA.

9.03   Defendant's conduct described above is also a deceptive trade practice under Subchapter E, Chapter 17 of the Texas Business and Commerce Code ("DTPA"), and is actionable under that subchapter actionable through the DTPA.

9.04   One or more of Defendant _____'s violations of the Texas Debt Collection Practices Act was a producing cause of damages to Plaintiff.

X. DAMAGES

10.01   Plaintiff has suffered actual damages as a result of one or more of Defendant's acts and omissions described herein.

[Continue with a description of the actual damages suffered by the plaintiff, such as:]

10.02   As a result of the strain and stress of the daily barrage of collection activities described above, Plaintiff has suffered severe emotional distress and mental anguish. Plaintiff has sought treatment for depression from a medical doctor and received prescriptions for medication she now uses to combat the symptoms. Defendant's actions forced Plaintiff to have to abruptly move from her apartment and to disconnect her telephone. As a result, Plaintiff became isolated from friends and family members who no longer knew how to contact her.

10.03   Further, as a result of the Defendant's inaccurate reports to credit bureaus, Plaintiff has not been prevented from obtaining credit on favorable terms to buy a house or even rent an apartment in a desirable area of town.

10.04   Plaintiff has been required to spend numerous hours of her time responding to Defendant's letters and telephone calls and trying to correct the inaccurate reporting with various credit agencies.

10.05   Plaintiff's damages are within the jurisdictional limits of this Court.

XI. ADDITIONAL AND STATUTORY DAMAGES

11.01   Further, Plaintiff seeks an award of statutory damages of $1,000.00 against Defendant _____ for its violation(s) of the Fair Debt Collections Practices Act, pursuant to 15 U.S.C §1692k(a)(2)(A).

11.02 Further, Plaintiff seeks an award of statutory damages of not less than $100.00 against Defendant _____ for its violation(s) of the Texas Debt Collection Practices Act in accordance with Texas Finance Code §392.403.

11.03 Further, Defendant's conduct in violation of the DTPA was committed knowingly or intentionally. Accordingly, Plaintiff seeks an award of additional damages under the DTPA of up to three times the amount of her actual damages.

XII. ATTORNEY'S FEES

12.01 As a result of Defendant's conduct, Plaintiff has been required to obtain the services of the undersigned attorney for the filing, prosecution and trial of this cause, and therefore seeks an award of reasonable and necessary attorney's fees pursuant to applicable law.

WHEREFORE, PREMISES CONSIDERED, Plaintiff respectfully prays that Defendant be cited to appear and answer herein, and that upon final trial hereof, Plaintiff recover from Defendant all of her actual damages, additional damages, pre-judgment and post-judgment interest as allowed by law, attorney's fees, costs of court and such other and further relief to which she may show herself justly entitled.

Respectfully submitted,

_____
ATTORNEY FOR PLAINTIFF

[b] FORM: Petition against bank on auto lease

NO. _____

_____ § IN THE DISTRICT COURT OF
§
vs. § _____ COUNTY, TEXAS
§
_____ § _____ JUDICIAL DISTRICT

PLAINTIFF'S ORIGINAL PETITION

NOW COMES _____, Plaintiff herein, complaining of _____, Defendant herein, and, for cause of action, would show unto the Court as follows:

I. DISCOVERY CONTROL PLAN DESIGNATION

1.01   By this action, Plaintiff seeks _____ [insert *appropriate designation under Rule 47(c), e.g.,* only monetary relief of $100,000 or less, including damages of any kind, penalties, costs, expenses, prejudgment interest, and attorney's fees]. The damages sought are within the jurisdictional limits of this court.

1.02   Discovery in this case is intended to be conducted under Level ___, pursuant to Rule 190.___, *Texas Rules of Civil Procedure.*

II. PARTIES

2.01   [*Plaintiff*] is a resident of _____ County, Texas.

2.02   Defendant is a foreign financial corporation, incorporated in [*location*], with its principal place of business in [*location*]. [*Defendant*] may be served by serving its registered agent for service, _____.

III. JURISDICTION AND VENUE

3.01   The Court has jurisdiction over the Defendant pursuant to Section 17.42 of the *Texas Civil Practice & Remedies Code.* By its actions described herein, Defendant has conducted commercial activities within the state of Texas.

3.02   Venue of this action is proper in _____ County, Texas because all or part of the events made a basis of Plaintiff's claims occurred, in whole or in part, in _____ County, Texas. Tex. Civ. Prac. & Rem. Code §15.002(a).

IV. CONDITIONS PRECEDENT

4.01   All conditions precedent to recovery by Plaintiff herein have been performed, have occurred, or have been excused.

V. AGENCY AND RESPONDEAT SUPERIOR

5.01   Unless otherwise stated, whenever it is alleged that Defendant committed an act, failed to perform an act or made a representation or a statement, it is alleged that Defendant acted or failed to act through its authorized agents, servants, employees or representatives acting with either expressed, implied, apparent, direct and/or ostensible authority, or [*defendant*] subsequently ratified these acts, failures to act, representations, statements or conduct.

VI. FACTS OF CASE

6.01   On _____, 20__, Plaintiff entered into an auto lease agreement with [*car dealership*]. The lease agreement specified that the lease would be immediately assigned to [*leasing trust of defendant*] or its successors and assigns. Subsequent to the execution of the lease, at a date unknown, the lease was in fact assigned to [*defendant*] d/b/a [*leasing trust of defendant*].

6.02   Plaintiff leased a used _____ for her personal use.

6.03   After Plaintiff made the final payment on the lease, Defendant wrongfully asserted that additional amounts were due under the lease, including but not limited to property taxes (from another Texas County) on the vehicle. In fact, Plaintiff's use of motor vehicle was for personal use and she had provided a proper exemption form to Defendant, but Defendant simply failed or refused to avail itself of the exemption. In any event, Defendant cannot charge Plaintiff for the property taxes because Plaintiff is not liable under state tax laws or the terms of the contract. Defendant failed or refused to give Plaintiff credit for other payments made by her to Defendant on the lease.

6.04   Plaintiff first notified Defendant of the errors regarding the billing on her account on _____, 20__. In that letter, she disputed the errors or her lease statement and informed Defendant that the property taxes for the vehicle have been wrongfully assessed to her account. She also asked for a refund of amounts which she had already paid in excess of what she owed.

6.05   Defendant refused to remove the charges for property tax from Plaintiff's account and proceeded with collection efforts on that account for the past due property taxes that Plaintiff was not obligated to pay. In its attempts to collect these amounts, Defendant made harassing phone calls to Plaintiff several times a day, including weekends. On _____, 20__ and again on _____, 20__, Plaintiff sent two (2) letters requesting that Defendant stop harassing her by making excessive phone calls to her residence and to stop trying to collect debts not actually owed.

6.06   Despite being notified of the legitimate dispute over the account, Defendant continued to make harassing phone calls, to send letters demanding payment, and to report to the credit reporting agencies Plaintiff's failure to make payments on the amounts not owed. Even after receiving notice of the dispute and a request to stop the harassing phone calls, Defendant continued to call Plaintiff several times a week to demand payment of the disputed charges.

6.07   Further, Defendant falsely reported to one or more credit-reporting agencies that Plaintiff was delinquent in her payments on the lease. Despite repeated requests, Defendant failed and refused to correct this information to these credit reporting agencies.

6.08   Plaintiff finally hired the undersigned counsel to intervene on her behalf. Even after being shown that Plaintiff had actually overpaid on her lease, Defendant continued with the harassing phone calls and refused to refund her the overpaid amount.

VII. FIRST CAUSE OF ACTION: TEXAS DEBT COLLECTION PRACTICES ACT

7.01   Plaintiff repeats and re-alleges the factual allegations in the preceding paragraphs.

7.02   Defendant, its employees, and agents are "debt collectors" as defined in *Texas Finance Code* §392.001(6).

7.03   Plaintiff is a "consumer" as defined in *Texas Finance Code* §392.001(1) and the transaction at issue in this suit concerns "consumer debt" as defined in *Texas Finance Code* §392.001(2).

7.04   The acts and omissions of Defendant, as set forth above, constitute violations of *Texas Finance Code* §392.302(4) which prohibits a debt collector from making repeated telephone calls to a consumer with the intent to harass the consumer.

7.05   The acts and omissions of Defendant, as set forth above, constitute violations of *Texas Finance Code* §392.304(a)(8) by misrepresenting the character, extent, or amount of a consumer debt allegedly owed by Plaintiff.

7.06   The acts and omissions of Defendant, as set forth above, constitute violations of *Texas Finance Code* §392.202 outlining certain actions to be taken and to not be taken in connection with reporting debts to credit-reporting agencies when the consumer disputes a debt.

7.07   One or more violations by Defendant of the Texas Debt Collection Practices Act was a producing cause of damages to Plaintiff for which she sues.

XIII. SECOND CAUSE OF ACTION: DECEPTIVE TRADE PRACTICES ACT

8.01   Plaintiff repeats and re-alleges the factual allegations in the preceding paragraphs.

8.02   Plaintiff is a consumer under the *Texas Deceptive Trade Practices - Consumer Protection Act, Texas Business & Commerce Code* §§17.41 *et seq.* ("the DTPA").

8.03   Defendant's violations of the Texas Debt Collections Practices Act are also deceptive trade practices under the Texas DTPA.

8.04   One or more Defendant's deceptive acts or practices were a producing cause of damages to Plaintiff, for which she sues.

8.05   Furthermore, because Defendant acted knowingly or intentionally under the DTPA, Plaintiff is entitled to a discretionary award of additional damages up to three times the amount of her actual damages.

IX. THIRD CAUSE OF ACTION: BREACH OF CONTRACT

9.01   Plaintiff repeats and re-alleges the factual allegations in the preceding paragraphs.

9.02   By the acts and omissions outlined above, Defendant has breached the automobile lease agreement between Plaintiff and Defendant.

9.03   Defendant demanded and Plaintiff paid more than the amounts owed under the lease. Despite demand, Defendant has failed and refused to refund the overpayments to Plaintiff.

9.04   As a result of one or more breaches of the lease contract by Defendant, Plaintiff has suffered damages for which she sues.

X. DAMAGES

10.01   Defendant's acts and omissions as described herein have been a producing and/or proximate cause of damages to Plaintiff.

10.02   Plaintiff is entitled to a refund of payments made over and above the payments required by the Lease.

10.03   Further, Plaintiff has suffered damages to her credit and credit reputation. Defendant has reported the false amounts allegedly owed to credit reporting agencies which have then published this information to their customers. As a result, Plaintiff has been denied credit on terms which she would have been offered had the true status of this account with Defendant been reported.

10.04   Further, Plaintiff has suffered mental anguish damages in an amount within the jurisdictional limits of this court.

10.05   Further, Plaintiff is entitled to compensation for the reasonable value of Plaintiff's time and expenses incurred in attempting to rectify the situation created by Defendant.

10.06   Further, Plaintiff is entitled to statutory damages under *Texas Finance Code* §392.403 of at least $100.00 for each statutory violation by Defendant.

XI. ADDITIONAL DAMAGES AND PUNITIVE DAMAGES

11.01   Defendant's conduct in violation of the DTPA was committed knowingly and/or intentionally as those terms are defined in the DTPA. Accordingly, Defendant is liable for additional damages under the DTPA.

11.02   Defendant acted with malice and in flagrant disregard of the rights of Plaintiff with actual awareness that Plaintiff would, in reasonable probability, suffer mental anguish and additional damages from its conduct. Defendant acted intentionally and knowingly. Defendant is thus liable for exemplary damages in an amount to be determined by the jury.

XII. ATTORNEY'S FEES

12.01   As a result of Defendant's conduct, Plaintiff has been required to obtain the services of the undersigned attorney for the filing, prosecution and trial of this cause, and therefore seeks an award of reasonable and necessary attorney's fees pursuant to applicable law.

XIII. PRAYER

WHEREFORE, PREMISES CONSIDERED, Plaintiff respectfully prays that Defendant be cited to appear and answer herein, and that upon final trial hereof, Plaintiff recover from Defendant as follows:

1. Actual damages;
2. Statutory damages;
3. Additional damages;
4. Exemplary damages;
5. Pre-judgment and post-judgment interest as allowed by law;
6. A permanent injunction pursuant to *Tex. Fin. Code* § 392.403(a)(1) prohibiting Defendant from ever again:
    A. misrepresenting the character, extent, or amount of Plaintiff's consumer debt;
    B. harassing Plaintiff by making repeated telephone calls to her; and/or
    C. falsely reporting to any credit-reporting agency or other third party that Plaintiff has not timely and fully paid Defendant all sums due under the lease in question.
7. Attorney's fees;
8. Costs of court; and,

9. Such other and further relief to which she may show herself justly entitled.

Respectfully submitted,

_____

ATTORNEY FOR PLAINTIFF

§5.27 Application for Injunctive Relief

DTPA claims occasionally involve the need for some form of extraordinary relief. This is particularly true when a consumer's property is threatened with foreclosure or repossession. In some cases, there may be a claim against the lender that would, if successful, have the effect of reducing the amount of the debt on which the foreclosure or repossession is threatened. *Cf. Irving Bank & Trust Co. v. Second Land Corp.*, 544 S.W.2d 684, 688 (Tex. Civ. App.—Dallas 1976, writ ref'd n.r.e.). When a foreclosure or repossession is threatened, injunctive relief also may be necessary in order to preserve certain remedies available under the DTPA such as rescission of the underlying transaction. *See Crossland Sav. Bank FSB v. Constant*, 737 S.W.2d 19, 22 (Tex. App.—Corpus Christi 1987, no writ). Consequently, some attention must be given to the availability of injunctive relief in DTPA cases.

The grant or denial of a temporary restraining order and temporary injunction is governed by TEX. R. CIV. P. 680 - 693. As a general proposition, a temporary restraining order or temporary injunction may be issued upon a showing by the applicant that he or she (1) has a "probable right" to the relief sought in the suit, (2) has suffered a "probable injury," and (3) that he has suffered an irreparable injury for which there is no adequate remedy at law. *Transport Co. of Texas v. Robertson Transports*, 261 S.W.2d 549, 552 (Tex. 1953). "The only question before the court is the right of the applicant to a preservation of the status quo of the subject matter of the suit pending a final trial on the merits." *Transport Co. of Texas v. Robertson Transports, supra* at 552. The applicant is only required to show a *probable* right and a *probable* injury; he is not required to show that he will prevail at the final trial. *Sun Oil Co. v. Whitaker*, 424 S.W.2d 216 (Tex. 1968); *Irving Bank & Trust v. Second Land Corp.*, 544 S.W.2d 684 (Tex. Civ. App.—Dallas 1976, writ ref'd n.r.e.).

In *Ballenger v. Ballenger*, 694 S.W.2d 72, 76 (Tex. App.—Corpus Christi 1985, writ ref'd. n.r.e.), the court reviewed the rules relating to the adequacy of the remedy at law and stated that the test for determining whether an existing remedy is adequate is whether the remedy is as complete and as practical and efficient to the ends of justice and its prompt administration as is equitable relief. *Ballenger, supra* at 76; *Brazos River Conservation & Reclamation District v. Allen*, 171 S.W.2d 847 (Tex. 1943). And, no adequate remedy at law exists, as a matter of law, if damages are incapable of calculation or if the defendant is insolvent or otherwise unable to pay damages. *Bank of Southwest N.A. v. Harlingen Nat'l Bank*, 662 S.W.2d 113, 116 (Tex. App.—Corpus Christi 1983, no writ).

The DTPA provides that upon proof of a violation of the statute, the court can enter, "an order enjoining such acts or failure to act," and "any other relief which the court deems proper." *See* DTPA §17.50(b)(2), (4). When a statute provides for injunctive relief, it is unnecessary for the applicant to establish that there is an inadequate remedy at law. Clearly, the DTPA authorizes a court to enjoin improper conduct; therefore, if the injunction is sought under the DTPA, the applicant should be able to dispense with proof that there is no adequate remedy at law.

Rule 680 requires that if a temporary restraining order is issued without notice, then it must specifically state, "why the order was granted without notice." TEX. R. CIV. P. 680.

Most commonly, there is insufficient time to notify the defendant and set a hearing on the application prior to the date the threatened conduct is to occur. Whatever the reason, it should be stated in the application and must be stated in the order. TEX. R. CIV. P. 680.

The request for injunctive relief can be contained in the original petition or in a separate document. The form which follows is intended as an insert in the original petition.

[a] FORM: —Petition for injunctive relief (general form)

Insert in original or amended petition:

[1.]

Application for Injunction Relief

Plaintiff seeks a temporary restraining order [without notice] and after hearing a temporary injunction.

(a) Defendant has threatened [*insert conduct that needs to be restrained*].

(b) Unless defendant is restrained from taking the action threatened, plaintiff will suffer irreparable harm, loss and injury for which there is no adequate remedy at law. In particular, [*describe harm, injury and loss*]. Further, DTPA §17.50(b)(2) and (4) provide statutory authority for the court to grant injunctive relief upon a showing that the statute has been violated.

(c) The action threatened by defendant is wrongful for the reason that [*describe manner in which conduct violates the DTPA or is otherwise wrongful*].

(d) Defendant's threatened action also will disrupt the status quo of this litigation for the reason that [*insert manner in which status quo will be disrupted*].

[(e) There is insufficient time within which to provide notice and hearing to defendant for the reason that [*describe why notice and hearing are impracticable*]. For this reason, plaintiff requests that the temporary restraining order be issued without notice.]

Insert in request for relief paragraph:

Plaintiff also asks that a temporary restraining order be issued without notice, and, after notice and hearing, a temporary injunction, restraining defendant, its officers, agents, servants, employees and attorneys, and such other persons in active concert or participation with it who have actual notice of the order by personal service or otherwise, from engaging in the following conduct: [*specify conduct to be restrained*].

[NOTE: An affidavit is required for the issuance of injunctive relief. *See* Tex. R. Civ. P. 682.]

[b] FORM: —Temporary restraining order (general form)

	NO. _____	
_____	§	IN THE DISTRICT COURT OF
	§	
vs.	§	_____COUNTY, TEXAS
	§	
_____	§	_____ JUDICIAL DISTRICT

<u>TEMPORARY RESTRAINING ORDER</u>

On this _____ day of _____, 20___, came on for hearing the application of _____, plaintiff, for a temporary restraining order, without notice, against _____ defendant.

It appears to the court that defendant intends to [*insert threatened conduct*]. It further appears to the court that plaintiff was notified of this threatened action by [*describe how plaintiff learned of threat*]. The court finds that defendant was given notice of this application. [*If advance notice was not given, insert the following*: Because of the immediacy of the threatened action by defendant and because there is no agent or counsel known to the court or the plaintiff for defendant, there is not sufficient time before the threatened action is to occur to notify this defendant of the filing of this application and to set a hearing on the application. Accordingly, plaintiff's application has been considered by this court and ruled on without notice to defendant.]

Having reviewed and considered plaintiff's verified petition, the court finds that plaintiff has shown a probable right to recover. That is, accepting plaintiff's verified petition as true for purposes of this application only, the court finds that [*insert findings that justify plaintiffs probable right to recover*]. The court further finds that if defendant [*insert conduct to be restrained*] before a hearing can be held on plaintiff's application, plaintiff will suffer irreparable injury, loss and damage for which there is no adequate remedy at law. The court further finds that Tex. Bus. & Com. Code §17.50(b)(2) and (4) authorize the court to grant this injunctive relief based on the facts established in this proceeding. The court further finds that the action threatened by defendant would disrupt the status quo of the parties to this litigation.

IT IS THEREFORE ORDERED by this court that the clerk shall issue a temporary restraining order restraining [defendant's name], its officers, agents, servants, employees and attorneys, and those other persons in active concert or participation with defendant who have actual notice of this order by personal service or otherwise from [*insert conduct to be restrained*].

IT IS FURTHER ORDERED that this temporary restraining order shall remain in full force and effect for a period of fourteen days from the date and time it is signed and shall then expire unless extended by this court or by agreement of the parties.

IT IS FURTHER ORDERED that a hearing on plaintiff's application for a temporary injunction is set for _____ o'clock __.M. on the _____ day of _____, 20___, in this courtroom which is located in the County Courthouse, _____ , _____ County, Texas. The clerk is directed to issue a notice to [defendant's name], together with a true and correct copy of this order and a copy of Plaintiff's Original Petition, advising this defendant of the time and place of the hearing in order that this defendant may show cause, if any there be, why a temporary injunction restraining the conduct described above should not be granted.

It further appears to the court that a bond in the amount of $_____ is sufficient and adequate security for plaintiff to file for issuance of the temporary restraining order. IT IS THEREFORE ORDERED that plaintiff shall, prior to the issuance of the temporary restraining order, file with the clerk a bond executed by it in the sum of $_____, payable to defendant, with good and sufficient surety, approved and conditioned as the law requires.

SIGNED this _____ day of _____, 20___ at _____ o'clock M. in the _____ Judicial District Courtroom in _____, _____ County, Texas.

[Signature of presiding judge]

[c] FORM: —Application for temporary injunction (threatened foreclosure)

```
                            NO. _____
_____                  §    IN THE DISTRICT COURT OF
                            §
vs.                         §    _____ COUNTY, TEXAS
                            §
_____                  §
and                         §
                            §
_____, Trustee         §    _____ JUDICIAL DISTRICT
```

APPLICATION FOR TEMPORARY INJUNCTION

TO THE HONORABLE JUDGE OF THE DISTRICT COURT:

_____, plaintiff in the above referenced cause, files this application for a temporary injunction to restrain foreclosure of a deed of trust by defendants _____ and _____, and as ground for the application will show:

1. Statutory authority. This application is made, in part, under the authority of Tex. Bus. & Com. Code §17.41 *et seq.*, commonly known as the Deceptive Trade Practices and Consumer Protection Act and cited in this application as the "DTPA."

2. *Defendants*. The defendants in this application are:

(a) _____, who is the substitute trustee under the deed of trust described in this application and who may be served with process at _____.

(b) _____, defendant herein, [who has been served with a copy of this application by hand-delivery to his [her] attorney of record, _____.]

3. Deed of Trust and Threatened Foreclosure.

On or about _____, plaintiff purchased a residential lot and house from defendant, which is more fully described as: [*insert legal description of property*].

In connection with the purchase, plaintiff executed a note which was payable to defendant and which was an interest bearing note in the principal sum of $_____. The note was due and payable in _____ but has not been paid for the reasons set forth in this application. Defendant has accelerated the note. Defendant has appointed a substitute trustee and has instructed him [her] to foreclose the deed of trust by selling the real property at a Trustee's Sale on the first Tuesday in _____, 20___, between the hours of 10: 00 a. m. and 4: 00 p. m. A true and correct copy of the notice received by plaintiff from _____ is attached hereto and incorporated herein as if fully set forth.

4. <u>Need for Injunctive Relief</u>.

(a) On _____, 20___, plaintiff filed suit against defendant because of numerous false representations made to him [her] in the purchase of the property described above. Defendant engaged in the following false, misleading and deceptive conduct in connection with the sale of the property, in violation of DTPA §17.46(b): [*insert false representations made, e.g.,*

(1). Defendant represented that the air-conditioning system recently had been serviced and was in good working order;

(2). Defendant represented that the roof did not leak;

(3). Defendant represented that the house was "exceptionally nice" and that it was listed below market;

(4). Defendant represented that the house would not need any major repair work done to it; and

(5). Defendant represented that the house had no latent defects].

(b) In truth and in fact, because of the defects in the house and the false, misleading and deceptive representations made by defendant, plaintiff must now pay at least the following amounts to repair defects that he [she] was not told about or was expressly told did not exist: [*insert repairs needed and costs*].

(c) The threatened foreclosure must be restrained in order to prevent defendant from taking inequitable and unconscionable advantage of plaintiff. In the event plaintiff prevails in his [her] suit against defendant, a judgment will be rendered against defendant for the damages set forth above, which damages are due to defendant's false representations at the time of sale. Such damages will be offset. against any debt owed to defendant by virtue of the sale. However, unless the threatened foreclosure is enjoined until the trial on the merits, plaintiff will suffer irreparable injury because he [she] will have lost his [her] home by the foreclosure because of a debt which is not owed since the amount of the debt is equal to or less than the amount of damages caused to plaintiff by defendant's conduct.

(d) The threatened foreclosure also will deprive plaintiff of the use and enjoyment of the property which now is used as his

[her] residence and homestead. Additionally, he [she] will lose the right to sell or mortgage the home at some future date, thus losing his [her] ability to obtain and take advantage of the appreciated value of the property. All of these facts threaten plaintiff with irreparable injury for which there is no adequate remedy at law. Further, DTPA §17.50(b)(2) and (4) specifically authorize the court to grant the injunction requested since defendant's conduct constitutes a violation of the DTPA.

5. Injunctive relief is equitable.

As stated above, there is no adequate remedy at law for plaintiff if the threatened foreclosure is allowed; and, as shown above, the injury to him [her] will be irreparable; however, with the temporary injunction, plaintiff will not suffer the irreparable injury now threatened, which injury would be severe. On the other hand, defendant will lose nothing and suffer no harm by the entry of such an order since the debt alleged to be owed will remain secured by the property in question and the bond required for the injunction requested will protect defendant from any other losses he [she] may suffer. Plaintiff is ready, willing and able, after final trial herein, to pay whatever amount is found to be due defendant after all offsets are allowed for the damages caused by defendant's conduct.

WHEREFORE, plaintiff requests that defendant _____, substitute trustee, be cited to appear and answer herein, and that after hearing, a temporary injunction be entered against defendant _____ and the substitute trustee, their officers, agents, servants, employees and those other persons in active concert or participation with them who receive actual notice of the temporary injunction by personal service or otherwise, restraining and enjoining such persons from foreclosing or attempting to foreclose on the deed of trust described above or by any other means selling or attempting to sell the above described property, except through judicial process, until a final trial herein.

Plaintiff further requests that this case be set for final trial on the merits.

Plaintiff further requests for such other and further relief to which he [she] may show himself [herself] entitled.

Respectfully submitted,

[Signature of attorney]

[Attach supporting affidavits]

NOTICE OF HEARING

A hearing on the foregoing application for temporary injunction has been set for the _____ day of _____, 20___ at _____o'clock ___.M. Docket call on this hearing will _____.

                        [Signature of attorney]

                        [Certificate of service]

[d] FORM: —Temporary Injunction

	NO. _____	
_____	§	IN THE DISTRICT COURT OF
	§	
vs.	§	_____COUNTY, TEXAS
	§	
_____	§	_____ JUDICIAL DISTRICT

TEMPORARY INJUNCTION

On this _____ day of _____, 20___, came on for hearing the application of plaintiff, _____, for a temporary injunction against defendants, _____ and _____, in the above entitled and numbered cause of action. All parties received actual notice of the hearing. Plaintiff appeared in person and by and through his [her] attorney of record and defendants appeared by and through their attorneys of record. The parties announced ready for hearing.

Having read the sworn pleadings of plaintiff, and having heard and considered the evidence and argument of counsel, it appears to the court that for the purposes of this hearing only, plaintiff has proven that certain representations were made about the quality of the property which is the subject of this suit; that such representations were false; and that plaintiff has suffered damages which were produced by such conduct. It further appears to the court that defendants will foreclose on the deed of trust which was obtained from plaintiff as security for a $_____ note for [part of] the purchase price of the real property, which foreclosure will result in a sale of the property on _____, 20___, unless restrained by this court. Plaintiff has proved by satisfactory evidence that he [she] has a probable right to injunctive relief; that he [she] has suffered a probable injury as a result of the representations made to him [her] and that he [she] will suffer irreparable harm if the foreclosure is not enjoined, for which there is no adequate remedy at law. The court further finds that Tex. Bus. & Com. Code §17.50(b)(2) and (4) authorize the entry of this order based on the evidence presented. The court further finds that the temporary injunction requested and hereinafter granted will preserve the status quo of the parties to this suit pending a final trial on the merits.

IT IS THEREFORE ORDERED by this court that after plaintiff has filed the necessary bond as described below, the clerk of this court shall forthwith issue a temporary injunction restraining defendants, their agents, servants, employees and attorneys, and those other persons in active concert or participation with him [her] who receive actual notice of this temporary injunction by personal service or otherwise, from engaging in the following acts:

INSTITUTING OR CONTINUING WITH FORECLOSURE PROCEEDINGS, EXCEPT THROUGH JUDICIAL PROCESS, AGAINST THAT PROPERTY OWNED BY _____ WHICH IS LOCATED AT [*insert address and legal description*].

This temporary injunction will remain in full force and effect pending a final trial of this cause or further orders of this court.

And, it further appears to the court that a bond in the amount of $_____ is sufficient and adequate for plaintiff to file upon issuance of the temporary injunction herein granted. It is therefore ordered that plaintiff shall, prior to the issuance of such writ of temporary injunction, file with the clerk a bond executed by him [her] in the sum of $_____, payable to defendant _____, with good and sufficient surety, approved and conditioned as the law requires.

In accordance with Rule 683 of the Texas Rules of Civil Procedure, the trial on the merits of the above entitled and numbered cause of action is hereby set for the _____ day of _____, 20___.

SIGNED THIS _____ day of _____, 20___.

[Signature of presiding judge]

§5.28 Pleading Discovery Rule to Avoid Limitations

Generally, lawsuits under the DTPA must be brought within two years after the date on which the false, misleading or deceptive act or practice occurred or within two years after the consumer discovered or in the exercise of reasonable diligence should have discovered the occurrence of the false, misleading or deceptive act or practice. DTPA §17.565.

In *Willis v. Maverick*, 760 S.W.2d 642 (Tex. 1988), the court held that when the defendant raises limitations as a defense and the plaintiff seeks to avoid the defense by the application of the discovery provision of the DTPA, then the *plaintiff* must plead and prove the date of discovery. This holding incorrectly shifts the burden of proof to the consumer by requiring the consumer to disprove that limitations bars the suit. *See* Curry, *Deceptive Trade Practices and Commercial Torts*, 43 Sw. L.J. 149, 165 (1989). In light of this holding, however, whenever the defendant pleads limitations, a supplemental or amended petition setting forth the facts which support the application of the discovery rule should, be filed. The allegation set forth below accomplishes this purpose.

[a] FORM: —Allegation invoking the discovery rule

```
Discovery rule. Plaintiff did not discover, and should not, in
the exercise of reasonable diligence, have discovered, the occur-
rence of the false, misleading or deceptive acts or practices
[or breach of warranty or unconscionable actions and courses of
action] alleged in this petition until less than two years before
this suit was filed.
```

§5.29 Petition for Unfair Debt Collection Practices

The following forms can be used by a consumer to assert claims against a debt collector for unfair debt collection practices in violation of both the FDCPA and the TDCPA. Because violations of the TDCPA are actionable under the DTPA, additional allegations have been included to assert liability under the DTPA through this tie-in statute.

[a] FORM: Petition for unfair debt collection practices

```
                         NO. _____
_____               §     IN THE DISTRICT COURT OF
                         §
vs.                      §     _____ COUNTY, TEXAS
                         §
_____               §     _____ JUDICIAL DISTRICT
```

PLAINTIFF'S ORIGINAL PETITION

NOW COMES _____, Plaintiff herein, complaining of _____ _____, Defendant herein, and for cause of action, would show unto the Court as follows:

I.

DISCOVERY CONTROL PLAN DESIGNATION

1.01 Discovery in this case is intended to be conducted under Level __ [1], pursuant to Rule 190.__[2], *Texas Rules of Civil Procedure*.

II.

PARTIES

2.01 _____, Plaintiff, is a resident of _____, _____ County, Texas.

2.02 _____, Defendant, is a [corporation/individual/partnership, etc.] [incorporated in _____ [state] with its principal place of business in _____ [city], _____ [state]. [Insert service allegations, such as: _____ [name of defendant] has no registered agent for service in Texas and can therefore be served by serving its statutory agent for service, the Texas Secretary of State, P.O. Box 12079, Austin, Texas 78711-2029, who should then forward a copy to _____ [name of defendant] at _____ _____ [address, city, state, zip code].]

[*Continue with similar paragraphs for any additional Defendants*]

III.

JURISDICTION & VENUE

3.01 The Court has *in personam* jurisdiction over Defendant pursuant to Section 17.42 of the *Texas Civil Practice and Remedies Code*. By [its/his/her] actions described herein, Defendant has conducted commercial activities within the State of Texas.

3.02 Venue of this action is proper in _____ County, Texas because all or part of the events made the basis of Plaintiff's claims occurred, in whole or in part, in _____ County, Texas and because _____ [name of plaintiff], a consumer under the Federal Debt Collection Practices Act, resides in _____ County, Texas at the time of the commencement of this suit.

IV.

CONDITIONS PRECEDENT

4.01   All conditions precedent to recovery by Plaintiff herein have been performed, have occurred, or have been excused.

V.

AGENCY [AND JOINT VENTURE]

5.01   Unless otherwise stated, whenever it is alleged that Defendant _____ committed an act, failed to perform an act, made a representation or a statement, or failed to make a disclosure, it is alleged that Defendant _____ acted or failed to act through [its/his/her] authorized agents, servants, employees or representatives acting with either expressed, implied, apparent, direct and/or ostensible authority, or Defendant _____ subsequently ratified these acts, failures to act, representations, statements or conduct.

[*Continue with similar paragraphs for any additional Defendants*]

[*If it is alleged that two or more Defendants acted in concert and should be vicariously liable for each other's actions, continue with the following:*]

5.02   Further, it is alleged that Defendants were engaged in a joint venture for their mutual benefit and acted as each other's agents with all express, implied, direct and/or ostensible authority to so act, and as such are vicariously liable for the acts, omissions, statements and conduct of the other as alleged herein.

VI.

FACTS OF CASE

[*Continue with a recitation of the facts giving rise to the plaintiff's cause(s) of action, such as:*]

6.01   In _____, Plaintiff opened a revolving charge account at _____ department store. On or about _____, 2009, Plaintiff purchased a dress using the credit card issued by _____. However, when she got the dress home, she discovered that the dress had a small tear in the fabric. On or about _____, 2009, Plaintiff returned the dress to the store and requested a reversal of the charges on her credit card for the purchase of the dress. At the time, the store clerk indicated to Plaintiff that her request would be honored, and Plaintiff thought no more about the incident for several weeks.

6.02   When Plaintiff received her credit card statement from _____ the next month, she noticed that the charge for the dress was still on her account and had not been reversed or removed. When she called _____ to inquire, she was told that the reversal of charges for returned items might take another "cycle" before it showed up, and that she should deduct the amount of the purchase from the balance on her check for payment of her balance. Plaintiff did as she was instructed and timely paid the balance of her credit card bill, less the amount for the returned dress.

6.03 However, in the following months, the credit card statements sent to Plaintiff continued to show the balance due for the returned dress and now included late fees and interest charges. When Plaintiff called to complain, she was then told that there was no record of her return, that the charges were valid, and that if she did not pay the balance of the credit card statements, with interest and late fees, she would be turned over to a collection agency.

6.04 Beginning on or about _____, 2010, Plaintiff began to receive reminder letters and phone calls from _____ trying to collect the balance of the disputed credit card bill. Beginning in _____, 2010, the tone of these collection efforts changed dramatically. In its effort to collect the disputed credit card debt, Defendant _____ relentlessly called Plaintiff, up to five times a day, and repeatedly sent demand letters threatening legal action. In phone calls to Plaintiff at all times of the day and night, Defendant' agents and representatives repeatedly harassed Plaintiff by calling her names such as "deadbeat," "low life" and "scum," by cursing and using profanity, and by calling back repeatedly after Plaintiff hung up from the calls.

6.05 In addition, in these phone calls, one or more of Defendant's agents made threats of legal action against Plaintiff, including threats to have her house taken away, her car repossessed and to have Plaintiff arrested for non-payment of the disputed bills.

6.06 On or about _____, 2010, Plaintiff notified Defendant _____ in writing that she disputes the validity of the debt and requested that Defendant _____ cease all communication with her.

6.07 Subsequent to receiving Plaintiff's written notice demanding that Defendant _____ cease and desist contacting Plaintiff in attempting to collect the alleged debt, Defendant _____ mailed to Plaintiff yet another letter demanding payment and threatening to pursue legal action, to report the account to all of the major credit bureaus, and to file a lien on her home. This demand letter from Defendant _____ sought to collect the total amount alleged due on the account, an amount of $_____.

6.08   Further, subsequent to receiving Plaintiff's written notice demanding that Defendant _____ cease and desist contacting Plaintiff, on or about _____, 2010, Defendant _____ sent a demand letter to Plaintiff seeking to collect the alleged debt due to _____ [*creditor*] in the amount of $_____. The letter also threatened that the account would be reported to credit reporting agencies.

6.09   On or about _____, 2010, within thirty days from the demand letter from Defendant _____, Plaintiff notified Defendant _____ in writing that she disputes the validity of the debt and demanded that they cease further communications with her. Plaintiff included with the letter to Defendant _____ her letter to Defendant _____ which demanded the cessation of collection efforts.

6.10   On or about _____, 2010, Defendant _____ sent yet another letter to Plaintiff attempting to collect the alleged debt. While this letter stated that Defendant _____ "verified" the amount of the debt, Defendant _____ did not provide Plaintiff any proof of the verification as required.

6.11   Despite Plaintiff's written requests that Defendant _____ cease communications with her, Defendant _____ continued to call Plaintiff at her home in an effort to collect the alleged debt. Defendant _____ called Plaintiff most recently on _____, 2010 and _____, 2010.

6.12   During all time that Defendant _____ attempted to collect an alleged debt from Plaintiff, Defendant _____ had not posted a bond in compliance with Texas Finance Code §392.101.

VII.

FIRST CAUSE OF ACTION: VIOLATION OF

FAIR DEBT COLLECTIONS PRACTICES ACT

7.01   Plaintiff repeats and realleges the factual allegations in the preceding paragraphs.

7.02   Defendant _____ is a "debt collector" as defined in 15 U.S.C. §1692a(6). Plaintiff is a "consumer" as defined in 15 U.S.C. §1692a(3).

[*Continue with a description of the statutory violations committed, such as:*]

7.03   One or more of Defendant _____'s actions in attempting to collect a debt were in violation of the Fair Debt Collection Practices Act, including:

(a) Engaging in harassment and/or abuse in connection with the collection of a debt [15 U.S.C. §1692d];

(b) Using false and/or misleading representations, threats and improper coercion in connection with the collection of a debt [15 U.S.C §1692e]; and,

(c) Communicating with a consumer with respect to the alleged debt owed after the consumer has given written notice that she wishes the debt collector to cease further communications [15 U.S.C.§1692c].

7.04   One or more of these violations resulted in actual damages to Plaintiff.

VIII.

SECOND CAUSE OF ACTION: VIOLATION OF TEXAS DEBT COLLECTIONS PRACTICES ACT

8.01   Plaintiff repeats and realleges the factual allegations in the preceding paragraphs.

8.02   Defendant _____ is a "debt collector" as defined in Texas Finance Code §392.001. Plaintiff is a "consumer" as defined in Texas Finance Code §392.001.

[*Continue with a description of the statutory violations committed, such as:*]

8.03   One or more of Defendant _____'s actions in attempting to collect a debt was in violation of the Texas Debt Collection Practices Act, including:

(a) Engaging in harassment and/or abuse in connection with the collection of a debt [Tex. Fin. Code §392.302];

(b) Using fraudulent, deceptive and/or misleading representations in connection with the collection of a debt [Tex. Fin. Code §392.304];

(c) Using threats and/or coercion in connection with the collection of a debt [Tex. Fin. Code §392.301]; and,

(d) Using unfair and/or unconscionable means in the attempted collection of a debt [Tex. Fin. Code §392.303].

[*Continue, if applicable, with allegations that a third party debt collector did not post a surety bond with the Texas Secretary of State as required*]

8.04   Further, Defendant _____, an agent working at the direction of _____ [*creditor and/or co-defendant debt collector*], did not have posted with the Texas

Secretary of State a bond required by Texas Finance Code §392.101 when attempting to collect the alleged debt from Plaintiff.

8.05   One or more of these violations resulted in actual damages to Plaintiff.

IX.

THIRD CAUSE OF ACTION: DTPA

9.01   Plaintiff repeats and realleges the factual allegations in the preceding paragraphs.

9.02   Plaintiff is a consumer entitled to bring this action for relief under the DTPA.

9.03   Defendant's conduct described above is also a deceptive trade practice under Subchapter E, Chapter 17 of the Texas Business and Commerce Code ("DTPA"), and is actionable under that subchapter actionable through the DTPA.

9.04   One or more of Defendant _____'s violations of the Texas Debt Collection Practices Act was a producing cause of damages to Plaintiff.

X.

DAMAGES

10.01   Plaintiff has suffered actual damages as a result of one or more of Defendant's acts and omissions described herein.

[Continue with a description of the actual damages suffered by the plaintiff, such as:]

10.02   As a result of the strain and stress of the daily barrage of collection activities described above, Plaintiff has suffered severe emotional distress and mental anguish. Plaintiff has sought treatment for depression from a medical doctor and received prescriptions for medication she now uses to combat the symptoms. Defendant's actions forced Plaintiff to have to abruptly move from her apartment and to disconnect her telephone. As a result, Plaintiff became isolated from friends and family members who no longer knew how to contact her.

10.03   Further, as a result of the Defendant's inaccurate reports to credit bureaus, Plaintiff has not been prevented from obtaining credit on favorable terms to buy a house or even rent an apartment in a desirable area of town.

10.04   Plaintiff has been required to spend numerous hours of her time responding to Defendant's letters and telephone calls and trying to correct the inaccurate reporting with various credit agencies.

10.05   Plaintiff's damages are within the jurisdictional limits of this Court.

XI.

ADDITIONAL AND STATUTORY DAMAGES

11.01   Further, Plaintiff seeks an award of statutory damages of $1,000.00 against Defendant _____ for its violation(s) of the Fair Debt Collections Practices Act, pursuant to 15 U.S.C §1692k(a)(2)(A).

11.02   Further, Plaintiff seeks an award of statutory damages of not less than $100.00 against Defendant _____ for its violation(s) of the Texas Debt Collection Practices Act in accordance with Texas Finance Code §392.403.

11.03   Further, Defendant's conduct in violation of the DTPA was committed knowingly or intentionally. Accordingly, Plaintiff seeks an award of additional damages under the DTPA of up to three times the amount of her actual damages.

XII.

ATTORNEY'S FEES

12.01   As a result of Defendant's conduct, Plaintiff has been required to obtain the services of the undersigned attorney for the filing, prosecution and trial of this cause, and therefore seeks an award of reasonable and necessary attorney's fees pursuant to applicable law.

WHEREFORE, PREMISES CONSIDERED, Plaintiff respectfully prays that Defendant be cited to appear and answer herein, and that upon final trial hereof, Plaintiff recover from Defendant all of her actual damages, additional damages, pre-judgment and post-judgment interest as allowed by law, attorney's fees, costs of court and such other and further relief to which she may show herself justly entitled.

Respectfully submitted,

_____

ATTORNEY FOR PLAINTIFF

[b] FORM: Petition against bank on auto lease

```
                              NO. _____
_____                §    IN THE DISTRICT COURT OF
                          §
vs.                       §    _____ COUNTY, TEXAS
                          §
_____                §    _____ JUDICIAL DISTRICT
```

PLAINTIFF'S ORIGINAL PETITION

NOW COMES _____, Plaintiff herein, complaining of _____, Defendant herein, and, for cause of action, would show unto the Court as follows:

I.

DISCOVERY CONTROL PLAN DESIGNATION

1.01   Discovery in this case is intended to be conducted under Level 1, pursuant to Rule 190.2, *Texas Rules of Civil Procedure.*

II.

PARTIES

2.01   [*Plaintiff*] is a resident of _____ County, Texas.

2.02   Defendant is a foreign financial corporation, incorporated in [*location*], with its principal place of business in [*location*]. [*Defendant*] may be served by serving its registered agent for service, _____.

III.

JURISDICTION AND VENUE

3.01   The Court has jurisdiction over the Defendant pursuant to Section 17.42 of the *Texas Civil Practice & Remedies Code*. By its actions described herein, Defendant has conducted commercial activities within the state of Texas.

3.02   Venue of this action is proper in _____ County, Texas because all or part of the events made a basis of Plaintiff's claims occurred, in whole or in part, in _____ County, Texas. Tex. Civ. Prac. & Rem. Code §15.002(a).

IV.
CONDITIONS PRECEDENT

4.01   All conditions precedent to recovery by Plaintiff herein have been performed, have occurred, or have been excused.

V.
AGENCY AND RESPONDEAT SUPERIOR

5.01   Unless otherwise stated, whenever it is alleged that Defendant committed an act, failed to perform an act or made a representation or a statement, it is alleged that Defendant acted or failed to act through its authorized agents, servants, employees or representatives acting with either expressed, implied, apparent, direct and/or ostensible authority, or [*defendant*] subsequently ratified these acts, failures to act, representations, statements or conduct.

VI.
FACTS OF CASE

6.01   On _____, 20__, Plaintiff entered into an auto lease agreement with [*car dealership*]. The lease agreement specified that the lease would be immediately assigned to [*leasing trust of defendant*] or its successors and assigns. Subsequent to the execution of the lease, at a date unknown, the lease was in fact assigned to [*defendant*] d/b/a [*leasing trust of defendant*].

6.02   Plaintiff leased a used _____ for her personal use.

6.03   After Plaintiff made the final payment on the lease, Defendant wrongfully asserted that additional amounts were due under the lease, including but not limited to property taxes (from another Texas County) on the vehicle. In fact, Plaintiff's use of motor vehicle was for personal use and she had provided a proper exemption form to Defendant, but Defendant simply failed or refused to avail itself of the exemption. In any event, Defendant cannot charge Plaintiff for the property taxes because Plaintiff is not liable under state tax laws or the terms of the contract. Defendant failed or refused to give Plaintiff credit for other payments made by her to Defendant on the lease.

6.04   Plaintiff first notified Defendant of the errors regarding the billing on her account on _____, 20__. In that letter, she disputed the errors or her lease statement and informed Defendant that the property taxes for the vehicle have been wrongfully assessed to her account. She also asked for a refund of amounts which she had already paid in excess of what she owed.

6.05   Defendant refused to remove the charges for property tax from Plaintiff's account and proceeded with collection efforts on that account for the past due property taxes that Plaintiff was not obligated to pay. In its attempts to collect these amounts, Defendant made harassing phone calls to Plaintiff several times a day, including weekends. On _____, 20__ and again on _____, 20__, Plaintiff sent two (2) letters requesting that Defendant stop harassing her by making excessive phone calls to her residence and to stop trying to collect debts not actually owed.

6.06   Despite being notified of the legitimate dispute over the account, Defendant continued to make harassing phone calls, to send letters demanding payment, and to report to the credit reporting agencies Plaintiff's failure to make payments on the amounts not owed. Even after receiving notice of the dispute and a request to stop the harassing phone calls, Defendant continued to call Plaintiff several times a week to demand payment of the disputed charges.

6.07   Further, Defendant falsely reported to one or more credit reporting agencies that Plaintiff was delinquent in her payments on the lease. Despite repeated requests, Defendant failed and refused to correct this information to these credit reporting agencies.

6.08   Plaintiff finally hired the undersigned counsel to intervene on her behalf. Even after being shown that Plaintiff had actually overpaid on her lease, Defendant continued with the harassing phone calls and refused to refund her the overpaid amount.

VII.

FIRST CAUSE OF ACTION: TEXAS DEBT COLLECTION PRACTICES ACT

7.01   Plaintiff repeats and re-alleges the factual allegations in the preceding paragraphs.

7.02   Defendant, its employees, and agents are "debt collectors" as defined in *Texas Finance Code* § 392.001(6).

7.03   Plaintiff is a "consumer" as defined in *Texas Finance Code* § 392.001(1) and the transaction at issue in this suit concerns "consumer debt" as defined in *Texas Finance Code* § 392.001(2).

7.04   The acts and omissions of Defendant, as set forth above, constitute violations of *Texas Finance Code* § 392.302(4) which prohibits a debt collector from making repeated telephone calls to a consumer with the intent to harass the consumer.

7.05   The acts and omissions of Defendant, as set forth above, constitute violations of *Texas Finance Code* § 392.304(a)(8) by misrepresenting the character, extent, or amount of a consumer debt allegedly owed by Plaintiff.

7.06   The acts and omissions of Defendant, as set forth above, constitute violations of *Texas Finance Code* § 392.202 outlining certain actions to be taken and to not be taken in connection with reporting debts to credit reporting agencies when the consumer disputes a debt.

7.07   One or more violations by Defendant of the Texas Debt Collection Practices Act was a producing cause of damages to Plaintiff for which she sues.

XIII.

SECOND CAUSE OF ACTION: DECEPTIVE TRADE PRACTICES ACT

8.01   Plaintiff repeats and re-alleges the factual allegations in the preceding paragraphs.

8.02   Plaintiff is a consumer under the *Texas Deceptive Trade Practices - Consumer Protection Act, Texas Business & Commerce Code* §§ 17.41 *et seq.* ("the DTPA").

8.03   Defendant's violations of the Texas Debt Collections Practices Act are also deceptive trade practices under the Texas DTPA.

8.04   One or more Defendant's deceptive acts or practices was a producing cause of damages to Plaintiff, for which she sues.

8.05   Furthermore, because Defendant acted knowingly or intentionally under the DTPA, Plaintiff is entitled to a discretionary award of additional damages up to three times the amount of her actual damages.

IX.

THIRD CAUSE OF ACTION: BREACH OF CONTRACT

9.01   Plaintiff repeats and re-alleges the factual allegations in the preceding paragraphs.

9.02   By the acts and omissions outlined above, Defendant has breached the automobile lease agreement between Plaintiff and Defendant.

9.03   Defendant demanded and Plaintiff paid more than the amounts owed under the lease. Despite demand, Defendant has failed and refused to refund the overpayments to Plaintiff.

9.04   As a result of one or more breaches of the lease contract by Defendant, Plaintiff has suffered damages for which she sues.

X.
DAMAGES

10.01   Defendant's acts and omissions as described herein have been a producing and/or proximate cause of damages to Plaintiff.

10.02   Plaintiff is entitled to a refund of payments made over and above the payments required by the Lease.

10.03   Further, Plaintiff has suffered damages to her credit and credit reputation. Defendant has reported the false amounts allegedly owed to credit reporting agencies which have then published this information to their customers. As a result, Plaintiff has been denied credit on terms which she would have been offered had the true status of this account with Defendant been reported.

10.04   Further, Plaintiff has suffered mental anguish damages in an amount within the jurisdictional limits of this court.

10.05   Further, Plaintiff is entitled to compensation for the reasonable value of Plaintiff's time and his expenses incurred in attempting to rectify the situation created by Defendant.

10.06   Further, Plaintiff is entitled to statutory damages under *Texas Finance Code* § 392.403 of at least $100.00 for each statutory violation by Defendant.

XI.
ADDITIONAL DAMAGES AND PUNITIVE DAMAGES

11.01   Defendant's conduct in violation of the DTPA was committed knowingly and/or intentionally as those terms are is defined in the DTPA. Accordingly, Defendant is liable for additional damages under the DTPA.

11.02   Defendant acted with malice and in flagrant disregard of the rights of Plaintiff with actual awareness that Plaintiff would, in reasonable probability, suffer mental anguish and additional damages from its conduct. Defendant acted intentionally and knowingly. Defendant is thus liable for exemplary damages in an amount to be determined by the jury.

XII.

ATTORNEY'S FEES

12.01   As a result of Defendant's conduct, Plaintiff has been required to obtain the services of the undersigned attorney for the filing, prosecution and trial of this cause, and therefore seeks an award of reasonable and necessary attorney's fees pursuant to applicable law.

XIII.

PRAYER

WHEREFORE, PREMISES CONSIDERED, Plaintiff respectfully prays that Defendant be cited to appear and answer herein, and that upon final trial hereof, Plaintiff recover from Defendant as follows:

1. Actual damages;
2. Statutory damages;
3. Additional damages;
4. Exemplary damages;
5. Pre-judgment and post-judgment interest as allowed by law;
6. A permanent injunction pursuant to *Tex. Fin. Code* § 392.403(a)(1) prohibiting Defendant from ever again:
   A. misrepresenting the character, extent, or amount of Plaintiff's consumer debt;
   B. harassing Plaintiff by making repeated telephone calls to her; and/or
   C. falsely reporting to any credit reporting agency or other third party that Plaintiff has not timely and fully paid Defendant all sums due under the lease in question.
7. Attorney's fees;
8. Costs of court; and,
9. Such other and further relief to which he may show herself justly entitled Plaintiff is entitled.

Respectfully submitted,

_____

ATTORNEY FOR PLAINTIFF

§5.30 Professional Services

[a] FORM: Petition for attorney's misrepresentations

	NO. _____	
_____	§	IN THE DISTRICT COURT OF
	§	
vs.	§	_____COUNTY, TEXAS
	§	
_____	§	_____ JUDICIAL DISTRICT

PLAINTIFF'S ORIGINAL PETITION

NOW COMES _____, Plaintiff herein, complaining of _____, Defendant herein, and respectfully shows as follows:

I.

DISCOVERY LEVEL

1.01   Pursuant to *Texas Rules of Civil Procedure* 190, Plaintiff intends to conduct discovery under a Level 2 Discovery Control Plan as defined in Rule 190.3.

II.

PARTIES

2.01   Plaintiff is an individual doing business under the assumed name of _____.

2.02.   Defendant is an individual residing in the State of Texas. He may be served with process at his residence which is [*address*].

II.

JURISDICTION

3.01   This Court has jurisdiction over this matter because the amount in controversy exceeds the minimum jurisdictional limits of this court.

IV.

VENUE

4.01   Venue is proper in _____ County, Texas because Defendant resides in _____ County, Texas.

IV.

CONDITIONS PRECEDENT

5.01   All conditions precedent to recovery have been performed, have occurred, or have been excused, including all notice required by any law upon which Plaintiff bases his claims.

VI.

BACKGROUND

6.01   Plaintiff owns and operates a tree farm in _____ County, Texas. On or about _____, 20__, _____ (an oil and gas company) negligently caused a fire at an oil well pad just south of [*plaintiff's*] property. The fire destroyed ____ acres of [*plaintiff's*] farm, and several hundred acres of adjoining land.

6.02   [*Plaintiff*] had an unassailable claim against [*company*] for the damages caused by the fire in question.

6.03   [*Plaintiff*] hired Defendant, who at all relevant times held himself out as an experienced trial lawyer to pursue his claims against [*company*].

6.04.   [*Defendant*] consulted with [*plaintiff*] and accepted representation of [*plaintiff*] against [*company*] no later than _____, 20__. [*Defendant*], an experienced trial lawyer, agreed to file a lawsuit on behalf of [*plaintiff*] against [*company*] and personally try and oversee the preparation of [*plaintiff*]'s case. At various times, when asked by [*plaintiff*] about the status of the case, [*defendant*] represented to [*plaintiff*] that [*defendant*] had filed suit on [*plaintiff*]'s behalf against [*company*], that the case was progressing, that [*defendant*] was in contact with opposing counsel about settlement, that the case was set for trial and pre-trial, and that [*defendant*] was "close to settlement." In fact, all of these statements were not true.

6.05   In reliance upon [*defendant's*] representations, [*plaintiff*] did not pursue his claims on his own. In reliance upon [*defendant's*] representations, [*plaintiff*] did not seek or retain competent counsel to pursue his claims. In reliance upon [*defendant's*] statements, [*plaintiff*] did not file suit against [*company*] within the applicable statute of limitations. Now [*plaintiff's*] claims against [*company*] are long barred by the statute of limitations.

6.06   The collectible damages to [*plaintiff's*] property from the [*company*] fire amount to $_____, and it is for these damages that he hired [*defendant*] to recover from [*company*], and now seeks to recover from [*defendant*].

VII.

FIRST CAUSES OF ACTION: DTPA

7.01 Plaintiff repeats and realleges the factual allegations in the preceding paragraphs.

7.02 Plaintiff is a consumer entitled to bring this action for relief under the *Texas Deceptive Trade Practices — Consumer Protection Act* (the "DTPA").

7.03 Defendant committed one or more acts in violation of the DTPA, including but not limited to:

a) Misrepresenting that services had characteristics or benefits which they did not have;

b) Failing to disclose information concerning services which was known at the time to induce a consumer into a transaction into which the consumer would not have entered had the information been disclosed; and/or

c) Engaging in unconscionable conduct and for an unconscionable course of conduct.

7.04 One or more of such violations by Defendant as described herein was a producing cause of damages to Plaintiff, for which he sues.

VIII.

SECOND CAUSE OF ACTION: PROFESSIONAL NEGLIGENCE

8.01 Plaintiff repeats and realleges the material allegations in the preceding paragraphs.

8.02 Defendant held himself out as competent and capable to pursue Plaintiff's claim against [*company*]. As an attorney engaged in the practice of law, Defendant owed Plaintiff a duty to act with the same care that an attorney of ordinary prudence would use under the same or similar circumstances. Thus, Defendant owed Plaintiff a duty to act as an attorney with knowledge under the same or similar circumstances.

8.03 Defendant breached these duties in one or more of the following ways:

a) Failing to timely and candidly advise Plaintiff of the status of Plaintiff's case;

b) Failing to timely file a lawsuit on Plaintiff's behalf; and/or

c) Failing to advise Plaintiff that a lawsuit had never been filed.

8.04   One or more of these acts or omissions separately or in combination, was a proximate cause of Plaintiff's damages for which he now sues.

IX.

DAMAGES

9.01   As a result of Defendant's conduct detailed above, Plaintiff has incurred substantial damages in the loss of recoverable compensation for fire damages to ____ acres of timber producing land totaling $_____.

X.

EXEMPLARY DAMAGES

10.01   Plaintiff would show that Defendant's conduct was grossly negligent and that Defendant, in committing that conduct was consciously indifferent to the interests of Plaintiff. Defendant owed Plaintiff a fiduciary duty of loyalty, honesty and the utmost of good faith; yet, Defendant lied to and deceived Plaintiff in the handling of the legal claim entrusted to Defendant. Defendant was actually and subjectively aware of the extreme degree of risk of harm to Plaintiff's interests of his conduct yet proceeded with conscious indifference and reckless disregard toward the rights of Plaintiff. Accordingly, Plaintiff seeks an award for exemplary damages from Defendant as punishment for engaging in such conduct and as a deterrence to others.

XI.

ATTORNEY'S FEES

11.01   In order to prosecute his claim against Defendant, the Plaintiff has retained the undersigned attorney and has agreed to pay his usual and customary fees. Plaintiff seeks all reasonable and necessary attorney's fees in this case which include the following: (a) preparation and trial of this lawsuit; (b) post-trial, pre-trial legal services; (c) an appeal to the Court of Appeals; (d) making or responding to an application for writ of error to the Supreme Court of Texas; (e) an appeal to the Supreme Court of Texas in the event application for writ of error is granted; and (f) post-judgment discovery and collection in the event the execution on the judgment is necessary.

XII.

REQUEST FOR DISCLOSURE

12.01   Pursuant to *Texas Rule of Civil Procedure*, Rule 194, Defendant is requested to disclose within fifty (50) days of service of this pleading, the information and material described in *Tex. R. Civ. P.* 194.2.

XIII.

JURY DEMAND

13.01   Plaintiff specifically requests a trial by jury of the matters herein.

XIV.

PRAYER

WHEREFORE, PREMISES CONSIDERED, Plaintiff prays that Defendant be duly cited to appear and answer herein, and that upon trial of this case, Plaintiff be awarded Judgment against Defendant for actual damages, including:

a. the lost recovery of his fire damages claim against [*company*];
b. exemplary damages;
c. pre- and post-judgment interest at the rates allowed by law;
d. costs of court;
e. attorney's fees; and
f. all other and further relief in law or in equity to which Plaintiff may be justly entitled.

Respectfully submitted,

_____

ATTORNEY FOR PLAINTIFF

§5.31 Residential Repair Services

[a] FORM: Misrepresentation re services performed

```
                        NO. _____
_____              §    IN THE DISTRICT COURT OF
                        §
vs.                     §    _____ COUNTY, TEXAS
                        §
_____              §    _____ JUDICIAL DISTRICT
```

PLAINTIFF'S ORIGINAL PETITION

NOW COMES _____, Plaintiffs herein, complaining of _____ and _____, doing business together under the assumed name of _____, Defendants herein, and for cause of action, would show unto the Court as follows:

I.

DISCOVERY CONTROL PLAN DESIGNATION

1.01   Discovery in this case is intended to be conducted under Level 1, pursuant to Rule 190.2, *Texas Rules of Civil Procedure*. Plaintiffs affirmatively aver that they seek only monetary relief aggregating $_____ or less, excluding costs, prejudgment interest and attorney's fees.

II.

PARTIES

2.01   [*Plaintiff 1*] is a resident of _____, Texas.

2.02   [*Plaintiff 2*] is a resident of _____, Texas.

2.03   [*Defendant 1*] is an individual who is doing business under the assumed name of [*company*], and resides and/or may be served at _____.

2.04   [*Defendant 1*] is an individual who is doing business under the assumed name of [*company*], and resides and/or may be served at _____.

III.

VENUE

3.01   Venue of this action is proper in _____, Texas because the events made a basis of Plaintiff's claims and causes of action occurred, in whole or in part, in _____, Texas.

IV.

CONDITIONS PRECEDENT

4.01   All conditions precedent to recovery by Plaintiff herein have been performed, have occurred, or have been excused.

V.

PARTNERSHIP

5.01   At all times relevant herein, [*defendants*] were engaged in business together as a general partnership under the assumed name of [*company*]. Where it is alleged herein that either Defendants committed an act, failed to perform an act, made a representation or statement or failed to make a disclosure, it is alleged that Defendants were acting in the course and scope of their partnership business with full authority, either express, implied, apparent or direct, or that Defendants subsequently ratified the acts and omissions of the other. Accordingly, Defendants are each vicariously liable for the acts, omissions, statement and conduct of the other as alleged herein.

VI.

FACTS OF CASE

6.01   On or about _____, 20__, Plaintiffs hired Defendants to repair the septic system at their residence in _____, Texas. For these services, Defendants charged Plaintiffs $_____.

6.02   Defendants did not inform Plaintiffs that the work they were doing required a permit. Defendants did not inform Plaintiffs that the work they were doing was illegal without a permit. Defendants failed to obtain a proper permit or approval of their plans from the _____ County Health Department in violation of *Texas Health and Safety Code* Section 366.051 *et seq.*

6.03   The work done by Defendants on Plaintiffs' septic system was substandard and did not meet the code requirements of _____ County or the State of Texas. As a result, Plaintiffs could not use the septic system and had to abandon it.

6.04   Plaintiffs were then required to completely replace their septic system at their home.

VII.
FIRST CAUSE OF ACTION: BREACH OF CONTRACT

7.01   Plaintiff repeats and realleges the material allegations in the preceding paragraphs.

7.02   Plaintiffs entered into a contract with Defendants for the improvement of their septic system and paid Defendants $4,000.00 for that work.

7.03   Defendants breached that contract by failing to perform the work as agreed.

7.04   Despite demand, Defendants have failed and refused to return the monies paid to Defendants for this work in the amount of $_____. By their actions as alleged herein, Defendants have breached one or more contracts with Plaintiffs resulting in damages to Plaintiffs for which they sue.

VIII.
SECOND CAUSE OF ACTION: DTPA

8.01   Plaintiff repeats and realleges the material allegations in the preceding paragraphs.

8.02   Plaintiffs are consumers within the definition of the *Texas Deceptive Trade Practices - Consumer Protection Act* ("the DTPA").

8.03   By their actions above, Defendants have engaged in one or more acts or omissions actionable under the DTPA which, together or separately, has been a producing cause of damages to Plaintiffs, including one or more of the following:

A. Representing the goods or services had approval, characteristics, uses or benefits which they did not have;

B. Representing the goods or services were of a particular standard, quality or grade when they were of another;

C. Failing to disclose information concerning goods or services which were known at the time of the transaction when such failure to disclose such information was intended to induce a consumer into a transaction in which the consumer would not have entered had the information been disclosed.

8.04   Further, Defendants committed actionable conduct under the DTPA by breaching the implied warranty that services would be performed in a good and workmanlike manner. The services performed by Defendants were inferior and did not pass inspection and was not the quality of work performed by a person who has the knowledge, training or experience necessary for the successful practice of repairing septic systems in Texas.

8.05   Further, by their conduct above, Defendants engaged in unconscionable conduct and/or an unconscionable course of conduct by taking advantage of Plaintiffs' lack of knowledge and experience to a grossly unfair degree.

8.06   One or more of Defendants' acts or omissions actionable under the DTPA was a producing cause of damages to Plaintiffs, for which they sue.

IX.

DAMAGES

9.01   As a result of the shoddy, unlicensed and unapproved work done by Defendants on Plaintiffs' septic system, they lost the use of their septic system completely. Further, Plaintiffs, in order to salvage the damage done, were required to install a replacement septic system. The reasonable cost to Plaintiffs for the repairs made to their septic system is $_____.

9.02   Further, Plaintiffs paid Defendants $_____ and received nothing of value in return.

9.03   Further, Plaintiffs have been forced to use their free time correcting and attempting to correct the problems with the septic system at their home. Plaintiffs therefore seek compensation for their time.

9.04   Further, Plaintiffs have suffered the loss of use of their home during the time that the repairs were being made. Plaintiffs therefore seek compensation for the loss of use of their home.

9.05   As described herein, Plaintiffs' damages exceed the minimum jurisdictional limits of this court.

X.

ADDITIONAL DAMAGES

10.01   Defendants' conduct in violation of the DTPA was committed knowingly or intentionally. Accordingly, Defendants are liable for additional, treble damages under the DTPA.

XI.

ATTORNEY'S FEES

11.01   As a result of Defendants' conduct, Plaintiffs have been required to obtain the services of the undersigned attorney for the filing, prosecution and trial of this cause, and therefore seeks an award of reasonable and necessary attorney's fees pursuant to applicable law.

XII.

REQUEST FOR DISCLOSURE

12.01   Pursuant to *Texas Rules of Civil Procedure*, Rule 194, Defendants are requested to disclose within fifty (50) days of service of this pleading, the information and material described in T.R.C.P., Rule 194.2.

WHEREFORE, PREMISES CONSIDERED, Plaintiffs respectfully pray that Defendants be cited to appear and answer herein, and that upon final trial hereof, Plaintiffs recover from Defendants, jointly and severally, all of their actual damages, additional damages, pre-judgment and post-judgment interest as allowed by law, attorney's fees, costs of court and such other and further relief to which they may show themselves justly entitled.

Respectfully submitted,

_____

ATTORNEY FOR PLAINTIFF

(This page intentionally left blank.)

Chapter 6

Defendant's Pleadings

§6.01 Pleas in Abatement
   §6.01.1 Inadequate Notice of Claim
      [a] FORM: Plea in abatement (inadequate notice of claim)
      [b] FORM: Order on plea in abatement
   §6.01.2 Refusal to Allow Inspection
      [a] FORM: Plea in abatement: no opportunity to inspect
      [b] FORM: Order on plea in abatement
   §6.01.3 Plea in Abatement—Mediation/Arbitration Agreements
      [a] FORM: Plea in abatement: mediation/arbitration
      [b] FORM: Order on plea in abatement
§6.02 [Reserved]
§6.03 Motion to Transfer Venue
   [a] FORM: Motion to transfer venue
   [b] FORM: Affidavit in support of motion to transfer venue
   [c] FORM: Order sustaining motion to transfer venue
§6.04 Original Answer
   [a] FORM: Original answer (general form)
§6.05 Special Exceptions: Inadequacy of Pleadings
§6.06 Affirmative Defenses: DTPA
   [a] FORM: Original answer with affirmative defenses
§6.07 Affirmative Defense: Waiver
   [a] FORM: Affirmative defense: waiver
§6.08 Affirmative Defenses: Residential Construction
§6.09 Affirmative Defense: Professional Opinion
   [a] FORM: Affirmative defense: professional opinion
   §6.09.1 Affirmative Defense: Claim Arises Out of Written Contract
      [a] FORM: Affirmative defense: claim arises out of written contract
   §6.09.2 Affirmative Defense: Transaction Exceeds DTPA's Dollar Limit
      [a] FORM: Affirmative defense: consideration paid exceeds DTPA's transactional cap
   §6.09.3 Affirmative Defense: "As Is" Purchases
      [a] FORM: Affirmative defense: "as is" real estate purchase
   §6.09.4 Affirmative Defense: Independent Investigation
      [a] FORM: Affirmative defense: independent investigation
   §6.09.5 Affirmative Defense: Reasonable Settlement Offer
      [a] FORM: Affirmative defense: reasonable settlement offer

§6.09.6 Affirmative Defense: Texas CRPC Chapter 33
 [a] FORM: Damages recovered must be reduced by value of settlement
§6.10 Counterclaim for Bad Faith and Harassment
 [a] FORM: Counterclaim for bad faith, harassment
§6.11 Leave to Designate Responsible Third Party
 [a] FORM: Motion for leave to designate responsible third party

§6.01 Pleas in Abatement

Pleas in abatement are authorized by the rules of civil procedure. *See* TEX. R. CIV. P. 85. A plea in abatement is a plea setting forth some obstacle to the further prosecution of the case, and, if sustained, the proper action is to abate the case until the impediment is removed. *See* 2 MCDONALD, TEXAS CIVIL PRACTICE, *"Pleading: Answer"* §9:12; *Union Pacific Fuels, Inc. v. Johnson*, 909 S.W.2d 130 (Tex. App.—Houston [14th Dist.] 1995, no writ). The purpose of a plea in abatement is not to dismiss the action in which it is filed; instead, the purpose is to delay the action until the occurrence of some other event on which the abatement is based. *Texas Highway Department v. Jarrell*, 418 S.W.2d 486, 488 (Tex. 1967). Generally, the party asserting the plea in abatement has the burden of proof, including the burden of introducing evidence to support the plea, unless the truth of the matter appears on the face of the plaintiff's pleadings. *Lake Country Estates, Inc. v. Toman*, 624 S.W.2d 677 (Tex. App.—Fort Worth 1981, writ ref'd, n.r.e.). It is important to distinguish cases in which a plea in abatement is filed as a means of enforcing an arbitration agreement. In these cases, once the agreement to arbitrate is established, the party seeking to avoid arbitration has the burden of proof. *Hearthshire Braeswood v. Bill Kelly Co.*, 849 S.W.2d 380 (Tex. App.—Houston [14th Dist.] 1993, writ denied). Proof either of the plea or the grounds to avoid arbitration must be by a preponderance of the evidence. *Atkinson v. Reid*, 625 S.W.2d 64 (Tex. App.—San Antonio 1981, no writ).

Although pleas in abatement are not on the list of pleadings that must be filed under oath (*see* TEX. R. CIV. P. 93), there is authority which holds that such pleas must be verified. *Sparks v. Bolton*, 335 S.W.2d 780 (TEX. CIV. APP.—Dallas 1960, no writ); *see also*, 2 MCDONALD, TEXAS CIVIL TRIAL PRACTICE "PLEADING: ANSWER" §9:8. And, as noted, under the 1995 amendments, abatement is "automatic" if no controverting affidavit is filed to a verified plea in abatement. For these reasons, any plea in abatement alleging improper notice should contain an affidavit supporting the plea.

A plea in abatement may be filed as a separate instrument or within the body of the original answer so long as the plea contains all of the requisite elements. In order to be sufficient, the plea must:

(1) describe the circumstances relied upon to justify abatement in detail; and

(2) provide the information necessary to apprise the plaintiff of the correct procedure that needs to be followed to cure the cause of the abatement.

See Bluebonnet Farms v. Gibraltar Sav. Ass'n, 618 S.W.2d 81 (Tex. Civ. App.—Houston [1st Dist.] 1980, writ ref'd n.r.e.).

As with any dilatory plea, a plea in abatement can be waived if it is not timely filed; however, the absence of a deadline fixed by law, courts are to examine the equities of the situation to determine whether a plea is timely. *Bluebonnet Farms v. Gibraltar Savings Ass'n*, 618 S.W.2d 81 (Tex. App.—Houston [1st Dist.] 1980, writ ref'd n.r.e.).

§6.01.1 Inadequate Notice of Claim

Statutory reference: DTPA §17.505(a); TEX. PROP. CODE §27.004(a)

Before a lawsuit is filed against a person under the DTPA, the plaintiff must give sixty days advance written notice of the claim. DTPA §17.505(a). The notice letter must include: (1) a statement of the complaint,

(2) a statement of the amount of damages sought (unless no monetary relief is or will be sought), and (3) a statement of the amount of expenses, including attorney's fees, if any, incurred by the consumer in asserting the claim. *See* DTPA §17.505(a); §3.02, §3.03 *supra*. As a result of the 1995 amendments, a consumer must specify the amount of economic damages, the amount of mental anguish damages and the expenses, including attorney's fees claimed. DTPA §17.505(a), as amended 1995.

When a lawsuit involves defective residential construction, the Property Code requires that plaintiff give defendant pre-filing notice. TEX. PROP. CODE §27.004(a). The notice must include a description of the defects "in reasonable detail." *Id.* The letter need not state an amount of damages or attorney's fees; however, if plaintiff brings suit under the DTPA, then plaintiff should follow the DTPA notice provisions.

The defendant's remedy for not receiving pre-suit notice is abatement, not dismissal. Moreover, the defendant cannot wait until the eve of trial to raise the plaintiff's failure to provide pre-suit notice. In *Hines v. Hash*, 843 S.W.2d 464 (Tex. 1992), the Supreme Court held that if no notice is given or if the notice which is given is insufficient, the defendant may file a plea in abatement, either with the answer or "very soon thereafter." By failing to do so, the defendant was held to have waived the right to the pre-suit notice. *Id.* at 469. In 1995, the DTPA notice provisions were amended to incorporate the rule announced in *Hines* and to specify the time period within which the plea in abatement must be filed. Section 17.505(c) of the statute now provides:

> A person against whom a suit is pending who does not receive written notice, as required by Subsection (a), may file a plea in abatement not later than the 30th day after the date the person files an original answer in the court in which the suit is pending. This subsection does not apply if [no notice is required].

DTPA §17.505(c), as amended 1995.

The 1995 amendment also provides that the court shall abate the suit if the court finds that "notice was not provided as required by this section." DTPA §17.505(d), as amended 1995. The RCLA similarly provides that the court shall abate the lawsuit if it finds that the claimant failed to provide the contractor with notice of the construction defects and an opportunity to inspect. TEX. PROP. CODE §27.004(d). Under both the DTPA and the RCLA, a defendant can obtain an "automatic" abatement of the suit, if the plea in abatement:

1. Is verified and alleges that the person against whom the suit is pending did not receive the written notice required by Subsection (a); and

2. Is not controverted by an affidavit filed by the consumer before the 11th day after the date on which the plea in abatement is filed.

DTPA §17.505(d), as amended 1995; Tex. Prop. Code §27.004(d); *see In Re Kimball Homes Texas, Inc.* 969 S.W.2d 522 (Tex. App — Houston [14th Dist.] 1998, no writ).

If the abatement is "automatic" under subsection (d), then it continues until the 60th day after the date that proper written notice is served. DTPA §17.505(e), as amended 1995.

Under the current version of the DTPA, the notice letter triggers an opportunity for the defendant to set up one or more defenses to the DTPA claim. By making a settlement offer that is substantially the same as or more than the damages found by the trier of fact, the defendant can limit the plaintiff's recovery to the lesser of the settlement offer or the damages found. DTPA §17.5052(g); *see* §4.01, *supra*. Additionally, a reasonable offer that includes an offer for attorney's fees that is substantially the same as or more than the amount actually incurred by the plaintiff up to the point of the settlement offer will limit the plaintiff's recovery of attorney's fees to the amount tendered in the settlement offer. DTPA §17,5052(h); *see* §4.01, *supra*. Further, by tendering the full amounts of damages claimed and the amount of attorney's fees reasonably incurred, the defendant will have a complete defense to the plaintiff's DTPA claim. DTPA §17.506(d).

If no notice letter is provided, these particular defenses are lost to the defendant. Timely abatement is therefore necessary for the defendant to set up these defenses at a point where the attorney's fees and expenses incurred by the consumer are significantly less than the amount of fees and expenses that will be incurred through trial. A defendant should therefore take advantage of the plea in abatement procedure provided by DTPA §17.505 in almost every instance when a recovery by the plaintiff under the DTPA is possible.

There will be circumstances when the plea in abatement for lack of pre-suit notice need not be asserted. The cost of obtaining an abatement should be measured against the benefit to be realized. When there is little doubt about the nature of the plaintiff's claim and, after consultation, the defendant has no intention of making a settlement offer, the right to an abatement can be intelligently waived by not filing a plea in abatement. The defendant will then save the expense required to prepare and file the plea and obtain a hearing.

If a notice letter has been given but it was not received until after the lawsuit was filed, it may be more efficient to simply respond to the letter rather than seeking an abatement and then responding. The Texas Supreme Court has held that it was not error for the trial court to refuse to abate the case when its abatement order was entered more than 60 days after the notice was received. *In Re Alford Chevrolet-Geo*, 997 S.W.2d 173 (Tex. 1999). The court held that the defendant had received the full sixty days opportunity to make a settlement offer; therefore, no further abatement was required.

In addition to the opportunity to set up the settlement defenses discussed above, other advantages may be gained from abatement. For example, the DTPA now requires that each defendant in a case involving goods be given the opportunity to inspect any claimed defects in the goods. *See* DTPA §17.505(a). A similar right of inspection is contained in the Property Code for cases involving residential construction. *See* Tex. Prop. Code §27.004(a). Unlike other DTPA cases, however, the Property Code also requires that the defendant be allowed to make an offer to repair residential construction defects. In either DTPA or residential construction cases, the "free" discovery provided by an inspection can provide substantial benefits either in evaluating the need for a possible settlement offer or in the litigation that may follow. In residential construction cases, an offer to repair made during the pre-filing notice period can possibly reduce the amount of damages that a plaintiff can recover. When substantial benefits such as these are available because of the plaintiff's failure to provide proper notice, defendant should file plea of abatement to require that notice be given in the manner and form required by DTPA §17.505(a). If the plaintiff fails to give notice after the lawsuit has been abated a reasonable amount of time for that purpose, the plaintiff's claim is subject to dismissal. *Hines*, 843 S.W.2d at 469 *(citing Miller v. Kossey*, 802 S.W.2d 873, 876-77 (Tex. App.—Amarillo 1991, writ den'd); *see Richardson v. Foster & Sear, L.L.P.*, 257 S.W.3d 782, 785 (Tex. App.—Fort Worth 2008, no writ).

In DTPA cases or those involving Chapter 27 of the Property Code, obviously the abatement is based on the plaintiff's failure to give pre-filing notice; therefore, the abatement should continue until notice is given and the appropriate statutory response period has expired. *See* DTPA §17.505(a); TEX. PROP. CODE §27.004(a).

[a] FORM: Plea in abatement (inadequate notice of claim)

```
                          NO. _____
_____              §    IN THE DISTRICT COURT OF
                          §
vs.                       §    _____COUNTY, TEXAS
                          §
_____              §    _____ JUDICIAL DISTRICT
```

PLEA IN ABATEMENT

TO THE HONORABLE JUDGE OF THE DISTRICT COURT:

_____, defendant, files this plea in abatement against _____, plaintiff, and will show the following:

1.

Plaintiff failed to give the pre-filing notice of this suit as required by law; therefore, this suit should be abated until such notice is given.

2.

Specifically, TEX. BUS. & COM. CODE §17.505(a), required plaintiff to give defendant written notice, at least sixty days before this suit was filed, advising defendant in reasonable detail of plaintiff's specific complaint(s) as well as the amount of damages and expenses, including attorney's fees, if any, reasonably incurred by plaintiff in asserting the claim against defendant.

[or]

Specifically, TEX. PROP. CODE §27.004(a) required plaintiff to give defendant written notice, at least sixty days before this suit was filed, advising defendant in reasonable detail of the alleged defects in the construction on which plaintiff's suit is based.

3.

Plaintiff failed to give any written notice to defendant before this suit was filed.

[*or*]

Although plaintiff sent defendant a letter in which a general complaint was made, the written notice failed to [*insert defects in notice, e.g.,* contain an amount of damages or expenses].

4.

Because of plaintiff's failure to comply with the statutory notice requirements, defendant has been deprived of any meaningful opportunity to resolve this matter prior to the filing of the lawsuit.

WHEREFORE, defendant requests that this suit be abated until such time as proper notice has been given and defendant has had [*insert response time allowed by statute, e.g.,* sixty] days from the date the notice is received to respond to it.

Respectfully submitted,

[Signature of attorney]

STATE OF TEXAS   §
                          §
COUNTY OF _____   §

AFFIDAVIT

BEFORE ME the undersigned Notary Public on this day personally appeared _____ who after having been by me duly cautioned and sworn did state to me upon his [her] oath that he [she] is the defendant in the above-referenced cause, has read the Plea in Abatement set forth above and that based on his [her] own personal knowledge, the facts contained in the plea and true and correct.

[Signature of affiant]

SUBSCRIBED AND SWORN TO before me on this ____ day of _____, 20___, to certify which witness my hand and official seal.

[Signature and seal of notary public]

[Certificate of service]

[b] FORM: Order on plea in abatement

```
                              NO. _____
                          §    IN THE DISTRICT COURT OF
_____              §
                          §
vs.                       §    _____COUNTY, TEXAS
                          §
_____              §    _____ JUDICIAL DISTRICT
```

ORDER ON PLEA IN ABATEMENT

On this _____ day of _____, 20___, came on for hearing defendant's Plea in Abatement; and it appears to the court that the plea is well taken and should be granted.

The court finds that the plaintiff failed to give notice of his [her] claim to defendant in writing more than sixty days before this suit was filed in the manner and form required by TEX. BUS. & COM. CODE §17.505(a) [or TEX. PROP. CODE §27.004(a)].

[or]

The court finds that defendant's plea in abatement was properly verified and that plaintiff has failed to file a controverting affidavit before the eleventh day after the plea in abatement was filed.

IT IS THEREFORE ORDERED that this suit is abated until sixty days after the day on which defendant receives proper written notice from plaintiff in which is contained in reasonable detail a statement of plaintiff's claim(s), as well as a statement of the amount of plaintiff's damages and expenses and the amount of attorney's fees incurred, if any, in the reasonable pursuit of plaintiff's claim [or in which is contained a list in reasonable detail of the claimed construction defects about which plaintiff complains].

SIGNED this _____ day of _____, 20___.

[Signature of presiding judge]

§6.01.2 Refusal to Allow Inspection

Statutory reference: DTPA §17.505(a); TEX. PROP. CODE §27.004(a)

As discussed in the preceding section, in addition to the DTPA notice requirement, a consumer must allow the prospective defendant the opportunity to inspect the "goods" that are involved in the claim (*see* DTPA §17.505[a]), and in the case of defective residential construction, the consumer must allow the prospective defendant the opportunity to inspect and to document the alleged defects. *See* TEX. PROP. CODE §27.004(a).

If a lawsuit is filed before an opportunity to inspect the property has been offered, a plea in abatement is proper if both of the following have occurred:

1. A written request for inspection has been made.

2. The request for inspection was timely.

Both DTPA §17.505(a) and TEX. PROP. CODE §27.004(a) require the prospective defendant to make a *written* request for an inspection. A written request to inspect the goods under the DTPA must be made during the sixty day period following receipt of the consumer's demand letter. DTPA §17.505(a). When the complaint involves defective residential construction, however, the opportunity to inspect must be requested during the thirty-five day period after the contractor receives the demand letter. TEX. PROP. CODE §27.004(a).

When a proper request has been made to inspect the goods or the residence but the request has either been refused or ignored, any lawsuit that is filed should be subject to a plea in abatement until the inspection occurs.

If the case proceeds to trial and still there has been no opportunity to inspect, the defendant has the burden of pleading and proving that he or she was denied a reasonable opportunity to inspect the goods or real property. *Smith v. Levine*, 911 S.W.2d 427 (Tex. App.—San Antonio 1995, writ denied).

[a] FORM: Plea in abatement: no opportunity to inspect

```
                NO. _____
_____       §     IN THE DISTRICT COURT OF
                 §
vs.              §     _____ COUNTY, TEXAS
                 §
_____       §     _____ JUDICIAL DISTRICT
```

PLEA IN ABATEMENT

TO THE HONORABLE JUDGE OF THE DISTRICT COURT:

_____, defendant, files this plea in abatement against _____, plaintiff, and will show the following:

1.

On _____, defendant received a demand letter from plaintiff concerning the transaction which is the subject of this suit. On _____, within sixty [thirty-five] days after the letter was received, defendant made a written request of plaintiff that defendant be allowed to inspect the claimed defects in the goods [residential property].

2.

Defendant's request was made under the authority of Tex. Bus. & Com. Code §17.505(a) [Tex. Prop. Code §27.004(a)] which, upon request, specifically requires that such an inspection be allowed as a condition precedent to filing suit.

3.

Plaintiff failed to respond to defendant's request for an inspection.

[or]

Plaintiff agreed to allow the inspection; however, plaintiff refused to schedule the inspection at a reasonable time so that it was impossible for the inspection to occur.

4.

Because of plaintiff's failure to comply with the statutory inspection requirements, defendant has been deprived of any meaningful opportunity to evaluate the condition of the goods [residential property] to determine whether it is possible to resolve this matter prior to the filing of a lawsuit.

WHEREFORE, defendant requests that this suit be abated until such time as the opportunity to inspect has been provided and defendant has had [thirty] days from the date the inspection is allowed to evaluate the findings and respond to plaintiff's demand letter.

Respectfully submitted,

[Signature of attorney]

STATE OF TEXAS   §
                        §
COUNTY OF _____   §

AFFIDAVIT

BEFORE ME the undersigned Notary Public on this day personally appeared _____ who after having been by me duly cautioned and sworn did state to me upon his [her] oath that he [she] is the defendant in the above-referenced cause, has read the Plea in Abatement set forth above and that based on his [her] own personal knowledge, the facts contained in the plea are true and correct.

[Signature of affiant]

SUBSCRIBED AND SWORN TO before me on this ____ day of _____, 20___, to certify which witness my hand and official seal.

[Signature and seal of notary public]

[Certificate of service]

[b]   FORM: Order on plea in abatement

```
                          NO. _____
_____          §      IN THE DISTRICT COURT OF
                          §
vs.                       §      _____ COUNTY, TEXAS
                          §
_____          §      _____ JUDICIAL DISTRICT
```

ORDER ON PLEA IN ABATEMENT

On this day came on for hearing defendant's Plea in Abatement; and it appears to the court that the plea is well taken and should be granted.

Specifically, the court finds that although requested in the manner and form required by law, plaintiff failed to give defendant a reasonable opportunity to inspect the claimed defects in the goods [residential property] which are the subject of this suit as required by Tex. Bus. & Com. Code §17.505(a) [Tex. Prop. Code §27.004(a)].

IT IS THEREFORE ORDERED that this suit is abated until [sixty] days after the day on which defendant is provided an opportunity to inspect the goods [residential property].

IT IS FURTHER ORDERED that defendant shall have the opportunity during this [sixty] day period to make an offer of settlement as provided by Tex. Bus. & Com. Code §17.505(c) [Tex. Prop. Code §27.004(b)] the same as if such offer had been made within the statutory notice period.

SIGNED this _____ day of _____ 20___.

[Signature of presiding Judge]

§6.01.3 Plea in Abatement Mediation/Arbitration Agreements

Arbitration is discussed in some detail in §8.01.5 *infra*.

In those cases in which arbitration agreements exist, a plea in abatement may be filed as a means of enforcing the arbitration agreement. The following forms may be used in this situation.

[a] FORM: Plea in abatement: mediation/arbitration

```
                              NO. _____
_____                    §       IN THE DISTRICT COURT OF
                              §
   vs.                        §       _____COUNTY, TEXAS
                              §
_____                    §       _____ JUDICIAL DISTRICT
```

PLEA IN ABATEMENT

TO THE HONORABLE JUDGE OF THE DISTRICT COURT:

_____, defendant, files this plea in abatement against _____, plaintiff, and will show the following:

1.

Plaintiff and defendant entered into an agreement on or about _____ in which the parties agreed to submit any disputes arising out of the transaction which is the subject of this suit to mediation [arbitration]. A copy of the agreement is attached to this plea as "Exhibit A" and is incorporated at this point as if fully set forth.

2.

Although defendant has requested that this dispute be submitted to mediation [arbitration], the mediation has not yet occurred for the reason that [the parties have been unable to agree on a date for the mediation *or* plaintiff has refused to participate in mediation].

[NOTE: The following paragraph should be added if interstate commerce is involved because the Federal Arbitration Act preempts the Texas statute in these situations].

3.

This transaction involves a contract evidencing a transaction involving interstate commerce.

WHEREFORE, defendant requests that this suit be abated until such time as mediation [arbitration] has occurred.

Respectfully submitted,

[Signature of attorney]

STATE OF TEXAS §
§
COUNTY OF _____ §

AFFIDAVIT

BEFORE ME the undersigned Notary Public on this day personally appeared _____ who after having been by me duly cautioned and sworn did state to me upon his [her] oath that he [she] is the defendant in the above-referenced cause, has read the Plea in Abatement set forth above and that based on his [her] own personal knowledge, the facts contained in the plea are true and correct.

[Signature of affiant]

SUBSCRIBED AND SWORN TO before me on this ____ day of _____, 20___, to certify which witness my hand and official seal.

[Signature and seal of notary public]

[Certificate of service]

[b] FORM: Order on plea in abatement

NO. _____

_____ § IN THE DISTRICT COURT OF
§
vs. § _____COUNTY, TEXAS
§
_____ § _____ JUDICIAL DISTRICT

ORDER ON PLEA IN ABATEMENT

On this day came on for hearing defendant's Plea in Abatement; and it appears to the court that the plea is well taken and should be granted.

Specifically, the court finds that there is an enforceable agreement between the parties to submit all disputes arising out of the transaction which is the subject of this lawsuit to mediation [arbitration]. The court further finds that such mediation [arbitration] has not yet occurred.

IT IS THEREFORE ORDERED that this suit is abated until such time as mediation [arbitration] has occurred as provided in the mediation [arbitration] agreement.

SIGNED this _____ day of _____ 20___.

[Signature of presiding Judge]

§6.02 [Reserved]

§6.03 Motion to Transfer Venue

A motion to transfer venue is governed by the due order of pleadings. The motion must be filed prior to or simultaneously with any other plea except a special appearance; otherwise, any complaint concerning venue is waived. TEX. R. CIV. P. 86(1).

Prior to the 1995 amendments to the Civil Practice and Remedies Code, venue under the DTPA could be sustained on the basis of the DTPA's own venue provision, see DTPA §17.56, or under any other general or special venue statute. The 1995 amendments to the DTPA and the Civil Practice and Remedies Code attempted to repeal the DTPA's venue provisions and require that, DTPA venue be controlled by Chapter 15 of the Civil Practice and Remedies Code. 1995 TEX. GEN. LAWS, Chap. 138 §7, p. 978. However, the 1995 legislature passed two versions of DTPA §17.56, *see* §5.14 *supra,* and the second version allows for alternate venue in the county in which the transaction was solicited. See DTPA §17.56(2), as amended by 1995 TEX. GEN. LAWS, Chap. 414 §9..

The defendant must specifically deny the venue facts pleaded by the plaintiff in the motion to transfer venue because, "[a]ll venue facts, when properly pleaded shall be taken as true unless specifically denied by the adverse party." Tex. R. Civ. P. 87(3)(a).

When the venue facts have been specifically denied, the party pleading the venue facts has the burden of making "prima facie proof" of the facts necessary to sustain venue in the county of suit. Tex. R. Civ. P. 87(3)(a).

Prima facie proof of venue facts is made by properly pleading venue facts and by filing one or more supporting affidavits in proper form. Tex. R. Civ. P. 87(3)(a). *See* §5.05 *infra*.

When the issues have been joined by pleadings and affidavits, the court shall determine proper venue by considering the pleadings, any stipulations between the parties, and such affidavits and attachments as have been filed. Tex. R. Civ. P. 87(3)(b).

It is important to note that affidavits made in support of transferring or retaining venue must be based on personal knowledge, set forth such facts as would be admissible in evidence, and show affirmatively that the affiant is competent to testify about the matters contained in the affidavit. Tex. R. Civ. P. 87(3)(a). When affidavits are required to be in this form, the affiant must state how he or she acquired the knowledge of the facts contained in the affidavit. *See e.g., Radio Station KSCS v. Jennings,* 750 S.W.2d 760 (Tex. 1988).

Under Rule 87(3)(b) and Rule 88, the court is specifically authorized to consider the product of any discovery that the parties may have completed, including answers to interrogatories, admissions, properly proved documents and deposition testimony. Tex. R. Civ. P. 87(3)(b), 88.

[a] FORM: Motion to transfer venue

```
                        NO. _____
                         §
_____               §      IN THE DISTRICT COURT OF
                         §
   vs.                   §      _____COUNTY, TEXAS
                         §
_____               §      _____ JUDICIAL DISTRICT
```

<u>MOTION TO TRANSFER VENUE</u>

TO THE HONORABLE JUDGE OF THE DISTRICT COURT:

_____, defendant, moves the Court to transfer venue of this action to _____ County, Texas, and as grounds for this motion will show the following:

Defendant specially denies that [*insert specific denial of venue facts, e.g.*, defendant had a fixed and established place of business in this county at the time suit was filed].

2.

The county in which this lawsuit has been filed is not a proper county with respect to venue.

[*or*]

Mandatory venue of this lawsuit is in _____ County, Texas as required by [*insert statute which mandates venue in another county, e.g.*, TEX. CIV. PRAC. & REM. CODE §_____].

3.

This action should be transferred to _____ County, Texas for the reason that [*insert venue facts to support transfer, e.g.* defendant is a resident of _____ County, Texas and has been during all of the transactions with plaintiff on which plaintiff's lawsuit is based].

[NOTE: If venue of the action is mandatory in another county, then the specific facts supporting mandatory venue should be stated.]

4.

Defendant further specially denies that there is any venue rule or law which applies to the facts alleged in plaintiff's petition under which venue can be maintained in the county of suit.

5.

Defendant requests a hearing on this motion to transfer venue.

[NOTE: The movant has the burden to request a setting for a hearing on the motion to transfer. TEX. R. CIV. P. 87(1).]

WHEREFORE, defendant requests that after hearing this court enter its order transferring venue of this action to _____ County, Texas, and that defendant be awarded costs as well as such other relief to which defendant may be entitled.

Respectfully submitted,

[Signature of attorney]

[Attach affidavits, if any]

[Certificate of service]

[b] FORM: —Affidavit in support of motion to transfer venue

[NOTE: The motion to transfer venue need not be verified. TEX. R. CIV. P. 86(3); however, an affidavit should be filed to support transfer of the lawsuit to a particular county.]

	NO. _____	
_____	§	IN THE DISTRICT COURT OF
	§	
vs.	§	_____ COUNTY, TEXAS
	§	
_____	§	_____ JUDICIAL DISTRICT

AFFIDAVIT

BEFORE ME the undersigned notary public on this day personally appeared _____, known to me to be the person whose name is signed below, who, after having been by me duly cautioned and sworn did state to me upon his [her] oath as follows:

"1. My name is _____. I am over the age of eighteen and am competent to make this affidavit.

"2. I have personal knowledge of the facts stated in this affidavit for the reason that [*insert basis of personal knowledge, e.g.*, I am the defendant in the above entitled lawsuit and I personally engaged in the transaction with plaintiff which is the subject of this suit].

"3. [*Insert facts which support transfer to a particular county, e.g.*, I reside in _____ County, Texas and have resided in this county for years. All of the transactions with plaintiff which are the subject of this suit occurred in the county in which I live. Further, none of the transactions which are the subject of this suit was solicited by defendant in the county in which this lawsuit was filed].

[Signature of affiant]

SUBSCRIBED AND SWORN TO before me on this _____ day of _____, 20__, to certify which witness my hand and official seal.

[Signature of notary public]

[c] FORM: Order sustaining motion to transfer venue

NO. _____

_____ § IN THE DISTRICT COURT OF
§
vs. § _____ COUNTY, TEXAS
§
_____ § _____ JUDICIAL DISTRICT

ORDER TRANSFERRING VENUE

On this _____ day of _____, 20___ came on for hearing defendant's motion to transfer venue of this action to _____ County, Texas, and, after hearing the evidence and argument of counsel, the court is of the opinion that plaintiff has failed to sustain the burden of making prima facie proof that venue of this action can be maintained in the county of suit [or mandatory venue of this action is in _____ County, Texas under [insert mandatory venue provision]; therefore, defendant is entitled to have this action transferred to _____ County, Texas which is [insert basis for transfer, e.g. the county in which the land which is the subject of this suit is located].

IT IS THEREFORE ORDERED that the clerk of this court shall transfer this cause and all papers associated with the cause to the _____ Judicial District Court of _____ County, Texas.

IT IS FURTHER ORDERED that all costs of transferring venue to _____ County, Texas shall be taxed against plaintiff.

SIGNED this _____ day of _____ 20___.

[Signature of presiding judge]

§6.04 Original Answer

The original answer in DTPA cases is governed by the same general rules applicable to answers in other cases. *See* TEX. R. CIV. P. 83.

As a result of the 1995 amendments to the DTPA, a plea in abatement which alleges that either no pre-suit notice or inadequate pre-suit notice was given must be filed "not later than the 30th day after the date the person files an original answer[.]" DTPA §17.505(c), as amended 1995.

The original answer which follows is in the form of a general denial only other pleadings and motions which are contained in this chapter may be inserted into this form as appropriate.

[a] FORM: Original answer (general form)

```
                          NO. _____
_____                §      IN THE DISTRICT COURT OF
                          §
vs.                       §      _____COUNTY, TEXAS
                          §
_____                §      _____ JUDICIAL DISTRICT
```

ORIGINAL ANSWER

TO THE HONORABLE JUDGE OF THE DISTRICT COURT:

_____, defendant, files this Original Answer [with Plea in Abatement] in response to plaintiff's petition, and will show the following:

1.

Defendant generally denies the allegations made in plaintiff's petition.

[*Insert other specific pleadings. See §§6.05 et seq. infra*]

WHEREFORE, defendant requests that plaintiff take nothing and that a judgment be entered awarding defendant his [*or* her] costs of court as well as such other relief to which defendant may be entitled.

                              Respectfully submitted,

                              [Signature of attorney]

[Certificate of service]

§6.05 Special Exceptions: Inadequacy of Pleadings

Special exceptions to pleadings are governed by TEX. R. CIV. P. 91. The function of a special exception is to identify defects in a pleading so that they may be cured, if possible, by amendment. *Horizon/CMS Healthcare Corp. v. Auld*, 34 S.W.3d 887, 897 (Tex. 2000). Generally, special exceptions address those defects which are shown on the face of the petition; consequently, when the defect can be established only by facts extrinsic to the petition, a special exception is inappropriate. *O'Neal v. Sherck Equipment Co.*, 751 S.W.2d 559 (Tex. App.—Texarkana 1988, no writ). Instead, if extrinsic facts must be relied on, the issue should be raised and dealt with by means of a plea in bar, a plea in abatement or motion for summary judgment. *Augustine v. Nusom*, 671 S.W.2d 112 (Tex. App.—Houston [14th Dist.] 1984, writ ref'd n.r.e.).

To be effective, a special exception must, "point out intelligibly and with particularity the defect, omission, obscurity, duplicity, generality or other insufficiency in the allegations in the pleading excepted to." TEX. R. CIV. P. 91.

Special exceptions may not be used to raise affirmative defenses. *Interfirst Bank San Antonio N.A. v. Murry*, 740 S.W.2d 550 (Tex. App.—San Antonio 1987, no writ). And, it is improper to use special exceptions as a means of questioning the jurisdiction of the court to hear a case. *Mahon v. Vandygriff*, 578 S.W.2d 144 (Tex. Civ. App.—Austin 1979, writ ref'd n.r.e.).

If no special exceptions to a pleading are filed, then any objection concerning the pleadings is waived. TEX. R. CIV. P. 90; *Troutman v. Traeco Bldg. Systems, Inc.*, 724 S.W.2d 385 (Tex. 1987) (failure to specially except to petition's general invocation of the DTPA waived any claim of defect). And, once special exceptions have been made, it is the duty of the party raising the exception to request a hearing and obtain a ruling on the exception; otherwise, the complaint is waived. TEX. R. CIV. P. 90; *see Hudspeth v. Hudspeth*, 756 S.W.2d 29, 34 (Tex. App.—San Antonio 1988, writ den'd.).

In a DTPA context, if the plaintiff fails to plead facts showing that he or she is a "consumer," a special exception should be filed. The plaintiff has the burden of pleading and proving consumer status. *Doe v. Boys Club*, 907 S.W.2d 472, 478 (Tex. 1995); *Farmers and Merchants State Bank v. Ferguson*, 617 S.W.2d 918, 920 (Tex. 1981).

§6.06 Affirmative Defenses: DTPA

As a general rule, common law defenses do not apply in DTPA litigation. *See* §2.02 *supra*; *Smith v. Baldwin*, 611 S.W.2d 611 (Tex. 1980). The only type of DTPA litigation in which common law defenses may apply is that which involves claims for damages arising out of defective residential construction. TEX. PROP. CODE §27.003.

A "business consumer" is defined as, "an individual, partnership or corporation who seeks or acquires by purchase or lease any goods or services for commercial or business use." DTPA §17.45(10). When a person is a "business consumer," standing to sue under the DTPA is taken away if that person has assets of $25 million or more, or if a company attempting to sue under the DTPA is owned or controlled by an entity with assets of $25 million or more.

In *Eckman v. Centennial Savings Bank*, 784 S.W.2d 672 (Tex. 1990), the Supreme Court held that the business consumer exception is an affirmative defense which must be pleaded and proved or it is waived.

Additionally, there are several statutory defenses to liability and damages which apply to DTPA litigation, whether it involves defective residential construction or other types of consumer transactions. Each of the statutory defenses provided in the DTPA are in the nature of affirmative defenses and must be pleaded and proved by the defendant. *See, e.g., American Petrofina, Inc. v. PPG Industries, Inc.*, 679 S.W.2d 740 (Tex. App.—Fort Worth 1984, writ dism'd by agr.).

The forms which follow are intended to illustrate pleading which raises each of the statutory defenses in DTPA litigation. Additional defenses which are provided by the Property Code in residential construction litigation are set forth in the sections which follow.

[a] FORM: Original answer with affirmative defenses

```
                                NO. _____
                                 §    IN THE DISTRICT COURT OF
_____                      §
                                 §
vs.                              §    _____COUNTY, TEXAS
                                 §
_____                      §    _____ JUDICIAL DISTRICT
```

ORIGINAL ANSWER

TO THE HONORABLE JUDGE OF THE DISTRICT COURT:

_____, defendant, files this Original Answer to plaintiffs petition and will show the following:

1. <u>Special exceptions</u>. [*See* §6.06 *supra*]

2. <u>General denial</u>. [*See* §6.04 *supra*]

3. <u>Special denials</u>. [*See* Tex. R. Civ. P. 93]

4. <u>Affirmative defenses</u>. Defendant asserts the following affirmative defense[s] in this lawsuit:

[(a)] <u>Conditions precedent not performed</u>. Plaintiff has not performed all conditions precedent necessary to maintain this lawsuit. Specifically, [*insert condition precedent that has not occurred*].

[(b)] Plaintiff has assets of $25 million or more or [Plaintiff is owned or controlled by an entity which has assets of $25 million or more] at the time that plaintiff's cause of action, if any, arose. For this reason, plaintiff does not have standing to sue under the DTPA, pursuant to Tex. Bus. & Com. Code 17.45(4).

[(c)] <u>Insufficient notice</u>. Plaintiff did not give notice to defendant, in writing, of plaintiff's claims, amount of damages, expenses and attorneys' fees at least sixty days before this suit was filed in the manner and form required by DTPA §17.505(a). [*See* §6.01 *supra*].

[(d)] Defects have been cured. The defects in the _____, about which plaintiff complains and seeks damages have been cured by defendant and were cured before this lawsuit was filed.

Authority: See Ramsey v. General Motors Corporation, 685 S.W.2d 15 (Tex. 1985) ("cure" is an affirmative defense which must be pleaded).

[(e)] Accord and satisfaction. Plaintiff and defendant have reached an accord and satisfaction with respect to the matters about which plaintiff complains in his [her] petition. Specifically, [*insert facts showing accord and satisfaction, e.g.*, upon receipt of the demand letter from plaintiff, defendant made an offer of settlement to plaintiff which was intended to resolve the dispute between plaintiff and defendant and which offer was accepted by plaintiff].

Authority: DTPA §17.506(d); *Jenkins v. Steakley Bros. Chevrolet Co.*, 712 S.W.2d 587 (Tex. App.—Waco 1986, no writ).

[(f)] No opportunity to inspect. Defendant made a written request to inspect the goods which are the subject of this lawsuit in a reasonable manner and at a reasonable time. This written request was made within sixty days after defendant received plaintiffs demand letter. In spite of this request, plaintiff failed and refused to respond and no opportunity to inspect the goods was offered. Plaintiffs failure to respond to defendant's written request for an opportunity to inspect the goods was unreasonable and violates TEX. BUS. & COM. CODE §17.505(a). Accordingly, plaintiff is prohibited from recovering two times any actual damages not exceeding $ 1,000 that may be found by the trier of fact.

[NOTE: As are result of the 1995 amendments, a consumer no longer is permitted to recover mandatory trebling of the first $1,000 in actual damages. *See* DTPA §17.50(b)(1), as amended 1995. For cases governed by the 1995 amendments, a plea in abatement should be used if the defendant is denied the opportunity to inspect the goods.]

Authority: DTPA §17.505(a) (repealed in part, 1995); *Smith v. Levine*, 911 S.W.2d 425, 434 (Tex. App.—San Antonio 1995, writ den'd.).

[(g)] Third Party Information. Plaintiff alleges that defendant made representations about the _____ that were false or inaccurate. Before the transaction which is the subject of this suit was consummated, and in a reasonable and timely manner, defendant gave written notice to plaintiff that defendant was relying on information obtained from another source. The information on which defendant relied was false and inaccurate. Defendant did not know that the information was false or inaccurate and could not reasonably have known of the falsity or inaccuracy of the information. The false or inaccurate written information on which defendant relied was a producing cause of damages to plaintiff.

No other conduct of defendant was a producing cause of damages to plaintiff.

Authority: DTPA §17.506(a)(2).

[NOTE: There are two other third party information defenses similar to that set forth above. The first concerns information obtained from official government records, DTPA §17.506(a)(1); and, the other deals with information concerning a test required or prescribed by a government agency. DTPA §17.506(a)(3).]

[(h)] <u>Statute of limitations</u>. The two years statute of limitations applicable to all Deceptive Trade Practice Act claims made in this case, as set forth in TEX. BUS. & COM. CODE §17.565, expired on plaintiffs claims before suit was filed. Specifically, plaintiff discovered, or in the exercise of reasonable diligence should have discovered, the claims that are the subject of this suit more than two years before _____, the date this suit was filed.

Authority: DTPA §17.565.

[NOTE: The plaintiff has the burden to plead and prove the application of the discovery rule, once a statute of limitations defense has been raised. *Willis v. Maverick*, 760 S.W.2d 642 (Tex. 1988).]

5. <u>Request for relief</u>. [*See* §6.04 *supra*]

                            Respectfully submitted,

                            [Signature of attorney]

[Affidavit, if necessary]

[Certificate of service]

§6.07 Affirmative Defense: Waiver

Prior to the 1995 amendments, waiver generally was not an issue since the statute provided that, "[a]ny waiver by a consumer of the provisions of this subchapter is contrary to public policy and is unenforceable and void." DTPA §17.42. The 1995 amendments now authorize waiver under certain circumstances. For a discussion of waiver under the DTPA *see* §2.02.02 *supra*.

[a] FORM: Affirmative defense: waiver

[NOTE: The following paragraph should be inserted in the original answer.]

Plaintiff has waived the application of TEX. BUS. & COM. CODE §17.41 *et seq*. to the claims asserted in its petition by executing a waiver in the manner and form required by the statute.

§6.08 Affirmative Defenses: Residential Construction

Forms for use in residential construction cases can now be found in Chapter 12. For a form of an answer with affirmative defense in a residential construction case, *see* §12.06.5[e], *infra*.

§6.09 Affirmative Defense: Professional Opinion

The 1995 amendments exclude from the DTPA a claim for damages "based on the rendering of a professional service, the essence of which is the providing of advice, judgment, opinion, or similar professional skill." DTPA §17.49(c), as amended 1995. The exclusion does not apply to,

(1) an express misrepresentation of a material fact that cannot be characterized as advice, judgment, or opinion;

(2) a failure to disclose information in violation of DTPA §17.46(b)(23);

(3) an unconscionable action or course of action that cannot be characterized as advice, judgment, or opinion; or

(4) the breach of an express warranty that cannot be characterized as advice, judgment, or opinion. DTPA §17.49(c).

If the exclusion applies, it includes any person who may be vicariously liable for the conduct of the "professional." DTPA §17.49(d), as amended, 1995. *See* §2.02.01 *supra*.

[a] FORM: Affirmative defense: professional opinion

```
In the transaction which is the subject of this suit, defen-
dant was providing a "professional service," as that term is
defined in TEX. BUS. & COM. CODE §17.49(c), the essence of which
was the providing of advice, judgment, opinion and similar pro-
fessional skills. Plaintiffs claim is for damages based on the
rendering of a professional opinion. For these reasons, the
Deceptive Trade Practices—Consumer Protection Act does not apply
to this lawsuit.
```

§6.09.1 Affirmative Defense: Claim Arises Out of Written Contract

The 1995 amendments also exclude certain claims which arise out of written contracts. Under §17.49(c), the DTPA does not apply if:

1. the contract relates to a transaction, a project, or a set of transactions related to the same project involving total consideration by the consumer of more than $100,000;

2. in negotiating the contract the consumer was represented by independent legal counsel (not identified, suggested or selected by the opposing party); and

3. the contract does not involve the consumer's residence.

DTPA §17.49(f), as amended 1995; *see* §2.02.02 *supra*].

[a] FORM: —Affirmative defense: claim arises out of written contract

```
The transaction about which plaintiff complains arises out of
a written contract which relates to a transaction [or project,
or a set of transactions related to the same project] involv-
ing a consideration paid by plaintiff which totaled more than
$100,000. Further, in negotiating the contract, plaintiff was
represented by independent legal counsel. Accordingly, this
transaction is excluded from the DTPA.
```

§6.09.2 Affirmative Defense: Transaction Exceeds DTPA's Dollar Limit

The 1995 amendments place a transactional "cap" on lawsuits filed under the DTPA if the cause of action arises out of a "transaction, a project, or a set of transactions relating to the same project," in which the consideration paid by the consumer exceeds $500,000. This exclusion does not apply to a cause of action involving the consumer's residence. DTPA §17.49(g), as amended 1995.

[a] FORM: —Affirmative defense: consideration paid exceeds DTPA's transactional cap

```
The transaction on which plaintiff's lawsuit is based involves
a project [or set of transactions relating to the same project]
in which the consideration paid by plaintiff exceeded $500,000.
Accordingly, pursuant to DTPA §17.49(g), this transaction is
excluded from the DTPA.
```

§6.09.3 Affirmative Defense: "As Is" Purchase

In *Prudential Ins. Co. of Am. v. Jefferson Assocs.*, 896 S.W.2d 156 (Tex. 1995), the Supreme Court held that if improved real estate is purchased "as is," and particularly if there is an acknowledgement by the buyer that he is not relying on any representations of the seller, then there is a break in causation between the allegedly wrongful conduct and any damages that the buyer may have suffered. See §2.02.04, *supra*, for discussion of "As Is" defense.

In residential real estate sales, the typical earnest money contract contains an "Acceptance of Condition" clause which is the functional equivalent of an as-is clause. *Larsen v. Carlene Langford & Assocs.*, 41 S.W.3d 245, 251 (Tex. App.—Waco 2001, pet. denied). The pleading set forth below is intended to raise the issue of an as-is purchase.

[a] FORM: Affirmative defense: "as is" real estate purchase

```
In the transaction which is the subject of this suit, plain-
tiff purchased the property "as is" by signing a contract which
contained an "Acceptance of Condition" clause. [If clause is
more explicit, quote it verbatim.] As a result of plaintiff's
agreement to purchase the property as is, there is no causation
between any allegedly wrongful conduct by this defendant and the
damages claimed by plaintiff.
```

§6.09.4 Affirmative Defense: Independent Investigation

If the consumer *actually discovers* the truth before entering the transaction through his own investigation, the element of reliance may be missing and the causal chain between the defendant's conduct and the plaintiff's damages broken. Sometimes referenced to as the "independent investigation" defense, the consumer's investigation and discovery of the truth is best understood as simply a negation of the element of reliance. For a full discussion of this inferential rebuttal issue, see §2.02.05, *supra*.

[a] FORM: Affirmative defense: independent investigation

```
Pleading further, if such defense be necessary, defendant
would show that, prior to the closing on the real estate pur-
chase which is the subject of this suit, plaintiff conducted his
own independent investigation regarding the existence and extent
of termite damage on the property. Specifically, plaintiffs
hired an independent termite inspector who provided a termite
inspection report to plaintiff which disclosed the existence of
the termite damage claimed to have been misrepresented by defen-
dant in this suit. As a result of plaintiff's independent inves-
tigation, plaintiff knew the true facts concerning the existence
of termite damage in the property and could not have relied upon
defendant's non-disclosure of termite damage to go forward with
the closing on the property at issue.
```

§6.09.5 Affirmative Defense: Reasonable Settlement Offer

[a] FORM: Affirmative defense: reasonable settlement offer

Pleading further, if such defense be necessary, Defendant would show that Plaintiff's claims are barred or diminished by the settlement offer made to Plaintiffs by Defendant in accordance with Section 17.5052, Texas Business & Commerce Code.

§6.09.6 Affirmative Defense: Texas CRPC Chapter 33

[a] FORM: Damages recovered must be reduced by value of settlement

	NO. _____	
_____	§	IN THE DISTRICT COURT OF
	§	
vs.	§	_____ COUNTY, TEXAS
	§	
_____	§	_____ JUDICIAL DISTRICT

DEFENDANT'S FIRST AMENDED ANSWER

TO THE HONORABLE JUDGE OF SAID COURT:

NOW COMES _____, one of the Defendants herein, and files this its First Amended Answer to the Petition and all amendments thereto filed by Plaintiffs, _____ and _____, and in support for such Answer would respectfully show unto the Court as follows:

I.

GENERAL DENIAL

Defendant generally denies each and every allegation contained in Plaintiffs' Original Petition and demands strict proof thereof pursuant to Rule 92, *Texas Rules of Civil Procedure*.

II.

AFFIRMATIVE DEFENSE: CHAPTER 33 AND SETTLEMENT CREDIT

Pleading further, if such defense be necessary, Defendant invokes the provisions of Chapter 33, *Texas Civil Practice & Remedies Code*. Plaintiffs have made joint allegations against all Defendants herein for the same harm and damages. Plaintiffs have now entered into a settlement agreement with [*other defendants*] by which Plaintiffs have released or will release them from all liability arising out of the factual premises made the basis of this suit in exchange for the payment of a sum of money to or on behalf of one or more of the Plaintiffs. Accordingly, any damages to be recovered by Plaintiffs against Defendant must be reduced by the dollar amount of the settlement described above.

WHEREFORE, PREMISES CONSIDERED, Defendant respectfully prays that the Court render judgment that Plaintiffs take nothing against Defendant, assessing all costs against Plaintiffs, and awarding all other relief to which Defendant may be entitled.

```
                              Respectfully submitted,


                              _____
                              ATTORNEY FOR DEFENDANT
```

§6.10 Counterclaim for Bad Faith and Harassment

Before the 1995 amendments, DTPA §17.50(c) provided:

> On a finding by the court that an action under this section was groundless and brought in bad faith, or for the purpose of harassment, the court shall award to the defendant reasonable and necessary attorneys' fees and costs.

The 1995 amendments revised §17.50(c) so that after the effective date of the amendments, it provides as follows:

> On a finding by the court than an action under this section is groundless in fact or in law or brought in bad faith, or brought for the purpose of harassment, the court shall award to the defendant reasonable and necessary attorneys' fees and court costs.

DTPA §17.50(c), as amended 1995. The effect of the amendments is two-fold. First, it is clear that bad faith attorney's fees are to be awarded whether the lawsuit is groundless because of a lack of evidence, or groundless because the evidence in hand fails to rise to the level of a recognized cause of action under the DTPA. Second, the amendment changes the law to allow bad faith attorneys' fees on a finding of *any* of the three elements (groundless, bad faith or harassment) rather than a requirement that there be a finding that the suit is groundless *and* either brought in bad faith or for harassment. DTPA §17.50(c), as amended 1995.

When a lawsuit has been filed by a consumer and the lawsuit is groundless and brought in bad faith or for the purpose of harassment, the defendant is authorized to file a counterclaim in order to recover his or her attorney's fees and costs. *Donwerth v. Preston II Chrysler-Dodge, Inc.*, 775 S.W.2d 6`34 (Tex. 1989).

A counterclaim can be included in the answer or it may be filed as a separate instrument. TEX. R. CIV. P. 85. While there is no charge for the filing of the answer, there is a separate charge from the district clerk for the filing of a counterclaim.

To determine whether a suit is groundless under the DTPA, the trial court must consider the totality of the tendered evidence to determine whether there is an arguable basis in fact or in law for the consumer's claim. *Davila*, 75 S.W.3d at 537, 543-544 (Tex. App.—San Antonio 2002, no pet.), *citing Splettstosser v. Myer*, 779 S.W.2d 806, 808 (Tex. 1989). Evidence that is otherwise inadmissible may be considered, provided that there is some good faith belief that the tendered evidence might be admissible or that it could reasonably lead to the discovery of admissible evidence. *Davila v. World Car Five Star*, 75 S.W.3d 537, *also citing New York Underwriters Ins. Co. v. State Farm Mutual Auto Ins. Co.*, 856 S.W.2d 194, 205 (Tex. App.—Dallas 1993, no writ): "Unless evidence is heard on the circumstances surrounding the filing of the pleadings and the signer's credibility and motives, the trial court has no evidence to determine that the party or its attorneys filed the pleading in bad faith or to harass."

Sanctions under DTPA §17.50(d) may be assessed against both the party and the party's attorney with sufficient proof of wrongdoing. *Davila v. World Car Five Star*, 75 S.W.3d 537.

[a] FORM: Counterclaim for bad faith, harassment

```
                              NO. _____
                           §    IN THE DISTRICT COURT OF
_____               §
                           §
vs.                        §    _____COUNTY, TEXAS
                           §
_____               §    _____ JUDICIAL DISTRICT
```

DEFENDANT'S COUNTERCLAIM

TO THE HONORABLE JUDGE OF THE DISTRICT COURT:

_____, counter-plaintiff, files this Counterclaim against _____, counter-defendant, and will show the following:

1. Service of citation. [See §5.03, supra].

[NOTE: In many cases, the attorney of record for the plaintiff may agree to accept service of citation; therefore, this paragraph should reflect that agreement as well as the name and address of the attorney or record.]

2. Statutory authority. This counterclaim is filed under the authority of TEX. BUS. & COM. CODE §17.41 et seq. commonly known as the Deceptive Trade Practices and Consumer Protection Act and cited in this counterclaim as the "DTPA."

3. <u>Actionable conduct</u>. Counter-defendant's lawsuit against counter-plaintiff is groundless and was brought in bad faith or for the purpose of harassment.

[NOTE: For lawsuit which are governed by the 1995 amendments, the word "and" between groundless and brought should be changed to "or."]

4. <u>Attorneys' fees</u>. Counter-plaintiff has retained the undersigned to defend the lawsuit filed by counter-defendant and to pursue this counter-claim. Counter-plaintiff has incurred and will continue to incur attorneys' fees which are reasonable and necessary under DTPA §17.50(c), and seeks to recover these fees from counter-defendant. These fees include:

(a) Preparation and trial of this lawsuit; and

(b) Post-trial, pre-appeal legal services; and

(c) An appeal to the Court of Appeals; and

(d) Making or responding to an application for writ of error to the Supreme Court of Texas; and

(e) An appeal to the Supreme Court of Texas in the event application for writ of error is granted.

5. <u>Request for relief</u>. Counter-plaintiff requests that after final trial, judgment be entered against counter-defendant for all of counter-plaintiffs reasonable and necessary attorneys' fees and costs, post-judgment interest at the highest lawful rate, and such other relief to which counter-plaintiff may be entitled.

                              Respectfully submitted,

                              [Signature of attorney]

[Certificate of service]

§6.11 Leave to Designate Responsible Third Party

In 2003, the legislature amended the proportionate responsibility provisions of the Texas Civil Practices and Remedies Code to provide a defense based upon the actionable conduct of a third party not joined by the plaintiff as a defendant in the suit. The provisions are expressly applicable to DTPA claims. Tex. Civ. Prac. & Rem. Code §33.002(a)(2). Through this new procedure, a defendant may seek leave of court to designate a person or entity as a "responsible third party," which means:

> [A]ny person who is alleged to have caused or contributed to causing in any way the harm for which recovery of damages is sought, whether by negligent act or omission, by any defective or unreasonably dangerous product, by other conduct or activity that violates an applicable legal standard, or by any combination of these. The term "responsible third party" does not include a seller eligible for indemnity under Section 82.002.

Tex. Civ. Prac. & Rem. Code §33.011(6).

Once properly designated, the fault of the responsible third party is then submitted to the jury to apportion, between the defendant(s) and responsible third party, the percentages of responsibility for causing the plaintiff's damages. Tex. Civ. Prac. & Rem. Code §33.003(a)(4). A finding that a responsible third party bares a percentage of the responsibility for causing the plaintiff's damages will reduce the defendant's responsibility and may reduce it below 51%, the threshold for joint and several liability. See Tex. Civ. Prac. & Rem. Code §33.013(b)(1). The responsible third party is not formally joined in the lawsuit unless the plaintiff acts to join him by proper service of citation. There is, therefore, no recovery allowed by the plaintiff from the responsible third party. Tex. Civ. Prac. & Rem. Code §33.003(i)(1).

Because the responsible third party is neither present nor represented by counsel, a responsible third party designation allows a defendant to blame an "empty chair" for causing the plaintiff's damages. The plaintiff is then forced to either join the responsible third party as a defendant or undertake to defend the alleged actions of the responsible third party in order to defeat the defendant's claims. The designation of a responsible third party can have a significant effect on the evidence admissible at trial. Evidence which tends to prove or disprove the fault of a responsible third party becomes relevant and admissible once leave to designate is granted. The responsible third party procedure offers a distinct advantage to the defendant who properly employs it.

The designation of a responsible third party is raised by a motion filed by the defendant at least 60 days prior to trial. Tex. Civ. Prac. & Rem. Code §33.004(a). The court must grant the motion and designate the person as a responsible third party unless the plaintiff files a timely objection within 15 days after the motion for leave is served. Tex. Civ. Prac. & Rem. Code §33.004(f). The motion can be challenged on the basis that it fails to plead sufficient facts establishing the legal responsibility of the responsible third party to the plaintiff. Tex. Civ. Prac. & Rem. Code §33.004(g). It is, therefore, important to allege facts sufficient to withstand a challenge by the plaintiff in the motion for leave.

Special rules apply to the designation of an unknown person as a responsible third party. In addition to the requirements of pleading one or more causes of action against the unknown responsible third party, the defendant must also plead facts sufficient for the court to determine that there is a reasonable probability that the act of an unknown person was criminal and all identifying characteristics of the unknown criminal, which were known to the defendant at the time of the answer. TEX. CIV. PRAC. & REM. CODE §33.004(j). The designation must also be made in the original answer or in an amended answer filed within 60 days of the defendant's original answer. TEX. CIV. PRAC. & REM. CODE §33.004(j).

The following form is for use by a seller of a used house to designate the buyer's real estate inspector who failed to discover and disclose, in a pre-closing inspection, hidden damage to a used home made the basis of the plaintiff's suit against the seller. The form should be adapted to meet the specific facts of each particular case.

[a] FORM: Motion for leave to designate responsible third party

```
                           NO. _____

_____              §   IN THE DISTRICT COURT OF
                          §
vs.                       §   _____COUNTY, TEXAS
                          §
_____              §   _____ JUDICIAL DISTRICT
```

MOTION FOR LEAVE TO DESIGNATE REPONSIBLE THIRD PARTY

TO THE HONORABLE JUDGE OF THE DISTRICT COURT:

_____, defendant, files this Motion for Leave to Designate Responsible Inspection Company as a responsible third party pursuant to TEX. CIV. PRAC. & REM. CODE §33.004, and will show the following:

1. In this suit, Plaintiff complains the Defendant should have disclosed the existence of foundation cracks in the house. Defendant inherited the house from her deceased mother and did not live in the house prior to sale and did not know of the foundation cracks prior to their discovery by Plaintiff.

2. Prior to the closing on the sale of the house, Plaintiff retained Responsible Inspection Company to inspect the house for defects or other conditions which might affect its value. Responsible Inspection Company performed an inspection of the house for Plaintiff and reported to Plaintiff that the foundation of the house was sound and free of defects. If Plaintiff's allegation that the foundation of the house had cracks in it prior to sale is true, then the report of Responsible Inspection Company to Plaintiff was false and Responsible Inspection Company failed

to exercise reasonable care in the performance of its inspection and reporting to Plaintiff. Plaintiff relied upon the inspection report prepared and presented by Responsible Inspection Company in deciding to purchase the house from Plaintiff.

3. Responsible Inspection Company is responsible, in whole or in part, for the damages claimed by Plaintiff in this suit. Responsible Inspection Company was negligent in the conduct of its inspection. Responsible Inspection Company made negligent misrepresentations to Plaintiff that were contained in its inspection report. Responsible Inspection Company violated one or more provisions of the DTPA laundry list section 17.46(b), including subsections (5), (7) and (24). These acts or omissions were a proximate and/or producing cause of the damages to Plaintiff made the basis of this suit.

4. Responsible Inspection Company is, therefore, a responsible third party as defined in TEX. CIV. PRAC. & REM. CODE §33.011(6).

5. [This Motion for Leave to Designate a Responsible Third Party is filed more than 60 days prior to trial.] or [Good cause exists to grant Defendant leave to designate a responsible third party within 60 days of trial because _____ *set forth facts that establish good cause, e.g., Defendant was relying on Plaintiff to join Responsible Inspection Company as a defendant in this action. Plaintiff amended her petition more than 60 days prior to trial to add Responsible Inspection Company as a defendant herein but has failed or refused to obtain service.*]

WHEREFORE, defendant requests leave of court to designate Responsible Inspection Company as a responsible third party in this suit.

          Respectfully submitted,

          [Signature of attorney]

[Certificate of service]

(This page intentionally left blank.)

Chapter 7

Discovery

§7.01 General Considerations
§7.02 Informal Discovery
§7.03 Corporation Information
§7.04 Assumed Names
§7.05 Financial Institutions
§7.06 Insurance Companies
§7.07 Insurance Agents
§7.08 Realtors
§7.09 Real Estate Inspectors
§7.10 Prior Lawsuits
§7.11 Prior Claims or Complaints
§7.12 Construction Information
§7.13 Manufactured Housing
§7.14 Formal Discovery
§7.15 [Reserved]
§7.16 Scope of Discovery
§7.17 Specific Discoverable Matters
§7.18 Potential Fact Witnesses and Parties
§7.19 Expert Witnesses
§7.20 Documents
§7.21 Tax Returns
§7.22 Financial Records
§7.23 Photographs
§7.24 Indemnity, Insuring and Settlement Agreements
§7.25 Medical Records
§7.26 Statements
§7.27 Wealth of Parties
§7.28 Other Claims
§7.29 Insurance Company Files
§7.30 Land
§7.31 Exemptions from Discovery
§7.32 Work Product

§7.33 Other Privileged Information
§7.34 Subpoenas
    [a] FORM: Subpoena
§7.35 Forms of Discovery
§7.36 Discovery Control Plan
§7.37 Level 1 Discovery
§7.38 Level 2 Discovery
§7.39 Level 3 Discovery
§7.40 Modification of Discovery Control Plan
    [a] FORM: Motion to modify discovery control plan
    [b] FORM: Order modifying discovery control plan
§7.41 Discovery Agreements
    [a] FORM: Rule 11 Agreement
  §7.41.1 Requests for disclosure
    [a] FORM: Request for Disclosure (general form)
    [b] FORM: Request for Disclosure (short form)
    [c] FORM: Supplemental Request for Disclosure (Level 1 expedited actions)
§7.42 Interrogatories
§7.43 Drafting Interrogatories
    [a] FORM: Interrogatories (general form)
§7.44 Additional General Questions to Plaintiff
    [a] FORM: —Additional questions (to plaintiff)
§7.45 Additional Questions for Specific Cases
    [a] FORM: Defective product (to defendant)
    [b] FORM: Defective product (to plaintiff)
    [c] FORM: Lender liability: unauthorized withdrawal of funds (to defendant)
    [d] FORM: Lender liability: unauthorized withdrawal of funds (to plaintiff)
    [e] FORM: Lender liability: false representation to extend credit (to defendant)
    [f] FORM: Lender liability: false representation to extend credit (to plaintiff)
    [g] FORM: Commercial lease (to defendant)
    [h] FORM: Commercial lease (to plaintiff)
    [i] FORM: Unfair debt collection practices (to defendant)
§7.46 Requests for Production of Documents and Things
§7.47 Drafting Requests for Production
    [a] FORM: Request for Production (general form)
  §7.47.1 Additional Requests for Specific Cases
    [a] FORM: Defective product (to defendant retailer)
    [b] FORM: Defective product (to plaintiff)
    [c] FORM: Unfair debt collection practices (to defendant)
§7.48 Requests for Admission
§7.49 Drafting Requests for Admission
    [a] FORM: Requests for Admission (general form)
    [b] FORM: Unfair debt collection practices (to defendant)

§7.50   Responding to Written Discovery Requests
   §7.50.1   Depositions on Written Questions
      [a] FORM: Notice of deposition of written questions
§7.51   Oral Depositions
§7.52   Notice of Oral Deposition
      [a] FORM: Notice of oral deposition (individual)
      [b] FORM: Notice of oral deposition (organization)
   §7.52.1   Depositions Before Suit
      [a] FORM: Petition for pre-suit deposition
      [b] FORM: Order for deposition before suit
§7.53   Deposition Checklists
§7.54   Preparing the Client for Deposition
      [a] FORM: Deposition preparation memorandum (plaintiff)
      [b] FORM: Deposition preparation memorandum (defendant)

§7.01 General Considerations

The key to the successful resolution of a case, by trial or settlement, is effective discovery. Historically, the goal of discovery has been to permit the parties to obtain full knowledge of the issues and facts prior to trial so that disputes may be decided by what is revealed, not what is concealed. *Jampole v. Touchy,* 673 S.W.2d 569 (Tex. 1984); *West v. Solito,* 563 S.W.2d 240 (Tex. 1978).

Effective January 1, 1999, the Texas Supreme Court substantially overhauled the existing rules regarding discovery. *See* 61 TEX. BAR. J. 1140 (1998). Depending on the type of case and the extent to which parties can agree on discovery, the effect of the rules may be to lessen significantly one's ability to compel information from an opponent.

From the advocate's point of view, the primary aims of discovery are to (1) marshal evidence that supports your client's claim, (2) discover all evidence that tends to rebut your client's case or prove a defense and (3) narrow the range of contested issues. In some instances informal discovery is effective, i.e. discovery obtained by interviewing witnesses, contacting third parties who may have had prior dealings with the parties, searching government records, etc. In virtually all cases, informal discovery must be supplemented with formal discovery. Even though there have been significant changes in the rules, counsel still must be prepared to file a proper and timely objection to improper discovery requests. Each of these matters is discussed in the sections that follow.

§7.02 Informal Discovery

Informal discovery in DTPA cases includes the usual techniques employed in all civil cases: (1) interviewing and obtaining witness statements from non-parties known to have knowledge of relevant facts, (2) inspection and photographing of the product or site, and (3) retrieval of appropriate records from the client, his agents (e.g., accountant), non-party witnesses, trade organizations and government agencies.

§7.03 Corporate Information

The name and address of the registered agent of a Texas or foreign corporation and its place and date of incorporation may be obtained by contacting the Secretary of State at Secretary of State, Corporation Division, P.O. Box 13697, Austin, Texas 78711, 512-463-5555. The Secretary of State may be found online at: www.sos.state.tx.us.

Ownership, location of agents, product lines, and general information about large corporations may be obtained from the Thomas Register, a large multi-volume set that has categories ranging from trade names to product type. The *Thomas Register* may be found in a public or college library or through Thomas Publishing Company, *Thomas Register,* Attn: Infocenter, 1 Penn Plaza, New York, NY 10117-0138. Some information may be available online at www.thomasregister.com. Basic facts concerning parent and subsidiary relationships or mergers and acquisitions can usually be found in the Directory of Corporation Affiliations, which is published by the National Register Publishing Company and updated annually. The company may be contacted at 312-256-6067.

Copies of filings with the Securities and Exchange Commission are available from S.E.C., 500 N. Capitol Street, Washington, D.C. 20549. The Commission's web site can be accessed at www.sec.gov.

§7.04 Assumed Names

Assumed name certificates for an unincorporated business or person must be filed in the county clerk's office in each county in which the business is maintained or conducted. TEX BUS. & COM. CODE §36.10 (*repealed eff.* April 1, 2009); TEX. BUS. & COM. CODE §71.054 (*eff.* April 1, 2009)

Any corporation doing business under an assumed name must file an assumed name certificate with the Texas Secretary of State and with the County Clerk of the county of its registered or principal office. TEX BUS. & COM. CODE §36.11 (*repealed eff.* April 1, 2009); TEX. BUS. & COM. CODE §71.103 (*eff.* April 1, 2009). Information concerning the Secretary of State's Office is available at www.sos.state.tx.us.

§7.05 Financial Institutions

The names of the officers and directors and a report of the resources and liabilities of Texas Banks is compiled in the *Texas Banking Red Book*, published by Bankers Digest, Inc., 6440 N. Central Expressway, Suite 215, Dallas, Texas 75206-4103. This information also is available from the Texas Banking Department, 2601 N. Lamar Blvd., Austin, Texas 78705, 877-276-5554. Their web site may be found at www.banking.state.tx.us.

For federally chartered banks, general information can be obtained from the Office of the Comptroller of the Currency. The Customer Assistance Group is located at 1301 McKinney Street, Suite 3450, Houston, TX 77010, 1-800-613-6743. The Comptroller's web site can be found at www.occ.treas.gov.

Information as to state banks, mortgage banks and mortgage brokers chartered by the State of Texas may be obtained by contacting the Texas Department of Savings and Mortgage Lending, 2601 N. Lamar, Suite 201, Austin, Texas 78705 512-475-1350.

General information on federally chartered thrift institutions or savings banks may be obtained from the Office of Thrift Supervision. The Office of Consumer Programs is 1700 G. Street, NW, Washington, DC 20552. Their web site may be found at www.ots.treas.gov.

§7.06 Insurance Companies

For a nominal fee, the *List of Authorized Insurance Companies* with update bulletins may be obtained from Publications, Texas Department of Insurance, 333 Guadalupe Street, Austin, TX 78701, 512-463-6169. This publication contains the full name, type of company, registered agent and address, as well as the licensing dates, capital, and net surplus for insurance companies authorized to do business in Texas.

Registered agent information for insurance companies also may be obtained from the Texas Department of Insurance by contacting the Company License Office at the Department's Austin address or by calling 1-800-252-3439.

The Texas Department of Insurance also maintains files of the annual statement that each licensed insurance company must provide to the Department. In addition to information concerning the company's financial condition, these reports contain the amount of annual legal expenses, paid, the number of claims disputed, each company's ownership, and each company's affiliates. The Corporate Activities Office in Austin will provide estimates of the cost to obtain copies. The information also is available for public inspection in Austin.

The Texas Department of Insurance web site may be found at www.tdi.state.tx.us.

§7.07 Insurance Agents

Information on insurance agents and adjusters can be obtained from the Agents and Adjusters Office at the Texas Department of Insurance in Austin. Among the types of information available are documents that establish whether an agent is registered as a local recording agent or as a soliciting agent for one or more insurance companies.

Contact information for the Texas Department of Insurance may be found in §7.06 *supra*.

§7.08 Realtors

The Texas Real Estate Commission maintains a file on each real estate agent or broker licensed in the State of Texas. This file generally contains the following types of information: school transcripts, certificates of course completion, and all applications for licensure showing the sponsoring broker and license.

Each agent's file is an open record, a copy of which may be obtained for a fee from the Texas Real Estate Commission by contacting the Commission at P.O. Box 12188, Capitol Station, Austin, Texas 78711, 512-459-6544. The Commission's web-site may be found at www.trec.state.tx.us.

§7.09 Real Estate Inspectors

Texas Occupations Code §1102.102 requires that any person who acts or attempts to act as a real estate inspector for a buyer or seller of real property must obtain a license from the 3Texas Real Estate Commission. A copy of each licensee's file generally contains the application, license and transcripts of the inspector. A copy of the file can be obtained for a fee from the Texas Real Estate Commission. For contact information see §7.08 *supra*.

§7.10 Prior Lawsuits

When a person has been involved in litigation before, the files at the county courthouse may contain a wealth of information. Although prior litigation will be asked about in formal discovery, it is often beneficial to check the records of the district and county clerk. Clerks' offices generally maintain an alphabetical index organized by year of filing. One shortcoming of such indexes is that frequently only the first named defendant will be listed. If the party in question was sued but not listed first in the style, it may be difficult to informally discover the case.

§7.11 Prior Claims or Complaints

Records of prior complaints against a Texas business may be obtained from at least two sources: the local Better Business Bureau and the headquarters or one of the regional offices of the Consumer Protection Division of the Texas Attorney General's Office. These offices are located in Austin, Dallas, San Antonio, Houston, El Paso, McAllen, and Lubbock. The web site of the Consumer Protection Division may be found at www.oag.state.tx.us/consumer/index.shtml.

For complaints about companies involved in interstate commerce, the Federal Trade Commission should be contacted. The FTC's address is Federal Trade Commission, CRC-240, Washington D.C. 20580. The FTC web site may be found at: www.ftc.gov.

§7.12 Construction Information

If a home is built within the city limits of a municipality, it will generally be subject to municipal building codes. Most, if not all, major municipalities require an application for a building permit, perform spot inspections during construction, and issue a certificate of occupancy. These records typically are maintained by the building inspection or building safety department of the city. Occasionally, the records will contain useful information. For example, the municipality may be able to confirm whether the contractor bypassed the municipal construction inspection process. It is important to remember that building codes are minimum standards and that some municipal inspections are generally less than thorough.

§7.13 Manufactured Housing

Chapter 1201 of the Texas Occupations Code, also known as the Manufactured Housing Standards Act, requires any manufacturer or retailer of new manufactured homes to be registered with the Department of Housing and Community Affairs. Information relating to the registration as well as licensing information supplied by the manufacturer or retailer and information on complaints that have been filed may be obtained from the Department. Its address is Department of Housing and Community Affairs, P.O. Box 13941, Austin, TX. 78711. Their website may be found at www.tdhca.state.tx.us/mh/index.htm.

§7.14 Formal Discovery

Formal discovery, that is, discovery pursuant to the Texas Rules of Civil Procedure, is indispensable in the preparation of any lawsuit, including DTPA litigation. Having said that, there may be practical, financial constraints on the amount of formal discovery you can undertake. The assumption, however, is that most formal discovery tools will be available to most attorneys in most cases.

Formal discovery involves consideration of four major areas:

- the scope of discovery

- the discovery tools available

- the procedures for protecting non-discoverable information

- the procedure for enforcing a party's right to discoverable information

§7.15 [Reserved]

§7.16 Scope of Discovery

Parties may obtain discovery regarding any matter that is not privileged and is relevant to the subject matter in the pending action, whether it relates to the claim or defense of the party seeking discovery or the claim or defense of any other party. TEX. R. CIV. P. 192.3(a). Since the "claim or defense" referred to in Rule 192.3(a) is defined, in large part, by the pleadings, care should be taken to plead those claims and defenses necessary to allow a party to obtain the broadest discovery possible.

It is not necessary for the information or documents sought to be admissible at trial if the information "appears reasonably calculated to lead to the discovery of admissible evidence." TEX. R. CIV. P. 192.3(a). *See Allen v. Humphreys*, 559 S.W.2d 798, 803 (Tex.

1977); *Jampole v. Touchy*, 673 S.W.2d 569, 573 (Tex. 1984); *Axelson, Inc. v. McIlhany* 798 S.W.2d 550 (Tex. 1990). Information falling within the general rule, if properly requested, is discoverable unless exempted from discovery. These exemptions are discussed below.

Through discovery and subject to certain limitations, a person has a right to obtain documents and tangible things, TEX. R. CIV. P. 192.3(b), the identity of persons who have knowledge of relevant facts, TEX. R. CIV. P. 192.3(c), the names, addresses and telephone numbers of any person who is expected to be called to testify at trial, TEX. R. CIV. P. 192.3(d), the identity, facts known to and mental impression and opinions of experts who will be called to testify, TEX. R. CIV. P. 192.3(e), the existence of indemnity and insuring agreements, TEX. R. CIV. P. 192.3(f), any settlement agreements, TEX. R. CIV. P. 192.3(g), the statements of persons who have knowledge of relevant facts (regardless of when the statement was made), TEX. R. CIV. P. 192.3(h), the identity of potential parties, TEX. R. CIV. P. 192.3(i), and the legal contentions and factual basis for those contentions, TEX. R. CIV. P. 192.3(j).

Discoverable information includes more than just "facts." Contentions, statements and opinions that relate to facts are discoverable. *Williamson v. O'Neill*, 696 S.W.2d 431, 432 (Tex. App.—Houston [14th] Dist.] 1985, no writ). The reach of the discovery rules extends to materials that are in the possession, custody or control of the person from whom discovery is sought. TEX. R. CIV. P. 192.3(b). "Possession, custody or control" means that a person either has the physical possession of the item or has a right to possession of the item that is equal to or superior to the person who has physical possession of the item. TEX. R. CIV. P. 192.7(b).

§7.17 Specific Discoverable Matters

The amount of discovery that can be conducted depends on the "level" of discovery applicable to the case. TEX. R. CIV. P. 190.1. Although the amount of allowable discovery varies, depending on the level of discovery applicable to the case, there are very few limits on the categories of discoverable matter. The limitations are discussed in succeeding sections; however, the discussion first will turn to those items that can be obtained through discovery.

§7.18 Potential Fact Witnesses and Parties

A party may discover the name, address and telephone number of potential parties to the litigation, TEX. R. CIV. P. 192.3(i), and all persons with knowledge of relevant facts. TEX. R. CIV. P. 192.3(c). In addition, for those persons with knowledge of relevant facts, a party may require the opponent to provide a brief statement of the person's connection with the case, *e.g.* "eyewitness," "chief financial officer," "treating physician,", etc. *Notes and Comments*, TEX. R. CIV. P. 192.3, 61 TEX. BAR J. 1150 (1998). Even if the potential witness does not have personal knowledge but only possesses second-hand information, his or her identity must be disclosed. *Sharp v. Broadway Nat. Bank*, 784 S.W.2d 669 (Tex. 1990); *see Jamail v. Anchor Mortgage Servs. Inc.*, 809 S.W. 2d 221 (Tex. 1991) (a person having knowledge of any discoverable matter has knowledge of relevant facts). A rebuttal witness whose use could have been anticipated prior to trial must be disclosed. TEX. R. CIV. P. 192.3(c). If the identity of fact witnesses and potential parties is requested in a request for disclosure, the exemptions to discovery in the rules of civil procedure do *not* apply, and this information is never protected from discovery. TEX. R. CIV. P. 194.5; *see also Giffin v. Smith*, 688 S.W.2d 112, 113 (Tex. 1985). If requested, a party may also be required to identify the witnesses that will be called to testify at trial. TEX. R. CIV. P. 192.3(d).

§7.19 Expert Witnesses

The only means by which a person can be required to designate and disclose information about testifying expert witnesses is through a request for disclosure under Rule 194. TEX. R. CIV. P. 195.1. Assuming that a proper request has been served, the responding party must provide the following information about the expert:

- the expert's name, address and telephone number;

- the subject matter on which the expert will testify;

- the facts known by the expert that relate to or form the basis of the expert's mental impressions and opinions formed or made in connection with the case in which the discovery is sought, regardless of when and how the factual information was acquired;

- the expert's mental impressions and opinions formed or made in connection with the case in which the discovery is sought, and any methods used to derive them;

- any bias of the witness;

- all documents, tangible things, reports, models, or data compilations that have been provided to, reviewed by, or prepared by or for the expert in anticipation of the expert's testimony;

- the expert's current resume and bibliography.

TEX. R. CIV. P. 192.3(e). As with fact witnesses, the identification of expert witnesses must be in writing; oral notification is insufficient. *Sharp v. Broadway Nat'l. Bank*, 784 S.W.2d 669 (Tex. 1990). A party may not require the opposing party to disclose the identity of purely consulting experts. TEX. R. CIV. P. 192.3(e).

The scope of the consulting expert exemption was modified by the 1990 amendments to former Rule 166b. Prior to the amendment, discovery pertaining to a consulting expert was permitted if the expert's work product formed "the basis either in whole or in part of the opinions of a [testifying] expert. " The amendments deleted that standard and substituted a test of whether the consulting expert's opinion or impressions had been "reviewed" by a testifying expert. This change is carried forward in the 1999 amendments to the rules. *See* TEX. R. CIV. P. 192.3(e).

It is important to note that the mental impressions and opinions of consulting experts whose work product was not reviewed by a testifying expert are shielded from discovery *only* when those mental impressions and opinions were acquired or developed in anticipation of litigation or in the course of the prosecution or defense of a claim. *Lindsey v. O'Neill*, 689 S.W.2d 400 (Tex. 1985); *Essex Crane Rental Corp. v. Kitzman*, 723 S.W.2d 241 (Tex. App.—Houston [1st Dist.] 1986, no writ). Thus, an employee who forms opinions based upon information acquired in the area of his employment would not qualify as a consulting expert because he was not employed in anticipation of litigation. *See Axelson, Inc.*

v. *McIlhany*, 798 S.W.2d 550 (Tex. 1990). On the other hand, an employee may qualify as a consulting expert if he was reassigned to another subject area specifically in anticipation of litigation arising out of an incident or transaction. *Id.*

The factual knowledge, as opposed to the mental impressions and opinions, of a consulting expert are discoverable unless the information was acquired solely through consultation. *Axelson, Inc. v. McIlhany, supra.*

In order to protect an expert's observations, impressions, and opinions from discovery under the consulting expert exemption, a party must positively state that the expert will not testify and will be used solely for consultation. *Barker v. Dunham*, 551 S.W.2d 41, 44 (Tex. 1977).

If a party is seeking affirmative relief, expert witnesses must be disclosed by the later of the following two dates: either 30 days after the request for the information is served, or 90 days before the end of the discovery period. TEX. R. CIV. P. 195.2. All other experts must be disclosed 60 days before the end of the discovery period. TEX. R. CIV. P. 195.2.

The rules do not dictate when a party must retain its testifying experts and do not require immediate identification after the expert is contacted.

It has been held under the old rules that the trial court may compel a party to determine whether an expert is a testifying or consulting expert by a specific date. *Loftin v. Martin*, 776 S.W.2d 145 (Tex. 1989). Under the new rules, the trial court has considerable discretion to fashion discovery orders for the case. TEX. R. CIV. P.191.1. Therefore, the court continues to have the power to require parties to decide who will and will not testify at trial by a date certain.

Parties occasionally re-designate a disclosed testifying expert with the hope of invoking the consulting expert privilege. However, the Texas Supreme Court has declared that such a re-designation is invalid when made as part of a bargain between settling adversaries to prevent another party from discovering the expert's opinions and impressions. *Tom L. Scott, Inc. v. McIlhany*, 798 S.W.2d 556 (Tex. 1990).

§7.20 Documents

Upon proper request, a party can be required to produce all documents that are within the scope of discovery. TEX. R. CIV. P. 196.1.

If a party seeks the discovery of electronic or magnetic data, the party making the request must specifically request the production of electronic or magnetic data and must specify the form in which the requesting party wants it produced. TEX. R. CIV. P. 196.4.

§7.21 Tax Returns

Tax returns are discoverable to the extent that they are relevant and material to the issues in the case. *Maresca v. Marks*, 362 S.W.2d 299 (Tex. 1962); *Narro Warehouse, Inc. v. Kelly*, 530 S.W.2d 146, 150 (Tex. Civ. App.—Corpus Christi 1975, writ ref'd n. re.). Because of the private nature of tax returns, the movant must show why the information contained in the returns is relevant and the court must conduct an in camera review to separate the relevant and irrelevant portions of the returns prior to disclosure. *Id.* The courts are reluctant to permit unnecessary discovery of federal income tax returns. *Sears, Roebuck & Co. v. Ramirez*, 824 S.W.2d 558 (Tex. 1992).

§7.22 Financial Records

All financial records are subject to discovery if they contain relevant information or are likely to lead to the discovery of relevant information. *See, e.g., Wielgosz v. Millard*, 679 S.W.2d 163, 167 (Tex. App.—Houston [14th Dist.] 1984, no writ) (bank records, invoices, receipts, financial statements); *Bottinelli v. Robinson*, 594 S.W.2d 112, 115 (Tex. Civ. App.—Houston [1st Dist.] 1979, no writ) (canceled checks, checkbook stubs, and financial statements). *See also* Longley & Kincaid, *Discovery and Sanctions for Discovery Abuse*, 18 ST. MARY'S L. J. 163, 171-172 (1986) for a comprehensive list of the types of records that are discoverable.

§7.23 Photographs

Photographs are discoverable, even if made in the investigation, prosecution or defense of a claim. *Houdaille Industries, Inc. v. Cunningham*, 502 S.W.2d 544, 549 (Tex. 1973); *Allen v. Humphreys*, 559 S.W.2d 798, 802 (Tex. 1977); *Terry v. Lawrence*, 700 S.W.2d 912, 913 (Tex. 1985). If photographs are part of the report of an expert, they take on the character of the report; that is, if the report is discoverable then the photographs are as well. *Allen v. Humphreys, supra.*

§7.24 Indemnity, Insuring and Settlement Agreements

The existence and contents of insurance policies under which the insuring company may be liable to satisfy all or part of a judgment in a case may be obtained by the opposing party. TEX. R. CIV. P. 192.3(f). The existence and contents of settlement agreements also are discoverable. TEX. R. CIV. P. 192.3(g). These documents must be produced in response to a request for disclosure under Rule 194. *See* TEX. R. CIV. P. 194.2(g).

§7.25 Medical Records

Medical records or an authorization to obtain medical records and bills that are reasonably related to any personal injury damages claimed, may be obtained through discovery. TEX. R. CIV. P. 194.2(j). And, if the medical records are obtained by the opponent through use of a medical authorization, the party providing the authorization is entitled to obtain copies of those records. TEX. R. CIV. P. 194.2(k).

Although relevant medical records may be obtained, a patient cannot be required to sign an authorization waiving all privilege as to unrelated medical treatments, nor can a patient be required to allow the opposing party to question his physician outside the presence of his attorney. *See Mutter v. Wood*, 744 S.W.2d 600 (Tex. 1988). An order compelling the discovery of medical records must be restrictively drawn to maintain the privilege with respect to records or communications not relevant to the medical or psychological claims at issue. *Groves v. Gabriel*, 874 S.W.2d 660 (Tex. 1994).

Although Rules 509 and 510 of the Texas Rules of Civil Evidence create a privilege for medical and mental health records respectively, there are a number of exceptions to the privilege. The most common is the "patient-litigant" exception. This exception applies when (1) the records sought to be discovered are relevant to the condition at issue, and (2) the condition is relied upon as a legally significant part of a party's claim or defense, meaning that the condition itself is a fact to which the substantive law assigns significance. *R.K. v. Ramirez*, 887 S.W.2d 836 (Tex. 1994). If both parts of the test are met, the trial court, if requested, should conduct an in camera inspection to assure that records produced are closely related in time and scope to the claims made. *Id.* However, it appears that even if the documents are privileged and not subject to the patient-litigant exception, they may still be subject to disclosure under the "offensive use" doctrine. *See Midkiff v. Shaver*, 788 S.W.2d 399 (Tex. App.—Amarillo 1990, no writ) (plaintiff's claim for mental anguish was sufficient to authorize discovery of information concerning treatment for that condition under the "offensive use" doctrine, even though the information was privileged under the Rules of Evidence and did not fall within the patient-litigant exception); *See R.K. v. Ramirez*, 887 S.W.2d at 841 (offensive use doctrine independent from patient-litigant exception).

§7.26 Statements

A party may obtain discovery of a witness statement, i.e. the statement of a person with knowledge of relevant facts, regardless of when the statement was made. A witness statement is defined in the rules as one that is:

1. A written statement signed or otherwise adopted or approved in writing by the person making it, or

2. A stenographic, mechanical, electrical or other type of recording of the witness's oral statement, or any substantially verbatim transcription of such a recording.

TEX. R. CIV. P. 192.3(h). Notes that are taken during an interview or conversation with a witness are not a witness statement under the rule. TEX. R. CIV. P. 192.3(h).

Any person may obtain, upon written request, any statements he or she has made concerning the lawsuit that are in the possession, custody or control of any party. TEX. R. CIV. P. 192.3(h).

§7.27 Wealth of Parties

Information regarding the wealth of parties is discoverable when relevant. For example, evidence of the defendant's net worth is discoverable when exemplary damages are sought. *Lunsford v. Morris*, 746 S.W.2d 471 (Tex. 1988). This rule is doubtless applicable to statutory additional damages under the DTPA. The amount of a *plaintiff's* assets may be relevant if the defendant raises the affirmative defense that the plaintiff is a "business consumer" as defined in DTPA §17.45(10). *See Eckman v. Centennial Sav. Bank*, 784 S.W.2d 672 (Tex. 1990).

§7.28 Other Claims

Information regarding other claims, lawsuits, and complaints against a defendant are discoverable when relevant or when likely to lead to the discovery of admissible evidence. For example, in a breach of warranty action, other complaints and warranty claims regarding the defendant's products are discoverable because they are relevant to the issues of the existence of a defect in a product, the cause of the injuries or damages, and the manufacturer's knowledge of problems in the product. *See Independent Insulating Glass/Southwest, Inc. v. Street*, 722 S.W.2d 798, 803 (Tex. App.—Fort Worth 1987, writ dism'd w.o.j.); *Allen v. Humphreys*, 559 S.W.2d 798, 803 (Tex. 1977). Prior claims are also relevant to show a plan, routine, scheme, or course of dealing on the part of a party, in that they tend to prove that the party acted in conformity with such pattern on the occasion in question. *See Independent Insulating Glass, supra; Aztec Life Ins. Co. v. Dellana*, 667 S.W.2d 911, 915 (Tex. App.—Austin 1984, no writ);

TEX. R. CIV. EVID. 406; *see also Underwriters Life Ins. Co. v. Cobb*, 746 S.W.2d 810, 815 (Tex. App.—Corpus Christi 1988, no writ). This type of information is often sought when a party's knowledge or state of mind is relevant, as for example when punitive or statutory additional damages are sought. *Id.*; TEX. R. CIV. EVID. 404(b).

§7.29 Insurance Company Files

In unfair claims settlement practices litigation, the insurance company's claim file is obviously relevant to the issue of the company's diligence in investigating the claim and its good faith in acting on it. The insurance company's "file" (i.e. all internal records pertaining to the claim) is thus discoverable except to the extent it may be covered by an exemption contained in the rules. For example, portions of claims files may be protected from discovery if they contain attorney work product. *See generally* TEX. R. CIV. P. 192.5; *Humphreys v. Caldwell*, 888 S.W.2d 469 (Tex. 1994). Note that the work product privilege is continuing. Therefore, the documents are privileged even if they are later sought in a subsequent third-party action. *Id.* In most cases, however, at least those documents generated before denial of the claim are discoverable. *See National Surety Corp. v. Dominguez*, 715 S.W.2d 67 (Tex. App.—Corpus Christi 1986, orig. proceeding); *Eckermann v. Williams*, 740 S.W.2d 23 (Tex. App.—Austin 1987, no writ); *Southern Casualty Co. v. Dyer*, 722 S.W.2d 548 (Tex. App.—Austin 1987, no writ); *Service Lloyds Ins. Co. v. Clark*, 714 S.W.2d 437 (Tex. App.—Austin 1986, no writ).

In a bad faith case that has been bifurcated, discovery of the claims file may be delayed until the underlying contract claim has been resolved. *Maryland Am. Gen. Ins. Co. v. Blackmon*, 639 S.W.2d 455 (Tex. 1982); *see Western Cas. & Sur. Co. v. Spears*, 730 S.W.2d 821, 823 (Tex. App.—San Antonio 1987, no writ).

§7.30 Land

Rule 196.7 expressly authorizes a party to obtain permission to enter upon and inspect land or other property under the possession, custody, or control of another party. TEX. R. CIV. P. 196.7(a). In addition to inspecting the property, a party may measure, survey, photograph, test, or sample the property or designated objects or operations on the property. *Id.*

§7.31 Exemptions from Discovery

The rules of civil procedure expressly exempt from disclosure two specific categories of information: (a) work product, which now includes the old party communication privilege, TEX. R. CIV. P. 192.5, and (b) by inference, certain consulting experts, TEX. R. CIV. P. 194.2(f).

Although "core" work product (that containing mental impressions, opinions, conclusions, or legal theories of the attorney or the attorney's representative) is never discoverable, all other work product may be discoverable if the party seeking discovery has a substantial need for the materials in preparing for trial *and* is unable to obtain the substantial equivalent by other means, without undue hardship. TEX. R. CIV. P. 192.5(b)(2).

§7.32 Work Product

Rule 192.5(a) defines work product as either material prepared or mental impressions developed in anticipation of litigation by or for a party or a party's representative, or, communications made in anticipation of litigation between or among the party and the party's representatives. TEX. R. CIV. P. 192.5(a). Under this rule, there is "core" work product and then there is any other kind of work product. "Core" work product is that work product of an attorney or attorney's representative that contains their mental impressions, opinions, conclusions, and legal theories. Core work product is not discoverable for any purpose. TEX. R. CIV. P. 192.5(b)(1). Any work product other than core work product is discoverable if the party seeking the discovery has a "substantial need" for the materials and is unable to obtain the substantial equivalent of the materials without undue hardship. TEX. R. CIV. P. 192.5(b)(2). Of course, the court has the power to take reasonable steps to protect a party from disclosing any core work product if the disclosure of non-core work product is ordered. TEX. R. CIV. P. 192.5(b)(4).

Certain items are not considered work product under any circumstances. These are:

- information on expert witnesses, fact witnesses, statements of witnesses, and a party's contentions that otherwise are discoverable under Rule 192.3

- trial exhibits (if they have been ordered disclosed under other rules)

- any photographic or electronic picture that depicts any underlying facts relevant to the lawsuit

- any work product that would be considered an exception to the attorney-client privilege in TEX. R. CIV. EVID. 503(d)

At first glance, Rule 192 appears to be a substantial departure from existing case law, which suggested that the work product privilege broadly included "specific documents, reports, communications, memoranda, mental impressions, conclusions, opinions, or legal theories prepared or assembled in actual anticipation of litigation." *National Tank Co. v. Brotherton*, 851 S.W.2d 193, 200 (Tex. 1993); *Humphreys v. Caldwell*, 888 S.W.2d 469, 471 (Tex. 1994); *Evans v. State Farm Mut. Auto. Ins. Co.*, 685 S.W.2d 765 (Tex. App.—Houston [1st Dist.] 1985, writ ref'd n.r.e.); *Brown & Root, Inc. v. Moore*, 731 S.W.2d 137, 140 (Tex. App.—Houston [14th Dist.] 1987, no writ); *see also Hickman v. Taylor*, 329 U.S. 495 (1947). However, the fundamental aim of the work production exemption has long been to protect the mental impressions and opinions of a party's attorney. *See, e.g., United States v. Nobles*, 422 U.S. 225 (1975). For example, before the amendments to the rules of procedure, it was suggested that the work product privilege applied to mental impressions and strategy, not the facts of the case. *Axelson, Inc. v. McIlhany*, 798 S.W.2d 550, 554, n. 8 (Tex. 1991)(dicta); *see also National Union Fire Ins. Co. v. Valdez*, 863 S.W.2d 458, 460 (Tex. 1993) (file memorandum not necessarily work product even though prepared by an attorney). Thus, even before Rule 192, there was no abuse of discretion in ordering the production of portions of an attorney's notes that were neutral recitals of facts, without commentary, prepared during a conference with a witness who died before his deposition could be taken. *Leede Oil and Gas, Inc. v. McCorkle*, 789 S.W.2d 686 (Tex. App.—Houston [1st Dist.] 1990, no writ). For these reasons, Rule 192 appears to be less a change in the law than a concise summary of the limited parameters that already had been placed on the work product exemption in recent years.

§7.33 Other Privileged Information

The rules do not change the privileges accorded in other statutes or rules. *See, e.g.,* TEX. R. CIV. EVID. 501-512; GOODE, WELLBORN, & SHARLOT, GUIDE TO THE TEXAS RULES OF EVIDENCE CIVIL AND CRIMINAL, 2ND ED., Chapter 5 (1993). Chief among these privileges are attorney-client communications, husband-wife communications, confidential communications to a clergyman, physician-patient communications, and mental health information.

§7.34 Subpoenas

A subpoena may be issued by any of the following persons:

1. The clerk of the appropriate district, county, or justice court, who must provide the party requesting the subpoena with an original and a copy for each witness that the party must then complete;

2. An attorney authorized to practice in the State of Texas as an officer of the court; or

3. An officer authorized to take depositions in Texas, who must issue the subpoena immediately on a request accompanied by a notice to take a deposition under either Rule 199 or Rule 200, or a notice under Rule 205.3, and who may also serve the notice with the subpoena.

TEX. R. CIV. P. 176.4.

Service of a subpoena may be accomplished by any sheriff or constable, or any person who is not a party and is 18 years of age or older. Proper service of a subpoena requires that a copy be delivered to the witness, together with any fee required by law. If the witness is a party and is represented by an attorney of record, then service may be made on the witness's attorney. TEX. R. CIV. P. 176.5(a).

In order to prove that the subpoena was served, either of the following documents may be filed with the court: (1) the witness's signed memorandum attached to the subpoena showing that the witness accepted the subpoena; or (2) a statement by the person who made the service stating the date, time, and manner of service, and the name of the person served. TEX. R. CIV. P. 176.5(b).

A subpoena may not command a person to produce documents or appear in a county that is more than 150 miles from where the person resides or is served. TEX. R. CIV. P. 176.3.

If a person is commanded only to produce documents or things, then he or she need not appear in person at the designated time and place so long as the documents or things are there. TEX. R. CIV. P. 176.6(c).

Objections to subpoena for documents or things may be made by serving written objections to producing all or any designated part of the materials requested on the party issuing the subpoena. The objections, however, must be delivered before the time specified for compliance in the subpoena. TEX. R. CIV. P. 176.6(d).

Anyone objecting to a subpoena for testimony, whether in deposition, hearing, or trial, as well as a person commanded to produce documents and things, may move for a protective order under TEX. R. CIV. P. 192.6(b) so long as the motion is filed before the time specified for compliance. The motion may be filed either in the court in which the action is pending or in the court in the county where service occurred. TEX. R. CIV. P. 176.6(e). In the event the subpoena is for a hearing or a trial, the person subpoenaed also has the option of objecting or moving for a protective order before the court at the time and place specified for compliance, rather than in advance of that date and time. TEX. R. CIV. P. 176.6(f).

A person causing a subpoena to issue must take reasonable steps to protect the person subpoenaed from incurring undue burden or expense. In this regard, upon ruling on any objections, the court must give the person subpoenaed "adequate time" for compliance, and the court may impose certain conditions so as to lessen the burden or expense, including compensating the witness for undue hardship. TEX. R. CIV. P. 176.7.

Subpoenas are enforced by contempt, and a person who fails to obey a subpoena without adequate excuse may be fined, imprisoned, or both. TEX. R. CIV. P. 176.8(a). These sanctions may be imposed only if all fees due the witness were paid or tendered. TEX. R. CIV. P. 176.8(b).

It is important to note that subpoenas may not be used to circumvent the discovery rules or the limitations on discovery contained in those rules. TEX. R. CIV. P. 176.3(b). This means that a deposition subpoena directed at a party is subject to the procedures set forth in Rules 196, 199, and 200, and a deposition subpoena to a non-party is subject to the procedures in Rule 205.

[a] FORM: Subpoena

```
                              NO. _____

_____             §    IN THE _____ COURT OF
                       §
                       §
vs.                    §    _____ COUNTY, TEXAS
                       §
_____             §    _____ [JUDICIAL DISTRICT]
```

THE STATE OF TEXAS

SUBPOENA [DUCES TECUM]

TO: _____ [*person subpoenaed*]
    _____ [*address*]

GREETINGS:

YOU ARE COMMANDED TO:

Attend and give testimony at a deposition [*or hearing or trial*] at [*insert address where witness is to appear*] on the _____ day of _____, _____, at __.m. then and there to give testimony in the case referenced above. You must remain at the place of

_____ [deposition, hearing or trial] from day to day until discharged by the court or by the party summoning the witness.

[*Optional. When subpoena is directed to organization*]

The matters on which examination is requested are: _____ [*explain, e.g.*, the practices and policies of the organization concerning the investigation of claims of patient abuse and the incident date *[date]*.] Under Texas Rule of Civil Procedure 176.6(b) you must designate one or more persons to testify on your behalf as to matters known or reasonably available to the organization.

YOU ALSO ARE COMMANDED TO:

Produce and permit inspection and copying of the documents or tangible things that are described on **Exhibit A**. The inspection and/or copying will occur at the same place, date and time that you have been directed to attend for the purpose of giving testimony.

[*or*]

YOU ARE COMMANDED TO deliver the documents or tangible things that are described on **Exhibit A** to this subpoena for inspection and copying by the party who requested that this subpoena be issued or that party's attorney and/or representative. The documents and/or tangible things shall be produced at [*insert address where documents are to be produced*] on the _____ day of _____, _____, at __.m.

Party directing issuance of subpoena: [*insert name of party at whose instance subpoena is issued*].

Attorney of record: [*insert name of attorney of record of party at whose instance subpoena is issued*].

A witness fee of $_____ is attached.

Date issued: [*insert date subpoena issued*]

ISSUED BY: _____

  [*Signature of person issuing subpoena*]

  [*typed/printed name of person issuing subpoena*]

PLEASE TAKE NOTICE that failure by any person without adequate excuse to obey a subpoena served upon that person may be deemed in contempt of the court from which the subpoena is issued or a district court in the county in which the subpoena is served, and may be punished by fine or confinement, or both. Texas Rule of Civil Procedure §176.8(a), (b).

Acknowledgment of Service

I acknowledge that the foregoing document was accepted by me on this _____ day of _____, at _____ o'clock __.m.

_____

[*signature of person served*]

Statement of Service

The foregoing subpoena was served by me on the person to whom this subpoena is directed on this _____ day of _____, at _____ o'clock ___.m. by hand delivery to the person named.

_____

[*signature of person making service*]

§7.35 Forms of Discovery

The Texas Rules of Civil Procedure recognize the following forms of discovery:

(A) Requests for disclosure

(B) Requests for production and inspection of documents and tangible things

(C) Requests and motions for entry upon and examination of real property

(D) Interrogatories to a party

(E) Requests for admission

(F) Oral or written depositions

(G) Motion for mental or physical examinations

TEX. R. CIV. P. 192.1. These forms of discovery may be used in any sequence that a party desires. They also may be combined in the same document. TEX. R. CIV. P. 192.2.

Not all of these discovery tools will be necessary in any particular case. Generally, DTPA cases can be fully prepared by using a request for disclosure, some interrogatories, a request for production, perhaps a request for admission, and one or more oral depositions. In most cases, the recommended practice is to initiate discovery with a request for disclosure. Then, depending on the information and documents obtained, the need for additional types of discovery can be determined.

Motions for production from third parties, depositions by written questions, formal requests for inspection of land and objects, and physical and mental examinations of persons are not frequently utilized in deceptive trade practice litigation. Accordingly, these discovery tools will not be discussed in this chapter.

The form of discovery selected dictates, to some extent, the breadth of the discovery requests that can be made using that form. For example, a request for production of documents must specify which documents or class of documents are sought. Otherwise, the request will be objectionable as overly broad. *Loftin v. Martin*, 776 S.W.2d 145, 148 (Tex. 1989). It has been suggested that greater latitude is allowed when the forms of discovery are either interrogatories or depositions. *See, e.g., Loftin v. Martin*, 776 S.W.2d 148: "[u]nlike interrogatories and depositions, Rule 167 is not a fishing rule." In *K-Mart Corp. v. Sanderson*, 937 S.W.2d 429 (Tex. 1996), however, the court stated unequivocally, "[w]e reject the notion that any discovery device can be used to 'fish.'" Thus, although interrogatories and depositions do not need to be as precise as requests for production, any discovery device is subject to an overly broad objection if it inquires into matters that have no bearing on the issues in question. As the court observed in *Sanderson*, "the burden of answering interrogatories [that are overly broad] is hardly less to K-Mart than producing documents containing the same information." *Id.* at 430.

The forms of discovery that may be used and as well as the extent to which the forms can be used is determined to a degree by the level of discovery applicable to the case based on the discovery control plan.

§7.36 Discovery Control Plan

For any case filed after January 1, 1999, a discovery control plan must govern the case. Misc. Docket No. 98-9196, *Approval of Revisions to the Texas Rules of Civil Procedure*, 61 TEX. BAR J. 1140 (1998). And, in the first numbered paragraph of all lawsuits filed after January 1, the plaintiff must state whether discovery is intended to be conducted under Level 1, Level 2 or Level 3 of Rule 190. TEX. R. CIV. P. 190.1.

The purpose of a discovery control plan is primarily to reduce the costs of litigation. *Explanatory Statement Accompanying the 1999 Amendments to the Rules of Civil Procedure Governing Discovery*, 61 TEX. BAR J. 1140 (1998). Costs savings are achieved by limiting the discovery that can be used and by limiting the amount of time that can be spent deposing witnesses. Also, the rules fix a period of time after a lawsuit is filed within which all discovery must be conducted. Procedurally, the amount of discovery that can be conducted is determined by the level of discovery applicable to the case. Each of these levels of discovery is discussed below.

By agreement, the parties can modify discovery control plans, and if done in the form of a Rule 11 agreement, the agreed upon modifications will be enforced. TEX. R. CIV. P. 191.1.

The limitations on discovery set forth in Rule 190 do not apply to discovery conducted under Rule 202 ("Depositions before suit or to investigate claims") or Rule 621a ("Discovery and Enforcement of Judgment"). However, Rule 202 cannot be used to circumvent the limitations in Rule 190. TEX. R. CIV. P. 190.6.

§7.37 Expedited Actions and Level 1 Discovery

In 2011, the Legislature amended section 22,004 of the *Texas Government Code* authorizing the Texas Supreme Court to adopt new rules of procedure to "promote the prompt, efficient, and cost-effective resolution of civil actions" in which the amount in controversy, inclusive of all costs, attorney's fees and damages of any kind, does not exceed $100,000.

Acts 2011, 82nd Leg., Ch. 203 (H.B. 274). In response, the Texas Supreme Court adopted significant amendments to Rules 47 and 190.2, as well as a completely new Rule 169 governing "Expedited Actions." Misc. Docket No. 12-9191 (Texas Supreme Court, Nov. 13. 2012).

Rule 190.2, defining the Level 1 discovery control plan, has been substantially re-written to provide a restricted discovery control plan for certain expedited actions governed by new Rule 169. Level 1 discovery rules govern any DTPA case in which the plaintiff pleads that he will seek only monetary relief aggregating $100,000 or less, inclusive of all damages, exemplary damages, costs, prejudgment interest, and attorney's fees. TEX. R. CIV. P. 169(a)(1). The parties will no longer be able opt out of Level 1 by agreement; rather, only the court can remove a case from a Level 1 discovery control plan, and then only upon a motion with a showing of "good cause." TEX. R. CIV. P. 169(a)(1).

Under Level 1, the discovery period opens on the day suit is filed and closes 180 days after the first discovery request is served. TEX. R. CIV. P. 190.2(b)(1). Thus, if a request for disclosure or other discovery request is included with the original petition, the discovery period closes 180 days after the suit is served.

Total deposition time under Level 1 is limited to no more than six hours per party. The parties may agree to expand this time up to ten hours total; however, any time over ten hours must be approved by the court. TEX. R. CIV. P. 190.2(b)(2). The court may modify the deposition hours so that no party is given an unfair advantage. It is suggested that when a plaintiff in a DTPA case must, of necessity, sue several persons or entities who may have identical interests, e.g. manufacturer and dealer, or real estate broker and real estate agent, it would create an unfair advantage if one side of the lawsuit is given twelve hours to depose persons whereas the plaintiff, who has the burden of proof, is limited to only six. In a situation such as this, the court should examine whether there is any need for discovery by a co-defendant that is over and above the needs of the other defendant, and the time for depositions should be allotted accordingly.

Interrogatories under Level 1 are limited to no more than 15, excluding any interrogatories asking a party to identify or authenticate specific documents. TEX. R. CIV. P. 190.2(b)(3). Each discrete subpart of an interrogatory is considered a separate interrogatory. TEX. R. CIV. P. 190.2(b)(3). Now, requests for production are limited no more than 15 separate requests. TEX. R. CIV. P. 190.2(b)(4). Further, requests for admissions are now limited to 15 separate requests. TEX. R. CIV. P. 190.2(b)(5).

A new discovery tool has also been added into Level 1 only: As part of the standard request for disclosure under Rule 194.2, a party may now request disclosure of all documents, electronic information and tangible items that the disclosing party has in its possession, custody or control and may use to support its claims or defenses. TEX. R. CIV. P. 190.2(b)(6). This part of the request for disclosure does not count towards the limit on requests for production. *Id.*

As noted above, the court can remove a case from the expedited action procedures and the Level 1 discovery control plan on motion showing good cause. Tex. R. Civ. P. 169(c). An expedited action may also be removed from the restrictions of Level 1 if any claimant (other than a counterclaimant) timely amends a claim to assert relief outside of the $100,000 or less monetary restriction. TEX. R. CIV. P. 169(c). To be timely, the pleading must be filed no later than 30 days after discovery is closed or 30 days before trial, whichever is earlier, unless leave of court is obtained. For instance, if the plaintiff amends to add a claim for declaratory relief or for an order of rescission and restitution, the suit is no longer for "only monetary relief" and is no longer properly considered an expedited action. In that case, the discovery period reopens, any trial date is continued and the suit is thereafter governed by the provisions of Level 2 or Level 3. Tex. R. Civ. P. Rules 169(c)(3), 190.2(c).

In expedited actions governed by Level 1, the admissibility of expert testimony may not be challenged before trial except in response to a motion for summary judgment. Tex. R. Civ. P. Rule 169(d)(4).

§7.38 Level 2 Discovery

Unless a case is governed by Level 1 discovery (no more than $100,000 total sought) or Level 3 discovery (court ordered plan), it will be governed by Level 2 discovery. Tex. R. Civ. P. 190.3(a).

Under Level 2, in DTPA cases, all discovery must be completed before the earlier of (a) 30 days before trial, or (b) nine months after the earlier of the date of the first oral deposition or the due date of the first response to written discovery. Tex. R. Civ. P. 190.3(b). It is important to remember that if one has the habit of attaching discovery to the original petition when it is filed, this act will fix the ending date within which all discovery must be completed, i.e. the deadline for discovery would be nine months after the due date for the responses to the discovery that is served with the petition.

Unlike Level 1 discovery that gives each *party* a certain amount of time for depositions, Level 2 discovery limits the time that may be spent in depositions to 50 hours *per side*. Tex. R. Civ. P. 190.3(b)(2). "Side" is defined in the rule as "all the litigants with generally common interests in the litigation." Tex. R. Civ. P. 190.3(b)(2). The exception to this rule is that if one side designates more than two experts, then the opposing side may have an additional six hours of deposition time for each additional expert designated. Tex. R. Civ. P. 190.3(b)(2). As with Level 1 discovery, the court may modify the total amount of deposition time allotted so as to not give one side an unfair advantage. Tex. R. Civ. P. 190.3(b)(2).

Interrogatories under Level 2 are limited to 25 questions, excluding interrogatories asking a party only to identify or authenticate specific documents. Tex. R. Civ. P. 190.3(b)(3). As with Level 1, each discrete subpart is considered a separate interrogatory. Tex. R. Civ. P. 190.3(b)(3).

§7.39 Level 3 Discovery

If a party makes a motion that a discovery control plan be fashioned for the particular needs of a case, then the court must grant that motion. Tex. R. Civ. P. 190.4(a). The court can also create a discovery control plan on its own motion. Tex. R. Civ. P. 190.4(a). If a motion is made, or if the court acts *sua sponte*, then any limitation contained in the rules of discovery can be changed. Tex. R. Civ. P. 190.4(b). The court's plan, however, must contain at least the following:

1. A date for trial or for a conference to determine a trial setting;

2. A discovery period during which either all discovery must be conducted, or all discovery requests must be sent, for the entire case or an appropriate phase of it;

3. Appropriate limitations on the amount of discovery; and

4. Deadlines for joining additional parties, amending or supplementing pleadings, and designating expert witnesses.

Tex. R. Civ. P. 190.4(b).

§7.40 Modification of a Discovery Control Plan

A court may modify a discovery control plan at any time, and must do so when the interests of justice requires. TEX. R. CIV. P. 190.5. Additionally, except in expedited actions governed by new Rule 169, the court must allow additional discovery under the following circumstances:

A. There are new or supplemental pleadings or new information disclosed in a discovery response or an amended or supplemental response. TEX. R. CIV. P. 190.5(a).

[NOTE: This exception applies only if the new or supplemental pleadings or responses were made either after the deadline for completion of discovery or so near the deadline as to deprive an adverse party of the opportunity to conduct discovery related to the new matters *and* the adverse party would be adversely affected without additional discovery. TEX. R. CIV. P. 190.5(a).]

B. Matters have changed materially after the discovery cut-off if trial is set or postponed so that the trial date is more than three months after the discovery period ends. TEX. R. CIV. P. 190.5(b).

[a] FORM: Motion to modify discovery control plan

```
_____          §    IN THE _____ COURT OF
                        §
vs.                     §    _____ COUNTY, TEXAS
                        §
_____          §    _____ [JUDICIAL DISTRICT]
```

MOTION TO MODIFY DISCOVERY CONTROL PLAN

TO THE HONORABLE JUDGE OF THE DISTRICT COURT:

_____, plaintiff [defendant] in the above entitled and numbered cause, moves the Court to modify the discovery control plan otherwise applicable to this lawsuit for the following reasons:

1. This motion is made pursuant to TEX. R. CIV. P. 190.5.

2. This is a suit under the Deceptive Trade Practices and Consumer Protection Act, TEX. BUS. & COM. CODE §17.41 et seq., cited in this motion as the "DTPA." Based on the pleadings, this case currently is governed by Level 1 discovery under TEX. R. CIV. P. 190.2.

3. [Insert specific grounds for motion, e.g. In this lawsuit, plaintiff has alleged that defendant "knowingly" engaged in the unlawful conduct that is alleged. Since plaintiff is a corporation, it will be necessary to depose each person who was involved in the decision making process that resulted in plaintiff being

the victim of a false, misleading and deceptive act or practice. Without deposition testimony from each of these witnesses, it would place an unjust burden on plaintiff and create an unnecessary obstacle in plaintiff's ability to prove that the corporation acted "knowingly"].

4. Plaintiff estimates that it will require an additional _____ hours of deposition time to obtain the necessary evidence.

5. Plaintiff also requests that the Court set a date for the trial of this case.

6. Plaintiff also requests that the Court set the discovery period for this case and that such period end _____ [insert deadline, e.g. thirty days before the date this case is set for trial].

7. Plaintiff also requests that this Court fix a deadline for adding parties, for amending or supplementing pleadings and for designation of expert witnesses.

8. This motion is made in the interest of justice and not merely for the purpose of obtaining additional deposition time.

WHEREFORE, plaintiff requests that this motion be granted.

_____
[Signature of attorney]

[Certificate of service]

[b] FORM: Order modifying discovery control plan

_____	§	IN THE _____ COURT OF
	§	
vs.	§	_____ COUNTY, TEXAS
	§	
_____	§	_____ [JUDICIAL DISTRICT]

ORDER MODIFYING DISCOVERY CONTROL PLAN

On this _____ day of _____, _____, came on for hearing the motion of plaintiff [defendant] to modify the discovery control plan applicable to this case. The court is of the opinion and so finds that the motion is well taken and should be granted.

IT IS THEREFORE ORDERED that the discovery control plan for this case is determined to be as follows:

Plaintiff estimates that it will require an additional _____ hours of deposition time to obtain the necessary evidence.

   A. The plaintiff shall have a total of _____ hours of deposition time; the defendant shall have a total of hours _____ of deposition time.

   B. This case is set for trial on the _____ day of _____, _____.

   C. The discovery period in this case shall end _____ [insert ending date for discovery, e.g., thirty days before the date this case is set for trial].

   D. No new parties shall be added to this lawsuit after the _____ day of _____, _____.

   E. The plaintiff shall amend or supplement pleadings no later than the _____ day of _____, _____; the defendant shall amend or supplement pleadings no later than the _____ day of _____, _____.

   F. The plaintiff shall designate all experts who will be called to testify at trial no later than the _____ day of _____, _____; the defendant shall designate all experts who will be called to testify at trial no later than the _____ day of _____, _____.

   SIGNED this _____ day of _____, _____.

                              _____
                              [*Signature of presiding judge*]

§7.41 Discovery Agreements

Most of the features of discovery control plans can be modified by agreement and are enforceable so long as they comply with Rule 11. Tex. R. Civ. P. 191.1. Under Rule 11, an agreement is enforceable so long as it is either (a) in writing, signed by the attorneys or parties and filed with the court, or, (b) made in open court and on the record. Tex. R. Civ. P. 11; *National Union Fire Ins. Co. v. Hudson Energy Co.*, 811 S.W.2d 552 (Tex. 1991).

[a] FORM: Rule 11 Agreement

```
[Date]

[Inside address]

    Re:[Cause no., style]

Dear _____:
```

This letter will confirm our agreement as follows: _____ [*Insert specific terms of agreement, e.g.* the plaintiff will have an additional thirty days within which to answer the request for disclosure served on him. This means that the responses to the request for disclosure will be due on _____].

If this letter accurately reflects our agreement, please sign in the space provided below, after which I will file the agreement with the court.

Thank you for your cooperation.

```
                          Sincerely,

                          [Signature of attorney]


[Signature line for opposing counsel]
```

§7.41.1 Requests for Disclosure

Historically, there have been standard interrogatories that are served on the opposing party in nearly every lawsuit. These interrogatories ask about such things as people with knowledge of facts, expert witnesses and insurance agreements. The discovery of basic facts can be delayed significantly when objections are made to these standard inquiries. In order to provide a more efficient means of allowing the parties to obtain basic information about the case without worrying whether their particular questions will be objected to, Rule 194 was written. *See* TEX. R. CIV. P. 194.1 - 194.6. This rule provides that a party to a lawsuit can serve a "Request for Disclosure" on other parties, using the exact language of the questions in the rule. If this is done, then "no objection or assertion of work product is permitted to a request" under Rule 194. TEX. R. CIV. P. 194.5. The following alternative forms may be used under Rule 194.

In 2013, Rule 190.2 was amended to create an additional request for disclosure. In suits governed by the expedited actions procedure and a Level 1 discovery control plan, a party may additionally request the disclosure of all documents, electronic information, and tangible items in the possession, custody or control of another party which the disclosing party may use in support of its claims or defenses. TEX. R. CIV. P. 190.2(b)(6) (effective March 1, 2013); *see* §5.01.1, *supra*. This request does not count toward the limit of requests for production. Forms [a] and [b] below can be modified as indicated to include this additional request for disclosure. Form [c] can be used as a supplemental request.

[a] FORM: Request for Disclosure (general form)

```
                    NO. _____

_____          §      IN THE DISTRICT COURT OF
                    §
    Vs.             §      _____ COUNTY, TEXAS
                    §
_____          §      _____ JUDICIAL DISTRICT
```

REQUEST FOR DISCLOSURE

TO: [*Opposing party, by and through attorney of record*]

Pursuant to Rule 194, you are requested to disclose, within 30 days of service of this request, the following information or material:

(a) The correct names of the parties to the lawsuit.

(b) The name, address, and telephone number of any potential parties.

(c) The legal theories and, in general, the factual bases of your claims or defenses.

(d) The amount of and method by which economic damages have been calculated.

(e) The names, addresses and telephone numbers of persons having knowledge of relevant facts, and a brief statement of each identified person's connection with the case.

(f) For any testifying expert: (1) the expert's name, address and telephone number, (2) the subject matter on which the expert will testify, (3) the general substance of the expert's mental impressions and opinions and a brief summary of the basis for them. If the testifying expert is not retained by, employed by, or otherwise subject to your control, then you are requested to produce documents reflecting the information in the three categories listed. If the expert is retained by, employed by, or otherwise subject to your control, then you are requested to produce the following: (1) all documents, tangible things, reports, models or data compilations that have been provided to, reviewed by or prepared by or for the expert in anticipation of the expert's testimony, and (2) the expert's current resume and bibliography.

(g) Any discoverable indemnity and insuring agreements described in Rule 192.3(f).

(h) Any settlement agreements described in Rule 192.3(g).

(i) Any witness statements described in Rule 192.3(h).

(j) [*In a suit alleging physical or mental injury and damages from the occurrence that is the subject of the case:* All medical records and bills that are reasonably related to the injuries or damages asserted or, in lieu thereof, an authorization permitting the disclosure of such medical records and bills].

(k) [*In a suit alleging physical or mental injury and damages from the occurrence that is the subject of the case:* All medical records and bills obtained by you by virtue of an authorization furnished by [the requesting party]].

(l) The name, address, and telephone number of any person who may be designated as a responsible third party.

[In expedited action cases, add the following]

[Pursuant to Rule 190.2(b)(6), *Texas Rules of Civil Procedure*, you are further requested to produce all documents, electronic information and tangible items that you have in your possession, custody or control and may use to support your claims or defenses in this action.]

           Respectfully submitted,

           [Signature of attorney]

[b] FORM: Request for Disclosure (short form)

```
                          NO. _____
_____                §      IN THE DISTRICT COURT OF
                          §
   vs.                    §      _____ COUNTY, TEXAS
                          §
_____                §      _____ JUDICIAL DISTRICT
```

REQUEST FOR DISCLOSURE

TO: [*Opposing party, by and through attorney of record*]

Pursuant to Rule 194, you are requested to disclose, within 30 days of service of this request, the following information or material described in Rule 194.2(a), (b), (c), (d), (e), (f), (g), (h), (i), (j), (k), and (l).

[In expedited action cases, add the following]

[Pursuant to Rule 190.2(b)(6), *Texas Rules of Civil Procedure*, you are further requested to produce all documents, electronic information and tangible items that you have in your possession, custody or control and may use to support your claims or defenses in this action.]

          Respectfully submitted,

          [Signature of attorney]

[c] FORM: Supplemental Request for Disclosure (Level 1 expedited actions)

```
                         NO. _____
_____               §       IN THE DISTRICT COURT OF
                         §
   vs.                   §       _____ COUNTY, TEXAS
                         §
_____               §       _____ JUDICIAL DISTRICT
```

SUPPLEMENTAL REQUEST FOR DISCLOSURE

TO: [*Opposing party, by and through attorney of record*]

Pursuant to Rule 190.2(b)(6), *Texas Rules of Civil Procedure*, Defendant is further requested to produce all documents, electronic information and tangible items that You have in Your possession, custody or control and may use to support Your claims or defenses in this action.

          Respectfully submitted,

          [Signature of attorney]

§7.42 Interrogatories

Written interrogatories can be an important tool for discovering facts inexpensively. They are useful in locating documents (including those that are not in the possession of the opposing party), extracting basic information about the transaction, and eliciting information that requires a search of files or records that may not be known to any particular agent or employee of a company and thus be difficult to obtain during oral deposition.

There are significant limitations on interrogatories. For cases that fall within Level 1, no more than 15 interrogatories (excluding any interrogatories asking a party only to identify or authenticate specific documents) may be sent to any other party. TEX. R. CIV. P. 190.2(b)(3). For Level 2 discovery control plan cases, no more than 25 interrogatories may be asked, excluding those interrogatories that ask a party to identify or authenticate specific documents. TEX. R. CIV. P. 190.3(b)(3). If a case is governed by Level 3 discovery, then the court may allow more interrogatories.

Within these limitations, a party may serve on another party, no later than thirty days before the end of the discovery period, written interrogatories to inquire about any matter within the scope of discovery, except those matters dealing with expert witnesses that are covered by Rule 195. Tex. R. Civ. P. 197.1.

An interrogatory may ask whether a party is making a specific factual or legal contention and may ask the responding party to state the legal theories and factual basis supporting that party's claims. Tex. R. Civ. P. 197.1. Interrogatories may not be used to require a party to marshal all of the party's evidence or to identify the proof that the party intends to offer at trial. Tex. R. Civ. P. 197.1.

An interrogatory can require a party to identify any person who is expected to testify at trial, except for rebuttal or impeaching witnesses who testimony cannot reasonably be anticipated before trial. Tex. R. Civ. P. 192.1(d).

Obviously, interrogatories are not the best tools for obtaining candid admissions or concessions from a party since the answers generally are reviewed by the answering party's attorney.

Interrogatory answers may be used against the answering party only. Tex. R. Civ. P. 197.3. Also, an answer to an interrogatory inquiring about matters described in Rule 194.2(c) and (d) (damages and legal theories as well as the factual bases for a party's claims) that has been amended or supplemented is not admissible and may not be used for impeachment. Tex. R. Civ. P. 197.3.

Interrogatories must be answered within thirty days from the date the interrogatories are served, unless they were served with the petition, in which event at least fifty days must be allowed. Tex. R. Civ. P. 197.2(a).

As noted, interrogatories may inquire into any matter that is discoverable. Accordingly, interrogatories should include broad inquiries designed to elicit the maximum amount of information per question. This is especially true since the rules are explicit that any "discrete subpart" of an interrogatory shall be considered a separate question. *See* Tex. R. Civ. P. 190.2(c)(3); 190.3(b)(3). Given the limitations on the number of interrogatories, it is tempting to rely upon requests for production to locate relevant documents and not to utilize interrogatories to inquire into the existence of such documents. One drawback to this approach, however, is that if an attorney relies upon requests for production, he may never learn of relevant documents that are not in the possession, custody or control of the opposing party.

§7.43 Drafting Interrogatories

Written interrogatories generally contain three components: (1) the notice and instructions to the receiving party, (2) the definitions, and (3) the questions. No particular arrangement of these components is mandated by the rules. One common approach is to attach the definitions and questions as an "exhibit" to the notice and instructions. The general form, which follows, utilizes this format.

Obviously the general form needs to be adapted to particular cases. For example, the term "product" is used for illustrative purposes only and should be changed to reflect the specific good or service in question. Depending upon the nature of the controversy, certain of the questions may be keyed to the "sale," "lease," "incident," "transaction" or "foreclosure." If so, those terms should be defined. In succeeding forms, specific inquiries applicable to different types of cases will be illustrated. Again, each of the illustrative questions should be revised to fit the facts of the case.

[a] FORM: Interrogatories (general form)

```
_____       §      IN THE _____ COURT OF
                     §
vs.                  §      _____ COUNTY, TEXAS
                     §
_____       §      _____ [JUDICIAL DISTRICT]
```

PLAINTIFF'S [DEFENDANT'S] INTERROGATORIES TO [OPPOSING PARTY]

TO: _____ , by and through his [her] attorney of record.

You are hereby directed to answer the interrogatories that are attached as Exhibit A. Your answers must be under oath except when your answers are based on information obtained from another person or when you are stating the names of persons with knowledge of relevant facts, trial witnesses and legal contentions. After your answers have been properly signed and notarized, you must deliver a true copy of your answers to the undersigned attorney, all of which must occur no later than thirty days after service of these interrogatories.

[NOTE: If the interrogatories are served with the original petition, then fifty days from service of the citation and petition must be allowed.]

If you object to any particular interrogatory or part of an interrogatory, answer all other interrogatories or portions of interrogatories to which no objection is made.

Respectfully submitted,

[*Signature of attorney*]

[*Certificate of service*]

EXHIBIT A

Definitions:

(a) Document(s) includes all writings (including notes, correspondence, memoranda, reports, computer print-outs, and journal entries), drawings, drafts, charts, photographs, tape or disc recordings (whether computer, sound, or video), and all other data compilations from which information can be obtained or translated, which are in your possession, custody, or control or which are known to you. Documents does not include the notes or memoranda of your attorneys made in connection with this case that contain your attorney's mental impressions or trial strategy, or correspondence between you and your attorney pertaining to this case.

(b) <u>Identify</u>, <u>identity</u>, <u>or identification</u> when used in reference to a natural person means to state his or her full name, the present or last known address of such person and his or her daytime telephone number; when used in reference to a corporation, agency or other entity means to state the full legal name of the corporation, agency, or other entity, its present or last known address, the name of the natural person in charge at that address and telephone number; when used in reference to a document, means to describe the document with sufficient particularity so as to distinguish it from all other documents by giving its date, a brief description of its subject matter and the natural person who authored the document.

(c) <u>Person</u> includes any individual, partnership, corporation, or other entity or group, however organized.

(d) You or your means [*name of answering party*], your [officers,] agents, servants, employees and representatives.

(e) Plaintiff refers to [*name of plaintiff*].

(f) Defendant refers to [*name of defendant*].

(g) Sale refers to [*insert description of sale, e.g.*, the sale by defendant to plaintiff of the product on or about [*date*]].

(h) Product means [*insert description of product, e.g.*, the 1998 Chevrolet Citation that is the subject of this suit].

<u>Interrogatories to be answered by you:</u>

1. Identify by category, all persons who have, claim to have or may have knowledge of any of the following matters:

(a) The sale, including any discussions or negotiations leading up to the sale;

(b) the condition of the product at the time of the sale;

(c) the cause of the malfunction of [*or* defect in] the product after it was sold to plaintiff;

(d) the manner and cost of repairing the alleged malfunction of [*or* defect in] the product;

(e) the type or amount of damages allegedly incurred by the plaintiff;

[**NOTE:** This information, generally, is supposed to be provided in response to a request for disclosure, Tex. R. Civ. P. 194.2(e); however, depending on the quality and quantity of the information received, it may be helpful to send this list of questions.]

4. Identify all documents, known to you, which pertain to [*name of party sending interrogatories*]. The documents are to be identified regardless of whether or not they are in your possession, custody or control. These documents include those pertaining to the sale and the product in question.

[**NOTE:** If the parties have dealt with each other on occasions other than the transaction in question the first sentence of this interrogatory may be unnecessarily broad. The following interrogatory may be more appropriate.]

[4. Identify all documents known to you that pertain to the sale or the product in question. These documents are to be identified regardless of whether they are in your possession, custody or control. These documents include all contracts, correspondence, loan documents, receipts, notes, and memoranda pertaining to the sale or the product.]

5. Identify any statement made by the plaintiff concerning the subject matter of this lawsuit.

6. Describe all conversations you have had with the plaintiff that concern the subject matter of this lawsuit. Include in your answer the following information:

(a) The date of the conversation; and

(b) The substance of the conversation; and

(c) The identities of all persons who participated in or overheard the conversation.

7. Identify all witnesses who will testify at this trial and give a brief description of each witness's connection to this case.

8. If you contend that the plaintiff is responsible, in whole or in part, for the damages or other losses that are claimed in this lawsuit, describe each and every act or omission by the plaintiff that you contend caused such damages, in whole or in part.

9. Identify all lawsuits filed against you since [*insert appropriate beginning date*] in which it was claimed that [*describe conduct*

alleged in lawsuit, e.g. you represented you would loan money to a person and failed to do so].

10. Identify all persons who have claimed, whether a lawsuit was filed or not, that you [*describe conduct alleged in lawsuit, e.g.* you represented you would loan money to a person and failed to do so].

11. Identify the person(s) executing the verification of these Interrogatories and who supplied the information used to provide your answers thereto.

12. To your knowledge, has any party or person with knowledge of facts relevant to this lawsuit ever been convicted of a felony or a crime involving moral turpitude? If so, state the nature of the charge and the date and place of arrest and conviction.

§7.44 Additional General Questions to Plaintiff

Additional general questions that defendants frequently ask include inquiries about the plaintiffs insurance coverage, if any, (to discover any subrogation claims), questions about the nature and extent of the plaintiff's damages, and prior claims that might involve the same damages.

[a] FORM: Additional questions (to plaintiff)

1. Identify all insurance policies under which you have or will submit a claim for any or all of the damages you claim in this lawsuit.

2. If any portion of the damages claimed by you consists of costs or expenses incurred or paid by or for you, then for each such cost or expense, state the amount, the person to whom it was paid or is owed, and a description of the good or service for which payment was made or is owed.

3. Identify each document pertaining to any cost or expense identified in response to the previous interrogatory.

4. Identify all persons from whom you have obtained an estimate of the cost to repair or replace the product involved in this suit or an opinion of the value of such product. For each, state the estimate or opinion and the date each was rendered.

[**NOTE:** Opinions of consulting experts are generally not discoverable.]

5. If you seek recovery of damages for mental anguish, then identify each doctor, psychiatrist, psychologist, counselor, or

other health care provider by whom you have been examined or from whom you sought or received treatment or advice for emotional or psychological problems during the last years.

6. If you seek recovery of damages for physical injuries, then identify each physician, hospital, clinic, doctor of osteopathy, chiropractor, therapist, or other health care provider by whom you have been examined or treated for any condition other than the common cold or influenza in the last years.

7. Identify by style, cause number, and county every lawsuit to which you are or were a party during the last years.

8. Specify the fee arrangement between you and your attorney and identify any written contract or fee agreement between you and your attorney.

9. If you contend or will contend that defendant was negligent or grossly negligent and that such negligence or gross negligence proximately caused all or any portion of the damages claimed by plaintiff, then, specify each way in which defendant was negligent or grossly negligent.

10. State the value of plaintiff's assets on [*the date of the transaction*]. If you contend that the value of plaintiff's assets was less than $25,000,000 on this date, then identify the following:

A. all financial statements, reports, or other documents indicating or tending to indicate the value of plaintiff's assets on that date; and

B. each person who has knowledge of the value of plaintiff's assets on that date.

[**NOTE:** This interrogatory is relevant to a party's status as a "business consumer." Such an interrogatory would be appropriate only if raised by appropriate pleading. *See Eckman v. Centennial Savings Bank,* 784 S.W.2d 672 (Tex. 1990).]

11. State all of the factors which were material to you in your decision to [*describe the plaintiff's complaint as necessary, e.g.,* purchase the house made the basis of your complaint].

§7.45 Additional Questions for Specific Cases

To the extent possible within the twenty-five question limit imposed by Rule 190.2 and Rule 190.3, questions may be added to the first set of interrogatories that are tailored to the particular transaction in question.

The forms in the following sections provide specific questions that are applicable to the following types of transactions:

- defective goods

- investments

- lender liability

- commercial leases

- unfair debt collection practices

Additional forms specific to those types of cases are located in the Chapters on Insurance (Chapter 11), Real Estate Sales (Chapter 12) and Residential Construction (Chapter 13). Separate questions for mobile home sales are not provided since the interrogatories relating to goods and residences, with slight modification, should apply. The interrogatories are illustrative in nature; it may be helpful to review all of the questions in forms [a] through [p] since a specific question in one case illustration may apply as well in other cases.

[a] FORM: Defective product (to defendant)

1. Identify by date each instance that the product was returned to you for inspection or repairs.

2. For each instance identified in response to the previous interrogatory, please provide the following information:

   A. the condition(s) of or defect(s) in the product for which the plaintiff sought repair or correction;

   B. the length of time that the product remained in your possession;

   C. the nature of the inspection or work performed on the product;

   D. the identity of the person(s) who performed the inspection or work;

   E. a description of any documents pertaining to the inspection or work; and

   F. the amount charged the manufacturer for the work performed.

3. State in detail what you contend or believe to be the cause of the [*describe the defect or malfunction, e.g.,* the water leaks inside the passenger compartment of the automobile].

4. State in detail what you contend or believe to be the nature of the repair work necessary to repair the [*describe defect or malfunction*].

5. State the retail cost of the work that you contend or believe is necessary to repair the [*describe the defect or malfunction*].

6. If you contend or believe that plaintiff has in any way created or contributed to the malfunction of the product or to the damage to the product, describe in detail the basis of that contention or belief.

7. Identify all bulletins, correspondence or other communications from the manufacturer that discuss or relate to [*describe condition or defect*] in all products sold by you that are of the same make or model as that purchased by plaintiff.

8. Identify all verbal or written warranties pertaining to the product or to the repair service.

[b] FORM: Defective product (to plaintiff)

1. What was the date on which you first noticed the [*describe defect, e.g.,* water leaking onto the floorboard] to which you refer in your petition.

2. Describe how you first discovered the [*describe defect*] and identify all persons who witnessed your discovery.

3. Identify each person, other than employees of defendant, who has inspected or worked on the product since it was purchased by you, and state the date of each instance of inspection or work.

4. For each instance identified in response to the previous interrogatory, please provide the following information:

    A. the conditions of the product for which plaintiff sought inspection or repair;

    B. the length of time that the product remained in possession of the party performing the inspection or repair;

    C. the nature of the inspection or the work performed on the product;

D. the cause of the condition for which repair was sought;

E. a description of any documents pertaining to the inspection of or work done on the product; and

F. the charge for the inspection of or work done on the product.

5. State in detail what you contend or believe to be the cause today of the [*describe the defect or malfunction*] in the product.

6. State in detail what you contend or believe to be the nature and cost of repair work necessary to repair the [*describe the defect or malfunction*].

7. Specify the terms of all express or implied warranties, other than written warranties, which you contend or believe were given by defendant in the course of the sale or subsequent repair work on the product.

8. Identify each written warranty that you contend or believe that defendant _____ ,gave to you in the course of the sale or subsequent repair work on the product.

9. Describe all statements by defendant, or any of his [or her] agents or employees that you contend or believe misrepresented any characteristic, condition, benefit, quality or quantity of product. For each such statement,

(a) identify the person who made the statement; and

(b) state the date on which it was made.

10. Identify each person who has operated [or used] the product since the date you purchased it.

[c] FORM: Lender liability: unauthorized withdrawal of funds (to defendant)

[**NOTE**: In the definitions section of the interrogatories, the phrase "account in question" should be defined.]

1. Identify by account name and number each signature card [and corporate resolution] pertaining to the accounts in question.

2. Identify the following persons:

(a) Your agent, employee, or representative who was present when each signature card [and corporate resolution] was presented to the bank by plaintiff or any person acting on plaintiff's behalf. Please specify which signature card [and corporate resolution] each such person was connected with; and

   (b) Your agent, employee, or representative who approved payment of plaintiff's checks numbered [*number of checks*], copies of which are attached to these interrogatories.

3. Identify the person or persons in charge of the accounts in question and the period of time for which they were in charge of or assigned to these accounts.

4. Describe in detail the procedure for reviewing checks drawn on accounts at your bank for determining whether signatures on the checks are authorized signatures and whether the required number of signatures are present. Also identify the person or persons in charge of that procedure during the following time period: _____.

5. Identify all memoranda, documents or manuals that set forth your procedures for (a) setting up checking accounts, (b) changing the authorized signatures on checking accounts, or (c) determining whether signatures on checks are the authorized signatures and whether the requisite number of authorized signatures are present on checks presented for payment.

6. Describe those facts that you contend authorized you to pay checks numbered [*number of checks*], copies of which are attached to these interrogatories.

7. Identify every term or provision of all documents that you contend justified your payment of checks numbered [*number of checks*], copies of which are attached to these interrogatories.

8. Identify which, if any, of the checks numbered [*number of checks*], copies of which are attached, that you contend benefited plaintiff. For each such check describe briefly the facts justifying your contention and identify the person with knowledge of those facts.

9. Identify which, if any, of the checks numbered [*number of checks*], copies of which are attached, for which you contend that payment was authorized by plaintiff. For each such check describe briefly the facts that justify your contention and identify the persons with knowledge of those facts.

[d] FORM: Lender liability: unauthorized withdrawal of funds (to plaintiff)

1. If you contend or believe that you received no benefit from the checks that form the basis of this suit, or that the checks were not used to pay your legitimate debts, state for each check the facts upon which you base your contention.

2. If you contend or believe that any officer, agent or employee of defendant represented to you that you had certain duties, rights or remedies under any agreement with the bank that you did not have, then for each such representation state the person who made the representation, the person to whom it was made, the date it was made and the substance of the statement.

3. Describe the factual basis for your contention that there exists a special relationship between you and defendant whereby defendant owed you a duty of good faith and fair dealing.

4. State in detail each way in which defendant allegedly failed to deal fairly and in good faith with you.

5. Identify each way in which defendant failed to exercise ordinary care in dealing with you.

6. State in detail all information or facts that you contend indicate that defendant knew that payment of the checks about which you complain had not been authorized.

7. For each check that you contend was wrongfully paid, how and when did you discover the allegedly unauthorized payment.

8. Identify the person who reviewed or whose responsibility it was to review the bank statements containing the checks in question.

9. Please state the job title and duties of [*insert name of person who actually signed checks*]. Include in your answer all authority this person has or has ever had to expend funds, sign checks or incur debt for you.

[e] FORM: Lender liability: false representation to extend credit (to defendant)

[**NOTE:** If a line of credit was revoked, use question number 1]

1. For the period of [*insert applicable time period*], describe the line of credit that you had extended to plaintiff and the period of time the line of credit was in effect. If the line of

credit was reduced during this period, indicate all factors that caused you to reduce the line of credit.

2. Identify all memoranda, notes or other documents discussing or pertaining to plaintiff's application for a loan [*or* the line of credit available to plaintiff].

3. Identify by date, persons present and topics discussed each meeting any officer, agent or employee of yours had with plaintiff in which the [*insert matter that forms basis of suit, e.g.*, loan application] was discussed.

4. Identify each and every reason you refused to make or fund a loan in the amount of to plaintiff [*or* refused to extend a line of credit in the amount of $_____ to plaintiff].

5. Identify all documents containing the criteria, factors, considerations or policies in effect during the months of [*insert appropriate time period*] that governed whether you would make loans [*or* extend a line of credit].

6. Identify every person on your loan committee(s) that reviewed, discussed or in any way considered the application or request of plaintiff for a loan [*or* line of credit]. State the dates of the meetings when such review, discussions or considerations took place and identify any notes, minutes, memoranda, summaries, recordings, or other documents reflecting the discussions or actions of the committee on those dates.

7. Identify all minutes and notes taken at all loan committee meetings and meetings of your Board of Directors that pertain to plaintiff.

8. Identify all documents created or circulated since [*insert appropriate date*] to the present that contain or refer to changes or modifications in your policies, standards, criteria or rules with respect to the making, renewal or extension of loans [*or* lines of credit].

[f] FORM: Lender liability: false representation to extend credit (to plaintiff)

1. Identify by date every promise or representation allegedly made by any officer, agent or employee of defendant to loan money or extend credit to you that loan or extension of credit was not made. For each promise or representation identify the person who made it, and identify any person who was present or has knowledge of such promise or representation.

2. A loan application dated [*date*], a copy of which is attached as Exhibit A, indicates your income was $_____ per month. State your actual monthly income for the following period of time from [*date*] to [*date*]. Identify by amount each source of that income.

3. A financial statement dated [*date*], attached as Exhibit B, indicates that your net worth is $_____. Please answer the following questions:

   (a)   what was your net worth on [*date*]; and

   (b)   how did you calculate your net worth as of that date.

[**NOTE:** The date that should be inserted in question number 3 should be either the date of the alleged promise, if changed circumstances are alleged, or the date of the financial statement if it is alleged that the information is false.]

4. Identify all appraisals, market analyses, and other documents stating or pertaining to the value of all of the real property that is listed on your financial statement that is attached as Exhibit B.

5. Identify every person, financial institution or other entity from whom you sought to borrow money during the period of time from [*date*] to [*date*]. For each institution or entity identified state the name and the position of the person with whom you dealt.

6. Identify all financial statements, loan applications, or credit applications prepared by you or on your behalf during or pertaining to the period of time from [*date*] to [*date*].

7. Identify each accountant, bookkeeper or financial advisor whom you have consulted or retained during the last _____ years.

8. Identify every source of income to you, from which you realized more than $_____ per year, for each of the following years: [*insert relevant years*].

9. Identify each reason given to you by defendant for not loaning you the money [*or extending you the line of credit*] as alleged in Plaintiff's Original Petition.

[g] FORM: Commercial lease (to defendant)

1. Identify by category all persons who have or claim to have knowledge of any of the following matters:

(a) The condition of the building [premises] including but not limited to the condition of the [*describe the defective element, e.g.*, roof] either prior to, during or after plaintiff's lease of the building [premises].

(b) Repair work done on or to the [*describe defective element*] the building prior to, during or after plaintiffs lease.

2. Identify the person or persons who:

(a) Built [or finished out] the building;

(b) Sold you the building;

(c) Performed any inspection of or work on [*describe defective element*] of the building since [*insert appropriate dates*].

(d) Leased the building from you or the previous owner prior to plaintiff [*if the premises were abandoned by the plaintiff, add the following*: or subsequent to plaintiff];

(e) Managed the building during plaintiff's lease and the three years prior to plaintiff's lease.

3. Identify all inspection reports, appraisals, leases, correspondence, repair proposals and invoices discussing or pertaining to [*describe defective element*] of the building.

4. Identify all complaints or notices from other tenants in the building concerning [*describe defective element*] that you received before [*date*].

5. Identify all agreements, leases, and correspondence between plaintiff and defendant.

6. If you contend or believe that any agreement between plaintiff and defendant or any provision in the lease required plaintiff to repair the [*describe defective element*], then identify with particularity the terms of such agreement or the provision of the lease.

7. If you have re-let the premises that were rented by plaintiff, identify the person to whom the premises have been re-let and describe the terms of the lease between you and this person.

8. If you contend or believe that plaintiff owes you any money under the lease or by virtue of any agreement between you and plaintiff or by virtue of plaintiff's abandonment of the premises,

identify the amount you claim is owed and describe all facts that support your claim.

[h] FORM: Commercial lease (to plaintiff)

1. Identify each alleged express or implied representation, promise and warranty that you contend was made or extended by defendant. For each such representation, promise or warranty, identify the person, documents and events making, extending or giving rise to the representation, promise or warranty.

2. With regard to the alleged defects in the building [premises], when (by day, month and year) did you first discover each such defect.

3. For each notice or complaint that you contend was given to defendant, state the following information:

   (a)   The date the notice or complaint was given;

   (b)   Whether the notice or complaint was written or oral;

   (c)   The substance of the notice or complaint;

   (d)   The person to whom the notice or complaint was given;

   (e)   The response, if any, given by the person who received the notice or complaint.

4. Identify all persons who have or claim to have knowledge of the alleged [*describe defective element*] in the building.

5. Identify any agent, broker, or other person who assisted you in relocating to other premises after you abandoned the building leased to you by defendant.

6. Describe the terms of your new lease and any compensation or benefits you received in connection with the relocation. Include in your answer any moving expenses, temporary free rent, or other such inducements or benefits.

7. Identify all documents pertaining to your new lease, including all listings, advertisements, proposals, draft or preliminary leases, final leases, and all other agreements with your lessor or any agent or broker who assisted you.

8. In connection with your claim for lost profits, provide the following information:

(a) Your income, by month, for the months prior to the date you abandoned the premises;

(b) Your expenses by month for the months prior to the date you abandoned the premises.

[**NOTE:** Include a sufficient time period to encompass both the pre-defect and post-defect periods under the lease.]

9. Identify each building and building owner from whom you have leased premises for the last _____ years.

[i] FORM: Unfair debt collection practices (to defendant)

1. State the name(s) of all software programs used by you when attempting to collect the Account.

2. Identify (by name, address and telephone number) all long distance telephone service providers that you used when attempting to collect the Account, as well as your primary billing address and telephone number(s) for such providers.

3. State the legal and assumed names; home addresses; date of birth; and gender of all natural persons who attempted to collect or assisted in attempting to collect the Account.

4. State all names, including assumed and trade names, under which you have conducted business for any period of time during the last five years.

5. Identify (by providing the name and state of information) all of your parent and subsidiary entities.

6. Identify (by style, court and cause number) all lawsuits which were filed during the last three years and in which it was alleged that you engaged in improper attempts to collect one or more debts.

§7.46 Requests for Production of Documents and Things

Requests for production of documents and things are another very important discovery tool. While interrogatories assist in locating potential trial testimony, requests for production are the most direct way to obtain relevant trial exhibits from the other side. Of course, a subpoena duces tecum accompanying a deposition notice is another way to obtain an opponent's documents prior to trial, but a request for production is preferred because it is more economical and because obtaining the documents well in advance of the deposition permits better deposition preparation.

At any time prior to thirty days before the end of the discovery period, any party may serve the other party with a request for production or for inspection. TEX. R. CIV. P. 196.1(a). The request can be for the purpose of copying documents or to inspect, sample, test, or photograph tangible things. TEX. R. CIV. P. 196.1(a). If sampling or testing is to be done, the item can not be destroyed or materially altered in the process. TEX. R. CIV. P. 196.5.

The request must specify the items to be produced or inspected, either by individual item or by category, and describe with reasonable particularity each item and category. TEX. R. CIV. P. 196.1(b).

The request must also specify a reasonable time and place for the inspection, testing or sampling that must be on or after the response date. TEX. R. CIV. P. 196.1(b). Further, if the item is to be sampled or tested, the request must describe the "means, manner and procedure" for testing or sampling with "sufficient particularity" to enable the responding party to know what is to be done. TEX. R. CIV. P. 196.1(b).

Mental health records and medical records can be obtained by means of a request for production. However, if a party requests another party to produce medical or mental health records on a non-party, the requesting party must serve a copy of the request on the non-party under the procedures set forth in Rule 21a. TEX. R. CIV. P. 196.1(c). The exceptions to this requirement are:

- A. The non-party signs a release of the records that is effective as to the requesting party; or

- B. The identity of the non-party whose records are sought will not directly or indirectly be disclosed by production of the records; or

- C. The court, upon a showing of good cause by the requesting party, orders that service is not required.

TEX. R. CIV. P. 196.1(c).

The response to a request for production must be served on the requesting party within 30 days after service, unless the request is served with the petition, in which case the response is due within 50 days after service. TEX. R. CIV. P. 196.2(a).

The content of the response must include with respect to each item or category of items requested, any objections made or privileges claimed. TEX. R. CIV. P. 196.2(b). If there are no objections or privileges to be asserted, then the response must state either:

- A. Production, inspection, or other requested action will be permitted as requested; or

- B. The requested items are being served on the requesting party with the response; or

C. Production, inspection, or other requested action will take place at a specified time and place, if the responding party is objecting to the time and place of production; or

D. No items have been identified, after a diligent search, that are responsive to the request.

TEX. R. CIV. P. 196.2(b).

More precision is required in a request for production than in an interrogatory. *See Loftin v. Martin*, 776 S.W.2d 145 (Tex. 1989). In Loftin the plaintiff requested, all notes, records, memoranda, documents and communications made that the carrier contends support its allegations [that the award of the Industrial Accident Board was contrary to the undisputed evidence].

The Texas Supreme Court affirmed a trial court ruling that the request was overly vague, broad and unclear. *Id.* The infirmity of the request in *Loftin* was that it did not seek "any particular class or type of documents" but merely requested all documentary evidence that the opposing party contended supported its case. *Id.* The teaching of *Loftin* appears to be that a request should be related to specific issues, persons, transactions, or types of documents, rather than being framed to encompass, in a single request, every possible document pertinent to any of the responding party's allegations. Thus, in *K-Mart Corp. v. Sanderson*, 937 S.W.2d 429 (Tex. 1996), the court held that the trial judge did not abuse his discretion in overruling K-Mart's objections that the following requests were overly broad and unduly burdensome:

(1) all documents that "relate to, touch on or concern the allegations of this lawsuit; (2) all documents "reflecting the incident made the basis of this lawsuit;" and (3) any document that relates in any way to this incident.

The court reasoned that while it would be better to be more specific, the document requests were related to an isolated incident and not all documents that supported a "position" or that related to "claims and defenses" that the court found objectionable in *Loftin*.

The guiding principle appears to be that discovery requests must reasonably be tailored to include only matters relevant to the case. *In re Alford Chevrolet-Geo,* 997 S.W.2d 173 (Tex. 1999). The courts will not permit a party to engage in a "fishing expedition" or to impose unreasonable discovery expenses on the opposing party. *Id.*

It is unclear whether a request for production can be used to obtain documents pertaining to expert witnesses. Rule 195.1 explicitly states, "[a] party may request another party to designate and disclose information concerning testifying expert witnesses only through a request for disclosure under Rule 194 and through depositions and reports as permitted by this rule." TEX. R. CIV. P. 195.1. Since this rule uses the terms "designate" and "information," and does not use the term "documents," there does not appear to be an express prohibition. Since Rule 194 specifically directs a party to produce "all documents, tangible things, reports, models, or data compilations" used by the expert; therefore, it would appear that the types of things a request for production might seek are provided for already in Rule 194; therefore, the intention of Rule 195.1 appears to be to limit discovery regarding testifying experts to the devices listed in Rule 195.1. The commentary to Rule 195.1 makes it clear, however, that, "[t]his rule does not limit the permissible methods of discovery concerning *consulting* experts whose mental impressions or opinions have been reviewed by a testifying expert." (Emphasis added).

Except for expert reports that may be ordered by the court, Tex. R. Civ. P. 195.5, or a request from a party to make a list of documents that have been withheld from discovery on the basis of a claim of privilege, Tex. R. Civ. P. 193.3(b), the rules of procedure do not require a party to create documents or reduce information to tangible form. *McKinney v. National Union Fire Ins. Co. of Pa.,* 772 S.W.2d 72 (Tex. 1989). Thus a request for production of the report of an expert witness or a list of persons with knowledge of relevant facts will be unavailing unless such a document already exists. *Id*; *Loftin v. Martin,* 776 SW.2d 145 (Tex. 1989).

Unlike interrogatories, the rules of procedure generally do not limit the number of sets of requests that may be served or the number of items that may be requested in a set. Of course, Rule 192.6. authorizes a party to seek a protective order to guard against discovery abuses. Tex. R. Civ. P. 192.6 (a). For expedited actions that fall within Level 1, there is now a limit to no more than 15 specific requests for production. Tex. R. Civ. P. 190.2(b)(4); *see* §5.01.1, *supra*.

A party's production of a document in response to written discovery authenticates the document for use against that party in any pretrial proceeding or at trial unless, within ten days (or a shorter time if ordered by the court) after the producing party learns that the document will be used, the party objects to the authenticity of the document, or any part of it, stating the specific basis for the objection. Tex. R. Civ. P. 193.7. The objection must be either in writing or on the record, and must have a good faith factual and legal basis. Tex. R. Civ. P. 193.7. If only part of the document is objected to, then the objection does not affect the remainder of the document. Tex. R. Civ. P. 193.7. If an objection is made, the party attempting to use the document must be given a reasonable opportunity to establish the authenticity of the document. Tex. R. Civ. P. 193.7.

§7.47 Drafting Requests for Production

Requests for production should contain three elements: (1) notice and instructions to the receiving party, (2) appropriate definitions, and (3) the specific requests. Although no arrangement of these elements is required by the Rules, one workable approach is to attach the definitions and requests as an exhibit to the notice and instructions. The general form that follows utilizes this format and contains requests that would be pertinent in most DTPA cases.

Each request for production should be as comprehensive as possible. Nevertheless, as discovery progresses, it may be necessary to send additional requests for production to obtain documents whose existence is discovered through depositions or otherwise.

Depending upon the nature of the case, certain requests may be keyed to the "sale," "lease," "incident," or "transaction" in question. Those terms should be defined.

The requests in the general form that follows are illustrative only, and, of course, should be tailored to each specific case.

[a] FORM: Request for Production (general form)

```
                          NO. _____
_____               §    IN THE DISTRICT COURT OF
                          §
vs.                       §    _____ COUNTY, TEXAS
                          §
_____               §    _____ JUDICIAL DISTRICT
```

PLAINTIFF'S [DEFENDANT'S] FIRST REQUEST FOR PRODUCTION

TO : _____, by and through his [her] attorney of record.

_____, plaintiff [defendant] requests that you produce for discovery under the provisions of Rule 196, Texas Rules of Civil Procedure, the items specified on Exhibit A that is attached.

The requested documents are to be produced on or before the expiration of thirty days after service of this request. The documents shall be produced at [*insert address*]. Delivery of the documents requested may be by mail if you so desire.

[**NOTE:** If the request is served with the original petition, then fifty days for response must be allowed.]

In the event you object to any of the items requested, you are instructed to furnish all other documents to which no objection is made.

Also note that Rule 196.3(c) provides that a party shall produce documents as they are kept in the usual course of business or shall organize and label them to correspond with the categories in this request.

[**NOTE:** The following paragraph may be added as an effort to give "actual notice" of an intention to use the documents that are to be produced at any hearing or trial. *See* Tex. R. Civ. P. 193.7. It would be advisable, however, to give actual notice again once the documents have been received so they can be more accurately described].

Please be advised that the undersigned intends to use the documents you produce in response to this request for production in any hearing or trial of this lawsuit.

> Respectfully submitted,
>
> [*Signature of attorney*]

Copy furnished to:

[*other parties*]

EXHIBIT A

Definitions:

A. Document(s) means all writings (including notes, correspondence, memoranda, reports, computer print-outs, journal entries), drawings, drafts, charts, photographs, tapes or disc recordings (whether computer, sound, or video), and all other data compilations from which information can be obtained or translated, which are in your possession, custody, or control, or that are known to you. "Documents" does not include the notes or memorandum of your attorneys made in connection with this case or correspondence between you and your attorney pertaining to this case.

B. You or your means [*insert name of responding party*], your agents, servants, employees and representatives.

C. Person means any individual, partnership, corporation or other group or entity however organized.

D. Plaintiff refers to [*name of plaintiff*].

E. Defendant refers to [*name of defendant*].

F. Sale refers to [*describe sale, e.g.,* the sale by defendant to plaintiff of the product on or about [*date*]].

G. Product means [*describe product, e.g.,* the automobile purchased by plaintiff from defendant on or about [*date*]].

With these definitions in mind, please produce the following documents:

1. All statements and recordings of plaintiff [defendant] or any person representing or purporting to represent this party.

2. The statement of any person containing facts relevant to any issue in this case.

3. All documents pertaining to the sale. This request includes but is not limited to [*describe specific categories of documents sought, e.g.*, all contracts, blueprints, design drawings, specifications, change orders, surveys, inspection reports, permits, and appraisals].

4. All documents pertaining to plaintiff [defendant]. This request includes but is not limited to [*describe types of documents likely to exist in case, e.g.*, all loan applications, loan extensions, loan renewals, correspondence, and memoranda of loan committee meetings].

5. All tax returns, or portion thereof, indicating the [*describe information sought, e.g.*, all of your income during the [*year*] tax year].

6. All photographs, films, videotapes and electronic recordings of any type of the [*describe subject of suit, e.g.*, house] that is the subject of this suit, or of plaintiff [defendant].

7. All documents on which are recorded or summarized any conversations you had with plaintiff [defendant] or his [her] agents or representatives.

8. All documents sent by plaintiff to defendant.

9. All documents sent by defendant to plaintiff.

10. All documents whose identity was requested in plaintiff's [defendant's] First Set of Interrogatories to you.

§7.47.1 Additional Requests for Specific Cases

In this manual, the discovery practice suggested is for the party to use interrogatories to request the identification of relevant documents and to then request the production of those identified documents in one or more requests for production, as in request no.10 in the preceding section. If that practice is followed, specifically tailored requests for production may be duplicative. However, an alternative may be necessary when the number of interrogatories propounded reaches the limit given by Rules 190.2(c)(3) and 190.3(b)(3) (*see §§7.37, 7.38, supra*). In that event, or if a different discovery practice is followed, case-specific requests for production of documents and tangible things can be propounded. The following requests are provided as suggestions for the types of documents and tangible things which may be relevant in specific cases. Additional forms specific to those types of cases are located in the Chapters on Insurance (Chapter 11), Real Estate Sales (Chapter 12) and Residential Construction (Chapter 13).

[a] FORM: Defective product (to defendant retailer)

1. All cash register tapes or other documents reflecting the sales made on [*date of purchase*] at your store.

2. All documents evidencing or containing complaints made to you regarding [*insert the product or type of product*] purchased during the months of [*insert relevant months*] at your store.

3. All video taped and audio taped recordings made at your store, both inside the store and outside the store, on [*insert date of purchase*].

4. All documents reflecting the scheduling of and hours worked by personnel employed by you in your store between [*insert relevant date*] and [*insert relevant date*].

5. All bulletins, correspondence or other communications from the manufacturer that discuss or relate to [*describe condition or defect*] in all products sold by you that are of the same make or model as that purchased by plaintiff.

6. All documents containing or reflecting the written warranties pertaining to the product or to the repair service.

[b] FORM: Defective product (to plaintiff)

1. All documents showing or tending to show when and/or where you purchased the [product] that you allege was defective.

2. All documents relating to any repairs necessitated by the allegedly defective product.

3. All documents showing or tending to show that the product that you purchased from Defendant was contaminated or defective.

4. All documents showing or tending to show any damages that you allege to have suffered as a result of the incidents made the basis of this law suit.

5. All documents showing or tending to show that any other consumers were damaged by the purchase of the allegedly defective product around the same time that you allege to have purchased the defective product.

6. Any and all fee agreements with your attorney herein.

[c] FORM: Unfair debt collection practices (to defendant)

1. Produce your records (typewritten, handwritten and computer-generated) of your attempts to collect the Account.

2. Produce all records (typewritten, handwritten and computer-generated) of the creditor's attempts to collect the Account.

3. Produce all recordings (including audio and video), and any transcripts thereof, that evidence your attempts to collect the Account.

4. Produce copies of all pages of your telephone long distance billing records that indicate calls placed by you when attempting to collect the Account.

5. Produce all agreements signed by the Plaintiff and which relate to this case.

6. Produce all agreements between you and anyone that you contend allowed you to attempt to collect the Account.

7. Produce copies of all documents containing or recording communications between you and Plaintiff or her attorneys during the relevant time period.

8. Produce all audio recordings of the Plaintiff and the Plaintiff's attorneys.

9. Produce all bonds and applications for bonds (with attachments, exhibits, schedules, and transmittal letters) that you have secured and/or applied for during the last five years and that you contend may meet the requirements of Texas Finance Code section 392.101.

10. Produce all bills, invoices, receipts, statements, agreements and other documents that evidence attorney's fees and costs for which you are seeking compensation in this case.

11. Produce the first page of all pleadings in all lawsuits in which you were a party during the last five (5) years, and in which it was alleged that you improperly attempted to collect an alleged debt.

12. Produce all documents evidencing the transmission of any information to or from any credit bureau and/or credit reporting agency regarding to the Account.

13. Produce the employment file(s) of all natural persons who attempted to collect the Account.

14. Produce all performance reviews of all natural persons who attempted to collect the Account.

15. Produce all records of commendation of and/or complaints against all natural persons who attempted to collect the Account.

16. Produce all records of disciplinary actions against all natural persons who attempted to collect the Account.

17. Produce all debt collection training records of all natural persons who attempted to collect the Account.

18. Produce all education records of all natural persons who attempted to collect the Account.

19. Produce all documents evidencing pay and/or bonus increases or decreases for all natural persons who attempted to collect the Account.

20. Produce copies of all Better Business Bureau complaints received by you during the last three years that included allegations that one of your employees or agents engaged in improper debt collection practices (as well as any responses you made to such complaints).

21. Produce all documents evidencing any felony conviction of any natural person who attempted to collect the Account.

22. Produce all form letters and telephone collection scripts you used to attempt to collect the Account.

23. Produce an organizational chart that reflects the personnel organizational structure of your debt collection department(s) during the relevant time period.

24. Produce all employees telephone extension lists used by you during the last two years.

25. Produce copies of all debt collector policies, procedures and techniques that you gave to persons who attempted to collect the Account.

26. Produce the user and programming manuals for collection software you used when attempting to collect the Account.

27. Produce all documents that list and define, or act as a key for, codes and abbreviations you used when attempting to collect the Account.

28. Produce all documents that indicate or suggest that the Plaintiff does not owe any monies for the Account.

29. Produce all documents that indicate or suggest that the Account was incurred for something other than personal, family or household purposes.

30. Produce all lists used by you during the relevant time period that include both the legal names and the assumed or fictitious names of all natural persons who attempted to collect the Account.

§7.48 Requests for Admission

Requests for admission are a useful tool for narrowing the scope and number of issues in a DTPA lawsuit, thereby facilitating the preparation and trial of the case. *See Fireman's Fund Ins. Co. v. Commercial Stand. Ins. Co.*, 490 S.W.2d 818, 825 (Tex. 1972).

Rule 198.1 provides that any party may request any other party to admit the truth of any matter within the scope of discovery, including the application of law to fact and mixed questions of law and fact, as well as the genuineness of documents served with the request, or otherwise made available for inspection and copying. TEX. R. CIV. P. 198.1. The request can be made at any time before the end of the discovery period. TEX. R. CIV. P. 198.1. Except for expedited actions, there is no limit on the number of requests for admissions that may be served. For expedited actions that fall within Level 1, no more than 15 requests for admissions may be served on any other party. TEX. R. CIV. P. 190.2(b)(5).

Like interrogatories and requests for production, requests for admissions can be served with the original petition. However, if served with the petition, then the time for response is fifty days. TEX. R. CIV. P. 198.2(a).

The proponent of the requests for admission must separately set forth each of the matters for which an admission is sought.

Unless an objection is made, the responding party must either specifically deny the matter or set forth in detail the reasons that the answering party cannot truthfully admit or deny the matter. A denial shall fairly meet the substance of the requested admission, and when good faith requires that a party qualify his answer or deny only a part of the matter of which an admission is requested, the party must specify so much of it as is true and qualify or deny the remainder. An answering party may not give lack of information or knowledge as a reason for failure to admit or deny unless he states that he has made reasonable inquiry and that the information known or easily obtainable by him is insufficient to enable him to admit or deny. TEX. R. CIV. P. 198.2(b). A party who considers that a matter of which an admission is requested presents a genuine issue for trial may not, on that ground alone, object to the request. TEX. R. CIV. P. 198.2(b).

Failure to respond results in the automatic admission of the matters set forth in the request, without the necessity of a court order. TEX. R. CIV. P. 198.2(c).

Any matter that is admitted under Rule 198 is conclusively established as to the admitting party. TEX. R. CIV. P. 198.3; *see also Standard Fire Ins. Co. v. Morgan,* 745 S. W. 2d 310, 312 (Tex. 1987); *Smith v. Home Indem. Co.,* 683 S.W.2d 559, 562 (Tex. App.—Fort Worth 1985, no writ). The trial court may, however, permit a party to withdraw or amend its response and may nullify a deemed admission upon a showing of good cause if the court finds that the party propounding the requests will not be unduly prejudiced and that it would promote a proper presentation of the merits. *Id; Stelly v. Papania,* 927 S.W.2d 620 (Tex. 1996). A party establishes good cause if its failure to answer was an accident or a mistake rather than intentional or the result of conscious indifference. *Id.* Furthermore, a party may waive his right to rely upon a Rule 198 admission by failing to object to the introduction of evidence that controverts the admission. *Marshall v. Vise,* 767 S.W.2d 699 (Tex. 1989).

One approach to preparing requests for admission is to outline those facts and opinions necessary to prove (or that tend to prove) an element of a cause of action or defense. Each of these elements is a candidate for inclusion in the requests. While requests for admission are good for outlining the issues in dispute, it is generally pointless to include those facts that an attorney already knows are disputed. Attorneys have been known, however, to include such requests in the hope that opposing counsel will stumble procedurally and fail to respond in a timely manner, thereby admitting each request.

The requests should seek admissions as to the authenticity of documents important to the case. Authentication of documents through requests for admission is especially helpful as to those documents created by the opposing party, since a witness who could authenticate the documents may not be present or available at trial. The requests should be sent far enough in advance of trial to leave time to follow-up with other discovery as to those matters that are denied, or, in the case of a bad faith or frivolous response, there must be time to seek a court order deeming the matters admitted.

The types of facts or issues for which it is particularly helpful to obtain admissions in DTPA cases include the following:

1. the receipt and sufficiency of pre-suit notice required by the DTPA;

2. the identity of the manufacturer or seller of the good or service;

3. the legal form of a party, e.g., corporation, partnership, etc.;

4. the date problems were first discovered with a product (for limitations purposes);

5. the nature and existence of prior claims that a product was defective;

6. that a person was or was not an agent of a party;

7. that a document was prepared by, sent to or received by a party;

8. that certain conduct was authorized by a party;

9. that certain disclosure statements or disclaimers were received by the consumer prior to the sale;

10. that a written offer to repair or of settlement was received by a party;

11. that verbal representations or warranties were or were not made by a party;

12. that a party did or did not know a certain fact at the time of the transaction; and

13. that a party did or did not disclose certain facts at the time of the transaction.

§7.49 Drafting Requests for Admission

Requests for admission are composed of three parts: (1) notice and instruction to the receiving party, (2) appropriate definitions, and (3) the requests. Additionally, when an admission as to the genuineness of documents is sought, copies of the documents in question should be attached to the request for admission as numbered exhibits.

The general form that follows utilizes a format similar to that recommended for interrogatories and requests for production. The definitions and requests are attached as "Exhibit A" to the notice and instructions. To avoid confusion, documents attached as exhibits should be identified numerically. Depending upon the nature of the case, certain requests will be keyed to the "sale," "lease," "incident" or "transaction" in question. Those terms need to be defined.

Requests for admission are even more "case specific" than interrogatories and requests for production. Accordingly, the requests in the general form are illustrative only.

[a] FORM: Requests for Admission (general form)

```
                         NO. _____
_____             §    IN THE DISTRICT COURT OF
                         §
vs.                      §    _____COUNTY, TEXAS
                         §
_____             §    _____ JUDICIAL DISTRICT
```

PLAINTIFF'S [DEFENDANT'S] REQUESTS FOR ADMISSION

TO: _____, by and through your attorney of record.

You are requested to admit the truth of the matters set forth on Exhibit A that is attached. You must answer in the form and manner required by Texas Rule of Civil Procedure 198. Each matter about which an admission is requested is admitted without the necessity of a court order unless within thirty days after service of this request, or within such time as the court may allow, you serve upon the undersigned a written response signed by you or your attorney of record as required by Rule 198.

[**NOTE:** If the requests are served with the original petition, then fifty days from service of the citation and petition must be allowed.]

                        Respectfully submitted,

                        [*Signature of attorney*]

Copy provided to:

[*Other attorneys of record*]

EXHIBIT A

Definitions:

A. You or your means [*insert name of party*], your agents, servants, employees and representatives.

B. Plaintiff refers to [*name of plaintiff*].

C. Defendant refers to [*name of defendant*].

D. [The house means that house located at [*address*], which is the subject of this suit].

With these definitions in mind, you are requested to admit the truth of the following matters:

[Illustrative requests to defendant]

1. You were the builder of the house.

2. On or about [*date*], you and plaintiff signed a sales contract pertaining to the house.

3. Exhibit 1, which is attached, is a true and correct copy of the sales contract between you and plaintiff pertaining to the house.

4. At the time the sales contract (Exhibit 1) was signed, you were doing business as [*business name*].

5. You represented in the sales contract (Exhibit 1) that construction of the house would be completed by [*date*].

6. You completed construction of the house after [*date*].

7. The sale of the house from you to plaintiff was closed on [*date*].

8. The Building Code of the City of _____, Texas, in effect between [*date*] and [*date*], required the grade beam of a house to extend _____ feet into undisturbed soil.

9. A portion of the grade beam of the house does not extend ____ feet into undisturbed soil.

10. The failure to extend the grade beam of the house in question _____ feet into undisturbed soil is not "good construction practices" as that phrase was used in the Sales Contract (Exhibit 1).

11. Exhibit 2 is a true and correct copy of a letter dated [*date*] from _____, attorney for plaintiff that was received by you on [*date*].

12. Exhibit 2 describes in reasonable detail plaintiff's complaints pertaining to the house.

13. Exhibit 2 states an amount of actual damages and expenses, including attorneys' fees.

14. A crack exists today in the grade beam and slab of the house.

15. To repair the crack in the grade beam and slab of the house, it will be necessary to place piers under the grade beam.

[Illustrative requests to plaintiff]

1. You purchased the house on [*date*].

2. In [*year*], you had a room added to the house.

3. Exhibit 1, a copy of which is attached, is a blueprint drawing that accurately depicts the location and size (relative to the remainder of the house) of the room (marked with an "X") that was constructed in [*location*].

4. Defendant did not build the additional room.

5. The additional room was built by [*contractor*].

6. Prior to construction of the additional room there were no visible cracks in the interior sheetrock of the house.

7. Prior to construction of the additional room, there were no indications of problems with or defects in the foundation of the house.

8. Within 90 days of the date the additional room was added to the house, you observed cracks in the interior sheetrock of the house.

9. Defendant made no oral warranties concerning the house.

10. After the sales contract was signed, you requested modifications in the original design of the house.

11. Exhibit 3, which is attached, is a change order signed by you on [*date*].

12. You were advised by defendant at the time the change order (Exhibit 3) was signed that the modification described in the change order would delay completion of the house.

[b] FORM: Unfair debt collection practices (to defendant)

1. Admit that the Plaintiff is not personally liable for any amount allegedly due on the Account.

2. Admit that you contend that the Plaintiff is liable for payment of the Account.

3. Admit that the Account is an obligation, or an alleged obligation, incurred primarily for personal, family or household purposes, and that it arose from a transaction or alleged transaction.

4. Admit that you are in the business of collecting or in soliciting for collection debts that are due or alleged to be due a creditor.

5. Admit that you do not own the Account.

6. Admit that the Plaintiff is a "consumer," as that term is defined by section 392.001(1) of the Texas Finance Code.

7. Admit that the Account is a "consumer debt," as that term is defined by section 392.001(2) of the Texas Finance Code.

8. Admit that you are a "debt collector," as that term is defined by section 392.001(6) of the Texas Finance Code.

9. Admit that you are a "third-party debt collector," as that term is defined by Section 392.001(7) of the Texas Finance Code.

10. Admit that you used a telephone autodialer in your attempts to collect the Account.

11. Admit that you left pre-recorded telephone messages in your attempts to collect the Account.

12. Admit that your current net worth exceeds $100,000.00.

§7.50 Responding to Written Discovery Requests

Perhaps the only trial preparation activity more tedious than preparing discovery requests is responding to the requests of another party. However, the emphasis today is on full and continuing discovery and the failure to live up to that standard can have very serious consequences.

A party has a duty to make a complete response to a discovery request, "based on all information reasonably available to the responding party or its attorney, at the time the response is made." TEX. R. CIV. P. 193.1. Each response must be preceded by the question or request to which it applies. TEX. R. CIV. P. 193.1.

The penalty for failing to respond to discovery requests or to appropriately amend and supplement discovery requests is severe, including the exclusion of the evidence that was not disclosed and the exclusion of testimony from witnesses not identified. TEX. R. CIV. P. 193.6(a). The court can allow the evidence or testimony only on a showing of either (a) good cause, or (b) that the failure to timely make, amend or supplement the discovery response will not unfairly surprise or unfairly prejudice the parties. TEX. R. CIV. P. 193.6(a). It also is important to note that the burden of proof is on the party who seeks to introduce the evidence or testimony. TEX. R. CIV. P. 193.6(b). In an effort to prevent a party from losing its day in court, however, the rules provide that even if a party fails to meet its burden of proof, the court may grant a continuance or temporarily postpone the trial to allow the response to be made, amended, or supplemented, and to allow opposing parties to conduct discovery regarding any new information provided by the response. TEX. R. CIV. P. 193.6(c).

Objections to discovery must be made within the time that the response is due. TEX. R. CIV. P. 193.2(a). The objections can be made in the response itself or in a separate document. Further, the party must state *specifically* the legal and factual basis for the objections and the extent to which the party is refusing to comply with the request. TEX. R. CIV. P. 193.2(a). *In re Alford Chevrolet-Geo*, 997 S.W.2d 173, 181 (Tex. 1999). Any objection made must have a good faith basis factual and legal basis at the time the objection is made. TEX. R. CIV. P. 193.2(c). Objections can be amended or supplemented if, at the time of the original response, the objection was inapplicable or was unknown after reasonable inquiry. TEX. R. CIV. P. 193.2(d).

An objection that is not made within the response time or that is "obscured by numerous unfounded objections" is waived, unless the court excuses the waiver for good cause. TEX. R. CIV. P. 193.2(e). *See Remington Arms Co., Inc. v. Canales*, 837 S.W.2d 624 (Tex. 1992).

If a privilege applies to the material or information requested, then in lieu of an objection, a party should assert the privilege as provided in Rule 193.3. *See* TEX. R. CIV. P. 193.2(f). The party may withhold production of the material or information; however, the party must state in the response or in a separate document that:

1. Information or material responsive to the request has been withheld;

2. The request to which the information or material relates; and

3. The privilege or privileges asserted.

TEX. R. CIV. P. 193.3(a).

Upon receipt of a response indicating that privileged material has been withheld, the party seeking discovery may serve a written request that the withholding party identify the information or material withheld. Tex. R. Civ. P. 193.3(b). Within fifteen days of service of that request, the withholding party must serve a response that:

1. Describes the information or materials withheld that, without revealing the privileged information or otherwise waiving the privilege, enables the other parties to assess the applicability of the privilege; and

2. Asserts a specific privilege for each item or group of items withheld.

Tex. R. Civ. P. 193.3(b). This procedure does not apply to privileged communications to or from a lawyer or lawyer's representative or a privileged document of a lawyer or lawyer's representative, if it was made at or after a time when the person was consulting the lawyer about possible litigation and it relates to the litigation in which the discovery is requested. Tex. R. Civ. P. 193.3(c).

If a party discovers, within ten days of delivering a response, that privileged material was disclosed inadvertently, then by amended response, the party can retain the privilege. If such an amendment is made, the requesting party must return the material that was inadvertently disclosed. Tex. R. Civ. P. 193.3(d).

If a party learns that the party's response to written discovery was incomplete or incorrect when made, or although complete and correct when made, is no longer complete and correct, the party must amend or supplement the response if:

1. The written discovery sought the identification of persons with knowledge of relevant facts, trial witnesses, or expert witnesses; and

2. To the extent that the written discovery sought other information, unless the additional information or corrective information has been made known to the other parties in writing, on the record at a deposition, or through other discovery responses.

Tex. R. Civ. P. 193.5(a).

An amended or supplemental response must be made "reasonably promptly" after the party discovers the need for an amendment or supplement. Tex. R. Civ. P. 193.5(b). *It is presumed* that an amended or supplemental response made less than 30 days before trial is not made reasonably promptly. Tex. R. Civ. P. 193.5(b). Further, a party must supplement the responses in accordance with any applicable discovery order or agreement of the parties. *See Mentis v. Barnard,* 870 S.W.2d 14 (Tex. 1994). If the original response had to be verified, then the amended or supplemental response must be verified; however, lack of verification will not make the amendment or supplement untimely unless the responding party fails to correct the defect within a reasonable time after notice. Tex. R. Civ. P. 193.5(b).

If there is an objection to part of a request, then the party must respond to the other parts of the request to which no objection is made unless it is unreasonable under the circumstances to do so. Tex. R. Civ. P. 193.2(b).

§7.50.1 Depositions on Written Questions

Many consumer cases, and in fact, most litigation, involve some type of business, medical or other records maintained by a third party. The records can be obtained and proved up by means of an oral deposition and subpoena duces tecum; however, the procedure is expensive, cumbersome, and time consuming for the parties and the third party. A much more efficient way of obtaining and proving up such information is by using a deposition on written questions.

A party may take the testimony of any person or entity by deposition on written questions before any person authorized by law to take depositions on written questions. TEX. R. CIV. P. 200.1. A deposition on written questions is, however, subject to the following specific rules:

1. A notice of intention to take a deposition on written questions must be served on all parties at least twenty days before the deposition is to be taken;

2. The deposition may be taken outside the discovery period only if the parties agree or if there is a court order; and

3. The party noticing the deposition must also deliver to the deposition officer a copy of the notice and all of the written questions to be asked during the deposition.

See TEX. R. CIV. P. 200.1(a).

Once the other parties to the case receive a copy of the notice containing the questions to be asked, they may either object to one or more questions or serve cross questions (which also must be served on all other parties). TEX. R. CIV. P. 200.3(a). The objections or cross-questions must be served within ten days after service of the notice and direct questions. *Id.* Within five days after cross-questions are served, any party may serve redirect questions. *Id.* Then, within three days of service of the redirect questions, the other parties may object or serve re-cross questions. *Id.*

In order to compel attendance and to obtain the documents normally sought through a deposition on written questions, a subpoena *duces tecum* can and should be issued to the witness. TEX. R. CIV. P. 200.2. *See* §7.34 *supra*.

The procedure for administering the deposition on written questions is similar to the procedure for taking an oral deposition in that the officer before whom the deposition is taken must do so at the time and place set forth in the notice, and must record the answers of the witness to the questions that are posed. The deposition transcript is then prepared, certified and delivered in accordance with Rule 203. TEX. R. CIV. P. 200.4.

[a] FORM: Notice of deposition of written questions

```
                        NO. _____
_____            §     IN THE DISTRICT COURT OF
                        §
vs.                     §     _____COUNTY, TEXAS
                        §
_____            §     _____ JUDICIAL DISTRICT
```

NOTICE OF DEPOSITION ON WRITTEN QUESTIONS

TO: [*Parties by and through attorneys of record*].

This is a notice that after twenty days from the service of this document, a deposition on written questions will be taken as follows:

Location of Deposition: [*insert office name and address*]

Person to be Deposed: [*insert name of deponent*]

Date of Deposition: [*insert date deposition is to be taken*]

Notice is further given that a subpoena *duces tecum* will be issued to the witness, and the officer authorized to take this deposition will cause it to be served on the witness, requiring the witness to attend the deposition, and to produce at the deposition for inspection and copying the original(s) or a true and correct copy of [*insert specific documents to be produced*] in the possession, custody or control of the witness, and to turn over all such records to the authorized officer so that copies of the documents may be made and attached to the deposition.

The questions to be asked of the witness are attached to this notice as Exhibit A.

Respectfully submitted,

[Signature of attorney]

Exhibit A

1. What is your full name, business address and title?

2. What is the name of your company?

3. Did you receive a subpoena for the production of records and other documents pertaining to [insert name of organization]?

4. Has [name of organization] made or caused to be made any memorandum, report, record or data compilation, in any form, of [insert subject matter, e.g. the complaints of persons who purchased a [name of product] from your company?

5. Are these memoranda, reports, records, or data compilations under your care, supervision, direction, custody and/or control?

6. Was it in the regular course of the business of your company for a person with knowledge of the acts, events, conditions, opinions or diagnoses recorded to make the record or transmit information about those things to be included in a record?

7. Were these memoranda, reports, or data compilations made or caused to be made by your company?

8. Were the entries of these memoranda, reports, records, or data compilations made at or shortly after the time of the transaction recorded on these entries?

9. Were these records kept in the ordinary course of business?

10. Please attach duplicates of the requested records to this deposition or hand exact duplicates of the requested records or the originals for photocopying to the notary public taking your deposition for attachment to this deposition. Have you done as requested?

11. If you have not done as requested in question # 9, identify for the notary public the records and documents you did not produce and explain why you did not produce them.

12. Have you been requested or directed by any person to withhold, conceal or destroy any part of the records requested, or, has it been suggested to you by any person that any part of the records requested be withheld, concealed or destroyed? If so, please state the name and address of the person who conveyed this information to you and when it occurred.

13. Do you have any reason to believe that any part of the records requested has been edited, purged, culled or in any way or other manner made different from the way the records existed when they were created? If so, please explain your knowledge or belief about any editing, purging or culling that may have occurred.

14. Are there any other locations for your company where any additional records pertaining to [*describe subject matter*] may be kept or stored? If so, identify the location or possible location of such records.

[NOTE: If the preference is to have the witness simply write answers in blank spaces following the questions, then the form should be created by inserting the style of the case at the beginning, and a title, "Deposition of Written Questions of _____," followed by each question and answer blanks. Then, at the end of the form, a signature block should be created for the witness, followed by the notary public's affidavit that the witness, under oath, made the answers recorded, and signed the document. The notary's affidavit also should state that the documents that are attached are exact duplicates of the originals, if the notary copied the originals].

§7.51 Oral Depositions

In many DTPA cases, oral depositions represent the culmination of the discovery process. Responses to interrogatories and requests for production and admissions provide useful information but it is often fragmented or incomplete; it also tends to be "sanitized" in that the responses are generally reviewed carefully by opposing counsel before they are delivered. Depositions provide an invaluable opportunity to (1) view both sides of the case as the jury will view it—through the testimony of the witnesses; (2) fill in the gaps in discovery and learn firsthand what is known by those witnesses "with knowledge of relevant facts;" (3) nail down an opponent's version of the facts and extract concessions or admissions; and (4) obtain documents from non-party witnesses through a subpoena duces tecum.

One major disadvantage of depositions as a discovery tool is the expense. Deposition costs can easily reach several thousand dollars in the average case, exclusive of attorney time and travel costs. Less expensive, but less satisfactory alternatives are available. For example, non-stenographic depositions and depositions by telephone are authorized by the rules. TEX. R. CIV. P. 199.1(b), (c).

Oral depositions may be taken without obtaining leave of the court at any time during the discovery period, and outside of the discovery period with leave of the court. TEX. R. CIV. P. 199.2(a). Notice of the oral deposition must be given to all parties and the witness a "reasonable time" before the deposition is taken. TEX. R. CIV. P. 199.2(a). The rules do not prescribe a specific number of days necessary to constitute "reasonable time;" however, it has been held that notice of less than a week is not unreasonable *per se*. For example, in *Bohmfalk v. Linwood*, 742 S.W.2d 518, 520 (Tex. App.—Dallas 1987, no writ) the court found that four days' notice was not unreasonable *per se;* and, in *Gutierrez v. Walsh*, 748 S.W.2d 27, 28 (Tex. App.—Corpus Christi 1988, no writ) the court found that six and eight days notice for depositions was reasonable.

Wholly apart from the question of whether the notice *required* by Rule 199 has been given is the consideration of professional courtesy. Although local customs may vary, it is always good practice to attempt to arrange all depositions by agreement with opposing counsel and to provide *at least* one week's notice except when a genuine need exists to take the deposition within a shorter period of time. It is important to note that if the deposition will be videotaped, then five days' written notice (by certified mail) must be given to all parties. TEX. R. CIV. P. 199.1(c).

Generally, when a person's oral deposition is taken, no "side" may examine or cross-examine the witness for more than six hours, excluding breaks. TEX. R. CIV. P. 199.5(c). For expedited actions governed by a Level 1 discovery control plan, each side is now limited to no more than six hours of deposition time for the entire case. TEX. R. CIV. P. 190.2(b)(2). This limitation may be extended by agreement to no more than 10 hours per side. *Id.*

No private conferences between a witness and his attorney are permitted during an oral deposition except (a) for the purpose of determining whether a privilege is applicable, or (b) during breaks and other agreed recesses. TEX. R. CIV. P. 199.5(d).

A written notice of deposition must state:

- the name of the deponent

- the time and place of the deposition

- a description of any documents that are to be produced by the deponent

- the identity of persons who will attend as required by Rule 199.5(a)(3)

- a statement as to whether non-stenographic means will be used to record the deposition

Tex. R. Civ. P. 199.2(b)

When the deponent is a corporation, partnership, association, or governmental agency, the notice should name the entity and describe with "reasonable particularity" the matters on which examination of the witness is sought. Tex. R. Civ. P. 199.2(b)(1). In a response made a "reasonable time" before the deposition, the organization shall designate one or more persons to testify on its behalf, and for each individual designated, those matters that will be addressed by the designated witnesses. Tex. R. Civ. P.199.2(b)(1).

The place of the deposition of a witness, other than a witness designated by an organization, shall be: (1) in the county of the witness' residence *or* (2) where the witness is employed or regularly conducts business *or* (3) in the instance of a non-resident or transient person, in the county in which he is served with the subpoena or within 150 miles of the place of service, *or* (4) at such other place directed by the trial court. Tex. R. Civ. P.199.2(b)(2).

The option of taking the deposition of an agent or employee of an organization in the county of suit applies only to those persons *designated by the organization.* When the party taking the deposition designates a particular agent or employee, the general rules concerning the location of the deposition apply. *Wal-Mart Stores, Inc. v. Street,* 754 S.W.2d 153, 155 (Tex. 1988).

No formal subpoena is necessary to compel the appearance (and the production of documents) of a party or an agent or employee subject to the control of a party. Tex. R. Civ. P. 199.3; *see also Wal-Mart Stores, supra* at 154. In these instances, service of the notice on the party or the party's attorney has the same force and effect as a subpoena served on the deponent. As to all other witnesses, a subpoena is required to compel their presence.

A party is not required to supplement the deposition testimony of a witness who changes the testimony. *See Titus City Hospital Dist. v. Lucus,* 998 S.W.2d 740 (Tex. 1998). However, Rule 195.6 provides that a party must amend or supplement the deposition testimony or written report of an expert witness retained or controlled by that party, but only with regard to the expert's mental impressions or opinions, and the basis for them. Tex. R. Civ. P. 195.6.

§7.52 Notice of Oral Deposition

The two forms that follow illustrate the notice of deposition appropriate for (1) a natural person and (2) an organization requiring designation of witnesses. As noted above, no subpoena is required if the deponent is a party, but a subpoena *is* required to compel the appearance of a non-party. The first form contains alternate language addressing both instances. Additionally, the first form contains alternate language to be used in the event the deposition will be videotaped.

[a] FORM: Notice of oral deposition (individual)

```
                              NO. _____
_____                    §    IN THE DISTRICT COURT OF
                              §
vs.                           §    _____ COUNTY, TEXAS
                              §
_____                    §    _____ JUDICIAL DISTRICT
```

NOTICE OF ORAL DEPOSITION

TO: _____, by and through your attorney of record.

The undersigned will take the oral deposition of the person named below at the place, date and time indicated:

WITNESS:

DATE:

TIME:

LOCATION:

The deposition will be taken before a certified court reporter.

The deposition will continue from day to day until completed.

[The deposition will be videotaped].

The witness is requested to bring to the deposition the documents that are listed on Exhibit A that is incorporated at this point as if fully set forth.

                        Respectfully submitted,

                        [*Signature of attorney*]

Copy furnished to:
[*Other attorneys of record*]

[b] FORM: Notice of oral deposition (organization)

```
                              NO. _____
_____                    §    IN THE DISTRICT COURT OF
                              §
vs.                           §    _____ COUNTY, TEXAS
                              §
_____                    §    _____ JUDICIAL DISTRICT
```

NOTICE OF ORAL DEPOSITION

TO: _____, by and through your attorney of record.

The undersigned will take the oral deposition of the organization named below at the place, date and time indicated:

ORGANIZATION:

DATE:

TIME:

LOCATION:

At this deposition, the undersigned will inquire into the following specific matters, for which you are requested to identify and produce one or more witnesses who will be asked to testify based on their own knowledge of based on information reasonably available to your organization: [*insert list of specific matters*].

The deposition will be taken before a certified court reporter.

The deposition will continue from day to day until completed.

[The deposition will be videotaped].

You are requested to bring to the deposition the documents that are listed on <u>Exhibit A</u>, which is incorporated at this point as if fully set forth.

        Respectfully submitted,

        [*Signature of attorney*]

Copy furnished to:
[*Other attorneys of record*]

§7.52.1 Depositions Before Suit

An oral deposition can be taken before a lawsuit is filed under two circumstances:

A. To perpetuate or obtain the person's testimony or that of any other person for use in an anticipated suit; or

B. To investigate a potential claim or suit.

TEX. R. CIV. P. 202.1(a), (b). In addition to the need to perpetuate the testimony of a witness or party who, for health or other reasons, is not expected to be available for trial, this rule recognizes that in some cases, there is value in obtaining testimony from potential witnesses who are in a position either to provide evidence of a claim, or, to provide evidence as to whether there is or is not a claim to be made. Courts throughout the state have different attitudes toward pre-suit depositions, with some resisting any attempts to depose a party before suit unless necessary to preserve testimony, while others embrace the procedure and willingly sign the requisite order upon proper application. It should never be assumed that courts will order presuit depositions simply because the rule says they can.

It has been held that Rule 202 does not authorize any type of presuit discovery other than depositions. *In re Akzo Nobel Chemical*, 24 S.W.3d 919, 921 (Tex. App.—Beaumont 2000, orig. proceeding).

In order to take a deposition before suit is filed, a petition must be filed in the manner and form outlined by the rule. First, the petition must be verified. TEX. R. CIV. P. 202.2(a). Second, the petition must be filed in a "proper court of any county," meaning, either in the county where venue of any anticipated suit would lie or in the county where the witness resides. TEX. R. CIV. P. 202.2(b). Third, the suit must be brought in the name of the petitioner. TEX. R. CIV. P. 202.2(c).

The petition must state either that the petitioner anticipates the institution of a suit in which the petitioner may be a party, or, that the petitioner seeks to investigate a potential claim by or against the petitioner. TEX. R. CIV. P. 202.2(d). Next, if a lawsuit is anticipated (although it is preferable to do so regardless), the petition must state the names of the persons that the petitioner expects to have interests adverse to the petitioner in the anticipated suit, and the addresses and telephone numbers of such persons, or, that the names, addresses and telephone of persons that petitioner expects to have adverse interests in the anticipated suit cannot be ascertained through diligent inquiry. In the latter instance, the persons must be described. TEX. R. CIV. P. 202.2(f).

Lastly, the petition must state the names, addresses and telephone numbers of the persons to be deposed, the substance of the testimony that the petitioner expects to elicit from the deponents, and the petitioner's reasons for desiring to obtain the testimony of each. TEX. R. CIV. P. 202.2(g). The petition should conclude with a request for an order authorizing the petitioner to take the depositions of the persons named. TEX. R. CIV. P. 202.2(h).

At least fifteen days before the date of the hearing on the petition, the petitioner must serve the petition and a notice of the hearing on the persons to be deposed, and, if suit is anticipated, on those persons who have interests adverse to petitioner. TEX. R. CIV. P. 202.3(a). The notice must be served in accordance with the procedures outlined in Rule 21a. If the persons who have interests adverse to the petitioner are not known, then notice can be by publication so long as the *first* published notice is given at least fourteen days before the hearing. TEX. R. CIV. P. 202.3(b)(1). The petition and notice must then be published once a week for two consecutive weeks, "in the county in which the petition is filed, or if no such newspaper exists, in the newspaper of broadest circulation in the nearest county in which a newspaper is published." TEX. R. CIV. P. 202.3(b)(1). If notice is given by publication, the subsequent deposition is subject to suppression by motion either in the proceeding or by bill of review. TEX. R. CIV. P. 202.3(b)(2).

If the court makes one of two findings, then it "must" order a deposition to be taken. These findings are: (1) allowing the petitioner to take the requested deposition may prevent a failure or delay of justice in an anticipated suit; or (2) the likely benefit of allowing the petitioner to take the requested deposition to investigate a potential claim outweighs the burden or expense of the procedure. TEX. R. CIV. P. 202.4(a). Thus, when drafting the court's order, it should reflect which of the two findings the court has made.

The language of the rule suggests that a court can order a presuit deposition even if it makes neither of the two findings. That is, the rule says that if the court makes either finding, it "must" order a deposition to be taken. TEX. R. CIV. P. 202.4(a). Presumably, therefore, even if neither finding is made, the court could order a deposition to be taken.

The court's order *must* state whether the deposition will be oral or written; the order *may* state the time and place of the deposition; however, if the order does not state the time and place, then the petitioner must notice the deposition as required by Rule 199 or 200. Further, the order should contain any protections that the court finds necessary or appropriate to protect the witness or any person who may be affected by the procedure. TEX. R. CIV. P. 202.4(b).

[a] FORM: Petition for pre-suit deposition

```
                                    NO. _____
                              §     IN THE DISTRICT COURT OF
                              §
In Re:                        §     _____COUNTY, TEXAS
                              §
_____                    §     _____ JUDICIAL DISTRICT
```

PETITION FOR PRE-SUIT ORAL DEPOSITION

TO THE HONORABLE JUDGE OF THE DISTRICT COURT:

_____, Petitioner, asks the Court for an order authorizing Petitioner to take the oral deposition of the witness[es] named below, for the purpose of [*insert purpose, e.g.* perpetuating or obtaining testimony] [*or investigating a potential claim*], and as grounds for this petition will show the following:

1. *Identity of petitioners*: Petitioner is _____ [*describe petitioner, e.g.* the purchaser of a new home which was built and sold by _____].

2. *Litigation is anticipated*: Petitioner believes that the unrepaired defects in Petitioner's home for which the builder is responsible will result in litigation. Based on this belief, Petitioner anticipates that a lawsuit will be filed against the builder pursuant to Tex. Bus. & Com. Code §17.50(a). In anticipation of litigation, Petitioner desires to perpetuate or obtain the testimony of [*identify person whose testimony is to be taken*_____] for use in an anticipated suit. Allowing Petitioner to take the requested deposition may prevent a failure or delay of justice in this anticipated suit.

[*or*]

2. *There is a potential claim*. Petitioner has a potential claim against [*identify person against whom petitioner has claim* _____]. Petitioner wishes to investigate this potential claim in order to determine whether there are grounds for a lawsuit. The likely benefit of allowing the Petitioner to take the requested deposition to investigate a potential claim outweighs the burden or expense of the procedure.

3. *Persons with adverse interests*: Petitioner believes that the following persons have interests adverse to Petitioner in the anticipated litigation [*or* claim] described above: [*identify all persons with adverse interest, including each person's name, address and telephone number*].

4. *Person to be deposed*: Petitioner wishes to depose the following person[s]: [*identify the person or persons to be deposed, giving each person's name, address and telephone number*]. The testimony which Petitioner expects to elicit from each witness is as follows: [*describe the anticipated testimony of each person to be deposed*].

WHEREFORE, Petitioner requests an order from this Court authorizing Petitioner to take the deposition of the person[s] named above, within the time and manner authorized by the Texas Rules of Civil Procedure. Petitioner requests such other relief to which Petitioner may be entitled.

Respectfully submitted,

[Signature of attorney]

AFFIDAVIT

STATE OF TEXAS §
COUNTY OF _____ §

BEFORE ME the undersigned authority on this day personally appeared _____ who, after having been by me duly cautioned and sworn did state to me upon his [her] oath that he [she] is the petitioner in the above entitled and numbered cause; that he [she] is over the age of eighteen and is competent to make this affidavit; that he [she] has read the foregoing petition and that each of the factual statements made in the petition are true and correct based on his [her] own personal knowledge.

[*Signature of affiant*]

SIGNED AND SWORN TO BEFORE ME on this _____ day of _____, 20__, to certify which witness my hand and official seal.

[*Signature of notary public*]

SEAL/ STAMP

NOTICE OF HEARING

A hearing on this petition to take a deposition before suit is filed has been set for the _____ day of _____, 20___ in the Judicial District Court of County, Texas which is located at [*insert street address of courthouse*].

[Signature of attorney]

CERTIFICATE OF SERVICE

I certify that a true and correct copy of the foregoing document was delivered to the following persons on this _____ day of _____ 20___, by certified mail, return receipt requested:

Persons served:
[*Insert names and addresses*]

[Signature of attorney]

[b] FORM: Order for deposition before suit

	NO. _____
	§ IN THE DISTRICT COURT OF
	§
In Re:	§ _____ COUNTY, TEXAS
	§
_____	§ _____ JUDICIAL DISTRICT

ORDER ON PETITION TO TAKE
A PRE-SUIT ORAL DEPOSITION

On this _____ day of _____, 20___, came on for hearing the petition of for an order to take the oral deposition of _____, before suit is filed.

The Court makes the following findings:

Allowing Petitioners to take a deposition before suit is filed may prevent a failure or delay of justice in an anticipated suit [*or* the likely benefit of allowing the petitioner to take the requested deposition to investigate a potential claim outweighs the burden or expense of the procedure];

Notice of this hearing was given in the time and manner prescribed by Tex. R. Civ. P. 202.3.

Based on these findings, the Court makes the following orders:

The deposition of will be taken on the _____ day of _____, 20___ at o'clock ___.m. at [*insert location of deposition*].

The deposition will be taken on oral examination [and will be video-taped].

SIGNED on this _____ day of _____, 20___.

[Signature of Judge]

§7.53 Deposition Checklists

Deposition checklists are useful starting points for deposition preparation, whether the deponent is a fact witness, a party, or an expert. The primary use of a deposition checklist is to eliminate the need to "reinvent the wheel" each time a deposition is taken. Instead, the checklist serves as an outline of questions that should be asked in all cases of a particular type, thereby allowing more time for structuring questions that are unique to the case at hand. Deposition checklists are especially important in view of the limitations on the number of hours that can be spent in depositions in any given case. *See* TEX. R. CIV. P. 190.

The following checklist provides a guide for taking depositions in deceptive trade practice cases. It is important to emphasize the need to supplement the checklist liberally in order to deal with specific transactions.

[a] Preliminary matters —Stipulations

(1) *Procedure*: Stipulations regarding depositions may be made by written agreement unless the court orders otherwise. An agreement that affects a deposition on oral testimony is enforceable if the agreement is recorded in the deposition transcript. TEX. R. CIV. P. 191.1.

(2) *Suggested stipulations*: The following matters should be dealt with by means of stipulations, if at all possible. If an opposing party refuses to enter into a stipulation on any of these matters, then questions should be posed to the appropriate witness to insure that necessary evidence will be admissible at trial:

- Authenticity of documents, particularly the business records of opposing parties.
- Receipt and adequacy of pre-suit notice letter(s).
- Written response(s) to pre-suit notice letter(s).
- The adequacy of the qualifications of expert witnesses who will testify at trial.

[**NOTE**: In *E. I. duPont de Nemours & Co., Inc. v. Robinson*, 923 S.W.2d 549, 557 (Tex. 1995), the Texas Supreme Court held that the admissibility of an expert witness's testimony should be evaluated on the basis of at least six, non-exclusive criteria: (1) the extent to which the expert's theory has been or can be tested; (2) the extent to which the technique relies upon the subjective interpretation of the expert; (3) whether the theory has been subjected to peer review or publication; (4) the technique's potential rate of error; (5) whether the underlying theory or technique has been generally accepted as valid by the relevant scientific community; and (6) the non-judicial uses that have been made of the theory or technique. *See generally* Boudreaux, *Cutting Edge Issues with Experts*, THE ADVOCATE, Vol. 15, No. 4, 1996 at 295-305. Should a *Robinson* challenge be made to the qualifications of an expert after the expert's deposition has been taken, particularly one who is scheduled to testify by deposition only, there is a considerable risk that the testimony of the expert may be lost. For this reason, it is important to determine at the time that the expert's deposition is taken, if possible, whether such a challenge will be made. If an opposing party is unable or unwilling to stipulate to admissibility, then the expert must be questioned closely during the deposition on each of the admissibility criteria.]

Signature of the witness.

[**NOTE:** Although it may not be necessary, it is helpful to obtain a stipulation that an unsigned copy of the deposition may be used at the time of any hearing or trial the same as if it had been signed.]

—Objections.

(1) *Procedure*: Objections to questions during oral examination are limited to "objection, leading," and "objection, form." Objections to testimony is limited to "objection, non-responsive." No other objections can be made and these objections are waived if not made as phrased. No other objections need to be made at the deposition in order to be heard by the court. If a party requests it, the party objecting must "give a clear and concise explanation of any objection" or it is waived. Argumentative or suggestive objections may be grounds for terminating the deposition or assessing costs or other sanctions. Tex. R. Civ. P. 199.5(e).

(2) *Substance*: For any witness who cannot or will not be at trial to testify, every effort should be made to secure an agreement that all objections to testimony will be made at the time the deposition is taken and that if no objection is made then any objection that could have been made is deemed waived. Without such an agreement, great care must be taken to ask "objection-proof" questions.

—Non-stenographic depositions.

(1) *Procedure*: Non-stenographic recordings of deposition testimony, including videotape, may be made without leave of the court and may be used at trial if: (a) all other parties are given five days notice by certified mail, return receipt requested, specifying the type of non-stenographic recording that is to be used. Tex. R. Civ. P. 199.2(b)(3).

[b] Beginning the deposition

A deposition should commence with the swearing of the witness and securing from the witness an agreement as to each of the following matters:

- If any question is asked that the witness does not understand, the witness will ask to have the question repeated or rephrased.
- The witness will give oral answers rather than a nod of the head.
- The witness will allow the questioner to finish asking a question before beginning an answer and the ques-

- tioner will endeavor to let the witness finish answering a question before asking a new one.
- The witness may take a break of consult with his or her attorney at any time; however, if a question has been asked but not answered, the witness will not take a break until the question has been answered.
- If no changes or additions are made by the witness to the deposition transcript, then it may be assumed that the witness intended to say what was said during the deposition.

[c] General questions of all witnesses

With rare exceptions, the following areas of questions should be asked of all witnesses who testify in a deposition:

- Name
- Other names ever used
- Business and home address
- Spouse's name, if any, and children's names, if any
- Business, occupation or profession (including the name of the employer, job title, job description, and beginning date of employment)
- Date of birth
- Driver's license state and number
- Social security number
- Names of family members (including in-laws) who reside in the county of suit
- Educational background
- Employment history (including names of employers, dates of employment, job titles, job descriptions, and reason for leaving each place of employment)
- Spouse's occupation (including name of employer, job title, job description, and beginning date of employment)
- Arrests or convictions
- Prior litigation (including parties, whether witness was plaintiff or defendant, county of suit, approximate date of filing and trial/ settlement, nature of suit, result of suit)
- Prior deposition or trial testimony (including parties, county of suit, approximate date testimony was given,

capacity in which person testified, and if an expert, on whose behalf witness was called to testify)

- Deposition preparation (including persons talked with, documents reviewed, discussions or other communications by non-party witness with opposing counsel)

[d] Sample questions of seller

In a transaction in which it is alleged that the seller made false representations about a good or service, the following questions should be included in the deposition:

- Identification of sale documents (including contract, brochures, advertising copy, warranties, etc.)
- Explanation of terms of sale
- Explanation of terms of warranty (including steps required of buyer to obtain warranty benefits)
- Location(s) of transaction
- Salesperson(s) involved
    - Training of salesperson(s)
    - Training materials used
    - When, where, and how long training was done
    - Identification of person who conducted training
    - Test scores, if any, of person trained
- All conversations with plaintiff (including approximate date(s), substance and participants)
- Similar consumer complaints received
    - Identification of complaint file(s)
    - Nature of complaint(s)
    - Resolution of complaint(s)
- Identification of all inspections or tests of product before or after sale
- If a problem with the product or service is acknowledged, a description of the problem and any necessary repair or replacement
- Governmental investigations/inquiries
    - When investigated and by whom
    - Reasons for and scope of investigation
    - Result of investigation

- Recalls on product, if any
  - Identification of recall documents
- Quality assurance programs, if any
  - Identification of person in charge
  - Types of files kept
  - Identification of files pertaining to product/service in question
  - Any changes in products/services brought about because of quality assurance program
- Responses made to plaintiff's complaint(s)
  - When, how responses were made
  - Substance of responses
- Statements made by plaintiff or anyone associated with plaintiff
  - Whether statements were recorded or documented
  - Identification of any witnesses to statements

1. Any conduct of plaintiff that contributed to damages claimed
   - Any conduct of any other person that contributed to plaintiff's problem or damages (including identity of person and description of how and why that party's conduct contributed to plaintiff's problem)

2. Any disciplinary action taken against persons who dealt with plaintiff
   - Identification of former sales/service employees
     - Names, addresses
     - Reasons for leaving
   - Identification of all persons with knowledge of product/ service or plaintiff's problem and description of the knowledge each person is believed to have

[e] Sample questions of buyer

In a transaction in which it is alleged that the seller made false representations about a good or service, the following questions should be included in the deposition of the buyer:

- Identification of sale documents (including contract, brochures, advertising copy, warranties, etc.)
- Identification of all persons with whom the consumer dealt (before, during, and after sale)

- Explanation of consumer's problems with the good or service
- Description of problem
- When problem was first noticed
- When problem was first called to seller's attention
- Complaints set forth in notice letter
- Complaints that are not mentioned in notice letter
- Identification of other complaint documents (letters, lists, complaints filed with any state agency)
- Steps, if any, consumer has taken to cure problems
- Current status of problems (still existing, cured or repaired)
- Alleged misconduct
- Representations alleged to have been made (when, what was said, by whom and the identification of any witnesses to misrepresentations)
- All oral warranties alleged to have been given (when, what was said, by whom and the identification of any witnesses to the making of the oral warranties)
- All facts that the consumer contends should have been disclosed but were not disclosed
- Any other conduct of seller about which consumer complains
- Identification of any recordings, notes or other writings referring to oral representations or warranties
- Relief sought
- Nature of relief sought (repair, replacement, refund)
- Basis for relief: conversations, reports, opinions, estimates
- Computation of damages (including evidence to support computation)
- Mental anguish damages (symptoms, when began, when ended, medications, identification of treating professional)
- Nature of attorney fee contract
- Identification of response(s) to notice of complaint
- Reasons seller's offer, if any, was not accepted
- Prior experience with goods or services

- Other similar goods or services purchased
- Other similar complaints (including lawsuits)
- Other parties to transaction with whom consumer has a complaint
- Identification of all persons with knowledge and explanation of what witness believes they know about transaction or its aftermath

§7.54 Preparing the Client for Deposition

The importance of preparing a client for his or her deposition cannot be overemphasized. Most clients have not had their deposition taken before and even those who have may have gotten bad advice, e.g. "Just answer 'yes' or 'no.'"

Deposition preparation obviously includes a review of key documents and answers to discovery, and an extended discussion about how the deposition will be taken and what to expect. Some attorneys engage in practice question and answer sessions, although other attorneys find that clients sometimes have a tendency to try and memorize answers to particular questions.

Although the process of deposition preparation will generally will include a face-to-face meeting, it is helpful for the client to have something in writing that can be reviewed from time to time before the deposition. The following client memorandum is one example of the first step used to prepare a client for the deposition.

[a] FORM: Deposition preparation memorandum (plaintiff)

```
MEMORANDUM TO CLIENT
(Date)
TO      :
FROM    :
SUBJ    :       PREPARING FOR YOUR DEPOSITION
```

As you may know, a deposition is an occasion when you are placed under oath by a court reporter and our opposing counsel is given the opportunity to ask you questions, the same as if you were testifying in court. To say the least, this is a very important part of our lawsuit. For this reason, I have prepared this rather lengthy memorandum to help you get ready for the deposition. Let's begin with the basics:

What are the purposes of a deposition?

There are two basic purposes of a deposition from our opposing counsel's point of view. The first purpose is to find out all that can be learned from you about the facts of our lawsuit.

The second purpose is to commit you, under oath, to the facts as you understand them so that it will be difficult to "change" your testimony later at trial.

What will be done to prepare me for the deposition?

I have begun your preparation for the deposition already by sending you this memorandum to read. Next, before the deposition, we will meet in order to review any questions you may have. I will not ask you all of the questions I think the other side will ask. Going over questions in detail causes people to try to memorize answers to questions, which is the last thing we want. Our clients tell us after a deposition that it was not as bad as they feared; nevertheless, you should expect some pre-game jitters and nervousness.

Some Deposition Rules

We have developed a number of "rules" for our clients to remember when they give their depositions. These rules and advice should not be memorized; instead, think about the reasons behind the rules and if needed, discuss the reasons with me. In this way, you will be better able to use this information to your advantage.

1. Always tell the truth to the best of your ability.

If you don't know the answer to a question, do not guess. Simply say you don't know.

2. Do not expect me to say very much at the deposition.

Unlike at trial, I rarely make objections at a deposition. The reason is that we can save our objections until the time of trial. Do not look to me for approval before you answer or expect me to object to questions. If an objection needs to be made, I will take care of it. In the event I do make an objection, please stop your testimony immediately—in mid-sentence if necessary.

3. Do not expect the other side's attorney to be unfriendly or abusive.

The opposing attorney is quite likely to be very friendly. Experience has taught attorneys that a witness will be less likely to freely give information to a hostile questioner. As a result, expect the opposing attorney to be very friendly and full of smiles. Remember, to some extent this ploy is used to get you off your guard. Do not be fooled. Remember that in spite of the smiles, the attorney is trying to spot weaknesses in the case.

4. Never get into a discussion with the opposing attorney before or after the deposition.

Be friendly. Say hello. But do not get into any extended discussions about anything.

> 5. *Never think you are smarter than the attorney asking you questions, even if you are.*

You are likely to be asked an easy series of questions at the beginning of the deposition to lull you into a false sense of security. The attorney may purposefully appear confused or unprepared in order to "bait" you into showing how much more you know about the case than he or she does. Do not take the bait. Just answer the questions that are asked.

> 6. *Do not look for a "trick" in every question.*

Very few, if any, "trick questions" will be asked in a deposition (or at trial for that matter). If you are not sure what a trick question is, a classic example is the question, "when did you stop beating your wife?" The question cannot be answered without admitting that you abuse your spouse, even if you have never done such a thing. Questions like this are fun to play with but very few lawyers waste time asking them. If you spend your time worrying about how to avoid trick questions, you will get confused and your testimony will be of less value to us. Let me worry about protecting you from trick questions. I will.

> 7. *Never lose your temper or joke around with the questioner.*

The opposing attorney may try to make you lose your temper. Under no circumstances, regardless of what question is asked, should you lose your temper. On the other hand, the questioner may try to get you to joke about something. We all value our senses of humor, but humor is not appropriate at a deposition. The jury may conclude that you think the case is funny.

> 8. *When a question is asked, listen carefully to the question, make sure you understand the question, think to yourself about your answer and then speak.*

In everyday conversation, we communicate with a combination of words, gestures, and other body language. Unlike any other type of communication we are used to, testimony requires that your answer be carefully thought out so that your words, when read, will be literally true. For example, imagine that you are sitting in a deposition in a body cast. The attorney asks you, "you're not really hurt, are you?" Sarcastically, you answer, "no, I'm not hurt!" By the time of trial, the body cast is gone and the cold, hard words on the page of your deposition read like an admission that you have sustained no injuries. The example may be silly, but it does illustrate the need to make sure your answers are literally true. Re-read the rule at the beginning of this paragraph. This is the most important rule you need to know.

9. Do not volunteer information.

In a deposition you must answer the questions asked but you are not required to volunteer information unless the information is <u>essential</u> to have your answer make sense. There is no judge or jury present to hear the volunteered information. Witnesses who volunteer information generally do so because they do not understand the question. Make a determined effort to listen to the question and answer only the question that is asked. Make the other side work for the testimony they get. At the same time, however, *never* try to hide or conceal information if the question fairly asks about it. If you are asked a question in deposition and you hold back information that was asked about, the judge may prevent you from offering that testimony at trial.

The line between answering fully and not volunteering information is a fine line to walk. If you are aware that the line exists, then you will do fine.

10. Remember to qualify your answers if you are not certain of your answers.

If you cannot remember a date but have an idea of the approximate date then answer truthfully, "I do not remember the exact date, but I think it was around _____." If you are certain of the answer, then say so, but if there is a chance you may be wrong or if you cannot give an answer as precise as the question seems to require, then give yourself some flexibility by using words such as "approximately" or "to the best of my memory." Normally, you should avoid using the words "always" and "never." In most situations, you may not remember the actual words used when you are asked about conversations with the opposing party. Very few of us have photographic memories or memories that are capable of recalling exact language. Do not let this concern you. Even though you may not remember the exact words used, you still remember what was "said."

11. Always admit that you have talked with me about your deposition.

I would be a poor attorney indeed if I did not prepare you for your deposition. Some people feel they should not admit this. Some attorneys try the old trick of asking, "What did your attorney tell you to say?" The only answer to this question is, "My attorney told me to tell the truth."

12. Read key documents.

The night before the deposition, re-read the petition we have filed in this case and your answers to interrogatories. You are likely to be asked about both at the deposition. If we made a mistake in any of the documents filed, do not hesitate to point that out. You should be able to back up each of the factual allegations in the documents (assuming they are accurate) but do not worry about trying to justify the words chosen.

13. Be wary of the "Is that all?" question.

After the opposing attorney has finished asking specific questions, you may be asked, "Can you think of anything else that supports your claims in this lawsuit?" You are not required to provide open-ended education to our opposing attorney; instead, you are required to fully and truthfully answer questions that are asked. For this reason, the appropriate type of response to this question is, "I have answered each of your questions to the best of my ability, but I will be happy to answer any other questions you may have."

14. Get some rest!

The night before the deposition, re-read this memorandum, read the petition and answers to interrogatories we filed in this lawsuit and then, when you have finished, get the best preparation possible: turn out the light and get a good night's sleep.

[b] FORM: Deposition preparation memorandum (defendant)

CLIENT MEMORANDUM

(Date)

TO   :
FROM   :
SUBJ   :   PREPARING FOR YOUR DEPOSITION

As you may know, a deposition is an occasion when you are placed under oath by a court reporter and our opposing counsel is given the opportunity to ask you questions, the same as if you were testifying in court. To say the least, this is a very important part of this lawsuit. For this reason, I have prepared this rather lengthy memo to help you get ready for the deposition. You may already be familiar with much of the information in this memorandum; even so, I encourage you to read the memorandum carefully to refresh your memory.

What are the purposes of a deposition?

There are two basic purposes of a deposition from our opposing counsel's point of view. The first purpose is to find out all that can be learned about the facts of this lawsuit from your point of view. The second purpose is to commit you, under oath, to the facts as you understand them so that it will be difficult to "change" your testimony later at trial.

What will be done to prepare me for the deposition?

I have begun your preparation for the deposition already by sending you this memorandum. Next, before the deposition, we will meet in order to review any questions you may have. I will not ask you all of the questions I think the other side will ask. Going over questions in detail causes people to try and memorize answers to questions, which is the last thing we want. Our clients tell us after a deposition that it was not as bad as they feared; nevertheless, you should expect some pre-game jitters and nervousness.

How should I answer the questions during the deposition?

We have developed a number of "rules" for our clients to remember when they give their depositions. These rules and advice should not be memorized; instead, think about the reasons behind the rules and if needed, discuss the reasons with us. In this way, you will be better able to use this information to your advantage.

(a) **Listen carefully to each question, make sure you understand the question, think to yourself about your answer and then speak.** In everyday conversation, we communicate with a combination of words, gestures and other body language. Unlike any other type of communication we are used to, testimony requires that your answer be carefully thought out so that your words, when read, will be literally true. For example, assume that a person is sitting at his deposition in a body cast, all broken and bruised. Should the other side's attorney ask him, "you're not really hurt are you?", the witness might be tempted to answer sarcastically, "no, I'm not hurt." Unfortunately, the written word does not convey the sarcasm, and months later when the body cast is gone and the bruises are healed, the sarcastic words used in the deposition become an admission that the witness is not hurting. This rule is perhaps the most important of all. Be sure you understand it fully.

(b) **Always tell the truth to the best of your ability.** If you don't know the answer to a question, do not guess—simply say you don't know. Although we all want to tell the truth, sometimes we keep ourselves from doing so. For example, years ago I was involved in a lawsuit about false representations in which one party was asked this question: "Now, Mr. _____, you don't actually remember the exact words that _____ spoke to you some two years ago, do you?" The party realized that he did not remember the exact words and so he answered, "No, I do not." The next question was, "so, you cannot sit here under oath today and tell us exactly what representations were made to you back then, can you?" The party thought for a minute and then answered, untruthfully, "no, I guess

I can't." The fact is, that person knew precisely what was said to him; he simply could not remember the exact words used to say it. The truthful answer to the question should have been, "yes, I do remember what was represented to me."

(c) **Qualify your answers if you are not certain of your answers**. If you cannot remember a date but have an idea of the approximate date then answer truthfully, "I do not remember the exact date, but I think it was around _____." If you are certain of the answer, then say so; but if there is a chance you may be wrong or if you cannot give an answer as precise as the question seems to require, then give yourself some flexibility by using words such as "approximately" or "to the best of my memory." Normally, you should avoid using the words "always" and "never."

(d) **Do not volunteer information**. In a deposition you must answer the questions asked but you are not required to volunteer information unless the information is necessary to make your answer *to the question* complete. Witnesses who volunteer information generally do so because they do not understand the question. Make a determined effort to listen to the question and answer only the question that is asked.

(e) **Make your answers complete**. Having just cautioned you to not volunteer information, you must also be sure that when a question is asked you answer the question fully. Never try to hide or conceal information if the question fairly asks about it. Some people decide that they will try to "save" a particularly damaging bit of testimony for trial, thinking that when it finally comes out the other side will really be hurt by it. Unfortunately, if you are asked a question and you hold back information fairly asked about, you may be prohibited by the Court from mentioning the information at trial.

Many questions call for short, "yes" or "no" type answers. For example, "have you ever been married?" The answer to the question is "yes" or "no." If you respond by saying, "I married Betty Sue in 1973," then you have not answered the question directly. The question was not "whom and when did you marry," the question was whether you have ever been married. By contrast, if you are asked, "tell me about the work you did to respond to the plaintiff's complaint," then you need to start talking and not stop until you have fully described each and every thing you did.

The line between not volunteering information and making your answers complete is a fine line to walk. If you are aware that the line exists, then you will do fine.

- - - - -

In addition to these "rules" about testifying, you also should keep in mind some additional rules about your conduct and thoughts during the deposition:

(a) **Do not expect the other side's attorney to be unfriendly or abusive.** The opposing attorney is quite likely to be very friendly. Experience has taught attorneys that a witness will be less likely to freely give information to a hostile questioner. As a result, expect the opposing attorney to be very friendly and full of smiles. Remember, to some extent this ploy is used to get you off your guard. Do not be fooled. Remember that in spite of the smiles, the attorney is trying to spot weaknesses in our side of the case. On the other hand, if the attorney is unfriendly or abusive, pay no attention to it. Some attorneys effect an attitude of resentment or sarcasm in order to get the hair up on the back of your neck. If you find yourself reacting emotionally to the attorney's attitude or tone of voice, it is time for a break and let me know.

(b) **Never get into a discussion with the opposing attorney before or after the deposition.** Be friendly. Say hello. But do not get into any extended discussions about anything.

(c) **Never think you are smarter than the attorney asking you questions, even if you are.** You are likely to be asked an easy series of questions at the beginning to lull you into a false sense of security. The attorney may purposefully appear confused or unprepared in order to "bait" you into showing how much more you know about the case. Do not take the bait. Just answer the questions that are asked.

(d) **Do not look for a "trick" in every question.** Not every question has a trap. In fact, very few questions are trick questions. If you spend your time worrying about how to avoid trick questions, you will get confused and your testimony will be of less value to us. Let me worry about protecting you from trick questions. I will.

(e) **Never lose your temper or joke around with the questioner.** As I mentioned earlier, the opposing attorney may try to make you lose your temper. Under no circumstances, regardless of what question is asked, should you lose your temper. On the other hand, the questioner may try to get you to joke about the case or the complaint. We all value our senses of humor, but humor is rarely appropriate from a witness at a deposition.

(f) **If asked, always admit that you have talked with me about your deposition.** We would be poor attorneys indeed if we did not prepare you for your deposition. Some people feel they should not admit this. Some attorneys try the old trick of asking, "What did your attorney tell you to say?" The only answer to this question is, "My attorney told me to tell the truth."

(g) **Be wary of the "Is that all?" question.** After the opposing attorney has finished asking specific questions, you may be asked, "Can you think of anything else that supports your defenses in this lawsuit?" You are not required to provide open-ended education to our opposing attorney; instead, you are required to fully and truthfully answer questions that are asked. For this reason, the appropriate type of response to this question is, "I have answered each of your questions to the best of my ability, but I will be happy to answer any other questions you may have." Should this question be asked, I will intervene in order to help keep you from leaving anything out.

- - - - -

As part of your preparation for the deposition, re-read the basic documents that pertain to this case. You are likely to be asked about these documents at the deposition. If I made a mistake in any of the legal documents filed (such as the answers to interrogatories), do not hesitate to point that out. You should be able to back up each of the factual allegations in the documents (assuming they are accurate) but do not worry about trying to justify the words chosen. Also, if there are particular documents that you believe are important to the lawsuit, you should review those documents carefully so that you will be familiar with them at the deposition.

Do not expect me to say very much at the deposition. Unlike at trial, I rarely make objections at a deposition. The reason is that we can save our objections until the time of trial. Do not look to me for approval before you answer or expect me to object to questions. In the event I do make an objection, please stop your testimony immediately—in mid-sentence if necessary.

The night before the deposition, after you have finished your review of the documents and this memorandum, get the best preparation possible: turn out the light and get a good night's sleep.

Chapter 8

Pre-Trial Proceedings

§8.01 General Considerations
 §8.01.1 Mediation
  [a] FORM: Motion to compel mediation
  [b] FORM: Order on motion to compel mediation
  [c] FORM: Mediation Settlement Agreement
 §8.01.2 When to Use Mediation
 §8.01.3 Preparing for Mediation
 §8.01.4 The Mediation Process
  §8.01.4.1 Avoiding Ethical Traps in Negotiation
 §8.01.5 Arbitration
 §8.01.6 Applicable Law
 §8.01.7 Defenses to Arbitration Agreement
  §8.01.7.1 Unconscionability
  §8.01.7.2 Waiver or Estoppel by Litigation
  §8.01.7.3 Plaintiff or Defendant Not a Party to the Agreement
  §8.01.7.4 Arbitration Procedure Under Texas Arbitration Act
 §8.01.8 Appeal of Arbitrator's Decision
  [a] FORM: Motion to compel arbitration
  [b] FORM: Order compelling arbitration
§8.02 Offer of Settlement
 §8.02.1 Invoking the Rule
  [a] FORM: Declaration for application of offer of settlement rule
 §8.02.2 Making Settlement Offer
  [a] FORM: Offer of settlement
 §8.02.3 Awarding Litigation Costs
 §8.02.4 "Litigation Costs"
§8.03 Obtaining Trial Setting and Giving Notice
  [a] FORM: Letter requesting trial setting
  [b] FORM: Certification of trial readiness
  [c] FORM: Letter providing notice of setting to parties
  [d] FORM: Letter providing notice of setting to witnesses
§8.04 Evidence by Affidavit
§8.05 Cost and necessity of services
  [a] FORM: Affidavit concerning cost and necessity of services

§8.06　Controverting Affidavit Concerning Cost and Necessity of Services
　　　[a]　FORM:　Counteraffidavit concerning cost and necessity of services
　　　[b]　FORM:　Request for leave of court to file counteraffidavit
　　　[c]　FORM:　Order granting leave to file counteraffidavit

§8.07　Business and Medical Records
　　　[a]　FORM:　Business or medical records affidavit

§8.08　Use of Criminal Convictions for Impeachment
　　　[a]　FORM:　Request for notice of use of criminal convictions for impeachment

§8.09　Visiting Judges
　　　[a]　FORM:　Objection to assignment of visiting judge

§8.10　Motions in Limine
　§8.10.1　Travis County Local Rule
　§8.10.2　Procedure
　　　[a]　FORM:　Motion in limine (general form)
　　　[b]　FORM:　Specific matters for plaintiff's motion in limine
　　　[c]　FORM:　Specific matters for defendant's motion in limine
　　　[d]　FORM:　Order on motion in limine

§8.11　Judicial Notice
　　　[a]　FORM:　Motion for court to take judicial notice
　　　[b]　FORM:　Order taking judicial notice

§8.12　Pre-Trial Conference
　　　[a]　FORM:　Motion for pre-trial conference
　　　[b]　FORM:　Order on pre-trial conference (general form)
　　　[c]　FORM:　Scheduling order

§8.13　Summary Judgment
　　　[a]　FORM:　Motion for summary judgment on independent investigation
　　　[b]　FORM:　Response to motion for summary judgment: independent investigation

§8.01 General Considerations

Everything in this book up to this point could be called a "pre-trial" proceeding in one form or another. The particular focus of this chapter, however, is on those matters that either should or must be taken care of before a case can be tried.

§8.01.1 Mediation

The 1995 DTPA amendments added a new section permitting a party to compel mediation. DTPA §17.5051, as amended 1995. The Texas Alternative Dispute Resolution Act, TEX. CIV. PRAC. & REM. CODE §§154.023 and 154.051-154.073, defines mediation as "a forum in which an impartial person, the mediator, facilitates communication between the parties to promote reconciliation, settlement, or understanding among them." TEX. CIV. PRAC. & REM. CODE §154.023. This statutory definition, while adequate for its purpose, is too abstract to fairly describe the mediation process or the role of the mediator. Mediation is more simply described as assisted negotiation. The mediator (an acceptable, impartial and neutral third party) provides a forum and a process for the parties to create, submit, receive, evaluate and respond to settlement proposals until, hopefully, a mutually acceptable settlement is achieved. The mediator oversees the process and assists the parties as necessary and appropriate; *see generally*, MOORE, THE MEDIATION PROCESS, 14-19 (Jossey-Bass 1987). The mediator does not render a decision, should not give legal or professional advice to the parties and, by statute, may not "impose his own judgment on the issues for that of the parties." TEX. CIV. PRAC. & REM. CODE §154.023.

Mediation pursuant to the DTPA serves dual purposes. First and foremost, mediation serves the same function that it serves in other cases: to facilitate settlement. Secondly, mediation establishes the time-frame for the defendant's post-suit response to presuit DTPA notice. See §4.01 supra. The DTPA now allows a defendant to tender an offer of settlement "during the period beginning on the day after the date that the mediation ends and ending on the 20th date after that date. " DTPA §17.5052(c), as amended 1995. In the absence of mediation, the second tender must be made within 90 days of the date an original answer is filed. See §4.01 supra.

To invoke the mediation process, a party may file a motion to compel mediation no later than the 90th day after service of a pleading which seeks DTPA relief. DTPA §17.5051(a). The Act provides that within 30 days after the motion is filed, the court *shall* enter an order setting the time and place of the mediation. DTPA §17.5051(b). Mediation shall be held within 30 days of the order unless the parties agree otherwise or the court determines that an additional time not to exceed an additional 30 days is warranted. DTPA §17.5051(d). Thus, in most instances, if mediation is invoked it will occur within five months of service of process. Unless all parties agree otherwise, each party who has appeared in the case shall participate in the mediation and shall share in the mediation fee. DTPA §17.5051(e). However, if the amount of economic damages claimed is less than $15,000, any party who compels mediation must pay its costs. DTPA §17.5051(f). The parties can agree on the mediator, but if they do not, the mediator shall be appointed by the court. DTPA §17.5051(c).

Although the process described by §17.5051 controls, the DTPA also provides that §§154.051 through 154.073 of the Texas Alternative Dispute Resolution Act generally apply to the appointment of the mediator and the mediation process. DTPA §17.051(g). Section 154.052 sets forth the minimum qualifications (40 hours of mediation training) for appointment by the court. TEX. CIV. PRAC. & REM. CODE §154.052. However, since DTPA §17.051(c) only calls for court appointment "[i]f the parties do not agree on a mediator," it appears that the parties can agree to use as a mediator someone who does not meet the qualifications set forth in §154.052.

Communications made by mediation participants are confidential and "may not be used as evidence against the participant in any judicial or administrative proceeding" unless disclosure is required by law (as for example, in instances of evidence of child or elder abuse) Tex. Civ. Prac. & Rem. Code §154.073. Except when authorized by the disclosing party, information given in confidence to the mediator may not be disclosed. Tex. Civ. Prac. & Rem. Code §154.053 (b). Even the conduct and demeanor of the parties is protected from disclosure. Tex. Civ. Prac. & Rem. Code §154.053 (c). *See generally*, RAU, SHERMAN & SHANNON, TEXAS ADR & ARBITRATION: STATUTES AND COMMENTARY, 21 (West 2000). Those black-letter rules notwithstanding, not all mediation information is protected from disclosure.

The ADR statute provides that oral and written information used in mediation (or another ADR proceeding) "is admissible or discoverable if it is admissible or discoverable independent of the procedure." Tex. Civ. Prac. & Rem. Code §154.073 (c). In other words, admissible and discoverable information does not become inadmissible or undiscoverable by virtue of the fact that it was utilized in mediation. In a questionable decision, one court relied on this exception to permit discovery of videotaped statements of a party's employees which were played at mediation even though they were prepared for mediation purposes. *In re Learjet, Inc.*, 59 S.W.3d 842 (Tex. App.—Texarkana 2001, orig. proceeding). Additionally, as alluded to above, when another law requiring disclosure conflicts with the statutory rule of mediation confidentiality a court may order the information disclosed (or may protect the information from disclosure) as warranted by "the facts, circumstances and context of the communications or materials." Tex. Civ. Prac. & Rem. Code §154.073 (e). This "other legal requirements" exception has been successfully invoked to permit testimony in two cases dealing with mediation communications relevant to *new* and *independent* torts allegedly committed *during* the mediation process. *See, Avary v. Bank of Am.*, 72 S. W. 3d 779 (Tex. App.—Dallas 2002, pet. denied) (testimony regarding an executor's breach of the fiduciary duty of full-disclosure during the mediation in a post-mediation claim made by beneficiary); *Alford v. Bryant*, 137 S.W.3d 916 (Tex. App.—Dallas 2004, pet filed) (testimony of mediator in action for attorney malpractice allegedly committed during the mediation). The bottom line is that while most mediation communications are confidential, the rule is not absolute.

If the parties reach a settlement and execute a written settlement agreement, it is enforceable in the same manner as any other written contract, and may be incorporated into the final decree disposing of the case. TEX. CIV. PRAC. & REM. CODE §154.071. If one party revokes its consent, the court cannot enter an agreed judgment on the settlement agreement; nevertheless, the agreement remains enforceable. *Compania Financiara Libano, S.A. v. Simmons*, 53 S.W.3d (Tex. 2001). The aggrieved party may enforce the agreement by pursuing a breach of contract claim in the underlying action or in a separate suit. *Mantas v. Fifth Court of Appeals*, 925 S.W.2d 656 (Tex. 1996). The party seeking to enforce the agreement is not entitled to an automatic judgment on the agreement, but must establish a breach of the agreement as in any other breach of contract claim. *Id.; Cadle Co. v. Castle*, 913 S.W.2d 627 (Tex. App. — Dallas 1995, writ denied). Although not explicitly required by the terms of TEX. CIV. PRAC. & REM. CODE §154.071, the court in *Mantas* strongly suggests that the agreement be filed with the court as dictated by Rule — to make it enforceable. Accordingly, if an action for breach of contract becomes necessary, the settlement agreement should be filed before its enforcement is sought. *See Padilla v. LaFrance,* 907 S.W.2d 454 (Tex. 1995).

For a sample mediation settlement agreement *see* Form [c] *infra.* This form is designed to be printed out and taken to mediation at which time the parties can fill in the blanks after a settlement has been reached.

Set forth below are a suggested motion to compel mediation in a DTPA case and a proposed order. Since the legislature has required the trial court to compel mediation, it is unlikely that a party will oppose the motion or that a court will refuse to grant it. Clearly it is in the interests of all parties to reach an agreement as to the date, time and place of the mediation and, of course, the mediator. Accordingly, in most cases the parties should file an agreed motion and order.

In those instances when the parties cannot agree, the court will be called upon to set the mediation and appoint the mediator. The proposed order also sets forth optional language which has proven helpful to the mediation process.

[a] FORM: Motion to compel mediation

```
                          §   IN THE DISTRICT COURT OF
                          §
vs.                       §   _____COUNTY, TEXAS
                          §
                          §   _____ JUDICIAL DISTRICT
```

PLAINTIFF'S [DEFENDANT'S] MOTION TO COMPEL MEDIATION

TO THE HONORABLE JUDGE OF THE DISTRICT COURT:

_____, plaintiff [defendant] files this Motion to Compel Mediation and would show the court the following:

1.

On _____ 20___ a pleading was served in this case seeking relief under the Texas Deceptive Trade Practices Act, Tex. Bus. & Com. Code §17.41 et seq., cited in this motion as the "DTPA." Pursuant to DTPA §17.5051 this motion is filed within 90 days of the service of such pleading.

2.

DTPA §17.5051(b) provides that by the thirtieth day after the filing of this motion the court shall sign an order setting the time and place of mediation. The parties have agreed to hold the mediation on _____ , 20___, beginning at ___ o'clock ___m. at the offices of the mediator. [or, The parties have not agreed upon a date, time and place and, accordingly, the movant requests that, pursuant to DTPA §17.505 1 (b) and (d), the court set the mediation for a date certain within [30] days of the date of the court's order at such time and place which the court deems proper].

[NOTE: DTPA §17.5051, as amended 1995, provides that the mediation shall be held within 30 days or such additional time as the court deems warranted not to exceed a total of 60 days of the date of the court's order.]

3.

The parties have agreed that _____ shall serve as mediator. [or, The parties do not agree on a mediator and, accordingly, movant requests the court to appoint one pursuant to DTPA §17.5051(c).]

4.

Movant requests that pursuant to DTPA §17.5051(e), all parties who have appeared in this action be ordered to participate in the mediation [except _____, who the parties agree need not participate]. Further, pursuant to that section, movant requests that the mediation fee be shared equally among the participants. [or, Further, pursuant to that section, movant agrees to pay the mediation fee.]

WHEREFORE, plaintiff [defendant] requests the relief set forth above and such other and further relief to which plaintiff [defendant] may be entitled.

Respectfully submitted,

[Signature of attorney]

[Certificate of service]

[b] FORM: Order on motion to compel mediation

```
                              NO. _____

_____               §    IN THE DISTRICT COURT OF

                         §

vs.                      §    _____ COUNTY, TEXAS

                         §

_____               §    _____ JUDICIAL DISTRICT
```

ORDER COMPELLING MEDIATION

The Motion to Compel Mediation is GRANTED.

Pursuant to the agreement of the parties, _____ shall serve as mediator for, The parties having failed to agree upon a mediator, the Court appoints _____ to serve as mediator].

 Pursuant to the agreement of the parties and the mediator, the mediation shall be held on _____, 20__, beginning at _ o'clock _m. [or, It is further ordered that the parties confer immediately with the mediator to establish a date for mediation. The mediation shall be held within 30 days of the date of this order, unless the parties agree otherwise. In the event the parties cannot agree upon a date available to the mediator within 10 days of the date of this order, it is ordered that the mediation be held on a date selected by the mediator.]

All parties who have appeared in this action, shall attend and participate in the mediation [except _____, pursuant to the agreement of all parties]. Named parties shall be present and each organization shall be represented by an officer or representative with authority to negotiate a settlement.

[If it is not practical for an agency or governmental entity to have a representative with settlement authority, the representative whose recommendation is most likely to be followed by the agency in determining whether to accept a proposed settlement in the case shall attend.]

The mediator's fees shall be divided and borne equally by the participating parties [or, shall be borne by _____], and shall be paid by the parties directly to the mediator.

No subpoenas, citation, writs or other process shall be served at or near the location of the mediation upon any person entering, leaving or attending any mediation session.

Upon completion of the mediation, the mediator shall file with the court a written statement indicating whether the parties attended the mediation and whether the case did or did not settle. As provided by Tex. Civ. Prac. & Rem. Code Ann. §154.053 and §154.073, all matters, including the conduct and demeanor of the parties and their counsel during the mediation process, are to remain confidential and will not be disclosed to anyone, including this Court. Except as may be permitted by Tex. Civ. Prac. & Rem. Code Ann. §154.073, neither the mediator nor the mediator's files shall be subject to a subpoena or to a request for production filed by any person.

The parties shall immediately serve a copy of this order on the mediator.

IT IS SO ORDERED this _____ day of _____, 20___.

_____
PRESIDING JUDGE

[c] FORM: Mediation Settlement Agreement

```
                          NO. _____

_____           §    IN THE DISTRICT COURT OF
                     §
vs.                  §    _____ COUNTY, TEXAS
                     §
_____           §    _____ JUDICIAL DISTRICT
```

<u>SETTLEMENT AGREEMENT</u>

The parties hereto agree to settle all claims and controversies between them, asserted or assertable in this case except _____ [*insert exceptions or write "none."*]

The consideration to be given for this settlement is as follows:

_____ shall receive the sum of _____ U.S. dollars, on or before _____, which sum will be paid by the following parties in the amounts stated: _____

_____ [*describe non-monetary consideration, if any*].

The above styled and numbered case shall be resolved by:

___ (a)   an agreed order of dismissal with costs taxed to _____ [*or*]

___ (b)   an agreed judgment providing as follows: [*describe specific terms of dismissal order*]

___ (c)   any agreed judgment shall be signed by the trial judge, but may not be abstracted or recorded or any collection effort made upon same so long as the following conditions are met: [*describe conditions, if any*].

The parties agree to release, discharge, and forever hold the other harmless from any and all claims, demands, or suits, known or unknown, fixed or contingent, liquidated or unliquidated whether or not asserted in the above case, as of this date, arising from or related to the events and transactions which are the subject matter of this case, except for the following: [*insert special terms, if any*]_____. This mutual release runs to the benefit of all attorneys, agents employees, officers, directors, shareholders and partners of the parties except [*list parties excluded from release, if any*] _____.

Each signatory, hereto warrants and represents:

___(a)   he or she has the authority to bind the parties for whom that signatory acts.

___(b)   the claims, suits, rights, and/or interests which are the subject matter hereto are owned by the party asserting same, have not been assigned, transferred or sold and are free of encumbrance.

_____ shall deliver drafts of any further settlement documents to the other parties by _____. The parties agree to cooperate with each other in the drafting and execution of such additional documents as are reasonably requested or required to implement the terms and spirit of this agreement.

If a dispute arise with regard to the interpretation and/or performances of this agreement or any of its provisions, and the parties are unable to resolve that dispute between themselves, the parties agree that before litigation is brought to construe or enforce this agreement they will attempt to resolve same by phone conference with the mediator who facilitated this settlement.

Other terms of this settlement are: [*insert any additional terms*] _____.

This agreement is made and performable in _____ County, Texas and shall be construed in accordance with the laws of the State of Texas.

Each signatory to this settlement has entered into same freely and without duress after having consulted with professionals of his or her choice. Each party has been advised by the Mediator that the Mediator is not the attorney for any party, that the mediator's comments were not intended as and should not be accepted as legal advice and that each party should have this agreement reviewed by that party's attorney prior to executing same.

Signed this ____ day of _____, 20____.

[Signature of Plaintiffs]

[Signature of Defendants]

§8.01.2 When to Use Mediation

It is generally recognized that ninety to ninety-five percent of all cases filed are resolved before trial. It is therefore obvious that the vast majority of cases will settle even without resort to mediation or other ADR process. Furthermore, although success rates in mediation are generally high, clearly not every case which is mediated will settle. Accordingly, it cannot be said that the mediation process is necessary or sufficient to settle every dispute. Sooner or later, generally later, most cases will settle. The issue, however, is whether there is a way to obtain that settlement while expending less time, money and anxiety.

In Travis County, by local rule, parties who are set for trial must submit their case to mediation no later than sixty days in advance of the trial setting in order to maintain their place on the docket. Accordingly, even if it is unlikely that a case can or will settle, mediation may still be a prerequisite to retaining a trial setting.

Although mediation is not always necessary or sufficient to settle a case, it is often necessary and is generally sufficient to settle a case short of the proverbial courthouse steps, and, therefore, before the completion of full blown discovery and trial preparation. An earlier settlement typically is obtained with less cost and greater client satisfaction. And, clearly there are cases, probably a significant number, which would go to trial but for mediation. See Low, An Alternative Solution: ADR, 56 Tex. Bar. J. 158, 160 (Feb. 1993).

Most experienced attorneys do not need help evaluating their cases nor do they need negotiation assistance. And, theoretically, two equally experienced and qualified attorneys with access to the same facts, representing opposing parties will arrive at roughly equivalent case evaluations making settlement relatively swift and easy. Typically, these cases will settle in due course without extensive discovery and without the need for alternative dispute resolution procedures.

Mediation can be helpful, however, when the attorneys do not have equivalent experience and expertise, or do not have access to the same facts, or when either lawyer has clients who have naive or unrealistic expectations about the outcome of the case. When the parties or their lawyers have a different perception of reality a settlement is not likely until they have acquired new facts, or a new perspective on old facts, sufficient to narrow that reality gap. Additionally, when one or both parties realize that the cost of acquiring new facts (through discovery) will exceed the value of their impact on negotiations, settlement becomes a priority.

Mediation is generally helpful in getting the parties to the point of settlement more quickly and with less cost. The mediation process shortens the lines of communication and gives each party an opportunity to present their view of the case to the other side. The mediator's job is to provide an orderly framework for that exchange of information, to serve as an "agent of reality" by testing the parties assumptions, and to assist the parties in formulating settlement alternatives. Mediation facilitates and shortens the search for a settlement range which both sides can accept. And since the cost of mediation is (or at least should be) less than the cost of an expert witness deposition, it is generally worth the expense.

Mediation may be premature when the parties do not yet have enough information to evaluate the case or when necessary or appropriate third parties have not been joined in the suit or otherwise involved in the negotiations. Of course, the parties should make an effort to resolve the case on their own prior to entering into mediation; if unsuccessful, the parties should assess if additional discovery or information is needed to meaningfully negotiate during mediation, or whether it makes sense to have potentially dispositive motions heard prior to mediation.

Coverage questions which turn on the interpretation of policy language should, to the extent possible, be resolved before mediation. If the coverage issue is set for summary judgment, or trial in a declaratory judgment action, it is generally advisable to have that heard first. Sometimes, however, one or both parties will want to mediate before the coverage issue is heard by the court; an adverse judicial construction of the policy may be one of the risks the party hopes to avoid by settling. This unsettled issue may, thus, promote settlement.

§8.01.3 Preparing for Mediation

An advocate should prepare himself, his client, the mediator and his opponent for mediation.

As with any negotiation the advocate must be thoroughly familiar with the facts of the case, the theory of recovery or defense, and the controlling law. The lawyer must "know" the case in sufficient detail to be able to succinctly and persuasively summarize his client's position and the basis for that position in the opening session of the mediation. Consideration should be given to whether exhibits, video tapes, or visual aids would be helpful. What evidence, statutory provisions or cases will persuade the opposing side that your evaluation of the case is correct? Most importantly the advocate should have completed his or her analysis and evaluation of the case. What are its strengths and weaknesses? What is the likelihood of success on the liability or defense issues? If liability is established, what is the range of probable damages? What are the anticipated out-of-pocket costs for preparing the case for trial? How much in attorneys' fees will be expended up to and through trial? What is the proposed settlement range and structure?

An advocate should discuss his or her analysis of the case, outlined above, with the client and confirm the settlement range. Explain that this is the goal but that the client and attorney should maintain an open mind and the flexibility to modify the range if warranted by the facts and arguments brought forth at the mediation. Emphasize the necessity of a sincere commitment to settling the case on a fair and reasonable basis and explain that patience and open-mindedness will be needed to attain that goal. Detail the mediator's role, the process and the important role the client will play. Let the client know that the mediator may ask him questions in the joint or separate caucuses but that he will not be cross-examined; explain clearly what will and will not be expected of the client. Finally, be certain to nail down any authority-to-settle issues.

Mediators should, and most mediators will, request a confidential pre-submission position paper from the parties. This enables the mediator to familiarize himself with the facts and to anticipate issues and problem areas which may arise. The lawyer should candidly advise the mediator of the strengths and weaknesses in the case, indicate who will be present, confirm that those present will have authority to settle, outline the negotiations to date and provide copies of any key documents. If there are special facts which may affect the possibility of settlement, such as the absence of insurance, extreme enmity between the parties, or the necessity of court approval of the settlement, bring these to the mediator's attention.

It is critically important to remember that an advocate needs to persuade the decision maker on the other side, not the mediator. Presumably some attempt, albeit unsuccessful, has been made to convince the other side to settle prior to mediation. If, however, no settlement demands or offers have been made, try at least one round before mediation. It is helpful to know just how far apart the parties are, or indeed if the case can be settled without mediation. Further, some defendants need to know the outer limits of the claim in order to determine the representatives with appropriate decision-making authority.

It can be extremely helpful for the parties to exchange settlement brochures prior to mediation. These are commonly used by plaintiffs to explain their theory of liability, itemize their damages and marshal critical evidence. This tool can be very effective. The value of settlement brochures are often overlooked by defendants. Defendants too should consider preparing a written presentation which combines supportive documents, deposition excerpts, expert witness reports and reports of jury verdicts in similar cases. All settlement brochures should be provided in advance of mediation.

§8.01.4 The Mediation Process

Although there are no hard and fast rules, most mediators mediating disputes in litigation utilize the joint session/caucus method. Under this approach, the parties will begin with a joint session. Each side will make a brief presentation of their view of the issues and evidence in the case. After clarifying questions are asked and answered, the parties split up into separate rooms for private meetings (caucuses) with the mediator. The mediator will then engage in shuttle diplomacy, carrying offers and information from one room to another. Occasionally, the mediator will bring the parties back together for another joint session or will hold a separate caucus with just the attorneys. When a settlement is reached, the parties, with the assistance of the mediator, draft a memorandum of agreement. The memorandum sets out the terms of the agreement and identifies the documents which will be signed to complete the settlement.

The opening session provides an opportunity for the lawyer to communicate directly to the other party without having it filtered by opposing counsel. The advocate should be firm but fair and should emphasize that their side is there in good faith and is willing to hear what the other side has to say. It is important for the lawyer to succinctly explain his or her client's position and the basis for that position. If the other party has suffered a loss which is the basis of the lawsuit, the lawyer should express sympathy for the other parties' situation, while respectfully explaining why they do not feel responsible (or fully responsible) for the injury. In appropriate cases, have the clients briefly express their view of the dispute, their hope that it can be resolved and, when appropriate, their sympathy or sorrow.

An advocate should never personally attack or insult the other side or back them into a corner whereby settlement will require a loss of face. In the opening session, a party should not discuss settlement ranges or the amount they want or will pay, and certainly should not discuss "bottom lines." If emotional or volatile issues are involved, be prepared for an outburst by the other side and exercise restraint and patience in the face of those statements.

In the private caucuses focus on analyzing the dispute, evaluating the respective claims of the parties and generating settlement proposals. The mediator will want to understand each parties' basis for their evaluation, and the strengths and weaknesses of each side's claim. It is important for each side to be objective; unless one and generally both sides are willing to reassess their position in light of the other side's information and arguments, the perception gap will not be narrowed. Similarly, if one side wants to alter the other side's view of "reality" they must be willing to share information and arguments with the other side. This creates a dilemma for some parties: should they disclose their "smoking gun" evidence or "dynamite" strategy with the hope that it induces a settlement, or save it for trial. In most instances the "smoking gun" or "dynamite" would be uncovered during discovery anyway; nevertheless, that is a judgment call that only the advocate can make and which the mediator must respect.

Inevitably, there will be one or more false impasses during the day. The mediator's job is to keep the parties working and find a way to "wire around" the problem. Often the perceived impasse is nothing more than a reflection of the differences in the parties'

negotiating styles: some parties need more time than others. Adding new elements to the proposal, switching to different issues, or revisiting the needs of the parties and the basis of the evaluations are approaches which often break through impasses. Most impasses will disappear in the face of patience, persistence, and creativity.

Is there a duty to mediate or negotiate in "good faith" or put differently, can a party be penalized for "bad faith" negotiations? Certainly, one of the common complaints heard by mediators is that "the other party is not negotiating in good faith."

The ADR statute does not expressly impose a good faith requirement. Nevertheless, at least one court of appeals has held that a trial court did not abuse its discretion in taxing costs against a party who had failed to mediate in good faith. *Texas DOT v. Pirtle*, 977 S.W.2d 657 (Tex. App.—Fort Worth 1998, writ ref'd). In that case a government agency attended the mediation but refused to participate, reasoning that it had a duty to the public not to settle disputed liability cases. The court held that even though the agency prevailed at trial, the trial court had the discretion to tax court costs against the agency because the agency had failed to object to the mediation (*see* TEX. CIV. PRAC. & REM. CODE §154.022), thereby causing the opposing party to incur the expense of mediating a case the agency had no intention of settling. There is contrary authority.

In *Decker v. Lindsay*, 824 S.W.2d 247 (Tex. App.—Houston [1st Dist.] 1992, no writ) the trial court ordered the parties to mediate the case over the objection of the plaintiff. Additionally, the court's order required the parties to "proceed in a good faith effort to try to resolve this case . . ." *Id.* at 248. On appeal, the court held that the trial court had not abused its discretion in ordering the parties to come together in mediation but had abused its discretion in ordering the parties to participate in good faith with the intention of settling. The court reasoned that the parties cannot be compelled to negotiate or settle a dispute unless they have voluntarily agreed to do so. *Accord, Hansen v. Sullivan*, 886 S.W.2d 467 (Tex. App.—Houston [1st Dist.] 1994, no writ); *see also, Gleason v. Lawson*, 850 S.W.2d 714 (Tex. App.—Corpus Christi 1993, no writ) (in a case in which the parties were not ordered to mediation, the trial court abused its discretion in assessing costs against a party for failing to voluntarily enter into good faith settlement negotiations).

The decision in *Texas Parks and Wildlife Dept. v. Davis*, 988 S.W.2d 370 (Tex. App. – Austin 1999, no writ) is particularly instructive. In *Davis*, the trial court rendered judgment for the plaintiff on a jury verdict and at the same time required the defendant to reimburse the plaintiff for costs and fees incurred in mediation on the grounds that the defendant had failed to negotiate in good faith during the mediation. The court of appeals held that the trial court was authorized to tax the mediation fee as costs to the losing party (*see* TEX. CIV. PRAC. & REM. CODE §154.054(b)) but abused its discretion in ordering the defendant to pay the plaintiff's attorney's fees incurred in mediation. The court distinguished *Pirtle, supra*, noting that the defendant in this case (unlike in *Pirtle*) did object to mediation but nevertheless attended and made an offer, *i.e.* participated. Relying on *Decker, supra*, the court held that while parties may properly be compelled to participate in mediation, they cannot be compelled to negotiate in good faith or settle their dispute. The court observed that:

> Furthermore, section 154.073 requires that communications and records made in an ADR procedure remain confidential; consequently, the manner in which the participants negotiate should not be disclosed to the trial court. See TEX. CIV. PRAC. & REM. CODE §154.073 (West 1977).

It is submitted that the *Davis* opinion exposes the flaw behind any attempt to impose a good faith mediation requirement. Putting aside the issue of what constitutes "good faith" negotiation, the question of whether a party who attended the mediation negotiated in good faith is the type of inquiry that cannot be explored without violating the principle of confidentiality. In other words, a party contending that the opposition abused the mediation process by failing to negotiate in good faith will in most cases be forced to abuse the mediation process by disclosing information which everyone understood to be confidential. *See, In re Acceptance Ins. Co.*, 33 S.W.3d 443 (Tex. App.—Fort Worth 2000, original proceeding). It is, of course, aggravating, disappointing and expensive to participate in a mediation in which one party refuses to compromise. Even so, alternative dispute resolution has never been about forcing your adversary to agree with you or even to compromise their position. For this reason, every attempt should be made to determine if both parties are sufficiently motivated to try to settle before agreeing to a mediation. The Texas Alternative Dispute Resolution Act provides an opportunity for a party to object to mediation when they believe the opposing party is not prepared to negotiate in good faith. *See* Tex. Civ. Prac. & Rem. Code §154.022 (West 1977).

Even if "bad faith" negotiations are not sanctionable by the court, they may under some conditions considered to be unethical. Disciplinary Rule 3.02 provides that "a lawyer shall not take a position that unreasonably increases the costs or other burdens of the case or that unreasonably delays resolution of the matter." Arguably, agreeing to mediate with no intention of settling the case falls within the provisions of this rule.

§8.01.4.1 Avoiding Ethical Traps in Negotiation

A lawyer who negotiates for a client or who advises a client in the course of negotiations has ethical obligations to the client and to the opposing party. These obligations arise from the attorney-client relationship and the lawyer's status as a member of the bar and an officer of the court. Attorneys and their clients may have additional duties which arise from participation in a mediation.

A. Obligations to the Client.

The Preamble to the Texas Rules of Professional Conduct provides a nice overview of the various functions of a lawyer, all of which are called into play in a mediation:

> As a representative of clients, a lawyer performs various functions. As advisor, a lawyer provides a client with an informed understanding of the client's legal rights and obligations and explains their practical implications. As advocate, a lawyer zealously asserts the client's position under the rules of the adversary system. As negotiator, a lawyer seeks a result advantageous to the client but consistent with requirements of honest dealing with others.

Preamble: A Lawyer's Responsibilities, TEX. DISCIPLINARY R. PROF. CONDUCT (1989). (The Rules of Professional Conduct can be accessed through the Texas Center for Legal Ethics and Professionalism website: www.txethics.org.) This discussion will focus on the primary guidelines that pertain to the negotiation process.

At the heart of the attorney-client relationship is communication. During the course of a negotiation, a lawyer should explain to the client what is going on, why it is going on, and what it means so that the client can make informed decisions. *See* Disciplinary Rule 1.03. The comments to Disciplinary Rule 1.03 counsel that "a lawyer negotiating on behalf of a client should provide the client with facts relevant to the matter, inform the client of communications from another party and take other reasonable steps to permit the client to make a decision regarding a serious offer from another party." TEX. DISCIPLINARY R. PROF. CONDUCT 1.03 comment 1 (1989). This includes promptly communicating offers of settlement from the opposing side unless from prior discussions with the client it is clear that the proposal would be unacceptable. *Id*. Full communication also includes explaining the terms of a settlement agreement presented to a client for approval.

The duty of a lawyer to avoid disclosing confidential information of a client without authorization is well established. *See* Disciplinary Rule 1.05. A lawyer is considered to have implied-in-fact authority to make disclosures when appropriate to carrying out the representation of the client, absent express instructions to the contrary. Disciplinary Rule 1.05, comment 6. Thus, for example, in negotiations a lawyer unless instructed otherwise, may disclose confidential information that facilitates a resolution satisfactory to the client. *Id*.

A lawyer has a responsibility to "tell it like it is" to the client by exercising independent judgment and by giving candid advice. Disciplinary Rule 2.10. This sometimes requires the lawyer to discuss unpleasant facts and alternatives. Disciplinary Rule 2.10, comment 1. Lawyers are admonished not to be deterred "by the prospect that the advice will be unpalatable to the client." *Id*. When purely technical legal advice is inadequate, the lawyer should not hesitate to refer to moral, ethical and practical considerations which may affect the outcome. *Id.* The mediator, while not in a position to give legal advice as such, can assist the lawyer in delivering "bad news" by illuminating the negative aspects of a strategy, position or outcome.

B. Obligations to Non-Clients

In the course of negotiating, parties make competing assertions about the facts, about the law, and about their intentions. In many cases the assertions of the parties cannot be reconciled and it is clear that at least one if not both assertions are incorrect. This does not mean that a party or it's lawyer has failed to act ethically. Absolute candor in negotiation is not required. Negotiation is part persuasion, part concession. To what extent can deception be employed to promote persuasion and to mask a willingness to make concessions?

It is appropriate to start with the proposition that:

> In the course of representing a client, a lawyer shall not knowingly:
>
> (a) make a false statement of material fact or law to a third person; or
>
> (b) fail to disclose a material fact to a third person when disclosure is necessary to avoid making the lawyer a party to a criminal act or knowingly assisting a fraudulent act perpetrated by a client.

Disciplinary Rule 4.01. Note that Disciplinary Rule 3.03 likewise prohibits knowingly false statements to a tribunal. The definition of tribunal includes mediators. *See* Rules of Professional Conduct, Terminology.

First, inaccurate but innocent misrepresentations of fact or law do not violate this provision, which prohibits "knowing" misconduct. A lawyer who believes his or her client's view of the facts is justified in advancing that view. Secondly, prohibited misrepresentations or non-disclosures must involve "material facts." Thus, the opinions of a lawyer (and the client) expressed during a negotiation are normally not considered to be unethical even if the opinions are unfounded or proven, ultimately, to have been incorrect. *See* Disciplinary Rule 4.01, comment 1. Examples of such opinions would be those pertaining to value, or to the credibility of a witness, the future action of a court, the appropriate application of a statute to a unique set of facts, or the outcome of a trial. Similarly, a party's litigation or settlement goals are not considered to be material facts: "under generally accepted conventions in negotiation, a party's supposed intentions as to an acceptable settlement of a claim may be viewed merely as negotiating positions rather than accurate representations of material fact." *Id.* Thus, untrue assertions that a particular number is the best offer, bottom line, non-negotiable, all that has been authorized or the like are considered acceptable negotiation tactics available to both sides.

The lawyer's duty to disclose is even more circumscribed. The rule essentially mandates disclosure by a lawyer only when failure to do so would make the lawyer a party to a crime or a knowing participant in a fraudulent act. Comment 3 to Disciplinary Rule 4.01 indicates that a lawyer has a duty to disclose material facts only when required by law or applicable rules of practice or procedure. Thus, a lawyer has a duty to truthfully disclose facts pursuant to formal discovery requests proffered by the other side. Note that the Rule does not require disclosure of relevant law to the other side, presumably because each side has equal access to the law and the state of the law is frequently a matter of opinion. However, Disciplinary Rule 3.03 seems to require the lawyer to disclose to the mediator known controlling authority directly adverse to the position of his or her client if such authority has not been disclosed by the other side. *See* TEX. DISCIPLINARY R. PROF. CONDUCT 3.03 (a)(4) (1989). Although the mediator would be bound to treat that information as confidential, it would provide a basis for private discussion with the disclosing party.

When the opposing party is unrepresented by counsel, care must be taken to make sure that the unrepresented party understands the lawyer's role in the matter. *See* TEX. DISCIPLINARY R. PROF. CONDUCT 4.03 (1989). Thus a lawyer should not lead the unrepresented party to believe that the lawyer is disinterested or neutral in the matter.

The rules discussed above obviously do not answer all of ethical questions that can arise in the course of negotiations—and the answers they do provide may not set the bar high enough to meet the standards of all lawyers. A lawyer's reputation is his or her most valuable asset. If the community of lawyers believes a tactic to be unethical, the fact that the conduct is not expressly prohibited by the disciplinary rules or indeed is expressly permitted will be of little moment. While lawyers should strive to passionately advance their client's interests, they are not required to compromise their personal integrity or reputation in do so.

§8.01.5 Arbitration

Arbitration has been defined as:

> A contractual proceeding by which the parties to a controversy or dispute, in order to obtain a speedy and inexpensive final disposition of the matter involved voluntarily select arbitrators or judges of their own choice, and by consent submit the controversy to such tribunal for determination in substitution for the tribunals provided by the ordinary processes of law.

Jack B. Anglin Co. v. Tipps, 842 S.W.2d 266 (Tex. 1992). The assumed facts on which the public policy favoring arbitration is based, e.g. "speedy," "inexpensive," "voluntary" selection of arbitrators, "consent to submit" the dispute to arbitration, etc., may be true of some commercial transactions, particularly those involving large businesses, *id.*, but it would appear that very few, if any, of these facts are either true or advantageous in consumer and small business disputes that are submitted to arbitration.

A. A "speedy" remedy

The first assumed fact about arbitration that does not ring true in consumer cases is its relative speed. The assumption *assumes* that the consumer (who stands to lose most in arbitration) pushes the other side into arbitration rather than waiting for the party who wants the matter arbitrated to take the first step. If the party who insists on arbitration fails to cooperate, the pace of arbitration can exceed that of a normal jury trial. *In re Bruce Terminix Co.*, 988 S.W.2d 702 (Tex. 1998), illustrates the point. In this case, a homeowner filed suit against Terminix for failing to rid a house of termites as promised and represented. A hearing was held on Terminix's motion to compel arbitration on September 26, 1994, which motion was granted. Almost a year and one-half later, Terminix still had done nothing to arrange the arbitration on which it insisted and so the homeowner sent Terminix a letter in March, 1996 asking for its assistance in getting the arbitration set up. Some additional correspondence was exchanged. Finally, the homeowner sent Terminix a completed form from AAA that required only its signature. The form was signed on July 5, 1996; however, it was never submitted to AAA. Believing that Terminix's unexplained delay in moving the case to arbitration constituted a waiver of its contractual right, the homeowner moved to vacate the trial court's earlier order. The trial court granted the motion. Terminix appealed, by way of mandamus, asking that the trial court's order compelling arbitration be reinstated. The Supreme Court reversed the court of appeals that had ruled in support of the trial court and held that even though Terminix had used the judicial process (a set of interrogatories and request for production of documents) and had done nothing to implement the arbitration process, it still had not waived its right to arbitration.

B. An "inexpensive" remedy

Except for any cost savings that may be achieved through limitations on discovery (which, as explained above is a double-edged sword for consumers and small businesses) arbitration generally is more expensive than the courthouse. However, recent introduction by the American Arbitration Association of a new body of procedures specific to home construction cases may reduce the burden on homeowner consumers. *See* HOME CONSTRUCTION ARBITRATION RULES AND MEDIATION PROCEDURES (AAA 2007), published on the AAA website at www.adr.org/sp.asp?id=32399.

Consider the case of a homebuyer who discovers that the slab is cracked because of poor workmanship and elects to pursue the rescission remedy provided in DTPA §17.50(b)(3). According to current fee schedules published by the American Arbitration Association, the following fees are imposed on the homeowner in cases involving home construction:

Amount of Claim	Filing Fee	Case Service Fee	Arbitrator Compensation
Level 1: $0 to $10,000	$125	-	-
Level 2: $10,000 to $75,000	$150	$100	$500
Level 3: $75,000 to $300,000	$525	$100	$900
Level 4: Above $300,000	$950	$150	$1,000*
Non-monetary claims	$550	$100	$1,000*
* One-day hearing only; more if additional days			

Of course, the parties must have agreed to use the new Home Construction Arbitration Rules in their arbitration agreement. Otherwise, arbitration fees under the more commonly used AAA Construction Industry Arbitration Rules and Mediation Procedures have increased effective September 1, 2007. (Available on AAA website at www.adr.org/sp.asp?id=22004.) Filing fees range from a minimum of $750 for claims up to $10,000 to $8,000 for claims from $1,000,000 to $5,000,000. In addition, for each hearing before a single arbitrator, each party must pay a "case service fee" ranging from $200 to more than $3,250, depending on the amount of the claim. *Id.* There also may be a fee for the rental of a hearing room. In traditional construction disputes, the fees paid to AAA do not include payment for the arbitrator's fees. The arbitrator or arbitrators are paid by the parties for their services similar to the way in which mediators are paid. A typical fee is at least $1,500 per day per party per arbitrator.

The fees set forth above are necessary just to get the matter heard. The fees of experts retained to provide evidence in the case still would have to be paid.

The filing fee that the plaintiff must pay when a lawsuit is filed, together with the fee for service of citation and a jury, rarely exceeds $350. This assures the plaintiff of a trial, regardless of length, presided over by a judge and heard by a jury. In arbitration under the traditional construction industry rules, the judge and jury is the arbitrator and the combined fees for a person seeking to rescind the sale of a $100,000 house would be $4,050 for a one day arbitration and if the arbitration extends to two days of hearing, the fee would be $5,500.

A multi-member arbitration panel can make arbitration prohibitively expensive. See *Olshan Foundation Repair v. Ayala*, 180 S.W.3d 212 (Tex. App.—San Antonio 2005, pet. den'd.) (holding that the $33,000 per party cost for an AAA arbitration to be unconscionable.)

Lastly, many arbitration agreements currently require that the parties mediate the dispute as a "condition precedent" to arbitration. Thus, in order to have a complete picture of the comparative costs, an additional $1,000 should be added for the cost of a one day mediation, bringing the total "fees" for a consumer in arbitration to $5,050 for a one day arbitration and $6,500 for a two day arbitration, or, *twenty times* the cost of a jury trial in district court. It is true that many courts now require mediation as a condition to keeping one's place on a docket, however, most counties schedule a "settlement week" during which parties can submit their cases for mediation free of charge.

C. Arbitrations are secret

The courthouse files provide a wealth of information for many litigants, particularly a consumer whose investigative resources may otherwise be limited. In these files, a person can locate and review prior lawsuits involving the same defendant and the verdicts in those cases and can obtain the names of other possible victims of the defendant and their lawyers. The jury reports published in many counties from these files provide invaluable assistance to attorneys seeking to determine what a case is "worth" so that the client can be advised about the economics of proceeding with the case and so that settlement offers can be assessed realistically. The rules of most organizations who provide arbitration services prohibit the release of any information about the arbitration proceedings that it conducts. There is an important public policy that is served by public access to information about litigation. With this information, the public can determine whether the judicial system is functioning as it should to resolve disputes fairly. Without this information, only the participants know how the system is performing and their views are likely to be influenced by the outcome.

D. Selection of arbitrators

Arbitrators typically are selected because of their familiarity with the business or profession involved in the arbitration. Thus, when a construction dispute is filed, the arbitration panel normally consists of builders, engineers and/ or the lawyers who represent them. As they currently are constituted, there are few arbitration panel members who would be considered a consumer's "peers." Additionally, other than the fees charged, much of the financial support for organizations like the American Arbitration Association is provided by business, professional and industry members. Obviously, if the arbitration proceedings result in awards that are not satisfactory to the members, it is logical to assume that financial support may decrease. There has been a considerable amount of public concern about the "appearance of impropriety" that results from large campaign contributions to judges by attorneys with cases before them. These same concerns arise when arbitration organizations who create the panels are supported, in part, by businesses or professions whose disputes with consumers are judged by these same organizations. When the fact that, except in very limited circumstances, the decisions of arbitrators may not be appealed, even when they are contrary to the evidence or the law, *see* §8.10.7 *infra,* there is no effective means for a consumer or small business to be assured of a fair hearing.

E. "Voluntary" arbitration

No statute or law commands arbitration; instead, in theory, arbitration is enforceable only if the parties "agree" to arbitrate. *Belmont Constructors v. Lyondell Petrochemical Co.,* 896 S.W.2d 352 (Tex. App.—Houston [1st Dist.] 1995, no writ); *Porter & Clements, L.L.P. v. Stone,* 935 S.W.2d 217 (Tex. App.—Houston [1st Dist.] 1996, no writ). In consumer transactions, however, the presumed willingness of a consumer to arbitrate may be illusory at best. *See e.g. Prima Paint Corp. v. Flood & Conklin Mfg. Co.,* 388 U.S. 395, 414, 87 S. Ct. 1801, 1811 (1967) (Black, Douglas, and Stewart, J., dissenting) *quoting* Senator Walsh in the debate on the Federal Arbitration Act: "such contracts 'are really not voluntarily [sic] things at all' because 'there is nothing for the man to do except to sign it; and then he surrenders his right to have his case tried by the court.'" Even if a party executes a contract containing an arbitration agreement under protest or, like the plaintiff in *In re RLS Legal Solutions, LLC,* 221 S.W.3d 629, 631 (Tex. 2007), as a condition to receiving her bi-weekly paycheck, expressly announcing she was signing the agreement "under duress," the arbitration agreement will be enforced to require her to arbitrate her defense of duress. *Id.* at 631.

The legislature has acted recently to provide homeowners some semblance of relief from boilerplate arbitration provisions buried in a builder's contract covered by the provisions of the Residential Construction Commission Act ("RCCA"). For builder's contracts signed on or after September 1, 2007, a provision for binding arbitration will not be enforceable unless it is "conspicuously printed" or typed or printed in at least 10-point bold type. RCCA §420.003 (2007). No similar provision is contained in the DTPA.

Historically, a waiver of a constitutional or even contractual right has not been enforceable when the waiver is contained in an adhesion contract. *Dillee v. Sisters of Charity of the Incarnate Word Health Care Sys.,* 912 S.W.2d 307, 309 (Tex. App—Houston [14th Dist.] 1995, no writ) (citing the Black's Law Dictionary definition of an adhesion contract: "a standardized contract form for consumer goods and services that are offered on a 'take it or leave it' basis without affording the consumer a realistic opportunity to bargain and under such conditions that a consumer cannot obtain the desired product or services except by acquiescing."). The Supreme Court has rejected this doctrine when the case involves arbitration. *In re Oakwood Mobile Homes, Inc.* 987 S.W.2d 571 (Tex. 1999), involved a consumer's attempt to sue a mobile home dealer for defects in the home. The Supreme Court appeared to accept as true (for purposes of the opinion) that the contract that contained the arbitration clause was forced on the consumer, i.e. "Oakwood represented that the sale would not go through if they did not sign the Agreement." There were other problems encountered by the consumer in that the mobile home dealer wholly failed to respond to the consumer's letters requesting arbitration. When the consumer gave up and filed suit, the mobile home dealer moved to stay the litigation and requested an order compelling arbitration. The Supreme Court reversed the trial court and the court of appeals and held that the arbitration provision, even under these facts, was enforceable. *In re Oakwood Mobile Homes, Inc.* 987 S.W.2d 571, 574 (Tex. 1999).

F. The decisions of the arbitrators

There is another critical distinction between a case handled through arbitration and one tried in court that should be considered in consumer cases. Judges and juries are bound to follow the law, including rules of evidence. If a mistake is made in either, the complaining party may appeal and have the error corrected. With arbitration, the rule is very different. Unless an arbitration agreement provides otherwise, the decisions of arbitrators can be against both the law and the evidence and still be upheld. As the court said in *Powell v. Gulf Coast Carriers, Inc.*, 872 S.W.2d 22, 24 (Tex. App. — Houston [14th Dist.] 1994, no writ), "a *mere* mistake of fact or law alone is insufficient to set aside an arbitration award." (Emphasis added). Based on this rule, the court refused to consider appellant's argument that the arbitrator's decision was "against the overwhelming weight of the evidence." *See also Johnson v. American Can Co.*, 361 S.W.2d 451, 453 (Tex. Civ. App. — Houston [1st Dist.] 1962, writ ref'd n.r.e.); *J.J. Gregory Gourmet Serv., Inc. v. Antone's Import Co.*, 927 S.W.2d 31, 35 (Tex. App. — Houston [1st Dist.] 1995, no writ).

Arbitration is an alternative method of dispute resolution that may work well when the parties involved make an arms' length agreement to arbitrate. This method can serve important interests of the parties, including a frequent business necessity to keep some matters confidential. There is cause for serious concern, however, when this method of dispute resolution is used in consumer and small business transactions.

§8.01.6 Applicable Law

Increasingly, consumer contracts contain arbitration clauses. Some even contain "med/arb" clauses, *i.e.*, contracts in which the parties agree to submit their controversy first to mediation and then, if mediation is not successful, to binding arbitration. The two general statutes that deal with arbitration are the Federal Arbitration Act, 9 U.S.C. §§1 - 16, sometimes referred to as the "FAA," and the Texas General Arbitration Act, TEX. CIV. PRAC. & REM. CODE §§171.001 -.023, sometimes referred to as the "TGA." Both Texas law and federal law "strongly" favor arbitration of disputes. *Prudential Sec., Inc. v. Marshall*, 909 S.W.2d 896 (Tex. 1995); *see Preston v. Ferrer*, ___ U.S. ___, 128 S.Ct. 978, 169 L.Ed.2d 917 (2008) ("FAA establishes a national policy favoring arbitration").

If the transaction in question is one that is "a transaction involving [interstate] commerce," then the Federal Arbitration Act will apply coextensively with the TGA. *Jack B. Anglin Co. v. Tipps*, 842 S.W.2d 266 (Tex. 1992); *see In re FirstMerit Bank, N.A.*, 52 S.W.3d 749 (Tex. 2001) ("interstate commerce" includes contracts "relating to" interstate commerce). In such cases, the FAA will preempt the TGA (and any other contrary state law) to the extent of any conflict. *In re Nexion Health at Humble, Inc.*, 173 S.W.3d 67 (Tex. 2008) (per curiam). The FAA has been broadly construed to further the federal policy favoring arbitration. Thus, for example, it has been held that the FAA overrides the consumer's statutory right to bring suit under the Magnuson-Moss Warranty Act. *In Re American Homestar of Lancaster, Inc.*, 50 S.W.3d 480 (Tex. 2001) (arbitration compelled absent clear legislative intent to override the FAA policy favoring enforcement of arbitration agreements). While the enforceability of arbitration agreements under both the FAA and TGA are essentially the same, a few substantive distinctions exist. More importantly, the invocation of the FAA allows the proponent of arbitration to rely on the extensive body of federal case law interpreting the FAA.

One major distinction is that, by its own terms, the TGA does not apply to any agreement for the acquisition by one or more individuals of property, services, money, or credit in which the total consideration to be furnished by the individual is not more than $50,000 unless (1) the parties to the agreement agree in writing to arbitrate; and (2) the agreement is signed by each party and the party's attorney. TEX. CIV. PRAC. & REM. CODE §171.002. While this provision would have the effect of shielding many consumer transactions from the coverage of the Texas statute because few consumer transactions include an attorney for the consumer, no similar consumer-friendly provision exists in the FAA. Because many, if not most, consumer transactions involve interstate commerce, an invocation of the FAA will render this provision inapplicable.

A second major distinction concerns the availability of interlocutory appellate review. Under the TGA, the trial court's decision denying a motion to compel arbitration under the TGA or granting a motion to stay arbitration on the basis that no enforceable agreement to arbitrate exists is reviewable by interlocutory appeal. TEX. CIV. PRAC. & REM. CODE §171.098. Under the FAA, however, there is a statutory prohibition against interlocutory appeals. *In re Palacios*, 221 S.W.3d 564, 565 (Tex. 2006) (applying FAA, 9 U.S.C. §16(b)(2)). As such, a trial court's refusal to compel arbitration under the FAA is only reviewable by mandamus. *See In re Weekley*, 180 S.W.3d 127, 130 (Tex. 2005). This distinction becomes important if appellate review is sought. The failure to properly invoke the FAA in the trial court will deprive the court of appeals of mandamus jurisdiction. *See In re Olshan Found. Repair Co. of Dallas, L.L.C.*, 192 S.W.3d 922 (Tex. App. — Waco 2006, orig. proceeding) (dismissing mandamus petition where FAA invoked first on appeal); *and compare In re Nexion*, 173 S.W.3d at 68-69 (mandamus available when FAA invoked first in trial court motion to reconsider). A determination on appeal that the FAA governs could result in the dismissal of an interlocutory appeal. Because of the risk of choosing incorrectly, parties often pursue both remedies at the same time.

§8.01.7 Defenses to Arbitration Agreement

Regardless of whether the FAA or the TGA governs, the party seeking an order compelling an opposing party to submit to contractually mandated arbitration has the burden of proof to show that an enforceable arbitration agreement exists and that the dispute between the parties fits within the scope of the agreement. *In re Oakwood Mobile Homes, Inc.*, 987 S.W.2d 571 (Tex. 1999). Both Texas and federal courts use state-law contract principles to determine the enforceability of an arbitration agreement. *J. M. Davidson, Inc. v. Webster*, 128 S.W.3d 223, 228 (Tex. 2003); *see First Options of Chicago, Inc. v. Kaplan*, 514 U.S. 938, 944, 131 L. Ed. 2d 985, 115 S. Ct. 1920 (1995). Thus, traditional contract defenses under state law—such as fraud, unconscionability and waiver—may be used to deny the enforceability of an arbitration agreement. And state-law contract principles will be used to determine whether to enforce an arbitration agreement against a third party beneficiary of a contract containing an arbitration clause.

Because the arbitration agreement is usually contained within a contract which is the subject of the dispute between the parties, the question arises as to who gets to determine the enforceability of the contract—the arbitrator or the trial judge? The answer depends on whether the defense goes to the entire contract as a whole or just to the arbitration clause in particular. Under both federal and Texas law, arbitration agreements may be set aside if the signing of the arbitration agreement was induced by fraud or on some other common law or equitable grounds that would allow a party to revoke the contract. TEX. CIV. PRAC. & REM. CODE §171.001; 9 U.S.C. §2. However, the grounds for revocation must be directed specifically to the arbitration provision and not to the contract as a whole. *Prima Paint Corp. v. Flood & Conklin Mfg. Co.*, 388 U.S. 395, 87 S. Ct. 1801 (1967); *In re FirstMerit Bank, N.A.*, 52 S.W.3d 749 (Tex. 2001). Challenges to the contract as a whole, such as an assertion that the contract as a whole was procured by fraud, are for the arbitrator to decide; only challenges specific to the arbitration clause or agreement itself will be heard by the court. *Buckeye Check Cashing, Inc. v. Cardegna*, 546

U.S. 440, 449, 126 S. Ct. 1204, 163 L. Ed. 2d 1038 (2006); *Perry Homes v. Cull*, 258 S.W.3d 580, 587 (Tex. 2008). An assertion of waiver is a question of law for the court to decide. *Perry Homes*, 258 S.W.3d at 587.

The following sections discuss some of the more commonly attempted defenses to an arbitration agreement. The list is by no means exclusive.

§8.01.7.1 Unconscionability

Arbitration agreements can be set aside if they were "unconscionable" at the time the agreement was made. TEX. CIV. PRAC. & REM. CODE §171.002; *Olshan Foundation Repair v. Ayala*, 180 S.W.3d 212, 214 (Tex. App. — San Antonio 2005, pet. denied). "Unconscionability includes two aspects: (1) procedural unconscionability, which refers to the circumstances surrounding the adoption of the arbitration provision, and (2) substantive unconscionability, which refers to the fairness of the arbitration provision itself." *In re Halliburton Co.*, 80 S.W.3d 566, 571 (Tex. 2002). The test for substantive unconscionability is whether, "given the parties' general commercial background and the commercial needs of the particular trade or case, the clause involved is so one-sided that it is unconscionable under the circumstances existing when the parties made the contract." *In re Palm Harbor Homes, Inc.*, 195 S.W.3d 672, 678 (Tex. 2006), *quoting In re FirstMerit Bank, N.A.*, 52 S.W.3d 749 (Tex. 2001).

The Texas Supreme Court has repeatedly demonstrated that the burden of avoiding an arbitration agreement on the grounds of unconscionability will be a heavy one. The mere fact that the arbitration agreement is found in a contract of adhesion will not render it substantively unconscionable. *Palm Harbor Homes*, 195 S.W.3d at 678; *In re AdvancePCS Health L.P.*, 172 S.W.3d 603, 608 (Tex. 2005). Nor does the fact that the parties are of greatly disparate bargaining power render the agreement unconscionable. *Id.* The fact that the consumer did not read or understand the arbitration agreement or clause is likewise of no consequence. A party who has the opportunity to read an arbitration agreement and signs it is presumed to know its contents. *EZ Pawn Corp. v. Mancias*, 934 S.W.2d 87, 90 (Tex. 1996).

However, upon proper proof, excessively large arbitration costs that keep a party from vindicating their rights can be a defense to the enforcement of an arbitration clause. *See Green Tree Fin. Corporation-Alabama v. Randolph*, 531 U.S. 79, 89 121 S.Ct. 513, 148 L.Ed.2d 373 (2000); *In re FirstMerit Bank*, N.A., 52 S.W.3d 749 (Tex. 2001). Thus, in *Olshan Foundation Repair v. Ayala*, an arbitration agreement contained in a contract between homeowners and a foundation repair company was held to be unconscionable and, therefore, unenforceable, when the homeowner's share of the arbitration cost—invoiced in advance by the American Arbitration Association—was over $33,000, an amount equal to 28% of the homeowners' combined annual gross income. 180 S.W.2d at 216.

PRACTICE POINT:

In order to claim the excessiveness of arbitration fees as an unconscionability defense, gather and submit detailed evidence of the expected arbitration expenses, not only the fees from the agency (such as AAA or NASD) but also the fees that can reasonably be expected to be paid to the arbitrators themselves (usually based on their hourly rates for all work done preparing for, traveling to and conducting the arbitration), travel expenses, location rental fees, court reporters, video-conferencing equipment, etc. If these expenses are substantial, the proponent of arbitration may want to consider offering to pay or at least to advance those expenses in order to diffuse this defense.

§8.01.7.2 Waiver or Estoppel by Litigation

It has been said that parties who "'conduct full discovery, file motions going to the merits, and seek arbitration only on the eve of trial' waive any contractual right to arbitration." *In re Vesta Ins. Group, Inc.*, 192 S.W.3d 759, 764 (Tex. 2006), *as quoted in In re Citigroup Global Mkts., Inc.*, 258 S.W.3d 623, 625 (Tex. 2008). However, whether less purposeful conduct would constitute a waiver of a right to arbitration is often contested. In 2008, the Texas Supreme Court decided several cases where one party was asserting that the opposing party had waived its right to arbitration, or should be estopped from asserting it late, based on that party's conduct in litigating the controversy before asking for arbitration. In *Perry Homes v. Cull*, 258 S.W.3d 580, 587 (Tex. 2008), the court held that a party may waive a right to arbitrate a particular dispute only by "substantially invoking" the judicial process to the other party's "detriment or prejudice." *Perry Homes*, 258 S.W.3d at 589-90. The burden to show such waiver is high, and what litigation conduct will "substantially invoke" the judicial process will be decided on a case-by-case basis and depend on the context. *Id.* at 591-93. In *Perry Homes*, the majority of a sharply divided court found the *plaintiffs* had waived the right to request arbitration where they had initially opposed arbitration and then, on the eve of trial and after having completed substantial discovery, decided to reverse course and demand arbitration themselves. *Id.* at 597.

In one of two cases decided shortly after *Perry Homes*, the court refused to find a waiver of the right to compel arbitration even though the defendant failed to pursue its arbitration demand for eight months while discussing a trial setting and allowing limited discovery. *In re Fleetwood Homes of Tex., L.P.*, 257 S.W.3d 692, 694 (Tex. 2008). And, in *In re Citigroup Global Mkts., Inc.*, 258 S.W.3d 623 (Tex. 2008), the court refused to find waiver even though the defendant had removed the case to federal court and sought consolidated with other, similar cases through the Judicial Panel on Multi-District Litigation for the purposes of streamlined discovery proceedings. *Id.* at 626. Thus, in practice, the court has demonstrated that the standard for *implied* waiver by litigation has been set extremely high. In these latter cases, the court left for another day the questions of what statements in pleadings or other court filings might constitute *express* waiver and whether a claim of express waiver would be decided under the same standard. *Citigroup* at 626; *Fleetwood Homes*, 257 S.W.3d at 694. Certainly stipulations to expressly waive arbitration filed in court should be enforced without a showing of prejudice by the other side. What kind of statements will be deemed to constitute an express waiver—without a showing of detriment or prejudice as required in *Perry Homes*—remains to be seen.

§8.01.7.3 Plaintiff or Defendant Not a Party to the Agreement

If the plaintiff did not sign an arbitration agreement, the agreement usually cannot be enforced against him. As the Supreme Court has stated in construing the FAA, "It goes without saying that a contract cannot bind a nonparty." *EEOC v. Waffle House, Inc.*, 534 U.S. 279, 294 122 S. Ct. 754, 151 L.Ed. 2d 755 (U.S. 2002). However, non-parties to a contract can, under some circumstances, be bound by a contractual arbitration clause. *In re Firstmerit Bank, N.A.*, 52 S.W.3d 749 (Tex. 2001) (litigant's suit based on the contract); *In re Weekley Homes, L.P.*, 176 S.W.3d 740 (Tex. 2005) (non-party tort plaintiff who purposely benefited from agreement); *In re Vesta Ins. Group*, 192 S.W.3d 759, 761-62 (Tex. 2006). As observed by the Texas Supreme Court, "federal courts [interpreting the Federal Arbitration Act] have recognized six theories, arising out of common principles of contract and agency law, that may bind non-signatories to arbitration agreements: (1) incorporation by reference; (2) assumption; (3) agency; (4) alter ego; (5) equitable estoppel; and (6) third-party beneficiary." *In re Kellogg Brown & Root, Inc.*, 166 S.W.3d 732, 739 (Tex. 2005). The Texas Supreme Court has held "that a person who seeks by his claim 'to derive direct benefit from the contract containing the arbitration provision' may be equitably estopped from refusing arbitration." *Meyer v. WMCO-GP, LLC*, 211 S.W.3d 302, 305 (Tex. 2006). However, when the suit is not based on the contract and the plaintiff does not seek to derive a direct benefit from the contract, the contractual arbitration provision will not control. *In re Kellogg Brown & Root, Inc.*, 166 S.W.3d 732 (Tex. 2005) (sub-contractor claim on *quantum meruit*).

The Texas Supreme Court has also allowed non-signatory parties to invoke the benefits of an arbitration agreement in certain circumstances. In *In re Merrill Lynch Trust Co. FSB*, 235 S.W.3d 185, 191 (Tex. 2007), the plaintiff apparently tried to get around its arbitration agreement with Merrill Lynch by suing Merrill Lynch's employee instead of Merrill Lynch directly. The court held that the employee could enforce his employer's arbitration agreement against the customer where the employer would be vicariously liable to the customer for the conduct at issue. *Id.* at 189. However, the court did not allow two separate but related corporate entities—ML Trust and ML Life—to invoke the benefits of the arbitration agreement with Merrill Lynch, even though there were allegations of "substantially interdependent and concerted misconduct," absent a showing that the plaintiff's claims against these two defendants sought "a direct benefit" from the contract containing the arbitration clause or the corporations were operated as the alter egos of each other. *Id.* at 192-194. Thus, the mere fact that the plaintiff's claim against a non-signatory party arises out of the same transaction or event as a claim which the plaintiff has agreed to arbitrate with another party is insufficient, without more, to require the plaintiff to arbitrate with the non-signatory party. *Id.*; see *Moses H. Cone Memorial Hospital v. Mercury Construction Corp.*, 460 U.S. 1, 19-20, 103 S. Ct. 927, 74 L. Ed. 2d 765 (1983) (hospital could not be forced to arbitrate with architect because its arbitration agreement was with builder only).

In consumer transactions, the seller has no duty to disclose the fact that the contract contains an arbitration provision, absent a fiduciary duty. *City of Emerald v. Peel*, 920 S.W.2d 398 (Tex. App. — Houston [1st Dist.] 1996, no writ). Therefore, whether or not the consumer is sophisticated enough to read and understand all of the language of a contract, the mere fact that the contract was signed by the consumer may be sufficient proof that there is an agreement to arbitrate. *Id.* Further, the fact that one of the parties has more bargaining power than the other does not mean that the agreement to arbitrate is unenforceable. *EZ Pawn Corp. v. Mancias*, 934 S.W.2d 87 (Tex. 1996).

§8.01.7.4 Arbitration Procedure Under Texas Arbitration Act

The burden is on the party making the claim to initiate the arbitration proceedings. *In re Oakwood Mobile Homes, Inc.*, 987 S.W.2d 571 (Tex. 1999). This is true even if the party who has the claim was forced to accept an arbitration provision in an adhesion contract prepared by the party resisting the claim. *In re Oakwood Mobile Homes, Inc.*, 987 S.W.2d 571 (Tex. 1999). This rule also applies when the party resisting the claim also refuses to cooperate with the consumer in submitting the matter to arbitration. *In re Bruce Terminix Co.*, 988 S.W.2d 702 (Tex. 1998).

When the arbitration agreement provides that mediation of the dispute is a condition precedent to arbitration, unless mediation occurs, one court has held that there is no right to arbitration. *Weekley Homes, Inc. v. Jennings*, 936 S.W.2d 16 (Tex. App. — San Antonio 1996, writ denied).

The arbitrators who will hear the case are determined either by the method set forth in the arbitration agreement, if any, or by application to the court. TEX. CIV. PRAC. & REM. CODE §171.041; *Mewbourne Oil Co. v. Blackburn*, 793 S.W.2d 735 (Tex. App. — Amarillo 1990, orig. proceeding). The decisions of the arbitrators (if more than one) are made by majority vote. TEX. CIV. PRAC. & REM. CODE §171.042.

Notice of an arbitration hearing must be "served" not less than five days before the date of the hearing and may be given either personally or by registered or certified mail, return receipt requested. TEX. CIV. PRAC. & REM. CODE §171.044. At the hearing, unless otherwise provided by the agreement, each party is entitled to (1) "be heard," (2) present evidence material to the controversy; and (3) cross-examine any witness. TEX. CIV. PRAC. & REM. CODE §171.044. The rules of evidence do not apply to arbitration proceedings unless the arbitration agreement so provides. *J.J. Gregory Gourmet Servs. v. Antone's Import Co.*, 927 S.W.2d 31 (Tex. App. — Houston [1st Dist.] 1995, no writ).

Attorney's fees may be recovered in arbitration only if the agreement to arbitrate so provides or if fees are provided for by law in a civil action in the district court in a cause of action on which any part of the award is based. TEX. CIV. PRAC. & REM. CODE §171.048. And, the arbitrator's fees and expenses can be "taxed" as part of the award. TEX. CIV. PRAC. & REM. CODE §171.055.

When the arbitrator's decision is confirmed by the court, a judgment shall be issued in conformity with the decision and enforced by the trial court as with other judgments. TEX. CIV. PRAC. & REM. CODE §171.016; *Holk v. Biard*, 920 S.W.2d 803 (Tex. App. — Texarkana 1996, no writ).

§8.01.8 Appeal of Arbitrator's Decision

If a party makes an application not later than the twentieth day after an arbitration conducted under the Texas Arbitration Act, the arbitrators can modify or correct the award that has been made. TEX. CIV. PRAC. & REM. CODE §171.054; *Teleometrics, Int'l, Inc. v. Hall*, 922 S.W.2d 189 (Tex. App. — Houston [1st Dist.] 1995, writ denied.

There are limited grounds upon which a party can appeal the decision of an arbitrator. For example, under the Texas Arbitration Act, an arbitrator's decision can be appealed only on proof of one of the following:

(1) the award is procured by corruption, fraud or other undue means;

(2) there was evident partiality by an arbitrator appointed as a neutral or corruption in any of the arbitrators or misconduct or wilful misbehavior of any of the arbitrators prejudicing the rights of any party;

(3) the arbitrators exceeded their powers;

(4) the arbitrators refused to postpone the hearing upon sufficient cause being shown therefor or refused to hear evidence material to the controversy or otherwise so conducted the hearing, contrary to the provision of Section 171.005, as to prejudice substantially the rights of a party; or

(5) there was no arbitration agreement and the issue was not adversely determined in proceedings under Section 171.002, and the party did not participate in the arbitration hearing without raising the objection; but the fact that the relief was such that it could not or would not be granted by a court of law or equity is not ground for vacating or refusing to confirm the award.

TEX. CIV. PRAC. & REM. CODE §171.014. Significantly, insufficiency of the evidence is not a ground for appeal; and, the "evidence" on which the decision is based need not be admissible under the Texas Rules of Civil Evidence. *J. J. Gregory Gourment Servs. v. Antone's Import Co.*, 927 S.W.2d 31 (Tex. App. — Houston [1st Dist.] 1995, no writ). As noted in the previous section, it has been held that a "mere mistake of fact or law" is not grounds to set aside an arbitrator's award. *TUCCO, Inc. v. Burlington N. R. R. Co.*, 912 S.W.2d 311 (Tex. App. — Amarillo 1995, no writ). If one of the listed grounds for appeal is not asserted and proved, the Texas statute provides that "the court, on application of a party, *shall* confirm the award. TEX. CIV. PRAC. & REM. CODE §171.087.

[a] FORM: Motion to Compel Arbitration

[**NOTE**: A plea in abatement may also be used to compel arbitration. See §6.02.3 supra].

```
                              NO. _____

_____              §    IN THE DISTRICT COURT OF
                          §
                          §
vs.                       §    _____COUNTY, TEXAS
                          §
_____              §    _____ JUDICIAL DISTRICT
```

MOTION TO STAY AND TO COMPEL ARBITRATION

TO THE HONORABLE JUDGE OF THE DISTRICT COURT:

_____, defendant in the above entitled action, moves the court to enter its order staying this lawsuit and compelling _____, plaintiff, to submit this case to arbitration.

1.

The transaction on which this lawsuit is based included a contract between plaintiff and defendant that contained a provision under which the parties agreed to submit any disputes to arbitration. Specifically, the clause provided: [*insert arbitration provision*].

2.

A true and correct copy of the contract referenced in paragraph 1 is attached as Exhibit A.

3.

As shown by the affidavit of _____, defendant's [*describe capacity, e.g.* sales manager] the contract attached as Exhibit A was explained to plaintiff, after which plaintiff signed the contract. Further, the contract has been performed by defendant.

4.

Defendant has not invoked the remedies and procedures available in this judicial proceeding other than filing an answer to plaintiff's petition. For these reasons, an order staying this lawsuit and compelling arbitration would not be prejudicial to plaintiff.

WHEREFORE, defendant requests that an order be entered by this court staying any further proceedings in this lawsuit; compelling plaintiff to submit this dispute to arbitration; and providing such other relief to which defendant may be entitled.

Respectfully submitted,

[Signature of attorney]

[*Attach affidavit*]

[*Certificate of Service*]

[b] Order Compelling Arbitration

```
                            NO. _____
_____            §    IN THE DISTRICT COURT OF
                      §
vs.                   §    _____COUNTY, TEXAS
                      §
_____            §    _____ JUDICIAL DISTRICT
```

ORDER GRANTING STAY AND COMPELLING ARBITRATION

On this _____ day of _____, 20___, came on for hearing the motion of _____, defendant, for an order staying any further proceedings in this lawsuit and compelling _____, plaintiff, to submit the claim to arbitration.

The Court has reviewed the evidence and argument of counsel and is of the opinion that the motion is well taken and should be granted.

IT IS THEREFORE ORDERED as follows:

1. Any further proceedings in this case are hereby stayed.

2. Any and all claims raised by _____, plaintiff, in this lawsuit are to be submitted, if at all, to arbitration in accordance with the terms of the contract between the parties.

[**NOTE:** If the contract specifies the arbitration organization and any other procedures, those matters can be spelled out in the order as well].

SIGNED this _____ day of _____, 20____.

[Signature of presiding judge]

[Approval as to form]

§8.02 Offer of Settlement

The 2003 amendments to the Civil Practices and Remedies Code mandate that the Texas Supreme Court adopt rules implementing an offer of settlement procedure in Texas, which rules are to become effective no later than January 1, 2004. TEX. CIV. PRAC. & REM. CODE §42.005(a). Although offer of settlement practice will be governed by the Supreme Court rule, the statute specifies the basic framework. Working within this framework, however, the Supreme Court must provide by rule for various deadlines (making declaration, making, accepting, rejecting offers, etc.), TEX. CIV. PRAC. & REM. CODE §42.005(b)(1) - (3), as well as specific procedures for making, accepting and rejecting offers, in single and multiple party cases. TEX. CIV. PRAC. & REM. CODE §42.005(b)(4).

In broad terms, the offer of settlement rule, when it applies, will shift some of the expense of litigation from the party (plaintiff or defendant) who makes a proper offer to the party (plaintiff or defendant) who rejects an offer improperly. TEX. CIV. PRAC. & REM. CODE §42.004(a).

The Achilles' heel of any offer of settlement rule is that it assumes that a litigant is capable of answering, before trial, an unanswerable question: how much will a jury award? There is nothing in the statute (and will be nothing in the rule) that makes this question any easier to answer, but the consequences of guessing wrongly can be dire.

The offer of settlement rule will apply to all civil litigation in which monetary damages are sought. TEX. CIV. PRAC. & REM. CODE §42.001(1) (defining "claim" as "a request, including a counterclaim, cross-claim, or third-party claim, to recover monetary damages," and "claimant" as "a person making a claim"). The only exceptions to the application of the offer of settlement rule are: (1) a class action, (2) a shareholder's derivative action, (3) an action by or against a governmental unit, (4) an action brought under the Family Code, (5) an action to collect workers' compensation benefits under Subtitle A, Tile 5, Labor Code, or (6) an action filed in a justice of the peace court. TEX. CIV. PRAC. & REM. CODE §42.001(1). The Supreme Court has been given some flexibility to designate other actions to which the offer of settlement rule will not apply. TEX. CIV. PRAC. & REM. CODE §42.005(d).

The rule will not prohibit a person from making an offer of settlement in a form that does not comply with the rule; nor does it prohibit a person from making an offer in a case to which the rule does not apply. TEX. CIV. PRAC. & REM. CODE §42.002(d). If an offer is made under either of these circumstances, the rule simply has no application as to the consequences of making, accepting or rejecting the offer.

§8.02.1 Invoking the Rule

The offer of settlement rule does not apply automatically. In order for the rule to apply, a *defendant* must file a declaration that the settlement procedure allowed by the offer of settlement rule "is available in the action." TEX. CIV. PRAC. & REM. CODE §42.002(c). In other words, the application of the rule is solely within the control of the defendant because a plaintiff has no authority to invoke it. Additionally, in cases in which there is more than one defendant, the rule must be invoked by *each* defendant, individually. TEX. CIV. PRAC. & REM. CODE §42.002(c). Since one defendant's declaration does not inure to the benefit of any other defendant, the provisions of the offer of settlement rule apply only to offers of settlement made or received by the defendant who filed a declaration. TEX. CIV. PRAC. & REM. CODE §42.002(c).

[a] FORM: Declaration for application of offer of settlement rule

[**NOTE**: The specific format for and contents of the declaration may be specified in the Supreme Court's rule when it is adopted. The following form merely tracks the statutory language.]

```
                            NO. _____
_____              §        IN THE DISTRICT COURT OF
                        §
vs.                     §        _____ COUNTY, TEXAS
                        §
_____              §        _____ JUDICIAL DISTRICT
```

DECLARATION ON SETTLEMENT PROCEDURES

_____, [a] defendant in the above entitled and numbered cause, files this Declaration that the settlement procedures set forth in Tex. Civ. Prac. & Rem. Code §42.001 et seq. are available in this action.

Respectfully submitted,

[Signature of attorney]

[Certificate of service]

§8.02.2 Making Settlement Offer

Although the Supreme Court's rule may specify additional elements, in order for a settlement offer to be made properly under the offer of settlement rule, it must:

(1) be in writing;

(2) state that it is made under Chapter 42 of the Civil Practice and Remedies Code;

(3) state the terms by which the claims may be settled;

(4) state a deadline by which the settlement offer must be accepted; and

(5) be served on all parties to whom the settlement offer is made.

TEX. CIV. PRAC. & REM. CODE §42.003. Clearly, the statute contemplates that the offer be sufficiently "formal" so as to call the plaintiff's attention to the fact that there may be serious consequences if careful consideration is not given. There is no statutory requirement that the offer of settlement be filed with the court. And, although the statute does not specify a method of service or delivery, whatever method is used should provide the means by which proof of receipt can be made.

[a] FORM: Offer of settlement

[**NOTE:** The specific format for and contents of the written offer of settlement may be specified in the Supreme Court's rule when it is adopted. The following form merely tracks the statutory language.]

```
[Certified mail, return receipt requested]

(Date)

(Inside address)

Re: Cause No. _____; _____ v. _____.

Dear _____:

This is a settlement offer, which is made to your client pursu-
ant to the provisions of Chapter 42 of the Texas Civil Practice
and Remedies Code.

The [plaintiff/ defendant] will settle all claims that have been
or could be made in the above referenced lawsuit on the follow-
ing terms: [insert specific terms of settlement, e.g. The plain-
tiff will dismiss this lawsuit with prejudice in exchange for the
payment of $_____ [insert amount to be paid and any terms of
payment]. In addition, the [plaintiff/defendant] is willing to
execute and exchange a mutual, global release of all claims that
have been or could be made in this lawsuit by the parties to this
settlement.

This offer of settlement must be accepted on or before the close
of business on _____, 20___. If the offer is not accepted by
that date and time, it will expire automatically.

                                        [Signature of attorney]
```

§8.02.3 Awarding Litigation Costs

When a settlement offer is made in a form that complies with the offer of settlement rule, and the offer is rejected, if the judgment to be rendered in the litigation is "significantly less favorable" to the rejecting party than the offer, then the offering party shall recover litigation costs from the rejecting party. TEX. CIV. PRAC. & REM. CODE §42.004(a). The statute specifies the meaning of "significantly less favorable": "A judgment will be significantly less favorable to the rejecting party than is the settlement offer if (1) the rejecting party is the claimant and the award will be less than 80 percent of the rejected offer; or (2) the rejecting party is the defendant and the award will be more than 120 percent of the rejected offer." TEX. CIV. PRAC. & REM. CODE §42.004(b). To illustrate, assume that a defendant offers to settle a case for $100,000 and the claimant (usually but not always the plaintiff) rejects the offer. In order for the defendant to recover litigation costs, the judgment to be rendered must be less than $80,000. If, on the other hand, the claimant offers to settle a case for $100,000 and it is rejected, the judgment to be rendered must be more than $120,000 in order for the claimant to recover litigation costs.

The litigation costs that may be recovered are limited to those costs incurred by the offering party *after* the date the rejecting party rejects the settlement offer. TEX. CIV. PRAC. & REM. CODE §42.004(c).

If a party is entitled to recover fees and costs under another law, then that party may not recover litigation costs in addition to whatever recovery the other law allows. TEX. CIV. PRAC. & REM. CODE §42.004(e). Assume, for example, that a claimant sues a defendant for breach of contract for which court costs and attorney's fees are recoverable by statute. *See e.g.* TEX. CIV. PRAC. & REM. CODE §38.001. In this circumstance, the claimant would not be entitled to a duplicate recovery of those same fees and costs under the offer of settlement rule.

There also is a restriction on the amount that can be included in the "amount to be recovered" when matching that amount against the settlement offer in that if the recovery of fees and costs is allowed under another law, the court may not include any fees or costs incurred by the claimant or defendant *after* the date of the rejection of the settlement offer when calculating the amount of the judgment to be rendered. TEX. CIV. PRAC. & REM. CODE §42.004(f).

Lastly, when litigation costs are to be awarded to the defendant, the costs should be awarded as an offset to the claimant's recovery. TEX. CIV. PRAC. & REM. CODE §42.004(g).

§8.02.4 "Litigation Costs"

Not all money spent or debt incurred in a lawsuit are considered "litigation costs." The term is defined to mean only "money actually spent and obligations actually incurred that are directly related to the case in which a settlement offer is made," TEX. CIV. PRAC. & REM. CODE §42.001(5), and is further limited to include only:

(1) court costs;

(2) reasonable fees for not more than two testifying expert witnesses; and

(3) reasonable attorney's fees.

TEX. CIV. PRAC. & REM. CODE §42.001(5)(A)-(C). The statute does not specify whether interest can be charged and collected on these expenses by the party who is entitled to recover litigation costs. And, the question as to how much is "reasonable" is left to the fact-finder.

There are further limitations on the amount of allowable litigation costs that can be recovered. Specifically, recoverable litigation costs may not be greater than an amount that is the product of a somewhat complicated formula:

A. Determine the sum of (1) 50% of the economic damages to be awarded in the judgment, (2) 100% of the non-economic damages to be awarded in the judgment, and (3) 100% of the exemplary or additional damages to be awarded in the judgment; and then

B. Subtract from the amount determined in (A), the amount of any statutory or contractual liens in connection with the occurrences or incidents giving rise to the claim.

§8.03 Obtaining Trial Setting and Giving Notice

The procedure for obtaining a trial setting varies from county to county, and sometimes varies between courts in a county. Generally, however, a case is set for trial by means of an oral or written request for a trial setting, made to the court coordinator or clerk of the court in which the case is pending. *See, e.g.,* Rule 1.5(a), *Local Rules of Practice in the Civil District Courts and County Courts at Law of Dallas County, Texas.* In those counties, such as Travis County, in which a central docket system is maintained, a case normally is set for trial by making a request to the court coordinator. *See, e.g.,* Rule 2.2, *Local Rules of Practice of the Travis County Judicial District Courts of Texas.* Still other counties have somewhat rigid rules that must be followed before a setting request will be honored. For example, in Jefferson County the local rules require a written request for a trial setting in which the attorney making the request certifies that seven specific conditions have been met, one of which is that, "all matters preliminary to trial have been accomplished[.]" Rule 4(B), *Jefferson County Local Rules of Practice.*

An agreed trial date from all the attorneys in the case obviously is preferred. If no agreement is possible, then at least there should be some confirmation that none of the parties' attorneys are already set for trial or have a vacation planned that would create a conflict.

The following alternative forms are for use in those counties in which a simple letter requesting a setting is sufficient (§[a]) and those counties in which a formal certification is required (§[b]).

[a] FORM: Letter requesting trial setting

```
(Date)

(Inside address)

Re: Cause no. _____; _____ vs. _____

Dear _____:

Please set the above referenced case for jury trial the week of
_____, 20___.
```

Under separate cover, a notice of the trial setting is being sent by certified mail, return receipt requested, to the attorneys of record who are listed below.

```
    Thank you for your cooperation.

                              Sincerely,

                              [Signature of attorney]

    cc: [Names and addresses of all attorneys of record]
```

[b] FORM: Certification of trial readiness

[**NOTE:** This form is intended to illustrate the requirements of those counties that require a certification that the case is ready for trial as a condition precedent to the request for a trial setting. The specific local rules of each county should be checked to insure that each element of the certification has been included.]

NO. _____

_____ § IN THE DISTRICT COURT OF
§
vs. § _____ COUNTY, TEXAS
§
_____ § _____ JUDICIAL DISTRICT

REQUEST FOR TRIAL SETTING

TO THE CLERK OF THE DISTRICT COURT:

_____, plaintiff [defendant] in the above referenced cause, requests that this case be set for jury trial for the week of _____, 20___.

1. The pleadings of the parties are in order and all parties have appeared and answered this lawsuit.

2. The attorneys who are named in the Certificate of Service below have not withdrawn from this case.

3. All agreements between the attorneys with respect to evidence and the taking of depositions have been filed.

4. All matters preliminary to trial have been accomplished.

5. All parties by and through their counsel of record have been furnished a copy of this request for a setting.

6. As far as is known to the undersigned, this case is ready for trial.

Respectfully submitted,

[Signature of attorney]

[Certificate of service]

Once a trial setting has been obtained, it is necessary to formally notify all parties of the setting. Some counties send notice of the setting to the parties who are of record; however, unless this form of notice is ordered by the court, Rule 21a of the Rules of Civil Procedure requires that notice be given either by personal service or by registered or certified mail. TEX. R. CIV. P. 21a. Because of the requirements of Rule 21a, it has been held that the notice which is mailed by the coordinators in some counties is ineffective as notice under Rule 21a. *P. Bosco & Sons Contracting Corporation v. Conley, Lott, Nichols Machinery Company*, 629 S.W.2d 142 (Tex. App.—Dallas 1982, writ ref'd n.r.e.) For this reason, whenever a trial setting is obtained, the attorney requesting the setting should immediately deliver a written notice of the setting to all parties in the case by certified or registered mail, or by hand delivery, retaining proof of delivery in the file.

In addition to notifying all parties of the setting, all witnesses also should be notified orally and in writing of the date the trial is to begin so there will be some assurance that the necessary trial days will be reserved by the witness. The letter should explain that the exact time the witness will be called to testify is unknown and unknowable. The letter should also prepare the witness for the fact that he or she may not know the time to come to the courthouse until the night before testimony is required. The more flexible a witness can keep a calendar during the time that the case will be in trial, the easier life is for the lawyer and the parties.

[c] FORM: Letter providing notice of setting to parties

```
Certified Mail, Return Receipt Requested

(Date)

(Inside address)

Re: Cause no. _____ ; _____ vs. _____

Dear _____ :
```

In accordance with our telephone conversation, I have set the above referenced case for jury trial as follows:

```
Date of setting: _____

Docket call: _____
```

It is my understanding that you have no conflict with this date. If a conflict with this setting develops, please notify me immediately.

```
                              Sincerely,

                              [Signature of attorney]
```

[d] FORM: Letter providing notice of setting to witnesses

(Date)

(Inside address)

Re: _____ vs. _____

Dear _____:

[As we discussed on the telephone,] The above referenced lawsuit has been set for jury trial beginning on [Monday], _____ 20___ at [9:00 a.m]. We expect the trial to last _____ days.

It is impossible to know precisely when you will be needed at the courthouse to testify. The first order of business will be the selection of a jury, after which opening statements will be made. No testimony will be taken until all of this is completed; therefore, I do not anticipate that you will be needed at the courthouse before _____. Some trials move very quickly; other trials move very slowly. For this reason, if at all possible, I need you to keep your calendar *very* flexible during the _____ days the case is expected to last.

Once the trial begins, we will try to give you as much advance warning as possible about when you should be at the courthouse; however, it sometimes happens that the best we can do is call you the night before you are needed and ask you to be in court the next morning.

I want to thank you again for your willingness to appear as a witness. Without your assistance, it would be impossible for us to show the jury what truly happened in this case.

Sincerely,

[Signature of attorney]

§8.04 Evidence by Affidavit

Two types of evidence frequently needed in DTPA cases may be proven by affidavit, if the affidavits are in proper form and if the affidavits are filed in a timely manner. The types of evidence are (1) the cost and necessity of services (*see* TEX. CIV. PRAC. & REM. CODE §18.001) and (2) business and medical records (*see* TEX. R. CIV. EVID. 902[10]).

§8.05 Cost and Necessity of Services

The cost of repairing consumer products ranging from automobiles to houses frequently is a major element of damages in DTPA litigation. The cost and necessity of such repair services may be proven by affidavit if the following requisites are met:

- The affidavit is taken before an officer with authority to administer oaths; and

- The affidavit is made by the person who provided the service, or the person in charge of records showing the service provided and the charge made; and

- The affidavit states that the amount that was charged for the service was reasonable at the time and place that the service was provided and that the service was necessary; and

- The affidavit includes an itemized statement of the service provided and the charges for the service.

See TEX. CIV. PRAC. & REM. CODE §18.001(b), (c).

The affidavit must be filed with the clerk of the court and a copy served on opposing counsel at least thirty days before the day on which evidence is first presented at the trial of the case. TEX. CIV. PRAC. & REM. CODE §18.001(d). If a controverting affidavit is not timely filed (*see* §8.06 *infra*), then the affidavit is sufficient to support a finding by the court or jury that the amount charged was reasonable and the service was necessary. TEX. CIV. PRAC. & REM. CODE §18.001(b).

[a] FORM: Affidavit concerning cost and necessity of services

```
                        NO. _____
_____              §    IN THE DISTRICT COURT OF
                        §
vs.                     §    _____COUNTY, TEXAS
                        §
_____              §    _____ JUDICIAL DISTRICT
```

AFFIDAVIT CONCERNING COST AND NECESSITY OF SERVICES

BEFORE ME the undersigned Notary Public on this day personally appeared _____ who after having been by me duly cautioned and sworn did state to me upon his [her] oath as follows:

1. My name is _____. I am over the age of eighteen; I have personal knowledge of the statements made in this affidavit; and I am competent to make this oath.

2. On _____, 20___, I provided services to _____ by [*insert type of repair work done*].

[*or*]

2. I am the person in charge of the records of [*insert company name*] which records show the services provided to _____ and the charges for those services on _____, 20___.

3. The specific services that were provided and the charges for those services were as follows:

Item	Charge
_____	$_____
_____	$_____
_____	$_____

4. The charges for the services itemized in paragraph 3 were reasonable in _____ County, Texas at the time they were made and the services were necessary.

[Signature of affiant]

SUBSCRIBED AND SWORN TO before me on this _____ day of 20___, to certify which witness my hand and official seal.

[Signature of notary public]

[Seal]
[Certificate of service]

§8.06 Controverting Affidavit Concerning Cost and Necessity of Services

When the plaintiff timely files an affidavit concerning the cost and necessity of services in proper form, the amount of the charges and the services performed can be controverted only if the opposing party files a counteraffidavit with the clerk of the court and serves a copy of the counteraffidavit on each party to the case. TEX. CIV. PRAC. & REM. CODE §18.001(e). The counteraffidavit must be filed within thirty days after the affidavit is received but no later than fourteen days before the day on which evidence is first presented at the trial of the case. TEX. CIV. PRAC. & REM. CODE §18.001(e)(1). In those cases where there are valid reasons why the counteraffidavit cannot be filed fourteen days prior to trial, with leave of the court, it may be filed at any time up to the commencement of the evidence. TEX. CIV. PRAC. & REM. CODE §18.001(e)(2).

In addition to the requirement that the counteraffidavit be filed in a timely manner, the counteraffidavit must satisfy the following criteria:

- It must give reasonable notice of the basis on which the party filing it intends at trial to controvert the claim reflected by the initial affidavit; and

- It must be taken before a person authorized to administer oaths; and

- It must be made by a person who is qualified, by knowledge, skill, experience, training, education, or other expertise, to testify in contravention of all or part of any of the matters contained in the initial affidavit.

See TEX. CIV. PRAC. & REM. CODE §18.001(f).

[a] FORM: Counteraffidavit concerning cost and necessity of services

```
                         NO. _____
_____            §    IN THE DISTRICT COURT OF
                      §
vs.                   §    _____COUNTY, TEXAS
                      §
_____            §    _____ JUDICIAL DISTRICT
```

COUNTERAFFIDAVIT CONCERNING COST AND NECESSITY OF SERVICES

BEFORE ME the undersigned Notary Public on this day personally appeared _____, who after having been by me duly cautioned and sworn did state to me upon his (her) oath as follows:

1. My name is _____. I am over the age of eighteen and I am competent to make an oath. I have personal knowledge of the statements made in this affidavit.

2. I have [insert educational background]. Following graduation, I have worked as a [insert employment history]. I am presently employed as a [insert current employment] and have been so employed for _____ years. This educational and employment background has given me the knowledge and experience necessary to evaluate the services provided to _____ as well as the cost of those services as reflected in the affidavit of _____ which is on file in this lawsuit.

3. In my opinion, the following services that are set forth in the affidavit were unnecessary for the reasons stated: [insert unnecessary services and reasons for the opinion, e.g., After the sheetrock cracks were repaired, the entire inside of the house was repainted even though sheetrock cracks existed in only two of the six rooms in the house].

4. In addition to the unnecessary repairs described in paragraph 3, in my opinion, the cost for such repair work was not reasonable for the following reasons: First, all of the charges for the unnecessary work described in the preceding paragraph

were not reasonable since the work did not need to be done in the first place. Second, for that work which was needed, the amount charged for the work was in excess of the customary charges for such work in _____ County, Texas. Specifically, [*insert specific charges and show what customary charges for that work would be, e.g.*, the total charge for painting the house was $_____. The customary charge for painting a house in _____ County, Texas of a similar size, using a similar quality of paint, was only $_____ at the time the house was painted].

[Signature of affiant]

SUBSCRIBED AND SWORN TO before me on this _____ day of 20___ to certify which witness my hand and official seal.

[Signature of notary public]

[Seal]

[Certificate of service]

[b] FORM: Request for leave of the court to file counteraffidavit

	NO. _____	
_____	§	IN THE DISTRICT COURT OF
	§	
vs.	§	_____ COUNTY, TEXAS
	§	
_____	§	_____ JUDICIAL DISTRICT

MOTION FOR LEAVE OF THE COURT TO FILE COUNTERAFFIDAVIT

TO THE HONORABLE JUDGE OF THE DISTRICT COURT:

_____, defendant, files this motion seeking leave of the court to file a counteraffidavit to the Affidavit on the Cost and Necessity of Services previously filed in this cause by _____, plaintiff.

1.

Leave of the court is necessary to file a counteraffidavit for the reason that the counteraffidavit would be filed less than fourteen days before the commencement of the evidence in this trial. TEX. CIV. (E).PRAC. & REM. CODE §18. 001 (e).

2.

The counteraffidavit which defendant requests leave of the court to file is attached to this motion as Exhibit A and incorporated at this point as if fully set forth.

3.

The counteraffidavit has not been filed more than fourteen days before trial because [*insert reasons for late filing*].

[4.]

[*Insert any other matters showing lack of surprise, etc., e.g.,* Immediately upon receipt of the affidavit from plaintiff, defendant advised plaintiff that the contents of the affidavit would be contested and that a counteraffidavit would be filed. Thus, although the actual counteraffidavit has not been delivered to plaintiff until the date this motion was filed, plaintiff has been aware that a counteraffidavit would be filed and its general contents since the date defendant received the initial affidavit.]

WHEREFORE defendant asks that this motion be granted and that leave be granted to file the counteraffidavit which is attached.

Respectfully submitted,

[Signature of attorney]

STATE OF TEXAS §
§
COUNTY OF _____ §

BEFORE ME the undersigned Notary Public on this day personally appeared _____ who after having been by me duly cautioned and sworn did state to me upon his [her] oath that he [she] has read the foregoing Motion for Leave to File and that each statement made in the motion is true and correct based on his [her] own personal knowledge.

[Signature of affiant]

SUBSCRIBED AND SWORN TO before me on this _____ day of 20___, to certify which witness my hand and official seal.

[Signature of notary public]

[Seal]

[Certificate of service]

[c] FORM: Order granting leave to file counteraffidavit

```
                            NO. _____
                        §
    _____          §    IN THE DISTRICT COURT OF
                        §
vs.                     §    _____COUNTY, TEXAS
                        §
    _____          §    _____ JUDICIAL DISTRICT
```

<u>**ORDER GRANTING LEAVE TO FILE**</u>

On this _____ day of _____, 20___, came on for hearing defendant's motion for leave to file a counteraffidavit in opposition to the initial affidavit on cost and necessity of services filed by plaintiff in this lawsuit. After considering the evidence and argument of counsel, it appears to the court that the motion is well taken and should be granted.

IT IS THEREFORE ORDERED that defendant is granted leave to file the counteraffidavit which is attached to defendant's motion as Exhibit A and such counteraffidavit shall have the same force and effect as if it had been filed more than fourteen days before the commencement of the evidence in this lawsuit.

SIGNED this _____ day of _____, 20___.

[Signature of presiding judge]

§8.07 Business and Medical Records

The records of regularly conducted businesses are frequent exhibits in DTPA litigation. Similarly, medical records generally are necessary exhibits when the mental or physical health of the plaintiff is alleged to have been adversely affected by the conduct of the defendant. Documents of this type can be properly authenticated through live testimony at trial of a sponsoring witness. TEX. R. CIV. EVID. 901(a). As an alternative, however, authentication may be made by affidavit. TEX. R. CIV. EVID. 902(10).

Authentication by affidavit is not advisable when the validity of the documents is seriously questioned, or when the conditions reflected in the documents are contested by the opposing party. In such cases, although it may be possible to admit the documents into evidence with a properly executed and filed affidavit, for the documents to be persuasive, the live testimony of a sponsoring witness is probably required. When, however, neither the genuineness of the documents nor the conditions reflected in the documents are open to serious question, the inconvenience and expense of summoning a sponsoring witness to court or to a deposition can be avoided by authenticating the documents with an affidavit. *See* TEX. R. CIV. EVID. 902(10).

Business records may be authenticated by affidavit only if the records and the affidavit are filed with the court no less than fourteen days before trial. TEX. R. CIV. EVID. 902(10)(a). The fourteen day filing requirement is mandatory and cannot be waived even if the opposing party is not surprised by the records. *Chemical Bank v. Commercial Industries Service Co., Inc.*, 662 S.W.2d 802 (Tex. App.—Houston [14th Dist.] 1983, writ ref'd n.r.e.). Further, all other parties in the lawsuit must be given "prompt notice" of the filing of the records and the affidavit. TEX. R. CIV. EVID. 902(10)(a). The notice must identify the name and employer of the person making the affidavit and should state that the records are available to all parties to the lawsuit for inspection and copying. TEX. R. CIV. EVID. 902(10)(a). The notice "shall be deemed to have been promptly given" if it is given in the manner contemplated by TEX. R. CIV. P. 21a. *See* TEX. R. CIV. EVID. 902(10)(a).

The form of the affidavit which follows is taken from TEX. R. CIV. EVID. 902(10)(b); however, the rule provides that any affidavit which substantially complies with the provisions of the rule will suffice.

[a] FORM: Business or medical records affidavit

```
                              NO. _____
    _____                §    IN THE DISTRICT COURT OF
                              §
    vs.                       §    _____ COUNTY, TEXAS
                              §
    _____                §    _____ JUDICIAL DISTRICT
```

<u>AFFIDAVIT</u>

BEFORE ME the undersigned authority, personally appeared _____, who, being by me duly sworn, deposed as follows:

My name is _____. I am of sound mind, capable of making this affidavit, and personally acquainted with the facts herein stated:

I am the custodian of the records of _____. Attached hereto are pages of records from _____. These said _____ pages of records are kept by _____ in the regular course of business of _____, and it was the regular course of business of _____ for an employee or representative of _____, with knowledge of the act, event, condition, opinion, or diagnosis, recorded to make the record or to transmit information thereof to be included in such record; and the record was made at or near the time or reasonably soon thereafter.

The records attached hereto are the originals or exact duplicates of the original.

[Signature of affiant]

SWORN TO AND SUBSCRIBED before me on the _____ day of _____ 20___. My Commission Expires:

[Typed Name of Notary]

Notary Public, State of Texas

§8.08 Use of Criminal Convictions for Impeachment

Criminal convictions are admissible for impeachment in very limited circumstances. TEX. R. CIV. EVID. 609 requires the following conditions to be met:

- The crime must be a felony or must involve moral turpitude; and

- The probative value of admitting the evidence of the conviction must outweigh its prejudicial effect to a party; and

- Generally, not more than ten years can have elapsed since the date of the conviction or the release from confinement, whichever is later.

See TEX. R. CIV. EVID. 609(a), (b).

Even if all of these conditions are satisfied, the conviction still may not be admissible if any of three situations exists. First, the conviction is not admissible if, based on a finding of rehabilitation of the person, the conviction has been pardoned, annulled or otherwise set aside by an equivalent procedure (so long as the person has not been subsequently convicted of a felony or other crime involving moral turpitude). Second, the conviction is not admissible if the person has satisfactorily served out his or her probation (again, so long as the person has not been subsequently convicted of another felony or a crime involving moral turpitude). And third, the conviction is not admissible if there has been a finding of innocence, on which basis the conviction has been the subject of a pardon, annulment or other equivalent procedure. *See* TEX. R. CIV. EVID. 609(c).

Lastly, evidence of a conviction of a felony or crime involving moral turpitude is not admissible for impeachment if the conviction was the result of a juvenile adjudication, TEX. R. CIV. EVID. 609(d), or if an appeal of the conviction is pending. TEX. R. CIV. EVID. 609(e).

There are few types of evidence more suited for discussion at a motion in limine hearing than evidence of prior convictions. The conditions under which the evidence is admissible are so limited and the potential damage to a party or witness is so devastating, that the question of admissibility should be disposed of before trial. And, therein lies the problem.

Nearly every trial attorney has been involved in one or more cases in which a witness or even the client has been convicted of a felony. And, in some cases, because the person's deposition was less thorough than it should have been, or perhaps not even taken, the attorney is unsure whether the fact of the conviction is known to the other side. If the conviction is known by the other side, then there is no harm in addressing the question of its admissibility in a motion in limine. However, if the attorney is unsure whether the conviction is known to the other side, then one has to decide whether disclosing the conviction in a motion in limine is worth the risk of informing the other side to the existence of the conviction. After all, the motion may be lost and in the process, the other side has been handed the means by which to seriously impair the credibility of an otherwise valuable witness.

The dilemma described in the preceding paragraphs can be avoided with some ease by following a procedure set out in the Rules of Evidence. TEX. R. CIV. EVID. 609(f) provides as follows:

Evidence of a conviction is not admissible if after timely written request by the adverse party specifying the witness or witnesses, the proponent fails to give to the adverse party sufficient advance written notice of intent to use such evidence to provide the adverse party with a fair opportunity to contest the use of such evidence.

In other words, if a proper written request is made, then the evidence cannot be introduced without "sufficient" advance warning. There have been no cases construing how much advance notice is required, but clearly the rule contemplates that enough time will be available so that the matter can be presented and dealt with at the motion in limine hearing.

Once the written request is made and assuming that no response is made, then a motion in limine should be filed to prevent the mentioning of any criminal convictions during trial. When there has been no written response to the request, this fact alone is a sufficient ground for sustaining the motion in limine so that there would be no need to reveal the existence of a conviction not previously asked about in discovery.

When the written request is made, it must list the names of each of the witnesses or parties asked about. To make sure that no one is left out, the names of all the witnesses who are called to testify should be included. Obviously, by listing all witnesses, the attorney avoids calling attention to the person or persons on the list who actually have a criminal conviction.

[a] FORM: Request for notice of use of criminal convictions for impeachment

CERTIFIED MAIL, RETURN RECEIPT REQUESTED

(Date)

(Inside Address)

Re: Cause No. _____; _____ vs. _____

Dear _____:

You are requested to give advance written notice to the undersigned of your intention to use any evidence of a felony conviction or a conviction of a crime involving moral turpitude with respect to any of the following individuals who may be called to testify at the trial of the above referenced lawsuit:

[Insert names of all witnesses]

                          Sincerely,

                          [Signature of attorney]

§8.09 Visiting Judges

The Government Code authorized the assignment of visiting judges to hear cases in order, "to dispose of accumulated business in the region." *See* TEX. GOV'T CODE §74.052(a).

Some attorneys disagree with the concept of assigning visiting judges to hear cases. One objection to such assignments, whether valid or not, is a concern that the visiting judge is less accountable to the local bar and citizens than the elected judge of the court. The lack of accountability, so the argument goes, leads to arbitrary rulings.

Another concern expressed by attorneys is that preparing a case for trial before a known judge is easier than preparing a case for trial before a visiting judge. With the elected judge, the attorney knows what to expect; with a visiting judge, the attorney finds out how the judge conducts trial only after the trial begins.

Still another concern about visiting judges is that they are perceived to be less likely to be up on the law than the elected judge since many of the judges who are assigned are retired.

In DTPA litigation, from the plaintiff's perspective, there is a special concern about some visiting judges hearing cases for the reason that DTPA litigation is a relatively new concept in the law and one which runs counter, in both substance and philosophy, to the common law under which most retired judges practiced.

When the power to assign visiting judges was given, the legislature recognized the concerns of some attorneys and provided a procedure by which an attorney can object to the assignment of a visiting judge. The Government Code provides that,

(a) When a judge is assigned under this chapter the presiding judge shall, if it is reasonable and practicable and if time permits, give notice of the assignment to each attorney representing a party to the case that is to be heard in whole or in part by the assigned judge.

(b) If a party to a civil case files a timely objection to the assignment, the judge shall not hear the case. Except as provided by Subsection (d), each party to the case is only entitled to one objection under this section for that case.

(c) An objection under this section must be filed before the first hearing or trial, including pretrial hearings, over which the assigned judge is to preside.

(d) A former judge or justice who was not a retired judge may not sit in a case if either party objects to the judge or justice.

TEX. GOV'T CODE §74.053. This section has been construed to permit a party to make one objection to an assigned judge and unlimited objections to an assigned former judge who is not a retired judge. *Flores v. Banner*, 932 S.W.2d 500 (Tex. 1996). If a party timely files an objection, the judge's disqualification is mandatory and any subsequent orders by the judge are void. *Id.*

Although the statute provides that the objection must be made before the first hearing or trial over which the visiting judge is to preside, local rules may further define the procedure necessary to object to the assignment of a visiting judge. Accordingly, to insure that an objection is properly made, local rules be consulted.

[a] FORM: Objection to assignment of visiting judge

```
                              NO. _____
_____                § IN THE DISTRICT COURT OF
                            §
vs.                         § _____ COUNTY, TEXAS
                            §
_____                § _____ JUDICIAL DISTRICT
```

<u>OBJECTION TO ASSIGNMENT OF VISITING JUDGE</u>

TO THE HONORABLE JUDGE OF THE DISTRICT COURT:

1.

_____, plaintiff [defendant], pursuant to the authority of TEX. GOV'T CODE §74.053, objects to the assignment of the following judge named to hear this lawsuit which is set for trial on _____, 20___:

[*Insert name of judge*]

[2.]

[A copy of this objection has been delivered to the office of the Court Administrator before docket call as required by local rules.]

                            Respectfully submitted,

                            [Signature of attorney]

[Certificate of service]

§8.10 Motions in Limine

Of all the pre-trial motions, a motion in limine is used more frequently that any other motion in a jury trial. 3 MCDONALD TEXAS CIVIL PRACTICE §19.3. There is no rule or statute that deals with motions in limine; instead, all of the law pertaining to the use of such motions has been developed through judicial decisions. O'CONNOR'S TEXAS RULES / CIVIL TRIALS, 227 (1998).

The purpose of a motion in limine is to "prevent the asking of prejudicial questions and the making of prejudicial statements in the presence of the jury with respect to matters which have no bearing on the issues in the case or the rights of the parties to the suit." *Bridges v. City of Richardson*, 354 S.W.2d 366, 367 (Tex. 1962). Although the violation of an order in limine may result in the imposition of sanctions, including contempt, *see e.g.*, TEX. GOV'T CODE §§21.001, 21.002, and may serve as the basis for the declaration of a mistrial, *Cody v. Mustang Oil Tool Co.*, 595 S.W.2d 214 (Tex. Civ. App.—Eastland 1980, writ ref'd n.r.e.), there is no appeal from the improper denial of a motion in limine unless the objectionable questions or evidence is in fact asked or offered. *Hartford Accident and Indem. Co. v. McCardell*, 369 S.W.2d 331, 335 (Tex. 1963); *Boswell v. Farm & Home Savings Ass'n*, 894 S.W.2d 761, 770 (Tex. App.—Fort Worth 1994, writ denied). In other words, a judge's decision on a motion in limine, even if erroneous, is never, in and of itself, reversible error. *Dailey v. Wheat*, 681 S.W.2d 747 (Tex. App.—Houston [14th Dist.] 1984, writ ref'd n.r.e.).

Accordingly, if a motion in limine is denied, the party making the motion must object at the time the objectionable evidence is offered, the question is asked or the argument is made and the failure to do so waives the objection. *Hartford Accident and Indemnity Co. v. McCardell*, 369 S.W.2d 331, 335 (Tex. 1963). Similarly, if a motion in limine is granted, the party whose evidence has been excluded must make an offer by way of a bill of exceptions or some similar procedure in order to preserve error. *Gaspard v. Gaspard*, 582 S.W.2d 629, 631 (Tex. Civ. App.—Beaumont 1979, no writ).

§8.10.1 Travis County Local Rule

On January 30, 1998, the judges of the Travis County District Courts issued a "Standing Order in Limine for Trial of Civil Jury Cases." *See* File No. 121,012. The apparent purpose of the order is to save the time required when the trial court has to hear and then rule on standard motions in limine that are made in nearly every case and are nearly always sustained. Thus, in all civil jury trials in Travis County, the matters listed below shall not be mentioned or referred to by the attorneys, the parties or their witnesses, without first approaching the bench and obtaining a ruling that authorizes the reference. In counties that do not have a similar standing order, the contents provide a useful guide for creating a motion in limine.

File No. 121,012

STANDING ORDER IN LIMINE FOR TRIAL OF CIVIL JURY CASES

During the trial of any civil jury case in the District Court, unless and except to the extent that the operation of this order shall have been suspended with reference to such specific trial, no attorney shall make mention, refer to or suggest any of the matters hereinafter set forth in the presence or hearing of the jury, the venire, or of any member of either without first approaching the bench and securing a ruling from the Court authorizing such reference. In addition, each attorney shall admonish the client, the client's representatives and all non-adverse witnesses the attorney may call to testify similarly to refrain from any such statement, reference or suggestion unless same is essential to respond truthfully to a question asked by opposing counsel.

The matters to which reference is prohibited by this order are as follows:

1. **Insurance**. Unless an insurance company is a named Defendant, that the Defendant is or is not protected, in whole or in part, by liability insurance, or that defense counsel was retained by, or all or any part of the costs of defense, or of any resulting judgment, are or will be paid by an insurance company, or any other matter suggesting an involvement of any insurance company with the defense of the case.

2. **Jurors' Connection with Insurance Industry**. Inquiring of potential jurors as to their present or past employment or connection with the insurance industry, or present or past connection of any family member with the insurance industry except that:

A. If a potential juror's juror information card discloses employment in the insurance industry, such potential juror may be questioned concerning same.

B. Inquiry may be made of potential jurors concerning their experience (or that of members of their family), if any, reviewing, adjusting or allowing/disallowing claims, as long as no express reference is made to "insurance."

3. **Liability or Non-Liability for Judgment**. That the named Defendant may or may not have to pay any resulting judgment.

4. **Collateral Source**. That any portion of the damages sought by Plaintiff have been, or will be, paid by any collateral source, including but not limited to:

A. Health and accident or disability insurance.

B. Any employee benefit plan, formal or informal, including payment of wages for time not actually worked.

C. Social security or welfare.

D. Veterans or other benefits.

E. Provisions of medical services free of charge or for less than reasonable and customary charges, provided that the foregoing does not prohibit reference to unpaid charges of any health care provider who actually testifies for Plaintiff (or whose medical records are offered by Plaintiff), or to any letter of protection securing any such charges.

5. **Retention of Attorney**. The time or circumstances under which either party consulted or retained an attorney provided that if any attorney referred a party to a health care provider who testifies in the case (or whose medical records are introduced by such party) such fact may be a subject of inquiry.

6. **Attorney's Fees**. That any party will have to pay attorney's fees, or any reference to the amount or basis of any attorney's fees, unless a claim for recovery of attorney's fees in the case will be submitted to the jury.

7. **Income Taxes**. That any recovery will or will not be subject to income taxes, in whole or in part.

8. **Independent Medical Examination**. That the plaintiff offered to, or was or is willing to, undergo an examination by an independent physician or psychologist.

9. **Criminal Offenses**. That any party or witness has been suspected of, arrested

for, charged with or convicted of any criminal offense unless there is evidence of a specific conviction that the Court has previously ruled is admissible in the case.

10. **Alcohol or Drug Use**. That any party or witness uses or abuses alcohol, tobacco, or any controlled substance, unless and until such alleged use or abuse is shown to be specifically relevant to the matters in controversy.

11. **Settlement Negotiations or Mediation**. Any negotiations, offers or demands with respect to any attempted settlement or mediation.

12. **Discovery Disputes**. Any reference to discovery disputes that arose during the preparation of the case for trial, any position taken by any party with respect thereto, or to the Court's rulings thereon.

13. **Prior Suits or Claims**. That any party has been a party to any prior lawsuit, or has asserted any prior claim, or that any prior claim has been asserted against a party; provided that this clause does not prohibit inquiry about a prior injury that may have been the subject of a claim, as distinguished from the claim, suit or settlement with reference thereto, if the nature of injuries claimed in the present suit make the same relevant.

14. **Ex Parte Statements of Witnesses**. Any reference to any *ex parte* statement of any witness or alleged witness, other than an adverse party or agent of an adverse party, unless and until such witness has been called to testify and has given testimony conflicting with such *ex parte* statement. A deposition or a statement in business or medical records that have been proved up as required by the Rules of Evidence is not an *ex parte* statement.

15. **Testimony of Absent Witnesses**. Any statement or suggestion as to the probable testimony of any witness or alleged witness who is unavailable to testify, or whom the party suggesting such testimony does not, in good faith, expect to testify in the trial. If the party is expected to testify by deposition, this provision does not apply to testimony contained in the deposition expected to be offered.

16. **Failure to Call Witness**. Any reference to the failure of an opposing party to call any witness.

17. **Hearsay Medical Opinions**. Any hearsay statement offered for the truth of the statement by an allegedly injured person concerning any diagnosis or medical opinions communicated to such person by a physician or other health care provider.

18. **Photographs and Visual Aids**. Showing any documents, photographs or visual aids to the jury, or displaying same in such manner that the jury or any member thereof can see the same, unless and until the same has been tendered to opposing counsel, and has been admitted in evidence or approved for admission or use before the jury, either by the Court or by all counsel.

19. **Requests for Stipulations**. Any request or demand in the presence of the jury for a stipulation to any fact, or that counsel admit or deny act fact.

20. **Requests for Files**. Any request or demand in the presence of the jury that opposing counsel produce any document or thing, or that opposing counsel or any party or witness exhibit, turn over or allow examination of the contents of any file or briefcase (except that a party may demand to see a document used by a witness on the stand to refresh his/her recollection, or that a witness testifies that he/she has used previously to refresh his/her recollection).

21. **Discrimination**. Any argument that a party should be treated more or less favorably because of such party's race,

gender, national origin, nationality, religion, marital status, occupation, or financial status (except in the second phase of a bifurcated trial).

22. **Social Cost of Award**. Any argument or suggestion that an award of damages will affect insurance premiums, the price of any goods or services, or the level of taxation.

23. **Hardship or Privation**. Any argument of suggestion that a failure to award damages will cause a Plaintiff privation or financial hardship.

24. **Golden Rule**. Any argument or suggestion that the jurors should put themselves in the position of a party.

25. **Counsel's Opinion of Credibility**. Any expression of counsel's personal opinion regarding the credibility of any witness.

26. **Effect of Answers to Jury Questions**. Any argument that any finding or failure to find in response to a particular jury question will, or will not result in a judgment favorable to any party. This provision does not bar argument by counsel that a particular jury question should be answered in a particular way.

27. **Evidence Not Produced in Discovery Response to a Proper Request**. Calling any witness, or offering any document in evidence, if the identity of such witness or the document has not been disclosed in response to a proper discovery request. If the party has a good faith basis to urge that such witness or document should be received either because (a) no discovery request property called for its disclosure, or (b) good cause existed for failure timely to disclose, such party shall first approach the bench and secure a ruling thereon. Counsel are advised that to the extent possible or predictable, such matters should be addressed and a ruling sought at pretrial once the case is assigned for trial.

28. **Objections to Evidence Not Produced in Discovery**. Any objection based on failure to discover evidence in pre-trial discovery. Any party desiring to urge any such objection shall request to approach the bench and urge such objection outside the hearing of the jury. To the extent possible or predictable, such matters should be addressed and a ruling sought at pretrial once the case is assigned for trial, although the objection may be urged for the record outside the hearing of the jury at the time such evidence is offered in the event the Court has overruled the objection at pretrial.

§8.10.2 Procedure

All motions are to be filed and served at least three days before the date of the hearing on the motion. TEX. R. CIV. P. 21. The general custom with respect to motions in limine, however, is that they frequently are filed and served just before the pre-trial proceedings begin. Local rules may vary the practice. A motion in limine can be made at any time the court will entertain it (even during trial), *City of Houston v. Watson*, 376 S.W.2d 23 (Tex. Civ. App.—Houston 1964, writ ref'd n.r.e.). so long as it is before the publication of the objectionable material to the jury because the error, if any, is not in overruling the motion but instead is in the admission of objectionable evidence or the making of objectionable argument.

There is no prescribed format for a motion in limine so long as it states the grounds for the motion and sets forth the relief or order sought. TEX. R. CIV. P. 21. It may be helpful to the court, however, to cite in the motion itself the authority for the exclusion of the evidence, testimony or argument and to have copies of the cases or statutes at hand.

[a] FORM: Motion in limine (general form)

```
                            NO. _____
_____              §      IN THE DISTRICT COURT OF
                        §
vs.                     §      _____ COUNTY, TEXAS
                        §
_____              §      _____ JUDICIAL DISTRICT
```

<u>PLAINTIFF'S [DEFENDANT'S] MOTION IN LIMINE</u>

TO THE HONORABLE JUDGE OF THE DISTRICT COURT:

_____, plaintiff [defendant] files this motion in limine as follows:

1.

This motion is filed before the commencement of the voir dire examination of the jury panel and within the time required by the local rules of court.

2.

Plaintiff moves the court to enter its order prohibiting defendant, defendant's counsel and all of defendant's witnesses, [*or* Defendant moves the court to enter its order prohibiting plaintiff, plaintiff's counsel and all of plaintiff's witnesses,] including those who may testify by deposition only, from making any mention or interrogation, directly or indirectly, in any manner whatsoever, of any of the matters set forth below, without first approaching the bench, outside the presence and hearing of the jurors, and obtaining a ruling by the court on the admissibility of such matters.

3.

Plaintiff [Defendant] requests that the court exclude the following matters:

(a) Any offers to settle or resolve this lawsuit or any settlement negotiations, for the reason that settlement negotiations and offers of settlement are not admissible as evidence. Tex. R. Civ. Evid. 408.

(b) Requesting that plaintiff's [defendant's] attorney produce any document from his [her] file or agree to do any thing or refrain from doing any thing.

(c) Calling as a witness any person who has not previously been disclosed, more than thirty days in advance of trial, in answer to plaintiff's [defendant's] interrogatories. TEX. R. CIV. P. 166(b); 215(5).

(d) Offering into evidence any document or other exhibit which was requested but has not previously been produced in response to plaintiff's [defendant's] Request for Production of documents. TEX. R. CIV. P. 215(5).

(e) Reading any question or answer from a deposition or playing any question or answer from a videotaped deposition to which question or answer an objection was made.

(f) Making reference to any criminal arrest or conviction of plaintiff [defendant] or any of plaintiff's [defendant's] witnesses for the reason that a written request under TEX. R. CIV. EVID. 609(f) was made for notice of an intention to use such evidence and no such notice was received [*or if such a request was not made*, Making reference to any conviction of plaintiff [defendant] for the reason that plaintiff [defendant] has never been convicted of a felony or crime involving moral turpitude]. TEX. R. CIV. EVID. 609(a).

(g) Any evidence which contradicts or tends to disprove the following matter: [*describe fact, e.g.*, that defendant built the house purchased by plaintiff] for the reason that such matter was admitted by defendant [plaintiff] [*or deemed admitted*] pursuant to TEX. R. CIV. P. 169.

(h) Making reference to plaintiff's [defendant's] failure to call a witness to testify if the witness was equally available to both parties. *Sanders v. St. Paul Fire & Marine Ins. Co.*, 429 S.W.2d 516, 521-523 (Tex. Civ. App.—Texarkana 1968, writ ref'd n.r.e.).

(i) Suggesting or inferring what the testimony of a witness would have been had that witness been called to testify. *Tex-Jersey Oil Corp. v. Beck*, 305 S.W.2d 162, 167 (Tex. 1957).

(j) Stating that this motion has been made or considered by the court and any ruling on the motion by the court.

[b] FORM: Specific matters for plaintiff's motion in limine

[Insert at end of paragraph 3, supra:]

[k] Stating that plaintiff has filed any prior claims, lawsuits or has received any prior settlements from such claims or lawsuits.

[l] Stating that any recovery by plaintiff in this case will not be subject to taxation. *Turner v. General Motors Corp.*, 584 S.W.2d 844, 853 (Tex. 1979).

[m] Making any reference to plaintiff's personal lifestyle or stating that plaintiff is [*insert specific matter to be excluded, e.g., homosexual*] for the reason that such matter is not relevant to any issue in this case.

[n] Stating that there are too many lawsuits, or that there has been a litigation explosion or words to that effect.

[o] Stating that a verdict in this lawsuit or any other similar lawsuit causes insurance rates to go up.

[p] Stating that any damages recovered by plaintiff are subject to automatic doubling or trebling for the reason that this is a matter for the court only.

In repair cases:

[q] Stating or inferring that the money recovered by plaintiff for cost of repairs may not actually be used to make the repairs.

In loss of use cases:

[r] Stating that plaintiff has not or will not actually rent [*insert replacement item, e.g.*, an automobile] with the money sought or found as damages for loss of use. *Luna v. North Star Dodge Sales, Inc.*, 667 S.W.2d 115, 118-119 (Tex. 1984).

In investment cases:

[s] Stating that plaintiff has lost money in prior [or subsequent] investments.

In house repair cases:

[t] Stating or inferring that defendant was denied an opportunity to repair plaintiff's [*describe item, e.g.*, house] for the reason that defendant did not avail himself [herself] of

the statutory right to offer repairs pursuant to TEX. PROP. CODE §27.004; accordingly, whether defendant was or was not given an opportunity to repair has no bearing on whether the implied warranty of good workmanship was breached and does not constitute a defense to any cause of action advanced by plaintiff.

If plaintiff is insured against loss:

[u] Making any reference to the fact that plaintiff is entitled to receive benefits from insurance for the reason that this is a collateral source of funds. *Brown v. American Transfer and Storage Co.*, 601 S.W.2d 931, 934 (Tex. 1980), *cert. denied*, 449 U.S. 1015 (1980); *Walker v. Missouri Pacific Railroad Co.*, 425 S.W.2d 462 (Tex. Civ. App.—Houston [14th Dist.] 1968, writ ref'd n.r.e.).

[c] FORM: Specific matters for defendant's motion in limine

[*Insert at end of paragraph 3, supra*:]

[k] Making any reference to the wealth of defendant for the reason that there is no claim for discretionary additional damages or exemplary damages in this case.

[l] Making any reference to insurance coverage in this case. TEX. R. CIV. EVID. 411.

[m] Making any reference to companies owned or controlled by defendant which are not involved in this litigation.

[n] Making any reference to prior claims made against defendant or prior settlements made by defendant.

[o] Making any reference to other lawsuits in which defendant has been involved or the results of those lawsuits.

[p] Making any reference to the response made to a demand letter for the reasons that (1) such a response is in the nature of a settlement offer and (2) the adequacy of the response is a question of law for the court [*in suits governed by the 1989 amendments to the DTPA, add the following*: and (3) because such matter is inadmissible under DTPA §17.505(d)].

[NOTE: Paragraph [p] probably would have no application in residential construction cases. *See* TEX. PROP. CODE §27.004. Also, if the response shows that the plaintiff is unreasonable, this paragraph obviously should not be inserted.]

[q] Making any reference to changes [*describe remedial measures taken, e.g.*, in the design of the computer disc drive] which were made after plaintiff's purchase of the product. Tex. R. Civ. Evid. 407(a).

[r] Making any prejudicial comments that defendant is a "large, out-of-state corporation" or words to that effect.

[d] FORM: Order on motion in limine

[NOTE: The form order set forth below can be used for either the plaintiff's or defendant's motion. Any specific matters added to the general motion in limine form should be included on the order with a space for the court's ruling.]

```
                              NO. _____
_____             §     IN THE DISTRICT COURT OF
                         §
vs.                      §     _____COUNTY, TEXAS
                         §
_____             §     _____ JUDICIAL DISTRICT
```

ORDER ON MOTION IN LIMINE

The court has considered Plaintiff's [Defendant's] Motion in Limine and in the opinion of the court those matters by which the court has indicated "granted" should be excluded from the hearing of the jury until a ruling on such matters is obtained.

IT IS THEREFORE ORDERED that defendant, defendant's attorney and any witness called by defendant to testify [*or* plaintiff, plaintiff's attorney, and any witness called by plaintiff to testify] are prohibited from making any mention or interrogation in the presence or hearing of the jury of the matters set forth below which have been granted by the court without first approaching the bench, out of the presence or hearing of the jury, and obtaining a ruling from the court on the admissibility of such matters:

1. Any offers to settle or resolve this lawsuit or any settlement negotiations.

Court's Ruling: _____ GRANTED _____ OVERRULED

2. Requesting that plaintiff's [defendant's] attorney produce any document from his [her] file or agree to do any thing or refrain from doing any thing.

Court's Ruling: _____ GRANTED _____ OVERRULED

3. Calling as a witness any person who has not previously been disclosed, more than thirty days in advance of trial, in answer to plaintiff's [defendant's] interrogatories.

Court's Ruling: _____ GRANTED _____ OVERRULED

4. Offering into evidence any document or other exhibit which was requested but not previously produced in response to plaintiff's [defendant's] Request for Production of documents.

Court's Ruling: _____ GRANTED _____ OVERRULED

5. Reading any question or answer from a deposition or playing any question or answer from a videotaped deposition to which question or answer an objection was made.

Court's Ruling: _____ GRANTED _____ OVERRULED

6. Making reference to any criminal arrest or conviction of plaintiff [defendant] or any of plaintiff's [defendant's] witnesses.

Court's Ruling: _____ GRANTED _____ OVERRULED

7. Offering any evidence which contradicts or tends to disprove that [*describe fact admitted pursuant to* TEX. R. CIV. P. *169, e.g.*, defendant built the house purchased by plaintiff].

Court's Ruling: _____ GRANTED _____ OVERRULED

8. Making reference to plaintiff's [defendant's] failure to call a person as a witness if that person was equally available to both plaintiff and defendant.

Court's Ruling: _____ GRANTED _____ OVERRULED

9. Suggesting or inferring what the testimony of a witness would have been if that witness had been called to testify.

Court's Ruling: _____ GRANTED _____ OVERRULED

10. Stating that this motion has been made or considered by the court and any ruling on the motion by the Court.

Court's Ruling: _____ GRANTED _____ OVERRULED

[*Insert other matters to be excluded*]

SIGNED this _____ day of _____, 19___.

[Signature of presiding judge]

§8.11 Judicial Notice

DTPA litigation occasionally involves violations of rules and regulations promulgated by state agencies such as the Motor Vehicle Commission or the State Board of Insurance. In cases involving ordinances that affect the value or use of goods or services sold, *e.g.*, flood plain ordinances, it will be necessary to prove the contents of the ordinances in order to establish all of the elements of the plaintiff's case.

When the content of state agency regulations or local government ordinances are at issue, the proper procedure is to request the court to take judicial notice of the rule or regulation.

TEX. R. CIV. EVID. 204 provides that:

A court upon its own motion may, or upon the motion of a party shall, take judicial notice of the ordinances of municipalities and counties of Texas, of the contents of the Texas Register, and of the codified rules of the agencies published in the Administrative Code. Any party requesting that judicial notice be taken of such matter shall furnish the court sufficient information to enable it properly to comply with the request. A party Is entitled upon timely request to an opportunity to be heard as to the propriety of taking judicial notice and the tenor of the matter noticed. In the absence of prior notification, the request may be made after judicial notice has been taken. The court's determination shall be subject to review as a ruling on a question of law.

TEX. R. CIV. EVID. 204.

[a] FORM: Motion for court to take judicial notice

```
                              NO. _____
_____                §    IN THE DISTRICT COURT OF
                            §
vs.                         §    _____COUNTY, TEXAS
                            §
_____                §    _____ JUDICIAL DISTRICT
```

MOTION FOR COURT TO TAKE JUDICIAL NOTICE

TO THE HONORABLE JUDGE OF THE DISTRICT COURT:

_____, plaintiff [defendant], moves the Court to take judicial notice of a rule of a state agency [*or* of a local government ordinance] as follows:

1.

This lawsuit involves questions of law and fact which relate to rules of the [*insert agency and rule citation, e.g.*, Texas State Board of Insurance which are entitled "Unfair Trade Practices Prohibited" and "Misrepresentation Defined; Standards for Determining Misrepresentation" and which are codified at

Tex. Admin. Code Title 28, §21.3 and §21.4 respectively]. A true and correct copy of the rules is attached to this motion as Exhibit A.

2.

Under the authority of Tex. R. Civ. Evid. 204, the court is respectfully requested to take judicial notice of these rules.

Respectfully submitted,

[Signature of attorney]

[Certificate of service]

[b] FORM: Order taking judicial notice

```
                           NO. _____
_____            §     IN THE DISTRICT COURT OF
                      §
vs.                   §     _____ COUNTY, TEXAS
                      §
_____            §     _____ JUDICIAL DISTRICT
```

ORDER ON REQUEST FOR JUDICIAL NOTICE

On this _____ day of _____, 20___, plaintiff [defendant] made a formal request that the court take judicial notice of [*insert rule, regulation, ordinance to be noticed*].

Notice of this request was served on opposing counsel, which notice has provided a reasonable opportunity to be heard.

After considering the request of plaintiff [defendant], the court has determined that judicial notice shall be taken as requested.

SIGNED this _____ day of _____, 20___.

[Signature of presiding judge]

§8.12 Pre-Trial Conferences

The authority to conduct a pre-trial conference is conferred on Texas courts by TEX. R. CIV. P. 166. At the conference, the court is empowered to consider any of the following matters:

(a) All pending dilatory pleas, motions and exceptions;

(b) The necessity or desirability of amendments to the pleadings;

(c) A discovery schedule;

(d) Requiring written statements of contentions of the parties;

(e) Contested issues of fact and simplification of the issues;

(f) The possibility of obtaining stipulations of fact;

(g) The identification of legal issues to be ruled upon;

(h) Exchange of a list of direct fact witness, including subject of testimony, the necessity of whose testimony cannot be determined before trial, and who will be called to testify;

(l) Expert witness lists indicating subject of testimony;

(j) Agreements and disagreements on issues of law;

(k) Proposed court's charge or findings of fact and conclusions of law;

(1) The marking and exchange of exhibits with stipulations as to their authenticity and admissibility;

(m) Written objections to exhibits;

(n) The settlement of the case;

(o) The advisability of referring certain issues to a master;

(p) Such other matters as may aid in the disposition of the case.

See TEX. R. CIV. P. 166.

The purpose of the rule is to provide a procedure to simplify and shorten trials and to limit the issues to those genuinely in dispute. *Provident Life & Acc. Ins. Co. v. Hazlitt*, 216 S.W.2d 805 (Tex. 1949). A court in a pre-trial conference cannot, however, adjudicate the merits of any issues raised by the pleadings without the agreement of the parties. *Mason v. Tobin*, 408 S.W.2d 243 (Tex. Civ. App.—Houston 1966, no writ).

A pre-trial conference can be called on motion of either party or on the court's own motion. TEX. R. CIV. P. 166; however, if a party moves the court to convene a pre-trial conference, the court has the discretion to deny the request. *Gaines v. Gaines*, 677 S.W.2d 727 (Tex. App.—Corpus Christi 1984, no writ). At the conclusion of the conference, the court may enter an order reflecting the rulings made at the conference. In DTPA cases, a pre-trial conference is a particularly appropriate forum for resolving questions that may be raised with respect to the adequacy of pre-filing notice and pleas in abatement that may have been filed as a result of a party's failure to allow another a reasonable opportunity to inspect the goods that are the subject of the lawsuit. *See* DTPA §17.505(a), as amended 1989.

Although a party generally is allowed to designate expert witnesses, "as soon as is practical, but in no event less than thirty (30) days prior to the beginning of trial," see Tex. R. Civ. P. 166b(6)(b), the court may order an earlier date for the disclosure of expert witnesses or any other matters relative to the trial, at the conclusion of a pre-trial conference. *Werner v. Miller*, 579 S.W.2d 455 (Tex. 1979); *see also* Tex. R. Civ. P. 166b(6)(c).

If a matter is considered at the pre-trial conference but is not ruled on by the court, then a party is at liberty to proceed as if no pre-trial conference on the question had occurred. *Mission Municipal Hospital v. Bryant*, 563 S.W.2d 293 (Tex. Civ. App.—Corpus Christi 1977) *on remand* at 575 S.W.2d 136 (Tex. Civ. App.—Corpus Christi 1978, no writ). For this reason, it is essential to obtain a ruling from the court on each matter presented and prepare an order for the court's signature at the conclusion of the hearing so that the time spent in the hearing will not be wasted.

[a] FORM: Motion for pre-trial conference

```
                              NO. _____
_____              §     IN THE DISTRICT COURT OF
                        §
vs.                     §     _____COUNTY, TEXAS
                        §
_____              §     _____ JUDICIAL DISTRICT
```

MOTION FOR PRE-TRIAL CONFERENCE

TO THE HONORABLE JUDGE OF THE DISTRICT COURT:

_____, plaintiff [defendant] requests that the court conduct a pre-trial conference in the above referenced lawsuit for the purpose of ruling on the following matters:

[*Insert matters to be considered, e.g.,*

1. Defendant's plea in abatement and the adequacy of plaintiff's pre-filing notice letter to defendant.

2. Defendant's special exceptions to plaintiff's Original Petition.

3. Plaintiff's special exceptions to defendant's Original Answer.

4. The admissibility of certain evidence.

5. The entry of a scheduling order with respect to:

   (a) Adding parties

(b) Designation of fact and expert witnesses

(c) Amending pleadings

(d) Completion of discovery

WHEREFORE, plaintiff [defendant] requests that a pre-trial conference be set for consideration of the matters listed above.

Respectfully submitted,

[Signature of attorney]

NOTICE OF PRE-TRIAL CONFERENCE SETTING

The pre-trial conference requested herein has been set for the _____ day of _____, 20___ at ___ o'clock __. m.

[Certificate of service]

[b] FORM: Order on pre-trial conference (general form)

	NO. _____	
_____	§	IN THE DISTRICT COURT OF
	§	
vs.	§	_____ COUNTY, TEXAS
	§	
_____	§	_____ JUDICIAL DISTRICT

ORDER

On the _____ day of _____, 20___, a pre-trial conference was held. At the conclusion of the conference and after hearing and considering the evidence and argument of counsel, the court is of the opinion and so finds that the following order should be entered;

IT IS THEREFORE ORDERED that:

1. [*Insert orders of the court*]

SIGNED this _____ day of _____, 20___.

[Signature of presiding judge]

[c] FORM: Scheduling order

```
                        NO. _____
                         §    IN THE DISTRICT COURT OF
_____             §
                         §
   vs.                   §    _____COUNTY, TEXAS
                         §
_____             §    _____ JUDICIAL DISTRICT
```

SCHEDULING ORDER

On this _____ day of _____, 20___, a pre-trial conference was held. At the conclusion of the conference and after hearing and considering the evidence and argument of counsel, the court is of the opinion and so finds that the following scheduling order should be entered;

IT IS THEREFORE ORDERED that:

1. All parties shall be joined no later than _____.

2. All expert witnesses shall be designated by the plaintiff no later than _____.

3. All expert witnesses shall be designated by the defendant no later than _____.

4. All discovery shall be completed no later than _____.

5. All pre-trial motions, except for motions in limine, shall be filed no later than _____.

6. A conference of attorneys shall be held no later than _____ for the purpose of determining whether any stipulations regarding the admissibility of evidence can be agreed upon.

This order shall remain in force unless modified for good cause shown.

SIGNED this _____ day of _____, 20___.

[Signature of presiding judge]

§8.13 Summary Judgment

If the material facts are not in dispute and the defendant is nevertheless entitled to judgment in his favor as a matter of law, the defendant should move for summary judgment. Under Rule 166a, *Texas Rules of Civil Procedure*, a defendant may move for summary judgment before trial if the undisputed evidence reflects that one or more of the elements of the plaintiff's cause of action is missing or if the undisputed facts establish a defendant's affirmative defense as a matter of law. *See Tex.R.Civ.P.* Rule 166a. Further, under Rule 166a(i), a defendant may move for summary judgment asserting that, despite having had an adequate opportunity to conduct discovery, the plaintiff still has "no evidence" to support one or more elements of his cause of action. *See Tex.R.Civ.P.* Rule 166a(i). A thorough review of the summary judgment procedure is beyond the scope of this treatise.

The following form for a motion for summary judgment based upon the affirmative defense that a plaintiff's independent investigation negates reliance as a matter of law, *see* §2.02.5, *supra*, may be modified as necessary to move for summary judgment on any other affirmative defense or to establish that one or more of the elements of the plaintiff's DTPA claim is lacking as a matter of law.

[a] Form: Motion for Summary Judgment on Independent Investigation

```
CAUSE No. _____
[Plaintiff 1] and [Plaintiff 2] §      IN THE DISTRICT COURT OF
PLAINTIFFS,                     §
V.                              §      _____ COUNTY, TEXAS
[Seller 1], [Seller 2],         §
[Defendant 1] AND               §
[Defendant 2] REALTORS          §
DEFENDANTS.                     §      _____ JUDICIAL DISTRICT
```

[DEFENDANT 1] AND [DEFENDANT 2] REALTORS' MOTION FOR SUMMARY JUDGMENT and NO EVIDENCE MOTION FOR SUMMARY JUDGMENT

TO THE HONORABLE JUDGE OF SAID COURT:

COME NOW [Defendant 1] and [Defendant 2] and hereby file their MOTION FOR SUMMARY JUDGMENT and in furtherance thereof would respectfully show unto this honorable Court as follows:

I. BACKGROUND

[Plaintiff 1] and his wife, [Plaintiff 2], have brought suit against Defendants alleging breach of express warranty, DTPA causes of action, breach of contract ([Sellers] only), statutory and common law fraud and negligent misrepresentation (Defendant 1] and [Defendant 2] only) arising out of the purchase of a home in _____, Texas. Defendants [Seller 1] and [Seller 2] owned the home that the Plaintiffs ultimately purchased. [Defendant 1] was the listing agent for the home and [Defendant 2] was [Defendant 1]'s broker in the transaction.

The Plaintiffs' case rests upon the MLS Listing Sheet that purports to represent that the [Sellers'] home has approximately 1,824 square feet of heated space. See Exhibit 1. The Plaintiffs do not allege that any defendant made verbal representations regarding the amount of square feet of the home. Both Plaintiffs conducted an independent investigation as to the accuracy of the square feet of the home—confirming through the _____ County Appraisal District's website that the square feet of the home on their rolls matched the square feet on the MLS Sheet. See Depo. of [Plaintiff 1] at pp. __,1. __ -__ and __,1.__ - p.__7,1.__, and Depo. of [Plaintiff 2] at p. __,1.__ -__ and p. __,1.__ -__). The Plaintiffs even lived in the home for 30 days before closing.

For the reasons more fully briefed below, Plaintiffs are unable to prevail on any cause of action asserted against [Defendant 1] or [Defendant 2] Realtors as a matter of law. Accordingly, this Court should grant summary judgment in Defendants' favor.

II. SUMMARY JUDGMENT STANDARDS

To prevail on a motion for summary judgment, the movant must establish that there is no genuine issue of material fact with regard to one or more essential elements of a particular cause of action. *See Brooks v. First Assembly of God Church*, 86 S.W.3d 793, 796 (Tex. App.—Waco 2002, pet. dismissed); *Larsen v. Carlene Langford & Assocs.*, 41 S.W.3d 245, 248-49 (Tex. App.—Waco 2001, pet. denied). When a trial court reviews a motion for summary judgment, three well-known principles apply: (1) the movant for summary judgment has the burden of showing that there is no genuine issue of material fact and that he is entitled to judgment as a matter of law; (2) in deciding whether there is a disputed material fact precluding summary judgment, evidence favorable to the nonmovant will be taken as true; and (3) every reasonable inference must be indulged in favor of the nonmovant and any doubts resolved in his favor. *Nixon v. Mr. Property Management Co.*, 690 S.W.2d 546, 548-49 (Tex. 1985). If the movant shows that no genuine issue of material fact exists and proves his entitlement to judgment, the burden shifts to the non-moving party to raise a fact issue to avoid summary judgment. *See Greene v. Thiet*, 846 S.W.2d 26, 29 (Tex. App.—San Antonio 1992, writ denied). If the nonmovant fails to raise a fact issue under those circumstances, the summary judgment must be granted. *Id.*

A no evidence motion for summary judgment may be filed after an adequate time for discovery has passed. *TEX. R. Civ. P.* 166a(i); *McClure v. Attebury*, 20 SW.3d 722, 727 (Tex. App.— Amarillo 1999, no pet.). When the motion is filed after the close of the discovery period set by pretrial order, there is a presumption that an adequate time for discovery has passed. *TEX. R. CIV. P.* 166a(i) Notes & Comments.

In the present instance, this no evidence motion for summary judgment is filed after a substantial amount of discovery has taken place, including the depositions of the Plaintiff and two representatives of the Defendants. Moreover, extensive written discovery has been exchanged, including disclosures, interrogatories, and requests for production. Accordingly, an adequate time for discovery has passed. When a movant files a no evidence motion for summary judgment, the burden shifts to the nonmovant to produce evidence sufficient to raise a genuine issue of material fact on the element(s) challenged. *In re Mohawk Rubber Co.*, 982 S.W.2d 494, 498 (Tex. App.—Texarkana 1998, orig. proceeding). If the nonmovant fails to meet this evidentiary burden, the motion must be granted. *Id.*

III. ARGUMENT AND AUTHORITIES

[Defendant 1] and [Defendant 2] are entitled to summary judgment on all claims asserted against them. Plaintiffs conducted an independent investigation into the square footage of the home, which negates any reliance they may have placed on the MLS Sheet. Moreover, the Plaintiffs signed a written statement which disclaimed any reliance on any statements, written or verbal, from [Defendant 1] and [Defendant 2]. For these reasons and those contained below, this Court should grant the Defendants' motion for summary judgment.

A. The Plaintiffs cannot prove reasonable reliance

The Plaintiffs are unable to prove, and are in fact barred from asserting, that they reasonably relied upon the purported statement in the MLS Sheet. Reasonable reliance is an element of every cause of action asserted against the [Defendant 1] and [Defendant 2] Defendants. *See Tex. Bus. & Com. Code* 17.50(a)(1)(B) (reliance essential element of DTPA laundry list actions); *Tex. Bus. & Com. Code* §27.01(a)(1)(B), (a)(2)(D) (reliance essential element of statutory fraud); *Schlumberger Tech. Corp. v. Swanson*, 959 S.W.3d 171, 182 (Tex. 1997) (same); *Haase v. Glazner*, 62 S.W.3d 795, 797-98 (Tex. 2001) (reliance essential element of fraudulent inducement claim); *Federal Land Bank Assn v. Sloan*, 825 S.W.2d 439, 442 (Tex. 1991) (reliance essential element of negligent misrepresentation claim).

1. Disclaimer Precludes Reasonable Reliance

The Plaintiffs executed a Disclaimer, attached hereto as Exhibit 4, which reads in pertinent part:

The Buyer is advised to verify all information important to him/her and to ask the appropriate questions of the appropriate authorities himself/herself or through an attorney with respect to important issues such as, but not limited to: . . . size of structure, size of rooms . . .

Having read the foregoing disclaimer, I/we, the prospective Buyer(s), by my/our signatures) below, state that I/we have not relied upon any statement given to me/us by the REALTOR and/or his/her associates with regard to the property, and my/our decision to make an offer on the property and to subsequently purchase the property is based on my/our independent decision with or without legal counsel. The foregoing disclaimer and this paragraph have been read by me/us or to me/us, and I/we freely sign my/our name(s) hereunder.

Id. Having so firmly and unequivocally disclaimed any reliance on the statements of [Defendant 1] and [Defendant 2], the Plaintiffs may not claim otherwise in this lawsuit.

2. The Plaintiffs' Independent Investigation Precludes Reasonable Reliance

In addition, the Plaintiffs are unable to prove reliance, an element for every cause of action against the [Defendant 1] and [Defendant 2], because they conducted their own independent investigation into the square footage of the home. [Plaintiff 1] testified that prior to closing he visited the _____ County Appraisal District's website and reviewed what the appraisal district listed as being the square footage of the home. See Depo. of [Plaintiff 1] at p. __, l.__ - p. __, l.__. The Plaintiffs admit that their decision to make an offer on the home and to subsequently purchase the property was based upon their own independent investigation. Id, at p. __,l. __ - p.__,l. _; see Depo. of [Plaintiff 2] at p. __,l.__ -__.

Texas courts have found in situations substantively identical to this case that the plaintiff's independent investigation precludes reliance upon statements made by a defendant. For example, in *Bartlett v. Schmidt*, 33 S.W.3d 35, 38 (Tex. Civ. App.—Corpus Christi 2000, pet. denied), the Corpus Christi court explained that:

Many courts have held that where false and fraudulent representations are made concerning the subject-matter of a contract, but the person to whom they are made, before closing the contract inspects and examines the subject of the contract, or conducts an independent investigation into the matters covered by the representations, which is sufficient to inform him of the truth, and which is not interfered with or rendered nugatory by any act of any other party, it is presumed that he places his reliance on the information acquired by such investigation and on his own judgment based on such facts, and not on the representations made to him, and therefore he cannot have relief because his bargain proves unsatisfactory to him.

Id. (*citing Marcus v. Kinabrew*, 438 S.W.2d 431, 432 (Tex. Civ. App.—Tyler 1969, no writ); *see also Kolb v. Texas Emp. Ins. Assn*, 585 S.W.2d 870, 872 (Tex. Civ. App.—Texarkana 1979, writ ref'd n.r.e.); *Lone Star Machinery Corp. v. Frankel*, 564 S.W.2d 135, 138 (Tex. Civ. App—Beaumont 1978, no writ); *M.L. Mayfield Petroleum Corp. v. Kelly*, 450 S.W.2d 104, 110 (Tex. Civ. App.—Tyler 1970, writ ref'd n.r.e.); *Mann v. Rugel*, 228 S.W.2d 585, 587 (Tex. Civ. App.—Dallas 1950, no writ)).

The common thread of these cases is that, regardless of the result of the independent investigation, the buyer's decision to undertake an independent investigation "indicates that he or she is not relying on the seller's representations." *Bartlett*, 33 SW.3d at 38. When the plaintiff investigates the information it received from the defendant, there is a presumption the plaintiff made his decision based on his own investigation instead of on the defendant's representation. *Id.*

In *Bartlett*, there was evidence that the buyer asked third parties to review conveyancing documents specifically to assure that no restrictions would interfere with his development of the property for his intended purpose. *Id.* He did this after specifically asking Bartlett about the very same thing. *Id.* The Corpus Christi court determined that this evidence sufficiently proved that the buyer did not rely on Bartlett's representations in making his decision to purchase the property. *Id.* As a matter of law, therefore, the court held that the buyer could not recover either negligent misrepresentation or fraud. *Id.*

The same is true here. Plaintiffs undertook to perform their own independent investigation into the square footage of the home. See Depo. of [Plaintiff 1] at p. __,1.__ - p. __, 1.__. In accordance with *Bartlett* and the other authorities cited above, this Court must therefore conclude as a matter of law that the Plaintiffs relied upon their own investigation and not upon any purported representation made by the Defendants. *Bartlett*, 33 S.W.3d at 38. As a matter of law, therefore, just like the plaintiff in *Bartlett*, the Plaintiffs are precluded from claiming any reliance on information provided by [Defendant 1] or [Defendant 2] regarding the square footage of the home. Without this element, all of Plaintiffs' claims fail.

V. CONCLUSION & PRAYER

All of the Plaintiffs' claims against [Defendant 1] and [Defendant 2] require the element of reliance. The summary judgment evidence establishes there is and can be no dispute that Plaintiffs conclusively disclaimed any reliance on Defendants' purported representations in deciding to purchase the house. Rather, Plaintiffs conducted their own independent investigation and as a result are barred from claiming reliance on Defendants as a matter of law. Accordingly, [Defendant 1] and [Defendant 2] would respectfully request that this Court enter judgment in favor of Defendants on all claims asserted against them by Plaintiffs in Defendants' favor and for any and all other relief, whether in law or in equity, to which Defendants may be justly entitled.

Respectfully submitted,

_____

[Attorney for Plaintiffs]

CERTIFICATE OF SERVICE

[b] Form: Response to Motion for Summary Judgment: Independent Investigation

	§	NO. _____
[PLAINTIFF 1] AND	§	IN THE DISTRICT COURT OF
[PLAINTIFF 2]	§	
Plaintiffs,	§	
	§	
VS.	§	XXXX COUNTY TEXAS
	§	
[SELLER 1], [SELLER 2]	§	
[DEFENDANT 1]	§	
AND [DEFENDANT 2]	§	
REALTORS	§	
Defendants.	§	XXXth JUDICIAL DISTRICT

<u>PLAINTIFFS' RESPONSE IN OPPOSITION TO DEFENDANTS'
MOTIONS FOR SUMMARY JUDGMENT</u>

TO THE HONORABLE JUDGE OF SAID COURT:

NOW COME [Plaintiff 1] and [Plaintiff 2], Plaintiffs herein, and make and file this their Response in Opposition to Defendants' Motion for Summary Judgment and No Evidence Motion for Summary Judgment, and for such, say unto the Court as follows:

I. SUMMARY OF ARGUMENT

Plaintiffs [Plaintiff 1] and [Plaintiff 2] bought a house in _____ in reliance upon statements contained in a written advertisement stating 1) that the house had 1,824 square feet, 2) that the price per square foot of the house was $65.52, and 3) that the house was priced "below market value." The MLS advertisement was prepared and distributed by [Defendant 1], a real estate agent with [Defendant 2] Realtors. In fact, the information was false: The correct square footage of the house is approximately 1,567 square feet and the resulting price per square foot was $76.26. There is ample summary judgment evidence that, at the express invitation of the Defendants, the Plaintiffs relied upon these statements, that they were material to their decision to purchase the house, and their reliance is not defeated, certainly not as a matter of law, by the arguments made. While the Plaintiffs disclaimed any reliance on their own real estate agent's [Buyers' Agent's] representations, the written disclaimer to that effect did not include these Defendants or their statements and does not "release" these Defendants from liability as claimed.

II. STATEMENTS OF FACTS

Plaintiffs entered into a standard TREC contract for the purchase of 2306 _____, a four bedroom single family residence in _____, Texas, on or about January 31, 2005. (Exhibit 9.) The sellers of that property, [Defendants Seller 1 and Seller 2], were represented by [Defendant 1], a real estate agent associated with and licensed through [Defendant 2] Realtors. (Deposition of [Defendant 1], p. __ l. __ to p. __, l.__; p. __, l.___ to p. __, l. __.) The [Plaintiffs], on the other hand, were represented by [Buyers' Agent], a real estate agent with [Buyer's Agency]. (Deposition of [Plaintiff 1], p. __ l. __ to p. __, l. __.)

The [Plaintiffs] first viewed the home on an afternoon in late January, 2005. When they entered the house, they found several copies of an MLS advertisement (Exhibit 1) prepared by [Defendant 1] on the kitchen bar along with her business cards. (Deposition of [Plaintiff 1], p. __, l. __ to p. __, l. __.) In looking for their first home to purchase, the [Plaintiffs] were very concerned that the home represent a good investment value. (Deposition of [Plaintiff 1], p. __, l. __ to p. __, l. __.) One indication of investment value they deemed extremely important was price per square foot. (Deposition of [Plaintiff 1], p. __, ll. __-__.) Thus, the written representations on the Defendants' advertisement that the house was priced at $65.52 per square foot (based upon $119,500 for 1,824 square feet) and was priced "below market value" were very material to them.

Unbeknownst to them, the house at 2306 _____ contained materially less square footage: just approximately 1,567 square feet. (Exhibit 12.) However, the Plaintiffs did not discover this discrepancy until after they had offered, contracted and closed on the house for a price of $119,200.00. (Deposition of [Plaintiff 1], p. __, ll. __-__.)

The written advertisement misstating the square footage and price per square foot of the house was prepared by [Defendant 1]. (Deposition of [Defendant 1], p. __, ll. __-__.) [Defendant 1] measured several rooms in the house with a digital/laser tool she has. (Deposition of [Defendant 1], p. __, l. __ - p. __, l. __.) She has testified that she obtained the amount of "1,824" for the approximate heated area from the _____ County Appraisal District's (____ CAD) website, and not from the [Seller Defendants] themselves. (Deposition of [Defendant 1], p. __, l. __ to p. __, l. __.) Although [Defendant 1] was provided with an opportunity to list ____ CAD as her source for this information, and routinely so qualifies such information, she did not do so on this advertisement. (Deposition of [Defendant 1}, p. __, l. __ to p. __, l.__.) As such, the amount of 1,824 was stated as unqualified fact without reference to its source. (Exhibit 1.) The $65.52 figure was automatically calculated by the software used to create the advertisement (Deposition of [Defendant 1], p. __, l. __ to p. __, l.__), but the remarks statement, "below market value," was a statement [Defendant 1] added on her own. (Deposition of [Defendant 1], p.___, ll.__-__.)

For their part, the [Plaintiffs] did not know and they were never informed that [Defendant 1] had obtained this (now known to be incorrect) information from the ____ CAD website. (Deposition of [Plaintiff 1], p. __, l. __ to p. __, l.__.) While [Plaintiff 1] visited the ____ CAD website to review tax information, he did not do so prior to entering into the contract to purchase the house nor within the option period given by that contract. (Deposition of [Plaintiff 1], p. __, l. ___to p.___, l.__.) [Plaintiff 1] did view ____ CAD's website prior to closing to look at the property tax history. (Deposition of [Plaintiff 1], p.__, ll.__-__.) While he saw that ____ CAD had the square footage listed at 1,824, he was not using ____ CAD's information to "independently investigate" that information (Deposition of [Plaintiff 1], p.___, ll. _-__) or to "verify" the square footage (Deposition of [Plaintiff 1], p. __, ll. __-__.). ____ CAD's website properly disclaims the accuracy of that type of information (Deposition of [Plaintiff 1], p.___, ll. __-__; p. __, ll. __-__.)

In conjunction with making their first offer on the house, the [Plaintiffs] were asked, by their agent, [Buyers' Agent], to execute a disclaimer from [Buyers' Agent's] Company, Inc. concerning statements made by [Buyers' Agent's] Company, Inc. and [Buyers' Agent]. (Exhibit 4; Deposition of [Plaintiff 1], p. __, ll.__ to p.___, l. __.) As explained to the [Plaintiffs] by [Buyers' Agent], the term "Realtor" in this document referred to [Buyers' Agent] and her company and "had nothing to do with the other real estate company involved." (Deposition of [Plaintiff], p. __, ll. __-__.) Specifically, the [Plaintiffs] and [Buyers' Agent] clearly understood that the term "Realtor" in that document did not refer to [Defendants]. (Deposition of [Plaintiff 1], p.___, ll. _-_.)

[Defendant 1] agrees that home buyers like the [Plaintiffs] are interested in price per square foot of a house when making a purchasing decision. (Deposition of [Defendant 1], p. __, l. __ to p. __, l.__.) At $65.52 per square foot, the [Sellers'] house was priced below the market value of other houses in its area. (Deposition of [Defendant 1], p. __, ll.__-__.) [Defendant 1] believes the [Plaintiffs] and their agent would be justified in relying upon the information in the MLS advertisement. (Deposition of [Defendant 1], p. __, ll. __-__.) She agrees that, without stating the source of the information, a buyer looking at the square footage figure on the MLS advertisement might think that she had measured it. (Deposition of [Defendant 1], p. __, l. __ to p. __, l.__.) [Defendant 1] attended the closing on the house. (Deposition of [Defendant 1], p. __, ll. __-__.) Nothing was said to or given to the [Plaintiffs] at or prior to the closing to let the [Plaintiffs] know that the square footage on the MLS advertisement at 1,824 square feet was incorrect. (Deposition of [Defendant1], p. __, l. __ to p. __, l. __.)

III. ARGUMENT AND AUTHORITIES

A. Occupations Code Section 1101.805 Not a Defense to [Defendant's] Misrepresentations.

Defendants' reliance upon *Texas Occupation Code* §1101.805 is misplaced. Section 1101.805(e) is designed to protect real estate agents from liability for misrepresentations made by their clients unless the real estate agent knows that the client has made a misrepresentation. Thus, Section 1101.805(e) protects a "license holder" from liability for a misrepresentation or concealment of a material fact made by a "party." "Party" is defined in Section 1101.551 to mean "a prospective buyer, seller, landlord, or tenant . . . ," and "does not include a license holder who represents a party." *Texas Occupation Code* §1101.551(2) (LEXIS 2006).

Here, the misrepresentation of the square footage was made in the MLS advertisement prepared by [Defendant 1] herself. (Deposition of [Defendant 1], p. __, ll. __-__; p. __, ll. __-__.) Thus, because the misrepresentation was "made by" [Defendant 1]—and not "made by" the [Sellers]—limitations of Section 1101.805 are unavailable to these Defendants. *Coldwell Banker Whiteside Assoc. v. Ryan Equity Partners, Ltd.*, 181 S.W.3d 879, 891 (Tex.App.—Dallas 2006, n.w.h.) (real estate agent was liable for its own misrepresentations despite Section 1101.805).

Because Section 1101.805 is inapplicable to shield these Defendants from their own misrepresentations, Defendants' no evidence motion with respect to actual awareness of the falsity of the misrepresentation also fails.

B. Disclaimer of Reliance on [Buyer's Agent's] Representations Ineffective to Disclaim Reliance on [Seller's Agent's] Misrepresentations.

In their zeal to hide behind the disclaimer executed by the [Plaintiffs] in favor of [the buyers' agents], Defendants misrepresent the nature of the document and completely disregard the facts surrounding its execution. First and foremost, neither [Defendant 1] nor [Defendant 2] are expressly named in this disclaimer. (Exhibit 4.) Rather, the form uses the term "REALTOR" as its beneficiary. (Exhibit 4.) To be certain that the term "REALTOR" referred only to [Buyers' Agents], the [Plaintiffs] specifically asked [Buyers' Agent]. (Deposition of [Plaintiff 1], p. __, ll. __-__; Deposition of [Plaintiff 1], p. __, ll.__-__.) The [Plaintiffs]' and [Buyers' Agent's] clear understanding was that the disclaimer had nothing to do with [Defendant 1] or [Defendant 2]. (Deposition of [Plaintiff], p. __, l.___ to p.___, l. __; Deposition of [Plaintiff 2], p.___, l.___ to p.___, l.__.) [Defendant 1] also understood that the disclaimer referred to [Buyers' Agents] and not her and [Defendant 2]. (Deposition of [Defendant 1], p. 39, l. 17 to p. 40, l. 14.) In fact, [Defendant 2] subsequently began using its own disclaimer form after this dispute arose. (Deposition of [Defendant 1], p. 40, ll. 16-23.)

[Defendant 1] and [Defendant 2] may strain their credibility by arguing to the jury in this case that this disclaimer applies to them as well. Their doing so, however, does nothing more than create a fact issue, and certainly does not defeat the [Plaintiffs'] reliance upon the MLS advertisement prepared by [Defendant 1] as a matter of law. Nor does it establish a "quasi-estoppel" as a matter of law. As such, summary judgment on either theory based upon this purported "release" is inappropriate.

C. No "Independent Investigation" Precludes Reliance as a Matter of Law.

Defendants rely upon *Bartlett v. Schmidt*, 33 S.W.3d 35 (Tex. App.—Corpus Christi 2000, pet. denied), for the proposition that a buyer's "independent investigation" negates reliance. Defendants then point to [Plaintiff 1's] visit to the _____ CAD website as a "independent investigation" negating reliance as a matter of law. (Motion at p. 7.) This argument is defective for several reasons.

First of all, the authority of *Bartlett* has been questioned by the Fourteenth Court of Appeals in *Warehouse Assocs. Corporate Ctr. II, Inc. v. Celotex Corp.*, 192 S.W.3d 225, 244 (Tex.App.—Houston [14th Dist.] 2006, pet. filed). In declining to follow *Bartlett,* the Houston Court of Appeals stated:

To the extent *Bartlett, Marcus [v. Kinabrew*, 438 S.W.2d 431 (Tex.Civ.App.—Tyler 1969, no writ)], or other cases cited therein hold that a buyer's independent investigation, without more, is sufficient as a matter of law to defeat an assertion that the seller fraudulently induced the buyer to enter into the contract, these cases are contrary to *Prudential [Ins. Co.*

of Am. v. Jefferson Assoc., Ltd., 896 S.W.2d 156 (Tex. 1995)], Schlumber [*Technology Corp. v. Swanson*, 959 S.W.2d 171 (Tex. 1997)], and cases cited therein.

Id. at 244-45. As such, *Bartlett's* draconian "independent investigation" holding is suspect.

Secondly, the language specifically quoted in *Bartlett* by Defendants actually defeats Defendants' own argument. Even *Bartlett* would require that this "independent investigation" be "sufficient to inform him [the claimant] of the truth . . ." *Bartlett*, 33 S.W.3d at 38. As posited by both [Plaintiff 1] (Deposition of [Plaintiff 1], p. __, l. __ to p. __, l. __) and [Defendant 2] in his first affidavit (Defendants' Motion, Tab 5), _____ CAD's website listed the square footage at "1,824," the exact misrepresented figure in the Defendants' MLS advertisement. (Exhibit 1.) In fact, Defendants go to some length to extol the virtuosity of _____ CAD's square footage information. (*See* Motion, Tab 7, Affidavit of [Defendant 2], and Tab 8, Affidavit of [Witness 2].) Clearly, _____ CAD's website was *not* sufficient to inform the [Plaintiffs] of the truth—their prospective house had more than 250 square feet less than as represented—and certainly not as a matter of law.

Thirdly, Defendants mischaracterize the summary judgment evidence in an attempt to squeeze it into the "independent investigation" concept championed in *Bartlett*. Defendants would equate the phrase in the [Buyers' Agents'] disclaimer, "independent decision with/without legal counsel" as the "independent investigation" described in *Bartlett*, presumably because they both use the word "independent." In *Bartlett*, the plaintiff was denied recovery because he in fact consulted a lawyer concerning the legal effect of some deed restrictions. *Id.* 33 S.W.3d at 37. Here, the [Plaintiffs] testified that they did *not* consult with a lawyer, but Defendants somehow insist their "independent decision" is now the same "independent investigation" described in *Bartlett*. (Motion at pp. 7, 9.)

A fairer reading of the [Plaintiffs'] deposition testimony reveals that they did not conduct an "independent investigation" sufficient to inform them of the true square footage of the house, and it certainly does not reflect that they did so as a matter of law. [Plaintiff] testified he did not conduct an independent investigation, that he did not consult the _____ CAD website to verify the square footage statements, and that the _____ CAD website disclaims accuracy and is not a method of verifying the square footage of a home. (Deposition of [Plaintiff 1], p.__, ll.__9-__.) For her part, [Plaintiff 2] also did nothing to verify or investigate the square footage of the house. (Deposition of [Plaintiff 2], p. __, ll.__-__.) For all of these reasons, the Defendants' argument that an "independent investigation" occurred which somehow precludes the Plaintiffs from establishing reliance on Defendants' MLS advertisement as a matter of law fails. At most, triable issues of fact exist on this issue which must be decided by the jury.

D. DTPA Section 17.506 Inapplicable Where No Notice Given to Plaintiffs.

Defendants assert that they gave reasonable and timely written notice to Plaintiffs of their reliance upon information from "official government records" (____ CAD) to establish the defense of DTPA Section 17.506 as a matter of law. To do so, Defendants again attempt to burrow themselves into the [Buyers' Agent's] disclaimer (Exhibit 4), despite the patent inapplicability of that document to them and the clear summary judgment evidence to the contrary. As set forth in Section III B of Argument and Authorities above, the [Buyer's Agent's] disclaimer does not apply to or benefit [Defendant 1] or [Defendant 2]. Moreover, the bare mention of "governmental authorities" in the [Buyers' Agent's] disclaimer is insufficient to meet the exacting standard given by Section 17.506(a)(1). [Defendant 1] had every opportunity to list _____ CAD as her source for the square footage stated on the MLS advertisement but did not do so. (Deposition of [Defendant 1], p. __, l. __ to p. ___, l. ___.) For all of these reasons, Defendants' attempt at summary judgment on Section 17.506 defense fails as a matter of law.

E. Mere Occupancy of House Does Not Equate to Perfect Knowledge of Square Footage

As explained by [Plaintiff 2], the [Defendant 3] asked the Bradfords to take over payments and rent the house from them prior to closing so that the [Defendant 3] could avoid another house payment. (Deposition of [Plaintiff 2], p.__, ll. __-__.) Even so, the [Plaintiffs] did not measure the house before closing to see if it conformed to the represented square footage. (Deposition of [Plaintiff 2], p. __, ll.__-__.) Defendants cite no legal precedent establishing that mere occupancy of a structure equates to perfect knowledge of the structure's square footage, as they apparently argue here. In the absence of any such authority, the best Defendants can salvage from this argument is the creation of a fact issue for the jury to decide.

IV. CONCLUSION AND PRAYER

For all of the foregoing reasons, Plaintiffs pray that Defendants' Motion for Summary Judgment and No Evidence Motion for Summary Judgment be, in all respects, denied, and for such other and further relief to which they may show themselves justly entitled.

>   Respectfully submitted,

>   _____

>   [Attorney for Plaintiffs]

CERTIFICATE OF SERVICE

Chapter 9

Trial: Part One — Voir Dire to Close of Evidence

§ 9.01 Jury Selection
§ 9.02 Challenges to Jurors
§ 9.03 Exemptions from Jury Service
§ 9.04 Voir Dire Examination
§ 9.05 Scope of Voir Dire Examination
§ 9.06 Sources of Information on Jurors
§ 9.07 Collecting the Information
§ 9.08 General Voir Dire Questions
§ 9.09 Communicating Concepts
§ 9.10 Introducing the Participants
§ 9.11 Opening Statement (Plaintiff)
§ 9.12 Opening Statement (Defendant)
§ 9.13 Objections in Voir Dire
    [a] CHECKLIST: Voir dire objections
§ 9.14 Preserving Error
§ 9.15 The Case-in-Chief
§ 9.16 Order of Testimony
§ 9.17 Direct Examination
§ 9.18 Cross Examination
§ 9.19 Objections to Evidence
    [a] CHECKLIST: Objections to evidence
§ 9.20 Proof of Attorney's Fees
  § 9.20.1 Keep Detailed Accurate Records
  § 9.20.2 Draft Fee Agreement to Support Award
  § 9.20.3 Present Attorneys as Expert Witnesses
    § 9.20.3.1 Independent Expert
    § 9.20.3.2 Trial Counsel as Witness
  § 9.20.4 Segregate DRPA Fees From Non-Recoverable Attorney's Fees
  § 9.20.5 Present *Arthur Andersen* Factors to Jury
  § 9.20.6 Contingency Fee and Lodestar Evidence
  § 9.20.7 Contingency Fee, Percentage of Recovery
  § 9.20.8 Attorney's Fees for Appeals
  § 9.20.9 Uncontroverted Testimony May Establish Amount of Recoverable Attorney's Fees as a Matter of Law
  § 9.20.10 Form – Outline for Narrative Testimony on Attorney's Fees

§9.01 Jury Selection

Although the title to this section is jury selection, the phrase actually is a misnomer. *Juror deselection* is a more appropriate description. From the first assembly of the jury panel until a jury ultimately is seated, a winnowing process occurs by which unqualified and as many otherwise unacceptable jurors are removed from the panel as possible.

There are a number of rules of thumb that attorneys have used through the years in selecting juries. Plaintiffs' juries generally are thought of as blue collar, *e.g.*, factory workers, union members, secretaries, and others on the lower end of the economic scale. Defense juries, on the other hand, generally are thought of as white collar, *e.g.*, bankers, doctors, and others on the upper end of the economic scale. Although doctors and bankers *probably* would make poor plaintiffs' jurors in any type of case, these rules of thumb cannot be trusted in DTPA litigation. Consumer transactions cut across too many social and economic lines to allow many stereotypes about DTPA jurors. A doctor who relies on an accounting firm for investment advice may be an ideal juror when the plaintiff has been defrauded by his accountant. A factory worker who must raise his or her family in a mobile home may be unsympathetic when the case involves construction defects in a ten bedroom mansion. The profile of a good or bad DTPA juror that will be used in juror selection must be developed on a case-by-case basis.

The selection (or deselection) of jurors is a two-step process which is begun by an examination of the panel by the court and concluded by an examination of the panel by the parties.

Prior to the selection of the panel for a particular trial, all panel members typically are gathered into one or two large courtrooms for the purpose of determining their basic legal qualifications to sit on a jury. The judge who conducts this examination normally will inquire into the eight criteria listed below. The fact that this is normal practice, however, does not relieve attorneys of the obligation to qualify jurors during the voir dire examination. *Guzman v. State*, 649 S.W.2d 77 (Tex. App.—Corpus Christi 1982, no writ); *Mitchell v. Burleson*, 466 S.W.2d 646 (Tex. Civ. App.—Beaumont 1971, writ ref'd n.r.e.).

The basic statutory qualifications are:

1. At least 18 years of age;

2. Citizen of Texas and of the county in which the juror is to serve;

3. Qualified to vote in the county in which the juror is to serve;

4. Of sound mind and good moral character;

5. Able to read and write [English];

[NOTE: Although the statute does not specify English, clearly this was the intent, and it has been held that if a juror cannot read and write the English language then the juror should be excused for cause. *Guzman v. State, supra.*]

6. Not served as a petit juror for six days during the preceding three months in the county court or during the preceding six months in the district court;

7. Has not been convicted of a felony; and

8. Is not under indictment or other legal accusation of misdemeanor theft or any other felony.

TEX. GOV'T CODE §62.102.

Legal blindness is not an automatic disqualification; however, if the needs of the particular case require sighted jurors, then the judge is empowered to disqualify a prospective juror who is legally blind. *See* TEX. GOV'T CODE §62.104.

§9.02 Challenges to Jurors

After a panel of individuals which meets the minimum qualifications for jury service has been assembled, the parties must determine during voir dire those individuals who are legally disqualified in the particular case, or who, in the opinions of the parties, demonstrate that they are inappropriate jurors for the particular case.

There are two types of challenges to jurors: challenges for cause and peremptory challenges. TEX. R. CIV. P. 227. A challenge for cause alleges facts demonstrating that the juror is legally disqualified or that he or she is otherwise unfit to serve on the jury. TEX. R. CIV. P. 228. Whether a juror who is not legally disqualified is, nevertheless, an "unfit person" to sit on a jury is left to the discretion of the court. See TEX. R. CIV. P. 228; *Compton v. Henrie*, 364 S.W. 2d 179, 182 (Tex. 1963).

There is no limit on the number of challenges for cause a party can make.

A peremptory challenge is a challenge other than "for cause" which does not assign any reason for the challenge. TEX. R. CIV. P. 232. Each side, as a general rule, is entitled to six peremptory challenges in state district court. TEX. R. CIV. P. 233.

The Texas Government Code lists other particular factors that will legally disqualify a prospective juror in a particular case and thus provide an opportunity for a successful challenge for cause. TEX. GOV'T CODE §62.105. These factors are:

1. The juror is or will be a witness in the case.

2. The juror is interested, directly or indirectly, in the subject matter of the case.

A typical example of a juror who has an "interest" in the case is a stockholder of a corporate defendant. *See Texas Power & Light Co. v. Adams*, 404 S.W.2d 930 (Tex. Civ. App.—Tyler 1966, no writ). Also, a person has an "interest" in the case if he or she carries insurance with a company and may be subject to a special assessment or fewer dividends if the company loses. *Texas Employers' Ins. Ass'n v. Lane*, 251 S.W.2d 181 (Tex. Civ. App.—Fort Worth 1952, writ ref'd n.r.e.).

3. The juror is related by consanguinity or affinity within the third degree to a party in the case.

This disqualification has been strictly construed. For example, a juror whose brother was married to the sister of the plaintiff's wife was held not to be related by "affinity" to the plaintiff. *Texas Employers' Ins. Ass'n v. McMullin*, 279 S.W.2d 699 (Tex. Civ. App.—San Antonio 1955, writ ref'd n.r.e.).

4. The juror has a prejudice in favor of or against a party in the case.

To disqualify a juror for bias or prejudice, it must be shown that the state of mind of the juror leads to a natural inference that he or she will not be impartial. *Compton v. Henrie*, 364 S.W.2d 179 (Tex. 1963). Once bias or prejudice is shown, however, the juror is disqualified as a matter of law and should be discharged even if the juror testifies that he can set the bias aside and provide a fair trial. *Carpenter v. Wyatt Constr. Co.*, 501 S.W.2d 748 (Tex. Civ. App.—Houston [14th Dist.] 1973, writ ref'd n.r.e.). Obviously, an employee of a party should be disqualified as a matter of law. *Preston v. Ohio Oil Co.*, 121 S.W.2d 1039 (Tex. Civ. App.—Eastland 1938, writ ref'd).

A juror may also be disqualified if he or she has a bias against the subject matter of the litigation. *Compton v. Henrie, supra; Ramirez v. Wood*, 577 S.W. 2d 278 (Tex. Civ. App.—Corpus Christi 1978, no writ). In DTPA cases, it is not unusual to encounter jurors who have had experiences very similar to those of the parties. A juror may own a house that has a cracked foundation and have personal experience with the frustration of trying to get a response from the builder or the insurer. A juror may have purchased a new automobile only to find that the automobile was a lemon. Some jurors who are business owners may have been sued under the DTPA and have a personal distaste for the statute and those that use it. Jurors who demonstrate bias toward the subject matter of the lawsuit should be removed since that bias inevitably will affect the juror's decisions during the trial.

5. The juror served as a petit juror in a former trial of the same case or in another case involving the same questions of fact.

TEX. GOV'T CODE §62.105.

Unlike challenges for cause, peremptory challenges are subjective in nature. They are "prompted by intuition, and are in spontaneous reaction to a juror's background, appearance, personality, prior contacts, and perceived attitude." *Patterson Dental Co. v. Dunn*, 592 S.W. 2d 914, 921 (Tex. 1979).

As discussed in §9.04 *infra*, one of the primary purposes of voir dire examination is to gain sufficient information to intelligently exercise peremptory challenges.

§9.03 Exemptions from Jury Service

Certain people may claim an exemption from jury service although they are under no compulsion to do so. Some of the exemptions presently allowed by law are:

1. Over 65 years of age;

2. Has legal custody of a child or children younger than 10 years of age and service on the jury requires leaving the child or children without adequate supervision;

3. Is a student of a public or private secondary school; or

4. Is enrolled and in actual attendance at an institution of higher education; and

5. Physical or mental impairment (requires a statement from a physician).

TEX. GOV'T CODE §62.106, §62.109.

The Government Code gives judges wide discretion in allowing people to avoid jury duty even though they may otherwise qualify to serve. This catch-all authority is provided in TEX. GOV'T CODE §62.1 10(a) which provides that ". . . a court may hear any reasonable sworn excuse of a prospective juror and release him from jury service entirely or until another day of the term." This authority frequently is exercised for teachers at the beginning of a school term, doctors whose patients' health may be affected by their absence, and others similarly situated. The exercise of the authority is discretionary with the judge.

One reason for avoiding jury duty given by some prospective jurors who otherwise are qualified to serve is economic necessity. For example, a small business owner who is called for jury duty may have no one to operate the business in his or her absence. Surprisingly, the statutes are not lenient with such a juror: each party of record must be present and must approve of the release of the juror when the basis for the release is economic necessity. TEX. GOV'T CODE §62. 1 10(c). It is difficult to imagine any plaintiff or defendant wanting such a person on a jury since the juror may be tempted to punish one side or the other, or may be too preoccupied with personal concerns to be attentive. For this reason, both parties usually are willing to agree to the release of the juror.

§9.04 Voir Dire Examination

The voir dire examination of the jury panel is a critically important part of the trial. Voir dire examination is important not only because of the information which can be gained *from* individual panel members, but also because of the information which can be communicated *to* panel members during the examination.

Voir dire examination has three primary purposes:

- Determine whether a juror is disqualified

- Provide information to attorneys and parties for the intelligent exercise of peremptory challenges

- Communicate favorably with the panel so that the jury ultimately selected will be receptive to the evidence and argument

The importance of voir dire is underscored by the belief of many experienced trial attorneys that strong juror opinions about the case frequently are formed during or by the end of the opening statements. If these early opinions are adverse to the client's case, the job of persuading the jury to find for the client is considerably more difficult. Thus, in addition to the purposes listed above, a fourth should be added and that is to *persuade* the jury.

§9.05 Scope of Voir Dire Examination

As stated above, the attorneys in each case have the responsibility to insure that each prospective juror possesses the minimum statutory qualifications so that jurors who do not may be removed from the panel for cause. See §§9.02, 9.03 *supra*. Additionally, however, each side in a jury case in district court generally has six peremptory challenges.

TEX. R. CIV. P. 233. Thus, voir dire provides the opportunity to obtain information so that peremptory strikes can be used intelligently. *Wise v. City of Abilene*, 141 S.W.2d 400 (Tex. Civ. App.—Eastland 1940, writ dism'd). For these reasons, broad latitude in questioning the jury panel is allowed. *Babcock v. Northwest Memorial Hospital*, 767 S. W. 2d 705, 709 (Tex. 1989); *Texas Employers Ins. Ass'n v. Loesch*, 538 S.W.2d 435 (Tex. Civ. App.—Waco 1976, writ ref'd n.r.e.).

There is no statute or rule of civil procedure that spells out directly the manner in which voir dire examinations are to be conducted. Thus, the legal principles which govern voir dire are drawn, for the most part, from case law. *See generally*, Bush, *Limitations on Voir Dire in Civil Cases*, 45 TEX. BAR. J. 1043 (1982).

Three primary legal principles related to voir dire examination deserve special consideration:

- The court has wide discretion in regulating voir dire

- Objections generally are essential to preserve error

- There are clear "stop signs" that an attorney may not run during voir dire

(1) *Discretion of trial court*

Wide discretion is vested in the trial court in the conduct of the voir dire examination. *Babcock v. Northwest Memorial Hospital*, 767 S.W. 2d 705, 709 (Tex. 1989); *Zeh v. Singleton*, 650 S.W.2d 518, 519 (Tex. App.—Houston [14th Dist.] 1983, no writ). The court's ruling during voir dire will be disturbed on appeal only if there is an abuse of discretion. *Texas & N.O.R. Co. v. Broadway*, 345 S.W.2d 814, 821 (Tex. Civ. App.—Beaumont 1961, no writ). For example, in *Zeh v. Singleton, supra*, the appellate court upheld the trial court's unusual approach of structuring the voir dire examination by directing the plaintiff and defendant to each give brief opening statements, followed by general questions by the plaintiff and then general questions by the defendant, and lastly, specific questions by the parties ("if necessary").

(2) *Preserving error*

In order to preserve error which may occur during voir dire, counsel must object. *Texas Employers' Ins. Ass'n v. Schanen* 263 S.W.2d 614 (Tex. Civ. App.—San Antonio 1953, no writ). Further, the voir dire examination must be transcribed in the statement of facts. *Lauderdale v. Insurance Co. of North America*, 527 S.W.2d 841 (Tex. Civ. App.—Fort Worth 1975, writ ref'd n.r.e.). Once error is shown, for it to be reversible error, the complaining party must demonstrate that it was reasonably calculated to and probably did cause the rendition of an improper judgment. *Texas Employers Ins. Ass'n v. Loesch*, 538 S.W.2d 435 (Tex. Civ. App.—Waco 1976, writ ref'd n.r.e.).

Objections may be required to preserve error; even so, objections during voir dire should be made only if absolutely necessary. If frequent objections are made, and especially if the objections are not sustained, the jury panel may resent the apparent interference with opposing counsel's voir dire.

(3) *"Stop signs"*

There are certain fixed rules that should not be violated during the voir dire examination. The prohibitions are clearly defined, for the most part, and violating these prohibitions unnecessarily risks reversal.

(a) *It is improper to seek a definite commitment from a juror to decide a case a certain way.*

See *Lassiter v. Bouche*, 41 S.W. 2d 88, 90 (Tex. Civ. App.—Dallas 1931, writ ref'd); *Postell v. State*, 663 S.W.2d 552, 555 (Tex. App.—Houston [1st Dist.] 1983, aff'd 693 S.W.2d 462 (Tex. Crim. App. 1985); *Campbell v. Campbell*, 215 S.W. 134, 136-138 (Tex. Civ. App.—Dallas 1919, writ ref'd).

This rule prohibits a voir dire question such as, "assuming that the evidence shows that the house has a crack In the foundation, will you find that it was not constructed in a good and workmanlike manner?" Conversely, however, there is no error in asking a juror whether, regardless of what the evidence shows, would he or she be unable to find that the house was not built in a good and workmanlike manner. An affirmative answer to this question is tantamount to a showing of bias or prejudice.

(b) *Questions which are designed to direct the attention of the jurors to a difference in the financial ability of the parties are improper.*

See *Texas & N.O.R. Co. v. Lide*, 117 S.W.2d 479 (Tex. Civ. App.—Waco 1938, no writ). This rule does not prohibit advising the jury of the wealth of the defendant when exemplary or punitive damages are sought. See *Lunsford v. Morris*, 746 S.W.2d 471 (Tex. 1988). Of course, a significant difference in wealth will be apparent to the jury without anything being said.

(c) *The mentioning of insurance coverage is error.*

See *Patterson v. East Texas Motor Freight Lines*, 349 S.W.2d 634 (Tex. Civ. App.—Beaumont 1961, writ ref'd n.r.e.). *A. J. Miller Trucking Co. v. Wood*, 474 S.W.2d 768 (Tex. Civ. App.—Tyler 1971, writ ref'd n.r.e.). Much creativity has gone into devising methods of getting around this rule. For example, "are any of the panel members in the business of adjusting *insurance* claims?". See *Dallas R. & T. Co. v. Flowers*, 284 S.W.2d 160 (Tex. Civ. App.—Waco 1955, writ ref'd n.r.e.). Or, "is anyone on the jury panel employed by an insurance company?". See *Johnson v. Reed*, 464 S.W.2d 689 (Tex. Civ. App.—Dallas

1971, writ ref'd n.r.e.). *cert. denied*, 405 U.S. 981 (1972). If a question is asked for the purpose of (or if it has the effect of) injecting insurance into the case, the question is improper. *Cf. Brown v. Poff*, 387 S.W.2d 101 (Tex. Civ. App.—El Paso, *writ ref'd n.r.e. per curiam*, 3 92 S.W.2d 113 (Tex. 1965). In *Brown*, the voir dire examination revealed that two jurors were employed in the insurance business. As a result of the examination, one juror was excused because of his inability to be free of bias. The court held that the examination did not necessarily focus the jury panel's attention on the fact that liability insurance may be involved; therefore, no mistrial was required.

In certain cases the jury panel may properly be questioned on the "liability insurance crisis" since this does not necessarily inject insurance into the case. *Babcock v. Northwest Memorial Hospital*, 767 S.W. 2d 705 (Tex. 1989).

(d) *Questions which advise the jury of the effect of their answers are improper.*

See Texas Emp. Ins. Ass'n v. Loesch, 538 S.W.2d 435 (Tex. Civ. App.—Waco 1976, writ ref'd n.r.e.).

(e) *Questions which show that a panel member has been convicted of an offense that disqualifies him or her, or that the panel member has been charged with theft or any felony are improper.*

See TEX. R. CIV. P. 230.

(f) *Matters that are not admissible in evidence may not be discussed.*

Inadmissible evidence should not be referred to In voir dire. Thus, for example, a comment during voir dire that a party has been indicted is reversible error. *Christie v. Brewer*, 374 S.W.2d 908 (Tex. Civ. App.—Austin 1964, writ ref'd n.r.e.).

Settlement agreements generally are inadmissible in evidence, *McGuire v. Commercial Union Ins. Co. of N.Y.*, 431 S.W. 2d 347, 352 (Tex. 1968); therefore, settlement offers, negotiations or agreements may not be discussed in voir dire. *Clayton v. Volkswagenwerk, A.G.*, 606 S.W.2d 15, 17-18 (Tex. Civ. App.—Houston [1st Dist.] 1980, writ ref'd n.r.e.). The exception to this general rule arises when two of the ostensibly adverse parties (normally a plaintiff and one of the defendants) have entered into a "Mary Carter" agreement under which the plaintiff has assigned to the settling defendant a percentage of the recovery. Obviously, the jury is entitled to hear the settling defendant's evidence and argument in light of the party's financial stake in the outcome of the case. *City of Houston v. Sam P. Wallace and Co.*, 585 S.W.2d 669, 673-674 (Tex. 1979).

(g) *Any matter excluded by an order on a motion in limine is prohibited.*

§9.06 Sources of Information on Jurors

There are occasional DTPA cases in which the amount in controversy justifies exhaustive research on the jury panel. There are firms available who are equipped to investigate the backgrounds of individual panel members, develop juror profiles for particular cases, determine community attitudes toward types of cases, conduct practice trials with individuals drawn from the community in which the actual trial will occur, and even place "shadow" jurors in the courtroom to monitor the effect of evidence and other events during the actual trial. There are some, but not many, DTPA cases in which such an investment is justified. Instead, in most DTPA cases, the type of juror desired will be determined from instinct, experience and common sense. And, information about individual panel members will be developed, if at all, in the courtroom after the case is called for trial.

There are three basic sources of information on prospective jurors:

- the juror information card

- personal knowledge of the attorneys or parties of individual panel members

- information developed and observations made during the voir dire examination

Most counties use juror information cards that are completed by panel members prior to or during the initial assembly with the judge. The cards contain a wealth of information and should be studied carefully. A commonly used juror information card contains the following information:

- Name, address and telephone number

- Age

- Marital status (and number and sex of children)

- Religious affiliation

- Occupation and length of employment

- Spouse's occupation

- Length of residency in county

- Relationship, if any, to law enforcement officers

- Prior jury service, civil and criminal

- Prior litigation experience as a party

- Prior involvement as an accused, complainant or witness in a criminal case

- History, if any, of bodily injury requiring medical attention

If any of the information listed above is not on the juror information card used in a particular county, the subjects omitted should be asked about during voir dire because each subject is important.

The parties and attorneys in a case should study each panel member carefully to determine whether the parties or attorneys have had any prior dealings with the juror. When an attorney is required to try a case outside his or her home county, local counsel can provide invaluable assistance in evaluating jurors and should *always* be consulted, and if possible, used during voir dire.

Of course, the primary source of information on jurors is that which is developed during the actual questioning of the panel members. The specific responses given by jurors, however, are only part of the information communicated by the juror. Particular attention also should be paid to each juror's body language, the level of attentiveness, demeanor, eye contact, and apparent intelligence.

§9.07 Collecting the Information

A well planned and executed voir dire examination will produce a considerable amount of important information about those panel members who are likely candidates for jury service. Unless the attitudes, opinions, observations and other data developed during voir dire are recorded in a systematic manner, relative comparisons of panel members will be difficult. *See generally*, SMITH & MALANDRO, COURTROOM COMMUNICATION STRATEGIES, §6.49 (1985).

The actual method used to gather and record the information is not important so long as the same type of information is gathered on each panel member.

One method of gathering data about panel members is to create pre-printed index cards on which are listed categories of information which are important to the case. Then, as information about a juror which bears on a particular category is developed, it is entered on that juror's card. The entry made should reflect a positive or negative evaluation of the information obtained as it relates to the lawsuit.

The categories of useful information vary somewhat with each case; however, the following categories, as set forth in SMITH & MALANDRO, COURTROOM COMMUNICATION STRATEGIES, *supra*, should be applicable to most cases:

Occupation

Age and sex

Ethnic or racial background

Religion

Party biases

Education

Personality type

Body type

Evaluation of non-verbal clues

Expressed biases

The pre-printed index cards (or whatever other system is used) should be completed by one or more assistants or co-counsel in the case and not by the attorney who is conducting the voir dire. Clearly, a successful voir dire is one in which, among other things, a favorable rapport is established with the panel members. Through a combination of story-telling (discussing the facts) and questioning the panel, a give-and-take rhythm is established by which the responses of the panel are used to carry the voir dire forward. The rapport which is established during a free flowing voir dire is difficult to achieve if the attorney asking the questions is constantly stopping to make notes.

In addition to being disruptive of the voir dire, notes which are made by the attorney doing the questioning frequently are incomplete at best and illegible at worst.

Even when an assistant or co-counsel is used during voir dire to record information, few attorneys can resist the temptation to make some notes during the examination. To make such notes useful and to reduce the amount of disruption that note-taking necessarily causes, a format should be developed ahead of trial that will enable the attorney to make key notes in some kind of shorthand fashion. Since it would be impractical for an attorney to shuffle through a set of index cards while conducting the voir dire examination, a different format is required.

Most attorneys use a seating chart as a reference during the voir dire examination. Such a chart can easily be adapted to accommodate a short-hand note taking system. Under this system, letter codes are used to identify certain juror characteristics that are important to the case. Unless an attorney has considerable experience in using all of the categories listed on the pre-printed index cards, a shorter or condensed list should be used by the attorney. The letter codes set forth below illustrate this method of making quick, understandable notes of observations about juror characteristics that should be made about each panel member.

The codes can be added to or subtracted from depending on those characteristics that are considered significant. During the examination, if a juror communicates positively in the area shown, *i.e.* "attentive," then the letter "A" is written in the box on the seating chart which contains the juror's name. If the juror is negative in this area, then the letter "A" is written with a line drawn through the letter.

Common Juror Characteristics:

A = Attentive

B = Body language

D = Demeanor

E = Eye contact

Ex = Expressed attitude

I = Intelligence

O = Occupation

S = Sympathetic

Illustration:

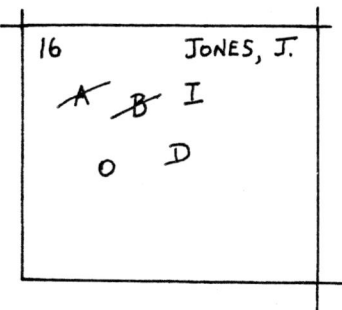

Regardless of the system used to record information about jurors, it is essential that some form of system is used so that valuable observations made during voir dire are not lost.

§9.08 General Voir Dire Questions

No system of collecting information will be of value unless the right questions are asked of the panel members. If carefully planned questions are asked, then the attorneys and parties will have sufficient information to fulfill the primary purpose of voir dire, *i.e.* to determine whether grounds exist for challenges for cause, and to allow an intelligent exercise of peremptory challenges. *Implement Dealers Mutual Ins. Co. v. Castleberry*, 368 S.W.2d 249 (Tex. Civ. App.—Beaumont 1963, writ ref'd n.r.e.).

The number of areas that should be explored during voir dire vary considerably with the type of DTPA case on trial. In general, however, the following areas should always be asked about in every DTPA case:

(1) *Relationship to or knowledge of the parties, attorneys and witnesses.*

See Gonzales v. Texas Employers' Ins. Ass'n 419 S.W.2d 203 (Tex. Civ. App.—Austin 1967, no writ); *Implement Dealers Mut. Ins. Co. v. Castleberry*, 368 S.W.2d 249 (Tex. Civ. App.—Beaumont 1963, writ ref'd n.r.e.). Questioning in this area should be designed to elicit a predisposition toward one side or the other as revealed by prior dealings with the parties or the law firms involved or any of the witnesses who may be called.

In DTPA cases it is far more likely that a panel member will have had prior contact with the defendant than might be the case in a personal injury lawsuit. The reason, quite simply, is that most DTPA defendants are businesses that sell goods and services to the public. In a personal injury case, it is unlikely that a panel member will know the person who ran over the plaintiff; It is far more likely in many DTPA cases that a panel member has done business with the defendant and has formed impressions and opinions based on that experience.

Challenges for cause based on previous contacts with the participants in the case are difficult unless the juror admits or otherwise shows clear signs of bias. For example, in *Texas Employers' Ins. Ass'n v. Godwin*, 194 S.W.2d 593 (Tex. Civ. App.—Dallas, rev'd on other grounds, 195 S.W.2d 347 (Tex. 1946), it was held that the fact that the defendant's attorney was then representing a juror's wife was not grounds, in and of itself, for disqualification. More than likely, the fact that a panel member has purchased goods or services from the defendant will not, in and of itself, provide sufficient grounds for disqualification for cause. Of course, if the panel member feels that he or she was treated unfairly by the merchant, a challenge for cause probably would be sustained because of the bias that the juror would bring to the case.

(2) *Relationship to subject matter of litigation.*

In many deceptive trade practice cases, the defendant may be in a line of business shared by some members of the jury panel. If selected, the juror may identify closely with the defendant resulting in a bias in favor of the defense.

There are instances, however, when a juror's relationship to the subject matter of the litigation works in favor of the plaintiff. For example, in a defective construction case, if the workmanship in question is particularly poor, and, the jury panel member takes obvious pride in his or her own construction work, that member may make a strong advocate in the jury room for the plaintiff's case. Conversely, in a house case, some members of the panel may own houses with construction defects equal to or even worse than that complained of by the plaintiff. Just because such jurors are similarly situated with the plaintiff, it is dangerous to conclude that there will be an automatic bias in the plaintiff's favor. The lesson to be learned is to pursue the relationship with careful questioning and make the decision to use or not use a strike only after further questioning has provided clear reasons.

(3) *Attitudes about litigation.*

Some members of the panel will have been involved in lawsuits, either as parties or witnesses. Based on that experience or the experiences of friends or relatives, a panel member may be biased against or for those involved in litigation. As a general rule, a panel member who has previously been a plaintiff in a civil lawsuit will better appreciate the need for litigation and will not be unfavorably disposed against it. The opposite generally is true when a person has been a defendant in a civil lawsuit involving something other than family law.

(4) *Occupation and education.*

The traditional plaintiff's juror is one who sees the broad picture and is not overly concerned with fine points and detail. The traditional defendant's juror is one who focuses on and examines the minutia of each and every bit of data developed during the trial. A plaintiff generally wants a jury to see the forest. A defendant normally wants the jury to see only a tree. These stereotypes are applicable in many DTPA lawsuits, but not all. One of the best keys to evaluating a juror's probable attitude toward a case is the juror's education and occupation. After all, aside from a person's family, one's education and job are the two activities, many times by choice, in which we spend most of our lives.

The background of each juror must be weighed in light of the type of case with which they will be confronted; however, from the plaintiff's perspective in nearly every DTPA case, there are several occupational and professional groups that seem incapable of seeing the forest except under the most unusual circumstances. At the top of many attorneys' lists are accountants, bankers, doctors, and engineers. Obviously, there are exceptions. A banker who takes his or her fiduciary obligations seriously may be incensed by a person who abuses a trust to achieve personal advantage. Thus, a banker's general reluctance to side with a plaintiff or to award a large verdict may be overcome by his or her personal sense of what is right and what is wrong. Few people should understand the obligations of a fiduciary relationship better than a bank officer in a trust department.

There also will be jurors who are employed in businesses, such as automobile dealerships, that are frequently involved in DTPA litigation. These individuals normally will resist a plaintiff's DTPA claim. Again, however, there are exceptions. Automobile dealers own houses and may have had such poor experiences in trying to get their own houses repaired that they would be moved to forget their general antagonism toward litigation.

In many cases, attorneys are equally high on either the plaintiff's or defendant's strike list. Again, however, the type of law practiced by the panel member is an important consideration. If an attorney's practice does not thrust the attorney into a traditional "plaintiff" or "defendant" role, or if it does not require the attorney to be aligned with those who typically are oriented toward one side of the docket or the other, then the fact that the juror is an attorney may have less significance that it otherwise would. For example, a legal aid attorney might be expected to lean toward a DTPA plaintiff; a real estate attorney could be expected to lean toward a DTPA defendant. An attorney employed by a state, county or city agency may lean in either direction and thus be as objective as any other juror.

In addition to determining the type of law practiced, however, it is also helpful to ascertain (if possible) whether the attorney is likely to be an active participant in the jury room.

In some cases an attorney will refrain from active participation out of a fear of unduly influencing the other jury members. Thus, whatever value the attorney may have had to either side is neutralized. In other cases, an attorney may so dominate the jury room that the other members of the jury are either alienated, or led wherever the attorney wants them to go.

From the defendant's point of view, unemployed persons, blue collar workers (especially union members), clerical workers, artists and musicians generally are considered poor risks for the defense. Like all stereotypes, however, these "truisms" should be considered, at most, merely the starting point in jury selection.

(5) *Religious affiliation.*

As a general rule, religious affiliation should not be asked about during voir dire. *See* 49 TEX. JUR. 3D *Jury* §73 (1986). Nevertheless, the information should be on the juror information card. Take special note of the affiliation, and if there is time, read up on or ask others about the tenets of that particular group's faith.

(6) *Family experience.*

A juror's family experiences should be questioned with caution, although the knowledge gained about a person's family history can be useful. For example, in a case where the plaintiff or a key witness is female, it would be helpful to know that one of the male panel members has been divorced three times. It would be equally helpful to know that a male panel member has three sisters, all of whom have pursued responsible careers in the work force or as homemakers. Family history is important in nearly every case; however, the questioning must be pursued with care to avoid appearing too personal, and thereby offending the prospective juror or the panel as a whole.

§9.09 Communicating Concepts

In DTPA cases, as in many other types of lawsuits, it is necessary to communicate concepts to the jury during voir dire, and through questioning, insure that the jury understands and can apply the concepts.

Each type of DTPA lawsuit involves one or more concepts that the jury may not have encountered before. For example, in a defective construction case, particularly residential construction, one of the major elements of damages for most plaintiffs is "stigma" damages, that is, after structural repairs have been made, property may still suffer a decrease in market value because of the "stigma" of the repair history. Another concept that must be dealt with in DTPA cases is that the total damages sought may equal or exceed the purchase price of the product. Superficially, it may seem unfair to make a seller pay more in damages than he or she was paid, especially when the consumer is allowed to keep the product.

Once the concept has been identified, then questions must be written that will (1) communicate the concept and (2) insure that the jury can apply the concept. Returning to the defective construction illustration just mentioned, it obviously is essential that the jurors be questioned about their understanding of the concepts of "market value" and "stigma" damages. Examples of the types of questions that probe this understanding are as follows:

> Assume you are about to purchase a house. Also assume that you have two houses to choose from, both identical in every respect except that one has a cracked slab. Which house would you choose?

> Assume that you are about to purchase a house. Also assume that you have two houses to choose from, both identical in every respect except that one has had a cracked slab but it has been repaired. Which house would you choose?

These questions, and the follow-up to them, acquaint the jurors with the concepts of market value and "stigma" which they must understand and apply if they are to be effective jurors in the case.

§9.10 Introducing the Participants

At the beginning of voir dire, it is customary to introduce the parties to the jury. Some courts will ask counsel to introduce their respective clients before the actual voir dire begins; others leave it entirely to counsel as to how the introduction is to be done. When the court allows counsel to control the introductions, plaintiff's counsel should always introduce not only his own clients but also the defendant and defendant's counsel, preferably asking each to stand while being introduced.

As each person is introduced, the panel should be asked whether they know the person. Frequently, the attorneys, if not the parties, will be known to someone on the jury panel; accordingly, follow-up individual questioning is essential to eliminate a juror who demonstrates bias as a result of the knowledge.

In addition to eliciting information about bias, the structure of the questions can be used to communicate information to the panel about the person, creating for that person an image that the attorney wants the jury to have. For example, if opposing counsel is from a large law firm, in order to find out if any jurors know the attorney, the question could be structured as follows:

> Mr. _____ is a senior partner in a law firm that has at least sixty partners and even more associates. I won't take the time to read all of their names, but does anyone on the jury panel know any members of this firm or Mr. _____?

The David and Goliath image is created without having to mention slingshots and such.

The initial introductions also provide counsel with the' opportunity to make his or her client as appealing as possible to the jury. Interesting facts from the client's background should be told to the jury so that he or she becomes a real person instead of just a party in a lawsuit. In a recent case, one of the plaintiffs was introduced along the following lines:

> Bill _____ was born in Colorado Springs, Colorado. He attended high school there and graduated in 1959. After high school he worked first as a cowhand on a large ranch in eastern Colorado and then worked as a roughneck in the Colorado oil fields. Bill has always had a thirst for learning, and so while he was working during the day, he was attending night school and taking correspondence courses in economics. When computers first began to come on the scene in the early 1960s, Bill taught himself how to program them with some help from a friend. Through the years he continued to work day and night whenever he could in programming so that by 1983 he was offered a job in Austin by Microelectronics Computer Technology Corporation as a principal researcher in the field of hypermedia information systems. Bill's work in computer programming was so successful that he was the 35th person hired by this company out of a research organization that ultimately employed 450 people.
>
> Now, with that introduction, does anyone on the jury panel know Bill _____?

The point is to make the client come to life in an impressive way so that by the time the client takes the stand, the jury already will feel favorably disposed.

Plaintiff's counsel may be allowed to introduce the defendant as well. Although the introduction should be courteous, the facts selected should create the desired image of the defendant. For example, if the defendant is a corporation, the attorney may want to say:

> Now XYZ Corporation is not a flesh and blood person. Since XYZ Corporation is not a live person, it cannot be here to sit in court and testify before you and so the testimony for the corporation will be from Mr. _____ who has been chosen as a representative of the corporation for this trial. Does anyone on the panel know Mr. _____ or has anyone had any dealings with XYZ Corporation?

§9.11 Opening Statement (Plaintiff)

When the introduction and preliminary questioning concerning knowledge of the parties and attorneys are completed, an opening statement should be given to acquaint jurors with the type of case before them and to provide a basis for subsequent questions that must be asked. The opening statement of the plaintiff should be prepared within the following guidelines:

(1) *It is improper to argue the case during the opening statement.*

Having stated the rule, it is important to distinguish between argument and *persuasion*. Among the writings of Mark Twain were two stories, *The Private History of the Campaign That Failed* and *The Mysterious Stranger*. Not a single sentence in these short stories "argue" against war, but a reader would be hard pressed to complete the stories without realizing that a war which turns brother against brother is insane. The *facts* of the stories compel the conclusion. The same is true of a good opening statement in voir dire. If the facts of the case are presented correctly, at the conclusion, the jury should be convinced that the cause is just and should prevail.

(2) *Tell the jury a story, not just the "facts."*

At the beginning of the opening statement, the jury panel should be told that what they are about to hear is not evidence; instead, it is a statement of what the evidence is expected to show. Once this disclaimer is clearly stated, the opening statement can and should be told in story form. *See* SMITH & MALANDRO, COURTROOM COMMUNICATION STRATEGIES, p. 627 (1985). The story should be *interesting* and *involving*. Compare the following two examples:

> In 1986, [the plaintiffs] bought a house.

> *or*

> Come back in time with me to 1986. Many of us remember what it was like when we bought our first home. Through the evidence, you will see [the plaintiffs] looking for weeks and even months, driving up and down countless streets and subdivisions trying to find the one house that was just what they wanted. We will see them saving and sacrificing and worrying about whether they could afford the payments. In the early months of 1986, this is where we will find [the plaintiffs] when they bought their home from [the defendant].

The first statement is sterile. The second statement invites juror involvement and relates experiences with which many on the panel will identify. When members of the jury panel begin to identify with one party or the other, the evidence which follows will have its most profound effect.

(3) *Develop a "theme" for the case.*

From the beginning of the opening statement until the last word of rebuttal, every opportunity should be used to develop the theme of the lawsuit. A lawsuit must have a theme. *See* CARLSON, SUCCESSFUL TECHNIQUES FOR CIVIL §6:9 (1983); PERDUE, WHO WILL SPEAK FOR THE VICTIM?, 6-7 (1989).

The type of theme a particular lawsuit should have depends entirely on the facts of the case. The most successful themes in deceptive trade practice cases appear to be those that contrast the plaintiff's (and jury's) reasonable expectations with what really happened in the transaction. For example, the following themes may be applied in many DTPA cases:

Type of case	*Theme*
Insurance	A consumer buys peace of mind; when insurance is needed, no one is there.
Banking	In good times, the bank is a friend; in bad times, the bank is a predator.
Defective construction	This was the consumer's first home, a dream home; now it's just a broken home.
Automobiles	The consumer bought the car in the brochure; they sold him the car in the garage.
Investments	What was a nest egg is now a goose egg.

A good theme is one which captures the essence of the problem in as few words as possible. Good themes are black and white, not shades of gray.

Although, many DTPA cases are similar, the theme selected for a particular case obviously must be an accurate reflection of the parties and the transaction. An attorney should never try to make the case fit a pre-selected theme; instead, the theme should be allowed to emerge naturally from the facts of the case. Once an accurate theme has emerged, the attorney should build the presentation of the evidence and argument around it.

(4) *The opening statement should defuse defenses.*

There are some bad facts on both sides of every case. the plaintiff should never allow the defendant to be the first to mention the weaknesses in the plaintiff's case. The facts are going to come out anyway. By discussing bad facts in the voir dire, they can be presented in the best light possible.

(5) *The opening statement should prepare the jury for conflicts in the evidence.*

In many deceptive trade practice cases, there not only will be conflicting expert testimony but also sharply conflicting testimony about the facts. One person will testify directly that something was said; the other will deny it. And, unlike skid marks at the scene of a collision, there may be little "objective" proof of who is telling the truth. The panel should be told about these conflicts in advance. Describing these conflicts (again in the best light possible) is a good way to illustrate the jury's most important function, *i.e.* to resolve conflicts in the evidence by judging the credibility of the witnesses and their respective memories.

(6) *Choose the target carefully.*

In every case, something or someone is on trial. Since the plaintiff has the right to go first, the plaintiff also has the opportunity to define the conflict for the jury. The temptation in DTPA cases is to characterize the lawsuit as one involving a poor, helpless consumer against a big, powerful company. If the case in fact has a poor, helpless consumer that was abused by a big, powerful company, then the correct target would be the company and the characterization would be correct. In most cases, however, the lines are not so clearly drawn. The "big, powerful company" may be a family owned business; the "poor, helpless consumer" may have an earned Ph.D. If the plaintiff and the defendant present equally sympathetic (or unsympathetic) images for the jury, then the focus needs to be shifted away from them.

Assume, for example, that the plaintiff owns a Rolls Royce (as his second car); that he was born wealthy; that he does not have a regular job but "dabbles" in antiques. The lawsuit is brought because the automobile was defective and the owner wants his money back. The target in this case should not be the company that made the car because between the company and the plaintiff, for the jury, there will be little difference. Instead, the Rolls Royce should be put on trial and the focus of the case should be in showing how the car purchased by the plaintiff fails to live up to the jury's expectations of what a Rolls Royce should be. The example admittedly is extreme; nevertheless, it illustrates that a properly chosen target should be one on which the jury can clearly and easily focus.

(7) *Explain the questions that will be asked.*

The jury should be made aware during voir dire exactly what is expected of them. That is, at the end of the trial they will be required to answer a series of questions based on what the evidence has shown. If possible, a chart should be used to illustrate one or more probable questions, assuming that the attorney is very confident that the question will, in fact, be asked. Naturally, the jury should be cautioned that the judge will have the final say as to the form and content of the questions that will be asked.

(8) *Talk about the amount of damages.*

There are conflicting views on whether the amount of damages should be specifically discussed during the opening statement. As a general proposition, however, it seems that the amount of damages not only should be mentioned in the opening statement, it also should be discussed during voir dire. A juror may be willing to find liability, but very reluctant to award the full measure of damages sought unless clear justification for the damages is presented.

Assuming that damages are to be discussed, the subject should not be presented until after the jury has been told what caused the damages (and hopefully has formed a favorable opinion of the plaintiff's side of the case). If the amount of damages is discussed before any justification for the amount is given, then the jury will have no basis upon which to agree or disagree that the amount sought is reasonable. Consequently, if the amount sought is high, the jury may form an impression that the plaintiff is greedy, an impression that may never have arisen if the reasons for the damages had first been discussed fully.

§9.12 Opening Statement (Defendant)

Many of the principles applicable to the plaintiff's opening statement in voir dire apply equally to the defendant's opening statement. Unlike the plaintiff, however, the defendant must be prepared not only to give his own statement of the case, but also to respond to the plaintiff's characterization of the case.

(1) *Establish the defense theme.*

When possible, the first sentence of the defendant's voir dire should establish the defense theme. By the time the defendant's attorney has the opportunity to speak, the plaintiff's attorney will have spent a considerable amount of time hammering home his or her theme of the case. In order to overcome the image created in the minds of the jury panel, the defendant's theme must be clear, sharply contrasting and to the point.

Assume that the plaintiff has sued for an amount that can fairly be labeled excessive. The first question of the panel might be:

> Members of the jury panel, how many of you believe it is wrong for one person to sue another for an amount of money that is far more than any loss they could possibly have suffered?

Commonly used defense themes in DTPA litigation include the following:

- No one should be forced to pay an excessive, unreasonable demand

- The plaintiff has a valid claim but the wrong defendant

- The plaintiff wanted a Cadillac but was only willing to pay for a Chevrolet

- Nothing in this world is perfect and yet the plaintiff demands perfection

- The plaintiff wants all of his money back but wants to keep what we sold him

- You've heard what the plaintiff says happened, now we'll tell you the rest of the story

The last theme is particularly effective when the plaintiff's attorney has been less than candid with the jury panel about the adverse testimony that will surely come in.

Obviously, the defendant's theme will depend, to some extent, on what the plaintiff's attorney does during voir dire. For this reason, several possible themes should be worked out in advance.

(2) *Remove the euphemisms from the plaintiff's case.*

In many DTPA cases, the plaintiff will allege that the defendant has "misrepresented" facts, and has done so "knowingly." In plain English, the defendant is accused of lying. Or, a defendant may be accused of "unconscionability." This means conduct that is *grossly unfair*. None of us enjoys labeling someone else a "liar," or accusing someone of being unfair, especially when we, like the jury panel, have just met the person. Even so, in many DTPA cases, these allegations are commonly made against defendants. Unless the evidence will bear out the harsh labels (in which case the lawsuit should have been settled), the defendant's counsel should emphasize the harshness of the charges and then point to the facts which demonstrate that the labels do not fit.

(3) *Draw attention to overstatements and misstatements of fact.*

Some plaintiff's counsel will overstate the evidence in an effort to score points early in the trial. Defense counsel should carefully and distinctly point out each overstatement made. Drawing attention to insupportable claims serves two purposes: (1) the credibility of opposing counsel is put in issue, and (2) the jury will be more likely to remember the exaggerated claims as the evidence begins to unfold.

When plaintiff's counsel makes a relatively minor misstatement of the evidence, such as giving the wrong date, the error should be politely corrected, if at all. If a correction is gently made, it will communicate to the jury the fact that defendant's counsel knows the case and is perhaps more prepared than his opponent.

(4) *Remind the jury that anyone can file a lawsuit.*

Some jurors are of the opinion that the fact that a lawsuit was filed must mean someone did something wrong. This tendency to believe that the mere filing of a lawsuit is some evidence of wrongdoing can be dealt with by counsel informing the jury that there is no one to "screen" the cases that are filed or that go to trial. *Lauderdale v. Insurance Co. of North America*, 527 S.W.2d 841 (Tex. Civ. App.—Fort Worth 1975, writ ref'd n.r.e.).

(5) *Commit the jury to wait on all of the evidence.*

One of the most important jobs confronting defense counsel in any lawsuit is to overcome the first impressions created by plaintiff's counsel in his or her presentation of the case, assuming that the first impression has been favorable. It is human nature to form quick impressions.

As mentioned above, one defense theme involves using the phrase, "the rest of the story." Paul Harvey, the radio commentator, has built a long-running segment of his program around the fact that first impressions are not always accurate. The segment is entitled, "The Rest of the Story" and on a daily basis sets up the listeners by relating a story that naturally leads to one impression, only to find that "the rest of the story" completely changes that impression. A jury's natural tendency to form quick impressions must be confronted by securing from the jury a commitment to wait until all the evidence is in before making a judgment. If a "rest of the story" theme happens to fit the case, then a dual purpose is served.

(6) *Explain the burden of proof.*

Jurors should be told that the plaintiff has the burden to prove his or her case-the defendant does not have to *disprove* anything. In fact, if there are no affirmative defenses in the case, the point can be emphasized by telling the jury that the defendant is not required to put on *any* evidence in order to win.

§9.13 Objections in Voir Dire

The decision to object during voir dire examination is difficult, at best. Objections may be seen by the jury panel as an unfair interference with opposing counsel, especially if the objections are overruled. Even so, on occasion, objections are necessary and should be made.

If improper questions are asked or if improper statements are made, *and*, if the improper voir dire can be cured by court instruction, then a prompt objection must be made or the error is waived. *Texas Employers Ins. Ass'n v. Loesch*, 538 S.W.2d 435 (Tex. Civ. App.—Waco 1976, writ ref'd n.r.e.).

Some conduct during voir dire is incurable and does not require an instruction to preserve error, *e.g.*, an argument that appeals to passion or prejudice, or one that suggests imaginary testimony not based on any evidence to be offered in the case. *See Otis Elevator Co. v. Wood*, 436 S.W.2d 324 (Tex. 1968); *American Home Assurance Co. v. Coronado*, 628 S.W.2d 818 (Tex. App.—Amarillo 1981, writ ref'd n.r.e.). There is a considerable risk, however, in assuming that an objection is not required to preserve error; therefore, if the conduct is of such a nature that an objection seems appropriate, it should be made.

The following checklist of objections can be used as a reminder of those objections that generally can be made in voir dire if the circumstances call for it.

[a] CHECKLIST: Voir dire objections

❑ Counsel is improperly arguing the case to the jury panel.

❑ Counsel is soliciting a promise from the jury panel to vote a certain way.

See Campbell v. Campbell, 215 S.W. 134 (Tex. Civ. App.—Dallas 1919, writ ref'd); §9.05 *supra*.

❑ Counsel is improperly inquiring into issues of law that are reserved for the court.

❑ Counsel is stating his or her personal belief in the merits of this case.

❑ Counsel is improperly referring to the difference in the financial condition of the plaintiff (or defendant).

See Texas & N.O.R. Co. v. Lide, 117 S.W.2d 479 (Tex. Civ. App.—Waco 1938, no writ); §9.05 *supra*.

❑ Counsel has made reference to insurance coverage (or the lack of it).

See A. J. Miller Trucking Co. v. Wood, 474 S.W. 2d 763 (Tex. Civ. App.—Tyler 1971, writ ref'd n.r.e.). §9.05 *supra*.

❏ Counsel has made reference to settlement discussions.

❏ Counsel is making statements that he or she knows will not be supported by the evidence at trial.

See e.g., *Christie v. Brewer*, 374 S.W.2d 908 (Tex. Civ. App.—Austin 1964, writ ref'd n.r.e.). §9.05 *supra*.

Violations of In-Limine Order:

❏ Objection. May we approach the bench? (Then, object to violation of order).

See §8.10 *supra*.

§9.14 Preserving Error

The voir dire examination should be recorded; otherwise, the rulings of the trial court are presumed valid. *Lauderdale v. Insurance Co. of North America*, 527 S.W.2d 841 (Tex. Civ. App.—Fort Worth, 1975, writ ref'd n.r.e.). If no record of the voir dire is made, then the error may be preserved by a bill of exceptions. *Tumlinson v. San Antonio Brewing Association*, 170 S.W.2d 620 (Tex. Civ. App.—San Antonio 1943, writ ref'd).

When the claimed error relates to the disqualification of a juror, special rules come into play. The record must establish that a specific, valid objection was made in a timely manner. *O'Day v. Sakowitz Brothers*, 462 S.W.2d 119 (Tex. Civ. App.—Houston [1st Dist.] 1970, writ ref'd n.r.e.). Further, the objection must be made before the exercise of peremptory challenges. *O'Day v. Sakowitz Brothers, supra*. And, in order for the error to be considered harmful, the objecting party must establish that (1) he or she would exhaust all peremptory challenges, and (2) that, after exercising all peremptory challenges, specific objectionable jurors would remain on the jury list. *Hallett v. Houston Northwest Medical Center*, 689 S.W.2d 888 (Tex. 1985).

§9.15 The Case-in-Chief

The most important ingredient of all trials is the evidence, whether in the form of testimony, exhibits, experiments or demonstrations. Obviously, the substance of the evidence presented is a primary consideration. It also is true, however, that the manner in which evidence is presented, as well as the time at which it is presented are perhaps equally important considerations.

§9.16 Order of Testimony

A jury trial is a dramatic production. Although it may sound crass, a jury trial should be planned as a drama: it is important to grab the attention of the jury as quickly as possible, expect there to be lulls in the action, carefully place the "show stopper," and plan for a strong finish.

In most cases (although not all) the plaintiff is the first witness. The thrust of the plaintiff's examination should be directed toward involving the jury in the personal aspects of the case. Although some plaintiffs are capable of giving testimony on technical matters, most plaintiffs are better suited for a "what happened next" type of examination.

The placement of experts in the order of testimony should be determined by the testifying ability of the expert. If the expert is dry and methodical, he or she should be sandwiched between more interesting witnesses. If the expert is interesting and alert, he or she should be used to pick up or perhaps conclude the plaintiff's or defendant's case.

The rules of evidence permit the plaintiff (or defendant) to cross examine a party opponent, regardless of who calls the witness to the stand. TEX. R. CIV. EVID. 611(c). The "adverse party rule" should be utilized fully by the plaintiff. Few things are more deflating to a defendant's case than to call the defendant during the plaintiff's case, preferably between two strong, plaintiff's witnesses. If an adverse party is called to testify during the plaintiff's case, however, the testimony must be developed fully. When the opponent's testimony is not fully developed, after the witness is passed, the opponent will gain momentary control of the case and can introduce areas not previously discussed in a manner most favorable to the defendant.

Deceptive trade practices litigation provides attorneys with the opportunity to testify about the reasonableness and necessity of their fees. Unless there is a clear reason not to do so, opposing counsel generally will stipulate to the fees. If no stipulation is made, then the opportunity to testify may be seized and used to its fullest effect, all for the purpose of showing that the fees sought are *reasonable* and *necessary*. Consider the probable effect of the following testimony on the jury:

> After my initial interview with my clients, we sent a letter, in March 1987, so we could notify him of our claim and hopefully resolve it without going to court. We did not get any response to our letter. We had no choice but to file suit since I could not advise my clients to just walk away from their losses. The process of preparing the letter took thirty minutes, or $75.00. The preparation of the documents necessary to file suit took an additional two hours or $300.00. The filing fee was $110.00 . . .

During the "self examination," an attorney can provide a lot of information favorable to the client while demonstrating that the time spent was required.

Having the jury hear the testimony of opposing counsel is probably worth the price if there are facts that can be developed through the attorney that will weaken the plaintiff's case or that will show that the fees sought are unreasonable. For example, if opposing counsel has not personally examined the goods or services in dispute, or personally inspected the house that is now claimed to be defective, this embarrassing fact can be driven home during the cross examination of the plaintiff's attorney.

When there is evidence that the lawsuit was filed in bad faith or for harassment, or when the damages actually proven are quite low in comparison to the cost of the trial, the cross examination of the plaintiff's attorney can also be used as an opportunity to explain to the jury the fact that once a lawsuit is filed, it must be answered and defended or a judgment by default will be rendered.

The order of testimony of the defendant's witnesses should be determined by the same considerations as those of the plaintiff. The first defense witness should always be strong, even if it means calling the defendant later in the trial. A strong first witness will assist in shifting the focus away from the theme that the plaintiff has worked hard to develop in order to give the defendant an opportunity to develop his or her own theme.

After the first witness, strong, interesting witnesses and weaker, less interesting witnesses should be balanced against each other so that the pace of the trial is developed and maintained in the most effective way possible.

When the defendant has been called to testify during the plaintiff's case-in-chief, he or she should always be recalled to testify when the defense is presented.

The purposes of recalling the defendant are twofold: (1) any evidence not yet developed can be presented; and (2) an opportunity will be presented to repair, to the extent possible, any damage that may have been done during the earlier testimony.

§9.17 Direct Examination

There are two purposes of direct examination:

- to present evidence that is legally sufficient to support each claim or defense

- to convince the jury of the truthfulness and accuracy of all the evidence supporting the claim or defense

The legal sufficiency of the evidence can only be evaluated by studying the substance of the testimony and exhibits on a case by case basis. However, the impact of direct testimony can be enhanced considerably by using certain techniques. *See generally,* SMITH & MALANDRO, COURTROOM COMMUNICATION STRATEGIES, §8.01 - §8.26 (1985).

(1) *Frame the questions carefully*

During direct examination, the witness will be asked certain "key" questions that relate directly to the questions the jury will be asked in the court's charge. Expert witnesses may also be asked questions on "ultimate facts" such as whether the conduct in question was a proximate or producing cause of damages. TEX. R. CIV. EVID. 704; *see, e.g., Louder v. DeLeon,* 754 S.W.2d 148 (Tex. 1988). This type of questioning can be most effective. When these key questions are framed, the words used, to the extent possible, should be the same words that will appear in the jury questions. For example, in a typical DTPA case involving an automobile, the jury will be asked,

> Did [defendant] represent that the automobile had certain characteristics that it did not have and if so was it a producing cause of damages to [plaintiff]?

In order to make the answer to the question crystal clear to the jury, whenever possible the same words should be used in questions asked of the witnesses.

A second technique for making the direct examination as persuasive as possible is to make the jury part of the team at every opportunity. One way of doing this during direct examination is to phrase questions as though the questioner and the jury are one. Instead of being asked to "tell the jury," the witness should be asked to "tell us."

Thus, using these suggestions, two of the key questions of the witness would be:

Q. Mrs. Jones, was anything said to you about the automobile before you bought it?

A. Yes.

Q. Then please tell us what [the defendant] represented to you about the characteristics of the car.

(2) Prepare the witness

Once the questions for a witness have been outlined, obviously, the attorney must review the questions with each witness so they will not come as a surprise to the witness at trial. Of course, the persuasive value of the witness' testimony may depend upon how the review is conducted.

Unless they are told not to, many witnesses will attempt to memorize the questions to be asked and the answers to be given. Such an approach courts disaster since the actual questions asked at trial may vary somewhat from the questions reviewed by the witness. More importantly, juries can easily spot memorized testimony. Because memorized testimony has no credibility, each witness must be cautioned against memorizing anything. The desired objective is to avoid surprise and misunderstanding through careful review, and yet preserve the witness' spontaneity.

Trial preparation also should include consideration of the courtroom environment in which the witness will testify. When a witness is prepared for the courtroom, the persuasive value of the witness' testimony is enhanced simply because the witness is able to testify more comfortably. Preparation for the courtroom appearance should acquaint the witness with both the courtroom environment as well as the manner in which the witness should relate to the jury. During the review sessions, each witness should be instructed, among other things, to:

- Look at the jury while testifying on direct

- Make sure every juror can hear every word

- Show confidence

A witness should always look at the jury while testifying on direct, except when answering questions that call for one or two word responses. People are distrustful of those who do not look them in the eyes during a conversation. Juries react the same way when a witness looks only at the attorney conducting the direct examination.

The witness must also make sure that every juror can hear every word. If there is a sound system, the witness should be reminded to use it. If there is no sound system, the witness should be told to talk to the last juror on the back row.

Of course, each witness must feel and show confidence in his or her testimony. The jury's perception of the character and truthfulness of a witness is formed, of necessity, during the brief time that the witness is on the stand. The only other sources of information are any comments that other witnesses may make. For this reason, each witness should be worked with for a sufficient amount of time to instill as much confidence as possible in the witness before he or she testifies.

(3) Prepare expert witnesses

Expert witnesses may require as much preparation and practice as lay witnesses. *See generally*, DOMBROFF, EXPERT WITNESSES IN CIVIL TRIALS (1987). Essentially the same techniques are used with both lay and expert witnesses. One problem that is encountered more with expert witnesses than with others is the "whose witness is it, anyway" syndrome. Even a seasoned expert can create problems if he or she fails to clearly understand the role of the expert witness in civil litigation.

When an expert witness is retained in a case, the expert's first job is to evaluate the facts and formulate an honest opinion based on those facts. If the expert's opinion is favorable, and the decision is made to call the expert to testify, it is essential for the expert to understand that he or she has a second, equally important job. The expert *must* assist the attorney in convincing the jury of the correctness of the opinion. The expert must be willing to be an advocate, not of the case as a whole, but of the opinion that he or she has reached. When the expert understands and accepts this dual role, the testimony given in court will be most effective.

A second feature of expert testimony that is different from that of other witnesses is the necessity of qualifying the witness to testify. Unfortunately, the process of qualifying an expert witness is one of the least interesting lines of questioning in a jury trial. This is especially true when a number of expert witnesses have testified, and when each of them has been qualified in essentially the same way. After one or two expert witnesses have testified, and the jury hears the first "qualification" question asked, some jurors have a tendency to give their minds a rest. As a result, important facts about the expert may never be heard by the jury.

When an expert witness has a particular qualification that will bolster an important opinion in the case, the jury obviously needs to hear the qualification. In this situation, consideration should be given to breaking up the qualification questions. That is, at the beginning of the expert's testimony, general, qualifying questions are asked. Then, after all other testimony is given, but just before the expert is asked for the opinion, the particular qualification of the expert is brought out for the first time. In this way, the probative and persuasive value of the qualification is less likely to be overlooked by the jury.

Expert witnesses frequently are most comfortable and effective when they are allowed to assume the role of a teacher in court. The expert should be encouraged to adopt this role. Also, visual aids should be used to assist the expert in the testimony to be given. Lastly, if the expert can do so comfortably, an attorney should take advantage of any opportunity to get the expert off the witness stand and in front of the jury. Presenting the witness in this manner will heighten the jury's perception of the expert as a teacher and someone to whom they should listen.

§9.18 Cross Examination

Cross examination is the most enjoyable part of a trial for most trial lawyers. Attorneys enjoy the mental duet; the opportunity to demonstrate powers of logic and deduction; the challenge of forcing a witness where he or she does not want to go, with words as the only weapon.

Effective cross examinations are not spontaneous; they are as carefully planned and practiced as any other phase of the trial.

Cross examination has three primary purposes:

- To test truthfulness and completeness of the direct testimony

- To repair or mitigate damage done during direct testimony

- To develop or reinforce necessary facts

(1) *Preparing the witness for cross examination*

Any witness who is to be cross examined must be prepared for the experience.

All witnesses are nervous about cross examination. Thorough preparation is required not only to reduce anxiety, but also to insure that the witness does not give away the case through careless answers to questions.

The first and foremost instruction to be given to a witness who is to be cross examined, whether in depositions or in trial, is to *listen carefully to the question asked.* The witness should not attempt to answer any question whose meaning is unclear. Next, the witness should be cautioned to never try and outsmart opposing counsel. Few witnesses are able to beat an attorney by anticipating where the attorney's questions are leading and "cutting him off at the pass." All too frequently, the witness is cut off, somewhere just above the knees.

The witness should be instructed to always control feelings of anger. An angry witness loses credibility.

All witnesses should be told to maintain eye contact with the questioner. Unlike direct examination where the witness should look at the jury while testifying, during cross examination, the witness should meet the adversary face to face so that the jury will not perceive that the witness is afraid of the questions.

Witnesses should be told to avoid answering questions with the words, "yes, but . . ." After a few of these answers, an impression is created that the witness cannot answer a question directly.

Many witnesses are afraid to testify about certain matters because they believe that a witness should never talk about facts that may hurt the case. This attitude must be dealt with because if the jury perceives that a witness is holding back or is shading testimony to make it more favorable, the witness' value to the case is lost. Most juries are fully capable of dealing fairly and easily with the truth. If testimony that is unfavorable is freely given by a witness when asked, then jurors know that they can believe the favorable testimony that comes from the same witness.

Sufficient time should be spent with all witnesses reviewing key questions that are likely to be asked on cross. Again, the purpose is not to memorize answers, but to provide an opportunity *prior to trial* to think through truthful answers to the tough questions.

(2) *Prepare for the cross examination*

Any witness can be made to say something good for either side of the case . . . if the right question is asked. By making the witness give favorable testimony on cross, some of the damage done during the direct examination can be mitigated.

The key to obtaining favorable testimony on cross is to ask questions which can truthfully be answered in only one, obvious way. If the answer is truthful, favorable testimony is obtained. If, for some reason, the witness chooses to give an obviously untruthful answer to a question, then the credibility of the witness is damaged, which may be as beneficial as any favorable testimony the witness could otherwise have provided.

To illustrate this technique, consider the following hypothetical cross examination of an expert witness in a lawsuit over a defective automobile:

Q. When you were testifying on direct for _____, you mentioned that you had sold cars for a time.

A. Yes, I did. For three or four years.

Q. Let's assume that one of your customers back then came in and you had two identical new cars sitting side by side, only one of them had been wrecked and repaired.

A. Ok.

Q. Which car would your customer choose if they both were the same price?

A. Does the customer know that the car has been wrecked?

Q. We'll assume you told them.

A. He'd choose the one that had not been wrecked.

Q. And in that situation, you would have to reduce the price of the wrecked car in order to sell it, wouldn't you?

A. Yes, you would.

Q. Unless, of course, you failed to disclose the fact of the wreck to your customer?

When the answers to the questions are obvious, the witness either will give the obvious answer or he will lose credibility by trying to avoid the obvious answer. Either way, the testimony is favorable.

There are many different styles of cross examining expert witnesses. The examination can be extensive, reviewing and challenging nearly every statement made on direct. The questions may, on the other hand, be limited to a few key areas. *See generally*, CARLSON, SUCCESSFUL TECHNIQUES FOR CIVIL TRIALS, §4.34 *et seq.* (1983). Regardless of the approach used, however, in nearly every case, it is helpful to initially ask a series of questions to which the witness must give a favorable answer.

If the expert is compelled to give answers which agree with the assertions made by the cross-examining attorney, the questions and answers can establish both a *rhythm* for the cross examination and a *pattern* of responding favorably to the attorney's questions. On the other hand, if the attorney begins his or her cross examination by challenging the expert's direct testimony, then a pattern of resisting the questioner is established.

An attorney should not overlook the opportunity to use "learned treatises" in the cross examination of an expert witness. It is no longer necessary that the witness acknowledge the authoritative standing of the treatise prior to its use; the testimony of another expert or judicial notice that the book is a reliable authority will suffice. TEX. R. CIV. EVID. 803(18).

(3) *Impeach with care*

Impeachment generally assumes one of two forms. First, the credibility of the witness as a witness may be attacked; or second, the specific testimony of a witness may be attacked.

It is important to note that any witness can be impeached by any party, including the party calling the witness. TEX. R. CIV. EVID. 607.

One generally effective way to challenge the trustworthiness of an expert witness is to establish that the person is a "professional witness." That is, among other ways, the credibility of the witness can be put in question by showing that:

- the witness frequently appears as an expert witness in similar cases (on the same side)

- the witness formed an opinion about the case before a thorough review of all of the evidence

- the witness is being paid a very large fee for the court appearance

The second method of impeachment involves an attack on particular testimony either because it is inherently unbelievable or because it contradicts previous testimony by the same witness. If impeachment involves contradictory statements made before trial, *i.e.* deposition testimony, then the strict requirements of Rule 613 of the Rules of Evidence must be met. Rule 613 provides:

> In examining a witness concerning a prior inconsistent statement made by him, whether oral or written, and before further cross-examination concerning, or extrinsic evidence of, such statement may

be allowed, the witness must be told the contents of such statement and the time and place and the person to whom it was made, and must be afforded an opportunity to explain or deny such statement. . . . If the witness unequivocally admits having made such statement, extrinsic evidence of same shall not be admitted. This provision does not apply to admissions of a party-opponent as defined in Rule 801(e)(2).

See TEX. R. CIV. EVID. 613(a).

(4) Re-emphasize direct testimony

A cross examination should never be structured so that the witness is given the opportunity merely to repeat damaging testimony that already has been given on direct. However, cross examination, particularly of expert witnesses, does provide an excellent opportunity to repeat favorable testimony that the attorney wants the jury to hear again. The favorable testimony is repeated by embodying it in the question asked of the witness. To illustrate, when laying the predicate for a question to a witness, an attorney might ask:

. . . there has been testimony that [the plaintiff's] house has a foundation that is cracked from side to side down the middle. Are you familiar with that evidence?

The question is legitimate because it focuses the attention of the witness on the particular subject matter about which he or she is to be questioned, or it serves as means of establishing a line of questions that will be used to impeach the witness. Either way, the repetition of key testimony reminds the jury of the important evidence in the case.

(5) Know when to stop

These are two hard and fast rules of cross examination:

- never ask a question if the answer the witness will give is unknown

- know when to stop

Except in rare instances, a cross examination should be ended if a telling point has been scored and there is no assurance of scoring another; or, if all of the planned cross examination has been exhausted and nothing has developed. In moments of frustration, an attorney may be tempted to continue with cross examination, hoping that something better will turn up. The better practice is to end the cross and move on to the next witness.

§9.19 Objections to Evidence

A thorough analysis of the validity of and authority for objections to evidence is beyond the scope of this volume. In any trial, however, it is helpful to have a guide to some of the more frequently made objections so that in the heat of battle they will not be forgotten or overlooked. Accordingly, the following checklist is intended as a brief review of frequently used evidence objections that can be scanned before or during trial.

[a] CHECKLIST: Objections to evidence

[1] *Witness*

>Not identified in answers to interrogatories

>Witness violated the Rule

[2] *Documentary evidence*

>Not produced in discovery

>Best evidence rule

>Parole evidence rule

>Hearsay

>Failure to establish necessary predicate

>Showing document to jury which is not in evidence

>Inflammatory; highly prejudicial

[3] *Testimony (questions)*

>Calls for hearsay response

>Leading

>Argumentative

>Asked and answered

>Assumes facts not in evidence

>Settlement discussions

>Best evidence rule

>Parole evidence rule

>Ambiguous

>Not supported by pleadings

Calls for expert opinion, witness not qualified

Compound question

Question calls for legal conclusion

Question calls for narrative response

Question invades privilege

Question misstates the evidence

Counsel is testifying

Personal attack

(At bench) Question violates In-limine order

[4] *Testimony (answers)*

Hearsay

Hearsay within hearsay

Failure to establish necessary predicate; therefore hearsay

Dead man's statute

Legal conclusion

Testimony from a document that is not in evidence

Document speaks for itself

Immaterial

Irrelevant

Non-responsive

Opinion testimony, witness not qualified

(At bench only) Answer violates In-limine order

§9.20 Proof of Attorney's Fees

The presentation of the evidence of recoverable attorney's fees requires appropriate preparation and forethought. On smaller cases, recoverable attorney's fees may far exceed the plaintiff's actual damages. *See, e.g., Hruska v. First State Bank of Deanville*, 747 S.W.2d 783,786 (Tex. 1988)(finding $12,500 fee reasonable to recover $2,900 in damages). The average consumer plaintiff is not going to be able to fund a lengthy court battle over a relatively modest claim, so a fee arrangement with at least some contingent aspect is likely the only way these consumers can get an attorney to represent them. The drafters of the Texas DTPA intended that the recoverability of attorney's fees would provide a dual incentive: for consumer plaintiffs to pursue DTPA meritorious claims even with relatively small damages, and for competent counsel to take such claims, even on a contingency fee basis. DTPA §17.44; *McKinley v. Drozd*, 685 S.W.2d 7, 9 (Tex. 1984); *see also* §1.02.28(D), *supra*. To make the most of these incentives, you must be prepared to properly present and prove your claim for attorney's fees at trial. The first two steps below—a timekeeping program and a proper fee contract form—are taken before you even agree to accept the case.

§9.20.1 Keep Detailed Accurate Records

While the Texas Supreme Court, in *Tony Gullo Motors I, L.P. v. Chapa*, 212 S.W.3d 299 (Tex. 2006), counseled that detailed time records will not be required as proof of attorney's fees, detailed time records are nevertheless extremely beneficial in presenting the claim for attorney's fees. If you intend to handle a significant amount of DTPA or other cases where attorney's fees are recoverable, I highly recommend that you obtain a computer billing program and diligently enter detailed records of your case-related activities.

Separate and apart from the multiple benefits to a law practice which come from such detailed recordkeeping, there are at least three distinct benefits for DTPA cases. First, being able to testify truthfully, accurately and convincingly as to the tasks performed and the amount of time expended on those tasks enhances your credibility with the jury. Second, properly redacted but detailed time records, when disclosed in discovery, can be a persuasive settlement tool when dealing with litigation-savvy defendants and insurance companies who are accustomed to reviewing such time records to justify payment to their own counsel. Third, the use of detailed time records prevents the inevitable underestimation (and perhaps overestimation) of the actual amount of time spent by counsel in handling a particular matter. I am consistently surprised, by the time a case gets to trial, by the amount of time I and my staff have spent on that particular case getting it ready for trial and presenting it to the trier of fact. Without detailed, accurate time records, I no doubt would have testified to less time, and thus recovered less in attorney's fees. Thus, while sufficient evidence of recoverable attorney's fees can be submitted to a jury without detailed time records, the discussion and forms that follow assume that you have and will use detailed time records in order to present your claim for recoverable attorney's fees.

§9.20.2 Draft Fee Agreement to Support Award

The next step in proving recoverable attorney's fees is to draft a fee contract that supports such an award. The standard personal injury-type contingency fee contract, where fees are not recoverable from the defendant and the fee is simply a straight percentage of the client's recovery, may not be flexible enough to allow you to make proof of and get paid for your efforts based on hourly or lodestar concepts. For instance, if the jury finds $10,000 in damages and $20,000 in attorney's fees, the client recovers a gross award of $30,000. Under a standard one-third contingency fee contract, the attorney's contractual fee is only $10,000 while the client receives a net recovery of $20,000. This unintended result can be easily avoided by including a provision in the fee contract for recovery of the amount of attorney's fees awarded by the judge or jury, if that amount is greater than a contingency fee based on percentage. The sample fee contract in §1.07(B) includes such a provision.

Furthermore, evidence of your fee contract with the plaintiff will be relevant, admissible and discoverable. Opposing counsel will be able to use a poorly drafted contingency fee contract to impeach an attempt to present evidence of the value of attorney's fees on an hourly or lodestar basis. In the example above, defense counsel could impeach your testimony regarding a $20,000 attorney's fee being reasonable and necessary with your written fee agreement limiting your attorney's fee to a simple one-third (*e.g.* $3,333) of the plaintiff's recovery. You do not want to address this issue for the first time sitting in the witness seat under cross-examination.

§9.20.3 Present Attorneys as Expert Witnesses

§9.20.3.1 Independent Expert

Under the DTPA, recoverable attorney's fees must be reasonable and necessary. DTPA §15.50(d). While the amount of time expended by the attorney and the tasks performed by the attorney are matters of fact which can be proven by a lay witness, the issues of whether the requested attorney's fees is "reasonable" is a matter of expert opinion which usually requires expert testimony from an attorney. *Thompson v. A. G. Nash & Co.,* 704 S.W.2d 822,824 (Tex. App.—Tyler 1985, no writ).

One practice which may lend credibility to your claim for attorney's fees is to use an attorney from a different firm who is not involved in the trial of the case to testify and give a legal opinion about the reasonableness and necessity of the claimed attorney's fees. With this strategy, you can often find someone in the venue where your case will be tried and whose opinion will be respected by the judge and jury. Try not to use someone whose personal friendship with you or other bias will overshadow their appearance of independence in testifying as an expert on your behalf. In such instances, the outside attorney must be made familiar with the trial preparation on the case and the amount of time involved in preparing and presenting it for trial. This familiarity can be gained through conversations with trial counsel and a review of the pleadings and discovery involved. *Amarillo v. Langley,* 651 S.W.2d 906, 915-16 (Tex. App.—Amarillo 1983, no writ).

> **Caution:**
> *No attorney-expert privilege.*
> Do not disclose privileged material to the outside attorney. Your conversations with this expert witness are discoverable to support or impeach the outside attorney's testimony.

§9.20.3.2 Trial Counsel as Witness

In every case, you should testify from your personal knowledge about the tasks performed by you and your office to prepare the case and present it for trial. Assuming you have established good rapport and credibility with the jury, you should not pass on the opportunity to testify from the witness stand regarding the efforts made and obstacles overcome to present the plaintiff and her case for trial. *See* §9.20(J), *infra*, for outline of testimony on attorney's fees.

Whether you present your evidence of attorney's fees yourself, through outside counsel, or both, you must timely disclose the attorney as an expert witness in compliance with any scheduling order, request for disclosure or other discovery requests from opposing counsel. *Sharp v. Broadway Nat'l. Bank*, 784 S.W.2d 669, 671-72 (Tex. 1990) (per curiam). Detailed time records may be reviewed prior to your testimony to refresh your recollection as to the number of hours spent on various subject matters and the tasks you performed. Production of the documents used to refresh your memory may be required if requested. *See Rotello v. Ring Around Prods., Inc.* 614 S.W.2d 455, 462-63 (Tex. App.—Houston [14th Dist.] 1981, writ ref'd n.r.e.) (objection to non-production waived when documents used to refresh memory not requested at time of testimony). If you plan to admit the billing records into evidence, you should timely disclose them with privileged material redacted in response to an appropriate discovery request. *See Montemayor v. Ortiz*, 208 S.W.3d 627, 663-64 (Tex. App.—Corpus Christi 2006, pet. filed) (on motion for reh'g.)

> **Practice Tip:**
> *Produce records not earlier than 30 days before trial.*
> There is certainly a tension here between the duty to disclose relevant evidence and the duty to protect the attorney-client and attorney work product privilege. Early disclosures of billing or time records will provide the other side a strategic advantage by showing them what you have done and what you haven't yet done to prepare your case for trial. I try to strike a balance between these two competing interests by agreeing to produce my billing and time records no earlier than 30 days prior to trial, and then redacting from them any references to privileged information.

§9.20.4 Segregate DTPA Fees From Non-Recoverable Attorney's Fees

The plaintiff is required to segregate the attorney's fees incurred pursuing the DTPA claims from those incurred pursuing related claims for which no recovery of attorney's fees is allowed, e.g., fraud or negligent misrepresentation. *See* §1.02.28(H) *supra*. For example, your time spent drafting the jury question on fraud and the jury question on negligent misrepresentation and your time spent drafting the paragraphs in your pleadings and discovery on those claims must be excluded. While detailed time records are not required for this effort (*Tony Gullo Motors I, L.P. v. Chapa*, 212 S.W.3d 299 (Tex. 2006)), such records may assist you in formulating an opinion as to the percentage of attorney time and effort expended solely pursuing these non-DTPA claims. After reviewing those records, you can then form an opinion as to what percentage of your time spent on the case would have been spent regardless of the existence of these non-DTPA claims, and reduce the total fees you claim accordingly.

Practice Tip:
Plan ahead; keep detailed time records from the beginning.
By keeping detailed time records of each task you performed and how long it took you to perform it, you will be in a much better position to accurately segregate your work between DTPA and non-DTPA claims. Thus, instead of recording, "Research Plaintiff's causes of action, 3.0 hours," record, "Research DTPA claim, 2.0 hours; Research negligent misrepresentation claim, 1.0 hours."

Failure to segregate recoverable attorney's fees from non-recoverable attorney's fees may be waived by the opposing party's failure to object. *Home Savings Ass'n v. Guerra*, 733 S.W.2d 134, 137 (Tex. 1987); *Aero Energy, Inc. v. Circle C Drilling Co.*, 699 S.W.2d 821, 823 (Tex. 1985). That objection, however, may come as late as an objection to the court's charge with a question on attorney's fees. *Stewart Title Guaranty Co. v. Sterling*, 822 S.W.2d 1, 10 (Tex. 1991). By that time, however, curing the objection would require re-opening the evidence to take additional testimony on attorney's fees.

Practice Tip:
If necessary, move to re-open evidence.
If you face a valid objection at the jury charge stage that you did not properly segregate, move the court to re-open the evidence to do so. See Tex. R. Civ. P. Rule 270. Point out that it would be reversible error to refuse to submit the jury question on attorney's fees and that remand and re-trial is the likely remedy should the court of appeals uphold the objection.

§9.20.5 Present *Arthur Andersen* Factors to Jury

In *Arthur Andersen & Co. v. Perry Equipment Corp.*, 945 S.W.2d 812, 818 (Tex. 1997), the Texas Supreme Court outlined the factors the court "must" consider in determining the reasonableness of an attorney's fee award:

1) the time and labor involved, the novelty and difficulty of the questions involved, and the skill required to perform the legal services properly;

2) the likelihood that the acceptance of the particular employment will preclude other employment by the lawyer;

3) the fee customarily charged in the locality for similar legal services;

4) the amount involved and the results obtained;

5) the time limitations imposed by the client or the circumstances;

6) the nature and length of the professional relationship with the client;

7) the experience, reputation, and ability of the lawyer or lawyers performing the services; and,

8) whether the fee is fixed or contingent on results obtained or uncertainty of collection before the legal services have been rendered.

Id., citing TEX. DISCIPLINARY R. PROF'L CONDUCT 1.04, *reprinted in Tex. Gov't Code,* Tit. 2, subtit. G app. A (TEXAS STATE BAR RULES art. X, §9).

Despite this admonition, the current pattern jury charge question does not mandate an instruction to the jury to consider these factors on the attorney's fees question. *See* §10:13. The inclusion of an instruction on the *Arthur Andersen* factors is discretionary. *Id.* Prior to *Arthur Andersen*, at least one court approved a refusal of an instruction to the jury listing these factors. *See Fox v. Boese*, 566 S.W.2d 682, (Tex. Civ. App.—Houston [1st Dist.] 1978, writ ref'd. n.r.e.). Regardless of whether or not an instruction on the *Arthur Andersen* factors is included in the jury question, your testimony and evidence on attorney's fees should address these factors.

Practice Tip:
Andersen *factors may confuse jury.*
I prefer the current pattern jury question—without reference to the *Arthur Andersen* factors—because it has less potential to confuse the jury. The outline of testimony in §9.20.10 is designed to present testimony on all of the *Arthur Andersen* factors.

§9.20.6 Contingency Fee and Lodestar Evidence

If the plaintiff has paid or is obligated to pay the attorney's fees on a flat fee basis or hourly fee basis, you can readily determine an exact amount of attorney's fees from those charges. In that instance, any effort to seek recovery in a higher amount would be subject to impeachment by evidence of the amount actually paid or payable. However, when your fee is contingent upon a recovery, and especially when a set percentage of the plaintiff's recovery would be inadequate under the *Arthur Andersen* factors, you should offer hourly rate—or "lodestar"—testimony to establish the reasonable value of your services.

Calculating an attorney's fee based upon the simple formula of hours of work multiplied by an hourly rate has gained almost universal acceptance. This method has been dubbed the lodestar method by federal courts, and that term is now in widespread use in Texas state court practice. *See, e.g., Johnson v. Georgia Highway Express, Inc.*, 488 F.2d 714, 717-19 (5th Cir. 1974); *City of Houston v. Levingston*, 221 S.W.3d 204 (Tex. App.—Houston [1st Dist.] 2006, no writ) (approving lodestar method for Whistleblower case); *Toshiba Machine Co., America v. SPM Flow Control, Inc.*, 180 S.W.3d 761 (Tex. App.—Fort Worth 2005, no pet.) (approving lodestar under Tex. Civ. Prac. & Rem. Code Ch. 38). The starting place for determining your "lodestar" may be your hourly rate for non-contingency matters or may be the hourly rate customarily charged by attorneys of similar training and experience in the locality.

Practice Tip:
Get the State Bar Hourly Rates Report:
One good resource for prevailing hourly rates can be found in the State Bar of Texas Department of Research & Analysis Hourly Rates Report, last published in September 2006 for hourly rates in 2005. This report is available online through the State Bar of Texas website, www.texasbar.com. If it is relied upon by the testifying attorney, a copy of the report should be disclosed in pretrial disclosures.

When the attorney's fee is contingent, you may want to offer testimony for an upward adjustment to your usual hourly rate to reflect the risk associated with accepting employment on contingency fee matters.

Other factors, known as the *Johnson* factors, are appropriately considered in making such an adjustment to the "lodestar" hourly rate. See *Johnson v. Georgia Highway Express, Inc.*, 488 F.2d 714, 717-19 (5th Cir. 1974). The *Johnson* factors include:

1) the time and labor required;

2) the novelty and difficulty of the questions;

3) the level of skill required;

4) the effect on other employment by the attorney;

5) the customary fees;

6) whether the fee is fixed or contingent;

7) time limitations imposed by the client or the circumstances;

8) the amount involved and the results obtained;

9) the experience, reputation and ability of the attorney;

10) the undesirability of the case;

11) the nature and length of the attorney's relationship with the client; and

12) awards in similar cases.

Id at 717-19.

Discussion of the application of the *Johnson* factors is often seen in federal courts where the judge must determine a reasonable attorney's fee under federal law. *See, e.g. Saizan v. Delta Concrete Prods. Co.*, 448 F.3d 795, 800 (5th Cir. 2006)(FSLA claim); *Camargo v. Trammell Crow Interest Co.*, 318 F. Supp. 2d 448, 449-50 (E.D. Tex. 2004) (state law contract claim). Use of the *Johnson* factors to adjust the hourly rate is likewise gaining acceptance in Texas state courts. *See, e.g. Dillard Department Stores, Inc. v. Gonzales*, 72 S.W.3d 398, 412 (Tex. App.—El Paso 2002, pet. denied) (TCHRA claim) *W. Telemarketing Corp. Outbound v. McClure*, 225 S.W.3d 658 (Tex. App.—El Paso 2006, pet. den'd.) (TCHRA claim); *City of Houston v. Levingston*, 221 S.W.3d 204 (Tex. App.—Houston [1st Dist.] 2006, no writ) (whistle-blower claim). While experienced trial judges are likely to be familiar with the "lodestar" concept and upward adjustments made in accordance with the *Johnson* factors, the average juror is not. As a result, care must be taken in asking a jury to accept an upwardly adjusted "lodestar" hourly rate in some multiple of the usual and customary hourly rates in the locality. For instance, if the "lodestar" rate for the plaintiff's attorney in the county of suit is $200.00 per hour, a local jury may be put off by a request for an adjusted hourly rate of $500.00 per hour, even if a similar adjustment might be readily accepted by a trial judge. Caution should therefore be exercised to educate the jury, through the attorney's testimony, that such adjustments are usual and appropriate in contingency fee cases.

Practice Tip:

Voir dire the jury panel on attorney's fees; use expert opinion from independent counsel.

1. Voir Dire. If you are going to ask the jury for fees based upon a lodestar rate adjusted upwards, you need to qualify them through voir dire as receptive to this idea. The jury panel should be questioned about their attitudes on considering evidence of contingent attorney's fees and your proposed upward "lodestar" adjustment as a reward for the contingency fee

risk. From the jury panel's responses to voir dire questions, you can refine your requested adjustment to be in line with the jury's expressed attitudes.

2. Independent Counsel. Here is where having independent counsel works well. Plaintiff's counsel can appear biased when testifying that his fees should be larger because of a risk multiplier. Eliminate the appearance of bias by using an independent expert who will not benefit from the finding on attorney's fees to explain this concept to the jury.

§9.20.7 Contingency Fee, Percentage of Recovery

Up to now, the discussion has focused on obtaining a finding on reasonable and necessary attorney's fees based upon a formula of hours spent times the hourly rate. What if you want to recover contingent attorney's fees under the traditional percentage of recovery method? Before the Texas Supreme Court's decision in *Arthur Andersen & Co. v. Equipment Corp.*, 945 S.W.2d 812, 818 (Tex. 1997), it was accepted practice to ask the jury to simply find a reasonable percentage of the plaintiff's recovery for the calculation of attorney's fees. If, for instance, the jury answered "40%" in response to this question, the court would calculate the dollar amount of attorney's fees awarded as 40% of the damages awarded to the plaintiff. *See, e.g., State Farm Fire & Cas. Co. v. Price*, 845 S.W.2d 427, 436 (Tex. App.—Amarillo 1992, writ dism'd by agr.) (40% finding); *March v. Thiery*, 729 S.W.2d 889, 897 (Tex. App.—Corpus Christi 1987, no writ) (33 1/3%); *Liberty Mut. Ins. Co. v. Allen*, 669 S.W.2d 750, 755 (Tex. App.—Houston [1st Dist.] 1987, writ ref'd n.r.e.) (33 1/3% finding); *Texas Gen. Indem.*

Co. v. Speakman, 736 S.W.2d 874, 885-86 (Tex. App.—Dallas 1987, no writ) (33 1/3% finding).

Although the Supreme Court in *Arthur Andersen* expressly rejected this process of finding reasonable attorney's fees, the court did not reject the concept that a reasonable attorney's fee may be calculated as a percentage of the plaintiff's recovery. *Id.*, 945 S.W.2d at 819. Rather than asking the jury to find a specific percentage, the *Arthur Andersen* court held that the jury must be asked to make a specific dollar amount finding. *Id.* at 819. Thus, in an appropriate case, specific dollar amounts can and should be offered based upon a percentage of the actual damages findings the attorney is expecting the jury to make. Then, these amounts should be discussed in connection with the *Arthur Andersen* factors and an opinion offered that the resulting fee amount (calculated as a percentage of the plaintiff's recovery) is reasonable in light of these factors.

Practice Tip:
Introduce evidence of both methods.
If a percentage of the plaintiff's expected recovery would be completely inadequate to compensate the attorney for the effort spent handling the DTPA claims, leave it out. If the percentage fee would be adequate, consider introducing evidence of attorney's fees both as a percentage of the plaintiff's expected recovery and as if paid on an hourly basis. Evidence of hourly fees can lend credibility to the percentage calculation and will also give the jurors an alternative basis for awarding attorney's fees.

§9.20.8 Attorney's Fees for Appeals

In order to recover attorney's fees on appeal, the plaintiff must obtain findings in the trial court. *Int'l Sec. Life Ins. Co. v. Spray*, 468 S.W.2d 347, 349 (Tex. 1971). Proof of attorney's fees on appeal can not be made after the appeal has been taken. *Varner v. Cardenas*, 218 S.W.3d 68, 70 (Tex. 2007). As such, you will want to offer testimony of reasonable attorney's fees in the event of appeals to the Court of Appeals and to the Texas Supreme Court. The pattern jury question on attorney's fees asks the jury to make such findings. See §10:13, *supra*. Proof of the reasonable and necessary fees recoverable for these appeals is governed by the same rules as attorney's fees through trial with the overriding requirement that the fees on appeal be "reasonable." *See, e.g., Valley Coca-Cola Bottling v. Molina*, 818 S.W.2d 146, 148 (Tex. App.—Corpus Christi 1991, writ denied); *City of Dallas v. Arnett*, 762 S.W.2d 942, 957 (Tex. App.—Dallas 1988, writ denied).

For your testimony on attorney's fees on appeal, you will need to rely upon your experience or the experience of other attorneys as to the amount of time necessary to pursue or defend appeals. Due consideration should be given to the time you anticipate to be necessary for 1) obtaining and reviewing the record, 2) drafting the party's primary brief and any reply brief, 3) preparing for any oral argument before the Court of Appeals, 4) presenting the argument to the Court of Appeals and 5) any post-submission motions or motions for rehearing. The factors discussed above for determining and perhaps adjusting the "lodestar" hourly rate apply equally to attorney's fees on appeal.

Your contingency fee contract with the plaintiff may establish an increase in the contingency fee percentage in the event of an appeal. In such instances, you should testify to one or more calculations of the resulting contingency fee on appeal based upon assumptions for the recovery of other damages. For instance, if the contingency fee percentage steps up from 40% to 45% in the event of an appeal, testimony on attorney's fees for appeal should be based upon 5% of the expected recovery.

Practice Tip:
Explain the appeals process to the jury.
I recently had a jury award "$0" for attorney's fees on appeal, despite testimony that a reasonable attorney's fee for an appeal would be $20,000. The jury forewoman later explained that the jury did not believe the case should be appealed and expected their judgment to be accepted by the Plaintiffs with finality. Obviously, I should have done a better job of explaining that the Plaintiffs would have no choice but to defend the appeal should the Defendant decide to appeal the jury's verdict. My lesson: Explain to the jury that the defendant can and often does appeal their verdict, and the plaintiff is the only one to defend their verdict on appeal. Explain also that the defendant gets two appeals, one to the Court of Appeals and then another one to the Texas Supreme Court. Then explain that the award of appellate fees is conditional: it will only be awarded if there is an unsuccessful appeal by the defendant. See, e.g., §9.20.10, Form - Outline for Narrative Testimony on Attorney's Fees.

§9.20.9 Uncontroverted Testimony May Establish Amount of Recoverable Attorney's Fees as a Matter of Law

When the testimony on attorney's fees is "clear, direct and positive, and not contradicted by any other witness or attendant circumstances," it is taken as true to establish the recoverable attorney's fee as a matter of law. *Ragsdale v. Progressive Voters League*, 801 S.W.2d 880, 882 (Tex. 1990). As such, it is improper for the judge or jury to disregard such testimony and award nothing or a nominal amount for attorney's fees. *Id.* On a motion to enter judgment disregarding this finding, the judge will be required to enter judgment in accordance with the undisputed evidence of attorney's fees as a matter of law. *McMillin v. State Farm Lloyds*, 180 S.W.3d 183, 210 (Tex. App.—Austin 2005, pet. denied). See §10.23[c], *infra*, for form of motion.

Practice Tip:
Ask for partial directed verdict.
If opposing counsel does not challenge your evidence of attorney's fees, ask the judge for a partial directed verdict on attorney's fees.

§9.20.10 Form – Outline for Narrative Testimony on Attorney's Fees

<u>Outline for Narrative Testimony on Attorney's Fees</u>

"Ladies and gentlemen of the jury, as you know, my name is ____ [name] ____.

I am a lawyer in ____[city]____.

I went to law school at ____[school]____ and graduated in ____ [date]____.

I took the bar exam and then was licensed to practice law by the Texas Supreme Court and admitted to the State Bar of Texas on ____[date]____. [I am admitted to practice before the Supreme Court of Texas, the United States Supreme Court, the United States Court of Appeals for the Fifth Circuit, the United States District Courts for the Western, Northern and Southern Districts of Texas and the District of Arizona.]

Since graduating from law school, I have worked for/with ____ [briefly describe work history]____.

I currently work with [the firm of] ____[firm]____ where I am ____[partner/associate, etc.]____.

[I am Board Certified in Consumer & Commercial Law by the Texas Board of Legal Specialization. This means that I have taken exams and proven to the Board that I am competent to hold myself out as a specialist in cases concerning consumer and commercial law—the type of case we are presenting to you today. Of all the lawyers in Texas, only about 200 are able to say they are Board Certified in Consumer & Commercial Law.]

I frequently handle cases involving the Texas Deceptive Trade Practices—Consumer Protection Act, one of the Texas statutes which governs the conduct at issue in this lawsuit. I have been handling cases in this area of the law for the last ____[#]____ years.

For all contingency fee cases, use the following;

[I offer my services to clients on both an hourly fee basis and on a contingency fee basis. I have a number of clients who pay me by the hour to do their work. I send them a bill for my services based upon the hours I spent working on their case, and they pay it. In those cases, my fee is not contingent upon any outcome I might obtain for them. Because I get paid, win or lose, my fee is not at risk with the client's outcome.]

[I also offer my services to some clients on a contingency fee basis. This means that my fee is paid only when I obtain a recovery for them. If there is no recovery, I don't get paid for my work. Why would anyone agree to take work on such a risky arrangement when there are plenty of paying clients willing to pay on an hourly basis? Part of the reason is that I hope to be rewarded for that risk by obtaining a result where the fees would be greater than what I would get on an hourly basis.]

[In this case, I took the Plaintiffs' case on a contingency fee basis. That means I don't get paid unless they recover money from this case. Under that arrangement, the fee could be a percentage of their recovery. We agreed that I would take 40% of what money we were able to collect from these Defendants in settlement; but, if it came to a point where I had to ask the judge or jury to find or make an award of the reasonable attorney's fees in this case, I would take that amount as my fee, whichever is greater. Certainly, on many occasions, I have found that the fee calculated on an hourly basis will be larger than on a percentage basis, and that is probably/certainly the case here.]

Continue with the following, if applicable:

For my entire career, it has been my habit and practice to keep detailed, written time records in fractions of an hour for the work I do on my clients' cases, whether that work is on an hourly basis or on a contingency fee basis. To do this, I fill out time sheets every working day to record what I have done and how long it took me to do it. Those written time records are then put into our computer billing system every day by my secretary. At any given time, I can pull up those records on the computer and see what all I have done on a particular matter. With these records, we can then print out a detailed, itemized bill to send to our clients if that is what is called for in our fee agreement.

I have reviewed my time records from our billing system up through yesterday. To handle this case up to this point, I have had to: [Describe tasks performed, e.g., initial client interview, investigation of facts, legal research, demand letter, pre-suit communications, drafting and filing of the lawsuit, discovery and any discovery disputes, gathering evidence, pre-trial motions filed and defended, interviewing and selecting witnesses, preparing pre-trial filings, jury selection and trial]. These tasks were unusually time-consuming/difficult because of ____ [i.e., documentation was held by defendants and defendants did not cooperate in discovery] ____.

If asking for fees on a lodestar or hourly basis, use the following:

[Since I first met the Plaintiffs, I have spent ____ hours working on their case getting it ready for trial and ____ hours since the trial began. I estimate I will spend another ____ hours trying this case while we go through the Defendants' evidence and witnesses and then ask you to make your decisions on the facts. If we go through [next Friday], that will be a total of ____ hours spent on this case.]

[I have handled a number of DTPA cases in this county and the surrounding counties. I am familiar with the hourly rates charged by lawyers in our community. Those rates vary depending on the skills of the lawyer, the age or experience of the lawyer, the lawyer's reputation for obtaining good results and the degree of expertise the lawyer and his law firm bring to the table. I currently charge my clients an hourly rate of $____ to handle matters of this nature. When I was a younger lawyer with less skills and expertise, I worked for less. My rate has increased over the years because of my experience and expertise. In my opinion, it is usual and customary for lawyers of my ability, training and experience to charge their fees based upon this hourly rate.]

If asking for a lodestar adjustment upwards, and you are not using independent counsel to testify, consider using the following:

[As I have described to you earlier, there is a huge difference in the risk I take between getting paid hourly as I go along and waiting for the case to be resolved before getting paid anything. The common way to compensate an attorney for taking that risk is to adjust the value of the hourly rate used to calculate the fee. Sometimes that adjustment may be two, three or four times the hourly rate usually charged by a lawyer to his regular hourly clients, so if a lawyer is accustomed to receiving $250 an hour from his hourly clients, he may be entitled to $1000 an hour for his work in a contingency fee case. Here, I believe an adjustment of ____% is appropriate to my normal hourly rate to account for the contingent fee risk.]

Continue with the following:

In my opinion, an hourly rate of $____ is a reasonable hourly rate in this community for lawyers of the same or similar experience and expertise as mine in handling cases of this nature on the same arrangements as I have on this case. With ____ hours in this case through the end of this trial, that works out to attorney's fees of $____ [hours X $hourly rate].

If asking for fees on a contingency fee basis, use the following:

[In this case, we believe the Plaintiff's damages resulting from the Defendants' conduct are $____, and at the end of this case, when the judge submits written questions to you about damages, I am going to ask you find, from the evidence, that $____ is the amount necessary to compensate the Plaintiffs for their damages. If you agree that the evidence shows compensable damages of $____, 40% of that is $____. In my opinion, $____ would be a reasonable amount for attorney's fees through the trial of this case.]

Address any other Arthur Andersen factors which impact the amount of the fee, such as taking this case against this defendant will keep them from hiring you in the future, time limitations imposed by the client or the court, whether this is a long-standing client or a one-time client, etc.

If segregation is an issue, use the following:

[As you know, we have made several allegations against the Defendants in this case. By law, attorney's fees are recoverable on the Deceptive Trade Practices claims but not the fraud claim. However, if we do work which moves the ball forward on both claims at the same time, the fees for that work are recoverable and properly included in the total. Having reviewed the records I keep, and being personally familiar with all of the work done to date to pursue these claims against these Defendants, only about ____ hours of our work I have described for you that was done on this case [Consider testifying about specific tasks, adjusting the level of detail as necessary] was not related to these non-DTPA claims. That amounts to about ____% of the work. In other words, ____% of the work done was related to pursuing the claims on which attorney's fees are recoverable by law. With that percentage,

$____ would be the reasonable attorney's fees necessary to pursue the DTPA claims in this case, in my opinion.]

For fees on appeal, use the following:

At the end of this case, you will be asked to make findings on attorney's fees through trial as well as findings as to attorney's fees for any appeals. So you will understand what I am about to say, you need to know a couple of things about the appeals process. First of all, an appeal involves taking all of the papers here in court, having the transcript of all of the testimony you have heard typed up and reviewed, sending that to the court of appeals in ____ and asking them to make a different decision on one or more issues than the decision made by the judge or the jury at trial. It is a time-consuming process which involves a lot of reading, writing, reviewing and researching, and one or more additional court appearances.

Either side can appeal. Even though the Plaintiffs may be completely satisfied with the results you reach from your deliberations, the Defendants and their lawyers could decide to challenge those decisions through an appeal. That is their right. But if they choose to exercise that right, the Plaintiffs and I will be the ones having to stand up for the decisions made by you and Judge ____ in this case in the Court of Appeals. That would be additional work which the attorney is required to do to adequately represent his client. By law, neither the court of appeals nor the Supreme Court of Texas can take testimony on attorney's fees. So, we have to estimate those fees now and ask you to make findings on those fees at this trial. The Plaintiffs and I will not get another opportunity to do that, so we have to do it here.

Based upon my experience, I would estimate an appeal of this case to the Court of Appeals would take another ____ hours of my time to perform the tasks necessary to present this case to the Court of Appeals for any decision they might be asked to make. [*Consider describing appellate tasks further.*]

[*If hourly:* At the hourly rate of $____ [*lodestar/hourly rate from before*], that would be attorney's fees of $____ for an appeal to the Court of Appeals.

[*If pure contingency:* In my opinion/based upon the fee agreement I have with the Plaintiffs, that would be another ____% *or* $____ in attorney's fees which would be reasonably necessary to handle an appeal to the Court of Appeals.]

Of course, the fact that we are asking you to make findings on attorney's fees on appeal does not mean that either side will in fact appeal or that I will get those fees if there is no appeal. If there is no appeal, no one will get these fees and no one will have to pay them. However, we won't know whether there will be an appeal until well after you all have gone home and forgotten everything you know about this case. These findings are just there as a backup in case an appeal is in fact taken.

In that same light, you will also be asked to find reasonable attorney's fees to handle a subsequent appeal to the Supreme Court of Texas. In addition to the right to appeal decisions of this court and jury to the Court of Appeals, either side will have the right to ask the Supreme Court of Texas to review any decisions made on appeal by the Court of Appeals. A lot of the same work goes into an appeal to the Supreme Court, but a lot of that work has already been done in the appeal to the Court of Appeals. As a result, it takes less work to present a case to the Supreme Court than to the Court of Appeals. Based upon my experience, I would estimate an appeal of this case to the Supreme Court of Texas would take another ____ hours of my time to perform the tasks necessary to present this case to the Supreme Court of Texas for any decision they might be asked to make.

[*If hourly*, At the hourly rate of $____ [lodestar/hourly rate from before], that would be attorney's fees of $____ for an appeal to the Supreme Court of Texas.

[*If pure contingency*, In my opinion/based upon the fee agreement I have with the Plaintiffs, that would be another ____% *or* $____ in attorney's fees which would be reasonably necessary to handle an appeal to the Supreme Court of Texas.]

Again, those findings are necessary simply as a precaution. Only if an appeal is actually taken to the Court of Appeals or on from there to the Supreme Court of Texas will these findings you make come into effect in this case.

To summarize, it is my opinion that $____ is a reasonable amount for attorney's fees necessarily incurred by the Plaintiffs in the pursuit of their Deceptive Trade Practices claims in this case through trial; that in the event an appeal is taken the Court of Appeals, an additional amount of $____ would be a reasonable amount for attorney's fees necessary for the Plaintiffs to handle that appeal; and that in the event a further appeal is taken to the Supreme Court of Texas, an additional amount of $____ would be a reasonable amount for attorney's fees necessary for the Plaintiffs to handle that appeal.

That concludes my testimony.

(This page intentionally left blank.)

Chapter 10

Trial: Part Two—
Court's Charge to Judgment

§10.01 The Court's Charge
   §10.01.1 Supported by Pleadings and Evidence
   §10.01.2 Governing Rules
   §10.01.3 Case Example
   §10.01.4 Form of the Jury Questions
      [a] FORM: Requested special charge
      [b] FORM: Ruling on requested question, instruction or definition
§10.02 General Definitions and Instructions
      [a] FORM: Producing cause
      [b] FORM: Market value
      [c] FORM: Good and workmanlike manner
      [d] FORM: Uninhabitable
      [e] FORM: Unconscionable action or course of action
      [f] FORM: Express warranty
      [g] FORM: Knowingly
      [h] FORM: Intentionally
      [i] FORM: Corporate agents
      [j] FORM: Alter ego
      [k] FORM: Agency
§10.03 DTPA "Laundry List" Questions
      [a] FORM: False, misleading, or deceptive act or practice
         [a.1] FORM: Broad form jury questions
         [a.2] FORM: Separate form jury questions
      [b] FORM: Description of goods or services
      [c] FORM: Quality or style of goods or services
      [d] FORM: Misrepresented and unlawful agreements
      [e] FORM: Work or services performed
      [f] FORM: Failure to disclose
      [g] FORM: Failure to disclose (Alternate)
§10.04 Breach of Duty of Good Faith and Fair Dealing
      [a] FORM: Breach of duty of good faith and fair dealing—cancellation of insurance coverage
      [b] FORM: Breach of duty of good faith and fair dealing—claim denial or delay
§10.05 Negligent Misrepresentation
      [a] FORM: Negligent misrepresentation

§ 10.06 Fraud
- [a] FORM: Common law fraud: general question
- [b] FORM: Common law fraud instruction: fraud by affirmative misrepresentation
- [c] FORM: Common law fraud instruction: misrepresentation
- [d] FORM: Common law fraud instruction: duty to disclose
- [e] FORM: Common law fraud instruction: duty to disclose whole truth
- [f] FORM: Statutory fraud in real estate or stock transaction: misrepresentation
- [g] FORM: Statutory fraud in real estate or stock transaction: false promise

§ 10.07 Breach of Warranty
- [a] FORM: Breach of warranty (broad form)
- [b] FORM: Breach of warranty (separate form)
- [c] FORM: Breach of warranty of merchantability
- [d] FORM: Breach of implied warranty on services
- [e] FORM: Breach of warranty of habitability and workmanship (new house) (governed by RCLA and not RCCA)
- [f] FORM: Breach of warranty of suitability of commercial lease space

§ 10.08 Unconscionability
- [a] FORM: Unconscionable action or course of action

§ 10.09 Chapter 541 of the Insurance Code
- [a] FORM: Chapter 541 of the Insurance Code (broad form)
- [b] FORM: Chapter 541 of the Insurance Code (separate form)

§ 10.10 Damages
- [a] FORM: Damages (general form)
- [b] FORM: Damages (alternative form)
- [c] FORM: Restoration of money or property

§ 10.11 Specific Elements of Damages
- [a] FORM: Cost to repair
- [b] FORM: Loss of use
- [c] FORM: Loss of value—benefit of the bargain
- [d] FORM: Stigma damages
- [e] FORM: Mental anguish

§ 10.12 "Knowing" and "Intentional" Conduct
- [a] FORM: "Knowing" conduct
- [b] FORM: "Intentional" conduct

§ 10.13 Additional and Exemplary Damages
- [a] FORM: Additional or exemplary damages
- [b] FORM: Exemplary damages predicate
- [c] FORM: Exemplary damages amount

§ 10.14 Attorneys' Fees
- [a] FORM: Attorneys' fees

§ 10.15 Defenses to DTPA and Residential Construction Actions
- [a] FORM: Third Party Information
- [b] FORM: Unreasonable rejection of settlement offer
- [c] FORM: No opportunity to repair
- [d] FORM: Negligence of another person

§ 10.16 Statute of Limitations
    [a] FORM: —Discovery Rule
§ 10.17 Proportionate Responsibility
    [a] FORM: —Proportionate responsibility
§ 10.18 Sample DTPA Charge
    [a] FORM: —Sample DTPA charge
§ 10.19 Jury Arguments
§ 10.20 General Legal Principles
§ 10.21 Contents of Jury Arguments
§ 10.22 Preserving Error
§ 10.23 Improper Jury Arguments
§ 10.24 Contents and Structure of Jury Argument
§ 10.25 Motions for Judgment
    [a] FORM: Motion for judgment on the jury verdict
    [b] FORM: Defendant's motion for judgment on jury verdict
    [c] FORM: Plaintiff's motion for judgment disregarding certain jury findings — attorney's fees
§ 10.26 Final Judgments
    [a] FORM: Final judgment for damages and attorneys' fees
    [b] FORM: Final judgment for restoration of money or property and rescission
    [c] FORM: Final judgment for defendant's attorney's fees
    [d] FORM: Alternative judgment for attorney's fees

§10.01 The Court's Charge

The court's charge represents the culmination of months and sometimes years of work on a lawsuit. Obviously, a party can prevail only by obtaining favorable answers to the jury questions contained in the court's charge. For this reason, the questions asked of the jury should be the focus of the entire trial.

It is impossible to draft the charge without a basic understanding of the legal principles that apply. The following discussion briefly highlights some of the more important legal considerations. After these general legal principles are reviewed, several forms are presented by which requested questions, instructions and definitions can be submitted to the court.

§10.01.1 Supported by Pleadings and Evidence

Questions submitted to the jury must be supported by both the pleadings and the evidence. TEX. R. CIV. P. 278; *Union Pacific R.R. v. Williams*, 85 S.W.3d 162, 166 (Tex. 2002); *Alaniz v. Jones & Neuse, Inc.*, 907 S.W.2d 450, 452 (Tex. 1995). If evidence has been introduced that supports a theory of recovery or defense but on which there are no pleadings, then a trial amendment should be requested so there will be a proper foundation for the applicable jury questions. TEX. R. CIV. P. 66.

Practice Tip:
Only those jury questions that control disposition of the case should be included in the charge. *Moore v. Kitsmiller*, 201 S.W.3d 147, 153 (Tex. App.—Tyler 2006, pet. denied). In DTPA cases, questions about "materiality" and "proximate cause" have no bearing on the outcome and should be omitted unless common law causes of action that contain these elements are included. See *Weitzel v. Barnes*, 691 S.W.2d 598, 600 (Tex. 1985); *Smith v. Baldwin*, 611 S.W.2d 611, 616 (Tex. 1980). This rule is of practical as well as legal significance. Juries often spend considerable time debating each question in the charge. They are told, in the charge, that no single question is more important than any other. If unnecessary questions are included, then any time spent by the jury on these questions will be wasted time, and, more significantly, there is a risk that the one or two unnecessary questions submitted will hang the jury.

§10.01.2 Governing Rules

The rules governing the submission of and objections to the court's charge have been described by the Texas Supreme Court as a "labyrinth daunting to the most experienced trial lawyer." *State Dep't. of Highways & Pub. Transp. v. Payne*, 838 S.W.2d 235, 240 (Tex. 1992) (describing complexities of charge procedures). The following basic rules will be noted.

The party who needs a question answered affirmatively in order to prevail has the responsibility of asking the court to submit the question in substantially correct form. TEX. R. CIV. P. 278, 279; *Willis v. Maverick*, 760 S.W.2d 642, 647 (Tex. 1988). Failure to properly submit the question to the court waives any error of the court in omitting the question unless the question is one relied upon by the opposing party. *Cf. Lester v. Logan*, 907 S.W.2d 452 (per curiam) (Tex. 1995). In the latter circumstance, a specific objection to the omission of the question or the tender of the omitted question in substantially correct form will preserve error. TEX. R. CIV. P. 278, 279; *Morris v. Holt*, 714 S.W.2d 311 (Tex. 1986).

If the court's charge omits a necessary definition or instruction, a party must tender to the court the instruction or definition in writing and in "substantially correct wording." TEX. R. CIV. P. 278; *Placencio v. Allied Indus. International, Inc.*, 724 S.W.2d 20, 21-22 (Tex. 1987); *Select Ins. Co. v. Boucher*, 561 S.W.2d 474, 479 (Tex. 1978). The definitions or instructions must be requested in connection with the question to which they pertain so that the trial court is made aware of the deficiency. *Universal Servs. Co. v. Ung*, 904 S.W.2d 638, 640 (Tex. 1995). An objection without a tender of the necessary instruction or definition is insufficient to preserve error. TEX. R. CIV. P. 274, 278; *Woods v. Crane Carrier Co., Inc.*, 693 S.W.2d 377, 379 (Tex. 1985).

Any complaint about the charge submitted to the jury is waived unless a specific objection is made, distinctly pointing out the objectionable matter and the grounds of the objection. TEX. R. CIV. P. 272, 274; *Castleberry v. Branscum*, 721 S.W.2d 270, 277 (Tex. 1983); *Spencer v. Eagle Star Insurance Co. of America*, 876 S.W.2d 154 (Tex. 1994) (objection is sufficient to preserve error in defective instruction). Whether made by oral objection to the charge or by submission of a properly worded written question or instruction, the objection will be deemed waived unless "the party made the trial court aware of the complaint, timely and plainly, and obtained a ruling." *State Dep't of Highways & Pub. Transp. v. Payne*, 838 S.W.2d 235, 241 (Tex. 1992).

When no element of a ground of recovery or defense is submitted to the jury, and when that ground of recovery or defense is not conclusively established under the evidence, that ground of recovery or defense is waived. TEX. R. CIV. P. 279. Different rules apply, however, when one or more elements of a ground of recovery or defense are submitted, but another element or elements is omitted. In these circumstances, the omitted element or elements can be "deemed" found by the court:

> When a ground of recovery or defense consists of more than one element, if one or more of such elements necessary to sustain such ground of recovery or defense, and necessarily referable thereto, are submitted to and found by the jury, and one or more of such elements are omitted from the charge without request or objection, and there is factually sufficient evidence to support a finding thereon, the trial court, at the request of either party, may after notice and hearing and at any time before the judgment is rendered, make and file written findings on such omitted element or elements in support of the judgment. If no such written findings are made, such omitted element or elements shall be deemed found by the court in such manner as to support the judgment.

TEX. R. CIV. P. 279.

§10.01.3 Case Example

Gulf States Utilities Co. v. Low, 79 S.W.3d 561 (Tex. 2002), considered the reach of Rule 279 when the meaning of the trial court's judgment is unclear. In *Low*, the plaintiff sued the utility company for wrongfully disconnecting his service. The jury found the plaintiff's damages to be $100 for spoiled food, $5,000 for past psychological treatment, and $20,000 for past mental anguish. The jury also found $150,000 to be reasonable attorney's fees. After considerable post-trial jockeying, the trial court sent a letter to counsel in which it overruled certain motions and announced that a judgment would be entered for the plaintiff for past mental anguish and spoiled food ($20,100), as well as $35,000 in attorney's fees. The court then signed a judgment that was quite different from its letter: the plaintiff was awarded $12,100 in actual damages and no award was made for attorney's fees. The suspicion on appeal was that the $20,000 award for past mental anguish was reduced by the plaintiff's percentage of responsibility (40%), but there was no clear indication one way or the other. The court of appeals reformed the trial court's judgment. According to the court, because there were findings made on some of the elements necessary to recover mental anguish under the DTPA (*i.e.* a finding of unconscionability), under Rule 279 the omitted element, a "knowing" violation, could be *deemed* found.

A sharply divided Texas Supreme Court disagreed with the court of appeals' analysis and held that deemed findings may only be used to support a trial court's judgment. Since the trial court did not enter judgment on the DTPA claim, there could be no deemed findings made under that theory of recovery: "The court of appeals misapplied Rule 279 to deem a finding, not to support the trial court's judgment, but to render a new judgment for actual damages in an amount nearly fifteen times the trial court's award." *Gulf States Utilities Co. v. Low*, 79 S.W.3d 564. The court also held that the plaintiff could not recover $100 for spoiled food since he failed to testify as to a dollar value for the food. In her dissent, Justice Hankinson observed that, "[t]he Court's insistence that the jury is incapable or unqualified to evaluate Low's testimony without a recitation of the price of a dozen eggs and a pound of bacon needlessly elevates form over substance." *Gulf States Utilities Co. v. Low*, 79 S.W.3d 570.

The Texas Supreme Court has indicated a desire to simplify these rules to one basic test: did the party make the trial court "aware of the complaint, timely and plainly" and did the court rule. *State Dep't of Highways & Pub. Transp. v. Payne*, 838 S.W.2d 241; *see Texas Dep't of Human Servs. v. Hinds*, 904 S.W.2d 629, 638 (Tex. 1995). Nevertheless, there are some specific guidelines for determining when and how to object which are summarized in the following table.

	Submitted Incorrectly	**Wrongfully Omitted**
Question you rely upon	Object	Tender Question
Question other party relies upon	Object	Object OR Tender Question
Instruction/Definition you rely upon	Object	Object AND Tender Question
Instruction/Definition other party relies upon	Object	Object AND Tender Question

§10.01.4 Form of the Jury Questions

The proper form of jury questions has been a source of debate and confusion since the first jury was impaneled in Texas. Initially, the questions were burdened by instructions which, although intended to be helpful to juries, accumulated to such an extent that an error-free charge became almost impossible. *Lemos v. Montez*, 680 S.W.2d 798, 801 (Tex. 1984). In 1913, the Legislature enacted a statute that was designed to move Texas away from a general charge burdened by countless instructions, replacing it with special issues. *Lemos v. Montez*, 680 S.W.2d 801. Unfortunately, by 1973, special issues had become so granulated (*i.e.* a separate question about every conceivable fact in the case) that the Supreme Court amended the rules to require the use of broad form issues. TEX. R. CIV. P. 277; *Mobil Chemical Co. v. Bell*, 517 S.W.2d 245 (Tex. 1974). In addition to broad form issues, the court also approved the submission of liability and causation in one question. *See Members Mutual Insurance Co. v. Muckelroy*, 523 S.W.2d 77 (Tex. Civ. App.—Houston [1st Dist.] 1975, writ ref'd n.r.e.); *Scott v. Atchison, Topeka & Santa Fe Ry. Co.*, 572 S.W.2d 273 (Tex. 1978).

The use of broad form jury questions was approved in DTPA cases in *Brown v. American Transfer & Storage Co.*, 601 S.W.2d 931, 937 (Tex. 1980). Specifically, the Court stated that jury questions should, to the extent possible, be submitted in the language of the statute. *Brown v. American Transfer & Storage Co.*, 601 S.W.2d 937.

Although the trial court has the discretion to submit questions to the jury in broad form by combining more than one element of a cause of action or more than one type of damage in a single question, care must be taken in choosing this approach. In *Crown Life Ins. Co. v. Casteel*, 22 S.W.3d 378 (Tex. 2000), the trial court submitted a single broad-form liability question incorporating several laundry list items. The Texas Supreme Court held that the plaintiff was not entitled to assert several of those subsections as a basis for liability. Since there was a single answer to the jury question, it was not possible to know whether one of the invalid theories formed the sole basis for the jury's answer. Accordingly, the Court held that submission of the question was reversible error. Thus, if there is a genuine question as to the plaintiff's right to invoke one or more grounds for liability, a separate submission of that ground or separate answers for each ground may be warranted. The same rule has been applied to submission of damages questions. The Court has held that submission of a broad form question on damages that includes an element without any evidentiary support is harmful error. *Harris County v. Smith*, 96 S.W.3d 230 (Tex. 2002); *see also Royal Maccabees Life Ins. Co. v. James*, 134 S.W.3d 906 (Tex. App.—Dallas 2004, no pet.) (improper to submit a damage question which included the element of mental anguish when that question was conditioned on an affirmative answer to several liability questions one of which was breach of contract, for which mental anguish is not recoverable).

If there is a question as to the evidentiary or legal support for a particular element of damage, separate answers for the damages elements should be obtained.

The following form, in conjunction with the form which follows, can be used to submit requested instructions, definitions and questions.

[a] FORM: Requested special charge

```
                        NO. _____
_____          §    IN THE _____ COURT OF
                    §
vs.                 §    _____ COUNTY, TEXAS
                    §
_____          §    _____ JUDICIAL DISTRICT
```

PLAINTIFF'S [DEFENDANT'S] REQUESTED SPECIAL CHARGE

TO THE HONORABLE JUDGE OF THE DISTRICT COURT:

_____, plaintiff [defendant], submits the following jury questions, instructions and definitions prior to the time that the court's charge is submitted to the jury and within the time required by the Local Rules.

The court is requested to endorse its ruling in the space provided on each requested question, instruction and definition if any requested question, instruction or definition is modified or refused.

In this request, TEX. BUS. & COM. CODE §17.41 *et seq.* is cited as the "DTPA."

                          Respectfully submitted,

                          [Signature of attorney]

[Certificate of service]

[b] FORM: Ruling on requested question, instruction or definition

[*Insert requested question, instruction or definition*]

This request is ____ refused/ ____ modified as shown and reflected in the court's charge to the jury as submitted.

JUDGE PRESIDING

§10.02 General Definitions and Instructions

There are several terms requiring definition which are common to deceptive trade practices litigation. Additionally, the 1995 amendments introduced some new terms, such as "intentional" which previously had not been a feature of this type of litigation. The alternative forms which are contained in this section contain many of these terms along with their approved definitions. The definitions are written so that those which are needed in a particular case can be inserted directly into separate request forms as shown in the preceding section. The authorities cited should be included in each request to the court.

[a] FORM: Producing cause

"Producing cause" means a cause that was a substantial factor in bringing about the damages, if any, and without which the damages would not have occurred. There may be more than one producing cause.

Authority: DTPA §17.50(a); *Ford Motor Co. v. Ledesma*, 242 S.W.3d 32, 46 (Tex. 2007).

[NOTE: The only distinction between "producing cause" and "proximate cause" is that the latter includes an element of foreseeability while the former does not. *Archibald v. Act III Arabians*, 755 S.W.2d 84, 88 (Tex. 1988) (Gonzalez, J., dissenting); *Pope v. Rollins Protective Services Co.*, 703 F.2d 197, 202 (5th Cir. 1983); *Rotello v. Ring Around Products, Inc.*, 614 S.W.2d 455 (Tex. Civ. App.—Houston [14th Dist.] 1981, writ ref'd n.r.e.). The approved definition of "proximate cause" is provided at 1 Texas Pattern Jury Charges §2.04 (2006); see §10.16 *infra*.]

[b] FORM: Market value

"Market value" means the amount of money which would be paid in cash by a willing buyer who desires to buy, but is not required to buy, to a willing seller who desires to sell but is under no necessity of selling.

Authority: *Exxon Corp. v. Middleton*, 613 S.W.2d 240, 246 (Tex. 1981).

[c] FORM: Good and workmanlike manner

"Good and workmanlike manner" is that quality of work performed by one who has the knowledge, training or experience necessary for the successful practice of a trade or occupation and performed in a manner generally considered proficient by those capable of judging such work.

Authority: *Melody Home Manufacturing Co. v. Barnes*, 741 S.W.2d 349, 354 (Tex. 1987).

[d] FORM: Uninhabitable

A house is uninhabitable if it is not suitable for human habitation, that is, if the house was constructed in such a manner as to subject its occupants to an unreasonable risk of danger or unreasonable discomfort.

Authority: *Humber v. Morton*, 426 S.W.2d 554, 559 (Tex. 1968); *Gupta v. Ritter Homes, Inc.*, 646 S.W.2d 168, 169 (Tex. 1983).

[e] FORM: Unconscionable action or course of action

An unconscionable action or course of action is an act or practice that, to a consumer's detriment, takes advantage of the lack of knowledge, ability, experience or capacity of the consumer to a grossly unfair degree.

Authority: DTPA §17.45(5); 4 TEXAS PATTERN JURY CHARGES §102.7 (2010).

[f] FORM: Express warranty

An "express warranty" is any affirmation of fact or promise made by [defendant] that relates to the goods [or services] and becomes part of the basis of the bargain [or Any description of goods [or services] which is made a part of the basis of the bargain] [or Any sample or model of the goods sold which is made part of the basis of the bargain]. It is not necessary that formal words such as "warrant" or "guarantee" be used or that there be a specific intent to make a warranty.

Authority: TEX. BUS. & COM. CODE §2.313; *see* 4 TEXAS PATTERN JURY CHARGES §102.09 (2010).

[NOTE: This definition of "express warranty" is applicable in connection with the sale of "goods" as that term is defined in the Uniform Commercial Code. This definition also is consistent with the courts' treatment of express warranties in transactions not governed by the UCC. *See Southwestern Bell Telephone Co. v. FDP Corp.*, 811 S.W.2d 572, 574 (Tex. 1991); *McCrea v. Cubilla Condominium Corp.*, 685 S.W.2d 755, 757 (Tex. App.—Houston [1st Dist.] 1985, writ ref'd n.r.e.). *Woods v. Littleton*, 554 S.W.2d 662, 666 n. 6 (Tex. 1977).]

[g] FORM: Knowingly

"Knowingly" means actual awareness, at the time of the act or practice complained of, of the falsity, deception, or unfairness of the act or practice giving rise to the consumer's claim, but actual awareness may be inferred where objective manifestations indicate that a person acted with actual awareness.

[or, in breach of warranty claims]

"Knowingly" means actual awareness of the act, condition, defect or failure constituting the breach of warranty, but actual awareness may be inferred where objective manifestations indicate that a person acted with actual awareness.

Authority: DTPA §17.45(9); 4 Texas Pattern Jury Charges §102.21 (2010).

[h] FORM: Intentionally

"Intentionally" means actual awareness of the falsity, deception, [or unfairness] of the act or practice [or the condition, defect or failure constituting the breach of warranty] giving rise to [plaintiff's] claim, coupled with the specific intent that [plaintiff] act in detrimental reliance on the falsity or deception [or in detrimental ignorance of the unfairness]. Intention may be inferred from objective manifestations that indicate that the person acted intentionally, or from facts showing that [defendant] acted with flagrant disregard of prudent and fair business practices to the extent that [defendant] should be treated as having acted intentionally.

Authority: DTPA §17.45(13); 4 Texas Pattern Jury Charges §102.21 (2010) (Comment).

[i] FORM: Corporate agents

You are instructed that a corporation can act or fail to act only through its agents, servants, employees and representatives.

Authority: *See Columbia Rio Grande Healthcare, L.P. v. Hawley*, 284 S.W.3d 851, 862-863 (Tex. 2009); *Underwriters Life Ins. Co. v. Cobb*, 746 S.W.2d 810, 821 (Tex. App.—Corpus Christi 1988, no writ).

[j] FORM: Alter ego

A corporation is an alter ego of a natural person(s) when there is such unity between the corporation and the individual that the separateness of the corporation has ceased and holding only the corporation liable would result in injustice. Alter ego is shown from the total dealings of the corporation, and the individual, including the degree to which corporate and individual property have been kept separately, the amount of financial interest, ownership and control the individuals maintain over the corporation and whether the corporation has been used for personal purposes.

Authority: *Castleberry v. Branscum*, 721 S.W.2d 270 (Tex. 1986).

[NOTE: The alter ego theory is now restricted to non-contractual obligations of a corporation. Tex. Bus. Org. Code § 21.223.]

[k] FORM: Agency

[NOTE: An instruction on agency may involve one or more of the four different kinds of authority possessed by agents, each of which is defined in this section.]

(1) *Authority of agent*

A party's conduct includes the conduct of another who acts with the party's authority or apparent authority.

Authority: *Celtic Life Ins. Co. v. Coats*, 885 S.W.2d 96, 98 (Tex. 1994); *Royal Globe Ins. Co. v. Bar Consultants*, 577 S.W.2d 688, 693-94 (Tex. 1979).

(2) *Actual authority*

"Authority" for another to act for a party must arise from the party's agreement that the other act on behalf and for the benefit of the party. If a party so authorizes another to perform an act, that other party is also authorized to do whatever else is proper, usual, and necessary to perform the act expressly authorized.

Authority: 4 TEXAS PATTERN JURY CHARGES §101.4 (2010); *Gaines v. Kelly*, 235 S.W.3d 179, 182-3 (Tex. 2007).

(3) *Apparent authority*

"Apparent authority" exists if a party (1) knowingly permits another to hold himself out as having authority or, (2) through lack of ordinary care, bestows on another such indications of authority that lead a reasonably prudent person to rely on the apparent existence of authority to his detriment. Only the acts of the party sought to be charged with responsibility for the conduct of another may be considered in determining whether apparent authority exists.

Authority: 4 TEXAS PATTERN JURY CHARGES §101.4 (2010); *Gaines v. Kelly*, 235 S.W.3d 179, 182-3 (Tex. 2007); *Baptist Mem. Hosp. Sys. v. Sampson*, 969 S.W.2d 945, 948 (Tex. 1998).

§10.03 DTPA "Laundry List" Questions

It has been established that DTPA liability questions should be submitted in the language of the statute, whenever possible, with only those modifications necessary to make the jury questions clear. *Brown v. American Transfer and Storage Co.*, 601 S.W.2d 931 (Tex. 1980), *cert. denied*, 449 U.S. 1015 (1980); *Spencer v. Eagle Star Ins. Co. of Am.*, 876 S.W.2d 154 (Tex. 1994). For example, if the representation pertains to future goods or services, the future tense should be used in the instruction. *See* 4 TEXAS PATTERN JURY CHARGES §102.2 (Comment) (2010); *Smith v. Baldwin*, 611 S.W.2d 611 (Tex. 1980). In addition, it has been suggested that in DTPA litigation both the liability and causation questions should be combined into one. *See, e.g.* 4 TEXAS PATTERN JURY CHARGES §102.1 (2010); *see generally*, TEX. R. CIV. P. 277.

The following format for submitting DTPA "laundry list" questions is generally recommended. The format is further illustrated in §10.16, *infra*. However, care must be taken in choosing this broad form approach. In *Crown Life Ins. Co. v. Casteel*, 22 S.W.3d 378 (Tex. 2000), the trial court submitted a single broad-form liability question incorporating several laundry list items. The Texas Supreme Court held that the plaintiff was not entitled to assert several of those subsections as a basis for liability. Since there was a single answer to the jury question, it was not possible to know whether one of the invalid theories formed the sole basis for the jury's answer. Accordingly, the Court held that submission of the question was reversible error. Thus, if there is a genuine question as to the plaintiff's right to invoke one or more grounds for liability, a separate submission of that ground or separate answers for each ground may be warranted.

[a] FORM: False, misleading, or deceptive act or practice

The following alternative forms illustrate the submission of DTPA cases. The first form is appropriate when there is evidence to support each, distinct "laundry list" violation; the second form is appropriate when there is an argument that one or more of the laundry list violations is not supported by the evidence:

[a.1] FORM: Broad form jury questions

```
Did [defendant] engage in any false, misleading, or deceptive
act or practice on which [plaintiff] relied to his [her] detriment
and that was a producing cause of damages to [plaintiff]?

"False, misleading or deceptive" means any of the following:
[insert all appropriate laundry list provisions, e.g., causing
confusion or misunderstanding as to [defendant's] affiliation,
connection, or association with another; or representing that an
agreement confers or involves rights or remedies which it does
not have or involve].

Answer "yes" or "no."

Answer _____
```

Authority: DTPA §17.46(b)(2), (12); see also 4 TEXAS PATTERN JURY CHARGES §102.1 (2010).

[a.2] FORM: Separate form jury questions

Did [defendant] engage in any of the following conduct on which [plaintiff] relied to his [her] detriment that was a producing cause of damages to [plaintiff]? Answer separately as to each:

	YES	NO
A. Causing confusion or misunderstanding as to [defendant's] affiliation, connection, or association with another.	____	____
B. Representing that an agreement confers or involves rights or remedies which it does not have or involve	____	____

[b] FORM: Description of goods or services

[NOTE: The following sample question demonstrates an alternative format for asking the question which tailors the question to the facts of the case, and which to some may be more readable.]

Did [plaintiff] rely to his [her] detriment on [defendant's] representation, if any, that the [house] had characteristics which it did not have [or that [defendant] had a sponsorship, affiliation, or connection which he did not] and if so, was it a producing cause of damages to [plaintiff]?

Answer "Yes" or "No."

Answer: _____

Authority: DTPA §17.50(a), §17.46(b)(5).

[c] FORM: Quality or style of goods or services

Did [defendant] represent that goods [or services] were of a particular standard, quality, or grade [or that goods were of a particular style or model] when they were of another, and if so, did [plaintiff] rely on this representation to his [her] detriment and, if so, was it a producing cause of damages to [plaintiff]?

Answer "Yes" or "No."

Answer: _____

Authority: DTPA §17.50(a), §17.46(b)(7).

[d] FORM: Misrepresented and unlawful agreements

Did [defendant] represent that an agreement conferred or involved rights, remedies, or obligations which it did not have or involve [or which were prohibited by law], on which [plaintiff] relied to his [her] detriment, and if so, was it a producing cause of damages to [plaintiff]?

Answer "Yes" or "No."

Answer: _____.

Authority: DTPA §17.46(b)(12).

[e] FORM: Work or services performed

Did [plaintiff] rely to his [her] detriment on [defendant's] representation, if any, that work or services had been performed on [or parts replaced in] goods when the work or services were not performed [or the parts were not replaced] and if so, was it a producing cause of damages to [plaintiff]?

Answer "Yes" or "No."

Answer: _____.

Statutory authority: DTPA §17.46(b)(21).

[f] FORM: Failure to disclose (See note below)

Did [defendant] fail to disclose information concerning goods [or services] which was known to [defendant] at the time of the transaction, and was the failure to disclose such information, if any, intended to induce [plaintiff] into a transaction into which [plaintiff] would not have entered had the information been disclosed, and if so, was it a producing cause of damages to [plaintiff]?

Answer "Yes" or "No."

Answer: _____.

Statutory authority: DTPA §17.46(b)(24).

[NOTE: As a result of the 1995 amendments, a consumer must prove detrimental reliance on the defendant's conduct. As shown in the form questions **[a]** through **[d]** above, inserting detrimental reliance into a laundry list question is not difficult. When the question involves a violation of subsection (b)(24), however, the task is problematic. On the one hand, a finding by the jury that a consumer would not have entered a transaction but for the failure to disclose seems to be the functional equivalent of detrimental reliance, especially when coupled with the producing cause inquiry. Stated differently, a jury finding that the consumer would not have entered the transaction but for the failure to disclose is the same as reliance; and, a finding that the failure to disclose was a producing cause of damages proves that the reliance was detrimental. For these reasons, the author believes that the form question in subsection [f] is sufficient and appropriate. There is, at this time, no authority other than logic to support this belief. An alternative, of course, is to use the general jury question in §[a] above which incorporates detrimental reliance into the question, followed by the language in DTPA §17.46(b)(24). *See* 4 Texas Pattern Jury Charges §102.1 and 102.5 (2010).]

[g] FORM: Failure to disclose (Alternate)

Did [defendant] fail to disclose information concerning goods [or services] which was known to [defendant] at the time of the transaction, and was the failure to disclose such information, if any, intended to induce [plaintiff] into a transaction into which [plaintiff] would not have entered had the information been disclosed, and if so, was it a producing cause of damages to [plaintiff]?

Answer "Yes" or "No."

Answer: _____.

Statutory authority: DTPA §17.46(b)(24).

§10.04 Breach of Duty of Good Faith and Fair Dealing

The Texas Supreme Court has recognized a cause of action for breach of the duty of good faith and fair dealing in insurance transactions. *Arnold v. National County Mut. Fire Ins. Co.*, 725 S.W.2d 165 (Tex. 1987); *Aranda v. Insurance Co. of N. Am.*, 748 S.W.2d 210 (Tex. 1988); *Union Bankers Ins. Co. v. Shelton*, 889 S.W.2d 278 (Tex. 1994).

Prior to the 1995 amendments, an insurance company's breach of the duty of good faith and fair dealing was actionable under Chapter 541 of the Texas Insurance Code (formerly Article 21.21). *See Vail v. Texas Farm Bureau Mut. Ins. Co.*, 754 S.W.2d 129 (Tex. 1988). The 1995 amendments limit actions under Chapter 541 to conduct specifically enumerated in Subchapter B of Chapter 541 or §17.46(b) of the DTPA. The common law action for breach of the duty of good faith and fair dealing was not included in the enumerated lists.

In *Universe Life Ins. Co. v. Giles*, 950 S.W.2d 48 (Tex. 1997), the Texas Supreme Court abandoned its longstanding definition of the duty of good faith and fair dealing and adopted, in its place, the "reasonably clear" standard of §541.060 (2)(A) (formerly Art. 21.21 §4(10)(ii)). An insurer now breaches the duty of good faith and fair dealing it owes to the insured in handling a claim when it fails to "attempt in good faith to effectuate a prompt, fair, and equitable settlement of a claim with respect to which the insurer's liability has become reasonably clear." *Universe Life Ins. Co. v. Giles, supra* at 55; *State Farm Lloyds v. Nicolau*, 951 S.W.2d 444 (Tex. 1997); *State Farm Fire & Cas. v. Simmons*, 963 S.W.2d 42 (Tex. 1998); As a result, the same conduct is actionable both at common law and under the Insurance Code.

The Court did not indicate a changed definition in policy cancellation cases. In *Union Bankers Ins. Co. v. Shelton*, 889 S.W.2d 278 (Tex. 1994), the Court held that an insurer breaches the duty of good faith and fair dealing when it "wrongfully cancels an insurance policy without a reasonable basis" and the insurer "knew or should have known of that fact." *Id.* at 283; *Rice v. Metro. Life Ins. Co.*, 324 S.W.3d 660, 672 (Tex. App.—Fort Worth 2010, no pet.). However, when an action for violation of Chapter 541 or for breach of the common law duty of good faith and fair dealing is based on the insurance company's failure to pay a claim, the absence of coverage under the insurance policy is a complete defense. *See, Progressive County Mutual Ins. Co. v. Boyd*, 177 S.W.3d 919 (Tex. 2005).

The first form that follows submits wrongful policy cancellation in accordance with the "no reasonable basis" test articulated in *Shelton*. The second form submits wrongful claim denial or delay in accordance with the "reasonably clear" standard articulated in *Giles*. These forms differ from the forms suggested in PJC by including the proximate cause element as an optional part of the liability question. See 4 TEXAS PATTERN JURY CHARGES 115.14. (2010) (including proximate cause element in damage question). The proximate cause element is optional because no causation element is required when the only damages sought are policy benefits. *Vail v. Texas Farm Bureau Mut. Ins. Co.*, 754 S.W.2d 129 (Tex. 1988) (policy benefits are damages caused by insurer's unfair refusal to pay claim as a matter of law).

[a] FORM: Breach of duty of good faith and fair dealing—cancellation of insurance coverage

Did [defendant] fail to fulfill its duty to act fairly and in good faith in connection with the cancellation of [plaintiff's] insurance coverage [and if so, was such failure a proximate cause of damages to [plaintiff]]?

You are instructed that an insurer fails to fulfill its duty to act fairly and in good faith in connection with the cancellation of an insured's coverage when:

(1) the insurer cancels the insurance coverage when there was no reasonable basis for doing so; and

(2) the insurer knew or should have known that there was no reasonable basis for such cancellation.

Answer "Yes" or "No."

Answer: _____

Authority: Union Bankers Ins. Co. v. Shelton, 889 S.W.2d 278 (Tex. 1994); *Rice v. Metro. Life Ins. Co.*, 324 S.W.3d 660, 672 (Tex. App.–Fort Worth 2010, no pet.).

[b] FORM: Breach of the duty of good faith and fair dealing—claim denial or delay

Did [defendant] fail to fulfill its duty to act fairly and in good faith in the handling of [plaintiffs] insurance claim [and if so, was such failure a proximate cause of damages to [plaintiff]]?

You are instructed that an insurer fails to fulfill its duty to act fairly and in good faith in the handling of an insured's claim when it:

(1) fails to attempt in good faith to effectuate a prompt, fair, and equitable settlement of a claim with respect to which the insurer's liability has become reasonably clear; or

(2) refuses to pay a claim without conducting a reasonable investigation.

Answer "Yes" or "No"

Answer: _____

Authority: *Universe Life Ins. Co. v. Giles*, 950 S.W.2d 48 (Tex. 1997); TEX. INS. CODE §541.060(a)(7); 4 TEXAS PATTERN JURY CHARGES §103.1 (2010).

§10.05 Negligent Misrepresentation

Negligent misrepresentation consists of the following elements:

1. A person is acting in the course of his business, profession or employment or has a pecuniary interest in the transaction; and

2. Supplies false information for the guidance of others in their business transactions; and

3. Fails to exercise reasonable care or competence in obtaining or communicating the information; and

4. Causes pecuniary loss to others because of their justifiable reliance upon the information communicated.

See RESTATEMENT (SECOND) OF TORTS §552.

Since recovery is restricted to "pecuniary loss," care must be taken to limit the damage question submitted to the jury. *See Federal Land Bank Ass'n v. Sloane*, 825 S.W.2d 439 (Tex. 1991); *D.S.A., Inc. v. HILLSBORO INDEP. SCH. DIST.*, 973 S.W. 2d 662 (Tex. 1998) (benefit of the bargain damages not available); *see generally* §10.11 *infra*.

[a] FORM: Negligent misrepresentation

Did [defendants] make a negligent misrepresentation on which [plaintiff] justifiably relied?

A negligent misrepresentation occurs when:

a. a party makes a representation in the course of *his/her* business or in a transaction in which he/she has a pecuniary interest, and

b. the representation supplies false information for the guidance of *another/others* in their business, and

c. the party making the representation did not exercise reasonable care or competence in obtaining or communicating the information.

Answer "Yes" or "No."

Answer:_____

Authority: 4 Tex. Pattern Jury Charges §105.19 (2010); *Federal Land Bank Ass'n of Tyler v. Sloane*, 825 S.W.2d 439 (Tex. 1991); see also *McCamish, Martin, Brown & Loeffler v. F.E. Appling Interests*, 991 S.W.2d 787, 791 (Tex. 1999).

§10.06 Fraud

A misrepresentation of fact, made with knowledge of its falsity or made recklessly without knowledge of whether it is true or false, may form the basis of a common law fraud action. *See Eagle Properties, Ltd. v. Scharbauer*, 807 S.W.2d 714 (Tex. 1990). Under some circumstances, statements of opinion and promises of future performance may also constitute actionable fraud. *See Formosa Plastics Corp. USA v. Presidio Eng'rs & Contrs.*, 960 S.W.2d 41 (Tex. 1998); *Trenholm v. Ratcliff*, 646 S.W.2d 927 (Tex. 1983); *Fina Supply, Inc. v. Abilene Nat'l Bank*, 726 S.W.2d 537 (Tex. 1987); *Spoljaric v. Percival Tours, Inc.*, 708 S.W.2d 432 (Tex. 1986). Additionally, when there is a duty to disclose information, the failure to do so may support a fraud cause of action. *See Bradford v. Vento*, 48 S.W.3d 749, 755 (Tex. 2001).

[a] FORM: Common law fraud: general question

Did [defendant] commit fraud in his [her] dealings with [plaintiff]?

[*Insert one or more of the following definitions of fraud*]

Answer "Yes" or "No."

Answer:_____

Authority: 4 Tex. Pattern Jury Charges §105.1 (2010); *Trenholm v. Ratcliff*, 646 S.W. 2d 927 (1983); *Spoljaric v. Percival Tours, Inc.*, 708 S.W.2d 432 (Tex. 1986).

[b] FORM: Common law fraud instruction: fraud by affirmative misrepresentation

You are instructed that a person commits fraud when:

a. that person makes a material misrepresentation; and

b. the misrepresentation is made with knowledge of its falsity or made recklessly without any knowledge of the truth and as a positive assertion; and

c. the misrepresentation is made with the intention that it should be acted upon by the other party; and

d. the other party acts in reliance upon the misrepresentation and thereby suffers injury.

Authority: 4 Tex. Pattern Jury Charges §105.2 (2010); *Trenholm v. Ratcliff*, 646 S.W.2d 927 (1983); *Spoljaric v. Percival Tours, Inc.*, 708 S.W.2d 432 (Tex. 1986).

[c] FORM: Common law fraud instruction: misrepresentation

You are instructed that "misrepresentation" means

[*insert as many of the following as are applicable*]:

a false statement of fact [*or*]

a promise of future performance with an intent not to perform as promised [*or*]

a statement of opinion based on a false statement of fact [*or*]

a statement of opinion that the maker knows to be false [*or*]

a statement of opinion that is false, made by one claiming or implying to have special knowledge of the subject matter of the opinion. "Special knowledge" means knowledge or information superior to that possessed by the other party and to which the other party did not have equal access.

Authority: 4 TEX. PATTERN JURY CHARGES §§105.3A-105.3E (2010); *Trenholm v. Ratcliff*, 646 S.W. 2d 927 (1983); *Spoljaric v. Percival Tours, Inc.*, 708 S.W.2d 432 (Tex. 1986); 4 TEX. PATTERN JURY CHARGES §105.01 - 105.025 (1992).

[d] FORM: Common law fraud instruction: duty to disclose

[*The following instruction is only appropriate if the court has found that there is a duty to disclose information as a matter of law.*]

For the purposes of this question you are also instructed that a person commits fraud when:

a. a person fails to disclose a material fact within the knowledge of that person, and

b. the person knows that the other party is ignorant of the fact and does not have an equal opportunity to discover the truth, and

c. the person intends to induce the other party to take some action by failing to disclose the fact, and

d. the other party suffers injury as a result of acting without knowledge of the undisclosed fact.

Authority: 4 TEX. PATTERN JURY CHARGES §105.4 (2010). *See Bradford v. Vento*, 48 S.W.3d 749, 755 (Tex. 2001); *Spoljaric v. Percival Tours, Inc.*, 708 S.W.2d 432 (Tex. 1986).

[e] FORM: Common law fraud instruction: duty to disclose whole truth

For the purposes of this question you are also instructed that a person commits fraud when he/she:

a. voluntarily discloses information, but fails to disclose the whole truth; *or*

b. makes a representation, but fails to disclose new information when that party is aware the new information makes the earlier representation misleading or untrue; *or,*

c. makes a partial disclosure and conveys a false impression.

Authority: 4 TEXAS PATTERN JURY CHARGES §105.4 (2010) (Comment); *see, e.g., Bradford v. Vento*, 48 S.W.3d 749, 755 (Tex. 2001); *Spoljaric v. Percival Tours, Inc.*, 708 S.W.2d 432 (Tex. 1986); *Columbia/HCA Healthcare Corp. v. Cottey*, 72 S.W.3d 735, 744-45 (Tex. App.-Waco 2002, no pet.); *Anderson, Greenwood & Co. v. Martin*, 44 S.W.3d 200,

212-13 (Tex. App.-Houston [14th Dist.] 2001, pet. denied); *Lesikar v. Rappeport*, 33 S.W.3d 282, 299 (Tex. App.-Texarkana 2000, pet. denied); *Hoggett v. Brown*, 971 S.W.2d 472, 487 (Tex. App.-Houston [14th Dist.] 1997, pet. denied); *Ralston Purina Co. v. McKendrick*, 850 S.W.2d 629, 636 (Tex. App.-San Antonio 1993, writ denied).

[f] FORM: Statutory fraud in real estate or stock transaction: misrepresentation

Did [defendant] commit fraud in his/her dealings with [plaintiff], and if so, was this a proximate cause of damages to [plaintiff]?

You are instructed that a person commits fraud when:

a. the person makes a false representation of a past or existing material fact, and

b. the false misrepresentation is made to another person for the purpose of inducing that person to enter into a contract, and

c. the false representation is relied on by that party in entering into that contract.

Answer "Yes" or "No"

Answer: _____

Authority: TEX. BUS. & COM. CODE §27.01; 4 TEX. PATTERN JURY CHARGES §§ 105.7, 105.8 (2010).

[g] FORM: Statutory fraud in real estate or stock transaction: false promise

Did [defendant] commit fraud in his/her dealings with [plaintiff], and if so, was this a proximate cause of damages to [plaintiff]?

You are instructed that a person commits fraud when:

a. the person makes a false promise to do an act, and

b. the promise is material, and

c. the promise is made with the intention of not fulfilling it, and

d. the promise is made to a person for the purpose of inducing that person to enter into a contract, and

e. that person relies on the promise in entering into that contract.

Answer "Yes" or "No"

Answer: _____

Authority: TEX. BUS. & COM. CODE §27.01; 4 TEX. PATTERN JURY CHARGES §§105.7, 105.9.

§10.07 Breach of Warranty

More than one warranty may apply in a given case. *See* §1.02.9 *supra*. Furthermore, certain of the warranties have multiple standards, the breach of any one of which constitutes a breach of warranty. *See, e.g.,* Tex. Bus. & Com. Code §2.314(b). For these reasons, a jury question which can accommodate the submission of multiple warranties (or standards) will be appropriate in many cases.

However, care must be taken in choosing this broad form approach. In *Crown Life Ins. Co. v. Casteel*, 22 S.W.3d 378 (Tex. 2000), the trial court submitted a single broad-form liability question incorporating several laundry list items. The Texas Supreme Court held that the plaintiff was not entitled to assert several of those subsections as a basis for liability. Since there was a single answer to the jury question, it was not possible to know whether one of the invalid theories formed the sole basis for the jury's answer. Accordingly, the Court held that submission of the question was reversible error. Thus, if there is a genuine question as to the plaintiff's right to invoke one or more grounds for liability, a separate submission of that ground or separate answers for each ground may be warranted.

The first form contains a format for submitting a breach of warranty jury question. In some cases, however, only a single warranty or single warranty standard will be involved. In these instances or for the reasons stated above, it may be preferable to depart from the suggested form and submit a question which focuses on the single warranty or standard which is involved. The forms which follow the general form in §[a] illustrate this approach.

[a] FORM: Breach of warranty (broad form)

Was the failure, if any, of [defendant] to comply with a warranty a producing cause of damages to [plaintiff]?

"Failure to comply with a warranty" means any of the following: [*insert all appropriate warranty standards, e.g.,* failing to comply with an express warranty, failing to perform services in a good and workmanlike manner, or selling goods that would not pass without objection in the trade under the contract description].

[*Insert definitions as applicable, see* §10.02 *supra.*]

Answer "Yes" or "No."

Answer: _____

Authority: 4 Tex. Pattern Jury Charges §§102.8-102.13 (2010).

[b] FORM: Breach of warranty (separate form)

Did [defendant] engage in any of the following conduct, and if so, was it a producing cause of damages to [plaintiff]?

[*Insert definitions as applicable, see §10.02 supra.*]

[*Insert various warranties that are alleged, e.g.*

		YES	NO
C.	Failure to install the roof in a good and workmanlike manner.	___	___
D.	Selling goods that do not pass without objection in the trade under the contract description.	___	___]

Authority: 4 Tex. Pattern Jury Charges §§102.8-102.13 (2010).

[c] FORM: Breach of warranty of merchantability

Was the __ unfit for the ordinary purpose for which __ are [is] used because of a defect, and if so, was this a producing cause of damages to [plaintiff]?

"Defect" means a condition of the goods that renders them unfit for the ordinary purpose for which they are used because of a lack of something necessary for adequacy [or because of the presence of something that renders them inadequate].

Answer "Yes" or "No."

Answer:_____

Authority: Tex. Bus. & Com. Code §2.314(b); *Plas-Tex, Inc. v. U.S. Steel Corp.*, 772 S.W.2d 442 (Tex. 1989); see 4 Texas Pattern Jury Charges §102.10 (2010).

[NOTE: The language of the form question and the definition has been modified from the specific language approved by the Supreme Court by the addition of the bracketed phrase. See *Plas-Tex, Inc. v. U.S. Steel Corp.*, supra. The bracketed phrase which is not found in the pattern jury charge was added because clearly there will be cases in which the wrong ingredient is added to or used in goods which makes the goods unfit. It should also be noted that the Supreme Court's language only pertains to one of the five elements that may cause goods to be unmerchantable. See Tex. Bus. & Com. Code §2.314. If the case involves one or more of the other elements, it is apparently unnecessary to incorporate the "defect" language. See 4 Texas Pattern Jury Charges §1.02.10 (2010) (comment).]

[d] FORM: Breach of implied warranty on services

Did [defendant] fail to perform [*specify service provided, e.g., the installation of the roof*] in a good and workmanlike manner, and if so, was this failure a producing cause of damages to [plaintiff]?

"Good and workmanlike manner" is that quality of work performed by one who has the knowledge, training or experience necessary for the successful practice of a trade or occupation and performed in a manner generally considered proficient by those capable of judging such work.

Answer "Yes" or "No."

Answer:_____

Authority: DTPA §17.50(b); *Melody Home Manufacturing Co. v. Barnes*, 741 S.W.2d 349, 354 (Tex. 1987).

[e] FORM: Breach of warranty of habitability and workmanship (new house) (governed by RCLA and not RCCA)

Did [defendant] fail to construct [plaintiff's] house in a good and workmanlike manner, and if so, was such failure a proximate cause of damages to [plaintiff]?

[*Insert definition of good and workmanlike manner, see §10.02(c) supra.*]

Answer "Yes" or "No."

Answer:_____

[NOTE: Most suits for breach of warranty of habitability and workmanship in new residential home construction are now governed by the RCLA, Tex Prop. Code §27.001 *et seq.* The RCLA precludes a consumer from recovering mental anguish damages in such suits and requires that recoverable economic damages be proximately caused by a construction defect. Tex. Prop. Code §27.004(g). For homes constructed between 2005 and 2009, the implied warranties are governed by the RCCA.]

Authority: *Gupta v. Ritter Homes, Inc.*, 646 S.W.2d 168 (Tex. 1983); *Melody Home Manufacturing Co. v. Barnes*, 741 S.W.2d 349 (Tex. 1987) (good and workmanlike manner).

[f] FORM: Breach of warranty of suitability of commercial lease space

Were the premises not suitable for their intended commercial purpose, and if not, was this a producing cause of damages to [plaintiff]?

"Suitable" means that there were no latent defects in the facilities that were vital to the use of the premises for their intended purpose, and that the essential facilities remained in a condition which made the property useable.

Answer "Yes" or "No."

Answer:_____

Authority: *Davidow v. Inwood North Professional Group-Phase I*, 747 S.W.2d 373 (Tex. 1988).

§10.08   Unconscionability

"Unconscionable action or course of action" is defined in DTPA §17.45(5) and is actionable under DTPA §17.50(a)(3).

[a] FORM: Unconscionable action or course of action

Did [defendant] engage in any unconscionable action or course of action in his [her] dealings with [plaintiff], and if so, was this a producing cause of damages to [plaintiff]?

[*Insert definition of "unconscionable action or course of action," see* §10.02(e) *supra.*]

Answer "Yes" or "No."

Answer:_____

Authority: DTPA §17.50(a)(3); §17.45(5); 4 Texas pattern Jury Charges §102.7 (2010).

§10.09 Chapter 541 of the Insurance Code

Many different forms of conduct are prohibited and their breach made actionable by §541.151 of the Texas Insurance Code. *See* §1.02.11 *supra*. The following question will permit submission of multiple violations actionable under Chapter 541 of the Insurance Code. *See generally* §§1.02.11 *et seq.*

However, care must be taken in choosing this broad form approach. In *Crown Life Ins. Co. v. Casteel*, 22 S.W.3d 378 (Tex. 2000), the trial court submitted a single broad-form liability question incorporating several laundry list items. The Texas Supreme Court held that the plaintiff was not entitled to assert several of those subsections as a basis for liability. Since there was a single answer to the jury question, it was not possible to know whether one of the invalid theories formed the sole basis for the jury's answer. Accordingly, the Court held that submission of the question was reversible error. Thus, if there is a genuine question as to the plaintiff's right to invoke one or more grounds for liability, a separate submission of that ground or separate answers for each ground may be warranted.

Although "producing cause" is the causation standard under the DTPA, Chapter 541 provides a cause of action to one who sustains damage "caused by the other person engaging in an act or practice" TEX. INS. CODE §541.151. Form [a], below, submits the "caused by" standard for use in connection with the damages question. Those wishing to submit producing cause out of an abundance of caution should ask the jury, "Did [defendant] engage in any unfair or deceptive act or practice that was a producing cause of damages to [plaintiff]?" Note that a causation element is not required when the only damages sought are policy benefits since *Vail v. Texas Farm Bureau Mut. Ins. Co.*, 754 S.W.2d 129 (Tex. 1988) held that an insurer's unfair refusal to pay a claim causes those damages as a matter of law.

[a] FORM: Chapter 541 of the Insurance Code (broad form)

Did [defendant] engage in any unfair or deceptive act or practice in the transaction in question that caused damages to [plaintiff]?

"Unfair or deceptive act or practice" means any of the following: [*insert all appropriate provisions of the Insurance Code, e.g.,* misrepresenting to [plaintiff] a material fact or policy provision relating to coverage at issue, or not attempting in good faith to effectuate a prompt, fair and equitable settlement of a claim with respect to which the insurer's liability has become reasonably clear].

Answer "Yes" or "No."

Answer: _____

Authority: TEX. INS. CODE §§541.151, 541.060(1),(2); see 4 TEX. PATTERN JURY CHARGES §§102.14-102.19 (2010).

[b] FORM: Chapter 541 of the Insurance Code (separate form)

```
Did [defendant] engage in any of the following and if so, were
such acts a cause of damages to [plaintiff]?
```

                                                                  YES   NO

```
A. Misrepresenting to [plaintiff] a material
   fact or policy provision relating to
   coverage at issue.                                        ____  ____

B. Not attempting in good faith to effectuate
   prompt, fair and equitable settlement of a
   claim with respect to which the insurer's
   liability has become reasonably clear.                    ____  ____
```

Authority: TEX. INS. CODE §541.060(1),(2); see 4 TEXAS PATTERN JURY CHARGES §§102.14, 102.18 (2010).

§10.10 Damages

Damages questions may be submitted conditionally on affirmative findings to liability questions. TEX. R. CIV. P 277. The advantage of this practice is that a jury will not spend time computing damages when the answer is immaterial. The disadvantage is that if, for some reason, the jury fails to find liability but the court disregards the jury's findings of law, that liability was proven, then a retrial is required.

The suggested damages question for suits under the DTPA is contained in the following form. As a result of the 1995 amendments to the DTPA, the elements of damages which can be recovered are limited to economic loss and mental anguish. See §1.02.14.3 *supra*.

If there is a genuine question as to the evidentiary support for a particular element of damages, separate answers for each damages element should be obtained. The Texas Supreme Court has held that submission of a broad form question on damages that includes an element without any evidentiary support is harmful error. *Harris County v. Smith*, 96 S.W.3d 230, 234 (Tex. 2002); *see also Crown Life Ins. Co. v. Casteel*, 22 S.W.3d 378 (Tex. 2000).

An alternative form is contained in §[b] for those cases in which multiple theories of liability are submitted, all of which employ the same measures of damages and causation. When both DTPA and non-DTPA causes of action are submitted, separate damage questions may be required. See §10.16, *infra*.

A third form is contained in §[c] which is intended for use in those cases in which relief is sought for restoration of money or property under the DTPA §17.50(b)(3).

[a] FORM: Damages (general form)

What sum of money, if any, if paid now in cash, would fairly and reasonably compensate [plaintiff] for his [her] damages, if any, that resulted from such false, misleading, or deceptive act or practice [or such unconscionable action] [or such failure to comply with a warranty] [or such unfair or deceptive act or practice].

Consider the following elements of damages, if any, and no others: [*insert appropriate elements of damages; see* §10.10 *infra*].

Do not include any amount for interest on past damages, if any.

Answer in dollars and cents, if any.

(a) [Economic damages element 1], if any.

Answer: $_____

(b) [Economic damages element 2], if any.

Answer: $_____

Authority: See 4 TEXAS PATTERN JURY CHARGES §115.9 (2010).

[b] FORM: Damages (alternative form)

What sum of money, if any, if paid now in cash would fairly and reasonably compensate [plaintiff] for his [her] damages, if any, that resulted from the conduct you have found to be a producing [*or* proximate] cause of damages to [plaintiff] in question number _____?

You may consider the following elements of damages and no others:

[*Insert instruction on damages; see* §10.10 *infra*.]

Do not include any amount for interest on past damages, if any.

Answer in dollars and cents, if any.

Answer: $_____.

Text reference. TEXAS CONSUMER LITIGATION 2D §8.02.

[c] FORM: Restoration of money or property

[NOTE: The following form should be submitted conditionally, based on an affirmative finding on a DTPA liability question.]

What sum of money, if any, was [or] Was the [*insert description of property, e.g.,* 10 acres of land in _____ County, Texas] acquired by [defendant] by the conduct, if any, found by you in answer to question number [*insert DTPA liability. question number*].

Answer in dollars and cents, if any.

Answer: $ _____ .

[or]

Answer "Yes" or "No."

Answer: _____ .

Authority: DTPA §17.50(b)(3); *Carrow v. Bayliner Marine Corp.*, 781 S.W.2d 691 (Tex. App.—Austin 1989, no writ).

Text reference: TEXAS CONSUMER LITIGATION 2D §8.12.

§10.11 Specific Elements of Damages

The specific elements of damages that should be listed in the general damages question depend on the losses proven in each case. The charge may contain more than one measure of damages. After the verdict, the plaintiff is entitled to elect the measure which affords the greatest recovery. *Kish v. Van Note*, 692 S.W.2d 463, 466 (Tex. 1985); TEXAS CONSUMER LITIGATION 2D §8.02. When multiple elements are submitted, from which the plaintiff can make an election, an instruction should be included so that the jury does not improperly adjust its answer, believing that the plaintiff will recover all of the damages found. *See* §10.16, *infra*

The instructions which follow include some of the more commonly used elements and measures of damages in DTPA litigation. While an instruction with a definition of "mental anguish" from another's death is included in the 2010 Pattern Jury Charges for General Negligence and Intentional Torts, the Pattern Jury Charges for Business an Consumer Cases has never contained a definition for mental anguish. *See, e.g.*, 1 TEXAS PATTERN JURY CHARGES §16.3 (2010), *and cf.* 4 TEXAS PATTERN JURY CHARGES §115.9 (Comment). In *Parkway Co. v. Woodruff*, 901 S.W.2d 434 (Tex. 1995), a consumer case involving damages to property only, the Texas Supreme Court suggested that giving the jury an instruction with the definition of mental anguish was appropriate. Id. at 444. However, the Court stopped short of approving the definition of "mental anguish" given there. In *Serv. Corp. Int'l v. Guerra*, 348 S.W.3d 239, 247 (Tex. App.—Corpus Christi 2009), rev'd on other grounds, 348 S.W.3d 221 (Tex. 2011), a case involving the mishandling of a corpse, the court of appeals approved of a definition of mental anguish which combined elements of the Pattern Jury Charge for general negligence death cases and the definition reviewed in *Parkway*. That definition is included in the form below.

[a] FORM: Cost to repair

The reasonable and necessary cost, if any, in _____ County, Texas, to repair the [*insert defects to be repaired, e.g.,* foundation of the house].

See 1 TEXAS PATTERN JURY CHARGES §11.3 (2006) (modified for DTPA cases); 4 TEXAS PATTERN JURY CHARGES §115.9 (2010) (Sample Instructions).

[b] FORM: Loss of use

The reasonable rental value of a [*insert good not used, e.g.,* house] in the same class as the [house] in question for the period of time, if any, [plaintiff] was deprived of the use of the [house] caused by the conduct found by you in answer to question number _____.

[*or*]

The reasonable and necessary expense incurred in renting a [*insert good not used, e.g.,* house] in the same class as the [house] in question for the period of time [plaintiff] was deprived of the use of the [house], if any, caused by the conduct found by you in answer to question number _____.

See 4 TEXAS PATTERN JURY CHARGES §115.9 (2010) (Sample Instructions); *Luna v. North Star Dodge Sales, Inc.*, 667 S. W. 2d 115 (Tex. 1984).

[c] FORM: Loss of value—benefit of the bargain

The difference, if any, in [*month and year of sale*] between the fair market value of the [*describe good, e.g.,* house] in the condition in which it was sold to [plaintiff] and the value it would have had if it had been as [warranted and represented].

See 4 TEXAS PATTERN JURY CHARGES §115.9 (2010).

[d] FORM: Stigma damages

The decrease, if any, on [*insert month and year of sale*] in the market value of the [*insert good, e.g.,* house] due to stigma, if any, associated with any [*describe defective condition, e.g.,* foundation defects], even though such defects, if any, have been repaired. Do not include the cost to repair, if any, in your answer.

See Ludt v. McCollum, 762 S.W.2d 575 (Tex. 1988); *Terminix International, Inc. v. Lucci*, 670 S.W.2d 657 (Tex. App.—San Antonio 1984, writ ref'd n.r.e.).

[NOTE: It is unclear what date should be used to determine the existence of stigma damages. Typically, loss of market value is measured as of the date of sale. *See Leyendecker & Associates, Inc. v. Wechter*, 683 S.W.2d 369, 373 (Tex. 1994). Stigma damages are in the nature of lost market value; however, they are measured as that decrease which will remain *after* repairs are completed, the cost of which typically is measured as of the date of the trial. The RCLA now expressly provides that reduction in market value is recoverable for structural failure defects and is determined after the repairs have been made. RCLA §27.004(g)(5).]

[e] FORM: Mental anguish

[*Insert condition instruction based on jury answer to "knowing" or "intentional" question, e.g.* Answer Question No. _____ if you have answered Question No. _____ "Yes"; otherwise, do not answer Question No. _____.]

What sum of money do you find would fairly and reasonably compensate [plaintiff] for his [her] mental anguish, if any, that resulted from the conduct found by you in answer to Question No. _____?

"Mental anguish" means emotional pain, torment and suffering. It is more than mere disappointment, anger, resentment or embarrassment, although it may include all of these. It includes a mental sensation of pain resulting from such painful emotions as grief, severe disappointment, indignation, wounded pride, shame, despair and/or public humiliation.

Do not include in your answer any amount for interest on past damages, if any. Answer in dollars and cents, if any.

(a) Mental anguish, if any, suffered in the past. $_____.

(b) Mental anguish, if any, which in reasonable probability will be suffered in the future.

$_____.

See Serv. Corp. Int'l v. Guerra, 348 S.W.3d 239, 247 (Tex. App.-Corpus Christi 2009), *rev'd on other grounds*, 348 S.W.3d 221 (Tex. 2011); *see Parkway Co. v. Woodruff*, 901 S.W.2d 434, 444 (Tex. 1995).

§10.12 "Knowing" and "Intentional" Conduct

A "knowing" or "intentional" violation must be proven if mental anguish damages are to be recovered under the DTPA. Additional damages (up to three times the amount of economic damages) may be awarded if a "knowing" violation is found. Mental anguish damages are subject to discretionary trebling only if an "intentional" violation is found.

The suggested forms for submitting a "knowing" and "intentional" violation are as follows:

[a] FORM: "Knowing" conduct

Did [defendant] knowingly engage in the conduct found by you in answer to question number [*insert number of question(s) that deals with wrongful conduct and on which there is evidence of a "knowing" violation*]?

[*Insert definition of "knowingly," §10.02(g), supra.*]

In answering this question, consider only the conduct you have found to be a producing cause of damages to [plaintiff].

Answer "Yes" or "No."

Answer: _____.

Authority: See 4 TEXAS PATTERN JURY CHARGES §102.21 (2010).

[b] FORM: "Intentional" conduct

Did [defendant] intentionally engage in the conduct found by you in answer to question number [*insert number of question(s) that deals with wrongful conduct and on which there is evidence of an "intentional" violation*]?

[*Insert definition of "intentionally," §10.02(h), supra.*]

In answering this question, consider only the conduct you have found to be a producing cause of damages to [plaintiff].

Answer "Yes" or "No."

Answer: _____.

Authority: DTPA §17.50(b)(1); see 4 TEXAS PATTERN JURY CHARGES §102.21 (2010).

[NOTE: In Insurance Code Chapter 541 cases, the appropriate causation standard should be substituted in the instruction for "producing cause." See §10.08 *supra*.]

§10.13 Additional and Exemplary Damages

As noted above, recovery of additional damages under the DTPA is predicated on a finding that the DTPA violation was committed "knowingly" or "intentionally." An award of additional damages is punitive in nature. An instruction to the jury to consider factors similar to those considered for an award of exemplary damages may therefore be necessary. *Transportation Ins. Co. v. Moriel*, 879 S.W.2d 10, 26-30 (Tex. 1994). The *Moriel* factors are included in both questions below.

Exemplary damages may be appropriate in common law fraud and bad faith cases. In order to even consider an award of exemplary damages, the jury must first find, unanimously and by clear and convincing evidence, that the injury to the plaintiff resulted from the defendant's malice, fraud or gross negligence. The forms below for exemplary damages are therefore broken into two parts in §§[b] and [c].

[a] FORM: Additional or exemplary damages

What sum of money, if any, in addition to actual damages should be assessed against [defendant] as additional damages?

"Additional damages" means an amount that you may in your discretion award as punishment of the wrongdoer and as a warning and example to the wrongdoer and others to deter the same or similar conduct in the future.

In determining the amount, you may consider:

(1) The nature of the wrong,

(2) The character of the conduct involved,

(3) The degree of culpability of the wrongdoer,

(4) The situation and sensibilities of the parties concerned,

(5) The extent to which such conduct offends a public sense of justice and propriety, and

(6) The size of an award needed to deter similar conduct in the future [or the net worth of the defendant].

Answer in dollars and cents, if any.

Answer: $_____.

Authority: 4 Texas Pattern Jury Charges §§115.11, 115.37 (2010).

[b] FORM: Exemplary damages predicate

Answer the following question only if you unanimously answered "Yes" to Question ____ [or Question ____, or Question ____]. Otherwise, do not answer the following question.

To answer "Yes" to [*any part of*] the following question, your answer must be unanimous. You may answer "No" to [*any part of*] the following question only upon a vote of ten or more jurors. Otherwise, you must not answer [*that part of*] the following question.

QUESTION ____

Do you find by clear and convincing evidence that the harm to [plaintiff] resulted from [*malice, fraud*, or *gross negligence*]?

"Clear and convincing evidence" means the measure or degree of proof that produces a firm belief or conviction of the truth of the allegations sought to be established.

"Malice" means a specific intent by [defendant] to cause substantial injury or harm to [plaintiff].

[*And/or use appropriate definition for "fraud" or "gross negligence"*]

Answer: _____

Authority: 4 Texas Pattern Jury Charges §115.36B (2010); Tex. Civ. Prac. & Rem. Code §41.003.

[c] FORM: Exemplary damages amount

What sum of money, if any, in addition to actual damages should be assessed against [defendant] as exemplary damages?

"Exemplary damages" means an amount that you may, in your discretion, award as punishment of the wrongdoer and as a warning and example to the wrongdoer and others to deter the same or similar conduct in the future.

In determining the amount, you may consider:

(1) The nature of the wrong,

(2) The character of the conduct involved,

(3) The degree of culpability of the wrongdoer,

(4) The situation and sensibilities of the parties concerned,

(5) The extent to which such conduct offends a public sense of justice and propriety, and

(6) The size of an award needed to deter similar conduct in the future [or the net worth of the defendant].

Answer in dollars and cents, if any.

Answer: $_____.

Authority: 4 TEXAS PATTERN JURY CHARGES §110.37 (2010); TEX. CIV. PRAC. & REM. CODE §41.011(A).

§10.14 Attorneys' Fees

Attorney's fees are recoverable under DTPA §17.50(c) for the defendant (for bad faith and harassment) and §17.50(d) for the plaintiff (for violations of the DTPA). Additionally, in many cases involving DTPA claims, other causes of action are submitted which may involve a right to recover attorney's fees under TEX. CIV. PRAC. & REM. CODE §38.001. The only difference between the proof requirements of the two statutes is that the DTPA requires a finding of "reasonable and necessary," while the Civil Practice and Remedies Code only requires a finding that fees are "reasonable."

The jury's answers to these questions should provide discrete amounts for the different stages of the appellate process in a manner so that any officer executing on the judgment can readily ascertain whether and how much of the attorney's fees on appeal should be collected. This form provides for separate findings of attorney's fees for making or responding to a petition for review in the Texas Supreme Court, a discrete activity within the control of at least one of the parties, and for briefing and for arguing to the Supreme Court if a petition is granted, less frequent activities entirely dependent on discretionary action by the Court. See TEX. R. APP. P. 53-56. The following form is suggested over the Texas Pattern Jury Charge because it authorizes the jury to find an amount of attorney's fees for "post-trial, pre-appeal and collection of judgment legal services," a time when often several thousands of dollars worth of legal services are provided. This part of the question may be modified or omitted if it appears that such post-judgment efforts will not be required.

Historically, consumers have been allowed to recover contingent attorney's fees in DTPA cases. *See, e.g., March v. Thiery*, 729 S.W.2d 889 (Tex. App.—Corpus Christi 1987, no writ); *Great Am. Ins. Co. v. North Austin Mun. Util. Dist. No.1*, 908 S.W.2d 415 (Tex. 1995). In *Arthur Andersen & Co. v. Perry Equip. Corp.*, 945 S.W.2d 812 (Tex. 1997), the Supreme Court held that under the DTPA, (1) a consumer must prove that the fees are both reasonable and necessary and (2) the jury must be asked to find a specific dollar amount as attorney's fees rather than a percentage of the plaintiff's recovery or damages. The opinion does not prohibit a contingent fee agreement between a consumer and the consumer's attorney, and, the opinion specifically allows a contingent fee agreement to be admitted into evidence; instead, it simply means that if attorney's fees are awarded under the statute, it must be based on an hourly fee. For the factors that the jury should consider in determining whether a fee is reasonable and necessary, see §1.02.28, *supra*.

Find the reasonable and necessary attorneys' fees for the legal services provided and to be provided to [plaintiff] in connection with this lawsuit. Answer in dollars and cents in the spaces provided below:

[a] FORM: Attorney's fees

```
Find the reasonable and necessary attorney's fees for the legal
services provided and to be provided to [plaintiff] in connec-
tion with this lawsuit. Answer in dollars and cents in the spaces
provided below:

(a) For the preparation and trial of this lawsuit in this court,
    including post-trial, pre-appeal legal services and legal
    services for collection of judgment: $_____

(b) For an appeal to the Court of Appeals:     $_____

(c) For representation at the petition for review stage in the
    Supreme Court of Texas: $_____

(d) For representation at the merits briefing stage in the
    Supreme Court of Texas: $_____

(e) For representation through oral argument and the completion
    of proceedings in the Supreme Court of Texas: $_____
```

Authority: See 4 Texas Pattern Jury Charges §115.46 (2010).

§10.15 Defenses to DTPA and Residential Construction Actions

There are several statutory defenses to DTPA actions contained in DTPA §17.5052 (offers of settlement), §17.506 (information from third parties and tender of amount of demand), and §17.565 (limitations). Additionally, the Texas Property Code contains certain defenses in residential construction cases. *See* Tex. Prop. Code §27.003. Some of these defenses are for the court only, *e.g.*, the adequacy of a tender. Others clearly are for the jury, *e.g.*, limitations.

[a] FORM: Third Party Information

Did [defendant], prior to the consummation of [the transaction in question] give reasonable and timely written notice of his/her reliance on the information contained in Exhibit _____ in making the representation, if any, found by you in Question ____?

You are instructed that you may answer this question "yes" only if all of the following are found by you:

1. [Defendant] gave written notice of his [her] reliance on the information to [plaintiff]; and

2. The written notice, if any, was given to [plaintiff] before the consummation of the transaction; and

3. The written notice, if any, was reasonable and timely; and

4. [Defendant] did not know and could not reasonably have known that the information was false or inaccurate; and

5. The information was a producing cause of the damages, if any, of [plaintiff].

Answer "Yes" or "No."

Answer: _____.

Authority: DTPA §17.506(a)(2).

[b] FORM: Unreasonable rejection of settlement offer

Was [defendant's] written offer of [date] concerning the construction defect[s] which is/are the subject of this suit reasonable?

Answer "Yes" or "No."

Answer: _____.

Authority: TEX. PROP. CODE §27.004(e),(j).

[c] FORM: No opportunity to repair

Did [plaintiff] fail to give a reasonable opportunity to repair the construction defect[s], if any, after accepting [defendant's] offer, if any, to repair the defect[s]?

Answer "Yes" or "No."

Answer: _____.

Authority: TEX. PROP. CODE §27.004(e).

[d] FORM: Negligence of another person

QUESTION NO. [1]

Was the negligence, if any, of [other person] a proximate cause of any or all of [plaintiffs] damages, if any, which were caused by the construction defect[s], if any?

Answer "Yes" or "No."

Answer: _____.

If you have answered Question No. [1] "yes," then answer Question No. [2]; otherwise, do not answer Question No. [2].

QUESTION NO. [2]

What percentage of [plaintiffs] damages, if any, were proximately caused by the negligence of [other person]?

Answer with a percentage.

Answer: _____.

Authority: TEX. PROP. CODE §27.003(a)(1).

[NOTE: There are four other statutory defenses listed in §27.003 of the Property Code, all of which can be submitted in the same format shown above. *See* TEX. PROP. CODE §27.003(a)(1)(A)-(E).]

§10.16 Statute of Limitations

A two-year statute of limitations applies in DTPA cases. DTPA §17.565. The limitations provision is keyed to the occurrence of the deceptive trade practice or the discovery by the consumer of the occurrence. *Id.* The DTPA limitations provision expressly incorporates the discovery rule. As long as the plaintiff pleads the discovery rule as an exception to the two-year limitations, the defendant has the burden of proof to establish the plaintiff's date of discovery of the wrongfully caused injury was more than two years before suit. *KPMG Peat Marwick v. Harrison County Hous. Fin. Corp.*, 988 S.W.2d 746 (Tex. 1999). The following jury question correctly places the burden of proof on the defendant. The jury question should be conditioned on affirmative findings of liability.

[a] FORM: Discovery Rule

Did [plaintiff] discover, or, in the exercise of reasonable diligence, should [plaintiff] have discovered [*insert actionable conduct, e.g.,* all of the false, misleading, or deceptive acts or practices] before [*insert date two years before suit was filed*]?

Answer: "Yes" or "No."

Answer: _____.

Authority: DTPA §17.565; *KPMG Peat Marwick v. Harrison County Hous. Fin. Corp.*, 988 S.W.2d 746 (Tex. 1999).

[NOTE: The Texas Pattern Jury Charge Committees adopted an alternative form for submitting the discovery rule. Texas Pattern Jury Charge §102.23 asks, "By what date should [plaintiff], in the exercise of reasonable diligence, have discovered all [the actionable conduct] of [defendant]?" The problem with this format, however, is that it requires a jury to find a specific date. If the court instructs the jury, "answer with a day, month, and year" and the jury is unable to determine the day, then the jury may conclude that it cannot answer the question. If the court says merely, "answer with a date," then the jury may put a year only, which answer probably would be insufficient. The ultimate fact is whether the plaintiff knew or should have known of the facts establishing the claim more than two years before the lawsuit was filed; therefore, by inserting the two year cut-off date into the question, a much simpler format is achieved. Note also that if there are different acts of misconduct resulting in distinctly different damages, it will be necessary to submit separate limitations questions in lieu of the foregoing instruction which addresses *all* of the false, misleading, or deceptive acts or practices.]

The Supreme Court approved the following submission of the little used statutory 180 day extension under the DTPA and the Insurance Code:

> Was Kenneco's (Armada's) failure to take action before December 15, 1986 [the date of the standstill agreement], caused by J & H's knowingly engaging in conduct solely calculated to induce Kenneco (Armada) to refrain from or postpone filing suit?

Johnson & Higgins, Inc. v. Kenneco Energy, 962 S.W.2d 507, 515 (Tex. 1998).

§10.17 Proportionate Responsibility

In 1995, the legislature amended Chapter 33 of the Texas Civil Practice and Remedies Code to make those provisions applicable to actions brought under the DTPA. TEX. CIV. PRAC. & REM. CODE §33.002(h). Unfortunately, there is no easy fit between the concept of proportionate responsibility set forth in Chapter 33 and the DTPA. Section 33.003 requires that the trier of fact determine the "responsibility" of designated persons for:

> causing or contributing to cause in any way the harm for which recovery of damages is sought, whether by negligent act or omission, by any defective or unreasonably dangerous product, by other conduct or activity that violates an applicable legal standard or by any combination of these.

TEX. CIV. PRAC. & REM. CODE §33.003.

Common law defenses such as contributory negligence will not bar a DTPA cause of action. *Smith v. Baldwin*, 611 S.W.2d 611

(Tex. 1981). The victim of false or fraudulent representations does not have a duty to use due diligence to suspect or discover the falsity of such statements. *Koral Industries v. Security-Connecticut Life Ins. Co.*, 802 S.W.2d 650, 651 (Tex. 1990). Moreover, the DTPA does not create an "applicable legal standard" by which to judge the consumer's conduct. As such, the existence of a legislatively created apportionment scheme, applicable to many causes of action, does not, without more, create new standards of conduct for consumers under the DTPA. It appears that the only function of Chapter 33 in DTPA litigation is to provide a vehicle for allocating responsibility among the liable defendants, settling persons and responsible third parties. In a straight DTPA case, the plaintiff's proportionate responsibility should not be submitted to the jury because the DTPA provides no "applicable legal standard" by which to judge the plaintiff's conduct. In any other case, the plaintiff's proportionate responsibility should only be submitted in this question if there has been an affirmative finding in a previous question that the plaintiff's conduct failed to meet an applicable legal standard. *See* 4 TEXAS PATTERN JURY CHARGES §115.35 (2010).

The following form assumes there have been affirmative liability findings against one or more defendants, a settling person and a properly designated responsible third party.

[a] FORM: Proportionate responsibility

If you have answered "Yes" to Questions _____ and _____ [*applicable liability questions*] for more than one of those named below, then answer the following question. Otherwise, do not answer the following question.

You should only assign percentages to those you find caused the damages. The percentages you find must total 100 percent. The percentages must be expressed in whole numbers. The percentage of responsibility attributable is not necessarily measured by the number of acts or omissions found.

QUESTION _____

For those found by you to have caused the damages to [*plaintiff*], find the percentage caused by:

a. [*Defendant*]   ____%

b. [*Settling defendant*]   ____%

c. [*Responsible third party*]   ____%

Total   100 %

Authority: 4 TEXAS PATTERN JURY CHARGES §115.35 (2010).

§10.18 Sample DTPA Charge

At the conclusion of the charge conference, the court's charge must be assembled. The completed charge is created by drawing together those special instructions, definitions, and questions that have been approved (or approved as modified) by the court and inserting them into general instructions required by the Rules of Civil Procedure. *See* TEX. R. CIV. P. 226a (III). When DTPA causes of action are submitted with non-DTPA causes of action, it has been held that a separate damages question must be submitted on the DTPA claim so that the court can determine the amount of damages that is subject to the additional damages features in DTPA §17.50(b)(1). *Lucas v. Nesbitt*, 653 S.W.2d 883 (Tex. App.—Corpus Christi 1983, writ ref'd n.r.e.). In these cases, an instruction should be included so that the jury does not adjust its answer to one damage question because of its answer to the other damage question. See 4 TEXAS PATTERN JURY CHARGES §100.12 (2010).

The following is a sample jury charge in a DTPA case that involves both DTPA and non-DTPA claims. This sample charge is intended simply to illustrate the manner in which the completed charge is assembled for submission to the jury. It assumes that no motion for bifurcated trial was granted. *See* §10.12, *supra.*

If there is a genuine question about the plaintiff's right to assert one of the grounds of recovery submitted to the jury, the broad form approach utilized in this sample charge should be supplemented with a separate submission of the questionable ground for liability. *See Crown Life Ins. Co. v. Casteel*, 22 S.W.3d 378 (Tex. 2000).

[a] FORM: Sample DTPA charge

```
                         NO. _____
                      §
_____          §    IN THE _____ COURT OF
                      §
vs.                   §    _____ COUNTY, TEXAS
                      §
_____          §    _____ JUDICIAL DISTRICT
```

CHARGE OF THE COURT

Members of the Jury [or Ladies & Gentlemen of the Jury]:

After the closing arguments, you will go to the jury room to decide the case, answer the questions that are attached, and reach a verdict. You may discuss the case with other jurors only when you are all together in the jury room.

Remember my previous instructions: do not discuss the case with anyone else, either in person or by any other means. Do not do any independent investigation about the case or conduct any research.

Do not look up any words in dictionaries or on the Internet. Do not post information about the case on the Internet. Do not share any special knowledge or experiences with the other jurors. Do not use your phone or any other electronic device during your deliberations for any reason. [I will give you a number where others may contact you in case of an emergency.]

[Any notes you have taken are for your own personal use. You may take your notes back into the jury room and consult them during deliberations, but do not show or read your notes to your fellow jurors during your deliberations. Your notes are not evidence. Each of you should rely on your independent recollection of the evidence and not be influenced by the fact that another juror has or has not taken notes.]

[You must leave your notes with the bailiff when you are not deliberating. The bailiff will give your notes to me promptly after collecting them from you. I will make sure your notes are kept in a safe, secure location and not disclosed to anyone. After you complete your deliberations, the bailiff will collect your notes. When you are released from jury duty, the bailiff will promptly destroy your notes so that nobody can read what you wrote.]

Here are the instructions for answering the questions.

1. Do not let bias, prejudice, or sympathy play any part in your decision.

2. Base your answers only on the evidence admitted in court and on the law that is in these instructions and questions. Do not consider or discuss any evidence that was not admitted in the courtroom.

3. You are to make up your own minds about the facts. You are the sole judges of the credibility of the witnesses and the weight to give their testimony. But on matters of law, you must follow all of my instructions.

4. If my instructions use a word in a way that is different from its ordinary meaning, use the meaning I give you, which will be a proper legal definition.

5. All the questions and answers are important. No one should say that any question or answer is not important.

6. Answer "yes" or "no" to all questions unless you are told otherwise. A "yes" answer must be based on a preponderance of the evidence [unless you are told otherwise]. Whenever a question requires an answer other than "yes" or "no," your answer must be based on a preponderance of the evidence [unless you are told otherwise].

The term "preponderance of the evidence" means the greater weight of credible evidence presented in this case. If you do not find that a preponderance of the evidence supports a "yes" answer, then answer "no." A preponderance of the evidence is not measured by the number of witnesses nor by the number of documents admitted in evidence. For a fact to be proved by a preponderance of the evidence, you must find that the fact is more likely true than not true.

7. Do not decide who you think should win before you answer the questions and then just answer the questions to match your decision. Answer each question carefully without considering who will win. Do not discuss or consider the effect your answers will have.

8. Do not answer questions by drawing straws or by any method of chance.

9. Some questions might ask you for a dollar amount. Do not agree in advance to decide on a dollar amount by adding up each juror's amount and then figuring the average.

10. Do not trade your answers. For example, do not say, "I will answer this question your way if you answer another question my way."

11. [Unless otherwise instructed:] The answers to the questions must be based on the decision of at least 10 of the 12 [5 of the 6] jurors. The same 10 [5] jurors must agree on every answer. Do not agree to be bound by a vote of anything less than 10 [5] jurors, even if it would be a majority.

As I have said before, if you do not follow these instructions, you will be guilty of juror misconduct, and I might have to order a new trial and start this process over again. This would waste your time and the parties' money, and would require the taxpayers of this county to pay for another trial. If a juror breaks any of these rules, tell that person to stop and report it to me immediately.

[NOTE: The following paragraph is a general instruction on *circumstantial evidence* that should be included in nearly every DTPA case, although it is not included in the general form contained in 4 TEXAS PATTERN JURY CHARGES §100.8.]

A fact may be established by direct evidence or by circumstantial evidence or both. A fact is established by direct evidence when proven by documentary evidence or by witnesses who saw the act done or heard the words spoken. A fact is established by circumstantial evidence when it may be fairly and reasonably inferred from other facts proved.

"Producing cause" is cause that was a substantial factor in bringing about the damages, if any, and without which the damages would not have occurred. There may be more than one producing cause.

"Proximate cause" is that cause which, in a natural and continuous sequence, produces an event, and without which cause such event would not have occurred. In order to be a proximate cause, the act or omission complained of must be such that a person using ordinary care would have foreseen that the event, or some similar event, might reasonably result therefrom. There may be more than one proximate cause.

"Ordinary care" means that degree of care that would be used by a person of ordinary prudence under the same or similar circumstances.

"Market value" means the amount of money which would be paid in cash by a willing buyer who desires to buy, but is not required to buy, to a willing seller who desires to sell, but is under no necessity of selling.

In answering questions about damages, answer each question separately. Do not increase or reduce the amount in one answer because of your answer to any other question about damages. Do not speculate about what any party's ultimate recovery may or may not be. Any recovery will be determined by the court when it applies the law to your answers at the time of judgment.

"Knowingly" means an actual awareness of the falsity, deception, or unfairness of the conduct in question. Actual awareness may be inferred where objective manifestations indicate that a person acted with actual awareness.

["The house" means that house purchased by plaintiff from defendant and which is the subject of this suit.]

QUESTION NO. 1

Did [defendant] engage in any false, misleading, or deceptive act or practice on which [plaintiff] relied to his [her] detriment and that was a producing cause of damages to [plaintiff]?

"False, misleading, or deceptive act or practice" means any of the following:

(a) Representing that the [house] had characteristics, uses, or benefits which it did not have, or

(b) Representing that the [house] was of a particular standard, quality, or grade when it was of another, or

(c) Failing to disclose information about the [house] that was known at the time of the transaction with the intention of inducing [plaintiff] into the transaction, which transaction [plaintiff] would not have entered had the information been disclosed.

Answer "Yes" or "No."

Answer: _____ .

If you have answered question number 1 "Yes," then answer question number 2; otherwise, do not answer question number 2.

QUESTION NO. 2

What sum of money, if any, paid now in cash would fairly and reasonably compensate [plaintiff] for his [her] damages, if any, that resulted from the conduct you have found in answer to question number 1?

Consider the following elements of damages, if any, and no others:

Do not include any amount for interest on past damages, if any.

Answer in dollars and cents, if any.

[*insert elements of damages, e.g.*:

(a) The difference, if any, in _____, 20__, between the market value of the house in the condition in which it was sold to (plaintiff) and the value it would have had if it had been as represented.

Answer: $ _____ .

[*or*] (a) The reasonable and necessary cost, if any, today in _____ County, Texas, to repair the (*insert defective condition, e.g.*, foundation defects), if any, in the house; and

Answer: $ _____ .

(b) The decrease, if any, on (*insert month and year of sale*) in the market value of the house due to the stigma, if any, associated with any (*insert defective conditions, e.g.*, foundation defects), even though such defects, if any, have been repaired. Do not include the cost to repair in your answer.]

Answer: $ _____ .

QUESTION NO. 3

Did [defendants] make a negligent misrepresentation on which [plaintiff] justifiably relied?

A negligent misrepresentation occurs when:

a. a party makes a representation in the course of *his/her* business or in a transaction in which he has a pecuniary interest, and

b. the representation supplies false information for the guidance of *another/others* in their business, and

c. the party making the representation did not exercise reasonable care or competence in obtaining or communicating the information.

Answer "Yes" or "No."

Answer: _____.

If you have answered question number 3 "yes," then answer question number 4; otherwise, do not answer question number 4.

QUESTION NO. 4

What sum of money, if any, paid now in cash would fairly and reasonably compensate [plaintiff] for his [her] damages, if any, that resulted from the conduct you have found in answer to question number 3?

You may consider the following elements of damages and no others: [*insert elements of damages*]

Do not include any amount for interest on past damages, if any.

Answer in dollars and cents, if any.

(a) The difference, if any, in _____ 20__, between the market value of the house in the condition in which it was sold to (plaintiff) and the value it would have had if it had been as represented.

Answer: $_____.

[*or*]

(a) The reasonable and necessary cost, if any, today in _____ County, Texas, to repair the (*insert defective condition, e.g.*, foundation defects), if any, in the house.

Answer: $_____.

(b) The decrease, if any, on (*insert month and year of sale*) in the market value of the house due to the stigma, if any, associated with any (*insert defective conditions, e.g.*, foundation defects), even though such defects, if any, have been repaired. Do not include the cost to repair in your answer.]

Answer: $_____.

QUESTION NO. 5

Did [defendant] knowingly engage in the conduct found by you in answer to question number 1?

Answer "Yes" or "No."

Answer: _____.

If you have answered question number 5 "yes," then answer question number 6; otherwise do not answer question number 6.

QUESTION NO. 6

What sum of money, if any, should be assessed against [defendant] as additional damages?

"Additional damages" means an amount of money that you may in your discretion award as punishment of the wrongdoer and as a warning and example to the wrongdoer and others to deter the same or similar conduct in the future.

In determining the amount, you may consider:

(1) The nature of the conduct.

(2) The character of the conduct involved.

(3) The degree of culpability of the wrongdoer.

(4) The situation and sensibilities of the parties concerned.

(5) The extent to which such conduct offends a sense of justice and propriety.

(6) The size of an award needed to deter similar conduct in the future.

Answer in dollars and cents, if any.

Answer: $ _____.

QUESTION NO. 7

Did [defendant], prior to the consummation of [the transaction in question] give reasonable and timely written notice of his/her reliance on the information contained in Exhibit _____ in making the representation, if any, found by you in Question ____?

You are instructed that you may answer this question "yes" only if all of the following are found by you:

1. [Defendant] gave written notice of his [her] reliance on the information to [plaintiff]; and

2. The written notice, if any, was given to [plaintiff] before the consummation of the transaction; and

3. The written notice, if any, was reasonable and timely; and

4. [Defendant] did not know and could not reasonably have known that the information was false or inaccurate; and

5. The information was a producing cause of the damages, if any, of [plaintiff].

Answer "Yes" or "No."

Answer: _____.

If you have answered question number 1 "yes," then answer question number 8; otherwise, do not answer question number 8.

QUESTION NO. 8

Find the reasonable and necessary attorney's fees for the legal services provided and to be provided to [plaintiff] in connection with this lawsuit. Answer in dollars and cents in the spaces provided below:

(a) For the preparation and trial of this lawsuit in this court, including post-trial, pre-appeal and collection of judgment legal services: $_____

(b) For an appeal to the Court of Appeals: $_____

(c) For representation at the petition for review stage in the Supreme Court of Texas: $_____

(d) For representation at the merits briefing stage in the Supreme Court of Texas: $_____

(e) For representation through oral argument and the completion of proceedings in the Supreme Court of Texas: $ _____

[*Insert other instructions, definitions and jury questions*].

After you retire to the jury room, you will select your own presiding juror. The first thing the presiding juror will do is have this complete charge read aloud and then you will deliberate upon your answers to the questions asked.

It is the duty of the presiding juror—

1. to preside during your deliberations,

2. to see that your deliberations are conducted in an orderly manner and in accordance with the instructions in this charge,

3. to write out and hand to the bailiff any communications concerning the case that you desire to have delivered to the judge,

4. to conduct all voting on the questions,

[NOTE: Instruction number 4 as contained in Pattern Jury Charges says: "to vote on the questions[.]" *See* 4 Texas Pattern Jury Charges §100.3 (2010) at 9. The literal language of the pattern charge instruction suggests that only the presiding juror should vote; therefore, instruction number 4 has been changed to make clear that the role of the presiding juror is to conduct the voting.]

5. to write your answers to the questions in the spaces provided, and

6. to certify your verdict in the space provided for the presiding juror's signature or to obtain the signatures of all the jurors who agree with the verdict if your verdict is less than unanimous.

You should not discuss the case with anyone, not even with other members of the jury, unless all of you are present and assembled in the jury room. Should anyone attempt to talk to you about the case before the verdict is returned, whether at the courthouse, at your home, or elsewhere, please inform the judge of this fact.

When you have answered all the questions you are required to answer under the instructions of the judge and your presiding juror has placed your answers in the spaces provided and signed the verdict as presiding juror or obtained the signatures, you will inform the bailiff at the door of the jury room that you have reached a verdict, and then you will return into court with your verdict.

_____
PRESIDING JUDGE

Certificate

We, the jury, have answered the above and foregoing questions as herein indicated, and herewith return same into court as our verdict.

(To be signed by the presiding juror if unanimous.)

_____
Presiding Juror

(To be signed by those rendering the verdict if not unanimous)

_____ _____

_____ _____

_____ _____

_____ _____

§10.19 Jury Arguments

A trial is divided into three basic parts: jury selection, presentation of evidence, and arguments. Stated differently, the first part of the trial (voir dire, opening statements) involves telling the jury what will be said; the second part is concerned with actually saying it; and, the third part of the trial (arguments) involves reminding the jury of what has been said.

There are several excellent, comprehensive works on jury arguments generally. Among these are:

Perdue, WHO WILL SPEAK FOR THE VICTIM?, State Bar of Texas, Austin, Texas 1989.

SMITH, MALANDRO, COURTROOM COMMUNICATION STRATEGIES, Kluwer Law Book Publishers, Inc., New York, New York, 1985 (1988 Cumulative Supplement).

Because of the in-depth treatment given by these and other texts to jury arguments, the following sections are limited to a review of general legal principles that apply to arguments and suggestions on how arguments can be approached in DTPA litigation to maximize their effectiveness.

§10.20 General Legal Principles

The manner in which jury arguments are conducted rests largely in the discretion of the court. TEX. R. CIV. P. 269(a). The discretion extends to nearly every aspect of *how* the argument is conducted, and to some degree, the subject matters that can be argued. For example, the court is empowered to regulate such things as the amount of time that will be allotted to each side, *Brownsville Medical*

Center v. Gracia, 704 S.W.2d 68 (Tex. App.—Corpus Christi 1985, writ ref'd n.r.e.), and, the court can determine when breaks will be taken during the argument. *Jarbet Co. v. Moore*, 397 S.W.2d 268 (Tex. Civ. App.—Beaumont 1965, writ ref'd n.r.e.).

Although the court's authority to regulate the subject matter of the argument is more limited, it has been held that a court can determine whether the party who opens can give further argument if the other side waives argument. *Medrano v. City of El Paso*, 231 S.W.2d 514 (Tex. Civ. App.—El Paso 1950, writ ref'd n.r.e.). The court may prevent plaintiff's counsel from raising new matters in the closing argument because of the rule that unless the plaintiff "opens fully," he or she is prohibited from mentioning a subject for the first time in closing. *Brownsville Medical Center v. Gracia, supra*. Closing is reserved for rebuttal. TEX. R. CIV. P. 269(b). It is left to the sound discretion of the court to determine whether the argument was opened fully. *Costa v. Storm*, 682 S.W.2d 599 (Tex. App.—Houston [1st Dist.] 1984, writ ref'd n.r.e.).

§10.21 Contents of Jury Arguments

There was a time when townspeople gathered in courtrooms to hear attorneys argue their cases. Arguments were entertaining, at least to the spectators. Although the days of great courtroom oratory are passing, they are not gone entirely. It still is proper for inspired counsel to weave into their arguments eloquent references to history, personal experience, anecdotes, Bible stories and even jokes. *Sheffield v. Lewis*, 287 S.W.2d 531 (Tex. Civ. App.—Texarkana 1956, no writ). As the court said in *Houston Lighting & Power Co. v. Fisher*, 559 S.W.2d 682, 684 (Tex. Civ. App.—Houston [14th Dist.] 1977, writ ref'd n.r.e.).

Counsel is not required to make such a luke-warm and sterile argument that the jury is unable to determine which side of the case he is on. Likewise, of course, counsel must be indulged in flights of oratory, and he is entitled to draw inferences from the evidence presented, whether reasonable or not.

Accordingly, it has been held that to tell the jury that it is the plaintiff's "last day in court" is not error. *Johnston Testers v. Rangel*, 435 S.W.2d 927 (Tex. Civ. App.—San Antonio 1968, writ ref'd n.r.e.). And, a statement by counsel that his client would rather have a hung jury than a verdict for less than the amount sought was proper in the circumstances of the case. *Tripp v. Bloodworth*, 374 S.W.2d 713 (Tex. Civ. App.—Eastland 1964, writ ref'd n.r.e.). *also see Texas Employers' Ins. Ass'n v. Mendenhall*, 334 S.W.2d 850 (Tex. Civ. App.—Fort Worth 1960, writ ref'd n.r.e.).

An attorney may ask the jury to answer the questions in a certain way, so long as the request is one which is based on counsel's stated view of what the evidence shows. *Cavnar v. Quality Control Parking, Inc.*, 678 S.W.2d 548 (Tex. App.—Houston [14th Dist.] 1984), *rev'd on other grounds*, 696 S.W.2d 549 (Tex. 1985).

Attorneys also enjoy considerable latitude in the use of materials to aid the argument. For example, an attorney may read from a memorandum of a witness' testimony rather than relying on memory so long as the memorandum is accurate. *Younger Bros. v. Moore*, 135 S.W.2d 780 (Tex. Civ. App.—El Paso 1939, writ dism'd judgmt cor.). Charts may be used in argument, showing damages or suggested jury findings. *Hernandez v. Baucum*, 344 S.W.2d 498 (Tex. Civ. App.—San Antonio 1961, writ ref'd n.r.e.).

During closing argument, an attorney obviously can draw deductions and inferences from the evidence and comment upon them.

Twin City Fire Ins. Co. v. Gibson, 488 S.W.2d 565 (Tex. Civ. App.—Amarillo 1972, writ ref'd n.r.e.). *Abramson v. City of San Angelo*, 210 S.W.2d 476 (Tex. Civ. App.—Austin 1948, writ dism'd).

However there *are* limits on the types of arguments counsel can make. As discussed below, a number of rules are clearly defined and should be scrupulously observed. One court has observed that:

> [b]rinksmanship in the field of jury argument is not to be commended. The careful advocate will better serve his profession—and his client—by following the acceptable standards governing counsel in his courtroom appearances.

Hemmenway v. Skibo, 498 S.W.2d 9, 14-15 (Tex. Civ. App.—Beaumont 1973, writ ref'd n.r.e.).

One clear limitation on jury argument is that attorneys are required to stay within the confines of the evidence heard by the jury and to arguments that are made by opposing counsel. TEX. R. CIV. P. 269(e); *Howsley & Jacobs v. Kendall*, 376 S.W.2d 562, 566 (Tex. 1964); *Plains Ins. Co. v. Evans*, 692 S.W.2d 952 (Tex. App.—Fort Worth 1985, no writ). Arguments outside the record are improper. *Id.* Other limitations are discussed in §10.21 *infra*.

§10.22 Preserving Error

Generally, if an improper argument is "curable," then in order to preserve error, it is necessary to object to the improper argument and ask for an instruction that it be disregarded. *Standard Fire Ins. Co. v. Reese*, 584 S.W.2d 835 (Tex. 1979); *Texas Emp. Ins. Ass'n v. Loesch*, 538 S.W.2d 435 (Tex. Civ. App.—Waco 1976, writ ref'd n.r.e.). The request for an instruction must be made at the time of the allegedly improper argument in order to give the trial court the opportunity to cure it. *Fowler v. Garcia*, 687 S.W.2d 517 (Tex. App.—San Antonio 1985, no writ).

The exception to the rule requiring an objection to preserve error arises when the improper argument cannot be cured by an instruction from the court. *Otis Elevator Co. v. Wood*, 436 S.W.2d 324 (Tex. 1968). The exception is easy to state but somewhat difficult to apply.

"Incurable improper jury argument" occurs when it is so inflammatory that its harmful or acutely prejudicial nature cannot be cured by an instruction to disregard. *Gannett Outdoor Co. of Texas v. Kubeczka*, 7 10 S. W. 2d 79 (Tex. App.—Houston [14th Dist.] 1986, no writ); *see also Hartford Acc. & Indem. Co. v. Thurmond*, 527 S.W.2d 180 (Tex. Civ. App.—Corpus Christi 1975, writ ref'd n.r.e.). Stated differently, incurable jury argument is a type of argument that brings to the attention of jurors matters that were not and could not have been presented in the case, and that are so prejudicial and inflammatory that their harmfulness cannot be eliminated by an instruction from the court. *Houston Lighting & Power Co. v. Fisher*, 559 S.W.2d 682 (Tex. Civ. App.—Houston [14th Dist.] 1977, writ ref'd n.r.e.). The rule is difficult to apply because no matter how many different ways it is stated, it tends to define itself in its own terms: incurable jury argument is improper jury argument that cannot be cured. Unless otherwise ruled upon by the trial court, a complaint of incurable jury argument must be made in a motion for new trial to preserve error for appeal. TEX. R. CIV. P. 324(b)(5).

§10.23 Improper Jury Arguments

Case law provides some examples of incurable, improper jury arguments. For example, in *Howard v. Faberge, Inc.*, 679 S.W.2d 644 (Tex. App.—Houston [1st Dist.] 1984, writ ref'd n.r.e.), the plaintiff claimed that Brut 33 Splash-On Lotion which he had poured on his hands and chest ignited when he accidentally "dropped a match into his waistband." During closing argument, in his zeal to demonstrate that the product was not flammable, defense counsel poured an unidentified and unauthenticated liquid (presumably his client's product) over his arm and tried to light it. Defendant's counsel then made a "plea to God to burn him, if he were wrong." The court held that this conduct was so objectionable that no objection was required to preserve error.

It also is error, although not necessarily incurable, to advise the jury of the effect of the answers to the questions or to ask jurors to answer questions in such a way as to produce a specific result. *Texas & N.O.R. Co. v. Perez*, 346 S.W.2d 369 (Tex. Civ. App.—Houston 1961, writ ref'd n.r.e.). *Brown v. Poff*, 387 S.W.2d 101 (Tex. Civ. App.—El Paso 1965, writ ref'd n.r.e.). It is improper, but not necessarily incurable, for an attorney to argue that just because a question was submitted to the jury, the court has found some evidence to support a finding. *Tucker v. Newth*, 157 S.W.2d 1010 (Tex. Civ. App.—Amarillo 1941, writ ref'd). And, it is improper to attack the professionalism or ethics of opposing counsel in closing argument. *American Petrofina, Inc. v. PPG Industries, Inc.*, 679 S.W.2d 740 (Tex. App.—Fort Worth 1984, writ dism'd by agr.).

Although there are cases that clearly define some types of improper jury argument, even when an argument is improper and a proper objection and request for instruction have been made, the test on appeal for reversal is quite stringent: whether the argument considered in its proper setting and in light of all of the evidence was reasonably calculated to and did cause such prejudice to the opposing party that a withdrawal by counsel or an instruction by the court, or both, could not eliminate the probability that it resulted in an improper verdict. *Texas Sand Co. v. Shield*, 381 S.W.2d 48 (Tex. 1964); *Standard Fire Ins. Co. v. Reese*, 584 S.W.2d 835, 839-841 (Tex. 1979).

The case of *Magic Chef, Inc. v. Sibley*, 546 S.W.2d 851 (Tex. Civ. App.—San Antonio 1977, writ ref'd n.r.e.). illustrates the point that improper jury argument must be very objectionable to lead to reversal. In *Magic Chef, Inc.*, plaintiff's counsel surprised the other side with a "school's out" argument:

> Then he tries to imply that I asked for sympathy. Well, I say to you that we've never asked for sympathy. And he says, 'They,' said this, and 'they' said that. Well, I'll tell you right now, if you don't find that this was a defective stove, if you don't find that it was, just go right down here and put zero, zero, zero because I will have failed in meeting my burden of proof. It will be the same thing. School's out. I say to you that we tilted the scales ever so slight, and we've got to have an 'It was,' answer to No. 1[.]

Magic Chef, Inc. v. Sibley, supra at 857. The court held that this argument was improper because it advised the jury of the effect of their answers; however, the court went on to hold that it could not say that the argument was reasonably calculated to and probably did cause the rendition of an improper judgment in the case. *Id.*

Some attorneys employ the "golden rule" argument in their summations. The golden rule argument is objectionable if it asks the jurors to step into the shoes of one of the parties to the case. *World Wide Tire Co. v. Brown*, 644 S.W.2d 144 (Tex. App.—Houston [14th Dist.] 1982, writ ref'd n.r.e.).

However, it is not improper to argue the golden rule if the attorney is merely asking the jury to look with equal solicitude on the rights of both the plaintiff and the defendant. *Texas Emp. Ins. Ass'n v. Thames*, 252 S.W.2d 228 (Tex. Civ. App.—Fort Worth 1952, writ ref'd n.r.e.).

It is important to note, however, that otherwise objectionable arguments may be permitted if opposing counsel has provoked or invited the improper argument. *Hartford Acc. & Indem. Co. v. Thurmond*, 527 S.W.2d 180 (Tex. Civ. App.—Corpus Christi 1975, writ ref'd n.r.e.). *Texas General Indem. Co. v. Moreno*, 638 S.W.2d 908, 913 (Tex. App.—Houston [1st Dist.] 1982, no writ).

§10.24 Contents and Structure of Jury Argument

The two, fundamental purposes of a jury argument are to (1) make the jury want to find for the client, and (2) tell the jury *how* to find for the client. *See* Keeton, *Trial Tactics and Methods*, Little Brown & Co., Boston, Mass. (1973) at 272-276. The first purpose is accomplished by framing the argument as an appeal to the jury's standards of fair play and its values. The second purpose is accomplished by walking the jury through the questions it will be asked and showing that the evidence allows, if not compels, the desired answer to each question.

The jury argument of the plaintiff consists of both an opening argument, or summation, and a closing argument, or rebuttal, after the defendant has argued. As discussed in §10.18 *supra*, it is improper for the plaintiff to "open" a topic after the defendant has concluded his or her argument; consequently, any aspect of the case that the plaintiff wants to argue must be presented in the first phase of the plaintiff's argument. TEX. R. CIV. P. 269(b).

Although the specific structure of jury arguments varies considerably from case to case, most jury arguments should accomplish at least the following:

- Restate the theme

- Remind the jury of voir dire promises kept

- Organize the evidence under the questions

- Address conflicts in the evidence

- Explain damages and attorneys' fees fully

- Motivate the jury to answer favorably

(1) *Restatement of the theme*. At the beginning of the trial, a theme for the case should have been established. The beginning of closing argument should restate the theme for the jury. To illustrate, in a lender liability case, one theme is that, "in good times a bank is a friend; in bad times (when a friend is needed) a bank is a predator." The following beginning of a jury argument illustrates one way in which the theme is restated in an attempt to convince the jury to *want* to find for the plaintiff:

> Ladies and gentlemen of the jury, [the plaintiff] and the bank were friends. You remember the testimony. [The plaintiff] and the bank officers played golf together, they ate together, they told jokes together, they talked business together. [The plaintiff] relied on his friends and they—that bank—encouraged that reliance. And can you hear the promise that the bank made? "If you will just do this, then we will loan you the money." Well, [the plaintiff] did what they asked, exactly as they asked. But then times began getting tough—and instead of just enjoying the friendship, [the plaintiff] began to need that friendship more than ever before in his life. And in his moment of need what did his friend, the bank,

do? The bank broke its solemn promise to [the plaintiff]. It refused to loan him the money. And then, after cutting off his only hope of survival, the bank became a predator. It swooped down and took his business; it seized all of his inventory and his land; it took his lake house; it devoured every dollar he had; and then it took the last and most valuable asset of all—it took his good name by forcing him into bankruptcy.

(2) *Remind jury of voir dire promises kept.* During voir dire and opening statement, the jury presumably was told what the evidence would be. After the theme has been restated, it is sometimes helpful to remind the jury that the evidence was, in fact, produced as promised. Reminding the jury of the promises made and kept not only serves to justify the jury's confidence in the attorney, it also provides a framework within which key evidence points can be restated. Using the lender liability example, such an argument would be:

> When this trial began, we reviewed with you what we believed the evidence would show. We told you then that we would prove that the bank made a promise to [the plaintiff] that it did not keep. And, we did that. [The plaintiff] testified under oath that the bank said, "If you'll do this, we will loan you the money." Even the bank admitted when its representative was on the stand that it made the promise. Was the promise kept? Absolutely not. Not one dollar of that promised money flowed into [the plaintiff's] account.

(3) *Organize the evidence under the jury questions.* One of the most important functions of closing argument is organizing the evidence for the jury so it can be applied by the jury to the questions that must be answered.

In cases in which multiple liability issues are presented involving essentially the same proof, it may be helpful to group jury questions together for the argument. For example, in DTPA litigation, the jury frequently will be asked more than one question dealing with misrepresentation, such as, a question drawn from the "laundry list" in DTPA §17.46(b), and a similar question drawn from the common law of negligent misrepresentation or, perhaps, fraud in real estate and stock transactions as set forth in TEX. BUS. & COM. CODE §27.01. The evidence under each of these questions essentially is the same; therefore, it is more efficient and understandable to argue the evidence which supports answers to all of the issues at the same time.

In arguing the evidence in support of each question, the attorney should (1) state the question (reading or paraphrasing the question makes sure the jury's attention is focused), and (2) specifically describe the evidence that supports the desired answer. Of course, this process is done in an argument style. Using the same lender liability example, the argument may follow this pattern:

> Members of the Jury, question number one asks, 'Did [the bank] represent to [the plaintiff] that its agreement with [him] conferred or involved certain rights and benefits which it did not have or involve? Answer "yes" or "no."' You and I both know what the evidence says about the answer to this question, but let me tell you why I think the evidence requires a "yes" answer. First, you heard [the plaintiff] and the bank testify about the agreement that they struck. There is no question but that there was an agreement to loan money. The bank claims that it did not have to give [the plaintiff] the money, but there is not any doubt that there was an agreement. Now, what was the representation about the agreement. [The plaintiff] testified that the bank *represented* to him that if he would do a certain thing, then it would deposit money into his account. In other words, [the plaintiff] would have a

right to the money and would receive the *benefit* of the money. Did the agreement really have or confer that benefit? Again, the answer is no, it did not. You heard the bank testify that [the plaintiff] really had no right to that money under the agreement. And [the plaintiff] surely did not realize any benefit from it. And so, the clear answer to this question under the evidence is "Yes."

Obviously, it is not advisable to review with the jury each and every piece of testimony or evidence that they have heard; nor is it advisable to go to the other extreme and talk in broad generalities about the evidence. Further, in discussing the testimony of witnesses, it is helpful to use the actual words contained in the jury questions as frequently as possible. In the example cited, the plaintiff testified that the bank *represented* certain things to him rather than saying that the bank said certain things. Since the jury question will ask what the defendant "represented," *see* §10.03 *supra*, that word should be used in the argument.

(4) *Address conflicts in the evidence*. Jury trials always involve conflicts between the testimony of witnesses. Obviously, if there is no conflict, there is no need for a trial. Dealing with conflicts in the evidence, however, is a very sensitive matter.

No human being that a person would want on a jury *enjoys* calling another human being a liar. When confronted with the need to decide, particularly in a group, many people reserve that harshest of all judgments until there is no reasonable alternative. Consequently, unless a witness has testified to facts that are demonstrably false, most jurors will give that person the benefit of the doubt. And, by giving the witness the benefit of the doubt, the force and effect of the opposing testimony is necessarily weakened.

The reluctance of people to assume that another person is not telling the truth suggests that an attorney had best stay clear of such arguments before the jury. Instead, every effort should be made to explain conflicts in testimony by encouraging the jury to consider who, among the witnesses, is most likely to have the best memory of the event. An illustration that is frequently used is to compare the witnesses to the participants in a wedding. The preacher who has married hundreds of couples before is not likely to have a clear memory of any particular wedding. The bride and groom, however, are likely to remember every detail of the wedding for the rest of their lives. In the same way, a salesperson who has sold hundreds of houses is unlikely to remember much, if anything, of any particular sale. The first time homebuyer, however, will be able to recall each word spoken for years after they have moved in, especially if the house is not what it was represented to be.

One should never stray from using clear evidence of false testimony to convince the jury that the witness lacks credibility; however, unless the evidence is clear, a different, less judgmental approach should be used.

(5) *Explain damages and attorneys' fees fully*. There is a natural inclination in most people to strive for fairness in dealings with other human beings. When this inclination is coupled with the very brief time that a jury has to get to know the parties to a lawsuit, the result is a tendency on the part of juries to compromise on the answers to questions so that each side gets something.

In liability questions, very little compromising is possible since only a "yes" or "no" answer can be given. There is no space for "maybe" or "probably." Consequently, the question that presents a jury with its long awaited opportunity to be "fair" is that on damages, where a great deal of compromising can be done.

Of course, a jury's natural good will toward both sides of a lawsuit can disappear quickly if the facts of the case are particularly egregious or if a party abuses the jury by lying to it. Since, however, few cases present the jury with clear justification for finding wholly in favor of one side and wholly against the other, the damages question remains the one inquiry that is likely to produce the greatest amount of give and take.

Interestingly, the tendency of many juries to compromise on the amount of damages does not appear to be limited to cases involving "soft" damages like pain and suffering or mental anguish where a great deal of juror discretion is encouraged. The same result is found in cases involving "hard" damages such as the cost to repair damaged goods where just a few dollars less than the amount asked means that the house does not get fixed.

Because of the difficulty the jury can be expected to have with the damages question in most trials, it is essential that the elements of damages and the evidence supporting the amount sought be explained and argued fully.

Perhaps the most effective way to present evidence of damages, particularly when there are multiple elements of damages is through the use of charts that clearly identify the type of damage and the amount that is supported by the evidence. When "hard" damages such as repair costs and medical bills are sought, the jury should be made to understand that anything less than the full amount will not do the job. In a residential construction case, this type of argument may be illustrated as follows:

> We know from the evidence that the foundation of this house needs to be stabilized. And in order to stabilize the foundation, [the witness] testified that eighteen piers are going to have to be drilled. He did not say seventeen and he did not say nineteen; he said eighteen. And the reason he said eighteen is that each pier must be located eight feet from the one next to it. Again, not nine feet and not seven feet, but eight feet. Years of engineering experience and study went into the opinion that you heard presented in this courtroom. Now, [another witness] testified that each pier that is drilled is going to cost $500. He can't do it for any less and he doesn't need any more. If you multiply these numbers out as I've done on the chart, you'll see that the cost to stabilize the foundation is exactly $9,000. If you find only $8,000 then it simply will not be enough to stabilize the foundation.

There are some jurors who resent the fees that attorneys are paid. With these types of jurors in mind, during argument the reasons why such fees can be recovered must be explained.

From the plaintiff's perspective, when two parties are unable to reach an agreement on who is responsible for a consumer's damages and who will pay, there is only one forum for resolving such disputes, a forum that is guaranteed by both the Texas and federal constitutions. That forum is the courthouse. Without an attorney, it would be impossible for the consumer to have his or her day in court.

When a bad faith claim is presented, and the defendant is asking for attorneys' fees, the defendant's attorney should explain to the jury that there was no choice about being in court since the consumer filed the suit. If the petition had not been answered and the lawsuit defended, the consumer would have recovered a default judgment. Since there was no choice about being in court, an attorney was required.

(6) *Motivate the jury to answer favorably.* The last function of closing argument is to use words, gestures and emotions that will motivate the jury to answer the questions favorably.

The defendant is the first to close. Since the plaintiff will have the last word, the defense attorney must not only motivate the jury to answer the defensive issues correctly, he or she must also anticipate and attempt to lessen the impact of the plaintiff's rebuttal.

Obviously, the key points made by the plaintiff's attorney during the opening argument must be rebutted with clear references to the evidence. Having answered each of the plaintiff's claims effectively, it is necessary to consider the impact of the plaintiff's opportunity to have the last word in rebuttal.

One method of reducing the impact of the plaintiff's rebuttal is to show the jury how "unfair" it is that the defense attorney will not have the opportunity to answer the plaintiff's closing argument. To accomplish this objective, the jury should be reminded that throughout the trial, the defense attorney has responded to each and every claim made by the plaintiff, particularly if the defendant's evidence has been convincing. An example of this line of argument is the following:

> Members of the jury, before I sit down, I want to ask you to think about something with me. In a few moments, the plaintiff's attorney will be allowed to get back up here and talk some more about what the evidence proved. And even though you know better than anyone in this courtroom what the evidence really has shown, the point I want to make is that under our rules, I will not be allowed to get up again and answer any of the claims that are about to be made. It has been this way throughout the trial. The plaintiff is allowed to go first and last because the plaintiff has to prove his case. Even though we had to wait our turn to speak, I think you will agree that we have answered every claim made by the plaintiff in this case with sound, credible evidence. Our job has been to tell you the rest of the story . . . filling in those gaps that the plaintiff left out because they don't help his side of the case. We won't have that chance any more, and so I ask you to remember how we've answered the plaintiff's claims throughout this trial and to know that we could do it again if we just had the chance.

An approach to motivating the jury to action is suggested in PERDUE, WHO WILL SPEAK FOR THE VICTIM?, *supra* at §10. 17, that will work equally well for the plaintiff or the defendant. The technique uses the phrase, "you know now what we knew then" followed by a restatement of the proof in the case on a particular point. The use of this or some similar phrase subtly asks the jury to join the team now that they have seen the evidence that the attorney knew all along was going to come in.

Lastly, to insure that whatever motivational skills the attorney has brought to bear continue working in the jury room, it may be helpful to call upon the "friendly" jurors to take up the argument in the jury room since the attorneys cannot be present:

> In a few moments the judge will excuse you to go into the jury room and begin your deliberations. At this point, there may still be some jurors who are unpersuaded how to answer the questions under the evidence. If you believe that we have met our burden of proof on these questions, stick by your beliefs. I will not be in the jury room to argue [the client's] case any more. It will be up to you to insist that each of these questions is answered correctly under the evidence.

By structuring a jury argument in a DTPA case so that it focuses on making the jury want to and then telling the jury how to answer the questions, the hard work put into presenting the case will stand its best chance of being rewarded with a favorable jury verdict.

§10.25 Motions for Judgment

A motion for judgment on the jury verdict is the standard procedure by which a court is asked to enter judgment after the conclusion of a jury trial. Motions for judgment in DTPA trials, however, serve an additional function in that they provide a vehicle for the plaintiff to "elect" between various theories of liability and elements of damages in order to obtain the maximum recovery.

DTPA lawsuits frequently involve several theories of recovery and, of necessity, several jury questions on damages to match the theories of recovery. For example, a case may be submitted on both negligence and deceptive trade practices or breach of warranty (under the DTPA). In a DTPA cause of action, a plaintiff is entitled to recover, "the greatest amount of actual damages alleged and factually established to have been caused by the deceptive practice[.]" *Kish v. Van Note*, 692 S.W. 2d 463, 466 (Tex. 1985). And, common law defenses that a jury may find against the plaintiff have no bearing on the DTPA action. *Smith v. Baldwin*, 611 S.W.2d 611 (Tex. 1980). Accordingly, when the jury finds a greater amount of damages under the DTPA question than any other, or, when the jury finds for the defendant on an affirmative defense that would adversely affect the plaintiff's ability to recover on a common law theory, an election by the plaintiff is necessary. The election should be made in the motion for judgment.

[a] FORM: Motion for judgment on the jury verdict

```
                        NO. _____
_____              §    IN THE _____ COURT OF
                        §
vs.                     §    _____ COUNTY, TEXAS
                        §
_____              §    _____ JUDICIAL DISTRICT
```

PLAINTIFF'S MOTION FOR JUDGMENT ON THE JURY VERDICT

TO THE HONORABLE JUDGE OF THE DISTRICT COURT:

_____, plaintiff, files this Motion for Judgment on the Jury Verdict and as grounds for the motion will show the court the following:

1. <u>Elections</u>. Plaintiff makes the following elections with respect to the jury's findings in its verdict:

(a) <u>Causes of action</u>

Plaintiff elects to recover judgment on the basis of the jury's answers to questions number _____, _____ [and

_____], which is the cause of action asserted by plaintiff under Tex. Bus. & Com. Code §17.50(a).

(b) <u>Measures of damages</u>

Plaintiff further elects to recover damages based on the jury's answer to question number _____ which is the proper measure of damages for an action under Tex. Bus. & Com. Code §17.50(b)(1).

2. <u>Judgment should be entered</u>. Judgment should be entered on the jury's answers to questions number _____, _____ [and _____] for the reason that there is evidence to support each finding and the findings, taken together, properly submit a cause of action for damages under Tex. Bus. & Com. Code §17.50(a).

3. <u>Prejudgment interest is recoverable</u>. The court also should enter judgment for prejudgment interest on the damages award in the highest amount allowed by law because prejudgment interest in such amount is recoverable in DTPA actions. *St. Paul Surplus Lines Ins. Co. v. Dal-Worth Tank Co.*, 974 S.W.2d 51, 54 (Tex. 1998).

4. <u>Additional damages should be awarded</u>. The court should also enter judgment that plaintiff recover the additional damages found by the jury in answer to question ____ because the jury found that the defendant's conduct was committed "knowingly" in answer to question ____, and the amount found by the jury does not exceed three times the amount of economic damages found by the jury in answer to question[s] ____ and ____. Tex. Bus. & Com. Code §17.50(b)(1); *Tony Gullo Motors I, L.P. v. Chapa*, 212 S.W.3d 299, 304 (Tex. 2006).

5. [*Insert other items on which judgment is requested*].

WHEREFORE, plaintiff requests that the court grant this motion and enter judgment on the jury verdict as set forth above and that plaintiff have general relief.

Respectfully submitted,

[Signature of attorney]

[Certificate of service]

[b] FORM: Defendant's motion for judgment on jury verdict

```
                              NO. _____
_____              §   IN THE _____ COURT OF
                          §
vs.                       §   _____ COUNTY, TEXAS
                          §
_____              §   _____ JUDICIAL DISTRICT
```

DEFENDANT'S MOTION FOR JUDGMENT ON THE JURY VERDICT

TO THE HONORABLE JUDGE OF THE DISTRICT COURT:

_____, defendant, files this Motion for Judgment on the jury verdict and as grounds for the motion will show the following:

1. The jury found against plaintiff on each of the questions necessary to establish any liability on the part of defendant.

2. Defendant has proven, by a preponderance of the evidence, that this lawsuit was motivated solely by bad faith and [or] was brought for the sole purpose of harassment. Accordingly, defendant asks that the Court make such a finding.

3. Further, defendant asks the Court to determine, as a matter of law, that plaintiff's claim was groundless.

4. Based on the requested findings and conclusions, defendant moves the Court to enter judgment on the jury's verdict with respect to defendant's attorneys' fees as contained in the jury's answer to question number _____.

WHEREFORE, defendant moves for judgment on the jury verdict that plaintiff take nothing and for further judgment against plaintiff for defendant's attorneys' fees in the amount found by the jury. Defendant also requests general relief.

                          Respectfully submitted,

                          [Signature of attorney]

[Certificate of service]

[c] FORM: Plaintiff's motion for judgment disregarding certain jury findings — attorney's fees

The following form is used when the plaintiff asks the trial court to disregard a jury's award of attorney's fees which is smaller than the undisputed testimony on attorney's fees. It also expressly elects for judgment on the jury's DTPA findings over concurrent findings under common law fraud because of the availability of attorney's fees.

PLAINTIFFS' MOTION FOR JUDGMENT DISREGARDING CERTAIN JURY ANSWERS

TO THE HONORABLE JUDGE OF SAID COURT:

NOW COME _____ Plaintiffs herein, and pursuant to Rule 301, *Texas Rules of Civil Procedure*, move the Court to enter judgment herein on the Jury's verdict, disregarding certain answers established otherwise as a matter of law, and for such, say unto the Court as follows:

I.

On _____, 2007, the Jury in this case returned its verdict with affirmative findings of liability in favor of Plaintiffs against Defendants _____, entitling Plaintiffs to the entry of judgment against them for damages, attorney's fees, pre-judgment interest, and taxable costs of court.

II.

However, the Jury answered Question No. 17A (regarding attorney's fees for preparation and trial) with "$54,000.00," Question No. 17B (regarding attorney's fees for an appeal to the Court of Appeals with $9,000.00," and Question No. 17C (regarding attorney's fees for an appeal to the Supreme Court of Texas) with "$4,500.00." The evidence conclusively established that the answers to these questions were $75,000.00 for 17A, $12,000.00 for 17B, and $6,000.00 for 17C.

III.

A Court should disregard the Jury's answer to a question if there is no evidence to support it or if the evidence established the fact to the contrary as a matter of law. *Best v. Ryan Auto Group, Inc.*, 786 S.W. 2d 670, 671 (Tex. 1990). And specifically, when evidence of attorney's fees is admitted without objection, cross-examination or evidence to the contrary, trial counsel's testimony regarding the reasonable and necessary attorney's fees establishes those amounts of attorney's fees as a matter of law. *Garcia v. Gomez*, 319 S.W.3d 638, 642 (Tex. 2010); *Ragsdale v. Progressive Voters League*, 801 S.W.2d 880, 882 (Tex. 1990).

IV.

Here, the undersigned counsel for Plaintiffs, testified without opposition or contradiction to reasonable attorney's fees through trial of $75,000.00, reasonable attorney's fees for an appeal to the Court of Appeals of $12,000.00, and reasonable attorney's fees for an appeal to the Texas Supreme Court of $6,000.00. These amounts were established conclusively as a matter of law. As such, the Jury's answers of "$54,000.00," "$9,000.00," and "$4,500.00" for each should be disregarded in findings by the Court made of $75,000.00, $12,000.00 and $6,000.00 for each of these matters, respectively.

V.

The remaining answers of the Jury in its verdict established Plaintiffs' right to recovery against Defendants under the theory of Deceptive Trade Practices Act violations and common law fraud. Plaintiffs elect to have judgment entered in the manner to provide them with the largest recovery: The Deceptive Trade Practices Act. Plaintiffs therefore pray that the Court enter its Judgment as set forth in Exhibit A attached hereto and incorporated herein by this reference.

WHEREFORE, Plaintiffs, _____, pray that the Court disregard the Jury's answers to Questions Nos. 17A, 17B and 17C, that the Court deem findings in the amounts established as a matter of law for these matters, and that Judgment be entered as set forth on the attached form of judgment, and for such other and further relief to which they may show themselves justly entitled.

Respectfully submitted,

[Signature of attorney]

[Certificate of service]

§10.26 Final Judgments

The final judgment forms which follow are appropriate for use in DTPA jury trials. The general format is the same as other final judgments in civil cases; however, the provisions for multiple damages and attorneys' fees in the plaintiff's judgment, as well as the court's finding that a lawsuit was groundless in one of the defendant's judgments, are generally found only in DTPA litigation.

Prejudgment interest in DTPA lawsuits that involve claims for "wrongful death, personal injury or property damage" had been governed by TEX. REV. CIV. STAT. art. 5069-1.05 §6(a); otherwise, the common law rules stated in *Cavnar v. Quality Control Parking, Inc.*, 696 S.W.2d 549 (Tex. 1985), have applied. However, in *Johnson & Higgins, Inc. v. Kenneco Energy*, 962 S.W.2d 507 (Tex. 1998), the Texas Supreme Court rewrote the *Cavnar* rule to conform it to the statute. The statutory language applies to all cases "in which judgment is rendered on or after December 11, 1997, and to all other cases currently in the judicial process in which the issue has been preserved." *Id.* at 284. Although the language of the statute is not in question, its location is uncertain. As noted by the Court, it is unclear whether the text of article 5069-1.05 is now found in the Finance Code §304.101 *et seq.* or whether it was reenacted as part of the Texas Credit Title Act. *Id.* at 284. For any judgment entered after September 1, 2003, prejudgment interest is not computed on future damages. TEX. FIN. CODE § 304.1045.

Statutory prejudgment interest begins to run 180 days after either the date suit is filed or the date that the defendant receives notice of the claim and continues to accrue until "the day preceding the date judgment is rendered." TEX. FIN. CODE § 304.104. Postjudgment interest begins to accrue on the day judgment is rendered and generally continues until the judgment is satisfied. TEX. FIN. CODE §304.005(a).

Postjudgment interest accrues on all amounts in the judgment, including attorney's fees, court costs, prejudgment interest or additional damages. TEX. FIN. CODE § 304. 003(a). However, interest on conditional awards of attorney's fees on appeal should not accrue until the appeal is taken. *See Law Offices of Windle Turley, P.C. v. French*, 164 S.W.3d 487, 493-494 (Tex. App.—Dallas 2005, no pet.) Therefore, the judgment should be drawn so that these amounts are segregated from those on which post judgment interest does accrue.

The statutory rate for both prejudgment and postjudgment interest is not less than 5% and not more than 15%, depending on the interest rate published by the Texas Consumer Credit Commissioner. TEX. FIN. CODE § 304.003.

[a] FORM: Final judgment for damages and attorneys' fees

```
                          NO. _____

_____           §      IN THE _____ COURT OF
                         §
vs.                      §      _____ COUNTY, TEXAS
                         §
_____           §      _____ JUDICIAL DISTRICT
```

FINAL JUDGMENT

On the _____ day of ___, 20___ the above referenced cause was called for trial at which time both plaintiff and defendant announced ready by and through their attorneys of record. A jury of twelve men and women were duly tested, selected, empaneled and sworn. The trial proceeded until the _____ day of _____ 20___, at which time the evidence of the plaintiff and defendant was closed. The court prepared its charge and the parties made their objections to the charge. The court then read its charge to the jury and counsel for both parties presented their arguments. The jury retired and deliberated and ultimately reached its verdict by a unanimous vote [by a vote of ___ to ___]. The jury returned its verdict to the court and it was received by the court and ordered filed among the papers of the cause. After this, the jury was discharged.

It appears to the court from the verdict of the jury and the law applicable to the verdict, that judgment should be entered in favor of plaintiff _____ and against defendant _____ for plaintiff's actual damages of $_____. It further appears to the court that plaintiff is entitled to judgment against defendant for $_____ in additional damages. And, it further appears to the court that plaintiff is entitled to attorneys' fees and costs of court as set forth below, which relief is authorized by TEX. BUS. & COM. CODE §17.50(d).

IT IS THEREFORE ORDERED, ADJUDGED AND DECREED that plaintiff _____ recover from defendant _____ the following sums:

1. The sum of $ _____ as actual damages; and

2. The sum of $ _____ as additional damages; and

3. Prejudgment interest on plaintiffs actual damages in the amount of $_____.

4. The sum of $ _____ as attorneys' fees; and

[NOTE: If attorney's fees on appeal are to be awarded, replace this paragraph with the alternative paragraph in §[d] *infra*.]

5. Postjudgment interest on these amounts at the rate of [5%] per annum, compounded annually, from the day this judgment is rendered until the judgment is satisfied.

IT IS FURTHER ORDERED that costs of court are taxed against defendant _____.

All writs and processes for the enforcement and collection of this judgment may issue as necessary.

All relief not granted by this judgment is denied.

SIGNED this _____ day of _____ 20___.

[Signature of presiding judge]

[b] FORM: Final judgment for restoration of money or property and rescission

```
                            NO. _____
_____       §    IN THE _____ COURT OF
                   §
vs.                §    _____ COUNTY, TEXAS
                   §
_____       §    _____ JUDICIAL DISTRICT
```

FINAL JUDGMENT

On the _____ day of _____, 20___ the above referenced cause was called for trial at which time both plaintiff and defendant announced ready by and through their attorneys of record. A jury of twelve men and women were duly tested, selected, empaneled and sworn. The trial proceeded until the _____ day of 20___ at which time the evidence of the plaintiff and defendant was closed. The court prepared its charge and the parties made their objections to the charge. The court then read its charge to the jury and counsel for both parties presented their arguments. The jury retired and deliberated and ultimately reached its verdict by a unanimous vote [by a vote of ____ to ____]. The jury returned its verdict to the court and it was received by the court and ordered filed among the papers of the cause. After this, the jury was discharged.

It appears to the court from the verdict of the jury and the law applicable to the verdict, that judgment should be entered in favor of plaintiff _____ and against defendant _____, canceling the [*insert obligation to be canceled, e.g.* purchase agreement between the parties] and restoring to plaintiff the sum of $_____, which relief is authorized by Tex. Bus. & Com. Code §17.50(b)(3) and (4). And, it further appears to the court that plaintiff is entitled to attorneys' fees and costs of court as set forth below, which relief is authorized by Tex. Bus. & Com. Code §17.50(d).

IT IS THEREFORE ORDERED, ADJUDGED AND DECREED that plaintiff shall have the following relief from defendant

1. The [*insert obligation to be canceled, e.g.*, purchase agreement between plaintiff and defendant dated 20___, is canceled and declared void, and

2. Plaintiff shall recover from defendant the sum of $_____, which constitutes money paid by plaintiff to defendant which should be restored to plaintiff; and

3. Prejudgment interest in the amount of $_____.

4. The sum of $_____ as attorneys' fees, and

[NOTE: If attorney's fees on appeal are to be awarded, replace this paragraph with the alternative form in §[d] *infra*.]

5. Postjudgment interest on these amounts at the rate of [5]% per annum, compounded annually, from the day this judgment is rendered until it is satisfied.

IT IS FURTHER ORDERED that costs of court are taxed against defendant _____.

All writs and processes for the enforcement and collection of this judgment may issue as necessary.

All relief not granted by this judgment is denied.

SIGNED this _____ day of _____ 20___.

[Signature of presiding judge]

[c] FORM: Final judgment for defendant's attorney's fees

	NO. _____	
_____	§ IN THE _____	COURT OF
	§	
vs.	§ _____	COUNTY, TEXAS
	§	
_____	§ _____	JUDICIAL DISTRICT

FINAL JUDGMENT

On the _____ day of _____, 20___ the above referenced cause was called for trial at which time both plaintiff and defendant announced ready by and through their attorneys of record. A jury of twelve men and women were duly tested, selected, empaneled and sworn. The trial proceeded until the _____ day of _____, 20___ at which time the evidence of the plaintiff and defendant was closed. The court prepared its charge and the parties made their objections to the charge. The court then read its charge to the jury and counsel for both parties presented their arguments. The jury retired and deliberated and ultimately reached its verdict by a unanimous vote [by a vote of ___ to ___]. The jury returned its verdict to the court and it was received by the court and ordered filed among the papers of the cause. After this, the jury was discharged.

The court has examined the pleadings of the parties, heard the evidence and argument of counsel and is of the opinion and so finds that plaintiff's lawsuit against defendant [insert one or more of the following: groundless in fact [or] groundless in law [or] was motivated solely by bad faith [or] brought for the sole purpose of harassment].

It appears to the court from the verdict of the jury, the findings of the court and the applicable law, that a take nothing judgment should be entered in favor of defendant and against plaintiff. It further appears to the court that judgment should be entered in favor of defendant _____ and against plaintiff _____ for defendant's attorneys' fees. It further appears to the court that defendant is entitled to recover costs of court from plaintiff, all of which is authorized by Tex. Bus. & Com. Code §17.50(c).

IT IS THEREFORE ORDERED, ADJUDGED AND DECREED that plaintiff take nothing on its suit against defendant.

IT IS FURTHER ORDERED, ADJUDGED AND DECREED that defendant _____ recover from plaintiff _____ the sum of $_____ as attorneys' fees.

[NOTE: If attorney's fees on appeal are to be awarded, replace this paragraph with §[d] *infra*.]

IT IS FURTHER ORDERED that costs of court are taxed against plaintiff _____.

All writs and processes for the enforcement and collection of this judgment may issue as necessary.

All relief not granted by this judgment is denied.

SIGNED this _____ day of _____ 20___.

[Signature of presiding judge]

[d] FORM: Alternative judgment for attorney's fees

[*Insert in final judgment*]

[3.] The sum of $_____ as attorney's fees; and, if this cause is not appealed, the judgment for attorney's fees will be credited with $_____, leaving $_____; and, if this cause is appealed to the court of appeals, but the appeal is not carried to the Supreme Court of Texas by appeal or writ of error, the judgment for attorney's fees will be credited with $_____, leaving a recovery of attorney's fees of $_____; and if application for writ of error is made but such application is denied, dismissed or refused, the judgment for attorney's fees will be credited with $_____, leaving a recovery of attorney's fees of $_____.

Chapter 11

Insurance Code Actions

§11.01　Introduction
§11.02　Texas Insurance Code Chapter 541
　§11.02.1　Standing Under the DTPA and Chapter 541
§11.03　Broad Grounds for Private Cause of Action Under Chapter 541
　§11.03.1　Misrepresentation of Insurance Policy
　§11.03.2　Unfair Settlement Practices as Grounds for Action
　§11.03.3　Damages and Attorney's Fees Under Chapter 541
§11.04　Duty of Good Faith and Fair Dealing
§11.05　Interpretation of Insurance Contracts
§11.06　Defenses Under Chapter 541
　§11.06.1　Settlement Offer Defense
　§11.06.2　Limitations
　§11.06.3　ERISA Preemption
　　§11.06.3.1　Attorney's Fees and ERISA
　§11.06.4　Counterclaim for Frivolous Action
§11.07　Providing Pre-Suit Notice Under Chapter 541
　　[a]　FORM: Notice letter: Chapter 541
§11.08　Plaintiff's Pleadings—Insurance Actions
　　[a]　FORM: Petition (Insurance Code Chapter 541)
　　[b]　FORM: Petition asserting ambiguity, breach of contract and Chapter 541 violations
§11.09　Defendant's Pleadings—Insurance Actions
　　[a]　FORM: Original Answer with specific denials, verified denials and affirmative-defenses—Insurance Code action
§11.10　Discovery—Insurance Code Actions
　§11.10.1　Interrogatories—Insurance Actions
　　　[a]　FORM: Insurance Code claim: denial of disability insurance benefits
　　　[b]　FORM: Insurance Code claim: homeowner's policy (to defendant)
　　　[c]　FORM: Insurance Code claim: homeowner's policy (to plaintiff)
　§11.10.2　Requests for Production—Insurance Actions
　　　[a]　FORM: Denial of insurance claim (to defendant insurance company)
　　　[b]　FORM: Insurance claim (to plaintiff)

§11.01 Introduction

This chapter provides resources for the representation of parties in connection with claims asserted under either the DTPA or under the Insurance Code for deceptive or unfair acts or practices in the business of insurance. The Texas statutes protecting consumers from unfair and deceptive insurance practices have been collected and codified in Chapters 541 through 560 of the Texas Insurance Code. Chapters 541 and 542 provide private, statutory causes of action for certain violations involving deceptive and unfair insurance practices and for the failure to promptly and fairly handle insurance claims.

§11.02 Texas Insurance Code Chapter 541

Chapter 541 of the Texas Insurance Code is a collection of prohibited unfair or deceptive acts or practices in the business of insurance. Chapter 541 was enacted effective April 1, 2005 as a recodification of a variety of prior statutes and regulations. It is derived mainly from former Article 21.21. The following chart shows the disposition of the former law and its place in the new Code.

A private cause of action may be brought through the DTPA by a "consumer" against a person who has committed one or more unfair or deceptive acts or practices in violation of Chapter 541. DTPA §17.50(a)(4). The DTPA

Disposition Table for Texas Ins. Code	
Former	Current
Art. 21.21 §1(a)	§541.001
Art. 21.21 §1(b)	§541.008
Art. 21.21 §2(a)	§541.002
Art. 21.21 §2(c)	§541.002
Art. 21.21 §3	§541.003
Art. 21.21 §4	§541.051-§541.061
Art. 21.21 §16(a)	§541.151
Art. 21.21 §16(b)	§541.152
Art. 21.21 §16(c)	§541.153
Art. 21.21 §16(d)	§541.162
Art. 21.21 §16(e), (f)	§541.154
Art. 21.21 §16(g)-(i)	§541.155
Art. 21.21 §16A(a)-(c)	§541.156
Art. 21.21 §16A(d)	§541.157
Art. 21.21 §16A(e)-(f)	§541.158
Art. 21.21 §16A(g)-(h)	§541.159
Art 21.21 §16A(k)	§541.160
Art.21.21 §16B	§541.161

cause of action is in addition to the private cause of action granted by Chapter 541. The private cause of action under Chapter 541 may also be predicated upon a violation of the DTPA laundry list relied upon by a "person" to his detriment. TEX. INS. CODE §541.151. With all of this cross-referencing, there is a tremendous amount of overlap between the two causes of action. Even so, subtle differences remain.

Chapter 542, Subchapter B, provides a cause of action for a statutory penalty of 18% per annum, together with attorney's fees, for an insurer's failure to pay a valid claim in full within certain deadlines. This cause of action may also be predicated upon the insurer's failure to promptly acknowledge a claim, as well as the failure to promptly initiate an investigation of a claim.

§11.02.1 Standing Under the DTPA and Chapter 541

A DTPA "consumer" who can show that a violation of Chapter 541 was a producing cause of his damages can recover under the DTPA. DTPA §17.50(a)(4). A "person" who can show a violation of the DTPA laundry list caused him damages can recover under Chapter 541. TEX. INS. CODE §541.151(2). A "person" who is also a "consumer" can maintain private causes of action under either the DTPA or Chapter 541, or both. *Allstate Ins. Co. v. Watson*, 876 S.W.2d 145, 149 (Tex. 1994); *Transport Ins. Co. v. Faircloth*, 898 S.W.2d 269, 273-74 (Tex. 1995); *Crown Life Ins. Co. v. Casteel*, 22 S.W.3d 378, 392 (Tex. 2000).

Most DTPA "consumers" will also be "persons" entitled to maintain a private cause of action under Chapter 541; however, not every "person" will qualify as a "consumer" under the DTPA. *See Crown Life v. Casteel*, 22 S.W.2d at 385-86 (insurance agent was a "person" but not a "consumer"). Whether a plaintiff may maintain a private cause of action under either the DTPA or Chapter 541, or both, for violations of Chapter 541 will depend on the plaintiff's status as either a DTPA "consumer" as defined by the DTPA or a "person" as defined by Chapter 541.

"Consumer" status under the DTPA requires showing that the plaintiff was seeking or acquiring goods or services. *See* §1.02.4, *supra*. The sale of insurance is the sale of a "service" as defined under the DTPA. *See, e.g., First Title Co. v. Garrett*, 860 S.W.2d 74 (Tex. 1993); *Chicago Title Ins. Co. v. McDaniel*, 875 S.W.2d 310, 311 (Tex. 1994); *3Z Corp. v. Stewart Title Guar. Co.*, 851 S.W.2d 933, 937 (Tex. App.—Beaumont 1993, writ denied). Consumer status is not limited to those who purchase insurance. One for whom insurance is purchased is a consumer since that person "acquired" the insurance services. *Kennedy v. Sale*, 689 S.W.2d 890 (Tex. 1985); *How Ins. v. Patriot Fin. Serv.*, 786 S.W.2d 533 (Tex. App.—Austin 1990, writ denied).

The cause of action for "unconscionability" in DTPA §17.50(a)(3) is available to a DTPA "consumer" but not to a "person" suing under Chapter 541 of the Insurance Code. *Transport Ins. Co. v. Faircloth*, 898 S.W.2d 269 (Tex. 1995) (discussing former Art. 21.21).

§11.03 Broad Grounds for Private Cause of Action Under Chapter 541

Chapter 541 provides a private cause of action to a "person" against another "person" who has caused the person damages by committing either: (1) an unfair or deceptive insurance act or practice as defined in Chapter 541, Subchapter B, or (2) a violation of the DTPA laundry list on which the plaintiff relied to his detriment. TEX. INS. CODE §541.151.

Standing to sue is broader under Chapter 541 than under the DTPA. Chapter 541 gives remedies for violation of DTPA §17.46, but it does not incorporate the DTPA consumer standing requirement. *Aetna Casualty & Surety. Co. v. Marshall*, 724 S.W.2d 770 (Tex. 1987). Section 541.151 provides that any person who "sustains actual damages may bring an action against another person for those damages caused by the other person." Thus, a person or entity other than the insured or beneficiary may maintain an action under Chapter 541. *Hermann Hospital v. National Standard Ins. Co.*, 776 S.W.2d 249 (Tex. App.—Houston [1st Dist.] 1989, writ denied).

Chapter 541 defines "person" to include any individual, corporation or other entity "engaged in the business of insurance." TEX. INS. CODE §541.002(2). Although the defendant in such cases will often be an insurance company, the term "person" is clearly broad enough to include an employee of an insurance company whose duties require him to engage in the business of insurance. *Liberty Mut. Ins. v. Garrison Contractors*, 966 S.W.2d 482, 485 (Tex. 1998) (insurance company employee is a "person" subject to suit under Chapter 541). Insurance business is broadly defined and includes taking or forwarding applications for insurance, collecting premiums, disseminating information as to coverage or rates, inspecting risks, and adjusting claims. TEX. INS. CODE §§101.002, 101.051.

Chapter 541, Subchapter B, prohibits a wide range of false advertising and unfair methods of competition in the sale of insurance. To illustrate the breadth of coverage, consider §541.052 which provides:

(a) It is an unfair method of competition or an unfair or deceptive act or practice in the business of insurance to make, publish, disseminate, circulate, or place before the public, or directly or indirectly cause to be made, published, disseminated, circulated, or placed before the public, an advertisement, announcement or statement containing an untrue, deceptive, or misleading assertion, representation, or statement regarding the business of insurance or person in the conduct of the person's insurance business.

(b) This section applies to an advertisement, announcement, or statement made, published, disseminated, circulated, or placed before the public:
   (1) in a newspaper, magazine or other publication;
   (2) in a notice, circular, pamphlet, letter or poster;
   (3) over a radio or television station; or
   (4) in any other manner.

TEX. INS. CODE §541.052 (formerly Art. 21.21 §4). Subchapter B prohibits other acts or practices such as defamatory conduct, boycotts or coercion, making false financial statements or keeping false records, engaging in unfair discrimination, and unlawfully paying rebates on the sale of certain insurance policies. *See* TEX. INS. CODE §§541.053 to 541.059.

§11.03.1 Misrepresentation of Insurance Policy

Section 541.061 (formerly Art. 21.21 §4(11)) broadly prohibits any misrepresentation of an insurance policy by:

(1) making an untrue statement of material fact;

(2) failing to state a material fact necessary to make other statements made not mis-

leading, considering the circumstances under which the statements were made;

(3) making a statement in a manner that would mislead a reasonably prudent person to a false conclusion of a material fact;

(4) making a material misstatement of law; or

(5) failing to disclose a matter required by law to be disclosed, including failing to make a disclosure in accordance with another provision of this code.

TEX. INS. CODE §541.061.

Violations of §541.061 by misrepresenting the terms of an insurance policy have been found where the policy's coverage or policy limits are misrepresented either at the point of sale or at the point a claim is made. *See, e.g., Crown Life Ins. Co. v. Casteel*, 22 S.W.3d 378, 392 (Tex. 2000) (number of life insurance premiums due misrepresented at time of application); *Celtic Life Ins. Co. v. Coats*, 885 S.W.2d 96 (Tex. 1994) (misrepresented limits on in-patient mental health coverage at time of sale); *Royal Globe Ins. Co. v. Bar Consultants, Inc.*, 577 S.W.2d 688, 694 (Tex. 1979) (misrepresented coverage for vandalism before repairs were made); *Colonial County Mut. Ins. Co. v. Valdez*, 30 S.W.3d 514, 527 (Tex. App. —Corpus Christi 2000, pet. denied.) (misrepresentation that vehicle was covered after transfer to family member); *see also Kennedy v. Sale*, 689 S.W.2d 890 (Tex. 1985) (DTPA claim for misrepresented policy benefits).

The misrepresentation of coverage must still be a producing cause of damages in order to support a cause of action under either Chapter 541 or the DTPA. The claim that an agent misrepresented the coverage of a policy as "full coverage" still requires proof that a "full coverage" policy was available which would have covered the claimed occurrence. *Metro Allied Ins. Agency, Inc. v. Lin*, 304 S.W.3d 830, 836 (Tex. 2009).

In *Tex. Mut. Ins. Co. v. Ruttiger*, 381 S.W.3d 430, 446 (Tex. 2012), the court confirmed that the private cause of action under Chapter 541 is still available to an injured employee against a workers' compensation carrier for violations of §541.061, but held that the evidence adduced at trial was insufficient to support a finding of misrepresentation of coverage in that case.

§11.03.2 Unfair Settlement Practices as Grounds for Action

Section 541.151 provides a private cause of action for the "unfair settlement practices with respect to a claim by an insured or beneficiary" as defined in §541.060. This includes: (1) misrepresenting a material fact or policy provision relating to coverage, (2) failing to attempt in good faith to settle a claim with respect to which liability has become reasonably clear, (3) failing within a reasonable time to affirm or deny coverage, and (4) refusing to pay a claim without conducting a reasonable investigation with respect to the claim. TEX. INS. CODE §541.060.

One of the most widely invoked provisions of Chapter 541 is Section 541.060(2)(A) (formerly Art. 21.21 §4(10)(a)(ii)), which requires an insurer to fairly settle a claim after liability has become reasonably clear. This provision has been applied primarily in cases involving allegations that an insured's claim against his insurance company was not promptly or fully paid. *See, e.g., Vail v. Texas Farm Bureau Mut. Ins. Co.*, 754 S.W.2d 129 (Tex. 1988) (suit by insured under homeowner's insurance policy). The Texas Supreme Court has confirmed that this provision provides an additional cause of action to an insured against his liability insurance company for failing to settle a third-party liability claim. *Rocor Int'l, Inc. v. National Union Fire Ins.*, 77 S.W.3d 253 (Tex. 2002). To establish liability in these cases, the insured must prove: (1) the policy covers the claim, (2) the insured's liability is reasonably clear, (3) the third party claimant has made a proper settlement demand within policy limits, and (4) the demand's terms are such that an ordinarily prudent insurer would accept it. *Id.*

The prohibitions against unfair settlement practices imposed by §541.060 are for first-party claims—claims against one's own insurance company—only. One of the most common insurance claims for Texas consumers is a third-party claim for property or personal injury damages resulting from an automobile collision. Injured parties often negotiate directly with the other driver's insurance company in order to settle their claim. In *Allstate Ins. Co. v. Watson*, 876 S.W.2d 145 (Tex. 1994), the Texas Supreme Court held that a third party injured in a car wreck did not have standing to sue the other driver's insurance company for prohibited unfair claims settlement practices under former Article 21.21, the predecessor of Chapter 541. As recodified in 2003, Chapter 541 now expressly excludes from coverage the handling of third party liability claims. TEX. INS. CODE §541.060(b).

What about first-party uninsured/underinsured motorist ("UM/UIM") insurance claims against one's own automobile insurance carrier? In *Brainard v. Trinity Universal Ins. Co.*, 216 S.W.3d 809 (Tex. 2006), the court held that the insurer's obligation to pay a UM/UIM claim did not accrue on UIM benefits in an auto policy until after the uninsured/underinsured driver's liability has been determined by judgment. As long as the insurer promptly pays any benefits owing after a proper judgment is rendered, no extra-contractual claim for damages, attorney's fees or statutory delay penalties will accrue under Chapter 541.

In 2012, the Texas Supreme Court concluded that the general duties imposed by §541.060 conflicted with the more specific duties imposed on a worker's compensation insurance carrier and held that the private cause of action under Chapter 541 is not available to an injured employee against a workers' compensation carrier for violations of §541.060. *Tex. Mut. Ins. Co. v. Ruttiger*, 381 S.W.3d 430, 451 (Tex. 2012).

§11.03.3 Damages and Attorney's Fees Under Chapter 541

In contrast to the DTPA's provision for the recovery of "economic damages," Chapter 541 provides for the recovery of "actual damages." TEX. INS. CODE §541.152. A plaintiff who prevails on a Chapter 541 claim may recover "the greatest amount of actual damages alleged and factually established to have been caused by the unfair or deceptive practice." *Harris v. Am. Prot. Ins. Co.*, 158 S.W.3d 614 (Tex. App.—Fort Worth 2005, no pet.) Case law giving expansive meaning to the recovery of "actual damages" under the pre-1995 version of the DTPA should apply to §541.152. *See* §1.02.14, *supra*.

When the limits of first-party insurance coverage are misrepresented, one measure of damages should be the difference between the benefits which would have been payable under the policy as represented and those payable under the policy as actually delivered. *See, e.g. Celtic Life Ins. Co. v. Coats*, 885 S.W.2d 96 (Tex. 1994); *Royal Globe Ins. Co. v. Bar Consultants, Inc.*, 577 S.W.2d 688, 694 (Tex.

1979); *Colonial County Mut. Ins. Co. v. Valdez*, 30 S.W.3d 514, 527 (Tex. App. —Corpus Christi 2000, pet. denied.); *see also Kennedy v. Sale*, 689 S.W.2d 890 (Tex. 1985) (DTPA claim for misrepresented policy benefits). If there is a question as to the availability of a policy with coverages or limits as represented, the plaintiff must prove that an insurance policy with such coverage was available in the marketplace. *Metro Allied Ins. Agency, Inc. v. Lin*, 304 S.W.3d 830 (Tex. 2009).

When an insurer wrongfully fails or refuses to pay an insured's claim, the measure of damages is the policy benefits improperly withheld as a matter of law. *Vail v. Texas Farm Bureau Mut. Ins. Co.*, 754 S.W.2d 129 (Tex. 1988); *Twin City Fire Ins. Co. v. Davis*, 904 S.W.2d 663, 666 (Tex. 1995).

Loss of credit reputation may result from the mishandling or refusal to pay an insurance claim; however, to be compensable, the insured must show that a necessary loan was either denied or a higher interest rate was charged. *St. Paul Surplus Lines Ins. Co. v. Dal-Worth Tank Co.*, 974 S.W.2d 51 (Tex. 1998).

It might have been assumed that "actual damages" under Chapter 541 includes mental anguish. In *State Farm Life Ins. Co. v. Beaston*, 907 S.W.2d 430 (Tex. 1995), the court held that in cases which do not involve a physical injury, mental anguish damages may be recovered under Chapter 541 only if a "knowing" violation is shown.

Like the DTPA, proof that a violation of Chapter 541 was committed knowingly allows the fact finder to award discretionary additional damages of up to three times the amount of actual damages. TEX. INS. CODE §541.152. One significant difference between the DTPA and Chapter 541 is that under §541.152, mental anguish damages may be trebled without a finding of intentional conduct.

In addition to damages, a prevailing plaintiff under Chapter 541 is entitled to recover reasonable and necessary attorney's fees. TEX. INS. CODE §541.152.

In *Arthur Andersen & Co. v. Perry Equip. Corp.*, 945 S.W.2d 812 (Tex. 1997), the court held that recovery of contingent attorney's fees in DTPA cases is not authorized by the statute. Presumably, the same rule applies in cases in which attorney's fees are sought under §541.152. The opinion does not prohibit a contingent fee agreement between a consumer and the consumer's attorney; instead, it simply means that if attorney's fees are awarded under the statute, it must be based on an hourly fee. See §1.02.15, *supra*.

§11.04 Duty of Good Faith and Fair Dealing

The Texas Supreme Court has recognized a common law cause of action for breach of the duty of good faith and fair dealing owed by the insurer to the insured in insurance claims. *Arnold v. National County Mut. Fire Ins. Co.*, 725 S.W.2d 165 (Tex. 1987); *Union Bankers Ins. Co. v. Shelton*, 889 S.W.2d 278 (Tex. 1994). The duty of good faith and fair dealing arises because of the disparity of bargaining power inherent in the insurer-insured relationship. *Stewart Title Guar. Co. v. Aiello*, 941 S.W.2d 68, 71 (Tex. 1997).

In *Universe Life Ins. Co. v. Giles*, 950 S.W.2d 48 (Tex. 1997), the Texas Supreme Court adopted the "reasonably clear" standard of §541.060 (2)(A) (formerly Art. 21.21 §4(10)(ii)) as the standard for discharging the duty of good faith and fair dealing. An insurer breaches the duty of good faith and fair dealing it owes to the insured in handling a claim when it fails to "attempt in good faith to effectuate a prompt, fair, and equitable settlement of a claim with respect to which the insurer's liability has become reasonably clear." *Id.* at 55; *State Farm Lloyds v. Nicolau*, 951 S.W.2d 444 (Tex. 1997); *State Farm Fire & Cas. v. Simmons*, 963 S.W.2d 42 (Tex. 1998). As a result, this same conduct is now actionable both as a common law tort and through the private causes of action under Chapter 541 and the DTPA.

In some cases, especially in life or disability insurance claims, the insurance company will deny a claim and cancel a policy based upon the claim that the insured falsified information on the application, such as smoking status or pre-existing conditions. In *Union Bankers Ins. Co. v. Shelton*, 889 S.W.2d 278 (Tex. 1994), the Court held that an insurer breaches the duty of good faith and fair dealing when it "wrongfully cancels an insurance policy without a reasonable basis" and the insurer "knew or should have known of that fact." *Id.* at 283. This articulation of the duty of good faith and fair dealing in that situation has no counterpart in §541.060, but remains actionable under the common law tort. *See, e.g., Rice v. Metro. Life Ins. Co.*, 324 S.W.3d 660, 672 (Tex. App. — Fort Worth 2010, no pet.).

In 1989, the Texas Legislature overhauled the Texas Worker's Compensation Act and imposed a series of affirmative duties and specific deadlines upon insurers for handling worker's compensation claims. *See* Tex. Labor Code §§401.001-506.002. In 2012, the Supreme Court held that, in light of these specific and potentially conflicting statutory duties and deadlines, there was no longer a need for a common-law duty of good faith and fair dealing to be imposed upon a workers' compensation carrier. *Tex. Mut. Ins. Co. v. Ruttiger*, 381 S.W.3d 430, 451 (Tex. 2012). The Court overruled *Aranda v. Insurance Co. of N. Am.*, 748 S.W.2d 210 (Tex. 1988), to that extent. *Id.*

When an action for violation of Chapter 541 or for breach of the common law duty of good faith and fair dealing is based on the insurance company's failure to pay a claim, the absence of coverage under the insurance policy is a complete defense to these types of extra-contractual claims. *Progressive County Mutual Ins. Co. v. Boyd*, 177 S.W.3d 919 (Tex. 2005).

Once a consumer obtains a judgment against an insurer who owed the duty of good faith and fair dealing, the relationship changes to that of a judgment creditor/judgment debtor and the duty dissolves. *Mid-Century Insurance Co. v. Boyte*, 80 S.W.3d 546 (Tex. 2002) (no duty of good faith settle a claim after judgment).

§11.05 Interpretation of Insurance Contracts

Insurance coverage claims and bad faith claims are independent claims; however, in most circumstances, an insured cannot prevail on a bad faith claim without first showing that the insurer breached the insurance contract. *Liberty National Fire Insurance Co. v. Akin*, 927 S.W.2d 627, 629 (Tex. 1996). For this reason, an understanding of how insurance contracts are interpreted to determine coverage is important.

The interpretation of an insurance policy is a question of law for the court. *New York Life Insurance Co. v. Travelers Insurance Co.*, 92 F.3d 336, 338 (5th Cir. 1996). The primary goal of the Court is to give effect to the written expression of the parties' intent. In order to ascertain this intent, all parts of the contract are read together, striving to give meaning to every sentence, clause and word to avoid rendering any portion inoperative. *Balandran v. Safeco Ins. Co. of Am.*, 972 S.W.2d 738, 741 (Tex. 1998).

Few consumers actually read every word of an insurance contract at the time it is first purchased; instead, if it is read at all, it is only after a possible claim arises. The courts get around this reality when searching for the "intention" of the parties by the use of a presumption that an insured is deemed to have read and know the contents of his or her insurance policy. *See e.g. Amarco Petroleum, Inc. v. Texas Pacific Indemnity Co.,* 889 S.W.2d 695 (Tex. App.—Houston [14th Dist.] 1994, writ denied). The presumption is especially interesting in light of the fact that the content of most insurance policies purchased by consumers in Texas is determined by the Texas Department of Insurance, rather than discussions between the company and the insured. *See e.g.* TEX. INS. CODE art. 5.06(1), providing that the Texas Department of Insurance, "shall adopt a policy form and endorsements for each type of motor vehicle insurance subject to this subchapter." For this reason, it has long been recognized that interpreting the terms of an insurance policy prescribed by the Department means, as a practical matter, determining the Department's and insurer's intention rather than that of the consumer. *Progressive County Mut. Ins. Co. v. Sink*, 107 S.W.3d 547, 551-52 (Tex. 2003), *quoting United States Ins. Co. of Waco v. Boyer,* 269 S.W.2d 340 (Tex. 1954).

As a general rule, insurance contracts are subject to the same rules of construction as are other contracts. *Balandran v. Safeco Ins. Co.,* 972 S.W.2d 738 (Tex. 1998). This means that if the policy language is clear and unambiguous, then it will be interpreted and applied as written. If, however, because consumers have virtually no input into the actual language of the policy, when it is susceptible to more than one reasonable interpretation, courts will adopt that construction which is most favorable to the consumer. *State Farm Fire & Cas. Co. v. Reed,* 873 S.W.2d 698 (Tex. 1993). It must be understood, however, that the rules of construction which favor the consumer do not come into play unless and until the provision of the policy in questions is determined to be ambiguous. And, the question of whether a policy provision is or is not ambiguous is for the court to decide. *State Farm Fire and Casualty Co. v. Vaughan,* 968 S.W.2d 931 (Tex. 1998).

Ambiguity in an insurance contract can be either patent or latent. A patent ambiguity is one that appears on the face of the policy, whereas a latent ambiguity is one that does not become apparent until the policy is applied to a particular situation. *National Union Fire Insurance v. CBI Industries,* 907 S.W.2d 517 (Tex. 1995). In either case, ambiguity does not exist merely because the parties advance conflicting interpretations of the policy language. *Kelley-Coppedge, Inc. v. Highlands Ins. Co.,* 980 S.W.2d 462 (Tex. 1998); instead, if the court can give a definite legal meaning to the provision in question, it is unambiguous as a matter of law. *Vaughan,* 968 S.W.2d at 933.

There are several rules that assist the court in determining whether an ambiguity exists. First, a policy provision is ambiguous if it is susceptible to more than one *reasonable* interpretation, each of which is fair and reasonable. *Quality Oil Field Products, Inc. v. Michigan Mutual Ins. Co.,* 971 S.W.2d 635 (Tex. App.—Houston [14th Dist.] 1998, no writ). Some of the best evidence of conflicting, reasonable and fair interpretations can be found when cases from varying jurisdictions give different meanings to the same policy language. *State Farm Fire & Cas. Co. v. Reed,* 873 S.W.2d 698 (Tex. 1993). Ambiguity also may exist when the interpretation advanced by the insured would require the court to render one or more policy provisions inoperable. *Baladran v. Safeco Insurance Co. of America,* 972 S.W.2d 738 (Tex. 1998). Once an ambiguity in policy language is found, the court must resort to other rules of insurance policy construction in order to determine which interpretation applies. *Barnett v. Aetna Life Insurance Co.*, 723 S.W.2d 663 (Tex. 1987).

If policy language is susceptible of more than one reasonable interpretation, then the court, "must resolve the uncertainty by adopting the construction that most favors the insured." *National Union Fire Ins. Co. v. Hudson Energy Co.*, 811 S.W.2d 552 (Tex. 1991) (the court must adopt the [construction urged by the insured] as long as the construction is not unreasonable). *See also, Balandran, supra.* Further, when an ambiguity involves an exclusionary provision of an insurance policy, the court, "must adopt the construction urged by the insured as long as that construction is not *unreasonable*, even if the construction urged by the insurer appears to be more reasonable or a more accurate reflection of the parties intent." *Balandran; National Union Fire v. Hudson Energy.*

§11.06 Defenses Under Chapter 541

As a companion statute, the statutory defenses in Chapter 541 are similar to the statutory defenses found in the DTPA. Likewise, common law defenses general applicable to contract or tort liability will not apply to purely statutory claims under Chapter 541. *See* §2.02.1, *supra.*

Not every statutory defense included in the DTPA has been duplicated in Chapter 541. For instance, there is no set of statutory exemptions, such as those for professional services or media defendants, like DTPA §17.49. *See* §§2.02.2, 2.02.8, *supra.* Likewise, there is no defense in Chapter 541 which could be invoked by giving notice to the consumer that the information at issue was received or obtained from third party or from governmental sources as in DTPA §17.506.

§11.06.1 Settlement Offer Defense

Like the DTPA, Chapter 541 provides a settlement offer defense to damages and attorney's fees. If the defendant timely offers the consumer an amount of money which is the same, substantially the same, or more than the actual damages found by the trier of fact, then the consumer may not recover an amount of damages that exceeds the lesser of (1) the amount tendered in the settlement offer, or (2) the amount of actual damages found by the trier of fact. TEX. INS. CODE §541.159.

Also like the DTPA, the windows of opportunity to make such a settlement offer are limited. The first window of opportunity is open for the 60 days after receiving a pre-suit notice. TEX. INS. CODE §541.156(a); *see* §11.03, *infra.* The time frame for the second window of opportunity depends on whether mediation is conducted pursuant to §541.161. If no mediation is conducted pursuant to §541.161, the opportunity to make a qualified settlement offer begins on the day the defendant answers the suit and ends 90 days afterwards. TEX. INS. CODE §541.156(b)(1). If mediation is conducted pursuant to §541.161, another opportunity to make a qualifying settlement offer extends from the day the mediation ends for 20 more days. TEX. INS. CODE §541.156(b)(2).

If the plaintiff files suit without giving notice, the defendant is entitled to have the suit abated until notice is provided in order to take advantage of the opportunity to make a qualifying settlement offer. TEX. INS. CODE §541.155; *see* §6.01 *supra.*

§11.06.2 Limitations

There is a two-year statute of limitations applicable to claims made under Chapter 541. TEX. INS. CODE §541.162. The limitations period begins when the unfair method of competition or unfair or deceptive act or practice occurred, or when the person bringing the action "discovered, or by the exercise of reasonable diligence, should have discovered that the unfair method of competition or unfair or deceptive act or practice occurred." TEX. INS. CODE §541.162(a). As with the DTPA, the two-year limitation period may be extended by 180 days if the plaintiff proves that his or her failure to timely commence the action "was caused by the defendant's engaging in conduct solely calculated to induce the plaintiff to refrain from or postpone commencement of the action." TEX. INS. CODE §541.162(b).

In cases in which coverage is denied or insurance is not renewed because of an allegedly unfair or deceptive practice, the limitations period typically begins to run from the date that the consumer is notified of the denial or refusal to renew. *Herrin v. Medical Protective Co.*, 89 S.W.3d 301, 310 (Tex. App.—Texarkana 2002, writ denied).

§11.06.3 ERISA Preemption

The Employee Retirement Income Security Act, 29 U.S.C. §§1001-1461 (1974) preempts state law claims made under either the DTPA or Chapter 541 of the Insurance Code against an insurer of an employer-provided or sponsored employee benefit plan. 29 U.S.C. §1144(a). ERISA preemption is an affirmative defense. *Metro. Life Ins. Co. v. Taylor*, 481 U.S. 58, 63, 107 S. Ct. 1542, 95 L. Ed. 2d 55 (1987). ERISA preemption also provides federal subject matter jurisdiction. Defendant claiming ERISA preemption may remove a case filed in state court to federal court under federal question subject matter jurisdiction. *Id.* As such, most of the case law concerning ERISA preemption of the DTPA and Chapter 541 has been decided by the federal courts.

The Fifth Circuit has repeatedly held that the DTPA and Chapter 541 claims by ERISA plan participants against the insurers of plan benefits are preempted by ERISA. *See, e.g., Ramirez v. Inter-Cont'l Hotels*, 890 F.2d 760, 763-64 (5th Cir. 1989) (stating "[w]e thus join three of our sister circuits and numerous district courts in holding that ERISA preempts state statutes that provide a private right of action for the improper handling of insurance claims," and dismissing DTPA and Insurance Code claims); *Hogan v. Kraft Foods*, 969 F.2d 142 (5th Cir. 1992); *Ellis v. Liberty Life Assur. Co.*, 394 F.3d 262 (5th Cir. 2004), *Ben. Recovery, Inc. v. Donelon*, 521 F.3d 326 (5th Cir. 2008).

At times, the Fifth Circuit has recognized exceptions to ERISA preemption as to the Chapter 541 and DTPA claims of hospitals, doctors and other medical care providers to whom misrepresentations about coverage have been made by plan insurers. *See, e.g. Transitional Hosps. Corp. v. Blue Cross & Blue Shield, Inc.*., 164 F.3d 952 (5th Cir. 1999), *and Memorial Hosp. Sys. v. Northbrook Life Ins. Co.*, 904 F.2d 236 (5th Cir. 1990) . At other times, the Fifth Circuit has found ERISA preemption. *See, e.g. Cypress Fairbanks Med. Ctr., Inc. v. Pan-American Life Ins. Co.*, 110 F.3d 280 (5th Cir. 1997); *Hermann Hosp. v. MEBA Med. & Benefits Plan*, 845 F.2d 1286 (5th Cir. 1988) ("Hermann I"), *and Hermann Hosp. v. MEBA Med. & Benefits Plan*, 959 F.2d 569 (5th Cir. 1992) ("Hermann II"). In *Access Mediquip, L.L.C. v. United Health Care Ins. Co.*, 698 F.3d 229 (5th Cir. 2012)(*en banc*), the Fifth Circuit, sitting en banc, reinstated the Chapter 541 claims of a medical device provider against the insurer of a group health plan who had represented that the devices would be paid out of policy benefits. In doing so, the full Fifth Circuit held that ERISA did not preempt the provider's Chapter 541, negligent misrepresentation and promissory estoppel claims and expressly overruled *Hermann I, Hermann*

II and *Cypress Fairbanks v. Pan-American* to the extent they were inconsistent with that holding. *Id.*

§11.06.3.1 Attorney's Fees and ERISA

Under ERISA, the court may in its discretion allow a reasonable attorney's fee and costs to either party. 29 U.S.C. §1132(g)(1). Since the award of attorney's fees is discretionary, any review of a district court's decision is based on whether the court abused its discretion. *Hardt v. Reliance Standard Life Ins. Co.*, ___ U.S. ___, 130 S. Ct. 2149, 2157-58, 176 L. Ed. 2d 998 (2010). The claim for attorney's fees under ERISA is not limited to a "prevailing party." 130 S. Ct. 2149, 2157-58. Rather, under §1132(g)(1), the court may award attorney's fees and costs if a party has achieved "some degree of success on the merits." *Id.* at 2158.

Once a court determines that a party is eligible for a fee award under §1132(g)(1), the court will consider whether fees are appropriate under the following factors:

1. The degree of the opposing parties' culpability or bad faith;

2. The ability of the opposing parties to satisfy an award of attorney's fees;

3. Whether an award of attorney's fees against the opposing party would deter other persons acting under similar circumstances;

4. Whether the parties requesting attorney's fees sought to benefit all participants and beneficiaries of any ERISA plan or to resolve a significant legal question regarding ERISA itself; and

5. The relative merits of the parties' position.

Hardt, 130 S.Ct. at 2158, fn. 8; *Wade v. Hewlett-Packard Dev. Co. LP Short Term Disability Plan*, 493 F.3d 533 (5th Cir. 2007) (referring to five factors as "*Bowen* factors").

If the court determines that a party is entitled to attorney's fees using the analysis set forth above, then the amount of the fee should be determined by using a lodestar calculation. *See generally, Hensley v. Eckerhart*, 461 U.S. 433, 103 S. Ct. 1933, 1939 (1983). This calculation is performed by multiplying the number of hours expended in a case by a reasonable hourly rate. *Wegner v. Standard Ins. Co.*, 129 F.3d 814, 822 (5th Cir. 1997); *Todd v. AIG Life Ins. Co.*, 47 F.3d 1448, 1459 (5th Cir. 1995).

§11.06.4 Counterclaim for Frivolous Action

Chapter 541 also provides that the defendant can recover its attorneys' fees and court costs on a finding by the court that the action was groundless or brought in bad faith or for the purpose of harassment. *See* DTPA §17.50(c); TEX. INS. CODE §541.153. In *Donwerth v. Preston II Chrysler-Dodge, Inc.*, 775 S.W.2d 634 (Tex. 1989), the Texas Supreme Court confirmed that the trial court, not the jury, determines the questions of groundlessness, harassment, and bad faith. To establish harassment, the defendant must prove that the action was brought solely for that purpose. "Groundlessness" under the DTPA has the same meaning as groundless under Texas Rule of Civil Procedure 13. *Id; see McCain v. NME Hosps., Inc.*, 856 S.W.2d 751 (Tex. App.—Dallas 1993, no writ).

§11.07 Providing Pre-Suit Notice Under Chapter 541

As with the DTPA, Chapter 541 of the Insurance Code requires 60 days' written notice to the prospective defendant before a suit for damages is filed under the statute. TEX. INS. CODE §541.154. The pre-filing notice requirement is essentially the same as that for the DTPA; however, under Chapter 541, there is no requirement that the notice letter state separately the claim for economic damages, mental anguish, and attorney's fees and expenses. *Id.*

Advance written notice is not required if the suit seeks a remedy other than damages. Thus, when only injunctive relief, a declaratory judgment or restitution is sought, advance notice need not be given. *Id.*

Advance written notice also is not required if the statute of limitations will run during the notice period or if the Insurance Code claim is asserted as a counterclaim. TEX. INS. CODE 541.154(c).

If a person files a suit for damages under Chapter 541 without giving notice, assuming that notice is required by §541.154, the defendant may file a plea in abatement to stop the proceedings until proper notice is given. TEX. INS. CODE §541.155. To be effective, the plea in abatement must be filed within 30 days after the date the original answer is filed. TEX. INS. CODE §541.155(a). *See* §6.01 *et seq., supra.*

The purpose of a notice letter under Chapter 541 is the same as the purpose under the DTPA: to encourage settlement of controversies without the need for litigation. In order to maximize the possibility of a pre-filing settlement of a claim, the letter should be a detailed, fair and factual statement of the wrongful conduct alleged and all of the damages suffered.

A person who receives a notice letter under Chapter 541 has 60 days within which to make a "tender" of an offer of settlement. TEX. INS. CODE §541.156. There is an additional provision which extends the period during which a "tender" of an offer of settlement may be made in the event mediation is not conducted pursuant to a motion to compel mediation which is filed within 90 days after service of citation. In this event, the recipient has 90 days within which to make a tender of an offer of settlement. TEX. INS. CODE §§541.156(b)(1). If mediation is conducted, the recipient has 20 days after the date mediation ends to make a tender of an offer of settlement. TEX. INS. CODE §541.156(b)(2).

The receipt of this pre-suit notice opens the door to the settlement offer defenses discussed above. *See* §11.02.1, *supra.*

[a] FORM: Notice letter: Insurance Code Chapter 541

CERTIFIED MAIL, RETURN RECEIPT REQUESTED

(Date)

(Inside address)

Re: (Client's name)

Dear _____:

[Notice of representation]

Our firm has [or I have] been retained to represent _____ with respect to a claim which he [she] has against you. Please direct all communications concerning this matter to me.

On _____, 20____, [insert description of loss, e.g., our client's home was destroyed by a fire]. The property was insured by your company under Texas Standard Homeowner's Policy no. _____. All payments on the policy were current, and the policy was in force on the date of the loss.

After the loss described above, our client submitted a claim to you. Although the claim was submitted in proper form and within the time specified in the insurance policy, you denied the claim. There was and is no justifiable basis for your denial.

[*Insert description of types of damages suffered, e.g.,* As a result of the fire, our client has lost virtually all of the personal property in the house, as well as the house itself. Additionally, as a result of the fire, our client was required to lease an apartment in which to live. Further, your wrongful denial of our client's claim has caused our client to suffer severe mental anguish since he [she] has had to live each day with the knowledge that short of legal action, there will be no compensation for the loss].

It is our contention that your conduct constitutes [insert statutory language, *e.g.*, unfair and deceptive acts or practices in the business of insurance in violation of Chapter 541 of the Texas Insurance Code, *such as:* Your failure to pay a claim which is properly presented and covered under the terms of an insurance policy is an unfair settlement practice prohibited by Chapter 541 and Chapter 542, Subchapter B, *Texas Insurance Code*].

[Statement of damages and expenses sought]

Based upon the information now available to us, and for purposes of this notice letter, we estimate that our client's damages are as follows:

Economic losses: $_____.

Mental anguish: $_____.

Expenses, including

attorney's fees: $_____.

Of course, we reserve the right to adjust these amounts to conform to the information and additional evidence that will be available to us at the time of trial, should litigation be necessary.

[Alternate statement of attorney's fees]

Our client has incurred reasonable and necessary attorney's fees in the pursuit of the claim stated in this letter. The amount of fees incurred as of the date of this letter is $_____ [or _____% of our client's total damages].

[Notice of contingent interest]

Under the contract of employment we have with our client, our firm has [or I have] been assigned an interest in the claim against you.

The purpose of this letter is to encourage you to resolve our client's claim in a fair and equitable manner without the need for further legal action. In the event you fail to respond to this letter with an offer of settlement that is acceptable to our client, we will have no alternative but to recommend to our client that a lawsuit be filed against you. The lawsuit will be filed under Chapter 541 of the Texas Insurance Code, among other authorities. In this lawsuit, rather than seeking only the amount of money we are asking of you at this time, we will seek to recover the full measure of our client's damages, expenses and attorney's fees as allowed by law. Additionally, as you may know, in this lawsuit, if the jury finds that you "knowingly" violated Chapter 541, our client may recover additional damages in an amount up to three times the amount of actual damages.

§11.08 Plaintiff's Pleadings—Insurance Actions

As stated above, the general rules of pleading applicable to DTPA actions are equally applicable to petitions under Insurance Code Chapter 541. *See* §5.01 *supra*. The following form petition incorporates (and substitutes) those allegations that are unique to most Chapter 541 cases.

[a] FORM: Petition (Insurance Code Chapter 541)

```
                          NO. _____

_____           §    IN THE DISTRICT COURT OF
                     §
vs.                  §    _____COUNTY, TEXAS
                     §
_____           §    _____ JUDICIAL DISTRICT
```

PLAINTIFF'S ORIGINAL PETITION

TO THE HONORABLE JUDGE OF THE DISTRICT COURT:

NOW COME _____ and _____, Plaintiffs herein, complaining of Insurance Company, Defendant herein, and for cause of action would show unto the Court as follows:

I. DISCOVERY CONTROL PLAN DESIGNATION

1.01 By this action, Plaintiff seeks _____ [*insert appropriate designation under Rule 47(c), e.g.,* only monetary relief of $100,000 or less, including damages of any kind, penalties, costs, expenses, prejudgment interest, and attorney's fees]. The damages sought are within the jurisdictional limits of this court.

1.02 Discovery in this case is intended to be conducted under Level _____ pursuant to Rule 190._____, *Texas Rules of Civil Procedure*.

II. PARTIES

2.01 _____ and _____ are residents of _____, _____ County, Texas.

2.02 _____ Insurance Company is an insurance company organized and existing under the laws of the state of Texas licensed and admitted to do business as a property and casualty insurer in the state of Texas and which may be served through _____, _____, _____ County, Texas, its registered agent for service of process in Texas.

III. VENUE

3.01 Venue of this action is proper in _____ County, Texas because the policy at issue was issued and delivered in _____ County, Texas, because the property insured is situated in _____ County, Texas, because Plaintiffs' losses occurred in _____ County, Texas, and because all or part of the events made the basis of this lawsuit and giving rise to Plaintiffs' claims and causes of action occurred in _____ County, Texas.

IV. CONDITIONS PRECEDENT

4.01 Defendant was given notice in writing of the claims made in this petition including a statement of Plaintiff's economic damages, mental anguish damages and expenses, including attorney's fees, more than 60 days before this suit was filed in the manner and form required by DTPA §17.505(a).

4.02 All conditions precedent to recovery have been performed, have occurred, or have been excused, including all notice required by any law upon which Plaintiffs base their claims.

V. AGENCY

5.01 Unless otherwise stated, whenever it is alleged herein that Defendant _____ committed an act, made a representation or statement, failed to perform an act, or failed to make a disclosure, it is alleged that _____ was acting or failing to act through its authorized agents, servants, employees, or representatives acting with either express, implied, apparent, direct and/or ostensible authority; or that _____ subsequently ratified these acts, failures to act, representations, statements or conduct.

VI. FACTS OF CASE

6.01 [*Describe factual basis for claims, e.g.,* Plaintiffs _____ own a home at [*insert property address*], _____ County, Texas.

6.02 On or about [date], Defendant _____ issued the Plaintiffs a Texas Family Home Policy ("the Policy") covering losses for the same house and personal property located at [address] County, Texas, with a policy period of [*insert policy period, e.g.,*: October 30, 2007 to October 30, 2008].

6.03 On or about _____, 20___, a date within the coverage period of the Policy, a catastrophic storm with tornado force winds blew through [*location*], causing one or more large tree(s) to topple onto the roof of the Plaintiffs' home. As a result, the roof of the Plaintiffs' home was severely damaged and was required to be replaced. Plaintiffs promptly gave notice to Defendant of this damage and made a claim for benefits and offered proof of their covered damages for $[*amount*] to Defendant.

6.04 The Policy clearly covers the cost to replace the roof on the Plaintiffs' house as a result of this storm damage.

6.05 Despite this coverage for the entire replacement cost of the roof under the Policy, Defendant refused to pay the claim [*if applicable*: wrongfully claiming, *e.g.,* that the Plaintiffs had a hail damage claim in March 2000 and had already been paid for the replacement of their roof at that time].

6.06 [*If applicable, continue with any false statements or misrepresentations about the Policy or the claims process, e.g.,* In denying Plaintiffs' claim, Defendant represented to the Plaintiffs:

(a) that their claim was not covered;

(b) that their Policy excludes coverage for property for which a previous claim on a previous policy has been paid; and

(c) that the Plaintiffs had a contractual obligation under either the current Policy and/or the prior policy to use the proceeds paid to repair their property exactly as specified in the estimate of Defendant's adjuster of their repair cost damages or they would lose the benefits payable under the Policy or future policies issued by Defendant.

6.07 In truth and in fact, these representations about the Policy and the prior policy were false. In truth and in fact, Plaintiffs' claim is covered under the Policy. In truth and in fact, the Policy does not exclude coverage for property for which a previous claim on a previous policy has been paid. In truth and in fact, neither the 2000 policy nor the current Policy imposes a contractual obligation or duty on the policyholder to make repairs to their property in the exact manner specified in the adjuster's estimate.]

6.08 In denying Plaintiffs' claim on bases not allowed under the Policy, Defendant has clearly elevated its own interest in profit over their policyholders' needs in the time of crisis. Defendant's actions as outlined above caused Plaintiffs damages for which they sue.

VII. FIRST CAUSE OF ACTION: BREACH OF CONTRACT

7.01 Plaintiffs repeat and re-allege the factual allegations in the preceding paragraphs.

7.02 The Policy is a contract binding Defendant to pay the benefits stated therein upon the occurrence of a covered event. The _____ 20___ storm was such a covered event, and the benefits claimed by Plaintiff are the benefits covered in and payable under the Policy.

7.03 Defendant breached the insurance contract at issue by denying and refusing to fully pay Plaintiffs' claim.

7.04 Defendant's breach has resulted in damages to Plaintiffs for which they sue.

VIII. SECOND CAUSE OF ACTION: UNFAIR INSURANCE PRACTICES

8.01 Plaintiffs repeat and re-allege the factual allegations in the preceding paragraphs.

8.02 By its conduct outlined above, Defendant committed unfair practices in the business of insurance prohibited by Chapter 541, *Texas Insurance Code,* and the statutes, rules and regulations incorporated therein.

8.03 Specifically, Defendant is guilty of the following unfair insurance practices which have been a producing cause of Plaintiffs' damages:

[*continue with specific actionable provisions of Chapter 541, such as:*]

(a) Defendant failed to, with good faith, effectuate a prompt, fair, and equitable settlement of the Plaintiffs' claim once the Defendant's liability became reasonably clear;

(b) Defendant failed to provide promptly to Plaintiff's a reasonable explanation of the basis in the policies, in relation to the facts or applicable law, for Defendant's denial of the claim or for the offer of a compromise settlement of the claim;

(c) Defendant refused to pay a claim without conducting a reasonable investigation with respect to that claim;

(d) Defendant breached its duty of good faith and fair dealing at common law;

(e) Defendant committed the following acts in violation of Texas Insurance Code §541.051: Defendant made, issued or circulated or caused to be made, issued or circulated an estimate, illustration, circular or statement misrepresenting with respect to the policy issued or to be issued:

    (1) the terms of the policy; and/or

    (2) the benefits or advantages promised by the policy.

(f) Defendant committed the following unfair methods of competition or deceptive acts or practices in the business of insurance in violation of Texas Insurance Code Section 541.061 by misrepresenting an insurance policy in one or more of the following manners:

    (1) Defendant made an untrue statement of material fact;

    (2) Defendant failed to state a material fact necessary to make other statements made not misleading considering the circumstances under which statements were made;

    (3) Defendant made a statement in a manner that would mislead a reasonably prudent person to a false conclusion of material fact; and/or

    (4) Defendant failed to disclose a matter required by law to be disclosed, including failing to make a disclosure in accordance with another provision of the Texas Insurance Code.

8.04 Defendant's conduct as described herein was a producing cause of damages to Plaintiffs for which they sue.

IX. THIRD CAUSE OF ACTION: DTPA

9.01 Plaintiffs repeat and re-allege the factual allegations in the preceding paragraphs.

9.02 Plaintiffs are consumers entitled to relief under the Texas Deceptive Trade Practices—Consumer Protection Act ("DTPA"). By its conduct outlined above, Defendant has engaged in the following violations of the DTPA which, together and separately, has been a producing cause of Plaintiffs' damages:

(a) Defendant made false representations about Plaintiffs' rights, remedies and obligations under the policies at issue. These statements were a misrepresentation of the insurance policies and their benefits in violation of §§17.46(b)(5), (7), (12) and (14), Texas Business & Commerce Code;

(b) Defendant failed to disclose information to Plaintiffs concerning the nature and extent of their insurance policies which was known by Defendant at the time for the purpose of inducing Plaintiff into transactions which they would not have otherwise entered in violation of §§17.46(b)(9) and (23), Texas Business & Commerce Code;

(c) Defendant's actions constitute an unconscionable course of conduct entitling Plaintiffs to relief under §17.50(a)(3), Texas Business & Commerce Code; and/or

(d) As described above, Defendant violated Chapter 541, *Texas Insurance Code*, entitling Plaintiffs to relief under §17.50(a)(4), Texas Business & Commerce Code.

9.03 Defendant's conduct as described herein was a producing cause of damages to Plaintiffs for which they sue.

X. FOURTH CAUSE OF ACTION: TEXAS INSURANCE CODE CHAPTER 542, SUBCHAPTER B DELAY IN PAYMENT

10.01 Plaintiffs repeat and re-allege the factual allegations in the preceding paragraphs.

10.02 Plaintiffs gave prompt notice of their claims to Defendant.

10.03 [*If applicable:*] Defendant failed to comply with the requirements of Chapter 542 by:

(a) Failing to acknowledge receipt of Plaintiffs' claim within 15 days of receiving notice of the claim;

(b) Failing to commence an investigation of the claim within 15 days after receiving notice of the claim; and/or

(c) Failing to request all of the items, statements and forms the Defendant reasonably believed at the time would be required from Plaintiffs to pay the claim within 15 days after receiving notice of the claim.

10.04 Plaintiffs provided all of the information requested by Defendant to Defendant as soon as Defendant requested it. Despite having all of the information requested, Defendant continued to delay and deny Plaintiffs' claim. Defendant has thus further failed to comply with Chapter 542 in one or more of the following manners:

[*Continue as applicable*:]

(a) Failing to notify Plaintiffs in writing, within 15 business days after receiving all of the items, statements, and forms required by the insurer to secure final proof of loss, of the acceptance or rejection of a claim; and/or

(b) Failing to pay Plaintiffs' claim within 60 days of receiving all of the items, statements, and forms required by the insurer to secure final proof of loss, of the acceptance or rejection of a claim.

10.05 Pursuant to *Texas Insurance Code* Chapter 542, Subchapter B, Plaintiffs are entitled to recover from Defendant the statutory penalty of 18% per annum on all amounts due on Plaintiff's claim, together with attorney's fees, for which they sue.

XI. FIFTH CAUSE OF ACTION: BREACH OF THE DUTY OF GOOD FAITH AND FAIR DEALING

11.01 Plaintiffs repeat and re-allege the factual allegations in the preceding paragraphs.

11.02 From and after the time the Plaintiffs' claims were presented to the Defendant, the Defendant's liability to pay the claims in accordance with the terms of insurance policies referenced above has been reasonably clear.

11.03 Despite there being no basis whatsoever on which a reasonable insurance company would have relied to deny payment for Plaintiffs' claims, the Defendant refused to accept the claims and pay the Plaintiffs as the policy required. At that time, the Defendant knew or should have known by the exercise of reasonable diligence that their liability was reasonably clear.

11.04 Defendant failed to conduct a reasonable and proper inspection of the claims and refused to rely on the true facts, resorting instead to producing faulty, incomplete and biased reasons to avoid paying a valid claim.

11.05 Through the actions described above, Defendant breached its duty to deal fairly and in good faith with the Plaintiffs.

11.06 Defendant's breach was a proximate cause of the losses, expenses and damages suffered by the Plaintiffs for which they sue.

XII. DAMAGES

12.01 Defendant's acts and omissions as particularly described above have been producing and/or proximate causes of damages to Plaintiffs.

12.02 Plaintiffs have suffered economic damages, including but not limited to unpaid policy benefits payable for the cost to repair the damages caused by storm in the amount of $_____.

12.03 Further, Plaintiffs have suffered actual damages, including mental anguish.

12.04 Plaintiffs' damages are in excess of the minimum jurisdiction limits of this court.

XIII. ADDITIONAL DAMAGES AND PENALTIES

13.01 Defendant's conduct in violation of *Texas Insurance Code* Chapter 541 and the DTPA was committed knowingly, as that term is defined by those statutes. Accordingly, Defendant is liable for additional damages under those statutes.

13.02 Defendant's refusal to pay the entire claim is a violation of one or more provisions of Chapter 542, Subchapter B, *Texas Insurance Code*, and as a result, Plaintiffs are entitled to recover statutory penalties of 18% per annum and attorney's fees.

XIV. ATTORNEY'S FEES

14.01 As a result of Defendant's conduct, Plaintiffs have been required to obtain the services of the undersigned attorneys for the filing, prosecution, and trial of this cause and therefore seek an award of reasonable and necessary attorney's fees pursuant to *Texas Insurance Code* Chapters 541 and 542, and DTPA §17.50.

14.02 Plaintiffs gave Defendant 30 days' notice of its claim. Accordingly, Plaintiffs are entitled to recovery of attorney's fees pursuant to Chapter 38, *Texas Civil Practice & Remedies Code*.

WHEREFORE, PREMISES CONSIDERED, Plaintiffs respectfully pray that Defendant be cited to appear and answer, and that upon final trial hereof, Plaintiffs recover from Defendant, all of their actual economic damages, statutory additional damages, attorney's fees, prejudgment and post-judgment interest as allowed by law, costs of court, and such other and further relief to which they may show themselves justly entitled.

> Respectfully submitted,
>
> [Signature of attorney]

[b] FORM: Petition asserting breach of ambiguous contract and Chapter 541 violations

Pleading is required to support a lawsuit on an insurance policy that is claimed to be ambiguous. The following petition for breach of contract is an example of such pleading.

```
                              NO. _____
_____              §   IN THE DISTRICT COURT OF
                        §
vs.                     §   _____ COUNTY, TEXAS
                        §
_____              §   _____ JUDICIAL DISTRICT
```

TO THE HONORABLE JUDGE OF THE DISTRICT COURT:

NOW COMES _____, Plaintiff herein, complaining of _____, Defendant herein, and for cause of action, would show unto the Court as follows:

I. DISCOVERY CONTROL PLAN DESIGNATION

1.01 By this action, Plaintiff seeks _____ [*insert appropriate designation under Rule 47(c), e.g., only monetary relief of $100,000 or less, including damages of any kind, penalties, costs, expenses, prejudgment interest, and attorney's fees*]. The damages sought are within the jurisdictional limits of this court.

1.02 Discovery in this case is intended to be conducted under Level _____, pursuant to Rule 190._____, *Texas Rules of Civil Procedure*.

II. PARTIES

2.01 _____ is a resident of _____, _____ County, Texas.

2.02 _____ Insurance Company is an insurance company organized and existing under the laws of the state of Texas licensed and admitted to do business as a property and casualty insurer in the state of Texas and which may be served through _____, _____, _____ County, Texas, its registered agent for service of process in Texas.

III. VENUE

3.01 Venue of this action is proper in _____ County, Texas because the policy at issue was issued and delivered in _____ County, Texas, because the property insured is situated in _____ County, Texas, because Plaintiffs' losses occurred in _____ County, Texas, and because all or part of the events made the basis of this lawsuit and giving rise to Plaintiffs' claims and causes of action occurred in _____ County, Texas.

IV. NOTICE; CONDITIONS PRECEDENT

4.01 Defendant was given notice in writing of the claims made in this petition including a statement of Plaintiff's economic damages, mental anguish damages and expenses, including attorney's fees, more than 60 days before this suit was filed in the manner and form required by DTPA §17.505(a).

4.02 All conditions precedent to recovery by Plaintiff herein have been performed, have occurred, or have been excused.

V. AGENCY

5.01 Unless otherwise stated, whenever it is alleged herein that Defendant _____ Committed an act, made a representation or statement, failed to perform an act, or failed to make a disclosure, it is alleged that _____ was acting or failing to act through its authorized agents, servants, employees, or representatives acting with either express, implied, apparent, direct and/or ostensible authority; or that _____ subsequently ratified these acts, failures to act, representations, statements or conduct.

VI. FACTS OF CASE

6.01 [*Describe factual basis for claims, e.g.*] Plaintiffs _____ own a home at [*insert property address*], _____ County, Texas.

6.02 On or about [*date*], Defendant _____ issued the Plaintiffs a Texas Family Home Policy ("the Policy") covering losses for the same house and personal property located at [*address*] County, Texas, with a policy period of [*insert policy period, e.g.,* October 30, 2007 to October 30, 2008].

6.03 The Policy insured Plaintiff against "direct physical loss or damage to the property...from any external cause[.]" The Policy also covered damages caused by "faulty or defective workmanship, material, construction or design."

6.04 On or about [*date*], a date within the coverage period of the Policy, Plaintiff that his insured home had suffered damages to its foundation and other parts, which damage was caused by an insured peril.

6.05 On _____, Defendant wrongfully denied the claim made by Plaintiff for the damages caused by insured perils.

6.06 Among other things, Defendant falsely represented material facts to Plaintiff, *i.e.*, that the damage caused to the foundation was not due to plumbing leaks in the sanitary sewer system; and that the differential movement in the foundations was due to seasonal changes in the moisture content in and consolidation of the soils. In fact, the damages were caused by insured perils.

6.07 Defendant claims that the phrase "external cause" in the exclusions section of the insurance policy means damage to the insured property from something that is not part of the property itself. Although Plaintiff believes that this is a strained interpretation of the policy language to the extent that it is advanced by Defendant as an interpretation of the meaning of the phrase "external cause," the phrase in the insurance policy is ambiguous. The phrase does not mean only losses from causes outside the physical boundaries of the insured property. Instead, the phrase includes fortuitous events, *i.e.* breakdowns, failures and conditions originating from within the insured property, and specifically includes losses caused by leaking sewer and water pipes, and the alleged interaction of tree roots and moisture on the foundation in question.

VII. FIRST CAUSE OF ACTION: BREACH OF CONTRACT

7.01 Plaintiff repeats and re-alleges the factual allegations in the preceding paragraphs.

7.02 The Policy is a contract binding Defendant to pay the benefits stated therein upon the occurrence of a covered event. The damage to Plaintiff's house was the result of a covered peril, and the benefits claimed by Plaintiff are the benefits covered in and payable under the Policy.

7.03 Defendant breached the insurance contract at issue by denying and refusing to fully pay Plaintiff's claim.

7.04 Defendant's breach has resulted in damages to Plaintiff for which he sues.

VIII. SECOND CAUSE OF ACTION: UNFAIR INSURANCE PRACTICES

8.01 Plaintiffs repeat and re-allege the factual allegations in the preceding paragraphs.

8.02 By its conduct outlined above, Defendant committed unfair practices in the business of insurance prohibited by Chapter 541, *Texas Insurance Code,* and the statutes, rules and regulations incorporated therein.

8.03 Specifically, Defendant is guilty of the following unfair insurance practices which have been a producing cause of Plaintiffs' damages:

[*Continue with specific actionable provisions of Chapter 541, such as:*]

(a) Defendant failed to, with good faith, effectuate a prompt, fair, and equitable settlement of the Plaintiffs' claim once the Defendant's liability became reasonably clear;

(b) Defendant failed to provide promptly to Plaintiffs a reasonable explanation of the basis in the policies, in relation to the facts or applicable law, for Defendant's denial of the claim or for the offer of a compromise settlement of the claim;

(c) Defendant refused to pay a claim without conducting a reasonable investigation with respect to that claim;

(d) Defendant breached its duty of good faith and fair dealing at common law;

(e) Defendant committed the following acts in violation of Texas Insurance Code §541.051: Defendant made, issued or circulated or caused to be made, issued or circulated an estimate, illustration, circular or statement misrepresenting with respect to the policy issued or to be issued:

    (1) the terms of the policy; and/or

    (2) the benefits or advantages promised by the policy.

(f) Defendant committed the following unfair methods of competition or deceptive acts or practices in the business of insurance in violation of Texas Insurance Code Section 541.061 by misrepresenting an insurance policy in one or more of the following manners:

    (1) Defendant made an untrue statement of material fact; and/or

    (2) Defendant made a statement in a manner that would mislead a reasonably prudent person to a false conclusion of material fact.

8.04 Defendant's conduct as described herein was a producing cause of damages to Plaintiffs for which they sue.

IX. THIRD CAUSE OF ACTION: DTPA

9.01 Plaintiffs repeat and re-allege the factual allegations in the preceding paragraphs.

9.02 Plaintiffs are consumers entitled to relief under the Texas Deceptive Trade Practices—Consumer Protection Act ("DTPA"). By its conduct outlined above, Defendant has engaged in the following violations of the DTPA which, together and separately, has been a producing cause of Plaintiffs' damages:

(a) Defendant made false representations about Plaintiffs' rights, remedies and obligations under the policies at issue. These statements were a misrepresentation of the insurance policies and their benefits in violation of §§17.46(b)(5), (7), (12) and (14), Texas Business & Commerce Code;

(b) Defendant's actions constitute an unconscionable course of conduct entitling Plaintiffs to relief under §17.50(a)(3), Texas Business & Commerce Code; and/or

(c) As described above, Defendant violated Chapter 541, *Texas Insurance Code*, entitling Plaintiffs to relief under §17.50(a)(4), Texas Business & Commerce Code.

9.03 Defendant's conduct as described herein was a producing cause of damages to Plaintiff for which he sues.

X. FOURTH CAUSE OF ACTION: TEXAS INSURANCE CODE CHAPTER 542, SUBCHAPTER B DELAY IN PAYMENT

10.01 Plaintiff repeats and re-alleges the factual allegations in the preceding paragraphs.

10.02 Plaintiff gave prompt notice of their claims to Defendant.

10.03 [*If applicable*:] Defendant failed to comply with the requirements of Chapter 542 by:

(a) Failing to acknowledge receipt of Plaintiff's claim within 15 days of receiving notice of the claim;

(b) Failing to commence an investigation of the claim within 15 days after receiving notice of the claim; and/or

(c) Failing to request all of the items, statements and forms the Defendant reasonably believed at the time would be required from Plaintiffs to pay the claim within 15 days after receiving notice of the claim.

10.04 Plaintiff provided all of the information requested by Defendant to Defendant as soon as Defendant requested it. Despite having all of the information requested, Defendant continued to delay and deny Plaintiff's claim. Defendant has thus further failed to comply with Chapter 542 in one or more of the following manners:

[*Continue as applicable*:]

(a) Failing to notify Plaintiff in writing, within 15 business days after receiving all of the items, statements, and forms required by the insurer to secure final proof of loss, of the acceptance or rejection of a claim; and/or

(b) Failing to pay Plaintiff's claim within 60 days of receiving all of the items, statements, and forms required by the insurer to secure final proof of loss, of the acceptance or rejection of a claim.

10.05 Pursuant to *Texas Insurance Code* Chapter 542, Subchapter B, Plaintiffs are entitled to recover from Defendant the statutory penalty of 18% per annum on all amounts due on Plaintiff's claim, together with attorney's fees, for which they sue.

XI. FIFTH CAUSE OF ACTION: BREACH OF THE DUTY OF GOOD FAITH AND FAIR DEALING

11.01 Plaintiff repeats and re-alleges the factual allegations in the preceding paragraphs.

11.02 From and after the time the Plaintiff's claims were presented to the Defendant, the Defendant's liability to pay the claims in accordance with the terms of insurance policies referenced above has been reasonably clear.

11.03 Despite there being no basis whatsoever on which a reasonable insurance company would have relied to deny payment for Plaintiffs' claims, the Defendant refused to accept the claims and pay the Plaintiffs as the policy required. At that time, the Defendant knew or should have known by the exercise of reasonable diligence that their liability was reasonably clear.

11.04 Defendant failed to conduct a reasonable and proper inspection of the claims and refused to rely on the true facts, resorting instead to producing faulty, incomplete and biased reasons to avoid paying a valid claim.

11.05 Through the actions described above, Defendant breached its duty to deal fairly and in good faith with the Plaintiffs.

11.06 Defendant's breach was a proximate cause of the losses, expenses and damages suffered by the Plaintiffs for which they sue.

XII. DAMAGES

12.01 Defendant's acts and omissions as particularly described above have been producing and/or proximate causes of damages to Plaintiff.

12.02 Plaintiff has suffered economic damages, including but not limited to unpaid policy benefits payable for the cost to repair the damages caused by storm in the amount of $_____.

12.03 Further, Plaintiff has suffered actual damages, including mental anguish.

12.04 Plaintiff's damages are in excess of the minimum jurisdiction limits of this court.

XIII. ADDITIONAL DAMAGES AND PENALTIES

13.01 Defendant's conduct in violation of *Texas Insurance Code* Chapter 541 and the DTPA was committed knowingly, as that term is defined by those statutes. Accordingly, Defendant is liable for additional damages under those statutes.

13.02 Defendant's refusal to pay the entire claim is a violation of one or more provisions of Chapter 542, Subchapter B, *Texas Insurance Code*, and as a result, Plaintiffs are entitled to recover statutory penalties of 18% per annum and attorney's fees.

XIV. ATTORNEY'S FEES

14.01 As a result of Defendant's conduct, Plaintiff has been required to obtain the services of the undersigned attorneys for the filing, prosecution, and trial of this cause and therefore seeks an award of reasonable and necessary attorney's fees pursuant to *Texas Insurance Code* Chapters 541 and 542, and DTPA §17.50.

14.02 Plaintiff gave Defendant 30 days' notice of its claim. Accordingly, Plaintiff is entitled to recovery of attorney's fees pursuant to Chapter 38, *Texas Civil Practice & Remedies Code*.

WHEREFORE, PREMISES CONSIDERED, Plaintiff respectfully prays that Defendant be cited to appear and answer, and that upon final trial hereof, Plaintiff recover from Defendant, all of his actual economic damages, statutory additional damages, attorney's fees, prejudgment and post-judgment interest as allowed by law, costs of court, and such other and further relief to which they may show themselves justly entitled.

Respectfully submitted,

[Signature of attorney]

§11.09 Defendant's Pleadings—Insurance Actions

With one notable exception, the rules governing a defendant's answer responsive to the plaintiff's petition are the same in Insurance Code cases as in other consumer law cases.

See §5.01 *supra.* The Insurance Code specifically provides that the insurer has the burden of proof on a written exclusion or limitation in an insurance policy and therefore has the obligation to affirmatively plead such exclusion or limitation or it is waived. TEX. INS. CODE §554.002; *Texas Farmers Ins. Co. v. Murphy*, 996 S.W.2d 873 (Tex. 1999). Moreover, the pleading by an insurer of a general denial has been deemed to waive any defenses based upon provisions in the policy sued upon. *Ford v. State Farm Mut. Auto. Ins. Co.*, 550 S.W.2d 663, 666 (Tex. 1977) (UM insurer waived consent clause by pleading general denial to suit for benefits).

In addition, the insurer may be required to verify certain defensive pleas. A denial that notice of a claim for insurance benefits and proof of the loss claimed to be covered must be alleged "specifically and with particularity" and verified by affidavit. TEX R. CIV. P. Rule 93(12). And a denial that an insured has complied with all of the provisions of a policy for uninsured motorist benefits must be verified to be effective. TEX R. CIV. P. Rule 93(15).

The following form provides a specific example of an answer by an insurer to petition for relief under Chapter 541.

[a] FORM: Original answer with specific denials, verified denials and affirmative defenses—Insurance Code Action

```
                                      NO. _____
_____                    §       IN THE DISTRICT COURT OF
                              §
vs.                           §       _____COUNTY, TEXAS
                              §
_____                    §       _____ JUDICIAL DISTRICT
```

ORIGINAL ANSWER

TO THE HONORABLE JUDGE OF THE DISTRICT COURT:

_____, defendant, files this Original Answer to plaintiff's petition and will show the following:

[*Admission as to insurance policy at issue, if applicable*]

1. Defendant admits that defendant issued a policy of insurance with coverage for uninsured motorist benefits.

[*Continue with modified general denial*]

2. Defendant otherwise generally denies the allegations made in plaintiff's petition.

[*Continue with any specific and verified denials as necessary*]

3. Defendant specifically denies that plaintiff has given proper notice of her claim under the policy and/or that plaintiff has provided the proof of loss required by the policy. The policy at

issue provides that proof of loss shall be in writing and verified under oath with details of the items the insured claims were damaged or destroyed, their date of acquisition or purchase and proof of the item's value. Plaintiff has not provided any of the information as required by the policy.

4. Defendant further specifically denies that plaintiff has complied with all of the terms of the policy as a condition precedent to maintaining this action on the policy. Plaintiff has not complied with the provisions of the policy requiring plaintiff to provide an examination under oath regarding the loss claimed as required by the terms of the policy.

[*Continue with any affirmative defenses, as applicable.*]

4. Pleading further and affirmatively, if such defense be necessary:

[(a)] Conditions precedent not performed. Plaintiff has not performed all conditions precedent necessary to maintain this lawsuit. Specifically, [*insert condition precedent that has not occurred*].

[(b)] Statute of limitations. The two-year statute of limitations applicable to all Insurance Code claims made in this case, as set forth in Texas Insurance Code §541.162, expired on plaintiff's claims before suit was filed. Specifically, plaintiff discovered, or in the exercise of reasonable diligence should have discovered, the claims that are the subject of this suit more than two years before the date this suit was filed.

Authority: Tex. Ins. Code §541.162.

[NOTE: The plaintiff has the burden to plead and prove the application of the discovery rule, once a statute of limitations defense has been raised. *Willis v. Maverick*, 760 S.W.2d 642 (Tex. 1988).]

[(c)] Plaintiff's claims are barred by the parol evidence rule.

[(d)] Plaintiff accepted the policy issued. Accordingly, his claims are barred by ratification, waiver and estoppel.

[(e)] Plaintiffs' claims are barred by the terms and conditions of the policies of insurance on which this action is based. Specifically, [*continue with terms of exclusions and/or limitations, e.g.,* the policy excludes coverage for "bodily injury to an insured with respect to which such insured, his legal representative or any person entitled to payment under this coverage shall, without written consent of the company, make any settlement with any person or organization who may be legally liable therefor." Plaintiff settled with the uninsured motorist without defendant's written consent.]

5. <u>Request for relief</u>. [*See* §6.04 *supra*]

                                      Respectfully submitted,

                                      [Signature of attorney]

Verification

STATE OF TEXAS   §

COUNTY OF _____   §

VERIFICATION

    BEFORE ME, the undersigned authority, on this day personally appeared _____, known to me to be the person whose name is subscribed below, and after being by me duly sworn, on his/her oath deposed and stated that he/she is over 18 years of age, that he/she is fully competent and authorized to make this affidavit, and that the foregoing Answers to Interrogatories are true and correct.

                                        _____

    SWORN TO AND SUBSCRIBED before me, the undersigned authority, on this _____ day of _____, 20__, to which witness my hand and seal of office.

                                        _____

                                        Notary Public in and for the
                                        State of Texas

[Certificate of service]

§11.10 Discovery—Insurance Actions

The following discovery requests may be tailored to fit a case involving a claim against an insurance company. See Chapter 7, *supra*, for general discovery forms.

§11.10.1 Interrogatories—Insurance Actions

[a] FORM: Insurance Code claim: denial of disability insurance benefits

The following is a full set of Interrogatories which can be used in a denial of benefits claim.

CAUSE NO. _____

_____	§	IN THE DISTRICT COURT OF
	§	
VS.	§	
	§	_____ COUNTY, TEXAS
_____ LIFE INSURANCE COMPANY,	§	
	§	
	§	_____ JUDICIAL DISTRICT

PLAINTIFF'S FIRST SET OF INTERROGATORIES TO DEFENDANT

TO: _____ LIFE INSURANCE COMPANY, DEFENDANT, BY AND THROUGH ITS ATTORNEY OF RECORD, _____

Pursuant to Rule 197, *Texas Rules of Civil Procedure*, Plaintiff, _____ (hereinafter "Plaintiff"), serves upon _____ Life Insurance Company (hereinafter "Defendant"), by and through its attorney of record, these Interrogatories.

Your answers to these Interrogatories shall be made separately and fully in writing under oath. Each Interrogatory shall be answered on the basis of all information available to You or reasonably ascertainable by You, in accordance with Rule 193.1, *Texas Rules of Civil Procedure*, and such answers delivered to the undersigned attorney not more than thirty (30) days after the service hereof.

Pursuant to Rule 193.4, *Texas Rules of Civil Procedure*, You have the additional duty to supplement from time to time the answers given to the Interrogatories herein. You are further advised that these Interrogatories and the sworn answers to them may be offered as evidence at the trial of or any hearing in the above cause.

Respectfully submitted,

_____

Counsel for Plaintiff

CERTIFICATE OF SERVICE

I hereby certify that a true and correct copy of the foregoing instrument was this _____ day of _____ 201_, forwarded by [✓] certified mail, return receipt requested, [ ] facsimile transmission, [ ] hand delivery, to:

_____

DEFINITIONS AND INSTRUCTIONS

1. "Person(s)" where used herein includes human beings, corporations, partnerships, associations, joint ventures, government agencies (federal, state, or local) or any other organization cognizable at law, and where any employee performs some task about which an inquiry is made herein as part of his employment, "Person(s)" includes both the employing and the employed person(s).

2. The terms "You," "Your," or "Defendant" refer to _____ Life Insurance Company, a Defendant in this cause, which is currently pending in the District Court of _____ County, Texas, and includes all employees, agents, trustees, representatives, and all other persons acting or purporting to act on behalf of _____ Life Insurance Company.

3. The terms "Policy" or "the Policy" refer to Policy No. _____ issued by _____ Life Insurance Company.

4. The terms "Plaintiff's Claim for Disability Benefits" and "Claim for Disability Benefits" refer to _____, 2011 Application for Disability Benefits submitted by Plaintiff and given Claim No. _____.

5. The term "Plaintiff" refers to _____, Plaintiff in this cause, which is currently pending in the District Court of

_____County, Texas, and includes all employees, agents, trustees, representatives, attorneys, and all other persons acting or purporting to act on behalf of Plaintiff.

6. The term "Document" and/or "Correspondence" as used herein shall mean all written, reported, recorded, or graphic matter, however produced, including but not limited to, drawings, designs, manuals, memoranda, reports, financial reports, notes, letters, envelopes, telegrams, messages (including reports, notes, and memoranda of telephone conversations and conferences), studies, analyses, books, articles, magazines, newspapers, booklets, circulars, bulletins, notices, instructions, stenographic or handwritten notes, records, studies, accounts, pamphlets, pictures, films, voice recordings, maps, reports, work papers, arithmetical computations, calendars, date books, minutes of all other communications of any type, including inter and intraoffice communications, purchase orders, questionnaires, and surveys, charts, graphs, audio and video tapes, or other recordings, punchcards, magnetic tapes, discs, drums, printouts, and other data compilations from which information can be obtained (translated if necessary into usable form), intra-corporate drafts of the foregoing, upon which notations and writings have been made which do not appear on the originals, which are subject to the control of, or within the knowledge of the party responding hereto, its counsel and any consultants, experts and investigators.

7. "Tangible Evidence" includes drawings, blueprints, charts, maps, graphs, photographs, still or moving picture films, models, and any physical object in the possession of, subject to the control of, or within the knowledge of Defendants, its counsel, and any consultants, experts or investigators.

8. If You are unable to answer any Interrogatory fully and completely after exercising due diligence to make inquiry and to secure information, You are to answer such Interrogatory as fully and completely as You can, and to:

A. Specify the portion which You are unable to answer in the Interrogatory;

B. State the facts on which You base the contention that You are unable to answer that portion;

C. State the knowledge, information, and belief You have concerning that portion; and

D. State the acts done and inquiries made by You in attempting to answer such Interrogatory.

9. The terms "Identify" or "Identification," when used in reference to a Document, mean to state the following:

A. Its date;

B. Identify its author;

C. Identify its addressee;

D. The type of Document, e.g., letter, memorandum, receipt, invoice, schedule, telegram, chart, photograph, salary production, etc.; and

E. Its present location; and

F. Identify its custodian.

You may produce the Document in lieu of identification. If any Document was, but no longer is, in Your possession or control, or in existence, explain why. If any of the foregoing information is not available, state any other available means of Identifying such Document.

10. The words "Identify" or "Identification" when used in reference to any "Person" means to state the following:

A. The Person's name;

B. The Person's most current home address;

C. The Person's most current business address;

D. The Person's most current home telephone number; and

E. The Person's most current business telephone number.

11. The terms "Identify" or "Identification" when used in reference to a communication, means to state the following:

A. The date of the communication;

B. Identify the Persons who participated in or overheard the communication;

C. The type of communication (telephone, written, face-to-face);

D. Identify all Documents which Mention, Concern, Relate to, or Evidence the communication; and

E. Provide a general summary of the substance of any verbal communication.

12. All Interrogatories are intended to include all information in the possession of Defendant, or subject to its custody or control, whether directly or indirectly. Information is deemed to be in the possession, custody, or control of Defendant if:

A. It is in the actual possession of Defendant; or

B. It is within the possession of any other person and Defendant has the right to compel the information from such person.

3. The terms "Evidence" or "Evidencing" shall mean proving, indicating, or probative of the existence or nature of.

14. The terms "Relate" or "Relating," or "Concern" or "Concerning," or "Mention" or "Mentioning," shall mean referring to, having any relationship to, pertaining to, Evidencing, or constituting Evidence of, in whole or in part, the subject matter of the Interrogatory.

15. For purposes of interpreting or construing the scope of the Interrogatories made herein, terms shall be given their most expansive and inclusive interpretation unless specifically limited by the language of the individual Interrogatory. This includes without limitation, the following:

A. Construing "and," as well as "or," in the disjunctive or conjunctive as necessary to make the request more inclusive;

B. Construing the singular form of the word to include the plural, and the plural form to include the singular; and

C. Construing the masculine to include the feminine, and the feminine to include the masculine.

16. Any term which is not given a special meaning within these definitions and instructions shall be given its ordinary meaning as commonly used by laypersons and as defined in the most recent edition of any recognized English dictionary, such as Webster's New Collegiate Dictionary or the New American Heritage Dictionary.

17. If any information is withheld because such information is stored electronically, identify the subject matter of the information and the place or places where such information is maintained and provide a suitable program or method of retrieving such information and provide a duplicate of the program and information on a CD-ROM if possible.

18. If any information requested herein is withheld on the basis of any claim of privilege, work product, or otherwise, You are requested to produce, in lieu of any such information, a written statement containing the following:

A. Identifying the Person or Persons who have knowledge of the information and stating how they became aware of the information;

B. Identifying the author, date, and recipients of all Documents alleged to be privileged;

C. Generally identifying the subject matter of the information being withheld without violating the claimed privilege;

D. Stating briefly why the information is claimed to be privileged or to constitute work product; and

E. If any information relates in any way to a meeting or to any conversation, Identify all Persons who were present at or participated in the meeting or conversation.

19. In those instances where the responding party chooses to answer a request for information by referring to a specific Document or record, it is requested that such specification be in such sufficient detail to permit the requesting party to locate and Identify the records and/or Documents from which the answer is to be ascertained, as readily as can the party served with the request.

20. If there is an objection to the number of Interrogatories, please notify opposing counsel immediately, so that either an agreement may be obtained or the matter may be set for hearing. ANY REQUESTS FOR EXTENSIONS OF TIME MUST BE IN WRITING.

21. These Interrogatories are ongoing. In accordance with Rule 193.4, Tex. R. Civ. P., Plaintiffs request that the answers to these Interrogatories be timely supplemented. For example: if individuals with knowledge of relevant facts come to the responding party's attention, after serving answers to these Interrogatories, or if any such individuals, employees or agents of the responding party change employment or move before trial, Plaintiffs request that it be timely informed of such developments.

22. IT IS REQUESTED THAT ALL DOCUMENTS AND/OR OTHER DATA COMPILATIONS WHICH MIGHT IMPACT ON THE SUBJECT MATTER OF THIS LITIGATION BE PRESERVED AND THAT ANY ONGOING PROCESS OF DOCUMENT DESTRUCTION INVOLVING SUCH DOCUMENTS CEASE.

PLAINTIFF'S FIRST SET OF INTERROGATORIES TO DEFENDANT

INTERROGATORY NO. 1: Please Identify each person providing answers or information used to compile answers to these Interrogatories, and for each such person Identified, please designate which Interrogatory(ies) each person assisted in answering.

INTERROGATORY NO. 2: Please Identify all persons whom You will call as witnesses at the trial of this cause.

INTERROGATORY NO. 3: Please Identify each and every misrepresentation You claim Plaintiff made to You.

INTERROGATORY NO. 4: Please Identify the written underwriting criteria in existence at the time Plaintiff's application for the Policy was received which would have disqualified Plaintiff from coverage under the Policy.

INTERROGATORY NO. 5: Please describe Your policy or practice, as it existed when Plaintiff's application was received, for requesting and reviewing medical records of applicant.

INTERROGATORY NO. 6: Please describe Your policy and/or practice, if any, as it existed at the time Plaintiff's application for disability benefits was received, concerning requesting medical records from the applicant.

INTERROGATORY NO. 7: Please Identify all persons who were involved in the underwriting of Plaintiff's application for the Policy.

INTERROGATORY NO. 8: Please Identify all persons who were involved in the decision to deny Plaintiff's Claim for Disability Benefits.

INTERROGATORY NO. 9: Why did You deny Plaintiff's Claim for Disability Benefits?

INTERROGATORY NO. 10: Please detail each step taken by You to investigate Plaintiff's Claim for Disability Benefits.

INTERROGATORY NO. 11: Please state each action and the date(s) taken by You to comply with Chapter 542, *Texas Insurance Code* in connection with Plaintiff's Claim for Disability Benefits.

INTERROGATORY NO. 12: Please describe the information and/or documentation obtained by You during Your investigation of Plaintiff's Claim for Disability Benefits from which You concluded that Plaintiff intentionally misrepresented her health status to You on her application.

[b] FORM: Insurance Code claim: homeowner's policy (to defendant)

The following are examples of additional questions to supplement the general form in §7.43, *supra*.

1. What is the full legal name of the company that issued the insurance policy?

2. Identify each person who made, participated in, or reviewed the decision not to pay plaintiff the benefits that plaintiff contends are payable under the insurance policy, and each person who gathered or supplied information provided to the person or persons who made or participated in such decision. For each person identified, identify the company for whom they were employed at the time of his or her activity described above.

3. Identify all documents and things known to you that pertain to (a) the policy of insurance, or (b) the claim for loss filed by plaintiff. These documents are to be identified regardless of whether or not they are in your possession, custody or control.

4. Identify all lawsuits filed in the State of Texas since [*insert date*] to which defendant was a party and in which it was claimed that defendant wrongfully failed or refused to pay a claim under a Texas Standard Homeowner's policy for [*describe type of loss, e.g.*, fire] loss to the insured property on the grounds that [*describe grounds for denial, e.g.*, the loss was a result of arson].

5. Identify all persons who, to your knowledge, have claimed or alleged since [*insert date*] that defendant wrongfully failed or refused to pay a claim under a Texas Standard Homeowner's policy for a [*describe type of loss, e.g.*, hail damage] loss to the insured property.

6. Identify every insurance claim that to your knowledge, information or belief, plaintiff has filed under any policy of insurance. Your answer should include, but not be limited to, any claims filed under policies issued by defendant.

7. Describe fully each and every reason defendant had on [*insert date of denial*] for denying plaintiffs insurance claim.

8. Describe fully each and every reason defendant has today for denying plaintiff's insurance claim.

9. Identify all documents (including, but not limited to, guidelines, memoranda, training or seminar materials or company manuals) discussing the process, procedures, standards or guidelines for handling or adjusting a [*describe type of loss, e.g.*, fire] loss claim under a Texas Standard Homeowner's policy issued by defendant. This request includes all standards or guidelines for determining whether a [*describe type of loss, e.g.*, fire] loss to a dwelling is a covered loss.

10. Identify all documents received, generated, or prepared on or before [*insert date of claim denial*] that were received, generated or prepared because of the insurance claim.

> [**NOTE:** Documents prepared after the date of denial may also be discoverable and a separate request for those documents should be made.]

11. Describe fully the type of statistical, anecdotal or other such information compiled or stored by defendant that pertains to [*describe the type of loss, e.g.*, fire] loss claims in the State of Texas under the Texas Standard Homeowner's policy.

12. Please identify each and every policy provision in the Policy which you claim supports your denial of the Claim.

13. When did you receive notice of the Plaintiffs' claim?

14. On which date did you take the following actions if any:

    (a)   acknowledge receiving Plaintiffs' claim?

    (b)   begin investigation of Plaintiffs' claim?

    (c)   ask Plaintiffs for all items you reasonably believed you would need to investigate the Plaintiffs' claim?

    (d)   after making an initial request, make any additional requests for information from Plaintiffs for information?

    (e)   Accept Plaintiffs' claim?

    (f)   Reject Plaintiffs' claim?

[c] FORM: Insurance Code claim: homeowner's policy (to plaintiff)

The following questions may be tailored for use by a defendant to a case involving a claim for homeowner's insurance benefits.

1. Identify the person from whom plaintiff purchased or received the insured dwelling, the date the dwelling was purchased or received, and, if applicable, the purchase price.

2. For all unscheduled personal property that plaintiff contends was lost or damaged, give the following information:

   (a)   the date the property was acquired,

   (b)   the person from whom it was acquired,

   (c)   the purchase price, if applicable,

   (d)   its value at the time of the loss,

   (e)   the amount you contend it will cost to repair such property, and

   (f)   the amount you contend it will cost to replace the property if you contend that repair is not feasible.

3. Identify (a) all documents that contain any of the information asked about in the preceding interrogatory, and (b) all photographs of the property asked about in the preceding interrogatory.

4. What is the amount you contend it will cost to repair the damage caused to the insured dwelling for which you have submitted a claim?

5. Identify all documents that contain information concerning the cost to repair the property asked about in the preceding interrogatory.

6. Describe in detail each act or omission of defendant in connection with your claim that you contend was (a) a failure to deal fairly or in good faith, (b) a violation of Art. 21.21 of the Texas Insurance Code or (c) a violation of the Deceptive Trade Practices Act. For each such act or omission, identify the natural person who did or failed to do the act complained of.

7. Identify all conduct of defendant concerning any claim other than the claim made the basis of this suit that you contend was

a violation of any of the laws listed in the preceding interrogatory.

8. Identify all documents, specifically including, but not limited to, all memoranda, correspondence, pleadings, responses to discovery, verdicts, and judgments, indicating that defendant engaged in the conduct asked about in the two preceding interrogatories.

9. Identify all claims made by plaintiff to any insurance company to recover insurance proceeds for property damage or loss, theft, or personal injury. For each such claim, identify the insurance company to which the claim was made, the date of the claim and describe the nature of the loss.

> [**NOTE:** If the claim denial involves an allegation that makes the plaintiffs financial condition relevant, e.g., arson, the following questions would be appropriate.]

10. Identify each bank account that (a) plaintiff currently has, and (b) that plaintiff had at the time of the loss.

11. For each of the accounts listed in answer to the preceding interrogatory, state the balances in the accounts on the date of the loss and on the date of service of these interrogatories.

12. Identify all outstanding loans and credit accounts that plaintiff (a) had on the date of the loss, and (b) has today. For each loan and credit account, state the amount owed on the date of loss and on the date of service of these interrogatories.

13. Identify by style, cause number, county and state, all judgments taken against plaintiff within the last 10 years.

14. Identify all sources of income plaintiff (a) had on the date of the loss, and (b) has today.

§11.10.2 Requests for Production—Insurance Actions

[a] FORM: Denial of insurance claim (to defendant insurance company)

The following is a complete Request for Production which can be used in a denial of benefits claim.

CAUSE NO. _____

_____	§	IN THE DISTRICT COURT OF
	§	
VS.	§	
	§	_____ COUNTY, TEXAS
_____ LIFE INSURANCE COMPANY,	§	
	§	
	§	_____ JUDICIAL DISTRICT

PLAINTIFF'S FIRST REQUEST FOR PRODUCTION TO DEFENDANT

TO: _____ LIFE INSURANCE COMPANY, DEFENDANT, BY AND THROUGH ITS ATTORNEY OF RECORD, _____

Pursuant to Rule 196, Texas Rules of Civil Procedure, Plaintiff, _____ (hereinafter "Plaintiff"), serves upon Defendant, _____ Life Insurance Company(hereinafter "Defendant"), by and through its attorney of record, these Requests for Production.

Defendant shall serve a written response to the Requests for Production as directed by Rule 196, Texas Rules of Civil Procedure, within thirty (30) days after the service of the Requests. Defendant is requested to produce the documents and tangible things identified within thirty (30) days after service of the Requests at _____ _____. Except as otherwise indicated, Defendant may attach copies of the requested documents to the written response. Defendant shall supplement its responses to the Requests for Production as required by Rule 193.5, Texas Rules of Civil Procedure.

NOTICE PURSUANT TO RULE 193.7. The requesting party hereby gives notice to the responding party that all documents produced by the responding party in response to this Request for Production may be used at the trial of this cause pursuant to Rule 193.7, Texas Rules of Civil Procedure.

Respectfully submitted,

_____

Counsel for Plaintiffs

CERTIFICATE OF SERVICE

I hereby certify that a true and correct copy of the foregoing instrument was this _____ day of _____ 201_ forwarded by [✓] certified mail, return receipt requested, [ ] facsimile transmission, [ ] hand delivery, to:

_____

DEFINITIONS AND INSTRUCTIONS

1. The terms "You," "Your," or "Defendant" refer to _____ Insurance Company and includes all employees, agents, trustees, representatives, and all other persons acting or purporting to act on its behalf.

2. The term "Plaintiff" refers to _____, and includes all employees, agents, trustees, representatives, attorneys, and all other persons acting or purporting to act on behalf of Plaintiff.

3. The terms "Policy" or "the Policy" refer to Policy No. _____ issued by _____ Life Insurance Company.

4. The terms "Plaintiff's Claim for Benefits" and "Claim for Benefits" refer to _____, 201__ Application for Benefits submitted by Plaintiff and given Claim No. _____.

5. The term "Document" and/or "Correspondence" as used herein shall mean all written, reported, recorded, or graphic matter, however produced, including but not limited to, drawings, designs, manuals, memoranda, reports, financial reports, notes, letters, envelopes, telegrams, messages (including reports, notes, and memoranda of telephone conversations and conferences), studies, analyses, books, articles, magazines, newspapers, booklets, circulars, bulletins, notices, instructions, stenographic or handwritten notes, records, studies, accounts, pamphlets, pictures, films, voice recordings, maps, reports, work papers, arithmetical

computations, calendars, date books, minutes of all other communications of any type, including inter- and intra-office communications, purchase orders, questionnaires, and surveys, charts, graphs, audio and video tapes, or other recordings, punchcards, magnetic tapes, discs, drums, printouts, and other electronic or magnetic data compilations from which information can be obtained (translated if necessary into usable form), intra-corporate drafts of the foregoing, upon which notations and writings have been made which do not appear on the originals, which are subject to the control of, or within the knowledge of the party responding hereto, its counsel and any consultants, experts and investigators.

6. "Tangible Evidence" includes drawings, blueprints, charts, maps, graphs, photographs, still or moving picture films, models, and any physical object in the possession of, subject to the control of, or within the knowledge of You, Your counsel, and any of Your consultants, experts or investigators.

7. The terms "Evidence" or "Evidencing" shall mean proving, indicating, or probative of the existence or nature of.

8. The terms "Relate" or "Relating," or "Concern" or "Concerning," or "Mention" or "Mentioning," shall mean referring to, having any relationship to, pertaining to, Evidencing, or constituting Evidence of, in whole or in part, the subject matter of the Request.

9. All Requests for Production of Documents are intended to include all information in Your possession, or subject to Your custody or control, whether directly or indirectly. Information is deemed to be in Your possession, custody, or control if:

A. It is in Your actual possession; or

B. It is within the possession of any other person and You have the right to compel the information or documents from such person.

If a Document was, but no longer is, in Your possession, or in existence, explain why.

10. For purposes of interpreting or construing the scope of the Requests for Production made herein, terms shall be given their most expansive and inclusive interpretation unless specifically limited by the language of the individual Request. This includes, without limitation, the following:

A. Construing "and," as well as "or" in the disjunctive or conjunctive as necessary to make the request more inclusive;

B. Construing the singular form of the word to include the plural, and the plural form to include the singular; and

C. Construing the masculine to include the feminine, and the feminine to include the masculine.

Any term which is not given a special meaning within these definitions and instructions shall be given its ordinary meaning as commonly used by laypersons and as defined in the most recent edition of any recognized English dictionary, such as Webster's New Collegiate Dictionary or the New American Heritage Dictionary.

11. For documents stored electronically, provide such documents along with a suitable program for retrieving such information on a CD-ROM.

12. If any information requested herein is withheld on the basis of any claim of privilege, work product, or otherwise, You are requested to produce, in lieu of any such information, a written statement containing the following:

A. Identifying the Person or Persons who have knowledge of the information and stating how they became aware of the information;

B. Identifying the author, date, and recipients of all Documents alleged to be privileged;

C. Generally identifying the subject matter of the information being withheld without violating the claimed privilege;

D. Stating briefly why the information is claimed to be privileged or to constitute work product; and

E. If any information relates in any way to a meeting or to any conversation, identify all Persons who were present at or participated in the meeting or conversation.

13. ANY REQUESTS FOR EXTENSIONS OF TIME MUST BE IN WRITING.

14. IT IS REQUESTED THAT ALL DOCUMENTS AND/OR DATA COMPILATIONS WHICH MIGHT IMPACT ON THE SUBJECT MATTER OF THIS LITIGATION BE PRESERVED AND THAT ANY ONGOING PROCESS OF DOCUMENT DESTRUCTION INVOLVING SUCH DOCUMENTS CEASE.

PLAINTIFF'S FIRST REQUEST FOR PRODUCTION TO DEFENDANT

REQUEST FOR PRODUCTION NO. 1: Please produce any and all documents containing correspondence between Plaintiff and Defendant.

REQUEST FOR PRODUCTION NO. 2: Please produce Your underwriting file on the Policy.

REQUEST FOR PRODUCTION NO. 3: Please produce Your claim file on Plaintiff's Claim for Benefits.

REQUEST FOR PRODUCTION NO. 4: To the extent not previously produced, any and all documents obtained by You during Your investigation of Plaintiff's application for the Policy.

REQUEST FOR PRODUCTION NO. 5: To the extent not previously produced, any and all documents obtained by You in connection with Your investigation of Plaintiff's Claim for Benefits.

REQUEST FOR PRODUCTION NO. 6: Please produce any and all audio recordings of Plaintiff.

REQUEST FOR PRODUCTION NO. 7: Please produce any and all audio recordings of any conversation between You and any third party regarding Plaintiff, the Policy, or Plaintiff's Claim for Benefits.

REQUEST FOR PRODUCTION NO. 8: Please produce any and all documents signed by or on behalf of Plaintiff concerning the application, Policy or Claim for Benefits.

REQUEST FOR PRODUCTION NO. 9: Please produce a true and correct copy of the Plaintiffs' policy.

REQUEST FOR PRODUCTION NO. 10: Please produce any and all documents containing estimates prepared or received by you concerning the losses sustained by Plaintiffs in connection with the claim.

REQUEST FOR PRODUCTION NO. 11: To the extent you used independent adjusters to work on Plaintiffs' claim, please produce any and all documents containing the contracts or terms of employment between you and each such person or that person's employer.

REQUEST FOR PRODUCTION NO. 12: Please produce all timesheets or invoices submitted to you by any outside contractor who worked on Plaintiff's claim.

REQUEST FOR PRODUCTION NO. 13: Please produce all diaries, notes, logs or journals kept by you or your outside adjuster(s) concerning any work in connection with Plaintiff's claim.

REQUEST FOR PRODUCTION NO. 14: Please produce Your complete underwriting file on any other policy of insurance you ever issued to Plaintiff.

REQUEST FOR PRODUCTION NO. 15: Please produce any and all documents reflection your receipt of notice of Plaintiff's claim.

[b] FORM: Insurance claim (to plaintiff)

REQUEST FOR PRODUCTION NO. 1: Please produce any and all diaries, calendars, notes or journals kept by you regarding the event made the basis of your claim.

REQUEST FOR PRODUCTION NO. 2: Please produce any and all estimates, bills and/or receipts for damages resulting from the loss made the basis of this suit.

REQUEST FOR PRODUCTION NO. 3: Please produce any and all documents reflecting expenses arising out of the loss incurred by you.

REQUEST FOR PRODUCTION NO. 4: Please produce any and all documents reflecting payment to you or on your behalf by any other insurance company that offered coverage with regard to the loss.

REQUEST FOR PRODUCTION NO. 5: Please produce any and all documents evidencing any settlement agreement or subrogation agreement you have reached concerning the loss.

(This page intentionally left blank.)

Chapter 12

Residential Construction

§12.01 History of Texas Residential Construction Law
§12.02 Applicability of the DTPA to New Home Construction
§12.03 Common Law Implied Warranties
    §12.03.1 New Home Construction
    §12.03.2 Repairs or Modifications to Existing Homes
§12.04 Residential Construction Commission Act (Historical)
    §12.04.1 RCCA—New Homes Purchased Prior to September 1, 2003
    §12.04.2 RCCA—New Homes Constructed between September 1, 2003 and June 1, 2005
    §12.04.3 RCCA—New Homes Constructed between June 1, 2005 and September 1, 2010
    §12.04.4 RCCA—2009 Sunset
    §12.04.5 RCCA—Third-Party Warranty Companies
§12.05 Residential Construction Liability Act ("RCLA")
    §12.05.1 RCLA—Definitions and Scope of Coverage
    §12.05.2 RCLA—Affirmative Defenses Available to Contractor
    §12.05.3 RCLA—Notice and Offer of Settlement Provisions
    §12.05.4 RCLA—Consequences of Failing to Provide Inspection or to Accept a Settlement Offer
    §12.05.5 RCLA—Consequences of Failing to Make Reasonable Settlement Offer or Initiate Repairs
    §12.05.6 RCLA—When Pre-Filing Notice Is Not Required
    §12.05.7 RCLA—Abatement for Failure to Give Pre-Suit Notice
    §12.05.8 RCLA—Limitations on Damages
§12.06 Forms
    §12.06.1 Checklists for Initial Interview
        [a] CHECKLIST: Purchase of new residence (Plaintiff)
        [b] CHECKLIST: Sale of new residence (Defendant)
    §12.06.2 Pre-Suit Notice Letters in Residential Construction Cases
        [a] FORM: Notice letter to builder/seller
        [b] FORM: Notice letter to engineer, architect
        [c] FORM: Notice letter on a home warranty claim
        [d] FORM: Notice letter to real estate broker/agent
    §12.06.3 Responses to Residential Construction Notice Letter
        [a] FORM: Letter requesting opportunity to inspect and photograph defects

[b] FORM: Letter to builder analyzing the notice letter
[c] FORM: Letter to subcontractor giving notice of claim
[d] FORM: Offer of settlement: repair of construction defects
[e] FORM: Offer of settlement: pay for repairs

§12.06.4 Petitions
[a] FORM: New house purchased from builder/seller (RCCA warranties)

§12.06.5 Defendant's Responsive Pleadings
[a] FORM: Plea in abatement (inadequate notice of claim)
[b] FORM: Order on plea in abatement
[c] FORM: Plea in abatement: no opportunity to inspect
[d] FORM: Order on plea in abatement
[e] FORM: Original answer with affirmative defenses (residential construction)

§12.06.6 Discovery in Residential Construction Cases
[a] FORM: Interrogatories to defendant
[b] FORM: Interrogatories to plaintiff
[c] FORM: Requests for Production to defendant (foundation repair)
[d] FORM: Requests for Production to plaintiff

§12.01 History of Texas Residential Construction Law

The single largest purchase most consumers make is the house in which they live, and unlike most purchases, this one is seen and used nearly every day of the year. A person's house also involves emotional attachments that other consumer purchases lack. Because houses have a special place in most people's lives, when things go wrong with houses, people are generally inclined to want to do something about it.

When the purchase is of a new residence, the opportunity for deception and resulting damages is great. It is no wonder that residential construction claims have been a major source of litigation under the DTPA. Historically, most residential construction defect claims have been predicated upon either a violation of the laundry list or upon the breach of an express or implied warranty. While the law governing laundry list and express warranties has changed little since the DTPA was first adopted in 1973, the law governing implied warranties has changed considerably. Generally, the law existing at the time of the purchase will determine whether and to what extent any warranties are implied in the new home purchase as a matter of law.

There have also been perceptions that the DTPA is ill-suited for resolution of many run-of-the-mill residential construction defect claims and that the DTPA has been abused by some to promote litigation over pre-suit resolution. As a result, there have been several significant changes made to the law governing residential construction claims by both the courts and by the Texas Legislature. In 1989, the Texas legislature enacted the Residential Construction Liability Act ("RCLA"), TEX. PROP. CODE §27.01 *et seq. See* §12.05, *infra.* In 2003, the Texas legislature enacted the Texas Residential Construction Commission Act ("RCCA"), creating the Texas Residential Construction Commission and imposing new implied warranties and building standards into the sale of new homes. *See* §12.04, *infra.* In 2009, the legislature allowed the RCCA to expire pursuant to the Sunset Act. After September 1, 2010, the Residential Construction Commission ceased to exist and the new home warranties and building standards it had created are no longer imposed by Texas law. The RCLA continues to control litigation against homebuilders and others.

Because the litigation of a residential defect claim may occur years after the sale, care must be exercised to determine which statutes and what version of them were in effect at the time of the sale. The date of the sale will usually determine which, if any, warranties will be implied into the sale as a matter of law. The historic review of prior statutes governing residential construction in this chapter should be consulted to determine if any prior law may yet govern a claim being brought or litigated today. The chart below summarizes the applicability of these legislative changes to residential construction defect claims in Texas law.

Before 1968	No implied warranties; *caveat emptor*
1968 to 1973	*Humber* implied warranties of habitability and construction in a good and workmanlike manner No DTPA
1973 to 1989	DTPA *Humber* implied warranties of habitability and construction in a good and workmanlike manner
1989 to 2003	DTPA *Humber* implied warranties of habitability and construction in a good and workmanlike manner
2003 to 2005	DTPA *Humber* implied warranties of habitability and construction in a good and workmanlike manner TRCCA (w/o warranties) RCLA
2005 to 2010	DTPA No *Humber* warranties TRCCA (w/ new TRCC 1, 2 and 10 year performance warranties and building standards and new warranty of habitability) RCLA
2010 to Present	DTPA *Humber* implied warranties of habitability and construction in a good and workmanlike manner RCLA No TRCCA

§12.02 Applicability of the DTPA to New Home Construction

The DTPA governs a consumer's purchase or acquisition of "goods' or "services." Expanding on the definition of "goods" found in the U.C.C., the DTPA defines "goods" to include "real property." DTPA §17.45(1). The DTPA has long been recognized to apply to a consumer's purchase of a new or used residence. *See, e.g., Flenniken v. Lonview Bank & Trust,* 661 S.W.2d 705 (Tex. 1983) (new home); *Cameron v Terrell & Garrett,* 618 S.W.2d 535 (Tex. 1981)(used home).

The desirability of DTPA protection of consumers in the purchase of a residence has led the Legislature to expressly exempt such purchases from the transaction limits imposed on other consumer transactions. See DTPA §17.49(f)(written contracts greater than $100,000); DTPA §17.49(g)(transaction greater than $500,000. See § 1.02.7.3.3, *supra*.

§12.03 Common Law Implied Warranties

§12.03.1 New Home Construction

In *Humber v. Morton*, 426 S.W.2d 554, 555 (Tex. 1968), the Texas Supreme Court rejected and discredited the common law doctrine of *caveat emptor* and recognized two implied warranties in the sale of a new house. Now referred to as the *Humber* warranties, the two warranties implied as a matter of law were: (1) the house has been constructed in a good and workmanlike manner, and (2) the house is suitable for human habitation. The *Humber* court reasoned that an ordinary purchaser of a home is not necessarily in a position to discover defects, but must instead rely on the builder, who is in the best position to know the condition of the house and how it was built. In the court's view, the caveat emptor doctrine did a disservice both to the purchaser, and to the industry because it encouraged "the unscrupulous, fly-by-night operator and purveyor of shoddy work." *Id.* at 562.

It has been held that the implied warranties recognized in *Humber* apply to completed construction as well as houses not yet finished. *See, e.g., March v. Thiery*, 729 S.W.2d 889 (Tex. App.—Corpus Christi 1987, no writ). Additionally, the *Humber* warranties extend "automatically" to subsequent purchasers of new homes. *Gupta v. Ritter Homes, Inc.*, 646 S.W.2d 168, 169 (Tex. 1983).

The concept of "good and workmanlike" construction is often defined as, "that quality of work performed by one who has the knowledge, training or experience necessary for the successful practice of a trade or occupation and performed in a manner generally considered proficient by those capable of judging such work." TEXAS PATTERN JURY CHARGES §102.12.

The meaning of "suitable for human habitation" is not so clear. In *Kamarath v. Bennett*, 568 S.W.2d 658, 661 (Tex. 1978), the court attempted to explain the concept by holding that in order for there to be a breach of the habitability warranty, it must be of such a nature "which will render the premises unsafe, or unsanitary, or otherwise unfit for living therein." Whether a house is unsafe or unsanitary is arguably susceptible to objective determination. For example, in *Humber* the fireplace was dangerously defective. It is unclear, however, exactly what "unfit for living" means. A cracked foundation may allow insects and other pests access to the interior of the house. One or two roaches or spiders would hardly render a house "unfit," but what about an infestation that cannot be removed until the cracks are sealed? Improper flashing may allow water to drip from windows or the ceiling. An occasional drip may cause little more than aggravation, but what if the leak is so severe that sheetrock gets soaked and begins to sag? And, is there a difference between what reasonably should be considered "unfit" in a house costing $1 million as opposed to one costing $75,000?

In *Centex Homes, Inc. v. Buecher*, 95 S.W.3d 266 (Tex. 2002), the court held that both of the implied warranties recognized in *Humber* can be waived, under certain circumstances. In order to waive the implied warranty of good workmanship, the agreement between the parties must provide for the "manner, performance or quality of the desired construction." If the agreement is sufficiently detailed, then a waiver is enforceable. On the other hand, the implied warranty of habitability may not be disclaimed "generally," but its application is now (a) restricted to only those defects which render the property so defective that it is "unsuitable for its intended use as a home," (b) applies only to latent defects, and (c) does not extend to any defects, even substantial ones, that are known by or expressly disclosed to the buyer. *Id.* at 275.

Although an implied warranty arises between a contractor and consumer, it has been held that there is no implied warranty between a subcontractor and consumer when the consumer has had no direct dealings with the subcontractor. *Codner v. Arellano*, 40 S.W.3d 666, 672-674 (Tex. App.—Austin 2001, no pet.); *Pugh v. Gen. Terrazzo Supplies, Inc.*, 243 S.W.3d 84, 89-90 (Tex. App.—Houston [1st Dist.] 2007, pet. denied); *J.M. Krupar Constr. Co. v. Rosenberg*, 95 S.W.3d 322, 332 (Tex. App.—Houston [1st Dist.] 2002, no pet.); *see also Raymond v. Rahme*, 78 S.W.3d 552, 563 (Tex. App.—Austin 2002, no pet.).

From 2003 to 2010, the *Humber* warranties were expressly superseded by four new implied warranties contained by Texas Residential Construction Commission Act of 2003. *See* §12.04.3, *infra*. With the sunsetting of the RCCA on September 1, 2010, the *Humber* warranties were resurrected for new home construction. For homes built between 2005 and 2010, the historical provisions and regulations of the RCCA, as described in the following section, should be consulted to determine whether the *Humber* warranties or the RCCA implied warranties apply.

§12.03.2 Repairs or Modifications to Existing Homes

An implied warranty that services in the repair or modification of existing tangible goods or property will be performed is a good and workmanlike performance was first recognized in *Melody Home Mfg. Co. v. Barnes*, 741 S.W.2d 349 (Tex. 1987), a case involving repairs to an existing home. This implied warranty has been applied to residential construction which modifies or repairs an existing residence. *See, e.g., McCrea v. Cubilla Condo. Corp.*, 769 S.W.2d 261, 264 (Tex. App.—Houston [1st Dist.] 1988, writ denied) (repairs to roof are covered by Melody Home implied warranty).

There is uncertainty as to whether the *Melody Home* warranty is actionable outside of the DTPA. In describing its newly created implied warranty, the Texas Supreme Court stated, "We hold that an implied warranty to repair or modify existing tangible goods or property in a good and workmanlike manner is available to consumers *suing under the DTPA.*" 741 S.W.2d at 354 (emphasis added). This phrasing of the *Melody Home* implied warranty has led some courts to limit its application to consumers suing under the DTPA while others have held the implied warranty is actionable outside of the DTPA. *Gonzales v. Southwest Olshan Found. Repair Co., LLC*, 400 S.W.3d 52n. 9 (Tex. 2013) *and cases cited therein*.

In *Melody Home*, the court held that this new implied warranty could be neither waived nor disclaimed as a matter of public policy. *Id.* at 355. Recently, however, the court modified this holding to allow written warranty provisions to supersede the implied warranty remedy if "the parties' agreement sufficiently describes the manner, performance or quality" of the services. *Gonzales v. Southwest Olshan Found. Repair Co., LLC*, 400 S.W.3d 52, 56 (Tex. 2013) (foundation repair company's written warranty promised lifetime adjustments and all work to be performed in a good and workmanlike manner).

When a homeowner hires a contractor to repair, remodel or even add on to his home, there often is no written contract to define the parties' expectations. In some instances, a written proposal or bid is the only written confirmation of the work to be done and the amount to be paid. Written warranties meeting the "manner, performance or quality of construction" (as contemplated by *Gonzales v. Southwest Olshan* and *Centex Homes, Inc. v. Buecher*) are the exception rather than the rule. In most other cases, the implied warranty is well-suited to fill the "gap" as to the parties' unexpressed intention as to the quality of workmanship expected in residential construction to repair or modify existing residential structures. *See Gonzales v. Southwest Olshan*, at 56.

§12.04 Residential Construction Commission Act (Historical)

[**NOTE:** The RCCA expired effective September 1, 2009. These provisions are included for historical reference because certain provisions may still apply to residential construction commenced between June 1, 2005 and August 31, 2010. For those cases, care must be taken to determine which law applies.]

The Texas Residential Construction Commission Act, TEX. PROP. CODE §401.001 *et seq.* ("RCCA") (repealed), enacted by the 2003 Legislature, created the Texas Residential Construction Commission as a new state agency with broad rule-making authority to implement the RCCA. The Commission was charged with establishing three new limited warranties and the detailed building performance standards for complying with them. The Commission was also responsible for overseeing a new alternative dispute resolution process for residential construction disputes. The RCCA expressly superseded the *Humber* implied warranties with its new one-year, two-year and 10-year limited warranties and building performance standards. RCCA § 430.006 (repealed). The RCCA also required home buyers to submit to a state-created inspection and non-binding dispute resolution process ("SIRP") as a prerequisite to filing a suit against the builder. The results of the SIRP were then admissible in subsequent legal proceedings. *See* RCCA § 426.005, *et seq.* (repealed). The Commission also certified third party inspectors and selected and employed state inspectors who served as the appeals panel in the dispute resolution process.

The RCCA expired effective September 1, 2009. RCCA §401.006 (repealed). From June 1, 2005 until its expiration, the statutory warranties for new home construction provided by the RCCA superseded the common law implied warranties which had been developed over the years in residential construction cases. *See* §12.04.3, *infra*. With the expiration of the RCCA, the *Humber* implied warranties again apply to the sale and construction of new homes and homeowners are no longer required to initiate an SIRP or otherwise comply with the RCCA as a prerequisite to filing a suit for damages. The full text of the expired RCCA provisions governing the SIRP process can be found in the Supplement.

Ascertaining which warranties and building standards apply to a home built in this time frame is not a simple matter. Consideration must be given to the effective date of the RCCA (September 1, 2003), the date construction begins on the home, the effective date of the Commission's statutory warranties (June 1, 2005), the expiration date of the RCCA (September 1, 2009) and the expiration date of the Commission's implied warranties and building standards (August 31, 2010).

§12.04.1 RCCA— New Homes Purchased Prior to September 1, 2003

For homes purchased prior to September 1, 2003, neither the RCCA nor its warranties and implied warranty exclusions would apply. These homes would be covered under the *Humber* common law implied warranties as well as any express warranty given by the builder. *See* §12.03 *supra*.

§12.04.2 RCCA—New Homes Constructed between September 1, 2003 and June 1, 2005

There was a significant lag time between the 2003 enactment of the RCCA and formal adoption of the actual limited warranties and building and performance standards by the Commission. The text of the RCCA did not itself establish the actual one-year, two-year and 10-year limited warranties, but rather directed the Commission to develop them and adopt building standards for complying with them "as soon as possible." RCCA §430.001 (b) (expired); *see* ACTS 2003, 78TH LEG., CH. 458, §1.03. The Commission did not adopt final limited warranty and building standards until June 1, 2005. 10 TEX. ADMIN. CODE §§304.1 (2005) *et seq.* (repealed), *published at* 30 TEX. REG. 669, *et seq.* (Feb. 11, 2005).

Recognizing there would be a lag time before their adoption, the 2003 Legislature directed that the TRCC's new warranties and building standards apply only to construction that "begins" on or after the standards' effective date. ACTS 2003, 78TH LEG., CH. 458, §1.03. The RCCA provided that the warranties and building and performance standards applicable to the construction before the effective date of the Commission's new warranties and building standards would continue to apply to construction commenced prior to that date (*i.e.*, June 1, 2005). *Id.* Thus, the *Humber* warranties were still implied as a matter of law into new homes constructed between September 1, 2003 to June 1, 2005.

§12.04.3 RCCA—New Homes Constructed between June 1, 2005 and September 1, 2010

For residential construction "commenced" on or after June 1, 2005, the rules and regulations of the Texas Residential Construction Commission imposed the following implied warranties into the construction and sale of new homes in lieu of the *Humber* warranties:

a) one-year warranty on all materials and workmanship,

b) a two-year warranty on plumbing, electrical, heating and air-conditioning delivery systems, and

c) a 10-year warranty on major structural components of the home.

10 TEX. ADMIN. CODE §§304.1 (2005) *et seq.* (repealed), *published at* 30 TEX. REG. 669, *et seq.* (Feb.11, 2005).

In addition, the RCCA imposed a statutory warranty of habitability. RCCA §430.002 (repealed). The RCCA warranty of habitability was defined as:

> "a builder's obligation to construct a home or home improvement that is in compliance with the limited statutory warranties and building and performance standards adopted by the commission under Section 430.001 and that is safe, sanitary, and fit for humans to inhabit."

RCCA §401.002(16) (repealed).

Significantly, the RCCA provided that the limited statutory warranties and the statutory warranty of habitability replaced all common law implied warranties:

> "The warranties established under this chapter supersede all implied warranties. The only warranties that exist for residential construction or residential improvements are warranties created by this chapter or by other statutes expressly referring to residential construction or residential improvements, or any express, written warranty acknowledged by the homeowner and the builder."

RCCA §430.006 (repealed). The TRCC's limited warranties and building performance standards applied to construction that "commenced" on or after June 1, 2005 and before September 1, 2010. *See* §12.04.4, *infra*. The TRCC defined the date construction commences as the earlier of the date of the agreement or the commencement of work. 10 TEX. ADMIN. CODE §304.1(b) (2005)(repealed), *published at* 30 TEX. REG. 669, 687 (Feb. 11, 2005). This approach may have conflicted with the legislative mandate that the standards apply only to construction that "begins" after the effective date of the standards. ACTS 2003, 78TH LEG., CH. 458, §1.03. Generally, the TRCC's rules address the responsibilities of builders and homeowners under the warranties, warranty periods, coverage and exclusions, and building component and system performance standards.

New homes for which construction began on or after June 1, 2005 thus came with the RCCA one-, two- and 10-year RCCA warranties (and building and performance standards), the statutory warranty of habitability and any express written warranty given by the builder. RCCA §430.006 (repealed). The RCCA's warranty periods began on the date of occupancy or the date title is transferred, whichever was earlier, unless the builder and the initial purchaser agreed otherwise. RCCA §430.001(f) (repealed). For home-improvement projects covered by the RCCA, the warranty periods began when the improvement was substantially completed. RCCA §430.001(g). By rule, the Commission defined "substantial completion" as the date the home was sufficiently complete that it could be occupied or the date of a final certificate of inspection or occupancy, whichever was later. 10 TEX. ADMIN. CODE §§304.1(c)(16) (2005)(repealed), *published at* 30 TEX. REG. 669, 688 (Feb.11, 2005).

The legislature did not give the new RCCA warranty of habitability a specified duration like the other RCCA limited warranties; however, the Commission's Rules described the warranty of habitability as a 10-year warranty. 10 TEX. ADMIN. CODE §§304.3(a)(4)(2005) (repealed), *published at* 30 TEX. REG. 669, 690 (Feb. 11, 2005); *cf.* RCCA §430.002(repealed). For a construction defect to be actionable as a breach of the RCCA warranty of habitability, the defect must

> "have a direct adverse effect on the habitable areas of the home and must not have been discoverable by a reasonable prudent inspection or examination of the home or home improvement within the applicable warranty periods adopted by the commission under Section 430.001."

RCCA §430.002 (b)(repealed). Thus, a condition which would be considered a breach of the one- or two-year implied warranties cannot be asserted later as a breach of the RCCA implied warranty of habitability unless it was not discoverable within the original one- or two-year warranty periods. For example, if a three-year-old home is rendered uninhabitable due to a plumbing leak, that breach would not be actionable as a breach of the RCCA warranty of habitability if the plumbing defect was discoverable through a reasonable inspection of the home during the duration of the two-year statutory warranty covering the plumbing system. This limitation did not exist with the *Humber* warranty of habitability.

The RCCA provided that the contract between the builder and the homeowner may not waive the limited statutory warranties, the building and performance standards, or the statutory warranty of habitability, nor may it limit the obligations of the builder under the statute. RCCA §§430.007, 430.011(repealed). This did not prevent a builder and homeowner for contracting for more stringent warranties and building standards. RCCA §430.007(repealed).

The RCCA provided that alternative warranty and building and performance standards applied in the colonias regions of South Texas. *See* RCCA §430.005(repealed).

The RCCA also declared that these limited residential construction warranties were not actionable under the DTPA. RCCA §430.011(c) (repealed). This statutory restriction on using the DTPA to sue for breach of the RCCA's limited warranties and warranty of habitability expired with the RCCA on September 1, 2009.

The one-year, two-year and 10-year implied warranties applied to residential construction through August 31, 2010, even though the RCCA expired effective September 1, 2009. *See* §12.04.4, *infra*.

§12.04.4 RCCA—2009 Sunset

The RCCA was enacted to be effective until September 1, 2009, unless continued in existence by a subsequent legislature. RCCA §401.006(repealed). What happened to the TRCC's limited warranties and building standards after September 1, 2009? The Texas Sunset Act provides that the rules and regulations promulgated by a state agency abolished by the Sunset Act in an odd-numbered year (*i.e.*, 2009) do not expire until the one year after the effective date of the agency's abolition. TEX. GOV'T CODE §325.017(a). Under this provision of the Sunset Act, the limited warranties and building standards adopted by the TRCC were therefore continued in effect for one year after September 1, 2009 and continued to apply to new home construction "commenced" prior to September 1, 2010. *Id.*

However, the statutory provisions of the RCCA—including the new statutory warranty of habitability and its supersession of the *Humber* warranties (*see* RCCA §430.006 (repealed)—were not extended by the Sunset Act. These statutory provisions expired, effective September 1, 2009. RCCA §401.006 (repealed). As of September 1, 2009, consumers can again use the DTPA to pursue a breach of one or more of the RCCA limited warranties. Homes constructed between September 1, 2009 and August 31, 2010 will come with the two *Humber* implied warranties, as well as the three RCCA implied warranties. And as of September 1, 2009, homeowners may once again be protected by the implied warranty that repair services were performed in a good and workmanlike manner in *Melody Home*.

§12.04.5 RCCA--Third-Party Warranty Companies

The RCCA's definition of "builder" included third-party warrantors and insurers. *See* RCCA §401.003(b)(repealed). The definition acknowledged the fact that many builders will attempt to meet their warranty obligations through a third-party warranty company. The company must have been approved by the Commission. *See* RCCA §430.008(repealed).

The third-party liability company could provide warranty standards in addition to the standards adopted by the Commission, but could not reduce the building and performance standards or the statutory limited warranty. *See* RCCA §430.010(repealed). However, the company was not required to provide a warranty of habitability. *Id.*

A builder who elected to provide a warranty through an approved third-party warranty company did not effectively transfer liability to the company unless the company agreed to perform the builder's obligations covered by the warranty *and* actually paid for or corrected any construction defects covered by the warranty. RCCA §430.009(repealed). In other words, if the third party warranty company failed to pay for or correct a construction defect, the builder remained responsible because the liability had not been successfully transferred. This protected the homeowner against the bankruptcy of the third-party warranty company, as happened with a nationwide company in the 1980s.

The RCCA gave the company all of the rights and obligations of the builder in connection with repair of construction defects. *Id.* By utilizing a third-party liability company, the builder could not avoid (and the company could not assume) liability for personal injuries or damage to personal property. And in instances where the company elected not to provide a warranty of habitability, the builder would obviously remain responsible under that warranty. *See* RCCA §430.010(repealed).

§12.05 Residential Construction Liability Act ("RCLA")

After home construction defect claims became a major source of litigation under the DTPA, homebuilders complained that the DTPA was being exploited by consumers to force cash settlements from builders without providing those builders with a reasonable opportunity to inspect the home and make or offer to make repairs in lieu of a cash settlement. In 1989, the Texas legislature enacted the Residential Construction Liability Act. TEX. PROP. CODE §27.001 *et seq.* (the "RCLA"). The RCLA prevails over the DTPA to the extent of any conflict between the two. RCLA §27.002(b). One purpose of the statute was to promote more non-monetary settlements between homeowners and contractors and to afford contractors the opportunity to repair their work in the face of dissatisfaction. *See In re Kimball Hill Homes Tex.*, 969 S.W.2d 522, 525 (Tex. App.—Houston [14th Dist.] 1998, orig. proceeding); *Bruce v. Jim Walters Homes, Inc.*, 943 S.W.2d 121, 123 (Tex. App.—Fort Worth 1997, writ denied). Another purpose of the statute was to create special defenses for homebuilders in order to limit their liability to consumers for residential construction defects. *See generally*, Whiteley, *The Scope of the Residential Construction Liability Act in Texas*, 36 HOUS. L. REV. 277, 279 (1999). Significantly, the RCLA supplants the DTPA pre-suit notice and settlement provisions in construction defect liability cases and provides its own statutory notice and offer of settlement scheme. RCLA §27.004. The RCLA also provides limitations on the damages recoverable in construction defect claims. RCLA §§27.003, 27.004.

The RCLA does not create a cause of action, but rather limits and controls existing causes of action as they apply to residential home construction. *See Sanders v. Construction Equity, Inc,* 42 S.W.3d 364 (Tex. App.—Beaumont 2001) *reh. overruled,* 45 S.W.3d 802 (2001, pet. denied). The statute applies to all cases involving defects in residential construction, whether or not the statute is raised or even mentioned in the plaintiff's pleadings. *In re Kimball Hill Homes, Texas, Inc.*, 969 S.W.2d 522, 526 (Tex. App.—Houston [14th Dist.] 1998, no writ). Even so, the RCLA does not preempt remedies available through the DTPA, and DTPA remedies remain viable and available to the homeowner after complying with the RCLA. *Gentry v. Squires*

Const., Inc., 188 S.W.3d 396, 405 (Tex. App.—Dallas 2006, no writ).

The RCLA does not apply to disputes arising out of fraud in a real estate transaction, a builder's wrongful abandonment of a project prior to completion, or misapplication of construction trust funds. RCLA §27.002(d).

§12.05.1 RCLA—Definitions and Scope of Coverage

The RCLA broadly applies to any action to recover economic damages arising out of a residential construction defect. RCLA §27.002(a). The RCLA applies to all types of residential housing, including a single family house, duplex, triplex, quadruplex or condominium unit. RCLA §27.001(7).

"Construction defect" is broadly defined to include not only the design, construction, or repair of a new residence, but also the alteration of or repair or addition to an existing residence. RCLA §27.001(4). Thus, a foundation repair company's installation of piers beneath a slab is an "alteration of" an existing residence which falls within the coverage of the RCLA. *O'Donnell v. Roger Bullivant of Texas, Inc.*, 940 S.W.2d 411, 417 (Tex. App.—Fort Worth 1997, writ denied).

The RCLA covers all claims for residential construction defects against a "contractor." RCLA §27.001(4). The term "contractor" is defined broadly to include traditional builders and general contractors as well as many persons who never lift a hammer and drive a nail, such as any owner, officer, director, shareholder, partner, or employee of the contractor; and any insurer that insures all or any part of a contractor's liability for the cost to repair a residential construction defect. RCLA §27.001(5).

§12.05.2 RCLA—Affirmative Defenses Available to Contractor

As originally enacted, one of the hallmark benefits to a consumer under the DTPA was that common law defenses simply did not apply. *Smith v. Baldwin*, 611 S.W.2d 611, 616 (Tex. 1980). It was recognized that such defenses were unnecessarily burdensome and restrictive on DTPA consumers and that the Texas legislature provided the provision of the DTPA to consumers in order to obtain relief in lieu of the traditional tort and contract remedial schemes. *Smith v. Baldwin*, 611 S.W.2d 616; *Alvarado v. Bolton*, 749 S.W.2d 47, 48 (Tex. 1988). The 1989 enactment of the RCLA represented a substantial departure from this rule of consumer litigation.

As a result of the enactment of the RCLA and subsequent amendments, any DTPA lawsuit, or any lawsuit brought under any other theory for residential construction defects, is now subject to the affirmative defenses contained in the RCLA. Specific affirmative defenses have been incorporated into the RCLA which were previously unknown at common law, and which normally would arise only in arguments about causation. Under the RCLA, a contractor is not liable for normal wear, tear and deterioration, damages caused by the contributory negligence of another person other than the contractor, failure to mitigate the damages, normal shrinkage due to drying or settlement of construction components, or the contractor's good faith reliance on written information obtained from a third party. RCLA §27.003(a).

In addition, the RCLA has its own provision dealing with frivolous suits under which a defendant can recover attorney's fees and costs. RCLA §27.0031.

§12.05.3 RCLA—Notice and Offer of Settlement Provisions

Building contractors are accustomed to having the opportunity to correct minor construction defects or warranty items after receiving notice without further charge. The DTPA, however, does not provide incentives for either the homeowner to allow repairs or for the contractor to perform repairs without charge. Rather, the DTPA only contemplates monetary demands and monetary offers of settlement. *See* §3.02, *supra*, one of the main purposes of the RCLA is to modify these notice and settlement provisions to promote resolution of homeowner complaints through prompt, corrective action, whether performed by the contractor himself or by another tradesman. *See In re Kimball Hill Homes Tex.*, 969 S.W.2d 522, 525 (Tex. App.—Houston [14th Dist.] 1998, orig. proceeding); *Bruce v. Jim Walters Homes, Inc.*, 943 S.W.2d 121, 123 (Tex. App.—Fort Worth 1997, writ denied).

The RCLA requires that a person seeking to recover damages from a residential construction defect provide pre-suit notice as follows:

> "before the 60th day preceding the date a claimant seeking from a contractor damages or other relief arising from a construction defect initiates an action, the claimant shall give written notice by certified mail, return receipt requested, to the contractor, at the contractor's last known address, specifying in reasonable detail the construction defects that are the subject of the complaint . . . ."

RCLA §27.004(a). Notice must be given prior to filing suit *or* initiating arbitration. *See* RCLA §27.001(1).

The RCLA notice provisions prevail over the DTPA which requires the pre-suit notice letter to state dollar amounts for economic losses, mental anguish, expenses and attorney's fees claimed. DTPA §17.505(a). The RCLA only requires "reasonable detail" of the "construction defects." However, in most cases, the construction defect claim will be asserted under the DTPA; therefore, all of the elements necessary in a DTPA notice letter normally should be included in a notice given under the RCLA, including monetary amounts for damages and attorney's fees incurred.

The RCLA contains additional notice requirements not found in the DTPA. If requested by the contractor, the claimant must provide "any evidence that depicts the nature and cause of the defect and the nature and extent of repairs necessary to remedy the defect, including expert reports, photographs, and videotapes, if that evidence would be discoverable under Rule 192 of the Texas Rules of Civil Procedure." RCLA §27.004(a). This pre-suit discovery provision in the RCLA is one-sided: there is no similar provision giving a claimant the right to examine evidence in the possession of the contractor either before or after a notice letter is sent. All of the claimant's discovery must wait until a lawsuit is filed.

During the 35-day period after the contractor receives notice of the claim, and if requested in writing, the claimant must give the contractor a reasonable opportunity to inspect and document the construction defects. RCLA §27.004(a).

Within 45 days after the contractor receives notice of the claim, the contractor may make a "written offer of settlement" to the claimant. RCLA §27.004(b). The offer must be sent to the claimant's "last known address" or to the claimant's attorney; and, as with the claimant's notice letter, the offer must be sent by certified mail, return receipt requested. RCLA §27.004(b).

The RCLA offer of settlement "may include either an agreement by the contractor to repair or to have repaired by an independent contractor partially or totally at the contractor's expense or at a reduced rate to the claimant any construction defect described in the notice," and, in that event, must include a statement "in reasonable detail" of the kind of repairs which would be made. RCLA §27.004(b). Alternatively, the contractor can make a monetary settlement offer or an offer to purchase the residence. RCLA §27.004(n).

Although the RCLA requires the offer to be made not later than the 45th day after receipt of the notice of the claim, if the notice letter expressly gives the contractor a longer period of time within which to make the offer, then the contractor can make the offer within the extended period and the offer will be considered timely. *O'Donnell v. Roger Bullivant of Texas, Inc.*, 940 S.W.2d 411, 419 (Tex. App.—Fort Worth 1997, writ denied).

A claimant then has 25 days after receipt of the contractor's repair offer, to accept the offer or the offer is deemed rejected. RCLA §27.004(i). However, the homeowner cannot simply reject the offer without further consequence. The RCLA places an additional obligation on the homeowner to advise the contractor as to why the offer was not acceptable and provide the contractor still another opportunity to make a settlement offer.

RCLA §27.004(b). The penalty for noncompliance is automatic abatement upon a properly filed motion. RCLA §27.004(d).

If repairs are to be made, they must be completed not later than the 45th day after the date the contractor receives written notice of the claimant's acceptance of the offer of repair. RCLA §27.004(b).

The following tables set forth the applicable time periods which govern the notice and offer of settlement provisions of the Residential Construction Liability Act:

TIME FOR NOTICE AND SETTLEMENT OFFERS UNDER RCLA

1. 60 days before suit is filed (or arbitration initiated)	• Written notice sent certified mail, return receipt requested to contractor at last known address • Specifying in reasonable detail • All construction defects
2. Any time	• Contractor can request, and claimant shall provide, any evidence discoverable pursuant to Rule 192 depicting construction defects
3. 35 days after receipt of Step 1 notice letter	• Contractor can request in writing to inspect the property to document construction defect(s)
4. 45 days after receipt of Step 1 notice letter	• Written offer of settlement, may include either: • Agreement to repair defect, or • Agreement to pay for repair of defect, and • Describe in detail repairs being offered; or • A monetary offer, or • An offer to re-purchase the residence
5. 60 days after Step 1	• Suit can be filed

6. 25 days after receipt of Step 4 settlement offer	• Claimant shall advise contractor in writing and in detail why offer is not acceptable
7. 10 days after receipt of Step 6 rejection explanation	• Contractor may make a supplemental written offer of settlement
8. 45 days after receipt of written acceptance of offer to repair	• Contractor makes all accepted repairs

§12.05.4 RCLA—Consequences of Failing to Provide Inspection or to Accept a Settlement Offer

Under the RCLA, if a claimant fails to allow a contractor an opportunity to inspect the construction defect or rejects a reasonable settlement offer, then the claimant's recovery in any subsequent litigation cannot exceed:

(a) the fair market value of the contractor's settlement offer, or

(b) the amount of a reasonable monetary settlement or purchase offer made under RCLA 27.004(n). Then, like the DTPA, attorney's fees will be limited to the amount of reasonable and necessary costs and attorney's fees incurred before the offer was considered rejected.

RCLA §27.004(e). The reasonableness of any settlement offer is a fact question for the jury or other trier of fact. RCLA §27.004(j).

It has been held that an offer to repair is reasonable only if it will, in fact, repair the construction defect. *O'Donnell v. Roger Bullivant of Texas, Inc.*, 940 S.W.2d 411, 419-420 (Tex. App.—Fort Worth 1997, writ denied). Under the logic of *O'Donnell*, a monetary offer which is inadequate to pay for repairs that will actually repair the construction defect is not reasonable.

§12.05.5 RCLA—Consequences of Failing to Make Reasonable Settlement Offer or Initiate Repairs

If a contractor fails to make a reasonable settlement offer after receipt of a proper notice letter, the contractor merely loses the settlement offer defense limiting the damages and attorney's fees recoverable. RCLA §27.004(f). In practice, there is no statutory penalty to the contractor for failing to make a reasonable offer. If a contractor fails to make a pre-suit settlement offer, then the damage limitations based upon a reasonable settlement offer would not apply in any event. The limitations on damages in RCLA §27.004(e) only apply when a claimant rejects a reasonable offer or refuses to permit performance of an accepted offer. Under the RCLA, the homeowner's remedies will be curtailed for his failure to permit a pre-suit inspection, accept a reasonable offer or explain the deficiencies of an unreasonable settlement offer, but the contractor suffers no penalty for failing to make a reasonable settlement offer.

If the consumer accepts the contractor's written offer to make repairs and the contractor then refuses to initiate repairs, the RCLA's limitations on damages will not apply. RCLA

§27.004(q). This provision only applies when the contractor refuses to *initiate* repairs after the homeowner accepts his offer. The choice of language suggests that if a contractor (1) initiates repairs, but does not complete them, or (2) completes the repairs, but does not do so in a good and workmanlike manner, then the limitations on damages would still apply.

§12.05.6 RCLA—When Pre-Filing Notice Is Not Required

Pre-filing notice is not required in two circumstances: (1) when the statute of limitations will expire during the notice period, or (2) when the claim is asserted as a counterclaim in a suit against the claimant by the contractor. RCLA §27.004(c). In these circumstances, however, the suit or counterclaim must specify in "reasonable detail" each of the construction defects on which the claim is based. RCLA §27.004(c). Upon written request, the contractor shall be given a reasonable opportunity to inspect the construction defects during the 75-day period after the suit, counterclaim or request for arbitration is served. RCLA §27.004(c). Additionally, under these circumstances the contractor has 60 days to make a §27.004(b) offer of settlement. *Id.*

The RCLA further provides that,

> "If, while a suit subject to this chapter is pending, the statute of limitations for the cause of action would have expired and it is determined that the provisions of Subsection (a) [relating to pre-suit notice] were not properly followed, the action shall be abated to allow compliance with Subsections (a) and (b) [relating to making an offer to repair]."

RCLA §27.004(c). Together with subsection (d) concerning mandatory abatement, this provision provides added protection for a contractor when an action is filed without pre-suit notice being given. At any time during the pendency of the action, a contractor can obtain an abatement to require that pre-suit notice and offer to repair procedures be followed.

§12.05.7 RCLA—Abatement for Failure to Give Pre-Suit Notice

The RCLA Act provides that if a person failed to give notice in advance of filing a lawsuit involving residential construction, on a motion by the defendant, the court shall abate the lawsuit if, after a hearing, the court finds that either the contractor was not given notice or the contractor was denied a reasonable opportunity to repair the construction defects. RCLA §27.004(d). Like the DTPA, the abatement can be invoked automatically, without a hearing, with a properly verified plea in abatement. RCLA §27.004(d); *see* §6.01.1, *supra.* A form for a verified plea in abatement under the RCLA can be found in §12.05.05, *infra.*

§12.05.8 RCLA—Limitations on Damages

The RCLA places limitations on the type and amount of damages that can be recovered in residential construction defect cases against contractors. In such cases, a claimant's recovery is limited to the following "economic" damages "proximately caused" by a construction defect:

(1) the reasonable cost of repairs necessary to cure any construction defect;

(2) the reasonable and necessary cost for the replacement or repair of any damaged goods in the residence;

(3) reasonable and necessary engineering and consulting fees;

(4) the reasonable expenses of temporary housing reasonably necessary during the repair period;

(5) the reduction in current market value, if any, after the construction defect is repaired if the construction defect is a structural failure; and

(6) reasonable and necessary attorney's fees.

RCLA §27.004(g).

The reference to the term "economic damages" reinforces the legislature's intent to limit claimants to the damages enumerated in RCLA §27.004(g). "Economic damages" is elsewhere defined as:

> "compensatory damages for pecuniary loss proximately caused by a construction defect. The term does not include exemplary damages or damages for physical pain and mental anguish, loss of consortium, disfigurement, physical impairment, or loss of companionship and society."

RCLA §27.001(6).

The RCLA does not apply to cases of fraud or where the contractor wrongfully abandons the construction project. In those cases, the RCLA will not act to restrict the damages, including exemplary damages, that may be recovered. *Bruce v. Jim Walters Homes, Inc.*, 943 S.W.2d 121, 123 (Tex. App.—San Antonio 1997, writ denied).

The RCLA allows a contractor to enter an agreement to buy back the residence at fair market value if the repairs needed exceed a certain percentage if its fair market value without defects. RCLA §27.0042. This election is not permitted if the home is more than 5 years old. If the contractor elects to purchase the residence the contractor must pay the original purchase price of the residence, closing costs, moving costs, reasonable attorney's fees and must reimburse the owner for permanent improvements made to the residence by the owner. RCLA §27.0042(c). This section further provides that an offer to purchase that complies with the statue is "considered reasonable absent clear and convincing evidence to the contrary." *See* RCLA §27.0042(d).

§12.06 Forms

The following forms have been developed for use in prosecuting or defending claims concerning residential construction defects made by consumers who desire or intend to invoke the provisions of the DTPA. Special care must be taken to comply with the provisions of the RCLA and, to the extent of any linger application, the limited warranty provisions and building standards promulgated pursuant to the now repealed RCCA.

§12.06.1 Checklists for Initial Interview

[a] CHECKLIST: Purchase of new residence (Plaintiff)

Client _____ Date of Interview _____

The property

☐ Location of property: Lot and block number; street address

☐ Tract house or custom home

    — If custom home, did client provide plans and specifications to builder?

[If client provided plans for house, then it will be necessary to determine whether defects are due to faulty design or construction or both.]

☐ Who is the seller?

The contract/representations

☐ When was the earnest money contract signed?

☐ Were any waivers contained in the contract?

☐ Who was the listing broker/agent?

☐ Who were the co-brokers/agents?

☐ Were any other licensed agents involved?

[If a licensed real estate agent or broker is involved, one source of recovering damages assessed against the agent or broker is the Real Estate Recovery Fund. *See* §13.02.7 *infra*.]

☐ Did contract permit/require property inspections; if yes, who inspected property?

[If property inspection was poorly performed and caused damages, one source of recovering damages assessed against the property inspector is the Real Estate Inspection Recovery Fund.]

☐ Was the seller also the builder?

☐ How much earnest money was paid?

☐ What representations were made about the house, by whom and when?

☐ Did client see advertising; if yes, where and when?

☐   Was client advised in writing that any information given to client was obtained from a third party?

[If information was obtained from third party, the person making the representation may have a defense under DTPA §17.506.]

Purchase information

☐   Date of closing and closing agent

☐   Purchase price

☐   Down payment

☐   Written warranties given

☐   HOW/HOME warranty given

☐   Did client receive a "Certificate of Participation" or other similar evidence of coverage?

[*See* Petition in §12.06.04, *infra*, for a review of the elements of a claim under a homeowner's warranty or insurance claim.]

☐   Who is the mortgage company?

☐   Type of mortgage: fixed or adjustable rate

☐   Interest rate/term of mortgage

☐   Monthly payments: how much principal, insurance, taxes

☐   Are payments current?

- If not, how delinquent?

- Have any demand letters, notice of acceleration, or notice of foreclosure been received?

[If client is delinquent, upon receipt of notice letter, the prospective defendant may file suit against client in an inconvenient forum. Consideration should thus be given to a "preemptive" common law action to fix venue and to insure that the client is the plaintiff.]

Construction

☐   When was the house built?

☐   Was house purchased (contract signed) before construction was complete?

☐   If construction was in progress,

- did client inspect property?

- did any person inspect property with or on behalf of client?

- what defects, if any, were noticed during construction?

☐ Were there any delays in construction: weather, strike, etc.?

☐ Who were the subcontractors on the job?

[If a list of subcontractors was not provided by the builder, one should be requested from the builder since subcontractors who actually did the faulty work may be equally liable to the plaintiff.]

☐ Improvements made by client: description, value

Construction defects in house

☐ When were the defects first noticed?

[The discovery rule will avoid the statute of limitations only if the client exercised "reasonable diligence." See DTPA §17.565.]

☐ How were the defects noticed, *e.g.*, did client simply see them or was there some event that prompted an investigation of problems in the house?

☐ What are *all* of the defects/symptoms of defects?

[TEX. PROP. CODE §27.004(a) suggests the need to include *all* defects in the notice letter to insure that damages can be recovered for all of the defects.]

☐ What are the workmanship and materials defects (one-year warranty)

☐ What are the defects in the plumbing, electrical, heating and air-conditioning delivery systems (two-year warranty)

☐ What are the defects in the foundations and major structural components (10-year warranty)

Notice of defects to builder

☐ Has builder been notified of defects in writing?

☐ Have defects been discussed verbally with builder; if so, when?

- ☐ Has builder inspected property?
- ☐ What was builder's response to the notice of defects?
- ☐ Did builder make an offer to repair or pay for repairs; if so,
    - Was the offer sufficiently detailed?
    - Has an independent expert examined the offer?
    - Will offered repairs cure the defect(s)?

[The offer to repair should be compared to the requirements of Tex. Prop. Code 27.004(b).]

- ☐ Did the client request an SIRP for the Residential Construction Commission?
- ☐ Was an SIRP inspection performed or scheduled?
- ☐ Has an SIRP report been issued?
- ☐ Has an SIRP appeal been commenced?

[See §12.04, *supra*, regarding any continued applicability of the Texas Residential Construction Commission Act.]

Repairs made

- ☐ Have any repairs been made; if so, by whom?
- ☐ Were repairs effective?
- ☐ Who paid for repairs?

Expectations of client

- ☐ What does client expect to accomplish through litigation?

Explanations to client

- ☐ Anticipated cost of litigation
- ☐ Attorney-client agreement
- ☐ Requirements of discovery; assistance with case
- ☐ Required attendance at depositions, trial
- ☐ Outcome of litigation is unpredictable

Documents to obtain from client

[Client should be advised to bring all documents that in any way relate to transaction; however, the following list is illustrative of the type of documents that must be provided if they exist.]

- ☐ Advertising seen
- ☐ Point of sale brochure and documents
- ☐ Earnest money contract
- ☐ Surveys of land
- ☐ Warranties, warranty brochures, certificate of participation
- ☐ Deed, deed of trust
- ☐ Any documents provided to or signed by client in connection with sale
- ☐ Closing statement
- ☐ Letters to or from anyone involved in transaction
- ☐ Report of experts
- ☐ All documents reflecting losses from transaction
- ☐ Repair estimates or invoices
- ☐ SIRP Reports or correspondence with TRCC

[b]　CHECKLIST: Sale of new residence (Defendant)

Client _____   Date of interview _____

Litigation

- ☐ Has a lawsuit been filed?
- ☐ If a lawsuit has been filed, what is the answer date?

The notice letter

- ☐ When was notice letter received?
- ☐ When is a response to the notice letter due?

☐ Does the notice letter contain sufficient information so that the claim can be evaluated; if not, what additional information is needed?

The property

☐ Legal description of property

☐ Street address of property

☐ Is this a custom home?

☐ If house was custom built, did the buyer provide plans and specifications to client?

[If buyer provided plans and specifications, the buyer's architect or engineer may be subject to a cross-action, and the client may have a defense to liability.]

Architects/Engineers

☐ Who drew the plans and wrote the specifications?

☐ Was a contract entered into between client and an architect/engineer?

[The standard AIA agreement contains an arbitration clause as well as numerous disclaimers of liability and some helpful language on the quality of services to be provided.]

☐ How much was paid to the architect/engineer?

☐ Did the architect/engineer supervise any aspect of the construction?

☐ Has the architect/engineer examined the house since construction to verify the existence of defects and to determine the cause?

☐ Has the architect/engineer provided any written reports on the construction?

The contract, representations

☐ When was the earnest money contract signed?

☐ How much earnest money was paid?

☐ Were any waivers contained in the contract?

☐ Who was the listing broker/agent?

☐ Who were the co-brokers, co-agents?

☐ Were any other licensed real estate brokers or agents involved in the transaction?

☐ Did the contract require/permit inspections of the property?

- If yes, who inspected the property and what was the result of the inspection?

[Real estate inspectors are licensed by the state and on occasion carry insurance to cover errors and omissions.]

☐ Was the client both the builder and the seller?

- If no, who was the seller and who was the builder?

[Depending on whether client was the builder or seller, a cause of action for contribution or indemnity may exist. See DTPA §17.555.]

☐ What representations were made to the buyer about the house (e.g., what was said, by whom, and when)?

☐ Did the buyer see a model home before purchase?

[A model home may create an express warranty that the house will conform to the model.]

☐ Did client use advertising to sell the house (either media or point of sale brochures)?

- If yes, when and where?

☐ Was the buyer advised in writing that any of the information given to him or her was obtained from third parties?

[If a person is given written notice that information used in a sales presentation was obtained from third parties, then a possible DTPA defense to liability exists. See DTPA §17.506.]

The purchase

☐ Date and place of closing

☐ Sales price

☐ Were any written warranties provided?

☐ Were any discounts given off of the sales price as compensation for any defects in house?

☐ Were any written warranties provided?

Construction

☐ When was construction of the house completed?

☐ Was house purchased before construction was completed?

☐ Were any defects in or problems with construction brought to client's attention during construction?

☐ Who were the subcontractors on the job and what specific work did each subcontractor perform?

Defects in house

☐ What are all of the known defects in the house?

☐ When were defects first noticed?

☐ How were defects first noticed?

Notice of defects to client

☐ Has client been notified by buyer in writing of defects?

[TEX. PROP. CODE §27.004(a) requires notice to the prospective defendant of all defects in the house.]

☐ Have the defects been discussed orally by buyer with client?

☐ What was client's response?

☐ Has client inspected the defects?

☐ Has a claim been made on the warranty?

– If yes, when, how and to whom was the claim made?

– What was the response?

☐ Is there an insurance policy issued by Home Owners Warranty Corporation or some similar company that may apply to the claimed defects in the house?

Repairs made

☐ Has the client offered to make any repairs?

– If yes, how was the offer made and what was included?

☐ Have any repairs been made?

- If yes, were the repairs effective?
- What was repaired and by whom?
- Who paid for the repairs?

Explanations to client

☐ Anticipated cost of litigation

☐ Attorney and client agreement

☐ Requirements of discovery, assistance with case

☐ Required attendance at depositions and trial

☐ Outcome of litigation is unpredictable

Documents to obtain from client

[Although client should be cautioned to provide *all* documents to the attorney that are, in any way, related to the transaction and its aftermath, the following documents *must* be obtained immediately.]

☐ All advertising and brochures on the house

☐ All construction plans and specifications

☐ Earnest money contract

☐ Inspection reports

☐ Closing statement

☐ Any document signed by client in connection with sale

☐ All warranties given on house

☐ Letters to client

☐ Letters from client

☐ Letters/claims filed on warranty or insurance policy

☐ Response to warranty or insurance claims

☐ Photographs

☐ Cost of repair estimates, reports of experts

☐ Home warranty documents provided by any third party warranty or insurance company

§12.06.2 Pre-Suit Notice Letters in Residential Construction Cases

The pre-suit notice procedures specified in the RCLA, discussed §12.05.3, *supra*, must be followed before initiating legal proceedings against a contractor. Like the DTPA, the RCLA requires that pre-suit notice be given at least 60 days before initiating suit unless excused. The RCLA notice must provide reasonable detail of the construction defect(s) alleged. RCLA pre-suit notice must be sent certified mail, return receipt requested, to the contractor's last known address. RCLA §27.004(a). In addition, to comply with the pre-suit requirements of the DTPA, the pre-suit notice must describe the consumer's specific complaint in reasonable detail and provide amounts claimed for economic damages, mental anguish and expenses incurred, including attorney's fees, if any. *See* §§3.01 *et seq., supra.*

The following forms provide examples of pre-suit notice letters designed to comply with both the DTPA and the RCLA where applicable.

[a] FORM: Notice letter to builder/seller

CERTIFIED MAIL, RETURN RECEIPT REQUESTED

(Date)
(Inside address)

Re: (Client's name)

Dear _____:

[Notice of representation.]

Our firm has [*or* I have] been retained to represent _____ with respect to a claim which he [she] has against you. Please direct all communications concerning this matter to me.

[Notice of claim.]

On or about __, 20__, our client purchased a house from you which is located at __.

[Written warranty:]

At the time our client purchased the house, a written warranty was provided by you [*insert general terms of warranty, e.g.*] under which you promised to repair any defects in materials or workmanship during the first year of ownership.

[Implied warranties under RCCA and common law, as applicable:]

Certain implied warranties arose as a matter of law when the house was sold. These warranties include a one-year warranty for workmanship and materials, a two-year warranty for plumbing, electrical, heating and air-conditioning delivery systems, and a ten-year warranty for structural components of the house.

In addition, at the time the house was sold, an implied warranty of habitability arose. Because of the defects listed below, [and other defects that our client suspects may exist in the house but cannot yet determine], the [written and] implied warranties were breached.

Among the defects in the construction of the house are the following:

[Insert detailed list of defects, e.g.]

The foundation of the house has failed in that there are cracks through the slab and beam in the living room, kitchen and master bedroom areas, at least. In addition to violating the warranty of workmanship, the foundation failure has had a direct, adverse effect on the habitable areas of the house. Further, this condition was not discoverable by a reasonably prudent inspection.

Much of the sheetrock in the living room, kitchen and master bedroom areas has cracked, as well as other hard surfaces.

The doors and windows in the areas affected by the foundation cracks do not open and close as they should.

[Note: RCLA §27.004(a) requires the disclosure, if requested by the contractor, of expert reports, photographs and other discoverable evidence depicting the nature of the defect and extent of repairs necessary; therefore, consider enclosing them with the demand letter with a variation of the following, if available: Enclosed is a copy of the engineering report obtained describing the defects observed, an estimate of the cost to perform the work necessary to correct these defects and/or photographs which show the defects listed above.]

Each of these defects was latent in that none of them were visible to us at the time the house was purchased.

Because of the defects in our client's house, our client has suffered very serious damages. The elements of our client's damages include, but are not necessarily limited to, the following elements:

(1) The cost to repair the defects.

(2) The decreased value of the house as a result of the defects in construction, a portion of which decrease will remain even after repairs are completed.

(3) The cost of substitute housing while repairs are being made.

(4) Engineering and other expert costs associated with evaluating and making the necessary repairs.

[If a suit is to be filed under the DTPA, the notice letter should include the following detail concerning the amount of damages:]

Because of the breach of warranties described above, our client's damages are as follows:

Economic damages, as described above:	$_____.
Mental anguish damages:	$_____.
Expenses incurred and to be incurred:	$_____.
Attorney's fees:	$_____.

[NOTE: Under the DTPA, a notice letter must include a statement of the consumer's damages, separately stating the amount of economic losses and the amount of mental anguish damages. See DTPA §17.505(a).]

[Notice of statutory violations.]

It is our contention that your conduct constitutes [*insert appropriate statutory language, e.g.,* false, misleading and deceptive acts in violation of §17.46(b)(5) of the Texas Deceptive Trade Practices—Consumer Protection Act].

[Descriptions of elements of damages, *see §1.02.14, supra.]*

[Statement of damages and expenses sought.]

Based upon the information now available to us, and for purposes of this notice letter, we estimate that the amounts reasonably necessary to compensate our client for her damages are as follows:

Economic losses:	$_____.
Mental anguish:	$_____.
Expenses, including attorney's fees:	$_____.

Of course, we reserve the right to adjust these amounts to conform to the information and additional evidence that will be available to us at the time of trial should litigation be necessary.

[Alternate statement of attorney's fees.]

Our client has incurred reasonable and necessary attorney's fees in the pursuit of the claim stated in this letter. The amount of fees incurred as of the date of this letter is $_____.

[**Notice of contingent interest.**]

Under the contract of employment we have with our client, our firm has [*or* I have] been assigned an interest in the claim against you.

[**Offer of settlement.**]

The purpose of this letter is to encourage you to resolve our client's claim in a fair and equitable manner without the need for further legal action. In the event you fail to take advantage of this opportunity to settle these claims without litigation, we [*or* I] will have no alternative but to recommend to our client that a lawsuit be filed against you under the Deceptive Trade Practices—Consumer Protection Act. In this lawsuit, rather than seeking only the amount of compensation we are asking of you at this time, we will seek to recover the full measure of damages to which our client is legally entitled as well as our client's expenses and attorney's fees as allowed by law.

[**Notice to insurance carrier.**]

In the event that you have insurance or a bond which you believe may cover all or any part of the claim made in this letter, you are requested to notify your insurance carrier or bonding company immediately.

[**Request for response.**]

If you are interested in resolving this matter without the necessity of litigation, please contact me within sixty days of your receipt of this letter.

Sincerely,

_____
[Signature of attorney]

[b] FORM: Notice letter to engineer, architect

[NOTE: Because of the "professional services" exemption in the DTPA, the following letter assumes that the claim against the engineer/architect is excluded from the DTPA. The facts giving rise to the claim should be examined closely to determine whether any of the exceptions to the professional services exclusion apply, in which case the requisite elements of the DTPA notice letter should be used. See generally § 2.02.2 supra.]

CERTIFIED MAIL, RETURN RECEIPT REQUESTED

[Date]

[Inside address]

Re: [Client's name]

Dear _____:

Our firm has [or I have] been retained to represent _____ in a claim which our client has against you. Please direct all communications concerning this claim to me.

On or about _____, 20___, our client purchased a house from _____. The house is located at _____.

It is our understanding that you provided engineering [architectural] services in connection with the construction of the house.

Our client has observed the following defects in the house since moving in:

[insert detailed list of defects, e.g.]

1. The foundation of the house has failed in that there are cracks through the slab and beam in the living room, kitchen and master bedroom areas, at least.

2. Much of the sheetrock in the living room, kitchen and master bedroom areas has cracked, as well as other hard surfaces that are clearly visible on inspection.

3. The doors and windows in the areas affected by the foundation cracks do not open and close as they should.

[Enclosed are photographs which show some of the defects listed above].

It is our client's contention that [*insert specific contention, e.g.,* your design of the foundation of the house was done in a negligent manner, failing to take into account the type of soils on which the house was to be built]. As a result of this negligence, our client has suffered the following damages which are known at this time:

1. The cost to repair the defects.

2. The decreased value of the house as a result of the defects in construction, a portion of which decrease will remain even after repairs are completed.

3. The cost of substitute housing while repairs are being made.

4. Engineering and other expert costs associated with evaluating and making the necessary repairs.

The total economic loss suffered by our client is estimated at this time to be $_____. [*Insert statement for amount of mental anguish damages, if claimed.*] Of course, we reserve the right to adjust this amount as additional information becomes known.

[Enclosed is a report from_____, a licensed engineer [architect] which discusses the acts of negligence involved in your design of the house.]

In the event that you have insurance or a bond that you believe may cover all or any part of this claim, you are requested to notify your insurance carrier or bonding company immediately.

If you are interested in resolving this matter without the necessity of litigation, please contact me within sixty days of your receipt of this letter.

                                          Sincerely,

                              _____
                              [*Signature of attorney*]

[c] FORM: Notice letter on a home warranty claim

[NOTE: This form may be used to satisfy the notice requirements of Tex. Ins. Code Chapter 541 when insurance coverage has been denied under a homeowner's warranty program.]

[Insert the following at "notice of claim," §12.06.2[a] *supra*]

On _____, 20___, our client purchased a new house from _____. At the time of purchase, our client received a new home warranty, which bears the number _____, and an enrollment date of _____, 20_____. The performance of the warranty was and is insured by your company.

As you are aware, when our client discovered certain defects in the house, a claim was made to you concerning those defects. You denied the claim. The claim submitted to you included the following construction defects that are apparent in the house:

[insert detailed list of defects, e.g.]

1. The foundation of the house has failed in that there are cracks through the slab and beam in the living room, kitchen and master bedroom areas, at least.

2. Much of the sheetrock in the living room, kitchen and master bedroom areas has cracked, as well as other hard surfaces that are clearly visible on inspection.

3. The doors and windows in the areas affected by the foundation cracks do not open and close as they should.

[Enclosed are photographs which show some of the defects listed above].

It is our client's contention that your denial of the claim was a breach of the insurance contract as well as a breach of your duty to deal fairly and in good faith with our client. Your conduct also constitutes unfair claims settlement practices.

Because of the defects in our client's house, and your unwarranted denial of the claim, our client has suffered very serious damages. The elements of our client's damages include, but are not necessarily limited to, the following elements:

1. The cost to repair the defects.

2. The decreased value of the house as a result of the defects in construction, a portion of which decrease will remain even after repairs are completed.

3. The cost of substitute housing while repairs are being made.

4. Engineering and other expert costs associated with evaluating and making the necessary repairs.

[If a suit is to be filed under Chapter 541, the notice letter should include the following detail concerning the amount of damages:]

Because of the construction defects described above and your denial of the claim, we estimate that the amounts reasonably necessary to compensate our client for his damages are as follows:

A. Economic damages, as described above: $_____.

B. Mental anguish damages: $_____.

C. Expenses incurred and to be incurred: $_____.

D. Attorney's fees: $_____.

[NOTE: Under the DTPA, a notice letter must include a statement of the consumer's damages, separately stating the amount of economic losses and the amount of mental anguish damages. *See* DTPA §17.505(a)]

[Continue with form notice letter, §12.06.2[a] *supra*]

[d] FORM: Notice letter to real estate broker/agent

[NOTE: The DTPA now contains an exemption for licensed real estate agents when their representations are not fairly considered advice, judgment or opinion. *See* §2.02.3 *supra*. Clearly, there are certain services rendered by a real estate agent or broker that will fall within the exemption; however, when an agent or broker strays outside the area of his or her expertise, such as making factual representations about the condition of a house, then the exemption should not apply. The notice letter to the agent should be written so as to make it clear the representations fall outside of this limited exemption for real estate agents.]

[Insert the following at "notice of claim," §12.06.02[a], *supra*]

On _____, 20____ our client purchased a house located at [insert address of house].

Prior to our client's purchase of the house, you made several important representations to our client about the house. Among the representations made were the following: [*insert representations made, e.g.*, (1) there were no latent defects in the house, (2) the roof was water-tight, (3) the house had 2,400 square feet of heated and air-conditioned space, etc.].

After our client purchased the house and moved into it, our client discovered that the representations listed above were false. Instead of the house being as represented, our client discovered the following conditions which have resulted in serious damages being sustained: [*insert complete list of defects in the house, e.g.*, the foundation of the house has failed; the sheetrock on several walls has cracked, and, as a result of the failed foundation, insects now enter the house through the cracks in the floor, etc.]. Had our client known that the representations were false, and that the conditions listed above existed, he [she] would not have purchased the house.

Because of the condition of the house, our client has suffered damages which include the following: [*insert elements of damages. See* §1.02.14, *supra*].

§12.06.3 Responses to Residential Construction Notice Letter

The analysis of a DTPA notice letter involving residential construction is similar in some respects to that required for other DTPA notice letters. *See* Chapter 4, *supra*. In addition, however, residential construction claims must be viewed in light of the procedures and special rights provided by the RCLA. *See* §12.05.3, *supra*.

Upon receiving a notice letter involving residential construction, the contractor has 35 days to inspect the property and document the defect(s) claimed and to determine the nature and extent of any repairs necessary. This inspection must be arranged upon written request. The contractor should request this inspection as soon as possible after receiving the notice letter to avail itself of this right of inspection during this relatively narrow time frame.

In addition, the RCLA allows the contractor to request and obtain from the claimant any discoverable evidence—such as expert reports, photographs, video recordings and repair estimates—depicting the nature and cause of the defect.

Residential construction cases also are different from other DTPA or Insurance Code cases in that in nearly every case independent subcontractors performed some, if not all, of the actual construction from which the homeowner's claim arises. For this reason, depending on the parts of the house that are claimed to be defective, the client may have a statutory claim for indemnity against the subcontractor. *See* DTPA §17.555. Because of this claim, the subcontractor or his or her insurance carrier may have an interest in assisting the client to resolve the claim before a lawsuit is filed. Notice of the homeowner's claim should be given to each subcontractor involved in the alleged defective construction as soon as possible to encourage their participation in any pre-filing settlement that may be made.

A contractor has 45 days from the date of receiving a notice letter to make a written settlement offer to make repairs or arrange for another to make the necessary repairs. The written settlement offer must be sent to the claimant or his attorney by certified mail, return receipt requested. The offer to repair the defects must describe the repairs to be made in "reasonable detail." RCLA §27.004(b). The amount of detail in the letter should be sufficient to enable the consumer or another contractor to evaluate whether the repairs will be effective. The letter should be as detailed as possible to remove any question as to whether the letter satisfies the statute.

In those instances where the contractor concludes that some (or all) of the claimed "defects" are not actual defects, the response should explain in detail why the claim is rejected so as to demonstrate the contractor's good faith.

The contractor will have 45 days after acceptance of his offer to make the repairs stated and should prepare accordingly.

[a] FORM: Letter requesting opportunity to inspect and photograph defects

```
[Note: The following form is designed to invoke these rights for a contractor under the
RCLA. It should be sent as soon as possible—and no later than 35 days—after the receipt
of the notice letter.]
```

CERTIFIED MAIL, RETURN RECEIPT REQUESTED

(Date)

(Inside address)

Re: [Consumer's name]

Dear _____:

We have received the letter you recently sent to _____, our client.

As you know, our client has a limited period of time in which to respond to your letter. In order to provide us the opportunity to evaluate your client's claims, we request that our client [and his engineer] be allowed to inspect the claimed defects in the [house] and that he [they] be allowed to photograph or otherwise document any findings and observations about the defects.

So that we may have sufficient time to analyze the claims made in your letter in light of our own inspection of the property, we request your permission to inspect the property on [*insert date and time of inspection*]. If this date and time is inconvenient to you or your client, we will attempt to accommodate your schedule as best we can so long as our client can conduct the necessary inspection as quickly as possible.

Prior to this inspection, please provide to us any evidence that depicts the nature and cause of the defect(s) claimed and the nature and extent of the repairs necessary to remedy that/those defect(s), including, but limited to, any photographs, video recordings, repair estimates, engineering reports and/or repair estimates in your possession or subject to your control.

We will require a reasonable amount of time after the inspection to evaluate your client's claims. For this reason, if it is necessary to delay the inspection in order to fully comply with this request or to accommodate your schedules, we would appreciate your agreement to extend the time within which we are required to respond to your letter.

This request is made under the authority of §27.004(a) of the Texas Property Code. I look forward to your prompt response.

Sincerely,

_____
[Signature of attorney]

[b] FORM: Letter to builder analyzing the notice letter

[Note: This is a form for use by an attorney to advise a contractor of its inspection ad settlement offer rights under the RCLA.]

(Date)

(Inside address)

Re: [Consumer's name]

[Address of property]

Dear _____:

I have reviewed the enclosed letter from _____ regarding the alleged defects in the construction of the residence listed above.

As you may know, the Deceptive Trade Practices Act ("DTPA") and the Residential Construction Liability Act ("RCLA") require that a "notice" letter be sent to you to give you the opportunity to resolve the claim before a lawsuit is filed. We should take advantage of the advance notice to evaluate the claim and prepare a carefully considered response.

Under the RCLA, you have the right to inspect the residence to determine the nature and extent of the claimed defect and any repairs necessary to remedy that defect. This opportunity will expire 35 days after your receipt of the notice letter. In addition, you have the right to obtain any evidence that depicts the nature and cause of the defect(s) claimed and the nature and extent of the repairs necessary to remedy that/those defect(s), including, but limited to, any photographs, video recordings, repair estimates, engineering reports and/or repair estimates.

If your investigation reveals the claim has merit, it is very important to consider seriously making an offer to repair the defects or to pay for the repairs. Under the RCLA, you have the right to make an offer to repair the claimed defects or to arrange for another contractor or provider to make necessary repairs. Your right to make such an offer expires 45 days after your receipt of the notice letter.

If your offer of repair is reasonable but is nevertheless rejected, it can be used to limit the claimant's recovery to just the fair market value of the rejected settlement offer and to the amount of his/her attorney's fees incurred up to the point the offer was rejected. In a claim under the DTPA, where there is a potential for treble damages and where the recovery of attorney's fees incurred through trial and any appeals is mandatory, the ability to limit your exposure in this manner is a valuable right which you should not pass up lightly.

Within the next [two weeks], we need to *complete* all of the following:

1. Make demand for the claimant to produce to you any evidence that depicts the nature and cause of the defect(s) claimed and the nature and extent of the repairs necessary to remedy that/those defect(s), including, but limited to, any photographs, video recordings, repair estimates, engineering reports and/or repair estimates.

2. Inspect the claimed defects; determine whether the defects exist; and if so, the probable cause.

3. If the claim has no merit, decide whether you want to reject the claim outright or make some type of "nuisance value" offer in an effort to avoid the cost of going further.

4. If any of the claim has merit, decide whether you want to offer to make repairs, and if so how, or whether, you want to offer to pay for the repairs.

5. If you decide to offer to do the repair work, prepare a detailed repair plan, including specifications or drawings and other supporting information so we can demonstrate that the proposed repairs will be effective.

6. If you decide to offer to pay for the repairs, obtain at least two bids for the proposed work so we will have "independent" support for the amount of the offer.

7. Make a written response to the notice letter, which must be delivered to the other side no later than _____, 20__.

Once you have had a chance to consider the approach you want to pursue, please give me a call.

                        Sincerely,

                        _____

                        [Signature of attorney]

[c] FORM: Letter to subcontractor giving notice of claim

[Statutory reference: DTPA §17.555]

(Date)

(Inside address)

Re: [Consumer's name; address of property]

Dear _____:

Enclosed is a notice letter which was received by our client _____, on 20___. Our client must respond to this letter no later than 20___.

As you can see from the letter, the claim [or one of the claims] arises from alleged defects in the construction of the _____. Since your company [or you] was [were] primarily responsible for the actual construction of this part of the house, we would appreciate you looking into this claim as quickly as possible so we can have the benefit of your observations and opinions before we respond to the notice letter.

We have scheduled an inspection of the house on _____ 20_ at ___.m. If it is possible, we would appreciate you going with us on the inspection. If it is not possible for you to attend the inspection as scheduled, please let me know immediately and I will try to get the inspection rescheduled to a more convenient time.

Sincerely,

_____
[Signature of attorney]

[d] FORM: Offer of settlement: repair of construction defects

Statutory reference: RCLA §27.004(b).

CERTIFIED MAIL, RETURN RECEIPT REQUESTED

(Date)

(Inside Address)

Re: [Consumer's name]

Dear _____:

This is in response to your letter dated _____, 20___ We have evaluated your [client's] claims regarding alleged construction defects in [your client's] house.

In order to resolve [your client's] claims amicably, we agree to repair the following items in the manner described below: [*insert list of items to be repaired and proposed method of repairs, e.g.,*

(1) Claimed defect: cracks in foundation

Method of repair: 21 drilled concrete piers will be placed around the perimeter of the foundation on 8' centers to a depth of 16 feet. The piers will be 16" in diameter and will have bell shaped bottoms. The foundation will be leveled to a tolerance of a 1/4" drop in 4'; however, leveling activity will stop if the superstructure of the house shows any signs of distress. The foundation cracks will be seated with an epoxy compound.

(2) Claimed defect: Sheetrock cracks in living room, bedrooms and kitchen

Method of repair: The cracks will be taped and floated and the wall on which the cracks are located will be spot painted to match, as close as is reasonably possible, the adjoining surface].

[With respect to your [client's] claim that the _____ is in need of repair, we disagree. Our inspection of the _____ revealed that it was designed and constructed in compliance with industry standards and that the condition about which your client complains is the result of _____.] [*List and explain any other claimed defects that will not be repaired.*]

This offer is contingent on your client executing a full and final release in favor of our client.

The repairs described above will be completed within forty-five (45) days after we receive written notice of your acceptance of this settlement offer.

The offer contained in this letter is made for the sole purpose of avoiding further, unnecessary expense associated with your client's claim. The offer is not intended to be and should not be considered by you or your client to be an admission of liability for your client's claim.

If you have any questions about this offer or need additional information, please contact me.

Sincerely,

_____
[Signature of attorney]

[e] FORM: Offer of settlement: pay for repairs

CERTIFIED MAIL, RETURN RECEIPT REQUESTED

(Date)

(Inside address)

Re: [Consumer's name]

Dear _____:

This is in response to your letter dated _____, 20___.

We have evaluated your [client's] claim regarding alleged construction defects in your [client's] house.

In order to resolve your [client's] claims amicably, we offer to pay the cost to repair up to a maximum of $_____ to a contractor of your choice. The funds will be paid on draw request which certify that the amount of work completed is the same as the percentage of the draw requested. Our client will expect both the contractor and your client to certify to us the percentage of the work completed each time a draw is requested. The repairs described above will be completed within forty-five (45) days after we receive written notice of your acceptance of this settlement offer.

As an alternative to paying for the work based on draw requests, we offer to pay to your client $_____ immediately.

These alternative offers are contingent on your client executing a full and final release in favor of our client.

If you have any questions about this offer or need additional information, please contact me.

The offer contained in this letter is made for the sole purpose of avoiding further unnecessary expense associated with your client's claim. The offer is not intended to be and should not be considered by you or your client to be an admission of liability for your client's claim.

Sincerely,

_____
[Signature of attorney]

§12.06.4 Petitions

In lawsuits involving new home construction, there normally will be the potential for multiple defendants. The builder/seller of the house is an obvious defendant. Additionally, however, many builders offer homebuyers long-term insurance protection through one of the companies that sell such programs. The form petition involves a new house; it assumes that the construction is defective and that the insurer providing the long-term warranty/insurance coverage has denied the claim. The form also assumes that the builder has failed to make an offer to repair the construction defects as provided in RCLA §27.004. The form also assumes that the RCCA warranties and building standards apply. When pleading the warranty applicable to the house, the language should track the statutory warranties that exist. See §12.04.3, *supra*.

In a suit for damages, a homeowner must file the petition on or before the expiration of any applicable statute of limitations. Caution must be taken to determine the applicable limitations deadline and suit filed accordingly.

[a] FORM: New house purchased from builder/seller (RCCA warranties)

[Note: The bracketed language in the form petition which follows contains terms of art used in some of the long-term warranty and insurance documents. These terms are illustrative only and care should be taken to conform the petition to the terms actually employed in the documents.]

NO. _____

_____	§	IN THE DISTRICT COURT OF
	§	
vs.	§	_____ COUNTY, TEXAS
	§	
_____	§	_____ JUDICIAL DISTRICT

PLAINTIFF'S ORIGINAL PETITION

NOW COMES _____, Plaintiff herein, complaining of _____, Defendant herein, and for cause of action, would show unto the Court as follows:

I. DISCOVERY CONTROL PLAN DESIGNATION

1.01 By this action, Plaintiff seeks _____ [insert appropriate designation under Rule 47(c), e.g., only monetary relief of $100,000 or less, including damages of any kind, penalties, costs, expenses, prejudgment interest, and attorney's fees]. The damages sought are within the jurisdictional limits of this court.

1.01 Discovery in this case is intended to be conducted under Level _____, pursuant to Rule 190._____, *Texas Rules of Civil Procedure*.

II. PARTIES

2.01 _____ is a resident of _____, _____ County, Texas.

2.02 _____ is a Texas corporation which may be served with process by serving _____, its registered agent, at _____, the corporation's registered address.

III. VENUE

3.01 Venue of this action is proper in _____ County, Texas because _____ reside in _____ County, Texas and the events made the basis of this lawsuit and giving rise to Plaintiff's cause of action occurred, in whole or in part, in _____ County, Texas.

IV. NOTICE; CONDITIONS PRECEDENT

4.01 Defendant was given notice in writing of the claims made in this petition including a statement of Plaintiff's economic damages, mental anguish damages and expenses, including attorney's fees, more than sixty days before this suit was filed in the manner and form required by DTPA §17.505(a).

4.02 All conditions precedent to recovery by Plaintiff herein have been performed, have occurred, or have been excused, including but not limited to the Residential Construction Liability Act, Tex. Prop. Code §§27.01 *et seq.*

[*If Applicable*: 4.03 This dispute was submitted to the Residential Construction Commission as required by Tex. Prop. Code §426.005. Following a state-sponsored inspection, the Commission ruled in favor of Plaintiff; therefore, pursuant to Tex. Prop. Code §426.008, a rebuttable presumption exists as to the existence of the defects described in this petition as well as the repair of those defects.]

V. AGENCY

5.01 Unless otherwise stated, whenever it is alleged that Defendant _____ committed an act, failed to perform an act, made a representation or a statement, or failed to make a disclosure, it is alleged that Defendant _____ acted or failed to act through its authorized agents, servants, employees or representatives acting with either expressed, implied, apparent, direct and/or ostensible authority, or _____ subsequently ratified these acts, failures to act, representations, statements or conduct.

VI. FACTS OF CASE

6.01 In _____, Plaintiff purchased a house from Defendant _____ ("Defendant Builder"). The house is located at _____. The purchase price of the house was _____.

6.02 By virtue of the sale, Defendant Builder impliedly warranted that [*insert exact language of statutory warranty, e.g.* that the house was safe, sanitary and fit for humans to inhabit].

6.03 Additionally, at the time the house was sold, Defendant Builder represented and warranted that the house had been constructed according to the statutory warranty standards promulgated by the Texas Residential Construction Commission.

6.04 However, Defendant Builder failed to construct the house in accordance with the applicable construction standards and warranties as required by Texas law. The resulting construction defects include: [*list defects, e.g.*, faulty wiring, uneven floors, inadequate heating, air conditioning and ventilation system, improper drainage, unfinished trim, cracked foundation, incomplete lawn sprinkler system, etc.]

6.05 [*If applicable*:] These construction defects render the house unsafe, unsanitary and/or unfit for human habitation.]

6.06 [*Describe how these defects breach the applicable warranty, e.g.* The defects described above have had a direct adverse effect on the habitable areas of the house and were not discoverable by a reasonable prudent inspection or examination of the home within the applicable warranty periods.] Plaintiff has made no alterations to the parts of the house which are defective or which caused or contributed to the structural defects existing in the house. The defects in the house were latent, that is, they existed from the date the house was constructed but did not become apparent and were not discovered although reasonable diligence was exercised, until after the purchase.

6.07 This lawsuit was filed [*insert applicable limitations period e.g.,* within two years of the date that Plaintiffs discovered the defects which are the subject of this suit *or* on or before the 45th day after the state-sponsored inspector made his [her] recommendations *or* within 45 days after the date the Commission issued its ruling on the appeal of the state-sponsored inspector's recommendations].

6.08 Defendant builder represented to Plaintiff through the documents provided to Plaintiff that the house was constructed in accordance with the statutory standards, and according to the plans and specifications agreed upon by the parties, when in fact it was not.

VII. CAUSE OF ACTION: DTPA

7.01 Plaintiff repeats and realleges the material factual allegations in the preceding paragraphs.

7.02 Plaintiff is a consumer entitled to bring this action for relief under the Texas Deceptive Trade Practices—Consumer Protection Act (the "DTPA"). The actions of Defendants outlined above constitute misrepresentations, breaches of warranties and unconscionable conduct, actionable under the DTPA.

7.03 Specifically, Defendant committed the following acts in violation of the DTPA "laundry list," one or more of which was a producing cause of damages to Plaintiff:

(a) Representing that the house had characteristics, ingredients, uses or benefits which it did not have;

(b) Representing that house was of a particular standard, quality or grade when it was of another;

(c) Representing that the purchase agreement conferred or involved rights, remedies or obligations which it did not or which are prohibited by law; and/or

(d) Failing to disclose information concerning the house which was known at the time in order to induce the Plaintiff to enter into a transaction which Plaintiff would not have otherwise entered.

7.04 Plaintiff relied on these representations to his [her] detriment.

7.05 Further, Defendant violated the DTPA by breaching one or more express or implied warranties.

7.06 Further, Defendants took advantage of Plaintiff's lack of knowledge about the condition of the property. Accordingly, Defendants violated the DTPA by engaging in unconscionable conduct and/or an unconscionable course of conduct.

7.07 Defendant's conduct as described herein was a producing cause of damages to Plaintiff.

7.08 Further, Defendant's conduct was committed knowingly, entitling Plaintiff to seek the trebling of his [her] actual damages in accordance with the DTPA.

VIII. DAMAGES

8.01 Defendant's acts and omissions as described herein have been a producing cause of damages to Plaintiff.

8.02 Plaintiff has suffered economic damages, including but not limited to: [*insert elements of damages, e.g.,* the reasonable and necessary cost to repair the [defects in the house, and the reasonable and necessary rental expenses that Plaintiff will incur while his [her] house is being repaired.] Defendants are jointly and severally liable for these damages. Additionally, Defendant [builder] is liable for the stigma damages, *i.e.,* the loss of value in the house because of the nature of the defects, even after the defects have been repaired. [*See* §5.16 *supra* for alternative allegations of economic damages].

8.03 These damages are within the jurisdictional limits of this Court.

IX. ADDITIONAL DAMAGES AND PUNITIVE DAMAGES

9.01 Defendant's conduct in violation of the DTPA was committed knowingly, as that term is defined. Accordingly, Plaintiff seeks an award of additional damages under the DTPA in an amount not to exceed three times the amount of his [her] economic damages.

X. ATTORNEY'S FEES

10.01 As a result of Defendant's conduct, Plaintiff has been required to obtain the services of the undersigned attorney for the filing, prosecution and trial of this cause, and therefore seeks an award of reasonable and necessary attorney's fees pursuant to applicable law.

WHEREFORE, PREMISES CONSIDERED, Plaintiff respectfully prays that Defendant be cited to appear and answer herein, and that upon final trial hereof, Plaintiff recover from Defendant all of his actual damages, additional damages, pre-judgment and post-judgment interest as allowed by law, attorney's fees, costs of court and such other and further relief to which he may show himself justly entitled.

Respectfully submitted,

_____
Attorney for Plaintiff

§12.06.5 Defendant's Responsive Pleadings

[a] FORM: Plea in abatement (inadequate notice of claim)

[Statutory reference: RCLA §27.004(a).]

```
                        NO. _____
_____                §      IN THE DISTRICT COURT OF
                          §
vs.                       §      _____COUNTY, TEXAS
                          §
_____                §      _____ JUDICIAL DISTRICT
```

PLEA IN ABATEMENT

TO THE HONORABLE JUDGE OF THE DISTRICT COURT:

_____, defendant, files this plea in abatement against _____, plaintiff, and will show the following:

1.

Plaintiff failed to give the pre-filing notice of this suit as required by law; therefore, this suit should be abated until such notice is given.

2.

Specifically, TEX. PROP. CODE §27.004(a) required plaintiff to give defendant written notice, at least 60 days before this suit was filed, advising defendant in reasonable detail of the alleged defects in the construction on which plaintiff's suit is based.

3.

Plaintiff failed to give any written notice to defendant before this suit was filed.

[or]

Although plaintiff sent defendant a letter in which a general complaint was made, the written notice failed to [*insert defects in notice, e.g.,* describe in sufficient detail the nature of all of the construction defects alleged].

4.

Because of plaintiff's failure to comply with the statutory notice requirements, defendant has been deprived of any meaningful opportunity to resolve this matter prior to the filing of the lawsuit.

WHEREFORE, defendant requests that this suit be abated until such time as proper notice has been given and defendant has had [*insert response time allowed by statute, e.g.,* 60] days from the date the notice is received to respond to it.

Respectfully submitted,

_____
[Signature of attorney]

STATE OF TEXAS   §
                      §
COUNTY OF _____ §

AFFIDAVIT

BEFORE ME the undersigned Notary Public on this day personally appeared _____ who after having been by me duly cautioned and sworn did state to me upon his [her] oath that he [she] is the defendant in the above-referenced cause, has read the Plea in Abatement set forth above and that based on his [her] own personal knowledge, the facts contained in the plea and are true and correct.

_____
[Signature of affiant]

SUBSCRIBED AND SWORN TO before me on this ____ day of _____, 20___, to certify which witness my hand and official seal.

_____
[Signature and seal of notary public]

[Certificate of service]

[b] FORM: Order on plea in abatement

```
                        NO. _____
_____                  §    IN THE DISTRICT COURT OF
                            §
vs.                         §    _____ COUNTY, TEXAS
                            §
_____                  §    _____ JUDICIAL DISTRICT
```

ORDER ON PLEA IN ABATEMENT

On this _____ day of _____, 20___, came on for hearing defendant's Plea in Abatement; and it appears to the court that the plea is well taken and should be granted.

The court finds that the plaintiff failed to give notice of his [her] claim to defendant in writing more than 60 days before this suit was filed in the manner and form required by Tex. Bus. & Com. Code §17.505(a) [or Tex. Prop. Code §27.004(a)].

[or]

The court finds that defendant's plea in abatement was properly verified and that plaintiff has failed to file a controverting affidavit before the 11th day after the plea in abatement was filed.

IT IS THEREFORE ORDERED that this suit is abated until _____ [60] days after the day on which defendant receives proper written notice from plaintiff in which is contained in reasonable detail a statement of plaintiff's claim(s), as well as a statement of the amount of plaintiff's damages and expenses and the amount of attorney's fees incurred, if any, in the reasonable pursuit of plaintiff's claim [or in which is contained a list in reasonable detail of the claimed construction defects about which plaintiff complains].

SIGNED this _____ day of _____, 20___.

_____
[Signature of presiding judge]

[c]   FORM: Plea in abatement: no opportunity to inspect

```
                        NO. _____
_____                §    IN THE DISTRICT COURT OF
                          §
vs.                       §    _____ COUNTY, TEXAS
                          §
_____                §    _____ JUDICIAL DISTRICT
```

PLEA IN ABATEMENT

TO THE HONORABLE JUDGE OF THE DISTRICT COURT:

_____, defendant, files this plea in abatement against _____, plaintiff, and will show the following:

1.

On _____, defendant received a demand letter from plaintiff concerning the transaction which is the subject of this suit. On _____, within 35 days after the letter was received, defendant made a written request of plaintiff that defendant be allowed to inspect the claimed defects in the residential property.

2.

Defendant's request was made under the authority of TEX. PROP. CODE §27.004(a) which, upon request, specifically requires that such an inspection be allowed as a condition precedent to filing suit.

3.

Plaintiff failed to respond to defendant's request for an inspection.

[or]

Plaintiff agreed to allow the inspection; however, plaintiff refused to schedule the inspection at a reasonable time so that it was impossible for the inspection to occur.

4.

Because of plaintiff's failure to comply with the statutory inspection requirements, defendant has been deprived of any meaningful opportunity to evaluate the condition of the residential property to determine whether it is possible to resolve this matter prior to the filing of a lawsuit.

WHEREFORE, defendant requests that this suit be abated until such time as the opportunity to inspect has been provided and defendant has had [30] days from the date the inspection is allowed to evaluate the findings and respond to plaintiff's demand letter.

Respectfully submitted,

_____
[Signature of attorney]

STATE OF TEXAS   §
                          §
COUNTY OF _____   §

AFFIDAVIT

BEFORE ME the undersigned Notary Public on this day personally appeared _____ who after having been by me duly cautioned and sworn did state to me upon his [her] oath that he [she] is the defendant in the above-referenced cause, has read the Plea in Abatement set forth above and that based on his [her] own personal knowledge, the facts contained in the plea are true and correct.

_____
[Signature of affiant]

SUBSCRIBED AND SWORN TO before me on this ____ day of _____, 20___, to certify which witness my hand and official seal.

_____
[Signature and seal of notary public]

[Certificate of service]

[d] FORM: Order on plea in abatement

```
                              NO. _____

_____                     §     IN THE DISTRICT COURT OF
                               §
vs.                            §     _____ COUNTY, TEXAS
                               §
_____                     §     _____ JUDICIAL DISTRICT
```

ORDER ON PLEA IN ABATEMENT

On this day came on for hearing defendant's Plea in Abatement; and it appears to the court that the plea is well taken and should be granted.

Specifically, the court finds that although requested in the manner and form required by law, plaintiff failed to give defendant a reasonable opportunity to inspect the claimed defects in the residential property which are the subject of this suit as required by Tex. Prop. Code §27.004(a).

IT IS THEREFORE ORDERED that this suit is abated until _____ [60] days after the day on which defendant is provided an opportunity to inspect the residential property.

IT IS FURTHER ORDERED that defendant shall have the opportunity during this ____ [60]-day period to make an offer of settlement as provided by Tex. Bus. & Com. Code §17.505(c) [Tex. Prop. Code §27.004(b)] the same as if such offer had been made within the statutory notice period.

SIGNED this _____ day of _____ 20___.

_____
[Signature of presiding Judge]

[e] FORM: Original answer with affirmative defenses (residential construction)

NO. _____

	§	IN THE DISTRICT COURT OF
_____	§	
vs.	§	_____ COUNTY, TEXAS
	§	
_____	§	_____ JUDICIAL DISTRICT

ORIGINAL ANSWER

TO THE HONORABLE JUDGE OF THE DISTRICT COURT:

_____, defendant, files this Original Answer to Plaintiff's Original Petition and as grounds for this answer will show the following:

1. <u>Special exceptions</u>. [*See* §6.06, *supra*]

2. <u>General denial</u>. [*See* §6.04, *supra*]

3. <u>Special denial</u>. [*See* TEX. R. CIV. P. 93]

4. <u>Affirmative defenses</u>. [*See* §6.07, *supra* as well as the following:]

[(a)] <u>Negligence of plaintiff</u>. The damages which plaintiff seeks to recover in this action were caused in whole or in part by plaintiff's own negligence. [*Insert facts which show negligence, e.g.*, Specifically, after the house was constructed, plaintiff negligently built an earthen dam around the back of the house which allowed rain water to run into, around, and under the house's foundation rather than away from the foundation as it was constructed by defendant. The action of this rain water eroded the soils around and beneath the foundation, which undermined support of the foundation, thereby proximately causing plaintiff's damages.]

[*Authority*: TEX. PROP. CODE §27.003(a)(1)].

[(b)] <u>Failure to mitigate damages</u>. Plaintiff failed to take any reasonable action to mitigate the damages which this lawsuit seeks to recover from defendant. Specifically, [*insert facts which show failure to mitigate, e.g.*, when the plumbing first developed a leak in plaintiffs house, plaintiff failed to contact defendant immediately to ask that it be repaired and plaintiff failed to contact a plumber to repair the leaks until several weeks had passed. The damage to plaintiff's flooring, tile work, and sheetrock for which plaintiff seeks a judgment in this lawsuit could have been prevented entirely if the leak had been repaired immediately].

[*Authority*: Tex. Prop. Code §27.003(a)(2).]

[c] <u>Normal wear, tear, and deterioration</u>. The alleged defects in plaintiffs house about which plaintiff complains in this lawsuit are the result, in whole or in part, of normal wear, tear, and deterioration and are not the result of any defects in construction.

[*Authority*: Tex. Prop. Code §27.003(a)(3).]

[(d)] <u>Normal shrinkage</u>. The alleged defects in plaintiffs house about which plaintiff complains in this suit are the result of normal shrinkage due to drying or settlement of construction components which are within the tolerance of building standards.

[*Authority*: Tex. Prop. Code §27.003(a)(4).]

[(e)] <u>Reliance on written information</u>. The actions of defendant, about which plaintiff now complains, were based on the defendant's reliance on written information relating to the residence [*or* appurtenance *or* real property on which the residence (or appurtenance) is affixed] that was obtained from official government records. Defendant will show that if the written information is proven to be false or inaccurate, the defendant did not know and could not reasonably have known of the falsity or inaccuracy of the information.

[*Authority*: Tex. Prop. Code §27.003(a)(5).]

[(f)] <u>Unreasonable rejection of settlement offer</u>. In response to a demand letter from plaintiff, defendant made an offer to repair [*or* pay for the repair] of the alleged defects about which plaintiff complains in this lawsuit. Plaintiff unreasonably rejected defendant's offer [*or* Plaintiff wholly failed to respond to defendant's offer]. Accordingly, any recovery by plaintiff in this lawsuit is limited to the reasonable cost of the repairs necessary to cure the construction defect, if any, and the reasonable and necessary attorney's fees and costs incurred before the offer was rejected.

[*Authority*: Tex. Prop. Code §27.004(e).]

[(g)] <u>Refusal to allow repairs</u>. In response to a demand letter from plaintiff, defendant made an offer to repair [*or* pay for the repair] of the alleged defects about which plaintiff complains in this lawsuit. The offer was accepted by plaintiff. After accepting the offer, plaintiff refused to permit defendant a reasonable opportunity to repair the defects. Accordingly, plaintiff's recovery is limited to the reasonable cost of the repairs necessary to cure the construction defect, if any, and the reasonable and necessary attorney's fees and costs incurred before the offer was rejected.

[*Authority*: Tex. Prop. Code §27.004(e).]

[(h)] <u>Repairs have been made</u>. In response to a demand letter from plaintiff, defendant made an offer to repair [*or* pay for the repair] of the alleged defects about which plaintiff complains in this lawsuit. The offer was accepted by plaintiff and the repairs were performed by defendant in a good and workmanlike manner. Accordingly, plaintiff is barred from recovering any damages for mental anguish.

[*Authority*: Tex. Prop. Code §27.004(e).]

5. <u>Request for relief</u>. [*See* §6.04 *supra*].

    Respectfully submitted,

                                      _____
                                      [Signature of attorney]

[Certificate of service]

§12.06.6 Discovery in Residential Construction Cases

[a] FORM: Interrogatories to defendant

[NOTE: These questions are for use in a suit against the first owner, builder, and home warranty insurance company when there is defective residential construction.]

[Questions to the builder]

[NOTE: Although a request for disclosure under Rule 194 is intended to elicit information on persons with knowledge of relevant facts, there is no requirement that the disclosure detail the specific type of knowledge the person possesses. For this reason, the following interrogatories may be useful.]

1. Identify the person or persons who:

    (a) designed the house or rendered any drawings or plans for the home; or

    (b) provided engineering review or consultation in connection with the construction of the house; or

    (c) built the [*describe defective component*].

2. Identify each sub-contractor who performed work on the house and describe the nature of the work (e.g., plumbing, site work, etc.) performed by each.

3. Identify all documents pertaining to the house including but not limited to plans, photographs, change orders, specifications, surveys, inspection reports, drawings, contracts, permits, invoices, engineering reports, appraisals, and correspondence.

4. If you have constructed any other houses in [*insert name of subdivision*] that have experienced or that any person has claimed have experienced problems related to [*describe defect*] then identify each such house and its owner.

5. What do you contend or believe is the cause of the [*describe defect*] in the house?

6. If you contend or believe that any act or omission by plaintiff caused or contributed to any of the problems in the house, then identify each such act or omission.

7. Identify the person or entity from whom you purchased the following materials or components: [*describe relevant materials or components, e.g.*, concrete, lumber, PVC pipe for the septic system, roofing tiles, exterior paint, HVAC system].

8. Was the [*describe defective component*] of the house constructed in conformity with the plans and specifications? If your answer is negative, identify each deviation from the plans and specifications and the purpose of the deviation.

9. Identify by street address and owner's name each house in [*identify subdivision or other geographic area*] involving alleged [*describe defective component, e.g.*, foundation] defects that was repaired by you or at your expense, or that was repurchased by you.

[**NOTE:** To avoid unnecessary objections, include any appropriate limiting instructions, e.g., This question pertains only to foundations with a post- tension design or to evaporation septic systems].

[Questions to insurer]

[NOTE: The phrase "major construction defect" is a term of art used in some home warranty insurance policies. If a different phrase is used to describe the covered conditions, then obviously that phrase should be substituted for the bracketed language. Also, in the definitions portion of the interrogatories, the term "policy" should be defined by policy or certificate number to refer to that particular policy issued to plaintiff.]

1. Identify each person who participated in the decision to deny plaintiff's claim for benefits under the policy. For each person, state the name of his or her employer.

2. Identify every basis for denying plaintiff's claim for benefits under the policy.

3. Please identify each inquiry, request, or claim made by or on behalf of plaintiff, and state the date received and the action that you took in response to each inquiry, request or claim.

4. Describe in detail the investigation and information gathering process, if any, that you used in making your decision on any claim made by plaintiff under the policy. Include in your description the identity of each person who conducted an investigation or gathered facts. For each such person, state the name of his or her employer.

5. Identify all lawsuits filed in Texas since [*insert appropriate date*] against you in which it was alleged that you failed to pay a claim for major construction defects under the policy or any similar policy issued by you.

6. If you have compiled any statistics or reports indicating the number or percentage of major construction defect claims granted or denied, provide those statistics or state the content of such report. (Note: In lieu of answering this question, you may attach a copy of such statistics or such report.)

7. Identify all adjusters, supervisors, managers, and other agents and employees of yours who reviewed plaintiff's claim under the policy.

8. Identify all documents discussing the factors to be considered in determining whether a home is [*insert policy language describing covered defects, e.g.*, unsafe, unsanitary or otherwise unlivable].

9. Identify all agreements between you and [*the builder*] pertaining to insurance coverage on homes constructed by [*builder's name*].

10. Identify all documents provided by you to [*builder's name*] or provided to you by [*builder's name*] to you pertaining to plaintiff's home or to plaintiff's claim for benefits under the policy.

11. Identify by date and location each training conference or symposium you have held or sponsored since [*insert date*] for claims representatives, independent adjusters, or engineers to educate or train them in evaluating claims under the policy or any similar policy you have issued. For each conference or symposium, describe the materials provided to attendees.

12. Identify all manuals and memoranda used or available for use to claims representatives that set forth guidelines, procedures, or standards for the evaluation of claims under the policy or any similar policy you have issued.

[Questions to the first owner]

1. Please provide the following information:

    (a)   the date that you purchased the house; and

    (b)   the name and address of the seller of the house; and

    (c)   the builder of the house; and

    (d)   the purchase price you paid for the house.

2. Identify the real estate sales agent and broker who assisted (a) you and (b) the seller in your purchase of the house.

3. Identify all persons who prior to or subsequent to your purchase, inspected the house to determine the existence or nonexistence of defects or items in need of repair.

4. Identify all appraisals that have been made of the value of the house.

5. Describe all modifications, repairs, or improvements that have been made to the house or that were suggested or recommended by any person. For each such improvement or repair, identify the person who made the improvement, modification or repair and the person who recommended it.

6. Identify all persons who signed a contract to purchase the house but did not close on the purchase.

7. Identify all advertisements and listings for the house.

8. Identify all persons who at any time during your ownership of the house rented or leased it from you.

[b] FORM: Interrogatories to plaintiff

[NOTE: The following questions are intended for use by the builder or the first owner in interrogatories to the plaintiff.]

1. Identify each alleged express or implied representation or warranty that you contend was made or extended by defendant. For each such representation or warranty, identify the person, document or event making, extending, or giving rise to the representation or warranty.

2. Describe in detail all alleged defects in design or workmanship that form the basis, in whole or in part, of your lawsuit.

3. With regard to each defect identified by you in the preceding interrogatory, when (by day, month and year) did you first discover each defect.

4. Identify by street address, apartment number (if applicable), city and state each dwelling you have occupied for the past _____ years. If you did not own the property, identify the person who owned the property at the time you lived there.

5. Describe in detail defendant's conduct that you contend constituted [*insert unlawful conduct alleged, e.g.*, an unconscionable action or course of action].

[**NOTE:** It may be advisable to consider sending additional interrogatories similar to those in the preceding section for the "first owner."]

[c] FORM: Requests for Production to defendant (foundation repair)

1. All documents provided to your employees during training on how to repair a foundation similar to the foundation of Plaintiffs' home.

2. All documents relating to the work you performed on Plaintiffs' home, including all drawings, notes, photographs, videos, memoranda and/or blueprints, whether prepared by you or not.

3. All documents which reflect materials, supplies, and equipment purchased for or used on Plaintiffs' home, including warranty information and manuals, if any.

4. Your job file(s) on the Plaintiffs' home.

5. All field notes, logs, journals and diaries which were made while the work was in progress concerning the work done by you at the Plaintiffs' home.

6. All invoices, bills, statements, draw requests and other requests for payment prepared by you in connection with your work on Plaintiffs' home.

7. All cancelled checks and receipts maintained by you concerning payment by you for materials, equipment, subcontractors or labor in connection with your work on the Plaintiffs' home.

8. All certificates issued to you regarding your license or qualification to perform the work on Plaintiffs' home.

9. All inspection reports and building permits obtained by you concerning your work on Plaintiffs' home.

10. All estimates for the costs to repair or complete the work on Plaintiffs' home.

[d] FORM: Requests for production to plaintiff

1. All estimates for the costs to repair the construction defects alleged to exist in the Plaintiffs' home.

2. All documents or tangible things which you contend support any damages you seek in this case.

3. All notes, reports, correspondence and working papers relating to or resulting from tests or studies run on Plaintiffs' home. This request includes but is not limited to soil tests, grading surveys and foundation tests.

4. All samples of materials taken from the Plaintiffs' home.

5. All documents relating to any communications between you and your insurance company relating to the insurance claim you filed for the house and damages at issue in this case.

(This page intentionally left blank.)

Chapter 13

Real Estate

§13.01   General Considerations
§13.02   Texas Law Affecting Real Estate Sales
   §13.02.1   Applicability of DTPA to Real Estate Transactions
   §13.02.2   Disclosures Required in Sale of Existing Residence
   §13.02.3   Statutory Real Estate Fraud
   §13.02.4   Standards of Conduct for Real Estate Brokers and Agents
   §13.02.5   Real Estate Brokers' and Agents' Exemptions from Liability
   §13.02.6   Affirmative Defense: "As Is" Purchase
   §13.02.7   Real Estate Funds to Satisfy Judgments
   §13.02.8   Real Estate Inspectors
   §13.02.9   Real Estate Inspector Recovery Fund
§13.03   Checklists for Initial Interview
   [a] CHECKLIST: Purchase of existing residence
   [b] CHECKLIST: Purchase of raw land (Plaintiff)
   [c] CHECKLIST: Sale of raw land (Defendant)
§13.04   Pre-Suit Notice Letters
   [a] FORM: Notice letter: raw land--no potable water on land
   [b] FORM: Notice letter: raw land in flood zone
§13.05   Sample Petitions
   [a] FORM: Unimproved land
   [b] FORM: Alternative claim for rescission and restitution
   [c] FORM: Existing house purchased from owner (failure to disclose defects)
   [d] FORM: Used house, suit against real estate agent
   [e] FORM: Used house, suit against real estate inspector
§13.06   Sample Affirmative Defenses in Real Estate Cases
   [a] FORM: Affirmative defense: transaction size limitation
   [b] FORM: Affirmative defense: real estate agent exemption
   [c] FORM: Affirmative defense: "as is" real estate purchase
   [d] FORM: Affirmative defense: independent investigation
§13.07   Sample Motions for Real Estate Recovery Trust Account
   [a] FORM: Motion for order directing payment out of the Real Estate Recovery Trust Account

　　　　[b] FORM: Affidavit of custodian of official records, Texas Real Estate Commission
　　　　[c] FORM: Order directing payment out of Real Estate Recovery Trust Account
§13.08　Discovery Requests for Real Estate Actions
　　§13.08.1　Interrogatories
　　　　[a] FORM: Plaintiff's interrogatories to defendant (sale of unimproved land)
　　　　[b] FORM: Defendant's interrogatories to plaintiff (sale of unimproved land)
　　　　[c] FORM: Plaintiff's interrogatories to defendant (sale of existing residence)
　　　　[d] FORM: Defendant's interrogatories to plaintiff (sale of existing residence)
　　§13.08.2　Requests for Production
　　　　[a] FORM: Plaintiff's Requests for Production to defendant (sale of unimproved land)
　　　　[b] FORM: Defendant's Requests for Production to plaintiff (sale of unimproved land)
　　　　[c] FORM: Plaintiff's Requests for Production to real estate agent defendant (sale of existing residence)
　　　　[d] FORM: Real estate agent defendant's Request for Production to plaintiff (sale of existing residence)

§13.01 General Considerations

A buyer of real estate, whether it is raw land, a house or a commercial building, is at a distinct disadvantage to obtain truthful and complete information necessary to negotiate fair purchase terms. The DTPA provides efficient and effective remedies to a consumer who receives false or deceptive information in connection with the purchase of real estate. The forms in this chapter are tailored for use in the more common cases between a real estate buyer against the seller, real estate agent and broker, and real estate inspector. The forms provided can be easily adapted to be used in cases involving other, less common parties.

§13.02 Texas Law Affecting Real Estate Sales

Several Texas statutes govern the more common consumer transactions in Texas real estate. The Texas Property Code provides for one or more mandatory disclosures in most real estate transactions. The Property Code also has extensive provisions governing the sale property through an executory contract, also known as a "contract for deed." The Texas Real Estate License Act, now recodified in Chapter 1101 of the Occupations Code, governs the licensing and conduct of real estate brokers and agents. Real estate inspectors are governed by Chapter 1102 of the Texas Occupations Code. And of course, the DTPA has wide applicability to consumer real estate transactions.

§13.02.1 Applicability of DTPA to Real Estate Transactions

The DTPA defines a consumer as one "who seeks or acquires, by purchase or lease, any goods or services . . . ." DTPA §17.45(4); *see* § 1.02.4, *supra*. "Goods" is then defined to include "real property purchased or leased for use." DTPA §17.45(1).

The DTPA has long been used with approval to provide relief for consumers against a seller of real estate who violates the DTPA. *See, e.g., Alvarado v. Bolton*, 749 S.W.2d (Tex. 1988); *Chastain v. Koonce*, 700 S.W.2d 579 (Tex. 1985)(unconscionable conduct in sale of residential lot). The DTPA also provides relief in real estate transactions against real estate agents and brokers (*see Cameron v. Terrell & Garrett, Inc.*, 618 S.W.2d 535 (Tex. 1981)(laundry list violations by agent in sale of existing home), real estate inspectors (*see Head v. U.S. Inspect DFW, Inc.*, 159 S.W.3d 731 (Tex. App.—Fort Worth 2005, pet. denied)(breach of warranty by real estate inspector), lenders (*see, e.g., Bohls v. Oakes*, 75 S.W.3d 473 (Tex.App.—San Antonio, pet. denied), and other service providers connected with the transaction (*see, e.g., National Bugmobiles, Inc. v. Jobi Properties*, 773 S.W.2d 616 (Tex. App.—Corpus Christi 1989, writ denied)(claims against termite inspector).

The DTPA expressly authorizes an order of restitution of property, real or personal, acquired in violation of the DTPA. DTPA §17.50(c)(3); *see* §1.02.14.5, *supra.* This remedy may be especially useful in real estate transaction when the aggrieved consumer would be better off returning the real estate to the seller and obtaining a refund rather than keeping the real state and trying to remedy the defects or re-selling it with the defects to another.

§13.02.2 Disclosures Required in Sale of Existing Residence

When offering an existing single family house for sale, the Texas Property Code requires that the seller complete a document entitled, "Seller's Disclosure of Property Conditions." TEX. PROP. CODE §5.008(a). The content of the form is mandated by statute. TEX. PROP. CODE §5.008(b). The document is intended to disclose to all prospective buyers the condition of the property, at least as known to the seller. If a contract is entered into without the seller providing the notice to the buyer, then the buyer may terminate the contract for any reason within seven days after the date that the notice is received. TEX. PROP. CODE §5.008(f).

The form for the Seller's Disclosure of Property Condition, prescribed by Section 5.008(b) can be found on the Texas Real Estate Commission's website at http://www.trec.state.tx.us/pdf/contracts/OP-H.pdf. Misrepresentations of fact and material omissions are often found by carefully reviewing the Seller's Disclosure.

§13.02.3 Statutory Real Estate Fraud

Whenever real estate is sold, an additional statutory cause of action is available under TEX. BUS. & COM. CODE §27.01. This statute relaxes the strict requirements of the common law remedy for fraud in real estate and stock sales. Section 27.01 makes actionable a false representation of fact or promise without the additional requirement of showing that the defendant knew the representation of fact or promise was false. TEX. BUS. & COM. CODE §27.01(a)(1),(2). Moreover, the defendant may be liable when he is found to have benefitted by not disclosing that a third party's representation or promise which he knew to be false. TEX. BUS. & COM. CODE §27.01(d). A significant benefit from pleading and proving a violation of this statute is that it provides for the recovery of attorney's fees, expert witness fees and costs of copies of depositions. TEX. BUS. & COM. CODE §27.01(e). A separate section alleging a cause of action under §27.01 is contained in the petition forms below. *See* 13.05[a], [d], *infra.*

§13.02.4 Standards of Conduct for Real Estate Brokers and Agents

Another important basis of liability for a real estate broker is the Real Estate License Act, now found in the Occupations Code. Real estate brokers and salespersons are licensed by the state, and cannot act as a broker or salesperson without a license. TEX. OCC. CODE §1101.351. The Code further provides that "a licensed broker is liable to the commission, the public, and the broker's clients for any conduct engaged in under this chapter by the broker or by a salesperson associated with or acting for the broker." TEX. OCC. CODE §1101.803. Thus, if a broker engages in conduct prohibited by the Code, which causes damages to his or her client, there is liability.

The Occupation Code prohibits a wide range of improper conduct. A broker or salesperson violates the Code if he or she, among other acts or omissions:

- acts negligently or incompetently;

- engages in conduct that is dishonest or in bad faith or that demonstrates untrustworthiness;

- makes a material misrepresentation to a potential buyer concerning a significant defect, including a latent structural defect, known to the license holder that would be a significant factor to a reasonable and prudent buyer in making a decision to purchase real property;

- fails to disclose to a potential buyer a defect described by Subdivision (3) that is known to the license holder;

- makes a false promise that is likely to influence a person to enter into an agreement when the license holder is unable or does not intend to keep the promise;

- solicits, sells, or offers for sale real property by means of a deceptive practice;

- acts in a dual capacity as broker and undisclosed principal in a real estate transaction;

- guarantees or authorizes or permits a person to guarantee that future profits will result from a resale of real property;

- withholds from or inserts into a statement of account or invoice a statement that the license holder knows makes the statement of account or invoice inaccurate in a material way;

- fails to advise a buyer in writing before the closing of a real estate transaction that the buyer should:

    (A) have the abstract covering the real estate that is the subject of the contract examined by an attorney chosen by the buyer; or

    (B) be provided with or obtain a title insurance policy;

TEX. OCC. CODE §1101.652(b).

Presumably, a violation of the Occupation Code by a broker does not, in and of itself, violate the DTPA since there is no cross-reference to the DTPA in the Code, unlike other statutes. Nevertheless, the standards of care set forth in the Occupations Code appear well-suited to support negligence per se cause of action. The unexcused violation of a statute setting an applicable standard of care constitutes negligence as a matter of law if the statute is designed to prevent injury to that class of persons to which the plaintiff belongs, even though the statute is silent on the issue of civil liability. *El Chico Corp. v. Poole*, 732 S.W.2d 306, 312 (Tex. 1987). Whether or not the underlying statute creates a civil cause of action is irrelevant to determining the applicability of the doctrine of negligence per se. *El Chico Corp. v. Poole*, 732 S.W.2d 312. The question instead is whether the statute creates a standard of care that is designed to protect people like the Plaintiff.

One of the purposes of the Real Estate License Act is to protect homebuyers from certain conduct by brokers or salespersons in the sale of residential property. The statute expressly provides that a licensed broker "is liable to the commission, *the public*, and the broker's clients for any conduct engaged in *under this chapter* by the broker or by a salesperson associated with or acting for the broker." TEX. OCC. CODE §1101.083. This section not only describes the class of people that the statute seeks to protect, but also creates a duty between a sales agent/broker and a homebuyer, even if the agent represents the seller.

Further proof of the intent of the statute to protect homebuyers may be found in those provisions which deal with the Real Estate Recovery Trust Account. *See* TEX. OCC. CODE §1101.601 *et seq*. This statute provides a fund from which "aggrieved persons" can recover some of their damages if the broker or salesperson is unable to pay. The statute defines those persons who are entitled to reimbursement from the fund to be those who are damaged because a broker or salesperson, "engages in conduct described by Section 1101.652(a)(3) or (b) or 1101.653(1), (2), (3), or (4)." TEX. OCC. CODE §1101.602.

§13.02.5 Real Estate Brokers' and Agents' Exemptions from Liability

In 2011, the DTPA was amended to provide an exemption for real estate brokers and agents similar to the exemption for "professionals" in DTPA §17.49(c). DTPA §17.49(i); see §§1.02.7.5, 2.02.3, supra. However, like the professionals' exemption, the exceptions to the real estate agent/broker exemption are broad. The exemption does not apply to express misrepresentations of fact or unconscionable actions that cannot be characterized as advice, judgment or opinion, nor to failures to disclose actionable under §17.46(b)(24). DTPA §17.49(i)(applicable to claims arising from conduct occurring after 2011).

Real estate salespersons and brokers act as agents for either the buyer or seller of real property. The Real Estate Code provides that a salesperson or broker is not liable for a misrepresentations or concealment of a material fact made by another party to the transaction unless the broker or salesperson knew of the falsity of the misrepresentation or concealment and failed to disclose the party's knowledge of the falsity of the misrepresentation or concealment. TEX. OCC. CODE §1101.805(e). Similar protection is provided to the seller if the licensed broker or salesperson makes misrepresentations or fails to disclose material facts. TEX. OCC. CODE §1101.805(d).

§13.02.6 Affirmative Defense: "As Is" Purchase

In *Prudential Ins. Co. of Am. v. Jefferson Assocs.*, 896 S.W.2d 156 (Tex. 1995), the Supreme Court held that if improved real estate is purchased "as is," and particularly if there is an acknowledgement by the buyer that he is not relying on any representations of the seller, then there is a break in causation between the allegedly wrongful conduct and any damages that the buyer may have suffered. See §2.02.04, *supra*, for discussion of "As Is" defense.

In residential real estate sales, the typical earnest money contract contains an "Acceptance of Condition" clause which is the functional equivalent of an as-is clause. *Larsen v. Carlene Langford & Assocs.*, 41 S.W.3d 245, 251 (Tex. App.—Waco 2001, pet. denied). The pleading set forth in §13.06[c] is intended to raise the issue of an as-is purchase.

§13.02.7 Real Estate Funds to Satisfy Judgments

Texas consumers who recover money judgments against either real estate agents or brokers may satisfy the judgments up to $50,000 from the Real Estate Recovery Trust Account under certain circumstances. TEX. OCC. CODE §1101.601 *et seq*. A similar fund exists for those persons who are damaged by the conduct of a licensed real estate inspector. TEX. OCC. CODE §1102.351 *et seq*. The maximum amount that can be recovered by any one consumer from the Real Estate Recovery Trust Account is $50,000 per transaction and $100,000 per agent or broker. *See* TEX. OCC. CODE §1101.610. The maximum amount that can be recovered from the Real Estate Inspector Recovery Fund is $12,500 per transaction and $30,000 per licensed inspector. TEX. OCC. CODE §1102.359.

The Real Estate Recovery Trust Account authorizes a recovery by a consumer when a real estate broker or real estate salesman, while selling, buying, trading, or renting property in his own name, engages in misrepresentation, or dishonest or fraudulent action. TEX. OCC. CODE §§1101.652 and 1101.653. In order to recover from the account, a final judgment must be entered in favor of the consumer and against the agent or broker, execution of the judgment must be returned *nulla bona,* and a judgment lien must be perfected. Then, upon filing a verified claim with the court and twenty days' notice to the Texas Real Estate Commission, the court may enter an order directing payment of the unsatisfied portion of the judgment (up to $50,000). TEX. OCC. CODE §1101.606. To be entitled to the order, however, the consumer must prove each of the following facts:

1. The judgment is based on facts allowing recovery under the Real Estate Recovery Trust Account; and

2. The consumer is not a spouse of the judgment debtor, or the personal representative of the spouse; and he is not a real estate broker or salesman, as defined by the statute, who is seeking to recover a real estate commission in the transaction or transactions for which the application for payment is made; and

3. The consumer has obtained a judgment that is not the subject to a stay or discharge in bankruptcy, stating the amount of the judgment and the amount still owing on the judgment; and

4. Based on the best available information, the judgment debtor lacks sufficient attachable assets in this state or any other state to satisfy the judgment; and

5. The amount that may be realized from the sale of real or personal property or other assets liable to be sold or applied in satisfaction of the judgment and the balance remaining due on the judgment after application of the amount that may be realized.

TEX. OCC. CODE §1101.607; *see Texas Real Estate Com'n v. Nagle,* 767 S.W.2d 691, 693 (Tex. 1989).

§13.02.8 Real Estate Inspectors

Whenever a used house is sold, and sometimes when a new house is sold, the buyer will retain the services of a real estate inspector to evaluate the condition of the component parts of the house, including appliances. A person cannot act as a real estate inspector unless that person is licensed by the state. TEX. OCC. CODE §§1102.102, 103.

A licensed "professional real estate inspector" must supervise, indirectly, the activities of a licensed "real estate inspector." TEX. OCC. CODE §1102.102(2). And, a licensed "apprentice inspector" can work only under the *direct* supervision of either a real estate inspector or professional real estate inspector. TEX. OCC. CODE §1102.101(2).

In order to promote consistency and reduce discrepancies, standardized forms must be used by all inspectors. TEX. OCC. CODE §1102.003.

Real estate inspectors, whether professional or otherwise, are liable to consumers for specified conduct, including the following:

(1) negligence and incompetence (TEX. OCC. CODE §1102.301);

(2) accepting employment which is contingent on producing a specific report, or acts in a manner that is otherwise dishonest, fraudulent, deceitful or a misrepresentation. (TEX. OCC. CODE §1102.302);

(3) acting as both an inspector and a principal or broker or salesperson. (TEX. OCC. CODE §1102.303);

(4) performing or agreeing to perform repairs or maintenance in connection with a real estate inspection under an earnest money contract. (TEX. OCC. CODE §1102.304).

(5) violating any rule of the Texas Real Estate Commission. (TEX. OCC. CODE §1102.305).

If licensed inspectors violate any of these prohibitions, an aggrieved consumer can apply to the Real Estate Inspection Recovery Fund for compensation, albeit limited. TEX. OCC. CODE §1102.351. Presumably, a violation of any of the prohibitions also creates negligence per se liability.

"Professional real estate inspectors" are entitled to the same exemption from the DTPA as doctors, lawyers, and accountants. *Retherford v. Castro*, 378 S.W.3d 29 (Tex. App.—Waco 2012, pet. denied); *see also Head v. U.S. Inspect DFW, Inc.*, 159 S.W.3d 731 (Tex. App.—Fort Worth 2005, pet. denied)(professional exemption assumed by both parties).

§13.02.9 Real Estate Inspector Recovery Fund

When a consumer has recovered a judgment against a real estate inspector, the fund is available to satisfy the judgment if the inspector did any of the following on which the judgment was based:

1. Accepts an assignment for real estate inspection if the employment or fee is contingent on the reporting of a specific, predetermined condition of the improvements to real property or is contingent on the reporting of specific findings other than those known by the inspector to be facts at the time of accepting such assignment; or

2. Acts in a manner or engages in a practice that is dishonest or fraudulent or that involves deceit or misrepresentation; or

3. Performs a real estate inspection in a negligent or incompetent manner; or

4. Acts in the dual capacity of real estate inspector and undisclosed principal in a transaction; or

5. Acts in the dual capacity of real estate inspector and real estate broker or salesman; or

6. Performs or agrees to perform any repairs or maintenance in connection with a real estate inspection pursuant to the provisions of any earnest money contract, lease agreement, or exchange of real estate; or

7. Performs a real estate inspection pursuant to a written contract for inspection which does not contain the required statutory disclosure statement in the contract for inspection in at least 10-point bold type above or adjacent to the signature of the purchaser of the real estate inspection; or

8. Violates the rules adopted by the commission, or any provision of Texas Occupations Code Chapter 1102.

TEX. OCC. CODE §1102.355.

The consumer's burden of proof is the same as that required for recovery from the Real Estate Recovery Fund. TEX. OCC. CODE §1102.356; *see* §5.21 *supra*. Thus, although the following forms specifically deal with a motion for payment from the Real Estate Recovery Trust Account, they may be modified with little effort for use in proceedings against the Real Estate Inspector Recovery Fund.

§13.03 Checklists for Initial Interview

[a] CHECKLIST: Purchase of existing residence

Client _____ Date of Interview _____

The property

☐ Location of property: Lot and block number; street address

☐ Who is the seller

☐ Were there any items of personal property conveyed with the purchase

The contract/ representations

☐ When was the earnest money contract signed

☐ Who was the listing broker/agent

☐ Who were the co-brokers/agents

[If a licensed real estate agent or broker is involved, one source of recovering damages assessed against the agent or broker is the Real Estate Recovery Fund. See §13.02.7]

☐ Did contract permit/require property inspections; if yes, who inspected property

[If property inspection was poorly performed and caused damages, one source of recovering damages assessed against the property inspector is the Real Estate Inspection Recovery Fund. See §13.02.9, supra.]

☐ Was the seller also the builder

[If there are construction defects, consider applicability of the RCLA. *See* Chapter 12, *supra*.]

☐ What representations were made about the house, by whom and when

☐ Did client see advertising; if yes, where and when

☐ Was client advised in writing that any information given to client was obtained from a third party

[If information was obtained from third party, the person making the representation may have a defense under DTPA §17.506.]

Purchase information

☐ Date of Closing and closing Agent

☐ Purchase price

☐ Down payment

☐ Written warranties given

☐ HOW/HOME Warranty given

☐ Who is the mortgage company

☐ Type of mortgage: fixed or adjustable rate

☐ Interest rate/term of mortgage

☐ Monthly payments: how much principal, interest, insurance, taxes

☐ Are payments current

　-If not, how delinquent

　- Have any demand letters, notice of acceleration, or notice of foreclosure been received

[If client is delinquent, upon receipt of notice letter, the prospective defendant may file suit against client in an inconvenient forum. Consideration should thus be given to a "preemptive" common law action to fix venue and to insure that the client is the plaintiff.]

Representations and Disclosures

☐ Did the Seller provide the Seller's Disclosure of Property Condition to the Buyer

- ☐ Are there any misrepresentations or omissions of material fact on the Seller's Disclosure
- ☐ What representations were made about the property by the seller
- ☐ What representations were made about the property by the real estate agents
- ☐ Was the property accepted "in present condition" or "as is"
- ☐ Was the buyer allowed to inspect the property prior to closing
- ☐ Was there a "walk-though inspection" prior to closing
- ☐ What documents were signed at the closing
- ☐ Was any damage done to the property between the signing of the contract and closing
- ☐ What correspondence has occurred

Complaints to seller, agents

- ☐ Has seller or agent been notified in writing of claim; if so, what was response
- ☐ Has client talked to seller or agent about claim; if so, what was said and by whom

Expectations of client

- ☐ What does client expect to accomplish through litigation

Explanations to client

- ☐ Anticipated cost of litigation
- ☐ Attorney-client agreement
- ☐ Requirements of discovery, assistance with case
- ☐ Required attendance at depositions, trial
- ☐ Outcome of litigation is unpredictable

Documents to obtain from client

[Client should be advised to bring *all* documents that in any way relate to transaction; however, the following list is illustrative of the type of documents that must be provided if they exist.]

- ☐ Advertising seen
- ☐ Point of sale brochures or documents
- ☐ Earnest money contract
- ☐ Inspection report from real estate inspector
- ☐ Termite inspection report
- ☐ Any other required disclosures: membership in a property owners association, home located within a public improvement district, warning about lead-based paint, notice of the presence of asbestos, notice of restrictive covenants, certificate of mold remediation
- ☐ Surveys of land
- ☐ Deed, deed of trust
- ☐ Any document signed by client in connection with sale
- ☐ Closing statement
- ☐ Letter to or from anyone involved in transaction
- ☐ Reports of experts
- ☐ All documents reflecting losses from transaction

[b] CHECKLIST: Purchase of raw land (Plaintiff)

Client _____ Date of interview _____

Litigation

- ☐ Has a lawsuit been filed
- ☐ If a lawsuit has been filed, what is the answer date

The notice letter

- ☐ When was the notice letter received

- ☐ When is a response to the notice letter due
- ☐ Does the notice letter contain sufficient information so that the claim can be evaluated; if not, what additional information is needed

The property

- ☐ Legal description of the property
- ☐ Size of tract
- ☐ Was client the developer
- ☐ Was client the seller
- ☐ Was a survey prepared
    - If yes, by whom
- ☐ Was a plat used in the sale of the property
- ☐ What was the purpose for which the property was bought
- ☐ Was the client aware of the purpose at the time of the sale

Representations; purchase

- ☐ Was an earnest money contract signed
    - If yes, when
    - How much in earnest money was paid
- ☐ Were any waivers contained in the earnest money contract
- ☐ Who was the listing broker/agent
- ☐ Who were the co-brokers/agents
- ☐ Were any other licensed real estate agents/brokers involved in the transaction
- ☐ Were any representations made about the property
    - If yes, what was said, by whom and when

[If unauthorized representations were made about property by any real estate agent or broker, client may have a cross-action against the agent or broker for indemnity. *See* DTPA §17.555.]

- ☐ Was advertising used to sell the property

    - If yes, what type, when was it seen, what did it say

- ☐ Was any information about the property obtained from a third party and passed on to the buyer

- ☐ Was the buyer advised in writing that any information about the property was obtained from a third party

[Information obtained from a third party and passed along to the buyer may allow for a defense to liability if certain procedures were followed at the time. See DTPA §17.506.]

- ☐ Was any important information not disclosed to the buyer that you believe would have caused the buyer not to purchase the property

The purchase

- ☐ Date and place of closing
- ☐ Was the purchase by deed or contract for sale
- ☐ What was the purchase price

Improvements made to land

- ☐ Has the buyer made any improvements to the land since the sale

    - If yes, what type of improvements have been made and when

- ☐ Was the client aware that improvements were being made
- ☐ Have any of the improvements become part of the real property or are they readily moved

[If improvements have been made by the buyer, then it may be necessary to reimburse buyer for the improvements if the transaction is cancelled.]

Complaints about land

- ☐ What are all of the defects in or complaints about the land which are known to client
- ☐ When were the defective conditions first noticed or brought to client's attention

- ☐ How were the defective conditions first noticed or brought to client's attention
- ☐ Can the defects be remedied
    - If yes, how and for how much,

Notice of claim

- ☐ Has client been notified of the claim
    - If yes, how and when
- ☐ What was client's response to the claim

Explanations to client

- ☐ Anticipated cost of litigation
- ☐ Attorney and client agreement
- ☐ Requirements of discovery, assistance with case
- ☐ Required attendance at depositions and trial
- ☐ Outcome of litigation is unpredictable

Documents to obtain from client

[Although client should be cautioned to provide all documents to the attorney that are, in any way, related to the transaction and its aftermath, the following documents must be obtained immediately.]

- ☐ Advertising for land
- ☐ Point of sale brochures, plats
- ☐ Earnest money contract
- ☐ Surveys of land
- ☐ Any document signed by client in connection with sale
- ☐ Closing statement
- ☐ Letters to parties involved in transaction
- ☐ Letters from parties involved in transaction
- ☐ Cost of cure estimates, reports of experts

[c] CHECKLIST: Sale of raw land (Defendant)

Client _____ Date of interview _____

Litigation

☐ Has a lawsuit been filed

☐ If a lawsuit has been filed, what is the answer date

The notice letter

☐ When was the notice letter received

☐ When is a response to the notice letter due

☐ Does the notice letter contain sufficient information so that the claim can be evaluated; if not, what additional information is needed

The property

☐ Legal description of the property

☐ Size of tract

☐ Was client the developer

☐ Was client the seller

☐ Was a survey prepared

– If yes, by whom

☐ Was a plat used in the sale of the property

☐ What was the purpose for which the property was bought

☐ Was the client aware of the purpose at the time of the sale

Representations; purchase

☐ Was an earnest money contract signed

– If yes, when

– How much in earnest money was paid

☐ Were any waivers contained in the earnest money contract

- ☐ Who was the listing broker/agent
- ☐ Who were the co-brokers/agents
- ☐ Were any other licensed real estate agents/brokers involved in the transaction
- ☐ Were any representations made about the property
    - If yes, what was said, by whom and when

[If unauthorized representations were made about property by any real estate agent or broker, client may have a cross-action against the agent or broker for indemnity. See DTPA §17.555.]

- ☐ Was advertising used to sell the property
    - If yes, what type, when was it seen, what did it say
- ☐ Was any information about the property obtained from a third party and passed on to the buyer
- ☐ Was the buyer advised in writing that any information about the property was obtained from a third party

[Information obtained from a third party and passed along to the buyer may allow for a defense to liability if certain procedures were followed at the time. See DTPA §17.506.]

- ☐ Was any important information not disclosed to the buyer that you believe would have caused the buyer not to purchase the property

The purchase

- ☐ Date and place of closing
- ☐ Was the purchase by deed or contract for sale
- ☐ What was the purchase price

Improvements made to land

- ☐ Has the buyer made any improvements to the land since the sale
    - If yes, what type of improvements have been made and when
- ☐ Was the client aware that improvements were being made

☐   Have any of the improvements become part of the real property or are they readily moved

[If improvements have been made by the buyer, then it may be necessary to reimburse buyer for the improvements if the transaction is cancelled.]

Complaints about land

☐   What are all of the defects in or complaints about the land which are known to client

☐   When were the defective conditions first noticed or brought to client's attention

☐   How were the defective conditions first noticed or brought to client's attention

☐   Can the defects be remedied

   – If yes, how and for how much,

Notice of claim

☐   Has client been notified of the claim

   – If yes, how and when

☐   What was client's response to the claim

Explanations to client

☐   Anticipated cost of litigation

☐   Attorney and client agreement

☐   Requirements of discovery, assistance with case

☐   Required attendance at depositions and trial

☐   Outcome of litigation is unpredictable

Documents to obtain from client

[Although client should be cautioned to provide all documents to the attorney that are, in any way, related to the transaction and its aftermath, the following documents must be obtained immediately.]

☐   Advertising for land

- ☐ Point of sale brochures, plats
- ☐ Earnest money contract
- ☐ Surveys of land
- ☐ Any document signed by client in connection with sale
- ☐ Closing statement
- ☐ Letters to parties involved in transaction
- ☐ Letters from parties involved in transaction
- ☐ Cost of cure estimates, reports of experts

§13.04 Pre-Suit Notice Letters

A notice letter involving the sale of real estate, whether for raw land or an existing building or residence, follows the same format as that for the sale of goods or services. The general form for a DTPA notice letter discussed in Chapter 3, *supra*, can be modified to provide the particular statement of claim. For the requirements of notice letters concerning residential construction cases, see §12.06.02, *supra*.

[a] FORM: Notice letter: raw land--no potable water on land

[*Insert the following at "notice of claim," §3.03[a] supra*]

On_____, 20__, our client purchased property from you for the purpose of building his [her] home on the property. The property is located at [*insert address or survey of property*].

At the time of the sale, you represented to our client that potable water would be available on the property in reasonable quantities for residential use [or At the time of sale, you failed to disclose to our client that potable water was not available on the property in reasonable quantities for residential use, even though this fact was known to you]. Because the property does not have potable water, the property has no value to our client as a residential homesite, which was the only purpose for which it was purchased. For this reason, you are now requested to cancel the sale of the property to our client and refund to him [her] all money that has been paid to you by our client.

You also are requested to reimburse our client for all reasonable and necessary expenses incurred in connection with our client's ownership of the property. The expenses incurred by our client include the following: [*insert itemized list of expenses*].

Our client also has made valuable improvements to the property which cannot now be removed without damage to the land, and as a result have no value to our client. These improvements and their costs are as follows: [*insert list of improvements and costs*].

We reserve the right to assert a claim for the full damages our client has suffered as a result of the purchase of the property if you fail to respond to this letter with an acceptable offer of settlement. These damages include, but are not limited to, the following: [*insert itemized damages, stating separately economic losses, mental anguish, attorney's fees and expenses*].

[*See §3.03[a] for other elements of letter*]

[b] FORM: Notice letter: raw land in flood zone

[*Insert the following at "notice of claim," §3.03[a] supra*]

On_____, 20___, our client purchased property from you for the purpose of building his [her] home on the property. The property is located at [insert address or survey of property].

At the time of the sale, you represented to our client that the property would be suitable for the construction of our client's home [or At the time of sale, you failed to disclose to our client that the property is located in a flood hazard zone, even though this fact was known to you]. Because the property is located in a flood hazard zone, it has no value to our client as a residential homesite, which was the only purpose for which it was purchased. For this reason, you are now requested to cancel the sale of the property to our client and refund to him [her] all money that has been paid to you by our client.

You also are requested to reimburse our client for all reasonable and necessary expenses incurred in connection with our client's ownership of the property. The expenses incurred by our client include the following: [*insert itemized list of expenses*].

Our client also has made valuable improvements to the property which cannot now be removed without damage to the land, and as a result have no value to our client. These improvements and their costs are as follows: [*insert list of improvements and costs*].

We reserve the right to assert a claim for the full damages our client has suffered as a result of the purchase of the property if you fail to respond to this letter with an acceptable offer of settlement. These damages include, but are not limited to, the following: [*insert itemized damages, stating separately economic losses, mental anguish, attorney's fees and expenses*].

[*See §3.03[a] for other elements of letter*]

§13.05 Sample Petitions

A deceived purchaser of real estate may seek either damages or restitution. *See* §13.02.1, *supra*. The form which follows asserts a claim for actual damages. Form [b], *infra*, provides a sample modification to assert a claim for rescission and restitution.

Whenever real estate is sold, an additional statutory cause of action is available under TEX. BUS. & COM. CODE §27.01. This statute augments the common law remedy for fraud in real estate and stock sales. The benefit in pleading and proving a violation of this statute is that it provides for the recovery of costs of copies of depositions and expert witness fees. TEX. BUS. & COM. CODE §27.01(e). A separate section alleging a cause of action under §27.01 is contained in the following petition.

The following form petition includes two defendants. The reason for multiple defendants is that whenever real estate is sold, normally there is a real estate agent or broker involved in the transaction who serves as a conduit for information or misinformation, as the case may be.

[a] FORM: Unimproved land

```
                              NO. _____
_____                §     IN THE DISTRICT COURT OF
                          §
                          §
vs.                       §     _____COUNTY, TEXAS
                          §
_____                §     _____ JUDICIAL DISTRICT
```

PLAINTIFF'S ORIGINAL PETITION

NOW COMES _____, Plaintiff herein, complaining of _____ Defendants herein, and for cause of action, would show unto the Court as follows:

I. DISCOVERY CONTROL PLAN DESIGNATION

1.01 By this action, Plaintiff seeks _____ [insert appropriate designation under Rule 47(c), e.g., only monetary relief of $100,000 or less, including damages of any kind, penalties, costs, expenses, prejudgment interest, and attorney's fees]. The damages sought are within the jurisdictional limits of this court.

1.02 Discovery in this case is intended to be conducted under Level _____, pursuant to Rule 190._____, *Texas Rules of Civil Procedure*.

II. PARTIES

2.01 _____ is a resident of _____, _____ County, Texas.

2.02 _____ is an individual who resides and may be served with process at _____, _____ County, Texas.

2.03 _____ is a Texas corporation which may be served with process by serving _____, its registered agent, at _____, the corporation's registered address.

III. VENUE

3.01 Venue of this action is proper in _____ County, Texas because _____ reside in _____ County, Texas and the events made the basis of this lawsuit and giving rise to Plaintiff's cause of action occurred, in whole or in part, in _____ County, Texas.

3.02 Since venue of this action in this county is proper as to Defendant _____ and no mandatory venue provision applies, venue is proper in this county as to all defendants.

IV. NOTICE; CONDITIONS PRECEDENT

4.01 Defendants were given notice in writing of the claims made in this petition including a statement of Plaintiff's economic damages, mental anguish damages and expenses, including attorney's fees, more than sixty days before this suit was filed in the manner and form required by DTPA §17.505(a).

4.02 All conditions precedents to recovery by Plaintiff herein have been performed, have occurred, or have been excused.

V. AGENCY AND JOINT VENTURE

5.01 Unless otherwise stated, whenever it is alleged that Defendant _____ committed an act, failed to perform an act, made a representation or a statement, or failed to make a disclosure, it is alleged that Defendant _____ acted or failed to act through its authorized agents, servants, employees or representatives acting with either expressed, implied, apparent, direct and/or ostensible authority, or _____ subsequently ratified these acts, failures to act, representations, statements or conduct.

5.02 Defendant _____ was the real estate broker representing the developer as the developer's duly authorized agent in the sale of the land. It is therefore further alleged that, at all times relevant hereto, Defendant _____ acted as the authorized agent of Defendant _____ with either expressed, implied, apparent, direct and/or ostensible authority, or that Defendant _____ subsequently ratified the acts, failures to act, representations, statements or conduct of Defendant _____.

5.03 Further, it is alleged that Defendants were engaged in a joint venture for their mutual benefit and acted as each other's agents with all express, implied, direct and/or ostensible authority to so act, and as such are vicariously liable for the acts, omissions, statements and conduct of the other as alleged herein.

VI. FACTS OF CASE

6.01 This lawsuit arises out of the purchase of certain unimproved real property by Plaintiff from Defendant _____.

6.02 Plaintiff purchased [*describe land, e.g.*, Lot _____, Block of _____, subdivision which is more particularly described in Vol. _____, page _____ of the Plat Records of _____ County, Texas].

6.03 The purchase price of the property was _____. Plaintiff made a down payment of _____ and financed the balance of the purchase price over a term of _____ years at _____ percent interest per annum.

6.04 At the time Plaintiff purchased the property, the following false, misleading and deceptive statements were made to Plaintiff about the property: [*insert false representations made, e.g.*,

    (a) That the land was suitable for use as a residential homesite; and

    (b) That a modular home could be constructed on the property].

6.05 Based on these representations, Plaintiff purchased the property.

6.06 The representations were false for the reason that [*describe why representations were false, e.g.,*

- (a) all of the land is located within a flood hazard zone and permanent construction of any type on the land is prohibited by county ordinance; and
- (b) even if construction was allowed, the deed restrictions applicable to the property prohibit the construction of modular homes, which is the type of house that Plaintiff told Defendants would be built].

6.07 Had Plaintiff known that the representations were false, he [she] would not have purchased the property. [*describe other facts on which claim is based*].

VII. FIRST CAUSE OF ACTION: DTPA

7.01 Plaintiff repeats and realleges the material factual allegations in the preceding paragraphs.

7.02 Plaintiff is a consumer entitled to bring this action for relief under the Texas Deceptive Trade Practices—Consumer Protection Act (the "DTPA"). The actions of Defendants outlined above constitute misrepresentations, breaches of warranties and unconscionable conduct, actionable under the DTPA.

7.03 Specifically, Defendant committed the following acts in violation of the DTPA "laundry list," one or more of which was a producing cause of damages to Plaintiff:

- (a) Representing that the land had characteristics, ingredients, uses or benefits which it did not have;
- (b) Representing that the land was of a particular standard, quality or grade when it was of another;
- (c) Representing that the purchase agreement conferred or involved rights, remedies or obligations which it did not or which are prohibited by law; and/or
- (d) Failing to disclose information concerning the land which was known at the time in order to induce the Plaintiff to enter into a transaction which Plaintiff would not have otherwise entered.

7.04 Plaintiff relied on these representations to his [her] detriment.

7.05 Further, Defendant violated the DTPA by breaching one or more express warranties.

7.06 Further, there is a gross disparity between the consideration paid by Plaintiff and the value he [she] received, and Defendants took advantage of Plaintiff's lack of knowledge about the condition of the property. Accordingly, Defendants violated the DTPA by engaging in unconscionable conduct and/or an unconscionable course of conduct.

7.07 Defendants' conduct as described herein was a producing cause of damages to Plaintiff.

7.08 Further, Defendants' conduct was committed knowingly, entitling Plaintiff to seek the trebling of his [her] actual damages in accordance with the DTPA. [See §5.15 and §5.15.1 infra for specific pleading forms]

VIII. SECOND CAUSE OF ACTION: STATUTORY FRAUD

8.01 Plaintiff repeats and realleges the material factual allegations in the preceding paragraphs.

8.02 By their conduct as described above, Defendants made one or more false representations of material fact and/or benefitted by not disclosing that a third party's representation of material fact was false, for the purpose of inducing Plaintiff into the contract for the purchase of the property.

8.03 Plaintiff relied upon the false representations of fact and entered into the contract for the purchase of the property, which resulted in actual damages to Plaintiff, for which he [she] sues.

IX. DAMAGES

9.01 Defendants' acts and omissions as described herein have been a producing and/or proximate cause of damages to Plaintiff. Plaintiff has suffered economic damages, including but not limited to: the difference in market value of the land as represented and its actual value at the time it was sold to Plaintiff, and Plaintiff's reasonable out-of-pocket expenditures which were made in connection with Plaintiff's ownership of the land in preparation for the use of the site for a modular home which is not, in fact, legal. [See §5.16, supra, for alternative allegations.]

9.02 These damages are within the jurisdictional limits of this Court.

X. ADDITIONAL DAMAGES AND PUNITIVE DAMAGES

10.01 Defendants' conduct in violation of the DTPA was committed knowingly, as that term is defined. Accordingly, Plaintiff seeks an award of additional damages under the DTPA in an amount not to exceed three times the amount of his [her] economic damages.

XI. ATTORNEY'S FEES

11.01 As a result of Defendants' conduct, Plaintiff has been required to obtain the services of the undersigned attorney for the filing, prosecution and trial of this cause, and therefore seeks an award of reasonable and necessary attorney's fees pursuant to applicable law.

WHEREFORE, PREMISES CONSIDERED, Plaintiff respectfully prays that Defendants be cited to appear and answer herein, and that upon final trial hereof, Plaintiff recover from Defendants, jointly and severally, all of his [her] actual damages, additional damages, exemplary damages, pre-judgment and post-judgment interest as allowed by law, attorney's fees, costs of court and such other and further relief to which he may show himself justly entitled.

Respectfully submitted,

_____
Attorney for Plaintiff

[b] FORM: Alternative claim for rescission and restitution

[For rescission as an alternative, insert the following into the Petition form 13.03.3[a], supra, as Paragraph IX.

IX. RESCISSION; DAMAGES

9.01 Because of the conduct described in the preceding paragraphs, Plaintiff asks that this court cancel the transaction by which the property was sold to Plaintiff and order Defendant to restore to Plaintiff all money, obtained by conduct which violates the DTPA. Plaintiff offers to credit Defendant with an offset for the reasonable rental value of the property during the time that Plaintiff has exercised ownership over the property.

9.02 Plaintiff also seeks to recover his [her] special damages or expenses which include [*insert expenses which are sought in addition to rescission, e.g.,* Plaintiff's reasonable out-of-pocket expenditures made as a result of the purchase of the house, interest expense incurred, and the reasonable value of the improvements made by Plaintiff to the house which cannot be removed from it].

9.03 As an alternative to the rescission remedy requested above, Plaintiff seeks to recover all of his [her] actual damages.

9.04 Defendant's acts and omissions as described herein have been a producing cause of damages to Plaintiff.

9.05 Plaintiff's damages include [*insert elements of damages, e.g.,* the reasonable and necessary cost to repair the defects in the house, and the loss in value of the house due to stigma, *i.e.,* the loss in value that the house will suffer after repairs are made because of the nature of the defects and repairs. [*See* §5.16 *supra* for alternative allegations].

9.06 These damages are within the jurisdictional limits of this Court.

[c] FORM: Existing house purchased from owner (failure to disclose defects)

The petition which follows concerns the purchase of a used home. There are no implied warranties given by the seller of the used house. For this reason, lawsuits against the seller typically involve allegations of false representations or failures to disclose material facts. *See* DTPA §17.46(b)(5),(7),(24); TEX. PROP. CODE §5.008 (seller's disclosure of property condition). The petition also includes pleadings which support rescission of the sale of the house, a remedy that buyers of defective houses frequently desire.

		NO. _____	
_____		§	IN THE DISTRICT COURT OF
		§	
vs.		§	_____COUNTY, TEXAS
		§	
_____		§	_____ JUDICIAL DISTRICT

PLAINTIFF'S ORIGINAL PETITION

TO THE HONORABLE JUDGE OF THE DISTRICT COURT:

NOW COMES _____, Plaintiff herein, complaining of _____, Defendant herein, and for cause of action, would show unto the Court as follows:

I. DISCOVERY CONTROL PLAN DESIGNATION

1.01 By this action, Plaintiff seeks _____ [insert appropriate designation under Rule 47(c), e.g., only monetary relief of $100,000 or less, including damages of any kind, penalties, costs, expenses, prejudgment interest, and attorney's fees]. The damages sought are within the jurisdictional limits of this court.

1.02 Discovery in this case is intended to be conducted under Level _____, pursuant to Rule 190._____, *Texas Rules of Civil Procedure*.

II. PARTIES

2.01 _____ is a resident of _____, _____ County, Texas.

2.02 _____ is an individual who resides and may be served with process at _____, _____ County, Texas.

III. VENUE

3.01 Venue of this action is proper in _____ County, Texas because _____ reside in _____ County, Texas and the events made the basis of this lawsuit and giving rise to Plaintiff's cause of action occurred, in whole or in part, in _____ County, Texas.

IV. NOTICE; CONDITIONS PRECEDENT

4.01 Defendant was given notice in writing of the claims made in this petition including a statement of Plaintiff's economic damages, mental anguish damages and expenses, including attorney's fees, more than sixty days before this suit was filed in the manner and form required by DTPA §17.505(a).

4.02 All conditions precedent to recovery by Plaintiff herein have been performed, have occurred, or have been excused.

V. AGENCY

5.01 Unless otherwise stated, whenever it is alleged that Defendant _____ committed an act, failed to perform an act, made a representation or a statement, or failed to make a disclosure, it is alleged that Defendant _____ acted or failed to act through its authorized agents, servants, employees or representatives acting with either expressed, implied, apparent, direct and/or ostensible authority, or _____ subsequently ratified these acts, failures to act, representations, statements or conduct.

VI. FACTS OF CASE

6.01 This lawsuit arises out of the following transaction, acts and events: On _____, Plaintiff purchased from Defendant a house which is located at [*insert street address*] and which is further described as [*insert legal description*].

6.02 The purchase price of the property was $_____ of which $_____ was paid at closing, with the balance financed over a period of _____ years.

6.03 Prior to the purchase of the house, Defendant represented that [*insert representations made, e.g.*, the house was in "good" condition; furthermore, in the Seller's Disclosure of Property Condition, Defendant represented that there were no latent defects in the house].

6.04 In _____, 20___, Plaintiff discovered for the first time that [*insert latent defect not disclosed, e.g.*, the foundation of the house was seriously defective and that it had been so at the time of the sale. Further, Plaintiff discovered that the true condition of the foundation was known to, but had been covered up and concealed by, Defendant. The false representations and concealment of the condition of the foundation was done in order to induce Plaintiff into purchasing the property. Had Plaintiff known the true condition of the foundation, he [she] would not have purchased the house].

6.05 As a result of [the defective condition of the foundation], Plaintiff has incurred and will continue to incur substantial repair costs.

6.06 Because of [the defective condition of the foundation of the house], the actual market value of the house is substantially less than the represented market value of the house (the purchase price).

VII. CAUSE OF ACTION: DTPA

7.01 Plaintiff repeats and realleges the material factual allegations in the preceding paragraphs.

7.02 Plaintiff is a consumer entitled to bring this action for relief under the Texas Deceptive Trade Practices—Consumer

Protection Act (the "DTPA"). The actions of Defendants outlined above constitute misrepresentations, breaches of warranties and unconscionable conduct, actionable under the DTPA.

7.03 Specifically, Defendant committed the following acts in violation of the DTPA "laundry list," one or more of which was a producing cause of damages to Plaintiff:

> (a) Representing that the house had characteristics, ingredients, uses or benefits which it did not have;
>
> (b) Representing that the house was of a particular standard, quality or grade when it was of another; and
>
> (c) Failing to disclose information concerning the house which was known at the time in order to induce the Plaintiff to enter into a transaction which Plaintiff would not have otherwise entered.

7.04 Plaintiff relied on these representations to his [her] detriment.

7.05 Further, Defendant violated the DTPA by breaching one or more express or implied warranties.

7.06 Further, Defendants took advantage of Plaintiff's lack of knowledge about the condition of the property. Accordingly, Defendants violated the DTPA by engaging in unconscionable conduct and/or an unconscionable course of conduct.

7.07 Further, Defendant's conduct was committed knowingly, entitling Plaintiff to seek the trebling of his [her] actual damages in accordance with the DTPA.

VIII. RESCISSION; DAMAGES

8.01 Because of the conduct described in the preceding paragraphs, Plaintiff asks that this court cancel the transaction by which the property was sold to Plaintiff and order Defendant to restore to Plaintiff all money, obtained by conduct which violates the DTPA. Plaintiff offers to credit Defendant with an offset for the reasonable rental value of the property during the time that Plaintiff has exercised ownership over the property.

8.02 Plaintiff also seeks to recover his [her] special damages or expenses which include [*insert expenses which are sought in addition to rescission, e.g.,* Plaintiff's reasonable out-of-pocket expenditures made as a result of the purchase of the house, interest expense incurred, and the reasonable value of the improvements made by Plaintiff to the house which cannot be removed from it].

8.03   As an alternative to the rescission remedy requested above, Plaintiff seeks to recover all of his [her] actual damages.

8.04   Defendant's acts and omissions as described herein have been a producing cause of damages to Plaintiff.

8.05   Plaintiff's damages include [*insert elements of damages, e.g.,* the reasonable and necessary cost to repair the defects in the house, and the loss in value of the house due to stigma, *i.e.,* the loss in value that the house will suffer after repairs are made because of the nature of the defects and repairs. [*See* §5.16 *supra* for alternative allegations].

8.06   These damages are within the jurisdictional limits of this Court.

IX. ADDITIONAL DAMAGES AND PUNITIVE DAMAGES

9.01   Defendant's conduct in violation of the DTPA was committed knowingly, as that term is defined. Accordingly, Plaintiff seeks an award of additional damages under the DTPA in an amount not to exceed three times the amount of his [her] economic damages.

X. ATTORNEY'S FEES

10.01 As a result of Defendant's conduct, Plaintiff has been required to obtain the services of the undersigned attorney for the filing, prosecution and trial of this cause, and therefore seeks an award of reasonable and necessary attorney's fees pursuant to applicable law.

WHEREFORE, PREMISES CONSIDERED, Plaintiff respectfully prays that Defendant be cited according to law to appear and answer this lawsuit, and that after a final trial, judgment be entered against Defendant and in favor of Plaintiff for the following relief:

(a) An order of the court cancelling the transaction by which the property was sold to Plaintiff, and, an order of the court directing Defendants to restore to Plaintiff all money obtained by Defendant through conduct described above, less an offset for the reasonable rental value of the property during the time that the property has been owned by Plaintiff. Additionally, Plaintiff seeks judgment for his [her] special damages as described above; or

(b) In the alternative, a judgment against Defendant for all of Plaintiff's actual damages as described above; and

(c) Under either alternative listed above, a judgment for attorneys' fees, prejudgment and post-judgment interest at the highest lawful rates, court costs, the cost of copies of depositions and expert witness fees; and

(d) Such other relief to which Plaintiff may be entitled.

Respectfully submitted,

_____
Attorney for Plaintiff

[d] FORM: Used house, suit against real estate agent

NO. _____		
_____	§	IN THE DISTRICT COURT OF
	§	
vs.	§	_____ COUNTY, TEXAS
	§	
_____	§	_____ JUDICIAL DISTRICT

PLAINTIFF'S ORIGINAL PETITION

TO THE HONORABLE JUDGE OF THE DISTRICT COURT:

NOW COMES _____, Plaintiff herein, complaining of _____, Defendant herein, and for cause of action, would show unto the Court as follows:

I. DISCOVERY CONTROL PLAN DESIGNATION

1.01 By this action, Plaintiff seeks _____ [insert appropriate designation under Rule 47(c), e.g., only monetary relief of $100,000 or less, including damages of any kind, penalties, costs, expenses, prejudgment interest, and attorney's fees]. The damages sought are within the jurisdictional limits of this court.

1.02 Discovery in this case is intended to be conducted under Level ___, pursuant to Rule 190.___, *Texas Rules of Civil Procedure*.

II. PARTIES

2.01 _____ is a resident of _____, _____ County, Texas.

2.02 _____ is an individual who resides and may be served with process at _____, _____ County, Texas.

III. VENUE

3.01 Venue of this action is proper in _____ County, Texas because _____ reside in _____ County, Texas and the events made the basis of this lawsuit and giving rise to Plaintiff's cause of action occurred, in whole or in part, in _____ County, Texas.

IV. NOTICE; CONDITIONS PRECEDENT

4.01 Defendant was given notice in writing of the claims made in this petition including a statement of Plaintiff's economic damages, mental anguish damages and expenses, including attorney's fees, more than sixty days before this suit was filed in the manner and form required by DTPA §17.505(a).

4.02 All conditions precedent to recovery by Plaintiff herein have been performed, have occurred, or have been excused.

V. AGENCY

5.01 Unless otherwise stated, whenever it is alleged that Defendant _____ committed an act, failed to perform an act, made a representation or a statement, or failed to make a disclosure, it is alleged that Defendant _____ acted or failed to act through its authorized agents, servants, employees or representatives acting with either expressed, implied, apparent, direct and/or ostensible authority, or _____ subsequently ratified these acts, failures to act, representations, statements or conduct.

VI. FACTS OF CASE

6.01 This lawsuit arises out of the following transaction, acts and events: On _____, plaintiff purchased a house which is located at [*insert street address*] and which is further described as [*insert legal description*]. Defendant _____ was the real estate broker and represented the sellers in the transaction.

6.02 Prior to the purchase of the house, defendant represented that [*insert representations made, e.g.,* the house had 4,500 square feet of livable space. Defendant also represented that there were no latent defects in the house].

6.03 In _____, 20___, plaintiff discovered for the first time that [*insert latent defect not disclosed, e.g.,* the foundation of the house was seriously defective and that it had been so at the time of the sale. Further, plaintiff discovered that the true condition of the foundation was known to, but had been covered up and concealed by, defendant. The false representations and concealment of the condition of the foundation was done in order to induce plaintiff into purchasing the property. Had plaintiff known the true condition of the foundation, he [she] would not have purchased the house. Plaintiff also discovered that the house has only 3,000 square feet of livable space].

6.04 As a result of [the defective condition of the foundation], plaintiff has incurred and will continue to incur substantial repair costs.

6.05 Because of [the substantially smaller size of the house than represented], the actual market value of the house is substantially less than the represented market value of the house (the purchase price).

VII. FIRST CAUSE OF ACTION: DTPA

7.01 Plaintiff repeats and realleges the material factual allegations in the preceding paragraphs.

7.02 Plaintiff is a consumer entitled to bring this action for relief under the Texas Deceptive Trade Practices—Consumer Protection Act (the "DTPA"). The actions of Defendants outlined above constitute misrepresentations, breaches of warranties and unconscionable conduct, actionable under the DTPA.

7.03 Specifically, Defendant committed the following acts in violation of the DTPA "laundry list," one or more of which was a producing cause of damages to Plaintiff:

   (a) Representing that the house had characteristics, ingredients, uses or benefits which it did not have;

   (b) Representing that the house was of a particular standard, quality or grade when it was of another;

(c) Representing that the purchase agreement conferred or involved rights, remedies or obligations which it did not or which are prohibited by law; and/or

(d) Failing to disclose information concerning the house which was known at the time in order to induce the Plaintiff to enter into a transaction which Plaintiff would not have otherwise entered.

7.04 Plaintiff relied on these representations to his [her] detriment.

7.05 Further, Defendant violated the DTPA by breaching one or more express warranties.

7.06 Further, Defendant took advantage of Plaintiff's lack of knowledge about the condition of the property. Accordingly, Defendants violated the DTPA by engaging in unconscionable conduct and/or an unconscionable course of conduct.

7.07 Defendant's conduct as described herein was a producing cause of damages to Plaintiff.

7.08 Further, Defendant's conduct was committed knowingly, entitling Plaintiff to seek the trebling of his [her] actual damages in accordance with the DTPA.

VIII. SECOND CAUSE OF ACTION: STATUTORY FRAUD

8.01 Plaintiff repeats and realleges the material factual allegations in the preceding paragraphs.

8.02 By its conduct as described above, Defendant made one or more false representations of material fact and/or benefitted by not disclosing that a third party's representation of material fact was false, for the purpose of inducing Plaintiff into the contract for the purchase of the property.

8.03 Plaintiff relied upon the false representations of fact and entered into the contract for the purchase of the property, which resulted in actual damages to Plaintiff, for which he [she] sues.

IX. THIRD CAUSE OF ACTION: NEGLIGENCE PER SE

9.01 Plaintiff repeats and realleges the material factual allegations in the preceding paragraphs.

9.02 Defendant _____ is a licensed real estate agent. Pursuant to Tex. Occupation Code §1101.652(a)(1), this defendant is prohibited from engaging in negligent conduct, and from making false representations of material facts, or failing to disclose material facts known to him in a real estate transaction.

9.03 Plaintiff is within the class of people that this statute was intended to protect, and the injury he [she] has suffered is the type of injury this statute was intended to prevent.

9.04 Accordingly, by engaging in the conduct set forth above, Defendant _____ was negligent per se.

X. DAMAGES

10.01 Defendant's acts and omissions as described herein have been a producing and/or proximate cause of damages to Plaintiff. Plaintiff has suffered economic damages, including but not limited to: *insert elements of damages, e.g.,* the reasonable and necessary cost to repair the defects in the house, and the reduced value of the house due to missing square footage [*See* §5.16 *supra* for alternative allegations].

10.02 These damages are within the jurisdictional limits of this Court.

XI. ADDITIONAL DAMAGES AND PUNITIVE DAMAGES

11.01 Defendant's conduct in violation of the DTPA was committed knowingly, as that term is defined. Accordingly, Plaintiff seeks an award of additional damages under the DTPA in an amount not to exceed three times the amount of his [her] economic damages.

11.02 The damages suffered by the Plaintiff resulted from fraud or gross neglect. Accordingly, Plaintiff alternatively seeks exemplary damages, not to exceed $_____, which in the opinion of the jury is necessary to punish Defendant and deter similar conduct in the future by Defendant and others.

XII. ATTORNEY'S FEES

12.01 As a result of Defendant's conduct, Plaintiff has been required to obtain the services of the undersigned attorney for the filing, prosecution and trial of this cause, and therefore seeks an award of reasonable and necessary attorney's fees pursuant to applicable law.

WHEREFORE, PREMISES CONSIDERED, Plaintiff respectfully prays that Defendant be cited according to law to appear and answer this lawsuit, and that after a final trial, judgment be entered against Defendant and in favor of Plaintiff for the following relief:

    (a) Judgment against Defendant for all of Plaintiff's actual damages as described above; and

    (b) Judgment for attorneys' fees, prejudgment and post-judgment interest at the highest lawful rates; and

    (c) Such other relief to which Plaintiff may be entitled.

Respectfully submitted,

_____
Attorney for Plaintiff

[e] FORM: Used house, suit against real estate inspector

```
                          NO. _____
_____                §    IN THE DISTRICT COURT OF
                          §
                          §
vs.                       §    _____ COUNTY, TEXAS
                          §
                          §
_____                §    _____ JUDICIAL DISTRICT
```

PLAINTIFF'S ORIGINAL PETITION

TO THE HONORABLE JUDGE OF THE DISTRICT COURT:

NOW COMES _____, Plaintiff herein, complaining of _____, Defendant herein, and for cause of action, would show unto the Court as follows:

I. DISCOVERY CONTROL PLAN DESIGNATION

1.01 By this action, Plaintiff seeks _____ [insert appropriate designation under Rule 47(c), e.g., only monetary relief of $100,000 or less, including damages of any kind, penalties, costs, expenses, prejudgment interest, and attorney's fees]. The damages sought are within the jurisdictional limits of this court.

1.02 Discovery in this case is intended to be conducted under Level _____, pursuant to Rule 190._____, *Texas Rules of Civil Procedure*.

II. PARTIES

2.01 _____ is a resident of _____, _____ County, Texas.

2.02 _____ is an individual who resides and may be served with process at _____, _____ County, Texas.

III. VENUE

3.01 Venue of this action is proper in _____ County, Texas because _____ reside in _____ County, Texas and the events made the basis of this lawsuit and giving rise to Plaintiff's cause of action occurred, in whole or in part, in _____ County, Texas.

IV. CONDITIONS PRECEDENT

4.01 All conditions precedent to recovery by Plaintiff herein have been performed, have occurred, or have been excused.

V. AGENCY

5.01 Unless otherwise stated, whenever it is alleged that Defendant _____ committed an act, failed to perform an act, made a representation or a statement, or failed to make a disclosure, it is alleged that Defendant _____ acted or failed to act through its authorized agents, servants, employees or representatives acting with either expressed, implied, apparent, direct and/or ostensible authority, or _____ subsequently ratified these acts, failures to act, representations, statements or conduct.

VI. FACTS OF CASE

6.01 On _____, Plaintiff purchased a house which is located at [*insert street address*] and which is further described as [*insert legal description*]. After an earnest money contract had been signed but before closing, Plaintiff retained Defendant _____ to perform an inspection of the property.

6.02 Defendant _____ is licensed by the state as a "professional real estate inspector." As a licensed professional real estate inspector, this defendant owed a duty to Plaintiff to do his job without negligence and in a competent manner (Tex. Occ. Code §1102.301), and to refuse to accept employment which is contingent on producing a specific report, or acts in a manner that is otherwise dishonest, fraudulent, deceitful or a misrepresentation. (TEX. OCC. CODE §1102.302);

6.03 In spite of the duties owed by Defendant to Plaintiff, Defendant failed to observe the following defects in the house, even though they should have been observable by him and were observable by a real estate inspector using ordinary prudence in the same or similar circumstances: [*insert conditions not noted in report, e.g.:*

- (a) <u>Rear addition</u>: There has been significant water penetration. Also, the slab for the rear addition of the house is inadequate in depth (less than 4"). Also, although gutters were clean during rain events, water poured over them indicating that they are non-functional.

- (b) <u>Electrical</u>: The main breaker box was dangerous (circuit breakers do not trip; moisture penetrates it; outside wiring had no ground fault protection, bare wires stapled and buried outside).

- (c) <u>HVAC</u>: Although only minor issues are noted with the HVAC, when the system was tested, it was found to be performing at less than 70% of expected system capacity. The entire system needed major repairs or replacement.]

6.04 As a result of [the defects in the house], Plaintiff has incurred and will continue to incur substantial, unexpected repair costs.

VII. CAUSE OF ACTION: NEGLIGENCE AND NEGLIGENCE PER SE

7.01 Plaintiff repeats and realleges the material factual allegations in the preceding paragraphs.

7.02 Defendant was negligent in the manner in which he [she] conducted the inspection of Plaintiff's house.

7.03 Defendant is a licensed real estate inspector. Pursuant to Tex. Occupation Code §1102.301, this defendant is prohibited from engaging in negligent conduct.

7.04 Pursuant to Tex. Occupation Code §1102.302, this defendant was obligated by law to refuse to accept employment which is contingent on producing a specific report, and to refrain from acting in a manner that is otherwise dishonest, fraudulent, deceitful or a misrepresentation. Plaintiff has reason to believe that Defendant violated both of these prohibitions and was, therefore, negligent per se.

VIII. DAMAGES

8.01 Defendant's acts and omissions as described herein have been a proximate cause of damages to Plaintiff. Plaintiff has suffered economic damages, including but not limited to: [*insert elements of damages, e.g.,* the reasonable and necessary cost to repair the defects in the house] [*See* §5.16 *supra* for alternative allegations].

8.02 These damages are within the jurisdictional limits of this Court.

WHEREFORE, PREMISES CONSIDERED, Plaintiff respectfully prays that Defendants be cited to appear and answer herein, and that upon final trial hereof, Plaintiff recover from Defendant all of his [her] actual damages, pre-judgment and post-judgment interest as allowed by law, costs of court and such other and further relief to which he may show himself justly entitled.

Respectfully submitted,

_____
Attorney for Plaintiff

§13.06 Sample Affirmative Defenses in Real Estate Cases

The following forms illustrate possible affirmative defenses that may be particularly applicable in DTPA cases involving real estate transactions. The general form for the Original Answer, §6.06[a], *supra*, can be modified to include one or more of the following affirmative defenses.

[a] FORM: Affirmative defense: transaction size limitation

The transaction about which plaintiff complains arises out of a written contract which relates to a transaction [*or project, or* a set of transactions related to the same project] involving a consideration paid by plaintiff which totaled more than $100,000/$500,000 and which was not the Plaintiff's residence. [*If relying on $100,000 limitation, add:* Further, in negotiating the contract, plaintiff was represented by independent legal counsel.] Accordingly, this transaction is excluded from the DTPA.

[b] FORM: Affirmative defense: real estate agent exemption

In the transaction which is the subject of this suit, defendant was acting as a real estate agent [or broker] licensed under Chapter 1101, *Texas Occupations Code*. Defendant is therefore exempt from liability under the DTPA by DTPA §17.49(i).

[c] FORM: Affirmative defense: "as is" real estate purchase

In the transaction which is the subject of this suit, plaintiff purchased the property "as is" by signing a contract which contained an "Acceptance of Condition" clause. [*If clause is more explicit, quote it verbatim.*] As a result of plaintiff's agreement to purchase the property as is, there is no causation between any allegedly wrongful conduct by this defendant and the damages claimed by plaintiff.

[d] FORM: Affirmative defense: independent investigation

Prior to the closing on the real estate purchase which is the subject of this suit, plaintiff conducted his own independent investigation regarding the existence and extent of termite damage on the property. Specifically, plaintiffs hired an independent termite inspector who provided a termite inspection report to plaintiff which disclosed the existence of the termite damage claimed to have been misrepresented by defendant in this suit. As a result of plaintiff's independent investigation, plaintiff knew the true facts concerning the existence of termite damage in the property and could not have relied upon defendant's non-disclosure of termite damage to go forward with the closing on the property at issue.

§13.07 Sample Motions for Real Estate Recovery Trust Account

[a]   FORM: Motion for order directing payment out of the Real Estate Recovery Trust Account

```
                            NO. _____

_____                  §      IN THE DISTRICT COURT OF
                            §
vs.                         §      _____COUNTY, TEXAS
                            §
_____                  §      _____ JUDICIAL DISTRICT
```

**MOTION FOR ORDER DIRECTING PAYMENT
OUT OF THE REAL ESTATE RECOVERY TRUST ACCOUNT**

TO THE HONORABLE JUDGE OF THE DISTRICT COURT:

This verified application is filed on behalf of _____, plaintiff in the above styled and numbered cause, pursuant to Occupations Code Chapter 1101, Subchapter M, requesting this court to enter an order directing payment of a final judgment out of the Real Estate Recovery Trust Account. Pursuant to this statute, plaintiff will show the following:

1.

On or about _____, 20___ plaintiff filed suit against defendant. By his [her] petition, plaintiff alleged that he [she] had suffered pecuniary damages as a result of misrepresentations, fraud and deceptive trade practices committed by in the course and scope of his [her] duties as a real estate agent.

2.

On or about _____, 20___ plaintiff obtained a final judgment against defendant in the amount of $_____ as actual damages, $_____ as statutory additional damages and $_____ as attorneys' fees, as well as all costs of court. The judgment was signed by the Honorable _____, Judge of the _____ Judicial District Court of _____ County, Texas, who found that plaintiff had proven the allegations of Plaintiff's Petition.

The judgment is based upon facts allowing recovery under Section 1101.607, *Texas Occupations Code*.

3.

The judgment is now final and nonappealable.

4.

No portion of the judgment in favor of plaintiff and against defendant has been satisfied as of the date of the filing of this claim.

5.

Plaintiff is not the spouse or personal representative of defendant.

6.

Defendant lacks sufficient attachable assets to satisfy the judgment.

7.

The plaintiff is aware of no real or personal property which may be seized by the Constable and sold or applied to the satisfaction of the judgment. The execution of the judgment in this case has been returned nulla bona.

8.

A judgment lien has been abstracted and perfected.

9.

Plaintiff requests that this court enter an order directing the Real Estate Commission to make payment to plaintiff pursuant to Section 1101.609, Texas Occupations Code.

WHEREFORE, plaintiff requests that the court enter an order as set forth above and for general relief.

Respectfully submitted,

_____
[Signature of attorney]

[Affidavit]
[Certificate of service]

[b] FORM: Affidavit of custodian of official records, Texas Real Estate Commission

THE STATE OF TEXAS   §

COUNTY OF _____   §

I, _____, Legal Counsel, Texas Real Estate Commission, and a lawful possessor and custodian of the official records of the Texas Real Estate Commission, after causing a search to be made of such records, do hereby certify that _____, license number _____, was a Texas-licensed real estate broker [or salesman] from _____, 20___ to _____, 20___ [, and that was under the sponsorship of _____, broker license number from _____, 20___ to _____, 20___].

IN TESTIMONY WHEREOF, I have hereunto signed my name officially and caused to be impressed hereon the seal of the Texas Real Estate Commission at my office in the City of Austin, Travis County, Texas, this the _____ day of _____ 20___.

_____
[Signature of legal counsel]

[c] FORM: Order directing payment out of Real Estate Recovery Trust Account

NO. _____

_____	§	IN THE DISTRICT COURT OF
	§	
vs.	§	_____ COUNTY, TEXAS
	§	
_____	§	_____ JUDICIAL DISTRICT

ORDER DIRECTING PAYMENT OUT OF
REAL ESTATE RECOVERY TRUST ACCOUNT

On this the _____ day of _____, 20___, came on to be heard Plaintiff's Application for Order Directing Payment out of the Real Estate Recovery Trust Account in satisfaction of a portion of that judgment, dated _____ 20___, rendered against pursuant to the provisions of the Real Estate License Act. The judgment creditor, _____, appeared by and through his [her] attorney of record, _____, and the commission appeared by its attorney, the Attorney General of Texas.

The court finds that it has jurisdiction of the parties and of the subject matter before it and that proper and sufficient notice of this hearing was afforded all parties.

The court finds [upon stipulation by the Texas Real Estate Commission] that the matters stated in Plaintiff's Application for Order Directing Payment out of the Real Estate Recovery Trust Account are true and correct. The court further finds that the judgment debtor, _____, was duly licensed as a real estate broker [or salesperson] by the State of Texas at the time the acts complained of in plaintiff's pleadings were committed. The court finds that the acts complained of were performed in the scope of activity which constitutes a broker or salesman as defined by the Real Estate License Act, *Texas Occupations Code* Chapter 1101.

After reviewing the judgment in this cause, the court finds that the judgment is based on facts allowing recovery under Section 1101.602, *Texas Occupations Code*, and that the judgment creditor is not the spouse of the debtor nor the personal representative of the spouse of the debtor, and that the judgment creditor has complied with the requirements of Section 1101.607, Texas Occupations Code, in that this action was instituted within two (2) years from the accrual of the cause of action and that proper notification to the commission of the granting of the Judgment has been made. The court further finds that the judgment creditor has obtained a judgment as required by Section 1101.606 and that the judgment is in the amount of $_____, as actual damages and $_____ as statutory additional damages, and $_____ as attorneys' fees, together with interest on the total amount at the rate of _____ percent (___%) per annum from _____ 20___, until paid and $_____ as costs of court.

The court further finds that execution on the judgment has been returned nulla bona and that a judgment lien has been abstracted and perfected. The court further finds that the judgment debtor has no real or personal property or other assets which can be sold or applied in satisfaction of the judgment and that therefore, the judgment debtor lacks sufficient assets to satisfy the judgment.

The court finds that Section 1101.610, *Texas Occupations Code*, restricts the amount which the commission must pay on plaintiff's verified claim to plaintiff's actual damages, interest thereon, reasonable attorneys' fees and costs of court, as reflected in the findings and judgment of the trial court; that the Act does not permit an aggrieved person to recover from the Real Estate

Recovery Trust Account any amount of the judgment representing exemplary damages or treble damages awarded by the trial court; and that the payment of claims are limited to $50,000 per transaction. The court finds further that those portions of plaintiff's verified claim which the commission must pay are now payable.

IT IS THEREFORE ORDERED, ADJUDGED and DECREED that the Texas Real Estate Commission is hereby directed to pay from the Real Estate Recovery Trust Account to _____, judgment creditor herein, the sum of $_____ for the claim of such judgment creditor, provided, however, that the aggregate of such payments hereby ordered shall in no event exceed the maximum amount payable from the Real Estate Recovery Trust Account in accordance with the limitations imposed by law. Plaintiff is hereby ordered to assign to the commission all his [her] right, title, and interest in the judgment up to the amount paid by the commission.

Signed this _____ day of _____ 20___.

_____
[Signature of presiding judge]

§13.08 Discovery Requests for Real Estate Actions

§13.08.1 Interrogatories

[a] **FORM: Plaintiff's interrogatories to defendant (sale of unimproved land)**

[Insert the following specific requests into the general form for Interrogatories, §7.43[a], supra.]

1. Identify all persons who have knowledge of the [*describe defect, e.g.*, availability or unavailability of potable water] on the property before and after you purchased it.

2. When did you purchase the property and from whom did you purchase it?

3. Identify all documents, including but not limited to listings, advertisements, inspection reports, appraisals, surveys, contracts, deeds, and documents executed or exchanged at closing, pertaining to your purchase and sale of the property.

4. Identify all permits or governmental approvals of any type that you sought or received that pertain to the property.

5. Identify all real estate agents, brokers or salespersons that you contacted to assist you in marketing or selling the property.

6. Identify all listings, advertisements or brochures pertaining to the property.

7. Identify all persons who made verbal or written offers to purchase the property from you.

[**NOTE:** If the lawsuit involves property that floods or other, similar latent defects, the following types of questions would be helpful in developing the history of the property.]

8. Has the property ever been covered, in whole or in part, with running water of a greater depth than 1" or inundated with standing water of greater than 1" depth? If so, please state the date of each such occurrence.

9. Describe fully all changes or modifications to the natural drainage of the land that you made or caused to be made to the property.

[b]   FORM: Defendant's interrogatories to plaintiff (sale of unimproved land)

[Insert the following specific requests into the general form for Interrogatories, §7.43[a], supra.]

1. Identify all persons who have knowledge of the [*describe defect in property, e.g.,* alleged propensity of the property to become inundated with water] before or after plaintiff purchased the property.

2. Identify all documents, including but not limited to, listings, advertisements, appraisal reports, surveys, contracts, and deeds pertaining to the property.

3. Identify all permits or governmental approvals of any type that you sought or received that pertain to the property.

4. Identify all real estate agents, brokers, or salespersons, architects, engineers, or other consultants you have consulted to assist you in using, developing or selling the property.

5. Identify the date on which and the manner in which you discovered the [*describe defect in property*].

6. Identify all persons who have or claim to have knowledge that [*describe defect in property*] existed prior to the date you purchased the property from defendant.

7. Identify all persons who have or claim to have knowledge that [*describe defect in property*] existed subsequent to the date you purchased the property from defendant.

8. Describe each improvement, alteration, modification or repair to the property since you purchased it.

9. Describe each action that you contend or believe is necessary to remedy the [*describe defect in property*].

10. State the market value of the property at issue just prior to the events made the basis of this lawsuit, and the current market value of the property.

11. State the market value of the property at issue as represented to You. If different, please state the market value of the property as delivered to You and state the basis for any difference.

[c] FORM: Plaintiff's interrogatories to defendant (sale of existing residence)

1. Please Identify the Person(s) from whom You purchased the Property and provide the date of such purchase.

2. Describe the condition of all the structures on the Property at the time You purchased the Property.

3. Please list all termite treatments on any structure located on the Property, and Identify the Persons provided such services and the date(s) of such service.

4. Identify all Persons employed by You to work on the Property since February 2002, please include each person's position, rate of pay, date of hire, and date of termination, if any, and job description.

5. Identify all Persons You have paid to do repair or remodeling work for You on the Property since Your purchase of the Property.

6. Please identify all communication between You and Bug Away Pest Control.

7. Please state the factual basis for the contention that Plaintiffs have failed to mitigate their damages as alleged in your Original Answer.

8. Please state the factual basis for the contention that Plaintiffs were contributorily negligent as alleged in your Original Answer.

9. Please state the factual basis for the contention that Plaintiffs waived any of the claims made in this lawsuit.

[d]   FORM: Defendant's interrogatories to plaintiff (sale of existing residence)

[Insert the following specific requests into the general form for Interrogatories, §7.43[a], supra.]

1. Please describe in detail the efforts you undertook, if any, to determine the actual square footage of the house.

2. State the month, day and year and time of day in which you first viewed the property.

3. State the month, day and year and time of day in which you viewed the property for the second time.

4. Describe in detail all conversations and communications you had with your real estate agent concerning price per square foot regarding the property.

5. State the factors which were material to you in your decision to purchase the property.

6. State the name, address, telephone number and contact individual for any entity, business or contractor which you paid to make any and all improvements on the property.

7. Describe in detail any effort or action which you claim defendant should have undertaken to verify the [misrepresented information, *e.g., square footage of the property, etc.*].

8. Describe in detail the complaints that you have allegedly suffered related to your claim for mental anguish.

9. State the addresses, square footage and asking price of each home which you viewed with your real estate agent prior to the purchase.

10. Please Identify all licensed professional counselors, psychologists, psychiatrists or other mental health professional who

have treated you as a result of the mental anguish which Plaintiff claims to have suffered due to the allegations in your Petition.

§13.08.2 Requests for Production

[a] FORM: Plaintiff's Requests for Production to defendant (sale of unimproved land)

[Insert the following specific requests into the general form for Requests for Production, §7,47, supra.]

1. All listings, advertisements or brochures pertaining to the property.

2. All maps, plats and/or surveys of the property.

3. All title commitments related to the property.

4. All abstracts of title related to the property.

5. All appraisals or other documents demonstrating the fair market value of the property.

6. Any and all documents reflecting property taxes paid by you on the property.

7. Any and all documents reflecting the legal description of the property.

[b] FORM: Defendant's Requests for Production to plaintiff (sale of unimproved land)

[Insert the following specific requests into the general form for Requests for Production, §7,47, supra.]

1. All documents demonstrating and/or evidencing any expenses or damages being claimed by you in this lawsuit.

2. All documents furnished to your insurance company or any insurance company as proof of the alleged injuries sustained by you as a result of any loss made the basis of this lawsuit.

3. All diaries, calendars and/or other lists or notes kept by you regarding or related in any way to the events made the basis of this lawsuit.

4. All documents you contend represent or contain admissions of Defendants or of any employees, agents and/or representatives of

Defendant, whether written, recorded or otherwise, that pertain to any of the events made the basis of this lawsuit.

5. All documents evidencing remediation or repairs made to the property at issue.

6. All documents demonstrating the diminished value of the property due to Defendant's alleged conduct.

7. All documents evidencing any safety standards, laws, regulations, ordinances, industry standards or building standards which you contend that any Defendant has violated with respect to the subject matter of this lawsuit.

8. Any and all listing agreements for any proposed sale of property at issue.

[c] FORM: Plaintiff's Requests for Production to real estate agent defendant (sale of existing residence)

[Insert the following specific requests into the general form for Requests for Production, §7,47, supra.]

1. Your file on the listing and/or sale of the Plaintiffs' home.

2. All listing agreements concerning the Plaintiffs' home.

3. All advertisements submitted by you for publicizing the sale of the Plaintiffs' home.

4. All multiple listing service listings concerning the Plaintiffs' home.

5. All materials received by you from the sellers concerning the home.

6. All written disclosures provided by you concerning the sale of the home.

7. All documents reflecting your investigation into the sellers' representations or disclosures concerning the sale of the home.

8. All documents reflecting your inspection or measurement of the home.

9. All documents containing correspondence between you and any inspector, contractor, lender, title company or other third party in connection with the sale of the home to Plaintiffs.

[d] FORM: Real estate agent defendant's Request for Production to plaintiff (sale of existing residence)

1. All documents containing or reflecting any representations of fact you contend you relied on in deciding to purchase the home.

2. All appraisals on the home.

3. All invoices, contracts, checks or other similar documents evidencing improvements made and/or work performed on the home since you purchase.

4. All ad valorem tax statements and notices of appraised value concerning the home.

5. All financial statements prepared by or for you which include the home as an asset.

6. All documents received by you from any real estate professional concerning the home.

7. All documents reflecting the inaccuracy of any statements made by defendant concerning the home on which statements you contend you relied upon in purchasing the home.

8. All documents reflecting the existence of defects in the home you contend were misrepresented or not disclosed.

9. All documents reflecting the cost to repair the conditions of the home made the basis of this lawsuit.

Chapter 14

New and Used Motor Vehicles

§14.01 General Considerations
§14.02 Specific Laundry List Provisions Applicable to Motor Vehicles
§14.03 Other Texas Laws Governing Sale of Motor Vehicles
    §14.03.1 Texas Lemon Law
    §14.03.2 Regulation of Motor Vehicle Advertising
    §14.03.3 Warranty Considerations
    §14.03.4 FTC Used Car Rule
§14.04 Defenses
§14.05 Initial Client Checklist
    [a] CHECKLIST: Purchase of new or used motor vehicle
§14.06 Pre-Suit Notice Letter to Seller of Motor Vehicle
    [a] FORM: —Notice letter (demanding rescission and/or damages)
§14.07 Plaintiff's Pleadings—New or Used Motor Vehicle
    [a] FORM: —New vehicle (with Holder-in-Due-Course Rule claim)
    [b] FORM: —Used motor vehicle (misrepresented/undisclosed condition)
§14.08 Defendant's Pleadings—Sale of New or Used Motor Vehicle
    [a] FORM: —Original answer with affirmative defenses—Sale of Used Motor Vehicle
§14.09 Discovery—Motor Vehicle Sales
    §14.09.1 Interrogatories
        [a] FORM: —Plaintiff's interrogatories to defendant car dealer
        [b] FORM: —Plaintiff's interrogatories to defendant manufacturer (recall)
        [c] FORM: —Defendant's interrogatories to plaintiff (claim of misrepresented defective vehicle)
    §14.09.2 Requests for Production
        [a] FORM: —Plaintiff's requests for production to defendant dealer/seller
        [b] FORM:— Defendant's requests for production to plaintiff

§14.01 General Considerations

Except for perhaps the purchase of a home, the purchase of a new or used car is likely the second largest purchase a consumer will make. My grandfather knew how to fix just about everything including his 1964 Rambler, which he bought from a salesman he knew and trusted. Past generations—by necessity--had a much better understanding of the various components and systems of a car. Today, rapidly-developing technology and the sheer complexity of present-day motor vehicles make it impossible for most consumers to evaluate anything more than the basic functions. Can you look under the hood of your car and tell why it is squeaking or knocking or how likely it is to leave you stranded in the middle of nowhere on your next trip out of town?

In this environment, the consumer is at the mercy of the seller to provide accurate and material information about a motor vehicle, new or used, to allow the consumer to make informed decisions about whether to purchase it, how much to pay for it and, quite often, how to finance that purchase. Unscrupulous sellers can take advantage of this disparity in knowledge and lead the consumer into an unfair bargain.

The DTPA is keenly suited to provide relief to consumers who have been the victim of deception in the purchase of an vehicle, whether new or used. Several DTPA laundry list provisions are applicable only to vehicle sales. The DTPA also enhances the ability of a consumer to obtain relief when a manufacturer's or dealer's warranty has been breached. In addition to the DTPA, other Texas laws provides regulatory and administrative protection to the consumer. The Texas Lemon Law, discussed in more detail below, is a powerful tool available to Texas consumers which can be used to force a manufacturer to re-purchase a new vehicle if repair attempts fail to conform it to the manufacturer's warranty.

The forms in this chapter have been tailored to apply to common motor vehicle purchase complaints and can be further customized for almost any DTPA case involving a new or used motor vehicle.

§14.02 Specific Laundry List Provisions Applicable to Motor Vehicles

The DTPA laundry list has a number of provisions which can be adapted to use in the sale or repair of a new or used motor vehicle. In addition to the general prohibitions of DTPA §§17.46(b)(5), (7) and (24), the following laundry list provisions are directly applicable to motor vehicle sales or service cases:

(12) Representing that an agreement [like a retail installment sales contract or limited warranty] confers or involves rights, remedies or obligations which it does not have or involve or which are prohibited by law;

(15) basing a charge for the repair of any item in whole or in part on a guaranty or warranty instead of on the value of the actual repairs made or work to be performed on the item without stating separately the charges for the work and the charge for the warranty or guaranty, if any;

(16) disconnecting, turning back, or resetting the odometer of any motor vehicle so as to reduce the number of miles indicated on the odometer gauge;

(20) representing that a guaranty or warranty confers or involves rights or remedies which it does not have or involve, provided,

however, that nothing in this sub-chapter shall be construed to expand the implied warranty of merchantability as defined in Sections 2.314 through 2.318 and Sections 2A.212 through 2A.216 to involve obligations in excess of those which are appropriate to the goods; and,

(22) representing that work or services have been performed on, or parts replaced in, goods when the work or services were not performed or the parts replaced.

Texas courts have routinely approved of the use of the DTPA in new and used motor vehicle sales. *See, e.g.Tony Gullo Motors I, L.P. v. Chapa*, 212 S.W.3d 299 (Tex. 2006) (affirming DTPA verdict against car dealer for delivering a Toyota Highlander "base" model after representing it was a "limited" model); *GJP, Inc. v. Ghosh*, 251 S.W.3d 854 (Tex. App.--Austin 2008, no writ) (seller's statements that used Jaguar "drove very well," "had no problems whatever," was "in fine running order," that "it's been very, very reliable," and that it had "strong mechanicals" were actionable representations of fact and not mere sales hype).

§14.03 Other Texas Laws Governing Sale of Motor Vehicles

The DTPA provides remedies for purchasers of new and used motor vehicles in claims arising out of false representations, breach of warranty and pricing. *See* DTPA §17.46(b). The DTPA practitioner should be familiar with other laws in Texas which may provide adequate remedies for aggrieved motor vehicle consumers. The Texas Occupations Code regulates the sellers and lessors of motor vehicles in Texas. The Texas Lemon Law is now part of the Occupations Code. In addition to statutory law, there is a body of administrative rules and regulations adopted by the Texas Department of Motor Vehicles Division under the Texas Occupations Code.

Although the notice letter requirements for a defective new vehicle are the same as for other products, a discussion of these alternative remedies is necessary to insure that early in the process, consideration is given to working through the Texas Department of Motor Vehicles.

The Texas Department of Motor Vehicles has the general power to regulate all aspects of the distribution, sale, and leasing of motor vehicles. TEX. OCC. CODE §2301.151. Included within this regulatory power are the powers to make investigations and conduct hearings on consumer complaints, TEX. OCC. CODE §2301.153, and in particular, the power to compel a dealer or manufacturer to comply with warranty obligations. TEX. OCC. CODE §2301.602.

§14.03.1 Texas Lemon Law

The Texas Lemon Law, now set forth in TEXAS OCCUPATIONS CODE Chapter 2301, Subchapter M, requires a manufacturer to repair a defect in a new motor vehicle purchased or leased from a Texas motor vehicle dealer so that it conforms with the manufacturer's warranty. TEX. OCC. CODE §2301.603. The definition of "motor vehicle" is expansive and includes cars, trucks, motor homes, motorcycles, all-terrain vehicles, towable recreational vehicles and neighborhood electric vehicles. TEX. OCC. CODE §2301.002(23). If the motor vehicle is still covered by the original manufacturer's warranty and has a defect or condition which creates a serious safety hazard, or substantially impairs the use or market value of the motor vehicle, and the manufacturer or dealer is unable to repair the vehicle "after a reasonable number of attempts," then the manufacturer must either "(1) replace the motor vehicle with a comparable motor vehicle; or (2) accept return of the vehicle from the owner and refund to the owner the full purchase price less a reasonable allowance for the owner's use of the vehicle and any other allowances or refunds payable to the owner." TEX. OCC. CODE §2301.604. The phrase "impairment of market value" means a "substantial loss in market value caused by a defect specific to a motor vehicle." TEX. OCC. CODE §2301.601.

The Code provides a rebuttable presumption that a "reasonable number of repair attempts" have been made if the following conditions are met:

(1) the same nonconformity has been subject to repair four or more times by the manufacturer or dealer, and two of the repair attempts have been made with the twelve month period following the date of delivery to the original owner, or 12,000 miles, whichever comes first;

(2) if the defect causes a substantial safety hazard, then only two repair attempts are required to create the presumption, so long as one of the attempts was made during the first 12 months or 12,000 miles, and at least one other attempt was made during the 12 months or 12,000 miles after the first repair was attempted; or

(3) if the vehicle is out of service for a cumulative total of 30 days or more in 24 months or 24,000 miles (whichever comes first), and at least two repair attempts were made in the first 12 months or 12,000 miles after delivery, and a nonconformity still exists which substantially impairs the vehicle's market value. TEX. OCC. CODE §2301.605.

The Board of the Texas Department of Motor Vehicles is empowered to order a manufacturer, distributor or converter to replace or re-purchase a defective motor vehicle ("lemon") from the purchaser. The first step in seeking this remedy is to file a complaint with the Department. The Department of Motor Vehicles has adopted regulations which govern its handling of consumer complaints. *See generally* 43 TEX. ADMIN. CODE §215.201 *et seq.*

The form (Form MVD-140 Lemon Law Complaint Form) for filing a Lemon Law complaint may be found on the Department of Motor Vehicles website at: http://txdmv.gov/motorists/consumer-protection/lemon-law. There is a $35 filing fee that is charged by the Department. TEX. OCC. CODE §2301.712. The Department of Motor Vehicles has a toll-free number for Lemon Law complaints (888-368-4689).

There is a relatively short time limit for filing for relief from the Department of Motor Vehicles under the Texas Lemon Law: The complaint must be filed with the Department within six (6) months after the earliest of: 1) the expiration of the express warranty term; 2) the dates on which 24 months or 24,000 miles have passed since the original delivery. For example, if the vehicle has been driven 24,000 miles in just 12 months, the deadline to file a Lemon Law complaint will be just 18 months after the original purchase and delivery.

If re-purchase is ordered by the Department, the manufacturer (or distributor or converter) must repay the consumer the full purchase price, including all taxes, title and license fees, but less a deduction for the reasonable value of the consumer's use of the vehicle during ownership. The value for reasonable use will be determined according to a formula which assumes a highway motor vehicle has a life expectancy of 120,000 miles and a towable motor vehicle has a life expectancy of 10 years. 43 TEX. ADMIN. CODE §215.208 (2012). In addition to this repurchase remedy, the purchaser is entitled to reimbursement from the manufacturer for "incidental expenses," which may include the cost of alternative transportation, towing, meals and lodging due to failure on out-of-town trips and accessories purchased and added to the vehicle. 43 TEX. ADMIN. CODE §215.209 (2012). Recovery of attorney's fees can also be included if the purchaser retains an attorney after notification the manufacturer is represented by counsel. *Id.*

It is unlikely the Lemon Law's repurchase or replacement remedy can be invoked in court without first timely filing a complaint with the Department of Motor Vehicles. The Lemon Law provides that the re-purchase or replacement remedy cannot be invoked by filing suit unless the purchaser has first exhausted his remedies with the Department of Motor Vehicles. TEX. OCC. CODE §2301.607. A right-to-sue letter may be obtained from the Department if no decision has been rendered on the complaint after it been on file for 150 days. TEX. OCC. CODE §2301.607(c). A violation of the Lemon Law (or any other provision of Subchapter M) can then be actionable as a tie-in statute violation under the DTPA. TEX. OCC. CODE §2301.607.

Any other judicial remedy seems to be limited to judicial review of the Department's final decision on the Lemon Law complaint, whether it be for or against the purchaser. TEX. OCC. CODE §2301.609.

§14.03.2 Regulation of Motor Vehicle Advertising

The provisions of the Occupations Code regulating the sale and leasing of motor vehicles contain express prohibitions against false advertising, TEX. OCC. CODE §2301.351. The Department of Motor Vehicles has adopted extensive regulations governing the advertising of motor vehicles for sale. *See, general*, 43 TEX. ADMIN. CODE Subch. H. For instance, Department regulations prohibit use of the terms "dealer's cost" or "invoice price," 43 TEX. ADMIN. CODE §215.252, and of the terms "lowest price," "best deal" or similar claims, 43 TEX. ADMIN. CODE §215.266 . The Department's advertising regulations are generally enforceable by administrative action for civil penalties initiated by the Department. TEX. OCC. CODE §§2301.801 *et seq.*

§14.03.3 Warranty Considerations

Department of Motor Vehicle regulations prohibit a dealer from failing to perform its warranty obligations, TEX. OCC. CODE §2301.353, and also prohibit a dealer from requiring a consumer to purchase, as a condition of the sale of a new vehicle, any special features, equipment, parts, or accessories not ordered or desired by the purchaser, unless they already are installed on a car at the time of sale. TEX. OCC. CODE §2301.352. Violations of these provisions of Subchapter M are actionable as a tie-in statute violation under the DTPA. TEX. OCC. CODE §2301.607.

§14.03.4 FTC Used Car Rule

Any person or business who sells or offers for sale more than five used vehicles in a 12-month period must comply with the Federal Trade Commission's Used Motor Vehicle Trade Regulation Rule, 16 C.F.R. Part 455. 16 C.F.R. §455.1. In addition to prohibiting the misrepresentation of the mechanical condition of the used vehicle and misrepresenting the terms of any warranty, the FTC's Used Car Rule mandates the prominent display of a completed Buyers Guide form on the vehicle in such a fashion that both sides are readily readable.

See https://www.consumer.ftc.gov/articles/pdf-0083-buyers-guide.pdf for an example of this form. The FTC-mandated Buyers Guide, as completed by the seller, should clearly disclose whether the motor vehicle is being offered with any warranty—full or limited—or whether the vehicle is being sold "AS IS – NO WARRANTY."

If the sale is conducted primarily in Spanish, the Buyers Guide must be printed in Spanish. 16 C.F.R. §455.5. The seller is prohibited from making statements, oral or written, to contradict the disclosures in the Buyers Guide. 16 C.F.R. §455.4. The Buyers Guide must be given to the buyer with the vehicle sold and is incorporated into the sale contract and overrides any contrary provisions in the contract. 16 C.F.R. §455.3.

§14.04 Defenses

Experienced motor vehicle dealers will take reasonable steps to reduce or eliminate exposure to claims of deceptive sales practices in connection with the sale of new or used motor vehicles. While the DTPA does not provide specific statutory defenses to motor vehicle dealers, the general concepts regarding "AS IS" disclaimers of express and implied warranties and written contractual provisions limiting or eliminating reliance on oral representations will apply to motor vehicle sales.

Prominent and conspicuous written disclosure that the seller is making no warranties or representations about the motor vehicle will raise the general affirmative defenses of disclaimer and independent investigation. *See* §§2.02.5-6, *supra*. Used motor vehicle dealers who comply with the FTC Used Car Rule and prepare the Buyers Guide to conspicuously disclaim any warranties should be entitled to the "as is" defenses under the U.C.C. and Texas common law. TEX. BUS. & COM. CODE §2.316(c)(all implied warranties excluded by expressions like "as is" and "with all faults").

Representations about the fuel economy of new motor vehicles can be misleading: Actual gas mileage is almost never as high as the mileage seen in advertisements. In this area, the Environmental Protection Agency (EPA) and the FTC have combined regulatory schemes that virtually assure deceptive representations about high fuel economy. See generally, 40 C.F.R. Part 600 (EPA's regulations for fuel economy testing, calculation labeling allowing (and in fact requiring) manufacturers to conduct their testing outside of normal driving parameters), and 16 C.F.R. Part 259 (FTC's regulations for fuel economy advertising requiring that fuel economy representations correspond with those derived in compliance with the EPA's testing regulations). However, the DTPA expressly exempts representations in advertisements specifically authorized by FTC regulations. DTPA §17.49(b). Motor vehicle sellers would therefore have an exemption defense to any action based upon misrepresentations about fuel economy in advertisements which comply with these EPA and FTC rules.

§14.05 Initial Client Checklist

[a] CHECKLIST: Purchase of new or used motor vehicle

Client _____   Date of Interview _____

The purchase

❑ What vehicle was purchased

❑ Date of purchase

❑ Who was the seller/dealership

❑ Who was the salesperson

❑ What was the purchase price

- Down payment

- Monthly payments

- Was there third party financing

- To whom are payments being made now

- Term of loan

- Interest rate

- Are payments current? If not, how far behind

[If payments are not current, then the prospective defendant may file suit against the client for the default in an inconvenient forum upon receipt of the pre-filing demand letter; therefore, consideration should be given to filing a "preemptive" common law claim against the seller to fix venue and to insure that the client is the plaintiff.]

❑ Was there any particular purpose for the purchase

❑ Why was it purchased from this seller

- Advertising

- Sales pitch

- Prior dealings between parties

- Other

❑ Was a written contract for the purchase used

❑ If a contract was used, is there an arbitration clause

[An arbitration clause may be enforceable if the Federal Arbitration Act applies to the transaction. See 9 U.S.C. §1, et seq.]

❑ If a contract was used, is there a holder-in-due course clause

[The Federal Trade Commission "holder-in-due course" and the "purchase money loan" rules extend liability for the seller's conduct to anyone who purchases the consumer's contract (if the purchase is for personal, family or household purposes) by requiring a holder in due course provision in the contract. *See* 16 C.F.R. 433.2(a); *see also Home Savings Association v. Guerra*, 733 S.W.2d 134 (Tex. 1987).]

- ❑ Were any written warranties given

[If express warranties were given, then federal law limits the effectiveness of disclaimers of implied warranties on goods purchased for personal, family or household purposes. *See* 15 U.S.C. §2308 ("Magnuson-Moss Warranty-Federal Trade Commission Act").]

- ❑ Is there an "as is" clause or disclaimer
- ❑ What was said about the quality or characteristics of the vehicle
- ❑ Did the mileage match the odometer statement
- ❑ Was any important information about the vehicle not disclosed to the client

Complaint about product/service

- ❑ What is the defect or deficiency in the vehicle
- ❑ When was the defect discovered

[The discovery rule applies to avoid the statute of limitations only if the client exercised "reasonable diligence." *See* DTPA §17.565.]

- ❑ How was the defect discovered
- ❑ Has the defect been repaired before
- ❑ Has the seller been notified of the defect; if so, how and when
- ❑ If seller has been notified, what was the response, if any
- ❑ Have repairs been attempted? If so, how and when
- ❑ Have any repairs been performed by any third parties

[Third party repairs may raise questions as to who is responsible for the condition of the vehicle.]

Use of vehicle

- ❑ How many miles has the vehicle been driven since it was purchased

[The seller may be entitled to a credit for miles driven if rescission is sought.]

- ❏ Has a replacement vehicle been rented or leased
- ❏ If so, how much has been paid for the rental or lease

Damages

- ❏ What is needed to fix the vehicle
- ❏ If vehicle cannot be fixed, what type of replacement is available
- ❏ How long was the vehicle not used
- ❏ Discuss each item of loss in questionnaire

Expectations of client

- ❏ What does client expect to accomplish through litigation

Explanations to client

- ❏ Anticipated cost of lawsuit
- ❏ Attorney and client agreement
- ❏ Requirements of discovery
- ❏ Must be present at depositions and trial
- ❏ Outcome of litigation is unpredictable

Documents to obtain from client

[Client should be advised to deliver *all* documents that in any way relate to transaction; however, the following list is illustrative of the type of documents that must be provided if they exist.]

- ❏ Advertising seen
- ❏ Point of sale brochures or documents
- ❏ Contract or receipts
- ❏ Odometer statement
- ❏ Warranties provided
- ❏ Service or repair orders
- ❏ Repair estimates
- ❏ Any document provided to or signed by client in connection with sale

❑ Letters to or from anyone involved

❑ Appraisals or valuation reports

❑ All documents reflecting losses from transaction

[NOTE: When a claim involves a new automobile that fails to conform to the warranties given on the automobile, administrative remedies are available to the owner under the Texas Lemon Law, TEX. OCC. CODE CHAPTER 2301, SUBCHAPTER M. The administrative remedy involves filing a complaint with the Director of the Board of the Texas Department of Motor Vehicles who has power to adjudicate the complaint and order corrective action by the dealer or manufacturer. *Id.* at §2301.602. The specific protection provided by the Code may not be used in litigation under the DTPA unless the owner of the automobile has first exhausted all administrative remedies. *Id.* at §2301.607. *See also* §3.05 *infra.*]

§14.06 Pre-Suit Notice Letter to Seller of Motor Vehicle

A DTPA notice letter involving a claim over a misrepresented sale of a new or used motor vehicle follows the same format as a notice letter for the sale of goods or services. See §§3.03, 3.04, supra.

[a]   FORM: —Notice letter (demanding rescission and/or damages)

CERTIFIED MAIL, RETURN RECEIPT REQUESTED

(Date)

(Inside address)

Re: (Client's name); [Date] Purchase of [motor vehicle]

Dear _____ :

Our firm has [or I have] been retained to represent _____ with respect to a claim which he [she] has against you. Please direct all communications concerning this matter to me.

As you are aware, on _____, 20___ our client purchased the above-referenced motor vehicle from your company. At the time of the purchase, [insert facts of transaction, e.g., you represented that the motor vehicle was in good working order and had not been in any major accidents. You presented our client with a written brochure which described various qualities and characteristics that the motor vehicle.] In fact, the motor vehicle does not conform to the descriptions you gave. In reality and contrary to your representations, [e.g., the motor vehicle has been in a major accident, the frame has been damaged and the odometer has been rolled back.] As time passes and additional investigation is done, additional defects may come to light.

Your actions in tis matter constitute false, misleading and deceptive acts in violation of the Texas Deceptive Trade Practices - Consumer Protection Act, including one or more of the following provisions:.

(5) representing that goods or services have sponsorship, approval, characteristics, ingredients, uses, benefits, or quantities which they do not have or that a person has a sponsorship, approval, status, affiliation, or connection which the person does not;

(6) representing that goods are original or new if they are deteriorated, reconditioned, reclaimed, used, or secondhand;

(7) representing that goods or services are of a particular standard, quality, or grade, or that goods are of a particular style or model, if they are of another;

(12) Representing that an agreement confers or involves rights, remedies or obligations which it does not have or involve or which are prohibited by law;

(15) basing a charge for the repair of any item in whole or in part on a guaranty or warranty instead of on the value of the actual repairs made or work to be performed on the item without stating separately the charges for the work and the charge for the warranty or guaranty, if any;

(16) disconnecting, turning back, or resetting the odometer of any motor vehicle so as to reduce the number of miles indicated on the odometer gauge;

(20) representing that a guaranty or warranty confers or involves rights or remedies which it does not have or involve;

(22) representing that work or services have been performed on, or parts replaced in, goods when the work or services were not performed or the parts replaced; and/or,

(24) failing to disclose information concerning goods or services which was known at the time of the transaction if such failure to disclose such information was intended to induce the consumer into a transaction into which the consumer would not have entered had the information been disclosed.

[Alternate 1: Rescission]

[Demand is hereby made that you cancel the transaction by which our client purchased the [motor vehicle]. Upon your agreement to cancel the transaction, our client will return the [motor vehicle] to you in exchange for a refund of all money paid by our client to you [less the reasonable rental value of the [motor vehicle] during the time that our client actually was able to use it].

[Additionally, as it was necessary for our client to finance the transaction, interest expense has been incurred in the amount of $. This interest expense must be included in the amount you agree to pay to our client.]

[Alternate 2: Damages]

Based upon the information now available to us, and for purposes of this notice letter, we estimate that our client's damages are as follows:

Difference in Value (between the motor vehicle as represented and the motor vehicle as delivered):	$ _____
Cost of Repair:	$ _____
Loss of Use:	$ _____
Mental Anguish:	$ _____
Expenses incurred (including attorney's fees):	$ _____

Of course, we reserve the right to adjust these amounts to conform to the information and additional evidence that will be available to us at the time of trial should litigation be necessary.

[Alternate statement of attorney's fees]

Our client has incurred reasonable and necessary attorney's fees in the pursuit of the claim stated in this letter. The amount of fees incurred as of the date of this letter is $_____ [or _____% of our client's total damages].

[Notice of contingent interest]

Under the contract of employment we have with our client, our firm has [or I have] been assigned an interest in the claim against you.

[Offer of settlement]

The purpose of this letter is to encourage you to resolve our client's claim in a fair and equitable manner without the need for further legal action. In the event you fail to take advantage of this opportunity, we [or I] will have no alternative but to recommend to our client that a lawsuit be filed against you under the Deceptive Trade Practices - Consumer Protection Act. In this lawsuit, rather than seeking only the amount of compensation we are asking of you at this time, we will seek to recover the full measure of damages to which our client is legally entitled and well as our client's expenses and attorney's fees as allowed by law.

[Notice to insurance carrier]

In the event that you have insurance or a bond which you believe may cover all or any part of the claim made in this letter, you are requested to notify your insurance carrier or bonding company immediately.

[Request for response]

If you are interested in resolving this matter without the necessity of litigation, please contact me within sixty days of your receipt of this letter.

[Copy to third party]

A copy of this letter is being sent to [insert name of third party], who, in our opinion, is subject to the same claims and defenses our client has against you.

[NOTE: In sending copies of notice letters to third parties, care must be taken in drafting the notice letter so as to avoid statements that may be actionable as defamatory.]

Sincerely,

[Signature of attorney]

§14.07 Plaintiff's Pleadings—New or Used Motor Vehicle

A DTPA petition which asserts a claim based on a defective new or used motor vehicle illustrates typical DTPA pleading involving the sale of goods or services.

The following petition illustrates application of the Federal Trade Commission "Holder-in-Due-Course" and "Purchase Money Loan" rules. These rules are discussed in more detail in §3.03, *supra*.

[a] FORM: —New vehicle (with Holder-in-Due-Course Rule claim)

```
NO. _____

_____      §      IN THE DISTRICT COURT OF
                §
vs.  §          _____ COUNTY, TEXAS
                §
_____      §      _____ JUDICIAL DISTRICT
```

<u>**PLAINTIFF'S ORIGINAL PETITION**</u>

NOW COMES _____, Plaintiff herein, complaining of _____ Defendants herein, and for cause of action, would show unto the Court as follows:

I. DISCOVERY CONTROL PLAN DESIGNATION

1.01 Discovery in this case is intended to be conducted under Level _____, pursuant to Rule 190._____, Texas Rules of Civil Procedure.

[NOTE: For a discussion of the levels of discovery, see §§7.37-7.39 supra.]

II. PARTIES

2.01 _____ is a resident of _____, _____ County, Texas.

2.02 _____ is an individual who resides and may be served with process at _____, _____ County, Texas.

2.03 _____ is a Texas corporation which may be served with process by serving _____, its registered agent, at _____, the corporation's registered address.

III. VENUE

3.01 Venue of this action is proper in _____ County, Texas because _____ reside in _____ County, Texas and the events made the basis of this lawsuit and giving rise to Plaintiff's cause of action occurred, in whole or in part, in _____ County, Texas.

3.02 Since venue of this action in this county is proper as to Defendant _____ and no mandatory venue provision applies, venue is proper in this county as to all defendants.

IV. NOTICE; CONDITIONS PRECEDENT

4.01 Defendant was given notice in writing of the claims made in this petition including a statement of Plaintiff's economic damages, mental anguish damages and expenses, including attorney's fees, more than sixty days before this suit was filed in the manner and form required by DTPA §17.505(a).

4.02 All conditions precedent to recovery by Plaintiff herein have been performed, have occurred, or have been excused.

V. AGENCY

5.01 Unless otherwise stated, whenever it is alleged that Defendant _____ committed an act, failed to perform an act, made a representation or a statement, or failed to make a disclosure, it is alleged that Defendant _____ acted or failed to act through its authorized agents, servants, employees or representatives acting with either expressed, implied, apparent, direct and/or ostensible authority, or _____ subsequently ratified these acts, failures to act, representations, statements or conduct.

VI. FACTS OF CASE

6.01 This lawsuit arises out of the purchase by Plaintiff from Defendant _____, of a new _____ vehicle identification number _____. At all material times, Defendant _____ was a merchant in the business of selling motor vehicles.

6.02 The sales price of the vehicle was _____, excluding finance charges. Plaintiffs made a down payment of _____, leaving an unpaid balance of _____.

6.03 The contract of sale was assigned to Defendant _____ (referred to as "lender"). The contract which was assigned contained the following provision:

"Any holder of this consumer credit contract is subject to all claims and defenses which the debtor could assert against the seller of goods or services obtained pursuant hereto or with the proceeds hereof. Recovery hereunder by the debtor shall not exceed amounts paid by the Debtor hereunder."

6.04 As a result of the sale of the vehicle by Defendant _____, an implied warranty of merchantability arose in the transaction which includes the following guarantees:

(1) that the vehicle would pass without objection in the trade under the contract description; and

(2) that the vehicle was fit for the ordinary purpose for which such an vehicle is purchased.

6.05 Subsequent to the sale, an implied warranty arose in connection with the repairs performed by Defendant _____. Specifically, Defendant _____ impliedly warranted that the repair work had been performed in a good and workmanlike manner.

6.06 In addition to the implied warranties that arose in the transaction, certain representations and express warranties were made, including the following [*insert express warranties made, e.g.*, that any malfunction in the vehicle occurring during a specified warranty period resulting from defects in material or workmanship would be repaired, and that repair work on the vehicle had, in fact, repaired the defects].

6.07 After the vehicle was purchased, [*insert facts on which lawsuit is based, e.g.*, Plaintiff discovered that the vehicle leaked water into the passenger compartment whenever the air conditioner was turned on]. This condition was discovered during the express warranty period. Plaintiff notified Defendant _____ of the condition and returned the vehicle to the dealership for repairs on numerous occasions, none of which were successful.

6.08 In addition to the condition described above, [*insert facts relating to other defects, e.g.*, the electrical system of the vehicle was and is defective such that the headlights, horn and blinker lights work only intermittently. Plaintiff notified Defendant _____ of the condition and returned the vehicle for repairs; however, Defendant never repaired the defects].

VII. FIRST CAUSE OF ACTION: DTPA

7.01 Plaintiff repeats and realleges the material factual allegations in the preceding paragraphs.

7.02 Plaintiff is a consumer entitled to bring this action for relief under the Texas Deceptive Trade Practices—Consumer Protection Act (the "DTPA"). The actions of Defendants outlined above constitute misrepresentations, breaches of warranties and unconscionable conduct, actionable under the DTPA.

7.03 Specifically, Defendant committed the following acts in violation of the DTPA "laundry list," one or more of which was a producing cause of damages to Plaintiff:

(a) Representing that the goods or services had characteristics, ingredients, uses or benefits which they did not have;

(b) Representing that goods or services were of a particular standard, quality or grade when they were of another; and

(c) Failing to disclose information concerning goods or services which was known at the time in order to induce the Plaintiff to enter into a transaction which Plaintiff would not have otherwise entered.

7.04 Plaintiff relied on these representations to his [her] detriment.

7.05 Further, Defendant violated the DTPA by breaching one or more warranties. Because of the inherent defects in the _____, which defects existed at the time the vehicle was sold although not discovered until later, the vehicle was not merchantable in that it would not pass without objection in the trade under the contract description and it was not fit for the ordinary purpose for which such vehicles are used.

7.06 Furthermore, Defendant _____ failed to perform the repair work in a good and workmanlike manner. This conduct by Defendant _____ constitutes a breach of the implied warranties described above, which breach is actionable under DTPA §17.50(a)(2).

7.07 When the vehicle was not repaired, the express warranties that it would be and had been repaired were breached. Defendant _____'s breach of the express warranties is actionable under DTPA §17.50(a)(2).

7.08 Further, Defendant violated the DTPA by engaging in unconscionable conduct and/or an unconscionable course of conduct. Defendant took advantage of Plaintiff's lack of knowledge, ability, experience and/or capacity to a grossly unfair degree. For this reason, this transaction was unconscionable and is actionable under DTPA §17.50(a)(3).

7.09 Defendant's conduct as described herein was a producing cause of damages to Plaintiff.

7.10 Further, Defendant's conduct was committed knowingly, entitling Plaintiff to seek the trebling of his [her] actual damages in accordance with the DTPA.

VIII. SECOND CAUSE OF ACTION: LENDER LIABILITY

8.01 Plaintiff repeats and realleges the material factual allegations in the preceding paragraphs.

8.02 Plaintiff is indebted to Lender as a result of his [her] purchase of the vehicle. Plaintiff is entitled to assert all claims and defenses stated above against Lender as a defense to the debt.

IX. DAMAGES; RESCISSION

9.01 Defendant's acts and omissions as described herein have been a producing and/or proximate cause of damages to Plaintiff. Plaintiff has suffered economic damages, including but not limited to:

(a) the reasonable and necessary cost to repair the vehicle;

(b) loss of use for the time that the vehicle has been unrepaired and, therefore, unusable;

(c) in the alternative, the diminished or lost value of the vehicle due to its defective condition.

[*See* §5.16, *supra*, for alternative allegations.]

9.02 These damages are within the jurisdictional limits of this Court.

[*If rescission is sought, insert the following:*]

9.03 Plaintiff seeks a damages remedy as an alternative to the remedy of rescission which is requested in the following paragraph. Plaintiff revokes his [her] acceptance of the vehicle for the reason that its defects substantially impair its value to Plaintiff and acceptance was based on Plaintiff's reasonable reliance on the false representations and warranties of Defendant _____ that the defects in the vehicle would be repaired.

9.04 Accordingly, Plaintiff seeks a cancellation of the vehicle purchase transaction and an order of the court restoring to him [her] the money obtained by Defendants as a result of the representations and breaches of warranty set forth above. Plaintiff also seeks cancellation of the debt and now offers to return the vehicle to Defendants. In this connection, Plaintiff also offers to credit Defendant with the fair rental value of the vehicle for the number of miles it was actually driven, calculated at the rate a vehicle in similar condition would have rented for during the time period in question.

X. ADDITIONAL DAMAGES AND PUNITIVE DAMAGES

10.01 Defendant's conduct in violation of the DTPA was committed knowingly, as that term is defined. Accordingly, Plaintiff seeks an award of additional damages under the DTPA in an amount not to exceed three times the amount of his [her] economic damages.

[*See* §5.17, *supra*, for alternative forms]

XI. ATTORNEY'S FEES

11.01   As a result of Defendant's conduct, Plaintiff has been required to obtain the services of the undersigned attorney for the filing, prosecution and trial of this cause, and therefore seeks an award of reasonable and necessary attorney's fees pursuant to applicable law.

WHEREFORE, PREMISES CONSIDERED, Plaintiff respectfully prays that Defendant be cited to appear and answer herein, and that upon final trial hereof, Plaintiff have judgment for:

(a)   An order of the court rescinding the vehicle purchase transaction and restoring to him [her] all money paid out in connection with the purchase, less a credit for Plaintiff's use of the vehicle. Plaintiff also seeks his [her] out-of-pocket expenses which include [*insert expenses sought in addition to rescission, e.g.,* Plaintiff's expenditure of funds for the repair of the vehicle].

(b)   In the alternative, Plaintiff seeks a judgment for all of his [her] economic and additional damages as described above.

(c)   Under either remedy, Plaintiff seeks prejudgment and post-judgment interest in the highest amount allowed by law, attorneys' fees, costs of court, and such other relief to which Plaintiff may be entitled.

Respectfully submitted,

_____

Attorney for Plaintiff

```
[NOTE: If the defendant's conduct reflects bad faith dealings with the plaintiff, it may
be appropriate to include a cause of action for breach of the duty of good faith under TEX.
BUS. & COM. CODE §1.203 since all contracts for the sale of goods under the UCC contain
a duty of good faith as a matter of law.]
```

[b] FORM: Used motor vehicle (misrepresented/undisclosed condition)

NO. _____

_____ §   IN THE DISTRICT COURT OF

§

vs.   §   _____ COUNTY, TEXAS

§

_____ §   _____ JUDICIAL DISTRICT

PLAINTIFF'S ORIGINAL PETITION

NOW COMES _____, Plaintiff herein, complaining of _____ Defendants herein, and for cause of action, would show unto the Court as follows:

I. DISCOVERY CONTROL PLAN DESIGNATION

1.01 Discovery in this case is intended to be conducted under Level _____, pursuant to Rule 190._____, Texas Rules of Civil Procedure.

[NOTE: For a discussion of the levels of discovery, see §§7.37-7.39 supra.]

II. PARTIES

2.01 _____ is a resident of _____, _____ County, Texas.

2.02 _____ is an individual who resides and may be served with process at _____, _____ County, Texas.

2.03 _____ is a Texas corporation which may be served with process by serving _____, its registered agent, at _____, the corporation's registered address.

III. VENUE

3.01 Venue of this action is proper in _____ County, Texas because _____ reside in _____ County, Texas and the events made the basis of this lawsuit and giving rise to Plaintiff's cause of action occurred, in whole or in part, in _____ County, Texas.

3.02 Since venue of this action in this county is proper as to Defendant _____ and no mandatory venue provision applies, venue is proper in this county as to all defendants.

IV. NOTICE; CONDITIONS PRECEDENT

4.01 Defendant was given notice in writing of the claims made in this petition including a statement of Plaintiff's economic damages, mental anguish damages and expenses, including attorney's fees, more than sixty days before this suit was filed in the manner and form required by DTPA §17.505(a).

4.02 All conditions precedent to recovery by Plaintiff herein have been performed, have occurred, or have been excused.

V. AGENCY

5.01 Unless otherwise stated, whenever it is alleged that Defendant _____ committed an act, failed to perform an act, made a representation or a statement, or failed to make a disclosure, it is alleged that Defendant _____ acted or failed to act through its authorized agents, servants, employees or representatives acting with either expressed, implied, apparent, direct and/or ostensible authority, or _____ subsequently ratified these acts, failures to act, representations, statements or conduct.

VI. FACTS OF CASE

6.01 This lawsuit arises out of the purchase by Plaintiff from Defendant _____, of a used _____ vehicle identification number _____. At all material times, Defendant _____ was a merchant in the business of selling vehicles.

6.02 The sales price of the vehicle was _____, excluding finance charges. Plaintiffs made a down payment of _____, leaving an unpaid balance of _____.

6.03 On or about _____, Plaintiff responded to an internet advertisement posted by Defendant for a "_____" [description of motor vehicle.

6.03 The advertisement described the vehicle as being in "great shape" and "good condition." When Plaintiff met with Defendant later that day to further discuss the vehicle, Plaintiff asked Defendant why he was selling the vehicle and whether Defendant had experienced any problems with it. Plaintiff specifically asked whether the vehicle had ever been in any collisions. In response, Defendant assured Plaintiff that the vehicle had been a good car for Defendant and that he had never been in a wreck with it. In reliance upon these and other assurances from Defendant, Plaintiff purchased the vehicle from Defendant for $_____.

6.04 After completing the purchase, Plaintiff attempted to secure comprehensive insurance coverage for the vehicle. The insurance company ran a history of the title and discovered that the vehicle was an assembled and salvaged vehicle which had been totaled in a previous collision. Because it is a rebuilt vehicle, the insurance company refused to issue full insurance without an appraisal and inspection of the vehicle.

6.05 Within a couple of days of possession of the vehicle, Plaintiff discovered that the vehicle was neither in "great shape" nor "good condition." Plaintiff further discovered that the vehicle had a persistent pull to the left indicative of a bent frame from a major collision.

6.06 In addition to the condition described above, [*insert facts relating to other defects, e.g.*, the electrical system of the vehicle was and is defective such that the headlights, horn and blinker lights work only intermittently. Plaintiff notified Defendant of the condition and returned the vehicle to Defendant for repairs; however, Defendant never repaired the defects].

VII. FIRST CAUSE OF ACTION: DTPA

7.01 Plaintiff repeats and realleges the material factual allegations in the preceding paragraphs.

7.02 Plaintiff is a consumer entitled to bring this action for relief under the Texas Deceptive Trade Practices—Consumer Protection Act (the "DTPA"). The actions of Defendants outlined above constitute misrepresentations, breaches of warranties and unconscionable conduct, actionable under the DTPA.

7.03 Specifically, Defendant committed the following acts in violation of the DTPA "laundry list," one or more of which was a producing cause of damages to Plaintiff:

(a) Representing that the goods or services had characteristics, ingredients, uses or benefits which they did not have;

(b) Representing that goods or services were of a particular standard, quality or grade when they were of another; and

(c) Failing to disclose information concerning goods or services which was known at the time in order to induce the Plaintiff to enter into a transaction which Plaintiff would not have otherwise entered.

7.04 Plaintiff relied on these representations to his [her] detriment.

7.05 Further, Defendant violated the DTPA by engaging in unconscionable conduct and/or an unconscionable course of conduct. Defendant took advantage of Plaintiff's lack of knowledge, ability, experience and/or capacity to a grossly unfair degree. For this reason, this transaction was unconscionable and is actionable under DTPA §17.50(a)(3).

7.06 Defendant's conduct as described herein was a producing cause of damages to Plaintiff.

7.07 Further, Defendant's conduct was committed knowingly, entitling Plaintiff to seek the trebling of his [her] actual damages in accordance with the DTPA.

VIII. DAMAGES; RESCISSION

8.01 Defendant's acts and omissions as described herein have been a producing and/or proximate cause of damages to Plaintiff. Plaintiff has suffered economic damages, including but not limited to:

(a) the reasonable and necessary cost to repair the vehicle;

(b) loss of use for the time that the vehicle has been unrepaired and, therefore, unusable;

(c) in the alternative, the diminished or lost value of the vehicle due to its defective condition.

[*See* §5.16, *supra*, for alternative allegations.]

8.02 These damages are within the jurisdictional limits of this Court.

[*If rescission is sought, insert the following:*]

8.03 Plaintiff seeks a damages remedy as an alternative to the remedy of rescission which is requested in the following paragraph. Plaintiff revokes his [her] acceptance of the vehicle for the reason that its defects substantially impair its value to Plaintiff and acceptance was based on Plaintiff's reasonable reliance on the false representations and warranties of Defendant _____ that the defects in the vehicle would be repaired.

8.04 Accordingly, Plaintiff seeks a cancellation of the vehicle purchase transaction and an order of the court restoring to him [her] the money obtained by Defendants as a result of the representations and breaches of warranty set forth above. Plaintiff also seeks cancellation of the debt and now offers to return the vehicle to Defendants. In this connection, Plaintiff also offers to credit Defendant with the fair rental value of the vehicle for the number of miles it was actually driven, calculated at the rate an vehicle in similar condition would have rented for during the time period in question.

IX. ADDITIONAL DAMAGES AND PUNITIVE DAMAGES

9.01 Defendant's conduct in violation of the DTPA was committed knowingly, as that term is defined. Accordingly, Plaintiff seeks an award of additional damages under the DTPA in an amount not to exceed three times the amount of his [her] economic damages.

[*See* §5.17, *supra*, for alternative forms]

X. ATTORNEY'S FEES

10.01 As a result of Defendant's conduct, Plaintiff has been required to obtain the services of the undersigned attorney for the filing, prosecution and trial of this cause, and therefore seeks an award of reasonable and necessary attorney's fees pursuant to applicable law.

WHEREFORE, PREMISES CONSIDERED, Plaintiff respectfully prays that Defendant be cited to appear and answer herein, and that upon final trial hereof, Plaintiff have judgment for:

(a) An order of the court rescinding the vehicle purchase transaction and restoring to him [her] all money paid out in connection with the purchase, less a credit for Plaintiff's use of the vehicle. Plaintiff also seeks his [her] out-of-pocket expenses which include [*insert expenses sought in addition to rescission, e.g.*, Plaintiff's expenditure of funds for the repair of the vehicle].

(b) In the alternative, Plaintiff seeks a judgment for all of his [her] economic and additional damages as described above.

(c) Under either remedy, Plaintiff seeks prejudgment and post-judgment interest in the highest amount allowed by law, attorneys' fees, costs of court, and such other relief to which Plaintiff may be entitled.

Respectfully submitted,

_____

Attorney for Plaintiff

§14.08 Defendant's Pleadings—Sale of New or Used Motor Vehicle

As noted above, the use of "AS IS" disclaimers and compliance with F.T.C. rules and regulations regarding advertising should be affirmative defenses to be pled by the defendant.

The form of the Defendant's Original Answer below includes these affirmative defenses and other defenses commonly found in the defendant's answer.

[a] FORM: —Original answer with affirmative defenses—Sale of Used Motor Vehicle

NO. _____

_____	§	IN THE DISTRICT COURT OF
	§	
vs.	§	_____ COUNTY, TEXAS
	§	
_____	§	_____ JUDICIAL DISTRICT

ORIGINAL ANSWER

TO THE HONORABLE JUDGE OF THE DISTRICT COURT:

_____, defendant, files this Original Answer to plaintiff's petition and will show the following:

[*general denial*]

1. Defendant generally denies the allegations made in plaintiff's petition.

[*Continue with any specific and verified denials as necessary*]

2. Conditions precedent not performed. Plaintiff has not performed all conditions precedent necessary to maintain this lawsuit. Specifically, [insert condition precedent that has not occurred].

[*Continue with any affirmative defenses, as applicable.*]

3. Pleading further and affirmatively, if such defense be necessary:

[(a)] Disclaimer of Warranties and Representations. Prior to offering the motor vehicle at issue for sale to the public, Defendant completed and conspicuously displayed the FTC Buyers Guide, disclosing to Plaintiff and others interested in purchasing the motor vehicle at issue that it was being offered "AS IS—NO WARRANTY." Defendant effectively disclaimed any warranties concerning the motor vehicle.

[(b)] In the transaction which is the subject of this suit, Plaintiff executed a contract which contained an "Acceptance of Condition" clause. [*If clause is more explicit, quote it verbatim.*] As a result of plaintiff's agreement to purchase the motor vehicle "as is," there is no causation between any allegedly wrongful conduct by this defendant and the damages claimed by plaintiff.

[(c)] Prior to the purchase of the motor vehicle which is the subject of this suit, plaintiff conducted his own independent investigation regarding the existence and extent of collision damage to the vehicle. Specifically, plaintiff took the vehicle to an independent repair shop to have the vehicle thoroughly inspected. As a result of plaintiff's independent investigation, plaintiff could not have relied upon any alleged misrepresentation or nondisclosure by defendant to go forward with the purchase of the vehicle.

[(d)] Statute of Limitations. The two years statute of limitations applicable to all DTPA claims made in this case expired on plaintiff's claims before suit was filed. Specifically, plaintiff discovered, or in the exercise of reasonable diligence should have discovered, the claims that are the subject of this suit more than two years before the date this suit was filed.

[(e)] Parol Evidence Rule. Plaintiff's claims are barred by the parol evidence rule.

4. Request for relief. [*See* §6.04 *supra*]

Respectfully submitted,

[Signature of attorney]

[Certificate of service]

§14.09 Discovery—Motor Vehicle Sales

The following discovery requests may be tailored to fit a case involving a claim against for deceptive acts in connection with the sale of a new or used motor vehicle. See Chapter 7, supra, for general discovery forms and introductory definitions.

§14.09.1 Interrogatories

[a] FORM: Plaintiff's interrogatories to defendant car dealer

The following are specific Interrogatories which can be included in a set sent to a motor vehicle dealer in connection with a claim that the vehicle was misrepresented at the time of the sale.

1. Identify the person answering these Interrogatories with the following information: full legal name, any prior names, address, social security number, driver's license number, date of birth and relationship to Defendant.

2. Identify all persons who personally interacted with Plaintiffs at the dealership, including but not limited to the salesman, finance manager and used car manager. For each conviction of a felony or crime of moral turpitude during the last ten (10) years for the persons identified in the previous interrogatories, please state the date, offense, court and sentence for each such conviction.

3. Please describe how You came into possession of the motor vehicle at issue in this case, including the date acquired, identity of prior owner(s), location of acquisition and identify of all persons involved in the acquisition.

4. Please describe the actions taken by You to inspect the vehicle prior to Your acquisition of it, including the identity of the persons involved in the inspection(s) or investigation(s).

5. Please identify all documents reviewed by You, Your employees, agents or representatives, prior to Your acquisition of the vehicle.

6. Please describe all action taken by You, Your employees, agents or representatives, to prepare the motor vehicle at issue for sale, including the identity of all persons involved in those actions.

7. How much did You pay for the vehicle when You acquired it?

8. How much did You spend to repair, improve and/or maintain the vehicle while it was in Your possession? To whom did You make these expenditures?

9. For each statement made by You or on Your behalf to Plaintiff about the condition of the vehicle prior to her purchase of it, please state the substance of the statement, who made it, the date and time made and all persons present when the statement was made.

10. Please describe all conversations You had with the Plaintiff concerning her decision to purchase the motor vehicle, including the substance of her statements, date made, to whom it was made and the identity of all persons who were there to hear the statement.

11. If You have inspected the vehicle since Plaintiff's purchase, please describe that inspection, including the date, persons involved and observations concerning the condition of the vehicle.

12. Did Plaintiff's vehicle come with a warranty? If so, please describe the general terms of the warranty and how the warranty was communicated to Plaintiff. If not, please describe how warranties were limited or disclaimed.

13. In Your opinion, what was the fair market value of the vehicle when it was sold to Plaintiff? What is the fair market value of the vehicle now?

14. What is the reasonable cost to repair the vehicle in order to put it [back] into the condition it was in at the time of Plaintiff's purchase?

[b] FORM: Plaintiff's interrogatories to defendant manufacturer (recall)

The following are specific Interrogatories which can be included in a set sent to a motor vehicle manufacturer in connection with a recall campaign.

1. Please describe the condition(s) which led to Your [XYZ] recall of the vehicle.

2. Please describe the effect(s) on the vehicle(s) caused by the conditions which led to Your [XYZ] recall.

3. Please describe the corrective action(s) to the vehicle(s) required by Your [XYZ] recall.

4. Do You contend that the symptoms reported by Plaintiff with his vehicle are within the normal specifications? If so, please state the factual basis of that contention.

5. Do You contend that any warranty, express or implied, regarding Plaintiff's vehicle has been waived or disclaimed, or otherwise excluded from covering Plaintiff's vehicle? If so, please state the factual basis of that contention.

6. Please state the factual basis of Your contention that Plaintiff has failed to mitigate his damages.

7. Please identify each act and/or omission relevant to this lawsuit You contend Defendant [Car Dealership] committed outside of the scope of its agency with You.

8. Please Identify each lawsuit filed against You in which the plaintiff has alleged a [year, make, model] vehicle experienced [the complaint alleged, e.g., stalling without warning while being driven].

9. Please Identify each Person who has lodged a written complaint with You concerning a [year, make, model] vehicle experienced [the complaint alleged, e.g., stalling without warning while being driven].

10. For each recall issued by You concerning a [year, make model] vehicle, please state the recall initiation date, identifying number or code, issue(s) of vehicle performance or condition causing the recall, and corrective action deemed required.

11. Please describe each and every investigation conducted by You, at your corporate facility, into the possibility of a common design or manufacturing defect of the [year, make, model] vehicle experienced [the complaint alleged, e.g., stalling without warning while being driven].

12. Please describe the process at [Defendant] by which customer complaints are collected and evaluated for the purpose of determining whether an issue requiring a recall has been identified.

13. Please describe the process at [Defendant] which led to the Recall Campaign No. ___.

14. Do You contend that Plaintiff's vehicle was damaged after the purchase? If so, please state the factual basis of that contention, including any testing.

[c] FORM: Defendant's interrogatories to plaintiff (claim of misrepresented defective vehicle)

The following are is a full set of Interrogatories to be sent by a motor vehicle manufacturer or dealer to the plaintiff when the plaintiff claims that the vehicle is defective and was misrepresented at the time of sale.

1. Please identify every item of advertising, including without limitation, print, radio, internet, billboard or television advertising–communicated by Defendant which You contend You relied upon in purchasing the vehicle, including the substance of such advertising, the date You saw, read or heard it, the media in which it was contained and why You relied upon it in deciding to purchase the vehicle.

2 Identify Yourself by Your full name, all previous names, social security number, date of birth, driver's license number and current address.

3. For each felony or crime of moral turpitude for which You have been convicted during the past ten (10) years, please state the date, crime, court, sentence and date of release.

4. Please describe each and every warranty, oral or written, express or implied, You contend You received from Defendant in connection with Your purchase of the vehicle.

5. Please state every problem, failure or defect in the vehicle You have experienced or that the vehicle has exhibited since Your purchase of the vehicle, including the date, failure, location where experienced or exhibited, and the identity of all persons who have witnessed or experienced the problem, failure or defect identified.

6. Please state who currently has possession of the vehicle and how it is currently being operated.

7. Please identify every repair You have made to the vehicle since You purchased it, stating the reason for the repair, the date, person or entity who made the repair, what repair was made, whether the repair was effective, the cost of the repair and who paid for the repair.

8. Please list every repair which has been made or attempted by Defendant, including the date, nature of the defect, repairs made, whether the repair was effective, and amount paid for the repair.

9. Please state the mileage on the vehicle as of the following dates:

    a) Your DTPA notice letter,

    b) when this lawsuit was filed, and

    c) the current mileage.

10. Please state the substance of any and all conversations or communications between You and any agent or employee of Defendant related to the vehicle which communications are the basis of Your complaint herein, including the date, identity of the persons involved and the substance of the communications.

11. Please identify every person or entity who has inspected the vehicle since Your purchase of the vehicle from Defendant, including the date of inspection, reason for inspection, identity of the personal entity making the inspection, written documentation obtained, general observations made and any amounts paid for the inspection.

12. What do You contend to be the fair market value of the vehicle in its current condition?

13. What do You contend to be the reasonable cost to repair the vehicle in order to put it into the condition as You believed it to be at the time of Your purchase of the vehicle?

14. Do You claim a loss of earnings from the vehicle in this lawsuit? If so, please identify the gross earnings in that profit earned by You with the vehicle monthly from the date of purchase through the present. Please state the nature of the business in which the vehicle was employed.

15. Please identify each and every modification You have made to the vehicle since You acquired it, specifying the date and nature of the modification, persons or entities who made the modification and amount paid by You for it.

16. For each incidents of maintenance made by You on the vehicle (such as tire rotation, oil change scheduled maintenance, etc.), please describe the date and action taken, with the person or entity performing the maintenance and the cost of doing so.

§14.09.2 Requests for Production

Insert the following specific requests into the general form for Requests for Production, §7.47, supra.

[a] FORM:— Plaintiff's requests for production to defendant dealer/seller

1. Please produce any and all documents executed by Plaintiff in connection with the purchase of the motor vehicle, including any Retail Installment Contract, bill of sale, buyer's order, title application, odometer statement, disclosure or receipt, including any drafts thereof.

2. Please produce any and all documents containing any warranty or warranty disclaimer concerning the vehicle purchased by Plaintiff.

3. Please produce any and all documents containing or evidencing Your advertisement of the vehicle sold to Plaintiff.

4. Please produce any and all documents executed or obtained by You in connection with Your acquisition of the vehicle.

5. Please produce any and all documents containing reports or information from third-party sources concerning the prior maintenance, repair, service or other condition of the vehicle prior to its sale to Plaintiff.

6. Please produce any and all documents reflecting Your maintenance, service or repair of the vehicle prior to its sale to Plaintiff.

7. Please produce any and all documents reflecting Your maintenance, service or repair of the vehicle after the sale to Plaintiff.

8. Please produce any and all documents reflecting Your purchase of parts for the vehicle prior to or subsequent to Your sale of the vehicle to Plaintiff.

9. Please produce any and all documents which reflect a record of the labor spent by Your employees inspecting, maintaining or repairing the vehicle prior to or subsequent to its purchase by Plaintiff.

10. Please produce any and all manufacturer's safety or repair bulletins received by You in connection with Plaintiff's vehicle.

11. Please produce any and all documents containing correspondence between You and Plaintiff concerning the vehicle.

12. Please produce any and all documents evidencing or reflecting the compensation received by Your employees in connection with the sale of the vehicle to Plaintiff.

[b] FORM:— Defendant's requests for production to plaintiff

1. Please produce any and all documents received by You from Defendant in connection with Your purchase of the motor vehicle.

2. Please produce any and all documents reflecting service, maintenance or repair of the vehicle since Your purchase of it.

3. Please produce any and all documents received by You from Defendant concerning the vehicle since Your purchase of the vehicle.

4. Please produce any and all repair estimates received by You in connection with the vehicle since Your purchase.

5. Please produce the owner's manual for the vehicle.

6. Please produce the warranty booklet for the manual.

7. Please produce any and all correspondence You received from the manufacturer of the vehicle concerning the vehicle since Your purchase.

8. Please produce any and all notes made by You concerning any conversation with any employee of Defendant concerning the vehicle.

9. Please produce any and all documents containing advertising You reviewed or relied upon in making the decision to purchase the vehicle.

10. Please produce any and all documents concerning any collision in which the vehicle may have been involved since Your purchase of it.

11. Please produce any and all documents which demonstrate or evidence the fair market value of the vehicle at any time.

12. Please produce any and all photographic or video representations of the vehicle Defendant's place of business or any of Defendant's agents or employees.

13. Please produce any and all audio records of any conversations or statements concerning the vehicle.

14. Please produce any and all parts, components or fluids removed from the vehicle.

15. Please produce any and all cancelled checks, credit card receipts or other evidence of payment for repairs by You to the vehicle.

16. Please produce any and all documents which evidence or reflect Your loss of income from the condition of the vehicle.

17. Please produce any and all documents reflecting Your payment of out-of-pocket expenses You claim as damages because of the condition of the vehicle.

18. Please produce any and all documents which evidence Your loss of time You claim as a result of the condition of the vehicle.

19. Please produce any and all documents demonstrating mental anguish You claim to have suffered as a result of the condition of the vehicle or the facts alleged in Your lawsuit.

20. Please produce any and all documents reflecting insurance claims for damages to the vehicle.

21. If this vehicle has been depreciated for tax purposes, please produce any and all tax schedules, returns, attachments or other documents reflecting Your deduction of depreciation or expenses associated with the vehicle for any year for which those claims were made.

22. Please produce any and all documents reflecting annual state inspections of the vehicle.

23. Please produce any and all documents received from the manufacturer concerning recall or service campaigns relating to the vehicle.

24. Please produce Your contract with Your attorney.

25. Please produce any and all documents reflecting the amount of attorney's fees incurred by You in connection with this lawsuit.

26. Please produce any and all advertisements You have placed or created for any sale or attempted sale of the vehicle.

(This page intentionally left blank.)

Chapter 15

Business Opportunities and Franchises

§15.01 Business Opportunities and Franchises—General Overview
§15.02 Texas Business Opportunity Act
§15.03 F.T.C. Franchise Rule Exemption
§15.04 Other Theories of Liability
§15.05 Pre-Suit Notice Letter to Seller of Business Opportunity
    [a] FORM: —Notice letter: business opportunity
§15.06 Plaintiff's Pleadings—Texas Business Opportunities Act
    [a] FORM: —DTPA, Texas Business Opportunity Act tie-in violations, fraud and bad faith
    [b] FORM: —Franchise investment
    [c] FORM: —Purchase of existing franchise
§15.07 Defendant's Pleadings—Sale of Franchise
    [a] FORM: —Original answer with specific denials, verified denials and affirmative defenses—Texas Business Opportunities Act Action
§15.08 Discovery—Business Opportunity Actions
  §15.08.1 Interrogatories
    [a] FORM: —Franchise investments (to defendant)
    [b] FORM: —Franchise investments (to plaintiff)
  §15.08.2 Requests for Production
    [a] FORM: —Franchisee to franchisor (misrepresentations regarding territory and profits)
    [b] FORM: —Franchisor to franchisee (misrepresentations in sale of franchise)

§15.01 Business Opportunities and Franchises— General Overview

In this age of rapid mobility and global media, we see the signs for the "same" restaurants, hotels or even fitness centers wherever we travel. Consumers have a good experience with a hotel or restaurant in one location and look for the same good experience from the hotel or restaurant under the same brand name and logo in another location. This consumer experience is the result franchising, a global phenomenon of the last 50 years which shows no sign of slowing down. According to *Entrepreneur* magazine (Jan. 2015), the top five U.S. franchises for 2015 are: 1) Hampton Hotels, 2) Anytime Fitness, 3) Subway, 4) Jack in the Box and 5) Supercuts. Because of franchising, many of these establishments are owned and operated as small businesses by single owners or family units.

After developing a successful branded product or service line, the owner may seek to sell that brand to an entrepreneur in a new location willing to pay for the goodwill and name recognition associated with that brand. Of course, the entrepreneur must agree to conduct his business in ways that promote the brand's goodwill. These entrepreneurs decide to buy into the franchise system in hopes that their hard work and investment, coupled with the brand owner's management of their product or service, would provide them a profitable return on their investment. On the other hand, the franchisor expects to profit from its development and maintenance of a brand that can be packaged sold into new markets with someone else shouldering the risk of failure.

Franchised businesses succeed (and fail) in new markets for a myriad of reasons: changing demographics, competitors entering or leaving the market, brand name recognition, market saturation, degree of brand preservation efforts, and changing consumer tastes to name a few. The caches information necessary to make an informed decision about purchasing a franchised product or service line—actual sales and income levels, costs of proprietary products, existing and proposed advertising support, supervision and litigation, for example--are closely guarded as trade secrets of the franchise brand owner/seller. The financial incentives in the marketing of franchise business opportunities to oversell the changes or degrees of expected success--or to hide information detrimental to the sale of the franchise--loom large.

§15.02 Texas Business Opportunity Act

Texas law recognizes that the prospective purchasers of these franchised "business opportunities" are deserving of many of the same protections afforded to consumers in more traditional consumer purchases. In 1997, the Texas Business Opportunity Act was enacted for the purpose of protecting persons against false, misleading or deceptive practices in the advertising, offering for sale or lease, and sale or lease of business opportunities, and to provide "efficient and economical" procedures to secure that protection. TEX. Bus. & COM. CODE §51.004. The statute applies to the sale or lease of any products, equipment, supplies, or services in which:

• the buyer pays at least $500 in initial consideration for products, equipment, supplies or services to begin a business; and

• the seller represents the buyer will earn or "is likely to earn" a profit; and

- the seller agrees to provide a sales, production, or marketing program; or to assist the buyer in finding locations for the use of the products; or to buy back products or equipment.

[TEX. BUS. & COM. CODE §51.003]

A "seller" who sells a business opportunity is prohibited from engaging in any of the following acts or practices:

(1) employing any representation, device, scheme, or artifice to deceive a purchaser,

(2) making any untrue statement of a material fact or omitting to state a material fact in connection with the documents and information required to be furnished to the secretary of state or prospective purchaser,

(3) representing that the business opportunity provides or will provide income or earning potential of any kind unless the seller has documented data to substantiate the claims and discloses this data to the purchaser at the time, or

(4) making any claim or representation in advertising or promotional material or in any oral sales presentation, solicitation, or discussion which is inconsistent with the information required to be disclosed by the Act.

[TEX. BUS. & COM. CODE §51.301]

The Business Opportunity Act does not provide its own cause of action for damages; however, the Business Opportunity Act is a "tie-in" statute and a violation of the Act can be brought through the DTPA. TEX. BUS. & COM. CODE §51.302.

In certain instances, a seller of a business opportunity is required to have a bond, trust account, or letter of credit established in the minimum amount of $25,000. TEX. BUS. & COM. CODE §51.101. Any person who is damaged by the seller's violation of the Act or breach of contract may bring an action against the bond, trust account, or letter of credit for the amount of actual damages sustained. TEX. BUS. & COM. CODE §51.102.

The Business Opportunity Act requires that, prior to offering any business opportunity for sale in Texas, the franchisor must file a copy its statutorily prescribed disclosure statement with the Texas Secretary of State. TEX. BUS. & COM. CODE §51.051. The detailed disclosure statement requirements are set out in Subchapter D of Chapter 51 and include accurate information about the financial performance of other franchisees and the nature and extent of litigation filed against the franchisor or its principals. TEX. BUS. & COM. CODE §§51.160, 51.161.

§15.03 F.T.C. Franchise Rule Exemption

The Federal Trade Commission has also adopted an extensive set of rules for franchise offerings in interstate commerce—the "Franchise Rule"—which can be found at 16 CFR Parts 436 and 437. The FTC's Franchise Rule requires the franchisor to prepare and deliver an extensive disclosure statement containing 23 specific items of information about the offered franchise, its officers, and other franchisees.

The existence of this parallel regulatory scheme results in two major consequences to the Texas Business Opportunity Act. First, the Texas Act carves out from the definition of a "business opportunity" any "franchise" offering defined by the F.T.C.'s Franchise Rule, so long as the franchisor: 1) complies in all material respects with the F.T.C.'s Franchise Rule, and 2) before offering any franchise for sale, files a notice with the Texas

Secretary of State containing the name of the franchisor, franchise name and franchisor's principal address. TEX. BUS. & COM. CODE §51.103(b)(8). Second, even if the franchisor does not avail itself of this exemption by filing this simple notice prior to offering the franchise in Texas, the Texas Business Opportunity Act allows a franchise seller to use a disclosure statement complying with the FTC Rule in lieu of the disclosure statement required by the Act, as long as it provides the information required by the Act. TEX. BUS. & COM. CODE §51.164.

§15.04 Other Theories of Liability

The person selling the business opportunity to the plaintiff may occupy a position of special influence or trust (*e.g.,* an accountant, an investment advisor, a banker, etc.). Or, a special relationship of trust and confidence may be encouraged by the person selling the business opportunity, a situation that arises with some frequency when franchises are marketed. Also, the seller of the business opportunity typically has superior knowledge about the product or service involved and is able to have a significant impact on the success or failure of the new venture. For example, a franchisor frequently has disparate control over the operation of the franchised business, resulting in unequal bargaining power between the parties. Therefore, a cause of action for breach of a fiduciary duty or a duty of good faith and fair dealing may exist.

The question of whether the franchisor owes a fiduciary duty or a duty of good faith and fair dealing to the franchisee must be examined on a case-by-case basis. Compare *Arnold v. Nat'l County Mutual Fire Ins. Co.*, 725 S.W.2d 165 (Tex. 1987) (insurer owes insured a duty of good faith and fair dealing) *with Crim Truck & Tractor v. Navistar Int'l*, 833 S.W.2d 591 (Tex. 1992) (finding no evidence that a confidential fiduciary relationship existed between the motor vehicle manufacturer and franchised dealer)(superseded by statute). An informal fiduciary relationship, may arise where one party trusts and relies on the other, "'whether the relation is moral, social, domestic or merely personal one.'" *Lee v. Hasson*, 286 S.W.3d 1, 14 (Tex. App.—Houston [14th Dist.], 2007, pet. denied) (*citing Crim Truck & Tractor Co. v. Navistar Int'l Transp. Corp.*, 823 S.W.2d 591, 594 (Tex. 1992)); *see also Meyer v. Cathey*, 167 S.W.3d 327, 330-31 (Tex. 2005). The question of whether a confidential relationship exists that gives rise to an informal fiduciary relationship is ordinarily one of fact, depending on the surrounding circumstances. *Meyer*, 167 S.W.3d at 331.

In at least one instance, the Texas Legislature has acted to impose a duty of good faith and fair dealing between a franchisor and franchisee. TEX. OCC. CODE § 2301.478 (motor vehicle manufacturer owes a duty of good faith to franchised motor vehicle dealer)("Each party to a franchise owes to the other party a duty of good faith and fair dealing that is actionable in tort."), *superseding Crim Truck & Tractor v. Navistar Int'l*, 833 S.W.2d 591 (Tex. 1992). On the whole, however, Texas courts have been reluctant to recognize a covenant or duty of good faith and fair dealing in arms-length transactions. *See, e.g., English v. Fischer*, 660 S.W.2d 521 (Tex. 1983) (no covenant of good faith and fair dealing in every contract); *Natividad v. Alexsis, Inc.*, 875 S.W.2d 695 (Tex. 1994) (insurance agent/insured); *Federal Deposit Ins. Corp. v. Coleman*, 795 S.W.2d 706 (Tex. 1990) (no duty of good faith in mortgagor/mortgagee or creditor/guarantor relationship); *Nautical Landings Marina, Inc. v. First Nat'l Bank*, 791 S.W.2d 293 (Tex. App.—Corpus Christi 1990, writ denied) (no good faith duty between lender and borrower); *Adolph Coors Co. v. Rodriguez*, 780 S.W.2d

477, 481 (Tex. App.—Corpus Christi 1989, writ denied) (supplier/distributor).

The seller or broker of the business opportunity may also have liability under a negligent misrepresentation theory. *See* RESTATEMENT (SECOND) OF TORTS §552; *Federal Land Bank Ass'n v. Sloane*, 825 S.W.2d 439 (Tex. 1991); *McCamish, Martin, Brown & Loeffler v. F.E. Appling Interests*, 991 S.W.2d 787, 791 (Tex. 1999).

Another cause of action available to an investor is common law fraud. A misrepresentation of fact, made with knowledge of its falsity or made recklessly without knowledge of whether it is true or false, may form the basis of a common law fraud action. *See Eagle Properties, Ltd. v. Scharbauer*, 807 S.W.2d 714 (Tex. 1990). Under some circumstances, statements of opinion and promises of future performance may also constitute actionable fraud. *See Formosa Plastics Corp. USA v. Presidio Eng'rs & Contrs.*, 960 S.W.2d 41 (Tex. 1998); *Trenholm v. Ratcliff*, 646 S.W.2d 927 (Tex. 1983); *Fina Supply, Inc. v. Abilene Nat'l Bank*, 726 S.W.2d 537 (Tex. 1987); *Spoljaric v. Percival Tours, Inc.*, 708 S.W.2d 432 (Tex. 1986). Additionally, when there is a duty to disclose information, the failure to do so may support a fraud cause of action. *See Bradford v. Vento*, 48 S.W.3d 749, 755 (Tex. 2001); *Trenholm v. Ratcliff*, 646 S.W.2d 927 (Tex. 1983). If a stock or real estate transaction is involved, a claim may exist for statutory fraud. *See* TEX. BUS. & COM. CODE §27.01.

§15.05 Pre-Suit Notice Letter to Seller of Business Opportunity

A DTPA notice letter involving a claim over a misrepresented business opportunity follows the same format as a notice letter for the sale of goods or services. *See* §§3.03, 3.04, *supra*. When special statutes apply to the business opportunity involved in the client's claim, the notice letter should be written to include any applicable theories of recovery that are provided by the special statutes.

[a] FORM: —Notice letter: business opportunity

[Insert the following at "notice of claim," §3.03[a], supra]

As you know, on _____, 20___, our client purchased a business opportunity from you. Prior to the time of purchase, you provided to our client certain written materials and brochures in which claims were made with respect to the benefits our client was to realize from the investment. Among the claims made were the following: [*insert claims made*].

The claims set forth in the preceding paragraph were false, misleading, and deceptive. [In addition, the investment you sold our client qualifies as a "business opportunity" under Texas law. As such, you were required by law to provide a disclosure statement to our client which met the requirements of TEX. BUS. & COM. CODE §51.001 *et seq.*, commonly known as the Texas Business Opportunity Act. The information you provided to our client does not satisfy the requirements of the statute. Had you provided all of the information that the law intended for our client to receive, our client would not have made the investment.

[*Insert other statutory claims, if any*]

Because of the conduct described above, our client has suffered substantial damages which include, but are not limited to, the following elements: [*insert elements of damages, e.g.*]

1. The amount of our client's investment; and

2. The interest expense incurred on the money borrowed to make the investment; and

3. The lost value of our client's time; and

4. The amount of the debts that our client has incurred with vendors as a result of the investment.

[*Continue with DTPA notice letter, §3.03[a] supra*].

§15.06 Plaintiff's Pleadings— Texas Business Opportunities Act

When a consumer has been victimized by a person selling investments, typically, several causes of action may be available in addition to the DTPA. See §§15.02-.04, supra. Form [a] below alleges DTPA causes of action, violations of the Texas Business Opportunity Act, negligent misrepresentation, and breach of fiduciary duty.

The franchise investment form (Form [b]) does not contain pleadings under the Texas Business Opportunity Act. The Act creates an exemption for a "franchise" (as that term is defined by the Federal Trade Commission in 16 C.F.R. §436.2) if the franchisor also complies with the applicable regulations and notice requirements specified by the F.T.C. Rule. See §15.03, supra. If the FTC requirements have not been met, then the Texas Business Opportunity Act pleadings in Form [a] can be added to the petition.

[a] FORM: —DTPA, Texas Business Opportunity Act tie-in violations, fraud and bad faith

```
        NO. _____

_____      §     IN THE DISTRICT COURT OF
        §
vs.     §     _____ COUNTY, TEXAS
        §
_____      §     _____ JUDICIAL DISTRICT
```

PLAINTIFF'S ORIGINAL PETITION

TO THE HONORABLE JUDGE OF THE DISTRICT COURT:

NOW COMES _____, Plaintiff herein, complaining of _____, Defendant herein, and for cause of action, would show unto the Court as follows:

I. DISCOVERY CONTROL PLAN DESIGNATION

1.01 Discovery in this case is intended to be conducted under Level _____, pursuant to Rule 190._____, *Texas Rules of Civil Procedure.*

II. PARTIES

2.01 Plaintiff _____ is a resident of _____, _____ County, Texas.

2.02 Defendant _____ is an individual who resides and may be served with process at _____, _____ County, Texas.

III. VENUE

3.01 Venue of this action is proper in _____ County, Texas because _____ reside in _____ County, Texas and the events made the basis of this lawsuit and giving rise to Plaintiff's cause of action occurred, in whole or in part, in _____ County, Texas.

IV. NOTICE; CONDITIONS PRECEDENT

4.01 Defendant was given notice in writing of the claims made in this petition including a statement of Plaintiff's economic damages, mental anguish damages and expenses, including attorney's fees, more than sixty days before this suit was filed in the manner and form required by DTPA §17.505(a).

4.02 All conditions precedent to recovery by Plaintiff herein have been performed, have occurred, or have been excused.

V. AGENCY; VICARIOUS LIABILITY

5.01 Unless otherwise stated, whenever it is alleged that Defendant _____ committed an act, failed to perform an act, made a representation or a statement, or failed to make a disclosure, it is alleged that Defendant _____ acted or failed to act through its authorized agents, servants, employees or representatives acting with either expressed, implied, apparent, direct and/or ostensible authority, or _____ subsequently ratified these acts, failures to act, representations, statements or conduct.

VI. FACTS OF CASE

6.01   In _____, 20¬__, Defendant contacted Plaintiff for the purpose of discussing an investment. The nature of the investment was [*describe type of investment, including a description of the goods and services purchased*]. [*If alleging violation of Business Opportunity Act insert facts showing standing under TEX. BUS. & COMM. CODE Section 51.001, e.g.,* Defendant represented that Plaintiff would earn a profit in excess of the initial consideration paid and further represented that he [she] would provide Plaintiff with a sales, production, or marketing program.]

6.02   While discussing the investment with Plaintiff, Defendant made several representations about the investment, among which are the following: [*state representations made*].

6.03   In addition to the representations described above, Defendant failed to disclose several material facts to Plaintiff, including but not limited to the following: [*state facts not disclosed*]. These facts were not disclosed for the purpose of inducing Plaintiff to enter into the transaction. Had the facts been disclosed, Plaintiff would not have agreed to participate in the investment.

6.04   Plaintiff further alleges that Defendant [*describe facts which allege violation of Business Opportunity Act, e.g.,* represented that the business opportunity would provide income of at least $_____ per month. However, Defendant did not disclose to Plaintiff any data to substantiate these representations at the time they were made].

6.05   Because of the representations made by Defendant and because of Defendant's failure to disclose certain material facts as described above, Plaintiff agreed to and did make the investment as requested by Defendant.

6.06   The representations made by Defendant to Plaintiff about the investment were misleading and deceptive in the following respects: [*insert reasons representations were false*].

6.07   The investment proved to be worthless [*or* worth far less than Defendant represented]; consequently, Plaintiff lost all [*or* substantially all] of the money invested and suffered other losses as well, which are described below.

VII. FIRST CAUSE OF ACTION: DTPA

7.01   Plaintiff is a consumer entitled to bring this action for relief under the Texas Deceptive Trade Practices—Consumer Protection Act (the "DTPA"). The actions of Defendant outlined above constitute misrepresentations, breaches of warranties and unconscionable conduct, actionable under the DTPA.

7.02   Specifically, Defendant committed the following acts in violation of the DTPA "laundry list," one or more of which was a producing cause of damages to Plaintiff:

(a) Causing confusion or misunderstanding as to the affiliation, connection or association with, or certification by, another;

(b) Representing that goods or services had characteristics, ingredients, uses or benefits which they did not have;

(c) Representing that goods or services were of a particular standard, quality or grade when they were of another;

(d) Representing that an agreement confers or involves rights, remedies, or obligations which it does not have or involve, or which are prohibited by law; and/or

(e) Failing to disclose information concerning goods or services which was known at the time in order to induce the Plaintiff to enter into a transaction which Plaintiff would not have otherwise entered.

7.04   Plaintiff relied on these representations to his [her] detriment.

7.05   Further, Defendant violated the Texas Business Opportunities Act, Chapter 51 of the *Texas Business & Commerce Code,* and such conduct is actionable under the DTPA pursuant to Section 51.302.

7.06   Further, Defendant took advantage of Plaintiff's lack of knowledge about the condition of the property. Accordingly, Defendant violated the DTPA by engaging in unconscionable conduct and/or an unconscionable course of conduct.

7.07   Defendant's conduct as described herein was a producing cause of damages to Plaintiff.

7.08   Further, Defendant's conduct was committed knowingly, entitling Plaintiff to seek the trebling of his [her] actual damages in accordance with the DTPA.

VIII. SECOND CAUSE OF ACTION: FRAUD

8.01   Plaintiff repeats and realleges the material factual allegations in the preceding paragraphs.

8.02   By the conduct described above, Defendant made representations of material facts to Plaintiff.

8.03   These representations were made knowing that they were false, or, in the alternative, they were made recklessly and as a positive assertion without knowledge of whether they were true or false.

8.04   Furthermore, Defendant failed to disclose material facts which were known to Defendant at the time of the transaction. The failure to disclose and the misrepresentations were done for the purpose of inducing Plaintiff to purchase the investment.

8.05   Plaintiff relied on the misrepresentations as well as the non-existence of the facts not disclosed. Had Plaintiff known the undisclosed facts, he [she] would not have made the investment.

8.06   For these reasons, Defendant's conduct constituted common law fraud, which was a proximate cause of damages to Plaintiff.

IX. THIRD CAUSE OF ACTION: BREACH OF FIDUCIARY DUTY

9.01   Plaintiff repeats and realleges the material factual allegations in the preceding paragraphs.

9.02   Defendant owed a fiduciary duty to Plaintiff at all times material to the claims made in this lawsuit. The duty arose out of the special relationship of the parties in that Defendant [*insert basis for duty, e.g.*, (a) acquired and used confidential information provided to the Defendant by Plaintiff, (b) encouraged Plaintiff to rely on Defendant's advice and counsel, and encouraged Plaintiff to place trust in Defendant, and (c) actively solicited a major investment by Plaintiff in a business enterprise, about which Defendant claimed to have special knowledge, and about which Defendant knew Plaintiff had no knowledge.

9.03   Because of the special knowledge that Defendant said he [she] had, combined with Plaintiff's lack of knowledge, and because of the trust and confidence Plaintiff placed in Defendant, Defendant exercised practical control over Plaintiff's decision to make the investment].

9.04   Defendant's conduct was calculated to and did create an advantage for him [her] while causing great losses to Plaintiff. Defendant was disloyal to Plaintiff, failed to act with utmost good faith, fairness, and honesty, and allowed his [her] interest to interfere and conflict with Plaintiff's best interests.

9.05   By engaging in the unlawful conduct described in this petition, Defendant has breached the fiduciary duty it owed to Plaintiff, which conduct was a proximate cause of damages to Plaintiff.

X. FOURTH CAUSE OF ACTION: NEGLIGENT MISREPRESENTATION

10.01   In the alternative, Plaintiffs allege as follows:

10.02   Defendant had a pecuniary interest in the sale of the investment and had a duty to exercise reasonable care and competence in obtaining and communicating the information about the investment.

10.03   Defendant knew or should have known that the representations made about the investment were false, and by virtue of Defendant's failure to provide material facts, the representations were misleading as well.

10.04   Defendant's false and misleading representations and failure to provide information to Plaintiff, on which Plaintiff reasonably relied, breached Defendant's duty to Plaintiff and thus, constituted negligence.

10.05 One or more of Defendant's negligent misrepresentations was a proximate cause of damages to Plaintiff.

10.06   Defendant's conduct created an extreme degree of risk of harm to Plaintiff. The Defendant had actual awareness of the extreme risk of harm created by its actions. Thus, Defendant acted with such an entire want of care as to establish that its acts or omissions were the result of a conscious indifference to the rights, safety, or welfare of Plaintiff. Defendant's conduct, therefore, was grossly negligent.

XI. DAMAGES

11.01   Defendant's acts and omissions as described herein have been a producing and/or proximate cause of damages to Plaintiff.

11.02   Plaintiff has suffered economic damages, including but not limited to: *insert elements of damages, e.g.*, the amount of money paid by Plaintiff for the investment, the debts owed by Plaintiff to third parties because of the investment, the interest paid on the money borrowed to make the investment, and damages to Plaintiff's credit ratings as a result of the losses suffered.

[alternate 11.02]   [The economic damages incurred by plaintiff include the amount of money paid for the business investment, less any net profits earned by plaintiff, as well as the reasonable out of pocket expenditures made by plaintiff in operating the business [and the interest expense incurred by plaintiff on the money borrowed to make the investment, less the value of the interest which reasonably could have been earned by plaintiff on the net profits of the business]. Plaintiff also seeks to recover damages for injury to plaintiffs credit reputation.]

11.03   These damages are within the jurisdictional limits of this Court.

XII. ADDITIONAL DAMAGES AND PUNITIVE DAMAGES

12.01   Defendant's conduct in violation of the DTPA was committed knowingly, as that term is defined. Accordingly, Plaintiff seeks an award of additional damages under the DTPA in an amount not to exceed three times the amount of his [her] economic damages.

12.02   The damages suffered by the Plaintiff resulted from fraud and/or gross negligence. Accordingly, Plaintiff alternatively seeks exemplary damages, not to exceed $_____, which in the opinion of the jury is necessary to punish Defendant and deter similar conduct in the future by Defendant and others.

XIII. ATTORNEY'S FEES

13.01   As a result of Defendant's conduct, Plaintiff has been required to obtain the services of the undersigned attorney for the filing, prosecution and trial of this cause, and therefore seeks an award of reasonable and necessary attorney's fees pursuant to applicable law.

WHEREFORE, PREMISES CONSIDERED, Plaintiff respectfully prays that Defendant be cited to appear and answer herein, and that upon final trial hereof, Plaintiff recover from Defendant all of his [her] damages, additional damages, exemplary damages, pre-judgment and post-judgment interest as allowed by law, attorney's fees, costs of court and such other and further relief to which he may show himself justly entitled.

> Respectfully submitted,
>
> _____
>
> Attorney for Plaintiff

[b] Form: —Franchise investment

```
    NO. _____

_____        §        IN THE DISTRICT COURT OF
                  §
vs.    §              _____COUNTY, TEXAS
                  §
_____        §        _____ JUDICIAL DISTRICT
```

PLAINTIFF'S ORIGINAL PETITION

TO THE HONORABLE JUDGE OF THE DISTRICT COURT:

NOW COMES _____, Plaintiff herein, complaining of _____, Defendant herein, and for cause of action, would show unto the Court as follows:

I. DISCOVERY CONTROL PLAN DESIGNATION

1.01   Discovery in this case is intended to be conducted under Level _____, pursuant to Rule 190._____, *Texas Rules of Civil Procedure.*

II. PARTIES

2.01   Plaintiff _____ is a resident of _____, _____ County, Texas.

2.02   Defendant _____ is a _____ Corporation with its principal place of business in _____ which is doing business in Texas but does not maintain a registered agent for service of process in Texas. Therefore _____ may be served with process by serving the Secretary of State of Texas, 1019 Brazos Street, P.O. Box 12079, Austin, Texas, 78711-2079, with instructions to forward the citation and other process to _____ at its home office address, _____ pursuant to Section 17.004, *Texas Civil Practice and Remedies Code.*

2.03   This Court has personal jurisdiction over Defendant _____ for the reason that [*insert detailed facts which show that jurisdiction is proper, e.g.,* Defendant was and is doing business in Texas, Defendant entered into contracts by mail with Texas residents, which contracts were and are to be performed in Texas, and Defendant has recruited Texas residents to serve as agents, franchisees and employees.]

2.04   Defendant _____ has appointed Defendant _____ to be its agent for the purpose of selling franchises in Texas, with the plan and knowledge that Defendant _____ would actively advertise and recruit individuals to purchase franchises. Defendant _____ is paid a franchise fee which is calculated not only on the basis of the franchise, but also on a percentage of gross sales of each franchise store in Texas. Accordingly, Defendant _____ realizes a profit from its business activities in Texas.

2.05   Defendant _____'s agents and employees regularly travel to Texas in connection with the management and operation of franchise stores in this state, and numerous, regular telephone calls are made into the state for the same purpose. Defendant _____, by its contracts with Texas residents, has provided itself access to Texas courts for the purpose of enforcing certain rights contained in those contracts.

2.06   Through the enactment of the DTPA, the Texas legislature has indicated a special interest in protecting Texas residents from the types of practices alleged in this petition.

2.07   For the reasons set forth above, this court's exercise of personal jurisdiction over Defendant does not offend traditional notions of fair play. Such jurisdiction may be exercised by virtue of Section 17.041, *Texas Civil Practice & Remedies Code*.

2.08 Defendant _____ is an individual who resides and may be served with process at _____, _____ County, Texas.

III. VENUE

3.01 Venue of this action is proper in _____ County, Texas because _____ reside in _____ County, Texas and the events made the basis of this lawsuit and giving rise to Plaintiff's cause of action occurred, in whole or in part, in _____ County, Texas.

IV. NOTICE; CONDITIONS PRECEDENT

4.01 Defendant was given notice in writing of the claims made in this petition including a statement of Plaintiff's economic damages, mental anguish damages and expenses, including attorney's fees, more than sixty days before this suit was filed in the manner and form required by DTPA §17.505(a).

4.02 All conditions precedent to recovery by Plaintiff herein have been performed, have occurred, or have been excused.

V. AGENCY

5.01 Unless otherwise stated, whenever it is alleged that Defendant 1 committed an act, failed to perform an act, made a representation or a statement, or failed to make a disclosure, it is alleged that Defendant 1 acted or failed to act through its authorized agents, servants, employees or representatives acting with either expressed, implied, apparent, direct and/or ostensible authority, or Defendant 1 subsequently ratified these acts, failures to act, representations, statements or conduct.

5.02 At all times during the transactions which are the subject of this lawsuit, Defendant 2 was the agent of Defendant 1. The agency is based on both express appointment and apparent authority. The express agency arose out of a written agreement between these Defendants under which Defendant 2 was empowered to act as a ['Regional Franchisor'].

5.03 The express and apparent authority of Defendant 2 also arose out of the following intentional acts of Defendant 1 [*insert conduct of principal showing apparent authority, e.g.,* allowing Defendant 2 to advertise under the name of Defendant 1 and supplying recommended texts for such advertising which clearly implied to Plaintiff that Defendant 2 was an agent]. Plaintiff reasonably relied on this conduct in forming his [her] belief that Defendant 2 was the agent of Defendant 1.

5.04   For the reasons stated above, whenever in this petition it is alleged that Defendant 2 did any act or thing, it is meant such act or thing was done by Defendant 1 as well.

5.05   Further, it is alleged that Defendants were engaged in a joint venture for their mutual benefit and acted as each other's agents with all express, implied, direct and/or ostensible authority to so act, and as such are vicariously liable for the acts, omissions, statements and conduct of the other as alleged herein.

VI. FACTS OF CASE

6.01   Defendant 1 is the owner of the national franchise and license for its business name and method of operation. As alleged above, Defendant 2 is licensed and authorized by Defendant 1 to sell its franchises.

6.02   Plaintiff met with Defendant 2 for the purposes of discussing an investment in a franchise. At that time, this Defendant made certain false representations to Plaintiff for the purpose of inducing Plaintiff to purchase a franchise.

6.03   Among these representations were [*insert false representations, e.g.*, (1) that Plaintiff would earn back the investment in the business in the first year and would be making a six-digit income within a few years, (2) that Defendant 2, as the area representative, was very knowledgeable about the business Plaintiff was purchasing and would train Plaintiff to operate the franchise as well as assist Plaintiff with any problems Plaintiff may have, and (3) that this was an excellent investment for Plaintiff to make].

6.04   Relying on the representations made by Defendants, Plaintiff agreed to and did purchase a franchise for a total investment of $_____.

VII. FIRST CAUSE OF ACTION: DTPA

7.01   Plaintiff repeats and realleges the material factual allegations in the preceding paragraphs.

7.02   Plaintiff is a consumer entitled to bring this action for relief under the Texas Deceptive Trade Practices—Consumer Protection Act (the "DTPA"). The actions of Defendants outlined above constitute misrepresentations, breaches of warranties and unconscionable conduct, actionable under the DTPA.

7.03   Specifically, Defendants committed the following acts in violation of the DTPA "laundry list," one or more of which was a producing cause of damages to Plaintiff:

(a) Causing confusion or misunderstanding as to the affiliation, connection or association with, or certification by, another

(b) Representing that goods or services had characteristics, ingredients, uses or benefits which they did not have;

(c) Representing that goods or services were of a particular standard, quality or grade when they were of another;

(d) Representing that an agreement confers or involves rights, remedies, or obligations which it does not have or involve, or which are prohibited by law; and/or

(e) Failing to disclose information concerning goods or services which was known at the time in order to induce the Plaintiff to enter into a transaction which Plaintiff would not have otherwise entered.

7.04   Plaintiff relied on these representations to his [her] detriment.

7.05   Further, Defendants took advantage of Plaintiff's lack of knowledge about the condition of the property. Accordingly, Defendants violated the DTPA by engaging in unconscionable conduct and/or an unconscionable course of conduct.

7.06   Defendants' conduct as described herein was a producing cause of damages to Plaintiff.

7.07   Further, Defendants' conduct was committed knowingly, entitling Plaintiff to seek the trebling of his [her] actual damages in accordance with the DTPA.

VIII. SECOND CAUSE OF ACTION: FRAUD

8.01   Plaintiff repeats and realleges the material factual allegations in the preceding paragraphs.

8.02   By the conduct described above, Defendants made representations of material facts to Plaintiff.

8.03   These representations were made knowing that they were false, or, in the alternative, they were made recklessly and as a positive assertion without knowledge of whether they were true or false.

8.04   Furthermore, Defendants failed to disclose material facts which were known to Defendant at the time of the transaction. The failure to disclose and the misrepresentations were done for the purpose of inducing Plaintiff to purchase the investment.

8.05   Plaintiff relied on the misrepresentations as well as the non-existence of the facts not disclosed. Had Plaintiff known the undisclosed facts, he [she] would not have made the investment.

8.06   For these reasons, Defendants' conduct constituted common law fraud, which was a proximate cause of damages to Plaintiff.

IX. DAMAGES

9.01   Defendants' acts and omissions as described herein have been a producing and/or proximate cause of damages to Plaintiff.

9.02   Plaintiff has suffered economic damages, including but not limited to: [*insert elements of damages, e.g.*, the difference between the value of the franchise as represented and its actual value, or alternatively, pursuant to DTPA §17.50(b)(3) and (4), all the money acquired by Defendants from Plaintiff, and, under either alternative, the amount of debt incurred by Plaintiff to third parties in the operation of the franchise, and Plaintiff's mental anguish which was suffered as a result of the conduct of Defendants as described in this petition]. [*See* §5.16, *supra*, for *alternative allegations*.]

9.03   These damages are within the jurisdictional limits of this Court.

X. ADDITIONAL DAMAGES AND PUNITIVE DAMAGES

10.01   Defendants' conduct in violation of the DTPA was committed knowingly, as that term is defined. Accordingly, Plaintiff seeks an award of additional damages under the DTPA in an amount not to exceed three times the amount of his [her] economic damages.

10.02   The damages suffered by the Plaintiff resulted from fraud. Accordingly, Plaintiff alternatively seeks exemplary damages, not to exceed $_____, which in the opinion of the jury is necessary to punish the Defendants and deter similar conduct in the future by the Defendants and others.

XI. ATTORNEY'S FEES

11.01   As a result of Defendants' conduct, Plaintiff has been required to obtain the services of the undersigned attorney for the filing, prosecution and trial of this cause, and therefore seeks an award of reasonable and necessary attorney's fees pursuant to applicable law.

WHEREFORE, PREMISES CONSIDERED, Plaintiff respectfully prays that Defendant be cited to appear and answer herein, and that upon final trial hereof, Plaintiff recover from Defendants, jointly and severally, all of his [her] damages, additional damages, exemplary damages, pre-judgment and post-judgment interest as allowed by law, attorney's fees, costs of court and such other and further relief to which he may show himself justly entitled.

Respectfully submitted,

_____

Attorney for Plaintiff

[c] FORM: —Purchase of existing franchise

NO. _____

_____	§	IN THE DISTRICT COURT OF
	§	
vs.	§	_____ COUNTY, TEXAS
	§	
_____	§	_____ JUDICIAL DISTRICT

TO THE HONORABLE JUDGE OF THE DISTRICT COURT:

NOW COMES _____, Plaintiff herein, complaining of _____, Defendant herein, and for cause of action, would show unto the Court as follows:

I. DISCOVERY CONTROL PLAN DESIGNATION

1.01 Discovery in this case is intended to be conducted under Level _____, pursuant to Rule 190._____, *Texas Rules of Civil Procedure*.

II. PARTIES

2.01 _____ is a resident of _____, _____ County, Texas.

2.02 _____ is an individual who resides and may be served with process at _____, _____ County, Texas.

III. VENUE

3.01 Venue of this action is proper in _____ County, Texas because _____ reside in _____ County, Texas and the events made the basis of this lawsuit and giving rise to Plaintiff's cause of action occurred, in whole or in part, in _____ County, Texas.

IV. NOTICE; CONDITIONS PRECEDENT

4.01 Defendant was given notice in writing of the claims made in this petition including a statement of Plaintiff's economic damages, mental anguish damages and expenses, including attorney's fees, more than sixty days before this suit was filed in the manner and form required by DTPA §17.505(a).

4.02 All conditions precedent to recovery by Plaintiff herein have been performed, have occurred, or have been excused.

V. AGENCY

5.01 Unless otherwise stated, whenever it is alleged that Defendant _____ committed an act, failed to perform an act, made a representation or a statement, or failed to make a disclosure, it is alleged that Defendant _____ acted or failed to act through its authorized agents, servants, employees or representatives acting with either expressed, implied, apparent, direct and/or ostensible authority, or _____ subsequently ratified these acts, failures to act, representations, statements or conduct.

VI. FACTS OF CASE

6.01   This lawsuit arises out of the following transaction, acts and events: [*describe transaction, e.g.* In _____, Plaintiff and Defendant entered negotiations for the purchase of a business in _____ known as _____, a fast food restaurant. The transaction included the sale of real property, fixtures and equipment, and promises of support and training to be provided by Defendant].

6.02   In the course of the transaction, Defendant engaged in the following unlawful conduct: [*insert specific allegations of wrongdoing, e.g.*

6.03   Plaintiff was aware that the store had been in operation for some time prior to the negotiations, and that the store had ceased operations. Plaintiff was told that the store was being remodeled, and that the previous operator had been terminated because he had failed to follow contractual guidelines for the operation of the business.

6.04   Plaintiff also was told that the store had been profitable in the past, and would have been profitable but for the acts and omissions of the previous owner.

6.05   Plaintiff requested financial information on the store; however, Plaintiff was told that such financial information did not exist. Plaintiff was then given financial information on Defendant's national business to demonstrate how profitable the business could be].

6.06   Defendant failed to disclose very material facts to Plaintiff, including but not limited to the following: [*insert material facts not disclosed*].

VII. FIRST CAUSE OF ACTION: DTPA

7.01   Plaintiff repeats and realleges the material factual allegations in the preceding paragraphs.

7.02   Plaintiff is a consumer entitled to bring this action for relief under the Texas Deceptive Trade Practices—Consumer Protection Act (the "DTPA"). The actions of Defendants outlined above constitute misrepresentations, breaches of warranties and unconscionable conduct, actionable under the DTPA.

7.03	Specifically, Defendant committed the following acts in violation of the DTPA "laundry list," one or more of which was a producing cause of damages to Plaintiff:

(a) Causing confusion or misunderstanding as to the affiliation, connection or association with, or certification by, another

(b) Representing that goods or services had characteristics, ingredients, uses or benefits which they did not have;

(c) Representing that goods or services were of a particular standard, quality or grade when they were of another;

(d) Representing that an agreement confers or involves rights, remedies, or obligations which it does not have or involve, or which are prohibited by law; and/or

(e) Failing to disclose information concerning goods or services which was known at the time in order to induce the Plaintiff to enter into a transaction which Plaintiff would not have otherwise entered.

7.04	Plaintiff relied on these representations to his [her] detriment.

7.05	Further, Defendant violated the Texas Business Opportunities Act, Chapter 51 of the *Texas Business & Commerce Code*, and such conduct is actionable under the DTPA pursuant to Section 51.302.

7.06	Further, Defendants took advantage of Plaintiff's lack of knowledge about the condition of the property. Accordingly, Defendants violated the DTPA by engaging in unconscionable conduct and/or an unconscionable course of conduct.

7.07	Defendants' conduct as described herein was a producing cause of damages to Plaintiff.

7.08	Further, Defendants' conduct was committed knowingly, entitling Plaintiff to seek the trebling of his [her] actual damages in accordance with the DTPA.

VIII. SECOND CAUSE OF ACTION: FRAUD

8.01	Plaintiff repeats and realleges the material factual allegations in the preceding paragraphs.

8.02	By the conduct described above, Defendant made representations of material facts to Plaintiff.

8.03   These representations were made knowing that they were false, or, in the alternative, they were made recklessly and as a positive assertion without knowledge of whether they were true or false.

8.04   Furthermore, Defendant failed to disclose material facts which were known to Defendant at the time of the transaction. The failure to disclose and the misrepresentations were done for the purpose of inducing Plaintiff to enter various contracts associated with the sale of the business.

8.05   Plaintiff relied on the misrepresentations as well as the non-existence of the facts not disclosed in entering into the transaction and related contracts. Had Plaintiff known the undisclosed facts, he [she] would not have entered the transaction and signed the contracts.

8.06   For these reasons, Defendant's conduct constituted common law fraud, which was a proximate cause of damages to Plaintiff.

IX. THIRD CAUSE OF ACTION: BREACH OF FIDUCIARY DUTY

9.01   Plaintiff repeats and realleges the material factual allegations in the preceding paragraphs.

9.02   Defendant owed a fiduciary duty to Plaintiff at all times material to the claims made in this lawsuit. The duty arose out of the special relationship of the parties in that the Defendant [*insert basis for duty, e.g.*, (a) acquired and used confidential information provided to the Defendant by Plaintiff, (b) encouraged Plaintiff to rely on Defendant's advice and counsel, and encouraged Plaintiff to place trust in Defendant, and (c) actively solicited a major investment by Plaintiff in a business enterprise, about which Defendant claimed to have special knowledge, and about which Defendant knew Plaintiff had no knowledge.

9.03   Because of the special knowledge that Defendant said he [she] had, combined with Plaintiff's lack of knowledge, and because of the trust and confidence Plaintiff placed in Defendant, Defendant exercised practical control over Plaintiff's decision to make the investment].

9.04   Defendant's conduct was calculated to and did create an advantage for him [her] while causing great losses to Plaintiff. Defendant was disloyal to Plaintiff, failed to act with utmost good faith, fairness, and honesty, and allowed his [her] interest to interfere and conflict with Plaintiff's best interests.

9.05   By engaging in the unlawful conduct described in this petition, Defendant has breached the fiduciary duty it owed to Plaintiff, which conduct was a proximate cause of damages to Plaintiff.

X. FOURTH CAUSE OF ACTION: NEGLIGENT MISREPRESENTATION

10.01   In the alternative, Plaintiff alleges as follows:

10.02   Defendant had a pecuniary interest in the sale of the investment and had a duty to exercise reasonable care and competence in obtaining and communicating the information about the investment.

10.03   Defendant knew or should have known that the representations made about the investment were false, and by virtue of Defendant's failure to provide material facts, the representations were misleading as well.

10.04   Defendant's false and misleading representations and failure to provide information to Plaintiff, on which Plaintiff reasonably relied, breached Defendant's duty to Plaintiff and thus, constituted negligence.

10.05   One or more of Defendant's negligent misrepresentations was a proximate cause of damages to Plaintiff.

10.06   Defendant's conduct created an extreme degree of risk of harm to Plaintiff. Defendant had actual awareness of the extreme risk of harm created by its actions. Thus, Defendant acted with such an entire want of care as to establish that its acts or omissions were the result of a conscious indifference to the rights, safety, or welfare of Plaintiff. Defendant's conduct, therefore, was grossly negligent.

XI. DAMAGES

11.01   Defendant's acts and omissions as described herein have been a producing and/or proximate cause of damages to Plaintiff.

11.02   Plaintiff has suffered economic damages, including but not limited to: *insert elements of damages, e.g.,* the amount of money paid by Plaintiff for the investment, the debts owed by Plaintiff to third parties because of the investment, the interest paid on the money borrowed to make the investment, and damages to Plaintiff's credit ratings as a result of the losses suffered. [*See* §5.16, *supra, for alternative allegations.*]

11.03   These damages are within the jurisdictional limits of this Court.

XII. ADDITIONAL DAMAGES AND PUNITIVE DAMAGES

12.01   Defendants' conduct in violation of the DTPA was committed knowingly, as that term is defined. Accordingly, Plaintiff seeks an award of additional damages under the DTPA in an amount not to exceed three times the amount of his [her] economic damages.

12.02   The damages suffered by the Plaintiff resulted from fraud and/or gross negligence. Accordingly, Plaintiff alternatively seeks exemplary damages, not to exceed $_____, which in the opinion of the jury is necessary to punish Defendant and deter similar conduct in the future by Defendant and others.

XIII. ATTORNEY'S FEES

13.01   As a result of Defendant's conduct, Plaintiff has been required to obtain the services of the undersigned attorney for the filing, prosecution and trial of this cause, and therefore seeks an award of reasonable and necessary attorney's fees pursuant to applicable law.

WHEREFORE, PREMISES CONSIDERED, Plaintiff respectfully prays that Defendant be cited to appear and answer herein, and that upon final trial hereof, Plaintiff recover from Defendant all of his [her] damages, additional damages, exemplary damages, pre-judgment and post-judgment interest as allowed by law, attorney's fees, costs of court and such other and further relief to which he may show himself justly entitled.

Respectfully submitted,

_____

Attorney for Plaintiff

§15.07 Defendant's Pleadings—Sale of Franchise

As noted above, the Texas Business Opportunity Act carves out from the definition of a "business opportunity" any "franchise" offering defined by the F.T.C.'s Franchise Rule, so long as the franchisor: 1) complies in all material respects with the F.T.C.'s Franchise Rule, and 2) before offering any franchise for sale, files a notice with the Texas Secretary of State containing the name of the franchisor, franchise name and franchisor's principal address. TEX. BUS. & COM. CODE

§51.103(b)(8). See §15.03, *supra*. Proving these facts should be an affirmative defense to be pled by the defendant.

Further, the Texas Business Opportunity Act allows a franchise seller to use a disclosure statement complying with the FTC Rule in lieu of the disclosure statement required by the Act, as long as it provides the information required by the Act. TEX. BUS. & COM. CODE §51.164. Proof of this action should also be an affirmative defense.

The form of the Defendant's Original Answer below includes these affirmative defenses and other defenses commonly found in the defendant's answer.

[a] FORM: —Original answer with specific denials, verified denials and affirmative defenses—Texas Business Opportunities Act Action

```
                                    NO. _____
_____                    §      IN THE DISTRICT COURT OF
                                §
vs.                             §      _____COUNTY, TEXAS
                                §
_____                    §      _____ JUDICIAL DISTRICT
```

<u>**ORIGINAL ANSWER**</u>

TO THE HONORABLE JUDGE OF THE DISTRICT COURT:

_____, defendant, files this Original Answer to plaintiff's petition and will show the following:

[*general denial*]

1. Defendant generally denies the allegations made in plaintiff's petition.

[*Continue with any specific and verified denials as necessary*]

2. <u>Conditions precedent not performed</u>. Plaintiff has not performed all conditions precedent necessary to maintain this lawsuit. Specifically, [*insert condition precedent that has not occurred*].

[*Continue with any affirmative defenses, as applicable.*]

3. Pleading further and affirmatively, if such defense be necessary:

[(a)] <u>Compliance with FTC Franchise Disclosure Rule</u>. Prior to offering the franchise opportunity to Plaintiff or to any other person in Texas, Defendant complied in all material respects in this state with the F.T.C. Franchise Rule, 16 C.F.R. Part 436, and each order or other action of the Federal Trade Commission; and, before offering or sale or selling a franchise in this state, filed with the Texas Secretary of State a notice containing: (i) the name of the franchisor; (ii) the name under which the franchisor intended to transact business; and (iii) the franchisor's principal business address. As such, Defendant's franchise offering was not a business opportunity as defined by the Texas Business Opportunity Act.

[(b)] <u>Statute of Limitations</u>. The two years statute of limitations applicable to all DTPA claims made in this case expired on plaintiff's claims before suit was filed. Specifically, plaintiff discovered, or in the exercise of reasonable diligence should have discovered, the claims that are the subject of this suit more than two years before the date this suit was filed.

[(c)] <u>Parol Evidence Rule</u>. Plaintiff's claims are barred by the parol evidence rule.

[(d)] Plaintiff accepted the policy issued. Accordingly, his claims are barred by ratification, waiver and estoppel.

[(e)] Plaintiffs' claims are barred by the terms, conditions and limitations contained in the franchise agreement on which this action is based. Specifically, [*continue with terms of exclusions and/or limitations*.]

5. Request for relief. [*See* §6.04 *supra*]

    Respectfully submitted,

    [Signature of attorney]

[Certificate of service]

§15.08 Discovery—Business Opportunity Actions

The following discovery requests may be tailored to fit a case involving a claim against a franchisor for deceptive acts in connection with the sale of a business opportunity. See Chapter 7, supra, for general discovery forms.

§15.08.1 Interrogatories—

[a] FORM: —Franchise investments (to defendant)

1. Identify each person authorized by you to describe, market, broker or sell a franchise in all or any part of Texas since [*insert appropriate date*].

2. Describe fully the terms of employment or engagement in effect on [*insert date of sale to plaintiff*] between you and [*insert name of broker or salesperson*]. Include in your answer, the terms of all written agreements between you and [*the salesperson*], or, in lieu of the description, you may attach a copy of all agreements. Also include those terms, express or implied, which pertained to this person's authorization to describe, market, sell or broker franchises in Texas.

3. State the amount of franchise fees (1) you received from plaintiff and (2) you contend you are or were entitled to receive from plaintiff.

4. If you contend or believe that plaintiff breached his [her] franchise agreement or breached any duty owed to you then describe specifically the actions, statements or inactions constituting the alleged breach and the date each allegedly occurred.

5. For each [*insert name of franchise*] franchise that has been granted by you in Texas, state the following:

    (a) each store number (or other identification) and street address; and

    (b) the date of each franchise agreement; and

    (c) the identity of the franchisee(s); and

    (d) the identity of each successor, franchisee or store owner and the dates each such franchise was granted or such ownership assumed.

6. For all stores franchised by you in Texas, what is the total amount of franchise fees you have received since [*insert appropriate date*]. Please list the amounts by store and by fiscal year.

7. State the date of all reviews of each of the stores franchised in Texas by you that were conducted by or for you and the results

of each such review. In lieu of stating the results you may attach a copy of all reports of such reviews.

8. State those facts and identify those portions of all documents that you contend or believe put plaintiff on notice that [*insert name of salesperson or broker*] was not your agent but was merely an independent contractor.

9. State the average net profit earned by each of your franchise stores in Texas for the following years: [*insert appropriate number of years*].

10. Identify all studies, reports, or data that would support the assertion that plaintiff's store could have been expected to earn net profits [or have gross sales] of $ [*amount*] during [*insert time period in question*].

11. Identify each disclosure statement or report prepared by or for you pursuant to regulations promulgated or enforced by the Securities and Exchange Commission or the Federal Trade Commission.

[b] FORM: —Franchise investments (to plaintiff)

1. Describe each meeting between you and [*insert name of salesperson or broker*] or defendant or defendant's agents, employees or representatives. Include in your description at least the following information:

    (a)   the date and location of each meeting;

    (b)   the identity of the persons present at the meeting;

    (c)   the substance of the discussions at each meeting; and

    (d)   the identity of all documents that contain notes or a record of the meetings.

2. Describe each conversation (other than those described in response to the previous interrogatory) between you and [*insert name of salesperson or broker*] or defendant, defendant's agents, employees or representatives. Include in your description at least the following information:

    (a)   the date of each conversation;

    (b)   the identity of all persons who participated in each conversation;

    (c)   the substance of each conversation; and

(d) the identity of all documents that contain notes or a record of the conversations.

3. Identify all documents you received or reviewed in connection with the advertisement, offering for sale, or sale of the franchise involved in this suit.

4. State each and every oral or written misrepresentation by defendant that you contend was a cause of loss or damage to you. For each such oral statement, identify the person making the statement, and the date that it was made. For each such written statement, identify the document in which it was contained.

5. Identify all information that you contend should have been but was not disclosed by defendant that you contend was a cause of loss or damage to you.

6. State the gross monthly income for the [*insert name of store*] store for the following years: [*insert appropriate period*].

7. State the net monthly profit for the [*insert name of store*] store for the years identified in the preceding interrogatory.

8. State the amount of income, whether denominated income, wages, salary, draws, distribution, advance, or repayment of loans that you received from the [*insert name of store*] store during the years identified in interrogatory no. 6.

9. Identify each bookkeeper, accountant or CPA who rendered bookkeeping or accounting services in connection with your franchise.

[NOTE: Many franchise cases involve allegations relating to a breach of a fiduciary duty. The following question is designed to explore the facts that the plaintiff contends relate to the relationship.]

10. In paragraph ____ of Plaintiff's Original Petition, you contend that a fiduciary relationship exists or existed between you and defendant. State in detail the facts that you contend or believe created that relationship and describe those acts or omissions of defendant that you contend or believe constitute a breach of the fiduciary duty.

§15.08.2 Requests for Production—

[a] FORM: —Franchisee to franchisor (misrepresentations regarding territory and profits)

1. All documents reflecting the basis for your statement in the promotional materials on your internet website that "_____ _____ is profitable with as few as _____ monthly customers."

2. All documents reflecting the basis for your statement in the promotional materials on your internet website that "_____-_____ ." [repeat as necessary for each claimed misrepresentation.]

3. All documents identifying the site selection criteria that you considered in approving each Plaintiff's site.

4. All documents reflecting the studies that you conducted in order to determine the viability of each Plaintiff's territory.

5. All documents such as promotional materials used and/or posted by you on the internet.

6. All documents reflecting your site selection criteria that you provided to each Plaintiff.

7. All documents identifying your "formula" regarding the population and demographics necessary to support a _____ franchise.

8. All documents reflecting the basis for your statement in the _____ edition of _____ magazine that "_____-_____ ."

9. The mapping program that you utilize to analyze franchise proximity and population density in an area prior to the opening and/or selling of a new franchise.

10. All documents reflecting the "formula" that you use to determine how many customers a new franchise can expect to have.

11. All documents reflecting the number of franchises that have _____ customers per month.

12. All documents reflecting that a town with a population of _____ can sustain _____ customers per month.

13. All documents reflecting the closings for your franchises.

14. All documents reflecting the formula of population, potential growth and proximity to other franchises that you utilize to determine where a franchise might succeed.

15. All documents reflecting the number of days that it takes for a franchisee to achieve the goal of _____ sales.

16. All documents reflecting the basis for the statement that the total out-of-pocket cost of a franchise is $_____.

17. All documents reflecting the basis for your statement that _____ of the true market population is the potential customer base for a franchise.

18. All documents reflecting the basis for your statement that _____% of the potential customer base is the sustainable percentage of members for a franchise.

19. All documents reflecting the basis for your statement that a franchise is profitable with as few as _____ customers.

20. All documents reflecting the average amount of time that it takes a franchise to break even.

21. All documents reflecting the average amount of time that it takes a franchise to make a profit.

22. All documents reflecting the compensation structure of your franchise sales force.

23. All documents reflecting the compensation structure of your corporate officers.

24. The minutes from Board of Director meetings for the following dates: _____.

25. The fee agreement between you and your counsel.

26. All documents reflecting the attorney's fees incurred by you in connection with the claims asserted in this case.

[b] FORM: —Franchisor to franchisee (misrepresentations in sale of franchise)

1. All documents identified, described or relied upon in formulating Your answers to Defendant=s First Set of Interrogatories.

2. If the signatory to the Franchise Agreement is an entity, produce all documents relating, referring or reflecting the formation of such entity, including documents reflecting its

members, shareholders, directors, officers, investors and/or other persons or entities having any interest in the entity.

3. All documents you reviewed during your study of the _____ industry prior to purchasing the franchise at issue.

4. All documents reflecting your experience in the _____ industry prior to becoming a franchisee.

5. All contracts, agreements, memoranda of understanding or other such documents containing or reflecting the terms and conditions of the contracts between You and Defendant.

6. All documents evidencing or reflecting Your negotiations with Defendant execution of the Franchise Agreement.

7. All documents You relied upon in making Your decision to enter into the Franchise Agreement.

8. All documents You received from Defendant prior to entering into the Franchise Agreement.

9. All documents containing or evidencing communications from Defendant to You which You contend were false statements, misrepresentations or false promises in connection with Your purchase of the Franchise at issue.

10. All screen shots of Defendant=s website or web pages which You consulted or relied upon in connection with entering into the Franchise Agreement.

11. All magazine, journal, website or other articles You read concerning the franchise opportunity prior to entering into the Franchise Agreement.

12. All documents which evidence or reflect the existence of a special relationship between You and Defendant giving rise to a fiduciary duty or a duty of good faith and fair dealing.

13. All documents which evidence or reflect communications to You from any accountant, consultants or advisors with whom You consulted prior to entering into the Franchise Agreement.

14. All documents which evidence or reflect communications between You and any representative of Defendant concerning the franchise, the Franchise Agreement or the operation of the franchise/business opportunity.

15. All documents reflecting any notice received from Defendant concerning Your noncompliance with the terms of the Franchise Agreement.

16. All documents evidencing or reflecting any notice from You to Defendant concerning Defendant=s noncompliance with the terms of the Franchise Agreement.

17. All documents evidencing or reflecting Your submission to Defendant for its approval Your exclusive territory.

18. All documents evidencing or reflecting Your submission to Defendant for its approval the location of Your store/restaurant.

19. All documents reflecting or evidencing Your marketing of the franchise opportunity for re-sale.

20. All documents evidencing or reflecting Your expenses incurred in the opening of the franchise.

21. All documents evidencing or reflecting the expenses incurred by You in operating Your franchise between _____ and _____.

22. All documents reflecting Your revenues generated from operating the franchise between _____ and _____.

23. All financial statements reflecting the income and financial condition of the franchise for any period between _____ and _____.

24. All documents reflecting Your advertising or marketing of the franchise to the public, including but not limited to screen shots of Your websites, web pages, print advertising and scripts and recordings of any television or radio advertising.

25. All photographs which depict any subject matter relevant to this lawsuit.

26. All audio or video recordings of any of Defendant=s employees, agents, officers or representatives concerning the allegations in this lawsuit.

27. All franchise offering circulars or any promotional materials Defendant provided to You at any time.

28. All franchise offering circulars or promotional materials regarding Defendant You received from any other party.

29. All tax returns filed by You or on Your behalf concerning Your operation of the franchise from its inception to the present.

30. All bank statements for bank accounts in which You deposited or spent money related to the operation of the franchise at any time from _____ to the present.

31. All documents evidencing or reflecting the damages You claim to have incurred as a result of the actions and omissions at issue in this lawsuit.

32. All documents evidencing or reflecting the agreement You have related to the compensation of Your attorney in this case, including, but not limited to, Your attorney fee contract and any invoices submitted to You by Your attorney in this case.

33. All documents reflecting the attorney's fees incurred by you in connection with the claims asserted in this case.

(This page intentionally left blank.)

Chapter 16

Manufactured Housing

§16.01 Texas Manufactured Housing Standards Act
   §16.01.1 Warranty Actions
   §16.01.2 Tie-In Statute Violation
   §16.01.3 Notice/Abatement
   §16.01.4 Manufactured Homeowners Recovery Fund
   §16.01.5 Action for Wrongfully Withheld Deposit

§16.02 Initial Client Checklist
   [a] CHECKLIST: —Manufactured housing

§16.03 Pre-suit Notice Letters
   [a] FORM: —Notice letter: manufactured housing
   [b] FORM: —Manufactured Homeowners' Recovery Trust Fund claim
   [c] FORM: —First demand for return of deposit
   [d] FORM: —Second demand for treble deposit and attorney's fees

§16.04 Sample Petitions—Manufactured Housing
   [a] FORM: —Manufactured home defects in workmanship and repairs
   [b] FORM: —Manufactured home retailer (refusal to refund deposit)

§16.05 Discovery in Manufactured Housing Cases
   §16.05.1 Interrogatories
      [a] FORM: —Interrogatories to defendant mobile home manufacturer
      [b] FORM: —Interrogatories to defendant wrongfully withholding deposit
   §16.05.2 Requests for Production
      [a] FORM: —Requests for Production to defendant manufacturer
      [b] FORM: —Requests for Production to defendant retailer (wrongfully withheld deposit)

§16.01 Texas Manufactured Housing Standards Act

Claims concerning manufactured housing or "mobile homes" are governed by a comprehensive statute entitled the Texas Manufactured Housing Standards Act. TEXAS OCCUPATIONS CODE CHAPTER 1201 *et seq.*, formerly TEX. REV. CIV. STAT. art. 5221f (the "MHSA"). The MHSA is administered by the Manufactured Housing Division of Texas Department of Housing and Community Affairs which has the authority to investigate complaints of inadequate or improper construction or installations of manufactured homes and to order action to correct any deficiencies found. As such, a consumer is expected to take advantage of the administrative remedies in the MHSA before seeking relief in court under the DTPA or other legal theories.

§16.01.1 Warranty Actions

The MHSA requires a one-year warranty from the manufacturer of a new manufactured home that:

(1) the home is constructed or assembled in accordance with all requirements prescribed by the United States Department of Housing and Urban Development (H.U.D.) under the National Manufactured Housing Construction and Safety Standards Act of 1974 (42 U.S.C. § 5401 *et seq.*); and,

(2) the home and all appliances and equipment included in the home are free from defects in materials or workmanship except for cosmetic defects. MHSA §1201.351.

If proper warranty service and repairs are not made, the customer may, at any time, without a fee, request a "consumer complaint home inspection" by the Manufactured Housing Division. MHSA §1201.355. A state inspector employed by the Division will then inspect the consumer's home and make written findings and orders with respect to each complaint made within 30 days of the request. MHSA §1201.333(c) As noted below, a "consumer complaint home inspection" must be requested in order to avoid an abatement of a warranty case, MHSA §1201.602; therefore, a letter requesting such an inspection and the DTPA notice letter should be sent at the same time if an inspection has not already been requested.

§16.01.2 Tie-In Statute Violation

A violation of the Act is a tie-in violation giving rise to a cause of action under the DTPA. MHSA §1201.603. *See* §1.02.12, *supra*.

In addition to prohibiting any of the conduct which is unlawful under the DTPA, the Manufactured Housing Act also contains express prohibitions against:

(1) retaining or converting money, property, or any other thing of value from consumers in the form of down payments, any sales or use taxes, deposits, or insurance premiums without lawful authorization [MHSA §1201.151]; and,

(2) failing to give or breaching any manufactured home warranty required by the statute, or by the Federal Trade Commission [MHSA §1201.352].

§16.01.3 Notice/Abatement

Before filing suit under the DTPA, a consumer is required to give written notice to the manufacturer, retailer and installer of any need for warranty service or repairs. MHSA §1201.353. A defendant who does not get this written notice before suit is filed is entitled to abatement of any lawsuit filed until an inspection is conducted by the state and the defendant is given an opportunity to comply with any orders from the state inspector or 150 days, whichever is earlier. MHSA §1201.602. A consumer's refusal to allow the manufacturer or retailer to perform warranty service in accordance with the state inspector's report will operate as a bar to any action for breach of express or implied warranties. *Id*. A DTPA lawsuit which alleges only non-warranty claims, *e.g.*, false representations, is not subject to abatement under the Act. *Id*.; *Holder v. Wood*, 714 S.W.2d 318 (Tex. 1986).

When the manufactured housing debt instrument has been assigned or sold to a third party, the consumer may assert any claims or defenses against the holder that he or she has against the retailer or manufacturer. MHSA §1201.601. Unless the holder is joined in the suit against the retailer or manufacturer, however, any judgment obtained against the retailer or manufacturer is neither binding nor admissible in a subsequent lawsuit against the holder. *Id*. For this reason, a copy of the pre-filing notice letter should be sent to the holder so that the holder can be sued at the same time as the retailer or manufacturer.

§16.01.4 Manufactured Homeowners Recovery Fund

Mobile home manufacturers are required to maintain a bond with which judgments obtained by consumers may be satisfied. MHSA §1201.105. Also, a Manufactured Homeowners Recovery Fund has been established to provide a further source of funds to satisfy a judgment. MHSA §1201.404 *et seq*. The purpose of the fund is to pay such claims up to a maximum of $35,000 for actual damages and an additional amount of no more than 20% of the actual damages for attorney's fees and expenses. MHSA §1201.405. The Recovery Fund is not available to pay claims for personal injury damages, mental anguish, additional damages or exemplary damages. *Id*. If payment is made by the Recovery Fund to a homeowner, the Department will seek reimbursement from the license holder's bond. MHSA §1201.409.

Under prior law, the homeowner was required to obtain a judgment against the license holder which remained unsatisfied before making a claim against the Recovery Fund. Under current law, no judgment is necessary. Rather, a verified claim must be submitted to the Manufactured Housing Division of the Texas Department of Housing and Community Affairs on the prescribed form. The deadline for submitting this claim is two (2) years from the date of the act or omission which caused the claimed damage or two (2) years from the act or omission giving rise to the claim. MHSA §1201.406. A copy of the form is referenced below in Form 16.03[b] below.

§16.01.5 Action for Wrongfully Withheld Deposit

A prospective buyer of manufactured housing is often requested to pay a substantial cash deposit to secure purchase and delivery of a manufactured home. The Manufactured Housing Standards Act provides the prospective buyer with a right to a full or partial refund of that deposit in many circumstances. If there is a written agreement for the special order of a manufactured home and the right to retain the deposit is conspicuously noted on the agreement, the seller may retain up to 5% of the price of the specially ordered home if it is in fact delivered and the buyer refuses to take delivery. MHSA §1201.151. In all other instances, the buyer is entitled to a refund of his deposit within 15 days of a written request. Id. If the seller fails or refuses to issue a refund of the a deposit within 15 days of this written request, the buyer can recover from the seller, in addition to any other damages or remedies, three times the amount of the deposit and attorney's fees. MHSA §1201.604. Forms 16.03[c] and [d] below are suggested letters for demanding the deposit refund and then, if not received, demanding the treble refund and attorney's fees.

§16.02 Initial Client Checklist

[a] CHECKLIST: Manufactured housing

```
Client _____        The purchase
Date of Interview _____
```

- ☐ Year, model and registration number of mobile home
- ☐ Date of purchase

[A consumer is required to inform the manufacturer, retailer, broker or installer and the Texas Department of Housing and Community Affairs in writing of any claim against a bond or security no later than two years after the date of purchase. See Tex. Occ. Code §1201.406.]

- ☐ Manufacturer's name, address
- ☐ Is the manufacturer registered with the Texas Department of Housing and Community Affairs
- ☐ Retailer's or broker's name, address
- ☐ Is the retailer (or broker) registered with the Texas Department of Housing and Community Affairs
- ☐ What was the purchase price
  - Down payment
  - Monthly payments
  - Was there third party financing; if so, by whom

[A person who holds a "debt instrument" on a mobile home sale is subject to the claims and defenses of the consumer against the retailer, broker or manufacturer. See Tex. Occ. Code §1201.601.]

- Term of loan
- Interest rate
- Are payments current; if not, how delinquent

❑ Was there an arbitration clause in the purchase contract

[An arbitration clause may be enforceable if the Federal Arbitration Act applies. *See* 9 U.S.C. §1 *et seq.*]

Representations and warranties made

❑ Why was the mobile home purchased from this company
- Advertising; if so, when, where
- Sales pitch
- Prior dealings between the parties
- Other

❑ What representations were made about the mobile home, by whom and when

❑ Of the representations made, which are untrue

❑ Was any important information about the mobile home not disclosed to the client; if so, what information was not disclosed

❑ Was a model home used in the sale

❑ Did the home delivered conform to the model

[Model homes may create express warranties that the home delivered would conform to the model. *See* Tex. Bus. & Com. Code §2.313(a)(3).]

❑ Is there a written warranty from the manufacturer that the house was constructed or assembled in accordance with all building codes, standards, requirements and regulations prescribed by the U.S. Department of Housing and Urban Development

❑ Is there a written warranty from the manufacturer that the house and all appliances and equipment are free from defects in materials and workmanship

[A manufacturer is required by law to give these warranties to the purchaser. *See* Tex. Occ. Code §1201.351.]

- ❏ Is there a written warranty from the retailer that the installation of the house will be completed in accordance with all standards, rules, regulations, administrative orders, and requirements of the Texas Department of Housing and Community Affairs
- ❏ Is there a written warranty from the retailer that all appliances installed by the retailer have been installed in accordance with the instructions or specifications of the manufacturer and are free from defects in materials and workmanship

[A retailer is required by law to give these warranties to the purchaser. *See* TEX. OCC. CODE §1201.352.]

- ❏ Did the retailer deliver to the client at the time the contract for sale was signed all of the following:
  - Manufacturer's warranty
  - Retailer's warranty
  - Warranties on all appliances and equipment
  - Name and address of the manufacturer and retailer to which the consumer is to give notice of warranty service requests

[The retailer is required to disclose each of these to the buyer. see TEX. OCC. CODE §1201.352.]

Defects

- ❏ What are all of the defects in the mobile home
- ❏ When were the defects discovered

[The discovery rule applies to avoid the statute of limitations under the DTPA if the consumer exercised "reasonable diligence," *see* DTPA §17.565; however if a consumer needs to make a claim on or against a bond or other surety, a written claim must be delivered to the manufacturer, retailer, broker or installer and the Texas Department of Housing and Community Affairs, "no later than two years after the purchase of the house." *See* TEX. OCC. CODE §1201.406.]

- ❏ How were the defects discovered
- ❏ Has a request for a "consumer complaint home inspection" been made to the Texas Department of Housing and Community Affairs; if so, has the inspection been performed and what were the findings

❑ Has notice of the defects been given in writing or verbally to the prospective defendant *and* to the Texas Department of Housing and Community Affairs

[Written notice is required to trigger application of the written warranty obligation to repair. See TEX. OCC. CODE §1201.353.]

Repairs made

❑ Have any repairs been made; if so, when and by whom

❑ Were the repairs effective

❑ Who paid for the repairs

❑ Has the mobile home been altered in any material way since delivery

[Alterations to the mobile home may affect the availability of the remedy of rescission and revocation of acceptance under TEX. BUS. & COM. CODE §2.608.]

Use of mobile home

❑ Has any alternative housing been required because of the defects; if so, when, how long and how much was spent on the housing

❑ How have the defects affected the use of the mobile home as a residence

Expectations of client

❑ What does client expect to accomplish through litigation

Explanations to client

❑ Anticipated cost of litigation

❑ Attorney-client agreement

❑ Requirements of discovery, assistance with case

❑ Required attendance at depositions, trial

❑ Outcome of litigation is uncertain

Documents to obtain from client

[The client should be advised to bring all documents that in any way relate to the transaction; however, the following list is illustrative of the type of documents that must be provided if they exist.]

- ❑ Advertising seen
- ❑ Point of sale brochures
- ❑ Purchase contract
- ❑ Financing agreement
- ❑ Manufacturer's warranty
- ❑ Retailer's warranty
- ❑ Warranties on any appliances or equipment that is defective
- ❑ Written complaints made
- ❑ Written responses to complaints
- ❑ Reports, correspondence from Texas Department of Housing and Community Affairs
- ❑ All documents that relate to losses sustained

§16.03 Pre-Suit Notice Letters

[a]   FORM: Notice letter: manufactured housing

[NOTE: This letter must be sent by certified mail, return receipt requested, and should be sent not only to the retailer or manufacturer but also to the holder, if any, of the debt instrument on that home.]

[Insert the following at "notice of claim," §3.03[a], supra]

On _____, 20___, our client purchased a manufactured house from _____. The house is a [describe model and year] and bears registration number _____.

At the time the mobile home was sold to our client, he [she] was told that [insert representations made, e.g., the house was free of defects in material and workmanship and that it was "exceptionally well-built"]. As the defects shown below demonstrate, these representations were false, misleading, and deceptive.

After our client moved into the house, the following defects were discovered: [insert complete list of defects].

The purpose of this letter is to notify you of the defects in the house and the need for warranty repairs.

If proper warranty service is not provided by you, we will request, on behalf of our client, a consumer complaint home inspection by the Texas Department of Housing and Community Affairs.

As a result of the false, misleading, and deceptive representations made to our client, and the breaches of warranty described above, our client has suffered substantial damages. These damages include, but are not limited to, the following elements: [*insert elements of damages*].

[*Insert the following in place of statement of damages and expenses in §3.03[a] supra*]:

In order to resolve this matter as quickly and inexpensively as possible, our client is willing to accept your repair of the house (assuming the repairs will be done properly), and $, which we believe to be only part of the actual damages and expenses our client has incurred. If proper warranty repairs are not made, then the amount of our client's economic loss will be $.

[b] FORM: Manufactured Homeowners' Recovery Trust Fund claim

The complaint form can be accessed from the Department's website by using the following link: http://www.tdhca.state.tx.us/mh/docs/cchform.pdf.

[c] FORM: First demand for return of deposit

Forms [c] and [d] are suggested letters for demanding the deposit refund under MHSA §1201.151 and then, if not received, demanding the treble refund and attorney's fees under MHSA §1201.604.

Via Facsimile

And Certified Mail, Return Receipt Requested

_____ Mobile Homes

_____

Waco, Texas

Re: Plaintiff 1 and Plaintiff 2

Dear Sir or Madam:

This letter will confirm my telephone request to you this afternoon that I represent [Plaintiff 1 and Plaintiff 2], and, on their behalf, I demand that you immediately return to them the $5,000.00 you are currently holding as a deposit on a potential mobile home purchase. Please make your check payable to [Plaintiff 1 and Plaintiff 2] in the amount of $5,000.00 and forward it to my attention.

If you believe there is any written agreement from the [Plaintiffs] authorizing you to deduct any amount from this $5,000.00, please fax it to my attention before doing so.

Yours very truly,

[d]   FORM: Second demand for treble deposit and attorney's fees

Via Facsimile

And Certified Mail, Return Receipt Requested

_____Mobile Homes

_____

Waco, Texas

Re: Plaintiff 1 and Plaintiff 2

Dear Sir or Madam:

As you will recall, we have spoken on the phone several times. I have requested copies of the paperwork, if any, signed by the [Plaintiffs] authorizing you to retain their deposit. Despite several promises, you have never produced, to me or to the [Plaintiffs], any documentation authorizing you to retain their deposit. As discussed in my last telephone conversation with you on _____, the clear inference from your failure to provide this paperwork is that you do not have it.

As a licensed retailer, broker and installer, you are no doubt familiar with the provisions of the Texas Manufactured Housing Standards Act which provides that it is unlawful for a retailer, salesperson or agent of the retailer to refuse to refund a consumer's deposit within 15 days following the receipt of written notice from the consumer requesting that refund. Further Section 1201.604 of that Act provides that a consumer may recover, cumulative of all other remedies, three times the amount of the deposit plus reasonable attorney's fees if a retailer, salesperson or agent of the retailer fails to make a refund within 15 days. Clearly, by failing to refund the [Plaintiffs'] deposit of $5,000.00 within 15 days of receiving my letter of _____, you have violated the provisions of this Act and are now liable to the Plaintiffs for $15,000.00, plus reasonable attorney's fees.

Demand is hereby made that you immediately pay to the [Plaintiffs] the sum of $15,000.00, plus reasonable attorney's fees in the amount of $2,000.00 in order to avoid the necessity of my filing suit against you for the full amount of the Plaintiffs' legal remedies and attorney's fees. I will allow you 30 days to resolve this matter by tendering a check to me in the amount of $17,000.00 made payable to "[Plaintiffs] and [their attorney]" If this matter is not so resolved within the next 30 days, suit will be filed.

Please direct any further correspondence regarding this matter to me and not to the [Plaintiffs].

Yours very truly,

§16.04 Sample Petition—Manufactured Housing

A petition involving a manufactured house is similar to that for the purchase of other goods, e.g., the causes of action may include false representations, unconscionability or breach of warranty (express or implied). *See* §17.01 *supra* TEX. OCC. CODE Chapter 1201 (the "MHSA"). For this reason, a modified version of the general form petition may be used as suggested in Form [a].

[a] FORM: Manufactured home defects in workmanship and repairs

```
        NO. _____

_____      §      IN THE DISTRICT COURT OF
                §
vs.             §      _____ COUNTY, TEXAS
                §
_____      §      _____ JUDICIAL DISTRICT
```

PLAINTIFF'S ORIGINAL PETITION

TO THE HONORABLE JUDGE OF THE DISTRICT COURT:

NOW COMES _____, Plaintiffs herein, complaining of _____, Defendant herein, and for cause of action, would show unto the Court as follows:

I. DISCOVERY CONTROL PLAN DESIGNATION

1.01   Discovery in this case is intended to be conducted under Level _____, pursuant to Rule 190._____, *Texas Rules of Civil Procedure.*

II. PARTIES

2.01   Plaintiff _____ is a resident of _____, _____ County, Texas.

2.02   Plaintiff _____ is a resident of _____, _____ County, Texas.

2.03   Defendant _____ is a Texas corporation which may be served with process by serving _____, its registered agent, at _____, the corporation's registered address.

III. VENUE

3.01   Venue of this action is proper in _____ County, Texas because _____ reside in _____ County, Texas and the events made the basis of this lawsuit and giving rise to Plaintiff's cause of action occurred, in whole or in part, in _____ County, Texas.

IV. NOTICE; CONDITIONS PRECEDENT

4.01   Defendant was given notice in writing of the claims made in this petition including a statement of Plaintiff's economic damages, mental anguish damages and expenses, including attorney's fees, more than sixty days before this suit was filed in the manner and form required by DTPA §17.505(a).

4.02   All conditions precedent to recovery by Plaintiff herein have been performed, have occurred, or have been excused.

V. AGENCY AND VICARIOUS LIABILITY

5.01 Unless otherwise stated, whenever it is alleged that Defendant _____ committed an act, failed to perform an act, made a representation or a statement, or failed to make a disclosure, it is alleged that Defendant _____ acted or failed to act through its authorized agents, servants, employees or representatives acting with either expressed, implied, apparent, direct and/or ostensible authority, or _____ subsequently ratified these acts, failures to act, representations, statements or conduct. Defendant _____ was the _____ manager of _____ in _____, _____ County, Texas. It is therefore further alleged that, at all times relevant hereto, Defendant _____ acted as the authorized agent of Defendant _____ with either expressed, implied, apparent, direct and/or ostensible authority, or that Defendant _____ subsequently ratified the acts, failures to act, representations, statements or conduct of Defendant _____.

VI. FACTS OF CASE

6.01 [*Insert factual basis for claims, e.g.*: In or around June or July, 20___, Plaintiffs _____ purchased a 20___ _____ Mobile Home from Defendant _____. The Home was placed upon Plaintiffs' property located at _____ in _____, _____ County, Texas. The purchase price was approximately $_____.

6.02 Defendant _____ provided an express limited warranty to the Plaintiffs that the mobile home would be "free from manufacturing defects in material or workmanship" for a period of one year following the date of original retail purchase. Defendant _____ further warranted that the mobile home was "designed and constructed in accordance with applicable Federal Manufactured Home Construction and Safety Standards." Defendant _____ further warranted and agreed that Defendant would repair or replace "without cost to the Owner" any "defective workmanship, part or parts within the scope of this warranty" as long as _____ received written notice of the defects.

6.03 Soon after moving into the mobile home, Plaintiffs began noticing that the roof leaked. Plaintiffs gave proper notice of this defect to Defendant _____, and Defendant _____, through its agents and employees, attempted to repair the leaking roof. Although the repairs fixed at least part of leaks, the repairs made caused a small amount of rain water to be channeled around a dormer window and into the attic space and down a wall in the mobile home. Thereafter, when it rained, rain water would leak around the dormer window and saturate nearby attic insulation. Further, the rain water would travel down an interior wall in one of the bedrooms and saturate the insulation and gypsum board structures inside the mobile home.

6.04 Because this leak was hidden from view by the walls and ceiling of the mobile home, Plaintiffs did not become aware of this condition until some time later. During the winter months of 20___ and the spring months of 20___, Plaintiffs noticed that an increasingly strong musty odor permeated the mobile home. As Plaintiffs later discovered, the damp insulation and gypsum board in their mobile home became a fertile breeding ground for a dangerous strain of black mold known as Stachybotrys as well as for Penicillium and Aspergillum molds.

6.05   After repeated requests, Defendant _____ finally agreed to make repairs to the damaged areas of Plaintiffs' mobile home under its warranty. However, despite knowing that the failure to fully remediate the existing mold infestation would only exacerbate the condition, Defendant's crew took only perfunctory steps to alleviate the mold. They then tried to cover up the mold infestation with new materials without testing it to determine if the mold had been fully removed. When Plaintiffs advised Defendant's crew that Plaintiffs would not accept repairs which did not comply with government mold remediation guidelines for testing the effectiveness of mold removal, Defendant simply withdrew its crew and left the repair job unfinished.

6.06   Subsequent testing done at Plaintiffs' expense revealed that the mold infestation continued to thrive inside the wall cavities, which Defendant attempted to cover up, as well as throughout Plaintiffs' mobile home. Since _____, Defendant has failed and refused to return to Plaintiffs' mobile home and make the necessary repairs.

VII. FIRST CAUSE OF ACTION: DTPA

7.01   Plaintiffs repeat and reallege the material factual allegations in the preceding paragraphs.

7.02   Plaintiffs are consumers entitled to bring a claim for relief under the Texas Deceptive Trade Practices-Consumer Protection Act, Texas Business & Commerce Code, §17.46 et seq. (the "DTPA").

7.03   Defendant committed one or more of the following acts or omissions in violation of the "laundry list" of the DTPA:

(a) representing that goods or services had characteristics, ingredients, uses or benefits which they did not have;

(b) representing that goods or services were of a particular standard, quality or grade when they were of another;

(c) failing to disclose information concerning goods or services which was known at the time of the transaction when such failure to disclose such information was intended to induce a consumer into a transaction into which the consumer would not have entered had the information been disclosed;

(d) advertising goods or services with the intent not to sell them as advertised;

(e) representing that an agreement confers or involves rights, remedies or obligations which it does not have or involve or which are prohibited by law;

(f) knowingly making false or misleading statements of fact concerning the need for parts, replacement or repair services;

(g) representing that a guarantee or warranty confers or involves rights or remedies which it does not have or involve; and/or

(h) representing that work or services have been performed on, or parts replaced in, goods when the work or services were not performed or the parts replaced.

7.04 Plaintiffs relied on these representations to their detriment.

7.05 Further, Defendant's breach of express and/or implied warranties concerning the mobile home and in connection with Defendant's service on the mobile home, as described above, is actionable through the DTPA.

7.06 Further, Defendant's conduct and course of action was unconscionable. Defendants took advantage of Plaintiffs' lack of knowledge, ability, experience or capacity to a grossly unfair degree.

7.07 One or more of the Defendants' violations of the DTPA was a producing cause of damages to Plaintiffs for which they sue.

7.08 Further, Defendant's conduct was committed knowingly, entitling Plaintiffs to seek the trebling of their actual damages in accordance with the DTPA.

VIII. DAMAGES

8.01 Defendant's acts and omissions as described herein have been a producing and/or proximate cause of damages to Plaintiffs. Plaintiffs have suffered economic damages, including but not limited to:

(a) the benefit of the bargain; that is the difference between the value of the mobile home as represented and the fair market value of the mobile home as delivered;

(b) the reasonable and necessary costs to Plaintiffs required in order to correct, remediate and repair the mobile home and bring it into conformance with the representations and warranties made;

(c) the value of Plaintiffs' time expended in attempting to correct Defendants' mistakes and wrong doings; and

(d) medical expenses incurred to treat the conditions caused from Plaintiffs being continuously exposed to toxic mold in their home.

8.02   Further, Plaintiffs have suffered mental anguish.

8.03   These damages are within the jurisdictional limits of this Court.

IX. ADDITIONAL DAMAGES

9.01   Defendant's conduct in violation of the DTPA was committed knowingly, as that term is defined. Accordingly, Plaintiffs seek an award of additional damages under the DTPA in an amount not to exceed three times the amount of their economic damages.

X. ATTORNEY'S FEES

10.01   As a result of Defendant's conduct, Plaintiffs have been required to obtain the services of the undersigned attorney for the filing, prosecution and trial of this cause, and therefore seeks an award of reasonable and necessary attorney's fees pursuant to applicable law.

WHEREFORE, PREMISES CONSIDERED, Plaintiffs respectfully pray that Defendant be cited to appear and answer herein, and that upon final trial hereof, Plaintiffs recover from Defendant all of their economic damages, mental anguish, additional damages, pre-judgment and post-judgment interest as allowed by law, attorney's fees, costs of court and such other and further relief to which they may show himself justly entitled.

Respectfully submitted,

_____

Attorney for Plaintiff

[b] FORM: Manufactured home retailer (refusal to refund deposit)

NO. _____

_____ § IN THE DISTRICT COURT OF

§

vs. § _____COUNTY, TEXAS

§

_____ § _____ JUDICIAL DISTRICT

PLAINTIFF'S ORIGINAL PETITION

TO THE HONORABLE JUDGE OF THE DISTRICT COURT:

NOW COMES _____, Plaintiffs herein, complaining of _____, Defendant herein, and for cause of action, would show unto the Court as follows:

I. DISCOVERY CONTROL PLAN DESIGNATION

1.01   Discovery in this case is intended to be conducted under Level _____, pursuant to Rule 190._____, *Texas Rules of Civil Procedure.*

II. PARTIES

2.01   Plaintiff _____ is a resident of _____, _____ County, Texas.

2.02   Plaintiff _____ is a resident of _____, _____ County, Texas.

2.03   Defendant _____ is a Texas corporation which may be served with process by serving _____, its registered agent, at _____, the corporation's registered address.

III. VENUE

3.01   Venue of this action is proper in _____ County, Texas because _____ reside in _____ County, Texas and the events made the basis of this lawsuit and giving rise to Plaintiff's cause of action occurred, in whole or in part, in _____ County, Texas.

IV. NOTICE; CONDITIONS PRECEDENT

4.01   Defendant was given notice in writing of the claims made in this petition including a statement of Plaintiff's economic damages, mental anguish damages and expenses, including attorney's fees, more than sixty days before this suit was filed in the manner and form required by DTPA §17.505(a).

4.02   All conditions precedent to recovery by Plaintiff herein have been performed, have occurred, or have been excused.

V. AGENCY AND VICARIOUS LIABILITY

5.01 Unless otherwise stated, whenever it is alleged that Defendant _____ committed an act, failed to perform an act, made a representation or a statement, or failed to make a disclosure, it is alleged that Defendant _____ acted or failed to act through its authorized agents, servants, employees or representatives acting with either expressed, implied, apparent, direct and/or ostensible authority, or _____ subsequently ratified these acts, failures to act, representations, statements or conduct. Defendant _____ was the _____ manager of _____ in _____, _____ County, Texas. It is therefore further alleged that, at all times relevant hereto, Defendant _____ acted as the authorized agent of Defendant _____ with either expressed, implied, apparent, direct and/or ostensible authority, or that Defendant _____ subsequently ratified the acts, failures to act, representations, statements or conduct of Defendant _____.

VI. FACTS

6.01 Defendant [Retailer] operates a business selling mobile homes to the public. Defendant [Manager] is employed by [Retailer] as its Manager and works at its _____ location.

6.02 On _____, Plaintiffs _____ visited [Retailer] and spoke with Defendant [Manager]. At that time, Defendant [Manager] offered to find Plaintiffs a mobile home site for their approval in the event Plaintiffs later decided to purchase a mobile home from Defendants. Defendant [Manager] represented that, in order to get this process started, Plaintiffs were required to deposit a substantial "down payment." Based upon the representations and at the urging of Defendants, Plaintiffs gave [Manager] a cash deposit of $5,000.00 on _____, 20__.

Even so, no contract was formed and no paperwork—other than the receipt for the $5,000.00 deposit—was prepared or signed.

6.03 During the next several months, Defendants were wholly ineffective in locating a suitable homesite for Plaintiffs. Only a few sites were ever suggested, and those sites were for various reasons unacceptable to Plaintiffs. Throughout the process, Defendants made various representations and promises to Plaintiffs to the effect that they would be in their new home "before summertime," "before school started," and later, "before Thanksgiving."

6.03 After six months of frustration, Plaintiffs realized that Defendants would never be able to provide them with a homesite and a mobile home satisfactory to them and suitable for their needs, and in _____ 20__ Plaintiffs asked Defendants [Manager] and [Retailer] for return of their $5,000.00 deposit. Defendant [Manager] gave Plaintiffs various excuses as to why the refund couldn't be made. After repeated requests, Defendant [Manager] began to avoid Plaintiffs by refusing to accept or return their phone calls and by having other employees of [Retailer] lie to Plaintiffs that Defendant [Manager] was not in the office when Plaintiffs visited.

6.05 On _____, 20__, the undersigned counsel, acting on behalf of Plaintiffs _____, following several weeks of telephone calls, formally requested a refund of the $5,000.00 deposit in writing to Defendants. A true and correct copy of that letter is attached hereto as Exhibit 1. Despite this formal written demand, Defendant [Manager] still refused to refund Plaintiffs' $5,000.00 deposit.

6.06 To prevent, deter and punish such shenanigans, the Texas Legislature has enacted the Texas Manufacturer Housing Standards Act, Texas Occupations Code Chapter 1201. Specifically, Section 1201.151 declares it unlawful for a retailer, salesperson or agent of a retailer to refuse to refund a consumer's deposit within 15 days following the receipt of written notice from the consumer requesting that refund. As a penalty, the Act provides the consumer with a civil action for damages in the amount of three times the amount of the deposit, plus reasonable attorneys' fees. As a result of the Defendants' conduct, Plaintiffs have been forced to avail themselves of the remedies under the Act.

6.07 In addition, Plaintiffs have been required to retain the services of the undersigned counsel in order to pursue this action against Defendants and have incurred attorney's fees and expenses. Plaintiffs therefore further sue for the recovery of their reasonable and necessary attorney's fees and expenses incurred in the prosecution of this action.

VII. FIRST CAUSE OF ACTION: TEXAS MANUFACTURED HOUSING STANDARDS ACT

7.01 Plaintiffs repeat and reallege the factual allegations in the preceding paragraphs.

7.02 Plaintiffs are "consumers" as defined by the Texas Manufactured Housing Standards Act. Defendants are "brokers," "retailers," and/or "salespersons" as defined by the Texas Manufactured Housing Standards Act.

7.03 Defendants refused to refund within 15 days following receipt of written notice from Plaintiffs of their request for a refund of their deposit in the amount of $5,000.00. Pursuant to *Texas Occupations Code* §1201.604, Defendants are liable to Plaintiffs, cumulative of other remedies, in the amount of three times the deposit amount of $5,000.00, for which they sue.

7.04 Further, Defendants are liable to Plaintiffs for their reasonable attorney's fees incurred in the prosecution of this action, for which they sue.

VIII. SECOND CAUSE OF ACTION: DTPA

8.01 Plaintiffs repeat and reallege the factual allegations in the preceding paragraphs.

8.02 Plaintiffs are consumers entitled to relief under the Texas Deceptive Trade Practices- Consumer Protection Act ("DTPA") by their conduct outlined above, Defendants have engaged in violations of the DTPA, which, together and separately, have been a producing cause of damages to Plaintiffs, including but not limited to:

a) violating the Texas Manufactured Housing Standards Act as outlined above; and/or

b) representing that an agreement confers or involves rights, remedies or obligations that did not have or involve.

8.03 Further, Defendants engaged in unconscionable conduct and an unconscionable course of conduct that was a producing cause of damages to Plaintiffs.

8.04 All of the above stated violations of the DTPA were committed knowingly by Defendants, and each of them, entitling Plaintiffs to recover treble damages for which they sue.

IX. ADDITIONAL DAMAGES

9.01 Defendant's conduct in violation of the DTPA was committed knowingly, as that term is defined. Accordingly, Plaintiffs seek an award of additional damages under the DTPA in an amount not to exceed three times the amount of their economic damages.

X. ATTORNEY'S FEES

10.01 As a result of Defendant's conduct, Plaintiffs have been required to obtain the services of the undersigned attorney for the filing, prosecution and trial of this cause, and therefore seeks an award of reasonable and necessary attorney's fees pursuant to applicable law.

WHEREFORE, PREMISES CONSIDERED, Plaintiffs pray at Defendants be cited to appear and answer herein, and that upon final trial hereof, Plaintiffs have judgment of and from Defendants, jointly and severally, for all actual damages, additional damages, civil penalties, prejudgment and post-judgment interest as allowed by law, attorney's fees, costs of court and such other and further relief to which they may show themselves justly entitled.

Respectfully submitted,

_____

§16.05 Discovery in Manufactured Housing Cases

§16.05.1 Interrogatories—

Insert the following specific requests into the general form for Interrogatories, §7.43[a], *supra*.

[a] FORM: —Interrogatories to defendant dealer

The following are specific Interrogatories which can be included in a set sent to a manufactured home dealer in connection with a claim that the home was misrepresented at the time of the sale.

1. Identify the person answering these Interrogatories with the following information: full legal name, any prior names, address, social security number, driver's license number, date of birth and relationship to Defendant.

2. Identify all persons who personally interacted with Plaintiffs at the dealership, including but not limited to the salesman, finance manager and manager. For each conviction of a felony or crime of moral turpitude during the last ten (10) years for the persons identified in the previous interrogatories, please state the date, offense, court and sentence for each such conviction.

3. Please describe how You came into possession of the manufactured home at issue in this case, including the date acquired, identity of prior owner(s), location of acquisition and identify of all persons involved in the acquisition.

4. Please describe the actions taken by You to inspect the manufactured home prior to Your acquisition of it, including the identity of the persons involved in the inspection(s) or investigation(s).

5. Please identify all documents reviewed by You, Your employees, agents or representatives, prior to Your acquisition of the manufactured home.

6. Please describe all action taken by You, Your employees, agents or representatives, to prepare the manufactured home at issue for sale, including the identity of all persons involved in those actions.

7. How much did You pay for the manufactured home when You acquired it?

8. How much did You spend to repair, improve and/or maintain the manufactured home while it was in Your possession? To whom did You make these expenditures?

9. For each statement made by You or on Your behalf to Plaintiff about the condition of the manufactured home prior to her purchase of it, please state the substance of the statement, who made it, the date and time made and all persons present when the statement was made.

10. Please describe all conversations You had with the Plaintiff concerning her decision to purchase the manufactured home, including the substance of her statements, date made, to whom it was made and the identity of all persons who were there to hear the statement.

11. If You have inspected the manufactured home since Plaintiff's purchase, please describe that inspection, including the date, persons involved and observations concerning the condition of the manufactured home.

12. Did Plaintiff's manufactured home come with a warranty? If so, please describe the general terms of the warranty and how the warranty was communicated to Plaintiff. If not, please describe how warranties were limited or disclaimed.

13. In Your opinion, what was the fair market value of the manufactured home when it was sold to Plaintiff? What is the fair market value of the manufactured home now?

14. What is the reasonable cost to repair the manufactured home in order to put it [back] into the condition it was in at the time of Plaintiff's purchase?

[b] FORM: —Interrogatories to defendant wrongfully withholding deposit

The following are specific Interrogatories to a manufactured home dealer in a claim that the dealer has wrongfully withheld the buyer's deposit after demand for its return.

1. Please Identify each Person providing answers or information used to compile answers, or in any way assisting in providing answers or information used to compile answers to these Interrogatories and designate which Interrogatory each Person assisted in answering.

2. Please Identify any statement in Your custody, possession, or control, of any and all Persons with knowledge of facts, including Plaintiff, which are or may be relevant to this lawsuit, and Identify the Person giving each statement.

3. Identify each communication between You and Plaintiffs Concerning Plaintiffs' potential purchase of a mobile home from Defendants.

4. Identify each communication between You and Plaintiffs Concerning Plaintiffs' cash deposit of $5,000.

5. Identify each communication between You and Plaintiffs Relating to Plaintiffs' cash deposit of $5,000 to You and state the result or action taken by You as a result of each communication.

6. Please state the dates and describe all correspondence and other communications between You and Plaintiffs.

7. Identify each person You will call as a witness in this cause.

8. Describe Your business and/or employment relationship with [Retailer].

9. State Your ownership interest in [Retailer], if any.

10. Please list all home sites You presented to Plaintiffs as potential mobile home sites from _____, 20__ until present.

11. Please Identify each and every document in Your possession signed by either Plaintiff.

12. Please state the reason(s) You would not return the Plaintiffs' $5,000 cash deposit to them within 15 days after the letter of _____, 20__ from Plaintiffs' counsel.

13. Please state the reason(s) You would not return the Plaintiffs' $5,000 cash deposit to them before _____, 20__.

§16.05.2 Requests for Production

[a] FORM: Requests for Production to defendant manufacturer

1. Produce any and all documents containing correspondence between Plaintiffs, or either of them, and Defendant.

2. Produce any and all documents containing correspondence between Plaintiffs, or either of them, and [Retailer] or [employee of Retailer].

3. Produce any and all documents delivered by You to Plaintiffs, or either of them, in connection with the Mobile Home.

4. Produce any and all documents received from Plaintiffs, or either of them.

5. Produce any and all documents recording the work done to install and/or set up the Mobile Home.

6. Produce any and all requests for service, service orders, work orders, invoices for work performed on the Mobile Home.

7. Produce any and all other documents recording or evidencing any and all repair work performed on the Mobile Home.

8. Produce any and all contracts, subcontracts, agreements or other documents reflecting the understandings in place between You and the persons or entities who performed service work on the Mobile Home.

9. Produce any and all photographs relating to the Mobile Home, the Plaintiffs or any issue in this lawsuit.

10. Produce any and all videotapes relating to the Mobile Home, the Plaintiffs or any issue in this lawsuit.

11. Produce any and all warranty and similar documents with regard to the Mobile Home, and any and all documents concerning its installation and any of its component parts.

12. Produce any and all documents relating to any repair, alteration or modification of the Mobile Home or any components in the Mobile Home including, but not limited to, any and all repair estimates, invoices, damage appraisals and repairs orders.

13. Produce any and all sales contracts and other documents concerning the purchase, mortgage loan and installation, including a copy of the title or deed, of the Mobile Home.

14. Produce any and all written contracts between the Plaintiffs and Defendant in this case involving the Mobile Home.

15. Produce any and all photographs, movies, videotapes or other photographic, digital, or electronic reproductions concerning any issue in this case.

16. Produce any and all written or recorded statements or any other written memorialization of any statement made by any director, officer, agent, representative or employee of [Manufacturer] relating to the Mobile Home or Plaintiffs prior to the receipt of the 60 day demand letter from Plaintiff's counsel.

17. Produce any and all correspondence, notes, memoranda or other documents passing between Plaintiffs and [Manufacturer] including but not limited to written requests for warranty service or complaints submitted in writing.

18. Produce any and all correspondence, notes, memoranda or other documents passing between You or your attorney and the retail dealer from whom Plaintiffs purchased the Mobile Home.

19. Produce any and all reports, inspection or investigation results prepared by You, or by someone on Your behalf, concerning the Mobile Home in question.

20. Produce any and all appraisals and evaluations on the Mobile Home.

21. Produce any and all documents relevant to any damages Plaintiffs have allegedly sustained as a result of the occurrence that is the subject of this suit.

22. Produce any and all documents, notes, memoranda or other writings concerning repair estimates and estimates for modifications to the Mobile Home, and any and all documents concerning any repairs and/or modifications actually made to the Mobile Home.

23. Produce any and all test results, reports, calculations and other documents generated pursuant to any and all tests performed on or in the home, including without limitation on any samples of air, water, soil or any other material or any components of the home.

24. Produce any and all articles, literature, tests, treatises, reports or other writings concerning any fungus or mold.

25. Produce any and all letters, correspondence, electronic mail, notes or other documents passing between or generated pursuant to You or Your counsel's communication with any government agency including the Texas Department of Housing and Community Affairs, the Texas Department of Health, the or United States Department of Housing and Urban Development regarding mold, the Mobile Home or Plaintiffs.

[b] FORM: Requests for Production to defendant (wrongfully withheld deposit)

1. Produce all Documents which Mention, Concern, Relate to or Evidence any of the communications between You and Plaintiffs.

2. Produce all Documents provided to You by Plaintiffs in connection with the subject matter of this suit.

3. Produce all Documents provided to You by any third party in connection with the subject matter of this suit.

4. Produce all Documents provided to Plaintiffs by You in connection with the subject matter of this lawsuit.

5. Produce all Documents provided to any third party by You Relating to Plaintiffs in connection with the subject matter of this lawsuit.

6. Produce all documents and taped recordings Mentioning, summarizing, containing, describing, or otherwise Relating to any communications between You and Plaintiffs.

7. Produce all tape recordings of any conversation between You and any third party relating to Plaintiffs.

8. Produce any Document signed or executed by or on behalf of Plaintiffs.

9. Produce all Documents which Reflect, Mention or Evidence interest earned on the $5,000 Cash Deposit.

10. Produce any and all Documents containing or Evidencing any and all employment or compensation contracts between [Manager] and [Retailer].

11. Produce any and all Documents Evidencing any and all compensation paid by I-35 Homes to You, including but not limited to any Forms W-2, Forms 1099, for the years 2000 and 2001.

12. Produce all Documents which reflect phone calls made to Your office from Plaintiffs or Plaintiffs' attorney since _____, 20__.

13. Produce all correspondence from You concerning Plaintiffs and/or the $5,000 Cash Deposit.

14. Produce all Documents which Reflect or Evidence advertisements You placed in any advertising media on behalf of [Retailer] from _____ to present, including, but not limited to [Craig's List/The Waco Tribune-Herald, etc.].

15. Produce all Documents which Reflect or Evidence any and all complaints which have been filed against You with the Manufacturing Housing Division of the Texas Department of Housing and Community Affairs since _____ 20___ to present.

16. Produce all Documents which Reflect or Evidence any lawsuits filed against You in the State of Texas since _____ 20__ to present, include the Cause Number, County in which the lawsuit was filed, and whether or not the lawsuit is pending.

17. Produce all Documents which Reflect or Evidence any demand letters You have received from [Retailer's] customers from _____ 201__ to present.

18. Produce any and all statements for the bank account(s) where Plaintiffs' $5,000.00 cash deposit was deposited by You for the months it was on deposit.

DTPA FORMS
AND
PRACTICE GUIDE

DESK BOOK
2016 Edition

**DECEPTIVE TRADE PRACTICES-
CONSUMER PROTECTION ACT**

CHAPTER 541

TEXAS INSURANCE CODE

(Selected provisions)

CHAPTER 542

TEXAS INSURANCE CODE

(Selected provisions)

**RESIDENTIAL CONSTRUCTION
LIABILITY ACT**

**TEXAS RESIDENTIAL CONSTRUCTION
COMMISSION ACT** (Expired)

(Selected provisions)

DIGEST OF SUPREME COURT OPINIONS
David G. Tekell

Contact us at (866) 72-JAMES or www.jamespublishing.com

Great care has been taken to reproduce accurately the text of the Deceptive Trade Practices – Consumer Protection Act, selected provisions of Chapter 541 of the Insurance Code, the Residential Construction Liability Act and the Residential Construction Commission Act. Naturally, however, we make no express or implied warranty with regard to the freedom from error or use of this publication. In the use of this booklet, each person ultimately must rely on the official texts of these statutes.

Copyright © 1989-2016
by
James Publishing Company
3505 Cadillac Ave.
Suite P-101
Costa Mesa, CA 92626

All rights reserved
ISBN 978-0-938065-87-6

STAFF

Managing Editor: Lisa J. Dunne, Esq.
Production: Amishi Sanghvi

CONTENTS

DECEPTIVE TRADE PRACTICES-CONSUMER PROTECTION ACT

§17.41	Short Title	1
§17.42	Waivers: Public Policy	1
§17.43	Cumulative Remedies	1
§17.44	Construction and Application	2
§17.45	Definitions	2
§17.46	Deceptive Trade Practices Unlawful	3
§17.461	Pyramid Promotional Scheme	6
§17.462	Listing of Business Location of Certain Businesses	7
§17.47	Restraining Orders	8
§17.48	Duty of District and County Attorney	9
§17.49	Exemptions	10
§17.50	Relief for Consumers	11
§17.501	Consumer Protection Division Participation in Class Action	12
§17.505	Notice; Inspection	12
§17.5051	Mediation	13
§17.5052	Offers of Settlement	14
§17.506	Damages: Defenses	15
§17.55	Promotional Material	15
§17.555	Indemnity	16
§17.56	Venue	16
§17.56	Venue	16
§17.565	Limitation	16
§17.57	Subpoenas	16
§17.58	Voluntary Compliance	17
§17.59	Post Judgment Relief	17
§17.60	Reports and Examinations	18
§17.61	Civil Investigative Demand	18
§17.62	Penalties	19
§17.63	Application	20

CHAPTER 541
TEXAS INSURANCE CODE
(Selected Provisions)

SUBCHAPTER A. General ions

§541.001. Purpose	21
§541.002. Definitions	21
§541.003. Unfair Methods of Competition and Unfair or Deceptive Acts or Practices Prohibited	21
§541.008. Liberal Construction	22

SUBCHAPTER B. Unfair Methods of Competition and Unfair or Deceptive Acts or Practices Defined

§541.051. Misrepresentation Regarding Policy or Insurer	22
§541.052. False Information and Advertising	22
§541.060. Unfair Settlement Practices	23
§541.061. Misrepresentation of Insurance Policy	23

SUBCHAPTER D. Private Action for Damages

§541.151. Private Action for Damages Authorized	24
§541.152. Damages Attorney's Fees, and Other Relief	24
§541.153. Frivolous Action	24
§541.154. Prior Notice of Action	24
§541.155. Abatement	25
§541.156. Settlement Offer	25
§541.157. Contents of Settlement Offer	25
§541.158. Rejection of Settlement Offer	26
§541.159. Limit on Recovery After Settlement Offer	26
§541.160. Effect of Settlement Offer	26
§541.161. Mediation	26
§541.162. Limitations Period	27

CHAPTER 542
TEXAS INSURANCE CODE
(Selected Provisions)

SUBCHAPTER A. Unfair Claim Settlement Practices

§542.001. Purpose	28
§542.002. Applicability of Subchapter	28
§542.003. Unfair Claim Settlement Practices Prohibited	28
§542.004. Examination of Tax Returns Prohibited	29

SUBCHAPTER B. Prompt Payment of Claims

§542.051. Definitions	29
§542.052. Applicability of Subchapter	30
§542.053. Exception	30
§542.054. Liberal Construction	31
§542.055. Receipt of Notice of Claim	31
§542.056. Notice of Acceptance or Rejection of Claim	31
§542.057. Payment of Claim	31
§542.058. Delay in Payment of Claim	32
§542.059. Extension of Deadlines	32
§542.060. Liability for Violation of Subchapter	32
§542.061. Remedies Not Exclusive	32

RESIDENTIAL CONSTRUCTION LIABILITY ACT

§27.001	Definitions	33
§27.002	Application of Chapter	34
§27.003	Liability	34
§27.0031	Frivolous Suit; Harassment	35
§27.004	Notice and Offer of Settlement	35
§27.0041	Mediation	38
§27.0042	Conditional Sale to Builder	38
§27.005	Limitations on Effect of Chapter	39
§27.006	Causation	39
§27.007	Disclosure Statement Required	39

DIGEST OF SUPREME COURT OPINIONS

CONTENTS

§1.00	General Provisions		40
	§1.01	Application and Effective Dates	40
	§1.02	Construction of the Act	41
§2.00	The Standing Requirement: Who Is a Consumer?		41
§3.00	Who Can Be Sued?		47
§4.00	False, Misleading or Deceptive Acts or Practices		51
§5.00	Breach of Warranty		57
§6.00	Unconscionability		59
§7.00	Article 21.21		62
§8.00	Causation		70
§9.00	Damages		73
	§9.01	Actual Damages	73
	§9.02	Treble Damages	78
§10.00	Attorney's Fees		79
	§10.01	Recovery by Plaintiff	79
	§10.02	Recovery by Defendant	81
§11.00	Jury Questions		82
§12.00	Defenses/Notice		83
§13.00	Contribution and Indemnity		91
§14.00	Other Decisions		91
	§14.01	Pleading	91
	§14.02	Assignment/Survival	91
	§14.03	Venue	92
	§14.04	Miscellaneous	92

TABLE OF SUPREME COURT OPINIONS   94

TOPICAL INDEX OF SUPREME COURT OPINIONS   98

DECEPTIVE TRADE PRACTICES-
CONSUMER PROTECTION ACT

(Texas Business and Commerce Code §17.41 - §17.63)

§17.41. SHORT TITLE

This subchapter may be cited as the Deceptive Trade Practices-Consumer Protection Act.

§17.42. WAIVERS: PUBLIC POLICY

(a) Any waiver by a consumer of the provisions of this subchapter is contrary to public policy and is unenforceable and void; provided, however, that a waiver is valid and enforceable if:

   (1) the waiver is in writing and is signed by the consumer;

   (2) the consumer is not in a significantly disparate bargaining position; and

   (3) the consumer is represented by legal counsel in seeking or acquiring the goods or services.

(b) A waiver under Subsection (a) is not effective if the consumer's legal counsel was directly or indirectly identified, suggested, or selected by a defendant or an agent of the defendant.

(c) A waiver under this section must be:

   (1) conspicuous and in bold-face type of at least 10 points in size;

   (2) identified by the heading "Waiver of Consumer Rights," or words of similar meaning; and

   (3) in substantially the following form:

   "I waive my rights under the Deceptive Trade Practices - Consumer Protection Act, Section 17.41 et seq., Business & Commerce Code, a law that gives consumers special rights and protections. After consultation with an attorney of my own selection, I voluntarily consent to this waiver."

(d) The waiver required by Subsection (c) may be modified to waive only specified rights under this subchapter.

(e) The fact that a consumer has signed a waiver under this section is not a defense to an action brought by the attorney general under Section 17.47.

§17.43. CUMULATIVE REMEDIES

The provisions of this subchapter are not exclusive. The remedies provided in this subchapter are in addition to any other procedures or remedies provided for in any other law; provided, however, that no recovery shall be permitted under both this subchapter and another law of both damages and penalties for the same act or practice. A violation of a provision of law other than this subchapter is not in and of itself a violation of this subchapter. An act or practice that is a violation of a provision of law other than this subchapter may be made the basis of an action under this subchapter if the act or practice is proscribed by a provision of this subchapter or is declared by such other law to be actionable under this subchapter. The provisions of this subchapter do not in any way preclude other political subdivisions of this state from dealing with deceptive trade practices.

§17.44. CONSTRUCTION AND APPLICATION

(a) This subchapter shall be liberally construed and applied to promote its underlying purposes, which are to protect consumers against false, misleading, and deceptive business practices, unconscionable actions, and breaches of warranty and to provide efficient and economical procedures to secure such protection.

(b) Chapter 27, Property Code, prevails over this subchapter to the extent of any conflict.

§17.45. DEFINITIONS

As used in this subchapter:

(1) "Goods" means tangible chattels or real property purchased or leased for use.

(2) "Services" means work, labor, or service purchased or leased for use, including services furnished in connection with the sale or repair of goods.

(3) "Person" means an individual, partnership, corporation, association, or other group, however organized.

(4) "Consumer" means an individual, partnership, corporation, this state, or a subdivision or agency of this state who seeks or acquires by purchase or lease, any goods or services, except that the term does not include a business consumer that has assets of $25 million or more, or that is owned or controlled by a corporation or entity with assets of $25 million or more.

(5) "Unconscionable action or course of action" means an act or practice which, to a consumer's detriment, takes advantage of the lack of knowledge, ability, experience, or capacity of the consumer to a grossly unfair degree.

(6) "Trade" and "commerce" means the advertising, offering for sale, sale, lease, or distribution of any good or service, of any property, tangible or intangible, real, personal, or mixed, and any other article, commodity, or thing of value, wherever situated, and shall include any trade or commerce directly or indirectly affecting the people of this state.

(7) "Documentary material" includes the original or a copy of any book, record, report, memorandum, paper, communication, tabulation, map, chart, photograph, mechanical transcription, or other tangible document or recording, wherever situated.

(8) "Consumer protection division" means the consumer protection division of the Attorney General's Office.

(9) "Knowingly" means actual awareness, at the time of the act or practice complained of, of the falsity, deceptive, or unfairness of the act or practice giving rise to the consumer's claim, or, in an action brought under Subdivision (2) of Subsection (a) of Section 17.50, actual awareness of the act, practice, condition, defect, or failure constituting the breach of warranty, but actual awareness may be inferred where objective manifestations indicate that a person acted with actual awareness.

(10) "Business consumer" means an individual, partnership or corporation who seeks or acquires by purchase or lease, any goods or services for commercial or business use. The term does not include this state or a subdivision or agency of this state.

(11) "Economic damages" means compensatory damages for pecuniary loss, including costs of repair and replacement. The term does not include exemplary damages or damages for physical pain and mental anguish, loss of consortium, disfigurement, physical impairment, or loss of companionship and society.

§17.46.

(12) "Residence" means a building:

    (A) that is a single-family house, duplex, triplex, or quadruplex or a unit in a multiunit residential structure in which title to the individual units is transferred to the owners under a condominium or cooperative system; and

    (B) that is occupied or to be occupied as the consumer's residence.

(13) "Intentionally" means actual awareness of the falsity, deception, or unfairness of the act or practice, or the condition, defect or failure constituting a breach of warranty giving rise to the consumer's claim, coupled with the specific intent that the consumer act in detrimental reliance on the falsity or deception or in detrimental ignorance of the unfairness. Intention may be inferred from objective manifestations that indicate that the person acted intentionally or from facts showing that a defendant acted with flagrant disregard of prudent and fair business practices to the extent that the defendant should be treated as having acted intentionally.

§17.46. DECEPTIVE TRADE PRACTICES UNLAWFUL

(a) False, misleading, or deceptive acts or practices in the conduct of any trade or commerce are hereby declared unlawful and are subject to action by the consumer protection division under Sections 17.47, 17.58, 17.60, and 17.61 of this code.

(b) Except as provided in Subsection (d) of this section, the term "false, misleading, or deceptive acts or practices" includes, but is not limited to, the following acts:

    (1) passing off goods or services as those of another;

    (2) causing confusion or misunderstanding as to the source, sponsorship, approval, or certification of goods or services;

    (3) causing confusion or misunderstanding as to affiliation, connection, or association with, or certification by, another;

    (4) using deceptive representations or designations of geographic origin in connection with goods or services;

    (5) representing that goods or services have sponsorship, approval, characteristics, ingredients, uses, benefits, or quantities which they do not have or that a person has a sponsorship, approval, status, affiliation, or connection which the person does not;

    (6) representing that goods are original or new if they are deteriorated, reconditioned, reclaimed, used, or secondhand;

    (7) representing that goods or services are of a particular standard, quality, or grade, or that goods are of a particular style or model, if they are of another;

    (8) disparaging the goods, services, or business of another by false or misleading representation of facts;

    (9) advertising goods or services with intent not to sell them as advertised;

    (10) advertising goods or services with intent not to supply a reasonable expectable public demand, unless the advertisements disclosed a limitation of quantity;

(11) making false or misleading statements of fact concerning the reasons for, existence of, or amount of price reductions;

(12) representing that an agreement confers or involves rights, remedies, or obligations which it does not have or involve, or which are prohibited by law;

(13) knowingly making false or misleading statements of fact concerning the need for parts, replacement, or repair service;

(14) misrepresenting the authority of a salesman, representative or agent to negotiate the final terms of a consumer transaction;

(15) basing a charge for the repair of any item in whole or in part on a guaranty or warranty instead of on the value of the actual repairs made or work to be performed on the item without stating separately the charges for the work and the charge for the warranty or guaranty, if any;

(16) disconnecting, turning back, or resetting the odometer of any motor vehicle so as to reduce the number of miles indicated on the odometer gauge;

(17) advertising of any sale by fraudulently representing that a person is going out of business;

(18) advertising, selling, or distributing a card which purports to be a prescription drug identification card issued under Section 19A, Article 21.07-6, Insurance Code, in accordance with rules adopted by the commissioner of insurance, which offers a discount on the purchase of health care goods or services from a third party provider, and which is not evidence of insurance coverage, unless:

(A) the discount is authorized under an agreement between the seller of the card and the provider of those goods and services or the discount or card is offered to members of the seller;

(B) the seller does not represent that the card provides insurance coverage of any kind; and

(C) the discount is not false, misleading, or deceptive;

(19) using or employing a chain referral sales plan in connection with the sale or offer to sell of goods, merchandise, or anything of value, which uses the sales technique, plan, arrangement, or agreement in which the buyer or prospective buyer is offered the opportunity to purchase merchandise or goods and in connection with the purchase receives the seller's promise or representation that the buyer shall have the right to receive compensation or consideration is contingent upon the occurrence of an event subsequent to the time the buyer purchases the merchandise or goods;

(20) representing that a guaranty or warranty confers or involves rights or remedies which it does not have or involve, provided, however, that nothing in this subchapter shall be construed to expand the implied warranty of merchantability as defined in Sections 2.314 through 2.318 and Sections 2A.212 through 2A.216 to involve obligations in excess of those which are appropriate to the goods;

(21) promoting a pyramid promotional scheme as defined by Section 17.461;

(22) representing that work or services have been performed on, or parts replaced in, goods when the work or services were not performed or the parts replaced;

(23) filing suit founded upon a written contractual obligation of and signed by the defendant to pay money arising out of or based on a consumer transaction for goods, services, loans, or extensions of credit intended primarily for personal, family, household, or agricultural use in any

county other than in the county in which the defendant resides at the time of the commencement of the action or in the county in which the defendant in fact signed the contract; provided, however, that a violation of this subsection shall not occur where it is shown by the person filing such suit that the person neither knew or had reason to know that the county in which such suit was filed was neither the county in which the defendant resides at the commencement of the suit nor the county in which the defendant in fact signed the contract;

(24) failing to disclose information concerning goods or services which was known at the time of the transaction if such failure to disclose such information was intended to induce the consumer into a transaction into which the consumer would not have entered had the information been disclosed;

(25) using the term "corporation," "incorporated," or an abbreviation of either of those terms in the name of a business entity that is not incorporated under the laws of this state or another jurisdiction;

(26) selling, offering to sell, or illegally promoting an annuity contract under Chapter 22, Acts of the 57th Legislature, 3rd Called Session, 1962 (Article 6228a-5, Vernon's Texas Civil Statutes), with the intent that the annuity contract will be the subject of a salary reduction agreement, as defined by that Act, if the annuity contract is not an eligible qualified investment under that Act or is not registered with the Teacher Retirement System of Texas as required by Section 8A of that Act;

(27) taking advantage of a disaster declared by the governor under Chapter 418, Government Code, by:

(A) selling or leasing fuel, food, medicine, or another necessity at an exorbitant or excessive price; or

(B) demanding an exorbitant or excessive price in connection with the sale or lease of fuel, food, medicine, or another necessity.

[Ed. Note: Two subsections (28) were added by the 2015 Legislature. Both are included here]

(28) using the translation into a foreign language of a title or other word, including "attorney," "lawyer," "licensed," "notary," and "notary public," in any written or electronic material, including an advertisement, a business card, a letterhead, stationery, a website, or an online video, in reference to a person who is not an attorney in order to imply that the person is authorized to practice law in the United States.

Text of subsection (28) as amended by Acts 2015, 84th Leg., H.B. 2573, §1, eff. Sept. 1, 2015.

(28) delivering or distributing a solicitation in connection with a good or service that:

(A) represents that the solicitation is sent on behalf of a governmental entity when it is not; or

(B) resembles a governmental notice or form that represents or implies that a criminal penalty may be imposed if the recipient does not remit payment for the good or service;

Text of subsection (28) as amended by Acts 2015, 84th Leg., H.B. 1265, §1, eff. Sept. 1, 2015.

(29) delivering or distributing a solicitation in connection with a good or service that resembles a check or other negotiable instrument or invoice, unless the portion of the solicitation that resembles a check or other negotiable instrument or invoice includes the following notice, clearly and conspicuously printed in at least 18-point type:

"SPECIMEN-NON-NEGOTIABLE"

(30) in the production, sale, distribution, or promotion of a synthetic substance that produces and is intended to produce an effect when consumed or ingested similar to, or in excess of, the

effect of a controlled substance or controlled substance analogue, as those terms are defined by Section 481.002, Health and Safety Code:

(A) making a deceptive representation or designation about the synthetic substance; or

(B) causing confusion or misunderstanding as to the effects the synthetic substance causes when consumed or ingested; or

(31) a licensed public insurance adjuster directly or indirectly soliciting employment, as defined by Section 38.01, Penal Code, for an attorney, or a licensed public insurance adjuster entering into a contract with an insured for the primary purpose of referring the insured to an attorney without the intent to actually perform the services customarily provided by a licensed public insurance adjuster, provided that this subdivision may not be construed to prohibit a licensed public insurance adjuster from recommending a particular attorney to an insured.

[Ed. Note: Both Subsections 28 and subsections 29, 30 and 31 were added by the 2015 Legislature and apply only to a cause of action that accrues on or after September 1, 2015. Acts 2015, 84th Leg. H.B. No. 1265, §§ 2, 3, and H.B. No. 2573, §§ 3,4.]

(c)(1) It is the intent of the legislature that in construing Subsection (a) of this section in suits brought under Section 17.47 of this subchapter the courts to the extent possible will be guided by Subsection (b) of this section and the interpretations given by the Federal Trade Commission and federal courts to Section 5(a)(1) of the Federal Trade Commission Act [15 U.S.C.A. §45(a)(1)].

(2) In construing this subchapter the court shall not be prohibited from considering relevant and pertinent decisions of courts in other jurisdictions.

(d) For the purposes of the relief authorized in Subdivision (1) of Subsection (a) of Section 17.50 of this subchapter, the term "false, misleading, or deceptive acts or practices" is limited to the acts enumerated in specific subdivisions of Subsection (b) of this section.

§17.461. PYRAMID PROMOTIONAL SCHEME

(a) In this section:

(1) "Compensation" means payment of money, a financial benefit, or another thing of value. The term does not include payment based on sale of a product to a person, including a participant, who purchases the product for actual use or consumption.

(2) "Consideration" means the payment of cash or the purchase of a product. The term does not include:

(A) a purchase of a product furnished at cost to be used in making a sale and not for resale;

(B) a purchase of a product subject to a repurchase agreement that complies with Subsection (b); or

(C) time and effort spent in pursuit of a sale or in a recruiting activity.

(3) "Participate" means to contribute money into a pyramid promotional scheme without promoting, organizing, or operating the scheme.

(4) "Product" means a good, a service, or intangible property of any kind.

(5) "Promoting a pyramid promotional scheme" means:

(A) inducing or attempting to induce one or more other persons to participate in a pyramid promotional scheme; or

(B) assisting another person in inducing or attempting to induce one or more other persons to participate in a pyramid promotional scheme, including by providing references.

(6) "Pyramid promotional scheme" means a plan or operation by which a person gives consideration for the opportunity to receive compensation that is derived primarily from a person's introduction of other persons to participate in the plan or operation rather than from the sale of a product by a person introduced into the plan or operation.

(b) To qualify as a repurchase agreement for the purposes of Subsection (a)(2)(B), an agreement must be an enforceable agreement by the seller to repurchase, on written request of the purchaser and not later than the first anniversary of the purchaser's date of purchase, all unencumbered products that are in an unused, commercially resalable condition at a price not less than 90 percent of the amount actually paid by the purchaser for the products being returned, less any consideration received by the purchaser for purchase of the products being returned. A product that is no longer marketed by the seller is considered resalable if the product is otherwise in an unused, commercially resalable condition and is returned to the seller not later than the first anniversary of the purchaser's date of purchase, except that product is not considered resalable if before the purchaser purchased the product it was clearly disclosed to the purchaser that the product was sold as a nonreturnable, discontinued, seasonal, or special promotion item.

(c) A person commits an offense if the person contrives, prepares, establishes, operates, advertises, sells, or promotes a pyramid promotional scheme. An offense under this section is a state jail felony.

(d) It is not a defense to prosecution for an offense under this section that the pyramid promotional scheme involved both a franchise to sell a product and the authority to sell additional franchises if the emphasis of the scheme is on the sale of additional franchises.

§17.462. LISTING OF BUSINESS LOCATION OF CERTAIN BUSINESSES

(a) A person may not misrepresent the geographical location of a business that derives 50 percent or more of its gross income from the sale or arranging for the sale of flowers or floral arrangements in the listing of the business:

(1) in a telephone directory or other directory assistance database;

(2) on an Internet website; or

(3) in a print advertisement.

(b) A person is considered to misrepresent the geographical location of a business for purposes of Subsection (a) if the name of the business indicates that the business is located in a geographical area and:

(1) the business is not located within the geographical area indicated;

(2) the listing fails to identify the municipality and state of the business's geographical location; and

(3) a telephone call to the local telephone number:

(A) listed in the directory or database routinely is forwarded or transferred to a location that is outside the calling area covered by the directory or database in which the number is listed; or

(B) provided on the Internet website or in a print advertisement routinely is forwarded or transferred to a location that is outside the calling area of the geographical area as indicated by the name of the business.

(c) A person may place a listing for a business described by Subsection (a) the name of which indicates that it is located in a geographical area that is different from the geographical area in which the business is located if a conspicuous notice in the listing states the municipality and state in which the business is located.

(d) This section does not apply to:

(1) a publisher of a telephone directory (or other publication) or a provider of a directory assistance service publishing, or providing, information about another business.

(2) an Internet website that aggregates and provides information about businesses;

(3) an owner or publisher of a print medium providing information about other businesses;

(4) an Internet service provider; or

(5) an Internet service that displays or distributed advertisements for other businesses.

(e) This section creates no duty and imposes no obligation upon anyone other than the business that is the subject of the advertisement or listing.

(f) A violation of this section is a false, misleading, or deceptive act or practice under this subchapter, and any public or private right or remedy prescribed by this subchapter may be used to enforce this section.

§17.47. RESTRAINING ORDERS

(a) Whenever the consumer protection division has reason to believe that any person is engaging in, has engaged in, or is about to engage in any act or practice declared to be unlawful by this subchapter, and that proceedings would be in the public interest, the division may bring an action in the name of the state against the person to restrain by temporary restraining order, temporary injunction, or permanent injunction the use of such method, act, or practice.

Nothing herein shall require the consumer protection division to notify such person that court action is or may be under consideration. Provided, however, the consumer protection division shall, at least seven days prior to instituting such court action, contact such person to inform him in general of the alleged unlawful conduct. Cessation of unlawful conduct after such prior contact shall not render such court action moot under any circumstances, and such injunctive relief shall lie even if such person has ceased such unlawful conduct after such prior contact. Such prior conduct shall not be required if, in the opinion of the consumer protection division, there is good cause to believe that such person would evade service of process if prior contact were made or that such person would destroy relevant records if prior contact were made, or that such an emergency exists that immediate and irreparable injury, loss, or damage would occur as a result of such delay in obtaining a temporary restraining order.

(b) An action brought under Subsection (a) of this section which alleges a claim to relief under this section may be commenced in the district court of the county in which the person against whom it is brought resides, has his principal place of business, has done business, or in the district court of the county where the transaction occurred, or, on the consent of the parties, in a district court of Travis County. The court may issue temporary restraining orders, temporary or permanent injunctions to restrain and prevent violations of this subchapter and such injunctive relief shall be issued without bond.

(c) In addition to the request for a temporary restraining order, or permanent injunction in a proceeding brought under Subsection (a) of this section, the consumer protection division may request a civil penalty to be paid to the state in an amount of:

(1) not more than $2,000 per violation, not to exceed at total of $10,000; or

(2) not more than $10,000 per violation, not to exceed a total of $100,000, if the consumer protection division determines that the act or practice that is the subject of the proceeding was calculated to acquire or deprive money or other property from a consumer who was 65 years of age or older when the act or practice occurred.

(d) The court may make such additional orders or judgments as are necessary to compensate identifiable persons for actual damages or to restore money or property, real or personal, which may have been acquired by means of any unlawful act or practice. Damages may not include any damages incurred beyond a point two years prior to the institution of the action by the consumer protection division. Orders of the court may also include the appointment of a receiver or a sequestration of assets if a person who has been ordered by a court to make restitution under this section has failed to do so within three months after the order to make restitution has become final and nonappealable.

(e) Any person who violates the terms of an injunction under this section shall forfeit and pay to the state a civil penalty of not more than $10,000 per violation, not to exceed $50,000. In determining whether or not an injunction has been violated the court shall take into consideration the maintenance of procedures reasonably adapted to insure compliance with the injunction. For the purposes of this section, the district court issuing the injunction shall retain jurisdiction, and the cause shall be continued, and in these cases, the consumer protection division, or the district or county attorneys with prior notice to the consumer protection division, acting in the name of the state, may petition for recovery of civil penalties under this section.

(f) An order of the court awarding civil penalties under Subsection (e) of this section applies only to violations of the injunction incurred prior to the awarding of the penalty order. Second or subsequent violations of an injunction issued under this section are subject to the same penalties set out in Subsection (e) of this section.

§17.48. DUTY OF DISTRICT AND COUNTY ATTORNEY

(a) It is the duty of the district and county attorneys to lend to the consumer protection division any assistance requested in the commencement and prosecutions of action under this subchapter.

(b) A district or county attorney, with prior written notice to the consumer protection division, may institute and prosecute actions seeking injunctive relief under this subchapter, after complying with the prior contact provisions of Subsection (a) of Section 17.47 of this subchapter. On request, the consumer protection division shall assist the district or county attorney in any action taken under this subchapter. If an action is prosecuted by a district or county attorney alone, he shall make a full report to the consumer protection division including the final disposition of the matter. No district or county attorney may bring an action under this section against any licensed insurer or licensed insurance agent transacting business under the authority and jurisdiction of the State Board of Insurance unless first requested in writing to do so by the State Board of Insurance, the commissioner of insurance, or the consumer protection division pursuant to a request by the State Board of Insurance or commissioner of insurance.

(c) In an action prosecuted by a district or county attorney under this subchapter for a violation of Section 17.46(b)(28), three-fourths of any civil penalty awarded by a court must be paid to the county where the court is located.

[Ed. Note: The 2015 Legislature added two "Sections 17.46(b)(28)." This subsection (c) was added by the 2015 Legislature in H.B. No. 2573, so the reference to "Section 17.46(b)(28)" should be read to reference §17.46(b)(28) as added by H.B. No. 2573.]

(d) A district or county attorney is not required to obtain the permission of the consumer protection division to prosecute an action under this subchapter for a violation of Section 17.46(b)(28), if the district or county attorney provides prior written notice to the division as required by Subsection (b).

[Ed. Note: Subsections (c) and (d) apply only to a cause of action that accrues on or after September 1, 2015. Acts 2015, 84th Leg. H.B. No. 2573, §§ 3,4.]

§17.49. EXEMPTIONS

(a) Nothing in this subchapter shall apply to the owner or employees of a regularly published newspaper, magazine, or telephone directory, or broadcast station, or billboard, wherein any advertisement in violation of this subchapter is published or disseminated, unless it is established that the owner or employees of the advertising medium have knowledge of the false, deceptive, or misleading acts or practices declared to be unlawful by this subchapter, or had a direct or substantial financial interest in the sale or distribution of the unlawfully advertised good or service. Financial interest as used in this section relates to an expectation which would be the direct result of such advertisement.

(b) Nothing in this subchapter shall apply to acts or practices authorized under specific rules or regulations promulgated by the Federal Trade Commission under Section 5(a)(1) of the Federal Trade Commission Act [15 U.S.C.A. 45(a)(1)]. The provisions of this subchapter do apply to any act or practice prohibited or not specifically authorized by a rule or regulation of the Federal Trade Commission. An act or practice is not specifically authorized if no rule or regulation has been issued on the act or practice.

(c) Nothing in this subchapter shall apply to a claim for damages based on the rendering of a professional service, the essence of which is the providing of advice, judgment, opinion, or similar professional skill. This exemption does not apply to:

(1) an express misrepresentation of a material fact that cannot be characterized as advice, judgment, or opinion;

(2) a failure to disclose information in violation of Section 17.46(b)(23);

(3) an unconscionable action or course of action that cannot be characterized as advice, judgment, or opinion;

(4) breach of an express warranty that cannot be characterized as advice, judgment, or opinion;

(5) a violation of Section 17.46(b)(26).

(d) Subsection (c) applies to cause of action brought against the person who provided the professional service and a cause of action brought against any entity that could be found to be vicariously liable for the person's conduct.

(e) Except as specifically provided by Subsections (b) and (h), Section 17.50, nothing in this subchapter shall apply to a cause of action for bodily injury or death or for the infliction of mental anguish.

(f) Nothing in the subchapter shall apply to a claim arising out of a written contract if:

(1) the contract relates to a transaction, a project, or a set of transactions related to the same project involving total consideration by the consumer of more than $100,000;

(2) in negotiating the contract the consumer is represented by legal counsel who is not directly or indirectly identified, suggested, or selected by the defendant or an agent of the defendant; and

(3) the contract does not involve the consumer's residence.

§17.50.

(g) Nothing in this subchapter shall apply to a cause of action arising from a transaction, a project, or a set of transactions relating to the same project, involving total consideration by the consumer of more than $500,000, other than a cause of action involving a consumer's residence.

(h) A person who violates Section 17.46(b)(26) is jointly and severally liable under that subdivision for actual damages, court costs, and attorney's fees. Subject to Chapter 41, Civil Practice and Remedies Code, exemplary damages may be awarded in the event of fraud or malice.

The 2011 addition of DTPA § 17.49(i) applies only to a claim arising from an act or omission that occurs on or after May 28, 2011. A claim arising from an act or omission that occurred before May 28, 2011 is governed by the law in effect on the date the act or omission occurred, and the former law is continued in effect for that purpose.

(i) Nothing in this subchapter shall apply to a claim against a person licensed as a broker or salesperson under Chapter 1101, Occupations Code, arising from an act or omission by the person while acting as a broker or salesperson. This exemption does not apply to:

(1) an express misrepresentation of a material fact that cannot be characterized as advice, judgment, or opinion;

(2) a failure to disclose information in violation of Section 17.46(b)(24); or

(3) an unconscionable action or course of action that cannot be characterized as advice, judgment, or opinion.

§17.50. RELIEF FOR CONSUMERS

(a) A consumer may maintain an action where any of the following constitute a producing cause of economic damages or damages for mental anguish:

(1) the use or employment by any person of a false, misleading, or deceptive act or practice that is:

(A) specifically enumerated in a subdivision of Subsection (b) of Section 17.46 of this subchapter; and

(B) relied on by a consumer to the consumer's detriment;

(2) breach of an express or implied warranty;

(3) any unconscionable action or course of action by an person; or

(4) the use or employment by any person of an act or practice in violation of Chapter 541, Insurance Code.

(b) In a suit filed under this section, each consumer who prevails may obtain:

(1) the amount of economic damages found by the trier of fact. If the trier of fact finds that the conduct of the defendant was committed knowingly, the consumer may also recover damages for mental anguish, as found by the trier of fact, and the trier of fact may award not more than three times the amount of economic damages; or if the trier of fact finds the conduct was committed intentionally, the consumer may recover damages for mental anguish, as found by the trier of fact, and the trier of fact may award not more than three times the amount of damages for mental anguish and economic damages.

(2) an order enjoining such acts or failure to act;

(3) orders necessary to restore to any party to the suit any money or property, real or personal, which may have been acquired in violation of this subchapter; and

(4) any other relief which the court deems proper, including the appointment of a receiver or the revocation of a license or certificate authorizing a person to engage in business in this state if the judgment has not been satisfied within three months of the date of the final judgment. The court may not revoke or suspend a license to do business in this state or appoint a receiver to take over the affairs of a person who has failed to satisfy a judgment if the person is a licensee of or regulated by a state agency which has statutory authority to revoke or suspend a license or to appoint a receiver or trustee. Costs and fees of such receivership or other relief shall be assessed against the defendant.

(c) On a finding by the court that an action under this section was groundless in fact or law or brought in bad faith, or brought for the purpose of harassment, the court shall award to the defendant reasonable and necessary attorneys' fees and court costs.

(d) Each consumer who prevails shall be awarded court costs and reasonable and necessary attorneys' fees.

(e) In computing additional damages under Subsection (b), attorney's fees, costs, and prejudgment interest may not be considered.

(f) A court may not award prejudgment interest applicable to:

(1) damages for future loss under this subchapter; or

(2) additional damages under Subsection (b).

(g) Chapter 41, Civil Practice and Remedies Code does not apply to a cause of action brought under this subchapter.

(h) Notwithstanding any other provision of this subchapter, if a claimant is granted the right to bring a cause of action under this subchapter by another law, the claimant is not limited to recovery of economic damages only, but may recover any actual damages incurred by the claimant, without regard to whether the conduct of the defendant was committed intentionally. For the purpose of the recovery of damages for a cause of action described by this subsection only, a reference in this subchapter to economic damages means actual damages. In applying Subsection (b)(1) to an award of damages under this subsection, the trier of fact is authorized to award a total of not more than three times actual damages in accordance with that subsection.

§17.501. CONSUMER PROTECTION DIVISION PARTICIPATION IN CLASS ACTION

(a) A consumer filing an action under Section 17.50 that is to be maintained as a class action shall send to the consumer protection division:

(1) a copy of the notice required by Section 17.505(a), by registered or certified mail, at the same time the notice is given to the person complained against; and

(2) a copy of the petition in the action not later than the earlier of:

(A) the 30th day after the date the petition is filed; or

(B) the 10th day before the date of any hearing on class certification or a proposed settlement.

(b) The court shall abate the action for 60 days if the court finds that notice was not provided to the consumer protection division as required by Subsection (a).

(c) The court, on a showing of good cause, may allow the consumer protection division, as representative of the public, to intervene in an action to which this section applies. The consumer protection division shall file its motion for intervention with the court before which the action is pending and serve a copy of the motion on each party to the action.

§17.505. NOTICE; INSPECTION

(a) As a prerequisite to filing a suit seeking damages under Subdivision (1) of Subsection (b) of Section 17.50 of this subchapter against any person, a consumer shall give written notice to the person at least 60 days before filing the suit advising the person, in reasonable detail, of the consumer's specific complaint and the amount of economic damages, damages for mental anguish, and expenses, including attorneys' fees, if any, reasonably incurred by the consumer in asserting the claim against the defendant. During the 60-day period a written request to inspect, in a reasonable manner and at a reasonable time and place, the goods that are the subject of the consumer's action or claim may be presented to the consumer.

(b) If the giving of 60 days' written notice is rendered impracticable by reason of the necessity of filing suit in order to prevent the expiration of the statute of limitations or if the consumer's claim is asserted by way of counterclaim, the notice provided for in Subsection (a) of this section is not required, but the tender provided for by Subsection (d), Section 17.506 of this subchapter may be made within 60 days after service of the suit or counterclaim.

(c) A person against whom a suit is pending who does not receive written notice, as required by Subsection (a), may file a plea in abatement not later than the 30th day after the date the person files an original answer in the court in which the suit is pending. This subsection does not apply if Subsection (b) applies.

(d) The court shall abate the suit if the court, after a hearing, finds that the person is entitled to an abatement because notice was not provided as required by this section. A suit is automatically abated without the order of the court beginning on the 11th day after the date a plea in abatement is filed under Subsection (c) if the plea in abatement:

   (1) is verified and alleges that the person against whom the suit is pending did not receive the written notice as required by Subsection (a); and

   (2) is not controverted by an affidavit filed by the consumer before the 11th day after the date on which the plea in abatement is filed.

(e) An abatement under Subsection (d) continues until the 60th day after the date that written notice is served in compliance with Subsection (a).

§17.5051. MEDIATION

(a) A party may, not later than the 90th day after the date of service of a pleading in which relief under this subchapter is sought, file a motion to compel mediation of the dispute in the manner provided by this section.

(b) The court shall, not later than the 30th day after the date a motion under this section is filed, sign an order setting the time and place of the mediation.

(c) If the parties do not agree on a mediator, the court shall appoint a mediator.

(d) Mediation shall be held within 30 days after the date the order is signed, unless the parties agree otherwise or the court determines that additional time, not to exceed an additional 30 days, is warranted.

(e) Except as agreed to by all parties who have appeared in the action, each party who has appeared shall participate in the mediation and, except as provided by Subsection (f), shall share the mediation fee.

(f) A party may not compel mediation under this section if the amount of economic damages claimed is less than $15,000, unless the party seeking to compel mediation agrees to pay the costs of the mediation.

DECEPTIVE TRADE PRACTICES–CONSUMER PROTECTION ACT　　　　　　　　　　§17.5052.

(g) Except as provided in this section, Section 154.023, Civil Practice and Remedies Code, and Subchapters C and D, Chapter 154, Civil Practice and Remedies Code, apply to the appointment of a mediator and to the mediation process provided by this section.

(h) This section does not apply to an action brought by the attorney general under §17.47.

§17.5052. OFFERS OF SETTLEMENT

(a) A person who receives notice under Section 17.505 may tender an offer of settlement at any time during the period beginning on the date the notice is received and ending on the 60th day after that date.

(b) If a mediation under Section 17.5051 is not conducted, the person may tender an offer of settlement at any time during the period beginning on the date an original answer is filed and ending on the 90th day after that date.

(c) If a mediation under Section 17.5051 is conducted, a person against whom a claim under this subchapter is pending may tender an offer of settlement during the period beginning on the day after the date that the mediation ends and ending on the 20th day after that date.

(d) An offer of settlement tendered by a person against whom a claim under this subchapter is pending must include an offer to pay the following amounts of money stated separately:

(1) an amount of money or other consideration, reduced to its cash value, as settlement of the consumer's claim for damages; and

(2) an amount of money to compensate the consumer for the consumer's reasonable and necessary attorney's fees incurred as of the date of the offer.

(e) Unless both parts of an offer of settlement required under Subsection (d) are accepted by the consumer not later than the 30th day after the date the offer is made, the offer is rejected.

(f) A settlement offer tendered by a person against whom a claim under this subchapter is pending that complies with this section and that has been rejected by the consumer may be filed with the court with an affidavit certifying its rejection.

(g) If the court finds that the amount tendered in the settlement offer for damages under Subsection (d)(1) is the same as, substantially the same as, or more than the damages found by the trier of fact, the consumer may not recover as damages any amount in excess of the lesser of:

(1) the amount of damages tendered in the settlement offer; or

(2) the amount of damages found by the trier of fact.

(h) If the court makes the finding described by Subsection (g), the court shall determine reasonable and necessary attorneys' fees to compensate the consumer for attorneys' fees incurred before the date and time of the rejected settlement offer. If the court finds that the amount tendered in the settlement offer to compensate the consumer for attorneys' fees under Subsection (d)(2) is the same as, substantially the same as, or more than the amount of reasonable and necessary attorneys' fees incurred by the consumer as of the date of the offer, the consumer may not recover attorneys' fees greater than the amount of fees tendered in the settlement offer.

(i) If the court finds that the offering party could not perform the offer at the time the offer was made or that the offering party substantially misrepresented the cash value of the offer, Subsection (g) and (h) do not apply.

(j) If Subsection (g) does not apply, the court shall award as damages the amount of economic damages and damages for mental anguish found by the trier of fact, subject to Sections 17.50 and 17.501. If Subsection (h) does not apply, the court shall award attorneys' fees as provided by Section 17.50(d).

(k) An offer of settlement is not an admission of engaging in an unlawful act or practice or liability under this subchapter. Except as otherwise provided by this section, an offer or a rejection of an offer may not be offered in evidence at trial for any purpose.

§17.506. DAMAGES: DEFENSES

(a) In an action brought under Section 17.50 of this subchapter, it is a defense to the award of any damages or attorneys' fees if the defendant proves that before consummation of the transaction he gave reasonable and timely written notice to the plaintiff of the defendant's reliance on:

(1) written information relating to the particular goods or service in question obtained from official governmental records if the written information was false or inaccurate and the defendant did not know and could not reasonably have known of the falsity or inaccuracy of the information;

(2) written information relating to the particular goods or service in question obtained from another source if the information was false or inaccurate and the defendant did not know and could not reasonably have known of the falsity or inaccuracy of the information; or

(3) written information concerning a test required or prescribed by a government agency if the information from the test was false or inaccurate and the defendant did not know and could not reasonably have known of the falsity or inaccuracy of the information.

(b) In asserting a defense under Subdivision (1), (2), or (3) of Subsection (a) of Section 17.506 above, the defendant shall prove the written information was a producing cause of the alleged damage. A finding of one producing cause does not bar recovery if other conduct of the defendant not the subject of a defensive finding under Subdivision (1), (2), or (3) of Subsection (a) of Section 17.506 above was a producing cause of damages of the plaintiff.

(c) In a suit where a defense is asserted under Subdivision (2) of Subsection (a) of Section 17.506 above, suit may be asserted against the third party supplying the written information without regard to privity where the third party knew or should have reasonably foreseen that the information would be provided to a consumer; provided no double recovery may result.

(d) In an action brought under Section 17.50 of this subchapter, it is a defense to a cause of action if the defendant proves that he received notice from the consumer advising the defendant of the nature of the consumer's specific complaint and of the amount of economic damages, damages for mental anguish, and expenses, including attorneys' fees, if any, reasonably incurred by the consumer in asserting the claim against the defendant, and that within 30 days after the day on which the defendant received the notice the defendant tendered to the consumer:

(1) the amount of economic damages and damages for mental anguish claimed; and

(2) the expenses, including attorneys' fees, if any, reasonably incurred by the consumer in asserting the claim against the defendant.

§17.55. PROMOTIONAL MATERIAL

If damages or civil penalties are assessed against the seller of goods or services for advertisements or promotional material in a suit filed under Section 17.47, 17.48, 17.50, or 17.51 of this subchapter, the seller of the goods or services has a cause of action against a third party for the amount of damages or civil penalties assessed against the seller plus attorneys' fees on a showing that:

(1) the seller received the advertisements or promotional material from the third party;

(2) the seller's only action with regard to the advertisements or promotional material was to disseminate the material; and

(3) the seller has ceased disseminating the material.

§17.555. INDEMNITY

A person against whom an action has been brought under this subchapter may seek contribution or indemnity from one who, under the statute law or at common law, may have liability for the damaging event of which the consumer complains. A person seeking indemnity as provided by this section may recover all sums that he is required to pay as a result of the action, his attorney's fees reasonable in relation to the amount of work performed in maintaining his action for indemnity, and his costs.

§17.56. VENUE

Text of section as amended by Acts 1995, 74th Leg., ch. 138, §7.

Except as provided by Article 5.06-1(8), Insurance Code, an action brought which alleges a claim to relief under Section 17.50 of this subchapter shall be brought as provided by Chapter 15, Civil Practice and Remedies Code.

§17.56. VENUE

Text of section as amended by Acts 1995, 74th Leg., ch. 414, §9

An action brought under this subchapter may be brought:

(1) in any county in which venue is proper under Chapter 15, Civil Practice and Remedies Code; or

(2) in a county in which the defendant or an authorized agent of the defendant solicited the transaction made the subject of the action at bar.

§17.565. LIMITATION

All actions brought under this subchapter must be commenced within two years after the date on which the false, misleading, or deceptive act or practice occurred or within two years after the consumer discovered or in the exercise of reasonable diligence should have discovered the occurrence of the false, misleading, or deceptive act or practice. The period of limitation provided in this section may be extended for a period of 180 days if the plaintiff proves that failure timely to commence the action was caused by the defendant's knowingly engaging in conduct solely calculated to induce the plaintiff to refrain from or postpone the commencement of the action.

§17.57. SUBPOENAS

The clerk of a district court at the request of any party to a suit pending in his court which is brought under this subchapter shall issue a subpoena for any witness or witnesses who may be represented to reside within 100 miles of the courthouse of the county in which the suit is pending or who may be found within such distance at the time of trial. The clerk shall issue a separate subpoena and a copy thereof for each witness subpoenaed.

§17.58.

When an action is pending in Travis County on the consent of the parties a subpoena may be issued for any witness or witnesses who may be represented to reside within 100 miles of the courthouse of a county in which the suit could otherwise have been brought or who may be found within such distance at the time of the trial.

The Texas Rules of Civil Procedure governing discovery were amended effective January 1, 1999 to provide, among other things, a subpoena range of 150 miles. In amending the Rules, the Texas Supreme Court ordered: "In accordance with Section 22.004(c) of the Texas Government Code, a statute is repealed as follows: Tex. Bus. & Com. Code § 17.57, to the extent that it conflicts with Rule 176.3(a)." Misc. Docket No. 98-9196 (6).

§17.58. VOLUNTARY COMPLIANCE

(a) In the administration of this subchapter the consumer protection division may accept assurance of voluntary compliance with respect to any act or practice which violates this subchapter from any person who is engaging in, has engaged in, or is about to engage in the act or practice. The assurance shall be in writing and shall be filed with and subject to the approval of the district court in the county in which the alleged violator resides or does business or in the district court of Travis County.

(b) The acceptance of an assurance of voluntary compliance may be conditioned on the stipulation that the person in violation of this subchapter restore to any person in interest any money or property, real or personal, which may have been acquired by means of acts or practices which violate this subchapter.

(c) An assurance of voluntary compliance shall not be considered an admission of prior violation of this subchapter. However, unless an assurance has been rescinded by agreement of the parties or voided by a court for good cause, subsequent failure to comply with the terms of an assurance is prima facie evidence of a violation of this subchapter.

(d) Matters closed by the filing of an assurance of voluntary compliance may be reopened at any time. Assurances of voluntary compliance shall in no way affect individual rights of action under this subchapter, except that the rights of individuals with regard to money or property received pursuant to a stipulation in the voluntary compliance under Subsection (b) of this section are governed by the terms of the voluntary compliance.

§17.59. POST JUDGMENT RELIEF

(a) If a money judgment entered under this subchapter is unsatisfied 30 days after it becomes final and if the prevailing party has made a good faith attempt to obtain satisfaction of the judgment, the following presumptions exist with respect to the party against whom the judgment was entered:

(1) that the defendant is insolvent or in danger of becoming insolvent; and

(2) that the defendant's property is in danger of being lost, removed, or otherwise exempted from collection on the judgment; and

(3) that the prevailing party will be materially injured unless a receiver is appointed over the defendant's business; and

(4) that there is no adequate remedy other than receivership available to the prevailing party.

(b) Subject to the provisions of Subsection (a) of this section, a prevailing party may move that the defendant show cause why a receiver should not be appointed. Upon adequate notice and hearing, the court shall appoint a receiver over the defendant's business unless the defendant proves that all of the presumptions set forth in Subsection (a) of this section are not applicable.

(c) The order appointing a receiver must clearly state whether the receiver will have general power to manage and operate the defendant's business or have power to manage only a defendant's finances. The order shall limit the duration of the receivership to such time as the judgment or judgments awarded under this subchapter are paid in full. Where there are judgments against a defendant which have been awarded to more than one plaintiff, the court shall have discretion to take any action necessary to efficiently operate a receivership in order to accomplish the purpose of collecting the judgments.

§17.60. REPORTS AND EXAMINATIONS

Whenever the consumer protection division has reason to believe that a person is engaging in, has engaged in, or is about to engage in any act or practice declared to be unlawful by this subchapter, or when it reasonably believes it to be in the public interest to conduct an investigation to ascertain whether any person is engaging in, has engaged in, or is about to engage in any such act or practice, an authorized member of the division may:

(1) require the person to file on the prescribed forms a statement or report in writing, under oath or otherwise, as to all the facts and circumstances concerning the alleged violation and such other data and information as the consumer protection division deems necessary;

(2) examine under oath any person in connection with this alleged violation;

(3) examine any merchandise or sample of merchandise deemed necessary and proper; and

(4) pursuant to an order of the appropriate court, impound any sample of merchandise that is produced in accordance with this subchapter and retain it in the possession of the division until the completion of all proceedings in connection with which the merchandise is produced.

§17.61. CIVIL INVESTIGATIVE DEMAND

(a) Whenever the consumer protection division believes that any person may be in possession, custody, or control of the original copy of any documentary material relevant to the subject matter of an investigation of a possible violation of this subchapter, an authorized agent of the division may execute in writing and serve on the person a civil investigative demand requiring the person to produce the documentary material and permit inspection and copying.

(b) Each demand shall:

(1) state the statute and section under which the alleged violation is being investigated, and the general subject matter of the investigation;

(2) describe the class or classes of documentary material to be produced with reasonable specificity so as to fairly indicate the material demanded;

(3) prescribe a return date within which the documentary material is to be produced; and

(4) identify the persons authorized by the consumer protection division to whom the documentary material is to be made available for inspection and copying.

(c) A civil investigative demand may contain a requirement or disclosure of documentary material which would be discoverable under the Texas Rules of Civil Procedure.

(d) Service of any demand may be made by:

(1) delivering a duly executed copy of the demand to the person to be served or to a partner or to any officer or agent authorized by appointment or by law to receive service of process on behalf of that person;

(2) delivering a duly executed copy of the demand to the principal place of business in the state of the person to be served;

(3) mailing by registered mail or certified mail a duly executed copy of the demand addressed to the person to be served at the principal place of business in this state, or if the person has no place of business in this state, to his principal office or place of business.

(e) Documentary material demanded pursuant to this section shall be produced for inspection and copying during normal business hours at the principal office or place of business of the person served, or at other times and places as may be agreed on by the person served and the consumer protection division.

(f) No documentary material produced pursuant to a demand under this section, unless otherwise ordered by a court for a good cause shown, shall be produced for inspection or copying by, nor shall its contents be disclosed to any person other than the authorized employee of the office of the attorney general without the consent of the person who produced the material. The office of the attorney general shall prescribe reasonable terms and conditions allowing the documentary material to be available for inspection and copying by the person who produced the material or any duly authorized representative of that person. The office of the attorney general may use the documentary materials or copies of it as it determines necessary in the enforcement of this subchapter, including presentation before any court. Any material which contains trade secrets shall not be presented except with the approval of the court in which the action is pending after adequate notice to the person furnishing the material.

(g) At any time before the return date specified in the demand, or within 20 days after the demand has been served, whichever period is shorter, a petition to extend the return date for, or to modify or set aside the demand, stating good cause, may be filed in the district court in the county where the parties reside, or a district court of Travis County.

(h) A person on whom a demand is served under this section shall comply with the terms of the demand unless otherwise provided by a court order.

(i) Personal service of a similar investigative demand under this section may be made on any person outside of this state if the person has engaged in conduct in violation of this subchapter. Such persons shall be deemed to have submitted themselves to the jurisdiction of this state within the meaning of this section.

§17.62. PENALTIES

(a) Any person who, with intent to avoid, evade, or prevent compliance, in whole or in part, with Section 17.60 or 17.61 of this subchapter, removes from any place, conceals, withholds, or destroys, mutilates, alters, or by any other means falsifies any documentary material or merchandise or sample of merchandise is guilty of a misdemeanor and on conviction is punishable by a fine of not more than $5,000 or by confinement in the county jail for not more than one year, or both.

(b) If a person fails to comply with a directive of the consumer protection division under Section 17.60 of this subchapter or with a civil investigative demand for documentary material served on him under Section 17.61 of this subchapter, or if satisfactory copying or reproduction of the material cannot be done and the person refuses to surrender the material, the consumer protection division may file in the district court in the county in which the person resides, is found, or transacts business, and serve on the person, a petition for an order of the court for enforcement of Sections 17.60 and 17.61 of this subchapter. If the person transacts business in more than one county, the petition shall be filed in the county in which the person maintains his principal place of business, or in another county agreed on by the parties to the petition.

(c) When a petition is filed in the district court in any county under this section, the court shall have jurisdiction to hear and determine the matter presented and to enter any order required to carry into effect the provisions of Sections 17.60 and 17.61 of this subchapter. Any final order entered is subject to appeal to the Texas Supreme Court. Failure to comply with any final order entered under this section is punishable by contempt.

§17.63.   APPLICATION

The provisions of this subchapter apply only to acts or practices occurring after the effective date of this subchapter, except a right of action or power granted to the attorney general under Chapter 10, Title 79, Revised Civil Statutes of Texas, 1925, as amended, prior to the effective date of this subchapter.

CHAPTER 541
TEXAS INSURANCE CODE

(FORMERLY KNOWN AS ARTICLE 21.21 TEXAS INSURANCE CODE)

TEXAS INSURANCE CODE Chapter 541 §541.001, §541.002, §541.003, §541.008, §541.051, §541.052, §541.060, §541.061, §541.151, §541.152, §541.153, §541.154, §541.155, §541.156, §541.157, §541.158, §541.159, §541.160, §541.161, §541.162

(Selected Provisions)

Ed. Note: *The Texas Insurance Code was recodified, effective April 1, 2005. Article 21.21, Unfair Competition and Unfair Practices, is now Chapter 541, Unfair Methods of Competition and Unfair or Deceptive Acts or Practices. Although the recodification was not intended to change the meaning or effect of the statute, it did change the section numbers, the format, and the wording. See also §1.03 of the practice guide for a disposition table that summarizes the changes to the sections discussed in the text.*

SUBCHAPTER A. GENERAL PROVISIONS

§541.001.   PURPOSE

The purpose of this chapter is to regulate trade practices in the business of insurance by:

(1) defining or providing for the determination of trade practices in this state that are unfair methods of competition or unfair or deceptive acts or practices; and

(2) prohibiting those trade practices.

§541.002.   DEFINITIONS

In this chapter:

(1) "Knowingly" means actual awareness of the falsity, unfairness, or deceptiveness of the act or practice on which a claim for damages under Subchapter D is based. Actual awareness may be inferred if objective manifestations indicate that a person acted with actual awareness.

(2) "Person" means an individual, corporation, association, partnership, reciprocal or interinsurance exchange, Lloyd's plan, fraternal benefit society, or other legal entity engaged in the business of insurance, including an agent, broker, adjuster or life and health insurance counselor.

§541.003.   UNFAIR METHODS OF COMPETITION AND UNFAIR OR DECEPTIVE ACTS OR PRACTICES PROHIBITED

A person may not engage in this state in a trade practice that is defined in this chapter as or determined under this chapter to be an unfair method of competition or an unfair or deceptive act or practice in the business of insurance.

§541.008. LIBERAL CONSTRUCTION

This chapter shall be liberally construed and applied to promote the underlying purposes as provided by Section 541.001.

SUBCHAPTER B. UNFAIR METHODS OF COMPETITION AND UNFAIR OR DECEPTIVE ACTS OR PRACTICES DEFINED

§541.051. MISREPRESENTATION REGARDING POLICY OR INSURER

It is an unfair method of competition or an unfair or deceptive act or practice in the business of insurance to:

(1) make, issue, or circulate, or cause to be made, issued or circulated an estimate, illustration, circular or statement misrepresenting with respect to a policy issued or to be issued:

(A) the terms of the policy;

(B) the benefits or advantages promised by the policy; or

(C) the dividends or share of surplus to be received on the policy;

(2) make a false or misleading statement regarding the dividends or share of surplus previously paid on a similar policy;

(3) make a misleading representation or misrepresentation regarding:

(A) the financial condition of an insurer; or

(B) the legal reserve system upon which a life insurer operates;

(4) use a name or title of a policy or class of policies that misrepresents the true nature of the policy or class of policies; or

(5) make a misrepresentation to a policyholder insured by any insurer for the purpose of inducing or that tends to induce the policyholder to allow an existing policy to lapse, or to forfeit, or surrender the policy.

§541.052. FALSE INFORMATION AND ADVERTISING

It is an unfair method of competition or an unfair or deceptive act or practice in the business of insurance to make, publish, disseminate, circulate, or place before the public, or directly or indirectly cause to be made, published, disseminated, circulated, or placed before the public, an advertisement, announcement or statement containing an untrue, deceptive, or misleading assertion, representation, or statement regarding the business of insurance or person in the conduct of the person's insurance business.

This section applies to an advertisement, announcement, or statement made, published, disseminated, circulated, or placed before the public:

(1) in a newspaper, magazine or other publication;

(2) in a notice, circular, pamphlet, letter or poster;

(3) over a radio or television station;

(4) through the Internet; or

(5) in any other manner.

§541.060. UNFAIR SETTLEMENT PRACTICES

(a) It is an unfair method of competition or an unfair or deceptive act or practice in the business of insurance to engage in the following unfair settlement practices with respect to a claim by an insured or beneficiary:

(1) misrepresenting to a claimant a material fact or policy provision relating to coverage at issue;

(2) failing to attempt in good faith to effectuate a prompt, fair, and equitable settlement of:

(A) a claim with respect to which the insurer's liability has become reasonably clear; or

(B) a claim under one portion of a policy with respect to which the insurer's liability has become reasonably clear to influence the claimant to settle another claim under another portion of the coverage unless payment under one portion of the coverage constitutes evidence of liability under another portion;

(3) failing to promptly provide to a policyholder a reasonable explanation of the basis in the policy, in relation to the facts or applicable law, for the insurer's denial of a claim or offer of a compromise settlement of a claim;

(4) failing within a reasonable time to:

(A) affirm or deny coverage of a claim to a policyholder; or

(B) submit a reservation of rights to a policyholder;

(5) refusing, failing or unreasonably delaying a settlement offer under applicable first-party coverage on the basis that other coverage may be available or that third parties are responsible for the damages suffered, except as may be specifically provided in the policy;

(6) undertaking to enforce a full and final release of a claim from a policyholder when only a partial payment has been made, unless the payment is a compromise settlement of a doubtful or disputed claim;

(7) refusing to pay a claim without conducting a reasonable investigation with respect to the claim;

(8) with respect to a Texas personal automobile insurance policy, delaying or refusing settlement of a claim solely because there is other insurance of a different kind available to satisfy all or any part of the loss forming the basis of that claim; or

(9) requiring a claimant as a condition of settling a claim to produce the claimant's federal income tax returns for examination or investigation by the person unless:

(A) a court orders the claimant to produce those tax returns;

(B) the claim involves a fire loss; or

(C) the claim involves lost profits or income.

(b) Subsection (a) does not provide a cause of action to a third party asserting one or more claims against an insured covered under a liability insurance policy.

§541.061. MISREPRESENTATION OF INSURANCE POLICY

It is an unfair method of competition or an unfair or deceptive act or practice in the business of insurance to misrepresent an insurance policy by:

(1) making an untrue statement of material fact;

(2) failing to state a material fact necessary to make other statements made not misleading, considering the circumstances under which the statements were made;

(3) making a statement in a manner that would mislead a reasonably prudent person to a false conclusion of a material fact;

(4) making a material misstatement of law; or

(5) failing to disclose a matter required by law to be disclosed, including failing to make a disclosure in accordance with another provision of this code.

SUBCHAPTER D. PRIVATE ACTION FOR DAMAGES

§541.151. PRIVATE ACTION FOR DAMAGES AUTHORIZED

A person who sustains actual damages may bring an action against another person for those damages caused by the other person engaging in an act or practice:

(1) defined by Subchapter B to be an unfair method of competition or unfair or deceptive act or practice in the business of insurance; or

(2) specifically enumerated in Section 17.46(b), Business & Commerce Code, as an unlawful deceptive trade practice if the person bringing the action shows that the person relied on the act or practice to the person's detriment.

§541.152. DAMAGES, ATTORNEY'S FEES, AND OTHER RELIEF

(a) A plaintiff who prevails in an action under this subchapter may obtain:

(1) the amount of actual damages plus court costs and reasonable and necessary attorneys' fees;

(2) an order enjoining the act or failure to act complained of; or

(3) any other relief the court determines is proper.

(b) Except as provided by Subsection (c), on a finding by the trier of fact that the defendant knowingly committed the act complained of, the trier of fact may award an amount not to exceed three times the amount of actual damages.

(c) Subsection (b) does not apply to an action under this subchapter brought against the Texas Windstorm Insurance Association.

§541.153. FRIVOLOUS ACTION

A court shall award to the defendant court costs and reasonable and necessary attorney's fees if the court finds that an action under this subchapter is groundless and brought in bad faith or brought for the purpose of harassment.

§541.154. PRIOR NOTICE OF ACTION

(a) A person seeking damages in an action against another person under this subchapter must provide written notice to the other person not later than the 61st day before the date the action is filed.

(b) The notice must advise the other person of:

(1) the specific complaint; and

(2) the amount of actual damages and expenses, including attorney's fees reasonably incurred in asserting the claim against the other person.

(c) The notice is not required if giving notice is impracticable because the action:

(1) must be filed to prevent the statute of limitations from expiring; or

(2) is asserted as a counterclaim.

§541.155. ABATEMENT

(a) A person against whom a suit is pending who does not receive the notice, as required by Section 541.154 may file a plea in abatement not later than the 30th day after the date the person files an original answer in the court in which the action is pending.

(b) The court shall abate the action if, after a hearing, the court finds that the person is entitled to an abatement because the claimant did not provide the notice as required by Section 541.154.

(c) An action is automatically abated without a court order beginning on the 11th day after the date a plea in abatement is filed if the plea:

(1) is verified and alleges that the person against whom the action is pending did not receive the notice as required by Section 541.154; and

(2) is not controverted by an affidavit filed by the claimant before the 11th day after the date on which the plea in abatement is filed.

(d) An abatement under this section continues until the 60th day after the date notice is provided in compliance with Section 541.154.

(e) This section does not apply if Section 541.154(c) applies.

§541.156. SETTLEMENT OFFER

(a) A person who receives notice under Section 541.154 may make a settlement offer during a period beginning on the date notice under Section 541.154 is received and ending on the 60th day after that date.

(b) In addition to the period described by Subsection (a), the person may make a settlement offer during a period:

(1) if mediation is not conducted under Section 541.161, beginning on the date an original answer is filed in an action and ending on the 90th day after that date; or

(2) if a mediation is conducted under Section 541.161, beginning on the day after the date the mediation ends and ending on the 20th day after that date.

§541.157. CONTENTS OF SETTLEMENT OFFER

A settlement offer made by a person against whom a claim under this subchapter is pending must include an offer to pay the following amounts, separately stated:

(1) an amount of money or other consideration, reduced to its cash value, as settlement of the claim for damages; and

(2) an amount of money to compensate the claimant for the claimant's reasonable and necessary attorneys' fees incurred as of the date of the offer.

§541.158. REJECTION OF SETTLEMENT OFFER

(a) A settlement offer is rejected unless both parts of the offer required under Section 541.157 are accepted by the claimant not later than the 30th day after the date the offer is made.

(b) A settlement offer made by a person against whom a claim under this subchapter is pending that complies with this subchapter and is rejected by the claimant may be filed with the court accompanied by an affidavit certifying the offer's rejection.

§541.159. LIMIT ON RECOVERY AFTER SETTLEMENT OFFER

(a) If the court finds that the amount stated in the settlement offer for damages under Section 541.157(1) is the same as, substantially the same as, or more than the amount of damages found by the trier of fact, the claimant may not recover as damages any amount in excess of the lesser of:

  (1) the amount of damages stated in the settlement offer; or

  (2) the amount of damages found by the trier of fact.

(b) If the court makes the finding described by Subsection (a), the court shall determine reasonable and necessary attorneys' fees to compensate the claimant for attorneys' fees incurred before the date and time the rejected settlement offer was made. If the court finds that the amount stated in the offer for attorneys' fees under Section 541.157(2) is the same as, substantially the same as, or more than the amount of reasonable and necessary attorneys' fees incurred by the claimant as of the date of the offer, the claimant may not recover any amount of attorneys' fees in excess of the amount of fees stated in the settlement offer.

(c) This section does not apply if the court finds that the offering party:

  (1) could not perform the offer at the time the offer was made; or

  (2) substantially misrepresented the cash value of the offer.

(d) The court shall award:

  (1) damages as required by Section 541.152 if Subsection (a) does not apply; and

  (2) attorney's fees as required by Section 541.152 if Subsection (b) does not apply.

§541.160. EFFECT OF SETTLEMENT OFFER

A settlement offer is not an admission of engaging in an act or practice defined by Subchapter B to be an unfair method of competition or an unfair or deceptive act or practice in the business of insurance.

§541.161. MEDIATION

(a) A party may, not later than the 90th day after the date a pleading seeking relief under this subchapter is served, file a motion to compel mediation of the dispute in the manner provided by this section.

(b) The court shall, not later than the 30th day after the date a motion under this section is filed, sign an order setting the time and place of the mediation.

(c) The court shall appoint a mediator if the parties do not agree on a mediator.

(d) The mediation must be held not later than the 30th day after the date the order is signed, unless:

  (1) the parties agree otherwise; or

  (2) the court determines that additional time not to exceed an additional 30 days is warranted.

§541.162.

(e) Each party who has appeared in the action, except as agreed to by all parties who have appeared, shall:

   (1) participate in the mediation; and

   (2) except as provided by Subsection (f), share the mediation fee.

(f) A party may not compel mediation under this section if the amount of actual damages claimed is less than $15,000 unless the party seeking to compel mediation agrees to pay the costs of the mediation.

(g) Except as provided by this section, the following apply to the appointment of a mediator and the mediation process provided by this section:

   (1) Section 154.023 Civil Practice and Remedies Code; and

   (2) Subchapters C and D, Chapter 154, Civil Practice and Remedies Code.

§541.162. LIMITATIONS PERIOD

(a) A person must bring an action under this chapter before the second anniversary of the following:

   (1) the date the unfair method of competition or unfair or deceptive act or practice occurred; or

   (2) the date the person discovered or, by the exercise of reasonable diligence, should have discovered that the unfair method of competition or unfair or deceptive act or practice occurred.

(b) The limitations period provided by Subsection (a) may be extended for 180 days if the person bringing the action proves that the person's failure to bring the action within that period was caused by the defendant's engaging in conduct solely calculated to induce the person to refrain from or postpone bringing the action.

CHAPTER 542
TEXAS INSURANCE CODE

Texas Insurance Code Chapter 542 §542.001, §542.002, §542.003, §542.004, §542.051, §542.052, §542.053, §542.054, §542.055, §542.056, §542.057, §542.058, §542.059, §542.060, §542.061

(Selected Provisions)

SUBCHAPTER A. UNFAIR CLAIM SETTLEMENT PRACTICES

§542.001. PURPOSE

This subchapter may be cited as the Unfair Claim Settlement Practices Act.

§542.002. APPLICABILITY OF SUBCHAPTER

This subchapter applies to the following insurers whether organized as a proprietorship, partnership, stock or mutual corporation, or unincorporated association:

(1) a life, health, or accident insurance company;

(2) a fire or casualty insurance company;

(3) a hail or storm insurance company;

(4) a title insurance company;

(5) a mortgage guarantee company;

(6) a mutual assessment company;

(7) a local mutual aid association;

(8) a local mutual burial association;

(9) a statewide mutual assessment company;

(10) a stipulated premium company;

(11) a fraternal benefit society;

(12) a group hospital service corporation;

(13) a county mutual insurance company;

(14) a Lloyd's plan;

(15) a reciprocal or inter-insurance exchange; and

(16) a farm mutual insurance company.

§542.003. UNFAIR CLAIM SETTLEMENT PRACTICES PROHIBITED

(a) An insurer engaging in business in this state may not engage in an unfair claim settlement practice.

(b) Any of the following acts by an insurer constitutes unfair claim settlement practices:

§542.004.

(1) knowingly misrepresenting to a claimant pertinent facts or policy provisions relating to coverage at issue;

(2) failing to acknowledge with reasonable promptness pertinent communications relating to a claim arising under the insurer's policy;

(3) failing to adopt and implement reasonable standards for the prompt investigation of claims arising under the insurer's policies;

(4) not attempting in good faith to effect a prompt, fair, and equitable settlement of a claim submitted in which liability has become reasonably clear;

(5) compelling a policyholder to institute a suit to recover an amount due under a policy by offering substantially less than the amount ultimately recovered in a suit brought by the policyholder;

(6) failing to maintain the information required by Section 542.005; or

(7) committing another act the commissioner determines by rule constitutes an unfair claim settlement practice.

§542.004. EXAMINATION OF TAX RETURNS PROHIBITED

(a) An insurer regulated under this code may not require a claimant, as a condition of settling a claim, to produce the claimant's federal income tax returns for examination or investigation by the insurer unless:

(1) the claimant is ordered to produce the tax returns by a court; or

(2) the claim involves:

(A) a fire loss; or

(B) a loss of profits or income.

(b) An insurer that violates this section commits:

(1) a prohibited practice under this subchapter; and

(2) a deceptive trade practice under Subchapter E, Chapter 17, Business & Commerce Code.

(c) A claimant affected by a violation of this section is entitled to remedies under Subchapter E, Chapter 17, Business & Commerce Code.

SUBCHAPTER B. PROMPT PAYMENT OF CLAIMS

§542.051. DEFINITIONS

In this subchapter:

(1) "Business day" means a day other than a Saturday, Sunday, or holiday recognized by this state.

(2) "Claim" means a first-party claim that:

(A) is made by an insured or policyholder under an insurance policy or contract or by a beneficiary named in the policy or contract; and

(B) must be paid by the insurer directly to the insured or beneficiary.

(3) "Claimant" means a person making a claim.

(4) "Notice of claim" means any written notification provided by a claimant to an insurer that reasonably apprises the insurer of the facts relating to the claim.

§542.052. APPLICABILITY OF SUBCHAPTER

This subchapter applies to any insurer authorized to engage in business as an insurance company or to provide insurance in this state, including:

(1) a stock life, health, or accident insurance company;

(2) a mutual life, health, or accident insurance company;

(3) a stock fire or casualty insurance company;

(4) a mutual fire or casualty insurance company;

(5) a Mexican casualty insurance company;

(6) a Lloyd's plan;

(7) a reciprocal or interinsurance exchange;

(8) a fraternal benefit society;

(9) a stipulated premium company;

(10) a nonprofit legal services corporation;

(11) a statewide mutual assessment company;

(12) a local mutual aid association;

(13) a local mutual burial association;

(14) an association exempt under Section 887.102;

(15) a nonprofit hospital, medical, or dental service corporation, including a corporation subject to Chapter 842;

(16) a county mutual insurance company;

(17) a farm mutual insurance company;

(18) a risk retention group;

(19) a purchasing group;

(20) an eligible surplus lines insurer; and

(21) except as provided by Section 542.053(b), a guaranty association operating under Chapter 462 or 463.

§542.053. EXCEPTION

(a) This subchapter does not apply to:

(1) workers' compensation insurance;

(2) mortgage guaranty insurance;

(3) title insurance;

(4) fidelity, surety, or guaranty bonds;

(5) marine insurance as defined by Section 1807.001; or

§542.054.   DTPA Forms and Practice Guide Desk Book

    (6) a guaranty association created and operating under Chapter 2602.

  (b) A guaranty association operating under Chapter 462 or 463 is not subject to the damage provisions of Section 542.060.

  (c) This subchapter does not apply to a health maintenance organization except as provided by Section 1271.005(c).

  (d) This subchapter does not apply to a claim governed by Subchapter C, Chapter 1301.

§542.054. LIBERAL CONSTRUCTION

This subchapter shall be liberally construed to promote the prompt payment of insurance claims.

§542.055. RECEIPT OF NOTICE OF CLAIM

  (a) Not later than the 15th day or, if the insurer is an eligible surplus lines insurer, the 30th business day after the date an insurer receives notice of a claim, the insurer shall:

    (1) acknowledge receipt of the claim;

    (2) commence any investigation of the claim; and

    (3) request from the claimant all items, statements, and forms that the insurer reasonably believes, at that time, will be required from the claimant.

  (b) An insurer may make additional requests for information if, during the investigation of the claim, the additional requests are necessary.

  (c) If the acknowledgment of receipt of a claim is not made in writing, the insurer shall make a record of the date, manner, and content of the acknowledgment.

§542.056. NOTICE OF ACCEPTANCE OR REJECTION OF CLAIM

  (a) Except as provided by Subsection (b) or (d), an insurer shall notify a claimant in writing of the acceptance or rejection of a claim not later than the 15th business day after the date the insurer receives all items, statements, and forms required by the insurer to secure final proof of loss.

  (b) If an insurer has a reasonable basis to believe that a loss resulted from arson, the insurer shall notify the claimant in writing of the acceptance or rejection of the claim not later than the 30th day after the date the insurer receives all items, statements, and forms required by the insurer.

  (c) If the insurer rejects the claim, the notice required by Subsection (a) or (b) must state the reasons for the rejection.

  (d) If the insurer is unable to accept or reject the claim within the period specified by Subsection (a) or (b), the insurer, within that same period, shall notify the claimant of the reasons that the insurer needs additional time. The insurer shall accept or reject the claim not later than the 45th day after the date the insurer notifies a claimant under this subsection.

§542.057. PAYMENT OF CLAIM

  (a) Except as otherwise provided by this section, if an insurer notifies a claimant under Section 542.056 that the insurer will pay a claim or part of a claim, the insurer shall pay the claim not later than the fifth business day after the date notice is made.

(b) If payment of the claim or part of the claim is conditioned on the performance of an act by the claimant, the insurer shall pay the claim not later than the fifth business day after the date the act is performed.

(c) If the insurer is an eligible surplus lines insurer, the insurer shall pay the claim not later than the 20th business day after the notice or the date the act is performed, as applicable.

§542.058. DELAY IN PAYMENT OF CLAIM

(a) Except as otherwise provided, if an insurer, after receiving all items, statements, and forms reasonably requested and required under Section 542.055, delays payment of the claim for a period exceeding the period specified by other applicable statutes or, if other statutes do not specify a period, for more than 60 days, the insurer shall pay damages and other items as provided by Section 542.060.

(b) Subsection (a) does not apply in a case in which it is found as a result of arbitration or litigation that a claim received by an insurer is invalid and should not be paid by the insurer.

(c) A life insurer that receives notice of an adverse, bona fide claim to all or part of the proceeds of the policy before the applicable payment deadline under Subsection (a) shall pay the claim or properly file an interpleader action and tender the benefits into the registry of the court not later than the 90th day after the date the insurer receives all items, statements, and forms reasonably requested and required under Section 542.055. A life insurer that delays payment of the claim or the filing of an interpleader and tender of policy proceeds for more than 90 days shall pay damages and other items as provided by Section 542.060 until the claim is paid or an interpleader is properly filed.

§542.059. EXTENSION OF DEADLINES

(a) A court may grant a request by a guaranty association for an extension of the periods under this subchapter on a showing of good cause and after reasonable notice to policyholders.

(b) In the event of a weather-related catastrophe or major natural disaster, as defined by the commissioner, the claim-handling deadlines imposed under this subchapter are extended for an additional 15 days.

§542.060. LIABILITY FOR VIOLATION OF SUBCHAPTER

(a) If an insurer that is liable for a claim under an insurance policy is not in compliance with this subchapter, the insurer is liable to pay the holder of the policy or the beneficiary making the claim under the policy, in addition to the amount of the claim, interest on the amount of the claim at the rate of 18 percent a year as damages, together with reasonable attorney's fees.

(b) If a suit is filed, the attorney's fees shall be taxed as part of the costs in the case.

§542.061. REMEDIES NOT EXCLUSIVE

The remedies provided by this subchapter are in addition to any other remedy or procedure provided by law or at common law.

RESIDENTIAL CONSTRUCTION LIABILITY ACT

Texas Property Code §27.001 - §27.007

§27.001. DEFINITIONS

In this chapter:

(1) "Action" means a court or judicial proceeding or an arbitration.

(2) "Appurtenance" means any structure or recreational facility that is appurtenant to a residence but is not a part of the dwelling unit.

(3) "Commission" means the Texas Residential Construction Commission.

(4) "Construction defect" has the meaning assigned by Section 401.004 for an action to which Subtitle D, Title 16, applies and for any other action means a matter concerning the design, construction, or repair of a new residence, of an alteration of or repair or addition to an existing residence, or of an appurtenance to a residence, on which a person has a complaint against a contractor. The term may include any physical damage to the residence, any appurtenance, or the real property on which the residence and appurtenance are affixed proximately caused by a construction defect.

(5) "Contractor":

  (A) means:

   (i) a builder, as defined by Section 401.003, contracting with an owner for the construction or repair of a new residence, for the repair or alteration of or an addition to an existing residence, or for the construction, sale, alteration, addition, or repair of an appurtenance to a new or existing residence;

   (ii) any person contracting with a purchaser for the sale of a new residence constructed by or on behalf of that person; or

   (iii) a person contracting with an owner or the developer of a condominium for the construction of a new residence, for an alteration of or an addition to an existing residence, for repair of a new or existing residence, or for the construction, sale, alteration, addition, or repair of an appurtenance to a new or existing residence; and

  (B) includes:

   (i) an owner, officer, director, shareholder, partner, or employee of the contractor; and

   (ii) a risk retention group registered under Article 21.54, Insurance Code, that insures all or any part of a contractor's liability for the cost to repair a residential construction defect.

(6) "Economic damages" means compensatory damages for pecuniary loss proximately caused by a construction defect. The term does not include exemplary damages or damages for physical pain and mental anguish, loss of consortium, disfigurement, physical impairment, or loss of companionship and society.

(7) "Residence" means the real property and improvements for a single family house, duplex, triplex, or quadruplex or a unit and the common elements in a multiunit residential structure in which title to the individual units is transferred to the owners under a condominium or cooperative system.

(8) "Structural failure" has the meaning assigned by Section 401.002 for an action to which Subtitle D, Title 16, applies and for any other action means actual physical damage to the load-bearing portion of a residence caused by a failure of the load-bearing portion.

(9) "Third-party inspector" has the meaning assigned by Section 401.002.

(10) "Developer of a condominium" means a declarant, as defined by Section 82.003, of a condominium consisting of one or more residences.

§27.002. APPLICATION OF CHAPTER

(a) This chapter applies to:

(1) any action to recover damages or other relief arising from a construction defect, except a claim for personal injury, survival, or wrongful death or for damage to goods; and

(2) any subsequent purchaser of a residence who files a claim against a contractor.

(b) Except as provided by this subsection, to the extent of conflict between this chapter and any other law, including the Deceptive Trade Practices-Consumer Protection Act (Subchapter E, Chapter 17, Business & Commerce Code), or a common law cause of action, this chapter prevails.

(c) In this section:

(1) "Goods" does not include a residence.

(2) "Personal injury" does not include mental anguish.

(d) This chapter does not apply to an action to recover damages that arise from: (1) a violation of Section 27.01, Business & Commerce Code; (2) a contractor's wrongful abandonment of an improvement project before completion; or (3) a violation of Chapter 162.

§27.003. LIABILITY

(a) In an action to recover damages or any relief arising from a construction defect:

(1) a contractor is not liable for any percentage of damages caused by:

(A) negligence of a person other than the contractor or an agent, employee, or subcontractor of the contractor;

(B) failure of a person other than the contractor or an agent, employee, or subcontractor of the contractor to:

(i) take reasonable action to mitigate the damages; or

(ii) take reasonable action to maintain the residence;

(C) normal wear, tear, or deterioration;

(D) normal shrinkage due to drying or settlement of construction components within the tolerance of building standards; or

§27.0031.   DTPA Forms and Practice Guide Desk Book

  (E) the contractor's reliance on written information relating to the residence, appurtenance, or real property on which the residence and appurtenance are affixed that was obtained from official government records, if the written information was false or inaccurate and the contractor did not know and could not reasonably have known of the falsity or inaccuracy of the information; and

 (2) if an assignee of the claimant or a person subrogated to the rights of a claimant fails to provide the contractor with the written notice and opportunity to inspect and offer to repair required by Section 27.004 or fails to request state sponsored inspection and dispute resolution under Chapter 428, if applicable, before performing repairs, the contractor is not liable for the cost of any repairs or any percentage of damages caused by repairs made to a construction defect at the request of an assignee of the claimant or a person subrogated to the rights of a claimant by a person other than the contractor or an agent, employee, or subcontractor of the contractor.

(b) Except as provided by this chapter, this chapter does not limit or bar any other defense or defensive matter or other defensive cause of action applicable to an action to recover damages or other relief arising from a construction defect.

§27.0031.   FRIVOLOUS SUIT; HARASSMENT

A party who files a suit under this chapter that is groundless and brought in bad faith or for purposes of harassment is liable to the defendant for reasonable and necessary attorney's fees and court costs.

§27.004.   NOTICE AND OFFER OF SETTLEMENT

(a) In a claim not subject to Subtitle D, Title 16, before the 60th day preceding the date a claimant seeking from a contractor damages or other relief arising from a construction defect initiates an action, the claimant shall give written notice by certified mail, return receipt requested, to the contractor, at the contractor's last known address, specifying in reasonable detail the construction defects that are the subject of the complaint. On the request of the contractor, the claimant shall provide to the contractor any evidence that depicts the nature and cause of the defect and the nature and extent of repairs necessary to remedy the defect, including expert reports, photographs, and videotapes, if that evidence would be discoverable under Rule 192, Texas Rules of Civil Procedure. During the 35-day period after the date the contractor receives the notice, and on the contractor's written request, the contractor shall be given a reasonable opportunity to inspect and have inspected the property that is the subject of the complaint to determine the nature and cause of the defect and the nature and extent of repairs necessary to remedy the defect. The contractor may take reasonable steps to document the defect. In a claim subject to Subtitle D, Title 16, a contractor is entitled to make an offer of repair in accordance with Subsection (b). A claimant is not required to give written notice to a contractor under this subsection in a claim subject to Subtitle D, Title 16.

(b) Not later than the 15th day after the date of a final, unappealable determination of a dispute under Subtitle D, Title 16, if applicable, or not later than the 45th day after the date the contractor receives the notice under this section, if Subtitle D, Title 16, does not apply, the contractor may make a written offer of settlement to the claimant. The offer must be sent to the claimant at the claimant's last known address or to the claimant's attorney by certified mail, return receipt requested. The offer may include either an agreement by the contractor to repair or to have repaired by an independent contractor partially or totally at the contractor's expense or at a reduced rate to the claimant any construction defect described in the notice and shall describe in reasonable detail the kind of repairs which will be made. The repairs shall be made not later than the 45th day after the date the contractor receives written notice of acceptance of the settlement offer, unless completion is delayed by the claimant or by other events beyond the control of the contractor. If a contractor makes a written offer of settlement that the claimant considers to be unreasonable: (1) on or before the 25th day after the date the claimant receives the offer, the claimant shall advise the contractor in writing and in reasonable detail of the reasons why the claimant considers the offer unreasonable; and (2) not later than the 10th day after the date the contractor receives notice under Subdivision (1), the contractor may make a supplemental written offer of settlement to the claimant by sending the offer to the claimant or the claimant's attorney.

(c) If compliance with Subtitle D, Title 16, or the giving of the notice under Subsections (a) and (b) within the period prescribed by those subsections is impracticable because of the necessity of initiating an action at an earlier date to prevent the expiration of the statute of limitations or if the complaint is asserted as a counterclaim, compliance with Subtitle D, Title 16, or the notice is not required. However, the action or counterclaim shall specify in reasonable detail each construction defect that is the subject of the complaint. If Subtitle D, Title 16, applies to the complaint, simultaneously with the filing of an action by a claimant, the claimant must submit a request under Section 428.001. If Subtitle D, Title 16, does not apply, the inspection provided for by Subsection (a) may be made not later than the 75th day after the date of service of the suit, request for arbitration, or counterclaim on the contractor, and the offer provided for by Subsection (b) may be made not later than the 15th day after the date the state-sponsored inspection and dispute resolution process is completed, if Subtitle D, Title 16, applies, and not later than the 60th day after the date of service, if Subtitle D, Title 16, does not apply. If, while an action subject to this chapter is pending, the statute of limitations for the cause of action would have expired and it is determined that the provisions of Subsection (a) were not properly followed, the action shall be abated in order to allow compliance with Subsections (a) and (b).

(d) The court or arbitration tribunal shall abate an action governed by this chapter if Subsection (c) does not apply and the court or tribunal, after a hearing, finds that the contractor is entitled to abatement because the claimant failed to comply with the requirements of Subtitle D, Title 16, if applicable, failed to provide the notice or failed to give the contractor a reasonable opportunity to inspect the property as required by Subsection (a), or failed to follow the procedures specified by Subsection (b). An action is automatically abated without the order of the court or tribunal beginning on the 11th day after the date a motion to abate is filed if the motion:

(1) is verified and alleges that the person against whom the action is pending did not receive the written notice required by Subsection (a), the person against whom the action is pending was not given a reasonable opportunity to inspect the property as required by Subsection (a), or the claimant failed to follow the procedures specified by Subsection (b) or Subtitle D, Title 16; and

(2) is not controverted by an affidavit filed by the claimant before the 11th day after the date on which the motion to abate is filed.

(e) If a claimant rejects a reasonable offer made under Subsection (b) or does not permit the contractor or independent contractor a reasonable opportunity to inspect or repair the defect pursuant to an accepted offer of settlement, the claimant:

(1) may not recover an amount in excess of:

(A) the fair market value of the contractor's last offer of settlement under Subsection (b); or

(B) the amount of a reasonable monetary settlement or purchase offer made under Subsection (n); and

(2) may recover only the amount of reasonable and necessary costs and attorney's fees as prescribed by Rule 1.04, Texas Disciplinary Rules of Conduct, incurred before the offer was rejected or considered rejected.

§27.004.

(f) If a contractor fails to make a reasonable offer under Subsection (b), the limitations on damages provided for in Subsection (e) shall not apply.

(g) Except as provided by Subsection (e), in an action subject to this chapter the claimant may recover only the following economic damages proximately caused by a construction defect:

   (1) the reasonable cost of repairs necessary to cure any construction defect;

   (2) the reasonable and necessary cost for the replacement or repair of any damaged goods in the residence;

   (3) reasonable and necessary engineering or consulting fees;

   (4) the reasonable expenses of temporary housing reasonably necessary during the repair period;

   (5) the reduction in current market value, if any, after the construction defect is repaired if the construction defect is a structural failure; and

   (6) reasonable and necessary attorney's fees.

(h) A homeowner and contractor may agree in writing to extend any time period described in this chapter.

(i) An offer of settlement made under this section that is not accepted before the 25th day after the date the offer is received by the claimant is considered rejected.

(j) An affidavit certifying rejection of a settlement offer under this section may be filed with the court or arbitration tribunal. The trier of fact shall determine the reasonableness of a final offer of settlement made under this section.

(k) A contractor who makes or provides for repairs under this section is entitled to take reasonable steps to document the repair and to have it inspected.

(l) If Subtitle D, Title 16, applies to the claim and the contractor's offer of repair is accepted by the claimant, the contractor, on completion of the repairs and at the contractor's expense, shall engage the third-party inspector who provided the recommendation regarding the construction defect involved in the claim to inspect the repairs and determine whether the residence, as repaired, complies with the applicable limited statutory warranty and building and performance standards adopted by the commission. The contractor is entitled to a reasonable period not to exceed 15 days to address minor cosmetic items that are necessary to fully complete the repairs. The determination of the third-party inspector of whether the repairs comply with the applicable limited statutory warranty and building and performance standards adopted by the commission establishes a rebuttable presumption on that issue. A party seeking to dispute, vacate, or overcome that presumption must establish by clear and convincing evidence that the determination is inconsistent with the applicable limited statutory warranty and building and performance standards.

(m) Notwithstanding Subsection (a), (b), and (c), a contractor who receives written notice of a construction defect resulting from work performed by the contractor or an agent, employee, or subcontractor of the contractor and creating an imminent threat to the health or safety of the inhabitants of the residence shall take reasonable steps to cure the defect as soon as practicable. If the contractor fails to cure the defect in a reasonable time, the owner of the residence may have the defect cured and may recover from the contractor the reasonable cost of the repairs plus attorney's fees and costs in addition to any other damages recoverable under any law not inconsistent with the provisions of this chapter.

(n) This section does not preclude a contractor from making a monetary settlement offer or offer to purchase the residence.

(o) A notice and response letter prescribed by this chapter must be sent by certified mail, return receipt requested, to the last known address of the recipient. If previously disclosed in writing that the recipient of a notice or response letter is represented by an attorney, the letter shall be sent to the recipient's attorney in accordance with Rule 21a, Texas Rules of Civil Procedure.

(p) If the contractor provides written notice of a claim for damages arising from a construction defect to a subcontractor, the contractor retains all rights of contribution from the subcontractor if the contractor settles the claim with the claimant.

(q) If a contractor refuses to initiate repairs under an accepted offer made under this section, the limitations on damages provided for in this section shall not apply.

§27.0041. MEDIATION

(a) If a claimant files suit seeking from a contractor damages arising from a construction defect in an amount greater than $7,500, the claimant or contractor may file a motion to compel mediation of the dispute. The motion must be filed not later than the 90th day after the date the suit is filed.

(b) Not later than the 30th day after the date a motion is filed under Subsection (a), the court shall order the parties to mediate the dispute. If the parties cannot agree on the appointment of a mediator, the court shall appoint the mediator.

(c) The court shall order the parties to begin mediation of the dispute not later than the 30th day after the date the court enters its order under Subsection (b) unless the parties agree otherwise or the court determines additional time is required. If the court determines that additional time is required, the court may order the parties to begin mediation of the dispute not later than the 60th day after the date the court enters its order under Subsection (b).

(d) Unless each party who has appeared in a suit filed under this chapter agrees otherwise, each party shall participate in the mediation and contribute equally to the cost of the mediation.

(e) Section 154.023, Civil Practice and Remedies Code, and Subchapters C and D, Chapter 154, Civil Practice and Remedies Code, apply to a mediation under this section to the extent those laws do not conflict with this section.

§27.0042. CONDITIONAL SALE TO BUILDER

(a) A written agreement between a contractor and a homeowner may provide that, except as provided by Subsection (b), if the reasonable cost of repairs necessary to repair a construction defect that is the responsibility of the contractor exceeds an agreed percentage of the current fair market value of the residence, as determined without reference to the construction defects, then, in an action subject to this chapter, the contractor may elect as an alternative to the damages specified in Section 27.004(g) that the contractor who sold the residence to the homeowner purchase it.

(b) A contractor may not elect to purchase the residence under Subsection (a) if:

(1) the residence is more than five years old at the time an action is initiated; or

(2) the contractor makes such an election later than the 15th day after the date of a final, unappealable determination of a dispute under Subtitle D, Title 16, if applicable.

(c) If a contractor elects to purchase the residence under Subsection (a):

(1) the contractor shall pay the original purchase price of the residence and closing costs incurred by the homeowner and the cost of transferring title to the contractor under the election;

(2) the homeowner may recover:

(A) reasonable and necessary attorney's and expert fees as identified in Section 27.004(g);

(B) reimbursement for permanent improvements the owner made to the residence after the date the owner purchased the residence from the builder; and

(C) reasonable costs to move from the residence; and

(3) conditioned on the payment of the purchase price, the homeowner shall tender a special warranty deed to the contractor, free of all liens and claims to liens as of the date the title is transferred to the contractor, and without damage caused by the homeowner.

(d) An offer to purchase a claimant's home that complies with this section is considered reasonable absent clear and convincing evidence to the contrary.

§27.005. LIMITATIONS ON EFFECT OF CHAPTER

This chapter does not create a cause of action or derivative liability or extend a limitations period.

§27.006. CAUSATION

In an action to recover damages resulting from a construction defect, the claimant must prove that the damages were proximately caused by the construction defect.

§27.007. DISCLOSURE STATEMENT REQUIRED

(a) A written contract subject to this chapter other than a contract between a developer of a condominium and a contractor for the construction or repair of a residence or appurtenance to a residence in a condominium, must contain in the contract a notice printed or typed in 10-point boldface type or the computer equivalent that reads substantially similar to the following:

"This contract is subject to Chapter 27 of the Texas Property Code. The provisions of that chapter may affect your right to recover damages arising from a construction defect. If you have a complaint concerning a construction defect and that defect has not been corrected as may be required by law or by contract, you must provide the notice required by Chapter 27 of the Texas Property Code to the contractor by certified mail, return receipt requested, not later than the 60th day before the date you file suit to recover damages in a court of law or initiate arbitration. The notice must refer to Chapter 27 of the Texas Property Code, and must describe the construction defect. If requested by the contractor, you must provide the contractor an opportunity to inspect and cure the defect as provided by Section 27.004 of the Texas Property Code."

(b) If a contract does not contain the notice required by this section, the claimant may recover from the contractor a civil penalty of $500 in addition to any other remedy provided by this chapter.

(c) This section does not apply to a contract relating to a home required to be registered under Section 426.003.

DIGEST OF SUPREME COURT OPINIONS

Scope Note

This digest contains all Texas Supreme Court opinions from the enactment of the Texas Deceptive Trade Practices Consumer Protection Act [Tex. Bus. & Com. Code §17.41 C 17.63 (cited as the "DTPA")] and Chapter 541 (formerly Article 21.21 §16) of the Texas Insurance Code through July. 1, 2015 in which there is a substantive consideration or holding by the Court under either statute.

Cases are listed in chronological order in each section. *See also* Table of Cases, p. **XXX**; Topical Index of Cases, p. **XXX**.

§1.00   GENERAL PROVISIONS

§1.01   APPLICATION AND EFFECTIVE DATES

Woods v. Littleton, 554 S.W.2d 662 (Tex. 1977). Plaintiffs, purchasers of a home from defendants, brought suit alleging that the home had a defective sewer system, and that the defendants had performed faulty repair work under a one year service contract. Although the home was purchased prior to the effective date of the Act (May 21, 1973) the jury found that subsequent to that date the defendants had engaged in a deceptive trade practice by misrepresenting that the sewer was in good working order. The Court held that since the acts giving rise to the cause of action occurred after the effective date of the DTPA, the Act applied, notwithstanding the fact that the sale which initiated the chain of events occurred prior to the effective date.

Stagner v. Friendswood Development Company, Inc., 620 S.W.2d 103 (Tex. 1981) (*per curiam*). Purchasers of homes brought suit against the sellers who had developed the subdivision. The Court affirmed a summary judgment for the defendants on the grounds that the purchasers adduced no summary judgment proof that the defendants committed any misconduct on or after the effective date (September 1, 1975) of the 1975 amendments to the DTPA. Prior to these amendments, the definition of "consumer" did not include a purchaser of real property.

English v. Fischer, 660 S.W.2d 521 (Tex. 1983). The plaintiffs purchased a home from the defendants in 1967. In 1979 the house was partially destroyed by fire and a dispute arose over application of the insurance proceeds. The Court affirmed the lower court denial of the plaintiffs' claim for damages under the DTPA. The Court noted that "unless [the plaintiffs] had been able to show some representation or warranty on the part of [defendants] which would have continued past the effective date of the DTPA (May 21, 1973), they are barred from any complaint as to the 1967 sale." *Id.* at 524. The Court went on the hold that the dispute was over the proceeds from an insurance policy which was neither "goods" nor "services" and that therefore the plaintiffs were not consumers.

Litton Indus. Products, Inc. v. Gammage, 668 S.W.2d 319 (Tex. 1984). This was a personal injury suit brought to recover damages as a result of a breach of warranty given in connection with the sale of a tool. The Court held that the plaintiff was not entitled to treble damages because he failed to allege or prove that the defendant did any act or practice after May 21, 1973, the effective date of the DTPA. In the absence of proof that the Act applied, the plaintiff was not entitled to recover damages pursuant to the Act.

La Sara Grain v. First Nat. Bank of Mercedes, 673 S.W.2d 558 (Tex. 1984). This action was brought to recover damages resulting from a bank's practice of honoring checks with fewer than the required number of signatures and failing to follow restrictive endorsements. Some of the checks were honored prior to May 23, 1977 the effective date of the amendment which deleted the phrase "for other than commercial or business use" from the definition of "services" under the DTPA. Other checks were honored after the effective date of this amendment. The Court held that it was error to apply the 1975 version of the DTPA to all of the checks. Checks honored after the effective date of the amendment were governed by that amendment.

In re Alford Chevrolet-Geo, et. al., Relators, 997 S.W.2d 173 (Tex. 1999). In this case the Court notes that whether the 1995 or 1996 version of the DTPA applies depends on the date the claims accrued. According to the statute, a DTPA claim accrues when "the consumer discovered or in the exercise of reasonable diligence should have discovered the occurrence of the false, misleading, or deceptive act or practice." DTPA §17.565.

§1.02 CONSTRUCTION OF THE ACT

Woods v. Littleton, 554 S.W.2d 662 (Tex. 1977). In holding that the DTPA applied to the misconduct in question and that the Act as originally passed provided for the recovery of mandatory treble damages, the Court relied upon the mandate of liberal construction in §17.44 of the DTPA.

Pennington v. Singleton, 606 S.W.2d 682 (Tex. 1980). In this case the Court summarized the principles applicable to construction of the DTPA:

The primary emphasis is on the intention of the Legislature, keeping in view "the old law, the evil and the remedy." The legislative intent should be determined from the language of the entire act and not isolated portions. The court is not necessarily confined to the literal meaning of the words used, and the legislative intent rather than the strict letter of the Act will control.

Smith v. Baldwin, 611 S.W.2d 611 (Tex. 1981). The Court gave the following guidance in construing the DTPA:

The DTPA does not represent a codification of the common law. A primary purpose of the enactment of the DTPA was to provide consumers a cause of action for deceptive trade practices without the burden of proof and numerous defenses encountered in a common law fraud or breach of warranty suit.

Jim Walter Homes, Inc. v. Valencia, 690 S.W.2d 239 (Tex. 1985). Relying upon *Pennington v. Singleton, supra*, the Court states that the purposes of multiple damages are twofold: (1) to encourage consumers to initiate litigation and (2) to deter sellers from violating the DTPA.

§2.00 THE STANDING REQUIREMENT: WHO IS A CONSUMER?

Riverside Nat. Bank v. Lewis, 603 S.W.2d 169 (Tex. 1980). The plaintiff Lewis sought to refinance a loan on his automobile through Riverside National Bank. A loan officer represented to the plaintiff that the loan had been approved but the bank subsequently refused to loan the money. As a result, the plaintiff's car was repossessed. The Court first held that in order to maintain a private action under §17.50 of the DTPA plaintiff must be a consumer as defined in §17.45(4). The Court rejected the contention that it was only necessary that the defendant's conduct constitute trade and commerce as defined in §17.45(b).

Next the Court addressed the question of whether Lewis had sought or acquired "goods" or "services." Section 17.45(1) defines goods as "tangible chattels" [or real property]. The Court concluded that the money Lewis sought to acquire was a "currency of exchange" rather than a tangible chattel and therefore did not constitute "goods" as defined in the DTPA.

The Court also held that the extension of credit sought by the plaintiff was not a "service." Referencing the definition of services in §17.45(2) as "work" or "labor" the Court held that seeking money or the use of money is not a seeking of work or labor.

The Court next considered Lewis' argument that in the course of extending credit the bank necessarily provided services to the plaintiff such as assistance in filling out the loan application, financial counseling and processing of the loan. Further, it was argued that services existed in the process of determining whether to lend money and in the actual lending of the money and that these were necessarily a part of the interest rate or purchase price of the loan. The Court noted that there was no *evidence* to support the existence of these activities or that the plaintiff sought to acquire these activities. Additionally, the plaintiff made no complaint about the quality of these activities but rather complained solely about the bank's failure to make a loan. In language that would loom large in later cases, the Court expressly reserved for future decision the question of whether activities collateral to the extension of credit may constitute a "service":

> [W]e do not pass upon the question of whether a bank's misrepresentation concerning its activities, such as the availability of financial counseling, the cost of processing a loan or the ability to pay a customer's monthly bills, could constitute a deceptive act in connection with the sale of "services." We only hold where those activities are not the subject of the complaint, then the presence of such collateral activities in a transaction otherwise not covered by the DTPA does not subject the parties to liability under the DTPA. Id. at 175.

Cameron v. Terrell & Garrett, Inc., 618 S.W.2d 535 (Tex. 1981). The purchasers of a house brought suit against the seller's real estate agent who misrepresented the number of square feet in the house in a MLS listing. The realtor argued that since his services had been purchased (through commission) by the sellers, the plaintiffs were not consumers because they had not sought or acquired services from the realtor. The Court rejected this argument. In so doing, the Court reaffirmed the requirements for standing as a consumer: (1) the person must have sought or acquired goods or services by purchase or lease and (2) the goods and services purchased or leased must form the basis of the complaint. The plaintiffs satisfied both elements since they sought or acquired the house in question and their complaint concerned the number of square feet in the house.

The Court rejected the argument that the defendant would have to be in the same chain of title as the person who furnished the good or service on which the complaint was based and refused to impose "any other similar privity requirement." *Id.* at 541. The Court concluded its analysis with the following discussion:

> [The definition of consumer] does not purport to define a consumer in terms of a person's relationship to the party he is suing. [It] does nothing more than describe the class of persons who can bring a suit for treble damages under Section 17.50 [citation omitted]. It does not say who a consumer can sue under §17.50 for a deceptive trade practice violation.... We therefore, hold that a person need not seek or acquire goods or services furnished by the defendant to be a consumer as defined in the DTPA. *Id.* at 541.

Farmers & Merchants State Bank v. Ferguson, 617 S.W.2d 918 (Tex. 1981). This case involved deceptive trade practices committed in connection with the wrongful dishonor of the plaintiff's checks drawn on his business account with the defendant bank. The court of appeals held that the plaintiff, who had been charged a service fee by the bank, had purchased a service from the bank, and was a consumer. The Court reversed, holding that the burden of proof is on the plaintiff to establish that he is a "consumer." The Court held that the plaintiff had failed to adduce evidence that the banking services were for other than "business use" so as to constitute a "service" as that term was defined prior to the 1977 amendments.

Stagner v. Friendswood Development Company, Inc., 620 S.W.2d 103 (Tex. 1981) (*per curiam*). The plaintiff, a purchaser of land, brought suit against the prior owner of the property who had sold it to the plaintiff's seller. The court of appeals had affirmed a take nothing judgment for the defendant based, in part, on the lack of contractual privity between the parties. In a *per curiam* opinion, the Court affirmed the take nothing judgment but disapproved of the lower court's holding that privity was required under the Act to qualify one as a consumer. In rejecting vertical privity, the Court relied upon *Cameron v. Terrell & Garrett, Inc., supra*.

Knight v. International Harvester Credit Corp., 627 S.W.2d 382 (Tex. 1982). The plaintiff in this case purchased a truck from a retailer. The plaintiff signed a retail installment contract which provided for payment over time with interest. The contract, prepared by IHCC, contained a misrepresentation as to the rights of the plaintiff under the agreement. The contract was assigned to IHCC which extended the credit for the transaction. The purchaser brought suit against both the retailer and IHCC alleging that IHCC had engaged in a deceptive trade practice by virtue of its misrepresentation in the contract. The court of appeals held that the purchaser was not a consumer as to IHCC because IHCC had merely extended credit which was neither a "good" nor a "service." The Supreme Court disagreed.

The Court held that the alleged misrepresentation did not deal solely with the extension of credit. The plaintiff sought to purchase a truck which clearly was a "good" under the Act. The contract pertained to the truck. The Court rejected the contention that the plaintiff was a consumer as to the retailer only and not to IHCC. The Court held that to argue that IHCC was involved only in the extension of credit ignored the realities of the transaction. IHCC had prepared the sales contract which contained the offending language. The contract provided not only for purchase of the truck but for payment over time with interest. Under these circumstances, the Court concluded that both the retailer and IHCC were so "inextricably intertwined in the transaction as to be equally responsible for the conduct of the sale." *Id.* at 389. The Court distinguished *Riverside Nat'l Bank v. Lewis, supra*, noting that in that case the bank had nothing to do with the sale of the vehicle. In *Knight*, the plaintiff's objective in the transaction was the purchase of a dump truck. Financing was merely the means of making that purchase. The alleged deceptive trade practice arose out of this purchase transaction. In the words of the Court, *Knight* was a "consumer" as to "all parties who sought to enjoy the benefits of that sale." *Id.*

English v. Fischer, 660 S.W.2d 521 (Tex. 1983). This case involved the dispute between a mortgagor and mortgagee over the proceeds of a homeowners insurance policy. Since the home was sold prior to the effective date of the DTPA, any misconduct in connection with the sale of the home which did not continue past the effective date was not covered by the DTPA. The Court concluded: "[The plaintiffs] seeks in this action the proceeds from an insurance policy which is neither 'goods' nor 'services'. Therefore they are not consumers[.]" *Id.* at 524.

Flenniken v. Longview Bank & Trust Co., 661 S.W.2d 705 (Tex. 1983). The Flennikens entered into a contract with a builder for construction of a residence. The Flennikens executed a mechanic's lien note secured by a deed of trust which were both assigned to the defendant bank in return for construction financing. The builder abandoned the contract after completing 20% of the work. The bank foreclosed on the property under the deed of trust. The jury found the foreclosure to be an unconscionable course of action, a finding which was not challenged by the bank on appeal. The court of appeals held that the Flennikens were not "consumers." The Supreme Court reversed and in the course of its opinion made the following points. First, the Court reiterated the rules set down in *Cameron v. Terrell & Garrett, Inc., supra*: It was not necessary for a person to seek or acquire goods or services *from* the defendant to meet the definition of consumer. Rather, a plaintiff establishes his standing in terms of his relationship to a transaction, not his relationship with a defendant. Second, the fact that the bank's unconscionable course of action occurred after the contract for the sale of the house was signed did not disqualify the Flennikens from bringing suit under the DTPA. In the words of the Court, "there is no requirement that the defendant's unconscionable act occur simultaneously with the sale or lease of the goods or services that form the basis of the complaint." Third, the court of appeals erred in holding that there were two transactions—one between the Flennikens and the homebuilder and another between the homebuilder and the bank. The Court noted that from the Flennikens' perspective there was only one transaction—the purchase of the house. The bank's unconscionable act arose out of the Flenniken's transaction with the builder. Relying upon *Knight v. International Harvester Credit Corp., supra*, the Court held that the Flennikens were "consumers as to all parties who sought to enjoy the benefits of that transaction." Finally, the Court distinguished *Riverside Nat'l Bank v. Lewis* noting that the house, not the bank's lending activities, formed the basis of the plaintiff's complaint.

Big H Auto Auction, Inc. v. Saenz Motor., 665 S.W.2d 756 (Tex. 1984). In a classic "man bites dog" fact situation, the plaintiff in this case was a used car dealer who brought an action for deceptive trade practices against the party from whom he bought an automobile. Naturally, the vehicle had been bought for resale and the question before the Court was whether a buyer of goods for resale was a "consumer." Specifically, the issue was whether goods purchased for resale constituted goods purchased "for use" as required by §17.45 of the DTPA. Relying upon legislative history and the mandate of liberal construction, the Court held that goods purchased for resale were purchased "for use" thereby qualifying the plaintiff as a consumer.

La Sara Grain v. First Nat. Bank of Mercedes, 673 S.W.2d 558 (Tex. 1984). This case involves a lawsuit between a customer and its bank in which the customer alleged that the bank had committed actionable misconduct under the DTPA by honoring checks which were not signed in accordance with the signature cards and in making an unauthorized loan to a renegade employee. In connection with the former allegations, the Court held that "the services provided by a bank in connection with a checking account are within the scope of the DTPA," citing the court of appeals' opinion in *Farmers and Merchants State Bank v. Ferguson, supra*. Although the Court found consumer status it went on to hold that no violation of the DTPA had occurred.

In connection with the allegation of unauthorized loans, the Court reviewed its prior holdings in *Riverside, supra, Knight, supra, Flenniken, supra* and *Cameron, supra*. The Court summarized *Knight* and *Flenniken* as follows: A lender may be subject to a DTPA claim if the borrowers "objective" is the purchase or lease of a good or service thereby qualifying the borrower as a consumer. Since in *La Sara* there was no evidence as to the borrower's purpose in seeking the loan or whether the loan was believed by the bank to be for the purchase or lease of goods or services, the Court held that the plaintiff had not shown itself to be a consumer.

Kennedy v. Sale, 689 S.W.2d 890 (Tex. 1985). This case involved a suit by an employee complaining of misrepresentations of the terms of a group insurance policy by the insurance salesman. The policy was purchased by the employer for the benefit of the employees. The court of appeals held that the employee was not a consumer because he did not "seek or acquire" by "purchase" the policy from Sale. The Court rejected this argument holding that while the employee did not seek the insurance policy he did acquire the benefits as a result of a purchase consummated for his benefit by his employer. The Court concluded there was nothing in the DTPA's definition of "consumer" to require that the consumer "must himself be the one who purchases or leases." The Court reiterated that privity was not a requirement under the DTPA.

Chastain v. Koonce, 700 S.W.2d 579 (Tex. 1985). The plaintiffs in this case were purchasers of residential lots from the defendants. Prior to purchase, the defendants represented that certain other lots in the area would be restricted for residential use only. After the plaintiffs purchased the lots, one of the other lots which had been represented to be restricted to residential use was actually used by its owner for commercial purposes; and, the lot had not been restricted to residential use as represented. The defendants argued that the plaintiffs did not qualify as consumers because their complaints concerned the use of property other than the lots they purchased and therefore the goods purchased by the plaintiffs did not form the basis of their complaint. A majority of the Supreme Court rejected this argument noting that misrepresentations had occurred during the transaction which resulted in the purchase of the plaintiffs' lots and the representations, if true, would have affected the desirability of the property being purchased. Thus, the plaintiffs were complaining about an aspect of the lots purchased in the transaction involved. Additionally, the floor debate in the Texas Legislature clearly indicated that type of transaction was contemplated as being encompassed by the DTPA.

Sherman Simon Enter. v. Lorac Service Corp., 724 S.W.2d 13 (Tex. 1987). An employee of a company rented a car from the defendant. The employee used a company credit card. The charges under the rental agreement were to be billed to a company of which the employer was a wholly owned subsidiary. The employee was involved in an automobile collision. The employer ultimately brought suit against the rental company alleging that the defendant misrepresented the existence of liability coverage under the rental agreement. The rental car company argued that the employer was not a consumer because there was no evidence that the employer was billed or paid for the rental car. These arguments were rejected by the Court which noted that §17.45(4) clearly indicates that a claimant can be a consumer if he "seeks" goods or services. It is therefore not necessary that a transaction be consummated (*i.e.* that the consumer actually pay for the goods or services). Furthermore, the employee was acting as an agent of the employer in acquiring transportation. It was the employer, therefore, that sought to acquire goods or services. The Court went on to hold that there was no misrepresentation and therefore no basis for liability.

Melody Home Mfg. Co. v. Barnes, 741 S.W.2d 349 (Tex. 1987). The Barnes purchased a modular home from Melody. After moving in the Barnes experienced continual problems with dampness and moisture in the home. Ultimately it was discovered that a sink was not connected to a drain in one of the walls and that the continual leak had caused severe damage to the home. Melody's employees attempted to repair the home on two occasions. Instead of correcting the problem, however, the repairs caused additional damages. The jury found that the workmen had failed to repair the home in a good and workmanlike manner. On appeal Melody contended that the Barnes were not consumers as to the repair services because they had not "purchased" them. The Court rejected this argument, holding that the absence of a cash payment for the repairs was not determinative. When the Barnes discovered the defects they were entitled to bring suit for damages resulting from Melody's breach of its obligation to build the home in a good and workmanlike manner. *See Humber v. Morton*, 426 S.W.2d 554 (Tex. 1968). The repairs were a continuation of the original purchase; accordingly, the Barnes had purchased the repair services. Put differently, their consumer status, originating with the purchase, continued.

Birchfield v. Texarkana Memorial Hospital, 747 S.W.2d 361 (Tex. 1987). In this case a minor's parents sued on their daughter's behalf to recover damages caused by hospital personnel, who improperly administered supplemental oxygen to her shortly after her birth. The parents sued on theories of negligence and deceptive trade practices. The hospital contended, on appeal, that the infant did not qualify as a consumer. The Supreme Court rejected this argument and reaffirmed that the Court defines a consumer in terms of his or her relationship to a transaction, rather than by his or her relationship to the defendant. The infant acquired goods and services sold by the hospital and thereby established her standing for purposes of the DTPA.

Eckman v. Centennial Savings Bank, 784 S.W.2d 672 (Tex. 1990). The Supreme Court ruled in this case that the defendant in a DTPA suit has the burden to plead and prove the applicability of the $25,000,000 exception to business consumer status as an affirmative defense. Recognizing that most claimants do not have assets of $25,000,000 or more, the Court reasoned that requiring every DTPA plaintiff to prove that he or she is not a multimillionaire would be an inefficient and uneconomical use of judicial resources. The Court stated further that imposing the burden of raising and negating the applicability of the $25,000,000 exception upon every business consumer would be unduly prejudicial.

Under the Supreme Court's holding, evidence concerning the consumer's financial status is irrelevant unless the defendant raises the issue. Once the issue is raised, such financial information will be discoverable to determine whether the exception applies. The Court cautioned that to avoid prejudicing the jury with evidence of the claimant's financial status, the parties should attempt to resolve the applicability of the exception before trial.

Transport Inc. v. Faircloth, 898 S.W.2d 269 (Tex. 1995). The plaintiff, the surviving minor daughter of a couple killed in a motor vehicle accident, received a quick settlement of all claims from the insurance company representing the driver of the other vehicle. Upon reaching majority, the plaintiff brought suit against the insurance company, among others, for unconscionable conduct and violations of Article 21.21. The Court held that the plaintiff did not seek to purchase any services of the insurance company and, hence, was not a consumer.

Arthur Anderson & Co. v. Perry Equipment Corp., 945 S.W.2d 812 (Tex. 1997). Perry Equipment Corporation (PECO) purchased another company, Maloney Pipeline Systems (Maloney). As a condition of the sale, PECO required audited financial statements. Maloney retained defendant Arthur Anderson & Co. (Anderson), for this purpose. The audit, which was relied upon by PECO, provided a false and misleading financial picture of Maloney. After the purchase turned out to be a total loss PECO brought suit claiming that Anderson had committed deceptive trade practices and recovered a judgment in the trial court.

On appeal Anderson argued that PECO was not a consumer because Maloney paid for the audit. The Court rejected this argument, holding that PECO had both sought and acquired Anderson's services. Following *Kennedy v. Sale*, 689 S.W.2d 890 (Tex. 1985), the Court reaffirmed that a consumer does not have to be the actual purchaser of the goods or services as long as it is the beneficiary of them. Here the audit was required by PECO and intended for PECO's benefit. The Court held that PECO was a consumer.

Insurance Co. of N. Am. v. Morris, 981 S.W.2d 667 (Tex. 1998). The plaintiffs were purchasers of oil and gas limited partnership interests. The purchase price included a down payment and a promissory note. The broker-dealers solicited the investments and assigned the notes to a bank to obtain production funds; INA issued bonds guaranteeing the notes. Prior to issuing the bonds, INA reviewed the documents and screened the investments. As part of the transaction, the plaintiffs agreed to indemnify INA in the event of default. The value of the investments were misrepresented by the broker-dealers and the investors ultimately defaulted on the notes. INA honored the bonds, paid the notes, and brought suit to obtain indemnification from the plaintiff-investors. The plaintiffs counterclaimed, alleging that INA was responsible for the misrepresentations of the broker-dealers. The Court held that because (1) the broker-dealers had only limited authority to act for INA—that authority extended only to representations concerning the insurance product and not to the investment product (2) INA's investment assessment was done for its own benefit not the investors and (3) INA's premiums were modest relative to the risk, the plaintiffs were consumers as to INA's "credit enhancement services" (bond issuance) but not to INA's pre-screening or investment-counseling services

DeWitt County Electric Cooperative, Inc. v. Parks et al., 1 S.W.3d 96 (Tex. 1999). The plaintiff homeowners entered into a service contract with the defendant electric cooperative for electrical service. At the same time, the plaintiffs signed a written agreement which gave the defendant an easement and the right to clear the easement of obstructions. When the defendant's employees cut down two of the plaintiff's trees and trimmed back another, the plaintiffs brought suit under the DTPA. The plaintiffs alleged that the defendant assured them that they would not remove any trees from the plaintiff's land. The defendant argued that the plaintiffs were not consumers as to the easement agreement. The Court disagreed, holding that since the easement agreement was made in connection with the service agreement (wherein the plaintiffs agreed to purchase electrical service from the defendant), the plaintiffs were consumers.

§3.00 WHO CAN BE SUED?

Pennington v. Singleton, 606 S.W.2d 682 (Tex. 1980). The question in this case was whether the DTPA applies to an isolated sale of a good by one who is not engaged in the business of selling that good (*e.g.* weekend garage sale). The Supreme Court after noting the broad definition of trade and commerce as well as the definition of "person" in §17.45(3) held that there was no indication in the DTPA that persons not in the business of selling were to be excluded. Section 17.49 does not contain such an exemption although other exemptions are allowed.

Cameron v. Terrell & Garrett, Inc., 618 S.W.2d 535 (Tex. 1981). Purchasers of a house brought suit against the sellers' real estate agent who misrepresented the number of square feet in the house. In the course of the opinion the Supreme Court had this to say about the class of individuals subject to suit under the DTPA:

The breadth of the Act is evidenced by Section 17.49 which sets out the exemptions to the DTPA. That section does not provide an exemption for deceptive trade practices by persons who do not furnish the goods or services on which the complaint is based....[I]f the Legislature had intended to place such a restriction on the class of persons who could be sued under the Act for deceptive trade practices, it could easily have done so by simply drafting the restriction into the definition of consumer or some other provision of the Act.... We find no indication in the definition of consumer in Section 17.45(4), or any other provision of the Act, that the Legislature intended to restrict its application only to deceptive trade practices committed by persons who furnished the goods or services upon which the complaint is based. Nor do we find any indication that the Legislature intended to restrict its application by any other similar privity requirement. *Id.* at 540-541.

Flenniken v. Longview Bank & Trust Company, 661 S.W.2d 705 (Tex. 1983). Plaintiff homebuyers brought suit alleging that a bank's wrongful foreclosure of a mechanic's lien constituted an unconscionable act or practice. The lien had been assigned to the bank by the builder of the plaintiffs' home, however the builder never completed the construction. In its discussion of the issue of whether the plaintiffs were consumers, the Court had this to say about the potential defendants under the DTPA: "Section 17.45(4), defining 'consumer' however, only describes the class of persons entitled to bring suit under Section 17.50; it does not define the class of persons subject to liability under the DTPA. The range of possible defendants is limited only by the exemptions provided in Section 17.49." *Id.* at 706.

Karl and Kelly Company, Inc. v. McLerran, 646 S.W.2d 174 (Tex. 1983) (*per curiam*). The plaintiffs, homebuyers, brought suit against the corporate builder of a home and the individual owners of the corporation for misrepresentations about the quality of the construction. A default judgment was taken against both the corporation and the individuals. The Supreme Court in a *per curiam* opinion held that while there was evidence of misrepresentation by the individual owners, there was no evidence that they were acting in their individual capacity or that the company was their alter ego. Accordingly, the Court concluded that the lower courts erred in rendering a personal judgment against the individuals.

Light v. Wilson, 663 S.W.2d 813 (Tex. 1983). In this suit, a sole owner of a construction company was held individually liable along with the corporate defendant for deceptive trade practices. The question before the Supreme Court was whether an individual could be held jointly and severally liable with his company. The Court held in the negative because (1) there were no alter ego pleadings to support piercing the corporate veil and (2) there was no finding of fact that the defendant, individually violated the Deceptive Trade Practices Act. The Court concluded "there being no finding of fact that [the defendant] violated the Deceptive Trade Practices Act, he cannot be personally liable." *Id.* at 814-815. In a concurring opinion, Justice Spears wrote that the rule in Texas has always been that an agent is personally liable for his own torts. He found no reason to treat agents differently when they violate the Deceptive Trade Practices Act.

In the view of the concurring opinion, the majority opinion recognized that the individual defendant would be liable if there were findings that he violated the Act and thereby implicitly overruled *Karl and Kelly Company, Inc. v. McLerran, supra.*

Weitzel v. Barnes, 691 S.W.2d 598 (Tex. 1985). This case involves a suit by purchasers of a remodeled home from a development company. One of the issues before the Court was whether corporate agents may be individually liable under the DTPA. After noting that the record contained evidence as to statements of the individuals upon which the trial judge could have concluded that they made oral misrepresentations, the Court distinguished *Light v. Wilson, supra,* as follows: "While it is true that in *Light v. Wilson,* 663 S.W.2d 813 (Tex. 1983), we exonerated a corporate agent from individual liability in a DTPA case...[i]mplicit in our holding in that case is that there can be individual liability on the part of a corporate agent for misrepresentations made by him." *Id.* at 601.

Home Savings Association v. Guerra, 733 S.W.2d 134 (Tex. 1987). In this case the lender was an assignee of a home improvement contract and note. The Court refused to hold the lender liable for the misconduct of the contractor, noting that a plaintiff must show that the defendant committed a deceptive act; a party's innocent involvement in a transaction was not grounds for liability. The Court explained that a creditor's liability is dependent on a showing of either direct creditor involvement in the sales transaction or some deceptive act relating to the financing. The Court distinguished *Knight v. International Harvester Credit Corp., supra*: The plaintiff could not recover against the lender because no evidence existed to show that the lender was "inextricably intertwined" with the contractor and the plaintiff had not advanced such a "theory of recovery."

Birchfield v. Texarkana Memorial Hospital, 747 S.W.2d 361 (Tex. 1987). In this case, the plaintiff accused the defendant hospital of committing deceptive trade practices in connection with medical services rendered to the plaintiff in 1974. The hospital argued that Article 4590i, §12.01, although not effective until 1977, evidenced a legislative intent to exclude health care providers from the DTPA's coverage. The Supreme Court ruled that nothing in the pre-1977 DTPA illustrated a legislative intent to exempt health care providers from liability under the DTPA.

Brown v. Galleria Area Ford, Inc., 752 S.W.2d 114 (Tex. 1988). In this suit, the plaintiffs took their vehicle to a car dealership for repairs. While the car was still in the shop, the dealership was sold. The plaintiffs sought to hold the successor dealership liable for the previous dealership's faulty repairs on the theory that the two dealerships were inextricably intertwined. The plaintiffs' standing as consumers was not an issue before the Court. The Court detailed the evidence that the consumers advanced in support of their inextricably intertwined argument but concluded that it was unnecessary to address the alternative theory of recovery because the successor dealer had itself engaged in unconscionable conduct.

Qantel Business Systems, Inc. v. Custom Controls Co., 761 S.W.2d 302 (Tex. 1988). Custom Controls, the purchaser of a computer system, brought suit against the retailer and Qantel Business Systems, Inc., the manufacturer. The trial court directed a verdict for Qantel on the grounds that Custom Controls presented no evidence that Qantel engaged, directly or vicariously, in any wrongful or misleading act. The court of appeals reversed and remanded the case to the trial court on the grounds that Custom Controls presented some evidence of a relationship that would provide a basis for liability. The Supreme Court reversed the court of appeals decision because the lower court applied an improper standard of review. In the course of its opinion the Court also rejected the implication that the inextricably intertwined doctrine was a theory of vicarious liability. The Court reaffirmed that the doctrine provided only a basis for establishing a party's status as a consumer and ratified its holding in *Home Savings Association v. Guerra, supra* that liability does not attach to a defendant based on his innocent involvement in a transaction. The Court concluded that the consumer may use the common law theories of vicarious liability under the DTPA and therefore, the Court had no need to expand derivative liability to parties who are inextricably intertwined.

Celtic Life Insurance Co. v. Coats, 885 S.W.2d 96 (Tex. 1994). In this case an insurance agent misrepresented the benefits available under an insurance policy. In its original opinion, the Court held that the authority to explain the policy did not authorize the agent to make misrepresentations about the policy, therefore, the insurer would not be liable for any misrepresentations of the agent outside the scope of the policy. *See* 36 Tex. Sup. Ct. J. 1259 (Sept. 10, 1993). However, on rehearing, the Court reversed its position and held that under common law principles of agency, an insurance company is liable for the misrepresentations of its agent if the agent is acting within the scope of his authority at the time of making the representations, even if the company did not authorize the specific misrepresentation made.

Sorokolit v. Rhodes, 889 S.W.2d 239 (Tex. 1994). Dr. Sorokolit performed a breast augmentation procedure on Mrs. Rhodes. Prior to surgery, Sorokolit told Rhodes that her breasts would look just like the ones she had selected from a magazine. When the result was not as promised, Rhodes sued for breach of warranty and misrepresentation under the DTPA. Sorokolit claimed that the Medical Liability and Insurance Improvement Act (Tex. Rev. Civ. Stat. Art. 4590i) precluded Rhodes' DTPA suit. Article 4590i §12.01(a) provides that the DTPA does not apply to claims resulting from the negligence of a physician. The Court held that the statute precludes negligence claims from being recast as DTPA claims. However, if the alleged DTPA claim is not based on the physician's breach of the accepted standard of care, but is instead based on some other cause of action, such as knowing breach of express warranty or knowing misrepresentation, then the action is not precluded by Article 4590i. Rhodes' claims that Dr. Sorokolit knowingly breached his express warranty and knowingly misrepresented his skills and the achievable results were not precluded.

Walden v. Jeffery, 907 S.W.2d 446 (Tex. 1995) (*per curiam*). The plaintiff brought suit against her dentist, claiming that the dentist knowingly misrepresented that he would provide her with properly fitting dentures in violation of §17.46. The Court held that the plaintiff's claim that the dentist provided ill-fitting dentures was simply a negligence action recast as a DTPA claim and, thus, barred by Article 4590i.

Gormley v. Stover, 907 S.W.2d 448 (Tex. 1995) (*per curiam*) The plaintiff brought suit against her dentist claiming that he misrepresented that he could perform surgery on her with no problems, that a skin graft would work as well as a bone graft, that a dentist would fit her with dentures which she would have no problem wearing, and that her post-surgery pain and numbness would cease in several months. The Court held that these representations were not actionable under the DTPA since they were "nothing more than an attempt to recast her malpractice claim as a DTPA action" in violation of Article 4590i.

Abbott Laboratories, Inc. v. Segura, 907 S.W.2d 503 (Tex. 1995). Parties who allegedly violate the Texas Free Enterprise and Antitrust Act are not subject to suit for such conduct under the DTPA. The bar to indirect purchaser recovery in antitrust suits also bars indirect purchasers from recovering for antitrust conduct under the DTPA.

Amstadt v. U.S. Brass Corp., 919 S.W.2d 644 (Tex. 1996). In this case, homeowners who purchased homes with defective plumbing systems brought suit against the manufacturers and component suppliers of the plumbing systems. The plaintiffs claimed and the jury found that defendants had engaged in deceptive trade practices and unconscionable conduct in marketing the systems to builders. Although there was evidence that building code officials and builders would not have approved and installed the plumbing systems but for the misrepresentations of one or more of the defendants, the Court held that the defendant's misrepresentations could not support DTPA liability because they were not made "in connection with" the plaintiffs' purchase of their homes. In the words of the Court: "the defendant's deceptive trade act or practice is not actionable under the DTPA unless it was committed in connection with the plaintiff's transaction in goods or services." The Court held that this requirement applies as well to unconscionable conduct.

MacGregor Medical Ass'n v. Campbell, 985 S.W.2d 38 (Tex. 1998). Plaintiff's husband became ill after ingesting a drink contaminated with formaldehyde. The plaintiff took her husband to the defendant clinic. He was not examined for approximately 45 minutes after which the doctor assured him that everything would be fine and advised him that the poisoning could be treated with Maalox. Approximately two and one-half years and two stomach surgeries later, he died. Plaintiff brought this lawsuit against the clinic but not within the time specified for a negligence claim under the Medical Liability and Insurance Improvement Act (MLIA). *See* Article 4590i, TEX. REV. CIV. STAT. ANN. The question presented was whether the Plaintiff's DTPA claim for misrepresentations fell within the MLIA and was, thus, similarly barred. The Plaintiff alleged that the clinic represented that it would provide "qualified personnel and resources," the best health services possible," and emergency service "24 hours a day." The Plaintiff complained that her husband had not been seen for almost an hour, that it was misrepresented that he would be fine and needed only Maalox, and that he was not advised of possible complications. The Court held that the Plaintiff's allegations that the defendant had failed to provide quality care as promised required the plaintiff to "prove a breach of the applicable standard of care for health care providers" and thus were nothing more than a negligence claim recast as a DTPA action. Citing *Walden v. Jeffrey and Gormley v. Stover, supra* and distinguishing *Sorokolit v. Rhodes, supra* the Court held that the Plaintiff's claim was covered, and thus barred, by the MLIA.

Earle v. Ratliff, 998 S.W.2d 882 (Tex. 1999). Ratliff sustained a back injury in June, 1991. The defendant physician inserted medical hardware in Ratliff's back in November, 1991 which caused Ratliff's condition to worsen. The defendant surgically removed and replaced the hardware in November, 1993. Ratliff's condition continued to worsen. Ratliff later learned of the risks associated with the hardware. In this suit, Ratliff alleged that the doctor violated the DTPA by misrepresenting and concealing the truth concerning the two surgeries, by telling him that he needed surgery, that he would get 95% better, that the pain was to be expected and that the hardware was safe. The Court held the representations were governed by the MLIA in that the "gist" of his claims were that the doctor "did not hold to the applicable standard of care."

Miller v. Keyser, 90 S.W. 3d 712 (Tex. 2002). In this case, the sales agent of a corporation misrepresented the characteristics of property sold to the plaintiffs. The question presented on appeal was whether an agent of a disclosed principal may be held personally liable under the DTPA for misrepresentations made in the course and scope of his employment. Following *Weitzel v. Barnes*, 691 S.W. 2d 598 (Tex. 1985), the Texas Supreme Court held that the defendant's status as an agent did not immunize him from liability under the DTPA. An agent who violates the DTPA is liable in the same manner as other violators; no special showing that the agent knew of the falsity of the representations is required. An agent who innocently passes along incorrect information supplied by his employer may seek contribution or indemnity from the employer to recoup his loss.

Nissan Motor Co. v. Armstrong, 145 S.W.3d 131 (Tex. 2004). As a matter of law, a car owner who purchased her allegedly defective car from her parents six years after they bought it from the manufacturer, did not have a claim for violation of the DTPA against the manufacturer because it had no involvement or pecuniary interest in her purchase transaction and there was no evidence of any manufacturer warranty or representation and the manufacturer did not have a duty to disclose.

PPG Industries, Inc. v. JMB/Houston Centers Limited Partnership, 146 S.W.3d 79, 89 (Tex. 2004). The Court recognized that UCC warranty claims are only actionable under the DTPA when the defendant has direct connection with the consumer. The Court observed that the "in-connection-with" requirement announced in *Amstadt v. U.S. Brass Co.*, 919 S.W.2d 644 (Tex. 1996), extended to warranty claims as well as laundry-list and unconscionability claims. Thus, an upstream seller of goods is not a proper defendant in a DTPA breach of implied warranty claim, even though it may be a proper defendant in a UCC breach of implied warranty action. The Court also recognized the implicit overrule of *Gupta v. Ritter Homes, Inc.*, 646 S.W.2d 168, 169 (Tex. 1983) on that point.

Murphy v. Russell, 167 S.W.3d 835 (Tex. 2005). Patient sued her anesthesiologist under the DTPA for administering a general anesthetic without her consent during a biopsy. The trial court dismissed her suit because she failed to file an expert report in accordance with the MLIIA. The Court of Appeals reversed, holding that the plaintiff's claims were not "health care liability claims." The Texas Supreme Court reversed holding that the plaintiff's claim that the doctor expressly represented and warranted that he would not sedate her was an attempt to "recast" a malpractice claim as a DTPA action because it had to do with the question of whether the defendant met the standard of care for anesthesiologists.

§4.00 FALSE, MISLEADING OR DECEPTIVE ACTS OR PRACTICES

Leal v. Furniture Barn, Inc., 571 S.W.2d 864 (Tex. 1978). In May of 1975 the plaintiffs purchased furniture from the defendant on a "lay-away" basis. By mid-summer the plaintiffs fell behind on their monthly payments and sought a refund of the down payment. In October of 1975 the defendant wrote a letter to the plaintiff which misrepresented the plaintiff's rights to a refund under the agreement. The Court held that letter constituted a violation of §17.46(b)(12) by misrepresenting the rights of the seller to forfeit the monies. [Note: The actual misrepresentation was made many months after the initial agreement of the parties. Thus, a deceptive trade practice does not have to occur at the time of the sale to be actionable].

Royal Globe Ins. Co. v. Bar Consultants, Inc., 577 S.W.2d 688 (Tex. 1979). This case involved a misrepresentation of coverage by an insurance company's local recording agent. The misrepresentation was made two times. It was made at the time the policy was originally purchased and was repeated after the loss had occurred. The Court held that the defendant's misrepresentation of coverage made at the time of the initial policy and impliedly repeated each time the policy was renewed violated subdivision 12 of §17.46 and adversely affected the plaintiff by misleading it to believe it was covered by the policy for the loss when it was not. The Court however held that the misrepresentation made after the loss occurred did not provide a basis for recovery because plaintiff was not damaged by this post-loss representation. The Court reasoned that the plaintiff would have repaired the damage to its business whether it was covered or not.

Pennington v. Singleton, 606 S.W.2d 682 (Tex. 1980). The purchaser of a boat brought suit for damages for misrepresentations, specifically, that the used boat was in "excellent condition," "perfect condition," and "just like new." The Supreme Court held that these representations violated subdivision 5 of §17.46(b). The Court rejected the defendant's argument that the representations concerned the boat's "condition" and did not concern the "characteristics," "uses" and "benefits" referred to subdivision 5. In the words of the Court: "A good may lack its claimed characteristics or fail to bring about its claimed uses or benefits because it is not in good mechanical condition, or for other reasons such as its design and manufacture." *Id.* at 687. The Court further held that the representations violated the prohibition in subdivision (7) against misrepresenting the "quality" of the goods. The boat's condition was in poor quality bringing it within the ambit of this subdivision. The Court summarized its holdings as follows: "The DTPA prohibits false, general descriptions about the good as well as misrepresentations pertaining to more specific information. Sometimes language only generally related to a product or its attributes will convey definite implications." *Id.* at 687.

The Court also rejected the contention that the DTPA would be unconstitutional unless an intent requirement was read into each laundry list item in §17.46(b). The Court contrasted the Legislature's intent to provide a scienter requirement for certain of the laundry list items with the balance of the laundry list, and concluded that it would not effectuate the legislative intent nor was it necessary for constitutional purposes to impose an intent requirement where it did not exist.

Smith v. Baldwin, 611 S.W.2d 611 (Tex. 1980). The defendant contracted to build a home for the plaintiff. The home buyer contended that the builder represented that the home would comply with VA standards and that this was a violation of subdivision 7 of §17.46(b). Two of the arguments advanced by the builder were that (1) subdivision (7) applied only to existing goods or services not to representations concerning goods or services not yet in existence and (2) if it did so apply, the plaintiff must show that the defendant did not intend to provide them as represented. The Court rejected both contentions. The Court noted that the language of the DTPA did not limit its provisions to existing goods, and it imposed an intent requirement only under specified circumstances. The Court concluded that §17.46(b)(7) does not require proof of an intentional misrepresentation and that this holding applies with equal force to representations of quality of both existing *and* future goods.

Robinson v. Preston Chrysler Plymouth, Inc., 633 S.W.2d 500 (Tex. 1982). The Robinsons alleged that they purchased a car and that the defendant had failed to disclose that the vehicle had previously been damaged and repaired. There was no evidence that the defendant knew the car had been wrecked however the plaintiffs contended that failure to disclose constituted a violation of the general prohibition against false, misleading or deceptive acts or practices in DTPA §17.46(a). The Supreme Court disagreed with the plaintiffs, holding that there is no liability for failure to disclose facts unknown to the seller: "when a seller makes representations to the buyer, he is under a duty to know if the statements are true. No such duty to know the facts are true arises when the seller does not make representations, but merely fails to reveal information which he does not know." *Id.* at 502.

Hurst v. Sears, Roebuck & Co., 647 S.W.2d 249 (Tex. 1983). This case involved a dispute over installation of a cooling system in Emma Hurst's home. A jury found that before the work began the defendant represented that it would secure a city permit to install the unit and would get the work inspected by city inspectors. It was undisputed that this was not done. The court of appeals held that these facts did not establish a violation of subdivision 7 of §17.46(b). The Supreme Court, relying upon *Smith v. Baldwin, supra*, held that a violation of Subdivision (7) was established: "Sears, like Baldwin, represented that it would obtain the approval of the appropriate governmental authority. The representation contained an implicit promise to comply with government standards. The failure to fulfill the representation was a violation of Section 17.46(b)(7) and was a per se deceptive trade practice." *Id.* at 252.

Parkins v. Texas Farmers Ins. Co., 645 S.W.2d 775 (Tex. 1983). Parkins brought suit against Farmers alleging that it committed a deceptive practice by representing that it would issue a policy insuring his dwelling in the event of fire when the policy carried an exclusion limiting coverage to owner occupied premises. The court of appeals held that Parkins was not entitled to recover because he failed to prove that his loss would have been covered by a standard fire policy then available from Farmers. The Supreme Court disagreed holding that Parkins need not prove a specific policy providing coverage in order to show that he was adversely affected. Liability is keyed to the misrepresentation not to the availability of coverage under existing policies. The Court went on to hold, however, that no misrepresentation had been made.

Ogden v. Dickinson State Bank, 662 S.W.2d 330 (Tex. 1983). The bank sought to foreclose on a mechanic's and materialman's lien after the homebuilder ceased construction and the prospective homeowners ceased payment. The majority of the Court ruled that the contract lien authorized the bank to begin foreclosure proceedings and therefore its conduct did not violate §17.46(b)(12) of the Act.

Ashford Development v. U.S. Life Real Estate Service, 661 S.W.2d 933 (Tex. 1983). This case involved a dispute over construction of a loan commitment agreement wherein the developer sought a refund of the prepaid commitment fee on the grounds that the lender was unwilling to loan money on the terms originally designated. The Court agreed with the developer and ordered the prepaid commitment fee returned. The Court however rejected the developer's DTPA claim on the grounds that "an allegation of mere breach of contract, without more, does not constitute a "false, misleading or deceptive act" in violation of the DTPA. *Id.* at 935.

Jim Walter Homes, Inc. v. Valencia, 690 S.W.2d 239 (Tex. 1985). Plaintiffs entered into a contract with a builder for construction of a house. The jury found that the builder had represented that the house was constructed in a good and workmanlike manner when it was not and that the builder had knowingly made these misrepresentations. The builder asserted that there was no evidence to support the finding that it knowingly violated the DTPA because there was no evidence that the builder did not intend from the outset to build the house in compliance with the contract. The Court rejected that contention with the following language: "The act or practice giving rise to the Valencias' cause of action was not the misrepresentations made to them at the time they entered into the contract; it was the act of building the house defectively after representing that the house would be built in a good and workmanlike manner.... The record contains evidence from which the jury could have inferred that Jim Walter Homes knew the house was defective at the time of construction." *Id.* at 242.

Weitzel v. Barnes, 691 S.W.2d 598 (Tex. 1985). This case followed *Smith v. Baldwin, supra,* 611 S.W.2d 611 (Tex. 1980), in holding that "trickery" artifice" and "device" are synonymous with intent to deceive, proof of which is not required to establish a violation of DTPA §17.46(b)(7).

Kennemore v. Bennett, 755 S.W.2d 89 (Tex. 1988). The Court held that the testimony and exhibits constituted "some evidence" that the builder violated DTPA §17.46(b)(5) and (7).

Woods v. William M. Mercer, Inc., 769 S.W.2d 515 (Tex. 1988). The Court held that an insurance company's failure to inform its insured that it had withdrawn the authority of an agent to issue an endorsement constituted "more than a scintilla of evidence" to support the jury's finding of a deceptive trade practice.

Donwerth v. Preston II Chrysler-Dodge, 775 S.W.2d 634 (Tex. 1989). In this case the purchaser of a used car claimed that the seller represented the vehicle was of a particular standard, quality or grade when it was of another. *See* DTPA §17.46(b)(7). The court of appeals found no evidence to support the jury finding of misrepresentation. The Supreme Court reversed, holding that evidence that the brakes began groaning within a few months of purchase, the odometer had been rolled back approximately 20,000 miles, and the brakes were "metal to metal" five months after the purchase established that the brakes were excessively worn and defective at the time of sale. Therefore, the salesman's statement that there was nothing wrong with the brakes misrepresented the standard, quality or grade of the vehicle.

Eagle Properties, Ltd. v. Scharbauer, 807 S.W.2d 714 (Tex. 1990). The opinion in this case dealt primarily with questions of collateral estoppel and res judicata. In the course of the opinion, however, the Court reaffirmed: (1) subdivisions (5) and (7) of §17.46(b) apply to both general and specific descriptions of goods and services (2) a violation of these subdivisions, as well as subdivision (12) may be established without proving that the defendant knew of the falsity of the misrepresentation or intended to deceive; subdivision (23), however does include an element of intent and (3) misrepresentations that do not constitute common law fraud may be actionable under the DTPA.

Black v. Victoria Lloyds Ins. Co., 797 S.W.2d 20 (Tex. 1990). Daniel used his truck in his employment by Wood Brothers. Wood Brothers obtained a liability policy from Victoria Lloyds that covered only business use. Victoria Lloyds supplied Daniel with an insurance card indicating that the policy "complies with the compulsory auto laws of the State of Texas." Daniel's daughter hit Black while driving the truck for personal use. Victoria Lloyds denied coverage based on policy language excluding personal use. Black, Daniel and Daniel's daughter sued the insurance company alleging, among other things, violations of Article 21.21. The trial court granted summary judgment for the insurer. The primary question before the Supreme Court was whether the evidence raised a fact issue of misrepresentation of the insurance coverage.

A divided Court held that sufficient evidence of a misrepresentation existed to defeat summary judgment. The Court noted that the insurance card did not contain any language which limited coverage to business use or excluded personal use. The "compulsory auto laws" do not distinguish between personal and business use. Daniel stated in his affidavit that he believed from conversations with his employer that the insurance covered both business and personal use, and that he understood the state laws required both types of coverage and believed the insurance card confirmed the existence of coverage. Taken together, the affidavit and the insurance card raised a fact issue concerning a misrepresentation of coverage.

Aguilar v. Autohaus, Inc., 800 S.W.2d 853 (Tex. 1991) (*per curiam*). Aguilar purchased a new Mercedes Benz from Autohaus and had numerous problems with the vehicle, including engine hesitation. Over a three year period, Aguilar took the car to Autohaus for repairs nineteen times. At trial Aguilar testified that the Autohaus salesman stated that Mercedes Benz is the best engineered car in the world, that the car probably would not have mechanical difficulties, that it probably would need servicing only for oil changes, and that it would be far superior to what Aguilar had previously driven. Based on this testimony, the trial court found that Autohaus violated DTPA §17.46(b)(5) and (7). A divided court of appeals reversed the judgment for Aguilar and held that the salesman's statements were mere puffing because they were "too general to be an actionable misrepresentation." 794 S.W.2d 459 (Tex. App.—Dallas 1990). The Supreme Court denied the Aguilar's application for writ of error noting that in doing so it was not approving or disapproving the court of appeals analysis of the puffing issue. 800 S.W.2d 853 at 854.

First Title Co. of Waco v. Garrett, 860 S.W.2d 74 (Tex. 1993). The plaintiffs contracted to purchase land for use as an automobile salvage yard. Although the land was encumbered with a deed restriction prohibiting such use, the title commitment stated:

THE POLICY WILL BE SUBJECT TO ... THE FOLLOWING MATTERS WHICH WILL BE ADDITIONAL EXCEPTIONS FROM THE COVERAGE OF THE POLICY:

THE FOLLOWING RESTRICTIVE COVENANTS OF RECORD ITEMIZED BELOW ... (INSERT SPECIFIC RECORDING DATA OR STATE "NONE OF RECORD"): NONE OF RECORD.

The Court held that a title company is responsible for an affirmative misrepresentation and concluded that the evidence supported the jury's finding that the title companies had misrepresented the state of the title. The majority rejected the dissent's argument that there was no affirmative misrepresentation of the title, but simply a promise to pay if there was a restrictive covenant on the property. *Compare, Chicago Title Insurance Company v. McDaniel*, 875 S.W.2d 310 (Tex. 1994) (issuance of policy without affirmative misrepresentations not DTPA violation).

Doe v. Boys Clubs of Greater Dallas, Inc., 907 S.W. 2d 472 (Tex. 1995). Three boys were sexually molested by Mullens who was a volunteer at the Boys Club. Mullens' volunteer service arose out of a DWI conviction which required him to do community service. The Boys Club had advertised that it provided a "wholesome environment." When one of the boys' grandparents contacted the club, she was assured the club thoroughly investigated its volunteers. When Mullens offered to take the boys on a private camping trip (not sponsored by the Boys Club), a grandparent asked the education director what he knew about Mullens. He replied that Mullens "seemed to be OK" but added that the club could not decide for the grandparent whether to let the boys go on the camping trip. The plaintiffs alleged "laundry list" misrepresentations and non-disclosure.

With regard to the misrepresentations, the Court held that the representation of a "wholesome environment" was not actionable as a matter of law because it constituted an opinion. The representation that Mullens "seemed to be OK" was determined by the Court to be true and, in any event, was not actionable because it did not induce the plaintiffs into doing business with the club and, thus, was not a producing cause of damages. Finally, the Court held that statement that the club "thoroughly checked out its volunteers" was not a producing cause of damages since the relationship between Mullens and the boys developed outside of the Boys Club; the representation did not cause the injury, but merely furnished "an attenuated condition that made the injury possible."

With regard to the non-disclosure claim the Court held that no violation of DTPA §17.46(b)(23) had been shown since the club did not know of Mullen's propensity to molest and, accordingly, had no duty to disclose that fact. Further, the club's non-disclosure of what it did know was not done for the purpose of inducing the plaintiffs into a transaction as required by that subdivision.

The Court affirmed a summary judgment for the defendant.

Transport Inc. v. Faircloth, 898 S.W.2d 269 (Tex. 1995). The plaintiff, the surviving minor daughter of a couple killed in a motor vehicle accident, received a quick settlement of all claims from the insurance company representing the driver of the other vehicle. Upon reaching her majority, the plaintiff brought suit against the insurance company, the adjustor, and her guardian under Article 21.21 for violations of §17.46 (23). Focusing on the language in subdivision (23) requiring that the non-disclosure concern "goods or services" and induce the "consumer" into the transaction, the Court held that no violation had been shown. The plaintiff did not qualify as a "consumer" and did not seek "services" defined as "work, labor or service *purchased or leased for use*." While the plaintiff had standing under Article 21.21 to sue for violations of DPTA §17.46, the subdivision in question imposed requirements the plaintiff could not meet.

Crawford v. Ace Sign, Inc., 917 S.W. 2d 12, (Tex. 1996). A "yellow page" representative told the plaintiff that his advertisement would be published if he paid the entire contract price up-front. He did pay but the ad was not published. The Court rejected the plaintiff's "laundry list" allegations holding that the statement was only a representation that the defendant would perform its contract. The failure to perform was a "mere breach of contract" and not actionable under the DTPA.

St. Paul Surplus Lines v. Dal-Worth Tank Co., 974 S.W.2d 51 (Tex. 1998). In this case the plaintiff alleged that its insurer committed deceptive trade practices in the handling of a third party claim resulting in the plaintiff suffering an adverse judgment and ultimate bankruptcy. The jury found that the insurer knowingly engaged in deceptive trade practices. On appeal, the insurer contended that there was no evidence to support this finding. The Texas Supreme Court agreed. Looking to the definition of "knowingly" in DTPA §17.45(9) the Court explained that:

> "[A]ctual awareness" does not mean merely that a person knows what he is doing; rather, it means that a person knows that what he is doing is false, deceptive or unfair. In other words, a person must think to himself at some point, 'Yes, I know this is false, deceptive or unfair to him, but I'm going to do it anyway.'" *Id.* at 382.

The Court confirmed that actual awareness is more than conscious indifference, holding that while the insurer did not do all that it should have done to determine whether the plaintiff had been sued, there was no evidence that the insurer knew that its actions were deceptive or unfair or that it was harming the plaintiff.

Brown v. Bank of Galveston, N.A., 963 S.W.2d 511 (Tex. 1998). A bank foreclosed on the plaintiff's home under a note given to finance construction. The plaintiff contended on appeal that the bank had misrepresented its right to demand full payment when the house was not complete. Following *Ogden v. Dickenson State Bank,* 662 S.W.2d 330 (Tex. 1983), the Court held that the bank did not misrepresent the plaintiff's rights in violation of DTPA §17.46(b) (12) because it had the right to demand full payment under the lien.

Douglas v. Delp, 987 S.W.2d 879 (Tex. 1999). Mr. and Mrs. Delp became involved in litigation with their business partners over control of several related corporations. The Delps were represented in that litigation by the defendant and his law firm. During a temporary injunction hearing, the parties to the underlying lawsuit negotiated a settlement agreement which the Delps signed on the advice of the defendant. The Delps became unhappy with the consequences of that settlement and brought suit against their lawyer alleging that the defendant misrepresented the characteristics and benefits of the agreement, as well as the Delps' their rights, remedies, and obligations under the agreement. As a result of a bankruptcy filed by Mr. Delp, only Mrs. Delp was able to pursue the claim. Mrs. Delp testified that while she could not remember specific statements the defendant made, she did recall that the defendant advised her to sign the settlement agreement. The court of appeals held that it could be inferred from the testimony that the defendant had represented that the agreement protected the Delps' interests. The Texas Supreme Court held that even assuming that such a representation could be inferred, such a statement is "too vague under the facts of this case" to support liability under the laundry list. *Id.* at 886. The Court reasoned that without evidence about the Delps "interests" which were to be protected by the agreement, the jury would have no standard by which to measure the truthfulness of the representation. The Court concluded that the representation constituted at most a "nonactionable opinion." *Id.*

DeWitt County Electric Cooperative, Inc. v. Parks et al., 1 S.W.3d 96 (Tex. 1999). The plaintiff homeowners entered into a service contract with the defendant electric cooperative for electrical service. At the same time the plaintiffs granted the defendant an easement which gave the defendant the right to clear the easement of obstructions. The defendant's policy was to clear the right of way, thus giving its employees the ability to remove all trees within the easement. When the defendant's employees cut down two of the plaintiff's trees and trimmed back another, the plaintiffs brought suit under the DTPA. The plaintiffs alleged that the easement did not give the defendant the right to cut the trees, thus constituting a representation that no such right existed; the plaintiffs alleged further that the defendant's action in cutting the trees constituted an actionable representation that the defendant had rights under the agreement that it did not have. *See* DTPA §17.46(b)(12). The Court rejected this argument, holding that the easement agreement gave the defendant the unambiguous right to cut the trees and, accordingly, there was no misrepresentation. The plaintiffs also contended that the defendants admitted failure to disclose the existence of its "clear the right of way" policy was actionable under DTPA §17.46(b)(23). The Court rejected that argument as well holding that it is not a DTPA violation for a party to fail to disclose that it intends to exercise its rights that an agreement expressly confers.

Crown Life Ins. Co. v. Casteel, 22 S.W.3d 378 (Tex. 2000). Casteel sold "vanishing premium" policies as an agent of Crown. When the premiums did not vanish, Casteel's clients brought suit against Casteel and Crown. Casteel, in turn, brought suit against Crown under Article 21.21 and the DTPA, alleging that he sold the policies in reliance upon false information provided by Crown. The jury found that Crown had knowingly engaged in deceptive and unfair trade practices that were producing causes of damages to Casteel. On appeal Crown challenged Casteel's right to recover under Article 21.21 for violations of the DTPA laundry list.

The Court rejected Crown's argument that because Casteel was not a consumer he could not recover for violations of the laundry list in DTPA §17.46(b). The Court acknowledged established law that Article 21.21 incorporated the laundry list but did not incorporate the consumer standing requirement. Further, the Court

§4.00   DTPA Forms and Practice Guide Desk Book

noted that some but not all of the laundry list items expressly referred to consumers. The Court had previously held that one such laundry list item, subsection 23, expressly referred to "consumers" and was only actionable by a party who qualified as such. *See Transport Inc. v. Faircloth,* 898 S.W.2d 269 (Tex. 1995).

In this case, the Court extended that same limitation to those laundry list items referencing "goods" and "services." The Court held that the only laundry list item invoked by Casteel upon which he could bring suit was DTPA §17.46(b)(12) which makes no reference to "consumer," "goods," or "service." Since the broad form jury charge contained laundry list items (other than subsection (b)(12)) as a ground for liability, the Court set aside the jury's verdict for Casteel.

Ken Petroleum Corp. v. Questor Drilling Corp., 24 S.W.3d 344 (Tex. 2000). The parties in this case each agreed to indemnify the other from claims made by their employees. The plaintiff brought suit to enforce the indemnity provision and under DTPA §17.46 (b) (12). The Court of Appeals held that the indemnity provision was void but that Ken Petroleum was entitled to proceed under the DTPA. The court rejected the argument that the "mere breach of contract" rule precluded a (b) (12) claim because the contractual provision in question was void.

The Court reversed holding that the indemnity provision was not void. The Court further opined that while the "mere breach of contract" rule would not automatically foreclose a DTPA action where all or part of the contract is void by operation of law, the fact that a portion of the contract is void does not, standing alone, constitute a violation of (b) (12). That DTPA provision requires a representation, for example, that the contract confers or involves rights that are prohibited by law. The contractual indemnity provision itself did not constitute such a representation but was only an agreement to indemnify.

Helena Chemical Co. v. Wilkins, 47 S.W.3d 486 (Tex. 2001). Farmers brought suit against a seed company contending that the defendant had misrepresented the tolerance and yield of the seed the farmers purchased. The jury found that the defendant had violated the DTPA and awarded damages for lost profits. The defendant contended on appeal that its statements were not actionable because they were puffing, and were, therefore, insufficient to support a jury verdict. The evidence included statements in the defendant's brochures that the seed was "one of the most durable, top yielding hybrids" with "an outstanding disease tolerance package," "excellent" yield potential, "excellent weatherability" and was a "good dry land variety and that it would hold up well under the dry land conditions." The court held that these statements (and others) constituted specific representations which amounted to more than mere puffing and supported jury findings of violations of DTPA §§17.46(b) (5) and (7).

Bradford v. Vento, 48 S.W.3d 749 (Tex. 2001). This case involved the purchase of a business located in a mall. The plaintiff buyer alleged that the seller and the mall engaged in deceptive trade practices. The seller had operated under a series of short term leases with the mall. There was evidence that after the buyer purchased the business in September, the mall representative represented that he would "take care of" the plaintiff in January, which the plaintiff understood to mean that they would work out a new lease at that time. The lease was not renewed in January and the plaintiff was forced to leave. The plaintiff contended on appeal that the defendant's representation violated DTPA §17.46(b) (5) and (12). The Court rejected the argument holding that the representative's statement "is simply too vague to provide a standard for the jury . . . to measure the accuracy of the representation; it is therefore nonactionable."

The plaintiff argued further that the defendant mall violated DTPA §17.46(b) (23) when it failed to disclose to the plaintiff that the lease was not assignable from the seller and that the buyer would be required to apply for a new lease. The court held, however, that subdivision (23) requires any failure to disclose to have been intended by the seller to induce the buyer into a transaction. Since there was no transaction into which the mall intended to induce the plaintiff there could be no violation even if there was the non-disclosure as alleged.

Tony Gullo Motors I, L.P. v. Chapa, 212 S.W.3d 299 (Tex. 2006). The Court affirmed a DTPA verdict against a car dealer for delivering a lesser model after promising a better model, over objection that the plaintiff's claims amounted to no more than "mere breach of contract." The court found that the evidence supported DTPA liability because of acts taken by the dealer separate and apart from merely failing to deliver a certain model of car as promised.

§5.00   BREACH OF WARRANTY

La Sara Grain v. First Nat'l Bank of Mercedes, 673 S.W.2d 558 (Tex. 1984). The customer of a bank contended that, as part of the depository contract, the bank impliedly warranted that it would only pay checks which complied with the dual-signature requirement adopted by the depositor. The Court wrote that if any such warranty existed its origin was independent of the DTPA: "The DTPA does not define the term "warranty." Furthermore, the Act does not create any warranty; therefore any warranty must be established independently of the Act." *Id.* at 565. The Court went on the hold that under the U.C.C., the bank's implied promise that it will not pay checks on an unauthorized signature was not a warranty but only an implied term of the contract. The bank's failure to conform with its implied promise was a "mere breach of contract" which did not violate the DTPA.

Melody Home Mfg. Co. v. Barnes, 741 S.W.2d 349 (Tex. 1987). This case involved a mobile home which was poorly built. The buyers requested the manufacturer to make the necessary repairs. The repair work was done poorly, as well, and resulted in even more damage to the home. The Court held that, as a matter of law, in consumer transactions involving the repair or modification of existing goods impliedly warranted that his services would be performed in a good and workmanlike manner. The Court defined good and workmanlike as:

> "that quality of work performed by one who has the knowledge, training, or experience necessary for the successful practice of a trade or occupation and performed in a manner generally considered proficient by those capable of judging such work."

The court further held that this implied warranty was actionable under DTPA §17.50 (a)(2) and could not be waived.

Parkway Co. v. Woodruff, 901 S.W.2d 434 (Tex. 1995). Parkway developed the Sugar Creek subdivision, a "master-planned" community. A builder bought a lot in section 24 and constructed a home on it. The plaintiffs were the third owners of the home. Later, in the course of developing another section of the subdivision, Parkway altered the drainage patterns of the land causing the plaintiffs' lot to flood. The jury found that Parkway breached an implied warranty.

The court of appeals had recognized the existence of an implied warranty to perform future development services in a good and workmanlike manner. The Texas Supreme Court reversed the DTPA portion of the judgment. Preliminarily, the Court affirmed that the DTPA "prohibits the breach of an express or implied warranty, but it does not create warranties" and noted further that "the *Melody Home* implied warranty extends only to services provided to remedy defects existing at the time of the relevant consumer transaction." The Court framed the issue as "whether consumers ...injured by substandard services can recover under an implied warranty theory when they neither sought nor acquired the services about which they complain." Focusing on the sale of the lot by Parkway, the Court held that the fact that the subdivision was "masterplanned" did not imply future development services. The Court concluded: "Because no services were included in the transaction, no service-related warranty was breached. ... [N]o implied warranty to perform future development services should be imposed in this case."

§5.00 DTPA Forms and Practice Guide Desk Book

Rocky Mountain Helicopters, Inc. v. Lubbock County Hosp. Dist., 987 S.W.2d 50 (Tex. 1998). The hospital district contracted with the defendant requiring the defendant to furnish operational and maintenance services for CareLink, the hospital's emergency patient transfer program. After refueling a CareLink helicopter, the defendant's employee failed to turn off the refueler permitting a significant quantity of fuel to spill on the hospital district's property. The district brought suit to recover the cost of the cleanup. The jury found that the district had violated the DTPA by, among other things, failing to perform its services in a good and workmanlike manner. A question presented on appeal was whether the law recognized an implied warranty to perform the services in question in a good and workmanlike manner. The Court held that no such warranty exists. Citing, *Melody Home Mfg. Co. v. Barnes, supra*, the Court noted that it had recognized an implied warranty for services "only when the services relate to the repair or modification of existing tangible goods or property". *Id.* at 52. Finding no compelling need to create a warranty governing the facts of this case, the Court held that "Texas law does not recognize an implied warranty that services incidental to helicopter maintenance will be performed in a good and workmanlike manner." *Id.*

Centex Homes v. Buecher, 95 S.W. 3d 266 (Tex. 2002). The question in this case was whether a homebuilder may properly disclaim the implied warranties of good and workmanlike construction and habitability that accompany the sale of a new home. The purchase agreement purported to limit the home buyers to a one-year limited express warranty. The Court held that different standards applied to each warranty. With regard to the implied warranty of good and workmanlike construction, the Court held that it may be disclaimed by agreement of the parties when "their agreement provides for the manner, performance or quality of the desired construction." The implied warranty of habitability, however, "may not be disclaimed generally." The Court noted that the warranty of habitability applies only to defects that render the property unsuitable for its intended use as a home and does not apply to defects known by or expressly disclosed to the buyer.

PPG Industries v. JMB/Houston Centers, 146 S.W.3d 79 (Tex. 2004). In this case, PPG manufactured and installed defective windows in a forty-six story building. All of the parties agreed that PPG issued a five-year warranty against defects in the windows. One of the issues on appeal was whether PPG had also extended a twenty-year warranty by virtue of an advertisement in a trade publication which represented that the PPG windows in question were warranted for twenty years against window seal failure. The lower courts held that this established a warranty as a matter of law and upheld a jury finding that such warranty had been breached.

On appeal, the Court held that the absence of any mention of the twenty-year warranty in the contract documents did not negate its existence as a matter of law because the UCC provides "express warranties may arise other than those stated in a contract." *Id.* at 99. By the same token, the warranty was not established as a matter of law because a fact issue existed on the question of whether the parties intended the warranty to be a basis of the bargain. On this issue, the Court noted that while no "particular" reliance on the advertisement was required, "something rather like it" was. *Id.* The building owner's architect's testimony that he relied on the advertisement was not enough to conclusively establish that the warranty was part of the basis of the bargain. The Court also held that there was a fact issue as to whether PPG had effectively withdrawn the warranty.

The Court's treatment of the limitations issues surrounding the warranties is summarized under Defenses/Notice *infra, §12.00*.

Man Engines & Components, Inc. v. Shows, 434 S.W.3d 132 (Tex. 2014). The UCC implied warranty of merchantability, as well as disclaimer thereof, passes with goods to subsequent purchasers: Doug Shows purchased a used yacht from a dealer in 2002. The yacht, which had been traded in by the original purchaser, was equipped with engines manufactured by Man Engines. One of the engines failed first in 2004 and then again in 2006. Shows sued Man Engines for breach of the implied warranty of merchantability. Although the yacht dealer sold it "as is," Man Engines failed to raise this defensive issue effectively at trial. On appeal, Man Engines claimed that the implied warranty of merchantability did not extend to subsequent purchasers of the product. HELD: The implied warranty of merchantability survives a re-sale of goods and extends to subsequent purchasers. However, it can be effectively disclaimed at the time of the original sale and such disclaimers will be effective against subsequent purchasers.

§6.00   UNCONSCIONABILITY

Hurst v. Sears, Roebuck & Co., 647 S.W.2d 24 (Tex. 1983). A homeowner alleged that Sears had represented that the installer of an air conditioning system would secure an installation permit and get the work inspected by city inspectors. The jury found that the failure of the installer to secure a permit and to have the inspection completed constituted an "unconscionable action or course of action." The installer had not obtained a permit because it was not properly licensed by the city; the city issued permits only to licensed installers. The court of appeals held that since it was not possible for the installer to obtain a permit its action could not be "unconscionable." The Supreme Court disagreed for two reasons. First, the Court noted that it was possible to obtain an inspection and a permit had Sears utilized a licensed installer. Second, impossibility of performance did not as a matter of law preclude unconscionable conduct. The Court noted that a person's failure to do the impossible could be unconscionable if he promised to perform services knowing they were impossible to perform.

Chastain v. Koonce, 700 S.W.2d 579 (Tex. 1985). The plaintiffs were purchasers of several residential lots in a subdivision. Prior to the purchase the developers represented that certain other lots in the subdivision would be likewise restricted for residential use only. After the plaintiffs purchased their property, the developers permitted a commercial use on one of the lots that was supposed to be restricted. When one of the plaintiffs complained, the developers threatened to put an even less desirable use near the plaintiffs' homes and ultimately threatened to "knock off" the head of one of the plaintiffs. Sensing they had reached an impasse, the plaintiffs filed suit and secured a jury finding that the defendants had engaged in unconscionable actions. At issue before the Supreme Court was whether there was evidence to support the jury finding of unconscionability. Focusing on part (b) of §17.45(5), which defines an unconscionable action as one which results in a gross disparity between the value received and the consideration paid, the Court held that the plaintiffs had failed to show any disparity between the value of the property at the time of purchase and the consideration paid. Accordingly, the Court held that plaintiffs had failed to meet the requirements of part (b). In reference to part (a) of §17.45(5), which defines an unconscionable action to be one which takes advantage of the lack of knowledge, ability or capacity of a person to a grossly unfair degree, the Court dealt first with the intent of the Legislature in requiring that the action be "grossly unfair." The Court rejected the analogy to gross negligence since this approach would focus attention on the mental state of the defendant, which was inconsistent with the legislative history of this provision and the structure of the statute as a whole. The Court concluded that the term "gross" should be given its ordinary meaning of "glaringly noticeable, flagrant, complete and unmitigated.... slight disparity between the consideration paid and the value received is not unconscionable; a glaring, flagrant disparity is." *Id.* at 583. The Court found no evidence to meet this standard. The Court rejected the threat made by the defendant because this conversation occurred one year after the alleged misrepresentations and did not reflect on the fairness of the original transaction between the purchasers and the defendants.

Brown v. Galleria Area Ford, Inc., 752 S.W.2d 114 (Tex. 1988). The Brown's took their damaged truck to LaMarque Ford of Texas for repair. While the vehicle was in the repair shop, three individuals contracted to purchase the dealership. The purchasers assumed full managerial authority for the day-to-day operations, but they remitted receipts from repair work already in progress to LaMarque. Shortly thereafter they formed a corporation, Galleria Ford, and conducted all operations under that name. Upon return of their vehicle the Browns found the repairs unsatisfactory and brought suit against Galleria under the DTPA for the faulty repairs. The Browns prevailed in the trial court. On appeal, the court of appeals reversed on the basis of no evidence that Galleria had engaged in any misconduct that would subject it to liability under the DTPA. The Supreme Court reversed and held that evidence presented at trial supported the jury findings that Galleria had engaged in an unconscionable act or course of action. The Court examined the evidence in relation to both definitions of unconscionability in the DTPA. Unrebutted evidence established that the truck was too dangerous to drive and that additional damage occurred during the repair work. The Court held such evidence established a gross disparity between the value received and the consideration paid, which violated the DTPA under the second half of the statutory definition. The Court also held that by representing itself to the parties as the company in charge of the dealership, Galleria took advantage of the Brown's lack of knowledge of the true responsibility of the parties involved in the dealership to a grossly unfair degree. As a result, the Court held that Galleria also violated the DTPA under the first half of the statutory definition. Finally, the Court rejected Galleria's contention that an agreement between LaMarque and itself that LaMarque would be responsible for deceptive trade practices committed in Galleria's name relieved Galleria of liability. The dissent argued that the record showed no evidence that any violation of the DTPA by Galleria was a producing cause of damages to the plaintiffs. The dissenters found no nexus between the confusion as to control of the dealership and the poor repair work as well as no evidence that Galleria performed the repairs.

Kennemore v. Bennett, 755 S.W.2d 89 (Tex. 1988). Bennett agreed to build the Kennemores a home. The Kennemores moved in upon completion, but refused to pay certain amounts that Bennett submitted on his bill because of alleged defects and plan deviations. Bennett instituted an action on the contract and for foreclosure. The Kennemores counterclaimed alleging that Bennett did not build the home in a good and workmanlike manner and that Bennett engaged in deceptive trade practices and unconscionable conduct. The Supreme Court held that Bennett's false assurances that he would personally supervise the work coupled with his continued failure to do so or to correct the defects resulting from his subcontractor's work constituted "some evidence that Bennett took advantage of the Kennemore's lack of knowledge of the construction business and lack of ability to correct the problems themselves." The Court held that this evidence would support a finding of unconscionability as defined in §17.45(5)(a). A consumer establishes a violation by producing evidence of unconscionability under either definition in §17.45(5).

Kinerd v. Colonial Leasing Co., 800 S.W.2d 187 (Tex. 1990). Radiator Aid sold radiator repair equipment to Colonial for $10,000. Colonial entered into a "lease agreement" with Kinerd. The jury was instructed that the lease was actually a sale by Colonial to Kinerd. The jury found that Colonial sold the equipment to Kinerd for $10,000 while the actual value of the goods was $2,000. The Court held that the fact that Colonial paid $10,000 for the equipment did not diminish the jury's finding that Colonial, in turn, overcharged Kinerd. The Court concluded that there was "some evidence" to support the jury's findings of unconscionability.

Parkway Co. v. Woodruff, 901 S.W.2d 434 (Tex. 1995). Parkway developed the Sugar Creek subdivision, a "master-planned" community. A builder bought a lot in section 24 and constructed a home on it. The plaintiffs were the third owners of the home. Later, in the course of developing another section of the subdivision, Parkway altered the drainage patterns of the land causing the plaintiffs' lot to flood. The jury found that Parkway engaged in an unconscionable practice.

The Court rejected the contention that Parkway's control over drainage on adjacent lots deprived the Woodruffs of the ability to protect their own interests. The Court held that "unconscionability requires that the seller take advantage of special skills and training *at the time of the sale*." (Emphasis added). The Court concluded that there was no evidence of this. The Court also rejected the finding of gross disparity between the value of the home and the amount paid reasoning that the amount of the disparity must be measured from the time of sale and cannot result from later events.

Abbott Laboratories, Inc. v. Segura, 907 S.W.2d 503 (Tex. 1995). The bar to indirect purchaser recovery in antitrust suits also bars indirect purchasers from recovering under the DTPA for antitrust violations couched as unconscionable conduct. A concurring justice writes that the price fixing alleged was not unconscionable under the DTPA.

State Farm Lloyds v. Nicolau, 951 S.W.2d 444 (Tex. 1997). The plaintiffs' home was insured by State Farm. The home suffered foundation damage that the plaintiffs believed to result from a plumbing leak, damage which is covered under the policy. The plaintiffs filed a claim under the policy for damage to their home. State Farm reimbursed the plaintiffs for the cost of locating and repairing the leak and for engineering and plumbing tests but denied the claim for foundation damage, contending that the foundation damage was unrelated to the leak. The plaintiffs brought suit against State Farm and recovered a judgment based in part on a jury finding of unconscionability. On appeal, State Farm contended that there was no evidence to support the jury finding.

The Court considered the definition of unconscionability available to consumers prior to the 1995 amendments in light of its prior holding that the unfairness or disparity must be gross, that is, "glaringly noticeable, flagrant, complete and unmitigated." *Id.* at 451. The Court was unpersuaded by the plaintiffs' argument that State Farm acted unconscionably by failing to conduct a more thorough investigation and failing to advise the plaintiffs about the additional living expense provision of the policy. Relying on the fact that the insurer had paid for the plumbing repairs and noting the plaintiffs' awareness of the policy provisions concerning foundation settlement, the Court held that there is no evidence that State Farm took advantage of the plaintiffs to a grossly unfair degree or that there was a gross disparity between what the plaintiffs paid and what they received under the policy.

Latham v. Castillo, 972 S.W.2d 66 (Tex. 1998). The Castillo's twin daughters were born prematurely and underwent surgery at the hospital. One twin died within a week and the other died approximately two years later. After the death of the first child, the Castillos brought suit against the hospital. Their lawyer settled the case for $70,000. After the death of the second child, the Castillos hired the defendant Latham to represent them in a legal malpractice suit against their first lawyer and a medical malpractice suit against the hospital for the death of their second twin child. Latham settled the legal malpractice case for $400,0000; the statute of limitations expired without the medical malpractice suit being filed. The Castillos then sued Latham alleging, among other things, that he had engaged in unconscionable conduct by representing that he had filed the medical malpractice lawsuit when he had not. The court of appeals reversed a directed verdict for Latham and remanded the case to the trial court. Applying the pre-1995 amendment DTPA, the Court affirmed the remand, holding that there was some evidence that Latham had taken advantage of the Castillos to a grossly unfair degree as described in DTPA §17.45 (A). The Court rejected the argument that the Castillos were required to prove that they would have prevailed in the medical malpractice case had it been filed as represented. The Court held that this "suit within a suit" requirement, applicable to negligence cases, did not apply to the DTPA; to do so would recast the Castillo's claim as a legal malpractice claim and subvert the purpose of the DTPA to deter deceptive business practices.

Insurance Co. of N. Am. v. Morris, 981 S.W.2d 667 (Tex. 1998). The plaintiffs were purchasers of oil and gas limited partnership interests. The purchase price included a down payment and a promissory note. The broker-dealers solicited the investments and assigned the notes to a bank to obtain production funds; INA issued bonds guaranteeing the notes. Prior to issuing the bonds, INA reviewed the documents and screened the investments. As part of the transaction, the plaintiffs agreed to indemnify INA in the event of default. The value of the investments were misrepresented by the broker-dealers and the investors ultimately defaulted on the notes. INA honored the bonds, paid the notes, and brought suit to obtain indemnification from the plaintiff-investors. The plaintiffs counterclaimed, alleging that INA had engaged in unconscionable conduct. The Court held that there was no evidence to sustain the allegation reasoning, in part, that INA could not be held responsible for the misrepresentations of the broker-dealers concerning the investment because INA gave them authority only in connection with the sale of the surety bonds.

The Court further indicated that while the use of unlicensed agents to sell the surety bonds violated the Insurance Code, that such violation was not a producing cause of damages to the plaintiffs.

Bradford v. Vento, 48 S.W.3d 749 (Tex. 2001). This case involved the purchase of a business located in a mall. The plaintiff buyer alleged that the seller and the mall engaged in unconscionable conduct The seller had operated under a series of short term leases with the mall. The plaintiff claimed to have bought out his partner in September, thus becoming the sole owner of the store. The defendant seller disputed that his interest had been bought out. There was evidence that after the alleged sale, the mall representative represented that he would "take care of" the plaintiff in January, which the plaintiff understood to mean that they would work out a lease at that time. A short time later the buyer and seller engaged in a heated discussion over ownership which resulted in the police being called to the store. The police asked the mall representative who owned the store, and there was evidence that the mall representative sided with the seller, resulting in the buyer being forced to leave the premises. Thereafter the mall signed a new lease with the seller and the buyer was forced to obtain a temporary injunction to regain control of the store. When the lease expired in January, the mall did not continue to lease to the plaintiff. The court held that there was no evidence to support the jury finding of unconscionable conduct reasoning that the evidence did not show that the mall took advantage of the plaintiff's lack of knowledge to a grossly unfair degree. The court noted that to be unconscionable the unfairness must be "glaringly noticeable, flagrant, complete and unmitigated."

§7.00   ARTICLE 21.21/CHAPTER 541

Royal Globe Ins. Co. v. Bar Consultants, Inc., 577 S.W.2d 688 (Tex. 1979). This case involved the purchase of an insurance policy by Bar Consultants, Inc., the operators of a bar. Prior to the purchase of the policy the defendant's local recording agent represented that the policy would cover loss caused by vandalism. The bar was vandalized and the day following the incident the agent advised the owner that the loss was covered and to have the work done. The insurance company refused to pay the claim. The bar owner brought suit under the DTPA and Article 21.21 alleging that the defendant had misrepresented the terms of the policy. The Supreme Court first reviewed the interplay between §16 of Article 21.21 and §17.46 of the DTPA. The Court next addressed the insurance company's contention that it could not be held liable for the misrepresentations of its agent absent actual authority. The Court rejected this contention holding: "an insurance company that authorizes an agent to sell its policies may not escape liability for the misrepresentations made by that agent which violate Article 21.21 and §17.46 merely by establishing that the agent had no actual authority to make any such misrepresentation." *Id.* at 693. The Court concluded that as a local recording agent for the insurance company, the agent had statutory authority under Article 21.02 and Article 21.14(2) to sell insurance policies and by necessary implication to represent the coverage afforded by such policies to the consumer. The insurance company was accountable for any misrepresentations made by the agent.

Hi-Line Elec. Co. v. Travelers Ins. Companies, 593 S.W.2d 953 (Tex. 1980) (*per curiam*). In this *per curiam* opinion the Court made clear that its action in refusing the application for writ of error n.r.e. should not be interpreted as approving the conclusion of the court of appeals that a private action under Article 21.21 must be based on the DTPA or that a person bringing suit pursuant to §16 must qualify as a consumer as defined in the DTPA.

Ceshker v. Bankers Comm'l Life Co., 568 S.W.2d 128 (Tex. 1978) (*per curiam*). This is another *per curiam* opinion in which the Supreme Court disapproved of a lower court holding which would limit persons entitled to bring suit under Article 21.21 to one engaged in the business of insurance.

Mayo v. John Hancock Mut. Life Ins. Co., 711 S.W.2d 5 (Tex. 1986). Steve Mayo was covered by a group insurance policy issued by the defendant. The defendant wrongfully denied Mayo's claim for maternity benefits. In Mayo's suit for breach of contract and violations of Article 21.21 and the DTPA, the trial court, over Mayo's objection, severed the breach of contract action and the action pursuant to Article 3.62 from the Article 21.21 and DTPA causes of action. After the Mayos recovered on their breach of contract and Article 3.62 causes of action the defendant filed a motion for summary judgment alleging that the remaining claims were barred because of the recovery of actual damages in the breach of contract and Article 3.62 claims. The Supreme Court reversed holding that the recovery of actual damages equal to the amount of medical expenses payable under the policy plus a 12% penalty for failure to timely pay the benefits did not bar a treble damage action under Article 21.21 §16 or the DTPA. The Court noted that the contractual cause of action and action for 12% penalty pursuant to Article 3.62 were based on different grounds than the action for violation of Article 21.21 and the DTPA. Therefore, recovery under both causes of action would not constitute recovery for the same act or practice as proscribed by §17.43 of the DTPA. The Court did note that in the event the Mayos prevailed at the trial of their claims, their judgment would be offset by the amount of actual damages recovered in the prior trial.

Aetna Cas. & Sur. Co. v. Marshall, 724 S.W.2d 770 (Tex. 1987). Plaintiff, Marshall, filed a workers compensation claim in 1976 and ultimately recovered a settlement including, among other things, a provision for payment by Aetna of future medical costs. This settlement agreement was incorporated into a judgment signed in 1978. After the settlement, the plaintiff had difficulties in obtaining payment for his medical expenses. Marshall brought suit pursuant to Article 21.21 on the basis that the defendant had represented that the agreed judgment contained medical benefits which it did not and that such misrepresentation was a producing cause of damages. The majority of the Supreme Court rejected the insurance company's argument that Marshall could not recover under Article 21.21 because he was not a consumer of goods or services and because a court judgment is not an insurance policy. In the words of the Court: "Article 21.21 does not incorporate the entire [DTPA] which would require that Marshall was a consumer of goods or services. Instead, Article 21.21 provides a cause of action to a person who has been injured by an insurance carrier who engages in an act proscribed by Section 17.46. Aetna's contention that a judgment is not an insurance policy is likewise irrelevant. The question is simply whether Aetna engaged in conduct prohibited by Section 17.46." *Id.* at 772.

Chitsey v. National Lloyds Insurance Co., 738 S.W.2d 641 (Tex. 1987). This suit involved a claim that the insured, Chitsey, had filed under his fire insurance policy. Chitsey alleged that the insurance company had failed to properly evaluate and investigate his claim and had therefore violated Article 21.21 and breached the insurance company's duty of good faith and fair dealing. With respect to the Insurance Code claim, Chitsey alleged that the jury's finding that the insurance company had failed to use due diligence in determining the amount of the plaintiff's loss established that the insurance company violated a State Board of Insurance order. The board order prohibits practices that constitute unfair methods of competition or unfair or deceptive acts or practices in the insurance business, as determined by law. The Court rejected Chitsey's claim, holding that the phrase *determined by law* in the board order refers to an agency or a legislative determination and that a jury finding, alone, does not constitute such a determination. The Court also held that Chitsey failed to prove that the insurance company had committed unfair practices with such frequency as to indicate a general business practice Ca requirement of another board order [28 TEX. ADMIN. CODE §21.203] invoked by Chitsey. [The Board Order has since been amended to delete this requirement]. The Court, however, did hold that based upon an affirmative jury finding, Chitsey could recover for the insurance company's breach of its common law duty of good faith and fair dealing in handling the claim. *See Arnold v. National County Mut. Fire Ins. Co.*, 725 S.W.2d 165 (Tex. 1987).

Vail v. Texas Farm Bureau Mutual Insurance Co., 754 S.W.2d 129 (Tex. 1988). The Vails brought suit under the DTPA alleging that Texas Farm Bureau had violated the Insurance Code by unfairly denying the Vails' claim under their fire insurance policy. The trial court rendered judgment for the Vails based upon jury findings that Texas Farm Bureau had failed to exercise good faith in processing the claim. The court of appeals affirmed in part and reversed in part. The Supreme Court, in a split decision, reversed and rendered judgment for the Vails.

At the outset the Court ruled that the DTPA incorporates the provisions of the Insurance Code in its entirety. Accordingly, any relief available pursuant to Insurance Code is available through the DTPA. Both provisions permit recovery for unfair claims settlement practices.

The Court also addressed the following alternative violations argued by the Vails in support of the judgment:

(1) Violation of §4(a) of Board Order 18663 [28 TEX. ADMIN. CODE §21.3]: This section prohibits those acts or practices defined by the Insurance Code or rules or regulations promulgated thereunder as unfair or deceptive. The Court held that a definition of unfair practices contained in Article 21.21-2 §2(d) of the Insurance Code, referred to as the Unfair Claim Settlement Practices Act, could form the basis for a cause of action under Article 21.21 of the Insurance Code and §17.50(a)(4) of the DTPA. The Court thereby dismissed Texas Farm Bureau's argument that one cannot incorporate the definition section of Article 21.21-2 into article 21.21 because Article 21.21-2 does not itself confer a private cause of action. The Court also rejected the argument that a plaintiff utilizing an Article 21.21-2 definition must establish that the defendant's conduct was committed with frequency; this is only a requisite in enforcement actions by the State Board of Insurance under Article 21.21-2.

(2) Violation of §4(b) of Board Order 18663 [28 TEX. ADMIN. CODE §21.3]: This section prohibits acts or practices that the law determines are unfair or deceptive. The Court had decided in *Chitsey v. National Lloyds Ins. Co.*, supra, that a jury finding did not constitute a determination by law. In *Vail* the Court held that the Court's own decisions did qualify as such a determination and specifically held that its opinions in *Arnold v. National County Mutual Fire Insurance Co.*, 725 S.W.2d 165 (Tex. 1987) and *Aranda v. Insurance Co. of North America*, 748 S.W.2d 210 (Tex. 1988) constituted legal determinations that an insurer's failure to exercise good faith was an unfair or deceptive act. Accordingly, the jury's finding that Texas Farm Bureau failed to exercise good faith in the handling of the Vails' claim established a violation of Board Order 18663 §4(b) as incorporated into Article 21.21 of the Insurance Code and was actionable under §17.50(a)(4) of the DTPA.

(3) Violation of §17.46(a) of the DTPA: A violation of §17.46 of the DTPA is actionable under Article 21.21 §16 of the Insurance Code. Article 21.21 includes violations of subdivision (a) of 17.46 which is not available to a consumer in a direct action under the DTPA. The Court held that the jury's finding that Texas Farm Bureau had failed to exercise good faith in its handling of the Vails' claim qualified as a finding that it had engaged in a deceptive act or practice prohibited by §17.46(a) of the DTPA. The violation was actionable through Article 21.21 of the Insurance Code and §17.50(a)(4) of the DTPA.

On the issue of damages, the Court held that when an insurer unfairly fails to pay an insured's claim, the insured as a matter of law, recovers damages of at least the amount of the policy benefits improperly withheld. Automatic treble damages were available under the Insurance Code, which the DTPA incorporated, justifying treble damages in the Vails' action under that provision.

Koral Industries v. Security-Connecticut Life Ins. Co., 802 S.W.2d 650 (Tex. 1990) (*per curiam*). Koral Industries obtained a one-million dollar life insurance policy from Security for one of its key employees, Lindsey. Lindsey did not disclose damaging medical history including prior hospitalization and treatment for alcohol abuse. When Lindsey died the insurance company refused to pay, asserting fraudulent inducement. Security tendered all premiums with interest to Koral Industries and declared the policy null and void. The jury found that Security had no reasonable basis for denying the claim. The jury also found that Lindsey had knowingly made false representations to Security to induce Security to issue the policy and that Security relied upon those representations. The jury also found that Security was aware of facts that would have caused a prudent person to make an inquiry, which if pursued with diligence would have uncovered Lindsey's fraud. The trial court rendered judgment for Koral Industries. The court of appeals reversed holding that the policy was properly voided for fraudulent inducement and that this precluded Koral Industries contractual and extra-contractual claims.

The Supreme Court denied Koral Industries' application for writ of error. In so doing the Court expressly disapproved the portion of the jury charge inquiring whether Security had information which, if investigated, would have led to discovery of the fraud. The Court held that failure to use due diligence to discover someone's fraud will not bar the defense of fraudulent inducement; Security's defense of fraudulent inducement and misrepresentation was a valid defense to the insured's breach of contract claim. The Court further held that "the jury's answers, as related to Security, negated any breach of good faith and fair dealing violations under the Insurance Code and any actions for unconscionability under the DTPA." *Id.* at 651.

Cathey v. Metropolitan Life Insurance Co., 805 S.W.2d 387 (Tex. 1991). The Supreme Court held in this case that ERISA preempts an insureds' claims under Article 21.21, Article 3.62, and the DTPA for wrongful denial under an employee group health insurance plan.

Pan American Life Ins. v. Erbauer Const., 805 S.W.2d 395 (Tex. 1991) (*per curiam*). Following *Cathey* the Court held that an employee's Insurance Code and DTPA claims under a group policy were preempted by ERISA since those claims "related" to an employee benefit plan. Citing *Gorman v. Life Ins. Co. of North America, infra,* the Court held that the ERISA defense in this case was jurisdictional and could be raised for the first time on appeal.

Gorman v. Life Ins. Co. of North America, 811 S.W.2d 542 (Tex. 1991). The Supreme Court held that when ERISA preemption is asserted as a defense to a claim within the concurrent jurisdiction of the state courts, it is an affirmative defense that must be timely pled and proven, or it is waived. This includes suits to (1) recover benefits due under the terms of the plan; (2) to enforce rights under the plan; or (3) to clarify rights to future benefits. Other claims relating to an ERISA plan fall within the exclusive jurisdiction of the federal courts; ERISA thus ousts a state court of jurisdiction. As such, this defense can be raised for the first time on appeal.

The Court also held that a de novo standard of review applied under ERISA, thus allowing the same recovery of policy benefits that would be allowed under state contract law. ERISA allows a claimant to recover attorneys' fees, prejudgment interest and costs but not mental anguish damages, delay penalties or exemplary damages.

Forbau v. Aetna Life Ins. Co., 876 S.W.2d 132 (Tex. 1994). This case involved claims by an employee under a health insurance policy. The employer paid all or part of its employees' premiums and collected and forwarded them to the insurance company. The Court did not reach the issue of whether ERISA preempted the employee's state law claims, including breach of contract. The Court noted, however, that it disapproved of the court of appeals' suggestion that the employee's remedies under ERISA and state contract law were identical. In the words of the Court: "The remedies available under ERISA are a declaratory judgment on entitlement to benefits, an injunction against a plan administrator's improper refusal to pay benefits, removal of a fiduciary, and an award of benefits due and attorneys' fees....ERISA's remedies are exclusive, and do not include extracontractual compensatory or punitive damages."

Allstate Insurance Company v. Watson, 876 S.W.2d 145 (Tex. 1994). Watson and another driver were involved in an automobile collision. Watson brought suit against the other driver alleging that the driver's negligence had caused the accident and Watson's injuries. In the same action, Watson sued the other driver's insurance company, Allstate, under Article 21.21 for unfair claims settlement practices. The trial court's summary judgment for Allstate was reversed by the court of appeals which held that Watson could bring an action under Article 21.21 against Allstate without first obtaining a judgment against Allstates' insured (the other driver).

The Court reversed the court of appeal's judgment, holding that a third party claimant, such as Watson, does not have a direct cause of action under Article 21.21. Initially, the Court discussed the statutory causes of action described in *Vail v. Texas Farm Bureau Mutual Ins. Co, supra*. Although its analysis departed from *Vail* on several points, the Court nonetheless concluded that "*Vail* remains the law as to claims for alleged unfair claim settlement practices brought by insureds against their insurers." In rejecting third party claims, the Court reasoned that the obligations imposed under *Vail* are "engrafted" onto the contract between the insurer and the insured. No such contract exists between the insurer and a third-party claimant; therefore, the third-party has no basis upon which to expect or demand the benefit of the extra-contractual obligations imposed by Article 21.21.

American Physicians Insurance Exchange v. Garcia, 876 S.W.2d 842 (Tex. 1994). This case is an appeal of a *Stowers* suit. The jury found that the insurer's failure to defend or to settle the original lawsuit constituted a "false, misleading, or deceptive act or practice" under Article 21.21 and the DTPA. Under *Stowers*, insurers are under an implied duty to accept reasonable settlement demands within policy limits. The Court held that the breach of the *Stowers* duty does not constitute a violation of Article 21.21 or the DTPA. The Court, in a footnote, stated that *Vail* is inapplicable since it concerned only a first-party insurance policy, and a *Stowers* suit necessarily involves a third-party claim. Since there was no evidence of any other unfair or deceptive acts or practices, the Court held that there was no violation of Article 21.21.

Celtic Life Insurance Co. v. Coats, 885 S.W.2d 96 (Tex. 1994). The Court held that a cause of action under Article 21.21 based on a misrepresentation of coverage accrues on the date the claim is denied, not the date on which the representation was made.

Transport Inc. v. Faircloth, 898 S.W. 2d 269 (Tex. 1995). The Court held that a claim for unconscionable conduct is not available in a suit brought under Article 21.21. That cause of action, created by DTPA §17.50(a)(3), is available only to consumers in suits brought under the DTPA. The Court also held that in order to invoke DTPA §17.46(b)(23) in an Article 21.21 action, the plaintiff must be a consumer since that laundry list item makes express reference to "the consumer."

Great American Ins. v. Austin Utility, 908 S.W.2d 415 (Tex. 1995). The Court holds that payment, performance and maintenance bonds issued by a commercial surety are not subject to Article 21.21: "[W]e conclude that suretyship, as historically understood in the insurance and suretyship fields, does not constitute the business of insurance under Art. 21.21."

Stewart Title Guar. Co. v. Aiello, 941 S.W.2d 68 (Tex. 1997). This case involves a claim that Stewart Title breached the common law duty of good faith and fair dealing. The Court held that no such duty was breached in this case and, therefore, the plaintiff's Article 21.21 action based on that claim failed as well. The Court noted further that "...to the extent *Vail* [*v. Texas Farm Bureau Mutual Insurance Company*, 754 S.W.2d 129 (Tex. 1988)] stands for the proposition that a failure to exercise good faith in processing insurance claims is an actionable deceptive trade practice, it does not control cases brought under the current version of article 21.21 because such behavior is not specifically enumerated in section 17.46(b) of the DTPA."

Johnson & Higgins of Tex. v. Kenneco Energy, 962 S.W.2d 507 (Tex. 1998). The Court holds that the two year statute of limitations applies to an Insurance Code cause of action that accrued prior to April 4, 1985, before there was a specific limitation provision in the Code.

Liberty Mut. Ins. v. Garrison Contractors, 966 S.W.2d 482 (Tex. 1998). The Court holds that insurance company employees, such as insurance agents, who engage in the business of insurance are "persons" under Article 21.21 and therefore subject to suit under Article 21.21 §16. The Court rejected the argument that the term "person" only included business entities and not their employees.

Provident Am. Ins. Co. v. Castaneda, 988 S.W.2d 189 (Tex. 1998). Castaneda filed a claim under a health insurance policy issued by the defendant. The defendant denied the claim, citing at varying times different exclusions. One of the exclusions was later admitted by at least one of the defendant's employees to be incorrect. The question presented on appeal was whether there was evidence to support the jury's findings of extra-contractual liability arising out of the defendant's handling of the claim. The jury charge submitted a number of counts including a version of the common law duty of good faith and fair dealing, and statutory claims under Article 21.21. The Court held that there was no evidence to support the jury findings, reasoning that (1) even if coverage was wrongfully denied, that alone was not evidence of bad faith: (2) evidence showing only a bona fide dispute about the applicability of an exclusion did not demonstrate the absence of a reasonable basis for denying the claim or that liability had become reasonably clear; (3) reliance on an incorrect basis for denying a claim was not actionable if there were other bases—even ones not yet articulated—that would lead another insurer to reasonably deny the claim; (4) the provisions of the Insurance Code prohibiting an insurer from offering an amount so clearly deficient as to be tantamount to denying a claim did not apply where the insurer offered no money on the claim; (5) a company's failure to properly investigate a claim may, in some circumstances, lead to extra-contractual liability but cannot be a basis for recovering policy benefits; (6) there was no evidence that the company had failed to adopt reasonable standards or respond with reasonable promptness; (7) the company's pre-approval of her surgery (and subsequent denial of benefits) was not an actionable misrepresentation because the company was not given key facts before the approval was given and there was no evidence that Castaneda relied on the pre-approval to her detriment since she would have had the surgery anyway and (8) none of the evidence regarding the handling of the claim supported a finding of unconscionability.

Crown Life Ins. Co. v. Casteel, 22 S.W.3d 378 (Tex. 2000). Casteel sold "vanishing premium" policies as an agent of Crown. When the premiums did not vanish, Casteel's clients brought suit against Casteel and Crown. Casteel, in turn, brought suit against Crown under Article 21.21 and the DTPA, alleging that he sold the policies in reliance upon false information provided by Crown. The jury found that Crown had knowingly engaged in deceptive and unfair trade practices that were a producing cause of damages to Casteel. On appeal Crown challenged Casteel's standing to bring suit under Article 21.21 and his right to recover under Article 21.21 for violations of the DTPA laundry list. Applying the pre-1995 version of Article 21.21, the Court held that an insurance agent, such as Casteel, had standing to bring an Article 21.21 claim because he met the definition of "person" in Article 21.21 §2(a) which expressly included "agents." The Court concluded that when an insurance agent meets the other elements of a cause of action under Article 21.21 §16(a), the agent has standing to bring a claim.

The Court next addressed Crown's argument that because Casteel was not a consumer he could not recover for violations of the laundry list in DTPA §17.46(b). The Court acknowledged established law that Article 21.21 incorporated the laundry list but did not incorporate the consumer standing requirement. Further, the Court noted that some but not all of the laundry list items expressly referred to consumers. The Court had previously held that one such laundry list item, subsection 23, expressly referred to "consumers" and was only actionable by a party who qualified as such. *See Transport Inc. v. Faircloth*, 898 S.W. 2d 269 (Tex. 1995). In this case, the Court extended that same limitation to those laundry list items referencing "goods" and "services". The Court held that the only laundry list item invoked by Casteel upon which he could bring suit was DTPA §17.46(b)(12) which makes no reference to "consumer," "goods," or "service." Since the broad form jury charge contained laundry list items (other than subsection (b)(12)) as a ground for liability, the Court set aside the jury's verdict for Casteel.

Rocor Intern. v. National Union Fire Ins., 77 S.W. 3d 253 (Tex. 2002). This case involved a suit by an insured against its excess liability carrier for attorney's fees and costs incurred as a result of the carrier's delay in settling a claim brought by a third party against the insured. The question before the Texas Supreme Court was whether the insured had a cause of action under Insurance Code art. 21.21. prior to its 1995 amendment adding §4(10)(a)(ii) which confers such a cause of action. The Texas Supreme Court, following the reasoning in *Vail v. Texas Farm Bureau Mutual Insurance Co.*, 754 S.W.2d 129 (Tex. 1988), held that the insured could assert an unfair settlement practices claim against its liability carrier when the carrier failed to attempt in good faith to effectuate a prompt, fair and equitable settlement of a claim once liability had become reasonably clear. The Court held further that to establish this cause of action an insured must prove that:

(1) the policy covers the claim;

(2) the insured's liability is reasonably clear;

(3) the claimant has made a proper settlement demand within policy limits; and

(4) the demand's terms are such that an ordinarily prudent insurer would accept it.

Rocor at 255. In this case, the Court held that the insured had not carried its burden of proof because the insured had not made a proper demand within policy limits.

Mid Century Ins. Co. of Texas v. Boyte, 80 S.W. 3d 546 (Tex. 2002). Boyte recovered a judgment against his insurer under the underinsured motorist (UIM) provisions of his automobile policy. The basis of that claim was that Mid Century had breached the UIM provision of the insurance policy by underpaying Boyte's claim for personal injuries. Mid Century appealed the claim and refused to pay the judgment (which had been superseded) while the appeal was pending. After the judgment had been affirmed in Boyte's favor, Boyte brought a new suit against Mid Century. In the second suit Boyte contended that Mid Century's failure to pay the judgment constituted bad faith and violated Insurance Code article 21.21 §4(10)(a)(ii), which prohibits a carrier from failing to attempt in good faith to settle a claim "with respect to which the insurer's liability has become reasonably clear." Boyte prevailed in the trial court and the court of appeals. The Supreme Court reversed, holding that upon entry of the money judgment Mid Century was transformed from insurer to judgment debtor. After judgment, Mid Century no longer owed a duty of good faith and could not be sued as an insurer under §4(10)(a)(ii) of the Insurance Code — at least as to those claims that had been reduced to judgment.

Progressive County Mutual Ins. Co. v. Boyd, 177 S.W.3d 919 (Tex. 2005). Insured brought suit against his automobile insurance company when the company denied his claim under his uninsured motorist coverage. The trial court severed the breach of contract and extra-contractual claims, including claims under Article 21.21. The trial court granted summary judgment for the insurer on the extra-contractual claims and the insurer won the breach of contract claim at trial. The Court of Appeals affirmed the take-nothing judgment on the contract but reversed the summary judgment on the extra-contractual claims. The Texas Supreme Court held that when all of the insured's claims are predicated on coverage under an insurance policy, an adverse finding on the insured's breach of contract claim defeats the insured's extra-contractual claims, as well.

Brainard v. Trinity Universal Ins. Co, 216 S.W.3d 809 (Tex. 2006). Here, the Court held that neither attorney's fees nor the prompt payment statute 18% penalties accrued on uninsured/underinsured motorist (UIM) benefits in an auto policy until after the uninsured/underinsured driver's liability has been determined by judgment. As long as the insurer promptly pays any benefits owing after the judgment is rendered, no claim for attorney's fees or statutory delay penalties will accrue under either Chapter 38, Texas Civil Practice & Remedies Code, or Chapter 541, Subchapter B (formerly Article 21.55), Texas Insurance Code.

State Farm Life Ins. Co. v. Martinez, 216 S.W.3d 799 (Tex. 2007). This was an interpleader action where the widow and ex-wife of the deceased insured filed competing claims for the death benefit of his life insurance policy. The Court held that the prompt payment of claims statute, formerly Article 21.55 and now Chapter 541, Subchapter B, Texas Insurance Code, applied to provide a penalty of 18% per annum and attorney's fees against the insurer for delaying payment past 60 days. However, once the death benefit was interpled and paid into the registry of the court, the penalty ceased accruing.

Lamar Homes, Inc. v. Mid-Continent Cas. Co., 242 S.W.3d 1 (Tex. 2007). The Court answered certified questions from the Fifth Circuit on the extent of coverage provided by a standard commercial general liability policy for construction defects alleged against the general contractor of a residence. The Court found that coverage was afforded "when 'property damage' results from the 'unexpected, unforeseen or undesigned happening or consequence' of the insured's negligent behavior." The Court also held that the insurer's wrongful failure to provide a defense upon demand by the insured resulted in liability for the 18% penalty under the prompt payment of claims statute, formerly Article 21.55 and now Chapter 541, Subchapter B, Texas Insurance Code. The court rejected the argument that claims for a defense and for indemnity were not first party claims under the statute.

Metro Allied Ins. Agency v. Lin, 304 S.W.3d 830 (Tex. 2009). In a DTPA case alleging failure to procure an insurance policy, the consumer must show that the misrepresented coverage was actually available. Plaintiff Lin paid Defendant Metro to procure a commercial general liability ("CGL") policy to cover his work as an electrical engineer on a construction contract. When he failed to adequately complete his work on the construction project, he was terminated and his performance bond surety was required to complete it for him. The surety then sued Lin to recoup what it had paid to complete the project. Metro had repeatedly assured Lin that Metro had procured Lin a CGL policy that would provide Lin coverage for the claims made by the bond surety. However, Metro in fact failed to write or procure any CGL policy for Lin. At trial, Lin did not present any evidence, either by expert testimony or by introduction of a particular CGL policy form, to prove that a CGL policy would have indemnified him from the bond surety's claims. Since Lin did not prove the existence of a CGL policy that would have indemnified him from the surety's claims, his DTPA claim failed as a matter of law. The Court acknowledged its departure from prior case law, which had held that the insurance consumer need not prove the existence of a specific policy in order to show liability under the DTPA (*Parkins v. Tex. Farmers Ins. Co.*, 645 S.W.2d 775, 776 (Tex. 1983); *Royal Globe Ins. Co. v. Bar Consultants, Inc.*, 577 S.W.2d 688, 694 (Tex. 1979)). The Court explained that the 1979 amendment to the DTPA changing the causation standard from "adversely affected" to "producing cause" resulted in a change in the proof necessary in failure to procure cases. In establishing this new standard for failure to procure cases, the Court observed that the "producing cause" standard is more stringent than the "adversely affected" standard under pre-1979 version of the DTPA.

Texas Mutual Ins. Co. v. Ruttiger, 381 S.W.3d 430 (Tex. 2012). In this workers' compensation insurance case, there was a dispute as to whether Ruttiger was injured on the job or, as contended by Texas Mutual, at a softball tournament. The workers' compensation claim was eventually settled in favor of Ruttiger. Ruttiger then sued Texas Mutual for damages resulting from its delay in paying his wage and medical benefits. He alleged unfair settlement practices under Insurance Code Chapter 541 and sought consumer status under the DTPA. The Court observed that specific and detailed provisions for dispute resolutions and remedies for failing to comply were built into the 1989 overhaul of the Texas Workers' Compensation Act (Tex. Labor Code §§ 401.001-506.002) and these specific provisions were at odds with a more general duties in Chapters 541 and 542 of the Insurance Code. The Court held that the Legislature could not have intended that injured workers have a cause of action for unfair settlement practices against their insurer under Insurance Code §541.060 or §542.003. The Court expressly overruled *Aetna Cas. & Sur. Co. v. Marshall*, 724 S.W.2d 770 (Tex. 1987) (*supra* p. 91) to the extent it held otherwise.

§8.00 CAUSATION

Parkins v. Texas Farmers Ins. Co., 645 S.W.2d 775 (Tex. 1983). Parkins brought suit alleging that the defendant represented that it would issue a policy insuring his dwelling in the event of fire, when it did not. The court of appeals rendered judgment for the defendant on the grounds that the insured had the burden of proving that his fire loss could have been covered under some policy *i.e.* that he prove the terms of a policy which could have been issued. The Supreme Court rejected the contention that the insured needs to prove a specific policy to show that he was adversely affected. It was enough that he was misled by the misrepresentation into believing such a policy existed. *Note:* The holding in this case was overruled in *Metro Allied Ins. Agency v. Lin*, 304 S.W.3d 830 (Tex. 2009).

Hurst v. Sears, Roebuck & Co., 647 S.W.2d 249 (Tex. 1983). The Supreme Court held that the jury question inquiring whether the defendant's conduct was a producing cause of damages was sufficient to satisfy the pre-1979 language in the statute authorizing recovery by consumers who had been "adversely affected."

Weitzel v. Barnes, 691 S.W.2d 598 (Tex. 1985). In this case the court of appeals held that before a consumer can recover it is necessary that he plead and prove that he *relied* upon the misrepresentations in question. The Supreme Court reversed, holding that subsection 1 of §17.50(b) only required that a consumer prove that a deceptive act or practice is a "producing cause" of actual damages. Noting the legislative history in which the word "reliance" was removed from an earlier draft of an amending bill, a majority of the Court reasoned that the Legislature had specifically rejected reliance as an element of recovery.

Brown v. Galleria Area Ford, Inc., 752 S.W.2d 114 (Tex. 1988). The dissent in this case argues that the evidence does not support a finding of producing cause.

Best v. Ryan Auto Group, Inc., 786 S.W.2d 670 (Tex. 1990) (*per curiam*). Best purchased a Harley-Davidson motorcycle dealership. The purchase included the inventory that was subject to a floor planning lien held by a third party. Best testified that at the time of the franchise sale, the seller misrepresented that Best would be able to buy inventory from Harley-Davidson. In fact, however, the dealership as sold did not include this right. After the purchase, the third party sued the seller and repossessed the inventory, which effectively put Best out of business. Best brought suit alleging that the seller had violated §17.46(b)(12) of the DTPA. The court of appeals found no evidence linking the misrepresentation to the lost profits damages awarded by the jury; rather, the damages resulted from the third party repossession. The Supreme Court disagreed, holding in a *per curiam* opinion that Best's testimony constituted legally sufficient evidence of a misrepresentation that produced his subsequent damages.

Prudential Ins. Co. v. Jefferson Associates, 896 S.W.2d 156 (Tex. 1995). This case involved a multi-million dollar recovery by the buyer of a building based upon the Prudential's failure to disclose the presence of asbestos in the building and its misrepresentation of the building's condition. The Court's opinion deals primarily with the effect of a comprehensive "as is" clause on the ability of a buyer to recover for misrepresentations.

In addition to the customary "as is" with all defects and no warranty language the "as is" clause provided that "Purchaser acknowledges that it is not relying upon any representation, statement or other assertion with respect to the property condition, but is relying upon the examination of the Property."

The Court held that the "as is" clause negated, as a matter of law, the causation necessary to sustain a cause of action, including a cause of action under the DTPA: "a valid 'as is' agreement ... prevents a buyer from holding the seller liable if the thing sold turns out to be worth less than the price paid because it is impossible for the buyer's injury on account of this disparity to have been caused by the seller."

The Court noted that an "as is" agreement is not universally determinative and suggested that it will not be given effect if fraudulently induced, if it was only an incidental part of the basis of a bargain between parties, or if the parties were of unequal bargaining power. Finally, the Court held that the "as is" clause did not contravene the "no waiver" provision in DTPA §17.42.

Haynes & Boone v. Bowser Bouldin, Ltd, 896 S.W.2d 179 (Tex. 1995). The plaintiff recovered judgment under the DTPA against its law firm for mishandling the defense of a lawsuit; the plaintiff claimed that the defendant's misconduct ultimately resulted in the foreclosure of plaintiff's property and the loss of a sales contract. The Court reversed the judgment, holding that there was no evidence that the defendant's DTPA violations were a producing cause of the foreclosure or lost sale.

Doe v. Boys Clubs of Greater Dallas, Inc., 907 S.W. 2d 472 (Tex. 1995). Three boys were sexually molested by Mullens who was a volunteer at the Boys Club. Mullens' volunteer service arose out of a DWI conviction which required him to do community service. Prior to enrollment, the grandparent of one of the boys contacted the club which assured her that it thoroughly checked out its volunteers. Some months later when Mullens offered to take the boys on a private camping trip (not sponsored by the Boys Club), a grandparent asked the education director what he knew about Mullens. He replied that Mullens "seemed to be OK" but added that the club could not decide for the grandparent whether to let the boys go on the camping trip. The plaintiffs' alleged "laundry list" misrepresentations.

The representation that Mullens "seemed to be OK" was determined by the Court to be true and, in any event, was not actionable because it did not induce the plaintiffs into doing business with the club and, thus, was not a producing cause of damages. The Court also held that statement that the club "thoroughly checked out its volunteers" was not a producing cause of damages. Producing cause requires an "unbroken causal connection" between the misrepresentation and the injury. The Court held that since the relationship between Mullens and the boys developed independently and outside of the Boys Club, the representation did not cause the injury, but merely "furnished an attenuated condition that made the injury possible."

Associated Indemnity Corp. v. Cat Contracting, 964 S.W.2d 276 (Tex. 1998). A contractor was in a dispute with the owner. The contractor's surety settled the claim and brought a contractual indemnity action against the contractor. The contractor counterclaimed for deceptive trade practices alleging that the surety interfered with the contractor's opportunity to arbitrate its dispute with the owner. The Court held that the actions of the surety were not a producing cause of the contractor's loss of contract claims.

Brown v. Bank of Galveston, N.A., 963 S.W.2d 511 (Tex. 1998). A bank foreclosed on the plaintiff's home under a note given to finance construction. The plaintiff appealed from an adverse judgment notwithstanding the verdict. The Court affirmed the take-nothing judgment, holding that there was no evidence that the actions of the bank were a producing cause of damages to the plaintiff. The Court noted that "producing cause" requires that the act be both a cause-in-fact and a substantial factor in causing the injuries.

Rocky Mountain Helicopters, Inc. v. Lubbock County Hosp. Dist., 987 S.W.2d 50 (Tex. 1998). The hospital district contracted with the defendant requiring the defendant to furnish operational and maintenance services for CareLink, the hospital's emergency patient transfer program. After refueling a CareLink helicopter, the defendant's employee failed to turn off the refueler, permitting a significant quantity of fuel to spill on the hospital district's property. The district brought suit to recover the cost of the cleanup. The hospital district alleged that defendant misrepresented its services by failing to abide by its written training policies concerning refueling. However, since there was no evidence that the hospital district was aware of the policies or that the policies had been communicated to anyone outside the defendant company, the Court held that there was no evidence that a misrepresentation was a producing cause of damages to the plaintiff.

Trinity Universal Ins. Co. v. Bleeker, 966 S.W.2d 489 (Tex. 1998). An insurance company's failure to inform its insured or his attorney of a third party claimant's settlement offer was not a producing cause of damages when there was no evidence that the insured would have accepted the offer.

DeWitt County Electric Cooperative, Inc. v. Parks, et al., 1 S.W.3d 96 (Tex. 1999). The plaintiff homeowners entered into a service contract with the defendant electric cooperative for electrical service. At the same time, the plaintiffs signed a written agreement which gave the defendant an easement and the right to clear the easement of obstructions. When the defendant's employees cut down two of the plaintiff's trees and trimmed back another, the plaintiffs brought suit under the DTPA. The plaintiffs alleged that the defendant assured them that they would not remove any trees from the plaintiff's land. The defendant responded that a clause in the service contract providing that the service contract represented the entire agreement between the parties and that the defendant's agents had made no representations not contained in the agreement foreclosed reliance on the alleged representations. The Court rejected this argument, noting that the language in the service contract could not be construed to foreclose reliance on any misrepresentations that were made about the easement agreement since obviously the parties did not consider the service contract to be the only agreement between the parties—if they did then the defendant had no easement and no right to cut the trees. Such a construction would be unreasonable.

Helena Chemical Co. v. Wilkins, 47 S.W.3d 486 (Tex. 2001). In this case involving misrepresentations in the sale of seed to farmers, the court summarized the rules pertaining to causation under the DTPA:

> To recover under the DTPA, the plaintiff must also show that the defendant's actions were the "producing cause" of actual damages. . . . This showing requires some evidence that the defendant's act or omission was a cause in fact of the plaintiff's injury. . . . Under this standard, it is not necessary to show that the harm was foreseeable.

Id. at 502. The court went on to hold that evidence of the seed unsuitability, performance of the plaintiff's crop, performance of their neighbor's crop, seed performance trials, expert testimony and rainfall statistics as well as evidence excluding other causes supported the jury's finding of producing cause.

Ford Motor Co. v. Ledesma, 242 S.W.3d 32, 46 (Tex. 2007). "Producing cause" is defined as "a cause that was a substantial factor in bringing about an injury, and without which the injury would not have occurred." Although this was not a DTPA case, the standard definition of "producing cause" in the TEXAS PATTERN JURY CHARGES has been changed as a result of this decision.

Metro Allied Ins. Agency v. Lin, 304 S.W.3d 830 (Tex. 2009). In a DTPA case alleging failure to procure an insurance policy, the consumer must show that the misrepresented coverage was actually available. Plaintiff Lin paid Defendant Metro to procure a commercial general liability ("CGL") policy to cover his work as an electrical engineer on a construction contract. Metro had repeatedly assured Lin that Metro had procured Lin a CGL policy that would provide Lin coverage for any claims made by the bond surety. However, Metro in fact failed to write or procure any CGL policy for Lin. At trial, Lin did not present any evidence, either by expert testimony or by introduction of a particular CGL policy form, to prove that a CGL policy would have indemnified him from the bond surety's claims. Since Lin did not prove the existence of a CGL policy that would have indemnified him from the surety's claims, his DTPA claim failed as a matter of law. The Court acknowledged its departure from prior case law, which had held that the insurance consumer need not prove the existence of a specific policy in order to show liability under the DTPA (*Parkins v. Tex. Farmers Ins. Co.*, 645 S.W.2d 775, 776 (Tex. 1983); *Royal Globe Ins. Co. v. Bar Consultants, Inc.*, 577 S.W.2d 688, 694 (Tex. 1979)). The Court explained that the 1979 amendment to the DTPA changing the causation standard from "adversely affected" to "producing cause" resulted in a change in the proof necessary in failure to procure cases. In establishing this new standard for failure to procure cases, the Court observed that the "producing cause" standard is more stringent than the "adversely affected" standard under pre-1979 version of the DTPA.

§9.00   DAMAGES

§9.01   ACTUAL DAMAGES

Duncan v. Luke Johnson Ford, Inc., 603 S.W.2d 777 (Tex. 1980). The purchaser of a motor vehicle sought to recover mental anguish damages in his suit under the DTPA. The Supreme Court disallowed any such recovery, holding: "In the present case there is no proof of a willful tort, gross negligence, willful disregard, or mental anguish causing physical damage. There is no evidence to support the award of damages for mental anguish." *Id.* at 779.

Brown v. American Transfer & Storage Co., 601 S.W.2d 931 (Tex. 1980). The plaintiffs alleged that the defendant moving company had misrepresented how they would pack, move and store the plaintiffs' household goods. Most of the items shipped were badly damaged or missing. Among other damages the plaintiffs sought recovery for mental anguish. The Supreme Court noted that the DTPA provides for recovery of actual damages. The Court held that actual damages mean those recoverable at common law. In line with two earlier Supreme Court cases, the Court concluded that "the Browns are not entitled to damages for mental anguish as there was no allegation that the wrongful action that caused the suffering was willful and there was no resulting physical injury." *Id.* at 939.

Farmers and Merchants State Bank v. Ferguson, 617 S.W.2d 918 (Tex. 1981). This case involved the wrongful dishonor of checks drawn on the defendant bank. The Court held that the plaintiff did not qualify as a consumer under the DTPA. The Court did find however a wrongful dishonor pursuant to TEX. BUS. & COM. CODE §4.402. The Court then considered whether the plaintiff was entitled to recover damages for mental anguish. The Court stated that damages for mental anguish cannot be recovered "absent a showing of an intentional tort, gross negligence, wilful and wanton disregard, or accompanying physical injury." 617 S.W.2d 921. Based upon a jury finding that the dishonor was malicious, the Court permitted the recovery of damages for mental anguish.

Luna v. North Star Dodge Sales, Inc., 667 S.W.2d 115 (Tex. 1984). The jury found that a car dealership had knowingly engaged in unconscionable conduct in the sale of a car to the plaintiff. The jury awarded the plaintiff damages for mental anguish and loss of use of the vehicle.

In considering the legal sufficiency of the evidence to support the mental anguish damages, the Court extended its prior holding that such damages are recoverable upon proof of a willful tort, willful and wanton disregard or gross negligence, to permit the recovery of these damages when the defendant's actions were committed "knowingly." The Court reasoned as follows:

> If a person commits a wrongful act with actual awareness of the falsity, deception or unfairness of the act, then this is a more culpable mental state than one who is grossly negligent. We are not attempting to equate the terms gross negligence, "knowingly," "willful" and intentional. These terms lie on a continuum with gross negligence being the lowest mental state and intentional being the highest. If grossly negligent conduct is sufficient to allow a plaintiff to recover mental anguish damages, then 'knowing' conduct is also sufficient.

Id. at 118.

The Court also set the standard for proof of damages for loss of use of a vehicle. The Court held that a plaintiff need not rent a replacement vehicle or spend money for alternative transportation to recover these damages because to do so would penalize those who did not have the financial ability to rent another car.

To prove up loss of use the consumer must only show the reasonable rental value, by day, week or month, of a substitute vehicle.

Leyendecker & Associates, Inc. v. Wechter, 683 S.W.2d 369 (Tex. 1984). This DTPA case involved, among other things, misrepresentations of the size of a residential lot. The Court noted that Texas courts have recognized two common law measures of damages for misrepresentation: the "out-of-pocket" measure and the "benefit of the bargain" measure. The Court held that the DTPA permits the plaintiff to recover either of these measures "whichever gives the consumer the greater recovery." *Id.* at 373.

Kish v. Van Note, 692 S.W. 463 (Tex. 1985). The plaintiffs in this case sought to recover damages for deceptive trade practices committed incident to the purchase of a pool. The Court set forth the following rules which govern the recovery of damages under the DTPA:

> The object of awarding a plaintiff recovery is to compensate for the actual loss sustained as a result of the defendant's conduct. The DTPA embraces this concept by permitting the injured consumer to recover the greatest amount of actual damages alleged and factually established to have been caused by the deceptive practice, including related and reasonably necessary expenses [citation omitted]... The amount of actual damages recoverable under the DTPA is determined by the total loss sustained as the result of the deceptive trade practice [citation omitted]. While the Act does not define "actual damages," the term has been construed to mean common law damages [citation omitted]. *Id.* at 466.

Farrell v. Hunt, 714 S.W.2d 298 (Tex. 1986). This was a suit for wrongful foreclosure under the DTPA. While acknowledging that the DTPA was intended to permit the consumer to recover the greatest amount of actual damages alleged and established, the Court held that the plaintiff did not prove actual damages according to any theory under common law and therefore was not entitled to recover.

Birchfield v. Texarkana Memorial Hospital, 747 S.W.2d 361 (Tex. 1987). An injured child's parents sued a doctor and a hospital for both negligence and deceptive trade practices in the treatment of the child. The jury verdict contained findings supporting both theories of recovery. On appeal the Court considered whether to allow the plaintiffs to recover both exemplary damages for gross negligence and treble damages under the DTPA. The Supreme Court held that because the jury found that the deceptive conduct and the negligent conduct resulted in the same damages, an award of both exemplary damages and statutory treble damages would constitute an impermissible double recovery of punitive damages. Accordingly, the Court permitted the plaintiffs to elect between the exemplary damages and treble damages under the DTPA. Further, the Court held that the plaintiffs did not waive their entitlement to treble damages by failing to make an election in the trial court. The Court explained that when the prevailing party does not elect a remedy, the trial court should render judgment for those damages affording the greatest recovery.

Jacobs v. Danny Darby Real Estate, Inc., 750 S.W.2d 174 (Tex. 1988). Jacobs purchased a tract of land from the defendant and made improvements upon it on the basis of the representation of the defendant that Jacobs was eligible for financing through the Texas Veterans Land Board. Jacobs did not obtain the financing and he brought suit seeking to recover his out of pocket expenses incurred in improving the land. He prevailed in the trial court but the court of appeals reversed and held that he had not offered evidence of the reasonableness and necessity of his expenses. The Supreme Court reversed the court of appeals. Despite the absence of specific testimony that the expenses were reasonable and necessary, the Court held that the evidence of the materials and services purchased for the improvements, most of which Jacobs did himself, supported the deemed finding that the expenses were reasonable and necessary. Finally, the Court noted that since the defendant did not preserve the issue of whether a consumer must establish the reasonableness and necessity of expenses in a DTPA action, the Court did not need to express an opinion on the issue. Justice Kilgarlin in his concurring opinion argued the additional point that the DTPA did not require proof of reasonableness and necessity because the statute did not specify such proof.

W. O. Bankston Nissan, Inc. v. Walters, 754 S.W.2d 127 (Tex. 1988). Walters, the plaintiff, purchased a pickup truck from W. O. Bankston Nissan, Inc. As part of the purchase price, Walters traded in his 280-ZX automobile at an agreed upon value of $7,700.00. After experiencing mechanical problems with the truck and upon learning that the truck was an older model than the year that Nissan represented, Walters demanded rescission of the sale and the return of his automobile. However, Nissan had already sold the 280-ZX. Walters then brought suit seeking recovery of the fair market value of his automobile on the date of the transaction. In the trial court the jury found for Walters, but the court rendered judgment notwithstanding the verdict. On appeal the court of appeals reversed. The Supreme Court reversed and sustained Nissan's contention that Walters failed to prove a compensable measure of damages. The Court stated that Walters may recover his damages with respect to the truck under either the out of pocket measure or the benefit of the bargain measure, whichever afforded the greater recovery. The Court also held that the value of the 280-ZX, which was the only damage issue submitted, was not the proper measure of damages. Justice Mauzy, in his concurring opinion, noted that while one could appropriately apply either the out of pocket or benefit of the bargain measures in this case, they were not the exclusive measure of damages available in DTPA cases.

Vail v. Texas Farm Bureau Mutual Ins. Co., 754 S.W.2d 129 (Tex. 1988). The Court held that when an insurer unfairly fails to pay an insured's claim, the insured, as a matter of law, is entitled to damages of at least the amount of the policy benefits improperly withheld.

Ludt v. McCollum, 762 S.W.2d 575 (Tex. 1988) (*per curiam*). The Supreme Court held that any residual loss of value in property after repairs are completed is compensable under the DTPA. The Court, however, refused to allow the plaintiff to recover both repair costs and loss in value because the trial court submitted a question to the jury that did not inquire as to the loss in value *after* repairs. The Court held that under these circumstances to have permitted recovery of both the cost of repair and reduction in value would result in a double recovery.

Mancorp, Inc. v. Culpepper, 802 S.W.2d 226 (Tex. 1990). Mancorp, the contractor, sued Culpepper, the owner, for failure to pay money owed under a construction contract. Culpepper counterclaimed alleging breach of warranty and deceptive trade practices. The trial court did not submit Culpepper's warranty and DTPA claims, but Culpepper claimed that the jury's finding regarding the cost of remedying defects in the building constituted a breach of warranty/damage finding and that, therefore, Culpepper was entitled to recover attorneys' fees. The Court disagreed, holding that the finding pertained to Culpepper's offset to Mancorp's breach of contract damages and did not constitute a finding of actual damages under the DTPA. Without such a finding, Culpepper was not entitled to recover attorneys' fees.

Henry S. Miller Company v. Bynum, 836 S.W.2d 160 (Tex. 1992). In this case, the Supreme Court rejected the argument that the "out of pocket" and "benefit of the bargain" rules are exclusive measures of damages recoverable under the DTPA. The Court explained that the DTPA permits recovery of actual damages, meaning "the total loss sustained [by the consumer] as a result of the deceptive trade practice." The Court gave several examples of available measures of damages, including related and reasonably necessary expenses, lost profits, interest, etc. and held that the plaintiff was properly permitted to recover his lost capital investment.

Boyles v. Kerr, 855 S.W.2d 593 (Tex. 1993). In this case the Court held that there is no cause of action for the negligent infliction of emotional distress. Noting that its holding left a claimant's right to otherwise recover mental anguish unaffected, the Court stated, in *dicta*, "mental anguish damages may not be recovered under the [DTPA]...absent proof of a willful or grossly negligent violation."

Parkway Co. v. Woodruff, 901 S.W.2d 434 (Tex. 1995). Parkway developed the Sugar Creek subdivision. A builder bought a lot in section 24 and constructed a home on it. The plaintiffs were the third owners of the home. Later, in the course of developing another section of the subdivision, Parkway altered the drainage patterns of the land causing the plaintiffs' home to flood. The jury awarded the Woodruffs damages for diminished value of their home and for mental anguish.

The Court reversed the award. As to the diminished value of the home, the Court held that awarding these damages in conjunction with cost of repairs constituted a double recovery since the diminution was calculated assuming no repairs to the home had been made. Diminution and repair costs are recoverable only when the diminution remains after repairs.

As to the mental anguish award, the Court stated that a jury finding of these damages will survive a no evidence challenge when there is "direct evidence of the nature, duration, and severity of [the] mental anguish, thus establishing a substantial disruption of the plaintiffs' daily routine." Without direct evidence of mental anguish, the court will look for evidence of "a high degree of mental pain and distress" that is more than "mere worry, anxiety, vexation, embarrassment or anger." The Court concluded that the plaintiffs did not present any testimony of emotions which rose to a compensable level; the fact that their house flooded would not support an inference that compensable mental anguish occurred ("flooding cannot be said to be beyond the vicissitudes of daily life" without additional evidence of a threat to personal safety).

State Farm Life Ins. Co. v. Beaston, 907 S.W.2d 430 (Tex. 1995). In this case involving a life insurance policy, the jury found that the insurance company and agent engaged in an unfair or deceptive act or practice causing mental anguish damages. The jury did not find that the defendant engaged in the misconduct "knowingly." At issue was whether a party can recover mental anguish damages under Article 21.21 of the Insurance Code in the absence of a "knowing" violation. The court, after noting that in DTPA cases not involving personal injury it had "required a threshold finding of a culpable mental state as one of the prerequisites for mental anguish damages," concluded that a similar finding was required under Article 21.21. The Court held that "mental anguish damages are not recoverable under Article 21.21 as an element of actual damages without an express finding of knowing conduct."

Arthur Anderson & Co. v. Perry Equipment Corp., 945 S.W.2d 812 (Tex. 1997). Perry Equipment Corporation (PECO) purchased another company, Maloney Pipeline Systems (Maloney). As a condition of the sale, PECO required audited financial statements. Maloney retained defendant Arthur Anderson & Co. (Anderson), for this purpose. The audit provided an incorrect financial picture of Maloney. Maloney was in bad financial condition when purchased and 14 months later, despite large cash infusions from PECO, filed bankruptcy. PECO brought suit against Anderson for deceptive trade practices. The damage question submitted to the jury asked the jury to determine the amount of the loss PECO had suffered as a result of Anderson's conduct and specifically asked the jury to determine (a) the purchase price of Maloney and (b) the amount of the costs and expenses incurred by PECO as a result of the purchase. Anderson appealed a judgment favorable to PECO, contending that the trial court improperly instructed the jury on the damage issue.

The Court first reviewed its earlier holdings that a consumer is entitled to recover those damages recoverable at common law in an amount which will compensate the consumer for the "total loss sustained as a result of the deceptive trade practice." Turning to the jury charge the Court held that the damage question was improper. The purchase price was an incorrect measure of direct damages because the evidence did not establish that Maloney was a total loss at the time of sale; the defendant was responsible only for that amount of the loss which occurred at the time of sale and any subsequent loss attributable to its misconduct and not any loss which PECO later suffered through no fault of the defendant. The Court noted also, that a consumer's recovery is limited by evidence that the consumer failed to mitigate its losses or by evidence of intervening causes.

Latham v. Castillo, 972 S.W.2d 66 (Tex. 1998). The Castillos twin daughters were born prematurely and underwent surgery at the hospital. One twin died within a week and the other died approximately two years later. After the death of the first child, the Castillos brought suit against the hospital. Their lawyer settled the case for $70,000. After the death of the second child, the Castillos hired the defendant Latham to represent them in a legal malpractice suit against their first lawyer and a medical malpractice suit against the hospital for the death of their second twin child. Latham settled the legal malpractice case for $400,000; the statute of limitations expired without the medical malpractice suit being filed. The Castillos then sued Latham alleging, among other things, that he had engaged in unconscionable conduct by representing that he had filed the medical malpractice lawsuit when he had not. The court of appeals reversed a directed verdict for Latham and remanded the case to the trial court. Applying the pre-1995 amendment DTPA, the Court affirmed the remand, holding that it was unnecessary for the Castillo's to prove economic damages as a predicate for the recovery of mental anguish damages. The Court further held that the plaintiff's testimony that the defendant's failure to file the lawsuit had made them "throw up," "sick, nervous, mad," "heartbroken" "devastated" and "physically ill" constituted some evidence that the defendant's conduct had caused the Castillo's the requisite "high degree of mental pain and distress" to support submission of mental anguish damages to the jury.

Gunn Infiniti, Inc. v. O'Byrne, 996 S.W.2d 854 (Tex. 1999). The plaintiff purchased an automobile from the defendant based upon the false representations that the vehicle had never been damaged. The plaintiff testified that after learning the truth and up until the time of trial he experienced mental anguish which he described as a "nightmare," "a constant mental sensation of pain or a rude awakening" and "severe disappointment both in myself and the dealership." He further explained that he had bragged about getting a new car, and had bought an Infiniti despite his friend's warnings, that he can see the imperfections in the car and its unreliability has caused him a lot of grief. He testified that "I felt like I'm publically humiliated. Yes, my friends give me a lot of grief," and "after putting up with ridicule from my friends, I feel embarrassed." The Court held that this was not legally sufficient evidence of mental anguish because it did not meet the high degree of mental distress required nor was there evidence of a substantial disruption of plaintiff's daily routine.

Gulf States Utilities Co. v. Low, 79 S.W. 3d 561 (Tex. 2002). Plaintiff brought a DTPA and negligence suit against an electrical utility company for wrongfully terminating his residential electric service. The jury found that the defendant had engaged in an unconscionable action and that both parties had been negligent. The jury awarded the plaintiff $100 for spoiled food, $20,000 for past mental anguish, $5,000 for psychological treatment and $150,000 in attorneys' fees. A question inquiring whether the defendant acted knowingly was not submitted to the jury. The trial court rendered judgment for the plaintiff in the amount of $12,100 with no mention of attorneys' fees.

On appeal the Texas Supreme Court held that the plaintiff was not entitled to recover under the DTPA because he had not proven any DTPA damages. The Court confirmed earlier decisions holding that even in pre-1995 DTPA cases (such as this one) a "knowing" finding was a necessary prerequisite to the recovery of mental anguish damages. The Court held that a "knowing" finding could not be deemed in support of the judgment because to do so would dictate a new judgment in an amount larger than the $12,000 trial court judgment. Without a finding that the defendant acted knowingly, the recovery of mental anguish damages could not stand.

The Court noted that the measure of damages for the destruction of household goods such as food is the "actual worth or value of the articles to the owner for use in the condition in which they were at the time of [the injury] excluding any fanciful or sentimental considerations." The jury may consider a number of factors including the original cost, the replacement cost (when appropriate), the use to which the property was put, and the testimony of qualified witnesses, including the owner. Although the plaintiff identified the items of food in the refrigerator, he did not place a monetary value on them. The Court held that without this testimony there was no evidence to support the finding. The jury was not entitled to answer the question based upon their own experience.

§9.02   DTPA Forms and Practice Guide Desk Book

Without supportable findings of damages the plaintiff was not entitled to recover his attorney's fees under the DTPA and was limited to his negligence cause of action.

Cruz v. Andrews Restoration, Inc., 364 S.W.3d 817 (Tex. 2012). The DTPA remedy of restoration requires showing by the consumer of actual damages and counter-restitution when feasible. Here, the consumer was able to show the defendant violated a tie-in statute, but the jury found he suffered no damages. He then sought judgment of restoration of the money he had paid the defendant. The Court analyzed the statutory remedy of restoration under the DTPA, concluding that it most closely resembled the common law remedy of rescission. Because common law rescission requires restoring both parties to their original positions, the court concluded that restoration is not available when the plaintiff is unwilling or unable to return valuable consideration received from the defendant.

§9.02   Treble Damages

Smith v. Baldwin, 611 S.W.2d 611 (Tex. 1980). The plaintiff brought suit for deficiencies in a house constructed by the defendant and recovered the cost of remedying the defects plus interim interest paid. The defendant was awarded an offset for the reasonable rental value of the house. The Supreme Court held that the applicable offsets should be deducted from the plaintiff's damages prior to trebling. Thus, the net recovery by the plaintiff is the amount to be trebled pursuant to §17.50.

Durham v. St. John, 645 S.W.2d 261 (Tex. 1983). This was a suit between a home remodeler and a homeowner in which the homeowner claimed entitlement to compensation for defective workmanship and the contractor claimed the right to an offset for what he was owed on the contract. The Supreme Court held that the damages awarded to the homeowner should be offset against the sum awarded to the contractor to determine whether the consumer had a net recovery which would be subject to trebling.

Martin v. E. McKee Realtors, Inc., 663 S.W.2d 446 (Tex. 1984). The Martins filed suit against their realtor for misrepresentations in connection with a real estate transaction. The jury found that the real estate agents knowingly made the misrepresentations in question. However, the plaintiffs failed to request a jury issue asking the jury to determine the amount, if any, of discretionary damages they should recover pursuant to §17.50(b)(l) as amended in 1979. The trial judge rendered judgment for the maximum amount of such damages permissible under the DTPA. The plaintiffs contended that the defendant's failure to object to the non-submission of an issue inquiring as to the amount of discretionary additional damages amounted to a waiver of that issue and entitled the plaintiffs to recover the maximum amount. The majority of the Supreme Court disagreed, holding that §17.50(b)(l) compelled the conclusion that in a jury trial, the plaintiffs who seek to recover discretionary damages must request a jury issue on such damages. The failure to do so results in waiver.

Jim Walter Homes, Inc. v. Valencia, 690 S.W.2d 239 (Tex. 1985). This case dealt with the construction of the language in §17.50(b)(l) of the DTPA which provides that a consumer who prevails may obtain:

> the amount of actual damages found by the trier of fact. In addition the Court shall award two times that portion of the actual damages that does not exceed $1,000.00. If the trier of fact finds that the conduct of the defendant was committed knowingly, the trier of fact may award not more than three times the amount of actual damages in excess of $1,000.00.

The Supreme Court rejected a calculation of additional damages pursuant to this provision that resulted in an award which was in excess of three times the amount of actual damages. The Court found no legislative intent to support an award of more than treble damages. The following breakdown illustrates the proper method of calculating damages pursuant to *Valencia:*

In a case involving $10,000 actual damages:

(1) three times the first $1,000 of actual damages = $3,000.00,

(2) not more than three times the amount of actual damages in excess of $1,000 = 27,000.00,

TOTAL: $30,000.00

Accord, Fairmont Homes, Inc. v. Upchurch, 711 S.W.2d 618 (Tex. 1986); *Capitol Brick v. Fleming Mfg. Co.,* 722 S.W.2d 399 (Tex. 1986).

Leonard & Harral Packing Co. v. Ward, 937 S.W.2d 425 (Tex. 1996). The Court held that the factual sufficiency review of punitive damages dictated by *Transportation Insurance Co. v. Moriel,* 879 S.W.2d 10 (Tex. 1994) should be conducted on the award of additional damages under the DTPA as well.

St. Paul Surplus Lines v. Dal-Worth Tank Co., 974 S.W.2d 51 (Tex. 1998). In this suit the insured recovered a judgment under the DTPA and Insurance Code that included prejudgment interest. The trial court trebled the prejudgment interest. The Texas Supreme Court reversed, citing *Vail v. Texas Farm Bureau Mut. Ins. Co.,*754 S.W.2d 129 (Tex. 1988), which held that prejudgment interest was not allowable on treble damages. The Court reasoned that trebling prejudgment interest was mathematically the same as awarding prejudgment interest on treble damages and, thus, was not permissible.

Tony Gullo Motors I, L.P. v. Chapa, 212 S.W.3d 299 (Tex. 2006). The Court affirmed a DTPA verdict against a car dealer for delivering a lesser model after promising a better model. The Court also may have caused confusion regarding the recoverability of additional damages, stating plainly, albeit in dicta, that treble additional damages are recoverable in addition to actual damages, paving the way for claims of quadruple damages in the future. In discussing the proper limits of the exemplary damages awarded by the jury for both fraud and "knowingly" findings, the Court observed, that Section 17.50(b)(1) limits the plaintiff's recoverable additional damages to "three times [plaintiff's] economic loss." Mathematically, the figures used by the Court reveal that the Court clearly assumed the plaintiff could recover additional damages of three times her economic damages in addition to her economic damages-or quadruple damages. While never decided under the 1995 revisions to the DTPA, similar language in the previous statute had been interpreted to limit the plaintiff's recovery to additional damages of two times actual damages. *See Jim Walter Homes, Inc. v. Valencia,* 690 S.W.2d 239 (Tex. 1985) (interpreting 1979 law); *and Dal-Chrome Co. v. Brenntag Sw., Inc.,*183 S.W.3d 133, 143-44 (Tex. App.-Dallas 2006, no pet.) (reducing award of quadruple economic damages to treble economic damages under post-1995 law). It remains to be seen if this was an intended result or a poor choice of wording.

§10.00 ATTORNEY'S FEES

§10.01 RECOVERY BY PLAINTIFF

McKinley v. Drozd, 685 S.W.2d 7 (Tex. 1985). The general contractor brought suit against his consumers seeking to recover the balance due on a construction contract. The consumers counterclaimed alleging deceptive trade practices. The jury found that the consumers owed the contractor $24,836.71 under the contract and that the contractor owed the consumers $11,650.00 in actual damages. The trial court awarded the contractor a net recovery of $13,186.00. The question on appeal was whether the consumers were entitled to attorneys' fees under the DTPA and specifically whether it was necessary for the consumers to receive a net recovery in the entire lawsuit to qualify for attorneys' fees. Relying upon the mandated liberal construction, the Supreme Court held that consumers are entitled to recover attorneys'

§10.01   DTPA Forms and Practice Guide Desk Book

fees under the DTPA in a successful claim for damages, even though the claim might be entirely offset by the claim of the opposing party.

Matthews v. Candlewood Builders, Inc., 685 S.W.2d 649 (Tex. 1985). Matthews purchased construction services from Candlewood. Candlewood sued Matthews on the construction contract and Matthews counterclaimed alleging breach of contract and four types of deceptive trade practices. The jury awarded the builder recovery under the contract and awarded Matthews damages for interim construction loan interest based upon the builder's failure to timely complete the residence. Following *McKinley* the Court held that Matthews was entitled to recover attorneys' fees even though the amount of damages awarded to him was entirely offset by the amount of damages awarded to Candlewood. Candlewood contended further that Matthews was not entitled to attorneys' fees because he had not proven which fees could be allocated to which claims; the jury question simply requested the jury to find attorneys' fees for the entire case rather than allocating the fees to each claim for which attorneys' fees could be awarded. The Court held that since Candlewood did not object, any complaint that the trial court allowed the jury to consider and award attorneys' fees not associated with Matthews' successful claim had been waived.

Stewart Title Guar. Co. v. Sterling, 822 S.W.2d 1 (Tex. 1991). The Court held that in a case involving multiple defendants, where one or more of the defendants have settled, the plaintiff must segregate the attorneys' fees owed by the non-settling parties in order to prove the reasonableness and necessity of the fees sought. An exception exists when the attorneys' fees are incurred in connection with claims out of the same transaction and are so interrelated that their "prosecution or defense entails proof or denial of essentially the same facts." In this circumstance, the party suing for attorneys' fees may recover all of the fees incurred. In this case, the Court determined that the attorneys' fees were capable of segregation. The plaintiff's failure to do so in the face of a proper objection required a remand for the presentation of evidence that segregated the fees sought.

Great American Ins. v. Austin Utility, 908 S.W.2d 415 (Tex. 1995). In this case the Court addressed the proper calculation of contingent attorney's fees. The Court held that the proper calculation is to give 33% of the face amount of the bond. The Court rejected the method of calculating a jury award of 33% of the "recovery" which would result in an attorney's fee award of 33% of the judgment.

Arthur Anderson & Co. v. Perry Equipment Corp., 945 S.W.2d 812 (Tex. 1997). The Court held that the award of contingent attorney's fees in DTPA cases is not allowed: "to recover attorney's fees under the DTPA, the plaintiff must prove that the amount of fees was both reasonably incurred and necessary to the prosecution of the case at bar and must ask the jury to award the fees in a dollar amount, not as a percentage of the judgment."

(The opinion does not prohibit a contingent fee agreement between a consumer and the consumer's attorney, only that if attorney's fees are awarded, it must be based on an hourly fee.)

Barker v. Eckman, 213 S.W.3d 306 (Tex. 2006). The Court remanded the issue of attorney's fees for a new trial when the damages award was reduced on appeal to one-seventh of the amount awarded by the jury and the jury clearly considered the amount of their award of actual damages in setting attorney's fees. Remand on attorney's fees will be required if the amount of actual damages recovered is substantially reduced on appeal and the appellate court "is not reasonably certain that the jury was not significantly influenced by the erroneous [damage award]."

Tony Gullo Motors I, L.P. v. Chapa, 212 S.W.3d 299 (Tex. 2006). The Court affirmed a DTPA verdict against a car dealer for delivering a lesser model after promising a better model over objection that the plaintiff's claims amounted to no more than "mere breach of contract." The Court also addressed the duty to segregate recoverable attorney's fees from attorney's fees incurred on claims where fees are not recoverable. The Court retreated substantially from the "inextricably intertwined" exception which has grown up after *Stewart Title Guar. Co. v. Sterling*, 822 S.W.2d 1 (Tex. 1991), stating that, while some attorney effort may advance all claims, in almost every case there remains an amount of work that will only advance a non-recoverable claim, even if it is a small percentage, and the proponent has a duty to segregate those fees out of the equation. The Court stopped well short of requiring the introduction of detailed time records: an estimated percentage will suffice.

§10.02   RECOVERY BY DEFENDANT

Jones v. Smith, 649 S.W.2d 29 (Tex. 1983) (*per curiam*). The plaintiff sought damages for misrepresentations under the DTPA. The defendant counterclaimed for attorneys' fees alleging that the suit had been brought in bad faith. Based on jury findings, the trial court rendered judgment for the plaintiff. The court of civil appeals reversed and remanded the cause for new trial. The court further rendered judgment that the defendant recover attorneys' fees. The Supreme Court, in a *per curiam* opinion, held that in the absence of the trial court finding referred to in §17.50(c), it was error for the court of appeals to award attorneys' fees to the defendant. *Accord, Ames v. Great Southern Bank*, 672 S.W.2d 447 (Tex. 1984).

Dairyland County Mut. Ins. v. Childress, 650 S.W.2d 770 (Tex. 1983). The defendant asserted that the filing of a DTPA claim without an allegation that the plaintiff purchased goods or services from the defendant constituted bad faith as a matter of law. The DTPA claim was subsequently deleted. The Court held that these facts did not prove bad faith as a matter of law. Since no evidence was presented on the issue of bad faith and no issues were requested the defendant waived its claim. The Court held that the party seeking bad faith attorneys' fees is required to offer evidence and secure a fact finding.

Leissner v. Schott, 668 S.W.2d 686 (Tex. 1984). In this case the court of appeals construed §17.50(c) as amended in 1979 to allow attorneys' fees to the defendant based upon (a) a finding of harassment, or (b) a finding that the suit was groundless and brought in bad faith. The Supreme Court refused the application for writ of error, finding no reversible error. In doing so, the Court reserved the question of whether the issues of bad faith and harassment are for the jury. The Court noted that although §17.50(c) refers to a "finding of the court," a number of lower court decisions have held that whether the suit is brought in bad faith or for the purpose of harassment is properly submitted to the jury. The Court concluded that the validity of this interpretation was not before it.

Donwerth v. Preston II Chrysler-Dodge, Inc., 775 S.W.2d 634 (Tex. 1989). In this case, the Supreme Court expressly held that the court, and not the fact finder, must make the determination of groundlessness, bad faith, or harassment. Reversing the decision of the court of appeals, the Court held that "groundless" under the DTPA has the same meaning as "groundless" under rule 13 of the Texas Rules of Civil Procedure. Under that rule, groundless means: "No basis in law or fact and not warranted by good faith argument for the extension, modification, or reversal of existing law." The Court held that the Donwerths' action as a matter of law was not groundless. The Court further stated that although Preston II had not preserved its contention that the Donwerth's action was brought for the purpose of harassment, Preston II probably could not have prevailed on that claim. The Court reasoned that since this provision requires that the suit be brought solely to harass, a case that was not groundless would not be likely to result in a finding of harassment. In the words of the Court: "Because any purpose for recovering money damages, however small, as a motivating factor would defeat such a finding, it is difficult to conceive of a case which was not groundless but was brought for the purpose of harassment." *Id.* at 638. In a concurring opinion, Chief Justice Phillips disagreed with this logic, reasoning that the language of the amended statute demonstrates that a finding of harassment alone will justify an award of attorney's fees.

Splettstosser v. Myers, 779 S.W.2d 806 (Tex. 1989). The Supreme Court relied on *Donwerth* to again reverse a court of appeals' judgment on bad faith attorney's fees. In holding that the action was not groundless as a matter of law, the court of appeals reasoned that when a plaintiff's DTPA cause survives a motion for directed verdict, neither the trial court nor an appellate court logically can find the lawsuit groundless. Expressly disapproving this standard, the Court remanded the case to the court of appeals to determine whether the evidence as a whole demonstrated an arguable basis in fact and law for the consumer's claim.

Klein v. Dooley, 949 S. W.2d 307 (Tex. 1997). When a DTPA plaintiff takes a voluntary non-suit the defendant's pending counterclaim for bad faith attorney's fees remains unaffected. TEX. R. CIV. P. 162. In this case the Court held that when the trial court rendered a judgment denying the counterclaim, the plaintiffs were not precluded by Rule 97(a) of the Texas Rules of Procedure from filing their claims in a second suit. The plaintiffs' claims were not compulsory counterclaims to the defendants claim for bad faith attorneys' fees within the meaning of that rule.

§11.00   JURY QUESTIONS

Spradling v. Williams, 566 S.W.2d 561 (Tex. 1978). This case was brought under the pre-1979 version of the DTPA which contained not only a "laundry list" of deceptive acts and practices but also a general prohibition against unlisted "false, misleading or deceptive acts or practices." *See* DTPA §17.46(a). The Court held that an unlisted act which is alleged to be deceptive requires the jury to find: (1) that the act or practice occurred, and (2) that it was a deceptive trade practice. Thus, two jury questions were required. The Court further held that to establish liability for a violation of one of the laundry list items, the jury is not required to find whether the act is false, misleading or deceptive since the statute declares those practices to be unlawful. Accordingly, it is not necessary to ask the jury whether the conduct is deceptive, simply whether it occurred.

Brown v. American Transfer & Storage Co., 601 S.W.2d 931 (Tex. 1980). The trial court submitted the following liability issues:

[Question No. 1]
Do you find...that the defendant...represented to the plaintiff...that the moving services of defendant... would include benefits and characteristics which they did not include?

[Question No. 2]
Do you find...that the defendant...represented to the plaintiff...that the moving services of defendant were of a particular standard, quality or grade when in fact they were not.

The defendant complained that the issues were too broad. The Supreme Court rejected this argument holding: "[I]ssues in deceptive trade practice cases for section 17.46(b) violations should be submitted in terms as close as possible to those actually used in the statute. The language of the statute may be altered somewhat to conform the issue to the evidence in the case." *Id.* at 937. The Court thus approved the submission of broad issues in DTPA cases. *Accord, Willis v. Johnson*, 603 S.W.2d 828 (Tex. 1980).

Spencer v. Eagle Star Insurance Co. of America, 860 S.W.2d 868 (Tex. 1993). In this suit for unfair claims handling practices the jury was asked:

Was the handling of the Spencers' claim for loss of earnings by Eagle Star an unfair practice in the business of insurance?

"Unfair practice" means any act or series of acts which is arbitrary, without justification, or takes advantage of a person to the extent that an unjust or inequitable result is obtained.

Answer "Yes" or "No"

The Court noted that the phrase "unfair practice in the business of insurance" was found in TEX. INS. CODE art. 21.21, §16(a) but held that the question itself was improper without an appropriate instruction limiting it to "those [practices] specified by certain other statutes and regulations." The Court held that the instruction was too broad and "ill-defined" to meet this requirement. Because the jury finding was defective, a new trial was required.

Johnson & Higgins of Tex. v. Kenneco Energy, 962 S.W.2d 507 (Tex. 1998). The Court approves the form of a jury question submitting the 180-day limitations extension available under Article 21.21 and the DTPA.

Stevens v. National Education Centers, Inc., 11 S.W.3d 185 (Tex. 2000) (*per curiam*). The defendant complained that the jury question on mental anguish was improperly submitted. One of the elements of damages the jury was permitted to consider was "mental anxiety, humiliation, and embarrassment." The Court, noting that the evidence necessary for an award of mental anguish damages was evidence of "a high degree of mental pain and distress" that is "more than mere worry, anxiety, vexation, embarrassment, or anger," concluded that the jury question was defective.

Crown Life Ins. Co. v. Casteel, 22 S.W.3d 378 (Tex. 2000). The Court held that an insurance agent was a person who had standing to bring an action under Insurance Code Article 21.21 (now Chapter 541) against the insurer for whom he sold life insurance even though he did not have standing as a consumer under the DTPA. Because the broad-form jury question submitted alternate definitions of unfair insurance practices, some of which were improper because of the agent's lack of DTPA standing, the Court reversed the finding of liability and remanded the case for a new trial. After *Casteel*, there must be legally sufficient evidence to support each alternate predicate of liability submitted in a broad-form jury question or the jury's finding will not be upheld. This case signals a retreat from-or at least the limit of-the Texas Supreme Court's long-standing preference for broad-form jury question submissions.

§12.00   DEFENSES/NOTICE

Brown v. American Transfer & Storage Co., 601 S.W.2d 931 (Tex. 1980). The Court held that 49 U.S.C. §20(11) regulating damages to freight shipped in interstate commerce did not preempt a DTPA claimed based upon misrepresentations made prior to the contract of carriage.

Smith v. Baldwin, 611 S.W.2d 611 (Tex. 1981). In this suit between a builder and a consumer the builder contended that a jury finding of substantial performance precluded liability under the DTPA. The Court rejected this contention holding that the doctrine of substantial performance was not relevant to a statutory cause of action under the DTPA. The DTPA cause of action was grounded on misrepresentations not upon the builder's failure to fulfill its contractual commitments. The Court noted that the remedy for breach of contract and those provided in the DTPA are cumulative and not mutually exclusive. Later in the opinion the Court rejected the imposition of an intent requirement into the DTPA and had this to say about common law requirements and defenses: "The DTPA does not represent a codification of the common law. A primary purpose of the enactment of the DTPA was to provide consumers a cause of action for deceptive trade practice without the burden of proof and numerous defenses encountered in a common law fraud or breach of warranty suit." *Id.* at 616.

Cail v. Service Motors, Inc., 660 S.W.2d 814 (Tex. 1983). The question in this case was whether a settlement offer made pursuant to §17.50A(b) must include an offer of reimbursement for attorneys' fees in order for the defendant to take advantage of the limitation on damages found in §17.50A(d). Relying upon the plain language of the statute, the Court held that §17.50A(c) specifically mandates that the settlement offer shall include an agreement to reimburse the consumer for reasonable attorneys' fees. Since the defendant's settlement offer failed to include such an agreement, it was insufficient as a matter of law.

Ramsey v. General Motors Corp., 685 S.W.2d 15 (Tex. 1985). This suit was brought under the pre-1979 DTPA for damages arising from the purchase of a defective pick-up truck. The retailer complained on appeal that the trial court had refused to submit an issue asking whether the defendant had cured the defect in the vehicle prior to initiation of the lawsuit. Section 17.50A(3) of the pre-1979 DTPA precluded treble damages if the defect was cured prior to the time suit was filed. The Supreme Court held that it was not error to refuse the requested issue because the defense of "cure" is an affirmative defense which the defendant failed to plead.

Cielo Dorado Development, Inc. v. Certainteed Corp., 744 S.W.2d 10 (Tex. 1988). The defendant pleaded that the plaintiff failed to give the pre-filing notice as required by the DTPA. The plaintiff's attorney testified at trial that the plaintiff had mailed a demand letter as required by the DTPA. The letter was not offered into evidence. No jury question concerning notice was requested or submitted and no objection to its nonsubmission was lodged. The trial court rendered judgment for the plaintiff on the verdict. A majority of the Supreme Court held that, even assuming that proof of notice was the plaintiff's burden, the defendant's failure to object to the non-submission of notice was deemed to support the judgment pursuant to rule 278 of the Texas Rules of Civil Procedure. The plaintiff's attorney's testimony, unobjected to by the defendant, constituted some evidence of proper notice. The dissent asserted that it is unequivocally the consumer's burden to prove proper notice. To discharge this burden the consumer must, in the dissent's view, prove that the notice was timely given, a question of fact. Second, the consumer must establish that the notice was legally sufficient, a question of law. The dissent argued that since this latter question, is one of law, as opposed to fact, a court cannot deem that the legal sufficiency requirement supports the judgment. Finally, the dissent argued that the testimony offered did not establish the sufficiency of the notice.

Ojeda de Toca v. Wise, 748 S.W.2d 449 (Tex. 1988). The plaintiff purchased a home from the defendant. The City of Houston had previously issued a demolition order for the home and the city filed the order in the Harris County deed records prior to the sale. The plaintiff was unaware of the demolition order, and the seller who knew of the order neglected to tell her. The plaintiff left town, and the city demolished the home while she was gone. The jury found that the defendant's failure to disclose was a deceptive trade practice and fraud. The court of appeals reversed and rendered judgment for the defendant on the ground that the plaintiff had constructive knowledge of the demolition order, which was a defense to her DTPA and fraud claims.

The Supreme Court reversed the judgment of the court of appeals. The Court opined that the purpose of the recording statute was to protect innocent purchasers from secret liens and encumbrances and not to protect those who would perpetuate a fraud. Accordingly, the Court held that imputed notice under the recordation statutes was not a bar to liability for fraud or a defense to a deceptive trade practice action.

Alvarado v. Bolton, 749 S.W.2d 47 (Tex. 1988). Bolton agreed to convey certain land to Alvarado. The earnest money contracts contained language constituting an express warranty that Bolton would convey the mineral interests. The warranty deeds, however, reserved the mineral interests and the jury found the reservation in the deed to be a breach of the express warranty. The court of appeals reversed and held that the doctrine of merger barred Alvarado's claim for breach of warranty. The Supreme Court reversed the court of appeals and held that merger is a common law defense that has no application to a statutory action under the DTPA.

In a strong dissent, four justices argued that, as a matter of law, no breach of warranty existed. The dissent reasoned that under the merger doctrine the deed extinguished the contractor's warranty. The merger doctrine was, therefore, not asserted as a defense to the breach of warranty action, but rather to negate the existence of a warranty. The dissent observed that had Alvarado alleged that Bolton had misrepresented a fact, the doctrine of merger would not have prevented proof of the misrepresentation.

Willis v. Maverick, 760 S.W.2d 642 (Tex. 1988). In this case, the Supreme Court primarily focused on the application of the statute of limitations in a common law cause of action for legal malpractice. The Court held that the discovery rule was applicable to legal malpractice actions and that the statute of limitations does not begin to run until the claimant, exercising reasonable care and diligence, discovers or should have discovered the facts that established his cause of action. The Court further held that since the discovery rule operates to avoid the statute of limitations, the claimant has the burden of pleading and proving when the operative facts were discovered or reasonably should have been discovered. Since the plaintiff had failed to request a proper issue submitting the discovery rule, she was unable to avoid the defendant's limitations defense.

In *Willis* the plaintiff also alleged a cause of action under the DTPA. The Court held that the plaintiff's cause of action was barred by the DTPA limitations provision. The Court reasoned that the DTPA "incorporates the discovery rule." The plaintiff's failure to request a properly worded discovery issue in connection with her DTPA claim waived her attempt to avoid the effect of limitations.

Kennemore v. Bennett, 755 S.W.2d 89 (Tex. 1988). Bennett agreed to build the Kennemores a home. The Kennemores moved in upon completion, but refused to pay certain amounts that Bennett submitted on his bill because of alleged defects and plan deviations. Bennett instituted an action on the contract and for foreclosure. The Kennemores counterclaimed alleging that Bennett did not build the home in a good and workmanlike manner and that Bennett engaged in deceptive trade practices. The Kennemores ultimately paid the amounts that Bennett demanded but nevertheless proceeded with their counterclaim under the DTPA. The trial court directed a verdict against the Kennemores and they appealed. The court of appeals affirmed the trial court's judgment on the ground that the Kennemores' payment to Bennett and possession of the home waived their claims and estopped them from asserting them. The Supreme Court reversed and held that in the absence of an express waiver of settlement, the consumers' payment for and acceptance of allegedly defective performance did not constitute a waiver of the DTPA claim. The Court reasoned that the waiver and estoppel theories that the lower courts relied on were applicable to contract actions, but were not controlling in this statutory action under the DTPA. The Court further noted that nothing in the language or policy of the DTPA requires consumers to withhold performance in order to avail themselves of the Act.

Aguilar v. Autohaus, Inc., 800 S.W.2d 853 (Tex. 1991) (*per curiam*). The Supreme Court expresses no opinion on the availability of the common law puffing doctrine to defeat liability.

Southwestern Bell Telephone Co. v. FDP Corp., 811 S.W.2d 572 (Tex. 1991). Bell's representative assured FDP that, despite previous mistakes, a new yellow page advertisement calling for multiple bold face listings, a display and cross references to the display, would be published correctly. When the directory was published the display was not included. FDP sued Bell and the jury found that Bell had breached an express warranty that it would publish FDP's advertisement. On appeal, the Supreme Court held that Bell's omission of the display was a deficit in its performance constituting a breach of warranty. The Court next addressed the effect of the following limitation in the written advertising contract:

> The applicant agrees that the Telephone Company shall not be liable for errors in or omissions of the directory advertising beyond the amount paid for the directory advertising omitted or in which errors occur, for the issue life of the directory involved.

The court of appeals had held this limitation invalid under §17.42 which prohibits waiver of a consumer's statutory rights. The Supreme Court disagreed holding that the contractual provisions which like the oral warranty was part of the basis of the bargain, served to limit the warranty. The Court reasoned that since the DTPA does not create warranties, their nature and extent are determined by common law principals and other statutory provisions. The Court noted that the UCC permits the disclaimer of implied warranties. The jury had failed to find that the limitation was unconscionable and that Bell had violated the DTPA. Finally, the Court stated that a limitation of liability would be invalid under §17.42 to waive liability for a deceptive trade practice as defined in §17.46(b).

Stewart Title Guar. Co. v. Sterling, 822 S.W.2d 1 (Tex. 1991). Sterling, the purchaser of a tract of land, brought suit alleging that the title to a portion of the land was misrepresented by the seller, a law firm and the title company. After trial began but before the case was submitted to the jury, Sterling settled with the seller and the law firm for $400,000. The jury found that the title company had knowingly engaged in deceptive trade practices which were a producing cause of $200,000 in actual damages. The damages were trebled by the trial court pursuant to Article 21.21 §16 of the Insurance Code. The primary issue on appeal was whether the title company was entitled to a credit for the $400,000 settlement Sterling made with the other defendants. The Court first determined that given the date the action was filed and the theories pleaded, the original contribution statute found in TEX. CIV. PRAC. & REM. CODE §32.001 *et seq.* applied. The Court held that the "one satisfaction" rule as developed under the original contribution statute was still viable and was applicable in this case, since the purchaser suffered a single injury. Accordingly, the title insurer was entitled to a dollar for dollar credit of the amount paid by the settling defendants. Significantly, the Court held that the credit was to be applied after the actual damages are trebled and not before. Consequently, the defendant still was required to pay $200,000.

Jack B. Anglin Company, Inc. v. Tipps, 842 S.W.2d 266 (Tex. 1992). A construction contract contained the following clause: "All questions subject to arbitration under this Contract may be submitted to arbitration at the choice of either party to the dispute." The court held that under the Federal Arbitration Act (applicable to transactions involving commerce among the states) the clause governed a DTPA claim for misrepresentation regarding the quality of services and materials used in the work. The Court further held that the federal statute preempts application of the "no-waiver" provision in DTPA §17.42. *See also, Capital Income Properties-LXXX, et. al v. Blackmon*, 843 S.W.2d 22 (Tex. 1992).

Hines v. Hash, 843 S.W.2d 464 (Tex. 1992). Hines sent a DTPA pre-suit notice letter by certified mail. Hash knew about the letter but never picked it up from the post office. The letter was returned unclaimed. The court of appeals reversed a judgment for Hines reasoning that the DTPA requires actual delivery of the notice. The Supreme Court reversed. The Court did not reach the issue of whether actual delivery is required, holding that Hash had waived the notice requirement by failing to request an abatement in the trial court. In the course of the opinion, the Court set forth the following rules: If a plaintiff files a DTPA action without first giving notice, a trial court, upon a timely request by the defendant, should abate the action for 60 days to permit proper notice. To be timely, a request for abatement must be made with the answer "or very soon thereafter." Failure to make a timely request waives any objection to lack of notice. If a plaintiff fails to give notice while the action is abated, the lawsuit should be dismissed.

First Title Co. of Waco v. Garrett, 860 S.W.2d 74 (Tex. 1993). The plaintiffs contracted to purchase land for use as an automobile salvage yard. Although the land was encumbered with a deed restriction prohibiting such use, the title companies represented that no such restriction existed. When the Garretts' use of the land was restrained by an adjoining landowner, they brought suit against the sellers and ultimately obtained a $69,000 settlement. The Garretts then sued the title companies and recovered a favorable jury verdict for $85,000, based upon findings of negligence and deceptive trade practices. The lower courts refused the defendants request that the $69,000 settlement be credited against the judgment.

The Court first addressed the title companies' argument that the following disclaimer constituted a complete defense: "The policy to be issued pursuant to this commitment does not guarantee that the insured property has adequate title to allow it to be used, sold, transferred, leased, or mortgaged for any purpose intended by the purchaser nor will it provide coverage for possible loss of opportunity or economic expectation." The Court rejected the title companies' argument: "[a]lthough we decline to disapprove all contractual caveats against reliance...when representations are made, a consumer cannot waive DTPA protection....Accordingly, we hold that the clause purporting to waive the Garretts' DTPA protection from affirmative misrepresentations is invalid." *Id.* at 78.

The Court next addressed the title companies' contention that it was entitled to a credit for the settlement. The Court first noted that because there had been findings of both negligence and DTPA violations, the case was governed by the contribution provisions found in TEX. CIV. PRAC. & REM. CODE §32.001-.003. Following *Stewart Title Guar. Co. v. Sterling*, 822 S.W.2d 1 (Tex. 1991), the Court held that in instances of an indivisible injury, a non-settling defendant is entitled to offset the amount of the judgment by the amount of a plaintiff's settlement with a joint tortfeasor. The defendant title companies, although not adjudicated joint tortfeasors, nevertheless established their right to an offset through introduction of the settlement agreement between the Garretts and the sellers. Because the settlement and the jury verdict both compensated the Garretts for an indivisible injury, the "one satisfaction" applied.

Prudential Ins. v. Jefferson Associates, 896 S.W.2d 156 (Tex. 1995). This case involved a multi-million dollar recovery by the buyer of a building based upon the Prudential's failure to disclose the presence of asbestos in the building and its misrepresentation of the building's condition. The Court's opinion deals primarily with the effect of a comprehensive "as is" clause on the ability of a buyer to recover for misrepresentations.

In addition to the customary "as is" with all defects and no warranty language the "as is" clause provided that "Purchaser acknowledges that it is not relying upon any representation, statement or other assertion with respect to the property condition, but is relying upon the examination of the Property."

The Court noted that an "as is" agreement is not universally determinative and suggested that it will not be given effect if fraudulently induced or if it was only an incidental part of the basis of a bargain between parties of relatively equal bargaining power. The Court refused to find fraud because there was no evidence that Prudential knew of the asbestos in this building or that its statement of no defects was made with knowledge of its falsity; the Court further concluded that the representations that the building was "superb," "super fine" and "one of the finest little properties in Austin" were mere puffing.

The Court held, further, that the "as is" clause did not contravene the "no waiver" provision in DTPA §17.42 because it did not waive rights, it only provided that there are no rights to waive. The Court explained: "[the] agreement does not say he cannot sue Prudential for violating the DTPA; it says he cannot win the suit."

Smith v. Gray, 907 S.W. 2d 444 (Tex. 1995) (*per curiam*). The Smiths purchased a house from the Grays. On February 6, 1989 the Smiths discovered major structural damage to the home. The Smiths filed suit against the Grays on July 11, 1991. In response to a motion for summary judgment alleging statute of limitations, the Smiths averred that they did not know and had no reason to know until late July, 1989 that the sellers had failed to disclose to them a sewer leak which was the cause of the structural damage. The court of appeals held that limitations began to run when the Smiths learned of the damage to the home in February, even though they did not know that the damage was caused by a sewer leak or that the Grays had known of the leak. The Supreme Court denied the application for writ of error but expressly noted that "the Court neither approves nor disapproves of the court of appeals' analysis of the statute of limitations under the DTPA."

Redman Homes v. Ivy, 920 S.W.2d 664 (Tex. 1996). The purchasers of a mobile home brought suit against the manufacturer for breach of warranty and deceptive trade practices. The defendant contended that the National Manufactured Home Construction and Safety Standards Act preempted the plaintiff's state law claims. The Court held that since the plaintiffs were not seeking to hold the defendant to a construction or safety standard different than those imposed by federal law their state claims were not preempted.

Arthur Anderson & Co. v. Perry Equipment Corp.,945 S.W.2d 812 (Tex. 1997). In remanding the case for retrial the Court notes that a plaintiff's recovery may be limited by "the defendant's evidence of the plaintiff's failure to reasonably mitigate losses or evidence of intervening causes."

Worthy v. Collagen Corp., 967 S.W.2d 360 (Tex. 1998). In this case the plaintiff brought suit under the DTPA for damages resulting from the injection of a collagen implant medical device that had received pre-marketing approval from the FDA under the Medical Device Amendments to the Food, Drug and Cosmetic Act. The Court held that the federal statute preempts such an action against the manufacturer.

KPMG Peat Marwick v. HCH, 988 S.W.2d 746 (Tex. 1999). KPMG was hired by HCH to insure that a trustee bank complied with the trust indenture. Unknown to HCH, KPMG had also been hired by the trustee to prepare a report about the assets. In February, 1993, KPMG filed suit against the bank alleging mismanagement of the trust funds. Later that year, in October 1993, HCH learned that KPMG had issued a report revealing irregularities in the bank's accounting of the trust assets and had advised the bank as to the amount of necessary reserve funds. HCH sued KPMG on July 14, 1995, asserting DTPA violations. KPMG moved for summary judgment asserting the DTPA two year limitations provision which provides for claim accrual when the consumer discovers or reasonably should have discovered the occurrence of the deceptive trade practice. *See* DTPA §17.565. HCH contended that the DTPA cause of action did not accrue until October, 1993, when it learned that KPMG knew of financial irregularities but failed to report them to HCH. The Court disagreed, holding that the cause of action accrued when HCH knew of the injury; it was not necessary that it know of the specific nature of each wrongful act causing the injury. The Court concluded that HCH's knowledge of the loss caused by the bank should have caused HCH to investigate KPMG's actions as auditor. When HCH sued the bank in February, 1993 it knew of the injury and that the injury had been caused by the misconduct of another. HCH's July 1995 lawsuit was filed too late.

Gunn Infiniti, Inc. v. O'Byrne, 996 S.W.2d 854 (Tex. 1999). The plaintiff purchased an automobile from the defendant based upon the false representations that the vehicle had never been damaged. After learning the truth, the plaintiff contacted the dealer. The parties made various offers and counteroffers back and forth but were unable to reach agreement. The plaintiff filed suit and at trial the defendant contended that it was entitled to a jury issue on as to whether the defendant's offers afforded an opportunity for the plaintiff to mitigate its damages. In the most extensive discussion to date of the application of the mitigation doctrine to DTPA case, the Court held that (1) the DTPA notice/offer provisions do not foreclose the application of the common law requirement that a plaintiff mitigate his damages if he can do so with minor expense or reasonable exertions; (2) for the defendant to claim that the plaintiff's failure to accept the defendant's offer constituted a failure to mitigate the offer must not require that the plaintiff release his claim; (3) a jury issue submitting the issue of whether the failure to accept the defendant's offer constituted a failure to mitigate is proper only when the offer was "clearly" one for mitigation rather than settlement and (4) the defendant's use of the terms "settlement" or "settle" implicitly, if not explicitly, required the plaintiff to release his claims and thus did not justify a jury submission on mitigation.

In re Alford Chevrolet-Geo, et al., Relators, 997 S.W.2d 173 (Tex. 1999). In this case the plaintiffs brought a class action lawsuit against 636 Texas motor vehicle dealerships, alleging that the dealerships violated the DTPA by passing on their inventory taxes to consumers as an itemized charge. The plaintiffs did not send a pre-suit notice of their DTPA claims but did send notice on behalf of the putative class after lawsuit was filed. The notice demanded that the dealerships reimburse all consumers who paid the tax since January 1994 for the taxes paid plus expenses incurred both before and after the lawsuit was filed. The defendants sought to abate the lawsuit on the grounds that the plaintiffs failed to send them proper notice under the DTPA.

Relying on the fact that the DTPA at one time contained its own provision dealing with class notification, the dealerships argued that when that provision was dropped in 1977, consumers lost the right to bring a DTPA class action. The Court rejected this argument noting that the DTPA class notification was repealed at the same time as Texas Rule of Civil Procedure 42, dealing with class actions, was revised. The rule revisions made the DTPA class notification provision unnecessary. Finding no obvious legislative intent to abolish DTPA class actions, the Court held that the DTPA permits a consumer to provide preliminary notice on behalf of a putative class.

The dealerships next argued that the consumer's DTPA notice was defective because it sought not only pre-suit damages and expenses but also attorneys' fees and costs "to date." The Court observed that this character complaint challenged only the reasonableness of the claim, not the validity. The inclusion of post-suit fees and costs did not impair the dealerships ability to tender those expenses and attorneys fees "reasonably" incurred by the consumers and thereby preserve their defense: a defendant's ability to assert a complete defense depends on the "reasonableness of the amount tendered to pay for the consumer's expenses, not on whether the tender matches or exceeds the consumer's claimed expenses."

Finally, the dealerships contended that notwithstanding the validity of the notices, the trial court should have granted their plea in abatement and abated the case for sixty days. The Court noted, however, that no formal abatement order was required because by the time the trial court issued its ruling more than sixty days had passed since the consumers sent their notice. Further, under the current version of the DTPA, a suit is automatically abated on the 11th day after the date a proper plea in abatement is filed if no controverting affidavit is filed. DTPA §17.505. With respect to the claims automatically abated, the trial court did not need to grant another abatement.

Underkofler v. Vanasek, 53 S.W.3d 343 (Tex. 2001). This is a legal malpractice suit in which the plaintiff sought to avoid the statute of limitations defense in DTPA §17.565 by invoking the tolling provision recognized in *Hughes v. Mahaney & Higgins,* 821 S.W.2d 154 (Tex. 1991). In *Hughes* the Court held that the running of limitations in a legal malpractice claim arising out of representation in litigation is tolled until all appeals of the underlying claim are exhausted. In this case the Court held that the *Hughes* tolling provision did not apply to a claim under the DTPA. The Court reasoned that the legislature incorporated a discovery rule exception and a fraudulent concealment exception into DTPA §17.565 and that to apply the *Hughes* rule would effectively rewrite the statute.

Helena Chemical Co. v. Wilkins, 47 S.W.3d 486 (Tex. 2001). This case involved the sale of seed to a farmer. The invoices, delivery tickets and seed label contained a "limitation of liability and remedies clause limiting the consumers damages to the purchase price. Relying on prior case law, the court held that such a limitation is effective under the DTPA as to warranties but is ineffective to limit damages for nonwarranty representations or unconscionability. *See* DTPA §17.42(a).

The court also dealt with the "puffing defense." The court held that statements that the defendant's seed was "one of the most durable, top yielding hybrids" with "an outstanding disease tolerance package," "excellent" yield potential, "excellent weatherability" and was a "good dry land variety and that it would hold up well under the dry land conditions" constituted specific representations which amounted to more than mere puffing. The court noted, in passing, that no appellate court had extended the puffing defense to violations of DTPA §17.46(b)(23) (non-disclosure) or DTPA §17.50 (a)(3) (unconscionable conduct). *See also Bradford v. Vento,* 48 S.W.3d 749 (Tex. 2001) (holding that a representation was too vague to be actionable but not mentioning the word "puffing").

Provident Life and Acc. Ins. Co. v. Knott, 128 S.W.3d (Tex. 2003). In this suit for misrepresentation and wrongful denial of disability benefits, one of the issues presented was whether the insurance company's letter constituted a denial of the claim sufficient to trigger the commencement of the limitations period, as a matter of law. The Court concluded that although the insurance company's letter in this case did not use the term "deny," it did meet the test of clearly conveying the company's decision to deny the claim and its reasons for that decision. As such, it qualified as an "outright denial," warranting a summary judgment on the limitations issue.

PPG Industries v. JMB/Houston Centers, 146 S.W. 3d 79 (Tex. 2004). This case concerns the statute of limitations on a breach of warranty claim and application of the discovery rule.

The original owner of a forty-six story building, completed in 1978, encountered problems with some of the building's windows manufactured and installed by PPG. PPG had issued a five-year warranty and when the owner complained in 1982, PPG replaced about twenty-five percent of the building's windows, a process that took three years. In 1989, the building was sold and, as part of the sale, all building warranties were assigned to the purchaser. When the purchaser encountered problems with the windows in 1991, it sued PPG under the UCC and the DTPA for breach of the five-year warranty and for breach of a PPG trade publication advertisement which the purchaser contended qualified as a twenty-year warranty. The purchaser prevailed in the lower courts on both warranties

On appeal the Court reversed the judgment for the purchaser, holding that the five-year warranty claim was barred by the four-year statute of limitations and was not saved by application of the discovery rule. The Court rebuffed the purchasers argument that the design defect which existed in all of the windows at the time of delivery was not discovered until many years after the 1982 window complaints: the Court held that, as a matter of law, even if it was not possible to spot problems with each window in 1982, the large number of failed windows put the purchaser or its predecessor on notice of a design defect. The Court also held that each window could not be treated as a separate product for limitation's purposes, that repairs such as those performed by PPG did not extend the limitations period for warranty claims, that there was no evidence that PPG gave false assurances to the owner that the problem had been repaired, and, finally, that PPG had no duty to be forthcoming and tell the building owner everything PPG knew about the window defects.

As for the twenty-year warranty, the existence of which was contested by PPG, the Court held that if such a warranty existed, it was a warranty against window seal failure during a twenty-year period; limitations would not run for any individual window until the failure of its seal was or should have been discovered; accordingly, if this warranty was established on remand, a breach of warranty claim would not be barred by limitations.

Mills v. Warner Lambert Co., 157 S.W.3d 424 (Tex. 2005). The Court holds that the Federal Food, Drug and Cosmetic Act did not have a forum preempting effect and did not vest exclusive jurisdiction of DTPA claims, concerning the efficacy of certain non-prescription head-lice remedies, in federal courts. The Court did not reach the issue of whether or not the FDCA, through ordinary preemption, provided a defense to the plaintiffs' claims.

Geodyne Energy Income Production Partnership I-E v. Newton Corp., 161 S.W.3d 482 (Tex. 2005). The Court holds that in a claim under the Texas Securities Act a quitclaim deed of the owner's interest in a mineral lease did not constitute a representation of the validity of the lease. In the course of the opinion, the Court wrote: "the merger doctrine may not prevent proof of prior misrepresentations under the Deceptive Trade Practices-Consumer Protection Act."

Gonzales v. S. W. Olshan Found. Repair Co., LLC, 400 S.W.3d 52 (Tex. 2013). The Court held that the common law doctrine of fraudulent concealment does not apply to DTPA claims. The DTPA limitations provision (DTPA §17.565) for fraudulent concealment tolls limitations for only 180 days, not until actual discovery of the fraudulent concealment. Even with the extra 180 days, Mrs. Gonzales's suit was not timely filed, and so her DTPA claims were all barred by limitations.

§13.00   CONTRIBUTION AND INDEMNITY

Swafford v. View-Caps Water Supply Corp., 617 S.W.2d 674 (Tex. 1981). The plaintiff sued the sellers of land who he alleged misrepresented the availability of a water tap from View-Caps. The sellers sought indemnity from View-Caps pursuant to §17.55A. The jury found View-Caps liable to the plaintiff but absolved the primary defendants. The Court held that the sellers were entitled to recover their attorneys' fees from View-Caps under §17.55A since View-Caps was found liable for the damaging event.

Plas-Tex, Inc. v. U.S. Steel Corp., 772 S.W.2d 442 (Tex. 1989). U.S. Steel manufactured and Plas-Tex sold allegedly defective goods to the plaintiff. The trial court rendered judgment against U.S. Steel for breach of warranty and violations of the DTPA and rendered a take-nothing judgment in favor of Plas-Tex, ruling that U.S. Steel should indemnify Plas-Tex for its attorney's fees pursuant to DTPA §17.55A (now §17.555). U.S. Steel appealed and the court of appeals reversed and remanded the entire case for new trial. The Supreme Court held that §17.55A was intended to incorporate into the DTPA "existing principals of contribution and indemnity law." The Court held that the court of appeals properly reversed Plas-Tex's award of indemnity for attorney's fees because the indemnitor, U.S. Steel, had not been found liable to the plaintiff (due to the court of appeals' reversal of the trial court's finding). Since under established law no right of indemnity exists against a defendant who is not liable to the plaintiff, Plas-Tex had to await the results of the remanded trial before seeking indemnification from U.S. Steel. *See also Stewart Title Guar. Co. v. Sterling*, 822 S.W.2d 1 (Tex. 1991); *First Title Co. of Waco v. Garrett*, 860 S.W.2d 74 (Tex. 1993).

§14.00   OTHER DECISIONS

§14.01   PLEADING

Troutman v. Traeco Bldg. Systems, Inc., 724 S.W.2d 385 (Tex. 1987). In this case, involving construction defects, the jury found that the defendant represented that its guarantee or warranty involved rights or remedies which it did not have or involve. The court of appeals held that the plaintiff did not plead a cause of action on a ground of recovery to support this jury question. The Supreme Court reversed holding that the petition alleged that the defendant represented that the roof would perform in a manner superior to its actual performance and prayed for damages in accordance with the DTPA. This pleading comported with subdivisions (12) and (19) of §17.46(b).

Bell v. Meeks, 725 S.W.2d 179 (Tex. 1987). Plaintiff brought suit against the defendant for negligence and breach of express and implied warranties. After all the evidence was in the plaintiffs sought to amend to include a claim for misrepresentation under the DTPA. After the jury returned the verdict the trial court granted the amendment. The court of appeals reversed holding that the trial court had abused its discretion. The Supreme Court held that the trial court did not abuse its discretion in permitting the trial amendment because the issue of misrepresentation was tried by consent. The Court noted that "we fail to see how the issue of misrepresentation would have been tried differently than the warranty issues." *Id.* at 180.

§14.02   ASSIGNMENT/SURVIVAL

Shell Oil Co. v. Chapman, 682 S.W.2d 257 (Tex. 1984). The Court reserves for later decision the question of whether a DTPA cause of action survives to the estate.

§14.03   DTPA Forms and Practice Guide Desk Book

PPG Industries v. JMB/Houston Centers, 146 S.W.3d 79 (Tex. 2004). This case concerns the issue of whether DTPA claims are assignable.

The original owner of a building encountered problems with the building's windows manufactured and installed by PPG. PPG replaced some but not all of the windows. Several years later the building was sold and, as part of the sale, all building warranties were assigned to the purchaser. When the purchaser encountered problems with the windows, it sued PPG under the UCC and the DTPA for breach of two express warranties: a five-year warranty given to the first owner and a twenty-year warranty advertised in a trade publication and relied upon by the architect. The jury found that both warranties had been breached and the purchaser recovered the cost of window replacement, which sum was trebled under the original version of the DTPA.

A divided Court reversed the judgment, holding that DTPA claims are not assignable. The Court indicated, however, that its holding did not prohibit an equitable assignment such as a contingent-fee interest assigned to a consumer's attorney. The questions of whether claims "that were created within and could not be brought without the DTPA" are assignable and whether DTPA claims survive to a consumer's heirs were reserved by the Court for another day.

§14.03   Venue

Legal Security Life Insurance Co. v. Trevino, 605 S.W.2d 857 (Tex. 1980). The Court held that venue is proper under the DTPA in a county in which the defendant "has done business" where the venue fact proved is the single transaction which is the basis of the suit.

Hodges v. Casey, 646 S.W.2d 175 (Tex. 1983). The Supreme Court held that §17.50 of the DTPA does not require proof of the cause of action as a predicate to maintain venue.

Wyatt v. Shaw Plumbing Co., 760 S.W.2d 245 (Tex. 1988). This case involved the requirement that a second suit, the subject matter of which is inherently interrelated to a prior filed suit, be abated pending disposition of the earlier litigation. In a concurring opinion, Justice Kilgarlin suggests that a consumer who gives §17.505 notice should be protected from losing venue to a seller who files a lawsuit during the notice period. In a dissenting opinion, Justice Gonzalez states that a consumer who files a DTPA lawsuit without giving the required notice is estopped from relying on a first-filed suit to abate a subsequent suit.

§14.04   Miscellaneous

Bonded Realty v. St. Paul Ins. Co., 583 S.W.2d 619 (Tex. 1979) (*per curiam*). The question before the Court was whether deceptive trade practices were covered under a liability policy which excluded coverage for "dishonesty, intentional fraud, criminal or malicious acts." In a *per curiam* opinion the Court disapproved of the lower court's opinion that all "unlawful" acts were excluded by the policy. The court affirmed the lower court's judgment denying coverage because all of the defendant's acts were either found to be knowing misrepresentations or intertwined with the knowing misconduct.

Pace v. State, 650 S.W.2d 64 (Tex. 1983). In this case, the Court held that treble damages are not payable from the Real Estate Recovery Fund, Tex. Rev. Civ. Stat. Article 6573a since they are in the nature of punitive damages.

Weitzel v. Barnes, 691 S.W.2d 598 (Tex. 1985). The Court held that the parol evidence rule did not prevent proof of an oral representation as to the quality of goods even when a written contract gives the buyer the right to inspect those goods.

Kish v. Van Note, 692 S.W.2d 463 (Tex. 1985). The Court rejects the lower court conclusion that recovery under the DTPA precluded recovery under other legal theories. Since recovery under the DTPA is generally cumulative, simultaneous recovery under the DTPA and the Consumer Credit Code is allowed.

State v. Bachynsky, 770 S.W.2d 563 (Tex. 1989). In this enforcement lawsuit brought by the Texas Attorney General's Office, the Court held that civil penalties may be imposed pursuant to §17.47(e) even without a showing of a "knowing" violation of the injunction.

Haney v. Purcell Co., Inc., 770 S.W.2d 566 (Tex. 1989). The Haneys purchased a house from the builder. The property had been a cemetery. The court of appeals held that since the property had been abandoned as a cemetery prior to the purchase there could be no cause of action under the DTPA. The Supreme Court held this to be a grave error. The Haneys' claims were not precluded by the fact of abandonment.

Subaru of America v. David McDavid Nissan, 84 S.W.3d 212 (Tex. 2002). The Texas Supreme Court held that before a party may bring a DTPA claim pursuant to and for violation of the Texas Motor Vehicle Commission Code he must exhaust his administrative remedies by obtaining Texas Motor Vehicle Board findings.

Gonzales v. S. W. Olshan Found. Repair Co., LLC, 400 S.W.3d 52 (Tex. 2013). In *Melody Home Manufacturing Co. v. Barnes*, 741 S.W.2d 349 (Tex. 1987), the Texas Supreme Court recognized an implied warranty that services rendered for the repair or modification of existing tangible goods will be performed in a good and workmanlike manner and held that, as a matter of public policy, this implied warranty could not be waived or disclaimed. In *Gonzales v. Olshan*, the jury found that Olshan did not breach its express warranty, but that Olshan breached the *Melody Home* implied warranty and engaged in unconscionable action under the DTPA. Olshan appealed. The Court held that the *Melody Home* implied warranty was superseded by Olshan's lifetime express warranty. Like the implied warranty of good workmanship in new construction recognized in *Humber v. Morton*, 426 S.W.2d 554, 555 (Tex. 1968), the implied warranty of good workmanship and repair services is a "gap-filler" or "default warranty," which can be superseded by an express warranty which "sufficiently describes the manner, performance or quality" of how the services are to be performed.

TABLE OF SUPREME COURT OPINIONS

Abbott Laboratories v. Segura	48, 60
Aetna Cas. & Sur. Co. v. Marshall	63
Aguilar v. Autohaus, Inc.	53, 85
Allstate Insurance Company v. Watson	65
Alvarado v. Bolton	84
American Physicians Ins. Exchange v. Garcia	66
Amstadt v. U.S. Brass Corp.	48
Arthur Anderson & Co. v. Perry Equipment Corp.	45, 76, 80, 88
Ashford Development v. U.S. Life Real Estate Service.	52
Associated Indemnity Corp. v. Cat Contracting	71
Barker v. Eckman	80
Bell v. Meeks	91
Best v. Ryan Auto Group, Inc.	70
Big H Auto Auction, Inc. v. Saenz Motor.	43
Birchfield v. Texarkana Memorial Hospital	44, 47, 74
Black v. Victoria Lloyds Ins. Co.	53
Bonded Realty v. St. Paul Ins. Co.	92
Boyles v. Kerr	75
Bradford v. Vento	56, 62
Brainard v. Trinity Universal Ins. Co.	68
Brown v. American Transfer & Storage Co.	73, 82, 83
Brown v. Bank of Galveston, N.A.	55, 71
Brown v. Galleria Area Ford, Inc.	47, 59, 70
Cail v. Service Motors, Inc.	84
Cameron v. Terrell & Garrett, Inc.	41, 46
Cathey v. Metropolitan Life Insurance Co.	65
Celtic Life Ins. Co v. Coats	48, 66
Centex Homes et al v. Buecher et al.	58
Ceshker v. Bankers Comm'l Life Co.	62
Chastain v. Koonce	43, 59
Chitsey v. National Lloyds Insurance Co.	63
Cielo Dorado Development, Inc. v. Certainteed Corp.	84
Crawford v. Ace Sign, Inc.	54
Crown Life Ins. Co. v. Casteel	55, 67, 83
Cruz v. Andrews Restoration, Inc., 364 S.W.3d 817 (Tex. 2012)	78
Dairyland County Mut. Ins. v. Childress	81
DeWitt County Electric Cooperative, Inc. v. Parks	45, 55, 72
Doe v. Boys Clubs of Greater Dallas, Inc.	53, 71
Donwerth v. Preston II Chrysler-Dodge, Inc.	52, 81
Douglas v. Delp	55
Duncan v. Luke Johnson Ford, Inc.	73
Durham v. St. John	78
Eagle Properties, Ltd. v. Scharbauer	52
Earle v. Ratliff	49
Eckman v. Centennial Savings Bank	44
English v. Fischer	39, 42
Farmers & Merchants State Bank v. Ferguson	41, 73
Farrell v. Hunt	74
First Title Co. of Waco v. Garrett	53, 86
Flenniken v. Longview Bank & Trust Co.	42, 46

Supreme Court Opinions

Forbau v. Aetna Life Ins. Co.	65
Ford Motor Co. v. Ledesma	72
Geodyne Energy Income Production Partnership I-E v. Newton Corp.	90
Gonzales v. S. W. Olshan Found. Repair Co., LLC	90, 93
Gorman v. Life Ins. Co. of North America	65
Gormley v. Stover	48
Great American Ins. v. Austin Utility	66, 80
Gulf States Utilities Co. v. Low	77
Gunn Infiniti, Inc. v. O'Byrne	77, 88
Haney v. Purcell Co.	93
Haynes & Boone v. Bowser Bouldin, Ltd.	71
Helena Chemical Co. v. Wilkins	56, 72, 89
Henry S. Miller Company v. Bynum	75
Hi-Line Elec. Co. v. Travelers Ins. Companies	62
Hines v. Hash	86
Hodges v. Casey	92
Home Savings Association v. Guerra	47
Hurst v. Sears, Roebuck Co.	51, 59, 70
In re Alford Chevrolet-Geo, et. al., Relators	40, 88
Insurance Co. of N. Am v. Morris	45, 66
Jack B. Anglin Company, Inc. v. Tipps	86
Jacobs v. Danny Darby Real Estate, Inc.	74
Jim Walter Homes, Inc. v. Valencia	40, 52, 78
Johnson & Higgins of Texas v. Kenneco Energy	66, 83
Jones v. Smith	81
Karl and Kelly Company, Inc. v. McLerran	46
Kennedy v. Sale	43
Kennemore v. Bennett	52, 60, 85
Ken Petroleum Corp. v. Questor Drilling Corp.	56
Kinerd v. Colonial Leasing Co.	60
Kish v. Van Note	74, 93
Klein v. Dooley	82
Knight v. International Harvester Credit Corp.	42
Koral Industries v. Security-Connecticut Life Ins. Co.	64
KPMG Peat Marwick v. HCH	88
La Sara Grain v. First National Bank of Mercedes	39, 43, 57
Lamar Homes, Inc. v. Mid-Continent Cas. Co.	69
Latham v. Castillo	61, 72
Leal v. Furniture Barn, Inc.	50
Legal Security Life Insurance Co. v. Trevino	92
Leissner v. Schott	81
Leonard & Harral Packing Co. v. Ward	79
Leyendecker & Associates, Inc. v. Wechter	74
Liberty Mutual Ins. v. Garrison Contractors	67
Light v. Wilson	46
Litton Indus. Products, Inc. v. Gammage	39
Ludt v. McCollum	75
Luna v. North Star Dodge Sales, Inc.	73
MacGregor Medical Ass'n v. Campbell	49
Man Engines & Components, Inc. v. Shows	58
Mancorp, Inc. v. Culpepper	75
Martin v. E. McKee Realtors, Inc.	78

Matthews v. Candlewood Builders, Inc.	80
Mayo v. John Hancock Mut. Life Ins. Co.	63
McKinley v. Drozd	79
Melody Home Mfg. Co. v. Barnes	44, 57
Metro Allied Ins. Agency v. Lin	69, 72
Mid Century Ins. Co. of Texas v. Boyte	68
Miller v. Keyser	49
Mills v. Warner Lambert Co.	90
Murphy v. Russell	50
Nissan Motor Co. v. Armstrong	49
Ojeda de Toca v. Wise	84
Ogden v. Dickinson State Bank	51
Pace v. State	92
Pan American Life Ins. v. Erbauer Const.	65
Parkins v. Texas Farmers Ins. Co.	51, 70
Parkway Co. v. Woodruff	57, 60, 76
Pennington v. Singleton	40, 46, 50
Plas-Tex, Inc. v. U.S. Steel Corp.	91
PPG Industries v. JMB/Houston Centers	49, 58, 90, 92
Progressive County Mutual Ins. Co. v. Boyd	68
Provident Am. Ins. Co. v. Castaneda	67
Provident Life and Acc. Ins. Co. v. Knott	90
Prudential Ins. Co. v. Jefferson Associates	70, 87
Qantel Business Systems, Inc. v. Custom Controls Co.	47
Ramsey v. General Motors Corp.	84
Redman Homes v. Ivy	88
Riverside Nat. Bank v. Lewis	40
Robinson v. Preston Chrysler Plymouth, Inc.	51
Rocky Mountain Helicopters, Inc. v. Lubbock County Hosp. Dist.	58, 71
Rocor Intern. v. National Union Fire Ins.	68
Royal Globe Ins. Co. v. Bar Consultants, Inc.	50, 62
St. Paul Surplus Lines v. Dal-Worth Tank Co.	54, 79
Shell Oil Co. v. Chapman	91
Sherman Simon Enter. v. Lorac Service Corp.	44
Smith v. Baldwin	40, 51, 78, 83
Smith v. Gray	87
Sorokolit v. Rhodes	48
Southwestern Bell Telephone Co. v. FDP Corp.	85
Spencer v. Eagle Star Ins. Co.	82
Splettstosser v. Myers	82
Spradling v. Williams	82
Stagner v. Friendswood Development Company, Inc.	39, 41
State v. Bachynsky	93
State Farm Life Ins. Co. v. Beaston	76
State Farm Life Ins. Co. v. Martinez	69
State Farm Lloyds v. Nicolau	61
Stevens v. National Education Centers, Inc.	83
Stewart Title Guar. Co. v. Aiello	66
Stewart Title Guar. Co. v. Sterling	80, 86
Subaru of America v. David McDavid Nissan	93
Swafford v. View-Caps Water Supply Corp.	91
Texas Mutual Ins. Co. v. Ruttiger	69

SUPREME COURT OPINIONS

Tony Gullo Motors I, L.P. v. Chapa	56, 79, 80
Transport, Inc. v. Faircloth	45, 54, 66
Trinity Universal Ins. Co. v. Bleeker	72
Troutman v. Traeco Bldg. Systems, Inc.	91
Underkofler v. Vanasek	89
Vail v. Texas Farm Bureau Mutual Insurance Co.	63, 75
Walden v. Jeffery	48
W.O. Bankston Nissan, Inc. v. Walters	75
Weitzel v. Barnes	47, 52, 70, 92
Willis v. Maverick	85
Woods v. Littleton	39, 40
Woods v. William M. Mercer, Inc.	52
Worthy v. Collagen Corp.	88
Wyatt v. Shaw Plumbing Co.	92

DTPA Forms and Practice Guide Desk Book

TOPICAL INDEX OF SUPREME COURT OPINIONS

ARTICLE 21.21/CHAPTER 541 62

    Aetna Cas. & Sur. Co. v. Marshall, 724 S.W.2d 770 (Tex. 1987)
    Allstate Insurance Company v. Watson, 876 S.W.2d 145 (Tex. 1994)
    American Physicians Insurance Exchange v. Garcia, 876 S.W.2d 842 (Tex. 1994)
    Brainard v. Trinity Universal Ins. Co., 216 S.W.3d 809 (Tex. 2006)
    Cathey v. Metropolitan Life Insurance Co., 805 S.W.2d 387 (Tex. 1991)
    Celtic Life Insurance Co. v. Coats, 885 S.W.2d 96 (Tex. 1994)
    Ceshker v. Bankers Comm'l Life Co., 568 S.W.2d 128 (Tex. 1978)
    Chitsey v. National Lloyds Insurance Co., 738 S.W.2d 641 (Tex. 1987)
    Crown Life Ins. Co. v. Casteel, 22 S.W.3d 378 (Tex. 2000)
    Forbau v. Aetna Life Ins. Co., 876 S.W.2d 132 (Tex. 1994)
    Gorman v. Life Ins. Co. of North America, 811 S.W.2d 542 (Tex. 1991)
    Great American Ins. v. Austin Utility, 908 S.W.2d 415 (Tex. 1995)
    Hi-Line Elec. Co. v. Travelers Ins. Companies, 593 S.W.2d 953 (Tex. 1980)
    Johnson & Higgins of Tex. v. Kenneco Energy, 962 S.W.2d 507 (Tex. 1998)
    Koral Industries v. Security-Connecticut Life Ins. Co., 802 S.W.2d 650 (Tex. 1990)
    Lamar Homes, Inc. v. Mid-Continent Cas. Co., 242 S.W.3d 1 (Tex. 2007)
    Liberty Mut. Ins. v. Garrison Contractors, 966 S.W.2d 482 (Tex. 1998)
    Mayo v. John Hancock Mut. Life Ins. Co., 711 S.W.2d 5 (Tex. 1986)
    Metro Allied Ins. Agency v. Lin, 304 S.W.3d 830 (Tex. 2009)
    Mid Century Ins. Co. of Texas v. Boyte, 80 S.W. 3rd 546 (Tex. 2002)
    Pan American Life Ins. v. Erbauer Const., 805 S.W.2d 395 (Tex. 1991)
    Progressive County Mutual Ins. Co. v. Boyd, 177 S.W.3d 919 (Tex. 2005)
    Provident Am. Ins. Co. v. Castaneda, 988 S.W.2d 189 (Tex. 1998)
    Rocor Intern. v. National Union Fire Ins., 77 S.W. 3d 253 (Tex. 2002)
    Royal Globe Ins. Co. v. Bar Consultants, Inc., 577 S.W.2d 688 (Tex. 1979)
    State Farm Life Ins. Co. v. Martinez, 216 S.W.3d 799 (Tex. 2007)
    Stewart Title Guar. Co. v. Aiello, 941 S.W.2d 68 (Tex. 1997)
    Texas Mutual Ins. Co. v. Ruttiger, ___ S.W.3d ___ , 54 Tex. Sup. J. 1642 (Tex. August 26, 2011)

    Texas Mutual Ins. Co. v. Ruttiger, 381 S.W.3d 430 (Tex. 2012)
    Transport Inc. v. Faircloth, 898 S.W. 2d 269 (Tex. 1995)
    Vail v. Texas Farm Bureau Mutual Insurance Co., 754 S.W.2d 129 (Tex. 1988)

ASSIGNMENT/SURVIVAL 91

    PPG Industries v. JMB/Houston Centers, 146 S.W.3d 79 (Tex. 2004)
    Shell Oil Co. v. Chapman, 682 S.W.2d 257 (Tex. 1984)

ATTORNEY'S FEES 79

Recovery by Plaintiff   79
    Arthur Anderson & Co. v. Perry Equipment Corp., 945 S.W.2d 812 (Tex. 1997)
    Barker v. Eckman, 213 S.W.3d 306 (Tex. 2006)
    Great American Ins. v. Austin Utility, 908 S.W.2d 415 (Tex. 1995)
    Matthews v. Candlewood Builders, Inc., 685 S.W.2d 649 (Tex. 1985)
    McKinley v. Drozd, 685 S.W.2d 7 (Tex. 1985)
    Stewart Title Guar. Co. v. Sterling, 822 S.W.2d 1 (Tex. 1991)
    Tony Gullo Motors I, L.P. v. Chapa, 212 S.W.3d 299 (Tex. 2006)

Supreme Court Opinions

Recovery by Defendant 81
Dairyland County Mut. Ins. v. Childress, 650 S.W.2d 770 (Tex. 1983)
Donwerth v. Preston II Chrysler-Dodge, Inc., 775 S.W.2d 634 (Tex. 1989)
Jones v. Smith, 649 S.W.2d 29 (Tex. 1983)
Klein v. Dooley, 949 S. W.2d 307 (Tex. 1997)
Leissner v. Schott, 668 S.W.2d 686 (Tex. 1984)
Splettstosser v. Myers, 779 S.W.2d 806 (Tex. 1989)

BREACH OF WARRANTY 57
Centex Homes v. Buecher, 95 S.W. 3d 266 (Tex. 2002)
Gonzales v. S. W. Olshan Found. Repair Co., LLC, 400 S.W.3d 52 (Tex. 2013)
Humber v. Morton, 426 S.W.2d 554, 555 (Tex. 1968)
La Sara Grain v. First Nat'l Bank of Mercedes, 673 S.W.2d 558 (Tex. 1984)
Man Engines & Components, Inc. v. Shows, 434 S.W.3d 132 (Tex. 2014)
Melody Home Mfg. Co. v. Barnes, 741 S.W.2d 349 (Tex. 1987)
Parkway Co. v. Woodruff, 901 S.W.2d 434 (Tex. 1995)
PPG Industries v. JMB/Houston Centers, 146 S.W.3d 79 (Tex. 2004)
Rocky Mountain Helicopters, Inc. v. Lubbock County Hosp. Dist., 987 S.W.2d 50 (Tex. 1998)
Tony Gullo Motors I, L.P. v. Chapa, 212 S.W.3d 299 (Tex. 2006)

CAUSATION 70
Associated Indemnity Corp. v. Cat Contracting, 964 S.W.2d 276 (Tex. 1998)
Best v. Ryan Auto Group, Inc., 786 S.W.2d 670 (Tex. 1990)
Brown v. Bank of Galveston, N.A., 963 S.W.2d 511 (Tex. 1998)
Brown v. Galleria Area Ford, Inc., 752 S.W.2d 114 (Tex. 1988).
DeWitt County Electric Cooperative, Inc. v. Parks, et al., 1 S.W.3d 96 (Tex. 1999)
Doe v. Boys Clubs of Greater Dallas, Inc., 907 S.W. 2d 472 (Tex. 1995)
Ford Motor Co. v. Ledesma, 242 S.W.3d 32, 46 (Tex. 2007)
Haynes & Boone v. Bowser Bouldin, Ltd, 896 S.W.2d 179 (Tex. 1995)
Helena Chemical Co. v. Wilkins, 47 S.W.3d 486 (Tex. 2001)
Hurst v. Sears, Roebuck & Co., 647 S.W.2d 249 (Tex. 1983)
Metro Allied Ins. Agency v. Lin, 304 S.W.3d 830 (Tex. 2009).
Parkins v. Texas Farmers Ins. Co., 645 S.W.2d 775 (Tex. 1983)
Prudential Ins. Co. v. Jefferson Associates, 896 S.W.2d 156 (Tex. 1995)
Rocky Mountain Helicopters, Inc. v. Lubbock County Hosp. Dist., 987 S.W.2d 50 (Tex. 1998)
Trinity Universal Ins. Co. v. Bleeker, 966 S.W.2d 489 (Tex. 1998)
Weitzel v. Barnes, 691 S.W.2d 598 (Tex. 1985)

CONTRIBUTION AND INDEMNITY 91
Plas-Tex, Inc. v. U.S. Steel Corp., 772 S.W.2d 442 (Tex. 1989)
Swafford v. View-Caps Water Supply Corp., 617 S.W.2d 674 (Tex. 1981)

DAMAGES 73

Actual Damages 73
Arthur Anderson & Co. v. Perry Equipment Corp., 945 S.W.2d 812 (Tex. 1997)
Birchfield v. Texarkana Memorial Hospital, 747 S.W.2d 361 (Tex. 1987)
Boyles v. Kerr, 855 S.W.2d 593 (Tex. 1993)
Brown v. American Transfer & Storage Co., 601 S.W.2d 931 (Tex. 1980)
Cruz v. Andrews Restoration, Inc., 364 S.W.3d 817 (Tex. 2012)
Duncan v. Luke Johnson Ford, Inc., 603 S.W.2d 777 (Tex. 1980)
Farmers and Merchants State Bank v. Ferguson, 617 S.W.2d 918 (Tex. 1981)

DTPA Forms and Practice Guide Desk Book

Farrell v. Hunt, 714 S.W.2d 298 (Tex. 1986)
Gulf States Utilities Co. v. Low, 79 S.W. 3d 561 (Tex. 2002)
Gunn Infiniti, Inc. v. O'Byrne, 996 S.W.2d 854 (Tex. 1999)
Henry S. Miller Company v. Bynum, 836 S.W.2d 160 (Tex. 1992)
Jacobs v. Danny Darby Real Estate, Inc., 750 S.W.2d 174 (Tex. 1988)
Kish v. Van Note, 692 S.W. 463 (Tex. 1985)
Latham v. Castillo, 972 S.W.2d 66 (Tex. 1998)
Leyendecker & Associates, Inc. v. Wechter, 683 S.W.2d 369 (Tex. 1984)
Ludt v. McCollum, 762 S.W.2d 575 (Tex. 1988)
Luna v. North Star Dodge Sales, Inc., 667 S.W.2d 115 (Tex. 1984)
Mancorp, Inc. v. Culpepper, 802 S.W.2d 226 (Tex. 1990)
Parkway Co. v. Woodruff, 901 S.W.2d 434 (Tex. 1995)
State Farm Life Ins. Co. v. Beaston, 907 S.W.2d 430 (Tex. 1995)
Vail v. Texas Farm Bureau Mutual Ins. Co., 754 S.W.2d 129 (Tex. 1988)
W. O. Bankston Nissan, Inc. v. Walters, 754 S.W.2d 127 (Tex. 1988)

Treble Damages 78
Durham v. St. John, 645 S.W.2d 261 (Tex. 1983)
Jim Walter Homes, Inc. v. Valencia, 690 S.W.2d 239 (Tex. 1985)
Leonard & Harral Packing Co. v. Ward, 937 S.W.2d 425 (Tex. 1996)
Martin v. E. McKee Realtors, Inc., 663 S.W.2d 446 (Tex. 1984)
Smith v. Baldwin, 611 S.W.2d 611 (Tex. 1980)
St. Paul Surplus Lines v. Dal-Worth Tank Co., 974 S.W.2d 51 (Tex. 1998)
Tony Gullo Motors I, L.P. v. Chapa, 212 S.W.3d 299 (Tex. 2006)

DEFENSES/NOTICE 83
Aguilar v. Autohaus, Inc., 800 S.W.2d 853 (Tex. 1991)
Alvarado v. Bolton, 749 S.W.2d 47 (Tex. 1988)
Arthur Anderson & Co. v. Perry Equipment Corp.,945 S.W.2d 812 (Tex. 1997)
Brown v. American Transfer & Storage Co., 601 S.W.2d 931 (Tex. 1980)
Cail v. Service Motors, Inc., 660 S.W.2d 814 (Tex. 1983)
Cielo Dorado Development, Inc. v. Certainteed Corp., 744 S.W.2d 10 (Tex. 1988)
First Title Co. of Waco v. Garrett, 860 S.W.2d 74 (Tex. 1993)
Geodyne Energy Income Production Partnership I-E v. Newton Corp., 161 S.W.3d 482 (Tex. 2005)
Gonzales v. S. W. Olshan Found. Repair Co., LLC, 400 S.W.3d 52 (Tex. 2013)
Gunn Infiniti, Inc. v. O'Byrne, 996 S.W.2d 854 (Tex. 1999)
Helena Chemical Co. v. Wilkins, 47 S.W.3d 486 (Tex. 2001)
Hines v. Hash, 843 S.W.2d 464 (Tex. 1992)
In Re: Alford Chevrolet-Geo, et al., Relators, 997 S.W.2d 173 (Tex. 1999)
Jack B. Anglin Company, Inc. v. Tipps, 842 S.W.2d 266 (Tex. 1992)
Kennemore v. Bennett, 755 S.W.2d 89 (Tex. 1988)
KPMG Peat Marwick v. HCH, 988 S.W.2d 746 (Tex. 1999)
Mills v. Warner Lambert Co., 157 S.W.3d 424 (Tex. 2005)
Ojeda de Toca v. Wise, 748 S.W.2d 449 (Tex. 1988)
PPG Industries v. JMB/Houston Centers, 146 S.W.3d 79 (Tex. 2004)
Provident Life and Accident Insurance Company v. Knott, 128 S.W.3d (Tex. 2003)
Prudential Ins. v. Jefferson Associates, 896 S.W.2d 156 (Tex. 1995)
Ramsey v. General Motors Corp., 685 S.W.2d 15 (Tex. 1985)
Redman Homes v. Ivy, 920 S.W.2d 664 (Tex. 1996)
Smith v. Baldwin, 611 S.W.2d 611 (Tex. 1981)
Smith v. Gray, 907 S.W. 2d 444 (Tex. 1995)
Southwestern Bell Telephone Co. v. FDP Corp., 811 S.W.2d 572 (Tex. 1991)

SUPREME COURT OPINIONS

    Stewart Title Guar. Co. v. Sterling, 822 S.W.2d 1 (Tex. 1991)
    Underkofler v. Vanasek, 53 S.W.3d 343 (Tex. 2001)
    Willis v. Maverick, 760 S.W.2d 642 (Tex. 1988)
    Worthy v. Collagen Corp., 967 S.W.2d 360 (Tex. 1998)

FALSE, MISLEADING OR DECEPTIVE ACTS OR PRACTICES 50

    Aguilar v. Autohaus, Inc., 800 S.W.2d 853 (Tex. 1991)
    Ashford Development v. U.S. Life Real Estate Service, 661 S.W.2d 933 (Tex. 1983)
    Black v. Victoria Lloyds Ins. Co., 797 S.W.2d 20 (Tex. 1990)
    Bradford v. Vento, 48 S.W.3d 749 (Tex. 2001)
    Brown v. Bank of Galveston, N.A., 963 S.W.2d 511 (Tex. 1998)
    Crawford v. Ace Sign, Inc., 917 S.W. 2d 12, (Tex. 1996)
    Crown Life Ins. Co. v. Casteel, 22 S.W.3d 378 (Tex. 2000)
    DeWitt County Electric Cooperative, Inc. v. Parks et al., 1 S.W.3d 96 (Tex. 1999)
    Doe v. Boys Clubs of Greater Dallas, Inc., 907 S.W. 2d 472 (Tex. 1995)
    Donwerth v. Preston II Chrysler-Dodge, 775 S.W.2d 634 (Tex. 1989)
    Douglas v. Delp, 987 S.W.2d 879 (Tex. 1999)
    Eagle Properties, Ltd. v. Scharbauer, 807 S.W.2d 714 (Tex. 1990)
    Helena Chemical Co. v. Wilkins, 47 S.W.3d 486 (Tex. 2001)
    Hurst v. Sears, Roebuck & Co., 647 S.W.2d 249 (Tex. 1983)
    Jim Walter Homes, Inc. v. Valencia, 690 S.W.2d 239 (Tex. 1985)
    Kennemore v. Bennett, 755 S.W.2d 89 (Tex. 1988)
    Ken Petroleum Corp. v. Questor Drilling Corp., 24 S.W.3d 344 (Tex. 2000)
    Leal v. Furniture Barn, Inc., 571 S.W.2d 864 (Tex. 1978)
    Ogden v. Dickinson State Bank, 662 S.W.2d 330 (Tex. 1983)
    Parkins v. Texas Farmers Ins. Co., 645 S.W.2d 775 (Tex. 1983)
    Pennington v. Singleton, 606 S.W.2d 682 (Tex. 1980)
    Robinson v. Preston Chrysler Plymouth, Inc., 633 S.W.2d 500 (Tex. 1982)
    Royal Globe Ins. Co. v. Bar Consultants, Inc., 577 S.W.2d 688 (Tex. 1979)
    Smith v. Baldwin, 611 S.W.2d 611 (Tex. 1980)
    St. Paul Surplus Lines v. Dal-Worth Tank Co., 974 S.W.2d 51 (Tex. 1998)
    Transport Inc. v. Faircloth, 898 S.W.2d 269 (Tex. 1995)
    Weitzel v. Barnes, 691 S.W.2d 598 (Tex. 1985)
    Woods v. William M. Mercer, Inc., 769 S.W.2d 515 (Tex. 1988)

GENERAL PROVISIONS 39

Application and Effective Dates   39
English v. Fischer, 660 S.W.2d 521 (Tex. 1983)
In Re Alford Chevrolet-Geo, et. al., Relators, 997 S.W.2d 173 (Tex. 1999)
La Sara Grain v. First Nat. Bank of Mercedes, 673 S.W.2d 558 (Tex. 1984)
Litton Indus. Products, Inc. v. Gammage, 668 S.W.2d 319 (Tex. 1984)
Stagner v. Friendswood Development Company, Inc., 620 S.W.2d 103 (Tex. 1981)
Woods v. Littleton, 554 S.W.2d 662 (Tex. 1977)

Construction of the Act   40
Jim Walter Homes, Inc. v. Valencia, 690 S.W.2d 239 (Tex. 1985)
Pennington v. Singleton, 606 S.W.2d 682 (Tex. 1980)
Smith v. Baldwin, 611 S.W.2d 611 (Tex. 1981)
Woods v. Littleton, 554 S.W.2d 662 (Tex. 1977)

JURY QUESTIONS 82

    Brown v. American Transfer & Storage Co., 601 S.W.2d 931 (Tex. 1980)

Johnson & Higgins of Tex. v. Kenneco Energy, 962 S.W.2d 507 (Tex. 1998)
Spencer v. Eagle Star Insurance Co. of America, 860 S.W.2d 868 (Tex. 1993)
Spradling v. Williams, 566 S.W.2d 561 (Tex. 1978)
Stevens v. National Education Centers, Inc., 11 S.W.3d 185 (Tex. 2000)

MISCELLANEOUS 92
Bonded Realty v. St. Paul Ins. Co., 583 S.W.2d 619 (Tex. 1979)
Haney v. Purcell Co., Inc., 770 S.W.2d 566 (Tex. 1989)
Kish v. Van Note, 692 S.W.2d 463 (Tex. 1985)
Pace v. State, 650 S.W.2d 64 (Tex. 1983)
Shell Oil Co. v. Chapman, 682 S.W.2d 257 (Tex. 1984)
State v. Bachynsky, 770 S.W.2d 563 (Tex. 1989)
Subaru of America v. David McDavid Nissan, 84 S.W.3d 212 (Tex. 2002)
Weitzel v. Barnes, 691 S.W.2d 598 (Tex. 1985)

PLEADING 91
Bell v. Meeks, 725 S.W.2d 179 (Tex. 1987)
Troutman v. Traeco Bldg. Systems, Inc., 724 S.W.2d 385 (Tex. 1987)

STANDING REQUIREMENT: WHO IS A CONSUMER?...40
Arthur Anderson & Co. v. Perry Equipment Corp., 945 S.W.2d 812 (Tex. 1997)
Big H Auto Auction, Inc. v. Saenz Motor., 665 S.W.2d 756 (Tex. 1984)
Birchfield v. Texarkana Memorial Hospital, 747 S.W.2d 361 (Tex. 1987)
Cameron v. Terrell & Garrett, Inc., 618 S.W.2d 535 (Tex. 1981)
Chastain v. Koonce, 700 S.W.2d 579 (Tex. 1985)
DeWitt County Electric Cooperative, Inc. v. Parks et al., 1 S.W.3d 96 (Tex. 1999)
Eckman v. Centennial Savings Bank, 784 S.W.2d 672 (Tex. 1990)
English v. Fischer, 660 S.W.2d 521 (Tex. 1983)
Farmers & Merchants State Bank v. Ferguson, 617 S.W.2d 918 (Tex. 1981)
Flenniken v. Longview Bank & Trust Co., 661 S.W.2d 705 (Tex. 1983)
Insurance Co. of N. Am. v. Morris, 981 S.W.2d 667 (Tex. 1998)
Kennedy v. Sale, 689 S.W.2d 890 (Tex. 1985)
Knight v. International Harvester Credit Corp., 627 S.W.2d 382 (Tex. 1982)
La Sara Grain v. First Nat. Bank of Mercedes, 673 S.W.2d 558 (Tex. 1984)
Melody Home Mfg. Co. v. Barnes, 741 S.W.2d 349 (Tex. 1987)
Riverside Nat. Bank v. Lewis, 603 S.W.2d 169 (Tex. 1980)
Sherman Simon Enter. v. Lorac Service Corp., 724 S.W.2d 13 (Tex. 1987)
Stagner v. Friendswood Development Company, Inc., 620 S.W.2d 103 (Tex. 1981)
Transport Inc. v. Faircloth, 898 S.W.2d 269 (Tex. 1995)

UNCONSCIONABILITY 59
Abbott Laboratories, Inc. v. Segura, 907 S.W.2d 503 (Tex. 1995)
Bradford v. Vento, 48 S.W.3d 749 (Tex. 2001)
Brown v. Galleria Area Ford, Inc., 752 S.W.2d 114 (Tex. 1988)
Chastain v. Koonce, 700 S.W.2d 579 (Tex. 1985)
Hurst v. Sears, Roebuck & Co., 647 S.W.2d 24 (Tex. 1983)
Insurance Co. of N. Am. v. Morris, 981 S.W.2d 667 (Tex. 1998)
Kennemore v. Bennett, 755 S.W.2d 89 (Tex. 1988)
Kinerd v. Colonial Leasing Co., 800 S.W.2d 187 (Tex. 1990)
Latham v. Castillo, 972 S.W.2d 66 (Tex. 1998)
Parkway Co. v. Woodruff, 901 S.W.2d 434 (Tex. 1995)
State Farm Lloyds v. Nicolau, 951 S. W.2d 444 (Tex. 1997)

Supreme Court Opinions

VENUE..92
> Hodges v. Casey, 646 S.W.2d 175 (Tex. 1983)
> Legal Security Life Insurance Co. v. Trevino, 605 S.W.2d 857 (Tex. 1980)
> Wyatt v. Shaw Plumbing Co., 760 S.W.2d 245 (Tex. 1988)

WHO CAN BE SUED? 46
> Abbott Laboratories, Inc. v. Segura, 907 S.W.2d 503 (Tex. 1995)
> Amstadt v. U.S. Brass Corp., 919 S.W.2d 644 (Tex. 1996)
> Birchfield v. Texarkana Memorial Hospital, 747 S.W.2d 361 (Tex. 1987)
> Brown v. Galleria Area Ford, Inc., 752 S.W.2d 114 (Tex. 1988)
> Cameron v. Terrell & Garrett, Inc., 618 S.W.2d 535 (Tex. 1981)
> Celtic Life Insurance Co. v. Coats, 885 S.W.2d 96 (Tex. 1994)
> Earle v. Ratliff, 998 S.W.2d 882 (Tex. 1999)
> Gormley v. Stover, 907 S.W.2d 448 (Tex. 1995)
> Home Savings Association v. Guerra, 733 S.W.2d 134 (Tex. 1987)
> Karl and Kelly Company, Inc. v. McLerran, 646 S.W.2d 174 (Tex. 1983)
> Light v. Wilson, 663 S.W.2d 813 (Tex. 1983).
> MacGregor Medical Ass'n v. Campbell, 985 S.W.2d 38 (Tex. 1998)
> Miller v. Keyser, 90 S.W. 3d 712 (Tex. 2002)
> Murphy v. Russell, 167 S.W.3d 835 (Tex. 2005)
> Nissan Motor Co. v. Armstrong, 145 S.W.3d 131 (Tex. 2004)
> PPG Industries, Inc. v. JMB/Houston Centers Limited Partnership, 146 S.W.3d 79, 89 (Tex. 2004)
> Pennington v. Singleton, 606 S.W.2d 682 (Tex. 1980)
> Qantel Business Systems, Inc. v. Custom Controls Co., 761 S.W.2d 302 (Tex. 1988)
> Sorokolit v. Rhodes, 889 S.W.2d 239 (Tex. 1994)
> Walden v. Jeffery, 907 S.W.2d 446 (Tex. 1995)
> Weitzel v. Barnes, 691 S.W.2d 598 (Tex. 1985)

Table of Cases

3Z Corp. v. Stewart Title Guar. Co., 851 S.W.2d 933, 937 (Tex. App. —Beaumont 1993, writ denied), §11.02.1

— A —

A. J. Miller Trucking Co. v. Wood, 474 S.W. 2d 763 (Tex. Civ. App.—Tyler 1971, writ ref'd n.r.e.), §9.13

Abbott Lab. (Ross Lab. Div.) v. Segura, 907 S.W.2d 503 (Tex. 1995), §1.02.7.4

Abramson v. City of San Angelo, 210 S.W.2d 476 (Tex. Civ. App.—Austin 1948, writ dism'd), §10. 19

Access Mediquip, L.L.C. v. United Health Care Ins. Co., 698 F.3d 229 (5th Cir. 2012), §11.06.3

Adolph Coors Co. v. Rodriguez, 780 S.W.2d 477, 481 (Tex. App.—Corpus Christi 1989, writ denied), §15.04

Aero Energy, Inc. v. Circle C Drilling Co., 699 S.W.2d 821 (Tex. 1985), §9.20.4

Aetna Casualty & Surety Co. v. Marshall, 724 S.W.2d 770 (Tex. 1987), §11.03

Aetna Casualty & Surety Co. v. Martin Surgical Supply Co., 689 S.W.2d 263 (Tex. App.—Houston [1st Dist.] 1985, writ ref'd n.r.e.), §1.02.104

Aetna Casualty & Surety Co. v. Taff, 502 S.W.2d 903, 904 (Tex. App.—Waco 1973, writ ref'd n.r.e.), §1.02.15

Aiken v. Hancock, 115 S.W.3d 26 (Tex. App.—San Antonio 2003, pet. denied), §2.02.1

Alaniz v. Jones & Neuse, Inc., 907 S.W.2d 450, 452 (Tex. 1995), §10.01.1

Allen v. Humphreys, 559 S.W.2d 798 (Tex. 1977), §§7.16, 7.23, 7.28

Allied Towing Service v. Mitchell, 833 S.W.2d 577 (Tex. App.—Dallas, 1992, no writ), §§1.02.4.1, 1.02.4.2

Allison v. Fire Insurance Exchange, 98 S.W.3d 227, 244 (Tex. App.—Austin 2002, no pet.), §5.14

Allstate Ins. Co. v. Watson, 876 S.W.2d 145, 149 (Tex. 1994), §§11.02.1, 11.03.2

Alvarado v. Bolton, 749 S.W.2d 47, 48 (Tex. 1988), §§1.02.8.3, 2.02, 2.02.2, 12.05.2, 13.02.1

Amarco Petroleum, Inc. v. Texas Pacific Indemnity Co., 889 S.W.2d 695 (Tex. App.—Houston [14th Dist.] 1994, writ denied), §11.05

Amarillo v. Langley, 651 S.W.2d 906 (Tex. App.—Amarillo 1983, no writ), §9.20.3.1

American Employers' Ins. Co. v. Aiken, 942 S.W.2d 156 (Tex. App.—Fort Worth 1997, no writ), §8.01.5

American Home Assurance Co. v. Coronado, 628 S.W.2d 818 (Tex. App.—Amarillo 1981, writ ref'd n.r.e.), §9.13

American Petrofina, Inc. v. PPG Industries, Inc., 679 S.W.2d 740 (Tex. App.—Fort Worth 1984, writ dism'd by agr.), §§6.06, 10.23

American Tobacco Co., Inc. v. Grinnell, 951 S.W.2d 420 (Tex. 1997), §2.02.6

Amstadt v. U.S. Brass Corp., 919 S.W.2d 644 (Tex. 1996), §§1.02.2, 1.02.7.1, 1.02.8

Anderson, Greenwood & Co. v. Martin, 44 S.W.3d 200 (Tex. App.—Houston [14th Dist.] 2001, pet. den'd), §10.06

Apple Imports, Inc. v. Koole, 945 S.W.2d 895 (Tex. App.—Austin 1997, writ den'd.), §1.02.8.2

Aranda v. Insurance Co. of N. Am., 748 S.W.2d 210 (Tex. 1988), §10.04, 11.04

Archibald v. Act III Arabians, 755 S.W.2d 84, 86 (Tex. 1988), §§1.02.9.2.3, 1.02.13, 10.02

Arnold v. Nat'l County Mutual Fire Ins. Co., 725 S.W.2d 165 (Tex. 1987), §§1.04, 10.04, 11.04, 15.04

Arthur Andersen & Co. v. Perry Equip. Corp., 945 S.W.2d 812, 818 (Tex. 1997), §§1.02.4.1, 1.02.4.2, 1.02.7.1, 1.02.15, 1.02.28, 2.02, 4.01, 9.20.5, 9.20.6, 9.20.7, 9.20.10, 10.14, 11.03.3

Arthur's Garage v. Racal-Chubb Sec., 997 S.W.2d 803 (Tex. App.—Dallas 1999, no writ), §1.02.9.2.4

Ashford Development, Inc. v. USLife Real Estate Services, 661 S.W.2d 933 (Tex. 1983), §1.02.8.1

Atkinson v. Reid, 625 S.W.2d 64 (Tex. App.—San Antonio 1981, no writ), §6.01

Augustine v. Nusom, 671 S.W.2d 112 (Tex. App.—Houston [14th Dist.] 1984, writ ref'd n.r.e.), §6.05

Austin Co. v. Vaughn Bldg. Corp., 643 S.W.2d 113, 115 (Tex. 1982), §1.02.9.1

Autohaus, Inc. v. Aguilar, 794 S. W.2d 459 (Tex. App.—Dallas 1990), §2.02

Avary v. Bank of Am., 72 S. W. 3d 779 (Tex. App.—Dallas 2002, pet. denied), §8.01.1

Axelson, Inc. v. McIlhany 798 S.W.2d 550 (Tex. 1990), §§7.16, 7.19, 7.32

Aztec Life Ins. Co. v. Dellana, 667 S.W.2d 911, 915 (Tex. App.—Austin 1984, no writ), §7.28

— B —

Babcock v. Northwest Memorial Hospital, 767 S. W. 2d 705 (Tex. 1989), §9.05

Bailey v. Gulf States Utilities Co., 27 S.W.3d 713 (Tex. App.—Beaumont 2000, no pet.), §1.02.5

Balandran v. Safeco Ins. Co. of Am., 972 S.W.2d 738, 741 (Tex. 1998), §11.05

Balandran; National Union Fire v. Hudson Energy, §11.05

Ballenger v. Ballenger, 694 S.W.2d 72, 76 (Tex. App.—Corpus Christi 1985, writ ref'd. n.r.e.), §5.27

Bank of Southwest N.A. v. Harlingen Nat'l Bank, 662 S.W.2d 113 (Tex. App.—Corpus Christi 1983, no writ), §5.27

Baptist Mem. Hosp. Sys. v. Sampson, 969 S.W.2d 945, 948 (Tex. 1998), §10.02

Barker v. Dunham, 551 S.W.2d 41 (Tex. 1977), §7.19

Barnett v. Aetna Life Insurance Co., 723 S.W.2d 663 (Tex. 1987), §11.05

Bartlett v. Schmidt, 33 S.W.3d 35 (Tex. Civ. App.—Corpus Christi 2000, pet. denied), §§2.02.6, 8.13

Belmont Constructors v. Lyondell Petrochemical Co., 896 S.W.2d 352 (Tex. App.—Houston [1st Dist.] 1995, no writ), §8.01.5

Ben. Recovery, Inc. v. Donelon, 521 F.3d 326 (5th Cir. 2008), §11.06.3

Benjamin Franklin Sav. Ass'n v. Kotrla, 751 S.W.2d 218 (Tex. App.—Houston [14th Dist.) 1988, no writ), §1:04

Bennett v. Bailey, 597 S.W.2d 532 (Tex. Civ. App.—Eastland 1980, writ ref'd n.r.e.), §1.02.104

Bentinck v. Franklin, 38 Tex. 458 (1873), §1.02.15

Bentwich v. Franklin and Galveston City Co., 38 Tex. 473, §1.02.15

Best v. Ryan Auto Group, Inc., 786 S.W.2d 670 (Tex. 1990), §10.25

Big H Auto Auction, Inc. v. Saenz Motors, 665 S.W.2d 756 (Tex. 1984), §1.02.5

Birchfield v. Texarkana Memorial Hospital, 747 S.W.2d 361, 367 (Tex. 1987), §§1.02.4.2, 1.02.14, 1.02.14.4, 5.17

Blackstock v. Dudley, 12 S.W.3d 131 (Tex. Amarillo 1999, no pet.), §§2.02.1, 2.02.2, 2.02.6

Blizzard v. Nationwide Mut. Fire Ins. Co., 756 S.W.2d 801, 806 (Tex. App.—Dallas 1988, no writ), §§1.02.15, 2.02.11

Bluebonnet Farms v. Gibraltar Sav. Ass'n, 618 S.W.2d 81 (Tex. Civ. App.—Houston [1st Dist.] 1980, writ ref'd n.r.e.), §6.01

Boales v. Brighton Builders, Inc., 29 S.W.3d 159 (Tex. App.—Houston [14th Dist.] 2000, no pet.), §1.02.7.4

Bohls v. Oakes, 75 S.W.3d 473 (Tex. App.—San Antonio 2002, pet. denied), §§1.02.4.1, 1.02.4.2, 13.02.1

Bohmfalk v. Linwood, 742 S.W.2d 518 (Tex. App.—Dallas 1987, no writ), §7.51

Boothe v. Dixon, 180 S.W.3d 915 (Tex.App.—Dallas, 2005, no pet.), §2.02.2

Bossier Chrysler-Dodge II, Inc. v. Riley, 221 S.W.3d 749, 752 (Tex. App.—Waco 2007, pet. denied), §1.02.14.2.2

Boswell v. Farm & Home Sav. Ass'n, 894 S.W.2d 761 (Tex. App.—Fort Worth 1994, writ denied), §8.10

Bottinelli v. Robinson, 594 S.W.2d 112 (Tex. Civ. App.—Houston [1st Dist.] 1979, no writ), §7.22

Boyles v. Kerr, 855 S.W.2d 593 (Tex. 1993), §§5.15, 10.12

Bradford v. Vento, 48 S.W.3d 749, 755 (Tex. 2001), §§1.02.8, 2.02, 10.06, 15.04

Brainard v. Trinity Universal Ins. Co., 216 S.W.3d 809 (Tex. 2006), §11.03.2

Brandon v. American Sterilizer Co., 880 S.W.2d 488, 492 (Tex. App.—Austin 1994, no writ), §1.02.4.2

Brazos River Conservation & Reclamation District v. Allen, 171 S.W.2d 847 (Tex. 1943), §5.27

Bridges v. City of Richardson, 354 S.W.2d 366, 367 (Tex. 1962), §8.10

Brooks v. First Assembly of God Church, 86 S.W.3d 793 (Tex. App.—Waco 2002, pet. dismissed), §8.13

Brown & Root, Inc. v. Moore, 731 S.W.2d 137, 140 (Tex. App.—Houston [14th Dist.] 1987, no writ), §7.32

Brown v. American Transfer & Storage Co., 601 S.W.2d 931 (Tex. 1980), §§1.02.7.4, 8.10.2 , 10.01.4, 10.03

Brown v. Galleria Area Ford, Inc., 752 S.W.2d 114 (Tex. 1988), §1.02.104

Brown v. Poff, 387 S.W.2d 101 (Tex. Civ. App.—El Paso 1965, writ ref'd n.r.e.), §§9.05 , 10.23

Brownsville Medical Center v. Gracia, 704 S.W.2d 68 (Tex. App.—Corpus Christi 1985, writ ref'd n.r.e.), §10.20

Bruce v. Jim Walters Homes, Inc., 943 S.W.2d 121, 123 (Tex. App.—San Antonio 1997, writ denied), §12.05.8

Bruce v. Jim Walters Homes, Inc., 943 S.W.2d 121, 123 (Tex. App.—Fort Worth 1997, writ denied), §12.05, 12.05.3

Buccaneer Homes of Ala., Inc. v. Pelis, 43 S.W.3d 586, 590 (Tex. App.—Houston [1st Dist.] 2001, no pet.), §§1.02.15, 2.02.11

Buckeye Check Cashing, Inc. v. Cardegna, 546 U.S. 440, 126 S. Ct. 1204, 163 L. Ed. 2d 1038 (2006), §8.01.7

Bugmobiles, Inc. v. Jobi Prop., 773 S.W.2d 616, 622 (Tex. App.—Corpus Christi 1989, writ denied), §1.02.9.1

Building Concepts, Inc. v. Duncan, 667 S.W.2d 897 (Tex. App.—Houston [14th Dist.] 1984, writ ref'd n.r.e.), §1.02.14.3

Bunting v. Fodor, 586 S.W.2d 144 (Tex. App.—Houston [1st Dist.] 1979, no writ), §1.02.9.1

Burk Royalty Co. v. Walls, 616 S.W.2d 911, 922 (Tex. 1981), §5.17

Burleson State Bank v. Plunkett, 27 S.W.3d 605 (Tex. App.—Waco 2000, no pet.), §1.02.14.1

Butterworth v. Kinsey, 14 Tex. 495 (1855), §1.02.15

— C —

C & H Nationwide, Inc. v. Thompson, 903 S.W.2d 315 (Tex. 1994), §2.02.1

Cadle Co. v. Castle, 913 S.W.2d 627 (Tex. App.—Dallas 1995, writ denied), §8.01.1

Camargo v. Trammell Crow Interest Co., 318 F. Supp. 2d 448 (E.D. Tex. 2004), §9.20.6

Cameron v. Terrell & Garrett, Inc., 618 S.W.2d 535 (Tex. 1981), §§1.02.4.1, 1.02.4.2, 1.02.7, 1.02.7.1, 1.02.7.5, 1.02.14.1, 12.02, 13.02.1

Campbell v. Campbell, 215 S.W. 134 (Tex. Civ. App.—Dallas 1919, writ ref'd), §§9.05, 9.13

Capital Income Properties - LXXX v. Blackmon, 843 S.W.2d 22 (Tex. 1992), §1.02.7.4

Capitol Life Ins. Co. v. Rutherford, 468 S.W.2d 535, 537 (Tex. Civ. App.—Houston [1st Dist.] no writ), §1.0.215

Carpenter v. Wyatt Constr. Co., 501 S.W.2d 748 (Tex. Civ. App.—Houston [14th Dist.] 1973, writ ref'd n.r.e.), §9.02

Carrow v. Bayliner Marine Corp., 781 S.W.2d 691 (Tex. App.—Austin 1989, no writ), §§1.02.14.1, 1.02.14.5, 10.10

Castleberry v. Branscum, 721 S.W. 2d 270 (Tex. 1986), §§2.01, 10.01.2, 10.02

Cathey v. Metropolitan Life Ins. Co., 805 S.W.2d 387 (Tex. 1991), §1.02.7.4

Cavnar v. Quality Control Parking, Inc., 678 S.W.2d 548 (Tex. App.—Houston [14th Dist.] 1984), *rev'd on other grounds*, 696 S. W. 2d 549 (Tex. 1985), §§10.21, 10.26

Celtic Life Ins. Co. v. Coats, 885 S.W.2d 96, 98 (Tex. 1994), §§10.02, 11.03.1, 11.03.3

Centex Homes, Inc. v. Buecher, 95 S.W.3d 266 (Tex. 2002), §12.03.1

Chamrad v. Volvo Cars of North Am., 145 F.3d 671 (5th Cir. 1998), §1.02.4.2

Chastain v. Koonce, 700 S.W.2d 579 (Tex. 1985), §§1.02.5, 1.02.104, 13.02.1

Chemical Bank v. Commercial Industries Service Co., Inc., 662 S.W.2d 802 (Tex. App.—Houston [14th Dist.] 1983, writ ref'd n.r.e.), §8.07

Chicago Title Ins. Co. v. McDaniel, 875 S.W.2d 310, 311 (Tex. 1994), §11.02.1

Christie v. Brewer, 374 S.W.2d 908 (Tex. Civ. App.—Austin 1964, writ ref'd n.r.e.), §§9.05, 9.13

Chrysler Corp. v. Schuenemann, 618 S.W.2d 799 (Tex. Civ. App.—Houston [1st Dist.] 1981, writ ref'd n.r.e.), §1.02.14.1

Church & Dwight Co. v. Huey, 961 S.W.2d 560, 568 (Tex. App.—San Antonio 1997, pet. denied), §1.02.9.1

Cielo Dorado Dev. v. Certainteed Corp., 744 S.W.2d 10 (Tex. 1988), §3.02

City of Dallas v. Arnett, 762 S.W.2d 942 (Tex. App.—Dallas 1988, writ denied), §9.20.8

City of Emerald v. Peel, 920 S.W.2d 398 (Tex. App.—Houston [1st Dist.] 1996, no writ), §8.01.7.3

City of Houston v. Levingston, 221 S.W.3d 204 (Tex. App.—Fort Worth 2005, no pet.), §9.20.6

City of Houston v. Sam P. Wallace and Co., 585 S.W.2d 669, 673-674 (Tex. 1979), §9.05

City of Houston v. Watson, 376 S.W.2d 23 (Tex. Civ. App.—Houston 1964, writ ref'd n.r.e.), §8.10.2

Clark Equip. Co. v. Pitner, 923 S.W.2d 117, 128 (Tex. App.—Houston [14th Dist.] 1996, writ den'd.), §1.02.4.2

Clayton v. Volkswagenwerk, A.G., 606 S.W.2d 15, 17-18 (Tex. Civ. App.—Houston [1st Dist.] 1980, writ ref'd n.r.e.), §9.05

Codner v. Arellano, 40 S.W.3d 666, 672-674 (Tex. App.—Austin 2001, no pet.), §12.03.1

Cody v. Mustang Oil Tool Co., 595 S.W.2d 214 (Tex. Civ. App.—Eastland 1980, writ ref'd n.r.e.), §8.10

Coldwell Banker Whiteside Assoc. v. Ryan Equity Partners, Ltd., 181 S.W.3d 879 (Tex. App.—Dallas 2006, n.w.h.), §8.13

Colonial County Mut. Ins. Co. v. Valdez, 30 S.W.3d 514, 527 (Tex. App. —Corpus Christi 2000, pet. denied.), §11.03.1, 11.03.3

Columbia/HCA Healthcare Corp. v. Cottey, 72 S.W.3d 735, 744–45 (Tex. App.—Waco 2002, no pet.), §10.06

Columbia Rio Grande Healthcare, L.P. v. Hawley, 284 S.W.3d 851, 862-863 (Tex. 2009), §10.02

Commercial Escrow Co. v. Rockport Rebel, Inc., 778 S.W.2d 532 (Tex. App.—Corpus Christi 1989, writ denied), §1.02.4.1

Compania Financiara Libano, S.A. v. Simmons, 53 S.W.3d (Tex. 2001), §8.01.1

Compton v. Henrie, 364 S.W.2d 179 (Tex. 1963), §9.02

Costa v. Storm, 682 S.W.2d 599 (Tex. App.—Houston [1st Dist.] 1984, writ ref'd n.r.e.), §10.20

Coulson v. Lake L.B.J. Mun. Util. Dist., 734 S.W.2d 649, 651 (Tex. 1987), §1.02.9.2.3

Crawford v. Ace Sign, 917 S.W.2d 12 (Tex. 1996), §§1.02.8.1, 2.02.1

Crown Life Ins. Co. v. Casteel, 22 S.W.3d 378, 392 (Tex. 2000), §2.02.11

Crim Truck & Tractor v. Navistar Int'l, 833 S.W.2d 591 (Tex. 1992), §15.04

Cronin v. Bacon, 837 S.W.2d 265 (Tex. App.—Fort Worth 1992, writ denied), §1.02.8.1

Crossland Sav. Bank FSB v. Constant, 737 S.W.2d 19, 22 (Tex. App.—Corpus Christi 1987, no writ), §5.27

Crown Life Ins. Co. v. Casteel, 22 S.W.3d 378, 392 (Tex. 2000), §§1.02.8, 10.01.4, 10.03, 10.07, 10.09, 10.10, 10.18, 11.02.1, 11.03.1

Cypress Fairbanks Med. Ctr., Inc. v. Pan-American Life Ins. Co., 110 F.3d 280 (5th Cir. 1997), §11.06.3

— D —

D.S.A., Inc. v. Hillsboro Indep. Sch. Dist., 973 S.W. 2d 662 (Tex. 1998), §10.05

D/FW Commercial Roofing Co., Inc. v. Mehra, 854 S.W.2d 182 (Tex. App.—Dallas 1993, no writ), §1.02.4.2

Dailey v. Wheat, 681 S.W.2d 747 (Tex. App.—Houston [14th Dist.] 1984, writ ref'd n.r.e.), §8.10

Dal-Chrome Co. v. Brenntag Sw., Inc., 183 S.W.3d 133, 143-44 (Tex. App.—Dallas 2006, no pet.), §1.02.14.2.2

Dallas R. & T. Co. v. Flowers, 284 S.W.2d 160 (Tex. Civ. App.—Waco 1955, writ ref'd n.r.e.), §9.05

David McDavid Pontiac, Inc. v. Nix, 681 S.W.2d 831 (Tex. App.—Dallas 1984, writ ref'd n.r.e.), §1.02.14.5

Davidow v. Inwood North Professional Group – Phase I, 747 S.W.2d 373 (Tex. 1988), §§1.02.9, 1.02.9.2.2, 1.04, 5.25, 10.07

Davies v. Texas Employers' Ins. Ass'n, 16 S.W.2d 524, 525 (Tex. Comm'n App. 1929, holding approved), §5.16

Davila v. World Car Five Star, 75 S.W.3d 537, §6.10

De Bakey v. Staggs, 605 S.W.2d 631, 633 (Tex. Civ. App.—Houston [1st Dist.] 1980, *writ ref'd n.r.e. per curiam*, 612 S.W.2d 924 (Tex. 1981), §§2.02.1

Decker v. Lindsay, 824 S.W.2d 247 (Tex. App.—Houston [1st Dist.] 1992, no writ), §8.01.4

Dennis v. Allison, 698 S.W.2d 94, 96 (Tex. 1985), §1.02.9.2.4

Detroit Automatic Scale Co. v. G.B.R. Smith Milling Co., 217 S.W. 198, 199 (Tex. Civ. App.—Dallas 1919, no writ), §1.02.9

Deutsch v. Hoover, Bax & Slovacek, LLP, 97 S.W.3d 179, 189 (Tex. App.—Houston [14th Dist.] 2002), §2.02.1

Dewitt County Elec. Coop., Inc. v. Parks, 1 S.W.3d 96 (Tex. 1999), §1.02.4.1

Dillard Department Stores, Inc. v. Gonzales, 72 S.W.3d 398 (Tex App.—El Paso 2002, pet. denied), §9.20.6

Dillard v. Texas Electric Cooperative, 157 S.W.3d 429 (Tex. 2005), §2.02.6

Dillee v. Sisters of Charity of the Incarnate Word Health Care Sys., 912 S.W.2d 307, 309 (Tex. App.—Houston [14th Dist.] 1995, no writ), §8.01.5

Diversicare General Partner Inc. v. Rubio, 185 S.W.3d 842 (Tex. 2005), §§2.02.2

Diversified, Inc. v. Gibraltar Sav. Asso., 762 S.W.2d 620, 622 (Tex. App.—Houston [14th Dist.] 1988, no writ), §1.02.9.2.4

Diversified, Inc. v. Walker, 702 S.W.2d 717, 723 (Tex. App.—Houston [1st Dist.] 1985, writ ref'd n.r.e.), §1.02.9.2.4

Dodecka, L.L.C. v. Garcia, ___ S.W.3d ___ 2011 Tex. App. LEXIS 8101 (Tex. App.—San Antonio, Oct. 12, 2011, no writ), §1.02.12.1

Doe v. Boys Clubs, 907 S.W.2d 472 (Tex. 1995) (discussing DTPA §17.46(b)(23), now (24)), §§1.02.08, 2.02, 6.05

Donnelley Marketing v. Lionel Sosa, Inc., 716 S.W.2d 598 (Tex. App.—Corpus Christi 1986, no writ), §1.02.9.1

Donwerth v. Preston II Chrysler-Dodge, Inc., 775 S.W.2d 634 (Tex. 1989), §§1.02.8.1, 2.02.4, 6.10, 11.06.4

Douglas v. Delp, 987 S.W.2d 879 (Tex. 1999), §§1.02.8.2, 1.02.8, 2.02

Dubow v. Dragon, 746 S.W.2d 857 (Tex. App.—Dallas 1988, no writ), §2.02.6

Durham v. St. John, 645 S.W.2d 261 (Tex. 1983), §1.02.14.3

— **E** —

EEOC v. Waffle House, Inc., 534 U.S. 279, 122 S. Ct. 754, 151 L.Ed. 2d 755 (U.S. 2002), §8.01.7.3

E.I. du Pont de Nemours & Co. v. Robinson, 923 S.W.2d 549, 558 (Tex. 1995), §1.02.13

EZ Pawn Corp. v. Mancias, 934 S.W.2d 87 (Tex. 1996), §§8.01.7.1, 8.01.7.3

Eagle Properties, Ltd. v. Scharbauer, 807 S.W.2d 714 (Tex. 1990), §§1.02.8, 10.06, 15.04

Earle v. Ratliff, 998 S.W.2d 882 (Tex. 1999), §2.02.1

Eckermann v. Williams, 740 S.W.2d 23 (Tex. App.—Austin 1987, no writ), §7.29

Eckman v. Centennial Sav. Bank, 784 S.W.2d 672 (Tex. 1990), §§1.02.4.1, 6.06, 7.27

Edwards v. Schuh, 5 S.W.3d 829, 833 (Tex. App.—Austin 1999, no pet.), §1.02.9.1

El Apple I, Ltd. v. Olivas, 370 S.W.3d 757, 763 (Tex. 2012), §1.02.15

El Chico Corp. v. Poole, 732 S.W.2d 306, 312 (Tex. 1987), §13.02.4

Ellis v. Liberty Life Assur. Co., 394 F.3d 262 (5th Cir. 2004), §11.06.3

Ellis v. Riddick, 78 S.W. 719, 722 (Tex. Civ. App. 1904, no writ), §1.02.9.1

Emerald v. Peel, 920 S.W.2d 398 (Tex. App.—Houston [1st Dist.] 1996, no writ), §8.01.5

English v. Fischer, 660 S.W.2d 521 (Tex. 1983), §15.04

Epps v. Ayer, 859 S.W.2d 107 (Tex. App.—Eastland 1993, writ denied), §1.02.7.4

Ernst & Young, L.L.P. v. Pacific Mutual Life Ins. Co., 51 S.W.3d 573 (Tex. 2001), §2.02.6

Erwin v. Smiley, 975 S.W.2d 335 (Tex. App.—Eastland 1998, writ denied), §2.02.2

Essex Crane Rental Corp. v. Kitzman, 723 S.W.2d 241 (Tex. App.—Houston [1st Dist.] 1986, no writ), §7.19

Evans v. J. Stiles, Inc., 689 S.W.2d 399 (Tex. 1985), §1.02.9.2.1

Evans v. State Farm Mut. Auto. Ins. Co., 685 S.W.2d 765 (Tex. App.—Houston [1st Dist.] 1985, writ ref'd n.r.e.), §7.32

Exxon Corp. v. Middleton, 613 S.W.2d 240, 246 (Tex. 1981), §10.02

— F —

Fairmont Homes, Inc. v. Upchurch, 704 S.W.2d 521 (Tex. App.—Houston [14th Dist.] *modified on other grounds*, 711 S.W.2d 618 (Tex. 1986), §4.01

Farmers & Merchants State Bank v. Ferguson, 617 S.W.2d 918 (Tex. 1981), §§1.02.4.1, 6.05

Federal Deposit Ins. Corp. v. Coleman, 795 S.W.2d 706 (Tex. 1990), §15.04

Federal Land Bank Ass'n v. Sloane, 825 S.W.2d 439 (Tex. 1991), §§15.04, 8.13, 10.05

Fernandez v. Schultz, 15 S.W.3d 648 (Tex. App.—Dallas 2000, no pet.), §2.02.6

Fina Supply, Inc. v. Abilene Nat'l Bank, 726 S.W.2d 537 (Tex. 1987), §10.05

Finger v. Ray, 326 S.W.3d 285, 298 (Tex. App.—Houston [1st Dist.] 2010, no pet.), §1.02.7.3.1

Fireman's Fund Ins. Co. v. Commercial Stand. Ins. Co., 490 S.W.2d 818, 825 (Tex. 1972), §7.48

First Bankers Ins. Co. v. Howell, 446 S.W.2d 711, 714 (Tex. Civ. App.—Amarillo 1979, no writ), §1.02.15

First Options of Chicago, Inc. v. Kaplan, 514 U.S. 938, 131 L. Ed. 2d 985, 115 S. Ct. 1920 (1995), §8.01.7

First Title Co. of Waco v. Garrett, 860 S.W.2d 74 (Tex. 1993), §§1.02.8.1, 2.02.1, 11.02.1

Fix v. Flagstar Bank, FSB, 242 S.W.3d 147, 159-160 (Tex. App.—Fort Worth 2007, pet. den'd.), §1.02.4.1

Flint & Assoc. v. Intercontinental Pipe & Steel, Inc., 739 S.W.2d 622, 624-25 (Tex. App.—Dallas 1987, writ denied), §1.02.15

Flenniken v. Longview Bank & Trust Co., 661 S.W.2d 705 (Tex. 1983), §§1.02.4.1, 1.02.5, 1.02.6, 1.02.7, 1.02.7.1, 1.02.104, 12.02

Flores v. Banner, 932 S.W.2d 500 (Tex. 1996), §8.09

Forbau v. Aetna Life Ins. Co., 876 S.W.2d 132 (Tex. 1994), §1.02.7.4

Ford Motor Co. v. Ledesma, 242 S.W.3d 32, 46 (Tex. 2007), §§1.02.13, 10.02

Ford v. State Farm Mut. Auto. Ins. Co., 550 S.W.2d 663, 666 (Tex. 1977), §11.09

Formosa Plastics Corp. USA v. Presidio Eng'rs & Contrs., 960 S.W.2d 41 (Tex. 1998), §§1.02.8.1, 10.06

Fowler v. Garcia, 687 S.W.2d 517 (Tex. App.—San Antonio 1985, no writ), §10.22

Frank B. Hall & Co. v. Beach, Inc., 733 S.W.2d 251 (Tex. App.—Corpus Christi 1987, writ ref'd n.r.e.), §1.02.14.4

Freeman Oldsmobile Mazda Co. v. Pinson, 580 S.W.2d 112 (Tex. Civ. App.—Eastland 1979, writ ref'd n.r.e.), §1.02.14.5

Frizzell v. Cook, 790 S.W.2d 41 (Tex. App.—San Antonio 1990, writ denied), §1.02.7.4

— G —

G. Prop. Mgmt. v. MultiVest Fin. Servs. of Tex., Inc., 219 S.W.3d 37 (Tex. App.—San Antonio 2006, no writ), §2.02.6

Gaines v. Gaines, 677 S.W.2d 727 (Tex. App.—Corpus Christi 1984, no writ), §8.12

Gaines v. Kelly, 235 S.W.3d 179, 182-3 (Tex. 2007), §10.02

Gannett Outdoor Co. of Texas v. Kubeczka, 710 S. W. 2d 79 (Tex. App.—Houston [14th Dist.] 1986, no writ), §10.22

Gano v. Jamail, 678 S.W.2d 152 (Tex. App.—Houston [14th Dist.] 1984, no writ), §1.07

Garcia v. Gomez, 319 S.W.3d 638, 642 (Tex. 2010), §10.25

Garcia v. Gutierrez, 697 S.W.2d 758 (Tex. App.—Corpus Christi 1985, no writ), §5.04

Garcia v. Texas Instruments, Inc., 610 S.W.2d 456, 465 (Tex. 1980), §1.02.9.1

Gaspard v. Gaspard, 582 S.W.2d 629, 631 (Tex. Civ. App.—Beaumont 1979, no writ), §8.10

Gentry v. Squires Const., Inc., 188 S.W.3d 396, 405 (Tex. App.—Dallas 2006, no writ), §12.05

Geodyne Energy Income Production Partnership I-E v. Newton Corp., 161 S.W.3d 482 (Tex. 2005), §2.02.2

Giffin v. Smith, 688 S.W.2d 112, 113 (Tex. 1985), §7.18

Gibson v. Ellis, 58 S.W.3d 818 (Tex. App.—Dallas 2001, no pet.), §2.02.2

Gill Sav. Ass'n v. Chair King, Inc., 783 S.W.2d 674 (Tex. App.—Houston [14th Dist.] 1989), *modified,* 797 S.W.2d 31 (Tex. 1990), §1.02.15

Gill Sav. Ass'n v. Chair King, Inc., 797 S.W.2d 31 (Tex. 1990), §1.02.28

GJP, Inc. v. Ghosh, 251 S.W.3d 854 (Tex. App.--Austin 2008, no writ), §14.02

Gleason v. Lawson, 850 S.W.2d 714 (Tex. App.—Corpus Christi 1993, no writ), §8.01.4

Goffney v. Rabson, 56 S.W.3d 186, 188-194 (Tex. App.—Houston [14th Dist.] 2001, pet. denied), §2.02.1

Gonzales v. Southwest Olshan Found. Repair Co., LLC, 400 S.W.3d 52, 56 (Tex. 2013), §§1.02.9.2.3, 12.03.2

Gonzales v. Texas Employers' Ins. Ass'n 419 S.W.2d 203 (Tex. Civ. App.—Austin 1967, no writ), §9.08

Goodyear Tire and Rubber Co. v. Portilla, 836 S.W.2d 664, 671-672 (Tex. App.—Corpus Christi 1992), *aff'd,* 879 S.W.2d 47 (Tex. 1994), §1.02.15

Gorman v. Life Ins. Co. of No. Am., 811 S.W.2d 542 (Tex. 1991), §1.02.7.4

Gormley v. Stover, 907 S.W.2d 448 (Tex. 1995), §2.02.1

Gourrier v. Joe Meyers Motors, 115 S.W.3d 570 (Tex. App.—Houston [14th Dist.] 2002), §1.02.13

Great Am. Ins. Co. v. North Austin Mun. Util. Dist. No.1, 908 S.W.2d 415 (Tex. 1995), §§1.02.15, 10.14

Green Tree Fin. Corporation-Alabama v. Randolph, 531 U.S. 79, 121 S.Ct. 513, 148 L.Ed.2d 373 (2000), §8.01.7.1

Greene v. Thiet, 846 S.W.2d 26 (Tex. App.—San Antonio 1992, writ denied), §8.13

Groves v. Gabriel, 874 S.W.2d 660 (Tex. 1994), §7.25

Guardian Royal Exchange Assurance, Ltd. v. English China Clays, P.L.C, 815 S.W.2d 223 (Tex. 1991), §5.08

Gulf States Utilities Co. v. Low, 79 S.W.3d 561 (Tex. 2002), §§1.02.14.1, 10.01.3, 10.12

Gunn Infiniti, Inc. v. O'Byrne, 996 S.W.2d 854 (Tex. 1999), §§1.02.14.1, 2.02.1

Gupta v. Ritter Homes, Inc., 646 S.W.2d 168, 169 (Tex. 1983), §§1.02.7.1, 1.02.9, 1.02.9.4, 1.02.14.1, 1.02.14.1, 10.02, 10.07, 12.03.1

Gutierrez v. Walsh, 748 S.W.2d 27, 28 (Tex. App.—Corpus Christi 1988, no writ), §7.51

Guzman v. State, 649 S.W.2d 77 (Tex. App.—Corpus Christi 1982, no writ), §9.01

G-W-L, Inc. v. Robichaux, 643 S.W.2d 392 (Tex. 1982), §1.02.9.2.3

Gym-N-I Playgrounds, Inc. v. Snider, 220 S.W.3d 905, 912 (Tex. 2007), §1.02.9.2.2

— H —

H. L. McRae Co. v. Hooker Construction Company, 579 S.W.2d 62 (Tex. App.—Austin 1979, no writ), §5.04

Haase v. Glazner, 62 S.W.3d 795 (Tex. 2001), §8.13

Hallett v. Houston Northwest Medical Center, 689 S.W.2d 888 (Tex. 1985), §9.14

Holloway v. Dannenmaier, 581 S.W.2d 765, 766 (Tex. Civ. App.—Fort Worth 1979, writ dism'd), §1.02.8.1

Hamra v Gulden, 898 S.W.2d 16, 19 (Tex. App.—Dallas 1995, writ dism'd w.o.j.), §§1.02.15, 2.02.11

Hansen v. Sullivan, 886 S.W.2d 467 (Tex. App.—Houston [1st Dist.] 1994, no writ), §8.01.4

Hardt v. Reliance Standard Life Ins. Co., ___ U.S. ___, 130 S. Ct. 2149, 2157-58, 176 L. Ed. 2d 998 (2010), §11.06.3.1

Harris v. Am. Prot. Ins. Co., 158 S.W.3d 614 (Tex. App. —Fort Worth 2005, no pet.), §11.03.3

Harris County v. Smith, 96 S.W.3d 230, 234 (Tex. 2002), §§10.01.4, 10.10

Harrison v. Dallas Court Reporting College, Inc., 589 S.W.2d 813 (Tex. App.—Dallas 1979, no writ), §§1.02.14.1, 1.02.15

Harroll v. McDuffie, 128 S.W. 1149, 1151 (Tex. Civ. App. 1910, no writ), §1.02.9.1

Hartford Acc. & Indem. Co. v. Thurmond, 527 S.W.2d 180 (Tex. Civ. App.—Corpus Christi 1975, writ ref'd n.r.e.), §§10.22, 10.23

Hartford Accident and Indem. Co. v. McCardell, 369 S.W.2d 331 (Tex. 1963), §8.10

Hash v. Hines, 796 S.W.2d 312 (Tex. App.—Amarillo 1990), §3.02

Hash v. Hines, 843 S.W.2d 464 (Tex. 1992), §6.01.1

Head v. U.S. Inspect DFW, Inc., 159 S.W.3d 731, 739 (Tex. App.—Fort Worth 2005, pet. den'd.), §2.02.2, 13.02.1, 13.02.8

Hearthshire Braeswood v. Bill Kelly Co., 849 S.W.2d 380 (Tex. App.—Houston [14th Dist.] 1993, writ denied), §6.01

Heintz v. Jenkins, 514 U.S. 291, 115 S Court 1489 (1995), §1.02.12.1

Helena Chem. Co. v. Wilkins, 47 S.W.3d 486 (Tex. 2001), §§1.02.8, 1.02.14.1, 2.02, 2.02.2, 2.02.4

Hemmenway v. Skibo, 498 S.W.2d 9, 14-15 (Tex. Civ. App.—Beaumont 1973, writ ref'd n.r.e.), §10. 19

Hennessey v. Skinner, 698 S.W.2d 382 (Tex. App.—Houston [14th Dist.] 1985, no writ), §1.02.5

Henry S. Miller Co. v. Bynum, 836 S.W.2d 160, 163 (Tex. 1992), §1.02.14.1

Hensley v. Eckerhart, 461 U.S. 433, 103 S. Ct. 1933, 1939 (1983), §§11.06.3.1, 11.06.3.1

Hermann Hosp. v. MEBA Med. & Benefits Plan, 845 F.2d 1286 (5th Cir. 1988), §11.06.3

Hermann Hosp. v. MEBA Med. & Benefits Plan, 959 F.2d 569 (5th Cir. 1992), §11.06.3

Hermann Hospital v. National Standard Ins. Co., 776 S.W.2d 249 (Tex. App.—Houston [1st Dist.] 1989, writ denied), §11.03

Hernandez v. Baucum, 344 S.W.2d 498 (Tex. Civ. App.—San Antonio 1961, writ ref'd n.r.e.), §10. 19

Herrin v. Medical Protective Co., 89 S.W.3d 301, 310 (Tex. App.—Texarkana 2002, pet. filed), §11.06.2

Hickman v. Taylor, 329 U.S. 495 (1947), §7.32

Hines v. Hash, 843 S.W.2d 464 (Tex. 1992), §§3.02, 5.13, 6.01.1

Hochheim Prairie Farm Mut. Ins. Co. v. Burnett, 698 S.W.2d 271, 277-278 (Tex. App.—Fort Worth 1985, no writ), §§1.02.15, 4.01

Hogan v. Kraft Foods, 969 F.2d 142 (5th Cir. 1992), §11.06.3

Hoggett v. Brown, 971 S.W.2d 472, 487 (Tex. App.—Houston [14th Dist.] 1997, pet. denied), §10.06

Holder v. Wood, 714 S.W.2d 318 (Tex. 1986), §16.01.3

Holk v. Biard, 920 S.W.2d 803 (Tex. App.—Texarkana 1996, no writ), §8.01.6

Holland Mortgage Inv. Corp. v. Bone, 751 S.W.2d 515 (Tex. App.—Houston [1st Dist.] 1987, no writ), §5.01

Holloway v. Dannenmaier, 581 S.W.2d 765, 766 (Tex. Civ. App.—Fort Worth 1979, writ dism'd), §1.02.8.1

Holmes v. P.K. Pipe & Tubing, Inc., 856 S.W.2d 530 (Tex. App.—Houston [1st Dist.] 1993, no writ), §2.02.4

Home Savings Ass'n v. Guerra, 733 S.W.2d 134 (Tex. 1987), §§3.03, 9.20.4

Honeywell v. Imperial Condominium Ass'n, 716 S.W.2d 75 (Tex. App.—Dallas 1986, no writ), §1.02.8.1

Horizon/CMS Healthcare Corp. v. Auld, 34 S.W.3d 887, 905 (Tex. 2000), §6.05

Houdaille Industries, Inc. v. Cunningham, 502 S.W.2d 544, 549 (Tex. 1973), §7.23

Houston Lighting & Power Co. v. Fisher, 559 S.W.2d 682 (Tex. Civ. App.—Houston [14th Dist.] 1977, writ ref'd n.r.e.), §§10. 19, 10.22

Houston Lighting & Power Co. v. Reynolds, 765 S.W.2d 784, 785 (Tex. 1988), §1.02.5

Houston Lighting & Power Co. v. Russo Properties, Inc., 710 S.W.2d 711, 715-716 (Tex. App.—Houston [1st Dist.] 1986, no writ), §1.02.15

Houts v. Barton, 657 S.W.2d 924 (Tex. App-Houston [1st Dist.] 1983, no writ), §1.02.15

How Ins. Co. v. Patriot Fin. Serv., Inc., 786 S.W.2d 533 (Tex. App.—Austin 1990, writ denied), §11.02.1

Howard v. Faberge, Inc., 679 S.W.2d 644 (Tex. App.—Houston [1st Dist.] 1984, writ ref'd n.r.e.), §10.23

Howell Crude Oil Co. v. Donna Refinery, 928 S.W.2d 100, 109 (Tex. App.—Houston [14th Dist.] 1996, no writ reported), §1.02.8.1

Howsley & Jacobs v. Kendall, 376 S.W.2d 562, 566 (Tex. 1964), §10. 19

Hruska v. First State Bank of Deanville, 747 S.W.2d 783 (Tex. 1988), §9.20

Hudspeth v. Hudspeth, 756 S.W.2d 29, 34 (Tex. App.—San Antonio 1988, writ den'd.), §6.05

Humber v. Morton, 426 S.W.2d 554 (Tex. 1968), §§1.02.9, 1.02.9.2.1, 10.02, 12.03.1

Humble Nat'l Bank v. DCV, Inc., 933 S.W.2d 224 (Tex. App.—Houston [14th Dist.] 1996, writ denied), §2.02

Humphreys v. Caldwell, 888 S.W.2d 469 (Tex. 1994), §§7.29 , 7.32

Hurst v. Sears, Roebuck & Co., 647 S.W.2d 249 (Tex. 1983), §§1.02.8.1, 1.02.8.2

Hyundai Motor Co. v. Rodriguez, 995 S.W.2d 661, 663 (Tex. 1999), §1.02.13, 1.02.15

— I —

Implement Dealers Mut. Ins. Co. v. Castleberry, 368 S.W.2d 249 (Tex. Civ. App.—Beaumont 1963, writ ref'd n.r.e.), §9.08

In re Acceptance Ins. Co., 33 S.W.3d 443 (Tex. App.—Fort Worth 2000, original proceeding), §8.01.4

In re AdvancePCS Health L.P., 172 S.W.3d 603 (Tex. 2005), §8.01.7.1

In re Akzo Nobel Chemical, 24 S.W.3d 919, 921 (Tex. App.—Beaumont 2000, orig. proceeding), §7.52.1

In re Alford Chevrolet-Geo, 997 S.W.3d 173 (Tex. 1999), §§1.02.1, 3.02, 4.01, 6.01.1, 7.46, 7.50

In re American Homestar of Lancaster, Inc., 50 S.W.3d 480 (Tex. 2001), §8.01.6

In re Bruce Terminix Co., 988 S.W.2d 702 (Tex. 1998), §§8.01.5, 8.01.6

In re Citigroup Global Mkts., Inc., 258 S.W.3d 623 (Tex. 2008), §8.01.7.2

In re FirstMerit Bank, N.A., 52 S.W.3d 749 (Tex. 2001), §§8.01.7, 8.01.7.1, 8.01.7.3

In re Fleetwood Homes of Tex., L.P., 257 S.W.3d 692 (Tex. 2008), §8.01.7.2

In re Halliburton Co., 80 S.W.3d 566 (Tex. 2002), §8.01.7.1

In re Kellogg Brown & Root, Inc., 166 S.W.3d 732 (Tex. 2005), §8.01.7.3

In re Kimball Hill Homes, Texas, Inc., 969 S.W.2d 522, 526 (Tex. App.—Houston [14th Dist.] 1998, no writ), §§6.01.1, 12.05, 12.05.3

In re Learjet, Inc., 59 S.W.3d 842 (Tex. App.—Texarkana 2001, orig. proceeding), §8.01.1

In re Merrill Lynch Trust Co. FSB, 235 S.W.3d 185 (Tex. 2007), §8.01.7.3

In re Mohawk Rubber Co., 982 S.W.2d 494 (Tex. App.—Texarkana 1998, orig. proceeding), §8.13

In re Nexion Health at Humble, Inc., 173 S.W.3d 67 (Tex. 2008), §8.01.6

In re Oakwood Mobile Homes, Inc. 987 S.W.2d 571 (Tex. 1999), §§8.01.5, 8.01.6, 8.01.7

In re Olshan Found. Repair Co. of Dallas, L.L.C., 192 S.W.3d 922 (Tex. App.—Waco 2006, orig. proceeding), §8.01.6

In re Palacios, 221 S.W.3d 564 (Tex. 2006), §8.01.6

In re Palm Harbor Homes, Inc., 195 S.W.3d 672 (Tex. 2006), §8.01.7.1

In re RLS Legal Solutions, LLC, 221 S.W.3d 629 (Tex. 2007), §8.01.5

In re Vesta Ins. Group, 192 S.W.3d 759 (Tex. 2006), §§8.01.7.2, 8.01.7.3

In re Weekley, 180 S.W.3d 127 (Tex. 2005), §8.01.6

In re Weekley Homes, L.P., 176 S.W.3d 740 (Tex. 2005), §8.01.7.3

Independent Insulating Glass/Southwest, Inc. v. Street, 722 S.W.2d 798 (Tex. App.—Fort Worth 1987, writ dism'd w.o.j.), §7.28

Indust-Ri-Chem Lab., Inc. v. Par-Pak Co., 602 S.W.2d 282, 287-88 (Tex. Civ. App.—Dallas 1980, no writ), §1.02.9.1

Interfirst Bank San Antonio N.A. v. Murry, 740 S.W.2d 550 (Tex. App.—San Antonio 1987, no writ), §6.05

International Security Life Ins. Co. v. Spray, 468 S.W.2d 347 (Tex. 1971), §9.20.8

Irving Bank & Trust Co. v. Second Land Corp., 544 S.W.2d 684, 688 (Tex. Civ. App.—Dallas 1976, writ ref'd n.r.e.), §5.27

— J —

J.J. Gregory Gourmet Servs. v. Antone's Import Co., 927 S.W.2d 31 (Tex. App.—Houston [1st Dist.] 1995, no writ), §§8.01.5, 8.01.6, 8.01.7

J. M. Davidson, Inc. v. Webster, 128 S.W.3d 223 (Tex. 2003), §8.01.7

J.M. Krupar Constr. Co. v. Rosenberg, 95 S.W.3d 322, 332 (Tex. App.—Houston [1st Dist.] 2002, no pet.), §12.03.1

J. Miller Trucking Co. v. Wood, 474 S.W.2d 768 (Tex. Civ. App.—Tyler 1971, writ ref'd n.r.e.), §9.05

Jack B. Anglin Co. v. Tipps, 842 S.W.2d 266 (Tex. 1992), §§1.02.7.4, 8.01.5, 8.01.6

Jack Roach Ford v. De Urdanavia, 659 S.W.2d 725 (Tex. App.—Houston [14th Dist.] 1983, no writ), §1.02.15

Jamail v. Anchor Mortgage Servs. Inc., 809 S.W. 2d 221 (Tex. 1991), §7.18

Jampole v. Touchy, 673 S.W.2d 569 (Tex. 1984), §§7.01, 7.16

Jarbet Co. v. Moore, 397 S.W.2d 268 (Tex. Civ. App.—Beaumont 1965, writ ref'd n.r.e.), §10.20

Jenkins v. Steakley Bros. Chevrolet Co., 712 S.W.2d 587 (Tex. App.—Waco 1986, no writ), §6.06

Jerman v. Carlisle, McNellie, Rini, Kramer and Ulrich LPA, 559 U.S. 573, 130 S.Ct. 1605, 1620-21 (2010), §1.02.12.1

Jim Walter Homes, Inc. v. Castillo, 616 S.W.2d 630, 635 (Tex. Civ. App.—Corpus Christi 1981, no writ), §§1.02.14.1,

Jim Walters Home, Inc. v. Samuel, 701 S.W.2d 351 (Tex. App.—Beaumont 1985, no writ), §1.02.14.5

Jim Walter Homes, Inc. v. Valencia, 690 S.W.2d 239, 242 (Tex. 1985), §§1.02.8.1, 1.02.14.2.2, 3.02

Johnson & Higgins, Inc. v. Kenneco Energy, 962 S.W.2d 507, 515 (Tex. 1998), §§10.16, 10.26

Johnson v. American Can Co., 361 S.W.2d 451, 453 (Tex. Civ. App.—Houston [1st Dist.] 1962, writ ref'd n.r.e.), §8.01.5

Johnson v. Georgia Highway Express, Inc., 488 F.2d 714 (5th Cir. 1974), §9.20.6

Johnson v. Reed, 464 S.W.2d 689 (Tex. Civ. App.—Dallas 1971, writ ref'd n.r.e.). *cert. denied*, 405 U.S. 981 (1972), §9.05

Johnson v. Willis, 596 S.W.2d 251 (Tex. Civ. App.—Waco 1980, writ ref'd n.r.e.), §5.12

Johnston Testers v. Rangel, 435 S.W.2d 927 (Tex. Civ. App.—San Antonio 1968, writ ref'd n.r.e.), §10. 19

Jordan Ford, Inc. v. Alsbury, 625 S.W.2d 1 (Tex. Civ. App.—San Antonio 1981, no writ), §1.02.14.1

Joseph v. PPG Indus., Inc., 674 S.W.2d 862 (Tex. App.—Austin 1984, writ ref'd n.r.e.), §1.02.15

— K —

Kamarath v. Bennett, 568 S.W.2d 658, 661 (Tex. 1978), §§5.25, 12.03.1

Kelley-Coppedge, Inc. v. Highlands Ins. Co., 980 S.W.2d 462 (Tex. 1998), §11.05

Kennedy v. Sale, 689 S.W.2d 890 (Tex. 1985), §§1.02.4.2, 11.02.1, 11.03.1, 11.03.3

Kennemore v. Bennett, 755 S.W.2d 89 (Tex. 1988), §§1.02.104, 2.02

Kerrville HRH, Inc. v. Kerrville, 803 S.W.2d 377, 387-388 (Tex. App.—San Antonio 1990, writ denied), §1.02.15

Kessler v. Fanning, 953 S.W.2d 515 (Tex. App.—Fort Worth 1997, no writ), §2.02

Kilgore Fed. Sav. & Loan v. Donnelly, 624 S.W.2d 933 (Tex. Civ. App.—Tyler 1981, no writ), §1.02.5

Kinerd v. Colonial Leasing Co., 800 S.W.2d 187 (Tex. 1990), §1.02.104

King v. Ladd, 624 S.W.2d 195 (Tex. Civ. App.—El Paso 1981, no writ), §1.02.15

Kish v. Van Note, 692 S.W. 2d 463, 466-67 (Tex. 1985), §§1.02.14, 10.11, 10.25

K-Mart Corp. v. Sanderson, 937 S.W.2d 429 (Tex. 1996), §§7.35, 7.46

Knight v. International Harvester Credit Corp., 627 S.W.2d 382 (Tex. 1982), §§1.02.4.1, 1.02.6, 1.02.7, 1.02.7.1

Kolb v. Texas Emp. Ins. Assn., 585 S.W.2d 870 (Tex. Civ. App.—Texarkana 1979, writ refd n.r.e.), §8.13

Koral Industries, Inc. v. Security-Connecticut Life Ins. Co., 802 S.W.2d 650, 651 (Tex. 1990), §§2.02.6, 10.17

KPMG Peat Marwick v. Harrison County Hous. Fin. Corp., 988 S.W.2d 746 (Tex. 1999), §10.16

— L —

La Sara Grain Co. v. First National Bank of Mercedes, 673 S.W.2d 558, 565 (Tex. 1984), §§1.02.6, 1.02.8.1, 1.02.9, 1.02.9.2, 1.02.9.2.4, 1.04

Lake Country Estates, Inc. v. Toman, 624 S.W.2d 677 (Tex. App.—Fort Worth 1981, writ ref'd, n.r.e.), §6.01

Lara v. Lile, 828 S.W.2d 536, 542 (Tex. App.—Corpus Christi 1992, writ denied), §1.02.4.2

Larsen v. Carlene Langford & Assocs., 41 S.W.3d 245, 251 (Tex. App.—Waco 2001, pet. denied), §§6.09.3, 8.13, 13.02.6

Lassiter v. Bouche, 41 S.W. 2d 88, 90 (Tex. Civ. App.—Dallas 1931, writ ref'd), §9.05

Latham v. Castillo, 972 S.W.2d 66 (Tex. 1998), §§1.02.3, 1.02.7.3.1, 1.02.8.1, 1.02.14.2.1, 1.02.104, 2.02.1

Lauderdale v. Insurance Co. of North America, 527 S.W.2d 841 (Tex. Civ. App.—Fort Worth 1975, writ ref'd n.r.e.), §§9.05, 9.12, 9.14

Law Offices of Windle Turley, P.C. v. French, 164 S.W.3d 487, 493-494 (Tex. App.—Dallas 2005, no pet.), §10.26

Lee v. Hasson, 286 S.W.3d 1 (Tex. App.—Houston [14th Dist.], 2007, pet. denied), §15.04

Leede Oil and Gas, Inc. v. McCorkle, 789 S.W.2d 686 (Tex. App.—Houston [1st Dist.] 1990, no writ), §7.32

Lemond v. Jamail, 763 S.W.2d 910 (Tex. App.—Houston [1st Dist.] 1988, writ denied), §1.08

Lemos v. Montez, 680 S.W.2d 798, 801 (Tex. 1984), §10.01.4

Lesikar v. Rappeport, 33 S.W.3d 282, 299 (Tex. App.—Texarkana 2000, pet. denied), §10.06

Lester v. Logan, 893 S.W.2d 570 (Tex. App.—Corpus Christi 1994), §2.02.4

Lester v. Logan, 907 S.W.2d 452 (per curiam), (Tex. 1995), §10.01.2

Lewis & Lambert Metal Contractors v. Jackson, 914 S.W.2d 584, 588 (Tex. App.—Dallas 1994), *vacated without reference to merits by*, 938 S.W.2d 716 (Tex. 1997), §1.02.4.2

Leyendecker & Assoc., Inc. v. Wechter, 683 S.W.2d 369 (Tex. 1984), §§1.02.14, 1.02.14.1

Liberty Mut. Ins. Co. v. Allen, 669 S.W.2d 750, 755 (Tex. App.—Houston [1st Dist.] 1983, writ ref'd n.r.e.), §§9.20.7, 1.02.15

Liberty Mut. Ins. v. Garrison Contractors, 966 S.W.2d 482, 485 (Tex. 1998), §11.03

Liberty National Fire Insurance Co. v. Akin, 927 S.W.2d 627, 629 (Tex. 1996), §11.5

Limitations on Voir Dire in Civil Cases, 45 Tex. Bar. J. 1043 (1982), §9.05

Lin v. Metro Allied Ins. Agency, 305 S.W.3d 1, 3-4 (Tex. App.—Houston [1st Dist. 2007] (mem. op.), §1.02.14.2.2

Lindsey v. O'Neill, 689 S.W.2d 400 (Tex. 1985), §7.19

Loftin v. Martin, 776 S.W.2d 145 (Tex. 1989), §§7.19, 7.35, 7.46

Lone Star Ford, Inc. v. McGlashan, 681 S.W.2d 720 (Tex. App.—Houston [1st Dist.] 1984, no writ), §1.02.14.1

Lone Star Machinery Corp. v. Frankel, 564 S.W.2d 135 (Tex. Civ. App.—Beaumont 1978, no writ), §8.13

Louder v. DeLeon, 754 S.W.2d 148 (Tex. 1988), §9.17

Lubbock Mortg. & Inv. Co. v. Thomas, 626 S.W.2d 611 (Tex. App.—El Paso 1981, no writ), §1.02.14.1

Lucas v. Nesbitt, 653 S.W.2d 883 (Tex. App.—Corpus Christi 1983, writ ref'd n.r.e.), §10.18

Lucas v. United States, 757 S.W.2d 687, 701 (Tex. 1988), §1.02.14.1

Ludt v. McCollum, 762 S.W.2d 575 (Tex. 1988), §10.11

Lukasik v. San Antonio Blue Haven Pools, Inc., 21 S.W.3rd 394, 402 (Tex. App.—San Antonio 2000, no pet.), §1.02.4.4

Luker v. Arnold, 843 S.W.2d 108 (Tex. App.—Fort Worth 1992, no writ), §§1.02.9

Luna v. North Star Dodge Sales, Inc., 667 S. W. 2d 115 (Tex. 1984), §§1.02.14.1, 5.15, 8.10.2

Lunsford v. Morris, 746 S.W.2d 471 (Tex. 1988), §§7.27, 9.05

— M —

M.L. Mayfield Petroleum Corp. v. Kelly, 450 S.W.2d 104 (Tex. Civ. App.—Tyler 1970, writ refd n.r.e.), §8.13

MacMillan v. Redman Homes, Inc., 818 S.W.2d 87 (Tex. App.—San Antonio 1991, writ denied), §1.02.7.4

Magic Chef, Inc. v. Sibley, 546 S.W.2d 851 (Tex. Civ. App.—San Antonio 1977, writ ref'd n.r.e.), §10.23

Mahan Volkswagen v. Hall, 648 S.W.2d 324, 332-33 (Tex. App.—Houston [1st Dist.], 1982, writ ref'd n.r.e.), §1.02.4.4

Mahon v. Vandygriff, 578 S.W.2d 144 (Tex. Civ. App.—Austin 1979, writ ref'd n.r.e.), §6.05

Mann v. Rugel, 228 S.W.2d 585 (Tex. Civ. App.—Dallas 1950, no writ), §8.13

Mantas v. Fifth Court of Appeals, 925 S.W.2d 656 (Tex. 1996), §8.01.1

Manufactured Housing Management Corp. v. Tubb, 643 S.W.2d 483 (Tex. App.—Waco 1982, writ ref'd n.r.e.), §6.05

March v. Thiery, 729 S.W.2d 889, 897 (Tex. App.—Corpus Christi 1987, no writ), §§9.20.7, 1.02.15, 4.01, 10.14, 12.03.1

Marcus v. Kinabrew, 438 S.W.2d 431 (Tex. Civ. App.—Tyler 1969, no writ), §2.02.6, 8.13

Maresca v. Marks, 362 S.W.2d 299 (Tex. 1962), §7.21

Marshall v. Vise, 76 7 S.W.2d 699 (Tex. 1989), §7.48

Maryland Am. Gen. Ins. Co. v. Blackmon, 639 S.W.2d 455 (Tex. 1982), §7.29

Mason v. Tobin, 408 S.W.2d 243 (Tex. Civ. App.—Houston 1966, no writ), §8.12

Matis v. Golden, 228 S.W.3d 301 (Tex. App.—Waco 2007, no writ), §2.02.6

Matthews v. Candlewood Builders, Inc., 685 S.W.2d 649 (Tex. 1985), §§1.02.15, 2.02.11

McCain v. NME Hosps, Inc., 856 S.W.2d 751 (Tex. App.—Dallas 1993, no writ), §§2.02.4, 11.06.4

McCamish, Martin, Brown & Loeffler v. F.E. Appling Interests, 991 S.W.2d 787, 791 (Tex. 1999), §§10.05, 15.04

McClure v. Attebury, 20 S.W.3d 722 (Tex. App.—Amarillo 1999, no pet.), §8.13

McCrea v. Cubilla Condominium Corp., 685 S.W.2d 755, 757 (Tex. App.—Houston [1st Dist.] 1985, writ ref'd n.r.e.), §1.02.9.1

McCrea v. Cubilla Condo. Corp., 769 S.W.2d 261, 264 (Tex. App.—Houston [1st Dist.] 1988, writ denied), §12.03.2

McGuire v. Commercial Union Ins. Co. of N.Y., 431 S.W. 2d 347, 352 (Tex. 1968), §9.05

McKinley v. Drozd, 685 S.W.2d 7 (Tex. 1985), §§1.02.15, 9.20

McKinney v. National Union Fire Ins. Co. of Pa., 772 S.W.2d 72 (Tex. 1989), §7.46

McKinley v. Drozd, 685 S.W.2d 7 (Tex. 1985), §2.02.11

McMillin v. State Farm Lloyds, 180 S.W.3d 183 (Tex. App.—Austin 2005, pet. denied), §9.20.9

Medrano v. City of El Paso, 231 S.W.2d 514 (Tex. Civ. App.—El Paso 1950, writ ref'd n.r.e.), §10.20

Melody Home Manufacturing Co. v. Barnes, 741 S.W.2d 349, 353 (Tex. 1987), §§1.02.4.1, 1.02.9, 1.02.9.2.3, 1.02.9.2, 10.02, 10.07, 12.03.2

Members Mutual Insurance Co. v. Muckelroy, 523 S.W.2d 77 (Tex. Civ. App.—Houston [1st Dist.] 1975, writ ref'd n.r.e.), §10.01.4

Memorial Hospital Systems v. Northbrook Life Ins. Co., 904 F.2d 236 (5th Cir. 1990), §11.06.3

Mendoza v. American National Ins. Co., 932 S.W.2d 605, 608 (Tex. App.—San Antonio 1996, no writ), §1.02.4.4

Mentis v. Barnard, 870 S.W.2d 14 (Tex. 1994), §7.50

Metro Allied Ins. Agency, Inc. v. Lin, 304 S.W.3d 830, 836 (Tex. 2009), §11.03.1, 11.03.3

Metro Ford Truck Sales, Inc. v. Davis, 709 S.W.2d 785 (Tex. App.—Fort Worth 1986, writ ref.d n.r.e.), §1.02.14.1

Metro. Life Ins. Co. v. Taylor, 481 U.S. 58, 63, 107 S. Ct. 1542, 95 L. Ed. 2d 55 (1987), §11.06.3

Mewbourne Oil Co. v. Blackburn, 793 S.W.2d 735 (Tex. App.—Amarillo 1990, orig. proceeding), §8.01.6

Meyer v. Cathey, 167 S.W.3d 327, 330-31 (Tex. 2005), §15.04

Meyer v. WMCO-GP, LLC, 211 S.W.3d 302 (Tex. 2006), §8.01.7.3

Mid-Century Insurance Co. v. Boyte, 80 S.W.3d 546 (Tex. 2002), §11.4

Midkiff v. Shaver, 788 S.W.2d 399 (Tex. App.—Amarillo 1990, no writ), §7.25

Miller v. Keyser, 90 S.W.3d 712 (Tex. 2002), §§1.02.7, 1.02.7.3, 1.02.8, 2.02.5

Miller v. Kossey, 802 S.W.2d 873, 876-77 (Tex. App.—Amarillo 1991, writ den'd), §6.01.1

Miller v. Presswood, 743 S.W.2d 275, 281 (Tex. App.—Beaumont 1987, writ denied), §5.13

Miller v. Soliz, 648 S.W.2d 734, 738 (Tex. Civ. App.—Corpus Christi 1983, no writ), §1.02.104

Mills v. Warner Lambert Co., 157 S.W.3d 424 (Tex. 2005), §1.02.7.4

Milt Ferguson Motor Co. v. Zeretzke, 827 S.W.2d 349 (Tex. App.—San Antonio 1991, no writ), §2.02

Mission Municipal Hospital v. Bryant, 563 S.W.2d 293 (Tex. Civ. App.—Corpus Christi 1977) *on remand* at 575 S.W.2d 136 (Tex. Civ. App.—Corpus Christi 1978, no writ), §8.12

Mitchell v. Burleson, 466 S.W.2d 646 (Tex. Civ. App.—Beaumont 1971, writ ref'd n.r.e.), §9.01

Mobil Chemical Co. v. Bell, 517 S.W.2d 245 (Tex. 1974), §10.01.4

Monday v. Cox, 881 S.W.2d 381 (Tex. App.—San Antonio 1994, writ denied), §1.02.15

Montemayor v. Ortiz, 208 S.W.3d 627 (Tex. App.—Corpus Christi 2006, pet. filed), §9.20.3.2

Moore v. Kitsmiller, 201 S.W.3d 147, 153 (Tex. App.—Tyler 2006, pet. denied), §10.01.1

Morris v. Holt, 714 S.W.2d 311 (Tex. 1986), §10.01.2

Moses H. Cone Memorial Hospital v. Mercury Construction Corp, 460 U.S. 1, 103 S. Ct. 927, 74 L. Ed. 2d 765 (1983), §8.01.7.3

Mother and Unborn Baby Care v. State, 749 S.W.2d 533 (Tex. App.—Fort Worth 1988, writ denied), §1.02.7.3

Munters Corporation v. Swissco-Young Industries, Inc., 100 S.W.3d 292, 298 (Tex. App.—Houston 2002), §2.02

Murphy v. Campbell, 964 S.W.2d 265 (Tex. 1997), §1.02.9.2.4

Murphy v. Russell, 167 S.W.3d 835 (Tex. 2005), §2.02.1

Murrary v. O&A Express, Inc., 630 S.W.2d 633 (Tex. 1982), §5.12

Mutter v. Wood, 744 S.W.2d 600 (Tex. 1988), §7.25

— **N** —

Narro Warehouse, Inc. v. Kelly, 530 S.W.2d 146, 150 (Tex. Civ. App.—Corpus Christi 1975, writ ref'd n. re.), §7.21

Nast v. State Farm Fire and Casualty Co., 82 S.W.3d 114 (Tex. App.—San Antonio 2002, no pet.), §2.02.1

National Bugmobiles, Inc. v. Jobi Prop., 773 S.W.2d 616, 622 (Tex. App.—Corpus Christi 1989, writ denied), §1.02.9.1, 13.02.1

National Surety Corp. v. Dominguez, 715 S.W.2d 67 (Tex. App.—Corpus Christi 1986, orig. proceeding), §7.29

National Tank Co. v. Brotherton, 851 S.W.2d 193, 200 (Tex. 1993), §7.32

National Union Fire Ins. Co. v. Hudson Energy Co., 811 S.W.2d 552 (Tex. 1991), §§7.41, 11.05

National Union Fire Ins. Co. v. Valdez, 863 S.W.2d 458, 460 (Tex. 1993), §7.32

National Union Fire Insurance v. CBI Industries, 907 S.W.2d 517 (Tex. 1995), §11.05

Nationwide Mut. Ins. Co. v. Holmes, 842 S.W.2d 335 (Tex. App.—San Antonio, 1992, writ denied), §1.02.104

Natividad v. Alexsis, Inc., 875 S.W.2d 695 (Tex. 1994), §15.04

Nautical Landings Marina, Inc. v. First Nat'l Bank, 791 S.W.2d 293 (Tex. App.—Corpus Christi 1990, writ denied), §15.04

Nelson v. Schanzer, 788 S.W.2d 81 (Tex. App.—Houston [14th Dist]. 1990, writ den'd.), §1.02.4.2

Netterville v. Interfirst Bank, 718 S.W.2d 921 (Tex. App.—Beaumont 1986, writ dism'd), §1.02.4.1

New York Life Insurance Co. v. Travelers Insurance Co., 92 F.3d 336, 338 (5th Cir. 1996), §11.05

New York Underwriters Ins. Co. v. State Farm Mutual Auto Ins. Co., 856 S.W.2d 194, 205 (Tex. App.—Dallas 1993, no writ), §6.10

Newman v. Tropical Visions, Inc., 891 S.W.2d 713 (Tex. App.—San Antonio 1994, no writ), §2.02.2

Nissan Motor Co. v. Armstrong, 145 S.W.3d 131 (Tex. 2004), §1.02.7.1

Nixon v. Mr. Property Management Co., 690 S.W.2d 26 (Tex. App.—San Antonio 1992, writ denied), §8.13

Nobility Homes of Texas, Inc. v. Shivers, 557 S.W.2d 77 (Tex. 1977), §§1.02.2, 1.02.7.1, 1.02.9.1, 1.02.14.1

Norwest Mortgage, Inc. v. Salinas, 999 S.W.2d 846 (Tex. App.—Corpus Christi 1999, no pet.), §1.02.14.2.1

— O —

O'Brien v. Lanpar Co., 399 S.W.2d 340 (Tex. 1966), §5.08

O'Day v. Sakowitz Brothers, 462 S.W.2d 119 (Tex. Civ. App.—Houston [1st Dist.] 1970, writ ref'd n.r.e.), §9.14

O'Donnell v. Roger Bullivant of Texas, Inc., 940 S.W.2d 411 (Tex. App.—Fort Worth 1997, writ denied), §§12.05.1, 12.05.3, 12.05.4

O'Neal v. Sherck Equipment Co., 751 S.W.2d 559 (Tex. App.—Texarkana 1988, no writ), §6.05

Oakes v. Guerra, 603 S.W.2d 371 (Tex. Civ.App.—Amarillo 1980, no writ), §1.02.14.1

Oakwood Mobile Homes, Inc. v. Cabler, 73 S.W.3d 363 (Tex. App.—El Paso 2002, pet. denied), §2.02.2

Olshan Foundation Repair v. Ayala, 180 S.W.3d 212 (Tex. App.—San Antonio 2005, pet. denied), §§8.01.5, 8.01.7.1

Orkin Exterminating Co., Inc. v. Lesassier, 688 S.W.2d 651 (Tex. App.—Beaumont 1985, no writ), §1.02.8.2

Osborne v. Jauregui, Inc., 252 S.W.3d 70 (Tex. App.—Austin 2008, pet. den'd.) (en banc), §§1.02.15, 2.02.11

Otis Elevator Co. v. Wood, 436 S.W.2d 324 (Tex. 1968), §§9.13, 10.22

— P —

P. Bosco & Sons Contracting Corporation v. Conley, Lott, Nichols Machinery Company, 629 S.W.2d 142 (Tex. App.—Dallas 1982, writ ref'd n.r.e.), §8.03

Padgett v. Bert Ogden Motor's, Inc., 869 S.W.2d 532 (Tex. App.—Corpus Christi, 1993, writ denied), §2.02

Padilla v. LaFrance, 907 S.W.2d 454 (Tex. 1995), §8.01.1

Padre Island Inv. Corp. v. Sorbera, 677 S.W.2d 90 (Tex. App.—San Antonio 1984, writ dism'd), §5.01

Pairett v. Gutierrez, 969 S.W.2d 512 (Tex. App.—Austin 1998, writ denied), §2.02.2

Palm Harbor Homes, 195 S.W.3d 678, §8.01.7.1

Pan Am. Life Ins. Co. v. Erbauer Constr. Co., 805 S.W.2d 395 (Tex. 1991), §1.02.7.4

Parkway Co. v. Woodruff, 901 S.W.2d 434 (Tex. 1995), §§1.02.9, 1.02.9.2.4, 1.02.14.2.1, 1.02.104, 10.11

Patterson Dental Co. v. Dunn, 592 S.W. 2d 914, 921 (Tex. 1979), §9.02

Patterson v. East Texas Motor Freight Lines, 349 S.W.2d 634 (Tex. Civ. App.—Beaumont 1961, writ ref'd n.r.e.), §9.05

Pecan Valley Nut Co., Inc v. E.I. du Pont de Nemours & Co., 15 S.W.3d 244 (Tex. App.—Eastland 2000, no pet.), §2.02.4

Pegasus Energy Group, Inc. v. Cheyenne Petroleum Co., 3 S.W.3d 112 (Tex. App.—Corpus Christi 1999, pet. denied), §1.02.15

Pennington v. Singleton, 606 S.W.2d 682 (Tex. 1980), §§1.02.7, 1.02.8.1, 1.02.14.1

Perry Homes v. Cull, 258 S.W.3d 580 (Tex. 2008), §§8.01.7, 8.01.7.2

Placencio v. Allied Indus. International, Inc., 724 S.W.2d 20, 21-22 (Tex. 1987), §10.01.2

Plains Ins. Co. v. Evans, 692 S.W.2d 952 (Tex. App.—Fort Worth 1985, no writ), §10. 19

Plas-Tex, Inc. v. U.S. Steel Corp., 772 S.W.2d 442, 446 (Tex. 1989), §§2.02.1, 10.07

Plaza Nat'l Bank v. Walker, 767 S.W2d 276 (Tex. App.—Beaumont 1989, writ denied), §1:04

Porter & Clements, L.L.P. v. Stone, 935 S.W.2d 217 (Tex. App.—Houston [1st Dist.] 1996, no writ), §8.01.5

Portland Sav. & Loan Assn. v. Bevil, 619 S.W.2d 241 (Tex. Civ. App.—Corpus Christi 1981, no writ), §1.02.5

Postell v. State, 663 S.W.2d 552, 555 (Tex. App.—Houston [1st Dist.] 1983, aff'd 693 S.W.2d 462 (Tex. Crim. App. 1985), §9.05

Powell v. Gulf Coast Carriers, Inc., 872 S.W.2d 22, 24 (Tex. App.—Houston [14th Dist.] 1994, no writ), §8.01.5

PPG Industries v. JMB/Houston Centers, 146 S.W.3d 79, 96 (Tex. 2004), §§1.02.4.3, 1.02.4.4, 1.02.7.1, 1.02.9.1

Preston v. Ferrer, ___ U.S. ___, 128 S.Ct. 978, 169 L.Ed.2d 917 (2008), §8.01.6

Preston v. Ohio Oil Co., 121 S.W.2d 1039 (Tex. Civ. App.—Eastland 1938, writ ref'd), §9.02

Preston v. Sears, Roebuck & Co., 573 S.W.2d 560 (Tex. Civ. App.—Texarkana 1978, writ ref'd n.r.e.), §1.02.9.1

Prima Paint Corp. v. Flood & Conklin Mfg. Co., 388 U.S. 395, 87 S. Ct. 1801 (1967), §§8.01.5, 8.01.7

Progressive County Mutual Ins. Co. v. Boyd, 177 S.W.3d 919 (Tex. 2005), §§10.04, 11.04

Progressive County Mut. Ins. Co. v. Sink, 107 S.W.3d 547, 551-52 (Tex. 2003)

Provident Life & Acc. Ins. Co. v. Hazlitt, 216 S.W.2d 805 (Tex. 1949), §8.12

Prudential Ins. Co. of Am. v. Jefferson Assocs., 896 S.W.2d 156, 161 (Tex. 1995), §§1.02.13, 2.02, 2.02.2, 6.09.3, 8.13, 13.02.6

Prudential Sec., Inc. v. Marshall, 909 S.W.2d 896 (Tex. 1995), §8.01.6

Pugh v. Gen. Terrazzo Supplies, Inc., 243 S.W.3d 84, 89-90 (Tex. App.—Houston [1st Dist.] 2007, pet. denied), §12.03.1

— Q —

Quality Oil Field Products, Inc. v. Michigan Mutual Ins. Co., 971 S.W.2d 635 (Tex. App.—Houston [14th Dist.] 1998, no writ), §11.05

Qantel Bus. Sys., Inc. v. Custom Controls Co., 761 S.W.2d 302 (Tex. 1988), §1.02.7.1

— R —

R.K. v. Ramirez, 887 S.W.2d 836 (Tex. 1994), §7.25

R.S. Assoc. Gen. Bldg. Contractors v. Devona, 610 S.W.2d 190 (Tex. Civ. App.—Houston [1st Dist.] 1980, writ ref'd n.r.e.), §1.02.104

Radio Station KSCS v. Jennings, 750 S.W.2d 760 (Tex. 1988), §6.03

Ragsdale v. Progressive Voters League, 801 S.W.2d 880 (Tex. 1990), §9.20.9, 10.25

Ralston Purina Co. v. McKendrick, 850 S.W.2d 629 (Tex. App.—San Antonio 1993, writ den'd), §10.06

Ramirez v. Inter-Cont'l Hotels, 890 F.2d 760, 763-64 (5th Cir. 1989), §11.06.3

Ramirez v. Wood, 577 S.W. 2d 278 (Tex. Civ. App.—Corpus Christi 1978, no writ), §9.02

Ramsey v. General Motors Corp., 685 S.W.2d 15 (Tex. 1985), §6.06

Ramsey v. Spray, No. 2-08-129-CV, 2009 Tex. App. LEXIS 9737, 2009 WL 5064539, at *1 (Tex. App.—Fort Worth Dec. 23, 2009, pet. denied), §1.02.14.2.2

Rauscher Pierce Refsnes, Inc. v. Koenig, 794 S.W.2d 514, 516 (Tex. App.—Corpus Christi 1990, writ denied), §1.02.15

Raye v. Fred Oakley Motors, Inc., 646 S.W.2d 288 (Tex. App.—Dallas 1983, writ ref'd n.r.e.), §1.02.14.1

Raymond v. Rahme, 78 S.W.3d 552, 563 (Tex. App.—Austin 2002, no pet.), §12.03.1

Redman Homes v. Ivy, 920 S.W.2d 664, 666-667 (Tex. 1996), §1.02.7.4

Reed v. Israel Nat'l. Oil Co., Ltd., 681 S.W.2d 228 (Tex. App.—Houston [1st Dist.] 1984, no writ), §1.02.4.1

Remington Arms Co., Inc. v. Canales, 837 S.W.2d 624 (Tex. 1992), §7.50

Rendon v. Sanchez, 737 S.W.2d 122 (Tex. App.—San Antonio 1987, no writ), §1.02.104

Retherford v. Castro, 378 S.W.3d 29 (Tex. App.—Waco 2012, pet. denied), §13.02.8

Rice v. Metro. Life Ins. Co., 324 S.W.3d 660, 672 (Tex. App.—Fort Worth 2010, no pet.), §10.04

Richardson v. Foster & Sear, 257 S.W.3d 782 (Tex. App.—Ft. Worth 2008, no pet.), §§3.02, 6.01.1

Rivera v. South Green Ltd. P'ship, 208 S.W.3d 12, 21 (Tex. App.—Houston 14th Dist. 2006, pet. den'd.), §1.02.4.1

Riverside Nat'l Bank v. Lewis, 603 S.W.2d 169 (Tex. 1980), §§1.02.5, 1.02.6, 1.02.7.4

Rocky Mountain Helicopters, Inc. v. Lubbock County Hosp. Dist., 987 S.W.2d 50 (Tex. 1998), §§1.02.8.1, 1.02.9.2.4

Rocor Int'l, Inc. v. National Union Fire Ins. Co., 77 S.W. 3d 253 (Tex. 2002), §11.03.2

Roof Sys., Inc. v. Johns Manville Corp., 130 S.W.3d 430, 440 (Tex. App.—Houston [14th Dist.] 2004, no pet.), §1.02.4.1

Rotello v. Ring Around Prod., Inc., 614 S.W.2d 455 (Tex. Civ. App.—Houston [14th Dist.] 1981, writ ref'd n.r.e.), §§1.02.14.1, 9.20.3.2

Rourke v. Garza, 530 S.W.2d 794 (Tex. 1975), §1.02.13

Royal Globe Ins. Co. v. Bar Consultants, Inc., 577 S.W.2d 688, 694 (Tex. 1979), §§1.02.8.1, 10.02, 11.03.1, 11.03.3

Royal Maccabees Life Ins. Co. v. James, 134 S.W.3d 906 (Tex. App.—Dallas 2004, no pet.), §10.01.4

RRTM Restaurant Corp. v. Keeping, 766 S.W.2d 804 (Tex. App.—Dallas 1988, writ den'd), §1.02.8.2

— S —

Saenz v. Fidelity & Guaranty Ins. Underwriters, 925 S.W.2d 607 (Tex. 1996), §1.02.14.2.1

Saizan v. Delta Concrete Prods. Co., 448 F.3d 795 (5th Cir. 2006), §9.20.6

Sanders v. Construction Equity, Inc, 42 S.W.3d 364 (Tex. App.—Beaumont 2001), *reh. overruled* 45 S.W.3d 802 (2001, pet. denied), §12.05

Sanders v. St. Paul Fire & Marine Ins. Co., 429 S.W.2d 516, 521-523 (Tex. Civ. App.—Texarkana 1968, writ ref'd n.r.e.), §8.10.2

Schlobohm v. Schapiro, 784 S.W.2d 355 (Tex. 1990), §5.08

Schlumberger Tech. Corp. v. Swanson, 959 S.W.2d 171 (Tex. 1997), §8.13

Scott v. Atchison, Topeka & Santa Fe Ry. Co., 572 S.W.2d 273 (Tex. 1978), §10.01.4

Sears, Roebuck & Co. v. Ramirez, 824 S.W.2d 558 (Tex. 1992), §7.21

Select Ins. Co. v. Boucher, 561 S.W.2d 474, 479 (Tex. 1978), §10.01.2

Serv. Corp. Int'l v. Guerra, 348 S.W.3d 239, 247 (Tex. App.—Corpus Christi 2009), rev'd on other grounds, 348 S.W.3d 221 (Tex. 2011), §§1.02.14.2.1, 10.11

Service Lloyds Ins. Co. v. Clark, 714 S.W.2d 437 (Tex. App.—Austin 1986, no writ), §7.29

Sharp v. Broadway Nat'l. Bank, 784 S.W.2d 669 (Tex. 1990), §§7.18, 7.19, 9.20.3.2

Sheffield v. Lewis, 287 S.W.2d 531 (Tex. Civ. App.—Texarkana 1956, no writ), §10. 19

Sherman Simon Enter., Inc. v. Lorac Serv. Corp., 724 S.W.2d 13 (Tex. 1987), §1.02.4.1

Sherrod v. Bailey, 580 S.W.2d 24, 28 (Tex. Civ. App.—Houston [14th Dist.] 1970, writ ref'd n.r.e.), §5.16

Siskind v. Villa Foundation for Education, Inc., 642 S.W.2d 434 (Tex. 1982), §5.08

Smith v. Baldwin, 611 S.W.2d 611 (Tex. 1980), §§1.02.8, 1.02.8.1, 1.02.14.1, 1.02.14.3, 2.02, 6.06, 10.01.1, 10.03, 10.25, 12.05.2

Smith v. Gray, 882 S.W.2d 103 (Tex. App.—Amarillo 1994, no writ), §2.02.4

Smith v. Gray, 907 S.W.2d 444 (Tex. 1995), §2.02.4

Smith v. Hennessey & Associates, Inc., 103 S.W.3d 567, 569 (Tex. App.—San Antonio 2003), §1.02.13

Smith v. Herco, Inc., 900 S.W.2d 852 (Tex. App.—Corpus Christi 1995, writ denied), §1.02.14.1

Smith v. Home Indem. Co., 683 S.W.2d 559, 562 (Tex. App.—Fort Worth 1985, no writ), §7.48

Smith v. Kinslow, 598 S.W.2d 910 (Tex. Civ. App.—Dallas 1980, no writ), §§1.02.14.1, 1.02.14.4

Smith v. Levine, 911 S.W.2d 425, 434 (Tex. App.—San Antonio 1995, writ den'd.), §6.06

Smith v. Levine, 911 S.W.2d 427 (Tex. App.—San Antonio 1995, writ denied), §6.01.2

Snyders Smart Shop, Inc. v. Santi, Inc., 590 S.W.2d 167 (Tex. Civ. App.—Corpus Christi 1981, no writ), §1.02.5

Sorokolit v. Rhodes, 889 S.W.2d 239 (Tex. 1994), §2.02.1

Southern Casualty Co. v. Dyer, 22 S.W.2d 548 (Tex. App.—Austin 1987, no writ), §7.29

Southwestern Bell Tel. Co. v. FDP Corp., 811 S.W.2d 572 (Tex. 1991), §§1.02.8.1, 1.02.9.1, 2.02.2, 2.02.4, 10.02

Southwestern Bell Tel. Co. v. Nash, 586 S.W.2d 647 (Tex. App.—Austin 1979, writ ref'd n.r.e.), §1.02.7.4

Sparkman v. Presley Olds-Cadillac, Inc., 616 S.W.2d 264, 265, fn. 1 (Tex. Civ. App.—San Antonio 1981, writ ref'd n.r.e.), §1.02.14.1

Sparks v. Bolton, 335 S.W.2d 780 (Tex. Civ. App.—Dallas 1960, no writ), §6.01

Spencer v. Eagle Star Ins. Co. of Am., 876 S.W.2d 154 (Tex. 1994), §§10.01.2, 10.03

Splettstosser v. Myer, 779 S.W.2d 806, 808 (Tex. 1989), §6.10

Spoljaric v. Percival Tours, Inc., 708 S.W.2d 432 (Tex. 1986), §§10.06, 15.04

St. Paul Surplus Lines Ins. Co. v. Dal-Worth Tank Co., 974 S.W.2d 51, 54 (Tex. 1998), §§1.02.14.2, 10.25, 11.03.3

Stafford v. Lunsford, 53 S.W.3d 906 (Tex. App.—Houston [1st Dist.] 2001, no pet.), §2.02.1

Standard Fire Ins. Co. v. Morgan, 745 S.W.2d 310, 312 (Tex. 1987), §7.48

Standard Fire Ins. Co. v. Reese, 584 S.W.2d 835 (Tex. 1979), §§10.22, 10.23

State Dept. of Highways v. Payne, 838 S.W.2d 235, 240, 241 (Tex. 1992), §§10.01.1, 10.01.2, 10.01.3

State Farm Fire & Cas. Co. v. Price, 845 S.W.2d 427 (Tex. App.—Amarillo 1992, writ dism'd by agr.), §9.20.7

State Farm Fire & Cas. Co. v. Reed, 873 S.W.2d 698 (Tex. 1993), §11.05

State Farm Fire & Cas. Co. v. Simmons, 963 S.W.2d 42 (Tex. 1998), §10.04, 11.04

State Farm Fire & Cas. Co. v. Vaughan, 968 S.W.2d 931 (Tex. 1998), §11.05

State Farm Life Ins. Co. v. Beaston, 907 S.W.2d 430 (Tex. 1995), §§5.15, 11.03.3

State Farm Lloyds v. Nicolau, 951 S.W.2d 444 (Tex. 1997), §§1.02.104, 10.04, 11.04

State National Bank of El Paso v. Farah Manufacturing Company, Inc., 678 S.W.2d 661 (Tex. App.—El Paso 1984, writ dism'd), §1:04

Stelly v. Papania, 927 S.W.2d 620 (Tex. 1996), §7.48

Stewart Title Guar. Co. v. Aiello, 941 S.W.2d 68, 71 (Tex. 1997), §11.04

Stewart Title Guar. Co. v. Cheatham, 764 S.W.2d 315, 318-319 (Tex. App.—Texarkana 1988, writ denied), §1.02.9.1

Stewart Title Guar. Co. v. Sterling, 822 S.W.2d 1 (Tex. 1991), §§1.02.28, 2.02.1

Stewart Title Guar. Co. v. Sterling, 772 S.W.2d 242, 248-49 (Tex. App.—Houston [14th Dist.] 1989), *rev'd*. 822 S.W.2d 1, 10 (Tex. 1991), §§1.02.15, 9.20.4

Stone v. Lawyers Title Ins. Corp., 554 S.W.2d 183 (Tex. 1977), §5.01

Sun Oil Co. v. Whitaker, 424 S.W.2d 216 (Tex. 1968), §5.27

Swafford v. View-Caps Water Supply Corp., 617 S.W.2d 674 (Tex. 1981), §2.02.1

— T —

Teleometrics, Int'l, Inc. v. Hall, 922 S.W.2d 189 (Tex. App.—Houston [1st Dist.] 1995, writ denied), §8.01.8

Terminix Int'l. Inc. v. Lucci, 670 S.W.2d 657 (Tex. App.—San Antonio 1984, writ ref'd n.r.e.), §10.11

Terry v. Lawrence, 700 S.W.2d 912, 913 (Tex. 1985), §7.23

Texas Mut. Ins. Co. v. Morris, 287 S.W.3d 401, 434 (Tex. App.—Houston [14th Dist.] 2009), §1.02.14.2.2

Tex. Mut. Ins. Co. v. Ruttiger, 381 S.W.3d 430, 446, 451 (Tex. 2012), §§11.03.1, 11.03.2

Texas & N.O.R. Co. v. Broadway, 345 S.W.2d 814, 821 (Tex. Civ. App.—Beaumont 1961, no writ), §9.05

Texas & N.O.R. Co. v. Lide, 117 S.W.2d 479 (Tex. Civ. App.—Waco 1938, no writ), §§9.05, 9.13

Texas & N.O.R. Co. v. Perez, 346 S.W.2d 369 (Tex. Civ. App.—Houston 1961, writ ref'd n.r.e.), §10.23

Texas Dep't of Human Servs. v. Hinds, 904 S.W.2d 629, 638 (Tex. 1995), §10.01.3

Texas DOT v. Pirtle, 977 S.W.2d 657 (Tex. App.—Fort Worth 1998, writ ref'd), §8.01.4

Texas Emp. Ins. Ass'n v. Loesch, 538 S.W.2d 435 (Tex. Civ. App.—Waco 1976, writ ref'd n.r.e.), §§9.05, 9.13, 10.22

Texas Emp. Ins. Ass'n v. Thames, 252 S.W.2d 228 (Tex. Civ. App.—Fort Worth 1952, writ ref'd n.r.e.), §10.23

Texas Employers' Ins. Ass'n v. Godwin, 194 S.W.2d 593 (Tex. Civ. App.—Dallas, rev'd on other grounds, 195 S.W.2d 347 (Tex. 1946), §9.08

Texas Employers' Ins. Ass'n v. Lane, 251 S.W.2d 181 (Tex. Civ. App.—Fort Worth 1952, writ ref'd n.r.e.), §9.02

Texas Employers' Ins. Ass'n v. McMullin, 279 S.W.2d 699 (Tex. Civ. App.—San Antonio 1955, writ ref'd n.r.e.), §9.02

Texas Employers' Ins. Ass'n v. Mendenhall, 334 S.W.2d 850 (Tex. Civ. App.—Fort Worth 1960, writ ref'd n.r.e.), §10.21

Texas Employers' Ins. Ass'n v. Schanen 263 S.W.2d 614 (Tex. Civ. App.—San Antonio 1953, no writ), §9.05

Texas Farmers Ins. Co. v. Hernandez, 649 S.W.2d 121 (Tex. App.—Amarillo 1983, writ ref'd n.r.e.), §1.02.15

Texas Farmers Ins. Co. v. Murphy, 996 S.W.2d 873 (Tex. 1999), §11.09

Texas First National Bank v. Ng, 167 S.W.3d 842 (fn. 24 (Tex. App.—Houston [14th Dist.] 2005 petition granted), §2.02.6

Texas General Indem. Co. v. Moreno, 638 S.W.2d 908, 913 (Tex. App.—Houston [1st Dist.] 1982, no writ), §10.23

Texas General Indem. Co. v. Speakman, 736 S.W.2d 874 (Tex. App.—Dallas 1987, no writ), §9.20.7

Texas Highway Department v. Jarrell, 418 S.W.2d 486, 488 (Tex. 1967), §6.01

Texas Parks and Wildlife Dept. v. Davis, 988 S.W.2d 370 (Tex. App.—Austin 1999, no writ), §8.01.4

Texas Power & Light Co. v. Adams, 404 S.W.2d 930 (Tex. Civ. App.—Tyler 1966, no writ), §9.02

Texas Real Estate Com'n v. Nagle, 767 S.W.2d 691, 693 (Tex. 1989), §13.02.7

Texas Sand Co. v. Shield, 381 S.W.2d 48 (Tex. 1964), §10.23

Texas Steel Co. v. Douglas, 533 S.W.2d I 11, 118 (Tex. Civ. App.—Fort Worth 1976, writ ref'd n. r. e.), §6.05

Tex-Jersey Oil Corp. v. Beck, 305 S.W.2d 162, 167 (Tex. 1957), §8.10.2

Thomas v. Oldham, 895 S.W.2d 352, 359 (Tex. 1995), §1.02.14.1

Thomes v. Porter, 761 S.W.2d 592, 593-594 (Tex. App.—Fort Worth 1988, no writ), §1.02.4.4

Thompson v. A. G. Nash & Co., 704 S.W.2d 822, 824 (Tex. App.—Tyler 1985, no writ), §9.20.3.1

Thrall v. Renno, 695 S.W.2d 84, 87 (Tex. App.—San Antonio 1985, writ ref'd n.re.), §1.02.9

Titus City Hospital Dist. v. Lucus, 998 S.W.2d 740 (Tex. 1998), §7.51

Todd v. AIG Life Ins. Co., 47 F.3d 1448, 1459 (5th Cir. 1995), §11.06.3.1

Tom L. Scott, Inc. v. McIlhany, 798 S.W.2d 556 (Tex. 1990), §7.19

Tony Gullo Motors I, L.P. v. Chapa, 212 S.W.3d 299, 304 (Tex. 2006), §14.02

Toshiba Machine Co., America v. SPM Flow Control, Inc., 180 S.W.3d 761 (Tex. App.—Fort Worth 2005, no pet.), §9.20.6

Townsend v. Memorial Medical Center, 529 S.W.2d 264 (Tex. Civ. App.—Corpus Christi 1975, writ ref'd n.r.e.), §6.05

Transitional Hosps. Corp. v. Blue Cross & Blue Shield, Inc.., 164 F.3d 952 (5th Cir. 1999, §11.06.3

Transport Co. of Texas v. Robertson Transports, 261 S.W.2d 549, 552 (Tex. 1953), §5.27

Transport Ins. Co. v. Faircloth, 898 S.W.2d 269, 273-74 (Tex. 1995), §§1.02.8, 11.02.1

Transportation Insurance Co. v. Moriel, 879 S.W.2d 10 (Tex. 1994), §§5.17, 10.13

Trenholm v. Ratcliff, 646 S.W.2d 927 (Tex. 1983), §§10.06, 15.04

Trinity Universal Ins. Co. v. Bleeker, 966 S.W.2d 489 (Tex. 1998), §1.02.104

Tripp v. Bloodworth, 374 S.W.2d 713 (Tex. Civ. App.—Eastland 1964, writ ref'd n.r.e.), §10. 19

Troutman v. Traeco Bldg. Systems, Inc., 724 S.W.2d 385 (Tex. 1987), §§5.01, 6.05

TUCCO, Inc. v. Burlington N. R. R. Co., 912 S.W.2d 311 (Tex. App.—Amarillo 1995, no writ), §8.01.8

Tucker v. Newth, 157 S.W.2d 1010 (Tex. Civ. App.—Amarillo 1941, writ ref'd), §10.23

Tumlinson v. San Antonio Brewing Association, 170 S.W.2d 620 (Tex. Civ. App.—San Antonio 1943, writ ref'd), §9.14

Turner v. General Motors Corp., 584 S.W.2d 844, 853 (Tex. 1979), §8.10.2

Tuthill v. Southwestern Public Serv. Co., 614 S.W.2d 205, 212-213 (Tex. Civ. App.—Amarillo 1981, writ ref'd n.r.e.), §1.02.15

Twin City Fire Ins. Co. v. Davis, 904 S.W.2d 663, 666 (Tex. 1995), §11.03.3

Twin City Fire Ins. Co. v. Gibson, 488 S.W.2d 565 (Tex. Civ. App.—Amarillo 1972, writ ref'd n.r.e.), §10. 19

— U —

U.S. Tire-Tech, Inc. v. Boeran, 110 S.W.3d 194, 197-198 (Tex. App.—Houston [1st Dist.] 2003), §1.02.9.1

Underkofler v. Vanasek, 53 S.W.3d 343 (Tex. 2001), §2.02.4

Underwriters Life Ins. Co. v. Cobb, 746 S.W.2d 810 (Tex. App.—Corpus Christi 1988, no writ), §§7.28, 10.02

Union Bankers Ins. Co. v. Shelton, 889 S.W.2d 278 (Tex. 1994), §10.04, 11.04

Union Pacific Fuels, Inc. v. Johnson, 909 S.W.2d 130 (Tex. App.—Houston [14th Dist.] 1995, no writ), §6.01

Union Pacific R.R. v. Williams, 85 S.W.3d 162, 166 (Tex. 2002), §10.01.1

United Postage Corp. v. Kammeyer, 581 S.W.2d 716 (Tex. Civ. App.—Dallas 1979, no writ), §§1.02.5, 1.02.14.5

United States Ins. Co. of Waco v. Boyer, 269 S.W.2d 340 (Tex. 1954), §11.05

United States Pipe and Foundry Co. v. Waco, 108 S.W.2d 432, 435-37 (Tex. 1937) cert. den. 302 US 749, §1.02.9.1

United States v. Nobles, 422 U.S. 225 (1975), §7.32

Universal Servs. Co. v. Ung, 904 S.W.2d 638, 640 (Tex. 1995), §10.01.2

Universe Life Ins. Co. v. Giles, 950 S. W.2d 48 (Tex. 1997), §§11.04, 10.04

— V —

Vail v. Texas Farm Bureau Mut. Ins. Co., 754 S.W.2d 129 (Tex. 1988), §§10.04, 10.09, 11.03.2, 11.03.3

Valley Coca-Cola Bottling v. Molina, 818 S.W.2d 146 (Tex. App.—Corpus Christi 1991, writ denied), §9.20.8

Valley Datsun v. Martinez, 578 S.W.2d 485 (Tex. Civ. App.—Corpus Christi 1979, no writ), §1.02.9.1

Varner v. Cardenas, 218 S.W.3d 68 (Tex. 2007), §1.02.15

Village Mobile Homes, Inc. v. Porter, 716 S.W.2d 543, 549-50 (Tex. App.—Austin 1986, writ ref'd n.r.e.), §1.02.14.1

— W —

W. Telemarketing Corp. Outbound v. McClure, 225 S.W.3d 658 (Tex. App.—El Paso 2006, pet. den'd), §9.20.6

W.O. Bankston Nissan, Inc. v. Walters, 754 S.W.2d 127 (Tex. 1988), §1.02.14

Wade v. Hewlett-Packard Dev. Co. LP Short Term Disability Plan, 493 F.3d 533 (5th Cir. 2007), §11.06.3.1

Waite Hill Servs. v. World Class Metal Works, 959 S.W.2d 182 (Tex. 1998), §1.02.14

Walden v. Jeffery, 907 S.W.2d 446 (Tex. 1995), §2.02.1

Walker v. Missouri Pacific Railroad Co., 425 S.W.2d 462 (Tex. Civ. App.—Houston [14th Dist.] 1968, writ ref'd n.r.e.), §8.10.2

Wal-Mart Stores, Inc. v. Street, 754 S.W.2d 153, 155 (Tex. 1988), §7.51

Warehouse Associates v. Celotex, 192 S.W.3d 225 (Tex. App.—Houston [14th Dist.] 2006, pet. filed), §§2.02.6, 8.13

Waterfield Mortgage Co., Inc. v. Rodriguez, 929 S.W.2d 641 (Tex. App.—San Antonio 1996, no writ), §1.02.12.1

Weekley Homes, Inc. v. Jennings, 936 S.W.2d 16 (Tex. App.—San Antonio 1996, writ denied), §8.01.6

Wegner v. Standard Ins. Co., 129 F.3d 814, 822 (5th Cir. 1997), §11.06.3.1

Weitzel v. Barnes, 691 S.W. 2d 598 (Tex. 1985), §§1.02.7, 1.02.8.3, 2.02, 5.01, 10.01.1

Wellborn v. Sears, Roebuck & Co., 970 F.2d 1420 (5th Cir. 1992), §§1.02.4.2, 1.02.4.4

Werner v. Miller, 579 S.W.2d 455 (Tex. 1979), §8.12

West v. Solito, 563 S.W.2d 240 (Tex. 1978), §7.01

Western Cas. & Sur. Co. v. Spears, 730 S.W.2d 821, 823 (Tex. App.—San Antonio 1987, no writ), §7.29

Western Cottage Piano & Organ Co. v. Anderson, 101 S.W. 1061, 1064 (Tex. Civ. App.—Ft. Worth 1907, writ denied), §2.02.6

Wheeler v. Box, 671 S.W.2d 75 (Tex. App.—Dallas 1984, no writ), §1.02.5

Whirlpool Corp. v. Texical, Inc., 649 S.W.2d 55 (Tex. App.—Corpus Christi 1982, no writ), §1.02.14.4

Whitsel v. Hoover, 120 S.W.2d 930 (Tex. Civ. App.—Amarillo 1938, writ dis'd d. f.w.o.j.), §2.02.6

Wielgosz v. Millard, 679 S.W.2d 163, 167 (Tex. App.—Houston [14th Dist.] 1984, no writ), §7.22

Williams v. Hills Fitness Center, Inc., 705 S.W.2d 189, 191-193 (Tex. App.—Texarkana 1985, writ ref'd n.r.e.), §§1.02.4.1, 3.02

Williams v. Trail Dust Steak House, Inc., 727 S.W.2d 812 (Tex. App.—Fort Worth 1987, no writ), §1.02.10

Williamson v. O'Neill, 696 S.W.2d 431, 432 (Tex. App.—Houston [14th] Dist.] 1985, no writ), §7.16

Willis v. Maverick, 760 S.W.2d 642, 647 (Tex. 1988), §§2.02.4, 5.28, 10.01.1, 11.09

Willowbrook Foods, Inc. v. Grinnell Corp., 147 S.W.3d 492 (Tex. App.—San Antonio 2004, no pet.), §1.02.8

Wise v. City of Abilene, 141 S.W.2d 400 (Tex. Civ. App.—Eastland 1940, writ dism'd), §9.05

Wolfson v. BIC Corp., 95 S.W.3d 527, 534 (Tex. App.—Houston [1st Dist.] 2002), §1.02.13

Woods v. Crane Carrier Co., Inc., 693 S.W.2d 377, 379 (Tex. 1985), §10.01.2

Woods v. Littleton, 554 S.W.2d 662 (Tex. 1977), §§1.02.1, 1.02.9

World Wide Tire Co. v. Brown, 644 S.W.2d 144 (Tex. App.—Houston [14th Dist.] 1982, writ ref'd n.r.e.), §10.23

Worthy v. Collagen Corp., 967 S.W.2d 360 (Tex. 1998), §1.02.7.4

— Y —

Young v. Neatherlin, 102 S.W.3d 415 (Tex. App.—Houston [14th Dist.] 2003, no pet.), §1.02.15

Younger Bros. v. Moore, 135 S.W.2d 780 (Tex. Civ. App.—El Paso 1939, writ dism'd judgmt cor.), §10. 19

— Z —

Zac Smith & Co. v. Otis Elevator Co., 734 S.W.2d 662 (Tex. 1987), §5.08

Zeh v. Singleton, 650 S.W.2d 518, 519 (Tex. App.—Houston [14th Dist.] 1983, no writ), §9.05

Index

[All references are to section numbers.]

For specific forms, see Table of Contents.

— A —

Abatement pleas, §6.01
    affirmative defenses (*See* Affirmative defenses)
    answer, original, §6.04
    arbitration agreements, §6.02.3
    counterclaim
    bad faith, §6.10
    harassment, §6.10
    defenses, affirmative, §6.06
    exceptions, §6.05
    forms
        affirmative defense (*See* Affirmative defenses)
        answer, original, §6.04
            arbitration agreements, §6.02.3
            bad faith, §6.10
            counterclaim, §6.10
            harassment, §6.10
            inadequate notice of claim, §6.01.1
            inspection, §6.01.2
            mediation, §6.01.3
            motion to transfer venue, §6.03
            notice of claim, inadequate, §6.01.1
            notice not given, §3.11
            order, §§6.01.1, 6.01.2, 6.01.3
            original answer, §§6.04, 6.08
            professional opinion, §6.09
            refusal to allow inspection, §6.01.2
            venue, motion to transfer, §6.03
            waiver, §6.07
            written contract, §6.09.1
    inadequacy of pleadings, §6.05
    inspection, refusal to allow, §§6.01, 6.01.2
    mediation, §6.01.3
    notice of claim, inadequate, §6.01.1
    original answer and affirmative defenses, §6.06
    residential construction, §6.01.1
    venue, motion to transfer, §6.03
Actions
    contract, §1.02.8.1
    residential construction, §10.15
    tort, §1.02.8.1

Acts. *See* specific acts
    arbitration (*See* Federal Arbitration Act)
    Deceptive Trade Practices Act (*See* Deceptive Trade Practices Act)
    Employee Retirement Income Security Act, §1.02.7
    MLIIA, §1.02.8
Actual damages (*See* Economic damages)
Adverse party rule, §9.16
Affidavit, §§6.01, 8.04, 8.05, 8.06
    rejection of settlement offer, §4.08
Affirmative defenses, §§2.02.1, 6.06
    dollar limit, exceeding, §6.09.2
    independent investigation §§6.09.4, 8.13
    original answer, §6.06
    professional opinion, §6.09
    reasonable settlement offer, §6.09.5
    residential construction, §6.08
    waiver, §6.07
    written contract, claims of, §6.09.1
Agreements
    arbitration, §6.02.3
        defenses to, §8.01.7
    attorney-client (*See* Attorney-client agreements)
    discovery, §7.41
    misrepresented, §10.03
    settlement, §7.24
    unlawful, §10.03
Alcohol use, §8.10.1
Alter ego, §10.02
Alternate dispute resolution, §8.01.1
Alternative Dispute Resolution Act (Texas), §8.01.1
American Arbitration Association, §8.01.5
Answer, §§6.04, 6.06, 6.08
Arbitration, §8.01.5
    agreements, §6.02.3
        defenses to, §8.01.7
        setting aside, §8.01.5
    appeal of decision of arbitrator, §8.01.8
    applicable law, §8.01.6

attorney's fees, §8.01.6
compelling, form, §8.01.8
decision of arbitrator, §8.01.5
    appeal, §8.01.8
defenses to agreement, §8.01.7
federal (*See* Federal Arbitration Act)
forms, §6.02.3
inexpensive remedy, §8.01.5
secrecy, §8.01.5
selection of arbitrators, §8.01.5
speedy remedy, §8.01.5
voluntary, §8.01.5

Article 21.21. *See* Insurance Code, Chapter 541

Assisted living facilities
    petition, §5.25.3[a]
    preparing a complaint against, §5.25.3

Assumed names, §7.04

Attorney's fees, §§1.02.15
    appeals, §9.20.8
    arbitration, §8.01.6
    bad faith, §6.10
    contingent fee, §1.02.28
    responding to notice letter, §4.01
    court's charge, §10.14
    damages, §§1.02.28, 10.14
    DTPA, §1.02.28
    final judgments, §10.26
    harassment, §6.10
    jury judgments, §10.26
    motions in limine, §8.01.1
    notice letter, §4.01
    original petition, §5.02
    proof of, §9.20
    reasonable, §1.02.28
    recovery, §1.02.28
    responding to notice letter, §4.01
    segregation of, §1.02.28
    testimony, §9.16

Attorney-client agreements, §§1.07-1.08
    hourly fees, §2.05

Attorney-client privilege, §7.33

Automobiles, *see* Chapter 14
    See also Motor Vehicles

— B —

Banking
    credit, false representation to extend, §5.23
    forms, §5.23
    unauthorized withdrawal of funds, §5.23

Breach of contract, §§5.23, 5.25
    ambiguous insurance, §5.25.2
    mere, §1.02.8.1

Breach of duty
    cancellation of insurance coverage, §10.04
    delay of claim, §10.04
    denial of claim, §10.04

Breach of warranty, §1.02.9
    commercial lease space, §10.07
    express (*See* Express warranty)
    implied (*See* Implied warranty)
    manufacturer, §5.14
    types of cases, §1.02.9

Burden of proof, §§5.28, 6.05

Business opportunities
    FTC franchise rule exemption, §15.03
    interrogatories, forms, §15.08.1
    overview, §15.01
    pleadings, defendant, §15.07
    pre-suit notice letter to seller, §15.05
    requests for production, forms, §15.08.2
    Texas Business Opportunity Act, §15.02
        discovery, §15.08
        pleadings, plaintiff, §15.06
    theories of liability, §15.04

Business records, §8.07

— C —

Causes of action
    general form, §5.15
    knowing conduct, §5.15

Chapter 541 (*See* Insurance Code, Chapter 541)

Checklists
    commercial real property, lease of, §2.04
    defendant (*See* Defendant client, initial contact with)
    deposition, §7.53
    evidence, §9.19
    goods and services, sale of, §2.04
    initial client interview
        defendant (*See* Defendant client, initial contact with)
        plaintiff (*See* Plaintiff client, initial contact with)
    interview, §2.04
    new residence, sale of, §2.04
    objections, §9.13
    evidence, §9.19
    plaintiff (*See* Plaintiff client, initial contact with)
    raw land, sale of, §2.04
    voir dire examination, objections to, §9.13

Citations, §5.03
    agents, service on, §5.11
    alleging statutory authority, §5.12
    Commissioner of Insurance, §5.07.1
    conditions precedent, §5.13
    corporations, §5.06

employees, service on, §5.11
forms
    corporations, §5.06
    individuals, §5.05
    insurance companies, §5.06
    long arm jurisdiction, §5.08
    notice given, §5.13
    partnerships, §5.05
    person in charge of business, §5.10
    Secretary of State, §5.07
    venue, §5.14
general venue rule, §5.14
individuals, §5.05
long arm jurisdiction, §5.08
multiple defendants, §5.15
non resident, suing, §5.08
notice given, §5.13
notice precedent, §5.13
partnerships, §5.05
person in charge of business, §5.10
prefiling notice, §5.13
proof of service, obtaining, §5.09
Secretary of State, §5.07
statutory authority, alleging, §5.12
venue, §§5.14, 5.15

Client interview and questionnaire, §1.03

Client contact
  defendant (*See* Defendant client, initial contact with)
  initial
    defendant (*See* Defendant client, initial contact with)
    plaintiff (*See* Plaintiff client, initial contact with)
  plaintiff (*See* Plaintiff client, initial contact with)
  solvency, §1.01

Collateral, §8.10.1

Commercial construction, §5.21

Commercial real property
  lease, §5.25

Common law fraud, §10.05

Conflict of interest
  prospective client, §1.01

Construction
  commercial, implied warranties for, §1.02.9.2.2
  new home, §1.02.9.2.1
  residential (*See* Residential construction)

Consumer
  business, §1.02.4
  defined, §1.02.4
  standing, §6.05
  transaction, §1.02.4
  after purchase, §1.02.4
  court's view, §1.02.4

Contingent fee, §4.01

Contracts
  actions, §1.02.8.1
  "As is" clause, §2.02.03
  breach (*See* Breach of contract)
  tort actions, distinguishing between, §1.02.8.1
  waiver/superseding clause, §2.02.03
  written, §6.09.1

Contribution, §2.02.9

Corporate agents, §10.02

Corporations, §§5.06, 7.03

Counteraffidavit, §8.06

Court's charge, §10.01
  breach of warranty, §10.07
  common law fraud, §10.05
  complaints, §10.01
  damages (*See* Damages)
  defenses (*See* Defenses)
  definitions, §10.02
    agency, §10.02
    alter ego, §10.02
    corporate agents, §10.02
    course of action, §10.02
    express warranty, §10.02
    good and workmanlike manner, §10.02
    intentionally, §10.02
    knowingly, §10.02
    market value, §10.02
    producing cause, §10.02
    unconscionable action, §10.02
    uninhabitable, §10.02
  description of goods and services, §10.03
  discovery rule, §10.16
  failure to disclose, §10.03
  false, misleading, or deceptive act, §10.03
  forms, §10.05
    additional damages, §10.13
    agency, §10.02
    alter ego, §10.02
    Chapter 541 of Insurance Code, §10.09
    attorney's fees, §10.14
    breach of warranty, §10.07
    commercial lease, §10.07
    corporate agents, §10.02
    course of action, §10.02
    damages, §§10.10, 10.13
    exemplary damages, §10.13
    express warranty, §10.02
    fraud, §10.05
    good and workmanlike manner, §10.02
    habitability and workmanship, §10.07

implied warranty, §10.07
intentional conduct, §10.12
intentionally, §10.02
knowing conduct, §10.12
knowingly, §10.02
market value, §10.02
merchantability, §10.07
negligent misrepresentation, §10.05
producing cause, §10.02
restoration of money or property, §10.10
statute of limitations, §10.16
unconscionable action, §§10.02, 10.08
uninhabitable, §10.02
good faith and fair dealing, breach of duty, §10.04
instructions, §10.02
Insurance Code, Chapter 541, §§1.02.11, 10.09
knowingly, §10.18
laundry list questions, §10.03
market value, §10.18
misrepresentation, §10.05
misrepresented agreements, §10.03
negligent misrepresentation, §10.05
objection, §10.01
ordinary care, §10.18
pecuniary loss, §10.05
producing cause, §10.18
proportionate responsibility, §10.17
quality of goods or services, §10.03
sample, §10.18
special charge, requested, §10.01
statute of limitations, §10.16
statutory fraud, §10.05
style of goods or services, §10.03
unconscionability, §10.08
unlawful agreements, §10.03
work or services performed, §10.03
Criminal convictions, §§8.08, 8.09
motions in limine, §8.10.1
Cross examination, §9.18

— D —

Damages, §10.10
actual (*See* Actual damages)
additional, §10.13
statutory, §5.17
attorney's fees, §§1.02.28, 10.14
banking, §5.23
commercial real property lease, §5.25
cost of repair, §10.11
elements, §10.11
exemplary, §10.13
forms, §10.10

actual, §5.16
additional, §§5.17, 10.13
additional statutory, §5.17
commercial real property lease, §5.25
discretionary additional, §5.17
exemplary, §§5.17, 10.13
intentional conduct, §§5.15.1, 10.12
knowing conduct, §10.12
lending, §5.23
mandatory treble, §5.17
personal injury, §5.17
wrongful death, §5.17
intentional conduct, §§5.15.1, 10.12
knowing conduct, §10.12
lending, §5.23
loss of use, §10.11
loss of value, §10.11
manufactured housing, §16.01
mental anguish (*See* Mental anguish)
special, §5.16
specific actions, pleading, §5.18
statutory, additional, §5.17
stigma, §10.11
treble, §§5.17, 10.12
Death, §5.17
Deceptive Trade Practices Act (DTPA)
amendments, 1995, §1.02.4
application, §1.02.1
assignability of claims, §1.02.4
construction, §1.02.2
cumulative remedies, §1.02.3
damages (*See* Damages)
defenses (*See* Defenses)
effective dates, §1.02.1
ERISA, §1.02.7
exemptions, limited, §1.02.7
forms (*See* Forms, subhead DTPA)
giving notice (See Notice letter, DTPA, §3.02)
goods defined, §1.02.5
laundry list questions, §10.03
limited exemptions, §1.02.7
mere breach of contract, §1.02.8.1
money lending, §1.02.6
notice letter (*See* Notice letter)
original answer affirmative defenses, §6.06
overview, §1.02
plaintiff, consumer, §1.02.4
pretrial proceedings, visiting judges in litigation, §8.09
remedies, cumulative, §1.02.3
resale goods, §1.02.5
sample charge, §10.18
services defined, §1.02.6
Smoke Detector Statute (Texas), §1.02.7

statute of limitations, §10.16
who can be sued, §1.02.7
Defective performance
   mere breach of contract, §1.02.8.1
Defendant client, initial contact with
   attorney-client agreements, §2.05
   checklists for initial interview, §2.04
      goods or services, §2.04
      real property, lease, §2.04
      sale of new residence, §2.04
      sale of raw land, §2.04
   claimant defined, §2.01
   client defined, §2.01
   form, §2.05
   general considerations, §2.01
   interview, initial, §2.04
   large transaction exemption, §2.02.12
   meeting, §2.01
   questionnaire, §2.03
   third party liability, §2.01
Defendant's pleadings
   abatement pleas (*See* Abatement pleas)
Defenses, §10.15
   affirmative (*See* Affirmative defenses)
   contribution and indemnity, §2.02.9
   dollar limit, §2.02.7
   DTPA, §10.15
   forms, §2.02.03
   indemnity and contribution, §2.02.9
   media exemption, §2.02.8
   overview, §2.02.1
   professional services exemption, §2.02.2
   puffing, §2.02.1
   real estate brokers and agents exemption, §2.02.3
   residential construction actions, §10.15
   settlement credit, §2.02.11
   statutory defenses, §2.02.7
   waiver, §2.02.4
Deposition
   before suit (§7.52.1)
      petition for, §7.52.1[a]
      order for, §7.52.1[b]
   oral, §7.51
   written questions, §7.50.1
Direct examination, §9.17
Disclosure
   failure, §10.03
Discovery
   agreements, §7.37
   considerations, §7.01
   control plans, §7.36
      modification of, §7.40
         form, §7.40

   exemptions, §7.31
      consulting experts, §7.19
      privileged information, §7.33
      work product, §7.312
      scope, §7.16
   forms
      allegations invoking discovery rule, §5.28
      drafting requests for production, §7.46
      requests for admission, §7.48
   informal (*See* Informal discovery)
   insurance code actions, §11.10
   interrogatories (*See* Interrogatories)
   Level 1, §7.37
   Level 2, §7.38
   Level 3, §7.39
   matters (*See* Matters of discovery)
   oral deposition (*See* Oral deposition)
   requests for admission, §7.48
      drafting, §7.49
      form, §7.49
   requests for disclosure, §7.41.1
   requests for production, §7.46
      drafting requests, §7.47
      requests, responding to, §7.50
      specific cases, §7.47.1
   subpoenas and, §7.34
   types, §7.35
      discovery agreements, §7.41
Discrimination, §8.10.1
Dollar limits, §2.02.7
   amounts, §6.09.2

— E —

Economic damages, §5.16
   forms, §5.16
   investment, §5.16
   product, §5.16
   residential construction, §5.16
   unimproved land, §5.16
Employee Retirement Income Security Act, see ERISA
   DTPA, §1.02.7
Employees
   service on, §5.11
ERISA, §1.02.7
Evidence, §§8.04, 9.15
   business records, §8.07
   checklist, §9.19
   cross examination, §9.18
   direct examination, §9.17
   experts, placement of, §9.16
   medical records, §8.07

objections, §9.19
records, §8.07
rules of evidence, §9.16
testimony, order of, §9.16
Exemptions, §1.02.7.3
   Personal injury claims, §1.02.7.3.2
   Professional services, §1.02.7.3.1
   Large transactions, §1.02.7.3.3
Expert witnesses, §7.19
Express warranty, §1.02.9.1
   special charge by court, §10.02

— F —

Fair dealing. *See* Good faith and fair dealing
False, misleading or deceptive acts or practices, §1.02.8
   form, §10.03
Federal Arbitration Act, §8.01.6
Fees
   agreements, §§2.01, 2.05
   attorney (*See* Attorney's fees)
   contingent, §4.01
Foreclosure, §5.25
Forms
   abatement pleas (*See* Abatement pleas, subhead forms)
   actual damages, §5.16
   arbitration, §6.02.3
   "as is" real estate purchase, §6.09.3
   attorney-client agreements (*See* Attorney-client agreement, subhead forms)
   banking, §5.23
   breach of duty, §10.04
   cause of action, §5.15
   citations (*See* Citations, subhead forms)
   commercial real property lease, §5.25
   consumer rights, waiver of, §2.02.4
   court's charge (*See* Court's charge, subhead forms)
   damages (*See* Damages, subhead forms)
   discovery (*See* Discovery, subhead forms)
   DTPA
     negligence of another person as defense, §10.15
     no opportunity to repair as defense, §10.15
     sample charge, §10.18
     third party information, §10.15
     unreasonable rejection of settlement offer, §10.15
   initial client contact
   defendant, §2.03
   injunctive relief, §5.27
   intentional conduct, §5.15.1
   interrogatories (*See* Interrogatories, subhead forms)
   jury judgments (*See* Jury judgments, subhead forms)
   knowing conduct, §5.15
   laundry list questions, §10.03
   mediation, §8.01.1
   notice letter (*See* Notice letter)
   oral deposition
     notice of, §7.51
     preparing the client for, §7.54
   original form for plaintiff's pleadings, §5.02
   plaintiff's pleadings
     citations, service of, §§5.06B5.08
     service of citations, §5.05
   pretrial conferences, §8.12
   pretrial proceedings (*See* Pretrial proceedings, subhead forms)
   requests for admission into discovery, §7.48
   requests for production, §7.46
   ruling on special court's charge, §10.01
   special court's charge, §10.01
   temporary injunction, §5.27
   temporary injunctive relief, §5.27
   temporary restraining order, §5.27
   venue, §§5.14, 6.03
   waiver of consumer rights, §2.02.4
Franchises, §§7.45
   See Business opportunities
Fraud, §10.05
FTC Purchase Money Loan Rule, §3.04

— G —

General Arbitration Act (Texas), §8.01.6
Gift Giveaway Act. *See* Contest and Gift Giveaway Act
Golden rule, §10.23
Good and workmanlike, §§1.02.9.2, 1.02.9.2.1
   commercial leasing/construction, §1.02.9.2.2
   defined, §1.02.9.2.1
   new homes, §1.02.9.2.2
   sale and goods, §1.02.9.2
   services, §1.02.9.2.3
Good faith and fair dealing, §10.04
   cancellation of insurance, §10.04
   delay of claim, §10.04
   denial of claim, §10.04
   description, §10.03
   inspection, §4.01
   notice letter, §4.01
   quality and style, §10.03
   sale, §2.04
Government Code (Texas)
   jury selection, challenges to jurors, §9.02

visiting judges, §8.09

— H —

Harassment, §§4.01, 6.10

Home Improvement Contracts. *See* Homestead: Sham Sales and Home Improvement Contracts

Husband-wife privilege, §7.33

— I —

Impeachment, §§8.08, 9.18
Implied representations, §1.02.8.2
Implied warranty, §1.02.9.2
    good and workmanlike (*See* Good and workmanlike)
    new homes, §1.02.9.2.1
    no, §1.02.19
    unconscionability, cause of action for, §1.02.10
Indemnity, §7.24
    contribution, §2.02.9
Independent investigation, §§6.09.4, 8.13
Informal discovery, §7.02
    assumed names, §7.04
    construction information, §7.12
    corporate information, §7.03
    financial institutions, §7.05
    insurance agents, §7.07
    insurance companies, §7.06
    manufactured housing, §7.13
    prior claims, §7.11
    prior complaints, §7.11
    prior lawsuits, §7.10
    real estate inspectors, §7.09
    Realtors, §7.08
Injunctive relief
    temporary, §5.27
Inspection
    refusal to allow, §6.02.2
Insurance
    cancellation of coverage, §10.04
Insurance Code, Chapter 541, §11.02-11.03
    defenses, §11.06
    form, §10.09
    pre-suit notice, §11.07
Insurance code actions
    Chapter 541, §§11.02-11.03, 11.06-11.07
    Defendant's pleadings, §11.09
    Discovery, §11.10
    Duty of good faith and fair dealing, §11.04
    Insurance contracts, §11.05
    Plaintiff's pleadings, §11.08
Insurance companies
    files and settlements, §7.29
Intentional conduct
    general forms, §5.15.1
Intentional violations, §5.15.1
Interrogatories, §7.42
    additional questions, §7.44
    commercial lease, §7.45
    defective goods, §7.45
    drafting, §7.42
    forms
        commercial lease, §7.45
        defective products, §7.45
        drafting, §7.42
        Insurance Code Claim; homeowner policy, §7.45
        lender liability, §7.45
        questions to defendant, §7.45
        questions to plaintiff, §7.45
        residential construction, §7.45
        unfair debt collection practices, §7.45
        unimproved land, §7.45
    insurance claims, §7.45
    Insurance Code Claim; homeowner policy, §7.45
    investments, §7.45
    lender liability, §7.45
    questions to defendant, §7.45
    questions to plaintiff, §7.45
    residential construction, §7.45
    sale of home with homeowner's warranty, §7.45
    sale of unimproved land, §7.45
    unimproved land, §7.45
Interviews
    initial client, §2.04
Invention Development Services
Investment
    actual damages, §5.16
    actual, §5.16
    interrogatories, §7.45
Investments and business opportunities, *see* Chapter 15

— J —

Judges
    visiting, §8.09
Judgments
    final, §10.26
    jury (*See* Jury judgments)
    motions for, §10.25

Jury arguments, §10.19
   closing arguments, §10.21
   contents, §§10.21, 10.24
   golden rule, §10.23
   improper, §10.23
   incurable improper, §10.22
   preserving error, §10.22
   principles, general legal, §10.20
   structure, §10.24
Jury duty
   categories, §9.07
   codes, §9.07
   exemptions, §9.03
   sources of information, §9.06
Jury judgments
   attorney's fees, §10.26
   damages, §10.26
   final judgments, §10.26
   forms
      attorney's fees, §10.26
      damages, §10.26
      defendant's motion, §10.25
      motions, §10.25
      rescission, §10.26
      restoration of money or property, §10.26
   motions, §10.25
   prejudgments, §10.26
   rescission, §10.26
   restoration of money and property, §10.26
   statutory prejudgments, §10.26
Jury questions, form of, §10.01.1
Jury selection, §9.01
   cause, challenges for, §9.02
   challenges, §9.02
   collecting information on jurors, §9.07
   communicating concepts, §9.09
   disqualification, §9.02
   exemptions from jury service, §9.03
   information on jurors, sources of, §9.06
   participants, introduction of, §9.10
   preemptory challenges, §9.02
   qualifications, §9.01

— K —

— L —

Land
   checklist, §2.04
   unimproved, §7.42
Large transactions
   Exemptions for, §1.02.7.3.3

Leases, commercial property
Leasing, §2.04
   commercial real property, §5.25
   implied warranty, §§1.02.9.2.2, 7.42
Liability, §§5.23, 7.42
   medical (*See* Medical Liability and Insurance Improvement Act (MLIIA))
Limited partnerships, §5.05
Long arm jurisdiction, §5.08

— M —

Manufactured housing
   discovery, §16.05
   initial client checklist, §16.02
   interrogatories, §16.05.1
   petition, defects in workmanship and repairs, §16.04[a]
   petition, retailer refusal to refund deposit, §16.04[b]
   pre-suit notice letters, §16.03
   requests for production, §16.05.2
   Texas Manufactured Housing Standards Act, §16.01
      Manufactured homeowners recovery fund, §16.01.4
      notice/abatement, §16.01.3
      tie-in statute violation, §16.01.2
      warranty actions, §16.01.1
      wrongfully withheld deposit, §16.01.5
Market value, §10.02
Matters of discovery, §7.16
   claims, §7.28
   documents, §7.20
   financial records, §7.22
   indemnity, §7.24
   insurance company files, §7.29
   insuring agreements, §7.24
   land, §7.30
   medical records, §7.25
   photographs, §7.23
   settlement agreements, §7.24
   statements, §7.26
   tax returns, §7.21
   wealth of parties, §7.27
   witnesses and parties
      experts, §7.19
      potential fact, §7.18
Mediation, §8.01.1
   ADR, §8.01.2
   ethical traps, avoiding, §8.01.4.1
   forms, §8.01.1
   preparation, §8.01.3

process, §§8.01.1, 8.01.4
   settlement agreement, sample, §8.01.1[c]
   when to use, §8.01.2
Medical records, §8.07
Mental anguish, §10.11
   award of, §5.15
Mere breach of contract
   defective performance, §1.02.8.1
Misrepresented fraud, §10.05
Mobile homes, see Manufactured housing supra
Motion for leave to designate responsible third party, §6.11
Motions in limine, §§8.10, 8.10.1
   absent witness, testimony, §8.10.1
   attorney's fees, §8.10.1
   attorney, retention of, §8.10.1
   collateral, §8.10.1
   cost of award, social, §8.10.1
   credibility, counsel's opinion, §8.10.1
   criminal offenses, §8.10.1
   denial, §8.10
   discovery disputes, §8.10.1
   discrimination, §8.10.1
   drug use, §8.10.1
   evidence not in discovery, §8.10.1
   ex parte statements of witness, §8.10.1
   failure to call witness, §8.10.1
   files, requests for, §8.10.1
   Golden Rule, §8.10.1
   hardship, §8.10.1
   income tax, §8.10.1
   insurance, §8.10.1
   juror's connection with insurance industry, §8.10.1
   jury questions, effect of, §8.10.1
   liability for judgment, §8.10.1
   mediation, §8.10.1
   medical examination, independent, §8.10.1
   medical opinions, hearsay, §8.10.1
   negotiation, §8.10.1
   photographs, §8.10.1
   prior suits or claims, §8.10.1
   privation, §8.10.1
   procedure, §8.10.2
   purpose, §8.10
   settlement, §8.10.1
   standing order for jury cases, §8.10.1
   stipulations, requests for, §8.10.1
   Travis County Local Rule, §8.10.1
   visual aids, §8.10.1
Motor vehicles, new and used
   advertising, regulation of, §14.03.2
   defenses, §14.04
   discovery, §14.09
   FTC used car rule, §14.03.4
   general considerations, §14.01
   initial client checklist, §14.05
   interrogatories, §14.09.1
   laundry list provisions, §14:02
   other Texas laws governing sale of, §14:03
   pleadings, §§14.07, 14.08
   pre-suit notice letter to seller, §14.06
   requests for production, §14.09.2
   Texas lemon law, §14:03.1
   warranty considerations, §14.03.3
Multiple defendants, §5.15

— N —

Negligence
   misrepresentation, §10.05
   withdrawal of funds, §5.23
New home construction, §1.02.9.2.1
Notice, DTPA, §3.01
   Objectives of notice, §3.02
   Pre-requisite to suit, §3.01
   Sufficiency of notice, §3.02
Notice letter, DTPA, §3.02
   Giving Notice
      client communications, §3.09
      elements of, §3.03
      exceptions to pre-filing notice requirement, §3.10
      general form, §3.03[a]
      method of delivery, §3.02
      products or services, §3.03
      residential construction, §3.09
      settlement offer, evaluation of, §3.10
   Responding
      additional information, requesting, §4.03
      additional time, letter requesting, §4.02
      analyzing claim, letter to client, §4.02
      attorney's fees, §4.01
      contingent fee, §4.01
      delivery, §4.01
      evaluation
         additional information, requesting, §4.03
         form, §4.02
         initial, §4.02
      evaluation, §4.02
      rejecting the claim, §4.07
      goods and services, §4.01
      initial evaluation, §4.02
         additional information, requesting, §4.03
         denial of liability, general statement, §4.04
         less than amount sought, §4.06
         letter rejecting claim, §4.07

offer of settlement, full amount, §4.05
offer of settlement, less than full amount, §4.06
offering full amount, §4.05
rejection of settlement offer, affidavit, §4.08
residential construction, §4.03
response to letter, §4.04
legal considerations, §4.02
letter requesting inspection of goods, §4.01
practical considerations, §4.02
purpose, §4.01
rejecting the claim
effect of, §4.08
form, §4.07
settlement offer, §4.01

— O —

Offer
settlement (*See* Settlement offer)
Offer to repair, residential construction, §3.09
Opening statement
defendant, §9.12
plaintiff, §9.11
Oral deposition, §7.51
checklists, §7.53
forms
preparing the client, §7.54
non-stenographic, §7.51
notice, §7.52
objections, §7.50
preparing the client, §7.51
Order of testimony, §9.6
Original petition, §5.02

— P —

Parol evidence rule
applicability of, §1.02.8.3
Partnerships, §5.05
Personal injury claims
Exemptions for, §1.02.7.3.2
Petition
actual damages, §5.02
additional damages, §5.02
assisted living facilities, §5.25.3[a]
attorney's fees, §5.02
causes of action, §5.02
contents of, §5.01
damages recovered must be reduced by value of settlement, §6.09.6[a]
demand for jury, §5.02

discovery and, §§5.01, 5.02, 5.18
expedited actions, §5.01.1
forms, §5.02
function, §5.04
knowing conduct, §5.02
notice, §5.02
original, §5.02
request for relief, §5.02
service of process, §5.02
statutory authority, §5.02
transaction, §5.02
venue, §5.02
Photographs, §§7.23, 8.10.1
work product, §7.32
Plaintiff client, initial contact with
client defined, §1.01
first meeting, §1.01
prospective defendant, §1.01
Plaintiff client, initial interview with, §1.01
Plaintiff's pleadings
causes of action, §5.18
citations (*See* Citations)
claim for relief, §5.12
damages (*See* Damages)
discovery, §5.28
fair notice, §5.12
forms
application for injunctive relief, §5.27
discovery, §5.28
warranty, §5.15
injunctive relief, §5.29
knowing conduct, §5.18
petition (*See* Petition)
remedies, §5.18
table for remedies, §5.18
temporary restraining order, §5.29
unfair debt collection practices, §5.26
warranty, §5.15
Pretrial conferences, §8.12
Pretrial proceedings
arbitration (*See* Arbitration)
business records, §8.07
conferences, pretrial, §8.12
considerations, §8.01
cost and necessity of services, §8.06
counteraffidavit, §8.06
criminal convictions used for impeachment, §8.08
evidence by affidavit, §8.04
business records, §8.07
cost of service, §8.05
medical records, §8.07
necessity of service, §8.05
service, §§8.05, 8.06

forms, §8.06
    business records, §8.07
    conferences, pretrial, §8.12
    criminal convictions used for impeachment, §8.08
    criminal convictions, request for notice of use to impeach, §8.09
    evidence by affidavit, service of, §§8.05, 8.06
    evidence of affidavit, §8.07
    judicial notice, §8.11
    letter requesting setting of trial, §8.02
    letters requesting setting of trial, §8.03
    medical records, §8.07
    order granted for leave to file, §8.06
    order taking, §8.11
    readiness, certification of trial, §8.02
    request for leave to file, §8.06
    services, cost and necessity of, §8.05
    setting of trial, §§8.02, 8.03
    visiting judges, §8.09
judicial notice, §8.11
mediation (*See* Mediation)
motions in limine (*See* Motions in limine)
setting of trial, §8.03
    date of obtaining, §8.02
    obtaining, §8.02
visiting judges, §8.09

Previous attorney, §1.01
Prima facie proof, §6.03
Products or services
Professional services
    Exemptions for, §1.02.7.3.1
Proof of attorney's fees, §9.20
Property
    Chapter 27, §1.02.2
    prefiling notice for residential construction, §6.02.1
    residential construction, §6.02.1
Puffing, §2.02.1

— R —

Raw land sales, §§5.16, 7.42
RCLA, *see* Residential Construction Liability Act, *infra*
Real Estate Agents & Brokers
    suits against, §1.02.7.5
Real Estate Commission (Texas)
    licensed Realtors, §7.08
Real Estate Inspector Recovery Fund
    suits against, §1.02.7.3

Real estate sales, Texas law affecting
    Affirmative defense, §§13.02.6, 13.06
    Brakers and agents exemptions from liability, §13.02.5
    Brokers and agents, standards of conduct, §13.02.4
    Disclosures, §13.02.2
    Discovery requests, §13.08
        Interrogatories, §13.08.1
        Requests for production, §13.08.2
    DTPA applicability, §13.02.1
    Inspectors, §13.02.8
    Inspector Recovery Fund, §13.02.9
    Motions for Real Estate Recovery Trust Account samples, §13.07
    Statutory real estate fraud, §13.02.3
Real property, commercial, §5.25
Requests for admissions, §7.48
Requests for disclosure, §7.41.1
Requests for production, §§7.46, 7.47
Residential construction, §§6.02.1, 12.01
    actual damages, §5.16
    affirmative defenses, §6.08
    commercial, §1.02.9.2.2
    common law implied warrants, §12.03
    damages, §5.16
    defenses, §§6.08, 10.15
        Notice, see Notice letter *supra*
    DTPA, applicability, §12.02
    Residential Construction Commission Act, §12.04
    Residential Construction Liability Act, §12.05
Residential Construction Commission Act, §12.04
Residential Construction Liability Act, §12.05
Restitution. *See* Rescission and restitution
Restraining order, temporary, §5.27
Rules of Civil Evidence (Texas)
    medical and health records, §7.25
Rules of Civil Procedure (Texas)
    work product exemption, §7.32

— S —

Secretary of State, §§5.05, 5.07
Securities Exchange Commission (SEC), §7.03
Segregation of attorney's fees, §1.02.28
Services. *See* Goods and services
Settlement offer
    Evaluation of, §3.10
    full amount, §4.05
    less than full amount, §4.06

offer of settlement rule, §8.02
   rejection, §§4.08, 10.15
   responding, §4.01
Settlement Credit, §2.02.11
Smoke Detector Statute (Texas)
   DTPA, §1.02.7
Soft damages, §1.01
Statements
   opening (*See* Opening statement)
Statute of limitations, §§1.02.3.1, 2.01, 10.16
   discovery rule, §5.28
   alleging, §5.12
Statutory cases of action
   tie-in statutes, §1.02.12
Statutory fraud, §10.05
Subpoena, §7.34
   discovery rules and, §7.34
   enforcement of, §7.34
   form, §7.34
   objections to, §7.34
   service of, §7.34
   who may issue, §7.34

— T —

Tables, §5.18
Temporary injunction, §5.27
Temporary restraining order, §5.27
Texas Lemon Law
   Notice letter, §3.03
   Purchase money loan rule, §3.03
Third party
   information, §10.15
   liability, §2.01
   responsibility, §§2.02.10, 6.11
Tort actions
   contract actions, distinguishing between, §1.02.8.1
Travis County Local Rule, §8.10.1
Treble damages
   Insurance Code, §10.12
   mandatory, §5.17
Trials
   beginning (*See* Beginning the case)
   closing argument, §10.21
   defendants (*See* headings under Defendant)
   discovery (*See* Discovery)
   notice of, §§8.03, 8.03[c], 8.03[d]
   plaintiffs (*See* headings under Plaintiff)
   pretrial (*See* headings under Pretrial)
   setting, §§8.03, 8.04
   voir dire (*See* Voir dire examination)

— U —

Unconscionability, §1.02.10
   banking, §5.23
   form, §10.08
Unfound lawsuit, §1.01
Unimproved land
   actual damages, §5.16

— V —

Venue
   forms, §6.03
   general, §5.14
   motion to transfer, §6.03
   multiple defendants, §5.15
   original petition, §5.02
   proper, §5.14
Violations
Visiting judges, §8.09
Visual aids, §8.10.1
Voir dire examination, §9.04
   case-in-chief, §9.15
   categories of collecting information on jury duty, §9.07
   codes on collecting information on jury duty, §9.07
   discretion of trial court, §9.05
   evidence (*See* Evidence)
   juror information, sources of, §9.06
   jury duty, collecting information on, §9.07
   jury selection
      concepts, communicating, §9.09
      participants, introduction of, §9.10
   objections, §9.13
   opening statement
      defendant, §9.12
      plaintiff, §9.11
   preserving error, §§9.05, 9.14
   questions, §9.08
      attitudes about litigation, §9.08
      education, §9.08
      family matters, §9.08
      knowledge of parties, attorneys and witnesses, §9.08
      occupation, §9.08
      prohibited, §9.05
      religion, §9.08
      subject matter of litigation, §9.08
   recording, §9.14
   scope, §9.05
   stop signs, §9.05

— W —

Waiver, §2.02.4
  affirmative defenses, §6.08
Warranties, §§1.02.9
  breach (*See* Breach of warranty)
  express (*See* Express warranty)
  implied (*See* Implied warranty)
Witnesses
  absent, §8.10.1
  cross examination, §9.18
  ex parte statements, §8.10.1
  expert, §7.19
  fact, §7.18
  failure to call, §8.10.1
  impeachment, §9.18
  knowledge of parties, §9.08
  potential fact, §7.17
  questions, §9.08
  statements, §§7.02, 7.33
Workmanlike. *See* Good and workmanlike
Written contracts, §§1.02.4, 6.09.1
Wrongful death, §5.17